T5-CRY-512

PATHS TO PEACE:

A CONTRIBUTION

DOCUMENTS OF THE HOLY SEE TO THE INTERNATIONAL COMMUNITY

PERMANENT OBSERVER MISSION OF THE HOLY SEE TO THE UNITED NATIONS

NEW YORK, 1987

Liturgical Publications, Inc.
1025 S. Moorland Road
Brookfield, WI 53005

Printed in the United States of America

ISBN 0-940169-01-0

FOREWORD

The volume which I have the pleasure to present is more than a valuable collection of statements by the Roman Pontiffs and the Holy See on some of the main contemporary issues which demand the consideration and concern of the international community. It witnesses to the abiding solicitude of the Church for the whole human family, of which the Church is and wishes to be an integral part.

The contemporary world, so vibrant in its achievements and expectations and yet so fragile in the face of catastrophic dangers, claims and deserves the concern of every person of good will. The Second Vatican Council, in the Pastoral Constitution "Gaudium et Spes", stated: "In wonder at their own discoveries and their own might, people are today troubled and perplexed by questions about current trends in the world, about their place and their role in the universe, about the meaning of individual and collective endeavor, and finally about the destiny of nature and of human beings". The Church, whose specific religious mission is not in the political, economic, or social order, "can find no more eloquent expression of its solidarity and affection for the whole human family, to which it belongs, than to enter into dialogue with it about all these different problems" (Ibidem).

The Second Vatican Council has been, in our century, a unique event which gave the Church an exceptional opportunity to reflect upon itself and to restate clearly, in language intelligible to the present generation, its own mission in the modern world. The Council documents, and particularly the above mentioned "Pastoral Constitution 'Gaudium et Spes' on the Church in the Modern World", have masterfully articulated the image and the role which the Church sees for itself vis a vis the world of today. Alongside the solemn pronouncements of the Council, the Church has, moreover, frequently addressed specific issues and problems facing the international community, which, in recent decades, has shown greater consciousness of its interrelatedness and mutual responsibilities. Thus the Church has had the opportunity to address itself to newly formed structures of international organizations, ever conscious of its duty to proclaim, always respectfully and yet confidently, its vision of a human family created and sustained by the love of its maker and called in Christ to a communion of lasting justice and peace.

The seemingly endless spectrum of topics and issues on which the Church has spoken, as evidenced by the documents collected in the present volume, should not surprise anyone, since "the joy and hope, the grief and anguish of the men of our time, especially of those who are poor or afflicted in any way, are the joy and the hope, the grief and the anguish of the followers of Christ as well. Nothing that is genuinely human fails to find an echo in their hearts." (Gaudium et Spes, 1).

Agostino Cardinal Casaroli
Secretary of State

The Vatican, 4 October 1986

PREFACE

The Permanent Observer Mission of the Holy See to the United Nations is making available, in this present collection, the most significant documents addressed by the Holy See to the United Nations and to the specialized organizations which constitute the United Nations system.

The purpose of this enterprise is twofold. On the one hand, this compilation underscores the Holy See's support for multilateral diplomacy, which, in the words of Pope Paul VI, is "the obligatory path that has to be taken for modern civilization and world peace" (Address to the 20th Session of the General Assembly of the United Nations, 4 October 1965. See below, par 10), and its encouragement for all efforts aimed at improving the United Nations structure toward a greater effectiveness and credibility. On the other, it witnesses the presence and activity of the Catholic Church in the international arena, which, with a view to building a better world based upon truth and justice, are directed to solicit, encourage and promote the pursuit of the universal common good and the integral good of man (cf. Paul VI, Address to the Holy See Representatives to International Organizations, 4 September 1974, L'Osservatore Romano, English Ed., 26 September 1974, page 3).

In such context, this book is addressed to:
- Scholars, researchers, students, and members of the United Nations and of International Organizations who wish to know the position of the Catholic Church and of the Holy See on issues before the international community;
- Catholics who, as members of the Church, seek to explore the dimensions of their responsibility and participation vis-a-vis the concerns of the human family.
- All those who, without being members of the Catholic Church, wish to be informed about the presence of the Church and of the Holy See in the international community.

In the years following World War II, the Holy See took part in the activities of international organizations even prior to the establishing of its office of Permanent Observer to the United Nations (21 March 1964). The Holy See had Permanent Observers to UNESCO and FAO from the time of their inception, and had followed the activities of the United Nations in New York, Geneva and Vienna through the Papal Representatives in the respective countries and through "ad hoc" delegates. From the time of the historical visit of Pope Paul VI to the United Nations Headquarters on 4 October 1965, however, the presence of the Holy See in the international organizations has assumed a larger dimension and its statements have been more frequent. Today, the Holy See has Permanent Observers to the United Nations Headquarters in New York and to the United Nations Office in Geneva; to the Food and Agricultural Organization (FAO) in Rome; to the International Labour Organization (ILO) and the World Health Organization (WHO) in Geneva; to the United Nations Educational, Scientific and Cultural Organization (UNESCO) in Paris; to the United Nations Industrial Development Organization (UNIDO) in Vienna, and a Permanent Representative to the International Atomic Energy Agency (IAEA) in Vienna. The Holy See, likewise, has Observers at other International Governmental Organizations, such as the Council of Europe, the Organization of American States, the International Committee of Military Medicine and Pharmacy, the World Tourism Organization, the International Institute for the Unification of Private Law.

The present collection contains the documents addressed by Popes Pius XII, John XXIII, Paul VI and John Paul II to the organizations which are part of the United Nations system; the statements of the Holy See delegations to the main International Conferences sponsored by the United Nations; selected statements of the Holy See Delegations to the General Conferences of UNESCO, to the Conferences of IAEA and UNIDO, to the Assemblies of WHO; some documents of the Holy See addressed to or published by the United Nations. Space limitations have precluded the inclusion of the many statements which the Permanent Observers in New York, Geneva, Rome, Paris and Vienna have made during the annual regular meetings of the various Organizations and Agencies.

The official sources are indicated for statements and documents issued by the Popes. For the other documents, some published here for the first time, we are indebted to the various Missions of the Holy See to the Organizations of the United Nations system and to the Pontifical Commission "Iustitia et Pax". To them we express sincere gratitude for their collaboration.

The texts are published in their entirety, with the omission of the occasional opening greetings. When a document did not originate in English, the non-official English translation was either obtained from the English edition of the "L'Osservatore Romano" or prepared by this Mission. A progressive numeration of paragraphs has been introduced to facilitate the references in the topical index. Whenever a document already carried a numeration in the original text, the same was maintained.

When making use of this collection, one should keep in mind the specific circumstances which have originated the documents. They do not, in fact, provide a systematic treatise on some of the most important issues concerning the human community. They are addresses and statements of the Roman Pontiffs or their representatives on specific occasions, such as the visits by Popes Paul VI and John Paul II to the headquarters of the International Organizations, the participation of the Holy See to International Conferences or Meetings, the observance of special occurrences, etc. For this reason, one will find repetitions as well as frequent references to previous statements. And yet, this very insistence on fundamental ethical principles demonstrates how the Holy See regards them as indispensable to solving problems which involve the human person, in its being and its activities, in its individual and social dimensions.

An extensive " topical index" has been prepared to serve as a guide to the systematic reading of this volume. It will facilitate its consultation and encourage a thorough study of the Church's statements by providing detailed references to specific documents as well as concise summaries of their content.

I cannot conclude these remarks without expressing profound gratitude to all who have collaborated in the realization of this book by the painstaking work of collecting the documents and by translating and editing the texts.

Archbishop Giovanni Cheli
Apostolic Nuncio
Permanent Observer of the Holy See
to the United Nations

New York, 25 October 1986

Having been called to succeed Archbishop Giovanni Cheli as the Permanent Observer of the Holy See to the United Nations, I have the distinguished pleasure to be the one who gives to the press the present collection of texts.

A unique kind of collection, one may call it, since it offers for the first time in the handy format of one volume almost all the statements addressed by the Holy See to the Organizations which constitute the United Nations system. Hopefully, it will be a conspicuous thesaurus, whose systematic reading and consultation will be made easy by the exhaustive topical- index.

I trust that the availability in this one volume of a whole series of significant documents will enhance the understanding of the mind of the Church on issues which are vital for the wellbeing of mankind at the present stage of its development and thus contribute to its progress on the paths of peace.

The present collection of documents reveals both the purpose and the mode of the presence of the Church in the international arena.

A presence of service, unassuming and yet forceful, for the Church believes that each human being is sacred because of God's personal love for him and that each one is urgently charged with the duty to contribute in the fashioning of a better world, in truth and in justice, for the good of all the earth's inhabitants, which the same love of God commands him to regard as his own brothers and sisters.

By transcending all limitations of particular and fragmented interests, the Church can and must speak only in the interest of all.

At the same time, the Church's presence is by its nature discreet and even humble, appealing as it does to the forces of reason and goodness, seeking to give rather than to receive, counting as success every step, however small, that is taken by individuals and nations toward the goal of peace.

I would be remiss if I did not add my own words of thanks to all who laboured diligently in making this publication possible, first among them the Counsellor of this Mission of the Holy See to the United Nations, Msgr. Antonio Franco, who has been the pivotal and undefatigable mainspring of the whole enterprise.

Archbishop Renato R. Martino
Apostolic Nuncio
Permanent Observer of the Holy See
to the United Nations

New York, 26 June 1987

ACRONYMS

AAS	"Acta Apostolicae Sedis", official gazette of the Holy See.
FAO	Food and Agriculture Organization of the United Nations.
IAEA	International Atomic Energy Agency.
ILO	International Labour Organization.
IMF	International Monetary Fund.
NPT	Treaty on the Non Proliferation of Nuclear Weapons.
UN	United Nations.
UNCTAD	United Nations Conference on Trade and Development.
UNDP	United Nations Development Programme.
UNEP	United Nations Environment Programme.
UNESCO	United Nations Educational, Scientific and Cultural Organization.
UNHCR	Office of the United Nations High Commissioner for Refugees.
UNICEF	United Nations Children's Fund.
UNIDO	United Nations Industrial Development Organization.
WHO	World Health Organization.

CONTENTS

CHAPTER I

SPECIAL ADDRESSES

a) At the Headquarters of the Organizations:

Paul VI:

John Paul II:

Cardinal Agostino Casaroli

CHAPTER II

HUMAN RIGHTS

Paul VI

John Paul II

CHAPTER IV

DISARMAMENT AND PEACE

CHAPTER V

DEVELOPMENT

CHAPTER VI

FOOD AND AGRICULTURE

5. Special concern of the Holy See for food problems:

THE UNIQUE ROLE OF THE HOLY SEE IN THE INTERNATIONAL COMMUNITY (*)

Original: Italian

(01) International conferences and meetings, the number and variety of which are one of the characteristic features of our age, are frequently attended by representatives of the Holy See, a fact which was unusual until a few decades ago. As participants on an equal footing with those of the States, or more often as Observers, these representatives demonstrate the concrete interest with which the Holy See follows the problems of the international Community, or directly share responsibilities for the discussions and efforts that are being made to solve these problems.

(02) Even though discussions at these meetings are not limited exclusively to questions of an ethical or juridical nature, the Holy See, when intervening, always regards the latter aspects essentially, while it remains on a plane of great discretion as regards the technical aspects, and holds itself aloof from exclusively political or military questions.

(03) If the participation of the Holy See in conferences and meetings of this kind is a modern phenomenon, so to speak, the recognition of its right to belong to the international community is, on the contrary, centuries old.

(04) The juridical and historical motivations and the various concrete expressions have been the object, and still are, of many doctrinal studies and interesting discussions. The fact itself is not denied by anyone: nor, on the other hand, would arguments be of avail against the attitude - it can be said - of all the States, including many which, on the bilateral plane, have no relations, or only strained and unfriendly ones, with the Holy See.

(05) Some people, in practice if not in theory, owing perhaps to insufficient knowledge of the terms of the problem, seem to confuse the Holy See with Vatican City, and they attribute to the Vatican City State recognition as a sovereign body admitted to the concert of States, having the same status and being juridically equal to other states, in spite of the very small size of its territory and population, and the peculiarities of its organization and action.

(06) This way of thinking can be detected especially in newly formed States which are not Catholic, and are less familiar, therefore, with a history and a reality - that of the Catholic Church and its centre - which was for many centuries exclusively or mainly European. It can explain and justify, in a certain sense, the resistance of the Popes to accepting the end of the Pontifical State and Pius XI's intransigence, on concluding the historic "Conciliation" (Lateran Treaty), with the Italian State, in demanding "a territorial sovereignty of some kind": "a condition that is universally considered indispensable - the Pope stated - for any real jurisdictional sovereignty." Therefore - he added - at least that minimum of territory necessary as a support for the sovereignty itself."

(07) Territorial sovereignty is a condition, therefore, that is more important psychologically than juridically: but a very important one, necessary, in practice, to give the world almost visual certainty of the sovereign independence of the Pope with regard to any other State, for the free exercise of his function as supreme Pastor of the Catholic Church. Even if, as Pius XI said further, it is just "that minimum of material territory which is indispensable (practically indispensable, he meant) for the exercise of a spiritual power entrusted to men for the benefit of men."

(08) The best doctrine, however - it could even be said the doctrine to which there is hardly an exception - is that which agrees in recognizing the attribution of sovereignty to the Holy See as the supreme organ of government of the Catholic Church.

(09) This appeared as something acceptable and was in fact accepted in the period from 1870, when the Holy See was deprived of the Pontifical States, until 1929, when it negotiated the creation of the new State of Vatican City. But it was true even before 1870, although the image was less clear; and it is even more obvious today, when (I am again quoting Pius XI's fine words in his

(*) The following is the text of a Lecture given to the Italian Society for International Organizations by His Eminence Cardinal Agostino Casaroli, when he was Secretary of the Council for the Public Affairs of the Church. Although delivered in January 1975, it has been chosen as an introduction to this collection because it states clearly and authoritatively the position of the Church in the International Community.

Address to the priests and Lenten preachers of Rome, on 11 February 1929) "the earthly terrain is reduced to such minimal terms that it, too, can and should be considered spiritualized by the immense, sublime and really divine spirituality that it is intended to support and serve."

(010) And in fact, even one who wished to attribute to the tiny Vatican State only the indispensable claim to enter the world concert of States (bringing the Holy See with it), could not help feeling - in comparison with small, average or large powers, and particularly the ones known as the "Superpowers" that he has before him an insignificant pedestal, on which, however, perches an independent and sovereign power, whose outstretched wings cover the entire globe. Whether that power be respected and esteemed, or suspected and combated, it imposes itself because of its stature, its history, its influence.

(011) It is actually this power, not its territory, which is recognized by the family of peoples as having the right to citizenship and to participation in their associated activities and collective effort in the service of mankind.

(012) A full member of the international community, on an equal footing with the States, the Holy See finds itself in a unique situation. Its sovereignty is spiritual in nature. Its authority - which is also spiritual and religious - extends over hundreds of millions of persons scattered all over the world and belonging to the most different peoples and countries. Its strength does not lie in armies, armaments, great material means - whatever people may have said - of persuasion or pressure. It arises from the respect that its words, its teaching, its policies enjoy in the conscience of the Catholic world (a respect that is widely shared by many people who do not belong to the Church.)

(013) Its *jus imperandi* - endowed, in fact, with all the characteristics of real sovereign jurisdiction (juridical *imperium*), manifested in laws and provisions of "government," has its practical affirmation more in the conscious and freely offered obedience of the faithful than by virtue of administrative or penal sanctions, which are in any case mainly moral (ecclesiastical, in any case) in nature.

(014) Its real kingdom is the kingdom of conscience. This does not prevent the Holy See to exercise a real influence, not infrequently a considerable one, in the life of the international community also but, rather, enables it to do so.

(015) This applies in a certain way also to other forces operating in the sphere of the spirit and conscience. I am thinking here, in particular, not so much of the personal influence of great thinkers and masters of life, but rather of the influence exercised, above all, by religious communities with their own organs of leadership and policy-making (I would not like to fail to recall very respectfully, in this connection, the World Council of Churches).

(016) But it applies preeminently to the Catholic Church and the Holy See: not only because of the numerical strength and world diffusion of Catholicism, but mainly because of the organized form of the Church. This form makes her an international *corpus*, juridically structured, an immense people united in faith and charity, but also, at the same time, in the acceptance of an authority at the summit of which there is the Sovereign Pontiff, the principle and visible foundation of a cohesion, that is also exterior, and which makes it possible for the Church to act as a unit, while maintaining the legitimate pluralism of traditions, customs, and concrete options in the fields in which plurality is permissible and, in fact, enriching.

(017) In Western Europe in the Middle Ages, the Church - in her supreme authority, the Pope - was regarded as a power not only independent of, but superior to, the civil power, personified by the Emperor. In a similar way religious values - represented by the one Church then recognized as true - were clearly considered superior to the values of earthly life, which, though lofty and noble, were subordinate, in the order of purposes, to the supreme ones of eternal life.

(018) These evaluations were subsequently modified, and the Holy Roman Empire replaced - in fact though not yet in law - by the multiplicity of national independent States. New peoples and States, the majority of which were non-Catholic, and not even Christian, gradually appeared on the world scene, so that the Holy See lost more and more its "medieval" position of preeminence with regard to civil society.

(019) But its spiritual and religious character continued to keep for it the place it had traditionally been recognized as having, not by virtue of the Pope's temporal sovereignty over the Pontifical States, but because he was the Head of the Catholic Church.

(020) The clear acceptance of the Holy See in the concert of Nations (even while its specific nature and, consequently, its special position in the international community is recognized), commits it particularly to full collaboration - in the specific nature of its aims and means - in order to carry out the aims of the community itself. Most of these aims, in fact, or at least certain aspects of them, correspond very well to the aims that, because of their very mission, the Catholic Church and the Holy See pursue as regards the earthly city.

(021) It is enough to reread the aims set out in the introduction to the Charter of the United Nations to see at once their broad parallelism with well-known pontifical and conciliar texts:
"To save succeeding generations from the scourge of war, which twice in our lifetime has brought untold sorrow to mankind, and
to reaffirm faith in fundamental human rights, in the dignity and worth of the human person, in the equal rights of men and women and of nations large and small, and
to establish conditions under which justice and respect for the obligations arising from treaties and other sources of international law can be maintained, and
to promote social progress and better standards of life in larger freedom."

(022) These solemn principles, rather than merely finding an echo in the concern of the Catholic Church and the Holy See, seem themselves an echo of the centuries-old Christian tradition.

(023) As I said above, the nature of the Holy See as a "moral power" does not prevent it from exerting a considerable influence in international life.

(024) Indeed, it would be more exact to affirm, by and large, that the moral influence is no less important for the international community than the influence exerted by States; it is, in every case, necessary, indispensable. In fact peace, the protection of the rights and dignity of the human person, justice in the relations between peoples, care for their social progress - though subordinate to a large extent, in their concrete implementation, to conditions over which man has no control - are, however, unthinkable without the generous, constant and intelligent effort of goodwill.

(025) Everything, therefore, that helps to strengthen and increase this goodwill, helps at the same time to ensure better conditions for the attainment of the aims of peace, justice and harmonious progress, which are the essential reasons why States and peoples live not only territorially juxtaposed on this "threshing-floor which makes us wax so fierce" (*Divina Commedia*, Paradise, Canto XXII), but connected and organized with bilateral or multilateral ties, even - as happens today - with ties which are worldwide, aimed at preventing destructive conflicts and fostering mutually beneficial cooperation.

(026) It is true that considerations, concerns and intentions of a moral nature are not in themselves alien to statesmen, and that these considerations and concerns receive much eloquent and effective support either through personal action, or through the action of non-governmental bodies and organizations, religious, ethical, humanitarian, or juridical in character.

(027) But it is also true that the States, owing to their responsibilities with regard to attaining these purposes, to protecting the interests of the political collectivity, and to defending it against external egoism or threats, are inclined to reason more in terms of "actual reality" than of moral principles, and to take as the criterion of behaviour more the "sacred egoism" of the nation or "reasons of State" than ethical norms.

(028) As for the other non-national or non-governmental organizations (and I refer particularly here to the important or less widespread religions, Christian and non-Christian), it would not be just or true to diminish the merits of their action, both in proclaiming principles, and in forming and guiding the consciences of so many leaders of public life, and in supporting just causes concretely or combating injustice.

(029) The fact is, nevertheless, that however we wish to explain and evaluate this fact, and whatever may be the opinions about other hypothetical, future possibilities, the international community - as has already been said - recognized only the Holy See, in its capacity as the central organ of government of the Catholic Church, as a full member of the community itself, admitting it to take its place and act in it like the States.

(030) This exceptional situation is not a reason for pride for the Holy See; but, while it considers it, in conformity with the concept that the Catholic Church has of herself, as recognition of a position that devolves upon it by native right, it makes it aware of a responsibility which, in a certain sense, extends beyond her frontiers.

(031) In the international community, in fact, the Holy See, in addition to carrying out its own specific function, feels almost obliged - very respectfully and without wishing to take the side of any other social body, far less to replace it - to represent in some way all the forces that aim at emphasizing moral values in the conduct of international affairs and in relations between the States. Such values, though specifically Christian, are nevertheless, to such a large extent and from so many points of view, common to the whole of mankind.

(032) Various authors point out how the Holy See is in some way recognized by the international community itself as being "representative," in the sense just specified.

(033) I would like to allude to a detail which may seem of secondary importance and which, actually, has no special value except that it signifies this recognition - which is certainly neither formal nor explicit. The attention paid in diplomatic life (and, if we are honest enough to admit it, not only in this field) to protocol precedence, is well-known even to those who are not very well acquainted with diplomacy and its rules (it has been and often is the object of ironical comments). In past centuries, in fact, an importance going far beyond mere problems of etiquette was attached to it. It implied claims, contestations and disputes about the rank and the importance of the Sovereigns represented. One norm was clearly accepted: the absolute precedence of the Representatives of the Pope and, after them, those of the Roman Emperor. In 1815 the Congress of Vienna, to end many useless discussions, decided to introduce the principle that, in each of the three classes into which diplomatic agents would be divided, they would take precedence among themselves according to the date of the official notification of their arrival to take up office.

(034) The Holy Roman Empire had been swept away by the Napoleonic cyclone: so that there was no problem here of any possible exception to the general rule.

(035) There remained the Pope. It is of a certain interest, for those who delve into diplomatic history, to reread the letters of Cardinal Consalvi, Secretary of State, present in Vienna from the end of 1814 to the first months of 1815 as Minister Plenipotentiary of Pope Pius VII, to Cardinal Pacca, who was acting as Pro-Secretary of State, on this subject. The Cardinal did not hide his embarrassment having to oppose the plan of the Congress, "since the Pope does not wish - he wrote - to accept what the Emperors of Austria and Russia, the Kings of France and Spain agree to accept"; and he mentioned the "disfavour with which it would be viewed by the mentality of these times should it appear that a priest wished to take first place, when the Emperors themselves had renounced their claims" (Consalvi to Pacca, 21 December 1814).

(036) In any case, he fought resolutely. And in his Note of 8 January 1815 to the Congress, after referring to the modesty of the Pope's territorial sovereignty, which, "far from putting him among the main Sovereigns, would certainly put him among those of inferior rank," Consalvi appealed to the "religious quality" of the Sovereign Pontiff, which put him, "so to speak, outside the ordinary line," pointing out that "it is for this main reason that precedence has always been granted to the Pope, as well as to his representatives."

(037) The matter ended with the approval of the clause that "the present Regulation (on the precedence of diplomatic agents) will not make any innovation as regards the Pope's representatives."

(038) Of the eight powers that signed the Vienna Regulation, four were non-Catholic (Russia, Prussia, Great Britain and Sweden).

(039) The question came up again one and a half centuries later, at the conference convened by the United Nations, also in Vienna, for the purpose of codifying diplomatic law. This time it was not just eight European and Christian powers that took part in the discussions and resolutions, but all the member states of the United Nations.

(040) The present author had then the honour - which, however, was something of an embarrassment for him, too - of presenting the point of view of the Holy See on a question still less in keeping with the "mentality of these times" than it was in Consalvi's days; and referring, in any case, to a specifically European tradition, subsequently adopted, without any difficulty, by the Catholic nations of Latin America, just because they were Catholic, but foreign to a majority of new States, which had had no part of any kind in this tradition.

(041) The International Law Commission of the United Nations had prepared a project of benevolent compromise, so to speak: respectful, that is, of the actual existing situation, where the precedence of the Pontifical Representative in the Diplomatic Corps was already recognized, but not open to future extensions.

(042) This solution seemed rather pragmatic and, so to speak, historicist; less corresponding, therefore, to the statement of principle which alone, in the judgment of the Holy See, can really justify recognition of the privileged situation previously reserved by the international community for the Pontifical Representatives (a privilege consisting, in itself, only in the possibility of making legitimately an exception to the general norm on precedence, should the accrediting State desire: as happened in fact by virtue of the 1815 Regulation).

(043) This statement of principle was recalled and "updated" in a Memorandum prepared by the Holy See on 23 February 1961, on the eve of the Vienna Conference. "Updating" was necessary because - before an Assembly composed of representatives of countries the majority of which were not Christian, and some of which were, in fact, committed to an officially non-religious ideology - the "religious quality" of the Sovereign Pontiff, to which Consalvi had effectively appealed at the Vienna Congress, could not have had much weight. The Holy See Memorandum pointed out, therefore, that "the fact is that among the Powers that make up the international Community, the Holy See - and it alone - is distinguished by its special nature and by the very particular characteristics of its aims and action: a nature, aims and action which refer directly to what is most lofty and respectable for all men and all peoples: spiritual and moral values. In this way the tribute traditionally paid to the Holy See and its representatives even by non-Catholic Powers, is a significant recognition of these common values, so noble and precious."

(044) There was no lack of discussion and some took very critical and negative stands. But in the end, thanks to the support not only of the representatives of countries of ancient Catholic tradition, but also of young African and Asian nations, the line of argument proposed by the Holy See, was accepted and paragraph 3 of Art. 15 of the Convention - which establishes that the general norm regarding the precedence of diplomatic agents "is without prejudice to any practice accepted by the receiving State regarding the precedence of the representative of the Holy See" - was approved with 59 votes against one negative vote and 17 abstentions.

Art. 15 as a whole subsequently obtained 71 positive votes, with no negative votes and 2 abstentions.

(045) Placed and accepted in this way, almost as the "conscience of humanity," within the international community, the Holy See gives it its willing and sincere cooperation.

(046) It does so not only by enunciating principles, proposing points of moral doctrine, the value of which is not only Christian but universal, and reminding everyone, but Catholics in particular, of the duty of observing them or exhorting and encouraging them to do so. To do this, membership in the concert of Nations would not even be indispensable. It could even be said that when it acts as a member of the international Community, finding itself in this way, so to speak, on a footing of equality with the other members of the Community, the Holy See, though without losing the specific characteristics of its own nature, finds itself obliged to use a certain "discretion" in carrying out the functions of ethical teaching which it can - and does - exercise with far greater freedom and solemnity in its primary capacity as the centre of the Church, "mother and teacher" of truth.

(047) Its capacity as travelling companion of the nations of the world is manifested rather in participation in the concrete concerns, problems, fears and hopes of peoples; sharing their legitimate intentions; supporting positive efforts; contributing practically, as far as it can, to overcoming the difficulties that arise and to carrying out initiatives, especially in the fields that are most congenial to it, such as education and culture, health care and humanitarian assistance in general, human promotion, and above all, peace.

(048) The Holy See is able to offer, in particular, a contribution that may be of considerable utility in the serene and objective study of the problems that afflict and often divide peoples. The more complex the problems are, the more necessary this careful dispassionate study is, for it is not possible to hope to solve problems with an effort of goodwill unless one has available an exact view of their deep reality, causes, foreseeable consequences, and possible and more suitable remedies.

(049) I do not mean, of course, that the Holy See always and necessarily has more complete data at its disposal on which to base its judgment, or that its men have greater capacities of analysis and synthesis than others. The multiplicity of its contacts, however, and the confidence it inspires in the conflicting parties, because it is above the disputes and opposed interests and can therefore view and evaluate things more dispassionately, usually put the Holy See in a more favorable situation to be of help in this field.

(050) There is another form of service that the Holy See may be able to render, at least in certain cases, more easily than others, just because it is not bound to party interests. This form, too, is of considerable importance. I mean to offer adversaries the possibility of a discreet, reserved and disinterested intermediary, for the beginning of a dialogue which would otherwise be extremely difficult, if not impossible, owing to obstacles of various kinds, starting with the difficulty of taking the first step, especially when feeling runs high and passions are explosive.

(051) Here, too, of course, it is not a question of a specific and exclusive position of the Holy See. Sometimes, in fact, the Holy See itself finds the way barred to dialogues in which it is interested; or else the conflicting parties do not give it much of a hearing, or it lacks the means of persuasion that would make its interventions more effective. We can see today also what can be done - though at the cost of great effort and not always with certainty - by any power, bent on bringing the conflicting parties closer to each other, if this power has, on the one hand, an outstanding capacity for disentangling complicated situations and driving home to the adversaries the requirements of mutual interests and common dangers; and, on the other hand - it must be said - the force of conviction that comes not only from the weight of arguments, but also from the military and economic power that great powers wield, for good and for evil.

(052) The Holy See certainly does not possess this power. But precisely because of the poverty of its material means, and the consequent fact that it does not eclipse anyone, and at the same time because of its widely recognized moral prestige, the trust its friendly attitude inspires, and its goodwill, free of selfish aims or concerns other than those prompted by healthy common interest, its readiness to act as a benevolent and respectful intermediary in difficult situations is, at least sometimes, of real benefit.

(053) The Holy See does not claim to play a role of "mediation" in the technical sense of the word on the international plane (unless it receives proposals to do so, as it was sometimes asked to "arbitrate"). But it does not refuse to accept requests, and does not itself hesitate to take initiatives of rapprochement and conciliation, being less concerned to safeguard a prestige exposed to the danger of failures than eager to contribute, to the best of its ability, to the welfare and peace of peoples, especially the weakest and most vulnerable.

(054) The Holy See is encouraged to play this part also by the special atmosphere - I would almost say one of real cordiality - that seems to characterize the relationship of the members of the international Community with it today.

(055) I do not say the whole international Community, or all its members respond in the same way. Some of them, in fact, maintain, at least for the present, positions of detachment or coldness which in some cases - altogether exceptional ones, actually - becomes open hostility.

(056) But one cannot help being impressed by the repeated manifestations of consideration and appreciation for the work carried out by the Holy See in the international field, and of confidence in what is expected from it in the future.

(057) In some cases, of course, this is to be attributed partly to politeness and - why not? - even to calculations of instrumentalization. But there can be no doubt, especially for those who have the fortune to witness these manifestations at first hand, particularly in the personal meetings of Heads of State and rulers with the Pope, that - with the due exceptions - the international Community as a whole sees in the Holy See today a power on whose resolute desire for good and on whose commitment all nations - Catholic or non-Catholic, Christian or non-Christian - can rely absolutely when it is a question of defending or promoting the great causes of mankind.

(058) This trust, it seems to me, finds its explanation and justification in the Holy See's attitude in its relations with States, an attitude made up of respect; understanding of the seriousness and difficulty of the tasks that devolve on those responsible for the government of the individual countries and the welfare of their community; interest and sympathy for their efforts; and readiness to cooperate, as I have already said.

(059) In this way, almost naturally, a dialogue is established. It develops, on the one hand, in the exercise, and, on the other hand, in the recognition and acceptance of an authority not involved in the inevitable conflicts of interest between peoples and States - everyone's friend. This is possible only for one who, without pursuing temporal interests of his own, is concerned about those legitimate ones that are common to all; lacking the material power to put others in the shade, but rich in a spiritual and moral influence, accepted by millions of persons, and respected even by non-Christians or non-believers.

(060) The Holy See is, I said, everyone's friend.
This is, as a matter of fact, one of the present day characteristics of the Holy See as regards the international community.

(061) In past centuries, the sovereignty that the Holy See exercised over the so-called "Church States" put the Pope in the condition of considering himself - not only as Head of the Catholic Church - but also as one of the Princes of Italy and Europe, and of having to act as such. This led him to take part in the quarrels and struggles between States and Sovereigns and to join their political and military alliances.

(062) Also on the ecclesial plane, the concept of "Christendom," as opposed to the non-Christian world, induced the Holy See even to promote wars and "Crusades" against the "infidels"; just as, later, the religious wars found the Holy See almost naturally aligned with the Catholic Princes.

(063) The end of the Pontifical State, replaced by that tiny and almost symbolic independent territory, Vatican City, relieved the Holy See from what it had considered for centuries the duty of defending the territorial patrimony handed down from Pope to Pope.

(064) The growing awareness on the part of the Catholic Church of the deep needs of her evangelizing mission, and the clear and strong growth of the ecumenical spirit (in its widest acceptance), make a "war of religion" almost unthinkable today.

(065) The spirit of dialogue proclaimed by the Catholic Church does not exclude even the most distant: even if, on the ideological plane, the difficulties - as Paul VI pointed out in the Encyclical *Ecclesiam Suam* - are so great as to seem almost impossible.

(066) When it is a question of problems that concern humanity as such, in the perspectives of its earthly life, the dialogue, as far as the Holy See is concerned, knows no limits except the ones imposed by a persistent refusal on the part of others.

(067) This attitude of the Holy See is inspired not only by a new sensitiveness as regards opening to the world, but also by the conviction that nowadays the great problems of mankind cannot be solved in a suitable way - or cannot be solved at all - without the contribution of all, because peoples and continents are now so closely connected and interdependent. In particular, world peace and development - which is the new name of peace, according to the well-known and happy expression of Paul VI - depend on a common effort of understanding, a convergence of will, and worldwide commitment.

(068) War is always to be deprecated, and by its very nature - being, as it is, a confrontation of forces that do not necessarily coincide with an equal force of right and reason - is an "a-rational" phenomenon. But today, as a result of modern scientific and technical progress, especially in the nuclear field, it constitutes an impending threat not only of evils and sufferings far greater than those of the past, but also of the destruction of a great part, if not all, of man's civilization, and his very existence.

(069) Christian conscience cannot avoid considering it a very serious moral duty to act to preserve mankind - or even just a part of it - from such a calamity.

(070) Only those who are not aware of the extreme seriousness of this moral imperative can be surprised - or pretend to be scandalized - if the Holy See does not refuse, but on the contrary desires and seeks dialogue, and offers its collaboration - however modest it may seem - to all those in charge of the destinies of peoples, and particularly to those whose responsibilities for peace and war in the world are greater, corresponding to the greatness of their power.

(071) The surprise - or the "scandal" - is due mainly to the fact that the Holy See offers dialogue and collaboration also to States where, for the Church, and for religion in general, serious and unresolved problems exist, and where dialogue aimed at their solution either is not progressing as is necessary and desirable or seems to have been rejected altogether.

(072) The position of the Holy See is clear and straightforward. It is aware, of course, that its first and fundamental duty is to protect and vigorously promote the cause of the Church, the rights of all believers to religious freedom, and respect for the fundamental rights of the human person and the individual conscience.

(073) No one can honestly doubt the effort made by the Holy See to carry out this duty. This is not the place - nor would there be time - to deal with the problem, or with the judgments, the questions about criteria, the means, the results, the perspectives of this indefatigable action to which the Holy See has given such deep thought.

(074) But I have no doubts about affirming that, despite the many difficulties and not infrequent incomprehension, the Holy See can entrust with a serene conscience the activity it is carrying out in the service of the Church, in one of the hardest and most dramatic periods of her life, to the severe but objective judgment of history.

(075) At the same time, however, the Holy See considers it part - a secondary but no less fundamental part - of its evangelical mission of love ("the second commandment is like the first one...") to operate in the service of peace and of a more just and brotherly social order, in and among all nations.

(076) I venture to make the forecast that history will record among the most memorable pages, in the long story of the Roman Pontificate - and with it of the whole Catholic Church - the one it is writing in this field.

(077) Memorable and really Christian! Unarmed, but backed by the support of millions of human beings, the Pope offers himself as an ally to all those with responsibilities regarding the great interests and great causes of mankind; and he courageously embarks on a dialogue with them, a dialogue not without uncertainties, but necessary. He has no illusions about the real possibilities of his making determinant contributions, but he is encouraged by the trust that is showered on him from the most different and opposite quarters, and he is impelled by an awareness of the urgency of uniting the efforts of everyone for such a cause.

(078) This does not prevent him from dealing freely, whenever it is necessary, and in the most suitable way, with the problems, the necessities, the tragedies and the rights of the Church. If anything, it gives him the opportunity to do so even with those whom, perhaps, he would not otherwise be able to reach.

(079) Another reason for perplexity about or objection to the activity of the Holy See in this area is what may seem to be a deliberate position of neutrality, of equidistance between the opposed parties or blocs: as if it does not want to compromise itself by expressing a judgment on the justice of the cause of either adversary, or, above all, by supporting one against the other.

(080) But, apart from the fact that very often - to quote Manzoni - right and wrong cannot be divided in a clear-cut way, it is certainly not the case that the Holy See fails to form its own moral judgment, or renounces manifesting it, even publicly and clearly when it is seen to be opportune. But normally - and except for special situations - its concern here, is not so much to "do justice" (which is often difficult to carry out completely, or - in seeking the "summum ius" - to carry out without inflicting suffering and perhaps even greater injustice); its concern is more specifically to "make peace": without neglecting, of course, but rather supporting in the best way possible not only the broad principles of justice but also the concrete reasons for pursuing it.

(081) And the desire to serve as a "bridge" that will bring opposing parties into a dialogue in an effort to reach a fair settlement certainly makes it necessary that the Holy See, when assuming a position in any dispute, must adopt a method and tone that is not counterproductive to its aim of establishing concord.

(082) Nor can it be forgotten that, even in this activity, the Pope always remains not a politician but a father. I have had the opportunity to note personally that this quality of his is "felt," at least in an indefinite way, even by non-Catholics, non-Christians and non-believers. This is perhaps the secret of why Statesmen - even the ones most accustomed to *realpolitik* - confess that they find a comforting source of moral and human "inspiration" in meetings with the Pope.

(083) There remains a last aspect for me to consider. It, too, concerns dialogue, but a multilateral one. It regards the above-mentioned participation of the Holy See in international organizations and conferences.

(084) As regards the latter, it is well known that the Holy See responds positively to invitations addressed to it, on the basis of qualifications recognized by the general norms that regulate the composition of these international meetings. Its presence is generally welcomed, its interventions listened to with interest, and the specific contributions that the Holy See's representatives make to the study of the questions dealt with are carefully examined.

(085) The frankly moral approach of the Holy See may sometimes seem disturbing; but it should be said that the spiritual inspiration that the Holy See - if not alone, at least preeminently - can bring to the work of the great international conferences, is not only received respectfully but positively appreciated. In any case, the sincerity of the Holy See's attitude and the recognized authority of its words, induce, if nothing else, more serious thought, which is always useful.

(086) The participation of the Holy See, as a member, in the organized forms of activity of the international Community is considerable, but not automatic, as is generally the case for States.

(087) In particular, it is not a member of the major organizations - including, particularly, the United Nations - having only a Mission as Permanent Observer attached to them.

(088) In view of the inevitability of continual political conflicts among the members of these organizations, and of the specific nature and functions of the Holy See in the life of the international community, it was considered more in keeping with its functions, and more calculated to permit an action - constant, but not committed to supporting or opposing the conflicting parties - to establish a discreet presence. Since this discreet presence would be more acceptable to various States, it would ultimately prove more effective than outright membership.

(089) The experience of a good many years, at the United Nations, UNESCO, FAO and other similar organizations, seems positive. Without making it an absolute principle, the Holy See continues, therefore, along this way.

(090) At the same time, the Holy See continues to proclaim, not simply the utility, but rather the necessity of a world organization of peoples, of an authority accepted by everyone and respected by everyone, to which everyone must contribute to give it life and strength, in order to replace the temptation of resorting to violence to impose aims of power and supremacy, or of resorting to the harsh law of the defence of honor - if not of one's legitimate interests or freedom or life itself - with the possibility of appealing to a just and impartial forum, endowed with sufficient capacity to ensure the rights and establish the duties of everyone.

(091) Among the many texts that could be quoted, I will just recall the expression of confidence in the Organization of the United Nations, which Paul VI delivered personally to the General Assembly of the U.N. on 5 October 1965. This memorable address conveyed to the world the Pope's thought about the idea inspiring the Organization, his appreciation of the efforts being made to put this idea into practice, his encouragement not to be disheartened by difficulties, but rather to keep on striving for more and more perfect achievements, as regards structures and activities, in order to provide humanity with better and better guarantees of peace in justice and beneficial cooperation: not through the dialectics of conflicts and wars (which were not infrequently regarded in the past as the driving power of history), but through the application of reason and law.

(092) Today humanity finds itself, dramatically, at a decisive turning point in its multimillenary history. Dramatically; but, I would venture to say, also providentially.

(093) Impelled by his restless curiosity for knowledge and an obscure exciting consciousness of being able to subdue, with his intelligence and tenacity, the mysterious but unintelligent forces which surround him and almost oppress him, man embarked over the centuries on his splendid adventure as king of the universe: "freudig (allow me to quote what I hold to be, perhaps, the finest line of poetry in the whole of German literature, great and rich though it is) freudig wie ein Held zum Siegen" - as joyful as a hero sweeping on to victory.

(094) But as he piles up one achievement after another, the latter often seem to revolt against him: like an apprentice-magician, he is no longer able to control them. Thus, at present, his breakthrough and technical progress in the field of nuclear energy could become the instrument of his destruction.

(095) A dramatic situation, as I said, but also a providential one. The danger, in fact, of misuse of the forces he has unleashed makes man more aware of realities and necessities which he is too inclined to forget in the intoxication of triumph.

(096) In his Address to the General Assembly of the U.N., on 5 October 1965, Paul VI recalled in fact: "It is not from progress or science that danger comes.... The real danger lies in man ...!" (See below, par. 33).

(097) It is not without a providential significance, therefore, that man is obliged, today more than ever, not to be content with subduing the forces of nature, but to try to control himself: his selfishness - on the plane of the individual, the nation, the group; his thirst for power; his lack of interest in the rights and needs of others, near or far away (but how can anyone be far away in a world of continents and peoples whose destinies are interdependent?).

(098) For the time being, we are still at the stage of the balance of terror. This balance is too unstable and precarious, sufficient perhaps - we all hope the margin is a wide one - to dispel the threat of irreparable catastrophes, but inadequate to create that spirit of collaboration which would render us eager to use the resources of nature and science in a way that will promote the development of peoples and, with their development, peace.

(099) Until man succeeds in making this qualitative leap from the static (even though unstable) equilibrium of cooperation, human civilization will remain exposed to the most serious threats.

(0100) It is a question, if we look at the deep reality of things, of making an effort of intelligence and will: a commitment, therefore, specifically of the moral order. An effort that is as titanic as it is indispensable.

(0101) The Holy See has too long an experience behind it to indulge in dreams and naive illusions, or to believe that it is easy to pass from what should be to what is. It has confidence, however, in man's capacity to understand the demands of reality and to meet them in the forms characteristic of his nature as a rational, moral being.

(0102) Is this not perhaps the phenomenon that has taken place over the centuries and has found expression in the gradual evolution of the relations between men? This evolution has given rise to forms of social organization intended to foster peaceful coexistence and reconcile conflicting interests under the aegis of law, thereby avoiding the necessity of reverting to individual or group force and discouraging temptations to oppress the weak.

(0103) However imperfect we consider what has been done so far in this field, it is undeniable that it has at least avoided recourse to the law of *bellum omnium contra omnes* within individual organized social groups. Would it be unreasonable to think that, in the light of the new situations, the organization of the international Community will also progress in such a way as to make it possible for the States to achieve - though with the imperfections that can hardly be avoided - what has already been obtained within the individual States or their federations and confederations?

(0104) Are we postulating an utopia? In any case, a utopia which today appears to be the only alternative to the destruction of man and the treasures of his civilization; to his enslavement by the strongest, who are able to survive and tyrannize over the others; and to his continual fear of being overpowered, with the consequent temptation - on all sides - to strengthen one's defences or pass to the attack, crushing one's real, feared or possible future enemies.

(0105) This utopia, if you wish to call it such, has the convinced support of the Holy See: on the plane not of an empty moralism but of a realistic - or, if you like, morally realistic - consideration of the present and future of mankind.

(0106) This is certainly one of the most challenging and difficult periods in the long history of humanity.

(0107) Today more than ever, therefore, the Holy See feels its ancient vocation to be not only the teacher of truths transcending the horizon of time and history, but also the travelling companion of peoples, sharing the responsibility of their rulers, as if it were the standard bearer and privileged spokesman of those common spiritual and moral values, without which it is impossible to build a real and worthy society of men.

(0108) As such, therefore, the Holy See still presents itself today, a friend - confident in the friendly response of all - to the Community of peoples; and it offers this Community its sincere and loyal contribution, in order that the deep aspiration of mankind may be fulfilled in a better and more certain way as a result of a joint effort: a peace established and strengthened in justice.

CHAPTER I

SPECIAL ADDRESSES

I - APPEAL FOR PEACE

Address of His Holiness Paul VI to the 20th Session of the General Assembly of the United Nations. New York, 4 October 1965.

Original: French (*)

(1) As we begin to speak to this audience that is unique in the whole world, we must first of all express our profound thanks to Mr. Thant, your Secretary General, who was kind enough to invite us to pay a visit to the United Nations on the occasion of the twentieth anniversary of this world institution for peace and collaboration between the nations of the whole world.

(2) We also want to thank the President of the Assembly, Signor Amintore Fanfani, who has had such kind words for us from the day on which he took over the office.

(3) We want to thank each of you here present for your kind welcome, and we offer you our cordial and respectful greetings. Your friendship has brought us to this gathering and admitted us to it. It is as a friend that we appear before you.

(4) In addition to our own respects, we bring you those of the Second Ecumenical Council of the Vatican, now meeting in Rome. The Cardinals who have accompanied us are its eminent representatives. In their name, as in our own, we pay honor to all of you and offer you greetings!

(5) This gathering, as you are all well aware, has a twofold nature: it is marked at one and the same time by simplicity and by greatness. By simplicity because the one who is speaking to you is a man like yourselves. He is your brother, and even one of the least among you who represent sovereign States, since he possesses - if you choose to consider us from this point of view - only a tiny and practically symbolic temporal sovereignty: the minimum needed in order to be free to exercise his spiritual mission and to assure those who deal with him that he is independent of any sovereignty of this world. He has no temporal power, no ambition to enter into competition with you. As a matter of fact, we have nothing to ask, no question to raise; at most a desire to formulate, a permission to seek: that of being allowed to serve you in the area of our competence, with disinterestedness, humility and love.

(6) This is the first declaration that we have to make. As you can see, it is so simple that it may seem insignificant for this assembly, which is used to dealing with extremely important and difficult affairs.

(7) And yet, as we were telling you, and you can all sense it, this moment bears the imprint of a unique greatness: it is great for us; it is great for you.

(8) For us, first of all. You know very well who we are, and whatever your opinion of the Pontiff of Rome may be, you know that our mission is to bring a message for all mankind. We speak not only in our own name and in the name of the great Catholic family, but also in the name of the Christian brethren who share in the sentiments we are expressing here, and especially of those who have been kind enough to designate us explicitly as their spokesman. This is the kind of messenger who, at the end of a long journey, is handing over the letter that has been entrusted to him. Hence we have an awareness of living through a privileged moment - brief though it be - when a wish borne in our heart for almost twenty centuries is being accomplished. Yes, you recall it. We have been on our way for a long time and we bring a long history with us. Here we are celebrating the epilogue to a laborious pilgrimage in search of an opportunity to speak heart to heart with the whole world. It began on the day when we were commanded: "Go, bring the good news to all nations." You are the ones who represent all nations.

(9) Permit us to say that we have a message, and a happy one, to hand over to each one of you.

(*) AAS 57(1965), 877-885.

(10) Our message is meant to be first of all a solemn moral ratification of this lofty Institution, and it comes from our experience of history. It is as an "expert on humanity" that we bring this Organization the support and approval of our recent predecessors, that of the Catholic hierarchy, and our own, convinced as we are that this Organization represents the obligatory path of modern civilization and world peace.

(11) In saying this, we are aware that we are speaking for the dead as well as the living: for the dead who have fallen in the terrible wars of the past, dreaming of world peace and harmony; for the living who have survived the wars and who in their hearts condemn in advance those who would try to have them repeated; for other living people too: the younger generation of today who are moving ahead trustfully with every right to expect a better mankind. We also want to speak for the poor, the disinherited, the unfortunate, those who long for justice, a dignified life, liberty, prosperity and progress. People turn to the United Nations as if it were their last hope for peace and harmony. We presume to bring here their tribute of honor and of hope along with our own. That is why this moment is a great one for you too.

(12) We know that you are fully aware of this. So listen now to the rest of our message, which is directed completely toward the future. This edifice that you have built must never again fall into ruins: it must be improved upon and adapted to the demands which the history of the world will make upon it. You mark a stage in the development of mankind. Henceforth, it is impossible to go back; you must go forward.

(13) You offer the many States which can no longer ignore each other a form of coexistence that is extremely simple and fruitful. First of all, you recognize them and distinguish them from *each other.* Now you certainly do not confer existence on States, but you do qualify each nation as worthy of being seated in the orderly assembly of peoples. You confer recognition of lofty moral and juridical value upon each sovereign national community and you guarantee it an honorable international citizenship. It is in itself a great service to the cause of mankind to define clearly and honor the nations that are the subjects of the world community and to set them up in a juridical position which wins them the recognition and respect of all, and which can serve as the basis for an orderly and stable system of international life. You sanction the great principle that relationships between nations must be regulated by reason, justice, law and negotiation, and not by force, violence, war, nor indeed by fear and deceit.

(14) This is as it should be. And permit us to congratulate you for having had the wisdom to open up access to this assembly to the young nations, the States that have only recently attained national independence and liberty. Their presence here is proof of the universality and magnanimity that inspire the principles of this Institution.

(15) This is as it should be. Such is our praise and our wish, and as you can see we are not reaching outside to find a basis for them. We are drawing them from within, from the very nature and spirit of your Institution.

(16) Your Charter goes even farther, and our message moves ahead with it. You are in existence and you are working in order to unite nations, to associate States. Let us use the formula: to bring them together *with each other.* You are an association, a bridge between peoples, a network of relations between States. We are tempted to say that in a way this characteristic of yours reflects in the temporal order what our Catholic Church intends to be in the spiritual order: one and universal. Nothing loftier can be imagined on the natural level, as far as the ideological structure of mankind is concerned. Your vocation is to bring not just some peoples but all peoples together as brothers. A difficult undertaking? Without a doubt. But this is the nature of your very noble undertaking. Who can fail to see the need and importance of thus gradually coming to the establishment of a world authority capable of taking effective action on the juridical and political planes?

(17) Again we repeat our wish: go forward! Even more, act in such a way as to bring back into your midst those who have separated themselves from you, and look for means to bring into your pact of brotherhood, honorably and loyally, those who do not yet belong. Act in such a way that those who are still outside will desire and deserve the confidence of everyone of you, and be generous in according it to them. And you who have the good fortune and honor to sit in this assembly of a peaceful community, listen to us: so act that this mutual confidence and trust that unites you and allows you to do great and good things may never be stained and never betrayed.

(18) The logic of this wish which pertains, you might say, to the structure of your organization leads us to complete it with other formulas, as follows. Let no one as a member of your organization be superior to others: *not one over the other.* This is the formula of equality. We know, of course, that there are other factors to be considered aside from mere membership in your organization, but equality is also a part of its constitution. Not that you are all equal, but here you make yourselves equal. And it may well be that for a number of you this calls for an act of great virtue. Permit us to tell you so, as the representative of a religion that works salvation through the humility of its divine Founder. It is impossible for someone to be a brother if he is not humble. For it is pride, as inevitable as it may seem, that provokes the tensions and struggles over prestige, over domination, over colonialism, over selfishness. It is pride that shatters brotherhood.

(19) Here our message reaches its culmination and we will speak first of all negatively. These are the words you are looking for us to say and the words we cannot utter without feeling aware of their seriousness and solemnity: *never again one against the other,* never, never again!

(20) Was not this the very end for which the United Nations came into existence: to be against war and for peace? Listen to the clear words of a great man who is no longer with us, John Kennedy, who proclaimed four years ago: "Mankind must put an end to war, or war will put an end to mankind." There is no need for a long talk to proclaim the main purpose of your Institution. It is enough to recall that the blood of millions, countless unheard-of sufferings, useless massacres and frightening ruins have sanctioned the agreement that unites you with an oath that ought to change the future history of the world: *never again war, never again war!* It is peace, peace, that has to guide the destiny of the nations of all mankind!

(21) All thanks and honor to you who have been working for peace for twenty years and have even given distinguished victims to this holy cause! All thanks and honor to you for the conflicts that you have prevented and for those that you have settled. The results of your efforts in behalf of peace right up to the last few days may not yet have been decisive, but still they deserve to have us step forward as spokesman for the whole world and express congratulations and gratitude to you in its name.

(22) Gentlemen, you have accomplished and are now in the course of accomplishing a great work: you are teaching men peace. The United Nations is the great school where people get this education and we are here in the assembly hall of this school. Anyone who takes his place here becomes a pupil and a teacher in the art of building peace. And when you go outside of this room, the world looks to you as the architects and builders of peace.

(23) As you know very well, peace is not built merely by means of politics and a balance of power and interests. It is built with the mind, with ideas, with the works of peace. You are working at this great endeavor, but you are only at the beginning of your labors. Will the world ever come to change the selfish and bellicose outlook that has spun out such a great part of its history up to now? It is hard to foresee the future, but easy to assert that the world has to set out resolutely on the path toward a new history, a peaceful history, one that will be truly and fully human, the one that God promised to men of good will. The pathways are marked out before you and the first one is disarmament.

(24) If you want to be brothers, let the arms fall from your hands. A person cannot love with offensive weapons in his hands. Arms, and especially the terrible arms that modern science has provided you, engender bad dreams, feed evil sentiments, create nightmares, hostilities, and dark resolutions even before they cause any victims and ruins. They call for enormous expenses. They interrupt projects of solidarity and of useful labor. They warp the outlook of nations. So long as man remains the weak, changeable, and even wicked being that he so often shows himself to be, defensive arms will, alas, be necessary. But your courage and good qualities urge you on to a study of means that can guarantee the security of international life without any recourse to arms.

This is an aim worthy of your efforts, and this is what peoples expect from you. This is what you have to achieve! And if it is to be done, everyone's confidence in this institution must increase and its authority must increase, and then, let us hope, its aim will be achieved. You will win the gratitude of the peoples of the world, who will be relieved of burdensome expenditures for armaments and delivered from the nightmare of ever-imminent war.

(25) We know - and how could we help rejoicing over this - that many of you have given favorable consideration to the invitation in behalf of peace that we issued to all nations from Bombay last December: to devote to the benefit of developing nations at least a part of the money that could be saved through a reduction of armaments. We want to repeat this suggestion now, with all the confidence inspired in us by your sentiments of humaneness and generosity.

(26) To speak of humaneness and generosity is to echo another constitutional principle of the United Nations, its positive summit: you are working here not just to eliminate conflicts between States, but to make it possible for States to work *for each other.* You are not content with facilitating coexistence between nations. You are taking a much bigger step forward, one worthy of our praise and our support: you are organizing fraternal collaboration between nations. You are establishing here a system of solidarity that will ensure that lofty civilizing goals receive unanimous and orderly support from the whole family of nations, for the good of each and all. This is the finest aspect of the United Nations Organization, its very genuine human side. This is the ideal that mankind dreams of during its pilgrimage through time; this is the greatest hope of the world. We would even venture to say that it is the reflection of the plan of God - a transcendent plan full of love - for the progress of human society on earth, a reflection in which we can see the Gospel message turning from something heavenly to something earthly. Here we seem to hear an echo of the voice of our predecessors, and especially of Pope John XXIII, whose message in *Pacem in Terris* met with such an honored and significant response among you.

(27) What you are proclaiming here are the basic rights and duties of man, his dignity, his liberty and above all his religious liberty. We feel that you are spokesmen for what is loftiest in human wisdom - we might almost say its sacred character - for it is above all a question of human life, and human life is sacred; no one can dare attack it. It is in your Assembly, even where the matter of the great problem of birth rates is concerned, that respect for life ought to find its loftiest profession and its most reasonable defense. Your task is so to act that there will be enough bread at the table of mankind and not to support an artificial birth control that would be irrational, with the aim of reducing the number of those sharing in the banquet of life.

(28) But it is not enough to feed the hungry. Each man must also be assured a life in keeping with his dignity, and that is what you are striving to do. Is this not the fulfillment before our eyes, and thanks to you, of the prophet's words that apply so well to your Institution:" They shall beat their swords into pruning-hooks" (Is. 2:4)? Are you not employing the prodigious forces of the earth and the magnificent inventions of science no longer as instruments of death, but as instruments of life for the new era of mankind?

(29) We know with what increasing intensity and effectiveness the United Nations Organization, and the world bodies dependent upon it, are working where needed to help governments speed up their economic and social progress.

(30) We know with what ardor you are working to conquer illiteracy and to spread culture in the world, to give men modern health service adapted to their needs, to put the marvelous resources of science, technology, and organization at the service of man. All this is magnificent and deserves everyone's praise and support including our own.

(31) We would also like to set an example ourself, even if the smallness of our means might prevent anyone from appreciating the practical and quantitative significance of it. We want to see our own charitable institutions undergo a new development in the struggle against hunger and toward meeting the main needs of the world. This is the way and the only way to build peace.

(32) One word more, Gentlemen, one last word. The edifice you are building does not rest on purely material and terrestrial foundations, for in that case it would be a house built on sand. It rests most of all upon consciences. Yes, the time has come for "conversion," for personal transformation, for interior renewal. We have to get used to a new way of thinking about man, a new way of thinking about man's community life, and, last of all, a new way of thinking about the pathways of history and the destinies of the world. As St. Paul says, we must "put on the new man, which has been created according to God in justice and holiness of truth" (*Eph.* 4:23).

(33) The hour has come when a pause, a moment of recollection, reflection, you might say of prayer, is absolutely needed so that we may think back over our common origin, our history, our common destiny. The appeal to the moral conscience of man has never before been as necessary as it is today, in an age marked by such great human progress. For the danger comes neither from progress nor from science; if these are used well they can, on the contrary, help to solve a great number of the serious problems besetting mankind. The real danger comes from man, who has at his disposal ever more powerful instruments that are as well fitted to bring about ruin as they are to achieve lofty conquests.

(34) To put it in a word, the edifice of modern civilization has to be built on spiritual principles, for they are the only ones capable not only of supporting it, but of shedding light on it and inspiring it. And we are convinced, as you know, that these indispensable principles of higher wisdom cannot rest on anything but faith in God. Is He the unknown God of whom St. Paul spoke to the Athenians on the Areopagus - unknown to those who, without suspecting it, were nevertheless looking for Him and had Him close beside them, as is the case with so many men of our times? For us, in any case, and for all those who accept the ineffable revelation that Christ has made to us of Him, He is the living God, the Father of all men.

II - PRESENCE OF THE CHURCH TO THE GREAT CAUSE OF WORK

Address of His Holiness Paul VI to the International Labour Organization on the occasion of its 50th anniversary. Geneva, 10 June 1969.

Original: French (*)

(35) 1. It is an honour and a joy for us to participate officially in this assembly in the solemn hour at which the International Labour Organization celebrates the fiftieth anniversary of its foundation. Why are we here? We do not belong to this international body, we are extraneous to the specific questions which have here their offices of study and halls of discussion, and our spiritual mission is not intended to intervene in matters outside its proper domain. If we are here, it is in order to respond to the invitation which you, Mr. Director-General, so kindly addressed to us. And we are happy to thank you publicly, to tell you how much we appreciated this very courteous gesture, how highly we rate its importance, and how great its significance appears to us.

(36) 2. Without any particular competence in the technical discussions on the defence and promotion of human labour, we are nevertheless no stranger to this great cause of labour for which this organization exists and to which you dedicate your energies.

(37) 3. From its very first page the Bible, of which we are the messenger, shows us creation as the result of the work of the Creator (*Gen.* 2:7), handed over to the work of His creature, whose intelligent efforts must develop it and perfect it, as it were, by humanizing it in his service (*Gen.* 1:29, *Populorum Progressio*, No. 22). Hence, according to the divine idea, work is the normal ac-

(*) AAS 61(1969), 491-502.

tivity of man (*Ps.* 105:23; *Eccl.* 7:15), and enjoying and rejoicing in its fruits is a gift of God (*Eccl.* 5:18), since each is quite naturally rewarded according to his works (*Ps.* 63:13 and 128:2; *Mt.* 16:27; *ICor.* 15:58; *IIThess.* 3:10).

4. Through the pages of the Bible, labour is seen as a basic fact of the human condition, so much so that, when He became one of us (*Jn.* 1:14), the Son of God also and at the same time became a worker, and was naturally referred to in His entourage by the profession of his family: Jesus was known as "the son of the carpenter" (*Mt.* 13:55). The labour of man thereby acquired the highest imaginable titles of nobility, and you have ensured their presence, in the place of honour at the headquarters of your Organization, in that admirable fresco by Maurice Denis, dedicated to the dignity of work, in which Christ brings the Good News to the workers who surround Him, who are themselves also sons of God and brothers to each other.

(38) 5. While there is no need for us to evoke the history of the birth and growth of your Organization, yet we cannot pass over in silence, in this hospitable land, the work of pioneers such as Bishop Mermillod and the Union of Fribourg, the admirable example given by the Protestant industrialist Daniel le Grand, and the fruitful initiative of the Catholic, Gaspard Decurtins, which was the first germ of an international conference on labour. And how could we forget that on the fortieth anniversary of Leo XIII.'s Encyclical on the condition of labour your first Director desired to render homage to "the tenacious workers for social justice, among them those who based themselves on the Encyclical *Rerum Novarum*" [Quoted by A. Le Roy: *Catholicisme social et Organisation Internationale du Travail* (Paris, Spes, 1937), p. 16]. And the officials of the International Labour Office, when drawing up the balance in *The International Labour Organization: The First Decade,* did not hesitate to recognize that "the great movement which was originated in the Roman Catholic Church by the Encyclical Rerum Novarum of 1891 has proved extremely fruitful" [*The International Labour Organisation: The First Decade* (London, Allen & Unwin, 1931), p. 359].

(39) 6. The sympathy of the Church towards your Organization, and for the whole world of labour, was unceasingly manifested from then on, most particularly in Pius XI's Encyclical *Quadragesimo Anno* (15 May 1931, No. 24), In Pius XII's address to the Governing Body of the International Labour Office (19 Nov. 1954), and in the Encyclical *Mater et Magistra* where John XXIII expressed his "heartfelt appreciation to the International Labour Organization, which... has been making its effective and precious contribution to the establishment in the world of a socio-economic order marked by justice and humanity, and one in which the lawful demands of the workers are recognized and defended" (15 May 1961, No. 103). We ourself had the pleasure of promulgating, at the close of the Vatican Ecumenical Council, the Pastoral Constitution *Gaudium et Spes* prepared by the bishops of the whole world. In it, the Church reaffirms the value of "the monumental amount of individual and collective effort", and also the primacy of the labour of men over "the other elements of economic life, for the latter have only the nature of tools", together with the inalienable rights and the duties which such a principle requires (Pastoral Constitution *Gaudium et Spes*, 7 Dec. 1965, Nos. 34, 67 and 68). Finally, our Encyclical *Populorum Progressio* took pains to make all aware that "the social question has become world-wide", and of the consequences that this involves for the integral and united development of peoples, that development which "is the new name for peace" (26 Mar. 1967, Nos. 3 and 76).

(40) 7. In other words, we are an attentive observer of the work you accomplish here, and more than that, a fervent admirer of the activity you carry on, and also a collaborator who is happy to have been invited to celebrate with you the existence, functions, achievements and merits of this world institution, and to do so as a friend. Nor do we wish to omit on this solemn occasion the other international institutions of Geneva, starting with the Red Cross, which are all well-deserving and laudable institutions to which we are glad to extend our respectful greetings and our warmest good wishes.

(41) 8. To us, who belong to an institution exposed to the wear of time for two thousand years, the fifty years untiringly dedicated to the International Labour Organization are a source of fruitful meditation. Everyone knows that such endurance is quite exceptional in the history of our century. The inevitable precariousness of human affairs, made even more evident and all-consuming by the acceleration of modern civilization, has not shaken your institution, to whose ideal we wish to render homage, namely "universal and lasting peace, based on social justice" (Constitution of the

International Labour Organization, Preamble). The ordeal of the disappearance of the League of Nations, to which it was organically bound, and the fact of the birth of the United Nations on another continent, far from taking away the needs for its existence, provided it rather with an opportunity, by means of the well-known Declaration of Philadelphia twenty-five years ago, to confirm and better define them, rooting them more deeply in the reality of society's progress. "All human beings, irrespective of race, creed or sex, have the right to pursue both their material well-being and their spiritual development in conditions of freedom and dignity, of economic security and equal opportunity" [Ibid. Annex, II *(a)*].

(42) 9. With all our heart we rejoice with you at the vitality of your fifty-year-old but still young institution, ever since its birth in the Peace Treaty of Versailles in 1919. Who can recount the work, the toil, the night watches so fruitful in courageous decisions of benefit to all workers as well as for the life of mankind, performed by all those who with great merit dedicated their talent and activity to this organization? Among all of these, we cannot omit to mention the first Director, Albert Thomas, and his present successor, David Morse. Nor can we omit to mention that at their request, and almost from the very beginning, a priest has always been included among those who constituted, constructed, sustained and served this outstanding institution. We are grateful to all for the work they have accomplished, and we express the wish that it may happily continue its complex and difficult mission which is truly providential for the greater good of modern society.

(43) 10. Those better informed than we are can say how great is the sum of the activities of the International Labour Organization during fifty years of existence, how imposing the results achieved by its 128 Conventions and its 132 Recommendations.

(44) 11. But there is a primordial fact of capital importance in this array of material which cannot be left unmentioned. Here - and this a decisive event in the history of civilization - here the labour of man is treated as a matter of basic concern. It was not always thus, as is well known, during the already long history of mankind. One may recall the ancient concept of labour (See, for example, Cicero: *De Officiis* 1:42), the disrepute it implied, the slavery it involved - that horrible plague of slavery which, unfortunately, has not yet entirely disappeared from the face of the earth. The modern concept, of which you are the heralds and defenders, is completely different. It is based on a fundamental principle which has been brought out conspicuously by Christianity: *in labour, it is man who comes first.* Whether he be an artist or an artisan, contractor, peasant or labourer, manual or intellectual, it is man who works, it is for man that he works. An end has been put to the priority of labour over the labourer, to the supremacy of technical and economical necessities over human needs. *Never again will work be superior to the worker, never again will work be against the worker; but always work will be for the worker, work will be in the service of man, of all men and of all of man.*

(45) 12. How can an observer avoid being impressed by seeing that this concept has been defined at the theoretically least favourable moment for the affirmation of the primacy of the human factor over the product of work, at the moment of the progressive introduction of the machine which multiplies inordinately the output of labour and tends to take its place? In an abstract vision of things, the work now accomplished by the machine and its energies, which are no longer supplied by the arm of man but by the formidable secret forces of tamed nature should, in the judgment of the modern world, so predominate as to eliminate concern for the labourer, who will often be freed from the extenuating and humiliating weight of a physical effort out of all proportion to his limited output. But this has not occurred. At the very moment of the triumph of technology and its gigantic effects on economic production, it is man who draws upon himself the concentrated attention of the philosopher, the sociologist and the politician. For in the final analysis there are no true riches but the riches of man. Now it is evident to all that the introduction of technique into the process of human activities would be to the detriment of man, if man did not always remain its master, and dominate its evolution. If "one must recognize in all justice the irreplaceable contribution made by the organization of labour and by the progress of industry to what development has accomplished" (*Populorum Progressio,* No. 26), still you recognize better than anyone else the evil results of what has been called the fragmentation of labour in contemporary industrial society [Cf. G. Friedmann: *Où va le travail humain* (Paris, Gallimard, 1950) and idem, *The anatomy of Work, The Implications of Specialization* (translated by W. Rawson)(London, Heinemann, 1961)]. Instead of helping man become more of a man it dehumanizes him; instead of expanding him, it stifles him under a cloak of heavy boredom. Work is still ambivalent, and its organization may easily depersonalize the one who performs it, if he becomes its slave, abdicates intelligence and freedom, and even loses his dignity through it (*Mater et Magistra,* No. 83; *Populorum Progressio,* No. 28). Who does not see that work, which gives rise to marvellous fruits when it is truly creative, can also (Cf. *Ex.* 1:8-14), when caught up in the cycle of arbitrary will, injustice, rapacity and violence, become a real social scourge, as is attested by those labour camps, organized as institutions, which have been the shame of the civilized world.

(46) 13. Who can describe the sometimes terrible drama of the modern worker, torn by his twofold destiny as the source of grandiose achievements, too often tormented by the intolerable sufferings of a miserable proletarian condition, in which hunger is joined to social degradation to create a state of real insecurity, both personal and family? You have understood this. It is labour as a human, prime and fundamental fact which constitutes the vital root of your Organization and makes it into a magnificent tree, which extends its branches throughout the whole world because of its international character, a tree which is the honour of our times, with an ever fertile root which nourishes it in continual organic activity. It is that same root which forbids you to favour particular interests and places you in the service of the common good. It constitutes your special genius and its fecundity; that of intervening always and everywhere to supply remedies for labour conflicts, avert them if possible, give spontaneous aid to victims, work out new protection against new dangers, improve the conditions of workers while respecting the objective equilibrium of real economic possibilities, struggle against any form of segregation which generates inferiority on any ground - slavery, caste, race, religion or class - in a word, to defend for all and against all, the freedom of all workers, and secure lasting victory for the ideal of brotherhood among men, all equal in dignity.

(47) 14. Such is your vocation. Your action is based, not on an unavoidable and implacable struggle between those who supply work and those who execute it, nor on the partiality of those who defend interests and functions. On the contrary, it is a freely organized and socially disciplined and organic participation in the responsibilities and in the profits of work. It has a single aim: not money, not power, but the good of man. It is more than an economic concept, it is better than a political concept: it is a moral and human concept which inspires you, namely social justice, to be built up, day by day, freely and of common accord. Discovering ever more completely whatever the good of the workers requires, you make others aware of it little by little, and propose it to all as an ideal. More than this, you translate it into new rules of social conduct, which impose themselves as norms of law. Thus you ensure a permanent passage from the ideal order of principles to the juridical order, that is, to positive law. In a word, you gradually refine and improve the moral conscience of mankind. This is an arduous and delicate task indeed, but it is so lofty and so necessary, and calls for the collaboration of all true friends of man. How then could we not give it our adherence and our support?

(48) 15. Along your way, obstacles to be removed and difficulties to be surmounted will not be lacking. But you have foreseen this, and to confront them you have recourse to an instrument and a method which could, of themselves, suffice as a justification for your institution. Your original and organic instrument is to bring together the three forces at work in the human dynamics of modern labour: men of government, employers, and workers. And your method, that has become a model, is to harmonize these three forces, so that they do not oppose each other, but combine "in a courageous and productive collaboration" (Pius XII, Address to the Governing Body of the ILO. See below, par. 324), by means of constant dialogue for the study and solution of ever renewed and recurring problems.

(49) 16. This excellent modern concept fully deserves to replace once and for all that concept which has unfortunately dominated our epoch, emphasizing efficiency at the cost of agitation which too often generates new sufferings and ruins, thus risking the loss rather than the consolidation of the results obtained at the price of sometimes dramatic struggles. It must be solemnly proclaimed: labour conflicts cannot be remedied by artificially imposed conditions which fraudulently deprive the worker and the whole social community of their first and inalienable human prerogative, which is freedom. Nor can they be remedied by solutions which result solely from the free play - as it is called - of the determinism of economic factors. Such remedies may indeed have an appearance of justice, but they do not possess its human reality. It is only when the deepest reasons of these conflicts are understood, and the just claims they express are satisfied, that you can avert their dramatic explosion and avoid its ruinous consequences. Let us repeat, in the words of Albert Thomas: "The social factor must take precedence over the economic factor; it must regulate and guide it, in the highest cause of justice" (*The International Labour Organization: The First Decade,* op. cit., Preface, p. XII). That is why the International Labour Organization offers today, in that closed arena of the modern world in which interests and ideologies are dangerously opposed, an open road towards a better future for mankind. Perhaps more than any other institution, you can contribute to this, quite simply, by being actively and inventively true to your ideal: *universal peace through social justice.*

(50) 17. It is for this reason that we have come here to give you our encouragement and our agreement, to invite you also to persevere tenaciously in your mission of justice and peace, to assure you of our humble but sincere fellowship. For it is the peace of the world which is at stake, and the future of mankind. This future can only be built up by peace among all the human families at work, between classes and peoples, a peace which rests upon an ever more perfect justice among all men (Cf. *Pacem in Terris; Populorum Progressio,* No. 76).

(51) 18. In this stormy hour of mankind's history, full of peril but also filled with hope, it is in large measure for you to build justice and thus to ensure peace. Do not think that your task is ended; on the contrary, it daily becomes more urgent. How many and what terrible evils, how many deficiencies, abuses, injustices, sufferings, laments, still rise up from the world of labour! Allow us in your presence to act as interpreter of all those who suffer unjustly, who are unworthily exploited, outrageously scorned in body and soul, debased by a degrading work systematically willed, organized and imposed upon them. *Hear this cry of sorrow which still rises up from suffering humanity*!

(52) 19. Struggle, courageously and untiringly, against the abuses which are ever reborn, the injustices ever renewed; induce particular interests to submit to the wider vision of the common good; adapt older provisions to new needs, develop new provisions, urge nations to ratify them; and take the means to ensure their respect, for "it would be vain to proclaim human rights if, at the same time everything were not done to ensure the duty of respecting them, *respect by everyone, at all times and for all men*" (Message to the International Conference on Human Rights, Teheran, 15 Apr. 1968. See below, Par. 413).

(53) 20. We presume to add this: *It is against himself that you must defend man,* for man is threatened with becoming only a part of himself, with being reduced, as has been said, to one dimension only [Cf. H. Marcuse: *One-Dimensional Man: Studies on the Ideology of Advanced Industrial Society* (Boston, Beacon Press, 1964)]. At all costs he must be prevented from becoming only the mechanized servant of a blind machine which devours the best of himself, or of a State tempted to subject all energies to its service alone. It is man that you must protect, man carried away by the formidable forces which he unleashes and, as it were, swallowed up by the gigantic progress of his work, man swept along by the irresistible current of his inventions and, as it were, stunned by the growing contrast between the prodigious increase of the goods at his disposal, and their distribution, so easily made unjustly, between men and between peoples. The myth of Prometheus casts its disquieting shadow over the drama of our times, when the conscience of man is failing to raise itself up to the level of his activity, and to assume its serious responsibilities, faithful to the design of God's love for the world. Have we forgotten the lesson of the tragic story of the Tower of Babel, when the conquest of nature by men forgetful of God was accompanied by the disintegration of human society? (*Gen.* 11:1-9).

(54) 21. Overcoming all the destructive forces of contestation and "babelization", it is the city of men which must be built up, a city of which the sole durable cement is fraternal love between races and peoples as well as between classes and generations. Through those conflicts which rend our era it is not so much a claim to *have,* as it is a lawful desire to *be,* which is ever more strongly affirmed (*Populorum Progressio,* Nos. 1 and 8). For fifty years you have woven an ever closer fabric of juridical rules which protect the labour of men, women and youth, ensuring its proper remuneration. Now you must take steps to ensure the organic participation of all workers, not only in the fruits of their labour, but also in the economic and social responsibilities upon which their future and the future of their children depend (Cf. *Gaudium et Spes,* No. 68).

(55) 22. You must also ensure the participation of all peoples in the building of the world, and take thought now for the less favoured, just as yesterday your first care was for the least favoured social categories. This means that *your legislative work must continue boldly and strike out resolutely along new paths,* to guarantee the common right of peoples to their integral development and enable in each instance "all peoples to become the artisans of their destiny" (*Populorum Progressio,* No. 65). This challenge is made to you today, at the dawn of the Second Development Decade. It is for you to take it up. It is for you to take the decisions which will avert the disappointment of such great hopes, and disarm the temptations of destructive violence. *You must express in rules of law that solidarity which is becoming ever more definite in the consciences of men.* Just as, yesterday, you guaranteed by your legislation the protection and survival of the weak against the power of the strong - for, as Lacordaire said long ago, "Between the strong and the weak, it is freedom which oppresses and law which sets free" [52nd Conference de Notre-Dame, Lent, 1848, in *Oeuvres,* of Fr. Lacordaire (Paris, Poussielgue, 1872), Vol. IV, p. 494] - so now and henceforth you must master the rights of strong peoples, and favour the development of weak peoples, by creating the conditions, not only theoretical but practical, *for a real international law of labour, as between the peoples.* Like each man, so too each people must be able by its work to develop itself, to grow in humanity, to pass from less humane conditions to more humane ones (Cf. *Populorum Progressio,* Nos. 15 and 20). For this, appropriate conditions and means are necessary, and a common will, of which your Conventions, freely worked out between governments, workers and employers could and should progressively provide the proper expression. Several specialized organizations are already at work to construct this great edifice. It is upon this path that you must advance.

(56) 23. In other words, even though technical arrangements are indispensable, yet they cannot bear fruit without an awareness of the universal common good which animates and inspires research and sustains efforts, without this ideal which urges all to rival each other in building a world of brotherhood. This world of tomorrow will have to be built up by the youth of today, but it is for you to prepare them for this. Many of them receive insufficient training, and have no real possibility of learning a trade and finding work. Many, too, have jobs which have no meaning for them, the monotonous repetition of which may indeed secure profit for them, but cannot suffice to give them a *reason for living,* to satisfy their lawful aspiration to take their place as men in society. Who has not sensed, in the rich countries, their anxiety at the invasion of technocracy, their rejection of a society which has not succeeded in integrating them into itself; and, in poor countries their lament that, for lack of sufficient training and fitting means, they cannot make their generous contribution to the tasks which call for it? In the present changing world, their protest resounds like a cry of suffering and an appeal for justice. Amid the crisis which shakes modern civilization, the expectation of youth is anxious and impatient: let us strive to open up for them the paths of the future, offer them useful tasks and prepare them for their performance. There is so much to be done in this domain. However, you are well aware of this, and we congratulate you on having included in the programme of your 53rd Session the study of special youth employment and training schemes for development purposes [ILO: *Special Youth Employment and Training Schemes for Development Purposes,* Report VIII (1), International Labour Conference, 53rd Session, Geneva 1969 (Geneva 1968)].

(57) 24. A vast programme, Gentlemen, well capable of arousing your enthusiasm and galvanizing all your energy, in the service of that great cause which is yours - and also ours - the cause of man. In this peaceful combat, the disciples of Christ intend to take part with all their heart. For, if it is important that all human forces work together for this promotion of man, then the spirit must be put in the place proper to it, in the first place, because the Spirit is Love. Is this not clear? This work of construction surpasses the strength of man alone. But, as the Christian knows, he is not alone with his brothers in this work of love, of justice and of peace, in which he sees the preparation and pledge of that eternal city which he awaits from the grace of God. Man is not left to himself in a lonely crowd. The city of men which he is building is that of a family of brothers, of children of the same Father, sustained in their efforts by a strength which animates and supports them, the force of the Spirit; a mysterious but real strength, not magic, nor totally unknown to our experience, both historical and personal, for it has expressed itself in human words. And its voice resounds more clearly than elsewhere in this house, which is open to the sufferings and anxieties of the workers, as well as to its achievements and its marvellous attainments; it is a voice whose ineffable echo unceasingly arouses, today as it did yesterday and ever will, the hope of men at work: "Come to me, all who labour and are heavy laden, and I will give you rest"; "Blessed are those who hunger and thirst for righteousness, for they shall be satisfied" (*Mt.* 11:28 and 5:10).

III - BROTHERLY LOVE AND SOLIDARITY CAN BRING ABOUT A NEW WORLD

Address of His Holiness Paul VI to the 15th Session of the Conference of the Food and Agriculture Organization, on the occasion of His visit to the Headquarters of the Organization. Rome, 16 November 1970.

Original: French (*)

(58) 1. It is a profound joy for us - also an honour - to bring in our turn to this rostrum the debt of gratitude and the cry of anguish and hope of millions of men and women, on this twenty-fifth anniversary of FAO. What a road has been travelled since that far-off day, the sixteenth of October 1945, when the representatives of forty-four States were invited to sign the act which set up the United Nations Organization for Food and Agriculture. Historians will point out the remarkable accomplishments of FAO, its progressive influence, its unflagging dynamism, the boldness of its views, the variety and breadth of its activities - since "it is above all else an institution orientated to action" (*FAO, son rôle, sa structure, ses activités*, Rome, Pub. FAO, 1970) - the courage of its pioneers and finally the love of man and the universal sense of brotherhood which are the driving force behind its undertakings. They will point out also the extraordinary challenge thrust at you today: as your efforts increase and become organized, so the number of men multiplies, the misery of many is intensified and while a small number of people is sated with ever-increasing and ever diversified resources, an ever greater part of mankind continues to hunger for bread and education and to thirst for dignity. The first decade of development - it would be vain to conceal it - was marked by a certain disenchantment of public opinion in the face of frustrated hopes. Would it thus be the case, as with Sisyphus, to grow tired of rolling the heavy stone and give in to despair?

(59) 2. Such an idea could not be expressed in these precincts, in this meeting of persons who face the future with the aims of harnessing it for the service of mankind, notwithstanding the obstacles which may present themselves along the way. From the time of his first meeting with FAO, our predecessor Pope Pius XII highly praised the deep insight "of your institution, specialized for food and agriculture, the magnanimity which characterizes its economy and application, and finally the wisdom and the circumspect method which determine its realization." (Allocution of 21 February 1948, *Discorsi e Radiomessaggi di S.S. Pio XII*, vol. IX, Tipografia Poliglotta Vaticana, p. 461). His successor, good Pope John XXIII, would seize every opportunity to express to you his sincere admiration. (Cf. in particular, Encyclical *Mater et Magistra*, 15 May 1961, AAS 53(1961), p. 439). For our part, we first knew the International Institute of Agriculture in its modest quarters in Villa Borghese, before seeing FAO "traverse the entire road which has led it to the magnificent developments which it knows today." (Address to the 12th International Conference of FAO. 23 November 1963. See below, Par. 2000). From that time on we have not ceased to follow with sympathetic interest your generous and disinterested initiatives - particularly the campaign against hunger - to render homage to your many activities and to call upon the Catholics of the entire world to collaborate generously therein, together with all men of good will. (Cf. in particular, En-

(*) AAS 62(1970), 830-838

cyclical *Populorum Progressio*, 26 March 1967, n. 46, AAS 59(1967), p. 280). Today we are happy to come to the headquarters of your Organization, situated within the very territory of our Diocese of Rome, and thus to return to FAO the many visits which the members of your working sessions have paid to the Vatican.

(60) How could the Church, solicitous for the true good of men, not be interested in an activity so clearly orientated as is yours to the alleviation of the greatest distress? How could the Church not be interested in your activity, which is engaged in a merciless combat to provide each man with enough to live - to live a truly human life, to be capable by his own work of guaranteeing the upkeep of his family and to be able through the exercise of his intelligence to share in the common good of society by a commitment freely agreed to and by an activity voluntarily assumed? (Cf., for example, Rev. L.-J. Lebret, O.P., *Dévelopment - Révolution Solidaire*, Paris, Editions Ouvrières, 1967). It is at this higher level that the Church intends to give you her disinterested support for the great and complex work which you carry out. Your work consists in stimulating international action for providing each person with the nourishment he needs, both in amount and quality, and thus promoting the progressive lessening of hunger, undernourishment and malnutrition. (Cf. for example, Josue de Castro, *Le livre noir de la faim*, Paris, Ed. Ouvrières, 1961). It means eliminating the cause of many epidemics, preparing trained labour and finding for it necessary employment so that economic growth may be accompanied by social progress without which there is no true development.

(61) 3. By what means do you intend to attain these goals, which we approve with all our heart? The absorbing study - as we can well describe it - of the many dossiers furnished us on your multiple activities have revealed to us the extraordinary and growing complexity of your efforts organized on a world-wide scale. A more intelligent utilization of basic physical resources, a better use of land and water, forest and oceans, an increased productivity from farming, livestock raising and fishing - all this certainly provides commodities in greater quantity and better quality. At the same time nutritional needs grow under the double pressure of a demographic increase - at times very swift - and of a consumption whose graphic curve follows the progression of income. The improvement of soil fertility, the intelligent use of irrigation, the redivision of plots of land, the reclaiming of marshes, the effort at plant selection and the introduction of high-yield grain varieties almost seem to fulfil the vision of the ancient prophet of the agricultural era: "The desert shall rejoice and blossom." (Cf. *Is.* 35:1). But the carrying out of these technical possibilities at an accelerated pace is not accomplished without dangerous repercussions on the balance of our natural surroundings. The progressive deterioration of that which has generally come to be called the environment, risks provoking a veritable ecological catastrophe. Already we see the pollution of the air we breathe, the water we drink. We see the pollution of rivers, lakes, even oceans - to the point of inspiring fear of a true "biological death" in the near future, if energetic measures are not immediately and courageously taken and rigorously put into practice. It is a formidable prospect which you must diligently explore in order to save from destruction the fruit of millions of years of natural and human selection. (Cf. *Cérès*, Revue FAO, vol. 3, No. 3, Rome, May-June 1970: *Environment: les raisons de l'alarme*). In brief, everything is bound up together. You must be attentive to the great consequences which follow on every intervention by man in the balance of nature, whose harmonious richness has been placed at his disposal in accordance with the living design of the Creator. (Cf., for example, *Ps.* 64: 10-14).

(62) 4. These problems surely are familiar to you. We have wished to evoke them briefly before you only in order to underline better the urgent need of a radical change in the conduct of humanity if it wishes to assure its survival. It took millennia for man to learn how to dominate, "to subdue the earth" according to the inspired word of the first book of the Bible (*Gen.* 1:28). The hour has now come for him to dominate his domination; this essential undertaking requires no less courage and dauntlessness than the conquest of nature itself. Will the prodigious progressive mastery of plant, animal and human life and the discovery of even the secrets of matter lead to anti-matter and to the explosion of death? In this decisive moment of its history, humanity hesitates, uncertain before fear and hope. Who still does not see this? The most extraordinary scientific progress, the most astounding technical feats and the most amazing economic growth, unless accompanied by authentic moral and social progress, will in the long run go against man.

(63) 5. Well-being is within our grasp but we must want to build it together: individuals for others, individuals with others and, never again, individuals against others. Over and above the magnificent achievements of these twenty-five years of activity is not the essential acquisition of your Organization this: the consciousness acquired by peoples and their governments of international solidarity? Are you not, sometimes without knowing it, the heirs of Christ's compassion before suffering humanity: "I feel sorry for all these people"? (*Mt.* 15:32). Do you not constitute by your very existence an effective denial of the discredited thought of ancient wisdom "Homo homini lupus"? (Plautus, *Asinaria*, II, 4,88). No, man is not a wolf to his fellowman; he is his compassionate and loving brother. Never in the millennial course of the inspiring adventure of man have so many peoples, so many men and women, delegated such a number of representatives with the unique mission of aiding men - all men - to live and to survive. For us this is one of the greatest motives of hope amidst the many threats that weigh upon the world. Those who in the years 2000 will bear the responsibility of the destiny of the great human family are being born into a world which has discovered, more to its advantage than to its disadvantage, its solidarity in good as well as evil, its desire to unite in order not to perish and, in brief, "to work together to build a common future for humanity." (Cf. Appeal in Bombay, 3 December 1964, AAS 57(1965), p. 132; repeated in *Populorum Progressio*, No. 43, AAS 59(1961), p. 447). We hope that soon the circle of your family will widen and that the peoples that are now absent from this meeting may also sit down at your table so that finally all may contribute together to the same unselfish goal.

(64) 6. Certainly in the face of the difficulties to be overcome there is a great temptation to use one's authority to diminish the number of guests rather than to multiply the bread that is to be shared. We are not at all unaware of the opinions held in international organizations which extol planned birth control which, it is believed, will bring a radical solution to the problems of developing countries. We must repeat this today: the Church, on her part, in every domain of human action encourages scientific and technical progress, but always claiming respect for the inviolable rights of the human person whose primary guarantors are the public authorities. Being firmly opposed to a birth control which according to the just expression of our venerable predecessor Pope John XXIII would be accomplished with "methods and means which are unworthy of man," (*Mater et Magistra*, AAS 53(1961), p. 447) the Church calls all those responsible to work with fearlessness and generosity for the development of the whole man and every man; this, among other effects, will undoubtedly favour a rational control of birth by couples who are capable of freely assuming their destiny. On your part, it is man whom you help and whom you support. And how would you ever be able to act against him, because you do not exist except through him and for him and since you cannot succeed without him?

(65) 7. One of the best assured invariable principles of your action is that the finest technical achievements and the greatest economic progress cannot effect by themselves the development of a people. However necessary they may be, planning and money are not enough. Their indispensable contribution, like that of the technology which they sponsor, would be sterile were it not made fruitful by men's confidence and their progressive conviction that they can little by little get away from their miserable condition through work made possible with means at their disposal. The immediate evidence of results creates, as well as legitimate satisfaction, the decisive commitment to the great work of development. In the long run, if nothing can be done without man, with him everything can be undertaken and accomplished; it is truly the spirit and the heart that first achieve true victories. As soon as those concerned have the will to better their lot, without doubting their ability to do it, they give themselves fully to this great cause, with all the gifts of intellect and courage, all the virtues of abnegation and self-sacrifice, all the efforts of perseverance and mutual help of which they are capable.

(66) 8. The young in particular are the first to give themselves with all their typical enthusiasm and earnestness to an undertaking which fits their capabilities and their generosity. The youth of the rich countries, bored because they lack an ideal worthy of claiming their support and galvanizing their energies, the youth of the poor countries, in despair at not being able to work in a useful way, because they lack the proper knowledge and the required professional training: there can be no doubt that the combination of these young resources can change the future of the world, if we adults can prepare them for this great task, show them how to approach it and furnish them with the means to give themselves to it with success. Is not this a plan that will claim the support of all young people, rich and poor, transform their outlooks, overcome enmity between nations, heal sterile divisions and finally bring about a new world: a world that will know brotherly love and solidarity in effort because it will be united in the pursuit of the same ideal - a fruitful world for all men?

(67) 9. A lot of money would be necessary, certainly. But will the world not finally grasp that it is a question of its future? "When so many peoples are hungry, when so many families are destitute, when so many men remain steeped in ignorance, when so many schools, hospitals, and homes worthy of the name remain to be built, all public and private expenditures prompted by motives of national or personal ostentation, every debilitating armaments' race becomes an intolerable scandal. It is our duty to denounce it. Would that those in authority would listen to us, before it is too late!" (*Populorum Progressio*, No 53, AAS 59(1967), p. 283). How is it possible not to experience a deep feeling of distress in face of the tragic absurdity which impels men - and whole nations - to devote vast sums to armaments, to fostering centres of discord and rivalry, to carrying out undertakings of pure prestige, when the enormous sums thus wasted would have been enough, if better employed, to rescue numbers of countries from poverty? It is a sad fate which weights so heavily upon the human race: the poor and the rich are for once treading the same path. Exaggerated nationalism, racism engendering hate, the lust for unlimited power, the unbridled thirst for domination: who will convince men to emerge from such aberrations? Who will be the first to break the circle of the armaments' race, ever more ruinous and vain? Who will have the good sense to put an end to such nonsensical practices as the brake sometimes applied to certain agricultural products because of badly organized transport and markets? Will man, who has learned how to harness the atom and conquer space, finally succeed in conquering his selfishness? UNCTAD - we like to hope - will succeed in putting an end to the scandal of rich countries buying at the lowest possible prices the produce of poor countries, and selling their own produce to these poor countries at a very high price. There is a whole economy, too often tainted by power, waste and fear, which must be transformed into an economy of service and brotherhood.

(68) 10. In view of the worldwide scale of the problem, there can be no fitting solution except on the international level. In saying this we do not in any way mean to belittle the many generous initiatives both private and public - suffice it to mention our indefatigable *Caritas Internationalis* - whose spontaneous appearance keeps alert and stimulates so much disinterested good will. Quite the contrary. But, as we said in New York, with the same conviction as our reverend predecessor John XXIII in his encyclical *Pacem in Terris*: "Who can fail to see the need and importance of thus gradually coming to the establishment of a world authority capable of taking effective action on the juridical and political planes?" [Address to the General Assembly of the UN, 4 October 1965, AAS 57(1965), p. 880. See above, Par. 16). This you have in fact understood, and you have undertaken this World Indicative Plan for agricultural development (PIM), which intended to integrate in one worldwide view all the various factors in this sphere. There is no doubt that freely entered into agreements between States will assist its being put into practice. Nor is there any doubt that the transition from selfish and exclusive profit-based economies to an economy which will voluntarily undertake the satisfaction of mutual needs calls for the adoption of an international law based on justice and equity, at the service of a truly human universal order. (Cf. M.F. Perroux, *De l'avarice des nations à une économie du genre humain*, in 39.e Semaine Sociale de France, *Richesse et Misère*, Paris, Gabalda, 1952, p. 195-212).

(69) It is therefore necessary to be brave, bold, preserving and energetic. So many lands still lie fallow, so many possibilities remain unexplored, so many human resources are as yet untapped, so many young people stand idle, so much energy is squandered. Your task, your responsibility and your honour will be to make these latent resources bear fruit, to awaken their powers and to direct them to the service of the common good. Here lie the breadth, the vastness, the urgency and the necessity of your role. Among responsible statesmen, publicists, educators, scientists, civil servants - indeed among all men - you must untiringly promote study and action on a world scale, while all believing men add their prayers to "God who gives the growth." (*ICor*. 3: 6-7) Already there are appearing important results, which yesterday were still unhoped for, but which today are the guarantee of solid hope. In these recent days who has not acclaimed as a symbol the award of the Nobel Prize for Peace to Norman Borlaug, "the father of the green revolution", as he is called? How true it is that if all men of good will throughout the world could be mobilized in a concerted effort for peace, the tragic temptation to resort to violence could then be overcome.

(70) 11. More than one, perhaps, will shake his head at such prospects. Yet, permit us to say it plainly, on the human, moral and spiritual level which is ours: no strategy of a commercial or ideological nature will soothe the complaint which rises from those who are suffering from "undeserved misery." (*Populorum Progressio*, No. 9, AAS 59(1967), p. 261) as the young, whose "protest resounds like a signal of suffering and an appeal for justice." (Address to the ILO, for its 50th anniversary, 10 June 1969, AAS 61(1969), p. 502. See above, Par. 56). If need and self-interest are powerful and often decisive motives for men's actions, the present crisis can only be surmounted by love. For, if "social justice makes us respect the common good, social charity makes us love it." (Rev. J.-T. Delos, O.P., *Le bien commun international*, in 24.e Semaine Sociale de France, *Le désordre de l'économie internationale et la pensée chretienne*, Paris, Gabalda, 1932, p. 210) "Charity, that is to say brotherly love, is the driving force behind all social progress." (Cardinal P.-E. Leger, in *Le pauvre Lazare est à notre porte*, Paris-Montreal, SOSFides, 1967, p. 13). Preoccupations of a military nature and motives of the economic order will never permit the satisfaction of the grave demands of the men of our time. There must be love for man: man devotes himself to the service of his fellowmen, because he recognizes him as his brother, as the son of the same Father; and the Christian will add: as the image of the suffering Christ, whose word moves man in his most hidden depths: "I was hungry and you gave me to eat...." (*Mt.* 25:35). This word of love is ours. We present it to you as our most precious treasure, the lamp of charity whose burning fire consumes hearts, whose shining flame lights the way of brotherhood and guides our steps along the paths of justice and of peace (*Ps.* 85: 11-14)

IV - DIGNITY OF HUMAN PERSON FOUNDED ON JUSTICE AND PEACE

Address of His Holiness John Paul II to the 34th Session of the General Assembly of the United Nations. New York, 2 October 1979.

Original: English (*)

(71) 1. I desire to express my gratitude to the General Assembly of the United Nations, which I am permitted today to participate in and to address. My thanks go in the first place to the Secretary General of the United Nations Organization, Dr. Kurt Waldheim. Last autumn, soon after my election to the Chair of Saint Peter, he invited me to make this visit, and he renewed his invitation in the course of our meeting in Rome last May. From the first moment I felt greatly honoured and deeply obliged. And today, before this distinguished Assembly, I also thank you, Mr. President, who have so kindly welcomed me and invited me to speak.

(72) 2. *The formal reason for my intervention* today is, without any question, the special bond of cooperation that links the Apostolic See with the United Nations Organization, as is shown by the presence of the Holy See's Permanent Observer to this Organization. The existence of this bond, which is held in high esteem by the Holy See, rests on the sovereignty with which the Apostolic See has been endowed for many centuries. The territorial extent of that sovereignty is limited to the small State of Vatican City, but the sovereignty itself is warranted by the need of the papacy to exercise its mission in full freedom, and to be able to deal with any interlocutor, whether a government or an international organization, without dependence on other sovereignties. Of course the nature and aims of the spiritual mission of the Apostolic See and the Church make their par-

(*) AAS 71(1979), 1143-1160.

ticipation in the tasks and activities of the United Nations Organization very different from that of the States, which are communities in the political and temporal sense.

(73) 3. Besides attaching great importance to its collaboration with the United Nations Organization, *the Apostolic See has always, since the foundation of your Organization, expressed its esteem for and its agreement* with the historic significance of this supreme forum for the international life of humanity today. It also never ceases to support your Organization's functions and initiatives, which are aimed at peaceful coexistence and collaboration between nations. There are many proofs of this. In the more than thirty years of the existence of the United Nations Organization, it has received much attention in papal messages and encyclicals, in documents of the Catholic episcopate, and likewise in the Second Vatican Council. Pope John XXIII and Pope Paul VI looked with confidence on your important institution as an eloquent and promising sign of our times. He who is now addressing you has, since the first months of his pontificate, several times expressed the same confidence and conviction as his predecessors.

(74) 4. This confidence and conviction on the part of the Apostolic See is the result, as I have said, not of merely political reasons but of the religious and moral character of *the mission of the Roman Catholic Church.* As a universal community embracing faithful belonging to almost all countries and continents, nations, peoples, races, languages and cultures, the Church is deeply interested in the existence and activity of *the Organization* whose very name tells us that it *unites and associates* nations and States. It unites and associates: it does not divide and oppose. It seeks out the ways for understanding and peaceful collaboration, and endeavours with the means at its disposal and the methods in its power to exclude war, division and mutual destruction within the great family of humanity today.

(75) 5. This is the real reason, *the essential reason*, for my presence among you, and I wish to thank this distinguished Assembly for giving consideration to this reason, which can make my presence among you in some way useful. It is certainly a highly significant fact that among the representatives of the States, whose *raison d'être* is the sovereignty of powers linked with territory and people, there is also today the representative of the Apostolic See and the Catholic Church. This Church is the Church of Jesus Christ, who declared before the tribunal of the Roman judge Pilate that he was a king, but with a kingdom not of this world (cf. *Jn.* 18:36-37). When he was then asked about the reason for the existence of his kingdom among men, he explained: "For this I was born, and for this I have come into the world, to bear witness to the truth" (*Jn.* 18:37). Here, *before the representatives of the States*, I wish not only to thank you but also to offer my special *congratulations*, since the invitation extended to the Pope to speak in your Assembly shows that *the United Nations Organization accepts and respects* the religious and moral dimension of those human problems that the Church attends to, in view of the message of truth and love that it is her duty to bring to the world. The questions that concern your functions and receive your attention - as is indicated by the vast organic complex of institutions and activities that are part of or collaborate with the United Nations, especially in the fields of culture, health, food, labour, and the peaceful uses of nuclear energy - certainly make it essential for us *to meet in the name of man in his wholeness*, in all the fullness and manifold riches of his spiritual and material existence, as I have stated in my encyclical *Redemptor Hominis*, the first of my pontificate.

(76) 6. Now, availing myself of the solemn occasion of my meeting with the representatives of the nations of the earth, I wish above all to send my greetings to all the men and women living on this planet. To every man and every woman, without any exception whatever. Every human being living on earth is a member of a civil society, of a nation, many of them represented here. Each one of you, distinguished ladies and gentlemen, represents a particular State, system and political structure, but what you represent above all are *individual human beings*; you are all *Representatives of men and women, of practically all the people of the world*, individual men and women, communities and peoples who are living the present phase of their own history and who are also part of the history of humanity as a whole, each of them a subject endowed with dignity as a human person, with his or her own culture, experiences and aspirations, tensions and sufferings, and legitimate expectations. This relationship is what provides the reason for *all political activity*, whether national or international, for in the final analysis this activity comes *from man*, is exercised *by man* and is *for man*. And if political activity is cut off from this fundamental relationship and finality, if it becomes in a way its own end, it loses much of its reason to exist. Even more, it can also give rise to a specific alienation; it can become extraneous to man; it can come to contradict humanity itself. In reality, what justifies the existence of any political activity is service to man, concerned and responsible attention to the essential problems and duties of his earthly existence in its social dimension and significance, on which also the good of each person depends.

(77) 7. I ask you, ladies and gentlemen, to excuse me for speaking of questions that are certainly self-evident to you. But it does not seem pointless to speak of them, since the most frequent pitfall for human activities is the possibility of losing sight, while performing them, of the clearest truths, the most elementary principles.

(78) I would like to express the wish that, in view of its universal character, the United Nations Organization will never cease to be the forum, *the high tribune from which all man's problems are appraised in truth and justice*. It was in the name of this inspiration, it was through this historic stimulus, that on 26 June 1945, towards the end of the terrible Second World War, the Charter of the United Nations was signed and on the following 24 October your Organization began its life. Soon after, on 10 December 1948, came its fundamental document, the *Universal Declaration of Human rights*, the rights of the human being as a concrete individual and of the human being in his universal value. This document is a milestone on the long and difficult path of the human race. The progress of humanity must be measured not only by *the progress of science and technology*, which shows man's uniqueness with regard to nature, but also and chiefly by *the primacy given to spiritual values* and by *the progress of moral life*. In this field is manifested the full dominion of reason, through truth, in the behaviour of the individual and of society, and also the control of reason over nature; and thus human conscience quietly triumphs, as was expressed in the ancient saying: *"Genus humanus arte et ratione vivit."*

(79) It was when technology was being directed in its one-sided progress towards goals of war, hegemony, and conquest, so that man might kill man and nation destroy nation by depriving it of its liberty and the right to exist - and I still have before my mind the image of the Second World War in Europe, which began forty years ago on 1 September 1939 with the invasion of Poland and ended on 9 May 1945 - it was precisely then that the United Nations Organization arose. And three years later the document appeared which, as I have said, must be considered a real milestone on the path of the moral progress of humanity - the *Universal Declaration of Human Rights*. The governments and States of the world have understood that, if they are not to attack and destroy each other, *they must unite*. The real way, the fundamental *way to this is through each human being*, through the definition and recognition of and respect for the inalienable rights of individuals and of the communities of peoples.

(80) 8. Today, forty years after the outbreak of the Second World War, I wish to recall the whole of the experiences by individuals and nations that were sustained by a generation that is largely still alive. I had occasion not long ago to reflect again on some of those experiences, in one of the places that are most distressing and overflowing with contempt for man and his fundamental rights - the extermination camp of Oswiecim (Auschwitz), which I visited during my pilgrimage to Poland last June. This infamous place is unfortunately only one of the many scattered over the continent of Europe. But the memory of even one should be *a warning sign* on the path of humanity today, in order that *every kind of concentration camp* anywhere on earth may once and for all *be done away with*. And everything that recalls those horrible experiences should also disappear forever from the lives of nations and States, everything that is a continuation of those experiences under different forms, namely, the various kinds of torture and oppression, either physical or moral, carried out under any system, in any land; this phenomenon is all the more distressing if it occurs under the pretext of internal "security" or the need to preserve an apparent peace.

(81) 9. You will forgive me, ladies and gentlemen, for evoking this memory. But I would be untrue to the history of this century, I would be dishonest with regard to the great cause of man, which we all wish to serve, if I should keep silent, I who come from the country on whose living body Oswiecim was at one time constructed. But my purpose in evoking this memory is above all to show what painful experiences and sufferings by millions of people gave rise to the Universal Declaration of Human Rights, which has been placed as the basic inspiration and *cornerstone* of the United Nations Organization. This Declaration was paid for by millions of our brothers and sisters at the cost of their suffering and sacrifice, brought about by the brutalization that darkened and made insensitive the human consciences of their oppressors and of those who carried out a real genocide. This price cannot have been paid in vain! The Universal Declaration of Human Rights - with its train of many declarations and conventions on highly important aspects of human rights, in favour of children, of women, of equality between races, and especially the two international covenants on economic, social and cultural rights and on civil and political rights - must remain the basic value in the United Nations Organization with which the consciences of its members must be confronted and from which they must draw continual inspiration. If the truths and principles contained in this document were to be forgotten or ignored and were thus to lose the genuine self-evidence that distinguished them at the time they were brought painfully to birth, then the noble purpose of the United Nations Organization could be faced with the threat of a new destruction. This is what would happen if the simple yet powerful eloquence of the Universal Declaration of Human Rights were decisively subjugated by what is wrongly called political interest, but often really means no more than one-sided gain and advantage to the detriment of others, or a thirst for power regardless of the needs of others - everything which by its nature is opposed to the spirit of the Declaration. "Political interest" understood in this sense, if you will pardon me, ladies and gentlemen, dishonours the noble and difficult mission of your service for the good of your countries and of all humanity.

(82) 10. Fourteen years ago my great predecessor *Pope Paul VI* spoke from this podium. He spoke memorable words, which I desire to repeat today: "No more war, war never again! Never one against the other", or even "one above the other", but always, on every occasion, "with each other."

(83) Paul VI was a tireless servant of the cause of peace. I wish to follow him with all my strength and continue his service. The Catholic Church in every place on earth proclaims a message of peace, prays for peace, *educates for peace*. This purpose is also shared by the representatives and followers of other Churches and Communities and of other religions of the world, and they have pledged themselves to it. In union with efforts by all people of good will, this work is certainly bearing fruit. Nevertheless, we are continually troubled by the armed conflicts that break out from time to time. How grateful we are to the Lord when a direct intervention succeeds in avoiding such a conflict, as in the case of the tension that last year threatened Argentina and Chile.

(84) It is my fervent hope that a solution also to the Middle East crises may draw nearer. While being prepared to recognize the value of any concrete step or attempt made to settle the conflict, I want to recall that it would have no value if it did not truly represent the "first stone" of a general overall peace in the area, a peace that, being necessarily based on equitable recognition of the rights of all, cannot fail to include the consideration and just settlement of the Palestinian question. Connected with this question is that of the tranquillity, independence and territorial integrity of Lebanon within the formula that has made it an example of peaceful and mutually fruitful coexistence between distinct communities, a formula that I hope will, in the common interest, be maintained, with the adjustments required by the developments of the situation. I also hope for a special statute that, under international guarantees - as my predecessor Paul VI indicated - would respect the particular nature of Jerusalem, a heritage sacred to the veneration of millions of believers of the three great monotheistic religions, Judaism, Christianity and Islam.

(85) We are troubled also by reports of the development of weaponry exceeding in quality and size the means of war and destruction ever known before. In this field also we applaud the decisions and agreements aimed at reducing the arms race. Nevertheless, the life of humanity today is seriously endangered by the threat of destruction and by the risk arising even from accepting certain "tranquillizing" reports. And the resistance to actual concrete proposals of real disarmament, such as those called for by this Assembly in a special session last year, shows that together with the will for peace that all profess and that most desire there is also in existence - perhaps in latent or conditional form but nonetheless real - the contrary and the negation of this will. The continual *preparations for war* demonstrated by the production of ever more numerous, powerful and sophisticated weapons in various countries show that there is a desire to be ready for war, and *being* *ready* means *being able to start it*; it also means taking the risk that sometime, somewhere, somehow, someone can set in motion the terrible mechanism of general destruction.

(86) 11. It is therefore necessary to make a continuing and even more energetic effort to do away with the very possibility of provoking war, and to make such catastrophes impossible by influencing the attitudes and convictions, the very intentions and aspirations of governments and peoples. This duty, kept constantly in mind by the United Nations Organization and each of its institutions, must also be a duty for every society, every regime, every government. This task is certainly served by initiatives aimed at international cooperation for the fostering of development. As Paul VI said at the end of his encyclical *Populorum Progressio*, "If the new name for peace is development, who would not wish to labour for it with all his powers?" However, this task must also be served by constant reflection and activity aimed at *discovering the very roots* of hatred, destructiveness and contempt - the roots of everything that produces the temptation to war, not so much in the hearts of the nations as in the inner determination of the systems that decide the history of whole societies. In this titanic labour of building up the peaceful future of our planet, the United Nations Organization has, undoubtedly, a key function and guiding role, for which it must refer to the just ideals contained in the Universal Declaration of Human Rights. For this Declaration has struck a real blow against the many deep roots of war, since the spirit of war, in its basic primordial meaning, *springs up and grows to maturity where the inalienable rights of man are violated.*

(87) This is a new and deeply relevant vision of the cause of peace, one that goes deeper and is more radical. It is a vision that sees the genesis, and in a sense the substance, of war in the more complex forms emanating from injustice viewed in all its various aspects: this injustice first attacks human rights and thereby destroys the organic unity of the social order, and it then affects the whole system of international relations. Within the Church's doctrine, the encyclical *Pacem in Terris* by John XXIII provides in synthetic form a view of this matter that is very close to the ideological foundation of the United Nations Organization. This must therefore form the basis to which one must loyally and perseveringly adhere in order to establish true *"peace on earth."*

(88) 12. By applying this criterion we must diligently examine *which principal tensions* in connection with the inalienable rights of man can weaken the construction of this peace which we all desire so ardently and which is the essential goal of the efforts of the United Nations Organization. It is not easy, but it must be done. Anyone who undertakes it must take up a totally objective position and be guided by sincerity, readiness to acknowledge one's prejudices and mistakes, and readiness even to renounce one's own particular interests, including political interests. Peace is something greater and more important than any of these interests. It is by sacrificing these interests for the sake of peace that we serve them best. After all, in whose "political interest" can it ever be to have another war? Every analysis must necessarily start from the premise that - although each person lives in a particular concrete social and historical context - every human being is endowed with a dignity that must never be lessened, impaired or destroyed but must instead be respected and safeguarded, if peace is really to be built up.

(89) 13. In a movement that one hopes will be progressive and continuous, the Universal Declaration of Human Rights and the other international and national juridical instruments are endeavouring to create general awareness of the dignity of the human being, and to define at least some of the inalienable rights of man. Permit me to enumerate some of the most important human rights that are universally recognized: the right to life, liberty and security of person; the right to food, clothing, housing, sufficient health care, rest and leisure; the right to freedom of expression, education and culture; the right to freedom of thought, conscience and religion, and the right to manifest one's religion either individually or in community, in public or in private; the right to choose a state of life, to found a family and to enjoy all conditions necessary for family life; the right to property and work, to adequate working conditions and a just wage; the right of assembly and association; the right to freedom of movement, to internal and external migration; the right to nationality and residence; the right to political participation and the right to participate in the free choice of the political system of the people to which one belongs. All these human rights taken together are in keeping with the substance of the dignity of the human being, understood in his entirety, not as reduced to one dimension only. These rights concern the satisfaction of man's essential needs, the exercise of his freedoms, and his relationships with others; but always and everywhere they concern man, they concern man's full human dimension.

(90) 14. Man lives at the same time both in the world of material values and in that of spiritual values. For the individual living and hoping man, his needs, freedoms and relationships with others never concern one sphere of values alone, but belong to both. Material and spiritual realities may be viewed separately in order to understand better that in the concrete human being they are inseparable, and to see that any threat to human rights, whether in the field of material realities or in that of spiritual realities, is equally dangerous for peace, since in every instance it concerns man in his entirety. Permit me, distinguished ladies and gentlemen, to recall a constant rule of the history of humanity, a rule that is implicitly contained in all that I have already stated with regard to integral development and human rights. The rule is based on the relationship between spiritual values and material or economic values. In this relationship, it is the spiritual values that are pre-eminent, both on account of the nature of these values and also for reasons concerning the good of man. The pre-eminence of the values of the spirit defines the proper sense of earthly material goods and the way to use them. This pre-eminence is therefore at the basis of a just peace. It is also a contributing factor to ensuring that material development, technical development and the development of civilization are at the service of what constitutes man. This means enabling man to have full access to truth, to moral development, and to the complete possibility of enjoying the goods of culture which he has inherited, and of increasing them by his own creativity. It is easy to see that material goods do not have unlimited capacity for satisfying the needs of man: they are not in themselves easily distributed and, in the relationship between those who possess and enjoy them and those who are without them, they give rise to tension, dissension and division that will often even turn into open conflict. Spiritual goods, on the other hand, are open to unlimited enjoyment by many at the same time, without diminution of the goods themselves. Indeed, the more people share in such goods, the more they are enjoyed and drawn upon, the more then do those goods show their indestructible and immortal worth. This truth is confirmed, for example, by the works of creativity - I mean by the works of thought, poetry, music, and the figurative arts, fruits of man's spirit.

(91) 15. A critical analysis of our modern civilization shows that in the last hundred years it has contributed as never before to the development of material goods, but that it has also given rise, both in theory and still more in practice, to a series of attitudes in which *sensitivity to the spiritual dimension of human existence is diminished* to a greater or less extent, as a result of certain premises which reduce the meaning of human life chiefly to the many different material and economic factors - I mean to the demands of production, the market, consumption, the accumulation of riches or of the growing bureaucracy with which an attempt is made to regulate these very processes. Is this not the result of having subordinated man to one single conception and sphere of values?

(92) 16. What is the link between these reflections and the cause of peace and war? Since, as I have already stated, material goods by their very nature provoke conditionings and divisions, the struggle to obtain these goods becomes *inevitable in the history of humanity.* If we cultivate this one sided subordination of man to material goods alone, we shall be incapable of *overcoming this state of need.* We shall be able to attenuate it and avoid it in particular cases, but we shall not succeed in eliminating it systematically and radically, unless we emphasize more and pay greater honour, before everyone's eyes, in the sight of every society, to *the second dimension of the goods of man*: the dimension that does not divide people but puts them into communication with each other, associates them and unites them.

(93) I consider that the famous opening words of the Charter of the United Nations, in which "the peoples of the United Nations, determined to save succeeding generations from the scourge of war" solemnly reaffirmed "faith in fundamental human rights, in the dignity and worth of the human person, in the equal rights of men and women and of nations large and small," are meant to stress this dimension.

(94) Indeed, the fight against incipient wars cannot be carried out on a merely superficial level, by treating the symptoms. It must be done in a radical way, by attacking the causes. The reason I have called attention to the dimension constituted by spiritual realities is my concern for the cause of peace, peace which is built up by men and women uniting around what is most fully and profoundly human, around what raises them above the world about them and determines their indestructible grandeur - indestructible in spite of the death to which everyone on earth is subject. I would like to add that *the Catholic Church* and, I think I can say, the whole of Christianity sees in this very domain *its own particular task.* The Second Vatican Council helped to establish what the Christian faith has in common with the various non-Christian religions in this aspiration. The Church is therefore grateful to all who show respect and good will with regard to this mission of hers and do not impede it or make it difficult. An analysis of the history of mankind, especially at its present stage, shows how important is the duty of revealing more fully the range of the goods that are linked with the spiritual dimension of human existence. It shows how important this task is for building peace and how serious is any threat to human rights. Any violation of them, even in a "peace situation," is a form of warfare against humanity.

(95) It seems that in the modern world there are two main threats. Both concern human rights in the field of international relations and human rights within the individual States or societies.

(96) 17. The first of these systematic threats against human rights is linked in an overall sense with the distribution of material goods. This distribution is frequently unjust both within individual societies and on the planet as a whole. Everyone knows that these goods are given to man not only as nature's bounty: they are enjoyed by him chiefly as the fruit of his many activities, ranging from the simplest manual and physical labour to the most complicated forms of industrial production, and to the highly qualified and specialized research and study. Various forms of *inequality in the possession of material goods*, and in the enjoyment of them, can often be explained by different historical and cultural causes and circumstances. But, while these circumstances can diminish the moral responsibility of people today, they do not prevent the situations of inequality from being marked by injustice and social injury.

(97) People must become aware that economic tensions within countries and in the relationship between States and even between entire continents contain within themselves substantial elements that restrict or violate human rights. Such elements are the exploitation of labour and many other abuses that affect the dignity of the human person. It follows that the fundamental criterion for comparing social, economic and political systems is not, *and cannot be*, the criterion of hegemony and imperialism: it can be, and indeed it must be, *the humanistic criterion*, namely the measure in which each system is really capable of reducing, restraining and eliminating as far as possible the various forms of exploitation of man and of ensuring for him, through work, not only the just distribution of the indispensable material goods, but also a participation, in keeping with his dignity, in the whole process of production and in the social life that grows up around that process. Let us not forget that, although man depends on the resources of the material world for his life, he cannot be their slave, but he must be their master. The words of the book of Genesis, "Fill the earth and subdue it" (*Gen.* 1:28), are in a sense a primary and essential directive in the field of economy and of labour policy.

(98) 18. Humanity as a whole, and the individual nations, have certainly made remarkable progress in this field during the last hundred years. But it is a field in which there is never any lack of systematic threats to and violations of human rights. Disturbing factors are frequently present in the form of the *frightful disparities* between excessively rich individuals and groups on the one hand, and on the other hand *the majority* made up of the poor or indeed of *the destitute*, who lack food and opportunities for work and education and are in great numbers condemned to hunger and disease. And concern is also caused at times by the radical separation of work from property, by man's indifference to the production enterprise to which he is linked only by a work obligation, without feeling that he is working for a good that will be his or for himself.

(99) It is no secret that the abyss separating the minority of the excessively rich from the multitude of the destitute is a very grave symptom in the life of any society. This must also be said with even greater insistence with regard to the abyss separating countries and regions of the earth. Surely the only way to overcome this serious disparity between areas of satiety and areas of hunger and depression is through coordinated cooperation by all countries. This requires above all else a unity inspired by an authentic perspective of peace. Everything will depend on whether these differences and contrasts in the sphere of the "possession" of goods will be systematically reduced through truly effective means, on whether the belts of hunger, malnutrition, destitution, underdevelopment, disease and illiteracy will disappear from the economic map of the earth, and on whether peaceful cooperation will avoid imposing conditions of exploitation and economic or political dependence, which would only be a form of neocolonialism.

(100) 19. I would now like to draw attention to *a second systematic threat* to man in his inalienable rights in the modern world, a threat which constitutes no less a danger than the first to the cause of peace. I refer to the various forms of injustice in the field of the spirit.

(101) Man can indeed be wounded in his inner relationship with truth, in his conscience, in his most personal belief, in his view of the world, in his religious faith, and in the sphere of what are known as civil liberties. Decisive for these last is equality of rights without discrimination on grounds of origin, race, sex, nationality, religion, political convictions and the like. Equality of rights means the exclusion of the various forms of privilege for some and discrimination against others, whether they are people born in the same country or people from different backgrounds of history, nationality, race and ideology. For centuries the thrust of civilization has been in one direction: that of giving the life of individual political societies a form in which there can be *fully safeguarded the objective rights of the spirit, of human conscience and of human creativity, including man's relationship with God*. Yet in spite of this we still see in this field recurring threats and violations, often with no possibility of appealing to a higher authority or of obtaining an effective remedy.

(102) Besides the acceptance of legal formulas safeguarding the principle of the freedom of the human spirit, such as freedom of thought and expression, religious freedom, and freedom of conscience, structures of social life often exist in which the practical exercise of these freedoms condemns man, in fact if not formally, to become a second-class or third-class citizen, to see compromised his chances of social advancement, his professional career or his access to certain posts of responsibility, and to lose even the possibility of educating his children freely. It is a question of the highest importance that in internal social life, as well as in international life, *all human beings* in every nation and country *should be able to enjoy effectively their full rights under any political regime or system*. Only the safeguarding of this real completeness of rights for every human being without discrimination can ensure peace at its very roots.

(103) 20. With regard to religious freedom, which I, as Pope, am bound to have particularly at heart, precisely with a view to safeguarding peace, I would like to repeat here, as a contribution to respect for man's spiritual dimension, some principles contained in the Second Vatican Council's Declaration *Dignitatis Humanae*: "In accordance with their dignity, all human beings, because they are persons, that is, beings endowed with reason and free will and therefore bearing personal responsibility, are both impelled by their nature and bound by a moral obligation to seek the truth, especially religious truth. They are also bound to adhere to the truth once they come to know it and to direct their whole lives in accordance with its demands" (*Dignitatis Humanae,* No 2).

(104) "The practice of religion of its very nature consists primarily of those voluntary and free internal acts by which a human being directly sets his course towards God. No merely human power can either command or prohibit acts of this kind. But man's social nature itself requires that he give external expression to his internal acts of religion, that he communicate with others in religious matters and that he profess his religion in community" (*Dignitatis Humanae,* No 3).

(105) These words touch the very substance of the question. They also show how even the confrontation between *the religious view of the world and the agnostic or even atheistic view*, which is one of the "signs of the times" of the present age, could preserve honest and respectful human dimensions without violating the essential rights of conscience of any man or woman living on earth.

(106) Respect for the dignity of the human person would seem to demand that, when the exact tenor of the exercise of religious freedom is being discussed or determined with a view to national laws or international conventions, the institutions that are by their nature at the service of religion should also be brought in. If this participation is omitted, there is a danger of imposing, in so intimate a field of man's life, rules or restrictions that are opposed to his true religious needs.

(107) 21. The United Nations Organization has proclaimed 1979 *the Year of the Child.* In the presence of the representatives of so many nations of the world gathered here, I wish to express the joy that we all find in children, the springtime of life, the anticipation of the future history of each of our present earthly homelands. No country on earth, no political system can think of its own future otherwise than through the image of these new generations that will receive from their parents the manifold heritage of values, duties and aspirations of the nation to which they belong and of the whole human family. Concern for the child, even before birth, from the first moment of conception and then throughout the years of infancy and youth, is the primary fundamental test of the relationship of one human being to another.

(108) And so, what better wish can I express for every nation and the whole of mankind, and for all the children of the world than *a better future* in which respect for human rights will become a complete reality throughout the third millennium, which is drawing near.

(109) 22. But in this perspective we must ask ourselves whether there will continue to accumulate over the heads of this new generation of children the threat of common extermination for which the means are in the hands of the modern States, especially the major world powers. *Are the children to receive the arms race from us* as a necessary inheritance? How are we to explain this unbridled race?

(110) The ancients said: *Si vis pacem, para bellum.* But can our age still really believe that the breathtaking spiral of armaments is at the service of world peace? In alleging the threat of a potential enemy, is it really not rather the intention to keep for oneself a means of threat, in order to get the upper hand with the aid of one's own arsenal of destruction? Here too it is the human dimension of peace that tends to vanish *in favour of ever new possible forms of imperialism.*

(111) It must be our solemn wish here for our children, for the children of all the nations on earth, that this point will never be reached. And for that reason I do not cease to pray to God each day so that in his mercy he may save us from so terrible a day.

(112) 23. At the close of this address, I wish to express once more before all the high representatives of the States who are present a word of esteem and deep love for all the peoples, all the nations of the earth, for all human communities. Each one has its own history and culture. I hope that they will live and grow in the freedom and truth of their own history. For that is the measure of the common good of each one of them. I hope that each person will *live and grow strong with the moral force of the community* that forms its members as citizens. I hope that the State authorities, while respecting the just rights of each citizen, will enjoy the confidence of all for the common good. I hope that all the nations, even the smallest, even those that do not yet enjoy full sovereignty, and those that have been forcibly robbed of it, will meet in full equality with the others in the United Nations Organization. I hope that the United Nations will ever remain the supreme forum of peace and justice, the authentic seat of freedom of peoples and individuals in their longing for a better future.

V - STRUGGLE AGAINST HUNGER: THE MOST SERIOUS AND URGENT PROBLEM

Address by His Holiness John Paul II to the 20th Session of the Conference of FAO, on the occasion of his visit to the Headquarters of the Organization. Rome, 12 November 1979.

Original: French (*)

(113) 1. My visit to you is, in a way, a prolongation of the one I paid to the United Nations Headquarters in New York, as happened in the case of my predecessor Paul VI.

(114) I am delighted that the Food and Agriculture Organization, established at Quebec on 16 October 1945, hence a little before the United Nations Organization, should be inspired by the same basic criteria, as well as by the Universal Declaration of Human Rights, while retaining the autonomy of action proper to any intergovernmental organization.

(115) Your Organization is of universal scope because it is open to the adhesion to its Constitution of all the peoples of the earth. Thus the number of its Member Nations has grown from the original forty-two to the one hundred and forty-six represented at this present Conference. It is therefore able to undertake joint action which derives from a real convergence between the countries of the world, whatever their economic systems and political structures.

(116) 2. FAO can pride itself on fulfilling an irreplaceable specialized function within the United Nations family. It has to tackle a sector - agriculture - which may be considered the most important sector in the world economy, that which supplies the food indispensable for the world and employs fifty percent of the world's population. It is also a sector for too long excluded from improvements in standards of living, a sector which the rapid and far-reaching social and cultural changes of our time affect in a particularly painful way, exposing the injustices inherited from the past, destroying the stability of individuals, families and societies, heaping up frustrations and provoking migrations, massive and chaotic.

(117) According to the preamble of your Constitution, FAO's purpose, which is to free the human family from hunger, entails a commitment by the Member Nations to raise levels of nutrition and better the condition of rural populations by improving efficiency in food production and distribution.

(118) 3. But I should like to underline also that, according to the same preamble, FAO aims at "furthering separate and collective action ... and thus contributing towards an expanding world economy" and the promotion of the common welfare.

(119) Its overall plan and the basic lines of its policy for development and international cooperation in the service of mankind are therefore in full accord with those of the United Nations, founded on the great principles on which I dwelt on 2 October last before the United Nations Organization.

(120) Here too we meet in the name of Man taken in his entirety, in the fullness and multiform richness of his spiritual and material existence (Cf. Address to the United Nations, No. 5. See above, Par. 75).

(121) 4. It is with particular satisfaction that I come to establish this direct contact with FAO. I have accepted the invitation to speak before the 20th Conference in this year which marks the 30th anniversary of the decision taken on 28 November 1949 to transfer FAO from its temporary site in Washington to these permanent headquarters in Rome - a decision which was put into effect in 1951.

(*) Insegnamenti di Giovanni Paolo II, vol. II, 2, 1133-1141.

(122) Your Organization thus effected what has been regarded as a return to its Roman origins. It was, in fact, preceded in a way by the International Institute of Agriculture, founded in 1905 under the inspiration of David Lubin and subsequently absorbed by FAO. Since that time Rome has become one of the centres of world agriculture and is now of new importance in this field, particularly after the decisions of the World Food Conference in November 1974.

(123) 5. Then there is a tradition of special relations between the Holy See and FAO. FAO is the first intergovernmental organization with which the Holy See established regular diplomatic relations, thanks to the far-sighted action of Msgr. Montini, then Substitute of the Secretariat of State. In fact, by unanimous vote the FAO Conference, on 23 November 1948, at its fourth session, accorded the Holy See the unique status of permanent observer, which guaranteed it the right to participate, not only in the Conferences of the Organization but also in the other fields of its activity, and to be allowed to speak on request, although not to vote. Such a position corresponds perfectly to the nature of the Church's religious and moral mission.

(124) Thus began the Holy See's collaboration with your Organization, the moral and humanitarian principles inspiring which Msgr. Montini took pleasure in underlining (see Letter of 16 November 1968 to Mr. Norris E. Dodd, Director-General of FAO).

(125) All FAO's activities and programmes demonstrate clearly in fact, that in the last analysis any technical and economic activity, like any political choice, implies a problem of morality and justice.

(126) The visit paid to your headquarters by Pope Paul VI on 16 November 1970, on the 25th anniversary of the creation of FAO, was a striking testimony to the continued growth in these relations of trust.

(127) 6. To these considerations is added another: it is with pleasure that I see FAO endeavouring to give concrete effect, in the field of food and agriculture, to an aspect of the world programme for economic and social development. Such a programme undoubtedly promotes peace by helping to remove tension and meet peoples' basic demands, demands connected with inalienable human rights.

(128) From this point of view, your specialized Organization refers more directly to the economic and social rights recognized in the Universal Declaration of Human Rights, which were subsequently formulated in a more precise and compelling way in the International Covenant on Economic, Social and Cultural Rights.

(129) But, as Pious XII said in his Christmas broadcast of 1942, development of the individual entails the establishment of social conditions which constitute the common assets of each national political community as well as of the international community as a whole. Such collective, organic and continuing development is the indispensable prerequisite for the concrete enjoyment of human rights, both those of an economic nature and those which directly concern spiritual values. If it is to be an expression of real human solidarity, however, such development must be obtained by calling on the free participation and the sense of responsibility of all, in the public and in the private sphere, both nationally and internationally.

(130) From this point of view, FAO appears as a concrete expression of the resolve to pass from declarations of principle to effective action and achievements, by calling on the free and active participation of all its Member Nations. It is to be hoped that the political will of each nation will ensure FAO of a collaboration which does not consist merely of supporting internal development projects and operations undertaken at the request of each government, and which is not content, either, with merely harmonizing self-centred nationalist interests. The joint action carried out within the framework of FAO requires an ever greater willingness to assume really continuing commitments by which each participates in an action decided upon by all.

(131) 7. Over the years FAO has acquired an even larger and better adapted structure as shown by the various programmes now under way and the documents submitted at this Conference. You are going not only to review the achievements of the past two years but also to fix the objectives to be achieved during the coming years and make the political choices necessary for this. You are already looking ahead to the year 2000 and the specific problems which agriculture has to overcome in order to cope with the requirements foreseen: accelerated increase of production, need to regulate trade and external assistance to the countries which need it to ensure their economic take-off. What has to be done is to take the steps which will ensure for all a better future in which the fundamental rights of each person will be respected. This present Conference can make an important contribution, as regards your Organization's sphere, to defining the most important objectives and fresh criteria which should make it possible to put the new international strategy for development into effect during the third United Nations Decade, which starts in the eighties.

(132) 8. But the world cannot be satisfied with theoretical speculations. The face of hunger becomes even more clearly defined, and concrete action must be taken by the Member Nations and the Organization as a whole. The fight against hunger can no longer be conducted by appeals to sentiment, by sporadic and ineffective outbursts of indignation: it is the praiseworthy resolve of your Organization to persist in seeking out the best ways and the methods adapted to the concrete conditions in each country and to make provision for their prudent application.

(133) It is over, the period of illusion when it was believed that the problems of underdevelopment and differences in growth between various countries could be automatically resolved by exporting the industrial models and the ideologies of the developed countries.

(134) It is over, in fact, the attempt to guarantee food for all by aid programmes based on donations of surplus goods or emergency aid programmes in exceptional cases.

(135) Your Organization is shifting towards a policy in which the effort made by each country for its own development has priority. This entails, of course, a requirement: if each country that needs them is to receive, without loss of dignity, the necessary international assistance and investments, while retaining control of the factors necessary to enable the farmers to play their proper role in the country's development, purely bilateral relations will have to be increasingly replaced by a multilateral system.

(136) 9. Another readjustment of development criteria and models which the present economic crisis makes even more necessary for the poor countries - and, indeed, for the more developed countries - is to set as the aim the satisfaction of real human needs, those which are really basic. It is these needs which should propel and guide the economy, not the artificial needs, partly created and always increased by publicity, by the play of market forces and by the positions of power acquired in the economic, financial and political fields. It is necessary to foresee and combat the dangerous consequences for men and women of certain technical and economic solutions, and to actively encourage their free and responsible participation in the choices and the work undertaken for the organic and programmed improvement of overall conditions in their own community.

(137) Contemporary experience makes it clear that the orderly and sustained growth of each country, like the effective guarantee of the basic human rights of individuals and peoples, necessitates organic and worldwide overall development. I note with interest how, in this field, the various technical cooperation and aid programmes launched by your Organization, the promotion of an international agreement to ensure the indispensable reserves of cereals, are slowly helping to transform the world economy.

(138) 10. However, of all the problems engaging your attention and the attention of the world, the most serious and the most urgent is that of hunger. The very existence of millions of people is endangered; every day many die because they do not have the minimum amount of food they need. And it must be recognized, alas, that as is being made cruelly evident at the moment, hunger in the world is not always due solely to unfavourable geographic, climatic or agricultural conditions, which you are attempting to remedy little by little; it is caused also by men themselves, by deficiencies in the organization of society which prevent personal initiative, even by terror and the oppression of inhuman ideological and practical systems.

(139) The search for the organic world development that all desire requires, then, that objective knowledge of human distress be included in the formation of individuals and groups to ensure authentic freedom and personal and collective responsibility.

(140) 11. The attainment of individual human development lies outside the scope of your Organization, of course. I know, however, that you are not indifferent to this aim. You promote it by endeavouring to diversify your technical models for assistance and development and to frame them in the light of the specific conditions, social and cultural as well as physical, of each country, thus taking into account the human, and hence also spiritual, values of peoples.

(141) These values include religious beliefs which express a vision of man, of his real needs, of the ultimate purpose of his activities: "Man does not live by bread alone", says the Gospel (*Mt.* 4:4). Technical development, however necessary it may be, is not everything; it has to find its place in a wider, fully human plan. Thus the spiritual realities force themselves on our attention. It is in this field too that the Church, which has always encouraged your efforts and which plays an effective part in man's harmonious development, wishes to go along with your efforts and collaborate with you for the good of mankind.

(142) 12. The work to be carried out is immense, and no-one should be discouraged if the goal to be attained sometimes seems to recede at the same rate as one makes efforts to achieve it. At this moment in world history, I rejoice to see FAO directing all its efforts in this essential field to promoting international cooperation for development. And we all hope that this development will spread from the technical and economic level to the personal and social progress of men and women.

(143) This will not happen unless human dignity and rights constitute, from the beginning, the active criterion inspiring and guiding all efforts. To overcome inertia and discouragement, to create the conditions for fresh thinking and sustained action, never lose sight of the fact that it is human beings who are at stake, real human beings, men and women who are suffering, men and women endowed with immense possibilities which must be set free.

(144) 13. I would add that the efforts you plan, undertake or encourage so that the earth will be cultivated, so that its riches, on land and sea, will be conserved and never wasted, better still increase, multiplying their potentialities without imprudently destroying the natural equilibrium which has served as the cradle for human life - in a word so that nature, at once respected and ennobled, may yield of its best in the service of humanity, all this connects, in a way, with God's design for creation, which the inspired text of Genesis describes to us in an archaic but suggestive manner: "God created man in his own image, male and female created He them. Fill the earth and subdue it ... And the Lord God took the man and put him into the Garden of Eden to dress it and to keep it" (*Gen.* 1: 27-28; 2: 16). Yes, the earth belongs to men, to all men, not forgetting the generations who will succeed us tomorrow and who must receive it from our hands, habitable and fruitful. Because it belongs first of all to God, the Creator, the Supreme Master, the stewards. It is in harmony with God's design that you are called on to work.

(145) Such is the wish I formulate for you as Pastor of the Universal Church. And it is in this spirit that I pray to Almighty God to bless the efforts you are making to serve the human family, to bless you and all those dear to you.

VI - THE FUTURE OF MANKIND DEPENDS ON CULTURE

Address by His Holiness Pope John Paul II on the occasion of His visit to the headquarters of the United Nations Educational, Scientific and Cultural Organization (UNESCO). Paris, 2 June 1980.

Original: French (*)

(146) 1. I wish first of all to express my most sincere thanks for the invitation extended to me on a number of occasions - initially on the first visit with which he has honoured me - by Mr. Amadou Mahtar M'Bow, Director-General of the United Nations Educational Scientific and Cultural Organization. There are many reasons why I am happy to be able to respond today to that invitation, which I deeply appreciate.

(147) For their kind words of welcome, I thank Mr. Napoleon LeBlanc, the President of the General Conference, Mr. Chams Eldine El-Wakil, the Chairman of the Executive Board and Mr Amadou-Mahtar M'Bow, the Director-General of the Organization. I also wish to greet all those assembled here for the 109th session of the Executive Board of UNESCO. It is with great joy that I see gathered together on this occasion so many delegates from nations throughout the world, so many outstanding personalities, such a wealth of talent and so many distinguished representatives of the world of culture and science.

(148) By this address, I shall attempt to make my own modest contribution to the edifice that you, ladies and gentlemen, are building with unfailing perseverance through your reflections and your resolutions in all UNESCO's fields of competence.

(149) 2. Let me begin by referring to the *Origins of your Organization.* The events which marked the foundation of UNESCO fill my heart with joy and gratitude towards Divine Providence: the signing of its Constitution on 16 November 1945; the coming into force of that Constitution and the establishment of the Organization on 4 November 1946; the agreement between UNESCO and the United Nations approved by the General Assembly of the United Nations that same year. Your Organization is indeed the creation of nations who, in the wake of the terrible Second World War, were impelled by what may be called a spontaneous desire for peace, union and reconciliation. Those nations sought ways and means of co-operation that might consecrate, deepen and perpetuate this new understanding. UNESCO thus came into being, like the United Nations, because the peoples of the world knew that great enterprises designed to promote peace and the progress of mankind throughout the earth must necessarily be founded on the *Union of Nations*, on mutual respect and on international cooperation.

(150) 3. Continuing the work, the thinking and the message of my great predecessor, Pope Paul VI, I had the honour of speaking to the General Assembly of the United Nations last October, at the invitation of Mr. Kurt Waldheim, the Secretary-General of the United Nations. Shortly afterwards, on 12 November 1979, I was invited by Mr. Edouard Saouma, the Director-General of the Food and Agriculture Organization of the United Nations in Rome. I have thus had divers opportunities to address myself to questions intimately linked with the whole range of problems relating to the peaceful future of man on earth. All those problems are indeed inextricably linked. We are faced, as it were, by a vast system of communicating vessels: the problems of culture, science and education do not arise, in the life of nations and in international relations, independently of the other problems of human existence, such as those of peace or hunger. The problems of culture are fundamentally affected by the other dimensions of human existence, just as they in turn influence those other dimensions.

(151) 4. There is however - as I stressed in my address to the United Nations when referring to the Universal Declaration of Human Rights - a fundamental dimension, which is capable of shaking to their very foundations the system within the whole of human lives, and of liberating human

(*) AAS 72(1980), 735-752

existence, both individual and collective, from threats that hang over it. This fundamental dimension is man, man in his entirety, man living simultaneously in the sphere of material values and in that of spiritual values. Respect for the inalienable rights of the human person underlies everything (cf. Address to the United Nations, Nos. 7 and 13. See above, Par. 77-79 and 89).

(152) Any threat to human rights, whether in the realm of spiritual or of material well-being, does violence to this fundamental dimension. For that reason, in my address to the Food and Agriculture Organization, I stressed that no man, no country and no system in the world can remain indifferent when confronted with the "geography of hunger" and the awesome threats which will result from it if the entire direction of economic policy and, in particular, the pattern of investments, are not substantially and radically changed. For this reason, too, I must stress, in referring to the origins of your Organization, the need to mobilize all those forces that serve to orient the spiritual dimension of human existence, that bear witness to the primacy of the spiritual in man - to what befits the dignity of his intelligence, his will and his heart - so that humanity shall not succumb again to the monstrous alienation of that collective evil which is always ready to employ material power in the lethal conflict of man against man and nation against nation.

(153) 5. UNESCO then, like the Universal Declaration of Human Rights, originates from these primary noble promptings of the human conscience, intelligence and will. I call to witness this origin, this beginning, these premises and these first principles. It is in their name that I have come to Paris today, to the headquarters of your Organization, bringing with me a plea that, at the close of a period of more than thirty years in your work, you should rally yet more closely around the ideals and principles that were there in the beginning. It is likewise in their name that I now propose to place before you some truly fundamental considerations for it is only in the light they cast that the significance of this institution, UNESCO, the United Nations Educational, Scientific and Cultural Organization, can be fully appreciated.

(154) 6. *Genus humanum arte et ratione vivit* (cf. Saint Thomas Aquinas, commenting on Aristotle, in *Post. Analyt.*, No. 1). These words from one of Christianity's greatest minds who, at the same time fruitfully carried further the thinking of the ancient world, have an impact that goes beyond the confines and contemporary significance of Western culture, be it Mediterranean or Atlantic. They bear a meaning which applies to the whole of humanity, in which the various traditions that make up its spiritual heritage and the different stages of its culture come together. According to St. Thomas Aquinas, the essential significance of culture lies in the fact that it is a characteristic of human life as such. *It is through culture that man lives a truly human life.* Human life is also culture in the sense that it is by culture that man is distinguished and differentiated from everything else that exists in the visible world: man cannot do without culture.

(155) Culture is a specific mode of man's "existing" and "being". Man always lives according to a culture of his own which, in turn, establishes among men a bond which is also, in itself, peculiar to them, determining the inter-human and social character of human existence. It is *in the unity of culture* as the distinctive mode of human existence that the *plurality of cultures* within which people live is rooted. Within this plurality, man develops without, however, losing the essential contact with the unity of culture as a basic and essential dimension of his existence and his being.

(156) 7. Man who, in the visible world, is *the only* ontic *subject of culture*, is also *its only object and its end.* It is through culture that man as a human being becomes more human, "exists" more fully and has more "being". And it is therein that the fundamental distinction between what man is and what he has, between being and having, is grounded. Culture is always essentially and necessarily related to what man is, while its relation to what he has, to his "possessions", is not only secondary, but entirely relative. All that man "possesses", is of importance for culture, and a factor creative of culture, only in so far as man, by virtue of what he "possesses", is also able to "be" more fully man, to become more fully man at all levels of his existence and in everything which marks out his humanity. The experience of the different periods of history, not excluding the present, shows that we think about culture and speak about it *first and foremost in connection with human nature*, and only *secondarily and indirectly, in connection with the world of human production.* This does not mean that we do not judge the phenomenon of culture by what man produces, or that at the same time we do not draw conclusions about man from it. This kind of approach - typical of *a posteriori* reasoning - also affords the possibility of working back towards the ontic-causal dependences. It is man, and man alone, who "acts" or "makes" culture, man, and man alone expresses himself in culture and finds his own balance in it.

(157) 8. All of us, present here today, meet *on the ground of culture, the fundamental reality* which unites us and which underlies the establishment of UNESCO and the Organization's purposes. We meet, by the same token, around man, and, in a sense, in him, in man. *Man,* who expresses and objectifies himself in and through culture, is *unique, complete and indivisible.* He is both the subject and the maker of culture. Consequently, he cannot be considered solely as the result of all the concrete conditions of his existence, as the result - to give one example - of the production relationships prevailing at any given time. Does this mean that the criterion of production relationships is in no way *a key to understanding* of the historic quality of man, to understanding of his culture and the manifold forms of his development? It is indeed a key, and even a very useful one, but it is not the basic, decisive key. There is no doubt whatever that human cultures reflect the various systems of production relationships; but culture originates, not in any particular system but in man, man who lives within the system, and accepts it or seeks to change it. It is impossible to conceive of a culture without human subjectivity or human causality; but in the field of culture *man is always the prime factor: he is the primordial and fundamental element of culture.*

(158) And man is always such in his wholeness: *in the entirety of his spiritual and material subjectivity.* While there is a real distinction between spiritual and material culture in terms of the nature and content of the products in which culture is expressed, it must also be noted that, on the one hand, works of material culture always reveal a *"spiritualization" of matter,* a subjection of the material element to the spiritual powers of man, in other words, to his intelligence and his will; and, on the other, works of spiritual culture specifically show a *"materialization" of the spirit,* an incarnation of what is spiritual. This dual characteristic appears to be both primordial and permanent in works of culture.

(159) Here then, by way of theoretical conclusion,we have a sufficient basis for understanding culture through man in his wholeness, through the entire reality of his subjectivity. Here too - in the field of action - we have a sufficient basis for seeking always in culture the whole man, man in his entirety, in all the truth of his spiritual and bodily subjectivity; a sufficient basis for *not superimposing preconceived divisions and oppositions* on culture, which is a genuinely human system, a glorious synthesis of mind and body. In point of fact, neither the absolutization of matter in the structure of the human subject, nor, conversely, the absolutization of the spirit in that structure, expresses man's truth or serves his culture.

(160) 9. I should like to dwell here on another essential consideration, of a very different kind. It is best approached by noting that the Holy See has a Permanent Observer accredited to UNESCO, whose presence is entirely in keeping with the very nature of the Apostolic See. On an even broader plane, this representation is consonant with the nature and mission of the Catholic Church and, indirectly, with that of Christianity as a whole. I should like to take the opportunity offered me here today to express a deep personal conviction. Although the representation of the Apostolic See in your Organization is also motivated by the specific sovereignty of the Holy See, the most important reason for it is the *organic and essential bond* between *religion* in general and Christianity in particular, on the one hand, and *culture,* on the other. This relationship takes in the manifold realities which must be defined as concrete expressions of culture at different stages of history and in all parts of the world. It would certainly be no exaggeration, for example, to maintain that, in a multiplicity of ways, all Europe - from the Atlantic to the Urals - testifies to the links between culture and Christianity in the history of each nation as well as in that of the community as a whole.

(161) In saying that, I do not wish in any way to detract from the heritage of other continents or from the uniqueness and value of that heritage, derived *from other sources of religious, humanistic and ethical inspiration.* If anything, I am moved to render the *most profound and heartfelt homage* to all the cultures of the great human family, from the most ancient to those of the present day. And I am thinking of all cultures as, with respect and admiration, I say to you here, in

Paris, at UNESCO's headquarters: "Behold the man!" I wish to proclaim my admiration for the rich creativity of the human mind, for its untiring efforts to fathom and affirm *the identity of man*, of that man who is always present in any form of culture.

(162) 10. On the other hand, in speaking of the *place of the Church* and the Apostolic See in your Organization, I am not thinking only of all the cultural works of the past two millennia by which men who had accepted Christ and the Gospel expressed themselves, or of the various institutions which were born of the same inspiration in the fields of education, instruction, charity, social aid, and so many others. I am thinking above all, ladies and gentlemen, of *the fundamental link between the Gospel, that is the message of Christ and of the Church, and man in his essential humanity.* For that link is indeed fundamentally creative of culture. For culture to be created, man must be viewed as a distinctive and autonomous value, as bearing in himself the transcendence of personality, with all that ultimately implies. *Man must be affirmed for his own sake*, and not for any other motive or reason: solely for himself! More than this, man must be loved because he is man, love is due to man by virtue of the special dignity which is his. All these affirmations concerning man lie in the very substance of the message of Christ and the mission of the Church, despite all that critics may have said on this score and all that may have been done by the various movements which are opposed to religion in general and to Christianity in particular.

(163) More than once, over the course of history, we have witnessed - and are still witnessing - *a process, a phenomenon of the greatest significance.* Wherever *religious institutions* have been suppressed, wherever the ideas and the activities born of religious inspiration and, in particular, of Christian inspiration, have been outlawed, men discover these same elements, *outside the institutional framework* when, in obedience to the truth and by their inner striving, they compare what constitutes their humanity with the content of the Christian message.

(164) You will not blame me, ladies and gentlemen, for this statement. I can assure you that it is not my intention to cause offence to anyone. I would merely ask you to understand that, in the name of what I stand for, *I could not refrain from bearing this testimony.* In fact it also contains a truth about culture which cannot be passed over in silence if we seek in culture all that is human, wherein man expresses himself and whereby he seeks to be the subject of his own existence. I wished too, in saying this, to *stress* even more my *gratitude* for the ties which unite UNESCO with the Apostolic See, ties that are reflected in a special way in my presence here today.

(165) 11. From what I have said, a number of major conclusions can be drawn. For the foregoing remarks point clearly to the fact that *the primary and indispensable duty of culture* in general - and of every culture - *is education.* To educate is to help man become ever more fully man, to enable him to "be" more, not only to "have" more, so that, through all he "has", through all he "possesses", man may become more fully capable of "being" man. If this is to come about, man must learn how to "be more" not only "with others" but also "for others". Education is of fundamental importance in developing human and social interrelationships. Here, too, I take up a set of axioms, in which there is a convergence of Christian traditions proceeding from the Gospel with the educational experience of all the men of goodwill and deep wisdom of whom there have been so many in every century. Our own times are not lacking either in *men who are seen to be great* simply because of their humanity, which they know how to share with others, and with young people in particular. At the same time, the symptoms of the crises of every kind to which the more affluent milieux and societies, as it happens, are succumbing and which affect, above all, the younger generations, are striking proof that the work of educating man *is not solely carried out by institutions*, by organized, material means, no matter how excellent they may be. These symptoms also show that what matters most is always *man*, man and *his moral authority*, deriving from the rightness of his principles and the conformity of his actions with those principles.

(166) 12. UNESCO, in its capacity as the world organization most competent to deal with all problems concerning culture, cannot neglect another cardinal question: What can be done to ensure man's education *above all within the family?*

(167) What state of public morality will give the family, and especially parents, the moral authority necessary for this purpose? What kind of instruction? What types of legislation uphold that authority or, on the other hand, weaken and destroy it? The causes of success or failure in man's education in the home are always found *at the very heart* of that basic culture-creating environment, the family, as well as *at a higher level*, that which lies within the province of the State and its agencies, on which they still depend. These problems cannot but give cause to reflection and concern in the forum where official State representatives gather together.

(168) There is no doubt that the prime and fundamental cultural factor is the spiritually mature individual, one who is fully educated, capable of educating himself and others. Neither is there any doubt that the prime and fundamental dimension of culture is sound morality: *ethical culture.*

(169) 13. There are, of course many specific questions in this field, but experience shows that everything is related and that these questions fall within systems which already clearly interact with each other. For example, in the whole process of education, and especially in school education, has there not been *a unilateral movement towards instruction in the narrow sense of the term*? If we consider the proportions that this phenomenon has assumed and the systematic growth of instruction exclusively geared to possession, is not the vision of man himself being increasingly obscured? The outcome is the literal *alienation of education*: instead of striving towards what man ought to "be", it operates only in terms of that to which man can lay claim in terms of "having" and "possessing". The next stage in this process of alienation is to accustom man, by depriving him of his own subjectivity, to becoming the *object of a host of manipulations*, whether these be ideological and political manipulations through public opinion; or manipulations operating through the monopoly or control of the media by economic forces or political powers; or indeed manipulations whereby people are taught that life is the specific manipulation of the self.

(170) Dangers such as these in education appear above all to constitute a threat to societies with a more highly developed civilization. These societies are having to contend with the *specific crisis of man*, in which *man has less confidence in his own humanity*, in the meaningfulness of being a man and in the sense of affirmation and the joy that stem therefrom and are a source of creativity. Present-day civilization attempts to impose on man a set of *apparent imperatives* which its spokesmen justify by appealing to the principle of development and progress. Respect for life, for example, is replaced by the "imperative" to snuff out and destroy life; love as the responsible communion of persons gives way to the "imperative" of maximum sexual enjoyment devoid of all sense of responsibility; and, instead of primacy being accorded to truth in a person's acts, "primacy" goes to the latest fashion in behaviour, to self-centredness and to instant success.

(171) All this amounts indirectly to the *wholesale and systematic abandonment* of the healthy ambition of being a man. Let us not delude ourselves: the system based on such false imperatives and fundamental denials may well dictate the future of man and of culture.

(172) 14. If, in the name of the future of culture, man's right to "be" more needs to be proclaimed, and if, for the same reason, the healthy *primacy of the family* in the whole process of educating man for genuine humanity needs to be demanded, the *right of the nation* also needs to be situated in the same line of thinking. It too must be situated at *the root of culture and education.*

(173) The Nation is indeed the broad community of men who are united by a variety of ties but are above all joined, in fact, by culture. The Nation exists *"by" culture and "for" culture*, and it is accordingly the main educative influence ensuring that men can "be more" within the community. It is that community which has a history going beyond the history of the individual and the family. It is also in that community, in terms of which every family acts as an educator, that the family starts its educational task with the simplest thing first, by imparting language and thereby enabling man in his early years to learn to speak, and thus to become a member of the community formed of his family and of his nation. All I am now saying and shall be dwelling on further reflects a specific experience and a *specific testimony.* I am the son of a Nation which has lived through the greatest vicissitudes of history, which its neighbours have condemned to death more than once, and yet which has survived and remained itself. It has kept its identity, and despite partition and foreign occupation, it has maintained its national sovereignty not by depending on the resources of physical force but solely by *relying on its culture*. In the case in point, that culture has proved more powerful than all other forces combined. Hence what I am saying here about the Nation's right to the fundamentals of its culture and its future in no way smacks of "nationalism": that right has been and always will be a stable factor in human experience and in the *humanist outlook for the development of man*. There is a fundamental sovereignty of society which is manifested in the culture of the nation. It is that sovereignty through which, at the same time, man is supremely sovereign. In expressing myself in these terms, I am also thinking, with deep personal emotion, of the *cultures of the many peoples of old* who did not yield when they were confronted with the civilizations of invaders. And those cultures are still the source of man's "being" in the innermost truth of his humanity. I am also thinking, with a sense of admiration, of the *cultures of the new societies* of those societies which are awakening to life in the community of their own Nation, just as my own Nation awoke to life ten centuries ago, and are struggling to maintain their own identity and their own values against the influences and pressures of models proposed from the outside.

(174) 15. To you, ladies and gentlemen, who, for more than thirty years now, have been meeting here in the name of primacy of the cultural realities of man, of human communities, peoples and nations, I should like to say this: use every means at your disposal to watch over the fundamental sovereignty possessed by every Nation by virtue of its own culture. Protect it! Do not allow fundamental sovereignty to fall prey to political or economic interests. Do not allow it to become the victim of totalitarianism, imperialism or hegemony, for which man is only an object of domination rather than the subject of his own human existence. To them, too, the Nation - whether it be their own Nation or that of others - is only an object of domination and a bait for different interests rather than the subject of the sovereignty deriving from the authentic culture which is its birthright. Are there not, on the map of Europe and the world, Nations which have a *marvellous historical sovereignty* born of their culture and yet which are at the same time deprived of their full sovereignty? Is not this an important point for the future of human culture, especially in our day and age, when it has become so urgent to banish the remnants of colonialism?

(175) 16. This sovereignty which exists and which has its origins in the specific culture of the Nation and society, in the primacy of the family in the task of education, and in the personal dignity of every individual, *must remain the fundamental criterion* in the approach to the problem of the *mass media* (and of the information bound up with them and of what we call "mass culture"), which is so crucial to mankind today. Since these media are the "social" means of communication, they cannot be the *means of domination over others* wielded by the agents of political or financial power who set out to dictate their own programmes and their own models. They must become the means - and a most important means - of *expression* for *society* which makes use of them and also keeps them in being. They must bear in mind the real needs of that society. They must take into account the Nation's culture and its history. They must *respect the family's responsibility in education*. They must have regard for man's well-being and his dignity. They must not be governed by the criteria of self-interest, sensationalism or immediate success, but, with due consideration for the requirements of ethics, must help to build a "more human" existence.

(176) 17. *Genus humanum arte et ratione vivit.* The basic assertion is that *man is man through truth*, and *becomes increasingly man through* an ever more perfect *knowledge of truth*. I should like here to pay tribute, ladies and gentlemen. to your Organization's outstanding work, and at the same time to the work of the States and institutions you represent and their commitment to the task of promoting *the general provision of education for the people at large*, at all grades and levels, and of eradicating illiteracy which reflects the non- existence of even the rudiments of instruction, a grievous deficiency not only from the point of view of the basic culture of individuals and their environment, but also in terms of socio-economic progress. There are alarming signs of disparities in this field, linked with an often acutely unequal and unjust distribution of wealth: we need only think of situations where a small plutocratic oligarchy coexists with starving multitudes living in extreme poverty. The disparity can be remedied, not through bloody struggles for power, but above all, by *systematically promoting literacy* through the widespread provision of education for the masses. This is the direction in which we must work if we wish afterwards to bring about the changes needed in the socio-economic domain. Man, who "is more" because, also, of what he "has", and what he "possesses", must *know how to possess*, that is to say, how to *deal with and administer* the resources in his possession, for his own good and for the common good. For this, education is essential.

(177) 18. The question of instruction has always been closely bound up with the *Church's Mission.* Over the centuries, the Church has founded schools at all levels; it brought into being the medieval universities in Europe: in Paris and Bologna, Salamanca and Heidelberg, Cracow and Louvain. It still offers the same contribution today, wherever its action in this field is sought and respected. May I here and now, *on behalf of Catholic families*, claim the right of all families to have their children educated in schools reflecting their own view of the world, and, in particular, the absolute right of believers not to have their children subjected to atheist-inspired curricula in their schools. This is one of the fundamental rights of man and the family.

(178) 19. The education system is organically linked to the system represented by the various policies followed as regards *the practice and popularization of science*, with which higher education institutions, universities and also, in the light of the present development of specialization and scientific methods, specialized institutes, are concerned. These are institutions of which it would be difficult to speak without feeling deeply affected. They are *the workshops*, where man's pursuit of knowledge and *the vital bond* between humanity *and truth* as the ultimate aim of knowledge become a daily reality, and, in a sense, become the daily bread of so many masters, revered leaders in science, and, around them, of young research workers dedicated to science and its applications, as well as the multitude of students enrolled in these centres of science and knowledge.

(179) We are, here, as it were, *on the uppermost rungs of the ladder* which man has, from the beginning been climbing towards understanding of the reality of the world around him and of the mysteries of his own humanity. This historical process has attained a *potential* in our time unknown in the past; it has opened up hitherto unsuspected *horizons* to human understanding. It would be difficult to go into details here, for, on the path to knowledge, specialist branches are as manifold as the development of science is rich.

(180) 20. Your Organization is a meeting-place, encompassing, in the broadest sense of the word, the whole, essential sphere of human culture. This forum is therefore an ideal place in which to *hail* all men of science, and pay tribute particularly to those who are here today and have received the highest recognition and the most outstanding world honours for their work. Allow me, then, to voice certain hopes which will, I have no doubt, find a sympathetic echo in the minds and hearts of the members of this distinguished assembly.

(181) Just as, in scientific work, we are edified - edified and profoundly gladdened - by that *progress in the disinterested knowledge of truth* which scientists serve with the utmost dedication, at times risking their health or even their lives, so also must we feel concern at everything which runs counter to the principles of disinterested objectivity, everything which would turn science *into an instrument* to attain goals which are quite alien to it. Yes, we must concern ourselves with everything that proposes and presupposes such non- scientific aims, when scientists are required to serve their purposes without having the opportunity of judging and deciding, quite freely, whether such aims are *honest in human and ethical terms*, or when they are threatened with the consequences if they refuse to have any part in them.

(182) Do these non-scientific goals of which I speak and the problem to which I refer need proof or comment? You know what I have in mind; suffice it to say that among those who were brought before the international courts at the close of the last world war, there were scientists. Ladies and gentlemen, please forgive me for uttering these words, but I should be false to my responsibilities if I did not give voice to them, in order not simply to hark back to the past, but to defend *the future of science and human culture*; what is more, to defend the future of man and the world! I think that Socrates, who with his exceptional moral rectitude maintained that science was also a moral virtue, would be less convinced if he were able to witness the experiments of our times.

(183) 21. We are well aware, ladies and gentlemen, that *the future of man and of the world is threatened* - very seriously threatened - despite the unquestionably lofty intentions of scholars and scientists. It is threatened because the wonderful results of their research ad discoveries, particularly in the natural sciences, have been and are still being exploited - to the detriment of ethical imperatives - for purposes which have nothing to do with the requirements of science, and indeed *for the purposes of destroying and killing*. Today, this has reached an unprecedented level and is causing inconceivable harm. Whereas science ought to be used for the good of human life, we find only too often that it is subjected to purposes destructive of the true dignity of man and of human life. Such is the case when scientific research itself is directed to such purposes or when its results are applied to ends contrary to the good of humanity. There is evidence of this both in the field of genetic manipulation and biological experiment and in that of chemical, bacteriological or nuclear armaments. Two considerations lead me to bring particularly to your attention the nuclear threat hanging over the world today, which could, if not averted, lead to the destruction of the fruits of culture and the products of the civilization built up over the centuries by successive generations of men who have believed in the primacy of the spirit and have spared neither their efforts nor their labours. The first consideration is this: reasons of geopolitics, economic problems on a world-wide scale, dreadful misunderstandings, wounded national pride, the materialism of our age and the decline of moral values have brought our world to a state of instability, a *delicate equilibrium* which is liable to be upset at any moment as a result of errors of judgement, information or interpretation.

(184) There is another consideration besides this disquieting prospect. Can we still be sure, nowadays, that disturbance of that equilibrium would not lead to war, and to a war in which nuclear weapons would be used without hesitation? Hitherto it has been said that nuclear weapons represented a deterrent which has prevented the outbreak of a major war; and this is very probably true. But at the same time we may wonder if it will always be so. Nuclear weapons, whatever their scale or type, are becoming more sophisticated year by year, and are being added to the arsenals of an ever-increasing number of countries. How can we be sure that the use of nuclear weapons, even for purposes of national defence or in limited conflicts, will not bring about an *unavoidable escalation* leading to destruction on a scale which mankind can never either contemplate or accept? However, there is no need for me to ask you, scientists and men of culture, not to close your eyes to what a nuclear war could mean for the whole of mankind (cf. Homily for the World Day of Peace, 1 January 1980).

(185) 22. Ladies and gentlemen, the world cannot go on like this much longer. No one who is aware of the situation and of what is at stake, and who is guided by an elementary sense of the responsibilities each individual bears, can avoid the conviction, which is also a *moral imperative*, that consciences must be called into play! The *efforts of people's consciences* must be increased to match the rising tension between good and evil to which men are being subjected at the close of the twentieth century. We must become convinced of the priority of the ethical over the technical, of the primacy of people over things and of the superiority of the spirit over matter (cf. *Redemptor Hominis*, No 16). The cause of mankind will be served if science and conscience are allied. Scientists will truly help mankind if they preserve "a sense of the transcendence of man over the world and of God over man" (Address to the Pontifical Academy of Science, 10 November 1979, No 4). Thus, availing myself of the opportunity afforded by my being here today at the headquarters of UNESCO, I, child of humanity and Bishop of Rome, address myself directly to you, men of science, to you assembled here who are the highest authorities in all the domains of modern science. And through you, I address myself to your colleagues and friends in all countries and on all the continents.

(186) I appeal to you in the name of this dreadful threat which hangs over mankind, and, at the same time, in the name of the future and the welfare of humanity throughout the world. I beseech you: *let us do our utmost* to institute and respect the primacy of ethics in all the spheres of science. Let us strive, above all, to preserve the family of man from the terrible prospect of nuclear war!

(187) I took up this subject before the General Assembly of the United Nations in New York on 2 October last year. Today I am speaking of it to you. I appeal to your minds and to your hearts, above and beyond all passions, ideologies and frontiers. I appeal to all those who, by their political or economic power, could be, and often are, called upon to determine scientists' *conditions of work* and the *lines they are to follow*. Above all, I appeal to each scientist individually and to the entire international scientific community.

(188) Together you have enormous power, the power of the intellect and of the conscience! Show yourselves to be more powerful than the most powerful in our contemporary world! Resolve to show the most noble form of solidarity with mankind: that which is based on the dignity of man. Build up peace on the foundation of *respect for all man's rights*, those bound up with his material and economic life as well as those connected with the spiritual and inner dimensions of his existence in this world. May wisdom inspire you! May love be your guide, that love which will overcome the growing menace of hatred and destruction! Men of science, pledge your full moral authority to save mankind from nuclear destruction!

(189) 23. Today I have accomplished *one of the most ardent desires of my heart*. I have been given the opportunity, here, of entering the Areopagus of the whole world. I have been given the opportunity of telling you all, members of the United Nations Educational, Scientific and Cultural Organization, who are working for good and for the reconciliation of men and peoples through all the fields of culture, education, science and information, of crying out to you, from the depths of my soul: Yes, the future on mankind depends on culture! Yes, world peace depends on the *primacy of the spirit*! Yes, peace in mankind's future depends on *love*!

(190) Your personal contribution, ladies and gentlemen, is important, indeed vital. It consists in adopting the *correct approach* to the problems with which you have to wrestle.

(191) My final word is this: Do not abandon the struggle! Continue it without ceasing!

VII - RESPONSIBILITIES OF SCIENCE AND TECHNOLOGY

Address of His Holiness John Paul II to Scientists and Representatives of the United Nations University. Hiroshima, 25 February 1981.

Original: English (*)

(192) 1. How can I express my feelings at this unique meeting, in Hiroshima, with the distinguished representatives of science, culture and higher learning? First of all, I would like to say that I feel very honoured to be among a group of such highly qualified men and women, who devote their energies to the business of Government and research, intellectual reflection and teaching. I am very grateful to the City and Prefecture of Hiroshima for welcoming me here today. I thank you sincerely for your cordial and benevolent welcome.

(193) I would like to offer a particular greeting to the representatives of the *University of the United Nations*, represented here by its Rector, Mr. Soedjatmoko, the Vice-Rectors, members of the Council, and the principal collaborators of the University. Your institution, which by its statutes is linked to the United Nations Organization and to UNESCO, is a completely original creation, founded to promote the lofty aims of the United Nations at the levels of research, advanced training and the dissemination of knowledge; it was deliberately established as a global and worldwide institution. My predecessor Paul VI and I have on more than one occasion expressed our esteem for this noble enterprise and our hopes for its future. It seeks to place science and research at the service of the great humanitarian ideals of peace advancement, development, the improvement of food resources, the proper use of natural resources and cooperation between the nations.

(*) AAS 73(1981), 420-428

(194) 2. Ladies and Gentlemen, we have gathered here today at Hiroshima: and I would like you to know that I am deeply convinced we have been given an historic opportunity to reflect together on the *responsibility of science and technology* at this period, marked as it is by so much hope and so many anxieties. At Hiroshima the facts speak for themselves, in a way that is dramatic, unforgettable and unique. In the face of an unforgettable tragedy which touches us all as human beings, how can we fail to express our brotherhood and our deep sympathy at the frightful wound inflicted on the cities of Japan that bear the names of Hiroshima and Nagasaki? That wound affected the whole of the human family. Hiroshima and Nagasaki: few events in history have had *such an effect on man's conscience.* The representatives of the world of science were not those least affected by the *moral crisis* caused throughout the world by the explosion of the first atomic bomb. The human mind had in fact made a *terrible discovery.* We realized with horror that nuclear energy would henceforth be available as a weapon of devastation; then we learned that this terrible weapon had in fact been used, for the first time, for military purposes. And then *there arose the question that will never leave us again*: will this weapon, perfected and multiplied beyond measure, be used tomorrow? If so, would it not probably destroy the human family, its members and all the achievements of civilization?

(195) 3. Ladies and gentlemen, you who devote your lives to the modern sciences, you are the first to be able to evaluate the disaster that a nuclear war would inflict on the human family. And I know that ever since the explosion of the first atomic bomb *many of you have been anxiously wondering about the responsibility of modern science and of the technology which is the fruit of that science.* In a number of countries, associations of scholars and research workers express the anxiety of the scientific world in the face of an irresponsible use of science, which too often does grievous damage to the balance of nature, or brings with it the ruin and oppression of man by man. One thinks in the first place of physics, chemistry, biology and the genetic sciences, of which you rightly condemn those applications or experimentations which are detrimental to humanity. But one also has in mind the social sciences and the human behavioural sciences when they are utilized to manipulate people, to crush their minds, souls, dignity and freedom. Criticism of science and technology is sometimes so severe that it comes close to condemning science itself. On the contrary science and technology are a wonderful product of God-given human creativity, since they have provided us with wonderful possibilities, and we all gratefully benefit from them. But we know that this potential is not a neutral one: it can be used either for man's progress or for his degradation. Like you, I have lived through this period, which I would call the "post-Hiroshima period", and I share your anxieties. And today I feel inspired to say this to you: surely the time has come for our society, and especially for the world of science, to realize that *the future of humanity depends as never before on our collective moral choices.*

(196) 4. In the past it was possible to destroy a village, a town, a region, even a country. Now, it is the whole planet which has come under threat. This fact should finally compel everyone to face *a basic moral consideration: from now on, it is only through a conscious choice and through a deliberate policy that humanity can survive.* The moral and political choice which faces us is that of putting all the resources of mind, science and culture at the service of peace and of the building of a new society, a society which will succeed in *eliminating the causes of fratricidal wars* by generously pursuing the total progress of each individual and of all humanity. Of course, individuals and societies are always exposed to the passions of greed and hate; but, as far as within us lies, let us try effectively to correct those social situations and structures which cause injustice and conflict. We shall build peace by building a more humane world. In the light of this hope, the scientific, cultural and university world has an eminent part to play. Peace is one of the loftiest achievements of culture, and for this reason it deserves all our intellectual and spiritual energy.

(197) 5. As scholars and researchers, you represent *an international community, with a task that can be decisive* for the future of humanity. But on one condition: that you succeed in defending and serving *man's true culture* as a precious possession. Your role is a noble one when you work towards man's growth in his being and not just in his possessions or his knowledge of his power. It is in the depths of his being that man's true culture lies. I tried to express this *fundamental aspect of our civilization* in an address that I gave to UNESCO on 2 June 1980: "Culture is a specific mode of man's 'existing' and 'being'.... And it is therein that the fundamental distinction between what man is and what he has, between being and having, is grounded.... All that man "possesses" is important for culture, and a factor creative of culture, only in so far as man, by virtue of what he "possesses", is also able to "be" more fully man, to become more fully a man at all levels of his existence and in everything which characterizes his humanity." (See above, Par. 155 and 156). This concept of culture is based upon a *total view of man*, body and spirit, person and community, a rational being and one ennobled by love: "Yes! the future of mankind depends on culture! Yes, world peace depends on the *primacy of the Spirit!* Yes, peace in mankind's future depends *on love!*" (*ibid.* See above, Par. 189). In truth, our future, our very survival are linked to the image that we shall make of man.

(198) 6. Our future on this planet, exposed as it is to nuclear annihilation, depends upon one single factor: *humanity must make a moral reversal.* At the present moment of history, there must be a general mobilization of all men and women of goodwill. Humanity is being called upon *to take a major step forward, a step forward in civilization and wisdom.* A lack of civilization, an ignorance of man's true values, brings the risk that humanity will be destroyed. We must become wiser. Pope Paul VI, in his Encyclical entitled *"The Development of Peoples"* (26 March 1967, No.20) stressed several times the urgent need to have recourse to the *wise men* in order to guide the new society in its development. In particular, he said that "if further development calls for the work of more and more technicians, even more necessary is the deep thought and reflection of wise men in search for a new humanism which would enable modern man to find himself anew by embracing the higher values of love and friendship, of prayer and contemplation".

(199) Above all, in this country of Japan, renowned for its creativity, both cultural and technological, a country with so many scientists, scholars, writers and religious thinkers, I take the liberty of making a very special appeal. I wish to address myself to the men and women of Japan, and through them to the wise men and women of the whole world, in order to encourage them to pursue ever more effectively the task of social and moral reconstruction which our world so ardently awaits. Work together to defend and to promote, among all the people of your nation and of the world, the idea of a just world, a world made to man's scale, a world that enables human beings to fulfil their capacities, a world that sustains them in their material, moral and spiritual needs.

(200) 7. Men and women dedicated to research and culture: your work has taken on a completely new importance in this age marked by the rise of science and technology. What an achievement for our time, *what intellectual and moral power, what a responsibility towards society and humanity!* Shall we be able to join in placing this scientific and cultural heritage at the service of the true progress of humanity, for the building of a world of dignity and justice for all? The task is enormous; some will call it an utopian one. But how can we *fail to sustain the trust of modernman*, against all the temptations to fatalism, to 1 and perm passivity and to moral dejection? We must say to the people of today: do not doubt, your future is in your own hands. The building of a more just humanity or a more united international community is not just a dream or a vain ideal. It is a moral imperative, a sacred duty, one that the intellectual and spiritual genius of man can face, through a fresh mobilization of everybody's talents and energies, through putting to work *all the technical and cultural resources of man.*

(201) 8. The people of our time possess, in the first place, *tremendous scientific and technological resources.* And we are convinced that these resources could be more effectively used for the development and growth of peoples; let us consider the progress made in agriculture, biology, medicine, the social communications media applied to education; then there are the social and economic sciences, and the science of planning, all of which could combine to direct in a more humane and effective way the process of industrialization and urbanization, and to promote the new models of international cooperation. If all the rich nations of the world wanted to, they could assemble an impressive number of specialists for the tasks of development. All this obviously presupposes political choices, and, more fundamentally, moral options. The moment is approaching when *priorities will have to be redefined.* For example, it has been estimated that about a half of the world's research-workers are at present employed for military purposes. Can the human family morally go on much longer in this direction?

(202) There is also the question of the *economic resources needed* for giving a decisive impulse to the integral advancement of the human family.

(203) Here too we are faced with choices. Can we remain passive when we are told that humanity spends immensely more money on arms than on development, and when we learn that one soldier's equipment costs many times more than a child's education?

(204) 9. Science and technology have always formed part of man's culture, but today we are witnessing the speedily increasing growth of a technology which seems to have *destroyed its equilibrium with the dimensions of culture* by acting as an element of division. Such is the great problem facing modern society. Science and technology are the most dynamic factors of the development of society today, but their intrinsic limitations do not make them capable, by themselves, of providing the power that would bind culture together. How then can a culture absorb science and technology, with their dynamism, without losing its own identity?

(205) There are *three temptations* to be avoided in this regard. The first is the temptation to pursue technological development for its own sake, the sort of development that has for its only norm that of its growth and affirmation, as if it were a matter of an independent reality that is properly human, imposing on man the inevitable realization of his ever new possibilities, as if one should always do what is technically possible. The second temptation is that of subjecting technological development to economic usefulness in accordance with the logic of profit or nonstop economic expansion, thus creating advantages for some while leaving others in poverty, with no care for the true common good of humanity, making technology into an instrument at the service of the ideology of "having". Thirdly, there is also the temptation to subject technological development to the pursuit or maintenance of power, as happens when it is used for military purposes, and whenever people are being manipulated in order that they may be dominated.

(206) 10. As men and women dedicated to culture, you enjoy *immense moral credibility* for acting upon all the centres of decision-making, whether private or public, that are capable of influencing the politics of tomorrow. Using all honest and effective means, make sure that a total vision of man and a generous idea of culture prevail. Work out persuasive arguments, so that everyone will be brought to understand that *peace or the survival of the human race is henceforth linked indissolubly with progress, development and dignity for all people*. You will succeed in your task if you restate your conviction that "science and technology find their justification in the service that they render to man and humanity"; and that rational science must be linked with a series of spheres of knowledge open wide to spiritual values. I urge all scientists, centres of research and universities to study more deeply *the ethical problems of the technological society*, a subject which is already engaging the attention of a number of modern thinkers. It is a question that is closely connected with the problems of the just sharing of resources, the use of technology for peaceful purposes, the development of nations.

(207) 11. The construction of a new social order presupposes, over and above the essential and technological skills, a lofty inspiration, a courageous motivation, a belief in man's future, in his dignity, in his destiny. It is man's heart and spirit that must be reached, beyond the divisions spawned by individual interests, selfishness and ideologies. In a word, *man must be loved for his own sake*. This is the *supreme value* that all sincere humanists, generous thinkers and all the great religions want to promote. Love for man as such is at the centre of the message of Jesus Christ and his Church: this relationship is indissoluble. In my speech to UNESCO, I stressed the fundamental link between the Gospel and the man in his very humanity: "That link is indeed fundamentally creative of culture. ... *Man must be affirmed for himself*... More than this, man must be loved because he is man, love is due to man by virtue of the special dignity which is his. All these affirmations concerning man lie in the very substance of Christ's message and of the mission of the Church" (No. 10. See above, Par. 162).

(208) All those who desire the defence and progress of man must therefore love man for his own sake; and for this *it is essential to count upon the values of the spirit*, which are alone capable of transforming hearts and deeply-rooted attitudes. All of us who carry in our hearts the treasure of a religious faith must share in a common work of man's development, and we must do it with clear-sightedness and courage. All Christians, all those who call upon God, all spiritual families should be invited to join in a common effort to sustain, spiritually and culturally, all those men and women who devote themselves to the total growth of man.

(209) 12. In this country one could not fail to evoke the great spiritual and religious traditions of Asia, traditions that have so enriched the worldwide heritage of man. Nor could one fail to wish for *closer dialogue and effective collaboration* between all those who believe in man's spiritual calling, his search for the Absolute, for justice, for fraternity, and, as we express it in our own faith, his thirst for redemption and immortality. Rational science and man's religious knowledge need to be linked together. You who devote yourselves to the sciences, are you not invited to study the link which must be established between scientific and technological knowledge and man's moral knowledge? Knowledge and virtue were cultivated together by the ancients, in the East as well as in the West. Even today, I know well, many scholars, even though they do not all profess one particular religion, are searching for an integration between their science and their desire to serve the whole man. Through their intellectual honesty, their quest for what is true, their self-discipline as scholars, and through their objectivity and respect before the mysteries of the universe, these people make up a great spiritual family. All who generously dedicate their knowledge to the progress of the people and all those who have faith in man's spiritual calling are invited to a common task: to constitute a *real science* for the total advancement of man.

(210) 13. In a word, I believe that our generation is faced by a great moral challenge, one which consists in harmonizing the values of science with the values of conscience. Speaking to UNESCO on 2 June 1980, I made an appeal that I put before you today: "A conviction, which is at the same time a *moral imperative*, forces itself upon anyone who has become aware of the situation... consciences must be mobilized! *The efforts of human consciences must be increased* in proportion to the tension between good and evil to which people at the end of the twentieth century are being subjected. We must convince ourselves of the priority of ethics over technology, of the primacy of the person over things, of the superiority of the spirit over matter (cf. *Redemptor Hominis*, No. 16). The cause of man will be served if science forms an alliance with conscience. The man of science will really help humanity if he keeps 'the sense of man's transcendence over the world and of God's transcendence over man' (Address to the Pontifical Academy of Sciences, 10 November 1979, No. 4)" (See above, par. 185).

(211) Ladies and Gentlemen, it is for you to take up this noble challenge.

VIII - A NEW SOLIDARITY BASED ON WORK

Address of His Holiness John Paul II to the International Labour Organization. Geneva, 15 June 1982.

Original: English (*)

(212) 1. First of all, I should like to tell you how happy I am to have this opportunity of being here today and addressing this illustrious assembly gathered here for the 68th Session of the International Labour Conference. As you know, events prevented me from responding to the Director-General's invitation to attend last year's session. I thank God for having preserved my life and restored my health. My inability to come to Geneva in 1981 further strengthened my determination to meet you, especially in view of the multiple ties that link me to the world of labour - not least among them the awareness of a special responsibility in regard to the many problems inherent in the reality of human work. These are important problems, often difficult; all are fundamental and

(*) AAS 74(1982), 992-1006.

they constitute the *raison d'être* of your Organization. The invitation which the Director-General reiterated even as I was recovering was therefore a source of particular joy to me. Meanwhile, I have published my Encyclical *Laborem Exercens* on human work, intended as a contribution to the development of the social doctrine of the Catholic Church, whose great texts, beginning with Pope Leo XIII's *Rerum Novarum*, were respectfully and favourably received by the International Labour Organization, keenly attuned as it has always been, throughout the various historic stages of its existence and activity, to the varied aspects of all the complex problems associated with human work.

(213) Allow me therefore to express my gratitude for your invitation and for the warm welcome extended to me. At the same time, I want to tell you how much I appreciate the kind words the Director-General has just spoken; they make it that much easier for me to address you now. As the guest of your Conference, I speak to you on behalf of the Catholic Church and the Apostolic See and within the framework of their universal mission, which is primarily and essentially a religious and moral one. From that point of view the Church and the Holy See share your Organization's concern for its basic objectives, just as they are at one with the entire family of nations in its fundamental purpose of promoting the progress of mankind.

(214) 2. In addressing you, Ladies and Gentlemen, I wish first of all, through you, *to pay tribute to human work,* whatever its nature and wherever in the world it may be performed - a tribute to all work, and to each and every man or woman engaged in it, irrespective of its specific content and including "physical" as well as "intellectual" work; irrespective, too, of its particular purpose, whether it be "creative" or "reproductive"; and irrespective of whether it consists of theoretical research providing a basis for the work of others, or an activity aimed at organizing the conditions and structure of such work or, again, the management or the actual performance, by workers, of the tasks involved in carrying out programmes. Work in any of its forms deserves particular respect because it represents the output of a human being and because behind it there is always a live subject: the human person. That is the source of its value, and its dignity.

(215) In the name of that dignity, which is a feature of all human work, I should also like to express my esteem for each of you, Ladies and Gentlemen, and for the concrete institutions - the organizations and authorities - which you represent here. In view of the universal character of the International Labour Organization, this occasion enables me to pay tribute to all the groups represented here and to praise the efforts of each of them to develop its own potential for promoting the common good of all its members - men and women united from generation to generation in their various jobs.

(216) 3. Finally - and here I think I am speaking not only for the Holy See but, in a sense, for all those present - I should like to express particular esteem and gratitude to the *International Labour Organization itself.* Your Organization occupies an important place in international life because of its age and its lofty objectives. Following its creation in 1919 under the Versailles Treaty, it undertook to contribute to lasting peace through the promotion of social justice, as stated by the opening words of the Preamble to its Constitution: "Whereas universal and lasting peace can be established only if it is based upon social justice...." This fundamental commitment to peace was quoted by the Director-General at the Symposium organized in Rome by the Papal Commission "Iustitia et Pax" at the beginning of April, when he referred to the parchment contained in the cornerstone of the International Labour Office building, with the inscription si vis pacem cole iustitiam - "if you want peace, cultivate justice."

(217) The merits of your Organization shine forth in its many international Conventions and Recommendations establishing international labour standards, these "new rules of social conduct" to compel "particular interests to submit to the wider vision of the common good" (Paul VI, Address to the ILO, nn. 14 and 19; AAS, 61(1969), pages 497 and 499. See above, par. 47 and 52). They are also evident in many other activities aimed at satisfying the new needs to which the evolution of social and economic structure has given rise. They are, finally, reflected in the persistent day-to-day efforts of the officials of the International Labour Office and the bodies it has created to strengthen its activities, such as the International Institute for Labour Studies, the International Social Association and the International Centre for Technical and Vocational Training.

(218) If I ventured to mention the International Labour Organization in my Encyclical *Laborem Exercens*, I did so both to draw attention to its many achievements and to encourage it to strengthen its activities *aimed at making work more human*. I also intended to highlight the fact that, in efforts to give human labour a truly moral basis consistent with the objective principles of social ethics, the aims of the International Labour Organization are very close to those which the Church and the Apostolic See are pursuing in their own sphere, with means adapted to their mission. This, indeed, has been stressed on several occasions by my predecessors Pius XII and John XXIII, and in particular by Paul VI when he visited the International Labour Organization in 1969 to take part in the celebration of the fiftieth anniversary of its founding. Today, as before, the Church and the Apostolic See take great joy in their excellent cooperation with the Organization, already half a century old, whose formal culmination was the accrediting in 1967 of a Permanent Observer to the International Labour Organization. In this way the Holy See sought to give stable expression to its desire for cooperation and to the lively interest of the Catholic Church in labour problems, stemming from its concern for the true good of man.

(219) 4. The message which you expect from me, Ladies and Gentlemen, is bound to be no different from that which I delivered to other gatherings of representatives of the peoples of all nations: the General Assembly of the United Nations, the United Nations Food and Agricultural Organization and the United Nations Educational, Scientific and Cultural Organization. My thinking aims at reflecting, in a coherent way, one fundamental idea and one basic preoccupation: *the cause of man, his dignity and the inalienable rights flowing therefrom*. Already in my first Encyclical *Redemptor Hominis*, I stressed the fact that "man is the first road which the Church must travel in fulfilling its mission; it is the first road and the fundamental road of the Church, mapped out by Christ himself...." That is also the reason why, in celebrating the 19th anniversary of *Rerum Novarum*, I felt I should devote a major document of my papacy to human labour, to man at work - homo laborem exercens. For not only does work bear the imprint of man, but it reveals to man the true meaning of his existence - work considered as a human activity regardless of its concrete content and circumstances. Work is endowed with "this basic dimension of human existence" through which "man's life is built up every day." From work "it derives its specific dignity but at the same time contains the unceasing measure of human toil and suffering and also of the harm and injustice which penetrate deeply into social life within individual nations and on the international level" (*Laborem Exercens*, n. 1).

(220) 5. The problems of work - problems that have repercussions in so many spheres of life and at all levels, whether individual, family, national or international - share one characteristic, which is at one and the same time a condition and a programme, and which I would like to stress before you today: *solidarity*. I feel impelled to place these considerations before you partly because solidarity is inherent in one way or another in the very nature of human work, and also because of the objectives of your Organization and above all the spirit which imbues it. The spirit in which the International Labour Organization has carried out its missions since its foundation is a spirit of *universalism*, which rests on the fundamental equality of nations and the equality of men, and which is perceived both as the starting point and the point of arrival of any social policy. It is also a spirit of *humanism*, which seeks to develop all of man's potentialities, both material and spiritual. Lastly, it is a *community spirit*, which is successfully reflected in your *tripartite structure*. At this juncture, I can only repeat the words pronounced here by Paul VI during his visit in 1969: "Your original and organic instrument is to bring together the three forces at work in the human dynamics of modern labour: men of government, employers and workers. And your method, that has become a model, is to harmonize these three forces, so that they do not oppose each other, but combine 'in a courageous and fecund collaboration' by means of constant dialogue for the study and solution of ever renewed and recurring problems" (Address to ILO, 10 June 1969, n. 15, AAS 61, p. 498. See above, par. 48). The fact that the solution to the problems of work has been seen to lie in a commitment by all the parties involved, and in peaceful bargaining aimed at the well-being of man at his work and peace between societies, shows that you are conscious of the need for solidarity, which unites you in a common effort transcending the real differences that exist and the divisions that may always occur.

(221) 6. This fundamental intuition which the founders of the International Labour Organization so strongly emphasized in the structure of the Organization itself and whose corollary is that the objectives it pursues can only be achieved through community and solidarity, reflects the *reality of human work*. For, in its fundamental characteristics, the reality of work is the same all over the world, in every country and in every continent; among men and women of every race and nation, who speak different languages and represent diverse cultures: among men and women who profess different religions or express their relationships with religion and with God in a variety of ways. The reality of work is the same behind a multiplicity of forms: manual work and brain work; work in farming and work in industry; work in the service sector and work in research; the work of the craftsman, the technician, the educator, the artist or the housewife; the work of the factory operative and the work of the supervisors and managers. Without concealing the specific differences which remain and which often quite sharply differentiate the men and women performing these very varied jobs, work - the reality of work - *unites all* in an activity which has the same significance and the same source. For all, work is a necessity, a duty, a task. For each and every one, it is a way of assuring alivelihood, family life and certain fundamental values. In the diversity and universality of its forms, human work unites men because every man seeks in work "to realize his humanity, to fulfil the calling to be a person that is his by reason of his very humanity" (*Laborem Exercens*, n. 6). Yes "work bears a particular mark of man and of humanity, the mark of a person operating within a community of persons" (*Laborem Exercens*, preamble). Work bears the stamp of unity and solidarity.

(222) Moreover, it is difficult - in dealing, before this Assembly, with such a vast, such a varied, and at the same time such a universal subject as the work of the entire human family - not to hear in the depths of one's heart the words of the Book of Genesis, in which work is given to man as a task so that he may subdue the earth and dominate it (cf. *Gen.* 1:28).

(223) 7. The fundamental reason why I single out the theme of solidarity lies therefore in the very nature of human work. The *problem of work* has a very profound link *with that of the meaning of human life*. Because of this link, work becomes and indeed is a problem of man's spiritual nature. This observation in no way detracts from the other aspects of work, which one might say are more easily measurable and which are related to the various patterns and operations of an "external" character, arising out of the organization; this same observation indeed enables us to set human work, in whatever way it is performed by man, within man himself, in other words, in his innermost being, in the essence of his nature, in what makes him a man and therefore destined to work. The conviction that there is an essential link between the work of every man and the overall meaning of human existence is the whole foundation of the Christian doctrine of work - one might say the foundation of the "gospel of work" - and it permeates the teaching and activities of the Church, in one way or another, at each stage of its mission throughout history. "Never again will work be against the worker; but always work will be ... in the service of man" - it is worth repeating today the words spoken in this same place in 1969 by Pope Paul VI (Address to ILO, 10 June 1969, n. 11, AAS 61, p. 495. See above, par. 44). If work must always serve the welfare of man, if the programme of progress can only be carried out through work, then there is *a fundamental right to judge progress* in accordance with the following criterion: *does the work really serve man?* Is it compatible with his dignity? Through it, does human life achieve fulfillment in all its richness and diversity?

(224) We have the right to conceive of human work in this way; and we also have a duty to do so. We have the right and the duty to consider man not according to *whether or not he is useful in his work*, but to consider *work in its relation to man*, to each man, *to consider work according to whether or not it is useful to man*. We have the right and the duty to take account, in our approach to work, of the various needs of man, in the spheres of both the spirit and the body, and to take this approach to human work in each society and in each system, in areas where well-being prevails, and even more so, in areas where destitution is widespread. We have the right and the duty to take this approach to work in its relation to man - and not the reverse - as a fundamental criterion for assessing progress itself. For progress always requires an assessment and a value judgement: one must ask whether a given progress is sufficiently "human" and at the same time sufficiently "universal"; whether it helps to level out unjust inequalities and to promote a peaceful future for the world; whether, in the work itself, fundamental rights are ensured, for each person, for each family and for each nation. In a word, one must constantly ask oneself whether the work helps to fulfil the meaning of human life. While seeking a reply to these questions when analyzing socio-economic processes as a whole, one must not overlook the aspects and the content which form man's inner self: *the development of his knowledge and his awareness*. The link between work and the very meaning of human existence bears constant witness to the fact that man *has not been alienated by work*, that he has not been enslaved. Quite the contrary, it confirms that work has become the *ally of his humanity*, which helps him to live in truth and freedom in a freedom built on truth which enables him to lead, in all its fullness, a life more worthy of man.

(225) 8. Confronted with the blatant injustices arising out of the systems of the last century, workmen, especially in industry, reacted and thereby discovered not only their common poverty, but the strength that comes from concerted action. As victims of the same injustices, they combined in a joint effort. In my Encyclical on human work, I called this reaction a "just social reaction"; this situation "caused the impetuous emergence of a great burst of solidarity between workers, first and foremost industrial workers. The call to solidarity and common action addressed to the workers - especially to those engaged in narrowly specialized, monotonous and depersonalized work in industrial plants, where the machine tends to dominate man - was important and eloquent from the point of view of social ethics. It was the reaction against the degradation of man as the subject of work.... This reaction united the working world in a community marked by great solidarity" (*Laborem Exercens*, n. 8). Despite subsequent improvements, despite the greater and more effective respect for workers' fundamental rights in many countries, various systems based on ideology and on power have allowed flagrant injustices to persist or have created new ones. Moreover, the enhanced awareness of social justice uncovers new situations of injustices which, because of their geographical extent or contempt for the inalienable dignity of the human person, are nothing less than challenges to mankind. The need today is to forge *a new solidarity based on the true significance of human work*. For it is only through a just concept or work that it will be possible to define the objectives of this solidarity and the various forms it should take.

(226) 9. The world of work, Ladies and Gentlemen, is the world of all the men and all the women who, through their efforts, are trying to respond to the call to dominate the earth for the benefit of all. The solidarity of the world of work will therefore be a solidarity that broadens horizons to include not only the interests of individuals and particular groups but the *common good of society as a whole*, whether nationally, internationally or worldwide. It will be a solidarity *for work*, manifesting itself in the struggle *for* justice and *for* the truth of social life. For what justification would there be for a solidarity that spent itself in uncompromising opposition to others, in a struggle against others? Of course, the struggle for justice must not ignore the legitimate interests of workers associated in the same occupation or suffering from certain forms of injustice. It cannot ignore the tensions between groups which are often liable to break into open conflict. True solidarity seeks to struggle for a just social order in which all tensions can be absorbed and in which conflicts - whether between groups or nations - can be settled more easily. In order to build a world of justice and peace,solidarity must remove the foundations of hatred, selfishness, and injustice, which have too often been erected into ideological principles or as a vital law of life in society. Within the same community of work, solidarity sets out to discover the *unity inherent in the nature of the work* rather than the forces making for division and opposition. It refuses to conceive of society in terms of a struggle "against" and of social relationships in terms of uncompromising opposition between classes. Solidarity, which derives its origin and its strength from the nature of human work, and therefore from the primacy of the human person over things, will create the machinery of dialogue and cooperation that is needed to resolve opposition without seeking to destroy the opponent. No, it is not utopian to assert that the world of work can also be made a world of justice.

(227) 10. The need for man to safeguard the reality of his work and to free it from any ideology in order to bring out once more the true meaning of human effort, becomes particularly apparent when one considers the world of work and the solidarity that it calls for *in the international context*. The problem of man at work today must be set against a worldwide background which can no longer be ignored. All the major problems of man in society are now world problems! They must be approached on a worldwide scale, in a realistic spirit of course, but in an innovative, critical spirit as well. Whether we are dealing with the problems of natural resources, development or employment, a satisfactory solution can be found only if the international aspect is borne in mind. As long as fifteen years ago, in 1967, Paul VI noted in his Encyclical *Populorum Progressio*: "Today, the major fact that everyone must grasp is that the social question has become worldwide in character" (n. 3). Since then, many events have borne out the truth of this observation. The world economic crisis, with its repercussions throughout the globe, compels us to recognize that the horizon of the problems is increasingly a world horizon. The hundreds of millions of starving or undernourished human beings, who also have the right to rise up out of their poverty, should make us realize that the fundamental reality today is mankind as a whole. There is a common good which can no longer be confined to a more or less satisfactory compromise between sectional demands or between purely economic requirements. New ethical choices are necessary; *a new world conscience must be created*; each of us, without denying his origins and his membership of his family, his people and his nation, or the obligations arising therefrom, must regard himself as a member of this great family, the world community.

(228) In other words, Ladies and Gentlemen, we must also seek a fresh significance in human work seen in a world context and therefore set ourselves fresh tasks. This also means that the worldwide common good requires a *new solidarity without frontiers*. In saying that, I do not wish to belittle the importance of the efforts that each nation must make, within the limits of its own sovereignty, its own cultural traditions and in accordance with its own needs, to achieve the type of social and economic development which respects the distinctive character of each of its members and of its entire people. Nor must it too readily be supposed that consciousness of solidarity is already sufficiently developed because of the simple fact that we are all aboard this space-ship, Earth. On the one hand, we must ensure that nations complement each other in their efforts to develop their own spiritual and material resources, and on the other, we must proclaim the demands made by universal solidarity and the structural consequences it implies. We must maintain this creative tension and in so doing, demonstrate how these two realities complement each other, for like the human person, the nation is distinctively individual and outward-looking at one and the same time.

(229) 11. Solidarity in the world of work, among men at work, has several facets. It means the solidarity *of the workers*; above all, in its deepest sense, it means solidarity *with work*, seen as a fundamental dimension of human existence, on which the meaning of that existence in fact depends. Taken in this sense, solidarity casts a special light on the problem of employment, *which has become one of the major problems* of our present society and one with harsh consequences for the workers which are too often overlooked, especially when they receive no assistance from society; with harsh and long standing consequences for the developing countries as a whole; with harsh consequences for rural workers whose lot is so often precarious whether they remain in the countryside where there is less and less work for them or whether they try to compete for the few jobs available in the towns; with harsh consequences for professional workers and indeed for all those who, in various categories and segments of the world of work, run the risk of a new form of proletarianization whenever their specific contribution is not appreciated at its true value because of changes in social systems or living conditions.

(230) As we know, the causes of involuntary unemployment may be, and indeed are, many and varied. One of these causes may lie in the improvement in the instruments of production which progressively curtails the direct share of man in the production process. This involves us in a new antimony which may well set human labour against "capital," defined as the means of production as a whole, comprising natural resources together with the means by which man appropriates this wealth which has been freely bestowed upon him and converts it to meet his needs. Thus we face a *new problem*, which is only beginning to reveal its scope and its consequences. To identify it, even in vague and imprecise outline, means being prepared to seek *a solution from the outset*, without waiting for it to force itself upon our attention by the harm it causes. The solution must lie in *solidarity with work*, in other words, in accepting the principle of the primacy of human work over the means of production, and the primacy of the individual at work over production requirements or purely economic laws. The human person is the first and ultimate criterion in the planning of employment; solidarity with work must be the overriding theme in any search for a solution and it opens a new field to man's ingenuity and generosity.

(231) 12. For this reason I ventured to say in *Laborem Exercens* that unemployment "in all cases is an evil and ..., when it reaches a certain level, can become a real social disaster. It is particularly painful when it especially affects young people..." (n. 18). Except in a very few privileged countries, mankind is now undergoing the painful experience of this sad reality. Is there always a proper appreciation of the tragedy it represents for so many young people who "see their sincere wish to work and their readiness to take on their own responsibility for economic and social development of the community sadly frustrated" (*ibid.*)? Can we tolerate a situation in which many young people may find themselves without any prospect of one day getting a job and which, at the very least, could leave them with lifelong scars? To this complex problem there are admittedly no easy answers - none, certainly, uniformly applicable in all situations and in all regions. The Director-General rightly points this out in his Report to this 68th Session of the International Labour Conference and, in the course of your deliberations, these problems will surely be explored in their full complexity. In the search for answers, whether at the national or international level, the guiding principle should be that human work is both a right and an obligation for everyone, not only reflecting, but enhancing the dignity of the human person. Moreover, this search for answers should be a matter of solidarity among all. Yes, here again, *solidarity is the key to the employment problem.* I say so emphatically: whether at the national or international level, a positive solution to the problem of employment, and more particularly employment for young people, presupposes solidarity of the highest degree within and among all peoples. All must be prepared to accept the necessary sacrifices, all must cooperate in the establishment of the programmes and agreements through which economic and social policy will become a tangible expression of solidarity, all must help in erecting the appropriate economic, technical, political and financial structures which the establishment of a *new social order of solidarity* indisputably requires. I refuse to believe that mankind today, with its prodigious scientific and technical prowess, is incapable of the kind of creative effort, inspired by the very nature of human work and solidarity among all living beings, which will yield fair and effective answers to the essentially human problem of employment.

(232) 13. A society of solidarity is built up day by day, first by creating and then by preserving the conditions on which the free participation of all in the common effort effectively depends. Any policy to achieve the common good must be the fruit of *organic and spontaneous cohesion of the forces of society.* This is another form of solidarity - solidarity as an imperative of social order, the kind that manifests itself typically through the existence and the work of associations of social partners. The right to associate freely is a fundamental one for all those who are connected with the world of work and who constitute the work community. It means that no working man need be either alone or isolated; it expresses the solidarity of all in the defence of the rights which are rightfully theirs and flow from the requirements of their work; it affords a normal channel for participating actively in the performance of work and everything related to it, *while being guided at the same time by a concern for the common Good.* This right presupposes that the social partners are truly free to form or join an association of their own choosing and to run it. Although *the right to freedom of association* seems beyond a doubt to be one of the basic rights most generally recognized, as attested by International Labour Convention No. 87 (1948), yet it is severely threatened, often flouted either in its principle or - more often - in one of the substantive aspects, with the result that freedom of association is disfigured. It seems essential to point out that cohesion among the forces of society, always desirable in itself, must be the outcome of free decisions by those concerned, taken in full independence from the political authorities and arrived at in full freedom as regards the determination of the internal organization of trade unions, their operating methods and their activities. The working man must assume responsibility for defending the truth, the true dignity of his work. He must not be prevented from exercising that responsibility, though also bearing in mind the good of the community.

(233) 14. Ladies and Gentlemen, I have tried, transcending systems, regimes and ideologies for regulating social relations, to suggest to you a way - the way of solidarity, *solidarity of the world of labour.* It is an open, dynamic concept based on the idea that human work derives its values, first and last, from the dignity of the human person, in keeping with God's own command. May such solidarity serve as your guide in your debates and achievements! The International Labour Organization already has to its credit a tremendous record of achievement within its field. You have drawn up many declarations and conventions and you will draw up more, to keep up with ever-changing problems and provide ever better answers. You have furnished guidelines and launched a multitude of programmes, and you have shown your determination to pursue that awesome adventure known as *making work more human.* In speaking for the Apostolic See, the Church and the Christian faith, I reiterate my most deeply heartfelt congratulations to your Organization for its accomplishments. At the same time I pray that its work, as well as all your efforts and all *your work,* will go on promoting the dignity of human labour and genuine human progress. May yours be a tireless contribution to the building up of a civilization of human labour, a civilization of solidarity and - even more than that - a civilization of human love. May man, by dint of mighty efforts of all kinds, achieve true dominion over the earth (cf. *Gen.* 1:28) and truly fulfil his destiny as a human being, as preordained by Eternal Wisdom and Eternal Love.

IX - AFTER GOD, MAN IS THE MEASURE AND END OF EVERY PROJECT

Address of His Holiness John Paul II to the International Organizations. Vienna, 12 September 1983.

Original: English (*)

(234) Distinguished Director General of the International Atomic Energy Agency, Director General of the United Nations Office and Executive Director of the United Nations Industrial Development Organization; Representatives and officials of the various International Organizations which have their headquarters here at United Nations City: to all of you I extend the expression of my respect and esteem. I do this all the more willingly, knowing that members of your families are also following this meeting of ours, and showing deep interest in it, as they do in all your worthy activities, which they support as only families can.

(235) 1. Allow me to express to you my sincere appreciation for the invitation to visit this place where so many *important agencies work to protect and promote life* in crucial areas of human endeavour: the peaceful use of nuclear energy, the promotion of industry especially in the developing world, trade law, social and humanitarian development and the serious questions of narcotics control.

(236) All these agencies and offices bear testimony to the pressing need we have in today's world *to work together* in order to deal constructively with sectors of human life that are complex and many- faceted. The treatment of these issues offers possibilities for good or for bad in ways that previous generations did not have to face.

(237) That is why the first obligation we share is the obligation of working together, of sharing our expertise, of building up a common consensus through *common effort and commitment.* Thus the agencies and offices grouped here participate in the same vision and spirit which is proper to the United Nations Organization as such, and which, as I said in New York in 1979, "unites and associates, it does not divide and oppose" (Address to the 34th General Assembly of UN, 2 October 1979, no. 4. See above, par. 74). The overriding characteristic that must mark the works you undertake should always be to unite and associate, not to divide and oppose. This characteristic stems from the spirit that called your organizations into existence. It is reinforced by the demands that the content of your fields of expertise makes on you.

(238) 2. In my Encyclical *Laborem Exercens,* I reflected on work in the objective sense and referred to the development of modern industry and technology in the richness of its expressions as "grounds for reproposing in new ways the question of work," and as "a whole set of instru-

---

(*) Insegnamenti di Giovanni Paolo II, Vol. VI/2, pp. 505-509.

ments which man uses in his work." I viewed the "correct affirmation of technology as a basic coefficient of economic progress" (*Laborem Exercens*, 5).

(239) Reflecting on this and applying it to your several concerns, you are being challenged to struggle in new ways *to explore and develop the relationship of man with technology.* For only when we examine the points of interaction between the human person and technology can we find the criteria to guide the present and future efforts you are called to make. To this end, and mindful that there are many elements to be examined in these points of interaction, I would like today to call your attention to two indispensable factors that must be brought constantly into consideration.

(240) 3. The very complexities of your subjects demand a level of training and education that, in terms of time and talent, can be all-absorbing. For example, to master even one of the disciplines that contribute to our knowledge of nuclear energy is a lifelong commitment and vocation. Because of this, the temptation can be great to let the content and the methodology of one discipline determine, in a total way, our vision of life, the values we espouse and the decisions we make. Because of this, because of the all-encompassing inner demands of these highly complex disciplines that offer so much to mankind, it is extremely important that we always maintain *the primacy of man as the criterion for our judgments and decisions.*

(241) Man is the subject of all work and of all our intellectual and scientific disciplines. *Man is, under God, the measure and end of all the projects* that we attempt in this world. Whether the object is industrial projects for developing countries, nuclear reactors, or programmes for the improvement of society, the human person is the guiding criterion. No project, however technically perfect or industrially sound, is justifiable if it endangers the dignity and rights of the persons involved. Every initiative of your agencies should be tested by the question: Does this advance the cause of man as man?

(242) Such a reflection will not always be easy to make, but it is necessary. No one would deny that the complexities of industry, technology, nuclear science and the many organizations of modern society must be approached with full respect for all the components which command our careful attention. In light of these realities and conscious of the potential they have, I can and must insist that the commitment and effort you rightly give to the intellectual, technological, scientific and educational aspects must always be matched by a sensitivity for and dedication to the cause of man who we proclaim is formed in the image of God and hence *worthy of total dignity and respect.*

(243) 4. The *second criterion* that I would mention briefly places us in the context of the world we live in. It is the concern we must have for the good of people as a whole, for the well being of society, for what we traditionally call *the common good.* For you it will mean seeing your work as a contribution not only for a specific project or for a certain government or agency. It will mean seeing your work as a contribution for all the peoples of the world. Thus you will measure the worth of a project by the impact it will have on cultural and other human values, as well as on the economic and social well being of a people or nation. In this way you place your work in the wide and challenging context of the present and future good of the world. You concern yourselves with *all the nations of this earth.* Promotion of the common good in your work demands respect for the cultures of nations and peoples coupled to a sense of the solidarity of all peoples and nations under the guidance of a common Father. The advancement of one nation can never be realized at the expense of another. The advancement of all in an equitable use of the expertise you have is the best guarantee of the common good that ensures that all people have what they need and deserve.

(244) 5. These few words of mine are offered to you today for your *encouragement.* As leader of the Catholic Church, whose members are found throughout the whole world, I wish to encourage all of you to be *servants of that world* which needs to be ever more united through the efforts each of us is called to make in our proper spheres. As *servants of the truth about man*, as well as servants of the truth of our disciplines, servants of the common good of all nations and peoples, may you be ever more intimately associated together in tasks that will utilize your talents and your knowledge to advance the well being, harmony and peace of all peoples for generations yet to come.

(245) 6. Permit me to allude to an extraordinary person of a former generation - one who is known and admired as an apostle of peace, one whose figure, so often reproduced in art, is familiar to so many of you, and whose ideas are crystallized in expressions that effectively manifest his spirit to the modern world. Yes, the ideals of Saint Francis of Assisi are a link spanning generations, uniting men and women of good will of all centuries in the quest for peace, whose spiritual goals are furthered by the honest efforts and hard and concerted work performed each day by the experts of so many fields and disciplines. It is in his spirit that I permit myself to speak of your contributions to the world, of what you are able to do for humanity, by working together, as brothers and sisters under the common Fatherhood of God: Lord, make us instruments of your peace! Where there is hatred - let us sow love! Where there is injury - pardon! Where there is sadness - joy! And where there is death, let us sow life! Where there is war - let us make peace! Lord, make us effective servants of humanity, servants of life, servants of peace!

X - PURSUE THE COMMON GOOD ON THE BASIS OF JUSTICE

Address of His Holiness John Paul II to the International Court of Justice. The Hague, 13 May, 1985

Original: English (*)

(246) 1. It is with a profound sense of respect and esteem that I have come today to the International Court of Justice. I am happy to have been able to include this meeting in the programme of my pastoral visit to the Netherlands, and I am pleased that it should take place in the presence of the members of the Permanent Court of Arbitration and of the Diplomatic Corps. Be assured that I am deeply grateful for the kind words of welcome that have been addressed to me. I feel honoured indeed to be with you in this historic Peace Palace, and to have this opportunity to speak to you.

(247) The Holy See attaches great importance to its *collaboration with the United Nations Organization and the various organisms* which are a vital part of its work. The Church's interest in the International Court of Justice goes back to the very beginning of this Tribunal and to the events that were linked to its establishment. I am thinking of the high degree of personal involvement of my predecessor, Leo XIII, with the Peace Conference held at The Hague in 1899, which paved the way for the Permanent Court of Arbitration, for the Permanent Court of International Justice and, eventually, for the International Court of Justice. As soon as Leo XIII learned of the initiative by Tsar Nicholas II, he encouraged it. He also gave it his support in an exchange of letters with Queen Wilhelmina, the monarch of the host country, the Netherlands. Even when it became apparent that the Holy See itself could not take part in the Peace Conference at The Hague, the interest of Leo XIII in the Peace Conference remained undiminished and he continued to encourage it. Through his Secretary of State, Cardinal Rampolla, he made it clear why he considered the Peace Conference to be so important, and his ideas have more than a merely historical value: "The international community lacks a system of moral and legal means to establish and maintain the rights of everyone. There is therefore no alternative but an immediate recourse to the use of force. This explains the rivalry between States to develop military strength... The establishment of mediation and arbitration would seem to be the most appropriate way of dealing with this disastrous situation; in every respect it satisfies the wishes of the Holy See" (11 January 1899).

(*) AAS 78(1986), 517-524.

(248) The Church has consistently supported the development of an *international administration of justice and arbitration as a way of peacefully resolving conflicts and as part of the evolution of a world legal system.* Traditionally the Holy See has played the role of mediator in disputes. It is worth recalling, for example, the mediation of Leo XIII in the controversy between Germany and Spain over the Caroline Islands. There were the repeated attempts by Benedict XV to mediate during the First World War, and his support for the creation of a League of Nations which would truly correspond to the exigencies of justice, peace and the promotion of the common good in international relations. Pius XII and his successors particularly welcomed and encouraged the creation and development of the United Nations Organization. John XXIII spoke of the issue in *Pacem in Terris,* while Paul VI personally expressed his support when he addressed the United Nations General Assembly on 4 October 1965; two years later, in *Populorum Progressio,* he reiterated his plea for "an order of justice which is universally recognized" (No. 78). I too was able to address the General Assembly of the United Nations in New York on 2 October 1979, and subsequently to reiterate support in my message to the Second Special Session of the General Assembly of the United Nations on Disarmament on 7 June 1982. I was also happy to speak to FAO in Rome in 1979, to UNESCO in Paris in 1980, to the International Labour Organization in Geneva in 1982, and to the International Organizations based in Vienna in 1983. In line with this record of continuous support and interest, I have accepted with great pleasure and an intense feeling of involvement the invitation of the President of the International Court of Justice, which, with the Permanent Court of Arbitration, has traditionally been based here in the Peace Palace. I hope that this visit will clearly show the *extent to which the Catholic Church wishes to support the efforts of these international bodies.*

(249) 2. If we turn from the historical background to the present situation, we have to recognize that there is today an even greater moral need than there was in past years for conflicts to be resolved peacefully on the basis of justice. In the first place, because of the existence of advanced weaponry, war in our time is increasingly coming to mean the total annihilation of the enemy. Every war threatens to become total war.

(250) The second reason is the new quality of *interdependence between nations.* More than ever before, the fates of individual nations are bound up with one another: the fact that many of their interests coincide is much more important than the fact that some are in conflict with one another. In addition, in our own time an organization of world peace has simply become a real possibility in a technical sense; the means of communication are available, and a large number of world organizations have already been developed. What is now required is *the will to achieve true peace.*

(251) At the present time it is both necessary and possible to promote worldwide peace. But the development of laws and mentalities in a community based on the principle of the absolute sovereignty of individual States has lagged behind other developments in an era in which destructive violence and all-embracing communications determine the picture of the world. We are still living too often with reflexes of suspicion and aggression which are detrimental to relations between nations.

(252) 3. Unfortunately, in today's world, even the peaceful settlement of disputes is often the province of a diplomacy determined more by self-interest than by the requirements of the common good of the international community - a common good based on what is right and just. This fact can have an inhibiting influence on the work of both the International Court of Justice and the Permanent Court of Arbitration. Nonetheless, these organizations have *an extremely important role* to play. The Permanent Court of Arbitration has contributed to *settling a number of conflicts* and to averting the use of armed force. The International Court of Justice has intervened in difficult areas and has managed to do more than simply apply existing law: it has also *contributed to the development of law.* The decisions of the Court have not infrequently had a wide-ranging scope because they are to be seen in the framework of the rules of international law and legal principles.

(253) The task of the International Court of Justice as well as the Permanent Court of Arbitration is to bring an element of impartiality and objectivity to bear on dealings between States. Their members have included many eminent lawyers. Together with the International Law Academy, the two organizations constitute an *international centre of distinguished legal activity.*

(254) 4. However, it is clear that the contribution of the International Court of Justice to the development of new norms of international law will be impeded as long as the States do not agree on the fundamental principles and general rules of international law. It is necessary to recall, in this regard, that, while progress has been made over the years, it has been limited. There is yet a long way to go - with trust and renewed determination.

(255) Strictly speaking, the present Court is no more - but it is also no less - than *an initial step* towards what we hope will one day be *a totally effective judicial authority* in a peaceful world. In the view of the Holy See, there are a number of ways in which the judicial element can play a wider role in international relations:

- by States and International Organizations making more intensive use of the International Court of Justice;
- by a wider acceptance of the so-called compulsory jurisdiction of the Court;
- by more frequent use of arbitration;
- by development of legal and political/humanitarian organizations at the regional level to supplement and support those at the world level;
- by development of the law of humanitarian and criminal responsibility towards the international community.

(256) These elements are clearly discernible in many recent developments: the international declarations and treaties on human rights; the work of organizations for human rights at regional and international levels; the work of the Red Cross and other agencies in the humanitarian sphere and particularly in aiding the victims of armed conflicts; the work of private organizations; and the extension of the role of the International Court as a result of requests from international organizations for advisory opinions. *A need to develop a world legal system* has also been expressed by the international community itself.

(257) 5. All of this deserves confirmation and support. The Catholic Church is involved in this field, as can be seen, for example, by her active participation in international organizations and by the many declarations of the Holy See in favour of them. In doing this, the Church points out *the criteria which the development of an international system of law must satisfy. In legal terms*, these can be expressed as the recognition of human rights: the right to life of every individual, the right to a decent existence worthy of human beings and the right to protection by the law; recognition of the right of peoples to self-determination and independence and their right to a fair share of the world's economic wealth. *Pacem in Terris* expresses the basic criteria *in moral terms* as truth, love, freedom, justice and solidarity.

(258) 6. These criteria must find expression in international relations in the form of *treaties* and in *the work of international organizations*, supported by a growing awareness among ordinary people of the duty to respect in all circumstances the fundamental rights of the human person. When this happens, the criteria will also have a further effect on the administration of international law and arbitration.

(259) The support of governments and public opinion is very important here. After all, developments in the world do not as a matter of course follow a straight line towards peace. They are influenced - often to a crucial extent - by *the clash of national interests, of cultures and ideologies*, by the attempts of one people or race to dominate another, and by the disregard of the rights of individuals and peoples. Even while the Court sits in the Peace Palace, the cries continue to ring out in many parts of the world of the imprisoned and the oppressed, the cries of people who are being exterminated, the cries of people whose cultural and spiritual freedom is being shackled - whose personal liberty is being denied.

(260) For Christians and for all who believe in a Covenant, that is, in an unbreakable bond between God and man and between all human beings, no form of discrimination - in law or in fact - on the basis of race, origin, colour, culture, sex or religion can ever be acceptable. Hence no system of *apartheid* or separate development will ever be acceptable as a model for the relations between peoples or races.

(261) Even the International Court of Justice comes under *pressure* designed to prevent it from transcending ideologies and interests. As international judges and magistrates, the members of the Court must give proof of the greatest independence and of perfect integrity. And it is for this reason that, before assuming their lofty role, they undertake a solemn commitment to exercise their functions with full impartiality and according to their conscience (cf. Art. 20 of the Statutes). They must resist such pressures and must be assisted in their efforts to do so. Against the politics of power struggles and self-interest we must set *a form of politics aimed at strengthening the values on which peace rests.*

(262) 7. Developing international law and extending and strengthening international organizations are vitally important tasks for humanity today. But what is absolutely essential in all of this is the pursuit of the common good on the *basis of justice*, according to the norms of a true world legal system. Without an understanding of *the source of law, the reasons for law and the object of law*, a proper legal system cannot exist. Without an understanding of *the criteria for the peaceful settlement of conflicts* such solutions do not come into being.

(263) The crux of the matter is that *man must love God above all else and love his neighbour as himself.* It is essential for human beings to realize that they have been created in God's image and that therefore they must respect one another instead of exploiting, torturing and killing one another. And so too States, as units in which people live together, must respect and support one another. Every lawyer and every ordinary person knows that man's law is not perfect. Legal formulations always leave something to be desired. There is always room for improvement and new developments and a need for legal institutions to be improved. This even applies to such basic documents as the declarations and treaties on human rights. The law of God written in peoples' hearts and proclaimed by the Church provides the norms and impulses for this improvement, for God's law transcends time. It speaks a language which everyone can understand, like the parable of the Good Samaritan. It provides an answer for man's desire for a meaning to life, a life which does not end with death. It expresses what people may expect from one another.

(264) Jesus Christ preached a Kingdom of truth, love and peace, three indivisible elements. People must want these elements to come into their lives and into their relations with others. Peace comes only *when human beings strive for truth and love in their dealing with one another*, when they discover who they really are and recognize one another's purpose. Peace is not born from fear of the bomb or the power of one over another. We should certainly be concerned about nuclear weapons, but our *first concern should be for people themselves*, for the way in which many people think and speak about life and society. There are few topics on which so much falsehood is spoken as peace; few are so susceptible to manipulation. This is the first threat.

(265) The Church speaks in the name of Him who will come one day to judge all people, to judge history on the basis of truth. Sent by Him, she wants *to help form the conscience and behaviour of human beings*. She wishes to show a way, a way that is difficult but sure - a way on which each individual gains strength to promote that peace which is both a fruit of human labour and a gift of God. It is a way on which everyone's endeavours are important, for the different fields of human activity and the different contexts in life are all closely related.

(266) Violence and criminal behaviour in nations and cultures encourage violence and criminal behaviour in international relations. The absence of *solidarity within a country* encourages a lack of *solidarity in the world*. Modern societies are characterized by increasing fragmentation and alienation. This leads to a situation in which people expect more of a system than they do of their own efforts and collaboration; and so dissatisfaction can turn them against systems and, as a result, society becomes more difficult to govern. A society seen as a mere system cannot provide people with a decent human existence. The more people become aware that society exists for man, the more they will be able to search for one another again and to discover a truly human inspiration for their dealings with one another. In so doing, they will be challenged *to look beyond national boundaries.*

(267) 8. Before concluding, I wish to express a word *of deep appreciation to the Netherlands,* which is strongly committed to playing host to the International Court of Justice and the Permanent Court of Arbitration. The Netherlands is a country with strong Christian traditions and a long history of freedom. It has given valuable service in the cause of the development of international law for peace, development, cooperation and human rights. It is a country in which ordinary citizens and private organizations have a strong involvement with the rest of the world. These efforts are worthy of esteem and they merit gratitude.

(268) Above all, I commend the efforts of the Judges of the International Court of Justice, of the Permanent Court of Arbitration and of all those who in their own love for justice work to promote it in the world. The Psalmist of the Old Testament says: "The just will flourish like the palm tree and grow like a Lebanon cedar" (*Ps.* 91/92:12).

(269) I pray that God will strengthen you in your efforts to be just and to promote justice. May he bless your work abundantly, so that it may help bring forth greater harmony in the world, and strengthen the foundations of a true and lasting peace.

XI - ENVIRONMENT PROGRAMMES TO ENSURE FOOD AND SETTLEMENT ARE CONCRETE WAYS TO FURTHER PEACE

Address of His Holiness John Paul II to the United Nations Centre for the Environment. Nairobi, 18 August 1985.

Original: English (*)

(270) 1. It is always an honour for me to visit one of the Agencies of the United Nations. The ever increasing importance of this prestigious Organization becomes more evident every year. At no time in history has there been a greater need for dialogue and collaboration at the international level, and for joint efforts by nations to promote integral human development and to further justice and peace - precisely the goals to which the United Nations Organization is dedicated.

(271) I am very grateful then for the invitation to come to this Centre today, an invitation which was extended to me by Dr. Mostafa K. Tolba, the Executive Director of *The United Nations Environment Programme.* In greeting him, I also greet the staff and all associated in the Agency's work. At the same time, I offer a cordial greeting to the staff of *Habitat: the United Nations Centre for Human Settlements,* also located here in Nairobi, and to its Executive Director, Dr. Alcot Ramachandron.

(272) 2. For many years now, *the Catholic Church* has taken an *active interest in questions concerning the environment.* A Delegation of the Holy See participated in the Conference on the Environment held in Stockholm in 1972, the meeting which prepared the way for the establishment of the United Nations Environment Programme. My predecessor, Pope Paul VI, sent a message to the Stockholm Conference, in which he said: "We would like to tell you and all the participants of the interest with which we follow this great enterprise. The care of preserving and improving the natural environment, like the noble ambition of stimulating a first gesture of world

(*) AAS 78(1986), 89-95.

cooperation in favour of this good, necessary for everyone, meets needs that are deeply felt among the people of our times" (1 June 1972. See below, par. 3093).

(273) The Church's commitment to the conservation and improvement of our environment is linked to a command of God. In the very first pages of the Bible, we read how God created all things and then entrusted them to the care of human beings who were themselves created in his image. God said to Adam and Eve: "Be fruitful and multiply, and fill the earth and subdue it; and *have dominion* over the fish of the sea and over the birds of the air and *over every living thing* that moves upon the earth" (*Gen.* 1:28).

(274) It is a requirement of our human dignity, and therefore a serious responsibility, to exercise dominion over creation in such a way that it truly serves the human family. Exploitation of the riches of nature must take place according to criteria that take into account not only the immediate needs of the people but also the needs of future generations. In this way, the stewardship over nature, entrusted by God to man, will not be guided by shortsightedness or selfish pursuit; rather, it will take into account the fact that all created goods are directed to the good of all humanity. The use of natural resources must aim at serving the integral development of present and future generations. Progress in the field of ecology, and growing awareness of the need to protect and conserve certain non-renewable natural resources, are in keeping with the demands of true stewardship. *God is glorified when creation serves the integral development of the whole human family.*

(275) 3. With the rapid acceleration of science and technology in recent decades, the environment has been subjected to far greater changes than ever before. As a result, we are offered *many new opportunities for development* and human progress; we are now able to transform our surroundings greatly, even dramatically, for the enhancement of the quality of life. On the other hand, this new ability, unless it is used with wisdom and vision, can cause tremendous and even irreparable harm in the ecological and social spheres. *The capacity for improving the environment* and *the capacity for destroying it* increase enormously each year.

(276) *The ultimate determining factor is the human person.* It is not science and technology, or the increasing means of economic and material development, but the human person, and especially groups of persons, communities and nations, *freely choosing* to face the problems together, who will, under God, determine the future. That is why whatever impedes human freedom or dishonours it, such as the evil of *apartheid* and all forms of prejudice and discrimination, is an affront to man's vocation to shape his own destiny. Eventually it will have repercussions in all areas requiring human freedom and as such can become a major stumbling block to the improvement of the environment and all of society.

(277) *Threats to the environment* today are numerous: deforestation, water and air pollution, soil erosion, desertification, acid rain and many more. Ecological problems are especially acute in the tropical regions of the world, and in particular here in Africa. Nearly all the nations affected by these problems are developing nations which are, with great difficulty, undergoing various stages of industrialization. A severe shortage of energy and natural resources impedes progress and results in harsh living conditions. And the problems are often complicated by the tropical environment which makes people especially susceptible to serious endemic diseases.

(278) Since every country has its own particular set of problems and varying amounts of natural resources, it is easy to see the difference between the problems faced by *developing nations* and those of *developed nations.* While modern industry and technology offer great hope of advancement, steps must be taken to ensure that the economic, material and social development which are so important include proper consideration of the impact on the environment, both immediate and in the future.

(279) 4. The Catholic Church approaches the care and protection of the environment from the point of view of *the human person.* It is our conviction, therefore, that all ecological programmes must respect the *full dignity and freedom* of whoever might be affected by such programmes. Environment problems should be seen in relation to the needs of actual men and women, their families, their values, their unique social and cultural heritage. For the ultimate purpose of environment programmes is to enhance the quality of human life, *to place creation in the fullest way possible at the service of the human family*.

(280) 5. Perhaps nowhere do we see more clearly the *interrelatedness of the world* today than in questions concerning the environment. The growing interdependence between individuals and between nations is keenly felt when it is a question of facing natural disasters such as droughts, typhoons, floods and earthquakes. The consequences of these stretch far beyond the regions directly affected. And the vastness and complexity of many ecological problems demand not only a combined response at local and national levels but also *substantial assistance and coordination from the international community*. As Pope Paul VI wrote to the Stockholm Conference: "Interdependence must now be met by joint responsibility; common destiny, by solidarity" (See below, par. 3097). One could hardly overstate the international character of ecological problems or the international benefits of their solution.

(281) These problems often require the expertise and assistance of scientists and technicians from industrialized countries. Yet the latter cannot solve them without the cooperation at every step of scientists and technicians from the countries being helped. *The transfer of technological skills* to developing countries cannot be expected to have lasting results if training is not provided for technicians and scientists from these countries themselves. *The training of local personnel* makes it possible to adapt technology in a way that fully respects the cultural and social fabric of the local communities. Local experts possess the necessary bonds with their own people to ensure a balanced sensitivity to local values and needs. They can evaluate the continuing validity of the newly transferred skills. Only when this trained personnel finally exists locally can one speak of full collaboration between countries.

(282) 6. I would now like to say a few words to those engaged in the work of the *United Nations Centre for Human Settlements*, and to all who are trying to improve the living conditions of the poor and provide shelter for the homeless. This work is of course closely related to the ecological problems of which I have been speaking. In fact it is at its very heart. As Pope Paul VI stated, in his message to the United Nations Conference on Human Settlements, in Vancouver in 1976: "The home, that is to say, the centre of warmth in which the family is united and the children grow in love, must remain the first concern of every programme relative to the human environment" (24 May 1976. Se below, par. 2782). For this reason, the Church's primary concern for the human person in problems of the environment includes the problems of housing and shelter as well.

(283) Those who believe in Jesus Christ cannot forget his words: "Foxes have holes, and the birds of the air have nests; but the Son of man has nowhere to lay his head" (*Mt.* 8:20). Thus *we see in the faces of the homeless the face of Christ the Lord*. And we feel impelled, by love of him and by his example of generous self-giving, to seek to do everything we can to help those living in conditions unworthy of their human dignity. At the same time, we gladly join hands with all people of good will in the worthy efforts being made to provide adequate housing for the millions of people in today's world living in absolute destitution. Nor can we remain passive or indifferent as the rapid increase of *urbanization and industrialization* creates complex problems of housing and environment. I assure you then of the Church's great interest in and support for your commendable endeavours to provide housing for the homeless and to safeguard the human dimension of all settlements of people.

(284) 7. Five years ago, on the occasion of my first Pastoral Visit to Africa, I went to Ouagadougou *in the heart of the Sahel region* and there launched a *solemn appeal* on behalf of all those suffering from the devastating drought. In the wake of that appeal there was a most generous response, so generous in fact that it became possible to set up a special programme to assist the suffering in a more formal way. Thus, the John Paul II Foundation for the Sahel was officially begun in February 1984. This Foundation is a sign of the Church's love for the men, women and children who have been stricken by this continuing tragedy. Even though the project seems small and inadequate in the face of such vast needs, nonetheless it is a concrete effort to help the people there and to contribute in some degree to the future of the African continent, a future which ultimately rests in the hands of the African peoples themselves.

(285) I wish to take this opportunity to renew my solemn appeal on behalf of the people of the Sahel and of other critical regions where the drought is still continuing and there is a clear *need for international assistance and solidarity* in order to provide food, drink and shelter and to solve the conflicts which are hindering efforts to help. Thus I repeat what I said in Ouagadougou five years ago: "I cannot be silent when my brothers and sisters are threatened. I become here the voice of those who have no voice, the voice of the innocent, who died because they lacked water and bread; the voice of fathers and mothers who saw their children die without understanding, or who will always see in their children the after-effects of the hunger they have suffered; the voice of the generations to come, who must no longer live with this terrible threat weighing upon their lives. I launch an appeal to everyone! Let us not wait until the drought returns, terrible and devastating! Let us not wait for the sand to bring death again! Let us not allow the future of these peoples to remain jeopardized for ever"! (10 May 1980). The solidarity shown in the past has proved, by its extent and effectiveness, that it is possible to make a difference. Let our response now be even more generous and effective.

(286) Two kinds of assistance are needed: assistance which meets the *immediate needs* of food and shelter, and assistance which will make it possible for the people now suffering to resume responsibility for their own lives, to reclaim their land and to make it once more capable of providing a stable, healthy way of life. Such *long-range programmes* make it possible for people to regain hope for the future and a feeling of dignity and self-worth.

(287) 8. Ladies and Gentlemen, as I speak to you today, I am reminded of the words of Paul VI which have become so well known: "Development is the new name for peace" (*Populorum Progressio*, 87). Yes, indeed, *integral development is a condition for peace*, and environment programmes for food and housing are *concrete ways of promoting peace*. All who serve the basic needs of their neighbours contribute building blocks to the great edifice of peace.

(288) *Peace is built* slowly through good will, trust and persevering effort. It is built by international agencies and by governmental and non-governmental organizations when they engage *in common efforts to provide food and shelter* for the needy, and when they work together *to improve the environment.*

(289) Peace is built by Heads of States and politicians when they rise above divisive ideologies and cooperate in joint efforts free of prejudice, discrimination, hatred and revenge. *Peace is the fruit of reconciliation*, and the peace of Africa depends also on the reconciliation of people in each individual country. It requires the solidarity of all Africans as brothers and sisters at the service of the whole African family and at the service of the integral development of all mankind.

(290) Peace is built up when national budgets are finally diverted from the creation of more powerful and deadlier weapons to provide food and raw materials to meet basic human needs. And peace is consolidated with each passing year as the use of nuclear weapons becomes a fading memory in the conscience of humanity. And today we thank God again that forty years have passed without the use of those weapons that devastated human life, together with its environment and shelter, in Hiroshima and Nagasaki - forty years of hope and determination, forty years in a new era for humanity.

(291) Peace is built by the men and women of *the mass media* when they bring to the attention of the public the facts about those who suffer, about refugees and the dispossessed, when they stir up in others a determination and generosity to respond to all those in need. Yes, *"development" and "a new heart" are new names for peace.* And those who make peace and promote conditions for peace shall for ever be called children of God!

XII - THE UNITED NATIONS: AN INSTRUMENT OF BROTHERHOOD BETWEEN NATIONS

Address of His Holiness Paul VI to H.E. U Thant, Secretary-General of the United Nations. The Vatican, 11 July 1963.

Original: English (*)

(292) The organization of the United Nations, of which you are the renowned and efficient Secretary General, is a historical reality of too great importance to leave us indifferent to this meeting with you, which is, on the contrary, a source of lively emotion.

(293) This is because, Mister Secretary General of the United Nations, the Holy See, which you are visiting today in our humble person, holds a very high conception of that international organism; it considers it to be the fruit of a civilization to which the Catholic religion, with its driving centre in the Holy See, gave the vital principles; it considers it an instrument of brotherhood between nations, which the Holy See has always desired and promoted, and hence a brotherhood intended to favour progress and peace among men; it considers the United Nations as the steadily developing and improving form of the balanced and unified life of all humanity in its historical and earthly order.

(294) The universality proper to the Catholic Church, with its pulsing heart here in Rome, seems in a way to be reflected from the spiritual sphere into the temporal sphere of the United Nations. The ideologies of those who belong to the United Nations are certainly multiple and diverse, and the Catholic Church regards them with due attention; but the convergence of so many peoples, so many races, so many States in a single organization, intended to avert the evils of war and to favour the good things of peace, is a fact which the Holy See considers as corresponding to its concept of humanity, and included within the area of its spiritual mission in the world.

(295) In recent years, the voice of the Popes, our Predecessors, was among the first to augur the formation of a body such as that of which you, Mister U Thant, guide the activities. In his own time, Pope Benedict XV desired it; its fundamental criteria were traced with happy foresight by Pope Pius XII in his Christmas message of 1939, and that of September, 1944; then its importance was underlined and its increasingly perfect functioning was encouraged by Pope John XXIII in his last Encyclical Letter, *Pacem in Terris*, the text of which, bearing the autograph signature of the Pontiff, was consigned to you, Mister Secretary-General, by Cardinal Suenens.

(296) We therefore derive consolation from your visit, and We avail ourself of the occasion to renew the expression of our esteem and of our hopes for the fundamental programme of the United Nations, especially in regard to the elimination of war, the assistance of developing peoples, and of those in need of defence and promotion, the lawful liberties of individuals and social groups, and the safeguarding of the rights and dignity of the human person.

(297) To these sentiments, then, we add our good wishes for the true prosperity of the great organization of the United Nations, and for the happy success of its activities, to which you, Sir, are so nobly dedicated.

(298) We pray Almighty God, our heavenly Father, to grant and fulfil these our good wishes.

(*) AAS 55(1963), 652-654.

XIII - PEACE AND HUMAN RIGHTS: DEEPEST CONCERN OF THE CATHOLIC CHURCH

Address of His Holiness Paul VI to the Secretary-General of the United Nations, Mr. Kurt Waldheim. The Vatican, 5 February 1972.

Original: French (*)

(299) We are very touched at the visit you have been kind enough to pay us and it is with the deepest satisfaction that we welcome you to the Vatican today.

(300) You have been Secretary General of the United Nations at a period of human history overshadowed with uncertainties and threats. There are, however, some signs of easing of tension and a more manifest resolution, in some areas, to reach, at last, peace among peoples, the first aim of your Organization, and the object, as you know, of the deepest concern of the Catholic Church. Although the planes and the means are different, your efforts and ours converge towards this aim, which corresponds to such a deep aspiration of the whole of mankind: peace!

(301) What we have tried to do in this field, in the course of the last few years, is well enough known to make it unnecessary to relate it to you in detail here. We mention it only to assure you of the attentive and constant interest with which we follow, and will continue to follow all the initiatives of the United Nations Organization to establish or to re-establish good understanding among all the nations on earth.

(302) There is yet another field, closely connected with that of peace, on which your action and ours meet: namely, the defence of the rights of man, the rights of human groups, and particularly of ethnical minorities. We cannot, without grave danger to society, resign ourselves to the infliction of so many and such painful wounds upon these rights today, in several countries, despite so many eloquent proclamations. The Church, concerned above all with the rights of God, can never dissociate herself from the rights of man, created in the image and likeness of his Creator. She feels injured when the rights of a man, whoever he may be, and wherever he may be, are ignored and violated.

(303) As a result of the choice that has been made of your person, you become the guarantor in a way, before the whole of mankind, of the respect for these rights.

(304) This is redoubtable responsibility, which imposes serious duties on you, but in which all men of feeling are at your side.

(305) As for us, we are anxious to reaffirm before you today what our presence within your Organization showed clearly in the past: we have faith in the United Nations, we have confidence in its possibilities of extending the domain of peace and the rule of law in our tormented world, we are ready to give it our whole moral support. The cause of peace and law is sacred. The obstacles it meets with must not discourage those dedicated to it. Whether they come from adverse circumstances or from the malice of men, they can and must be overcome.

(306) What may seem beyond human forces becomes possible with God's help. We warmly invoke it upon you, Mr. Secretary-General, and on your noble and difficult task, for which you are assured our benevolence, encouragement and prayer.

(*) AAS 64(1972) 214-215.

XIV - IRREPLACEABLE ROLE OF UNITED NATIONS

Address of His Holiness Paul VI to the Secretary-General of the United Nations, H.E. Mr. Kurt Waldheim. The Vatican, 9 July 1977.

Original: French (*)

(307) You are welcome in this house, with all those who accompany you. We are always happy to receive you. We wish to listen to the voice of the authorized representative of the United Nations Organization. We like to witness the efforts of this Organization and gather the fruit of your daily experience, that is, the echo of the concerns of Governments and peoples, of their hopes and also of obstacles to peace. It seems to us equally important to let you know our thought on the problems of which Catholics, and the Holy See in particular, are most deeply aware, and to assure you of our efforts, to support the human work of justice, peace and development which remains the ideal of the United Nations.

(308) We have unceasingly manifested our esteem and our trust for the way opened up by this Organization, in a spirit of free negotiation and collaboration among all peoples. Oh, certainly, we are conscious of the limits, of institutional or practical order, which reduce its possibilities of effective intervention in difficult situations. We would also like the resolutions, taken by the delegates of the States at the headquarters of the Organization, to be determined always by the objective good of all, above all of the populations most affected by want, hunger, injustice or ill-usage, and not by selfish or nationalistic perspectives or by purely economic interests. This is to suppose a political will of the States, impartial and clear-sighted, firmly resolved to prevent conflicts or find reasonable solutions for them, and to put into practice, effectively, what is demanded by human rights and solidarity. Should not this will be shared by everyone?

(309) But all this merely emphasizes more the beneficial and irreplaceable role of the United Nations Organization and its specialized institutions. We are happy to pay tribute to the way in which you yourself carry out your heavy and delicate task, as Secretary General, in which you have recently been reconfirmed.

(310) We know the patience you show, your multiple and tenacious efforts of mediation, according to the mandate received and to the whole extent permitted, to unravel the tangled skein of violence or mistrust, or to cause the humanitarian sense to prevail, in numerous critical points of our globe. We are also following with interest the preparation of the extraordinary session of the General Assembly of the United Nations on disarmament, in order to make the latter more effective, in the overall framework of the efforts already undertaken for the same purpose. We hopefully wish that the Organization's possibilities of action may be further improved, thanks to juridical mechanisms more calculated to carry out effectively, in legitimate respect of the sovereignty of peoples, what the universal common good requires. Above all, we wish the United Nations to be *par excellence* the expression and the rampart of the human rights it so solemnly proclaimed nearly thirty years ago.

(311) An extra effort of conscience would be necessary to make these rights the criterion of a really human civilization, and really to bring about, not excluding any race or any people, the solidarity that is necessary among brothers, all created in God's image. You know the efforts and intentions of Christians consistent with their faith in this field: the Church wishes to exert herself unceasingly to improve consciences and open hearts. And this work is inseparable from the prayer that we raise to God to obtain his Spirit, without whom men cannot succeed in becoming friends and in living together in respect and love.

(312) We are happy to make known to you again in this way, Mr. Secretary-General, our esteem and encouragement, our wishes and our hopes. We pray to the Lord to bless you and those who cooperate with you.

(*) AAS 69(1977), 544-546.

XV - ESSENTIAL LINK BETWEEN THE ORGANIZATION OF THE INTERNATIONAL COMMUNITY AND THE SAFEGUARDING OF PEACE

Address of His Holiness John Paul II to H.E. Mr. Javier Pérez de Cuéllar, Secretary-General of the United Nations. The Vatican, 6 April 1982.

Original: Spanish (*)

(313) I am deeply grateful for this visit which you have so graciously granted me only a few months after assuming your important duties as Secretary-General of the United Nations. Truly, it is very gratifying for me to have the opportunity to meet you personally. I am also happy to reiterate my best wishes as you undertake your weighty tasks, and to express to you my desire to continue and to deepen the cordial and respectful dialogue between the Catholic Church and the United Nations, whose development I consider of such great importance.

(314) The position that you, Mr. Secretary-General, hold in the United Nations and in the international community is unique. Called as you are to direct the General Secretariat of so complex an organization, you must fulfill effectively very important functions of an administrative type but, at the same time, discharge a delicate task of political nature through representative, diplomatic and operational means.

(315) The international character of your office is at the service of the universality of the United Nations, and aims at achieving very high goals: peace and cooperation among all peoples, the safeguarding of the dignity of human rights, and international justice. The mere naming of these duties and objectives highlights the importance of the burden which is yours and the service you can render to the entire human family.

(316) Mr. Secretary-General, on this occasion I wish to repeat what you already know well: the Holy See through successive Popes, has demonstrated, in a clear and serious way, its moral support for the institutional principles and the basic goals of the United Nations. My predecessor Paul VI, in his memorable discourse of October 4, 1965, spoke of the United Nations as "the obligatory path of modern civilization and of world peace" (See above, par. 10).

(317) I myself at the 34th General Assembly of the United Nations, October 2, 1979, affirmed the confidence and the attitude of my predecessors in that same institution. The reasons for such trust, Mr. Secretary-General, are not accidental, they are intentional. They are based on deep convictions: the need to organize international society globally, given its present degree of interdependence among peoples, in order to achieve a common international good and to realize the need for a world authority; and thus the conviction of the intimate - I would even say, essential - link between the world organization and the safeguarding of peace and concord among all the peoples of the earth.

(318) In our day public concern converges on many points of tension. There is the very delicate situation between Argentina and Great Britain. In a more generalized way, and with good reason, there is the terrible and imminent threat of nuclear war. This threat is increasingly more real because of the determination of some to proliferate the manufacture of arms, already too numerous, and also because of the tremendous obstacles encountered by those governments responsible for initiating realistic and effectual negotiations on various types of armaments.

(319) Mr. Secretary-General, the Holy See is more concerned than ever because of the renewed outbreak of international tension and it is its fervent hope that the next Extraordinary Assembly on disarmament will help allay fears. But we are also amazed at how much the issues which more immediately touch the industrialized nations tend to obscure the dramatic situation of two-thirds of the world's peoples who live in misery. How important it is that the activities of the United Nations for the development of peoples continue to be the main concern of the govern-

(*) AAS 74(1982), 711-714.

ments of the more affluent nations. In view of the ever-widening disparities, it would be sad indeed if the economic crisis that affects the northern hemisphere were to serve as a pretext to keep us from fulfilling our duty of solidarity. As for you, Mr. Secretary-General, I praise and encourage your efforts to awaken the consciousness of the more materially favored by reminding them of their grave responsibilities towards the more needy.

(320) Though needed and essential in the historical journey of the human family, such goals and common good are also very complex and difficult to attain in any permanent way. Today, as never before, the collaboration of all is necessary; it is necessary to go beyond individualistic views and self-interest in order to be open to a truly universal concept of the common good.

(321) Conscious of the sublimity of these ideals and the difficulties encountered in attaining them, I wish, Mr. Secretary-General, most sincerely to encourage you and all your colleagues to work with trust, courage and with the great sense of responsibility, which is your hallmark, to overcome the tensions and crises which cloud the international horizon and to strengthen and to perfect the institution of the United Nations, which, after tragic events, was set up to serve the highest interests of nations and peoples.

(322) In the realization of so important a task for the destiny of the whole of humanity, the Holy See is prepared, within the limits of its specific mission, to continue to offer the United Nations and you, Mr. Secretary-General, its loyal collaboration, above all in those matters which most especially serve the cause of peace, the defence of the dignity and the rights of human beings, international justice and the development of peoples, and particularly peoples of the Third World, those most destitute and those who, in their just aspirations for liberty are most oppressed or menaced.

It is with these sentiments that I invoke upon you and your office, Mr. Secretary-General, the assistance, protection and blessings of the Almighty.

XVI - THE CHURCH AND THE INTERNATIONAL LABOUR ORGANIZATION

Address of His Holiness Pius XII to the International Labour Organization. The Vatican, 19 November 1954.

Original: French (*)

323) During the course of the year, we have frequently had occasion to converse with representatives of a great variety of different professional associations and to express to each our interest and regard. Now it is with special pleasure that we welcome the delegates of the International Labour Organization, which certainly represents a vast number of workers, with their cares, their difficulties, and especially their aspirations for a better, a more just world.

(324) For more than thirty years you have patiently, untiringly built up a work of which you are justly proud, not only because you have contributed to forwarding social legislation in different States, but especially because you have brought together governments, employers and workers in courageous and productive collaboration. You have led them to rise above passion, above feelings of bitter vindictiveness, above the obstinate refusal to acknowledge unavoidable change in order to listen to one another, to weigh calmly the givens of an extremely complex problem and, with common accord, to propose needed improvements. In this way, you have opened up a sort of international forum, a locus for exchange where all kinds of indispensable information and use-

---

(*) AAS 46(1954), 714-718.

ful suggestions are received, examined, and disseminated. After a long process of formulation involving discussion and rigorous criticism, the General Conference has worked out conventions which, without having the force of law in the different member States, always required consideration and can, with ratification, become actual international treaties.

(325) A comparison of contemporary labor legislation with its status at the time of World War I suffices to make us appreciate the extent of the work accomplished. Even during the last century, people were urging the necessity for a coordinating organization capable of unifying workers' struggles so that they could extricate themselves from the inhuman situations in which they were mired. Indeed it was realized that measures of defense and social protection would impose economic burdens and would therefore lower the status of any country that decided to put these into effect.

(326) Our predecessor Leo XIII had an acute perception of the great importance of workers engaging in international collaboration. As early as 1890, a year before the publication of the encyclical *Rerum Novarum*, the International Conference was scheduled to meet in Berlin to find ways of ameliorating the conditions of the working classes. At that time Leo XIII wrote of the meeting that it was an answer to one of his dearest wishes and added: "A conformity of views and laws insofar as these allow for different circumstances in different places and countries, will be of a nature to greatly advance matters towards a just solution" (Letter to William II, 14 March 1890, Leonis XIII P.M. Acta, Vol. X, Roma 1891, pp. 95-96). Shortly afterwards, in 1893, he gave his approval to the proposed congress of worker delegates without discrimination because of nationality or political adherence.

(327) In 1900 the International Association for the Legal Protection of Workers was formed, but war soon interrupted its proceedings. It was still only a matter of private initiative. Greater hopes could be placed in an institution officially recognized by the different States. Finally, in 1919, the universal desire was fulfilled and from that time on the International Labor Organization has continued to respond ever more aptly to the expectations of workers and of all those with a sincere love for justice.

(328) The central structure of the International Labor Organization is as follows: A General Conference, a Governing Body with an International Labor Office, which through its special organizations - regional conferences and industrial commissions - has enabled the ILO to give effective support to workers syndicates [unions] in their efforts to remedy working conditions. While the International Labor Code, concentrating chiefly on the elimination of abuses, set up your organization's main objectives during its foundational period, the Philadelphia Declaration, formulated in 1944, adapted these to new circumstances. The struggle that went on between the two World Wars made it more evident that positive solutions were needed and some of the primary elements of these were put forward: the limitation of work hours; the regulation of the work of women and adolescents; protective measures against illness, unemployment, and accidents; a call for an organic unity of projects capable of being included in formulas for social security and full employment. Among all the areas in which your efforts are being exercised, the relations between workers and employers need your attention, as here we find one of the touchiest spots in the evolution of modern society. The International Labour Organization is already engrossed in collective agreements, in conciliation and arbitration and in the collaboration of employers and workers in planning their enterprise. At the present time, the human factor, its role too long neglected - but not, however, in Catholic social doctrine - is attracting attention, especially of sociologists, and we know that you want to place it in the forefront of your considerations.

(329) The authority and effectiveness of your institution arises in the main from its respect for the high ideal animating those who press for a civilization completely open to the just aspirations of workers. The International Labour Organization has no desire to represent only one social class or to become an expression of any exclusive bias. It welcomes everything constructive, everything that responds to the real needs of a harmoniously formed society; because of this, our predecessor Pius XI did not hesitate to call attention to the remarkable coincidence of the principles set forth in the Labor Code with those in the encyclical *Rerum Novarum.* Christian movements, for their part, wholeheartedly accept the International Labour Organization and are honored to participate in its deliberations, hoping by so doing to reach their social goals more surely and more quickly. These propose, first of all, to establish living conditions that will safeguard inviolable human rights contained in the natural law or formulated in positive law. By itself, however, law is an inanimate norm, a barrier to fend off deviations; what is essential is the spirit that animates those who defend human rights, the impetus that goes beyond existing perspectives. These are, no doubt, better than those of the past, but they are still lackluster in many respects and always encumbered by the uncertainty of human weakness. To engage with enthusiasm in building a temporal city where private initiative may flourish without fear; where, in full respect for all persons, the aptitudes and resources of each may unfold and flower; where people can wholeheartedly adhere to higher principles, both moral and religious, it is important to believe in spiritual values and to have a firm expectation that they will be victorious over all the forces of dissolution and discord.

(330) Here we are dealing not just with the interests of the working class and the access of workers to the full exercise of their responsibilities but with the future of the whole human society. The labor movement cannot content itself with material successes, with achieving a perfect system of guarantees and insurances, with acquiring a greater share of influence in the economic sphere. It cannot conceptualize its future as consisting in opposition to other social classes or to the undue ascendancy of the State over the individual. It must seek an end on the same plane where your organization places yours - that is, on the universal level - as the encyclical *Quadragesimo Anno* envisions it, in a social order where material prosperity is engendered by sincere collaboration by all for the general good and support is given to the highest values of culture and, above all, to a consummate union of minds and hearts.

(331) We wish you well as you bring to a close the work of the one hundred and twenty-seventh session of your Administrative Council. Keep up your tireless study of the problems of the labor world so that you can add to the material already in place, additions that will complete and consolidate the whole. May the Master of all, who became a divine Worker in order to announce his message of peace and brotherhood, continue to watch over your activities and to give you the courageous perseverance to overcome the obstacles in your path. As a sign of his loving kindness and an evidence of our high regard, we accord you and all who collaborate with the International Labour Organization our apostolic blessing.

XVII - COMMON GOOD OF NATIONS AND COMMON GOOD OF MAN

Message of His Holiness Paul VI to H.E. U Thant, Secretary-General of the United Nations Organization, on the occasion of the 25th anniversary of the United Nations. The Vatican, 4 October 1970.

Original: French (*)

(332) At this time when the United Nations Organization is celebrating the twenty-fifth anniversary of its foundation, we are happy to convey to it, through your good offices, our confident good wishes, and the assurance of our good-will and our support for its worldwide mission. Today we wish once more to repeat the words which we had the honour to pronounce on 4th October 1965 from the tribune of your Assembly "This Organization represents the path that has to be taken for modern civilization and for world peace." [AAS. 57(1965), p. 878. See above, par. 10]

(333) Is not an anniversary such as this a propitious occasion for assessing and reflecting upon the results which it has been possible to achieve in the course of this first quarter of a century? If it has not been possible to fulfil the expectations and hopes which were raised when your institution came into being, it must at least be recognized that it is within the United Nations Organization that the desire of governments and peoples to work together efficaciously for the establishment

(*) AAS 62(1970), 683-687.

of brotherly unity is most surely followed up. Where else, moreover, could these governments and peoples better find a bridge to link them, a table around which they can gather, and a tribunal where they may plead the cause of justice and peace? Even if the sources of violence still smoulder, flaring up here and there into fresh conflagrations, the conscience of humanity still makes itself heard no less clearly in this privileged forum where, going beyond selfish rivalries, men find once more that inalienable part of themselves which unites them all - the human element in man.

(334) Is it not so as to assure, ever more firmly, respect for this human element that your Assembly has rightly taken pains to lay down in appropriate texts, pacts or declarations, the conditions of dignity, of freedom and of security which must be guaranteed "by all, in all places and for all?" [Message to the Teheran Conference, AAS, 60(1968), p. 285. See below, par. 413]. At this agonizing hour of their history, the peoples are more vividly aware than ever of the gap which separates these generous resolutions from their effective implementation. In the face of so many inextricable situations, conflicting interests, deeply rooted prejudices and the tragic series of conflicts, discouragement lies in wait for even the best, as they witness the collapse of the hope of peaceful coexistence by obstinately hostile forces. Let us presume to say this: there will be no lasting peace until a new spirit impels individuals, social groups and nations to true reconciliation. That is why we must strive untiringly to substitute relationships based on force with relationship of deep understanding, mutual respect and creative collaboration.

(335) Proclaimed more than twenty years ago by your Assembly, the Charter of Human Rights remains in our view one of its greatest claims to fame. To ask that all, without distinction of race, age, sex or religion should be able to enjoy human dignity and the conditions necessary for its exercise - is not this to express strongly and clearly the unanimous aspiration of men's hearts and the universal witness of their consciences? No violation in practice can stifle the recognition of this inalienable right. But in circumstances of prolonged oppression, who will prevent those who are humiliated from succumbing to the temptation of what seems to them to be the solution of despair?

(336) In spite of inevitable setbacks and the many obstacles placed in the way of such a vast body by its very complexity, it must be the honoured task of your Assembly to lend its voice to those who are not able to make themselves heard, to denounce, without care for ideologies, all oppression, whatever its source, and to ensure that cries of distress receive a hearing, just requests be taken into consideration, the weak be protected against the violence of the strong and the flame of hope thus be kept burning in the breast of the most humiliated section of mankind [Cf. Address to the ILO, AAS, 61(1969), pp. 479, 499]. It is to the heart of each man - "for the real danger comes from man" [Address to United Nations, AAS, 57(1965), p. 885. See above, par. 33] - that is necessary to repeat untiringly: "What have you done to your brother?" (Cf. *Gen.* 4: 10), that brotherly integral development of man and that interdependent development of mankind to which we have boldly invited them, in the name of a "full-bodied humanism," in our Encyclical *Populorum Progressio* (Cf. n. 42).

(337) As the Second Development Decade dawns, who better than the United Nations Organization and its specialized agencies will be able to take up the challenge presented to all mankind? It is a question of ensuring that the nations, while preserving their identity and original way of life, shall agree at least on the means to be taken to support their common will to live, and, in the case of some of them, to assure their survival. Let us recognize this fact: the common good of the nations, be they large or small, demands that States should rise above their merely nationalistic interests, so that the most brilliant schemes may not remain a dead letter and that well ordered dialogue structures may not be dislocated by plans capable of putting all mankind in peril. Is it not surrendering mankind to an uncertain and perhaps catastrophic future to continue to throw away on war budgets the most astonishing opportunities for progress that mankind has ever known? Has not the hour struck for reason to take stock of that terrifying future which so much wasted energy risks preparing for the world? "They will hammer their swords into ploughshares, their spears into sickles" (*Is.* 2:4). May your untiring perseverance, placed at the service of all plans for reciprocal and controlled disarmament, ensure in our industrial age the realization of those words of this ancient prophet of the agricultural era. May it ensure that the resources thus made available are employed for scientific progress, for the harnessing of the immense resources of land and sea and for the sustenance of the ever growing numbers of the members of the human race. May the work of the living never be used against life; on the contrary, let it be used to feed that life and to make it truly human. With imagination, courage and perseverance, you will thus enable all peoples peacefully to take their rightful place in the concord of nations.

(338) To move forward, this new dynamism requires, it must be said, a radical change of attitude, in order to acquire "a new way of thinking about the pathways of history and the destinies of the world" [Address to the United Nations, AAS, 57(1965), p. 884. See above, par. 32]. There is scarcely need to emphasize the fact that spiritual progress does not stem from material progress - to which however it alone gives true meaning - as the effect from its cause. Technical achievements, however admirable, do not of themselves bring moral advance. When science advances from success to success, its use places ever greater demands upon the conscience of the man who sets it to work. The modern world, troubled in its most dynamic and most youthful elements by the gravest question that has ever assailed it, the question of its survival, hesitates between fear and hope, and desperately searches for a meaning to give its arduous ascent, to make it genuinely human.

(339) It is thus of capital importance that your Organization has recognized among the fundamental rights of the human person what our venerable predecessor John XXIII called man's right "of being able to worship God in accordance with the right dictates of his own conscience, and to profess his religion both in private and in public" [*Pacem in Terris*, AAS, 60(1963), p. 260]: this is religious freedom, the complete value of which was fully affirmed by the Church in the Ecumenical Council (Declaration *Dignitatis Humanae*, n. 2). But alas, this most sacred of all rights is for millions of men, innocent victims of intolerant religious discrimination, ridiculed with impunity. And so we turn with confidence towards your distinguished Assembly, in the hope that it will be able to promote, in a domain so fundamental to the life of man, an attitude in conformity with the insuppressible voice of conscience, and to ostracize conduct incompatible with the dignity of mankind.

(340) How great is the hope reposed in your Organization that it may achieve that community of free men which is the ideal of humanity; how great is the vigour it must show to bring such a programme to fulfillment. But, as a great contemporary thinker has so rightly observed: "The more difficult this immense task, the more it must attract men. People are not moved to act except for difficult things." (J. Maritain, *Christianisme et Democratie*, Paris, Hartmann, 1947, p. 71)

(341) There exists in effect a common good of man, and it is up to your Organization, because of its dedication to universality, which is its reason for being, to promote it untiringly. In spite of permanent tensions and unceasingly recurring oppositions, the unity of the human family shows itself more and more in the very rejection of injustice and war and in the very hope of a world of fraternity where people and communities can freely develop themselves according to their material, intellectual and spiritual potentialities. In the midst of the worst confrontations there appears ever more strongly the aspiration towards a world where force - especially that of the strongest - no longer dominates with its blind and selfish weight, but where force is the exercise of a larger and higher responsibility at the service of a free and healthy cooperation among all human groups, in mutual respect for their own proper values.

(342) Is not the task of the United Nations that of strengthening States against the temptations and helping peoples on the road towards a society where each one may be recognized, respected, and supported in his efforts to achieve spiritual growth towards a greater mastery of self in genuine freedom? Yes, the work of men and the conquests of human genius meet the design of God the Creator and Redeemer provided that his intelligence and his heart rise to the level of his science and his technology and are able to eliminate the forces of division, that is of dissolution, which are always at work in the human race.

(343) So we renew our confidence that your Organization will be able to meet the immense hope of a world fraternal community in which each one can live a really human life. As disciples of him who gave his life to reunite the scattered children of God, Christians for their part, buoyed up by the hope, which is drawn from the message of Christ, intend to take an energetic part in this great work in collaboration with all men of good will. May the United Nations, in the unique position it occupies, apply itself resolutely to this task and go forward with confidence and courage. Upon this generous future in the service of all men and of all peoples, we invoke from our heart the blessing of the Almighty.

XVII - INTENSIFY SERVICE TO PEACE AND BROTHERHOOD

Message of His Holiness John Paul II to His Excellency Jaime de Pinies, President of the 40th General Assembly of the United Nations on the occasion of the 40th anniversary of the coming into force of the Charter of the United Nations. The Vatican,14 October 1985.(*)

Original: French (**)

(344) In associating itself with the celebration of the fortieth anniversary of the coming into force of the Charter of the United Nations signed in San Francisco, the Holy See desires to reaffirm its moral support and its offer of collaboration in the noble aims that "the Peoples of the United Nations" set themselves in the aftermath of the Second World War, and to encourage them to take up, thanks to the lessons of accumulated experience and a better knowledge of the difficulties still to be overcome, the fresh challenges of international collaboration.

(345) 1. Following the footsteps of my predecessors John XXIII and Paul VI, I have already had the honour when I personally addressed, on 2 October 1979, this eminent Assembly, to recall all the esteem with which the Holy See accompanies the activities which the Charter of the United Nations of 26 June 1945 assigns to the Nations which "determined to unite their strength" in order to promote the supreme goods of peace, justice and solidarity between them.

(346) Without being a member of your organization, for very understandable reasons, the Holy See is associated in its work and the objectives which it pursues, to the extent that these latter are in accordance with the demands of its own mission in the world. Its presence, through the intermediary of a Permanent Observer at the headquarters in New York as also in Geneva and at the specialized organisms in Rome, Paris and Vienna, attests to its interest in the work of the United Nations and emphasizes the convergence of the aims pursued, each in the sphere proper to it, by your organization with its worldwide nature on the one hand, and by the religious community with a worldwide vocation which is the Catholic Church on the other. The latter is well aware of the specific nature of its possible contribution, which is essentially that of appealing to the conscience of humanity in the face of the forces which divide individuals and nations, in order tirelessly to seek new paths to peace, understanding and cooperation between peoples and communities.

(347) Between your organization and the Catholic Church collaboration is moreover all the more easy and fruitful by reason of the fact that they both refer to the fundamental principle, solemnly affirmed in the preamble to the "Universal Declaration of Human Rights" of 1948, and which the Holy See itself forcefully teaches, according to which "the recognition of the personal dignity and equal and inalienable rights of all the members of the human family is the foundation of freedom, justice and peace in the world."

(348) 2. The Holy See, as you know, has considered the United Nations Organization, from its beginning, as an irreplaceable institution in the present phase of the history of humanity. My pre-

---

(*) The Message was delivered to the General Assembly by His Eminence Cardinal Agostino Casaroli, Secretary of State, on 18 October 1985.

(**) Insegnamenti di Giovanni Paolo II, Vol. VIII,2, 982-988.

decessor Paul VI did not hesitate to see in it "the obligatory path of modern civilization and world peace", going as far as to call it "the last hope for peace and harmony" (Address to the United Nations, AAS 57 (1965), pp. 878 and 879. See above, par. 10 and 11). This constant support on the part of the Holy See was born of the Church's conviction that the nations form one solid unity and have the duty,in spite and even by reason of the repeated setbacks of the past and the present, to discover and bring to ever greater perfection the institutional mechanisms, which ensure their peaceful relationships.

(349) As far back as August 1917, Benedict XV, in his famous appeal to the belligerents, proposed general disarmament and the setting up of an international authority capable of acting as an arbiter and of imposing sanctions (cf. AAS 9(1917), pp. 417-420). In a similar context of war, Pius XII already in 1939 was calling for an international organization really able to stand up to the arbitrary actions of States (cf. Encyclical *Summi Pontificatus*, AAS 31(1939), p. 498). In his Christmas Message of the same year, he indicated the conditions whereby the worst could still be avoided and a lasting peace envisaged: one of these conditions was the creation of a new world organization, on the basis of international law (cf. AAS 32 (1940), pp. 5-15). John XXIII, in his unforgettable Encyclical *Pacem in Terris*, for his part stated that the natural moral order requires the setting up of "a public authority of universal competence" in order to promote "the recognition, respect, protection and promotion of the rights of the person" everywhere in the world (AAS 55(1963), pp. 293-294). Such an authority, he said, since it cannot be imposed by force, would have to be freely set up and agreed to by the sovereign States. Its purpose is to serve the universal common good, that is to say the supreme interests of the world community as such, the final criterion of which always remains respect for and promotion of the universal and inalienable rights of the human person. Your organization seems to bring together all the conditions for constituting in an ever more effective manner this necessary regulating authority. This is what my predecessor Paul VI and myself have had the opportunity of emphasizing before your noble Assembly (cf. AAS 57(1965), p. 880 and AAS 71(1979), p. 1160).

(350) 3. Forty years are of course a short period when it is a question of reversing the immemorial tendency of individuals and peoples to settle their conflicts by force and defend their interests by violence. It is also a short period, unfortunately, in regard to the final aim being pursued: a civilization of peace. National self-interest, ideological rigidity, self-absorption, a reluctance or even refusal to have recourse to international bodies in cases of crisis, the temptation to manipulate these same bodies for purposes of selfish propaganda - these are dangers very difficult to avoid. But forty years of experience have shown how much the objectives which are common to the Holy See and to the United Nations must absolutely be pursued, in spite of possible setbacks and numerous disappointments. Our faith in the God of the Bible, while reminding us that the perfection of peace and justice cannot be attained on earth by human efforts alone, assures us that it is precisely permanent striving towards that ultimate goal which gives meaning and greatness to the whole human adventure.

(351) It would be unjust to pass over in silence everything that the United Nations has achieved in the course of this first period of its existence. We must ask ourselves what the history of the world might have been like without your Organization, during the forty years since the Second World War: these times so rich and so tumultuous, full of promise yet full of questions too, times which have known the almost total end of colonialism and an unparalleled growth in the number of nations gaining independence, times which have seen the development of so much progress in the domain of science and technology, side by side with so much dangerous tension - very particularly the deep ideological division of the planet - tensions and divisions which are certainly not the fruit of the United Nations, but the United Nations have often been able to contain the most troublesome developments thereof. Dysfunctions, which are hard to avoid but are always surmountable, must not be a reason for discouragement but rather an indication of the direction of efforts and of corrections to be made.

(352) The more the old reflexes of recourse to force remain the order of the day, the clearer it becomes that one risks going towards a total failure not only of the international cooperation that people have been patiently trying to build up during the last forty years but also of the whole of human civilization. As far back as the eve of the Second World War, Pius XII solemnly recalled that "with peace nothing is lost, but everything can be lost with war" (AAS 31(1939), p. 334). Today, the prospect of what a nuclear war would be like leaves us no choice. It obliges us, some would say it condemns us, to create a new sort of future in which the solutions of law and justice are victorious over the law of the most powerful. Forty years after the signing of the Charter of the United Nations, the stakes of peace and the human rights must be treated with a more acute sense of responsibility than before. The commitments solemnly entered into by the signatories of this Charter must be respected and carried out according to its spirit and letter.

(353) 4. In a particular way, I am pleased to recall, in this context, the vast amount of work done by your organization over the last forty years, devising juridical instruments which make explicit and develop the protection of the fundamental rights of the human person. In this domain, which is that of the creation of a veritable jurisprudence of the universal rights of man and of international justice, important progress has been made. In this long and patient work of alerting universal consciousness and of progressively building up a more just world order, the Holy See and the Catholic Church, as you are well aware, have not failed to offer their own contribution.

(354) Your organization is not a world government; it has no true sovereignty of its own. It is meant to be an association of sovereign States. Though it has no power of constraint, it nevertheless possesses an authority based upon the highest moral values of humanity and upon the law. The events of the last forty years seem to confirm the need that such an authority should be endowed with juridical and political means enabling it to promote ever more effectively the universal common good and to bring about the triumph of the solutions of law and justice when conflicts threaten to break out between nations. The Holy See cannot encourage the United Nations too strongly to intensify this role of the service of peace which is their *raison d'être*, and to seek, in common accord, appropriate means of dissuasion and intervention when member States are tempted to have recourse, or unfortunately actually do have recourse, to the force of arms in order to settle their conflicts. By its nature and vocation your organization is the world forum where problems have to be examined in the light of truth and justice, with a renunciation of narrow egoism and threats of recourse to force.

(355) 5. There is one current international problem in which the Holy See shares the concern of the members of your organization, for it also presents an ethical and humanitarian aspect: this is the question of the external debt of the Third World, and in particular of Latin America.

(356) There exists today a consensus on the fact that the problem of the Third World's global indebtedness and of the new relationships of dependence which it creates cannot be posed solely in economic and monetary terms. It has become more widely a problem of political cooperation and economic ethics.

(357) The economic, social and human cost of this situation is often such as to bring whole countries to the brink of breakdown. Moreover, neither the creditor countries nor the debtor countries have anything to gain from the development of situations of despair that would be uncontrollable. Justice and the interests of all demand that, at the world level, the situation should be envisaged in all its aspects and dimensions, not just the economic and monetary aspects and dimensions but the social, political and human ones too.

(358) Your organization certainly has a front-line part to play in the coordination and animation of the international effort which the situation calls for, in a well-understood spirit of equity which is also in harmony with a realistic appreciation of things.

(359) 6. In conclusion, I would stress that the Holy See shares with your organization the feeling that the priority objectives of common action must be:

- in the immediate situation, an intensification of the process of general, balanced and controlled disarmament;
- a strengthening of the moral and juridical authority of the United Nations for the safeguarding of peace and international cooperation in favour of the development of all the peoples;
- the carrying out of the agreements signed and the defence of the fundamental rights of the human person;

- the effective recognition by all member States of the principles of law and of the accepted rules contained in the 1945 Charter, the 1948 "Universal Declaration of Human Rights" and the other international juridical instruments.

(360) The international community cannot tolerate that States that are members of this organization should systematically and openly violate fundamental human rights, by practicing racial discrimination, torture, political and ideological repression, stifling of the freedoms of opinion and conscience. This goes not only for the interests of individuals and peoples but also for the cause of peace in the different parts of the world.

(361) In order to achieve these objectives, it is essential that there should be established a greater confidence between the nations of the different social and political systems, and in the first place between the Great Powers which have, in this regard, a particular responsibility.

(362) The United Nations will carry out their lofty mission all the more effectively if in the member States and among their leaders there develops a conviction that to govern people is to serve a design that is greater than they. The vision full of hope and courage of those who drew up the Charter of 1945 has not been betrayed by difficulties and obstacles, and it cannot be, so long as all the peoples of the world are determined to overcome them together. This is the encouragement that I address to you; this is the fervent good wish that I formulate and that I entrust to the protection of God.

XIX - THE CULTURE OF PEACE

Homily of His Eminence Cardinal Agostino Casaroli, Secretary of State, at a Mass in St. Patrick's Cathedral on the occasion of the 40th anniversary of the coming into effect of the Charter of the United Nations Organization. New York, 20 October 1985.

Original: English (*)

(363) 1. We have gathered here in this Cathedral of Saint Patrick in order to remember before God the Fortieth Anniversary of the coming into force of the Charter of the United Nations, on October 24th, 1945.

(364) On June 26 of that same year, the Representatives of fifty-one States had signed it in San Francisco, "to save generations from the scourge of war ... and to reaffirm faith in fundamental human rights, in the dignity and worth of the human person, in the equal rights of men and women and of nations large and small, and to establish conditions under which justice and respect for the obligations arising from treaties and other sources of international law can be maintained, and to promote social progress and better standards of life in larger freedom".

(365) Not a few of those persons who like to consider themselves "realists" certainly accompanied that act with a hidden smile of scepticism; in fact, it could be seen as a fresh manifestation of good will linked with that capacity for Utopian idealism which has accompanied humanity throughout its millenary and chequered history. That comes to the fore particularly and more fully at certain moments of its journey: that is, when the peoples, exhausted by the bloody efforts of a great war and fearful of their own power to destroy themselves, feel more keenly the desire and need for security and tranquillity. At such moments their ears are better attuned to the voices of idealistic

(*) L'Osservatore Romano, Engl. Ed. 4 November 1985, pp. 5 and 12.

and generous spirits, which have ever dreamed of the never-ending reign of justice and peace in the world.

(366) At the end of the second and terrible World War, not only the vanquished but the victors too could not fail to note, with a sense of dismay, a truth which a few years later President John Kennedy was to express in terms that made him a faithful interpreter of the universal feeling: "Humanity must put an end to war, or war will put an end to humanity." On the stage of human history, already oppressed by so many instruments of death, the apocalyptic shadow of atomic destruction, dark and menacing, had already made its appearance.

(367) One cannot therefore doubt the sincerity of those who then signed, and were to sign subsequently, up to our own day, the Charter of the United Nations. But would that sincerity suffice, will it suffice, in order to secure peace for the world?

(368) 2. Forty years from that fundamental date in human history the people of the United Nations commemorate it, celebrate it, but cannot avoid at the same time making of it an examination of conscience: what has become of the hopes that impelled and continue to impel the Nations of the earth (which now number over 150) to bind themselves together in that Pact and to repeat their commitment to peace? Various voices make themselves heard in these present days, from the lofty tribune of the United Nations Organization, by turns optimistic and pessimistic, praising or criticizing, encouraging or admonishing.

(369) We too this morning have gathered here, together with our brothers and sisters of other beliefs or simply of good will, in order to reflect; in order to make a commitment; and - for those who believe in God - in order to pray. For those who have faith in a higher Providence cannot forget that *"peace is a gift of God entrusted to everyone."*

(370) The Popes who have lived through the last forty years of history together with humanity have made no secret of their esteem for the institution and purposes of the United Nations, which Benedict XV and later Pius XII, during the great conflict, had hoped would come into being.

(371) The names of Pius XII, John XXIII, Paul VI and the present Pontiff will remain forever linked with this organization by reason of their words of recognition and appreciation.

(372) 3. This does not mean that these Popes have not seen, together with the highly positive aspects, also the shortcomings of this collective effort of the peoples, and have suffered the disappointments which have marked its development. But the voice of the Apostolic See continues still today to be a voice of support, encouragement, and even of exhortation, if such is the case, to do more and better.

(373) The Holy See, placed like a sentinel on a high post, from which with a friendly and fraternal eye it embraces the whole world scene, can affirm in the words of the Prophet Isaiah, before God as before humanity: "Upon a watchtower I stand, O Lord, continually by day, and at my post I am stationed whole nights" (*Is.* 21:8).

(374) We ask it, in the name of all our sisters and brothers, scattered and anxious in every corner of the world: "*watchman, what time of night*? Watchman, what time of night?" (*ibid.*, 11).

(375) How much longer shall we have to wait before the darkness of fear is dispersed and there finally shines forth the dawn of security and hope?

(376) Unfortunately, without wishing to forget the many positive aspects of our time, a glance at the world as it actually is suffices to show how far we are from that "culture of peace" which alone can guarantee the survival of humanity and its civilization.

(377) 4. One could say, indeed, that there exist here and there signs of a dangerous worsening of situations already grave and menacing.

(378) a) The expectations, hopes and fears of the world are still dependent upon the relationships between the Great Powers, especially in connection with the problems of nuclear weapons and the threat which these present for humanity. It is the great fear which hangs over humanity and which essentially conditions its mode of conduct. This fear acts as an impulse to that "arms race" or rather the quest for the balance of armaments which is now seen almost as the sole guarantee of mutual security, but which at the same time could be the prelude to a still more radical catastrophe.

(379) b) But beyond this aspect, there remains the deep division between two worlds that are ideologically and politically opposed, the division which has marked in such a damaging fashion the history of this postwar world.

(380) It is *the great distrust*, based on the fear (or the conviction) of the wish to exercise power, or of a "crusading" spirit, on the part of one or other of the blocs.

(381) Overcoming this damaging attitude, in justice and general security, remains one of the most vital challenges for peace and international collaboration in our times.

(382) c) No less serious or perilous than the great fear and great distrust is what we could call the *great selfishness* - even though the relationships between rich countries and poor countries, between the States which can make loans and those which need them, between the peoples of affluence and those which are suffering from hunger or which lack the necessary means in the spheres of health and education, between North and South, as people say (in parallel with the East-West relationship), do not always depend on a conscious and deliberate selfish choice. All too often there are grave objective obstacles and the inability to overcome them in an organized and effective manner. International collaboration for common progress is one of the great objectives of the United Nations. It ought to give real content to the affirmation of the juridical equality of all the member States, and permit a victorious counteroffensive against endemic or occasional natural calamities such as drought, desertification, floods, earthquakes, and the like, yet it is still far from becoming effective.

(383) d) And what is one to say of the *great injustice* which constitutes in our days too, even more than in other periods of history, the violation of the rights of individuals and peoples? And this in spite of the approval, by the United Nations, of that *Universal Declaration of Human Rights* which, as Pope John Paul II said when addressing the Representatives of the U.N. on October 2, 1979, "is to be considered a real milestone on the path of the moral progress of humanity"? (See above, par. 79).

(384) The abuses in this field are so numerous and blatant that it is superfluous even to list them all. Certainly, one can admit that the concept of human dignity may in some way be influenced by the differences in social and cultural contexts; but the priority of the human person over every political or ideological system, the equality of every human being and every nation, great or small, solemnly affirmed in the great Acts of the United Nations, must be accepted and respected by all and everywhere.

(385) e) Numerous local wars continue to take their toll of innocent victims. Often they are the result of conflicts of interests or ideologies of other countries acting behind the belligerents. The production and export of arms to developing countries are a permanent incitement to have recourse to the path of violence. Thus situations have been created, such as the one in the Middle East, to mention only this one, for its lengthiness, complexity and gravity, from which it seems that neither the good will of mediators nor the wisdom of political leaders enables one to glimpse a way out that conforms to justice and reason.

(386) f) As a consequence of wars, revolutions, the denial of human rights, the persecution of minorities and uncertainty about the future, the flow of refugees is daily increasing in most parts of the world. Nations that grant asylum are often no longer in a position to provide them with adequate shelter and help them to fit into society. Uncontrolled immigration has become a major cause of social unrest on a world scale.

(387) g) Finally, partly as a consequence of a society which does not offer enough space and hope to the weak and the poor, we are witnessing a worldwide spread of violence among individuals and groups for political or other motives. Terrorism, sometimes with the backing of public powers, has become one of the plagues of our society. It is often linked with the commerce of drugs and the explosion of sordid violence of all kinds, before which political communities often stand helpless.

(388) 5. In the face of such situations must we conclude that the United Nations have to a great extent failed in the accomplishment of the noble aims which they had set themselves?

(389) From his watchtower, must the watchman therefore reply to the expectations of the peoples that the night is still dark, that the hoped-for dawn is still far off, and perhaps will never come?

(390) There are two extremes to be avoided: A blind optimism or an unenlightened and certainly not Christian pessimism.

(391) It is true, the present situation of the world shows that some of the great myths of our modern times are collapsing. Our civilization was partly based on the assumption that scientific and technical progress would automatically bring moral and human progress. We know now that this is not true. There is no social or human engineering that could definitively resolve human problems. In their common background, some of the modern ideologies share the assumption that we can achieve complete happiness, peace, justice - in a word paradise on earth - merely through the rational planning and organization of society. Some of them add that it is in the power of the State to eliminate the contradictions within every person and establish a perfectly reconciled society on earth. These dreams have now begun to fade from the collective consciousness.

(392) The Promethean myth has been disproved. People cannot be liberated merely by changes in their external conditions of life.

(393) On the other hand, we know that God has given us a reason and a will that enable us to overcome the instincts of selfishness which cause us to seek our own interest even against justice and the rights of othérs, to hate the neighbor who stands in our way or who is simply different from us: that selfishness which is the root of divisions and wars.

(394) Peace - as the Popes repeat in the face of the defeatism of so many pessimists - peace is possible: difficult, indeed very difficult, but possible. It requires a higher wisdom, a sense of humanity, perseverance which does not flag or become discouraged. It requires (why not?) awareness of one's own interests, especially when - and this is the case today - war means not only the destruction of others but self-destruction.

(395) The real difficulty, obviously, is to direct the common will towards this common aim.

(396) But I would dare to say that the present situation of the world, with all its negative and frighteningly dangerous aspects, can and must be transformed into a providential opportunity to find finally, or perhaps to impose, the reaching of an understanding, not only in order to avoid the logic of war which today cannot fail to bring about the annihilation of entire regions of the earth, of whole civilizations, but also we must set about, realistically and generously, *building peace*. The enterprise is historically gigantic, but not beyond the capacity of humanity.

(397) The United Nations, with the inadequacies regretted by many and for which corrective steps must be taken, is a special place for this effort which the evolution of the world and its potentials of death demands as a condition for human survival. The moral law imposes this as an obligation of the human conscience.

(398) 6. Believers, on their part, are sustained in this by awareness of the presence and the action of God in history. They are comforted by the confidence of being able to have recourse to a higher and definitive aid, through prayer, which finds an ear that listens to it and a heart that responds. Faith supports hope, and at the same time it sharpens in the heart the sense of one's own moral responsibilities and the consequent personal commitment.

(399) 7. The Christian, then, has altogether special reasons for commitment and hope.

(400) Fraternity among all individuals and peoples, the duty therefore of respect, indeed of love, for every member of the great human family, assumes for the Christian a specific motivation and strength: every person is called to be not only sister or brother in Christ, but a member of the very Body of Christ, animated by the one Spirit who is the Spirit of the Father and of the Son: "One body and one spirit ... just as you were called to the one hope that belongs to your vocation.... One faith, one baptism, one hope" (*Eph.* 4:4-5).

(401) This feeling of unity is an essential part of the "fire" which Christ came to bring to the world. And what does he desire but that it be then kindled? (cf. *Lk.* 12:49).

(402) This must mean the beginning, in the earthly life of humanity, of that eschatological Kingdom in which truth and grace, holiness and life, justice, love and peace will reign without hindrance and without end. That Kingdom Christ has won with his sacrifice and his Resurrection, conquering death and the dark powers of sin and hatred.

(403) Unflinching faith, unshakable hope, even "against hope," invincible courage, generosity and love which are not halted even in the face of the "enemy" - these are the specific strengths of the Christian in the face of the challenges of the present life, including there the forces of selfishness, of hatred and of war.

(404) The especial strength of the Christian is prayer: that God will not deny the gift of peace but will move the heart, the will, the wisdom, the sense of responsibility of the people to whom this gift is entrusted.

(405) For this reason we are gathered here today, to pray, as we renew our personal commitment to do everything - little or much - that each of us is able to do.

Domine, dona nobis pacem! Lord, grant us peace!

CHAPTER II

HUMAN RIGHTS

I - HUMAN RIGHTS CANNOT BE ATTACKED WITH IMPUNITY WITHOUT UNDERMINING THE VERY FOUNDATIONS OF LIFE IN SOCIETY

Message of His Holiness Paul VI to the President of the International Conference on Human Rights, held in Teheran, Iran, on 22 April-13 May 1968, to mark the 20th anniversary of the Universal Declaration of Human Rights. The Vatican, 15 April 1968

Original: French (*)

(406) We have learned with keen satisfaction that the United Nations Organization, wishing to commemorate fittingly the twentieth anniversary of the Declaration of Human Rights, has decided to hold an international conference for this purpose. Gladly responding to the invitation that you have given us, we have appointed a delegation to represent us, headed by our dear son, Theodore Hesburgh, President of the University of Notre Dame.

(407) If the declaration of human rights proved capable of stirring up controversy and becoming the object of justifiable objections, as Pope John XXIII saw it, there is no doubt, nevertheless, that it marked an important step towards the establishment of a juridico-political organization of the world community, as that unforgettable Pontiff equally emphasized, noting that it recognizes the dignity of all human persons without exception and affirms the right of each individual freely to seek the truth, to follow the norms of morality, to practice the duties of justice, to demand living conditions in conformity with human dignity and to exercise those other human rights that are inseparable from these.

(408) Our venerated Predecessor in his encyclical *Pacem in terris*, a veritable and well remembered spiritual testament, could legitimately speak of the declaration as one of the "signs of the times." (N. 143) He immediately and realistically added, "May the day come as quickly as possible when every human being will find therein an effective safeguard for the rights which derive directly from his dignity as a person and which are therefore universal, inviolable and inalienable rights." (*Pacem in Terris*, N. 145)

(409) We ourself, at the time when the Vatican Council was meeting in Rome, had the honor of making this United Nations program our own at the very rostrum of the Organization:"... the ideal which humanity dreams about during its pilgrimage through time ... the greatest hope of the world ... the basic rights and duties of man, his dignity, his liberty and above all, his religious liberty." (See above, par. 26 and 27).

(410) The Church, which shares the hope, the grief and the anguish of people of our time, firmly insists that "forms of social or cultural discrimination in basic personal rights on the grounds of sex, race, color, social conditions, language or religion must be curbed and eradicated as incompatible with God's design." (*Gaudium et Spes*, N. 29)

(411) Who does not see how vast is the distance to be covered before these declarations of intent are put into effect, before constant and numerous violations of principles rightly called "universal, inviolable, and inalienable" are eliminated? We ourselves have judged it our duty, a fulfillment of the responsibility entrusted to us, to echo, in our encyclical on the development of peoples, the legitimate aspirations of the people of our day, not hesitating to call action for the realization of that end" a ferment of the Gospel in the human heart." (*Populorum Progressio,* N. 32)

(412) Together with all people of good will, we will be following with great interest the conference in Teheran, which plans to formulate a program of measures to be taken to extend the year of human rights. Racial discrimination brings on so many troubles - social injustice, economic misery, and ideological oppression as well as revolutions, because the temptation is great to respond with violence to such wrongs to human dignity. It has to be said, nevertheless, that "a real evil should not be fought against at the cost of greater misery." (*Populorum Progressio* N. 30, N. 31) May all peo-

(*) AAS 60(1968), 283-286.

ple of good will band together not only to proclaim the principles of the United Nations but to put them into effect and may States not only promulgate them in their constitutions but have public authorities put them into operation so that every person can live a life worthy of the same.

(413) The extent and urgency of the action needed demands that all of us cooperate with one another. What means can we find to make international resolutions effective among the world's peoples? How are we to insure that basic human rights are observed when they are being flouted? In a word, how are we to intervene to save the human person, threatened everywhere? How do we make leaders aware that the essential patrimony of humanity is at stake and that it cannot be attacked with impunity without attaining what is most sacred in the human being and without, by so doing, undermining the very foundations of life in society? These are all grave problems that cannot be ignored; it would be vain to proclaim human rights if, at the same time, everything were not done to ensure the duty of respecting them, respect by all, in all places and for all.

(414) To speak of human rights means asserting a common good for all human beings, entails working to build a fraternal community, includes striving to establish a world "where each one is loved and helped as a neighbor, a brother." (*Populorum Progressio*, N. 82) The golden rule reads "So always treat others as you would like them to treat you..." (*Matt.* 7:12) In fidelity to this teaching of her divine Founder, the Church reaffirms it during this year of human rights, desiring to cooperate with all people of good will to build "a world where every person no matter of what race, religion, or nationality can live a fully human life... where freedom is not an empty word..." (*Populorum Progressio*, N. 47)

(415) As we said yesterday in our Easter message, this peaceful enterprise of affirming human rights in the clearest, most authoritative and most effective way deserves to be emulated by all people of good will. The Teheran Conference is, no doubt, making its felicitous contribution to this end. We ourself rejoice that it is taking place among a people zealously pursuing the elimination of illiteracy and the elevation of women to their rightful place in society. With a full heart, we call down upon all the participants, as well as upon their noble hosts, the abundant blessings of the Almighty.

II - HUMAN RIGHTS AND PEACE

Message to H.E. Mr. Emilio Arenales Catalan, President of the XXIII General Assembly of the United Nations, on the occasion of the 20th Anniversary of the Universal Declaration of Human Rights. The Vatican, 4 December 1968.

Original: English (*)

(416) In 1948, the United Nations, after the tragic experience of the Second World War, solemnly published its "Universal Declaration on Human Rights", and during the past year this precious document has been placed before universal mankind as an ideal for the community of man. The realization of this goal, as urgent as ever, is still the principal aim of the United Nations, and it remains the basis of effective brotherly collaboration among men without which a true peace can never be achieved. In Our unforgettable visit to the General Assembly, We associated Ourself with the program of the United Nations in this important field by calling in the ideal of which the human race dreams in its pilgrimage in time and the greatest hope for the world. We stated that "you are proclaiming here the basic rights and duties of man, his dignity, his liberty and above all his religious liberty."(See above, par. 27). In substance, you have placed before the world ideals which dedicated men have striven to achieve, a fundamental principle expressed in the Constitution of the United States - "All men have been created equal; they have been endowed by the Creator with inalienable rights, among which are life, liberty and the pursuit of happiness".

(417) This Universal Declaration on Human Rights is equally important today; it has indicated a course that cannot be abandoned if mankind sincerely wishes to achieve peace. The events of our days, unfortunately, make it evident that this brotherly collaboration in an atmosphere of respect and understanding is still cruelly contradicted in many parts of the world, by racial, ideological and religious discrimination, by the forceful subjection of weaker nations, by political regimes which deprive citizens of just freedom, by recourse to threats and violence instead of recourse to negotiations to resolve conflicts of self-interest. There is a direct relation between human rights and peace. It is impossible to have true and lasting peace where human rights are unrecognized, violated and trampled upon.

(418) The Catholic Church will not remain indifferent to responsibility towards the unity of the human family. She seeks not to impose new structures or establish juridic norms for the City of Man, but she does insist that these norms be inspired by the principle of respect for human rights and by the promotion and preservation of these same rights. On January 1st, the universal Church will sponsor a World Day of Peace, and she will emphasize the theme that promotion of human rights is the path towards peace. In this we follow closely the example of Christ who has given to the Church the message of love, from which the norms of moral life derive and which sanctions fully the respect owed to the human person.

(419) We call upon you, Your Excellency, and your colleagues, who represent the aspirations of all men, not to cease your efforts to make the Universal Declaration on Human Rights a reality which will bring about the peace so desired by men everywhere. For Our part, by prayer, in season and out, We shall beg God's blessings upon the efforts of the United Nations for men, brothers of one human family and children of one God.

III - CHURCH'S CONCERN FOR HUMAN RIGHTS

Message of His Holiness Paul VI to H.E. Mr. Leopoldo Benites, President of the 28th General Assembly of the United Nations, for the 25th anniversary of the Universal Declaration of Human Rights. The Vatican, 10 December 1973.

Original: French (*)

(420) Impelled by the consciousness of our mission to render immediate, living and actual to men the message of salvation which Christ proclaimed, we have not failed during our Pontificate repeatedly to offer our moral support to the United Nations' activities in favour of all the peoples of the world.

(421) As this eminent international Assembly now prepares to commemorate the Twenty-fifth Anniversary of the Universal Declaration of Human Rights, we desire once more to express to you our great confidence and at the same time our firm approval of the continuing commitment of the United Nations Organization to promote, in an ever clearer, more authoritative and more effective manner, respect for the fundamental human rights.

(422) As we stated on another occasion, the Declaration of Human Rights "in our view remains one of the greatest claims to fame" [Message for the Twenty-fifth Anniversary of the United Nations Organization. AAS 62(1970), p.684. See above, par. 335] for your Organization, especially when one evaluates the importance which is attributed to it as a *sure path to peace.* In reality, peace and rights are two benefits directly related to each other as cause and effect. There can be no peace where there is no respect for, defence and promotion of human rights. While promotion of the rights of the human person leads to peace, at the same time peace contributes towards the realization of this aim.

(423) We cannot, then, remain indifferent in the face of the urgent need to construct a human coexistence which will everywhere guarantee to the individual, to communities, and particularly to minority groups, the right to life, to personal and social dignity, to development in a safe and improved environment, and to an equitable division of nature's resources and the fruits of civilization.

(424) "The Church, concerned above all with the rights of God", as we said last year to the Secretary General, Dr. Kurt Waldheim, "can never dissociate herself from the rights of man, created in the image and likeness of his Creator. She feels injured when the rights of a man, whoever he may be, and wherever he may be, are ignored and violated." (*Address to the Secretary-General of the United Nations Organization*, AAS 64(1972), p. 215. See above, par. 302).

(425) For this reason the Holy See gives its full moral support to the common ideal contained in the Universal Declaration, as also to the progressive affirmation of the human rights which are expressed in it.

(426) The human rights are based upon the recognition of the dignity of all human beings and upon their equality and brotherhood. The duty of respecting these rights is a duty which is universal. The promotion of these rights is a factor for peace and their violation is a cause of tensions and disturbances even in the international sphere.

(427) If it is in the interest of States to cooperate in scientific, economic, technological and ecological matters, it is even more in their interest to collaborate in the safeguarding and promotion of human rights. The United Nations Charter expressly obliges them to pursue this objective.

(428) The objection is sometimes raised that this collaboration of all States in promoting human rights constitutes interference in internal affairs. But surely it is true that the most certain means for

(*) AAS 65 (1973), 673-677.

a State to avoid external interference is precisely for it to recognize and ensure that, in the territories under its jurisdiction, fundamental rights and liberties are respected.

(429) Without wishing to enter into the merits of the individual formulations, we consider that this outstanding document remains the expression of a more mature and more definite awareness of the question of the rights of the human person, and continues to represent the secure basis for the recognition of every man's title to worthy citizenship in the community of peoples.

(430) It would, indeed, be deplorable for mankind if this solemn pronouncement were to be reduced to an empty recognition of values or to an abstract doctrinal principle without a concrete and increasingly coherent application in the contemporary world, as you yourself rightly pointed out when you assumed the Presidency of this honourable Assembly.

(431) We are well aware that such application on the part of the public authorities is not without difficulties, but a concerted effort is required in order to ensure that these rights are respected and promoted by those with the power and the duty to do so, and that awareness of the fundamental rights and liberties of man is steadily developed among peoples. The cooperation of everyone must be sought to ensure that these principles are respected "by all, in all places and for all" (Message to the Teheran Conference for the Twentieth Anniversary of the Declaration of Human rights, AAS 60 (1968), p. 285. See above, par. 413). Is it really possible, then, without grave danger for the peaceful coexistence of peoples, to remain indifferent in the face of the many grave and often systematic violations of those human rights clearly proclaimed in the Declaration as universal, inviolable and inalienable?

(432) We cannot conceal our serious anxiety at the persistence and aggravation of situations which we bitterly deplore - situations such as racial and ethnic discrimination; obstacles to the self-determination of peoples; the repeated violations of the sacred right to religious liberty in its various aspects and the absence of an international agreement supporting this right and specifying its consequences; the inhumane treatment of prisoners; the violent and systematic elimination of political opponents; other forms of violence, and attacks on human life, especially on life in the womb. To all the silent victims of injustice we lend our voice of protest and of entreaty. But mere denunciation, often too late or ineffective, is not sufficient. There must be an analysis of the deep-rooted causes of such situations and a firm commitment to face up to them and resolve them correctly.

(433) It is encouraging, however, to note that the men of our time are showing that they are not insensible to the fundamental values contained in the Universal Declaration. Is not the ever increasing number of denunciations and of recriminations, in fact, a significant symptom of this increasing sensibility in the face of the multiplication of offences against the inalienable liberties of man, both as an individual and in the community?

(434) We have learned with lively interest and deep satisfaction that this General Assembly, on the occasion of the Twenty-fifth Anniversary of the Universal Declaration, will hold a special session at which there will be proclaimed the Decade of Struggle against Racism and Racial Discrimination. This preeminently human undertaking will once again find the Holy See and the United Nations in close accord - albeit on different levels and with different means - in a common effort to defend and protect the freedom and dignity of every person and of every group, without distinction of race, colour, language, creed or any particular social condition.

(435) In this Message we also wish to underline the value and importance of the other documents on human rights previously approved by the United Nations. These documents, which came into being in accordance with the spirit and on the basis of the Universal Declaration of Human Rights, represent a sure step forward in the promotion and concrete safeguarding of certain of those rights, and seek to guarantee their careful and faithful application. Their ratification will ensure their effectiveness in both national and international circles. The Holy See gives its moral adherence and offers its support to the legitimate and praiseworthy aspirations to which these documents are directed.

(436) While the fundamental human rights represent a common good for the whole of mankind on its path towards the conquest of peace, it is necessary that all men, ever more conscious of this reality, should realize that, in this sphere, to speak of rights is the same as spelling out duties.

(437) Thus we reiterate our good wishes to your noble and eminent Assembly, convinced as we are that it will continue tirelessly to promote among the Nations respect for and application of the principles solemnly enunciated in the Universal Declaration, with a sincere effort to transform the human family into a world community of brothers in which all the sons of men can lead a life worthy of the sons of God.

IV - THE RECOGNITION OF INHERENT DIGNITY OF EACH PERSON IS THE FOUNDATION OF FREEDOM, JUSTICE, PEACE

Message of His Holiness John Paul II to H.E. Mr. Kurt Waldheim, Secretary-General of the United Nations, on the occasion of the 30th Anniversary of the Universal Declaration of Human Rights. The Vatican, 2 December 1978.

Original: English (*)

(438) The signal occasion of the thirtieth anniversary of the Universal Declaration of Human Rights gives the Holy See the opportunity of proclaiming once again to people and to nations its constant interest and solicitude for fundamental human rights whose expression we find clearly taught in the Gospel message itself.

(439) With this in mind I want to greet you, Mr. Secretary-General, and through you the President and members of the General Assembly of the United Nations who have gathered to commemorate this anniversary. I want to express to all of you my firm agreement to "the continuing commitment of the United Nations Organization to promote, in an ever clearer, more authoritative and more effective manner, respect for the fundamental human rights" (Paul VI, Message for the 25th Anniversary of the Declaration of Human Rights, 10 December 1975, AAS 65(1973), p. 674. See above, par. 421).

(440) In these past thirty years significant steps have been taken and some outstanding efforts made to create and support the juridical instruments which would protect the ideals set out in this Declaration.

(441) Two years ago the International Covenant on Economic, Social and Cultural Rights and the International Covenant on Civil and Political Rights came into effect. By them, the United Nations marked a significant step forward in making effective one of the basic principles which it has adopted as its own from the very foundation of the organization: namely, to establish juridically binding means for promoting the human rights of individuals and for protecting their fundamental liberties.

(442) Certainly, it would be a desirable goal to have more and more States adopt these Covenants in order that the content of the Universal Declaration can become ever more operative in the world. In this way the Declaration would find greater echo as the expression of the firm will of people everywhere to promote, by legal safeguards, the rights of all men and women without discrimination of race, sex, language or religion.

(443) It should be noted that the Holy See - consistent with its own identity and at various levels - has always sought to be a faithful collaborator with the United Nations in all those initiatives which

---

(*) AAS 71(1979), 121-125.

would further this noble but difficult task. The Holy See has always appreciated, lauded, and supported the efforts of the United Nations, endeavouring to guarantee in an ever more efficient way the full and just protection of the basic rights and freedoms of the human person.

(444) If a review of the past thirty years gives us all reason for real satisfaction at the many advances that have been made in this field, still we cannot ignore that the world we live in today offers too many examples of situations of injustice and oppression. One is bound to observe a seemingly growing divergence between the meaningful declarations of the United Nations and the sometimes massive increase of human rights violations in all parts of society and of the world. This can only sadden us and leave us dissatisfied at the current state of affairs.

(445) Who can deny that today individual persons and civil powers violate basic rights of the human person with impunity: rights such as the right to be born, the right to life, the right to responsible procreation, to work, to peace, to freedom and social justice, the right to participate in the decisions that affect people and nations?

(446) And what can be said when we face the various forms of collective violence like racial discrimination against individuals and groups, the use of physical and psychological torture perpetrated against prisoners or political dissenters? The list grows when we turn to the instances of the sequestration of persons for political reasons and look at the acts of kidnapping for material gain which attack so dramatically family life and the social fabric.

(447) In the world as we find it today, what criteria can we use to see that the rights of all persons are protected? What basis can we offer as the soil in which individual and social rights might grow? Unquestionably, that basis is the dignity of the human person. Pope John XXIII explained this in *Pacem in Terris*: "Any well-regulated and profitable association of men in society demands the acceptance of one fundamental principle: that each individual is truly a person... As such he has rights and duties which together flow as a direct consequence from his nature. These rights and duties are universal and inviolable and, therefore, altogether inalienable" (n. 9).

(448) Quite similar is the preamble of the Universal Declaration itself when it says: "the recognition of the inherent dignity and of the equal and inalienable rights of all members of the human family is the foundation of freedom, justice and peace in the world".

(449) It is in this dignity of the person that human rights find their immediate source. And it is respect for this dignity that gives birth to their effective protection. The human person, even when he or she errs, always maintains inherent dignity and never forfeits his or her personal dignity. (*Pacem in Terris*, n. 158).

(450) For believers, it is by allowing God to speak to man that one can contribute more truly to the strengthening of the consciousness that every human being has of his or her destiny, and to the awareness that all rights derive from the dignity of the person who is firmly rooted in God.

(451) I now wish to speak of these rights themselves as sanctioned by the Declaration, and especially of one of them which undoubtedly occupies a central position: the right to freedom of thought, of conscience and of religion (cf. Article 18).

(452) Allow me to call the attention of the Assembly to the importance and the gravity of a problem still today very keenly felt and suffered. I mean the problem of religious freedom, which is at the basis of all other freedoms and is inseparably tied to them all by reason of that very dignity which is in the human person.

(453) True freedom is the salient characteristic of humanity: it is the fount from which human dignity flows; it is "the exceptional sign of the divine image within man" (*Gaudium et Spes*, N. 17). It is offered to us and conferred on us as our own mission.

(454) Today men and women have an increased consciousness of the social dimension of life and, as a result, have become ever more sensitive to the principle of freedom of thought, of conscience and of religion. However, with sadness and deeply felt regret we also have to admit that, unfortunately, in the words of the Second Vatican Council, in its Declaration on Religious Freedom, "forms of government still exist under which, even though freedom of religious worship receives constitutional recognition, the powers of government are engaged in the effort to deter citizens from the profession of religion and to make life difficult and dangerous for religious communities" (*Dignitatis Humanae*, n. 15).

(455) The Church strives to be the interpreter of the thirst modern men and women have for dignity. So I would solemnly ask that, in every place and by everyone, religious freedom be respected for every person and for all peoples. I am moved to make this solemn appeal because of the profound conviction that, even aside from the desire to serve God, the common good of society itself "may profit by the moral qualities of justice and peace which have their origin in man's faithfulness to God and to his holy will" (*Ibid.*, n. 6). The free exercise of religion benefits both individuals and governments. Therefore, the obligation to respect religious freedom falls on everyone, both private citizens and legitimate civil authority.

(456) Why then is repressive and discriminatory action practiced against vast numbers of citizens, who have had to suffer all sorts of oppression, even death, simply in order to preserve their spiritual values, yet who, despite all this, have never ceased to cooperate in everything that serves the true civil and social progress of their country? Should they not be the objects of admiration and praise rather than considered as suspects and criminals?

(457) My predecessor, Paul VI, raised this question: "Can a State fruitfully call for entire trust and collaboration while, by a kind of 'negative confessionalism', it proclaims itself atheist and, while declaring that it respects within a certain framework individual beliefs, takes up positions against the faith of part of its citizens?" (Paul VI, Address to the Diplomatic Corps, 14 January 1978, AAS 70 (1978), p. 170).

(458) Justice, wisdom and realism all demand that the baneful positions of secularism be overcome, particularly the erroneous reduction of religion to the purely private sphere. Every person must be given the opportunity within the context of our life together to profess his or her faith and belief, alone or with others, in private and in public.

(459) There is one last point which deserves attention. While insisting - and rightly so - on the vindication of human rights, one should not lose sight of the obligations and duties that go with those rights. Every individual has the obligation to exercise his basic rights in a responsible and ethically justified manner. Every man and woman has the duty to respect in others the rights claimed for oneself. Furthermore, we must all contribute our share to the building up of a society that makes possible and feasible the enjoyment of rights and the discharge of the duties inherent in those rights.

(460) To conclude this message, I wish to extend to you, Mr. Secretary-General, and to all those who, in whatever capacity, serve in your Organization, my heartfelt good wishes, with the hope that the United Nations will continue tirelessly to promote everywhere the defence of the human person and of his dignity in the spirit of the Universal Declaration.

V - INFORMATION

1. Address of His Holiness Pius XII to the United Nations Coordinating Committee for Public Information. The Vatican, 24 April 1956

Original: French (*)

(461) Gentlemen, in response to your wish to have us speak, we want to say a few words about the importance that we attach to the office of public information, which is yours under various titles, for you must indeed accomplish a work of communication with influence and repercussions that can be considerable.

(462) To supply exact information about international affairs is not an assignment of little importance. It demands intellectual and moral qualities of a high order. There is no question of simply publishing facts, statistics, the raw data of investigations: their objectivity has to be verified, their causes indicated, their consequences, if not measured, at least considered. In a word, data have to be clarified with apt commentary. Such delicate procedures presuppose intelligent prudence, capable of locating and identifying sources of possible errors, patience and perseverance in research, absolute honesty in exposition and the art of presentation that points up essentials without damaging truth or concealing what ought to be said or taking unfair advantage of people's ignorance or good faith. The moral aspect of all publication must never be passed over because the most objective report involves value judgments and influences decisions. An informant worthy of the name should not ruin anyone but try to understand and make understood mistakes and even misconduct. To explain need not mean to excuse but rather to suggest a remedy and consequently, to accomplish something positive and constructive.

(463) Gentlemen, such is your noble work, we would almost say, your vocation, for everything that has to do with truth and the preservation of peace, which depends so directly upon truth, has a certain sacred character. That is why, in expressing our encouragement to you, we call down upon you the light and strength of Most High. Receive our apostolic blessing for yourselves, your families, and all who are dear to you.

2. Address of His Holiness Paul VI to the United Nations Regional European Seminar on the Freedom of Information. The Vatican, 17 April 1964.

Original: French (**)

(464) Thank you for leaving your meeting a few moments to come here. You have judged correctly that the theme of your work "freedom of information" could give us the opportunity to reflect usefully with you on what the Church thinks about so serious and current a subject and on the directions that the teaching authority is able to give to those who, like you, are attending to these questions at levels of high responsibility.

(465) It is very evident, although hardly necessary to note it, that due to the evolution of society, the problem of information appears in today's world extremely different from what it was in past centuries. Information henceforth is recognized unanimously as a "universal, inviolable, and inalienable" right of the modern person; it responds to a profound need of human social nature; according to the words even of our revered predecessor Pope John XXIII, in the justly celebrated encyclical *Pacem in Terris*, "Each human being has the right to objective information."

(466) Since it concerns a right founded in the nature of the human being, obviously proclamation in theory is not enough; we must still acknowledge it in practice, defend and serve it, and guide its

(*) Discorsi e Radiomessaggi di Sua Santità Pio XII, Vol. XVIII, 137-138.

(**) Insegnamenti di Paolo VI, Vol. II, 253-255.

exercise so that it remains consistent with its end. It is a right both active and passive: the pursuit of information and the possibility for all to receive it.

(467) Here, the importance of the informant's duty becomes clearly visible: it allows each one, by the information provided, to know situations better and with better knowledge of the facts, to be able to make decisions as a person responsible in solidarity, a member of a human group.

(468) The activities of the informant thus benefit not only individuals but all society. Appealing to the delegates of American enterprises in the press and radio on 21 July 1945, our predecessor Pope Pius XII was not afraid to assert: "It is an invaluable service that your profession renders to society" (*Discorsi e Radiomessaggi*, VII, 125).

(469) From this goal of information, which is to assist the human being to better undertake its own destiny and that of the human community, spring forth moral laws: respect for them is the surest guarantee of their healthy practice. Information must be true and honest in fidelity to the event in order to fill its social role, and it will do so only if the informant has a lasting concern for objectivity.

(470) It follows that information must first of all respond to truth. Hence, no one has the right knowingly to spread false information or to present it in a way which distorts comprehension. No one has the right either to choose information in an arbitrary fashion, by spreading only what is in agreement with personal opinions and by keeping silent about the rest; moreover, truth can be offended by deliberate omissions as well as by inaccurate assertions.

(471) It does not suffice that information is objective. Necessarily, information must impose upon itself limits demanded by a higher good; for example, how to respect the rights of others to their good reputation and how to stop before the lawful privacy of their personal lives. How many infractions there are today on these two points. You know it, as we do. Further, information must be respectful of others and of their personal well-being, and even more so perhaps of the common good. Who would dare assert that all information, whatever it may be, is equally beneficial or harmless at all times and in all circumstances? Consider, for example, the sensitive and vulnerable sector that is youth! To do so is to indicate limits which dignity itself demands of information for dissemination, not because of externally and arbitrarily imposed interdicts, but by virtue of the demands of its noble social mission.

(472) These brief notes have shown you what attentive interest we take in the freedom of information and its actual practice.

(473) There could be much yet to say about the professional conscience of informants with regard to public authorities vis-a-vis individuals and about the rights and duties of public authorities in the matter of information and informants.

(474) The Church, as you know, also gives its attention to a slightly different problem, but one which is not unlike the present object of your pursuits: that of religious freedom. That is a question whose importance and scope are such that the Ecumenical Council has taken it up. On this subject, it can rightfully be expected the publication of a text which will be of great import not only for the Church but for all those, and they are innumerable, who will feel affected by an authorized declaration on this topic.

(475) Gentlemen, in closing we offer you our best wishes for a successful conclusion of your work, on which we petition wholeheartedly, as well as on you and your families, the most generous blessings.

VI - FREEDOM OF CONSCIENCE AND OF RELIGION

1. Letter of His Holiness John Paul II to the Heads of the Nations who signed the Helsinki Final Act. The Vatican, 1 September 1980.

Original: French (*)

(476) 1. Because of her religious mission, which is universal in nature, the Catholic Church feels deeply committed to assisting today's men and women in advancing the great cause of justice and peace so as to make our world ever more hospitable and human. These are noble ideals to which people eagerly aspire and for which governments carry a special responsibility. At the same time, because of the changing historical and social situation, their coming into effect - in order to be ever more adequately adapted - needs the continued contribution of new reflections and initiatives, the value of which will depend on the extent to which they proceed from multilateral and constructive dialogue.

(477) If one considers the many factors contributing to peace and justice in the world, one is struck by the ever increasing importance, under their particular aspect, of the widespread aspiration that all men and women be guaranteed equal dignity in sharing material goods, in effectively enjoying spiritual goods, and consequently in enjoying the corresponding inalienable rights.

(478) During these last decades the Catholic Church has reflected deeply on the theme of human rights, especially on freedom of conscience and of religion; in so doing, she has been stimulated by the daily life experience of the Church herself and of the faithful of all areas and social groups. The Church would like to submit a few special considerations on this theme to the distinguished Authorities of the Helsinki Final Act's signatory countries, with a view to encouraging a serious examination of the present situation of this liberty so as to ensure that it is effectively guaranteed everywhere. In doing so, the Church feels she is acting in full accord with the joint commitment contained in the Final Act, namely "to promote and encourage the effective exercise of civil, political, economic, social, cultural, and other liberties and rights, all deriving from the dignity inherent in the human person, and essential for his free and integral development"; she thus intends to make use of the criterion acknowledging "the universal importance of human rights and fundamental liberties, the respect of which is an essential factor of peace, justice, and welfare necessary to the development of friendly relationships and cooperation among them and among all States."

(479) 2. It is noted with satisfaction that, during the last decades, the international Community has shown interest in the safeguarding of human rights and fundamental liberties and has carefully concerned itself with respect for freedom of conscience and of religion in well-known documents, such as:

a) the *UN Universal Declaration of Human Rights* of 10 December 1948 (article 18);

b) the *International Covenant on Civil and Political Rights* approved by the United Nations on 16 December 1966 (article 18);

c) the *Final Act of the Conference on European Security and Cooperation*, signed on 1 August 1975 ("Questions related to security in Europe, 1, a). Declaration on the principles governing mutual relationships among participating States: VII. Respect for human rights and fundamental liberties, including freedom of thought, conscience, religion or conviction").

(480) Furthermore, the Final Act's section on cooperation regarding "contacts among persons" has a paragraph wherein the participating States "confirm that religious cults, and religious institutions and organizations acting within the constitutional framework of a particular State, and their representatives, may, within the field of activity, have contacts among themselves, hold meetings and exchange information."

(481) Moreover, these international documents reflect an ever growing worldwide conviction resulting from a progressive evolution of the question of human rights in the legal doctrine and public

---

(*) AAS 72(1980), 1252-1260.

opinion of various countries. Thus, today, most State Constitutions recognize the principle of respect for freedom of conscience and religion in its fundamental formulation as well as the principle of equality among citizens.

(482) On the basis of all the formulations found in the foregoing national and international legal instruments, it is possible to point out the elements providing a framework and dimension suitable for the full exercise of religious freedom.

(483) First, it is clear that the starting-point for acknowledging and respecting that freedom is the dignity of the human person, who experiences the inner and indestructible exigency of acting freely "according to the imperatives of his own conscience" (cf. text of the *Final Act* under (c) above). On the basis of his personal convictions, man is led to recognize and follow a religious or metaphysical concept involving his whole life with regard to fundamental choices and attitudes. This inner reflection, even if it does not result in an explicit and positive assertion of faith in God, cannot but be respected in the name of the dignity of each one's conscience, whose hidden searching may not be judged by others. Thus, on the one hand, each individual has the right and duty to seek the truth, and, on the other hand, other persons as well as civil society have the corresponding duty to respect the free spiritual development of each person.

(484) This concrete liberty has its foundation in man's very nature, the characteristic of which is to be free, and it continues to exist - as stated in the Second Vatican Council's Declaration - "even in those who do not live up to their obligation of seeking the truth and adhering to it; the exercise of this right is not to be impeded, provided that the just requirements of public order are observed" (*Dignitatis Humanae* , 2).

(485) A second and no less fundamental element is the fact that religious freedom is expressed not only by internal and exclusively individual acts, since human beings think, act and communicate in relationship with others; "professing" and "practising" a religious faith is expressed through a series of visible acts, whether individual or collective, private or public, producing communion with persons of the same faith, and establishing a bond through which the believer belongs to an organic religious community; that bond may have different degrees or intensities according to the nature and the precepts of the faith or conviction one holds.

(486) 3. The Catholic Church has synthesized her thinking on this subject in the Second Vatican Council's Declaration, *Dignitatis Humanae* , promulgated on 7 December 1965, a document which places the Apostolic See under a special obligation.

(487) This Declaration had been preceded by Pope John XXIII's Encyclical *Pacem in Terris* , dated 11 April 1963, which solemnly emphasized the fact that everyone has "the right to be able to worship God in accordance with the right dictates of his conscience."

(488) The same Declaration of the Second Vatican Council was then taken up again in various documents of Pope Paul VI, in the 1974 Synod of Bishops' message, and more recently in the message to the United Nations Organization during the papal visit on 2 October 1979 (see above, par. 103-104), which repeats it essentially: "In accordance with their dignity, all human beings, because they are persons, that is, beings endowed with reason and free will and therefore bearing a personal responsibility, are both impelled by their nature and bound by moral obligation to seek the truth, especially religious truth. They are also bound to adhere to the truth once they come to know it and to direct their whole lives in accordance with its demands" (*Dignitatis Humanae* , 2). "The practice of religion by its very nature consists, primarily, of those voluntary and free internal acts by which a human being directly sets his course towards God. No merely human power can either command or prohibit acts of this kind. But man's social nature itself requires that he give external expression to his internal acts of religion, that he communicate with others in religious matters and that he profess his religion in community" (*Dignitatis Humanae* , 3).

(489) "These words", the United Nations address added, "touch the very substance of the question. They also show how even the confrontation between the religious view of the world and the agnostic, or even atheistic, view, which is one of the 'signs of the times' of the present age, could preserve honest and respectful human dimensions without violating the essential rights of conscience of any man or woman living on earth" (Address to the 34th General Assembly of the United Nations, no. 20. See above, par. 105).

(490) On the same occasion, the conviction was expressed that "respect for the dignity of the human person would seem to demand that, when the exact tenor of the exercise of religious freedom is being discussed or determined with a view to national laws or international conventions, the institutions that are, by their nature, at the service of religion should also be brought in." This is because, when religious freedom is to be given substance, if the participation of those most concerned in it and who have special experience of it and responsibility for it is omitted, there is a danger of setting arbitrary norms of application and of "imposing, in so intimate a field of man's life, rules or restrictions that are opposed to his true religious needs" (Address to the UN 34th General Assembly, no. 20. See above, par. 106).

(491) 4. In the light of the foregoing premises and principles, the Holy See sees it as its right and duty to envisage an analysis of the specific elements corresponding to the concept of "religious freedom" and of which they are the application insofar as they follow from the requirements of individuals and communities, or insofar as they are necessary for enabling them to carry out their concrete activities. In fact, in the expression and practice of religious freedom one notices the presence of closely interrelated individual and community aspects, private and public, so that enjoying religious freedom includes connected and complementary dimensions:

(492) a) *At the personal level*, the following have to be taken into account:

- freedom to hold or not to hold a particular faith and to join the corresponding confessional community;
- freedom to perform acts of prayer and worship, individually and collectively, in private or in public, and to have churches or places of worship according to the needs of the believers;
- freedom for parents to educate their children in the religious convictions that inspire their own life, and to have them attend catechetical and religious instruction as provided by their faith community;
- freedom for families to choose the schools or other means which provide this sort of education for their children, without having to sustain directly or indirectly extra charges which would, in fact, deny them this freedom;
- freedom for individuals to receive religious assistance wherever they are, especially in public health institutions (clinics and hospitals), in military establishments, during compulsory public service, and in places of detention;
- freedom, at personal, civic or social levels, from any form of coercion to perform acts contrary to one's faith, or to receive an education or to join groups or associations with principles opposed to one's religious convictions;
- freedom not to be subjected, on religious grounds, to forms of restriction and discrimination, vis-a-vis one's fellow-citizens, in all aspects of life (in all matters concerning one's career, including study, employment or profession; one's participation in civic and social responsibilities, etc.).

(493) b) *At the community level*, account has to be taken of the fact that religious denominations, in bringing together believers of a given faith, exist and act as social bodies organized according to their own doctrinal principles and institutional purposes.

(494) The Church as such, confessional communities in general, need to enjoy specific liberties in order to conduct their life and to pursue their purposes; among such liberties the following are to be mentioned especially:

- freedom to have their own internal hierarchy or equivalent ministers freely chosen by the communities according to their constitutional norms;
- freedom for religious authorities (notably, in the Catholic Church, for bishops and other ecclesiastical superiors) to exercise their ministry freely, ordain priests or ministers, appoint to ecclesiastical offices, communicate and have contacts with those belonging to their religious denomination;
- freedom to have their own institutions for religious training and theological studies, where candidates for priesthood and religious consecration can be freely admitted;

- freedom to receive and publish religious books related to faith and worship, and to have free use of them;

- freedom to proclaim and communicate the teaching of the faith, whether by the spoken or the written word, inside as well as outside places of worship, and to make known their moral teaching on human activities and on the organization of society: this being in accordance with the commitment, included in the Helsinki Final Act, to facilitate the spreading of information, of culture, of exchange of knowledge and experiences in the field of education; which corresponds moreover in the religious field to the Church's mission of evangelization;

- freedom to use the media of social communication (press, radio, television) for the same purpose;

- freedom to carry out educational, charitable, and social activities so as to put into practice the religious precept of love for neighbour, particularly for those most in need.

(495) Furthermore:

- With regard to religious communities which, like the Catholic Church, have a supreme Authority responsible at world level (in line with the directives of their faith) for the unity of communion that binds together all pastors and believers in the same confession (a responsibility exercised through magisterium and jurisdiction): freedom to maintain mutual relations of communication between that authority and the local pastors and religious communities; freedom to make known the documents and texts of the magisterium (encyclicals, instructions, etc.);

- at the international level: freedom of free exchange in the field of communication, cooperation, religious solidarity, and more particularly the possibility of holding multinational or international meetings;

- also at the international level, freedom for religious communities to exchange information and other contributions of a theological or religious nature.

(496) 5. As was said earlier, freedom of conscience and of religion, including the aforementioned elements, is a primary and inalienable right of the human person; what is more, insofar as it touches the innermost sphere of the spirit, one can even say that it upholds the justification, deeply rooted in each individual, of all other liberties. Of course, such freedom can only be exercised in a responsible way, that is in accordance with ethical principles and by respecting equality and justice, which in turn can be strengthened, as mentioned before, through dialogue with those institutions whose nature is to serve religion.

(497) 6. The Catholic Church is not confined to a particular territory and she has no geographical borders; her members are men and women of all regions of the world. She knows, from many centuries of experience, that suppression, violation or restriction of religious freedom have caused suffering and bitterness, moral and material hardship, and that even today there are millions of people enduring these evils. By contrast, the recognition, guarantee and respect of religious freedom bring serenity to individuals and peace to the social community; they also represent an important factor in strengthening a nation's moral cohesion, in improving people's common welfare, and in enriching the cooperation among nations in an atmosphere of mutual trust.

(498) In addition, the wholesome implementation of the principle of religious freedom will contribute to the formation of citizens who, in full recognition of the moral order, "will be obedient to lawful authority and be lovers of true freedom; people, in other words, who will come to decisions on their own judgment, and, in the light of truth, govern their activities with a sense of responsibility, and strive after what is true and right, willing always to join with others in cooperative effort" (*Dignitatis Humanae* , 8).

(499) Moreover, if it is properly understood, religious freedom will help to ensure the order and common welfare of each nation, of each society, for when individuals know that their fundamental rights are protected, they are better prepared to work for the common welfare.

(500) Respect for this principle of religious freedom will also contribute to strengthening international peace which, on the contrary, is threatened by any violation of human rights, as pointed out in the aforementioned United Nations address, and especially by unjust distribution of material goods and violation of the objective rights of the spirit, of human conscience and creativity, including man's relation to God. Only the effective protection of the fullness of rights for every individual, without discrimination, can guarantee peace down to its very foundations.

(501) 7. In this perspective, through the above presentation the Holy See intends to serve the cause of peace, in the hope it may contribute to the improvement of such an important sector of human and social life, and thus of international life also.

(502) It goes without saying that the Apostolic See has no thought or intention of failing to give due respect to the sovereign prerogatives of any State. On the contrary, the Church has a deep concern for the dignity and rights of every nation; she has the desire to contribute to the welfare of each one and she commits herself to do so.

(503) Thus, the Holy See wishes to stimulate reflection, so that the civil authorities of the various countries may see to what extent the above considerations deserve thorough examination. If such reflection can lead to recognizing the possibility of improving the present situation, the Holy See declares itself fully available to open a fruitful dialogue to that end, in a spirit of sincerity and openness.

2. Statements by the Rev. Fr. René Coste, Head of the Delegation of the Holy See, at the "Seminar on the encouragement of understanding, tolerance and respect in matters relating to freedom of religion or belief", organized by the United Nations Centre for Human Rights. Geneva, 3-14 December 1984.

Original: French

I - HUMAN DIGNITY AND UNIVERSAL SOLIDARITY

(504) 1. As stated in the working paper of the Holy See, the latter "considers that the organization of this international seminar is a good initiative of the United Nations and hopes that this important meeting may be an auspicious occasion for making a contribution to the defense, respect and promotion of religious freedom in the world at present."

(505) The advantage of a seminar is that all participants can express themselves personally, speaking from their deepest convictions, in an atmosphere of listening and dialogue and a common concern for the search for truth which implies the willingness to open up to new perspectives and to change an initial point of view. You all know that, above all since Pope John XXIII and since Vatican II, the Catholic Church wishes to be *the church of dialogue*, using the expression of Paul VI in his encyclical *Ecclesiam Suam*. It seeks this dialogue, first of all with other Christian churches - particularly those in the World Council of Churches - but also with other religions, above all the monotheistic ones which, as do Christians, regard Abraham as their father in faith, and with all people of good-will, believers and non-believers alike.

(506) Does not the practice of tolerance, which we shall have to discuss, presuppose as an indispensable condition a respect for and an effort to listen to and speak with the other?

(507) You also know that at Vatican II, with the Declaration *Dignitatis Humanae*, the Catholic Church vigorously, and without any reticence, took a position in favor of the promotion of religious liberty, and also of all the other human rights. Many times it has expressed its profound respect for the Universal Declaration of Human Rights and the other similar texts drawn up by the United Nations.

(508) Our present Pope, John Paul II, is universally recognized as one of the most ardent, unprejudiced champions of the cause of human rights. Many Catholics along with many other Christians, often endangering their freedom and even their lives, are actively engaged almost everywhere in the world in fighting for the defense and in promotion of human rights. There are innumerable witnesses to this fact.

(509) I freely acknowledge that in the past Christians and even church institutions did not always promote tolerance and even contributed to intolerance. But I would like to say two things:

a) Let us not judge the past on the basis of the present and let us know how to evaluate it with a great concern for historic truth;

b) It is evident that the Church of Vatican II radically renounces any behaviour that could be resented outside the Church as manifesting hegemony, and it profoundly respects, in theory and in practice, each person's religious and philosophical convictions and also the freedom of personal conduct of each individual.

(510) 2. It would seem to be appropriate to recall the two basic reasons for the struggle by the Catholic Church, in close alliance with the other Christian churches, for the promotion of human rights, and particularly, religious freedom: *the eminent dignity of the human being* (of all human beings) *and the necessary interpersonal solidarity based on our universal fraternity* .

(511) This eminent dignity of the human being is based, in the eyes of the Christian faith, on the conviction that human persons were created in the image and likeness of God, according to the well-known statement in Genesis, and that every human being is called by grace to become a son or daughter of God.

(512) Christians fully understand that others may not share their faith in God the Creator and in Jesus of Nazareth whom they consider God's Son, and in the Holy Spirit, i.e., their faith in the Triune God, who is One, but they ask that those who do not share this faith accept this manner of speaking of the relationship between man and God as the highest expression of the superior worth of all human beings.

(513) Seen from this angle, a basic agreement can be arrived at, even if others express it differently. It is such an agreement with all persons of good will that the Catholic Church is trying hard to bring about: the will to advance all persons and all that is human because of the fact alone that they are human beings.

(514) The necessary interpersonal solidarity derives, as an essential requirement, from the Christian belief that all human beings are brothers and sisters because they have a single Creator and Father. In our age of armaments of mass destruction which threaten the very existence of humanity, the promotion of this universal solidarity is more needed than ever. It is the precondition for the future of the human race.

(515) 3. It is from the eminent dignity of the human persons, as the working paper proposed by the Holy See states, that "flow human rights, among which freedom occupies a central place, because of the essential relations which this right establishes between human being and the Creator."

(516) I personally would like to appropriate the following axiom formulated in the working paper of the International Association for the Defense of Religious Liberty: "Freedom of thought, of conscience, of religion or of belief is the most important of the human freedoms and is at the base of all human freedoms."

(517) The originality of this axiom is that it synthesizes into one single indissoluble freedom the four freedoms of thought, conscience, religion and belief. This corresponds perfectly to the spirit of the international documents and to Catholic doctrine. I sincerely hope that this synthesis will be fully accepted and considered fundamental to theory and to fact.

(518) 4. The need for interpersonal solidarity derived from our universal fraternity clearly leads to the conclusion that all of international society is directly concerned by the violation of human rights, particularly religious liberty, regardless of where it occurs, and in promoting these rights. Governments do not have the right to invoke their sovereignty in order to evade practicing the basic requirements of the United Nations Charter and the great documents on human rights connected with it.

(519) *The Declaration of the Elimination of all Forms of Intolerance and Discrimination based on Religion or Belief* has marked a big step forward.

(520) In spite of certain divergent views, it seems desirable to me personally that, following on new studies and possible improvements, this Declaration might become an *International Convention* properly speaking and stipulate institutions for enforcement. The Holy See is of course extremely interested in everything which would further the implementation of human rights.

II - THE CHURCH IS DEFENDING THE HUMAN PERSON

(521) As a representative of the Holy See, I am not here to make accusations regarding the nature and dimensions of contemporary manifestations of intolerance of religion or belief, but to examine the facts objectively with the participants of this seminar and to explain the comportment of the Catholic Church concerning them.

(522) 1. The contemporary manifestations of intolerance are numerous and often very serious in many areas of the planet. Sometimes, unfortunately, they emanate from people who call themselves Christians, directed against other Christians. In other cases, the persons responsible are nonbelievers or members of other religions, and the victims are those who refuse to bend to a manner of thought or action which is contrary to their conscience.

(523) In many cases, the facts are undeniable. The Catholic Church, which has members in all countries, knows them on the basis of incontestable testimony.

(524) When the Church denounces them, what is it doing, first of all, other than informing world public opinion, whereas those responsible for manifestations of intolerance are only interested in keeping people in ignorance or spreading misinformation?

(525) These are *facts*. For instance, John Paul II, in his speech in Ottawa on September 19, 1984, explained: "Religious liberty is a right that directly concerns what is essential in the human person and what fully manifests his or her dignity: the relationship to God, the Creator and the ultimate destiny of every human being. It is all the more reprehensible - he continued - that various forms of denial of religious freedom and of discrimination against believers and the whole community of the Church still take place, notwithstanding the existence of constitutional legislation and international instruments which guarantee the right to religious liberty."

(526) In the working paper of the Holy See presented to you, you may read a long list of very serious contemporary instances of intolerance contained in a speech by John Paul II himself, given on August 14, 1983 (*). Nothing in this list is invented. Nothing is exaggerated.

(*) Here are the very words of the Pope:

> "Today, during my pilgrimage to Lourdes, I would like to reach out in thought and with the heart of the Church to all those who suffer *persecution in our days* ...
>
> Persecutions today are often similar to those described in the Martyrology of the Church for past centuries. They include various types of discrimination against believers and against the whole community of the Church. Such forms of *discrimination* are often practiced at the same time as is recognized the right to religious liberty and to freedom of conscience, and this in the laws of individual countries as well as in declarations of an international nature.
>
> Must I be more specific?
>
> In the persecutions of the early centuries, the usual penalties were death, deportation and exile.

(527) We could add many other serious matters. I will only list a few:

(528) In some countries, very serious hindrances to religious instruction of children and young people; very serious restrictions against the use of mass media (in a country with a heavy Catholic majority, the Catholic press succeeds in printing a total of barely half a million copies per week, while the official press prints 41 million); refusal, in some places, to permit appointments to the episcopacy; restrictions on the number of seminarians in the few existing seminaries; use of churches for non-religious purposes and refusal of permits to build new places of worship; discrimination in fact against believers in certain professional activities, etc.

(529) In other countries, not only are Christians forbidden to build houses of worship, but it is practically impossible for them to obtain the benefits of the ministry of religious assistance. No entry visas are given the ministers of the Christian religion, and the few priests and pastors present can only function as employees in certain enterprises. Religious functions can be held only in secret in private places where only small groups have access, and must avoid attracting attention.

(530) I repeat: these are only a few manifestations of religious intolerance. Our files are voluminous. Truth and solidarity with the victims require us to denounce what makes them suffer unjustly.

(531) The working paper of the Holy See tells the truth when it affirms that the Catholic Church "knows from experience over the centuries, that the suppression, violation or restriction of religious freedom has caused suffering and hardship, moral and material trials and that even today there are millions of persons who are suffering because of it."

(532) 2. The preoccupations of the Catholic Church do not concern only manifestations of intolerance which victimize its own members. This would manifest a narrowness of spirit and heart, because, from the point of view of the Christian faith, all human beings are brothers and sisters; it matters little whether the victims of intolerance are Catholics, Protestants, Orthodox, Jews, Moslems, Hindus, communists, atheists - or anything else - by the mere fact that they are suffering unjustly, Christ is crucified in them. If I did not experience solidarity with them, if I did not do all I could to help them, I would be contravening the essence of my faith. The God of the Christians is a liberating God and calls on all believers to struggle against all exploitation, all oppression of any person by another.

Today, besides prison, concentration camps, forced labour camps and expulsion from one's country, there are other punishments less well known but more subtle: not *violent* death, but a kind of *civil* death; not only isolation in prisons or in camps, but social discrimination or permanent restriction of personal liberty.

There are today hundreds upon hundreds of thousands of witnesses to the faith, all too often ignored or forgotten by public opinion whose attention is drawn elsewhere. They are often known to God alone. They suffer daily hardships, in various parts of every continent.

They include believers forced to meet in hiding because their religious community is not legally authorized.

They include bishops, priests and religious who are forbidden to exercise their sacred ministry in churches or in public gatherings.

They include nuns who have been dispersed and cannot live their consecrated life.

They include young women who are denied the possibility of consecrating themselves to a common life dedicated to prayer or to works of charity.

They include parents who are refused the right to have their children educated according to their faith.

They include men and women, manual workers, intellectuals, or those carrying out other occupations, who, simply because they profess their faith, run the risk of being deprived of interesting opportunities for their careers or their studies.

To these cases can be added the serious and distressing condition of prisoners, internees and exiles, not only among Catholics and other Christians, but also among other believers (cf. *Redemptor Hominis* , 17). Their plight is like a hymn which rises continually to God from the sanctuary of their conscience, like a spiritual offering certainly pleasing to God."

(533) It is human being whom the Church is defending. If it attributes such importance to the defense of religious freedom, it is because in its eyes, this is vital for all human beings. As John Paul II said on January 14, 1984, to the diplomatic corps accredited to the Holy See: "The Church sides with what is essential and inviolable in the human person: conscience, and relationship to God. She knows that a regime which tries to extirpate faith in God cannot safeguard respect for the human person and the human fraternity. It does not cease to call for religious liberty as a basic right."

(534) By this very fact, it defends freedom of thought and of conscience for everybody. It respects the different beliefs and convictions. What it cannot allow is the attempt to impose them by force, for that is the worse violation: an attack on the inviolability of conscience.

(535) 3. How to explain the manifestations of intolerance we are discussing?
The causes are evidently many. We would have to examine each case. But it seems to me that there are only two basic causes: ideology and the fear of differences.

(536) By ideology, I mean all systems of ideas - based on more or less philosophical beliefs or convictions - which are used to justify undertakings set up to attain objectives which are considered absolute and whose preferred instrument is propaganda, i.e., indoctrination of the masses without concern for either their real freedom or the truth.

(537) As for the fear of differences, it evokes an instinctive feeling of rejection of everything which brings disorder into the familiar universe. This fear, which can be found in individuals and collectivities, alone explains many manifestations of intolerance and discrimination recorded by history.

(538) It remains an important factor at present. It is all the more dangerous as it can easily be exploited by ideologies. A long, complicated education is often required to overcome it, especially where it engenders passionate reactions over a long history.

(539) Referring to a remark made this morning, I cannot agree that all religions, in spite of themselves, contain the germ of intolerance. It is true that some of them can become intolerant to the extent that they are transformed into ideologies in the sense I have used this word. But this development is neither inevitable nor general.

(540) As regards Christianity, I can state that intolerance is absolutely contrary to the Gospel and that, to the extent that Christians and church institutions are sincerely based on it, by that mere fact they adopt an attitude of deep respect, understanding and dialogue with others. This is what the Second Vatican Council wanted for the contemporary Catholic Church.

(541) 4. However brief, this analysis is meant to point a finger at the fact that the authors of intolerance are not necessarily only individuals - possibly a bureaucracy - but also, in some cases, large sections of a population in proportion to the minorities of belief or conviction. Even each of us can be found intolerant of the person who is different.

(542) We will have to examine these mass or hidden manifestations of intolerance in points 3 and 4 of our seminar and to supply educational models and programs to purge them.

(543) I will only add here that when the acts of intolerance are due to governments, the Catholic Church first of all appeals to the conscience of the rulers and to the responsibility of the international community. In the same speech given on January 14, 1984, after evoking "the arbitrary procedures, torture, disappearances, banishments, forced emigrations of families, executions after hasty trials" John Paul II added: "This is not worthy of self-respecting sovereign States and one can ask if the international community - whose principles and charter they have accepted - could not denounce this illogical fact more plainly and have it remedied. As far as we are concerned, we solemnly appeal to the conscience of these rulers before God and before their people."

(544) Like Jesus Christ, the Church is unarmed. Like Him and because of Him, its strength is that of the truth, of solidarity with all victims of intolerance, of protection of conscience and even of those who practice intolerance, so that they may renounce it.

(545) Perhaps we should point out that the Catholic Church does not have any *a priori* feelings or prejudices against any political regime. It can adapt to the diversity of cultures and to changes in historic movements.

(546) What counts for the Church are not formal criteria, but objective ones, essentially the manner in which a specific political regime effectively assures respect and promotion of human rights for all of its population, including racial, ethnic or religious minorities, above all, the freedoms and fundamental rights, but also civic and political, economic, social and cultural rights which lead to the need to struggle against poverty and to advance the working classes, and to the real effort to contribute to the development of peace in the world, and in an industrialized country, solidarity with developing countries.

III - LEARNING TO RESPECT OTHERS AND TO DIALOGUE

(547) During this whole seminar, I have been listening with keen interest to the information from the representatives of the various States on the efforts by their countries to combat intolerance and, by that very fact, to encourage understanding, tolerance and respect for religion and belief. I am delighted with the progress made in that direction.

(548) Nonetheless, very serious problems remain and in certain areas we can even see a distressing regression. I take the liberty of reminding you of the painful facts stated by John Paul II on August 14 of last year, which you can read in the working paper presented by the Holy See and in the listing - by no means exaggerated - of very serious contemporary examples of intolerance which I outlined in my previous intervention. Even during the course of our work here, press agencies have revealed some very regrettable judicial or administrative measures of this type.

(549) Thus considerable progress remains to be made. I think it is essential that our seminar be deeply conscious of this and that it firmly express this essential ethical requirement in the conclusion of its work. We are certainly facing a fundamental human problem: one of the most basic of our own period of history.

(550) As has been said quite rightly here, the question is basically a "cultural problem"; i.e., a problem which concerns the values or lack of values that are the basic inspiration for religions, ideologies, and cultures and which manifest themselves also in legislation, legal, and administrative practices and in the daily behavior of individuals and social groups.

(551) Critical discernment in the light of international texts on human rights, which texts represent great human wealth, is imperative. Adjustments may be necessary which will bring freedom and, therefore, liberation from present oppression in the domain of freedom of thought, conscience, religion, and belief. As the previous speaker so aptly said, we must promote a "moral society."

(552) As previously mentioned by several persons during this seminar, this calls for a world-wide program of educating conscience and behavior, and even a "precocious education" as a participant said very exactly, because the essential traits of character are formed at a very early age, as shown by recent studies in psychology.

(553) The fourth point in today's agenda which deals with educational programs designed to promote tolerance of religion or belief is therefore a key factor. I will try to outline briefly the specific contribution which the Catholic Church has made to this immense undertaking we face of educating consciences and behaviors.

(554) 1. I have already had the opportunity to say that the Catholic Church of today, the Church of Vatican II, has chosen to become the *church of dialogue* . The texts of the Council are very clear in this regard, and they are binding on all Catholics.

(555) I need not quote those that concern the promotion of communication and cooperation with other Christian churches, because it is evident how much progress has been made in this direction, almost everywhere in the world. Even if doctrinal divergences subsist between us, we respect each other deeply, and our ties are more and more close and fraternal.

(556) With regard to other religions, the Council stated the following: "The Catholic Church rejects nothing that is true and holy in these religions. It regards with sincere respect those ways of behavior and living, those rules and doctrines which, although different in many aspects from those to which it adheres and promulgates, nonetheless often bring a ray of truth that illuminates all human beings."

(557) And it adds: "It therefore urges its sons and daughters so that with prudence and love, through dialogue and collaboration with those who follow other religions, and all the time giving evidence of their Christian belief and life, they recognize, preserve and develop the spiritual, moral and cultural values which are in them" (Declaration *Nostra Aetate* on the Church's relations with non-Christian religions, No. 2).

(558) Needless to say - but it is good to recall this - very strong ties unite Christians to Judaism, since its fundamental holy books - what we call the Old Testament - are also ours, in addition to those from the apostolic Church (the New Testament). The Council said it unambiguously: "The Church ... deplores hatred, persecution and all manifestations of antisemitism directed against Jews, regardless of when and by whom" (*Op. cit* ., No. 4).

(559) Special ties also unite us with Islam. The Council solemnly states that: "The Church regards ... with esteem all Moslems who worship the one God, Who is alive and Who exists, is merciful and omnipotent, the Creator of heaven and earth, Who has spoken to human beings," and the Council urges Christians and Moslems to forget the past and to strive sincerely for mutual understanding" (*Op. cit* ., No. 3).

(560) During our Seminar, several Moslem speakers eloquently explained the requirement for tolerance stated in the heart of their faith. May they be assured that the Christian faith also calls for the deepest respect of others.

(561) Indeed we Christians cannot stop giving evidence of our belief through our words and deeds, as do of course the convinced members of other religions. But they may rest assured: testimony is not proselytizing in the present, current, negative sense of this word. The Catholic Church firmly rejects all proselytizing understood in this way, as stated by the Council: "In propagating the faith and introducing religious practices, we must always refrain from all forms of behavior that have about them a whiff of coercion, dishonesty or insincere persuasion, especially with people without their own culture or resources. Such behavior must be regarded as abusing one's rights and violating the rights of others" (Declaration *Dignitatis Humanae* on religious freedom, No. 4).

(562) If, unfortunately, one or another incident of Catholic proselytizing in the sense just defined occurs somewhere, let it be known that it is inconsistent with the official directives of the Church.

(563) The same attitude of respect and dialogue is advocated towards unbelievers and atheists. As demanded by Vatican II: "The Church, while absolutely rejecting atheism, nonetheless declares, without ulterior motive, that all human beings, believers and non-believers, must work towards the right building up of this world in which they live together; this is certainly only possible by frank and prudent dialogue" (Pastoral Constitution *Gaudium et Spes* on the Church in the Modern World, No. 21, p. 6).

(564) At the beginning of our work here, Professor Munkata, the representative from Japan, invited us in a stimulating way to rediscover authentic values which generate religions and belief and to seek those which they have in common.

(565) This was precisely the big undertaking of Vatican II in the Catholic Church both with regard to the Gospel which is at its source and with regard to all the authentic values of the different religions and beliefs: the search for a common heritage of humanity on which it would be possible to build a future of justice, solidarity, and peace.

(566) What I have just said is echoed in the official documents of the Church, in the sermons, the catechesis, in the books, in meetings of all kinds, in Catholic schools, in many encounters with other Christians, members of other religions, and non-believers.

(567) The Catholic Church is convinced that through the education of its own members and its many outside contacts it is already making a very positive contribution to the promotion of tolerance and respect, esteem and friendship in pluralist societies. And all its internal dynamism urges the Church to work ever more intensely in that direction.

(568) 2. It is in this spirit that, with its internal dynamism of faith and willingness to dialogue and collaborate with everyone, whenever these conditions are met, the Catholic Church emphasizes the education of its members and proposes to all religions and faiths that they promote the "integral development of man" and the "development of the whole man," according to the famous statements by Paul VI in his encyclical letter *Populorum Progressio* .

(569) That is why one of the most important documents of Vatican II, the Constitution *Gaudium et Spes* , is addressed to "all people" (No. 2 and 1) and that is why what the Council intended was precisely "to address itself to all, to throw light on the mystery of human being and to help humanity to find the solution to major problems of our time" (No. 10 and 2).

(570) Likewise, John Paul II wrote in his encyclical letter *Redemptor Hominis* : "Man in the full truth of his existence, of his personal being and also of his community and social being ... this man is the primary route that the Church must travel in fulfilling her mission: he is the primary and fundamental way for the Church...." (No. 14).

(571) "The dignity and value of the human person" proclaimed by the Preamble to the Charter of the United Nations which constitutes the basic inspiration of the texts on human rights is clearly one of the root convictions of the Christian faith at the basis of every educational effort by the contemporary Catholic Church.

(572) 3. True coexistence between social groups is only possible if everyone recognizes *some fundamental ethical values* . At a time like ours when all humanity has become interdependent, this need is felt on a world-wide scale. It is imperative and urgent to arrive at a unanimously shared recognition of some basic ethical criteria.

(573) For a long time I have been among those who think that one can find them, for the most part, in the international texts concerning human rights and that their study should be considered everywhere as one of the essential bases for educating conscience and behavior.

(574) Don't they in effect propose that certain of the most fundamental ethical values such as dignity of the human person, freedom, equality, fraternity, etc. and also certain essential political, economic, social and cultural conditions be concretely adhered to?

(575) Catholic doctrine has always been engaged in looking for ethical criteria that could be recognized by all. Since John XXIII, it has not ceased to express its esteem for the enormous practical value of the international texts concerning human rights. What it expressly and insistently demands is that in these texts recognition be given to the moral and universal imperative that genuine respect of rights implies an obligation in conscience on the part both of political powers and individuals.

(576) 4. In monotheistic religions, God alone is the absolute, and it is God Who is the final foundation for ethical values which have to be respected by everyone under all circumstances.

(577) Such a belief makes it possible to relativize some human values (for instance, the homeland, the nation, the State, the social class, money, sex, comfort) which, while they are respectable in themselves, become very dangerous when they are made absolute and sacred, i.e., when those who champion them do not hesitate to use any means to reach their objective. The same would happen with religion if it were transformed in this way.

(578) Far from being the opiate of the people, authentic faith places human objectives in their true proportions and thus preserves them from the inhuman aims and greatly stimulates unfailing respect of basic ethical values which are indispensable to true coexistence between people. It is thus revealed as a very positive factor of a highly human education of conscience.

(579) 5. As a human being and as a Christian, I believe that *learning respect for others and for dialogue* is one of the essential components of an education worthy of human persons.

(580) Such education will erase aggression aroused by fear of differences, for such fear will be overcome. In the history of humanity, making conflicts sacred and deliberately denigrating the enemy - often in the form of making the opponent a "demon" or "satan" - have been at the root of frightful hatred and confrontations. Such behavior unfortunately is far from disappearing. When fundamental conscientization occurs, inevitably it brings with it a reversal of tendencies.

(581) Speaking positively, we must promote at the same time a civilization of the universal as well as a dialogue of cultures, for each has its own wealth from which others may and must benefit.

(582) 6. Finally, I will place at the basis of the education which our seminar wishes to promote, the advancement of *interpersonal solidarity* beside that of the dignity of the human being. They form the inseparable centers of the universal ethic which must be championed.

(583) I am formulating this requirement while being fully aware of the seriousness of conflicts which may separate social groups and also of the importance of the structural changes which demand clarity and courage in planning in order to promote justice and solidarity.

(584) Nonetheless, all of humanity has in fact become interdependent, and, if we do not deliberately promote solidarity, we shall be incapable of resolving the great problems we must face. The Christian name for solidarity is fraternity. It is mentioned, as I recall, in the first article of the Universal Declaration of Human Rights.

IV - CONSIDERATIONS AND SUGGESTIONS

(585) In the name of the delegation of the Holy See with regard to future activities to be promoted to further the freedom of religion and belief, I wish to express the following considerations and suggestions:

(586) 1. We are anxious to publicly express our high appreciation for the *"Declaration on the Elimination of all Forms of Intolerance and Discrimination based on Religion and Belief,"* and, in conformity with what has been expressed right here by a certain number of speakers, our desire to begin immediately the steps and the work necessary to change this Declaration into an actual International Convention.

(587) 2. We appreciate very much the information paper drawn up by Mrs. E. Odio Benito (HR/Geneva 1984/80.2) (*). In our opinion, all the steps that she suggests constitute a solid base for the effective promotion of freedom of religion and belief.

(588) We would have wished that, in its history section, this document would have better expressed the remarkable originality of Christianity with regard to the promotion of freedom of religion and belief, and even more fundamentally, of human freedom, an originality to which the Vatican Council II gave special tribute.

(589) 3. In reference to the first article of the "Declaration on the Elimination of All Forms of Intolerance and Discrimination based on Religion and Belief," we would wish that in a convention draft, there would be a return explicitly to the important formulation contained in Article 18 of the *Universal Declaration of Human Rights*, a formulation that stipulates that the "right to freedom of thought, conscience and religion ... implies freedom to change religion or belief."

(590) 4. With reference to Article 5 of the "Declaration on the Elimination of All Forms of Intolerance and Discrimination based on Religion or Belief," we would wish that for a draft convention the stipulations in Article 5 of the *Charter of the Rights of the Family*, presented by the Holy See on October 22, 1983, would be considered. In order that everyone can immediately weight the importance of this article as to the effective promotion both of the family and of freedom of religion and belief, I am taking the liberty of reading it to this group:

> "Since they have conferred life on their children, parents have the original, primary and inalienable right to educate them; hence they must be acknowledged as the first and foremost educators of their children.
>
> a) Parents have the right to educate their children in conformity with their moral and religious convictions, taking into account the cultural traditions of the family which favour the good and the dignity of the child; they should also receive from society the necessary aid and assistance to perform their educational role properly.
>
> b) Parents have the right to choose freely schools or other means necessary to educate their children in keeping with their convictions. Public authorities must ensure that public subsidies are so allocated that parents are truly free to exercise this right without incurring unjust burdens. Parents should not have to sustain, directly or indirectly, extra charges which would deny or unjustly limit the exercise of this freedom.
>
> c) Parents have the right to ensure that their children are not compelled to attend classes which are not in agreement with their own moral and religious convictions. In particular, sex education is a basic right of the parents and must always be carried out under their close supervision, whether at home or in educational centres chosen and controlled by them.
>
> d) The rights of parents are violated when a compulsory system of education is imposed by the State from which all religious formation is excluded.
>
> e) The primary right of parents to educate their children must be upheld in all forms of collaboration between parents, teachers and school authorities, and particularly in forms of participation designed to give citizens a voice in the functioning of schools and in the formulation and implementation of educational policies.
>
> f) The family has the right to expect that the means of social communication will be positive instruments for the building up of society and will reinforce the fundamental values of the family. At the same time the family has the right to be adequately protected, especially

---

(*) Special Rapporteur of the United Nations Sub-Commission on Prevention of Discrimination and Protection of Minorities.

with regard to its youngest members, from the negative effects and misuse of the mass media."

(591) 5. Finally, we would like to state emphatically our wish that all constitutions, legislations and judicial and administrative practices in all States conform with the stipulations of the international texts concerning human rights. In the name of all victims of intolerance wherever they may be in this world, it is our duty to mention that this is far from being so in many States, even in several of those officially represented in our Seminar.

(592) As John Paul II said in his encyclical letter *Redemptor Hominis* , when he referred to the fact that in our world today, there is no program that puts the human being first: "If, despite such premises, human rights are violated in various ways, if in practice we see before us concentration camps, violence, torture, terrorism, and discrimination in many forms, this must then be the consequence of the other premises, undermining and often almost annihilating the effectiveness of the humanistic premises of these modern programmes and systems. This necessarily imposes the duty to submit these programmes to continual revision from the point of view of the objective and inviolable human rights."

(593) The Catholic Church gladly accepts invitations to increase the promotion of authentic freedom - i.e., freedom that is responsible and in solidarity as well as respectful of others and truly dialogic. But the Church considers that its duty of truth and disinterested service to humanity impels us to remind you of all concrete demands of human rights and, in particular, because of the theme of our Seminar - genuine freedom of thought, conscience, religion, or belief.

VII - RACIAL DISCRIMINATION

1. Deep ethical roots for the rejection of racism

Statement of the Holy See Delegation at the meeting of government representatives organized by UNESCO in Paris on 13-20 March 1978 to work out the draft of a declaration on racial prejudices.

Original: French

(594) The Holy See Delegation wishes to express its agreement on the appropriateness of this Declaration because it does not repeat declarations and prior conventions of the United Nations and of UNESCO, because it is happily set in the framework of the main aims of UNESCO and because it seems suitable to offer a basis for its action in this field.

(595) The Holy See Delegation is also anxious to say how much it appreciates the clarity and vigour of this condemnation of racism in its various aspects.

(596) But as regards the justifications of this condemnation, offered by the draft in question, it seems to us that they need, from certain standpoints, a better presentation which would give them more weight and greater validity and might dispel certain ambiguities of the text. The Declaration would gain by making room for a fundamental view.

(597) By associating ethics and science very closely in many passages, the text of the draft runs the risk of letting it be understood that when all is said and done the condemnation of racism must be sought in science (biology, human sciences). Now, however considerable may be the contribution of recent scientific works - especially in genetics - to the condemnation of racism, it is, nevertheless, particularly in views independent of the conclusions of positive sciences, subjected, moreover, to changes which may not, perhaps, be negligible, that justification of this condemnation must be sought. This means the acceptance of the conviction derived from a fundamental reflection on the human condition, according to which the essential unity of the human species is affirmed - and this even without appealing to its unity of origin - and also its consequence, the equality of all human beings and of all peoples. How would it be possible to base on science alone the ethics of solidarity, brotherhood and peace in which the condemnation of racism must be set, if it is desired to give it all the force necessary to permit its effective application?

(598) 2. These views are certainly present in the document. But they have as their sources, on the one hand the norms of international law, especially the international Declaration on Human Rights, and on the other hand the social consensus of the peoples.

(599) Now this condemnation, as also the norms themselves, have a deeper inspiration which is to be sought in an ideal, an ethic, a concept of nature and of the vocation of man and of humanity that is far more important than purely social norms.

(600) Let us add that these more important views, which find their expression today in the framework of the United Nations Organization, are also found, and have been found for a long time, in philosophies, moralities, religions, realities which, moreover, were taken into consideration, as such, in UNESCO's colloquium on "Convictions and Peace" in May 1974. There is here a state of things which it would have been desirable to have mentioned in the draft of the Declaration.

(601) As regards the Catholic Church, there have been many stands against racism: as early as the sixteenth century, by Las Casas, for example, and by Pope Paul III. And very recently in a particularly firm and explicit manner in the Constitution *Gaudium et Spes* of the Second Vatican Council. "Forms of social or cultural discrimination in basic personal rights on the grounds of sex, race, colour, social conditions, language or religion, must be curbed and eradicated as incompatible with God's design" because "all men are endowed with a rational soul and are created in God's image; they have the same nature and origin...; there is here a basic equality between all men and it must be given ever greater recognition".

(602) In this perspective it would not be out of place to stress the more important role of education for the elimination of racism, so rightly noted in the text of this draft. This education, which will not be just information, but a formation of consciences, will establish this condemnation of racism in the deepest recesses of men's hearts.

2. "Liberation for human fulfillment and authenticity"

Statement by the Rev. Fr. Roger Heckel, Under-Secretary of the Pontifical Commission "Justice and Peace", Head of the Delegation of the Holy See, at the World Conference on the Struggle against Racism and Racial Discrimination, held in Geneva, Switzerland, on 14-25 August 1978. Geneva, 22 August 1978.

Original: French

(603) Since his historic visit of 4 October 1965, Pope Paul VI has supported the United Nations actively and ceaselessly with the moral authority of the Holy See and of the spiritual and doctrinal patrimony of the Catholic Church. In a warm and personal commitment, he presented himself to the General Assembly in New York as a "friend", a "brother", an "expert on humanity", uniquely concerned to serve disinterestedly as a witness of the living God who loves all human persons and confers on all an equal and indelible dignity (cf. Address to the 20th Session of the General Assembly of the United Nations, 4 October 1965, AAS 57(1965), 878. See above, par. 1-10). The Delegation of the Holy See wishes to contribute to the success of this World Conference on the Struggle against Racism and Racial Discrimination in the spirit of the late great Pope.

(604) Sometimes, persons and peoples who have gravely suffered injustice for a long time attain an exceptional human profundity. Then they are preoccupied in effectively assisting others to extract themselves from the same troubles, but they sense that the means to be implemented must already carry the mark of human fraternity that they wish to institute. In congratulating you on your election, Mr. President, the Holy See delegation wishes that, in the courageous, sad experience of so many people including your own who are represented here and under your competent direction, this assembly will find new ways to relinquish chains of hatred and scorn and to lead into understanding, mutual respect and friendship.

(605) From the beginning, Paul VI expressed his "great interest" and his "lively satisfaction" in the Decade of the Struggle against Racism and Racial Discrimination which the 28th General Assembly was preparing to proclaim. In a Message to the President of the Assembly, he wrote: "This preeminently human undertaking will once again find the Holy See and the Unite Nations in close accord - albeit on different levels and with different means - in a common effort to defend and protect the freedom and dignity of every person and every group, without distinction of race, color, language, creed or any particular social condition" [AAS 65(1973), 673-677. See above, par. 434]. In an allocution on 22 May 1974 addressed to the United Nations Special Committee on *apartheid,* Pope then explained the firm, constant doctrine of the Church on the equal dignity of human persons, with, correlatively, the unequivocal condemnation of everything which injures or denies this equality (see below, par. 635-648). He came back to the topic again at the beginning of this year in the discourse to the Diplomatic Corps on human rights.

(606) Delegations of the Holy See have taken an active part in the works of the Conference of Lagos for action against *i* in August 1977 (see below, par. 663-674) as well as at the meeting organized in Paris last March by UNESCO to draw up a draft declaration on race and racial prejudices (see above, par. 594-602).

(607) Such steps emphasize how much the Holy See is resolutely committed, according to its appropriate mission and competencies, in the common effort of this Decade, while Christian communities, more than once at the cost of the liberty and the very life of the faithful and of pastors, witness to Gospel love and the message of universal brotherhood at the heart of the most difficult situations.

(608) In the important context of the celebration of the 25th anniversary of the Universal Declaration of Human Rights, the 28th General Assembly launched the Decade of the Struggle against Racism and Racial Discrimination, showing thereby that human rights are indivisible: the effective struggle on one particularly threatened point calls for a similar effort on all the others.

(609) This broadening of perspective, which the Holy See has always encouraged, allows an attack against the multi-faceted causes producing and supporting behaviours of racial discrimination. Besides, by maintaining attention on the range of political, economic, cultural, and religious discriminations, each person, each country, each group is invited by the Holy See to remain aware of their own weaknesses in one or the other domain; what it loses eventually in rigidity and bias, the struggle against racism gains in moral credibility and in real strength.

(610) The interdependence of all forms of aggressiveness and of discrimination does not thereby signify confusion. If all these forms can produce and maintain racist tensions according to different contexts and receive a more or less intense racist tint, they do not thereby lose their specificity: each calls for an appropriate treatment to be defined in the context of relevant meetings. With even greater clarity these necessary distinctions bring out the particularly odious and injurious character of racism, the necessity of eliminating it in all its forms, those above all established and hardened by institutionalization.

(611) This Conference is resolutely oriented to action for the effective eradication of racism and racial discrimination. Very wisely, efficacy is sought less in a new proliferation of texts than in a resolute implementation of the instruments with which the United Nations is already equipped at various levels. A party to the International Convention on the Elimination of All Forms of Racial Discrimination and to the common effort of the Decade on the Struggle against Racism and Racial Discrimination, the Holy See intends to assume the relevant responsibilities fully according to its nature and its own mission. Its appropriate presence in the international meetings signifies the interest it brings to all aspects of work here and its will to cooperate. But no one expects the Holy See to abandon its specificity and its particular contribution which the international community looks for. To obtain the desired result, it gives without hesitation its moral support, sometimes clarified in a formal, international, juridical agreement, to the great orientations of this Decade and to the Conventions by which the promotion of human rights receives an indispensable structure binding in international law; but it generally does not have the competence to appreciate the more technical and conditional aspects of the most effective policies, given the complexity and diversity of situations. Therefore, a preference, in conferences where these aspects dominate, for the status of observer.

(612) This is not evasion, but awareness of limits and respect for the competency of others; and also, a condition necessary to exercise its specific mission more resolutely with all. In a debate like this on racism, the education of mentalities and of consciences plays an irreplaceable role. It is also an action. Here, the Holy See and the Church it represents can help the common work most effectively. As has been emphasized often right here, the struggle against racial discriminations must be able to count on the simple dynamism of enlightened consciences really convinced of the fundamental equality of all persons and carried by a spontaneous movement to reject all practices and all justifications which could be an obstacle to that equality.

(613) Now, we are obliged to state that this essential dynamism is often distorted or uncertain. The sciences are not enough to right it. Assuredly they contribute a great deal to undo much of the false evidence sought to cover up the justification for racist behaviours or defer necessary transformations. But, by their very method, they refrain from saying the final word on humanity or from defining those universal moral laws of unconditionally binding moral character. The highest expressions of philosophy, of morality and of religions are the irreplaceable witness and educators here.

(614) Thus, while emphasizing the necessity of giving a juridical and political expression, always perfectible, to the equal dignity of all human persons and all peoples, Catholic doctrine puts forth the religious and moral meaning of such equality. On last 14 January, Paul VI, witness to this doctrine which is born and grows in the constant confrontation of the evangelical inspiration with the aspirations of peoples while giving a privileged attention to the poorest, said to the Diplomatic Corps: "For those who believe in God, all human beings, even the least favored, are children of the universal Father who created them in his image and guides their destinies with an attentive love. The paternity of God means fraternity among human persons: this is a strong point in Christian universalism, a point held in common also with other great religions and an axiom of the highest human wisdom of all times, that which reveres human dignity. For a christian, no person is excluded from the possibility of being saved by Christ and of enjoying the same goal in the Reign of God. It is inconceivable, therefore, for anyone who receives the Gospel message, even taking into account physical, intellectual or moral differences, to deny fundamental human equality in the name of a pretended superiority of one race or one ethnic group." (L'Osservatore Romano, 15 January 1978).

(615) Constraint would be an inadmissible as well as ineffective interference in dealing with these most intimate convictions and with their formation. Instead, minds must be helped to liberate by themselves their own movements toward human fulfillment and authenticity. At the external levels of collective mentalities, behaviors and social structures oppressing human persons and groups in various ways, political authorities and the world community legitimately seek effective ways within the framework of laws and of binding conventions to eliminate injustices and to uphold efforts that the oppressed themselves undertake to have their rights recognized. The Holy Father has always encouraged such peaceful efforts and, when obstinate refusal of necessary reforms provokes, alas, violent revolt, he devotes himself, in the measure of his means, to restrict the exacerbation of hatreds, to warn against the self-interested exploitation of conflictive situations, always directing minds toward the search for peace in justice.

(616) The contribution of the Holy See is therefore many-sided: participation in international conferences bringing its own specific contribution; encouragement of Christians to act in civil society according to the ordinary conditions of political, economic and cultural action; coordination and stimulation of educative efforts on the part of christian communities everywhere in the world. Where the racial problem suffers particular intensity and where christians, like others, must struggle against the imposition on them of traditions, structures and collective mentalities penetrated by racism, the bishops and the Episcopal Conferences have multiplied realistic, precise, demanding interventions to harmonize convictions and behaviours with the Gospel. Still, these extreme cases invite a wider and more constant effort to combat racism in its most latent or more widespread forms and to prevent its appearance. This explains the constant attention of the Holy See and of christian communities to the situation of migrants and minorities.

(617) No one is excluded from the educational effort which the Holy see and the Church ceaselessly continue and renew in the most diverse situations. Charity and patience towards all do not in any way weaken the resolute commitment to the victims of racial discrimination. Risking much misunderstanding, the Christian community shares their fate, loans them its voice, nourishes their hope, contributes to their advancement in every way, frees moral and spiritual energies permitting them to become the principal artisans of their true liberation, their full development in solidarity with the human family.

3. Fundamental equality of all human persons

Statement of Msgr. Giuseppe Bertello, Head of the Holy See Delegation at the Second World Conference on Racism and Racial Discrimination, held in Geneva, Switzerland, on 1-12 August 1983. Geneva, 8 August 1983.

Original: French

(618) The Second World Conference on Racism and Racial Discrimination gives the Holy See, once again, the timely opportunity to add its contribution to the considerations of the international community on a drama which cannot but worry all men of good will, inviting them to unite their efforts to eradicate this scourge from the life of man.

(619) You can well understand the interest of my Delegation for this great debate which reflects in an acute and honest way the conscience of the world on this problem. Against racism, as against other social evils, the Catholic Church and the Holy See, always basing themselves on the principles of Christian universality, have developed their thinking and directed their action in a constantly changing historical context and an unending confrontation with the aspirations and experiences of nations, while always paying particular attention to the poorest.

(620) It would suffice to recall the mediation of the Popes at the time of the first contacts between Europe and the peoples of the New World; or, almost a hundred years later, at the beginning of the 17th century, the foundation of the Congregation for the Propagation of the Faith, one of whose goals was to free the Church from interference by colonial powers; or again, the activity in favour of the freeing of slaves; right up to the important pontifical documents of our day which emphasize the merits of native cultures and the yearning of individuals and nations for equal dignity and its realization in all walks of life.

(621) As His Holiness Pope John Paul II stated in his Message to the President of the 11th Special Session of the General Assembly of the United Nations, the Catholic Church believes it has its own part to play in proceedings of this kind. It does not foresee bringing practical solutions to complex situations which are not of its competence; but when fitting, it will speak up during such debates, so as to give witness of its concern for all that touches upon the human condition and to present a vision of man and society. It will also offer useful criteria so that human values and the merits of nations and cultures will not be used, by mistake, to pursue goals unworthy of the person and the society which we seek to promote.

(622) Today, more than ever before, we are especially concerned about the sharing of material wealth, equality in educational opportunity and democracy in the exercise of authority. And all the more do we feel the oppression of man, his subjection, his exploitation, the manipulations of which he is both the object and the outcome. We have before us various forms of discrimination which attack the rights of persons and groups as well as social peace. There is discrimination when individuals and entire populations are deprived of religious liberty, when one is punished in his social and professional life for his religious belief, when the rights of minorities are disregarded, when the migrant worker is treated as a second-class citizen and the poor condemned to inhuman living conditions.

(623) But at the present time, among all these unjust practices, racial discrimination is very much in the news because of the tension which it creates both within certain countries and at the international level. Quite reasonably, people hold as unjustifiable and reject as inadmissible, attempts to introduce or maintain legislation or behaviour based entirely on racial prejudice.

(624) This condemnation of racism is not only the result of scientific conclusions which are better known today because of a higher level of education, the improvement of information media, or a greater awareness of the evils of modern times. Rather, it is fully justified by a moral philosophy, an ideal, a conception of humanity which asserts the basic unity of the human race and the equality of all men and of all nations.

(625) The Catholic Church makes its contribution at this level especially, in drawing attention to the religious and moral meaning of the equality of all men more than to its juridical or political aspect.

(626) In his address to the diplomats accredited to the Holy See, at the beginning of 1978 Pope Paul VI thus summarized the doctrine of the Church: "For those who believe in God, all human beings, even the least favored, are children of the universal Father who created them in his image and guides their destinies with an attentive love. The paternity of God means fraternity among human persons: this is a strong point in Christian universalism, a point held in common also with other great religions and an axiom of the highest human wisdom of all times, that which reveres human dignity. For a Christian, no person is excluded from the possibility of being saved by Christ and of enjoying the same goal in the Reign of God. It is inconceivable, therefore, for anyone who receives the Gospel message, even taking into account physical, intellectual or moral differences, to deny fundamental human equality in the name of a pretended superiority of one race or one ethnic group." And, after recalling the situation in certain African countries, he added: "The Church cannot be silent concerning her teaching that all racist theories are contrary to the faith and Christian love" (L'Osservatore Romano, 15 January 1978).

(627) At the same time as they are a solemn declaration in modern language of the doctrinal basis for human rights, these words of the Sovereign Pontiff also constitute the starting point of action in this vast field.

(628) In ratifying the International Convention on the eradication of all forms of racial discrimination and in participating in the common project of the Decade Against Racism and Racial Discrimination, the Holy See, in line with its own nature and mission, wants to make an honest contribution to building a community of life which guarantees to individuals and to groups everywhere the right to life, to personal and social dignity, to development, to a just sharing of natural wealth and the advantages of civilization, convinced as it is that moral and religious questions cannot be separated from today's economic, political and social realities.

(629) My Delegation does not think it necessary to recall here the many initiatives launched by the Holy See and the bishops during these last years to combat all forms of racial discrimination. The mass media, for example, have often reported the declarations and decisions of the bishops of South Africa, and the stand in favour of migrants and minorities.

(630) However, we would like to recall the efforts of the Church in educating to brotherhood, justice and peace while respecting different cultures and civilizations. As its very name indicates, Christian universality requires the abolition of classes and discrimination, and the conquest of individual and collective egoism, so as to achieve full social solidarity and to seek the good of the world community. *"Every man is my brother,"* the theme of a World Day of Peace, should not be just a good slogan.

(631) This deep spirit of brotherhood, which appeals to conscience and is the result of constant interior renewal, makes man very sensitive to everything which offends his dignity and to all forms of injustice. It forces him to try to change attitudes which cause so much suffering and to alter structures so as to satisfy the legitimate aspirations of oppressed peoples.

(632) In the search for greater justice and in reconciling conflicting interests, man must not let himself be drawn down to hatred and brute force, in thinking that the best way to resolve problems is armed struggle. Experience teaches us that this solution only increases the gap between social groups and intensifies tensions and conflicts, making it impossible to realize the aspirations which are at the root of these very claims. True commitment to justice and to effective participation in social and political life requires the setting up of relationships motivated by reciprocal collaboration and by constructive sincerity which give rise, on the world level, to honest negotiations with the help of international organizations to which the community of nations is asked to give authority, effectiveness and confidence.

(633) In its work of education, finally, the Church does not ignore the merits and characteristics special to each nation. On the contrary, it respects, protects and honours the heritage of values which they possess and wants to contribute to its development in cultural, social and political expressions which are always truly human. Allow me to repeat a few words from the address of His Holiness John Paul II to Indians during his visit to Central America: "Your Indian cultures are the wealth of peoples... They deserve the greatest respect, the highest esteem, the greatest sympathy and full support from all of humanity".

(634) The celebration of the Decade Against Racism and Racial Discrimination finds the Holy See and the United Nations together once again in a common effort to defend and protect the freedom and the dignity of each individual and of each group without distinction. My Delegation hopes that these few thoughts will help this Assembly to better identify the various forms of racial discrimination, especially where they are fixed or structured into *apartheid* , and will help individuals and governments to act more clearly in an effort to exert effective pressure which is more constructive than violence.

X - *APARTHEID*

1. Discrimination denies Christ's message

Address of His Holiness Paul VI to the United Nations Special Committee on *Apartheid*.
The Vatican, 22 May 1974.

Original: English (*)

(635) We have responded willingly to the request for an audience by the Committee of the United Nations on *Apartheid*. We are happy to have this occasion to restate the Church's position on the great crucial themes of human dignity and the fundamental equality of all men, and, in particular, on the issue of discrimination. This teaching reflects a whole Christian concept of man himself, who is created in God's likeness and redeemed by Christ. It was he who left us both a heritage and a challenge when he said: "You are all brothers." (*Matth.* 23:8)

(636) Our predecessors in the See of Peter, the Vicars of Christ throughout the years, have repeatedly given expression to his teaching in the defence of man. It was Paul III who promoted the dignity of the native peoples of the Americas: their freedom, their right to property (*Pastorale Officium*, 29 May 1537: DS 1495; cf. also Gregory XVI, *In Supremo Apostolatus Fastigio*, 24 December 1839: DS 2745). In modern times our great predecessors Pius XII and John XXIII steadfastly reaffirmed the priceless Gospel heritage (cf. Radio Message, 24 December 1942: AAS 35(1943), p. 19; *Pacem in Terris*, 11 April 1963: AAS 55(1963), pp. 259-260].

(637) Thus we unhesitatingly proclaim once again the dignity of the human person and the brotherhood of all men. True brotherhood takes into account the common origin, nature and destiny of all members of the human family and the equality of their fundamental rights. We find it as relevant today as seven years ago to state: "This equality demands an ever more explicit recognition in civil society of every human being's essential rights... Consequently, the aspirations of all men desiring to enjoy those rights which flow from their dignity as human persons are wholly legitimate." [Message to Africa: AAS 59(1967), p. 1082]

(638) And yet as we note with pleasure that there is indeed a growing awareness of the exalted dignity proper to the human person, and that civilization marches towards the recognition of equality and the freedoms demanded by reason of this human dignity and equality, we must all admit that one of the great paradoxes of our time is that in fact these freedoms are all too frequently restricted, violated and denied.

(639) Various forms of discrimination militate against the rights of individuals and communities and the harmony of society. Antagonisms and rivalries obscure the effective realization of the one united human family under the fatherhood of God. Hatred existing in the hearts of men and manifested in strife still imperils the security, peace and prosperity of peoples.

(640) As we warn of the dangers concomitant with abuses against human dignity, equality and liberty, we reiterate the Church's often-repeated appeal to banish all discrimination, in law or in fact, which is based on "race, origin, colour, culture, sex or religion." [*Octogesima Adveniens*, 16: AAS 63(1971), p. 413]

(641) Discrimination takes on many forms. It is present when individuals and entire populations are not granted the right of religious freedom, the "free and normal expression of that most jealously guarded right of the human spirit." [Message for the Day of Peace 1972: AAS 63(1971), p. 413]. It is likewise present, for example, when the equal dignity of women is not respected. It is present

---

(*) AAS 66(1974), 342-346.

when the migrant worker is looked down upon, when the poor are held down to inhuman conditions of life.

(642) As we rightly recognize the importance of each of these categories, we willingly state that "racial discrimination possesses at the moment a character of very great relevance by reason of the tension which it stirs up both within certain countries and on the international level. Men rightly consider unjustifiable and reject as inadmissible the tendency to maintain or introduce legislation or behaviour systematically inspired by racial prejudice." [*Octogesima Adveniens*, 16: AAS 63(1971), p. 413]. What we are repeating now we had said even before, as we stood on African soil: "We deplore the fact that, in certain parts of the world, there persist social situations based upon racial discrimination and often willed and sustained by systems of thought; such situations constitute a manifest and inadmissible affront to the fundamental rights of the human person...." [Address to the Parliament of Uganda: AAS 61(1969), p. 585].

(643) Conditions in the world today prompt us once again to repeat with the same measure of conviction what we said before: "Within a country which belongs to each one, all should be equal before the law, find equal admittance to economic, cultural, civic and social life and benefit from a fair sharing of the nation's riches." [*Octogesima Adveniens*, 16: AAS 63(1971), p. 413]. All men must participate in the life of the nation. Power, responsibility and decision-making cannot be the monopoly of one group or race or segment of the people. The message which we offer - and it is at the same time advice, counsel and injunction for Christian consciences - to every group or State or nation is what we have learned from him whom we represent: "You are all brothers."

(644) In advocating the recognition of the dignity of all men and the protection of their fundamental rights, the Christian message calls for integral human development, which - we have insisted - is "the new name of peace" [*Populorum Progressio*, 87: AAS 59(1967),p. 299] and "the indisputable exigency of justice." [Address to the Parliament of Uganda: AAS 61(1969), p. 582]. The Church realizes that the development of peoples involves, besides the equality of races, "the right to aspire to their own legitimate autonomy." (Ibid. p. 584). Our thought on this complex issue is no secret to you. We expressed it when we explained that freedom means "civil independence, political self-determination, emancipation from the domination of other powers..." (*ibid.* p. 582).

(645) In the quest for the attainment of this full measure of human dignity, men must indeed proceed in certain circumstances and historical situations with particular prudence and wisdom. The degree of the gradualness with which they proceed must be in proportion to the urgency; there must be a precise plan with a definite time-table. But the cause is urgent and the hour is late. "Yes," as we said last year, "as long as the rights of all the peoples, among them the right to self-determination and independence, are not duly recognized and honoured, there cannot be true and lasting peace, even though the abusive power of arms may for a time prevail over the reactions of those opposed. For as long as, within the individual national communities, those in power do not nobly respect the rights and legitimate freedoms of the citizens, tranquillity and order (even though they can be maintained by force) remain nothing but a deceptive and insecure sham, no longer worthy of a society of civilized beings." [Address to the College of Cardinals, 21 December 1973: AAS 66(1972), p. 21]. Therefore, from our vantage point we earnestly call upon all men of good will to recognize this and to give heed to the just yearnings of individuals and peoples.

(646) In the solution of these pressing problems, the only possible means are the means indicated by the Christian message, which claims without reservation the need to give witness to promote and effect justice, as brotherhood, love and the inventive capacity of man suggest, but with violence excluded. On another occasion we noted: "In the face of deplorable delays, or even of continuous disregard of the problems, the temptation to violent means ... may become very strong. But violence as a solution is illusory. Moreover, it is difficult to reconcile violence with the righteousness that it is intent upon proclaiming or defending." [Letter to Cardinal Conway, 6 March 1972: AAS 64(1972), p. 312-313]. No, we repeat, violence is not an acceptable solution. It must give way to reason, mutual trust, sincere negotiations and fraternal love.

(647) The subject of our consideration today has vast ramifications and it is not possible to speak of all of them. The theme we have touched upon calls to mind also the need to terminate class struggle and hatred at every level and in every form. The rights of minorities call out for protection as do the rights of the poor, the handicapped, the incurably ill and all those who live at the margin of society and are without voice. Above all the precious right to life - that most fundamental of all human rights - must be affirmed anew, together with the condemnation of that massive aberration which is the destruction of innocent human life, at whatever stage it may be, through the heinous crimes of abortion or euthanasia.

(648) Yes, it is our mission to call upon all men to give recognition to God's dominion - to whom be glory for ever and ever (*Gal.* 1,5) - and to banish all discrimination in recognition of the dignity of every man. To all men of good will we repeat again, and yet again: "You are all brothers."

2. The system of *apartheid* contrary to the dignity of individuals and whole communities

Address of His Holiness John Paul II to the Chairman of the United Nations Special Committee against *Apartheid*, H.E. Major-General J.N. Garba. The Vatican, 7 July 1984.

Original: English (*)

(649) 1. I have accepted very willingly your request to be received in audience, for I have seen in it a sign of your appreciation of what the Catholic Church is doing to *defend the dignity of the human person*, and in particular to combat all forms of racial discrimination.

(650) Your Committee is no stranger to this place, and it is familiar with the often reaffirmed teaching of the Church and the position of the Holy See on racial discrimination and *apartheid*.

(651) Ten years ago, on 22 May 1974, my predecessor Paul VI received your Committee and indicated the bases of the Christian commitment to the cause of promoting human dignity. Today's meeting gives me an opportunity to emphasize once more the principles governing this commitment. Man's *creation by God* "in his own image" (*Gen.* 1:27) confers upon every human person an eminent dignity; it also postulates *the fundamental equality of all human beings*. For the Church, this equality, which is rooted in man's being, acquires the dimension of an altogether special brotherhood trough the Incarnation of the Son of God, whose sacrifice redeemed all people. In *the Redemption* effected by Jesus Christ the Church sees a further basis of the rights and duties of the human person. Hence every form of discrimination based on race, whether occasional or systematically practised, and whether it is aimed at individuals or whole racial groups, is absolutely unacceptable. The Apostle Saint Paul says very clearly: "Here there cannot be Gentile and Jew, circumcised and uncircumcised, barbarian, Scythian, slave, free man, but Christ is all, and in all" (*Col.* 3:11).

(652) 2. Unfortunately, as I had to note on the occasion of the celebration of the International Day for the Elimination of Racial Discrimination: "... the scourge of racial discrimination, in all its many forms, still disfigures our age. It denies the fundamental equality of all men and women, proclaimed by the different Declarations of the United Nations, but above all rooted in God" (21 March 1984).

(653) I would also like to recall the fact that Paul VI, in his last address to the Diplomatic Corps accredited to the Holy See, spoke about the racial conflict in Africa and mentioned "the attempt to create juridical and political structures in violation of the principles of universal suffrage and the self-determination of peoples" (14 January 1978).

(*) Insegnamenti di Giovanni Paolo II, VII,2 (1984) 35-39.

(654) The Holy See is following with close attention the *development of the situation in Southern Africa,* and has repeatedly shown its concern that the rights of the individuals and peoples living there be respected.

(655) 3. In this context, I would like to make reference to two particular aspects of the problem that exists in that part of the world. It is a question of two aspects that raise questions which are complex, serious and difficult, but which are fundamental for the future of the region and for the well-being of the people living there. I am speaking of the problem of *the independence of Namibia,* which I referred to in my address to the Diplomatic Corps last January 14th, and the problem of the *displacement of vast numbers of people in South Africa.*

(656) My reason for mentioning these two issues today is not that the Holy See wishes to put forward proposals of a political nature. The Holy See is not unaware of the numerous political implications surrounding these issues, but its interest is on another level: *the level of the human person.* And it is at this level that these matters cause deep disquiet, for the weight of suffering affecting the individuals and communities concerned is very heavy. The Catholic Church, faithful to her mission in the world, shares these sufferings and cannot pass them over in silence, for if she did, her witness of love and service to man would be compromised. The Good News which she received from her divine Founder obliges the Church to proclaim the message of salvation and human dignity and to condemn injustices and attacks on human dignity.

(657) As for Namibia, the Holy See expresses the hope that it will be possible for the negotiations, which have been going on for a long time, to be translated, without too much delay, into clear decisions which will recognize without ambiguity *the right of this nation* to be sovereign and independent. This will be an important contribution towards restoring peace in the region, and a valuable sign of reconciliation between the different peoples that live there. It will similarly be an exemplary application of the principles of international law which cannot fail to extend its positive influence to other conflicts on the African continent and also elsewhere.

(658) The recent agreements which have marked relations between different countries in Southern Africa seem to constitute an advance in this direction. In the meantime, it is of capital importance that the conduct of the civil and military authorities in Namibian territory should be inispired by *respect for the rights of the inhabitants*, even in the situations of confrontation that may exist.

(659) Concerning the second issue that I have mentioned, namely the displacement of vast numbers of South African citizens to the places of residence assigned to them by the Government, *the local Catholic Church has already expressed its protest*, since this procedure represents a grave violation of the rights of the human person, and at the same time is deeply damaging to family life and the social fabric.

(660) *A joint ecumenical initiative* has been taken by the Southern Africa Catholic Bishops' Conference and the South African Council of Churches, in order to draw the attention of the public and of international organizations to these facts, which are a *consequence of the system of apartheid.* The Holy See, for its part, expresses its concern at procedures contrary to the dignity of individuals and whole communities. It earnestly hopes that a different policy will be established, in order that a population already so sorely tried and whose right to be treated without discrimination is systematically flouted may be spared further painful and tragic experiences. It likewise desires the revision of such a policy so that other catastrophic consequences can be avoided in the future, for the true good of all who live in the region and for the sake of world peace.

(661) 4. My dear friends: your delicate work demands *firmness in the defence of principles* and *prudence in the choice of means* suitable for attaining your purpose. I assure you that the Church, keeping in mind her own level of responsibilities and competencies, is at your side as you travel your difficult road, and she is ready *to support every effort aimed at removing the temptation to violence* and at helping to solve the problem of *apartheid* in *a spirit of dialogue and fraternal love* that respects the rights of the parties involved.

(662) May Almighty God inspire good will in all people concerned, and help those in positions of responsibility to make wise decisions, so that in that region of the world justice and peace may prevail. What is at stake is *the dignity of the human person and the well-being of all mankind.*

3. The Church supports non-violent efforts for action against *apartheid*

Statement of H.E.Msgr Girolamo Prigione, Head of the Holy See Delegation, to the World Conference for Action against *Apartheid* held in Lagos, Nigeria, from 22 to 26 August 1977. Lagos, 25 August 1977.

Original: English

(663) By participating in this World Conference, the Holy See intends to offer its contribution, and that of the whole Church, to support common non-violent efforts against what is commonly referred to as *apartheid.*

(664) The Holy See deplores the social situations directly resulting from *apartheid,* an unjust system based upon racial discrimination, and considers them as a manifest and inadmissible affront to the fundamental rights of the human person.

(665) Because it offends human dignity, arbitrarily limiting basic freedoms, *apartheid* must be eliminated. The opposition of the Holy See and of the entire Church to *apartheid* does not stem from political motives, or from hostility towards persons. The opposition derives rather from the incompatibility existing between systematic racial discrimination and basic beliefs of christianity, according to which all men and women are equal by reason of their common origin, nature and destiny.

(666) In particular, christianity professes that all people are created in the image and likeness of the same God and endowed by their creator with the same human nature; all are redeemed by the Son of God made man; all are invited to the same destiny of eternal happiness and fulfillment. Sharing humanity in common, all people are equal in human dignity.

(667) In the concrete, this equality of dignity must find expression in civil life and be manifested through the social, economic and political activity of free citizens, unhampered by reason of colour or race.

(668) His Holiness Pope Paul VI emphasized the importance of this concept and the fundamental motivation behind it when addressing the President and members of the United Nations Special Committee on *apartheid,* on 22 May 1974. On that occasion he stated: "All men must participate in the life of the nation. Power, responsibility and decision-making cannot be the monopoly of one group or race or segment of people. The message which we offer - and it is, at the same time, advice, counsel and injunction for Christian consciences - to every group or State or nation is what we have learned from him whom we represent: 'You are all brothers'." (See above, par. 643).

(669) No system can be justified that violates this universal brotherhood by impeding the exercise of the natural rights of marriage or by prohibiting normal family life on the grounds of colour or race. No system can be vindicated that deprives the workers of their just rights and of their personal and corporate dignity by reason of their colour or race.

(670) The christian stand against racism, against its applications and against its systematic embodiment has been expressed not only in many documents of the Popes and the Holy See but also in the teaching of the Church on the local level The Southern Africa Catholic Bishops Conference has recently stated: "...we again profess our conviction, so often repeated, that the only solution of our racial tensions consists in conceding full citizen and human rights to all persons in the Republic, not by choice on the false grounds of colour, but on the grounds of the common humanity of all men, taught by our Lord Jesus Christ." (Statement on Current Situation, 10 February 1977).

(671) The Holy See is keenly aware of the fact that the violation of basic rights and freedoms constitutes moreover a threat to true peace. Under these conditions the abusive power of arms may prevail for a while. But, in the words of Paul VI: "...as long as, within the individual national communities, those in power do not nobly respect the rights and legitimate freedoms of the citizens, tranquillity and order (even though they can be maintained by force) remain nothing but a deceptive and insecure sham, no longer worthy of a society of civilized beings" (Address to the College of Cardinals, 21 December 1973).

(672) Precisely in this context the Holy See repeats the appeal of Paul VI: "...the cause is urgent and the hour is late." (Address of 22 May 1974. See above, par. 645). At the same time being convinced of the irreversible tide of history in this sector affecting human dignity, the Holy See views its condemnation of *apartheid* as a salutary warning, which, if heeded, will later be seen to be, what in reality it is: an act of charity that would spare those at present engaged in oppression the recriminations that history will perhaps not be in a position to ward off, or that moderate men may not succeed in restraining.

(673) Having wished to raise a prophetic voice in order to avert bloody recrimination and further useless suffering, the Holy See, after repudiating *apartheid* and urging its elimination, above all by renunciation, wishes to express the witness of its own conviction that the struggle to banish this system will not succeed in effectively promoting human dignity if hatred is nurtured or if violence is resorted to. Justice must be effected; and brotherhood, love and the inventive capacity of man must find the means. But violence is not among them; violence as a solution is illusory. Paul VI has clearly expressed the position of the Church: "...violence is not an acceptable solution. It must give way to reason, mutual trust, sincere negotiations and fraternal love" (Address of 22 May 1974. See above, par. 646).

(674) This Delegation reserves its last word - one of charitable appeal before the conscience of humanity and the witness of history - to those who still have the means to change the system, thus giving the hope of human dignity to millions of people, and procuring the blessings of peace to a tormented area. To them, above all, this Delegation repeats again the words of Paul VI: "...the cause is urgent and the hour is late."

CHAPTER III

CULTURE AND EDUCATION

I - EDUCATIONAL WORK INDUCES DEVELOPMENT, IS A FOUNT OF PEACE BETWEEN MEN AND NATIONS

Message of His Holiness Paul VI to Mr. René Maheu, Director-General of UNESCO, to mark the closing of the International Year of Education. The Vatican, 8 December 1970.

Original: French

(675) We have often had occasion to inform you of our great regard for UNESCO's Work for Education, Science and Culture.

(676) The Holy See welcomed the happy idea of an International Education Year with pleasure, and Catholics on their part, intend to collaborate generously in the grand designs of this campaign, convinced that all educational work induces development and is a fount of peace between men and nations.

(677) On this occasion, the Holy See considers it opportune to stress some of the major aspects of this subject, and We hope to please you by acquainting you with them, our only concern being to make a useful contribution to this great cause. (*)

(678) Our heartfelt desire is to see UNESCO, faithful to its noble aims, extend its peaceful activities for human development, which is of prime importance for the future of the world.

(*) NOTE OF THE HOLY SEE on the occasion of the International Year of Education.

I

(679) All men and all nations have always been concerned with the transmission of life, the means of existence and ways of living to succeeding generations. Moreover, in various ways according to place and time, education has always been considered as a work of primary importance, one which assures the transmission of knowledge and behaviour, and which tends to make man more humane by having him share all those things in nature and in history which can enrich his life ... and to use the forces of the physical world as instruments for his freedom (cf. J. Maritain, *L'humanisme intégral*, Paris, Aubier, 1936, p. 10-11).

(680) This primordial task is being fulfilled today in thousands of ways, among ancient peoples and in young nations. But the profound changes that disturb our times render communication between generations more difficult. Furthermore, communication requires a continuous formation which is intended to help adults bring their knowledge up to date and profit by the progress made in knowledge and in techniques for their daily life as well as their professional activity.

(681) While inequalities between the rich and the poor increase in a world narrowed down by modern means of social communication, the imbalance becomes more pronounced in the presence of "overdeveloped means and underdeveloped ends" (Paul VI, Address to the International Seminar of Catholic European Periodicals and the African Society of Culture, Osservatore Romano, 2 October 1969). Humanity hesitates, uncertain before fear and hope, in confused consciousness that a brilliant material and technical success can be on a par with a sort of moral failure (cf. Paul VI, Address to the FAO, 16 November 1970, n. 4, in Osservatore Romano, 17 November 1970. See above, par. 62), and that adults often seem frustrated when faced with the anxious and impatient expectation of youth. "Who has not sensed, in rich countries, their anxiety at the invasion of technocracy, their rejection of a society which has not succeeded in integrating them into itself; and, in poor countries, their lament that, for lack of sufficient training and fitting means, they cannot make their generous contribution to the tasks which call for it?" (Paul VI, Address to the ILO in Geneva, 10 June 1969, n. 23, in AAS, 61 [1969], p. 502. See above, par. 56).

UNESCO AND THE INTERNATIONAL YEAR OF EDUCATION

(682) "Hunger for education is no less depressing than hunger for food." (Encyclical *Populorum Progressio*, 26 March 1967, n. 35). The UNESCO, established by the Organization of the United Nations as an agency for specialization in education, science and culture, has given rise to legitimate hopes. The Church, on her part, has never ceased to collaborate with this deserving institution, and will continue to do so, particularly during this international year of education. Thus, for example, in the more traditional forms of teaching which harmonize closely with the programmes of the civil authorities to whom it is fitting to render homage, we have seen in young Christian nations the development of functional reading and writing, and the use of modern means of social communication for larger sectors of rural populations. Moreover, technical progress continues to be made in this field, and will make possible in the future what still seemed impracticable in the past. Who does not see, for example, the boundless possibilities offered to educators by satellite transmissions and film recorders?

(683) This shows that present scientific and technical changes and their repercussions on daily life call for the constant study of methods of education always better adapted to the changing needs of a world in perpetual evolution. Knowledge is no longer something acquired once and for all. The amount of available information constantly increases, while methods and techniques continually change. The student of today knows that in the future he will be faced with innovations, the emergence of which his teachers hardly suspect. In addition to the necessary transmission of knowledge, educators must use all possible means to develop the faculties of judgment and discernment, and give to those concerned the desire and the means to pursue their own education by themselves later on. In short, learn to learn.

(684) In this hour so important for the future of mankind, the Church on her part, in her own way and without ever losing sight of her purpose which is to proclaim the Gospel of Christ the Saviour, (cf. Vatican Council II, Dogmatic Constitution *Lumen Gentium*, 21 November 1964, n. 1 and 8) intends to pursue her task as "mother and teacher" (*) in countries where she has taken roots since her very beginnings. This is a requirement of "faith working through love" (*Gal.* 5:6). Eager to help young people and adults, not only for the needs of their physical and intellectual life, but also for those of their moral and spiritual life, "her missionaries have built, not only Churches, but also hostels and hospitals, schools and universities" (Paul VI, *Populorum Progressio*, n. 12). Moreover, far from restricting herself to educational establishments, the Church has founded numerous communities of education - let it suffice to recall the works of Don Bosco, Cardinal Cardijn and Saint John Baptist de La Salle - works destined to help young people develop their personality by integrating themselves freely in social life.

(685) This educational effort, which has varied throughout the ages and history, has been applied particularly on behalf of the poor of all categories, and today in a special way to the physically and mentally handicapped and maladjusted. Numerous educators - religious men and women in the first place - have largely contributed, on their part and in many countries, to the advancement of the least favoured, and notably of women. In thousands of ways the educational task of the Church continues all over the world where she contributes "to the authentic development, a development which is for each and all the transition from less human conditions to those which are more human" (*ibid.* n. 20). By so doing, as Pope Paul VI stated at the close of the recent ecumenical Council in Rome, the Church has but one aim: "to serve man" (AAS, 58[1966], pp. 55-59).

(686) If it is true, according to the famous saying of an eminent philosopher, "that a developed body requires the supplement of a soul, and that the mechanical would require the mystical" (H. Bergson, *Les deux sources de la morale et de la religion*, Paris, Alcan, 17th ed., 1934, p. 335), the Church believes that her contribution to education, in its specific aspects (**) can help the men of

---

(*) Familiar expression of the Fathers of the Church and used by John XXIII for the title of his Encyclical *Mater et Magistra*, 15 May 1961, in AAS, 53[1961], pp. 401-464.

(**) Among the documents for reference in this matter are: Benedict XV, Apostolic Letter *Communes Litteras*, 10 April 1919, in AAS 11 (1919), p. 172 and ff.; Pius XI, Encyclical Letter *Divini Illius Magistri*,

our times realize to the full their most noble aspirations: to build a fraternal world wherein all the members of the great human family, from the youngest to the oldest, working with enthusiasm to realize this project so worthy of giving renewed life to their energies, will gradually succeed in controlling the forces of nature, in developing harmoniously the possibilities of education, and, respecting legitimate diversities, will promote a world civilization wherein all men can live as free and responsible persons, according to the image of the God of love who is their father.

II

COMPLETE HUMANISM AND INTEGRAL DEVELOPMENT

(687) "What must be aimed at is complete humanism. And what is that if not the integral development of the whole man and of all men? ... There is no true humanism but that which is open to the Absolute and is conscious of a vocation which gives human life its true meaning..Man can only realize himself by reaching beyond himself." These statements of the encyclical *Populorum Progressio* (n. 14) indicate clearly the fundamental objectives of the Church's activity in education. The Church is anxious to respect the balance between nature and grace, to help men recognize that they are brothers in a humanity advancing towards its full development.

(688) "Walk as children of light" (*Eph.* 5:8). This recommendation of the Apostle Paul engages Christians in a zealous search for the truth. Far from leading them astray, faith stimulates their search in every field. They discover the multiform activity of man in the continued activity of the Creator. The Creator is not an embarrassing rival of his creature, since the scientific and technical achievements of the creature are accomplished in conformity with the designs of the Creator (cf. *Gen.* 1:8). Is not the increasing ascendancy of man over the forces of nature in direct line with his vocation, similar to the control of the economy and the political adjustment of society? Is it not one of the primordial tasks of education to spread this creative enthusiasm, to share "the patrimony of civilization won by immense sacrifice," (Paul VI, Christmas Message of 1968, in AAS 61[1968], p. 56) and in this way, open wide the avenues of the future?

(689) Such a discovery of educational manifestations and technical progress, which have characterized the life of man, opens the mind, enriches the heart, leads to respect and thoughtful admiration, and becomes the school of responsible freedom. In this process towards the conquest of truth, the personality of the educator is irreplaceable, for his task is no longer only a matter of transmitting knowledge, but of communicating values and discovering truth - an unlimited field whose gradual conquest broadens the mind and develops the person in search of perfection.

YOUTH IN QUEST OF TRUTH

(690) This rising generation in quest of truth, athirst for authenticity and distrustful of all authority, often rebellious to lessons of the past, especially the recent past - does not this generation seek knowledge that teaches us how to live rather than knowledge which is continually undergoing

---

(continued from page 115)
31 December 1929, in AAS, 22(1930), p. 49 and ff.; Pius XII, many documents among which the most important are in AAS (1939-1958) and conveniently put together until 1954 in *Les enseignements pontificaux, L'Education*, Paris, Desclée, 1955, or Pius XII, *L'Education, la science et la culture*, Paris, Fleurus, 1956; John XXIII, Message for the 30th anniversary of *Divini Illius Magistri*, 30 December 1959, in AAS, 52(1960), p. 57 and ff.; Vatican Council II, Declaration on Christian Education, 28 October 1965, in AAS, 58(1966), p. 728 and ff.; Paul VI, numerous texts in AAS, 55(1963 ff.).

evolution and whose limitations are keenly perceived by this generation? Who would remain indifferent in the face of these demands of our times? The best educational reforms, though indispensable, would not give us the satisfactory answer. What we need is a testimony of life. Always prepared, according to the recommendation of the Apostle Peter, "to make a defence to anyone who calls you to account for the hope that is in you" (*1Pt.* 3:15), educators will experience with joy the words of Christ to Nicodemus: "he who does what is true comes to the light" (*Jn.* 3:21).

(691) Education, which is rooted in a living experience that communicates, unwearyingly pursues its goal: form men, teach them how to live, train them to discover how imprudent it is to act without knowledge, but that to know and not to act would be cowardice. For the acquisition of knowledge and the training of the will are directly focused on personal and social action. There is no education without the application of all the human faculties, nor without the harmonious development of the mind and body. Moreover, is not the one who benefits from education also its principal agent, whose interior dynamism has to be awakened, nourished and directed? Far from restricting man to a situation of passivity, we have to initiate him without delay into assuming responsibilities by gradually entrusting to him tasks to fulfil and decisions to make.

(692) There is no education for the sake of education, but education is an effort undertaken by men to help other men take their proper place in the community where they live, and in this community exercise in their turn their free and responsible activity. To educate does not mean to transmit abstract knowledge, but to instill a way of life in a particular civilization, and provide the means to realize it: rudimentary knowledge, to be sure, but with the intention to open up avenues for an adaptable formation and help a person learn a trade, perform a useful professional task, and work as a citizen. Therefore, educators are not those who are set in their knowledge which has nothing to do with life and are fixed in stereotyped formulas. True educators are those who are stimulated by a constant concern for study, research and adaptation, who are preoccupied in preparing a future, and who are always alert to the demands of the times and events: inventions, initiatives, and even contestations in order to give these a positive objective, without depriving them of their stimulating function.

(693) To fulfil their task properly, educators must become thoroughly integrated within the community in order to be imbued with "its traditions, its needs, its level of culture, its orientations and tendencies ... its requirements ... interpreted at the school level, by individuals and organized groups, by educational or religious institutes, whose specific goal is to prepare youth for their future tasks." (Letter of the Secretariat of State on the occasion of the 45th Social Week in France, on "*L'Enseignement, problème social*", in the Report of the Week, Lyon, Social Chronicle of France, 1958, p. 6). A certain intellectual individualism has caused so much havoc that we strongly feel the need for a broader diffusion of education throughout the world (cf. Message to René Maheu, Director-General of UNESCO, for the International Year of Education).

III

EDUCATION, A JOINT EFFORT

(694) More than ever before, education is a community task which must mobilize to its advantage all the dynamic forces of the community of men: the family in the first place, the teachers at all levels with their specific contribution, the socio-cultural groups and the professional associations, the ecclesial communities, all working generously and unselfishly for the advancement of this great work in the service of the common good whose guarantors are the civil authorities (cf. John XXIII, Encyclical *Pacem in Terris*, p. 301 and ff.).

(695) As the first educators of their children, parents should be aware of the leading trends in the field of teaching. Their important and irreplaceable influence must be joined harmoniously to those of specialists in order to assure the success of this difficult task of educating youth and preparing them to face their future tasks. For, in order to be successful, education must be considered not as a substitution but as a complement to that of the family. Is it not the practically unique role of parents to assure the harmonious development of the affective faculties of the child? Does not the moral integrity witnessed in the home imprint on man an indelible mark and, at the same time, provide him with a model norm to which he unceasingly has recourse? Because adults are more and more disconcerted when faced with the pressing and sometimes contradictory demands of rising generations, parents and teachers must devise together a common plan which will help them to assure the indispensable transmission of the cultural heritage, to assimilate the ever increasing treasures of sciences and techniques, and finally to prepare today's student to undertake his future professional tasks and civil engagements as a responsible person in the world we are building (Cf. John XXIII, Encyclical *Mater et Magistra*, p. 450 and ff.).

SEGREGATION MUST BE BANISHED

(696) The divisions which too often separate men from each other are the result of a history marked by egoism, ambition, a spirit of domination, personal and collective sin. The child and the adolescent ask for nothing more than to live in mutual relationship with their equals, whatever be their race and social origin, beyond the differences arising from wealth and power. It is therefore of capital importance that all segregation be banished from educational environment, and that this educational environment contribute to the development of the best potentials of each person in a fervid atmosphere of fraternal competition and fruitful friendship.

(697) Integration in a distinct culture is on a par with respect due to others. While men discover their differences, they become aware that they complement each other. Their readiness to serve is an essential factor of their formation, so true is it that the command of the judgment and the ability to adapt are particular characteristics of true culture (cf. Vatican Council II, Pastoral Constitution *Gaudium et Spes*, n. 13). All over the world exchanges increase, relations are established, joint interests are formed, and groups of people who were formerly strangers to each other suddenly become familiar. At the same time, we see harmful inequalities and flagrant injustice, which stimulate the temptation to revolt against the inefficiency of institutions. In fact, do we not see persons and social groups - even entire nations - continue to enrich themselves in a selfish way, while others - the great majority - find themselves doomed to stagnation or even regression?

EDUCATION FOR DEVELOPMENT

(698) The International Year of Education, combined with the Second Development Decade, offers the providential occasion for a responsible examination of this unworthy phenomenon of a civilized humanity. At a time when development in education is mobilizing ever greater forces, these forces would fail in their purpose if they were not to serve education in development with all the means in their power. Indifference and inactivity are no longer acceptable in the face of this drama of our times, denounced with anguish in the encyclical *Populorum Progressio*. A "conscientiousness," as has been rightly said, becomes indispensable, and we can hope that it will blossom like an irrepressible source of hope throughout the world athirst for justice.

(699) By developing minds and molding wills, education awakens consciences and calls for action. Such an effort requires the harmonious cooperation of divers human communities. The Church, on her part, has no other ambition than to continue to contribute to this effort. Claiming no other purpose than to serve (Vatican Council II, Declaration on Religious Freedom, n. 13), Catholic educators wish to work in close relationship with all educators, in loyal collaboration with those who are responsible for the common good of the community. They strive to banish every temptation to narrow self-interest or aggressive rivalry. There will never be enough men of good will to accomplish successfully the task of education which imposes its pressing need on men today, if men are to assure the harmonious development of what is human in man and in society.

AUTHENTIC HUMAN FORMATION

(700) At a time when everyone wishes to see a renewal in educational programmes and methods, the Church, faithful to spiritual requirements, exhorts all her children to work with competence, discernment and responsibility - parents, educators, animators - for an authentic human formation. In her own centres of education, the Church strives while imparting necessary knowledge and developing socio-professional abilities, to inculcate a just concept of true values, to form men in personal and social virtues, and to transmit a love for man and a faith in Christ. Wherever Catholics are employed in educational tasks, the Church asks them to distinguish themselves by their generous contribution to the common good, by their unselfishness, their concern to promote fraternal communities, to develop harmoniously all the potentials of persons entrusted to them, and to foster true values.

(701) An immense task confronts men today. They will not accomplish it in a spirit of disenchantment. Taking a closer look at the needs of the future, where we can discern the major trends and the means to respond to them, the International Year of Education provides the occasion for all responsible men to deepen their convictions and go forward with enthusiasm. Beyond the legitimate differences of convictions among men, they must come to an agreement on a common plan: build together a society of free and responsible men, so true is it that "the most crucial problem in our educational system is not a problem of education, but a problem of civilization." (J. Maritain, *Pour une philosophie de l'éducation*, Paris, Fayard, 1969, p. 155) The ultimate goal of all authentic education is wisdom, composed of knowledge and conscience. By knowledge, man who was the last creation of God on earth but the only creature endowed with intelligence, penetrates the secrets of nature; by conscience, man marshals his conquests for the service of the human family. Established as lord of creation, man discovers, in his collaboration with the divine plan and in his domination of nature, his dignity as a human person, the foundation of a true fraternal society. What a lofty task for all educators: help men as men to accomplish their marvellous destiny!

II - EDUCATION, SCIENCE AND CULTURE FOR THE INTEGRAL DEVELOPMENT OF THE HUMAN PERSON

Message of His Holiness Paul VI to Mr. Rene' Maheu, Director-General of UNESCO, on the occasion of the 25th Anniversary of the Organization. The Vatican, 1 November 1971.

Original: French (*)

(702) The Twenty-fifth anniversary of the Organization of the United Nations for education, science and culture affords us the opportunity to express to you, with our satisfaction for the work accomplished, our best wishes for its fruitful development. Are not the great international institutions privileged centres of creative exchanges for the future of man? According to its charter of foundation, UNESCO has principally the vocation of "contributing to peace and security by promoting collaboration among the nations through education, science and culture."

(*) AAS 63(1971), 837-840.

(703) Such a purpose could not leave the Church indifferent. So as soon as your Organization was created, the Holy See manifested all its interest in it by choosing in the person of Mons. Roncalli - the future John XXIII - its first Permanent Observer, and by maintaining close and trusting relations ever since. Then, too, numerous International Catholic Organizations collaborate with you in the framework of Non-Governmental Organizations and quite recently the International Year on Education gave us the opportunity to make clear the specific contribution of the Church to this great work: "to enable men to fulfil, as men, their marvellous destiny" (Note from the Holy See on the occasion of the International Year of Education, on 8 December 1970. See above, par. 701 and previous).

(704) A deeper conviction, in fact, animates the Church: "It is a fact bearing on the very person of man that he can come to an authentic and full humanity only through culture, that is, through the cultivation of natural goods and values" (*Gaudium et Spes*, n. 53). This ideal implies passing from a society in which education was the appanage of privilege to a world marching towards its universal promotion. This immense enterprise, owing to its very aim, must take place on the international plane, the plane on which you are operating with means that increase continually, but are always insufficient in view of the scope of the task to be carried out.

(705) Partitioned by political frontiers and divided by ideological tensions, the world is nevertheless traversed by a deep desire for unity, which these divisions make even keener. It is the vocation of UNESCO to meet this aspiration. Education forms man, science provides him with the means to act, culture brings him full development by making him familiar with the past, rooting him in the present and opening him to the future. On these three planes, your means of action are in the service of the great human family.

(706) While culture is not limited to mere possession of a patrimony inherited from the past, yet the great experiences of mankind, in its multimillenary progress, with the testimonies of art, thought, literatures, religions, sciences and technologies, are nevertheless an essential component of it. To deprive oneself of them would be to cut oneself off from one's roots; to renounce them, would be to mutilate oneself gravely. So the action of UNESCO in this field must call for the gratitude of all men worthy of the name. Let us just recall here the chain of solidarity to which the campaign to preserve the works of art of Nubia gave rise. At the moment when the genius of man is beginning to master new spaces, there is no doubt but that the rediscovery of his past will be for him a lesson of life and wisdom, and at the same time a source of legitimate pride.

(707) It is necessary, furthermore, that all men may be able to take part in this development of the spirit. Undoubtedly past centuries had some means of allowing the masses to benefit from the cultural riches of the intellectual elite. But today reading and writing are regarded as indispensable elements of social integration as well as personal enrichment, and therefore necessary to make man capable of fulfilling himself completely. Only this basic education makes it possible to ensure development. We repeat forcefully: "Hunger for education is no less debasing than hunger for food: an illiterate is a person with an undernourished mind" (*Populorum Progressio*, n. 35. See above, par. 682).

(708) The declarations of the highest international authorities - Universal Declaration of Human Rights, 10 December 1948, art. 26 and 27; Rights of the Child solemnly and unanimously proclaimed on 20 November 1959 by the General Assembly of the United Nations, principles 2 and 7 - and those of the Vatican Council - pastoral Constitution *Gaudium et Spes*, Chap. II, the proper development of culture, n. 60 - we are glad to stress, agree on this point. But what would be the use "of proclaiming rights, if every effort were not made at the same time to ensure the duty of respecting them, by everyone, everywhere, and for everyone?" [Message to the International Conference on Human Rights at Teheran, on 15 April 1968, in AAS 60(1968). See above, par. 413]. With what satisfaction, therefore, the Church sees private initiatives and public projects combine in this field, under the active impetus of UNESCO. She herself, moreover, has long been making an effort in this direction, with a conviction all the more firm in that it is rooted in the great certainties that constitute her *raison d'être*.

(709) For, let us be quite clear on this point, such an undertaking, in fact, can be sustained only by an ideal, the humanism that inspired the action of so many of our predecessors: it is not enough to give a taste for knowledge and the means of power, it is also necessary to add reasons for living. You very rightly said so yourself on the occasion of the "Meeting of cultures" organized at the headquarters of your Organization "under the sign of collaboration and peace" immediately after Vatican II: "There is no organization of cсllective intellectual work without spirituality ... that is what UNESCO is essentially: both an instrument and a spiritual experience of the universal in mankind" (Closing address by Mr. René Maheu). Beyond instruction, this is the aim of education: to form men, teach them to live, bring the young, in search of truth, thirsting for authenticity, more than knowledge in perpetual evolution, a wisdom that is a project of life rooted in a specific civilization; give them at the same time the means of implementing it, fecundate intelligence, forge wills, awaken consciences and prepare for action: in short "to build a fraternal world wherein all the members of the great human family ... will gradually succeed in controlling the forces of nature, in developing harmoniously the possibilities of education, and, respecting the legitimate diversities, will promote a world civilization wherein all men can live as free and responsible person" (Note from the Holy See on the occasion of the International Year of Education. See above, par. 686).

(710) UNESCO has thus the vocation of working for the complete development of man, who is responsible for his destiny before his brothers and before history, and is called to solve the numerous antinomies with which he is confronted: multiplied cultural exchanges and preserved ancestral wisdom, expansion of a new culture and living faithfulness to the heritage of traditions, harmonization of the old classical culture and the new scientific and technical culture, multiplication of specialized disciplines and synthesis of knowledge, development of the inventive genius and flourishing of contemplation, symbiosis between the masses and the elites, legitimate autonomy of culture and respect for religious values. These fundamental questions (cf. *Gaudium et Spes*, n. 56) can be solved only by a common desire to respect and welcome the values that are the honour of the cultures brought forth by mankind, in their very diversity: "Between civilizations, as between persons, sincere dialogue indeed creates brotherhood" (*Populorum Progressio*, n. 73).

(711) Our personal representative at the commemorative ceremonies that will mark the twenty-fifth anniversary of UNESCO, our dear son Cardinal Jean Danielou, will bring you this wish, which we would have liked to express to you by word of mouth, if circumstances had allowed us to accept your respectful invitation.

(712) It is with these sentiments of deep esteem and trust that we warmly call the abundance of divine blessings upon the tireless efforts you are making to hasten the advent of a more just and more fraternal society.

III - THE JOHN XXIII INTERNATIONAL PEACE PRIZE TO UNESCO

1. Peace, aim of UNESCO

Statement by H.E. Mgr. Giovanni Benelli, Substitute of the Secretary of State, at the 18th General Conference of UNESCO announcing the award of the Prize. Paris, 14 November 1974.

Original: French

(713) I should like first of all, in paying my respects to the President of this Assembly and to the delegates present here today, to stress what an honour I feel it to be, to be amongst you all today and to say a few words to you on a subject which preoccupies us all, the promotion of peace.

(714) I should also like to emphasize the Holy See's particular interest in the work of this 18th General Conference whose proceedings it is following through the intermediary of its delegation. You have our best wishes for a successful outcome to the deliberations of this meeting and for the effective implementation of the decisions you are about to take. In addition, I feel very happy at finding myself once again within these precincts where I was privileged, a few years ago, as the Holy See's Permanent Observer, to meet a great many of you in the course of carrying out our common task.

(715) I hope that you, Mr. Director-General, will allow me - and I feel sure that the General Conference agrees with my request - to pay my very special respects to you, and to associate myself with the tribute which has been paid to you after your long years of devoted service to UNESCO. My memories of a lengthy period of cooperation, based on dialogue and mutual confidence, adds, as you will no doubt be aware, a note of deep emotion to the respectful greetings which I venture to bring to you from Pope Paul VI.

(716) But the main reason for my being here with you today is as follows: Pope Paul VI has asked me to announce to this Assembly that he has decided to pay tribute to UNESCO's humanitarian work and to its work for peace by awarding the Organization the John XXIII Peace Prize. This Prize, which, as you are no doubt aware, is being awarded for the second time, was created by Pope John XXIII, who was the Holy See's first Permanent Observer at UNESCO, and whose memory will always be linked to a document which is held dear by all those who work for peace: *Pacem in Terris*, that peace between the nations which he thought ought to be based on liberty, justice, truth and love.

(717) Peace! Who can deny that Pope Paul VI is obsessed with it when his constant desire to promote this supreme benefit to mankind with all his strength is obvious to anyone who reads his speeches, follows his activities and knows of the intercessions he has made? Paul VI, aware as he is that such a cause can only be won through collective action and support, is heedful of the work of all those who are sincerely and courageously working for peace. He desires to encourage them, support them, and provide them with proof of his solidarity.

(718) The active desire, manifested by UNESCO, to promote everything which, on the natural plane, is capable of ensuring the grandeur and dignity of mankind, appeared to him to be a supreme factor in promoting peace.

(719) The privileged position in which UNESCO finds itself today is due to the fact that the Organization has kept faith with its Constitution which laid down that its aim should be "to contribute to the maintenance of peace by strengthening the links between the nations, through education, science and culture, so as to ensure that universal respect for justice, human rights and fundamental liberties for all men, irrespective of differences of race, sex, language or religion, which the United Nations Charter acknowledges to be the rightful due of all nations".

(720) Of course, there is still some room for improvement in the methods and measures employed by UNESCO, as in those employed by any other organization, and a great deal more use will need to be made of the creativity and generosity of every individual person if UNESCO is to realize the aims laid down for it in its Constitution to the fullest extent. Your Organization must establish and extend its activities in all areas if these aims are to be realized to an adequate degree.

(721) This is not the appropriate place and time to catalogue the ways in which UNESCO has, since its inception, gone about the business of achieving the fundamental aims which provide the inspiration and guidelines for its programmes. But I hope I may be allowed at least to point out the specific link which, to my way of thinking, connects some of the essential points of these programmes to the dynamics of peace.

(722) "Development is a new name for peace": in making this statement, Paul VI was not thinking only in terms of the development, growth and distribution of material resources. He was thinking first and foremost of the organization of a world in which all men would be able to become the responsible agents of their own development. He knows that man's deepest aspirations cannot be satisfied by means of benefits bestowed on them from outside sources. He is certain that no true peace is possible so long as millions of humans beings remain prisoners of their ignorance, of their inability to communicate with others, and to decide on their own destiny.

(723) It is stated in the encyclical *Pacem in Terris* that one of the four basic requirements for peace is liberty. UNESCO's activities are without shadow of doubt orientated towards this primarily cultural and spiritual liberation of those people who are shut up inside the walls of under-development. UNESCO desires to develop its activities according to intentions and lines of action which correspond closely to the preoccupations expressed by Paul VI in his *Populorum Progressio* when he called for programmes capable of "liberating man from his bonds, making it possible for him to be, himself, the craftsman responsible for the improvement of his own material well-being, for his moral progress and for his spiritual development". Here I should like to mention the World Literacy Campaign as being a particularly significant undertaking from this point of view.

(724) Another essential condition for peace, according to *Pacem in Terris* and to Paul VI, is justice. There can be no peace without justice, without acknowledgement and respect for fundamental equality between men, whatever their race, beliefs, cultural level or social position. And if there is one constant factor in UNESCO's outlook, it seems to me that it is the one demonstrated in the Organization's activities on behalf of human rights, in its unceasing fight against all forms of racial discrimination, oppression and nationalist domination, and against everything which undermines the dignity and integrity of the human individual. No one here is likely to contradict me when I say that the most advanced civilizations collapse when they no longer either respect or protect the individual.

(725) In its self-imposed role as the guardian of civilization, UNESCO is concerned not only with the defence of man but also with his promotion. Thus, in its educational and cultural programmes, it sets out to encourage the formulation of all the individual's higher potentialities and values. Deciding to give precedence to "being more" the Organization invites men not to become - in his search after "having more" - a prey to selfish appetites, generators of conflicts of interests and ever-deepening rifts.

(726) There is no doubt that UNESCO, too, is involved in the work of reducing the scandalous inequalities between the rich countries and the impoverished countries, between the well-to-do groups and those whose poverty renders them dependent and vulnerable. But it thinks that this work on behalf of justice should not be limited simply to the search for equality so far as material things are concerned. What really matters to it is that man should transcend himself by his own efforts so as to dominate his aggressive and possessive instincts and to give the necessary breadth and priority to the life of his spirit. At this higher level of his being, man can become aware of his liberty, thus putting himself in a position where he is able to control his own life and to orientate it towards constructive tasks, towards tasks propitious to peace. The more man advances into the realms of "being more", the more he becomes an agent and factor for peace.

(727) I should also like to remind you that truth is an essential ingredient of peace, as is stated in the encyclical *Pacem in Terris* and as Paul VI has repeated on several occasions. What mankind stands particularly in need of today, to my way of thinking, is precisely this truth, a loyal adherence to ideas common to all nations concerning man's paramount needs.

(728) Ideas rule the world, as we say. Yes, but which ideas? UNESCO has the noble mission of encouraging the growth of ideas capable of enlightening mankind and of helping man to prove by his actions that he has a constant concern for truth and objectivity. UNESCO does this by stimulating scientific research, by evaluating the chances of implementing it given the cultural realities existing in the various nations, by encouraging the comparing of ideas, and by helping to formulate a vital process of thought suitably adapted to the real needs of men. In this way, UNESCO helps to set mankind on the road to truth, seeing to it that the yearnings after happiness and peace do not remain unfulfilled, or worse still, receive only an illusory satisfaction as a result of the tricks to which propagandists of all types resort.

(729) Paul VI, following up *Pacem in Terris*, constantly appeals to men to meet each other in an atmosphere of sincere love, and I think, therefore, that of all the methods used by UNESCO, the most effective so far as the establishing of peace is concerned, is perhaps the one which consists of inviting men from every cultural and ideological background to meet together to pursue a particular problem of research. By assembling such men around the same work table, the Organization is encouraging the clarification of theories and projects calculated to contribute to the general well-being; but above all, it is giving representatives of the human race who differ from one another as to race, culture or philosophy, the opportunity of getting to know each other, of listening to each other, of trying to understand and value each other; thus, it is possible to put the most diverse cultures and mentalities face to face, and to discover whatever common factors there may be in men's aspirations and, in the long run, what is capable of uniting them.

(730) Of course, the meetings organized by UNESCO have precise scientific or cultural aims. But it is no less true, nevertheless, that, from the point of view of peace, each one of these meeting encourages a universal rapprochement through dialogue and thus is of capital interest.

(731) If I may be allowed to say so, I should like to see the representatives of every nation in the world without exception and without any considerations of a political or social nature, seated round this table, with a guarantee that each one of them will be able to take part freely and to an increasing extent in the interchange which help to ensure mankind's cultural progress. If this wish was not granted, how, I ask you, could UNESCO still remain in all truth one of the focal points of universal rapprochement?

(732) The most constant, and the most current, preoccupations of the Church and of its head, are associated with the views which I have just been describing, and it was this which motivated Pope Paul VI's gesture towards your organization. Pope Paul VI wished, by this gesture, to emphasize the convergence which exists between the preoccupations of the Church and those of UNESCO, and to show that, as Mr. Maheu said on the occasion of the Organization's 25th anniversary, there exists between the two institutions "a community of intentions in their concern over the destiny of mankind on Earth".

(733) Of course, the Church and UNESCO are two very distinct realities, which, in some respects - whether essential or minor - differ greatly from each other; but although each has its own specificity and pursues its own particular mission, they both meet up on the common ground of the disinterested spirit in which they serve mankind; the mission of both of them is, in fact, to accomplish a task of an intrinsically dedicated nature, which, if it is not to come to grief, can have precious little truck with calculations, manoeuverings or actions aimed at serving any particular interests.

(734) Another point of convergence between the Church and UNESCO is to be found in the priority which they both accord to the development of that element in man which is responsible for his grandeur and for his superiority over other living things; that is to say, his spirit. They are both convinced that, in every man, whatever appearances may suggest to the contrary, the mind is alive, waiting perhaps to be freed from the accidental impediments which imprison it.

(735) So far as the Church is concerned, the work of UNESCO - even though it is a-denominational and religiously neutral - is supremely valid and worthy of respect, because it aims, through its encouragement of education, culture and science, at putting man in a position where he can put the higher faculties of his being to use. In so doing, UNESCO helps to make him more receptive, more understanding, more responsible, freer and more universal. It makes it possible for him to fulfil himself, to set out on the road to perfection, that perfection which to believers, is called God.

(736) I do not claim, of course, to be the first person to stress the fact that UNESCO's work rests on a veritable code of ethics, and Mr. Maheu will allow me to borrow from him the words in which he stated, at a meeting organized in this very place about Vatican II, that "there can be no organization of collective intellectual work without spirituality".

(737) Servants of man in the task of enabling him to be a living, aware and active member of society, UNESCO and the Church come together in this gigantic and I would say almost superhuman effort to recombine the unity of the human family. It is this grandiose view of things which actuates and stimulates within each of them, according to their individual universalist vision, their efforts on behalf of dialogue, encounter, defence and promotion. For the Church, as for UNESCO, a human being is not an individual shut away within his own destiny: he is an essentially social person, member of a universal community within which he has the right to be recognized, listened to and respected, because he is an irreplaceable, active element of that community.

(738) Thus, it is also because he is aware of this convergence of the ideas and projects of the Church and of UNESCO in the service of international understanding, that Pope Paul VI wished to acknowledge, by awarding the Prize to this Organization, the value which the Holy See places on the Organization's work on behalf of peace. He sends his thanks to all those who play a part, at whatever level, in the activities of the Organization - from the General Conference to the Executive Board and to those officials working in the field throughout the world: to all of them, the Pope owes his gratitude. You will allow me, nevertheless, I hope, to emphasize that this gratitude is directed in particular to Mr. René Maheu who has worked, over the past twelve years, with so much lucidity, intellectual vigour, administrative skill, conviction and generosity, to set UNESCO on the paths which lead to peace in order to serve mankind. The Pope is full of confidence and hope that what has been accomplished thus far will continue to develop in accordance with the same spirit of allegiance to the true needs of mankind.

(739) The Holy Father, wishing to stress these two sentiments born of an objective observation of the past and a confident vision of the future, would like, in awarding this Prize, to address his remarks both to Mr. René Maheu to whom UNESCO owes so much, and to Mr. Maheu's successor to whom he sends his warmest good wishes for the successful tenure of his high office.

(740) Madam President, Ladies and Gentlemen, may the awarding of this Prize be a sign of hope to you all: that is what the Pope wishes it to be. In choosing UNESCO, the Holy See certainly had no pretensions to setting itself up as the judge of the activities of one of the United Nations agencies, but it considered that the moment was opportune to inform world opinion that the head of the Catholic Church, which has two thousand years of experience behind it and might thus be considered as "an expert on humanity", acknowledges UNESCO's contribution to the cause of peace, and hopes that this tribute, paid to such a difficult and thereby such an ennobling work, will result in other organizations being brought into the service of mankind and of peace.

2. The Apostolic See and UNESCO meet along the road to peace

Address of His Holiness Paul VI on awarding the John XXIII International Peace Prize to UNESCO, represented by its Director-General Mr. Amadou Mahtar M'Bow. The Vatican, 30 November 1974.

Original: French(*)

(741) We are all the more happy and honoured by your presence, and appreciative to have you not only as spectators but as participants in the act that we have just performed, inasmuch as this audience takes on for us a particular significance, in our opinion far more valuable that the prize, which in truth is more of a symbolic than economic value. In the memory and spirit of our venerated and lamented Predecessor Pope John XXIII, we have presented this prize, dedicated to the promotion of Peace, to UNESCO, that is the United Nations Educational, Scientific and Cultural Organization, in the illustrious persons of the two Directors of that now celebrated and worthy world institution, the outgoing Director and his successor. The former is well known to us, Mr. René Maheu. During the twelve years of the exercise of his high office we had the occasion to meet him personally, to listen to him in interesting conversation on themes of common interest, and to ad-

(*) AAS 66(1974), 704-709.

mire him for the breadth and noble inspiration of his activity. The latter is most welcome, Mr. M'Bow, former Minister of Public Instruction in his own Country, Senegal. Here then we have a pleasing and not unexpected testimony, in the context of international civilization, of the indigenous originality and already consolidated cultural maturity of the great and young continent of Africa.

(742) The particular significance of the presentation of this prize seems to us to spring from the meeting of two bodies, namely the Apostolic See and UNESCO, along the road to Peace. Each travelling along the path proper to it, here they are, as though at a meeting point, to celebrate together this lofty ideal, which ever more resembles a light-house guiding civilization - Peace.

(743) That this Apostolic See should be in an original, fitting and constitutional way dedicated to the promotion of peace in the world will surprise no one, we think, if one remembers whence the Catholic Church and this centre, "the perpetual and visible principle and foundation" of her unity, take their origin. They take it from that Christ whose coming into the world was greeted by the heavenly announcement of peace. A new peace this, linked to the fruitful and inexhaustible relationship with a transcendent divine fatherhood; established upon the messianic, paradoxical but henceforth invincible principle of a universal brotherhood, and always actively affirming and regenerating itself in the mysterious and inexpressible but most benign animation of a Spirit that permits the most diverse tongues of men to express themselves and understand one another in a friendly and harmonious colloquy.

(744) This of course is the epiphany of the Catholic Church in the world - an ancient and dynamic reality, which experiences within itself a double stimulus to manifest itself as living and present. In the first place there is the stimulus of its own history. In the recent Ecumenical Council the Church became more urgently aware of her native vocation to be the teacher of universal peace: there must be no delay in proclaiming that peace among men, for they are men, that is, members all of one same family - mankind. In the second place, there is the stimulus of the anxiety that men themselves manifest to solve the dominant problem of their living together in the world in harmonious and organic concord. This living together by men has all the more need of being untiringly actuated to the extent that the maturing of its progress shows how, on one hand, peace is logical and necessary and how war is criminal and absurd, and on the other hand, how always unstable and fragile is that "tranquility of order" that precisely defines it.

(745) Peace, we said, is necessary; peace is possible; human dogmas these, that finally appear as clearly deriving from that religion which the Church finds the reason for her existence.

(746) Peace, therefore, especially after the Christmas messages of Pope Pius XII and after *Pacem in Terris* of Pope John XXIII, has become the programme of our apostolic presence in the world; and the voice with which we proclaim it intends to be all the more limpid and persuasive to the extent that it is more free and unhampered in its regard, and also in the ever rising, fevered and contrasting play of human interests. Since we are and must be strangers to the temporal and political kingdom, therefore we dare, as humble prophets and persuasive poets, to make peace our customary and cordial greeting, to all of you, the people of the earth: Peace!

(747) And so here is the meeting. It is a meeting at the highest level of ideas. And it is precisely on this level of ideas that we have met UNESCO - met it with our support and with our admiration for the principle on which it is founded and from which it derives its many-sided and provident activity, the principle that "peace must be built on the foundation of the intellectual and moral solidarity of mankind". But let us say straight away that when today's meeting was arranged the episode which has recently upset such a large part of the world of culture was not foreseen. We are speaking of certain deliberations of the recent General Conference of UNESCO.

(748) We are hence unexpectedly faced with a fact which upsets in public opinion the serenity of this happy moment. Thus all the more we express the wish that this unforeseen case may find a speedy solution, trusting as we do in the common desire for justice and peace of the parties concerned. And we hope for this with the thought that the first to rejoice at it will be the illustrious guests whom we have the honour to have present here today, the Directors and exponents, that is, of UNESCO, by reason of the universal and peaceful character and - as it has been said - the spirit of tolerance which characterizes it, extraneous as it is to political rivalries and always consistent in its own educational, scientific and cultural aims, as witness its concern for the values of history, of art and of religion of a territory which is most dear and sacred to all of us.

(749) Here we are thus brought back again by this memory - to which similar ones should be associated by special mention, such as those for instance of the interventions of UNESCO in favour if Nubia and of Venice - brought back again, we say, to the proven merits of the peacemaking activity of UNESCO itself, activities linked not only with geographical places but even more to moral situations, where the needs of humanity hail and greet as wise and providential the work of this great institution, dedicated, as we know, to the advancement of education, of science and of culture. It suffices to recall the worldwide campaign in favour of literacy.

(750) But an ample account of these merits of UNESCO, which typify it also in our eyes, eager as they are to find in the human panorama signs of forces working for peace, has already been given by our diligent collaborator, Archbishop Giovanni Benelli, a former Observer of the Holy See to UNESCO, who a short time ago went to Paris to announce to the General Conference of UNESCO, meeting in plenary session, the awarding of the peace prize named after Pope John to UNESCO in recognition of its work. You will certainly all have heard the echoes of this.

(751) One could therefore think that, at least for the chief leaders, everything that suffices to justify this friendly gesture of ours has already been said: what you are in regard to peace, illustrious and valiant members of UNESCO, and what you are doing and have already accomplished for its cause deserves from the recognition represented by the prize named after our great and venerated Predecessor, Pope John XXIII. But it is precisely his name that authorizes us not only to look at your past and your present to find it worthy of this significant award, but likewise this blessed name impels us to look forward to your future, which for us and for all who know you is a promise no less meritorious of applause and encouragement than the years already passed. You are a hope for peace in the future of mankind and civilization; this is said in the charter setting up your Organization. You are sent forward, as harbingers of peace, into future history. You make of education, science and culture powerful and wonderful factors for the universal spiritual fusion of peoples. Politics, which you leave to other bodies to promote, especially the United Nations Organization, from which you take inspiration and strength, will succeed, we trust, in establishing a peaceful cohesion, an organic juridical and economic relationship, a balanced and ordered harmony between the Nations; yes, but you work to form a communion, you strive for the brotherhood of the peoples of the earth. You seek to give mankind a common thought; you promote a uniform sociology of culture; you render possible an identical civil language among men.

(752) "UNESCO", writes Mr. Maheu, "is an understanding for the organization of international relationships concerning the activities of the mind with a view to promoting human rights of man and collaborating for the establishment of a regime of just and lasting peace" (cf. *Dans l'Esprit des hommes*, UNESCO, 1971, p. 313). In doing this, you carry out a work of silent but prodigious mobilization of minds, which on the contrary seem by the very progress of civilization to be arming themselves psychologically and technically for a terrible and apocalyptic war, which should never happen, but, alas becomes still possible and horribly easier. For your part you dissipate the nightmare of such a deplorable and unthinkable fate. You make once more serene the horizon of future history; today you restore Peace once more to the world, making it safe for tomorrow.

(753) Is there anything at all more deserving among the community of peoples? And is there any better title for bringing your Organization close to ours, which is called the assembly of men who are brothers? Such in fact is the name "Church" etymologically, and we trust and strive to our utmost that it may be so in reality. Is the road we travel parallel to yours? Yes, on different levels, at this moment we see that it is. Parallel in the sense of reciprocal independence, of the respective common end, and we can also say, in the happy possibility of being associated with one another in certain times, without losing our individual identities. Ours is a religion of peace. Yours is a work on behalf of peace.

(754) And may this concluding observation serve to explain the reason for this prize, which despite its smallness in comparison with the cause for which it is destined aims to take on a deep significance, as it were a Biblical echo, that of the celebration of an idea which is a light, of an idea which is strength - peace; that of the proclamation of an urgent and universal duty - peace; that of the announcement of a positive and inexpressible hope - peace.

(755) Allow us then to leave the last word to him whose good and prophetic name this prize bears, Pope John XXIII, who in his Encyclical *Pacem in Terris*, as though in his last testament, thus admonishes us: "There is an immense task incumbent on all men of good will, namely the task of restoring the relations of the human family in truth, in justice, in love and in freedom; the relations between citizens and their respective political Communities; between political Communities themselves; between individuals, families, intermediate associations and political Communities on the one hand and the world Community on the other, for it is the task of bringing about true peace in the order established by God" (AAS, 1963, pp. 301-301).

IV - UNESCO: A CONTRIBUTION TO PEACE

Letter of His Holiness Paul VI to Mr. Amadou Mahtar M'Bow, Director-General of UNESCO, on the occasion of the 30th Anniversary of the Organization. The Vatican, 3 November 1976.

Original: French(*)

(756) In this year which marks the thirtieth anniversary of UNESCO, we are happy to unite ourselves with all those who look confidently to this international Organization. We hope that, over and above the diversity of mentalities and immediate interests, it will be able to continue to promote effectively for all men the education, science and culture capable of affording their spirit more substantial nourishment, a more universal outlook on affairs and an elevation worthy of their spiritual vocation. Doing so, UNESCO is thus able to make an important contribution to mutual understanding, peace and cooperation among peoples. We willingly renew our hearty encouragement to its leaders to take this eminent task further and further, in an impartial spirit.

(757) We add special wishes for the work of this nineteenth session of the General Conference. We are convinced that the promotion of free, exact and widely spread information, as well as the international exchanges it calls for, are quite compatible with the authority and responsibility of rulers, rightly concerned with the common good of their own countries, and with the elimination of all propaganda in favor of war, violence, racism and *apartheid*. Expressing to you once more our satisfaction at seeing these problems dealt with at the level of UNESCO, we recommend to Almighty God the efforts undertaken at present for concerted progress towards more truth and brotherhood.

(*) AAS 68(1976), 655-656

V - THE PROGRESS OF CULTURE FOR A MORE JUST AND A MORE FRATERNAL WORLD

Message of His Holiness John Paul II to Mr. Amadou Mahtar M'Bow, Director-General of UNESCO, for the World Conference on Cultural Policies held in Mexico City on 26 July-6 August 1982. The Vatican, 24 July 1982.

Original: French (*)

(758) 1. The Conference on cultural policies, an international gathering organized by UNESCO and about to open in Mexico City, is an event of great importance. It will be an excellent opportunity to make an assessment of the experience gained regarding policies and practices in the field of culture since the Intergovernmental Conference on the Institutional, Administrative and Financial Aspects of Cultural Policies organized by UNESCO in 1970.

(759) And it must, in fact, be plain to all. The decade which has passed since the Venice Conference has seen important changes take place in the life of mankind. And the time has come to initiate some careful reflection on the basic problems of culture in today's world. Let me simply emphasize the need to strengthen cultural cooperation on an international scale, and also the cultural dimension of development. For it is becoming more and more obvious that cultural progress is closely connected with the construction of a more just and more fraternal world.

(760) Knowing what your Conference may mean for the future, and because of the close ties which unite the Catholic Church to the Organization which you head with such competence and devotion, the Holy See will be represented at the Mexico Conference by a team of Observers, desiring thereby to express its interest, its esteem, and also its warmest good wishes for a wholly successful meeting.

(761) 2. Ever since the birth of UNESCO, the Catholic Church has always followed its programmes with close attention, particularly in the field of culture, and has constantly shown its willingness to cooperate in every possible way. It intends to continue to behave in the same way in the future, ungrudgingly, without reservations, with great open-mindedness, and with the certainty that it will continue to find the same attitudes on the part of UNESCO.

(762) 3. To reflect on the Church and its relations with culture means to discover in its thousand-year past reason to be justly proud, to find in its present activities important evidence of the value of its mission, and to involve all its sons in the exciting task of preparing and formulating its programme for the future. To think about UNESCO's work in support of culture means to see the nations of the world shaking hands across their frontiers and, recognizing the immense value of every culture, wishing to encourage the development of mutual understanding together with joint and fruitful progress aimed at the integral betterment of mankind.

(763) 4. The relations between the Church and UNESCO quite rightly find their place amidst the vast network of relations which the Church maintains with the world and the international organizations. This network, which you know well, involves not only the Holy See but also the living grass-roots of the Church itself.

(764) It is the needs of mankind, seen in the light of God, which are appealing to the intelligence and charity of Christians for a worldwide initiative involving the responsibility of the Church vis-a-vis men, and more specifically the responsibility of Christians in whatever sectors they work. And these Christians will be in evidence in all their richness of soul; they will make an exceptionally valuable contribution to the construction of the future, by acting in accordance with their Christian conscience, knowing that organization is not everything but that there must be an absolute respect for the innermost law of life.

(*) AAS 74 (1982), 1179-1181.

(765) 5. Man is the centre, the focal point, to which all observations about culture refer and are addressed. It is impossible to set up a dividing line between the concept of man and the promotion of culture. And it is impossible to have this concept of man without coming back to the spiritual and moral dimension of man himself. It is precisely this spiritual dimension, intrinsic in the human individual in all his depth, which can make it possible to avoid biased and incomplete definitions of culture and enable culture to serve the real good of men and of society, and the promotion of ever higher standards in life, in the individual, and in society.

(766) All this helps us to understand that a valid cultural policy must be concerned with man and his entirety, that is to say, in all his personal dimensions - not forgetting the ethical and religious aspects - and in his social dimensions. From this it follows that cultural policies cannot leave out of account the spiritual vision of man, in promoting culture. In future years, therefore, they should pursue the following aims in a more decisive manner:

- a more marked orientation of culture towards a disinterested search for truth and human values; rediscovery of those values as an answer to modes of life which are more advanced in appearance only;
- promotion of a type of culture which puts increasing emphasis on the dignity of the individual, of human life, on respecting it and defending it, that is to say, a culture which actually conduces to the promotion of human life and not to its destruction;
- putting technology back into its proper place, making it quite clear that it exists to serve mankind. There is an urgent need for people to embark on reflection on the ethics involved in this subject. Any scientific and technological development which was bent on dispensing with ethical values would gradually turn against the destiny of man himself.

(767) 6. To end this message I should like, Mr. Director-General, to send my respectful and cordial greetings to you yourself and to all your colleagues in UNESCO, and also my very best wishes for the work of the Mexico City Conference.

(768) May God bless UNESCO and its commendable initiatives!

VI - SUPPORT FOR LITERACY ACTIVITIES

1. Literacy must be integrated in the overall process of development of the individual

Message of His Holiness Paul VI to Mr. René Maheu, Director General of UNESCO for the World Congress of Ministers of Education. The Vatican, 26 August 1965.

Original: French

(769) We greatly appreciate your courteous letter inviting the Holy See to participate in the World Congress of Ministers of Education for the eradication of illiteracy, which, according to the resolution of the General Conference of UNESCO, is to be held at Teheran in the near future. In choosing to represent us at this Congress a delegation headed by Monsignor Giovanni Benelli, Permanent Observer of the Holy See to UNESCO, we wish to manifest the importance in which we hold this Congress, and express our ardent hope that it may mark a decisive step forward in the fight against one of the great plagues of our times. We assure you that the Catholic Church, while accomplishing her religious mission, will not cease to work to raise the cultural and social standards of all men to whom she presents her message without distinction of race, class or origin.

(770) Even if, in the past, peoples have been able to attain a true culture without the aid of writing, and if to-day the means of audio-visual communication offer in this domain vast possibilities, who can deny the irreplaceable contribution offered by literacy? Literacy is an incomparable source of progress both for the individual and for society. For man, it is a means of the utmost importance to social integration, personal enrichment, professional achievement, and lasting education. Literacy is, at the same time, a privileged instrument of economic progress and development for society. It is also worthy of note that, without literacy, man cannot tap the vast treasures of Oriental and Western literatures, and every one knows the special place the Bible holds among these. Man will not be able to come to that ability of judgement and that mastery of thought reflection, which renders him truly free, capable of assuming his destiny and playing his role in social life in a completely lucid and deliberate manner.

(771) For the full attainment of its goals, literacy must not be an isolated process, a purely technical objective, but ought to be integrated within an overall movement for the development of the individual. This ideal has inspired the action of the Church down through the centuries, and has succeeded - not without effort or sacrifice - in furthering reading and writing at the same time as announcing the Gospel of Christ. It is also with joy that to-day the Church co-operates with national and international organizations, and in a special way with UNESCO, in bringing to the illiterate masses of the world the possibilities of a human and social blossoming now beyond them. It is a question of the full development of man and humanity which opens to all the way of truth; the truth of science - a major factor of cultural, technical and economic progress - as well as moral and spiritual truth, which alone is capable of fulfilling man's highest aspirations.

(772) The Congress of Teheran will provoke, without a doubt - and this is our ardent wish - by its work and its repercussions on international public opinion, a stimulus to the awareness of this grave problem, and will give rise to a common desire to solve it with appropriate measures. It is to the honour of UNESCO to have convened this Congress, and all peoples will ever be grateful to His Imperial Majesty the Shahinshah Mohammed Reza Shah Pahlavi, Emperor of Iran, for having been its promoter, and for having enabled it to be realized.

(773) It is from our heart that we send our best wishes to you, Mr. Director-General of UNESCO, to the President of the Congress, to the noble nation that hosts it, to the highly qualified delegations that compose it, and we wish an abundance of celestial blessings on these efforts made for the eradication of illiteracy.

2. International cooperation to combat illiteracy

Letter of His Holiness Paul VI to Mr. René Maheu, Director-General of UNESCO on the occasion of the 8th International Literacy Day (*) . The Vatican, 7 September 1974.

Original: French (**)

(774) At the moment when UNESCO, at the end of its ten years' world programme, is starting a new phase of its struggle against illiteracy, we wish to repeat how interested the Church and the Holy See are in this world problem, thus confirming the action pursued in the course of the centuries and in many regions for the cultural promotion of peoples,among adults as well as young people.

(775) Man naturally desires to know: knowledge gives him access to a new relationship with nature; above all, it offers him renewed possibilities of dialogue with his fellow men. The general dif-

---

(*) The following are some of the messages sent each year, since the first International Literacy Day (8 September 1968), by the Sovereign Pontiffs to the Secretary-General of UNESCO.

(**) AAS 66(1974), 496-498.

fusion of a basic education aims, therefore, at putting right inequalities and social discriminations, at opening up access to responsibilities in private and collective life, at encouraging better understanding between the generations, thus contributing to establishing conditions of real communication among men.

(776) In spite of the efforts already made, the problem is a grave and urgent one, owing to the population growth and the increased burdens that the requirements of a more thorough effort to ensure literacy imposes on all nations. Certainly, the important work carried out by UNESCO in the course of the last few years provides a solid basis of research and experimentation. Taking advantage of the experience acquired, it is now opportune to promote a wider action, aimed without discrimination at all categories of peoples. The responsibility for these enterprises then belongs especially to the national authorities. It is for them to direct investments and educational priorities, while remaining wide open to the collaboration of initiatives which offer to contribute, in a disinterested way, to the joint effort. The Church has long taken her part in this service of the underprivileged, particularly where poverty prevails, where there is no hope of material profit, but where the joy of seeing man, with his head erect, become a participant in his own education, and himself improve the quality of his life and finally discover its ultimate meaning, is the only reward for those who recognize, in every human being, an image of the creator.

(777) In this privileged field of human collaboration, needs are immense. Their satisfaction should be a priority aim of national policy and of international cooperation. How ,then, can we fail to be astonished when we consider the importance that so many countries - even among the developing ones - attach one-sidedly to the pursuit of purely material economic growth, or to an even greater extent, disastrously, to military expenses which so often contribute to making peace and security precarious? How can we fail to recall, above all, the serious moral obligation, for the rulers of rich nations, to make their fellow countrymen become aware of their important duty of solidarity with the underprivileged peoples, to help them in a disinterested way and include this aid in their economic programmes instead of trying constantly, on the national or international plane, to get the most profit for the investments?

(778) International cooperation must therefore be carried out in a spirit of sincerity and disinterested service, with respect for the cultural differences of every people, with the determination to avoid everything that would be undue attempt at influencing or a subtle form of domination. That is why we hail and encourage the proposed creation of an "International Literacy Fund". We hope it will make it possible to bring to the underprivileged, in the framework of the Second Development Decade, the disinterested help they need, while giving the richest countries a means of acting that avoids, as much as possible, the spirit of rivalry or domination.

(779) In these perspectives, we take the opportunity of the celebration of the International Literacy Day to renew our best wishes for the development of this great work of human brotherhood, on which we invoke, as well as on all its workers, the abundance of the divine blessings.

3. Literacy, a basic precondition for genuine human development

Letter of His Holiness Paul VI to Mr. Amadou Mahtar M'Bow, Director-General of UNESCO, on the occasion of the 9th International Literacy Day. The Vatican, 29 August 1975.

Original: French (*)

(780) In this tenth year after the Teheran Conference which marked the starting point of world action to eliminate illiteracy, we wish specially to stress the major part which has already been

(*) AAS 67(1975), 548-550.

played by UNESCO in this field for many years now, not only in making world opinion aware of the seriousness of this problem but also in drawing up and implementing appropriate programmes effectively catering to the needs of mankind and of development.

(781) We reaffirm the support which the Holy See intends to continue to give to these efforts. Indeed the educational action of the Church is aimed, through literacy work, at the moulding of the individual as a whole and at his human and social advancement, seeking thus to integrate individual men and women, deliberately and in a responsible manner, into the society to which they belong. In this way they will be able to enjoy their right to participate in the culture of their people, and will also become aware of their own mission in society.

(782) Those in position of responsibility in the Catholic world, in collaboration also with their brothers of other religions or those who share other convictions, have already made a valuable contribution to the success of this noble campaign, through a great number of undertakings as varied as they are original. In connection with this, the ninth International Literacy Day, they will not fail to redouble their efforts, with renewed dedication, to secure the recognition of literacy as a basic precondition for all genuine human development and all economic and social progress. May we also be allowed to insist on one aspect of these efforts, which is perhaps a special one but is of growing importance, namely literacy programmes for migrant workers.

(783) Large numbers of workers are being forced, for economic reasons, to leave their countries for long periods of time. Urgent measures are required to enable them in the first place to participate fully in the culture of their own home country, and then to integrate with social and professional activities in the host country. A genuine literacy campaign will frequently be necessary to achieve both of these aims, since otherwise migrant workers are likely to find themselves helpless and at the mercy of all kinds of exploitation. We know how many generous spirits have already set to work in this field, but much still remains to be done.

(784) It is true that it is for nations themselves to define and promote literacy through appropriate policies. It is with great satisfaction that we note the development along these lines of manifold activities which can serve as an example and a model. The problem is however a vast one, and necessitates the collaboration of all, going beyond cultural and territorial boundaries. A sense of international community calls for the prevision of useful aid of all kinds, particularly to the least favoured countries, whether by directly supporting the implementation of clearly defined programmes or by sharing with them the fruits of experience, thus enabling them to improve their methods or make an accurate assessment of the results achieved. We know and we appreciate the persevering action conducted on these lines by UNESCO, and it is for this reason that we shall follow with special interest the implementation of the projects and programmes drawn up for the next few years with a view to finding an over-all solution to the serious problem of literacy work throughout the world.

(785) In connection with the celebration of this International Literacy Day we reiterate to you our good wishes for this noble task, which so appropriately finds its place in UNESCO's specific mission and which, transcending many grievous divisions, manifests mankind's common desire to achieve more genuine fulfillment for individual men and women.

4. Renewed spirit of cooperation in the struggle against illiteracy

Message of His Holiness Paul VI to Mr. Amadou Mahtar M'Bow, Director-General of UNESCO, on the occasion of the 10th International Literacy Day. The Vatican, 28 August 1976.

Original: French (*)

(786) On sending to you, last year, our message on the occasion of the 1975 World Literacy Day, we repeated to you the satisfaction with which the Holy See had welcomed the initiative of such a "Day", which reaches its tenth celebration this year.

(787) During these ten years, we have followed with interest UNESCO's activity in its struggle against the scourge of illiteracy. We have encouraged the specific programmes it has undertaken, for example, on behalf of the young, on women and of migrants. On various occasions, too, we affirmed the warm support of the Holy See for these meritorious initiatives and we reminded Catholics insistently how important it was for them to intensify their efforts in favour of literacy campaigns, in faithfulness to a long tradition of cultural assistance, the contribution of which has been and remains considerable.

(788) A tenth anniversary suggests drawing up a balance sheet. Is it not opportune to try to make a thorough and serene evaluation of the aims attained, in order to draw from them new impetus for new commitments? Illiteracy, in fact, a scourge which is far from being circumscribed, still causes an increase every year in the millions of men, including a great many young people, who are cut off from the vital stream of complete development and who, for that reason, are unable to hold their rightful place in society. So we think that the struggle against illiteracy should be intensified in a renewed spirit of cooperation, even, in a certain sense, a new one, which will unite the individual, the family and local community, public and private infrastructures, governments, and, beyond them, the whole international community.

(789) That is why it seems to us that efforts are called for in two directions. It is necessary, on the one hand, to drive home to illiterates more and more the justification of the action undertaken. On the other hand, it is expedient to make public opinion, both national and international, more and more aware of its real responsibilities in this work of cooperation. What perseverance in action can be hoped for if the latter be not based on personal conviction? In a number of cases, it would be opportune, therefore, to undertake, among the beneficiaries of literacy movements, a campaign to convince them deeply that the efforts asked of them serve their own progress. They must also be persuaded that, to the right of receiving from the responsible organism all possible assistance to help them to shake off the heavy yoke of illiteracy, there corresponds the duty of continuing perseveringly their effort towards spiritual, moral and cultural enrichment; that the improvement of their living conditions must entail a proportionate effort to contribute to improving the quality of life for the whole community and its social progress.

(790) There are, however, deplorable situations which prove to be very difficult to change. As the result of age, the weight of habit, or a certain fear to involve oneself in change, a certain number of the members of a community do not feel the necessary energy to emerge from their situation. Campaigns of collective information should appeal to them, too, in order to convince them at least not to hinder the development of instruction, and even to inspire in them the desire to help those who can benefit from it. We are thinking here particularly of the young, who must leave illiteracy behind them, and women, who are frequently victims of actual situations or habits. It is to be hoped that efforts already made to assure them, even the poorest, of the right to education, will be continued and strengthened. One must think, in fact, that women in particular can become, thanks to their educative action among their children, very effective agents for the promotion of literacy.

(*) AAS 68 (1976), 563-565.

(791) How could we fail to point out also the importance of the "day" and of information campaigns as regards public opinion? It is important to make known in a more and more complete and detailed way the scope of the problem of illiteracy and its consequences. It is essential, furthermore, to raise consciousness of the unity of mankind in order to perceive clearly the precise duties imposed by solidarity, not only within the local or national community, but also on the universal plane, beyond the frontiers between countries or continents. A public opinion formed in this way will be able to convince itself of its duty of cooperation, in spite of the sacrifices imposed. It will even support new initiatives taken by public authorities to solve this problem better, both on the domestic plane and in the field of collaboration between the privileged countries and those that need help.

(792) Presenting these few thoughts to you, we express to you our fervent wishes for the full success of the tenth World Literacy Day and of the new efforts to combat illiteracy. This task is one of those that reflect greatest credit on the Organization of which you are at present the Director-General and which unites, with the dedication and experience of your various collaborators, the agreement and unanimous support of all men of goodwill.

5. Responsible participation of all in the task of achieving literacy

Message of His Holiness Paul VI to Mr. Amadou Mahtar M'Bow, Director-General of UNESCO, on the occasion of the 11th International Literacy day. The Vatican, 30 August 1977.

Original: French (*)

(793) In the effort for the liberation as well as for the complete and united development of men and peoples, literacy remains a very special task. Thanks to the initiative and persevering efforts of UNESCO, it has now its annual Day. The celebration of its success and of the personal and social values which it promotes, contributes to deepening convictions and to awakening new energies, which will bring forth new progress. We share in this celebration wholeheartedly, aware of the service which, in the name of the Lord Jesus and of his inexhaustible goodness for all the needs of men, we owe to the whole human family.

(794) It is right to celebrate, first of all, these innumerable men and women who, at the cost of particularly meritorious efforts, wish to learn to read and write. In this way they open up for themselves irreplaceable opportunities to become more clearly aware of what they are living and of what they are; to communicate among themselves and take a more active part in social life and their changes; to discover other cultures and to make their presence more felt in the venture of the whole human family. Stress is legitimately laid nowadays on the necessity of constructing a new world order on the foundation of the responsible participation of all. Literacy, not only by its results, but already by the experience it constitutes, sets in motion the immense crowd of the underprivileged and prepares them to bring precious reserves of creativity to the common work.

(795) It is right too, to celebrate those who, within each people and among peoples, undertake to help this effort of their brothers. The highlighting of their example becomes an appeal to all men of goodwill, in favour of the increasingly wide and better supported action against the great misery of illiteracy, which, in spite of the progress made, remains a very worrying problem. How many men and women, young people and adults could, in fact, join this vast movement, though with modest means and actuated by simple motivations. But remaining faithful to these motivations, they will understand by themselves that through the communication of knowledge they undergo a human experience, capable of transforming them, in their turn, on contact with those whom they help and who very often manifest astonishing riches of courage and wonder. In this way they acquire a new

(*) AAS 69(1977), 544-546.

sensitivity which teaches them to respect, with the tact that arises from friendship, personalities eager to study their own identity, at the very moment when they discover unsuspected horizons.

(796) UNESCO is concerned to gather these spontaneous experiences, to invite them to confront one another, to improve pedagogical methods which will make them more efficient and guard them against discouragement and deviations. It endeavours to call new forces unceasingly to the service of the task, the scope of which increases from year to year. It endeavours also to bring in the indispensable financial means.

(797) Not long ago we ourselves asked, in our address to journalists in Bombay, for a world fund to be set up, supplied by part of the military expenses, in order to assist the most underprivileged: such a fund should serve especially the priority task of achieving literacy. The centuries-old experience of the Church has not ceased to stimulate access to reading and writing in order to enable the masses to develop their personality and their culture, as well as to make them fruitful by opening them to the common heritage of mankind.

(798) It falls to us to call especially upon Catholics to join all men in celebrating International Literacy Day, in thanksgiving and in amazement at the progress already made. And we pray God that UNESCO's initiative, to which you, Mr. Director-General, bring tenacious and inventive dedication, may release new energies for an enterprise particularly in keeping with the advancement of man and with brotherhood among men.

6. Through the literacy of parents we prepare a future for the children

Letter of His Holiness John Paul II to Mr. Amadou Mahtar M'bow, Director-General of UNESCO, on the occasion of the 13th International Literacy Day. The Vatican, 29 August 1979.

Original: French (*)

(799) On the occasion of the celebration of the International Literacy Day 1979, I send you my warmest good wishes for the complete success of this day, hoping that it will strengthen the literacy campaign launched by UNESCO more than a decade ago in close collaboration with its activities for the total and harmonious development of man and respect of his dignity.

(800) With these wishes and congratulations I am happy to give evidence of the interest of the Holy See and my own personal interest in such an important activity for the future of many human beings. Very much preoccupied as was my predecessor Pope Paul VI with the vastness and gravity of the plague of illiteracy in the world, I would like to encourage all those involved in literacy programmes who devote their energy to this problem and whose efforts give so much hope.

(801) The theme "Through the literacy of parents, we prepare a future for the children" was chosen in conjunction with the International Year of the Child. As it proclaimed, it concerns both the parents who are the immediate beneficiaries of literacy who will then have the tools to exercise the inalienable rights and to fulfil more efficiently their role as educators, and the children themselves who will benefit from the cultural development of their parents.

(802) The literacy campaign this year is therefore addressed primarily to the family where both parents and children enjoy rights and assume special duties, founded on those higher values which give its full meaning to their common life. Thus they will be led to evaluate material goods with more objectivity, to profit by them without compromising their dignity, to share the family circle and with all the members of the society to which they belong.

(*) Insegnamenti di Giovanni Paolo II, II,2 (1979) 203-204.

(803) It is to be hoped then that, without neglecting the schooling of children and continuing the efforts exerted up to now, special attention will be given to the literacy of parents. This will be an effective way to assuring both the individual and the collective development of the family, the fundamental cell of society. The latter will also be interested in this since the parents, when they have become literate, can give their children the irreplaceable basic education which reaches its full development in the formation given in the schools and can also increase their chances of promotion.

(804) In this hope, I am happy to have this opportunity of the International Literacy Day 1979, to renew my wishes to all those who are devoting themselves to this great work of human fraternity, and I pray the Omnipotent God to shower abundant blessings on them and their efforts.

7. Appeal for a new international order

Message of His Holiness John Paul II to Mr. Amadou Mahtar M'Bow, Director-General of UNESCO, on the occasion of the 15th International Literacy Day. The Vatican, 2 September 1981.

Original: French (*)

(805) The 1981 International Literacy Day occurs at the beginning of last twenty years which separate mankind from the year 2000 and during which UNESCO hopes to be able to reap the final results of its efforts to bring literacy to every human being in the world. This hope is shared by all those who have at heart the peaceful progress of the human community.

(806) Everyone has an equal right to be free, or to be freed, from the painful and humiliating condition of being illiterate, a condition which is not a negligible cause of the poverty and handicaps that weigh on the least advanced peoples.

(807) Thanks to literacy, every human being becomes more of a man, in himself and with others, but also for others; thanks to it, he can achieve his complete and harmonious development, on the spiritual, cultural and material plane, and learn to possess this fundamental asset to develop it and use it always for his own good and that of the community.

(808) The literacy effort must ensure nearly a billion persons a great hope that cannot be disappointed by those who, having already attained a higher level of global development, have the duty to make others share in it. It is a question of a service which man renders to man and in which each one must do its utmost to enable all to grow as human beings. In this way everyone will be able to lead a more human life in freedom and respect for their dignity and their transcendence.

(809) I am sure that these affirmations coincide with the thought and the convictions of the vast majority of men and women of good will, who launch a justified and energetic appeal in view of a general commitment, both on the national plane and on that of world cooperation, to bring about the changes required by a new international order as well as for an increased search for, and the best possible use of, all the means necessary for this very noble struggle.

(810) Knowing the results already achieved, I am anxious to congratulate you, Mr. Director-General, as well as those who are working, with generosity, tenacity and effectiveness,in the area of literacy. I also wish to renew my warm encouragement and my most fervent wishes for everyone.

(*) AAS 73(1981), 561-562.

8. Need to "demarginate" the illiterate

Letter of His Holiness John Paul II to Mr. Amadou Mahtar M'Bow, Director-General of UNESCO, on the occasion of the 16th International Literacy Day. The Vatican, 25 August 1982.

Original: French (*)

(811) The 16th anniversary of the International Literacy Day, which you have invited us to celebrate on 8 September, demonstrates the perseverance with which UNESCO is working in this essential domain to promote the growth of the human person, beginning with his most basic needs. All men and their institutions must indeed take notice and contribute to this work as far as their means allow.

(812) Does not the new international order which men of good will propose to institute imply that even the most disadvantaged should fully take their place in society, and no longer be treated as second class citizens?

(813) The illiterate are highly disadvantaged in their cultural progress, their daily relations, their different social environments, and in their potential for employment. This is a major handicap for the whole of society in those developing countries where a high percentage of the population is illiterate. And it is a considerable problem as well for the illiterate persons themselves and their families in the more prosperous countries: having needs and abilities out of step with those of the general population, they are all the more neglected in their general development. The question on the conscience of modern man is: how to "demarginate" the illiterate?

(814) Certainly,there have been remarkable achievements in this field in the last fifteen years through the use of new materials and technical devices to make teaching more effective. And you rightly encourage, Mr. Director-General, the pursuit of these methods. But must one not also insist on legal measures and on attitudes for the existence of the illiterate as a separate and disadvantaged group to be taken into account by all those responsible in the various areas?

(815) And then there is still room for consciousness- raising initiatives - by governments, public and private institutions, and individuals - geared to serve the young, but also to serve those adults who have not had a chance to learn or need to familiarize themselves with new means of communication because they have left their native country or social group, their specialized field. Yes, adults must be given this opportunity, just as in some societies today they are offered opportunities of training for professional advancement.

(816) The elimination of illiteracy thus stands more and more as a process of adaptation to the more technical world where, in order to survive and be respected in one's rights, one must know how to read and write. The illiterate are victims of a too-wide discrepancy between their own traditions and the new institutions to which they must adapt.

(817) But the elimination of illiteracy has an importance beyond its utilitarian and practical aspect. Literacy is the first name of education and culture. Today, it is the initial stage of all the awakening process of man's personality in his relations with others. And it also facilitates the development of the abilities of mind and soul and the reflection each man is called on to make on the meaning of his life and on his transcendent destiny.

(818) One must hope that the elimination of illiteracy be considered not only as a kind of assistance for marginals, but as a natural duty of justice. And how could those for whom religion creates this duty of solidarity with our less privileged brethren be insensitive to this primary right? God bless all those who work towards this sharing of the good of the spirit!

(*) AAS 74(1982), 1184-1185.

(819) It is thus, Mr. Director-General, that I express wishes for the full success of this sixteenth International Literacy Day, in the service of real progress of man through man and his desire for peace in fraternity.

9. Elimination of illiteracy essential for the promotion of human dignity

Letter of His Holiness John Paul II to Mr. Amadou Mahtar M'bow, Director-General of UNESCO, on the occasion of the 17th International Literacy Day. The Vatican, 5 September 1983.

Original: French (*)

(820) On 8 September, for the seventeenth consecutive year, you invite us to celebrate International Literacy Day. The way in which the leaders and members of UNESCO, year after year, without discouragement, but rather with firm determination, tackle this problem which is so difficult to overcome shows the strength of their conviction that the elimination of illiteracy is essential for the promotion of human dignity, that it is possible to do much more in this field, and that a greater awareness of the situation must be developed so as to produce new, generous and wise commitments.

(821) The many and varied aspects of this problem of illiteracy have already been widely studied and debated, and the programmes set in motion have produced tangible results which will get even better, thanks to public and private efforts, and this will happen especially if everyone, both the contributors to these efforts and the recipients, understand that the dignity of man is at stake here, since it is a question of a right and of a duty.

(822) One naturally thinks of the right of the disadvantaged to receive schooling, education, culture and preparation for the world in which they must play a full and active role. And there is also the duty of the more fortunate to share what they have received, in reality largely through personal good luck and the efforts of their predecessors.

(823) But the illiterate also have the duty to require of themselves first, and of others also, that the initial steps be taken in this basic education and to take an active part in it.

(824) Should not this International Literacy Day make men even more convinced of the great principles which order their rights and duties?

(825) For example, all rights are indissolubly linked together; and, in so far as this right to literacy is still neglected, it is the struggle for other human rights which is equally delayed or minimized.

(826) Moreover, all men are brothers; and, in so far as some of them, somewhere in the world or in some aspect of their lives, see their rights flouted, it is the dignity of the entire human race which is wounded.

(827) Finally all rights are linked to duties; and, if a duty is not carried out, the corresponding right is left begging; if there is a right to life, there is a duty to favour and protect life; if there is a right to peace, there is a duty to make peace; if there is a right to freedom, there is a duty to make men free; if there is a right to literacy, there is a duty to eliminate illiteracy and to seek this basic education.

(828) It is to be hoped, Mr. Director-General, that nations will widely react to the celebration of the seventeenth International Literacy Day of your Organization, for which I offer wishes of success.

(*) Insegnamenti di Giovanni Paolo II, Vol VI,2 (1983), 408-410.

May they find the means of making public opinion aware of the enormous suffering which illiteracy represents for adults and children alike, much like malnutrition is in terms of body health, and equally dramatic! May people commit themselves to seek and develop, at home and in the least favoured countries, adequate national and international initiatives! I hope that this day and these efforts will help to enable a large number of people to overcome the handicap of not being able to read or write, so as to allow them to participate more fully in the culture and life of society, and also to find better access to the spiritual realities which are themselves so well expressed in the sacred writings. I know that such progress is part of God's plan.

VII - EDUCATION, INFORMATION, POPULATION

Statement by H.E. Msgr. Giuseppe M. Sensi, Head of the Delegation of the Holy See, at the 17th Session of the General Conference of UNESCO. Paris, 30 October 1972.

Original: French

(829) I should like first of all to emphasize our appreciation of the efforts UNESCO is making in its present programme (cf. Documents 17 C/4 and 17 C/5) to deal with the changes in society and the crises these bring in their wake. In the fields of education, science, culture and information, more than in the technical and economic fields, the evolution which is taking place brings with it far-reaching changes which assail man himself.

(830) Awareness of this, which is widely agreed on here, marks the last of Pope Paul VI's documents on social problems, in which he stated, in May 1971: "In the changes taking place at the present time, so far-reaching and so rapid, man discovers himself anew, each day, and he queries the meaning of his own being and of his collective survival" (*Octogesima Adveniens*, 7). If man questions things thus, it is because, through the development of the human sciences, he is becoming, in his turn, the subject of a science, and a science which criticizes in radical fashion all the knowledge acquired up to now; he can also become the subject of manipulations which guide his desires and his needs, change his behaviour and even his system of values. "There is no doubt that herein lies a grave danger for the Society of tomorrow and for man himself. For, although everyone is agreed on constructing a new society which would be the service of men, we still need to know what sort of man is envisaged" (*Octogesima Adveniens*, 39).

(831) Behind our scientific approaches to a knowledge of man, in the educational methods to be employed, is there not, finally, a deeper choice to be made concerning what man is, so far as his future rather than his past is concerned, and with regard to his collective destiny just as much as to his personal existence. This search for identity is common to us all; and even though we arrive at a solution by different routes, a dialogue between us ought to bear fruit. Pope Paul VI pointed out one way when he said: "...Doubtful about drawing lessons from a past which he considers over and done with and too different, man nevertheless has need to shed light on his future - which seems to him as uncertain as it is changing - by means of permanent, eternal verities, which are beyond his grasp, certainly, but traces of which he can discover for himself, if he really wants to" (*Octogesima Adveniens*, 7).

(832) One of the fundamental subjects brought into question today is that of scientific and technical progress. The efforts made by man to procure for himself the most hidden resources of the universe, are accompanied by a search for a better understanding of creation; creation remains, however, the essential mystery which science is managing to pinpoint better, without ever being able to solve it or evaluate it. Nobody would deny the very positive results achieved by science; but all at once, by an unexpected *volte-face*, this very success has become disquieting: "By his thoughtless exploitation of nature, man is in danger of destroying it and of being, in his turn, the victim of this destruction" (*Octogesima Adveniens*, 21). It is not only the material environment that is being attacked but the human environment itself; and will not man be building an intolerable universe for himself? Here, we link up with Mr. Maheu's statement at the Stockholm Conference on the Environment: "Man is discovering his power, and even more his desire, to denature himself and the world with him."

(833) In this far-reaching work of discovery, each science should learn to recognize its limits, in its own field; it cannot claim a monopoly so far as the meaning of man is concerned; it must respect other approaches and remain open to the possibility of a transcendent factor (cf. *Octogesima Adveniens*, 40).

(834) I am particularly glad to note the place which UNESCO intends to give to young people in its future plans. The young feel more than others the contradictions evident in society, since they are particularly concerned about the future; their aspirations, utopian though they sometimes are, betray the desire to go beyond a society of simple well-being where the essential task would consist of producing and consuming; they also show a refusal to become part of a world of dominant interests and egotistical violence. Does not this search of theirs, vague though it is as yet, express hopes whose appeal must be welcomed? It is an appeal for a world freed from the obsession with quantitative growth, aspiring to fraternity and sharing, looking for ways leading to the solidary development of mankind.

(835) Although nations and men are continually rent by dissensions and war, nevertheless there is always an immense aspiration for peace in everyone's heart, for social peace as well as for international peace, for peace based on justice and on the recognition, in all his rights and in his development, of the dignity of man. Peace is possible, because it is inscribed in the hearts of men.

(836) I am also very pleased to see that UNESCO intends to give priority attention to the least favoured. So far as the developing countries are concerned, the work undertaken, in agreement with the UNDP, happily lays the emphasis on aid programmed, according to countries and thought of as a "policy," which affords greater respect for the specific cultural characteristics and encourages the autonomous progress of each nation. In this way, too, a wider diffusion of the values of the spirit is brought about, an effective modernization and even democratization of knowledge. Here, of course, I am touching on a delicate subject. Although international aid should be imbued with respect for indigenous cultures, especially the aid given by UNESCO in the realms of education, culture and information, this principle should not lead to countries isolating themselves; on the contrary, a more lively feeling of solidarity among the nations must be encouraged. But this solidarity must not lead to the domination of certain countries by certain other countries, especially where the transfer of scientific and technological knowledge is concerned, fields in which the developed countries are further ahead. It is more a matter of a meeting of cultures, in the course of which each one receives something from the other and gives something to the other at the same time. Although it has proved possible to denounce economic, financial or political forms of imperialism, cultural or ideological domination would be a much more subtle and redoubtable thing, because it touches the spirit of man more directly.

(837) To these general views, I should like to add, if I may, a few brief remarks on three subjects: education, information and population problems.

(838) 1. I greatly appreciate the studies undertaken by UNESCO on behalf of a renewal of education. This effort is reflected throughout UNESCO's programme, and in particular, in the report of the International Commission on Education.

(839) The accent is put on a global approach which suggests a new concept of education for mankind, based principally on lifelong education and on the idea of the "educative community." This requires first of all, the harmonization of the systems of formal education and those of what is called "parallel" education. All sections of society are being asked to coordinate their educational facilities. The State certainly has its own role to play, but it must respect, in addition, the rights of the family, a legitimate pluralism, which guarantees fundamental liberties and becomes at the same time a source of fecund creativity and initiative.

(840) Within this global and united background, the exercise of responsibility by parents must not only be preserved but encouraged, for a child's education cannot leave out of account the most fundamental of its spheres of activity. So as to acquit themselves well in this task, parents themselves must continually keep up to date with the advance of knowledge and of educational methods.

(841) While making a distinction between young people and adults, *lifelong education* brings to the forefront, in a most opportune manner, a concept of life seen as a continuous process of improving one's self. It is important that all should be made aware of this duty and of this right. Pope Paul VI wrote, in his letter on the development of the peoples: "...In God's design, every individual is destined to develop his potentialities.... Endowed with intelligence and freedom, he is responsible for his own growth.... This human growth is not optional, however, ... it constitutes, as it were, the sum and substance of our duties" (cf. *Populorum Progressio*, 15 and 16).

(842) As for *integral education*, explicitly advocated in UNESCO's programme for the future, it will be founded first and foremost on a better balance between the various types of education - scientific education will be linked up with emotional and aesthetic education, intellectual education will be linked with practical education. To succeed in this, the acquisition of knowledge, even over a long period of time, is not enough; individuals must learn to dominate themselves and to serve others, to an equal and reciprocal extent. It would seem essential today to stress the aspect of justice and solidarity so far as education is concerned. Such education, undertaken from the earliest age, should be lifelong, since it is true that each individual is tempted to retire within himself, defending his own interests, asserting his rights rather than his duties. Isn't it the same with the nations? This is why education from the standpoint of justice should be international in scope; it is the most difficult, but also the most urgent.

(843) Moral education, based on the spiritual dimension of man, should characterize the whole process: in this way the child will "learn to be."

(844) 2. I note with satisfaction the place given to *information* in UNESCO's programme. Nobody is ignorant of "the increasing expansion of the role of the communications media and of their influence on the changes in mental habits, knowledge, organizations and even society itself" (*Octogesima Adveniens*, 20). Through their power and capacity to penetrate both minds and distance, the communications media manage to constitute a new sort of potency. "The men who possess this power have serious moral responsibilities with regard to the truth of the information which they have to put out, with regard to the needs and reactions which they bring to birth, with regard to the values which they uphold" (*Octogesima Adveniens*, 20).

(845) Let me speak first of all about the content of information. it is still too much a means of dominating, an instrument for instigating violence, war, social hatred, moral degradation. It should shape things rather than misshape them; it can be an efficient means of widening everybody's horizons, it can weave solidarity, it can develop a peaceful spirit among the nations and contribute to the spiritual and material progress of all.

(846) I should also like to remind you that the right to information is a fundamental right and that it proceeds directly from the vocation of man in his capacity as a spirit thirsting after truth and knowledge. Information only takes on its full significance if it is true, competent, coherent and comprehensible. The right to information also entails the free flow of information, and we all know of UNESCO's practical and efficacious achievements in this field - achievements which the Organization intends to develop still more in the years to come.

(847) Technical innovations in broadcasting by satellite will have a favourable effect on the free flow of information, on the expansion of education and on the development of cultural exchanges. Such progress must be encouraged, but it should also give rise to some thought on the growing power of these media, and therefore on the responsibilities of those in possession of such powers. The setting up of an international agency guaranteeing human rights and fundamental liberties in this field, would be desirable.

(848) 3. *Population problems.* According to its programmes on population, UNESCO intends to pursue its researches, within its fields of competence, particularly where the International Population Year and the 1974 United Nations Conference are concerned. In this way, UNESCO will collect better data and thus be able, to quote its very words, "to fulfill its responsibilities in this field with active efficacy, based on more solid foundations" (Draft medium term plan for 1973-78, 0208).

(849) Nobody questions the fact that, faced with the urgent and difficult problems which have arisen, solid, scientific foundations are indispensable, on condition that the work is carried out with total objectivity, and without any a priori. A scientific study requires that, for each population, the complex totality of data should be taken into account: the geographic, economic, cultural, historical, social and religious data. To leave out of account the moral principles which actuate the conscience, principles concerning the right to life, respect for all human beings, the relations between men and women, the family ... would be to adopt a questionable positivist attitude which would compromise the reliability of the studies undertaken.

(850) To put the question, as indicated in the document 17 C/4 (0204), in terms of "present and potential conflicts between demographic conditions and trends, and values and aims linked to the well-being of individuals and communities" would be to place one's self straightaway on a quantitative plane, that is to say to put in opposition to each other the growing world population and a restricted availability of material goods; this means taking as a starting point a definition of well-being in which material factors are predominant; it means allowing one's self to be confined within the ideology of a sort of progress which is measured and recognized first and foremost on a quantitative basis. Concerning this sort of progress, said Paul VI, "There are doubts today on its value and on its consequences" (*Octogesima Adveniens*, 41).

(851) In the methods suggested for studying demographic evolution - indicators, simulation aids, evaluation criteria - I should like to emphasize that they are often based on subjacent philosophical and ideological suppositions which should be clarified and the choice of which should be justified.

(852) I am very aware of the fact that these questions are very important and very complex. But "like all other problems which concern human life, the problem of the birthrate must be considered from a standpoint far beyond fractional outlooks - whether biological, psychological, demographic or sociological - in the light of an integral vision of man and of his vocation, not only his natural and terrestrial vocation but his supernatural and eternal vocation" (*Humanae Vitae*, 7).

(853) My speech was intended to show the interest which the Holy See takes in the work of UNESCO and the help we are ready to give within the limits of our strength and competence.

(854) The spirit which animates us is expressed in Paul VI's letter on the development of the peoples: "to help mankind to attain its full development" (*Populorum Progressio*, 13).

VIII - RESPECT FOR HUMAN RIGHTS, PROGRESS OF KNOWLEDGE, CULTURAL PLURALISM AND INTERNATIONAL SOLIDARITY

Statement by H.E. Msgr. André-Jacques Fougerat, Head of the Delegation of the Holy See, at the 18th Session of the General Conference of UNESCO. Paris, 28 October 1974.

Original: French

(855) Our delegation has studied with the greatest interest and attention the very rewarding documents, document 18 C/4 in particular, which we have been asked to consider and on which the Director-General, Mr. Rene Maheu commented in such masterly fashion.

(856) At the end of a term of office lasting 13 years and so rich in undertakings and achievements, which allows us to have a great deal of hope for the future, it would be impossible for us not to offer him an expression of our profound gratitude.

(857) The members of our delegation have had two feelings strengthened by this study: a feeling of anxiety, faced with the importance which the cultural crisis is taking on, a crisis which is at one and the same time the cause and the result of the other crises (energy, money, food) which are shaking the world; and a feeling of the responsibilities, full of promise as they are, which all UNESCO's members are jointly assuming in order to cope with this state of affairs.

(858) Without underestimating the importance of the programme and budget proposed for 1975 and 1976 (18 C/5), our delegation was particularly interested in the outlook for the future described in document 18 C/4: "Analysis of problems and chart of aims serving as a basis for medium-term planning (1977-1982)".

(859) Over and beyond the four groups of problems and the precise aims we are asked to consider, I should like to put forward one or two basic thoughts which, to our mind, dominate and orientate these various processes of research.

(860) We are told (18 C/4) that this first area of reflection constitutes one of the original and fundamental bases on which UNESCO has been built - and that recent changes which have taken place in the world have only increased the value and primacy of this ideal. We have no difficulty in agreeing with this way of looking at things and of judging them.

(861) Nevertheless, it seems to us that something is lacking from the full strictness of the affirmations and the appeals for justice and peace, born of respect for human rights. To this word, respect, we give a much wider meaning than that of esteem and mutual tolerance. It is a matter of making a positive affirmation that these rights exist, a matter of total commitment not to infringe them, a matter of making every effort to promote and extend them. The more one affirms their nobility and the need for them, the more one increases the moral obligation to respect them.

(862) Several distinguished speakers have mentioned this "moral obligation" in the course of their remarks. But one is still surprised at the hesitancy of thought and pen in the face of an evocation of this idea and in the face of the conscious or unconscious repugnance which many people show when confronted with the idea of "duty" and with the word itself. An explanation may be found in a too abstract form of educational moralism. Nevertheless, there is no escaping that positive genesis of "duties" which has its origins in the community life of men and women, and which is engendered by the social existence of men and women, all of whose rights are solemnly affirmed.

(863) We are then faced with the ineluctable question: on what grounds am I in duty bound to respect, always and everywhere, the dignity of the individual human being? But even if we put to one side this question of justifying one's duties, a question which some think can never be solved and which others think can be understood in a variety of ways, it is necessary to affirm the existence of these duties in order to arrive at some form of concentrated and concerted action. To our mind, this affirmation of duties, correlative as it is to the noble affirmation of rights, is not mentioned often enough.

(864) It is obvious that the Holy See's delegation is not holding itself aloof from the joint efforts which are being made, and in this it is holding fast to its convictions and its ideals. Its profound attachment to the promotion of human dignity on a worldwide scale and to the advent of justice and peace, is well-known. But it remains of the opinion that no moral authority able to convince men of the need for all men to benefit from integral justice, and of the need to respect this justice, and to put it into practice in positive fashion, is actually in a position to affirm this except in the name of something which transcends man.

(865) For us, this absolute has its source in God. In saying this, we are not getting away from the common ideal; we are simply complementing and strengthening it.

(866) Shall I add that this cult of justice which is part of the Christian heritage is implanted within an adhesion to a higher moral and spiritual reality: by which I mean Love, Charity and Fraternity. To see that justice is done is one of the first duties of Love, which would otherwise be nothing but hypocrisy: this places the strict exercise of justice within an atmosphere of equity and attentive human warmth: it also confers on respect for the individual a quality of fundamental spiritual brotherhood, inherited from the One who said: "Love one another...". Living out this ideal in no way diminishes our communion of heart and mind in esteeming and working for the common good of all mankind, in concert with everyone else.

(867) And it is this that makes us so attentive and so sympathetic towards the completion and growth of knowledge amongst all nations of which we would like to say something now.

(868) Document 18 C/4 states: "Men are coming more and more to consider that the discovery of more detailed knowledge about man himself and about the universe is essential for the improvement of their individual and collective well-being". This document also states: "The solution to all problems, whatever they may be, must necessarily make use of the objective progress of knowledge".

(869) Learning has its own grandeur and nobility quite apart from its beneficent practical applications. It searches for the truth and expands the human spirit, enriching it with knowledge. And when it produces techniques which benefit human well-being, it adds an irreplaceable social blessing to its primary mission of finding out the truth and enriching man's intelligence by this knowledge, at the same time enriching his heart with the joy of knowing.

(870) This great tribute of admiration and gratitude which we owe to our savants, research workers and technicians, should, nevertheless, form part of a global vision of reality and of a concern for the integral promotion of men. UNESCO, by its very name, and by its ideals, links learning and the sciences closely to education and culture.

(871) Having asserted the legitimate autonomy of learning in its capacity as a systematic body of scientific truth, and recognized the autonomy proper to these truths, so long as no claim is made to change into normative rules what should remain the simple acknowledgment of what actually is - may I be allowed to remind you - that learning and all that goes with it is, in actual practice, the savants and all that goes with them.

(872) The savant is a man who, in pursuing his scientific research work, must always remain faithful to a professional code of loyalty and justice. When he carries out scientific experiments on a human being, body and mind, he knows that he must respect human rights which he does not come up against in material things or in things endowed with non-human life.

(873) These standards apply to all savants at the ordinary level of their research work. But to this must also be added the spirit of awareness which is at present laying hold of the community of savants, the new sense of the responsibilities of science, the generous concern over cooperation in development. The savants who work with UNESCO are engrossed in this major preoccupation: their mission must therefore become increasingly extensive, but must increasingly form part of the whole process of human progress.

(874) So far as knowledge is concerned, there are different degrees of learning because there are several fields of reality (juxtaposed or on a hierarchical system). The immense field of experimental realities which can be formulated into more or less approximate scientific laws, is a field of reality which is constantly being enlarged. But there is also the reality vis-a-vis the sphere of quality, the reality of beauty, the reality of friendship and love, the reality of suffering, the reality of the mystery of death and of what follows after: these kinds of reality have their own private approach roads. There is all that immense Reality, supra-human and supra-terrestrial, to which the philosophers, and the religious even more so, are attached: it, too, has its approach roads. It is with all these aspects of the human, part and parcel of education and culture, that learning should unashamedly fraternize.

(875) So far as action is concerned, it is no longer a question of learning, but of making use of learning. Technology is taking over from science. The achievements of technology, like those of science, enjoy a legitimate autonomy so long as they do no harm: but with the putting into practice of these techniques come, because of mankind's freedom, the possibilities of providing the extraordinary benefits proper to a civilization of well-being (I do not say a civilization of happiness), and the very grave dangers inherent in the misuse of the applied sciences. Our delegation, like everyone else, rejoices over the former and goes in fear of the latter. Moral imperatives then come into play vis-a-vis the social and material activities of technology "confronted by these powers which are so easily misused".

(876) This concise reminder of these great problems requires a more discriminating and more precise form of research work: this is the aim of the work of the Commissions. We wished simply to say that although "scientific knowledge is one of the foundations of the evolution of society", it is not the only one - and that although it is one of the essential values of a modern form of humanism, it is not simply serving one exclusively scientific form of humanism, but humanism plain and simple, in the absolute meaning of the term.

(877) Finally, in hoping that technology will be widely diffused in the service of the less favoured nations, the Holy See's delegation is in full agreement over the danger of the transference of poorly-adapted technologies, imposed on a country to the detriment of the nation's original culture, and used with the aim of dominating that country.

(878) After affirming the principle of cultural identity (18 C/4, no: 133) and the right of other cultures to be appreciated (18 C/4, no: 6), the document on medium-term planning reminds us that "That recognition of cultural *pluralism* as a basis for international cooperation based on mutual respect, and the equality of rights between the nations, has now become an essential aspect of UNESCO's programme". Should we not go further and speak not only of cooperation between the nations but of *solidarity*, international solidarity, and try to promote, as document 18 C/4 says "an intellectual and social solidarity of all mankind". So as not to leave things vague and not to have too many formulas, the two ideas, pluralism and solidarity, should be the subject of theoretical and practical reflection. Pluralism rests on the distinguishing factors and specificity of each culture; solidarity presupposes a desire to recognize common factors, complementary aspects, points of convergence; a march towards unity based on mutual respect; a permanent desire to communicate; the awareness of a common responsibility vis-a-vis the challenges of the future.

(879) At the present time, international solidarity - even though a great deal is said about it - is progressing too slowly so far as actual behaviour and decision-making is concerned. It should result, in part, from the education of the moral conscience, encouraging it to transcend particularisms which are often narrow even though legitimate, in order to discover the vocation of every man, of every nation, and to take up, together with other people, a point of view which is more universal in nature. This transition to the universal view of humankind may seem utopian, abstract or premature, since mankind is only just finishing organizing itself into national entities concerned about their independence and their own identity. Nevertheless, the appeal for a more universal form of solidarity should already be given a hearing.

(880) One culture has succeeded another throughout the centuries; up to the present, they were spread about in distant parts. Now that the world has become complete, and is crisscrossed with innumerable means of communication, these cultures naturally meet up with each other; and each one has had a tendency, in order to safeguard its identity, to assert itself, and even to pit itself against others. Apart from this, the meeting of cultures seems likely to be no more peaceful than the meeting of interests; it is possible for it to remain at the stage of mere co-existence. But is there not a need, today, for us to discover together a new kind of humanism which transcends and at the same time recognizes cultural differences and open them up to wider forms of solidarity?

(881) We have just been talking about the convergence, the constructive convergence of cultures. This word "convergence" is used in the preamble to document 18 C/4, which tells us that the four areas we are asked to think about and work on, though they are not placed in any hierarchical system are nevertheless orientated towards the same point of convergence,the quality of life.

(882) It is a well-chosen term, engaging and fashionable. The quality of life of individuals - the quality of life of nations - the quality of life of mankind. What a programme! But this wonderful ideal would no doubt be a falsely clear idea if it covered only ambiguities. The road which leads from well-being to happiness is difficult to define because of the diverse types of mentality, of their freedom of choice and of their personal destinies. Education which, for lack of time, we shall deal with at greater length in the Commissions, has as its object the full development of the individual and the fraternal commitment to serve others. All educational activities are thus two-fold creators of the quality of life. And provided this ideal remains receptive to the temporal and eternal values of the soul, the Holy See's delegation supports it and hopes to see it achieved in the noblest, widest and most beneficial ways. But this widening of the horizons of the "interior landscape", as it has been called, must not diminish the common values necessary to the progress of the entire human family which are truly fortified, truly served and truly hailed with joy and hope when they expand.

(883) These few more basic reflections, which are the product of an attentive reading of the documents of the 18th session of our General Assembly, do not make us forget about the more special and already vast problems with which we are asked to deal, and in particular: the orientation of development, the advancement of women, migrant workers, the growth of literacy, indispensable as it is, the development of life-long adult education, the remarkable contribution to research work on an international scale which the creation of the United Nations University constitutes. But these must all be put back again into a more universal and forward-looking vision of things, and to this we have tried to make our own specific contribution. Is not this more spiritual outlook on the future in fact essential? The destiny and happiness of mankind is at stake here.

IX - "MAN, THE CENTRE OF DEVELOPMENT"

Statement of H.E. Msgr Agostino Cacciavillan, Head of the Delegation of the Holy See, at the 19th Session of the General Conference of UNESCO. Nairobi, 3 November 1976.

Original: English

(884) In the name of the Holy See, I present my warmest good wishes for the full success of this General Conference, which, for the first time in the history of the Organization, is being held in Africa, whose powerful natural forces may be considered a symbol of the generous energy with which her sons take their place, every day more fully, in the universal community, in order to collaborate towards the complete progress of mankind and towards the establishment of the true spirit of reconciliation and justice, the foundation of peace.

(885) Side by side with this African and universal springtime - a vision both ideal and real, in which one sees the new economic and social international order - we find the wonderful realization of the satellite "Symphonie", a significant example of collaboration among countries and also of the service which science and technology should render towards the progress of all.

(886) The good wishes of the Holy See are a part of the sincere interest it has always shown for the ideals and activities of UNESCO. The Holy See, in fact, is aware of and attentive to the many ways in which the services of UNESCO, in its competence and its achievements, correspond to the mission which the Church accomplishes for the benefit of man and peoples.

(887) The Holy See finds in this 19th General Conference a very special reason for expressing, at least on certain major points, the attention it pays to the action of UNESCO and to the spirit that animates it. This reason is found in the great care which the Organization manifests in order to give its action a better foundation, making it a more suitable answer to the great problems of the modern world. The effective answer that UNESCO wants to give, is envisaged in the two converging documents: the mid-term plan for the six-year period 1977-1982, and the book *Moving towards change.*

(888) Of these great problems, so aptly expressed in the Project of a mid-term plan 19 C/4, especially in the remarkable and very penetrating introduction that the Director General has given it, we would wish to recall three aspects which seem to us to merit particular attention, and which correspond to the preoccupations of the Holy See, as many documents show, as for example, the Encyclical Letter of Pope Paul VI, published in 1967, *Populorum Progressio* which we know had a very favourable reception on the part of the United Nations and of its specialized agencies, and particularly UNESCO.

(889) First, there is question of the race for development, which threatens to lead to unrestrained consumption, bringing about also the degradation of nature and the exhaustion of its resources, with the added danger of the degradation of man himself. Facing this development, which appears not to know where it is leading, if not to make material satisfaction, often artificially created, predominate for man, to the extent of making him forget his spiritual destiny, we must ask the question which is clearly formulated in the introduction to 19 C/4: "What are the objectives of development, what kind of man do we envisage as the result of this process?".

(890) By putting the theme "Man, as the centre of development" among the ten great problems constituting the basis of its action, UNESCO is helping to contribute to that rectification which is necessary if we are to prevent humanity from bringing about its own ruin. Evidently such rectification implies, not a halt to development, which of itself is necessary and good for all peoples, but the moderation of this development, accepted in principle by the wealthier countries but still far from being put into practice, and a harmonization of its own growth with that of others, in each country.

(891) The second major question, closely linked with the first: the inequalities, not only economic but also social and cultural, within each nation, and in a much more serious way, between the privileged countries and those less privileged. It is to these inequalities that we particularly direct our attention. In spite of generous efforts to reduce them, efforts in which UNESCO in its thirty years of existence has played a very notable part, we notice that those inequalities continue and even increase. That is why we must rejoice at seeing this preoccupation written into the future programme of UNESCO, more explicitly than in the past, especially because of the place given to rural populations, which still remain those who derive the least benefit from progress.

(892) In order that the sacrifices, which this profound transformation of the attitude of countries requires, may be understood and accepted, a very profound motivation is necessary, a motivation which can only come from a recognition of the unity of the human species, of its "catholicity" in the Greek sense of the word, of the true and effective brotherhood which should unite all mankind. These are realities which are the common patrimony of all humanity, whose foundation is seen by believers to be God, and which Christians see in their faith in Christ, the saviour of all men.

(893) The third major question to which we wish to draw attention is that of the human rights. This preoccupation is also happily retained as one of the ten great problems of the mid-term plan project. We must recall the sad gap that exists between so many obligations subscribed to, and their implementation. Man has need of liberty. There is no respect for his dignity, for his vocation as a person, artisan and master of his destiny, if the rights which guarantee his liberty are not acknowledged. Just as collaboration cannot exist among the international community without each nation being free, similarly within a country it is difficult to require the collaboration of all if this is not given by individuals who are completely free.

(894) Certainly, the problem of human rights exceeds the competence of UNESCO; but, within the field of its activity, the Organization is charged with the defence and the promotion of the rights to education, to culture, to freedom from racial and religious discrimination. Important progress has been made, notably through the action of UNESCO, but how many men still suffer cruelly and sometimes are subjected to humiliating life conditions, just because those rights are not respected. Such violations of human rights injure their dignity in its most profound and sacred nature.

(895) In order to give effect to the requirements we have just mentioned and which coincide with those which UNESCO, in its mid-term plan, sets down as the basis for the definition and direction of its action, it would appear that two very special conditions must be met:

(896) Firstly, an exceptional educational effort is required. We will not realize a world truly suitable for man, a world which recognizes the fullness of his destiny, which is above all spiritual; we will not achieve a true international order, unless appropriate dispositions and attitudes are found in each individual. Education must be the first to contribute to this, but on the condition that it must be thought of, not as just teaching, but also involving a formation which proposes and makes understood and esteems the values of life, the true values and their proper hierarchy.

(897) A second condition for the realization of the requirements so happily inserted in mid-term plan, is that all those who, by whatever title, work in the institutions whose mission it is to contribute to the realization of those objects, must fully assume their responsibility with a spirit of service, evaluating the nobility and importance of the tasks entrusted to them, far removed from all ambition for power. This particularly concerns the elites. In this regard, we cannot refrain from paying homage to their courage, especially in the developing countries, for they must undertake duties, which, however attractive, are very difficult.

(898) These are the reflections which we have thought it opportune to present to this conference, which also marks the thirtieth year of the existence of the Organization. They will allow you to understand better the extent to which the Church and its Head, Pope Paul VI, have at heart the tasks accomplished by UNESCO.

X - INDIVIDUAL HUMAN RIGHTS AND THE RIGHTS OF THE COLLECTIVITY

Statement of H.E. Msgr. Ernesto Gallina, Head of the Delegation of the Holy See at the 21st Session of the General Conference of UNESCO. Belgrade, 30 September 1980.

Original: French

(899) 1. The Holy See Delegation is anxious in the very first place to express sentiments of deep gratitude for the delicate and warm welcome that UNESCO recently bestowed on His Holiness Pope John Paul II.

(900) His visit will have contributed to a high degree to drawing closer the relations that have already been established for long years between the Holy See and UNESCO, to emphasizing the broad community of views that unites them, and to strengthening their collaboration.

(901) Our Delegation is authorized to confirm, on the occasion of this General Conference, the esteem in which the Holy Father holds UNESCO and its noble ideal, and his firm intention to continue to encourage and stimulate all initiatives that deserve a common commitment.

(902) 2. In the same spirit that marked this visit, and taking into account the views expressed by the Director-General in the remarkable introduction he gave to the draft programme and budget for 1981-1983, as well as in his preliminary report, so inspiring, on the intermediate term plan for 1984-1989, allow me to present some brief reflections on some of the numerous themes contained in this programme. We chose them because of their particular importance.

(903) 3. You will not be surprised that the question of human rights takes first place among these reflections. This is due to the more important place that the Organization gives it, as well as to the many painful situations in which they are actually challenged and even ignored today. Among the problems raised at present by the investigation of UNESCO, so happily increased in the field of human rights, we wish to stress the circumspection with which the widening of the concept of human rights, in itself such a good thing, must be met. This widening is such that there is talk of new human rights. Two points deserve particular attention in this regard. The first concerns possible conflicts between human rights that are individual ones, and human rights that could be classified as rights of collectivities, mainly of nations. A harmonizing of these two types of rights must be reached, so that the exercise of the inalienable rights of the human person will not be prevented in any way.

(904) The second point concerns the rights called those of the second kind, which involve services on the part of the collectivity: the right to education, to culture, to information, to health. However legitimate they may be, we must take into account the possibilities of the collectivity which will often be able to meet these requirements only imperfectly owing to its poor means. But to the extent to which it will be able to do so, it will have to be according to criteria which take into account, on the one hand, an authentic hierarchy of values, and on the other, the imperative requirements of justice, which call for special solicitude for the underprivileged.

(905) 4. Man's formation remains one of the problems in which UNESCO plays a leading role within the United Nations. Like the problem of human rights, it constitutes a question in which there are at stake the most fundamental values that UNESCO has the mission to preserve and promote.

(906) We would like merely to make some brief remarks on this subject. Certainly, the adaptation of man's formation to his future occupation, to which UNESCO gives increasing importance in its programme, conditions both man's fulfillment in his professional life, and development, which, as numerous examples show, is a question of men even more than of goods.

(907) But UNESCO adds to this subject, as regards the school, that of general education. This is to recognize that man's formation cannot be limited to preparation for a job.

(908) Allow me to express the wish that the organization give even more expression to this broad view of man's formation, according to which man must be prepared not only for a productive function, but also for his future family life, so charged with responsibilities, for his role as an active and enlightened citizen, for use of his leisure time which, far from leading to a life of apathy - when it is not, as is too often the case, real degradation - brings about a real fulfillment.

(909) 5. With regard to culture, we would like to recall the problems, often very serious ones, that cultural pluralism raises in many countries. The whole question lies, in a word, in the fact that a certain lack of realism sometimes impedes the reconciliation of two equally valuable aspects: the unity of the nation, on the one hand, the common good for which the State is responsible, and also, for the oldest nations, of bonds woven by a common past. On the other hand, the preservation, respect, esteem, and promotion of the cultures of the various groups that compose them, whether it is a question of language, religion, numerous traditions, and many other features. We know what a difficult task this reconciliation represents and the often serious conflicts that have their source in the opposition of these two requirements, the question of cultural identity, so happily taken into consideration by UNESCO, being only one side of this problem.

(910) 6. I would also like to mention all the importance that the Holy See attaches to UNESCO's action with a view to better recognition of the growing solidarity that unites peoples, playing a specific role in this connection with regard to its member States. The stress laid on this solidarity has as its main source the progress of science and technology, while this progress, if rightly conceived, and if everyone can benefit from it, will strengthen this solidarity.

(911) Such solidarity will be better understood and pursued even more ardently if men realize more clearly that they belong to one humanity and that they are all fundamentally equal - we again find here the foundation of human rights; and even more, allow me to say, if, believing, they are able to recognize one another as brothers, being created by God. This appears so forcefully for Christians in the message of Jesus Christ, who told us what store he set by the unity of men, a unity which cannot be conceived without mutual love in the image of the love that God bears us.

(912) 7. This sense of the unity of mankind, and of the solidarity which has actually been established today on a worldwide scale, has already been manifested by UNESCO for a long time by working to safeguard the finest monuments, recognized by everyone as the heritage of humanity; and it is a good thing that the Organization has recently extended this enterprise of safe-keeping to the most remarkable beauty spots in the world.

(913) But however significant this may be, it is only a partial expression of the concept of the heritage of mankind. It must be widened to reach the idea, expressed repeatedly in Holy See documents, of the universal destination of all goods, whether it is a question of natural resources, or of creations of the human spirit, works of art, certainly, but also scientific discoveries and techniques. Realism makes it a duty for us, here too, to ensure the reconciliation of this requirements with the sovereignty of Nations over their natural resources and over their collective or individual creations, and, more widely, all goods directly connected with their territory and, more fundamentally, their being as a nation.

(914) Are we not here at the heart of this elaboration of a new economic order in which UNESCO sees one of the most fundamental ideas of its programme? May the Organization, in the sphere of its competence, contribute to such a reconciliation which presupposes - let us not be afraid to say so - substantial sacrifices on the part of those who have more, in favour of those who have less, but also fair terms of trade, promoting the good of all.

(915) 8. A precise analysis of UNESCO's vast programme would lead to touching too many points whose importance no one doubts.

(916) The themes of cooperation are at once fascinating and dramatic, in all areas of the activity of the spirit, to go beyond all vestiges of unjust dominations, as well as to suppress discriminations that still persist, move in the direction of a judicious abandonment of arms, and ensure the gradual strengthening of real peace.

(917) It is important to take advantage of the new media of communication which create bridges for thought and speech, making trenches of fire useless and dangerous. Christianity is based on the "good communication" of an eternal "Word": the Gospel of the Word of God.

(918) The network of international conventions, which gather the peoples of the world in a deeper and deeper understanding, must also be encouraged. The Holy See intends to exercise a role of presence and promotion here for it knows that its supranational character frees it from geographical conditionings, but also that its mission binds it to every place where people are working for concord, love, and peace.

(919) 9. Allow me to conclude by recalling some words of Christ: "You will be sorrowful, but your sorrow will turn into joy. When a woman is in travail she has sorrow because her hour has come; but when she is delivered of the child, she no longer remembers the anguish, for joy that a child is born into the world" (*Jn.* 16:20-21).

(920) Our world is living a time of toil and suffering, but also of great hope.

(921) May UNESCO again contribute this time, through its 21st General Conference, to the coming of a better mankind in a renewed world!

XI - EDUCATION, CULTURE, COMMUNICATION FOR DEVELOPMENT

Statement of H.E. Msgr. Angelo Felici, Head of the Holy See Delegation, at the 22nd Session of the General Conference of UNESCO. Paris, 5 November 1983.

Original: French

(922) Before making some brief remarks on several major points of UNESCO's program, the Delegation of the Holy See wishes to emphasize our appreciation for the role of this Organization as the place for the exchange of ideas and thoughts amid a diversity of convictions and ways of thinking, but within a context of listening and mutual respect. UNESCO already assures an unequalled role for this within the spheres of its competence.

(923) We also want to say how much we feel UNESCO's ever-increasing concern to respond to serious problems of great contemporary interest with well-determined, wisely chosen and carefully conceived actions by means of greatly varied methods: meetings of specialists, consultations to many relevant activities, publications. Concerning the latter, we would hope that they are distributed more widely, appropriate to the quality and service they can offer.

(924) We also appreciate that the pursuit of peace is the basis of all UNESCO's actions, particularly at a time when we see it compromised, threatened and even very seriously disputed in so many regions. Indeed, is it necessary to repeat it?, this Organization is not competent to treat peace in its political aspects, but how right and opportune for UNESCO to work for peace by influencing the spirit and heart of human persons.

(925) In this very place, last October 5 in the presence of the Director-General, the 20th anniversary of Pope John XXIII's encyclical *Pacem in Terris* was celebrated. In this major document, as well as in a number of other pontifical works, notably the Messages for the Day of Peace, it was clearly recalled that true peace is associated only with liberty and justice. In other words, the concept of peace is inseparable from that of human rights, essentially those drawn up in the Universal Declaration of 1948, and in the two International Covenants of 1966, the one pertaining to economic, social and cultural rights, and the other, to civil and political rights. On this occasion, let us note here to-day that the rights of the individual and the rights of peoples are connected, as was already found in Pacem in Terris. Therefore, the emphasis is on the fact that a person is not only an individual, but also a social being, marked by relationships to others and at the heart of numerous social groups, particularly of nations. This parallel, this complementarity must not make us disregard the primacy, the uniqueness of the human being, which collective interest should not harm in any way.

(926) Further, to understand peace in all its ramifications and to give it full reality, it must be seen as the fruit of universal reconciliation, more specifically, of universal brotherhood, a brotherhood called for by a condition shared by all humanity and by its close solidarity. Fraternity is the great teaching which Christians received from Christ. This brotherhood will only be effective if individuals and peoples pursue this effort of mutual understanding that UNESCO has so rightly associated to its search for peace, implying openness of each one to the other, the desire to know others as they are, their authentic selves, their particular characteristics and their deepest aspirations.

(927) Concerning the program of education, we would like to address two points of major importance. One is the training of teachers. Educational programs and the progress of educational planning could be very excellent; they would be so only if the school prepares teachers truly conscious of their duties. Of course, teachers should be competent and capable of transmitting knowledge, but they must also be educators in the true sense of the word. Although this latter task falls first upon the family, educators will have to make their contribution to the development of individuals, not only to their intelligence, but also to their character and will, by means of various methods according to their disciplines. They must make known and appreciated the values which, today, (if not, alas, always practiced in real life) are largely recognized beyond the diversity of beliefs as the common heritage of humanity. These are values which proceed fundamentally from the recognition of the dignity and the grandeur of humanity and of the relations between human persons, united in a common project of the advancement of everything which comprises the value of human life. The second aspect of the education program on which we would like to present some reflections is adult education, not only that dimension of education specifically so named but numerous other aspects which, without being so called, directly refer to it. Under these different modes, UNESCO apparently attaches an increasing importance to it. Indeed, at the moment adult education increasingly attracts the attention of the Organization, since under its auspices, the 4th International Conference on Adult Education will reconvene in 1985. And rightly so, not only because of deficiencies and even the absence of education unfortunately still so widespread, but also because of the very rapid evolution of our civilization, of life styles, and of technology. Without minimizing in any way, the specific role of the school, which remains irreplaceable, adult education appears as a major demand of our times. Without a doubt its aims are practical, but undeniably it constitutes a factor of great bearing on the personal advancement of human being.

(928) We discern here two fundamental modes: on the one hand, literacy. When it is well-planned, it constitutes, especially among the excessively passive people principally in rural areas of developing countries, an essential requirement for an awakening, which therefore should allow them full participation in the social and political life of their country. On the other hand, there is professional training, without which a country cannot control its own destiny, make its own constructive society, and assure its own growth. In this area, to its action in academic and university technical education, UNESCO in different ways makes an addition hardly known outside a circle of a few specialists, but of great scientific and technical programs relating to oceanography, hydrology, and environmental education.

(929) Concerning culture, the Holy See is attentive to the activities of UNESCO which match its own. It is sufficient to recall the discourse made here on June 2, 1980 by Pope John Paul II and the recent contacts made with UNESCO by the Pontifical Council for Culture, established last year by Pope John Paul II.

(930) UNESCO had the great merit of immediately recognizing the new perspective in which culture appeared in the modern world, particularly at the time of the Conference on Cultural Policies in Mexico in 1982. No longer is culture reserved only to an elite group; it is offered to all; all can claim it because it appears not as a luxury, as a superfluity, but as an essential part of the being of each person and people, as a major factor of their affirmation, advancement, development, and spiritual growth. And what is new, culture is now recognized as a major component of progress. In a large measure, specific to each people, it calls for exchange and mutual appreciation. And to a great degree, it also includes elements common to all of humanity. Among these, we note scientific and technical culture.

(931) As for Information and Communication, the Delegation of the Holy See wishes to express all its appreciation for UNESCO's extensive and innovative efforts in many respects in this complex and diversified area which aims at gathering and synthesizing the program of the New World Information and Communication Order. In first place, and rightly so, there is the universal right to information and the freedom of communication which to-day is so threatened; with these, the concern for authentic communication as a source of communion among all and implying honesty founded on truth.

(932) But isn't it appropriate to underline two dangers for information and communication. On the one hand, a lack of quality - let us be realistic enough to recognize the mediocrity of too many of the "messages"; and, alas!, also, many times, the moral degradation that they favor. On the other hand, an excess of "messages", not certainly in all countries - many of which suffer cruelly from a lack of information and communication - but above all in the developed countries. This excess is the source of fragmentation and of an "exteriorization" which affects that interior of human persons without which they cannot be in control of life, directing it according to a clearly recognized and desired plan, and really fulfilling it.

(933) Allow me to take advantage of these remarks to bring to mind another problem, which, I know, has the full attention of UNESCO, although it is not designated as the subject for a large program, since it underlies all; that is, the problem of youth which will be on the agenda particularly because 1985 will be the International Youth Year. May UNESCO consider this problem in all its gravity, which lies essentially in the agony of youth - the term is not too strong. Agony in the face of unemployment of which there is little hope of seeing any diminishment, agony before the madness of armaments and their increasingly fearsome power; more fundamentally, agony in facing a life to which so many young people are unable to give a meaning. Certainly UNESCO alone cannot respond to this problem. But it can contribute much by its action, principally in those areas which we have mentioned.

(934) Undoubtedly, this Assembly, having gathered together such remarkable and qualified personalities so devoted to UNESCO and its work, will be able to give to the program of the Organization all the value and efficacy called for by the great fundamental problems which the Organization confronts in the world today.

XII - UNIVERSALITY MUST BE TRANSLATED IN TERMS OF SOLIDARITY

Statement by H.E. Msgr. Luigi Poggi, Head of the Delegation of the Holy See, at the 23rd Session of the General Conference of UNESCO. Sophia, 11 October 1985.

Original: French

(935) Forty years ago, almost to the month, UNESCO, specialized agency of the Organization of the United Nations for education, science and culture, began its journey and its work to arouse in the minds of men the defence of peace.

(936) Today, in these moments when UNESCO is experiencing difficulties, our delegation is anxious to express the esteem the Holy See bears to the Organization because of the major role it recognizes as belonging to it and because of the convergence, in a number of fundamental questions, of the objectives of UNESCO with the mission of the Holy See.

(937) We do not wish to repeat here what the Holy See has frequently had occasion to say on this subject, particularly through the voice of Popes John XXIII, Paul VI and John Paul II, as well as in the interventions of our delegation at the preceding General Conferences. We will say only, with regard to UNESCO, that the position of the Holy See remains as clear and as firm as in the past in affirming the validity of the objectives of UNESCO.

(938) We are of course aware of the difficult problems confronting the Organization today. It is not our task to recall these here in detail. But we would like to underline the work pursued by UNESCO, by its Director-General, by its Executive Council, in view of resolving them, and the measures that have already been taken in this direction. And we would like to insist on what constitutes, in our view, the fundamental issue at stake in the crisis of the Organization, for we fear that discussions, necessary in large measure to be sure, can cause this to be lost sight of, or at least relegated to the distant horizon.

(939) We are speaking of an aspect of the ideal and of the activity of UNESCO, as of the United Nations itself and its other specialized agencies, but here with a special and more marked accent, by reason of the specific competence of UNESCO. Such an aspect must be constantly recalled and given top priority. We refer to the aspect of the *universality* of its objectives. To prejudice this aspect is to fail to recognize the imposing reality of the unity of humanity, of the community of destiny common to all men over and beyond their legitimate divisions into independent nations. Of this order of the things of the spirit, a necessary expression, and one of the most invaluable as well. Are we not living at present in a world where this universality, which was always an issue, is beginning to show itself in increasingly concrete ways and accordingly calling more and more for concerted efforts and projects of universal scope?

(940) This universality should not remain at a purely speculative level. It does not reach its full actualization, its full efficacy unless it is translated in terms of *solidarity*. We understand by this term those exchanges, that cooperation, those acts of mutual assistance by which, simultaneously, each people brings to the others what can help them realize their development, their expansive growth, and receives from them similar assistance. This is especially urgent at a time when people which, in great numbers, have recently acceded to independence, are appealing to this very universality in order to achieve better recognition and to affirm themselves in their individuality.

(941) To weaken the universality of UNESCO would be to compromise seriously the exercise of solidarity, especially of multilateral cooperation, of whose limitations we are surely aware, but which has benefits that would not be offered to the same degree by bilateral cooperation alone, necessary and valuable as this may be.

(942) By its very nature an organization of universal character, UNESCO saw itself entrusted in this perspective, through its constitutive Act, with a work of *peace*. Here again we do not need to repeat what the Holy See has many times taken pains to bring out: the major importance of this objective. Suffice it to recall what was said in this regard at length, in depth and with relevance, notably in the encyclical *Pacem in Terris*, by Pope John XXIII: "Peace is not only absence of war; it is above all absence of the fear of war; it has also other synonyms such as: reconciliation, international cooperation, development and integral progress of mankind".

(943) May it be better understood that UNESCO will truly accomplish this work of peace only within the precise domain of its competence, above all by its investigations and its achievements regarding education, science, culture, and now communication; tasks which, in fact and for a long time now, constitute by far the largest part of its activities and available resources, and on whose importance its member States unanimously agree! In this regard, it seems to us that vague dissertations and discourses are of much less importance and often even a source of danger to unity. Moreover, they only repeat old points of view already many times expressed and which are a source of ambiguities and fruitless meetings.

(944) It would be extremely regrettable if polarization on such questions and the controversies they engender were to compromise the pursuit of the work of UNESCO, in itself so constructive and of such great importance; or if such questions were to lead to misunderstanding. This is unfortunately already often the case among agencies which have the mission, by various titles, to treat of the affairs of UNESCO. It also applies to a notable part of public opinion, which is not always well informed.

(945) Without committing itself to a detailed evaluation of the programme submitted to the General Conference, the delegation of the Holy See would like to underline its very particular interest in the programme concerning culture and in the project of a world decade of cultural development.

(946) Alongside the fundamental work UNESCO has pursued since its foundation in the domains of education and science, a work which has been rendered more suitable and effective through long years of experience-though not sufficiently recognized-and without forgetting the domain of communication, the domain of culture appears to us as that called to experience the most significant growth and extension and as that where the newest problems are being posed. It constitutes a sector whose importance for man's full development and happiness, whose spiritual interest, appear increasingly better recognized. This was especially evident in the reception UNESCO gave to the speech delivered within its walls by Pope John Paul II, who was calling for a determination, in its most profound aspects, of the nature and the significance of culture.

(947) We would like in concluding to underline the fact that the emphases apparent in our intervention are above all inspired by the attitude the Catholic Church has always maintained with regard to the objectives of the Organization. It does not belong to it to interfere in the practical and purely temporal aspects of its activity, but it regards it as its duty to evaluate it in the name of its spiritual mission and of morality. The Holy See earnestly desires that the member States of the Organization be ever more aware of this higher interest of the objectives of UNESCO and ever better recognize the importance of its role. They would have to look more closely at their responsibility in this regard. It is to be hoped that they will show ever more concern for its future.

(948) Then, in spite of so many concerns, difficulties, inevitable differences with which the Organization is today confronted, we can have hope - not naive but firm and enlightened - as we watch UNESCO pursue and better accomplish the tasks set out for it, in a spirit of cooperation and dialogue presupposing and aiming at a full and true understanding and an ever increasing mutual openness among its member States.

CHAPTER IV

DISARMAMENT AND PEACE

I - NECESSITY FOR CONTROLLED LIMITATION OF ARMAMENTS

Letter of His Holiness Paul VI to H.E. U Thant, Secretary General of the United Nations, on the occasion of the resumption in Geneva of the work of the "Committee of Eighteen for Disarmament". The Vatican, 24 January 1966.

Original: French (*)

(949) You are aware with what attention we have been following the efforts of the United Nations in favour of peace.

(950) At this moment when the "Committee of Eighteen for Disarmament" is resuming its activities in Geneva, we wish to convey to you an urgent appeal, motivated by the desire to see the work of this Committee attain a positive, concrete result and thus mark a new stage in the realization of disarmament, the hope and desire of all mankind.

(951) We feel encouraged in this step by the recent position taken by more than two thousand Catholic bishops, meeting for the Ecumenical Council, in Rome. We are also encouraged by the echo which our appeal from Bombay found among the Members the Disarmament Commission, and the favorable reception by world opinion of our speech at the United Nations.

(952) In raising our voice in favor of the great cause of disarmament, we are aware of faithfully following the path delineated by our predecessors. To cite only the most recent ones, we know how clearly Pius XII immediately recognized the problem during the first wartime Christmas of his pontificate. Calling for order in conformity with justice which should succeed the ruins of war, he said:

(953) "For order thus established to have the tranquility and duration which are the foundation of real peace, nations must be liberated from the oppressive servitude of the arms race and from the danger that physical force instead of serving as a guarantee of justice may on the contrary become a tyrannic instrument for violation of justice. Peace treaties, which do not attribute basic importance to mutually agreed, organic, progressive disarmament, in the practical and spiritual order, and which would not work to realize it faithfully, would sooner or later reveal their precarious and inconsistent nature." (Discorsi e Radiomessaggi, I, 441). "Justice, wisdom, and a sense of humanity," proclaimed by John XXIII in the memorable encyclical *Pacem in Terris*, "demand the halt of the arms race; they require disarmament duly obtained by joint agreement and effective controls."

(954) In intervening in this area now, we do not intend to ignore the complexity of the problem or to overlook the enormous difficulties which the relevant organizations of the United Nations have faced since their foundation with a consistency and competence to which in all fairness we render homage.

(955) But it cannot be denied: that every passing day shows more clearly that no stable peace can be established among men until there is effective, general, controlled armament reduction. Every passing day also establishes more painfully and dramatically the contrast between the enormous sums invested in the production of ammunitions and the immense, ever increasing material distress of more than half of mankind, which is waiting to witness the satisfaction of its most elementary needs.

(956) We are indeed confident, Secretary-General, that you will accept this intervention from us as a testimony of the esteem in which we hold the authority of the United Nations and the great capability of the members of the Committee of Eighteen for Disarmament.

(957) We trust you will also herein discern an echo of the ardent hope of mankind, at this time when, in the name of the Ecumenical Council, recently held in Rome, We have thought it opportune and obligatory in fact to approach your kind self.

(*) AAS 58(1966), 479-480.

(958) It is in this sentiment that we extend our most ardent wishes for the complete success of the coming deliberations in Geneva, and We invoke for them and for all participants the blessing of the Almighty God.

II - A STRATEGY OF PEACE AGAINST THE SCANDAL OF ARMS

Message of His Holiness Paul VI to the First Special Session of the United Nations General Assembly dedicated to Disarmament, delivered on 6 June 1968 by H.E. Archbishop Agostino Casaroli, Secretary of the Council for the Public Affairs of the Church. The Vatican, 24 May 1978.

Original: French (*)

(959) On the occasion of the Special Session which the General Assembly of the United Nations has decided to devote to the problem of disarmament, there exists a widespread expectation, and its echo has reached us. Does not the Holy See have something to say on a subject of such burning relevance and such vital importance for the future of the world?

(960) Without being a member of your Organization, the Holy See follows its many activities with greatest attention and with profound understanding, sharing its preoccupations and its generous intentions. We cannot remain insensitive to an expectation such as this.

(961) We therefore very willingly accept the opportunity that has been given to us to address once again a message to the General Assembly of the United Nations, as we had the honour to do, in person, in that already distant October of 1965. The present circumstance is in effect absolutely exceptional in the life of your Organization and for the whole of humanity.

(962) 1. We come to you once again today, in the spirit and with the sentiments of our first meeting, the remembrance of which is always vivid and dear to our heart. Please accept our respectful and cordial greeting.

(963) We come to you as the representative of a Church that is made up of hundreds of millions of people spread throughout all the continents. But at the same time we have the consciousness of giving a voice to the aspirations and hopes of other hundreds of millions of people, Christians and non-Christians, believers and non-believers: we would like to gather them together, as in an immense choir ascending towards God and towards those who have received from God the responsibility for the destiny of the nations.

(964) 2. Our message is meant to be, first of all, a message of congratulations for your having resolved to confront decisively, in this lofty forum, the problem of disarmament. Yours is an act of courage and wisdom. It is the response to an extremely grave and urgent need.

(965) Our message is also a message of understanding. We know the exceptional difficulties that you must face, and we fully realize the weight of your responsibilities, but we have confidence in the seriousness and sincerity of your commitment.

(966) Our message is meant to be above all - if you permit me to say so - a message of encouragement.

(*) AAS 70(1978), 399-407

(967) 3. The peoples are manifesting such interest in the theme of your discussion because they believe that to disarm is, first of all, to deprive war of its means: peace is their dream, their deepest aspiration.

(968) The desire for peace is also the noble and profound motive that has brought you to this Assembly. But, in the eyes of statesmen, the problem of disarmament presents itself under a much more articulated and much more complex form.

(969) Faced with the situation as it is, the statesman asks himself, not without reason, if it is just and if it is possible not to recognize the right of the members of the International Community to make their own provisions for the legitimate defence, and hence to procure the means necessary for such a goal.

(970) And the temptation is strong to ask oneself if the best possible protection for peace does not in fact continue to be ensured, basically, by the old system of the balance of forces between the different States or groups of States. A disarmed peace is always exposed to danger; its very weakness is an incentive to attack it.

(971) Against this background one can and must - it is said - develop, in a parallel way, efforts aimed on the one hand at perfecting the methods and bodies for preventing and resolving peacefully conflicts and confrontations; and on the other hand to render less inhuman those wars that are not successfully avoided. At the same time, one can and must endeavour to reduce mutually the arsenals of war, in a way that does not destroy the existing balances, but lessens the temptation to have recourse to weapons and lightens the enormous military budgets.

(972) Such seems to be the path of political realism. It claims justification in reason and experience. To go further seems to many people a useless or indeed dangerous effort.

(973) 4. Let us say at once that all substantial progress towards improving the mechanism of preventing conflicts, towards eliminating particularly dangerous and inhumane weapons, and towards lowering the level of armaments and military expenditure, will be hailed by us as an extremely valuable and beneficial result.

(974) But this is still not enough. The question of war and peace, in fact, presents itself today in new terms.

(975) It is not that the principles have changed. Aggression by one State against another was illicit yesterday just as it is today. Even in the past, an "act of war directed to the indiscriminate destruction of whole cities or vast regions with their inhabitants" was "a crime against God and humanity itself" (*Gaudium et Spes,* 80). And war, although one must honour the heroism of those who sacrifice their lives to the service of their native land - has always been, in itself, a supremely irrational and morally unacceptable means of regulating the relationships between States, though without prejudice to the right of legitimate defence.

(976) But today, war has at its disposal means which have "immeasurably magnified its horrors and wickedness" (*ibid.*).

(977) The logic underlying the quest for the balances of power impels each of the adversaries to seek to ensure a certain margin of superiority, for fear of being left at a disadvantage. This logic, in conjunction with the amazing progress of humanity in the spheres of science and technology, has led to the discovery of ever more sophisticated and powerful instruments of destruction. These instruments have accumulated, and, by virtue of an almost autonomous process, they tend to self-perpetuate unendingly, in a continual escalation both in quantity and quality, with an immense expenditure of men and means, to the point of reaching today a potential amply capable of wiping out all life on the planet.

(978) Developments in nuclear armament make up a special chapter, and certainly the most typical and striking one, of this quest for security through the balance of power and fear. But can one forget the "progress" that has also been made and that, alas, might still be made in the sphere of other arms of mass destruction or with the capacity to produce particularly damaging effects - arms that are considered to have, for that very reason, a special power of "dissuasion"?

(979) But even though the "balance of terror" has been able to avoid the worst and may do so for some time more, to think that the arms race can thus go on indefinitely, without causing a catastrophe, would be a tragic illusion.

(980) Certainly, the subject above all concerns, at least directly, the Great Powers and the countries forming their blocs, but it would be very hard for the other countries not to feel concerned.

(981) Humanity therefore finds itself forced to turn back on itself and ask itself where it is going, or rather, what it is plunging into. It is forced above all to ask whether the point of departure is not mistaken and should therefore be radically altered.

(982) The reasons for a change of this kind - whether moral reasons, or reasons of security or of particular and general interest - are certainly not lacking.

(983) But, is it possible to find a substitute for the security - however uncertain and costly it may be - that each is trying to ensure by acquiring the means of his own defence?

(984) 5. Few problems appear today so inevitable and difficult as the problem of disarmament. Few problems respond so much to the needs and expectations of the peoples, and at the same time so readily provoke mistrust, scepticism and discouragement. It seems to be a problem situated at the level of a prophetic vision open to the hopes of the future. And yet one cannot really face this problem without remaining solidly based upon the hard and concrete reality of the present.

(985) Disarmament therefore calls for an extraordinary effort of intelligence and political will on the part of all the members of the great family of nations, in order to reconcile demands that seem to contradict one another and cancel one another out.

(986) The problem of disarmament is substantially a problem of mutual trust. It would therefore be largely useless to seek possible solutions of the technical aspects of disarmament if one were to fail to cure at its source the situation that serves as fertile soil for the proliferation of armaments.

(987) Even the terror of new weapons runs the risk of being ineffective, to the extent that other guarantees are not found for the security of States and for the solution of the problems capable of bringing those States into confrontation on points vital to them.

(988) If one wishes - as one must - to make substantial progress along the road to disarmament, it is therefore essential to find means of replacing "the balance of terror" by "the balance of trust".

(989) But, in practice, is it possible? And to what extent? Certainly, a first step consists in trying to improve with good faith and good will the atmosphere and the reality of international relations, especially between the Great Powers and the blocs of States. In this way the fears and suspicions that today divide them can lessen, and it will be easier for them to believe in the real desire for mutual peace. It involves a long and complicated effort, but one that we would like to encourage with all our power.

(990) Detente in the real sense, that is to say, founded upon a proven willingness to exercise mutual respect, is a condition for setting in motion a true process of disarmament. In turn, balanced and properly supervised disarmament measures assist detente to progress and grow stronger.

(991) However, the international situation is too exposed to the ever possible changes and caprices of tragically free wills. Solid international trust therefore also presupposes structures that are objectively suitable for guaranteeing, by peaceful means, security and respect for or recognition of everyone's rights, against always possible bad will. In other words, such trust presupposes an international order capable of giving everyone what each is today seeking to ensure for himself by the possession and threat of arms, if not by their use.

(992) But is there not a risk of thus slipping into utopianism? We think that we can and must resolutely answer no. It is true that the task in question is extremely arduous, but it is not beyond the tenacity and wisdom of people who are aware of their own responsibilities before humanity and history - above all before God. This means the need for a higher religious awareness. Even those who do not take God into account can and must recognize the fundamental exigencies of the moral law that God has written in the depths of human hearts and that must govern people's mutual relationships on the basis of truth, justice and love.

(993) At a time when humanity's horizons are widening far beyond the confines of our planet, we refuse to believe that man, animated by such an awareness, is not capable of exorcising the demon of war which threatens to destroy him, even if this demands of him immense efforts and a reasonable renunciation of old-fashioned concepts that continue to set peoples and nations ad odds.

(994) 6. In making our own and expressing to you the hope and anguish of humanity aspiring to the peace it needs, we are aware that the path which must lead to the coming of a new international order capable of eliminating wars and the causes of wars and thus making arms superfluous cannot in any case be as short as we would like it to be.

(995) It will therefore be indispensable in the meantime to plan and promote a strategy of peace and disarmament - a step-by-step strategy but one that is at the same time almost impatient, a strategy that is balanced yet courageous - always keeping our eyes and our wills fixed on the final goal of general and complete disarmament.

(996) We do not have the competence or authority to indicate to you the methods and mechanisms for such a strategy, which in any case presupposes the setting up of reliable and effective international controls systems. We believe however that there is common agreement with you on the need to lay down some principles in the effort aimed at halting the arms race and reducing the amount of existing arms.

(997) a) Nuclear weapons certainly have first place: they are the most fearsome menace with which mankind is burdened. We appreciate very much the initiatives that have already been taken in this area, but we must encourage all countries, particularly those which have the chief responsibility for it, to continue and to develop these initiatives, with the final goal of completely eliminating the atomic arsenal. At the same time means must be found for giving all peoples access to the immense resources of nuclear energy for their peaceful use.

(998) b) Next comes already existing or possible weapons of mass destruction, such as chemical, radiological, and all other such weapons, and those that strike indiscriminately or, to use an expression that is itself rather cruel, weapons with excessively and needlessly cruel effects.

(999) c) Mention must also be made of trade in conventional weapons, which are, so to speak, the principal fuel for local or limited wars. In comparison with the immensity of the catastrophe that a war resorting to the whole arsenal of strategic and other weapons would mean for the world or for whole continents, such conflicts may seem of minor importance, if not negligible.

(1000) But the destruction and suffering that they cause to the peoples that are their victims are no less than those that would be brought about on quite a different scale by a general conflict. Furthermore, the increase in arms budgets can stifle the economy of countries that are often still at the developing stage. Besides, account must be taken of the danger that in a world which has grown small and in which different interests interfere and clash a local conflict could gradually provoke much wider conflagrations.

(1001) 7. The arms race is a matter of scandal; the prospect of disarmament is a great hope. The scandal concerns the crying disproportion between the resources in money and intelligence devoted to the service of death and the resources devoted to the service of life. The hope is that, by cutting down on military expenditure, a substantial part of the immense resources that it now absorbs can be employed in a vast world development project.

We feel the scandal. We make the hope our own.

(1002) In this same hall where you are gathered today we renewed on 4 October 1965 the appeal we made to all States on the occasion of our journey to Bombay the previous December: "to devote to the benefit of developing nations at least a part of the money that could be saved through a reduction of armaments".

(1003) We now repeat this appeal with still more force and insistence, calling on all countries to study and put into operation an organic plan within the framework of the programmes for the fight against inequality, underdevelopment, hunger, disease and illiteracy. Justice demands it; the general interest recommends it. For progress by each of the members of the great human family will be to the advantage of progress by all and will serve to give a more solid foundation to peace.

(1004) 8. Disarmament, a new world order, and development are three obligations that are inseparably bound together and that by their essence presuppose a renewal of public outlook.

(1005) We know and understand the difficulties presented by these obligations. But it is our will and our duty to remind you strongly, as people who are conscious of responsibility for the destiny of mankind, of the very serious reasons that make it necessary to find means of overcoming these difficulties. Do not depart without having laid the foundations and given the indispensable impulse to the solution of the problem that has brought you here together. Tomorrow may be too late.

(1006) But, you will ask, what contribution can and will the Holy See make to this immense common effort for disarmament and peace?

(1007) It is a question you have a right to ask. It places us in our turn face to face with our responsibilities, with respect to which our means are much inferior to our will.

(1008) The Holy See is not a World Power, nor has it political power. It has declared in a solemn treaty that "it wishes to remain and will remain extraneous to all temporal disputes between States and to international congresses held for such objects, unless the contending parties make concordant appeal to its mission of peace; at the same time reserving the right to exercise its moral and spiritual power" (Lateran Treaty, Article 24).

(1009) Sharing your problems, conscious of your difficulties, and strong by our very weakness, we accordingly say to you with great simplicity: If you ever think that the Holy See can help overcome the obstacles blocking the way to peace, it will not shelter behind the argument of its "non-temporal" character nor shy away from the responsibilities that could be involved in interventions that have been desired and asked for. For the Holy See greatly esteems peace and greatly loves it.

(1010) In any case, we shall continue to proclaim aloud, untiringly and without losing courage, the duty of peace, the principles that govern its dynamism, and the means of gaining and defending it through renouncing by common accord the weapons that threaten to kill it while claiming to serve it.

(1011) We know the strength of public opinion when it is upheld by solid ideals, convictions firmly rooted in consciences. We shall therefore continue to cooperate in order to educate dynamically for peace the new humanity. We shall continue to recall that there will be no disarmament of weapons if there is no disarmament of hearts.

(1012) We shall continue to pray for peace. Peace is the fruit of the good will of men and women, but it remains continually exposed to perils that good will does not always succeed in controlling. That is why peace has always appeared to mankind as above all else a gift from God. We shall ask him for it: Grant us peace. And we shall ask him to guide your work, in order that its results, both immediate and future, will not disappoint the hope of the peoples.

III - NEGOTIATION: THE ONLY REALISTIC SOLUTION TO THE CONTINUING THREAT OF WAR

Message of His Holiness John Paul II to the Second Special Session of the United Nation General Assembly dedicated to disarmament, delivered on 11 June 1982 by His Eminence Cardinal Agostino Casaroli, Secretary of State. The Vatican, 7 June 1982.

Original: French (*)

(1013) 1. In June 1978, my predecessor Pope Paul VI sent a personal message to the First Special Session of the United Nations devoted to Disarmament, in which he expressed his hopes that such an effort of good will and political wisdom by the international community would bring the result that humanity was looking for.

(1014) Four years later you are gathered here again to ask yourselves if those initiatives have been - at least partially - realized.

(1015) The answer to that question seems neither very reassuring nor very encouraging. If one compares the situation in the area of disarmament four years ago with that of today, there seems to be very little improvement. Some in fact think that there has been a deterioration at least in the sense that hopes born of that period could now be labeled as simple illusions. Such a stance could very easily lend itself to discouragement and impel those who are responsible to seek elsewhere for the solution to these problems - general or particular - which continue to disturb the lives of people.

(1016) That is in fact how many see the current situation. Figures from various sources all point to a serious increase in military expenditures represented by a greater production of different kinds of weapons along with which, according to specialized institutes, there is a new rise in the sale of weapons. Recently the news media has given a great deal of attention to research and use on a wider scale of chemical weapons. Moreover new kinds of nuclear weapons have also come into existence.

(1017) Before an Assembly as competent as this one, there is no need to repeat the figures which your own Organization has published on this subject. It is sufficient, as an indication, to refer to the study according to which the sum total of military expenditures on the planet corresponds to a mean of $100 per person per year, a figure which for many people who live on this earth is all they would have annually to survive.

(1018) Faced with these facts, I willingly want to express my satisfaction that the United Nations Organization has proposed to confront the problem of disarmament once again and I am grateful for the courtesy so graciously extended to me to address some words to you on this occasion.

(1019) While it is not a member of your Organization, for some time the Holy See has had a Permanent Mission of Observer, a post which allows it to follow your daily activities. No one is unaware of how much my predecessors valued your work. I myself, especially at the time of my visit to the Headquarters of the United Nations, have had the opportunity of making my own their words of appreciation for your Organization. Like them I understand the difficulties. And while I am ever hopeful that your efforts be crowned with even more important and better results, I recognize its precious and irreplaceable role in helping ensure a more tranquil and peaceful future for the world.

(1020) This is the voice of one who has no interests nor political power, nor even less military force. It is a voice which is heard here again in this hall thanks to your courtesy. Here where practically all the nations, great and small, of the world come together, my words are meant to be the echo of the moral conscience of humanity "in the pure sense," if you will grant me that expression.

(*) AAS 74(1982), 872-883.

My words bear with them no special interests or concerns of a nature which could mar its witness value and make it less credible.

(1021) A conscience illumined and guided by Christian faith, without doubt, but which is by the fact none the less profoundly human. It is therefore a conscience which is shared by all men and women of sincerity and good will.

(1022) My voice is the echo of the concerns and aspirations, the hopes and the fears of millions of men and women who, from every walk of life, are looking toward this Assembly asking, as they hope, if there will come forth some reassuring light or if there will be a new and more worrisome disappointment. Without claiming a mandate from all these people, I believe I can make myself the faithful interpreter to you of the feelings which are theirs.

(1023) I neither wish nor am I able to enter into the technical and political aspects of the problem of disarmament as they stand before you today. However, I would like to call your attention to some ethical principles which are at the heart of every discussion and every decision that might be looked for in this field.

(1024) 2. My point of departure is rooted in a statement unanimously agreed upon not only by your citizens but also by the governments that you lead or you represent: the world wants peace: the world needs peace.

(1025) In our modern world to refuse peace means not only to provoke the sufferings and the loss that - today more than ever - war, even a limited one, implies; it could also involve the total destruction of entire regions, not to mention the threat of possible or probable catastrophes in ever vaster and possibly even universal proportions.

(1026) Those who are responsible for the life of peoples seem above all to be engaged in a frantic search for political means and technical solutions which would allow the results of eventual conflicts "to be contained." While having to recognize the limits of their efforts in this direction, they persist in believing that in the long run war is inevitable. Above all this is found in the spectre of a possible military confrontation between the two major camps which divide the world today and continues to haunt the future of humanity.

(1027) Certainly no power, and no statesman, would be of a mind to admit to planning war or to wanting to take such an initiative. Mutual distrust, however, makes us believe or fear that because others might nourish designs or desires of this type, each, especially among the great powers, seems to envisage no other possible solution than through necessity to prepare sufficiently strong defense to be able to respond to an eventual attack.

(1028) 3. Many even think that such preparations constitute the way - even the only way - to safeguard peace in some fashion or at least to impede to the utmost in an efficacious way the outbreak of wars, especially major conflicts which might lead to the ultimate holocaust of humanity and the destruction of the civilization that man has constructed so laboriously over the centuries.

(1029) In this approach one can see the "philosophy of peace" which was proclaimed in the ancient Roman principle: "*si vis pacem, para bellum*". Put in modern terms, this "philosophy" has the label of "deterrence" and one can find it in various guises of the search for a "balance of forces" which sometimes has been called, and not without reason, the "balance of terror."

(1030) As my predecessor Paul VI put it: "The logic underlying the request for the balances of power impels each of the adversaries to seek to ensure a certain margin of superiority, for fear of being left at a disadvantage." (Message to the United Nations General Assembly, 24 May 1978. The Teachings of Pope Paul VI, vol. 11, 1978, p. 202. See above, par. 977).

(1031) Thus in practice the temptation is easy - and the danger always present - to see the search for balance turned into a search for superiority of a type that sets off the arms race in an even more dangerous way.

(1032) In reality this is the tendency which seems to continue to be prevalent today perhaps in an even more accentuated fashion than in the past. You have taken as your specific purpose in this Assembly to search how it could be possible to reverse this trend.

(1033) This purpose could seem to be in a sense "minimalist," but it is of vital importance. For only a real renewal can raise the hope that humanity will commit itself on the road that leads to the goal that everyone so much desires; even if many still consider it a utopia: total disarmament, which is mutual and surrounded by such guarantees of effective controls that it gives to everyone confidence and necessary security.

(1034) In addition this Special Session surely reflects another truth: like peace, the world wants disarmament; the world needs disarmament.

(1035) Moreover, all the work which has gone on in the Committee for Disarmament, in the various commissions and sub-commissions and within governments, as well as the attention of the public, all give witness to the importance that is being placed today on the difficult question of disarmament.

(1036) The actual convocation of this Meeting indicates a judgment: the nations of the world are already overarmed and are overcommitted to policies that continue that trend. Implicit in this judgment is the conviction that this is wrong and that the nations so involved in these actions need to re-think their positions.

(1037) However, the situation is a complex one where a number of values - some of the highest order - come to play. It is one where there are divergent viewpoints that can be expressed. We must therefore face up to these problems with realism and honesty.

(1038) That is why, before all else, I pray to God that he might grant you the strength of spirit and good will that will be needed for you to complete your task and further the great cause of peace which is the ultimate goal of all your efforts at this Special Session.

(1039) That is why my every word is intended to be a word of encouragement and of hope: encouragement that you may not let your energies weaken at the complexities of the questions or at the failures of the past and unfortunately the present; hope because we know that only people who build in hope can have the vision necessary to progress patiently and tenaciously towards goals that are worthy of the best efforts and the common good of all.

(1040) 4. Perhaps no other question of our day touches so many aspects of the human condition as that of armaments and disarmament. There are questions on the scientific and technical level; there are social and economic questions. There are deep problems of a political nature that touch the relations between States and among peoples.

(1041) Our world-wide arms systems impinge in great measure on cultural developments. But at the heart of them all there are present spiritual questions which concern the very identity of man, and his choices for the future and for generations yet to come. Sharing my thoughts with you, I am conscious of all the technical, scientific, social, economic, political aspects, but especially of the ethical, cultural and spiritual ones.

(1042) 5. Since the end of the Second World War and the beginning of the "atomic age," the attitude of the Holy See and the Catholic Church has been clear. The Church has continually sought to contribute to peace and to build a world that would not have recourse to war to solve disputes. It has encouraged the maintenance of an international climate of mutual trust and cooperation. It has supported those structures which would help ensure peace. It has called attention to the disastrous effects of war. With the growth of new and more lethal means of destruction, it has pointed to the dangers involved and, going beyond the immediate perils, it has indicated what values to develop in order to foster cooperation, mutual trust, fraternity and peace.

(1043) My predecessor Pius XII, as early as 1946, referred to "the might of new instruments of destruction" which "brought the problems of disarmament into the centre of international discussions under completely new aspects." (Address to the College of Cardinals, 24 December 1946)

(1044) Each successive Pope and the Second Vatican Council continued to express their convictions, introducing them into the changing and developing situation of armaments and arms control. If men would bend to the task with good will and with the goal of peace in their hearts and in their plans, then adequate measures could be found, appropriate structures erected to ensure the legitimate security of every people in mutual respect and peace; thus the need for these grand arsenals of fear and the threat of death would become superfluous.

(1045) The teaching of the Catholic Church in this area has been clear and consistent. It has deplored the arms race, called nonetheless for mutual, progressive and verifiable reduction of armaments as well as greater safeguards against possible misuse of these weapons. It has done so while urging that the independence, freedom and legitimate security of each and every nation be respected.

(1046) I wish to reassure you that the constant concern and consistent efforts of the Catholic Church will not cease until there is a general verifiable disarmament, until the hearts of all are won over to those ethical choices which will guarantee a lasting peace.

(1047) 6. In turning to the current debate that concerns you, and to the subject at hand, we must recognize that no element in international affairs stands alone and isolated from the many-faceted interests of nations. However it is one thing to recognize the interdependence of questions; it is another to exploit them in order to gain advantage in another. Armaments, nuclear weapons and disarmament are too important in themselves and for the world ever to be made part of a strategy which would exploit their intrinsic importance in favour of politics or other interests.

(1048) 7. Therefore it is important and right that every serious proposal that would contribute to real disarmament and that would create a better climate be given the prudent and objective consideration it deserves. Even small steps can have a value which would go beyond their material or technical aspects. Whatever the area under consideration, we need today freshness of perspective and a capacity to listen respectfully and carefully to the honest suggestions of every responsible party in this matter.

(1049) In this context there is what I would call the phenomenon of rhetoric. In an area already tense and fraught with unavoidable dangers, there is no place for exaggerated speech or threatening stances. Indulgence in rhetoric, in inflamed and impassioned vocabulary, in veiled threat and scare tactics can only exacerbate a problem that needs sober and diligent examination.

(1050) On the other hand governments and their leaders cannot carry on the affairs of State independent of the wishes of their peoples. The history of civilization gives us stark examples of what happens when that is tried. Currently the fear and preoccupation of so many groups in various parts of the world reveal that people are more and more frightened about what would happen if irresponsible parties unleash some nuclear war.

(1051) In fact just about everywhere peace movements have been developing. In several countries, these movements which have become very popular are being supported by an increasing sector of the citizenry from various social levels, different age groups and backgrounds, but especially by youth. The ideological bases of these movements are multiple. Their projects, proposals and policies vary greatly and can often lend themselves to political exploitation. However, all these differences of form and shape manifest a profound and sincere desire for peace.

(1052) May I also join myself to the spirit of your draft appeal to public opinion for the birth of a truly universal consciousness of the terrible risks of war. May that consciousness in its turn lead to a general spirit of peace.

(1053) 8. In current conditions "deterrence" based on balance, certainly not as an end in itself but as a step on the way toward a progressive disarmament, may still be judged morally acceptable. Nonetheless in order to ensure peace, it is indispensable not to be satisfied with this minimum which is always susceptible to the real danger of explosion.

(1054) What then can be done? In the absence of a supranational authority of the type Pope John XXIII sought in his Encyclical *Pacem in Terris*, one which one would have hoped to find in the United Nations Organization, the only realistic response to the threat of war still is *negotiation*. Here I would like to remind you of an expression of Saint Augustine which I have already cited in another context: "Destroy war by the words of negotiations but do not destroy men by the sword." Today once again before you all I reaffirm my confidence in the power of true negotiations to arrive at just and equitable solutions. Such negotiations demand patience and diligence and must notably lead to a reduction of armaments that is balanced, simultaneous and internationally controlled.

(1055) To be even more precise: the development of armaments seems to lead to the increasing interdependence of kinds of armaments. In these conditions, how can one countenance a balanced reduction if negotiations do not include the whole gamut of arms? To that end the continuation of the study of the "Complete Programme of Disarmament" that your Organization has already undertaken, could facilitate the needed coordination of different forums and bring to their results greater truth, equity and efficacy.

(1056) 9. In fact nuclear weapons are not the only means of war and destruction. The production and sale of conventional weapons throughout the world is a truly alarming and evidently growing phenomenon. No negotiations about armaments would be complete if they were to ignore the fact that 80 per cent of the expenditures for weapons are devoted to conventional arms. Moreover, the traffic in these weapons seems to be developing at an increasing rate and seems to be directed most of all toward developing countries. Every step taken to limit this production and traffic and to bring them under an ever more effective control will have been an important contribution to the cause of peace.

(1057) Recent events have sadly confirmed the destructive capacities of conventional weapons and the sad plight of nations tempted to use them to solve disputes.

(1058) 10. To focus, however, on the quantitative aspects of armaments, nuclear and conventional, is not enough. A very special attention must be paid to the qualitative improvement of these arms because of new and more advanced technologies. Here one confronts one of the essential elements in the arms race. To overlook this would be to fool ourselves and to deal dishonestly with those who desire peace.

(1059) Research and technology must always be at the service of man. In our day, the use and misuse of science and technology for other purposes is a too well known fact. In my address to UNESCO on 2 June 1980, I spoke extensively with men of culture and science on this subject. May I be allowed today at least to suggest that a significant percentage of the research that is currently being expended in the field of arms technology and science be directed towards life and the welfare of man.

(1060) 11. In his address to the United Nations Organization on 4 October 1965, Pope Paul VI stated a profound truth when he said: "Peace, as you know very well, is not built merely by means of politics or the balance of power and interests. It is built with the mind, with ideas, with works of peace." (See above, par. 23). The products of the mind, ideas, the products of culture, and the creative forces of peoples are meant to be shared. Strategies of peace which remain on the scientific and technical level and which merely measure out balances and verify controls will never be sufficient for real peace unless bonds that link peoples to one another are forged and strengthened. Build up the links that unite people together. Build up the means that will enable peoples and nations to share their culture and values with one another. Put aside all the narrow interests that leave one nation at the mercy of another economically, socially or politically.

(1061) In this same vein, the work of many qualified experts plumbing the relationship between disarmament and development is to be commended for study and action. The prospect of diverting material and resources from the development of arms to the development of peoples is not a new one. Nonetheless, it is a pressing and compelling one which the Catholic Church has for a long time endorsed. Any new dynamism in that direction coming from this Assembly would be met with the approbation and support of men and women of good will everywhere.

(1062) The building of links among peoples means the rediscovery and reassertion of all the values that reinforce peace and that join people together in harmony. This also means the renewal of what is best in the heart of man, the heart that seeks the good of the other in friendship and love.

(1063) 12. May I close with one last consideration. The production and the possession or armaments are a consequence of an ethical crisis that is disrupting society in all its political, social and economic dimensions. Peace, as I have already said several times, is the result of respect for ethical principles. True disarmament, that which will actually guarantee peace among peoples, will come about only with the resolution of this ethical crisis. To the extent that the efforts at arms reduction and then of total disarmament are not matched by parallel ethical renewal, they are doomed in advance to failure.

(1064) The attempt must be made to put our world aright and to eliminate the spiritual confusion born from a narrow-minded search for interest or privilege or by the defense of ideological claims: this is a task of first priority if we wish to measure any progress in the struggle for disarmament. Otherwise we are condemned to remain at face-saving activities.

(1065) For the root cause of our insecurity can be found in this profound crisis of humanity. By means of creating consciences sensitive to the absurdity of war, we advance the value of creating the material and spiritual conditions which will lessen the glaring inequalities and which will restore to everyone that minimum of space that is needed for the freedom of the spirit.

(1066) The great disparity between the rich and the poor living together on this one planet is no longer supportable in a world of rapid universal communications, without giving birth to a justified resentment that can turn to violence. Moreover the spirit has basic and inalienable rights. For it is with justice that these rights are demanded in countries where the space is denied them to live in tranquility according to their own convictions. I invite all those struggling for peace to commit themselves to the effort to eliminate the true causes of the insecurity of man of which the terrible arms race is only one effect.

(1067) 13. To reverse the current trend in the arms race involves, therefore, a parallel struggle on two fronts: on the one side, an immediate and urgent struggle by governments to reduce progressively and equally their armaments; on the other hand, a more patient but nonetheless necessary struggle at the level of the consciences of peoples to take their responsibility in regard to the ethical cause of the insecurity that breeds violence by coming to grips with the material and spiritual inequalities of our world.

(1068) With no prejudice of any kind, let us unite all our intellectual and spiritual forces, those of statesmen, of citizens, of religious leaders, to put an end to violence and hatred and to seek out the paths of peace.

(1069) Peace is the supreme goal of the activity of the United Nations. It must become the goal of all men and women of good will. Unhappily still in our days, sad realities cast their shadows across the international horizon, causing the suffering of destruction, such that they could cause humanity to lose the hope of being able to master its own future in harmony and in the collaboration of peoples.

(1070) Despite the suffering that invades my soul, I feel empowered, even obliged, solemnly to reaffirm before all the world what my predecessors and I myself have repeated so often in the name of conscience, in the name of morality, in the name of humanity and in the name of God:

(1071) Peace is not a utopia nor an inaccessible ideal nor an unrealizable dream.

(1072) War is not an inevitable calamity. Peace is possible.

(1073) And because it is possible, peace is our duty: our grave duty, our supreme responsibility.

(1074) Certainly peace is difficult; certainly it demands much good will, wisdom, and tenacity. But man can and he must make the force of reason prevail over the reasons of force.

(1075) That is why my last word is yet a word of encouragement and of exhortation. And since peace, entrusted to the responsibility of men and women, remains even then a gift of God, it must also express itself in prayer to him who holds the destinies of all peoples in his hands.

(1076) May I thank you for the activity you undertake to make the cause of disarmament go forward: disarming the engines of death and disarming spirits. May God bless your efforts and may this Assembly remain in history a sign of reassurance and hope.

IV - BLOODSTAINED LEBANON AWAITS THE END OF ITS SUFFERING

Message of His Holiness John Paul II to Mr. Javier Pérez de Cuéllar, Secretary-General of the United Nations. The Vatican, 7 May 1985.

Original: French (*)

(1077) The particular concern I bear towards Lebanon and the alarming news that continues to come from this bloodstained land once again induce me to address myself to Your Excellency.

(1078) After so many years of assaults which have sowed only devastation, intolerance and sorrow, it appears that still more tragic events are to be feared.

(1079) Every day, bloody combats, unspeakable stories of human suffering and appeals for help coming from all parts and from all the communities can only revive a profound sorrow in my heart.

(1080) The Lebanese population, tried by this long state of war, seems to have reached the extreme limit of endurance, and no one can remain insensitive to so much suffering and destruction. It is impossible to remain passive before the profoundly moving spectacle of these families compelled to leave their homes and their property, pursued and as it were doomed to reprisals of every kind.

(1081) What is happening in the south of the country - I am thinking in particular of the Christian populations and of the risks incurred by all those who have found refuge at Jezzine - the indiscriminate bombings that are battering Beirut and the anarchy that is gradually taking hold of all sectors of social life lead one to believe that such a situation, if it continues, could become fatal to the survival of this country.

(1082) In this context, one can only share the fears of the Lebanese people themselves - Christian and Múslim - when they see the gulf widening between the various communities, the extreme positions becoming more embittered and the whole identity of the nation on the verge of disappearing.

(*) Insegnamenti di Giovanni Paolo II, Vol. VIII,1 (1985), 1209-1211.

(1083) Convinced that such an outcome is not inevitable, knowing the Lebanese will to live and confident in the solidarity of so many men of good will, I continue to spare no effort in appealing to the conscience of the nations and of their leaders regarding this matter, so that Lebanon may once again become itself. I see this as a commitment that derives of course from my mission as Shepherd, concerned first of all for so many of his sons who are prey to the greatest afflictions and who often have the feeling of being misunderstood and forgotten.

(1084) Also involved here is a duty of fidelity towards the One who proclaimed for all men the beatitude of peace and who desires in this way to help toward a discernment capable of inciting all those who have any power of decision - in Lebanon as elsewhere - to concretely involve themselves in discouraging enmities, fear and violence.

(1085) The Organization of the United Nations, by reason of its size and its international responsibilities, appears to be a platform particularly suited for broadcasting an appeal which would in some sense be the voice of all the Lebanese people who are tempted to despair: do not abandon Lebanon; help its people to lay the foundations of a clear dialogue for the building of a truly renewed country!

(1086) I am confident, Mr. Secretary-General, that the United Nations Organization, up to its highest agencies, will accept my overture and will set in motion every possible measure aimed at coordinating the concrete and urgent initiatives required by such a complex situation. I am persuaded, moreover, that this same Organization will not hesitate to intensify its participation in the establishment of peace on the field, by way of an extended presence of the forces it has maintained in Lebanon for some years now and which assume a particularly important mission.

(1087) In sharing these reflections and these aspirations with the Secretary-General of the United Nations Organization, I cherish the hope that they will reach a large audience and that thereby a stimulus will be given to the good will of all those who, in the society of the nations, still believe in the values represented by Lebanon and who truly desire to see the end of its long agony. Moreover, confidence and courage will be restored to so many Lebanese people who aspire, in their own country as in the whole of the Middle East, to a future of coexistence based on mutual understanding among the communities and the people of the region.

(1088) Counting on your influence and your moral authority, I ask you, Mr. Secretary General, to kindly accept the renewed assurance of my sentiments of highest regard.

V - PEACE IS THE RESULT OF JUSTICE

Address by His Eminence Cardinal Agostino Casaroli, Secretary of State, at a UNIDO Day of Peace Celebration. Vienna, 6 March 1986.

Original: French

(1089) 1. It has been particularly pleasing to me to accept the invitation to take part today in the celebration of the Day of Peace, traditionally organized by the Permanent Mission of the Holy See to the Agencies of the United Nations in Vienna.

(1090) The City of Vienna alone, for what it has been and for what it is today, and above all for what it has represented for me at especially significant moments of my life, would be enough to make me value the opportunity which has been once more offered to me to pay it a visit.

(1091) Another reason, no less vivid, for satisfaction is that I find myself in a company that I shall venture to call familiar: the company of the United Nations. The fact that sponsorship of the manifestations has this year been assumed by UNIDO seems to me to have a great significance, for it remind one that, in the words of the great Pope Paul VI, "development is the new name of peace".

(1092) The time-limit which has rightly been suggested for my intervention does not allow me - even in a context devoted to "development" - to develop at too great length my address on the theme of peace, which nevertheless would amply lend itself thereto.

(1093) Be that as it may, I would like to extend a respectful greeting to the illustrious personalities honouring this meeting with their presence.

(1094) To you in particular, Herr Bundesprasident, I wish to repeat also on the present occasion my feeling of profound esteem and - if you will permit me - of friendship dating from many years ago, and which the passage of time has merely made deeper. Please accept, together with my respects, my most sincere good wishes for your person and your activity.

(1095) 2. The present stage of relations between East and West seem to me an invitation to think about the insight of the Prophet Isaiah when he declared that peace is the result of justice - "*opus iustitiae pax*" (*Is.* 32:17), in an expression that indicates at one and the same time people's profound aspiration and the price they must pay in order that it may be achieved.

(1096) Whether it is a question of relations between individuals, social groups or nations, peace is never a state of perfection achieved once and for all, but rather a dynamic balance between diverging interests, obeying values and rules accepted by all. It is clear that a balance of this sort remains subject to possible changes of position on the part of those concerned who are free to choose it or to call it into question. Moreover, a "peace" imposed by victors on vanquished would be nothing more than an apparent peace. History shows well enough that a lasting peace can only be built upon justice, that is to say upon the recognition and respect on the part of all the parties concerned of the inalienable rights which belong to them as human beings and as peoples.

(1097) A balance in justice is secured on the social level, within one nation, to the extent that the law guarantees rights and lays down the duties of citizens, and when the relationships of production, exchange and the redistribution of resources are negotiated and ordered in the framework of institutions capable of reconciling the legitimate interests of individuals and the demands of the common good. Conflicts which are difficult to avoid then find solutions whose acceptance depends on the extent to which they are solved according to the principles and rules of equal justice for all. Justice is always the higher norm which the law is entrusted with interpreting and sanctioning. In fact, a society lives in peace when it has reached a consensus on the transcendent and unassailable character of justice itself.

(1098) 3. It can be said that the same criterion is applicable to relations between nations. The latter have learned as a result of terrible ordeals, that they cannot live in peace unless they develop their cooperation on the basis of law and with the help of joint institutions. Their coming together within the United Nations Organization and the adoption of fundamental norms such as the *Universal Declaration of Human Rights* are the expression and guarantee of a desire for peace in respect of what is right and just.

(1099) a) The principles of justice establish the juridical equality of all States, but also the right of peoples to self-determination, the right to give themselves institutions and a freely chosen government, to develop their production and exchanges according to rules which secure justice for their own interests while respecting the rights and legitimate interests of their partner.

(1100) In order for there to be peace between nations, justice must first preside over their economic relations, in a fair division of international work, and a setting of fair prices for raw materials, agricultural or industrial products and of wages. Relationships of dependence and exploitation foster frustrations and reactions which are at the root of many wars of liberation or of internal revolts.

(1101) b) Aid to development - that is to say the economic and social expansion of every people and of all peoples - which is an exigency of justice, is a factor *par excellence* of promotion and peace. In effect, this exchange is no less beneficial for the investor than for the receiver. Again, this aid must not take on the forms of neo-colonialism, but must concentrate on the sectors vital for social progress. Its goal should be progressively to lead developing countries to a position of self-reliance (cf. "Iustitia et Pax" Commission, *Self-Reliance. Compter sur soi. Vers la troisième décennie du développement. Pour un monde plus solidaire, des peuples plus responsables.* 15 May 1978). The financial blind alleys into which a number of debtor countries of the Third World have been led today invite the governments involved and the international organizations concerned to take stock of the gravity of the situation, to recognize the objective mechanisms which have been the cause of this, and to evaluate the mistakes which have been made, so as to cooperate in a search for solutions which are in conformity with justice and true common interest.

(1102) c) General peace is still constantly endangered by the extension that local conflicts can take on. The great or the less great Powers do wrong to justice and take considerable risks when, instead of preventing these conflicts from spreading, they keep them going by providing the belligerents with arms. The arbitrary sale of arms, especially to poor countries, remains one of the gravest threats to peace at the present time.

(1103) In order to neutralize all threats to peace, the Holy See has always considered - this is well known and has often been judged unrealistic - that only a world public Authority would be capable of ensuring respect for law and negotiation when conflicts break out between nations. In the meantime, the Holy See favours the development and improvement of the existing international bodies, by inviting them to promote ever more extensive world cooperation.

(1104) 4. Between the law and reality, the gap is still far too obvious. Humanity find itself today in a precarious situation. Between East and West, instead of this balance which is constituted by cooperation in justice, there reigns a "peace" based upon the balance of nuclear terror. Yet ethical reflection must convince us that such a balance - which itself evokes objections of a moral nature - remains full of unforeseeable developments. In fact, this situation cannot satisfy the potential adversaries themselves. Moreover, they find themselves on common ground when they each consider a nuclear war as collective suicide and an absolute evil to be avoided. The strategy of mutual dissuasion is thus considered, at the best, as a strategy of peace, but of a precarious and uncertain peace resting simply upon the fear of reprisals, with the risk that this peace could, at a given moment, give way to despair or to the folly of rash adventure.

(1105) It may be considered a lesser evil that the parties, as long as they remain enclosed within the perspective of dissuasion, should apply to the very concept of dissuasion a few clear and mutually accepted ethical criteria. Thus, the consensus which exists on the unacceptable character of the actual use of nuclear weapons ought logically to be extended to the threat to have recourse to them. For to argue that the threat can be associated with a desire for their non-use would be to remove its *raison d'être* and its power of dissuasion. One sees today more clearly than ever that justice and the interest of peace demand a rapid abandonment of the mentality of relations based upon the fear of mutual destruction.

(1106) 5. The Holy See has constantly recalled the fact that the strategy of dissuasion can be envisaged only as a stage in the process aimed at disarmament, even of a progressive nature (cf. John Paul II, Message to the United Nations General Assembly, 11 June 1982, No. 8. See above, par. 1053-1055). So long as it is taken as an end in itself, dissuasion encourages the protagonists to ensure a constant superiority over one another, in a ceaseless race for over-arming (cf. Pope Paul VI, Message to the United Nations General Assembly, 24 May 1978, No. 4. See above, par 973-983). It fails to initiate that beginning of trustful dialogue which would enable both sides to persuade each other more convincingly of their mutual intentions.

(1107) Justice demands that the real problem - mutual, simultaneous and controlled disarmament, down to the lowest level of conventional armament - should be courageously envisaged, negotiated and applied. Recent developments in the East-West negotiations give the world fresh reasons to hope. The mutually agreed elimination of other weapons of extermination, such as chemical weapons, can be achieved here and now. The progressive destruction of nuclear weapons, called for by both sides, must remain the final goal. The security of all countries, particularly in the sensitive area of Europe, could then be secured, for instance, by a level of conventional armament acceptable to all.

(1108) Peace is to be found at the end of an indispensable process of rapprochement by the parties involved, desirous as they are of basing their relations upon a new balance of cooperation and trust. The chances of achieving such a balance will depend on the extent to which both sides will permit themselves to be guided no longer by fear which divides but rather by the quest for that justice which is the supreme norm of all human and international coexistence.

VI - QUESTION OF JERUSALEM

1. Note addressed by the Holy See to the Commission established on 22 March 1979 by United Nations' Security Council Resolution 446 (1979) "to examine the situation relating to settlements in the Arab territories occupied since 1967, including Jerusalem". The document was published by the Security Council on 4 December 1979 (S/13679).

Original: English

(1109) 1. It is commonly felt that the failure to find a solution to the question of Jerusalem, or an inadequate solution, or even a resigned postponement of the problem could bring into question the settlement of the whole Middle East crisis. The Holy See also considers it important that in this matter there should not be created irreversible situations which prejudice the desired solution.

(1110) 2. In his speech of 21 December 1973, His Holiness Pope Paul VI expressed the confident hope that the Holy See would fittingly be able to make its voice heard when the problem of Jerusalem became the subject of concrete discussions in the context of the peace negotiations for the Middle East.

(1111) On his part, His Holiness Pope John Paul II, in his address to the General Assembly of the United Nations on 2 October 1979, stated: "I also hope for a special statute that, under international guarantees - as my predecessor Paul VI indicated - would respect the particular nature of Jerusalem , a heritage sacred to the veneration of millions of believers of the three great monotheistic religions, Judaism, Christianity and Islam." (See above, par. 84).

(1112) It hardly seems necessary to emphasize that the Holy See's interest in this question has a spiritual, historical and juridical basis, that its nature is not political but religious and that its aims are conciliation and peace. The intention of the Holy See is to preserve and guarantee to the Holy City its identity as a religious centre, unique and outstanding in the history of the world, in such a way that it may become a stable place of encounter and concord for the three great monotheistic religions (Judaism, Christianity and Islam).

(1113) Needless to say, on this subject the Holy See endeavours to keep in contact not only with the religious authorities of the various Christian Churches but also with the principal leaders of Islam and Judaism.

(1114) 3. The ideal and historical reality of the Holy City is manifested in the fact that Jerusalem has been and continues to be the most important centre of all three great monotheistic religions, inasmuch as the City is the seat of three religious communities that live together there and is the site of shrines and memorials venerated by the followers of these religions, who, numbering almost a billion and a half throughout the world, regard Jerusalem as a common sacred patrimony.

(1115) This composite presence in Jerusalem of various groups means that an equitable stable and peaceful solution of the problem of Jerusalem implies, above all, the recognition of an historical and religious pluralism, to be put into practice by according all of the three religions, in their particular expression as communities, full enjoyment of their respective rights, excluding positions of predominance and, indeed, favouring the prospect of a useful human and religious dialogue.

(1116) 4. The Holy See's view is that such considerations are of primary and determining importance with regard to the problem of political sovereignty itself. That is to say: whatever solution be found to the question of sovereignty over Jerusalem (not excluding the hypothesis of the "internationalization" of the City), the satisfying and safeguarding of the above-mentioned requirements must be ensured, and at the same time, the international community ought to be the guarantor of interests that involve numerous and diverse peoples.

(1117) This does not mean, however, that any solution of the political problem of the sovereignty of Jerusalem can be considered irrelevant to the global settlement of the question. Rather, the Holy See, the more because of the particular character of Jerusalem, acknowledges the need for a solution that will be based on the principles of justice and attained by peaceful means.

(1118) 5. This perspective gives rise to the need for a "special statute, internationally guaranteed" for Jerusalem, which the Holy See is earnestly hoping for.

(1119) (a) Parity, for three religious communities, of freedom of worship and of access to the Holy Places; of protection of rights of ownership and of other rights acquired by the individual communities; of the preservation and safeguarding of the historical and urban aspects proper to the City.

(1120) (b) Equal enjoyment of the rights of the three religious communities, with guarantees for the promotion of their spiritual, cultural, civil and social life, including adequate opportunities for economic progress, education, employment etc.

(1121) It will be necessary, furthermore, to define the territory and list the Holy Places, as well as provide for the guarantees and for the supervision which the international commitment and of the accord of the interested parties.

(1122) 6. In many localities of the Holy Land apart from Jerusalem there are important Shrines and Holy Places of one or other religious confession. Suitable guarantees, analogous to those for the City of Jerusalem and in some way linked to an international juridical protection, should be provided for these places also.

2. Editorial by "L'Osservatore Romano" (30 June 1980), published as a document of the United Nations Security Council (S/14032) on 30 June 1980.

Original: Italian

(1123) In his speech to the President of the United States of America, Mr. Jimmy Carter, on Saturday 21 June 1980, the Holy Father spoke of Jerusalem in these terms: "The question of Jerusalem, which during these very days attracts the attention of the world in a special way, is pivotal to a just peace in those parts of the world, since this Holy City embodies interests and aspirations that are shared by different peoples in different ways. It is my hope that a common monotheistic tradition of faith will help to promote harmony among all those who call upon God".

(1124) In His Holiness's words we find references to permanent historical features (the "common monotheistic tradition of faith"), to present facts (the "interests and aspirations that are shared by different peoples") and to a "hope" for Jerusalem (that "harmony among all those who call upon God" may be promoted in Jerusalem, in the Middle East and throughout the world).

(1125) Throughout the centuries Jerusalem has been endowed with deep religious significance and spiritual value for Christians, Jews and Moslems.

(1126) The Holy City is the object of fervent love and has exercised a constant appeal for the Jewish people, ever since David chose it as his capital and Solomon built the temple there. Within it much of the history of Judaism took place, and the thoughts of the Jews were directed to it down the centuries, even when scattered in the "diaspora" of the past and the present.

(1127) There is no ignoring either the deep attachment of the Moslems to Jerusalem "the Holy", as they call it. This attachment was already explicit in the life and thoughts of the founder of Islam. It has been reinforced by an almost unbroken Islamic presence in Jerusalem since 638 A.D., and it is attested by outstanding monuments such as the Aksa Mosque and the Mosque of Omar.

(1128) There is no need to point out that Jerusalem also belongs spiritually to all Christians. There the voice of Christ was heard many times. The great events of the redemption, the passion, death and resurrection of the Lord, took place there. It was there that the first Christian community sprang up, and there has been, even if at times with great difficulty, a continuous ecclesiastical presence. Numerous shrines indicate the places connected with Christ's life and, ever since the beginnings of Christianity, there has been a constant flow of pilgrims to them. Saint Jerome is one of the most illustrious witnesses to the Christian presence. In the picture of the world presented by Dante Alighieri in his "Divina Commedia" Jerusalem is seen as the centre of the earth.

(1129) At present all three communities, the Christian, the Jewish and the Moslem, are part of the Holy City's population and are closely linked with its life and sacred character. Each community is the "guardian" of its shrines and holy places. Jerusalem has a whole network of organizations, reception centres for pilgrims, educational and research institutes and welfare bodies. These organizations have great importance for the community they belong to and also for the followers of the same religion throughout the world.

(1130) In short, the history and contemporary reality of Jerusalem present a unique case of a city that is in itself deeply united by nature but is at the same time characterized by a closely intertwined religious plurality. Preservation of the treasures of the significance of Jerusalem requires that this plurality be recognized and safeguarded in a stable concrete manner and therefore publicly and juridically, so as to ensure for all three religions a level of parity, without any of them feeling subordinate with regard to the others.

(1131) The three religious communities of Jerusalem, the Christian, the Jewish and the Moslem, are the primary subjects interested in the preservation of the sacred character of the city and should be partners in deciding their own future. No less than the monuments and holy places, the situation of these communities cannot fail to be a matter of concern for all. As regards the presence of the Christians, everyone is aware of the importance, both in the past and still today, not only of the Catholic community with its various rites, but also of the Greek Orthodox, the Armenian and the other eastern communities, not forgetting the Anglican groups and others springing from the Reformation.

(1132) In short, the Jerusalem question cannot be reduced to mere "free access for all to the holy places." Concretely it is also required: (1) that the overall character of Jerusalem as a sacred heritage shared by all three monotheistic religions be guaranteed by appropriate measures; (2) that the religious freedom in all its aspects be safeguarded for them; (3) that the complex of rights acquired by the various communities over the shrines and the centres for spirituality, study and welfare be protected; (4) that the continuance and development of religious, educational and social activity by each community be ensured; (5) that this be actuated with equality of treatment for all three religions; (6) that this be achieved through an "appropriate juridical safeguard" that does not derive from the will of only one of the parties interested.

(1133) This "juridical safeguard" corresponds, in substance, to the "special statute" that the Holy See desires for Jerusalem: "this Holy City embodies interests and aspirations that are shared by different peoples". The very universalism of the three monotheistic religions, which constitute the faith of many hundreds of millions of believers in every continent, calls for a responsibility that goes well beyond the limits of the States of the regions. The significance and value of Jerusalem are such as to surpass the interests of any single State or bilateral agreements between one State and others.

(1134) Furthermore, the international community has already dealt with the Jerusalem question; for instance, UNESCO very recently made an important intervention with the aim of safeguarding the artistic and religious riches represented by Jerusalem as a whole, as the "common heritage of humanity".

(1135) As early as its second session, the General Assembly of the United Nations approved on 29 November 1947 a resolution on Palestine of which the third part was devoted to Jerusalem. The resolution was confirmed in the next two sessions, on 11 December 1948 and 9 December 1949 while on 14 April 1950 the Trusteeship Council approved a "special statute" for the city on the basis of the Assembly's decisions. The solution proposed by the United Nations envisaged the setting up of a "corpus separatum" for "Jerusalem and the surrounding area", administered by the Trusteeship Council of the United Nations.

(1136) The "territorial internationalization" of Jerusalem was not of course put into effect, because in the 1948 conflict the Arab side occupied the eastern zone of the city and the Israeli side, the western. The position of the United Nations does not appear at least as yet to have been formally revoked. The General Assembly, as well as the Security Council, has repeatedly, beginning with the resolution of 4 July 1967, insisted on the invalidity of any measure taken to change the status of the city.

(1137) The Holy See considers the safeguarding of the Sacred and Universal character of Jerusalem to be of such primary importance as to require any Power that comes to exercise sovereignty over the Holy Land to assume the obligation, to the three religious confessions spread throughout the world, to protect not only the special character of the City, but also the rights connected, on the basis of an appropriate juridical system guaranteed by a higher international body.

(1138) In his address to President Carter, the Holy Father referred to the fact that the question of Jerusalem "during these very days attracts the attention of the world in a special way".

(1139) The positions of the two sides on the question of sovereignty over Jerusalem are known to be very far apart; any unilateral act tending to modify the status of the Holy City would be very serious. The Holy Father's hope is that the representatives of the nations will keep in mind the "common monotheistic tradition of faith" and succeed in finding the historical and present day reality of Jerusalem reasons for softening the bitterness of confrontation and for promoting "harmony among all those who call upon God". The aim will be to ensure that Jerusalem will no longer be an object of contention but a place of encounter and brotherhood between the peoples and believers of the three religions and a pledge of friendship between the peoples who see in Jerusalem something that is part of their very soul.

VII - EDUCATION, DIALOGUE, SOLIDARITY: A PROGRAMME FOR PEACE.

Note of the Holy See in preparation for the International Year of Peace, published as United Nations General Assembly document A/38/413. The Vatican, 2 May 1983.

Original: French

(1140) 1. It would be fitting to choose topics that would serve as a catalyst and guide the activities to be developed in preparation for the International Year of Peace and during its observance. These topics could be grouped around three concepts which, taken together, provide as it were, a teaching programme for peace: *education*, *dialogue* and *solidarity*.

(1141) 2. *Education* counts first, because it is the human heart that gives birth to the attitudes of tension, aggressiveness and violence which, at a more generalized level, may take the form of threats to peace. Accordingly, there is a need to train minds to understand and adopt those values which inspire peace, not a peace viewed negatively as a mere absence of conflict, but a peace which assumes its full positive dimension through four key elements: truth, justice, love and freedom. This task of education should be aimed specifically at the younger generation and should receive special attention during the International Youth Year scheduled for 1985, one of the themes of which is precisely that of peace. In this way, the Year of Peace could be effectively prepared through the observance of the International Youth Year.

(1142) 3. *Dialogue* represents a condition for peace. In the present-day world, there is a clash of different cultural, ideological, political and economic systems. Against this background, there is a need not only to respect legitimate pluralism but also to go beyond the level of coexistence in order to achieve co-operation of the kind inspired by the conscience and the common destiny of the human family. In this delicate, difficult and often arduous exercise, an essential condition for laying solid foundations for peace in our time is to establish an authentic dialogue at all levels, conducted with patience and tenacity in full knowledge of and respect for reciprocal positions. The Holy See, in the desire to do its part in bringing about such a dialogue, proposed in 1983 the theme for the International Day of Peace which the Catholic Church has been celebrating each year since 1968, namely, "The dialogue for peace: a challenge for our time". This theme was fully illustrated by Pope John Paul II in his Message on that occasion.

(1143) 4. *Solidarity* may be regarded as a step along the path of peace, as the outcome of a dialogue and as a universal appeal which, being both specific and imperative in nature, makes a noteworthy contribution to the cause of peace. Human beings are called upon to live, not as solitary individuals, but in a society, and the world is becoming increasingly aware of the mutual dependence of all people and the obligations which flow from that dependence. Indeed, the sense of international solidarity constitutes one of the positive values of modern culture. Solidarity strengthens the freedom of those who engage in the service of their community and represents one of their main duties. Pope John Paul II, in his speech to the International Labour Organization on 15 June 1982, emphasized that "... the world-wide common good requires a new solidarity without frontiers". (See above, par. 228). Solidarity is a pledge of peace.

(1144) 5. The United Nations should encourage Governments to carry out appropriate programmes at the national level in which all would cooperate. It would seek to promote, in all sectors of society, a renewed awareness of their responsibility to pledge themselves for peace. In particular, an effort should be made to involve the international non-governmental organizations in the activities for the Year, especially those already deeply involved in efforts to educate the public about peace.

(1145) The Holy See intends to participate through appropriate initiatives in the observance of the Year. It nourishes the hope that this Year will produce the desired results and will mark a significant stage in bringing about peaceful relations among peoples and nations in a spirit of international reconciliations and universal brotherhood. The Holy See is convinced that "peace on earth, which men of every era have so eagerly yearned for, can be firmly established only if the order laid down by God be dutifully observed" (Encyclical letter, *Pacem in Terris*, Pope John XXIII).

VIII - MIDDLE EAST: NO JUST PEACE IS POSSIBLE IF THE RIGHTS OF ALL THE PEOPLES CONCERNED ARE NOT RECOGNIZED

Statement by Rev. Fr. Raymond Roch, for the Delegation of the Holy See, at the International Conference on the Palestinian Question. Geneva, 4 September 1983.

Original: French

(1146) Conscious of its unique and lofty humanitarian role, the Holy See pays particular attention to the Near East as a whole, that part of the world which is especially tormented today.

(1147) Called to be, especially for believers, a centre of peace and brotherly understanding which ought above all to favour comprehension and cooperation among its various components, this region has suffered repeated violence. It constitutes a case "typical in the extent of its disasters, in the harshness of the problems to be resolved and in the multiplicity of the communities involved..." (John Paul II, Address to the Diplomatic Corps, 15 January 1983).

(1148) Consequently, the Sovereign Pontiff and the authorities of the Apostolic See follow with unflagging interest all the constructive efforts of the international community, whether on the part of heads of State, intergovernmental or non-governmental organizations, Churches, communities of believers or humanitarian societies, in view of restoring peace by finding the best means to preserve the often fragile equilibrium of the region and to eliminate all causes of violence.

(1149) However, if, on the one hand, the troubles in this region not only attract the attention of the Holy See but also cause it very great concern, it turns its thoughts very sadly to the Holy Land where there is so much suffering, with tragic consequences even on the surrounding countries and areas.

(1150) The Palestinian Question does not leave the international community indifferent. But has it sufficiently understood its own responsibility in the matter?

(1151) The Delegation of the Holy See thinks that, beyond verbal indignation certainly founded on undeniable facts, beyond condemnation often well deserved, it is to the building of a comprehensive peace process that the representatives of the nations should give priority. The recourse to arms and to violence of all kinds, to terrorism and to reprisals, degrades man and is unworthy of his rational nature and of his calling to a destiny beyond himself.

(1152) The most urgent problem is not only to stop the obvious abuses by condemning them; rights must be restored so that these abuses will cease. The restoration of rights requires, not only on the part of the people and communities involved, but also and especially of their leaders, a change of political will and an objective appreciation of men and of situations so that the respect of the other and of his rights may once again get the consideration it deserves. In other words, "the Holy See is convinced that there can be no true peace without justice; and that there will be no justice if there are not recognized and accepted, in a stable, adequate and equitable way, the rights of the peoples concerned. Among these rights, one that is primordial and cannot be set aside is that of existence and of security on its own territory while safeguarding the proper identity of each one" (John Paul II, Address at the general audience of 15 September 1982).

(1153) The Palestinian Question involves many various aspects all linked together, but my Delegation would like to say a few words about only the human aspect of the problem. The inhabitants of the occupied territories are subject to harsh and highly regrettable constraints. Many times the United Nations, and in particular the Security Council, have condemned measures which tend to be repeated, such as expropriation of land, not to mention political, psychological and administrative pressure. Such measures oppress the people and, in the long run, force them to leave their place of residence. It is high time that this exodus be ended which spares neither the Muslim nor the Christian communities, and that the intellectual, cultural and religious development of these communities no longer be delayed or prevented, in their proper civil and civic context.

(1154) We also cannot remain silent about the Palestinian refugees who expect so much from this Conference. My Delegation will refrain from describing their sorrowful plight, so well known to the entire world. We would like only to voice their hope of finally seeing at least the beginning of the end of their plight. The wish of the refugee is not only to live with dignity in the land which receives him; it is especially that of no longer being a refugee and of returning home with the certainty that all of his rights will surely be recognized. For the "Palestinians", the end of their existence as refugees depends on the solution of other serious problems which in fact are causing the number of refugees to increase even more rather than to remain stable. That is why Pope John Paul II, on several occasions, praying to God Almighty and addressing all believers, has stated: "...Let us pray for the Palestinian people, that an end be put to their sufferings, and their rights be recognized, as it is just that it be so for all the peoples of the region..." (Appeal at the "Angelus" of 27 June 1982).

(1155) In concluding this intervention, Mr. President, the Delegation of the Holy See would like to recall that the Apostolic See, particularly touched by the sufferings of mankind so often called to mind during this Conference, has not only offered suggestions of a religious or ethical nature.

(1156) To meet not only the problem of suffering but also the hope of greater justice and the promotion of human dignity, the Holy See, among other things, created a Special Mission which, since 1949, operates in conjunction with other organizations of the Catholic Church according to the specific mandate of each component. Thus, some concrete help is provided in the educational, social and religious fields for individuals and for communities alike. Even though they do not cover all needs, these efforts give witness to the constant concern of the Holy See for human advancement without distinction of race or religion.

(1157) My Delegation hopes that this Conference will give due attention to the problems we have just recalled. We would hope that this declaration will contribute to the work of this Assembly which should reach a truly positive solution in justice, for peace not only in the Near East but in the entire world.

IX - A DISARMAMENT VICTORY IS A VICTORY FOR PEACE

Statement by Archbishop Achille Silvestrini, Secretary of the Council for the Public Affairs of the Church, at the 1984 Session of the Disarmament Conference. Geneva, 15 March 1984.

Original: French

(1158) 1. I am honoured and delighted this morning to be able to address such a qualified and competent gathering as that constituted by the participants in this 1984 Session of the Disarmament Conference which is the only "multinational forum for negotiation" and which has as its objective the achievement of a consensus on the essential matters concerning peace and collaboration among peoples.

(1159) In a special way, I wish to greet Mr. Datcou, the Rumanian Ambassador, and wish him every success in exercising his role as Conference President for the month of March. Similarly, I wish to thank Mr. Turbanski, the Ambassador of Poland, for the manner in which he discharged the same role with competence and effectiveness as the first President of the Conference.

(1160) 2. This meeting is invested with particular importance by the very mandate entrusted to it: to promote general and complete disarmament, subject to effective international inspection. Lengthy progress by the Disarmament Conference has enabled the agenda to include the elaboration of a draft for an international treaty banning nuclear weapons testing and also a draft of an international agreement on the complete and effective banning of the preparation, manufacture and stockpiling of all chemical weapons containing moreover, terms to assure the destruction of stockpiles.

(1161) We are dealing here with a task of great importance of which the Holy See is able to appreciate the significance and value. Pope John Paul II, that tireless apostle of peace, expressly entrusted to me his concern to convey to this Conference evidence of the interest which he devotes to its work, and each of its members, whose mandated responsibility motivates their desire to create the opportunity for man today to develop his marvelous talents far from the besetting spectre of conflicts which one might fear to be irreparable.

(1162) Moreover, in encouraging the efforts of all those who strive for the building of a genuine peace and in frequently calling to mind that peace is the duty of all, the Pope is conscious of being in some way the spokesman of millions of men and women, young and adult, near and far, who refuse to live in a world where war seems to be avoided only by a precarious balance of terror.

(1163) 3. Truth to tell - despite the tensions that still exist, this year's work has begun under auspices that can be considered encouraging: the Stockholm Conference was concerned with lighting a path which could foster mutual trust in Europe, and one hopes to see the speedy resumption in Vienna of the negotiations on the reduction of conventional weapons.

(1164) A great deal more remains to be accomplished, however, at the level of determining measures for averting the peril of nuclear war, as the Pope recalled in his address at Hiroshima on 25 February 1981, on the very spot where there was revealed in all its horror the terrifying reality of what a nuclear holocaust could be. "In the face of the man-made calamity that every war is, one must affirm and reaffirm, again and again, that the waging of war is not inevitable or unchangeable... Clashes of ideologies, aspirations and needs can and must be settled and resolved by means other than war and violence" (n. 4). Thanks to the good offices of the Venezuelan Delegation, this text has been inserted into the official documents of this Conference, and I hope that it will be for the Conference a reference point.

(1165) In this context, the Holy See, without wishing to pronounce on the technical aspects of the work and discussions, desires, in a spirit of solidarity and service, to share some of its convictions, which are inspired by the message of Christ, who enlightens the human conscience in a specific manner.

(1166) 4. It is certainly a fundamental objective of this session to prevent nuclear war and to deal with all the questions relating to this. There can be no doubt that this is a matter of the most basic necessity. More and more numerous are our brothers in humanity who have the terrible feeling of living on top of a volcano, which, at any moment, could become active, unleashing devastating forces, extending deathly pall over our planet and placing a final "full-stop" to the course of human history.

(1167) Let us think of the frustration this feeling can engender, particularly among young people. In this world, so full of the danger of death, those who wish to live, to understand, to love and to build are asking themselves what existence means and what does human activity matter if total war seems more and more to be its inevitable and calamitous fate? Even though it still bears the seeds of creative hope for humanity and for the future, the feeling of parenthood itself is not spared this "crisis of meaning": young couples are beginning to question the future of their offspring, terrified by the thought that their children are sooner or later destined to be victims.

(1168) Tired of rhetoric about peace, public opinion is attentive to the slightest initiative, no matter how modest, which might become the seed of a more reassuring world and might restore to many the hope of a more serene tomorrow.

(1169) This is why the concluding of a treaty banning nuclear testing would doubtlessly constitute a guarantee that all States are willing to commit themselves to a new direction.

(1170) It is regrettable that the terms of the treaty concerning the non-proliferation of nuclear weapons, to which the Holy See became a party in 1971, have not yet succeeded in releasing all the dynamic energy which inspired its stipulation, both because it has not yet obtained the universal adherence which it had every right to anticipate, and because the commitments solemnly made by the nuclear powers who promoted the Treaty are far from being fulfilled; that is, to halt the arms race and ensure their gradual reduction by appropriate inspection, until complete disarmament is achieved.

(1171) Quite the contrary, not only has it not been possible to bring about the agreed balances at the lowest possible level, but the door has been left open for an even more unbridled and dangerous arms race. In his Message for the World Day of Peace 1984, Pope John Paul II emphasized that the leaders of nations must be convinced that "war is in itself irrational, and that the ethical principle of the peaceful settlement of conflicts is the only way worthy of man". He specified: "...the dreadful risks of the arms of massive destruction must lead to the working out of processes of cooperation and disarmament which will make war in practice unthinkable" (n.4).

(1172) Simultaneous progressive disarmament, including the acceptance and implementation of genuine international inspection, would create a new climate, a climate of confidence which would have beneficial repercussions not only at strategic levels, but even more so in the economic and social domain.

(1173) As Pope John Paul II stated in his homily of 1 Jan., on the occasion of the 1984 World Day of Peace: "Today's world is ever more marked by contrasts, caught up by tensions which are manifested in a harrowing manner and in opposing directions in the relations between East and West, and North and South".

(1174) It is more precisely in the North-South direction, adds the Pope, that "the most important aspect is represented by the resulting contrasts in peoples' conditions. In rich countries health and nourishment improve, whereas in the poor countries the means of nourishment for survival are lacking and the mortality rate soars, especially among infants".

(1175) Several concomitant factors combine to create this gap separating rich and poor countries. But there is no doubt that it becomes wider by reason of the dissipation of economic resources squandered on expensive armaments: resources which should rightly be devoted to the assistance of less favoured peoples. In this situation, it should come as no surprise, emphasized the Holy Father, that the menace of nuclear catastrophe and the plague of famine in numerous countries are intimately connected. Like the Four Horsemen of the Apocalypse, they are a terrifying spectre on the horizon of peace.

(1176) 5. Similar considerations can be made in the case of the other forms of war which are called "conventional", and which are reputed to be more controllable. In their regard, one cannot pass over in silence the commercial trade in conventional arms, which is governed by the laws of the market, just as if it were a matter of products for everyday use. Neither must it be forgotten that the greater part of countries' military budgets is spent on this type of armament. What is to be thought of a humanity which employs in such a disproportionate fashion its best resources in the manufacture and spread of death-dealing machines, often without distinguishing between defence needs and intentions which are more or less acknowledged as aggressive? In light of the fact that so many praiseworthy efforts are being made to combat certain epidemics, terrorism, or the scourge of drugs, and that every country takes care to regulate the carrying and use of arms within its own territory, is it too far-fetched to ask why the international community does not arrive at an agreement to establish terms which would permit effective control of the reduction and spread of conventional weapons? For the moment, unfortunately, we see conflicts that have become chronic, being ceaselessly fed by the purveyors of death-machines, opening up a veritable competition to supply their "clients", and at an ever greater profit.

(1177) 6. In the face of this complex reality, which the Holy See recognizes in all its seriousness, without minimizing the competence with which this Conference addresses it, I would like here and now to insist on a certain number *of priorities which are likely to lead to effective disarmament, and hence to a stronger peace.*

(1178) First: never refuse to *negotiate*. In the absence of a supranational authority, negotiation for progressive, simultaneous and internationally controlled arms reduction remains an imperative need, which must not be allowed to elude us. Every agreement on immediate measures, no matter how modest, would contribute to a considerable reduction in the risk of conflict.

(1179) Second: restore *trust*. Mutual loyalty and esteem must always inspire the communication and evaluation of information, thus favouring a sincere and fruitful dialogue.

(1180) Finally: strive to place *science* and *technology* at the service of *life*, instead of war. You have before you the "Declaration on the consequences of the use of nuclear arms" (see below, par. 1204-1220), published by the Pontifical Academy of Sciences, a copy of which Pope John Paul II wished to be conveyed personally (in 1981) to the Heads of those States which possess nuclear arms. This document presents in a startling way the horrible consequences which the use of certain weapons would cause to civilian populations and to the environment. It has become a matter of extreme urgency to recall that scientific research is at the service of man. How is it possible not to desire, as does the Pope, that a "significant percentage of the research that is currently being expended in the field of arms technology and science be directed towards life and the welfare of man" (Message to the Second Special Session of the General Assembly of the United Nations on Disarmament, 11 June 1982, n.10. See above, par. 1059).

(1181) This aspect of the relations between "science" and "armaments" seems to me to be particularly important when one speaks of weapons in outer space, radiation weapons or chemical weapons. In reference to the latter, which this Conference is discussing in these very days, it is greatly to be hoped and a matter of urgency that existing agreements calling for their total banning should be carried out and become a reality. An adequate and effective system of inspection must be carefully worked out. The Holy See, which signed the Geneva Protocol of 1925 banning bacteriological and chemical weapons, will continue to lend its moral support to every initiative contributing to the definitive elimination of the horrors of total war, in accordance with the solemn Declaration of the Second Vatican Council which, in this regard, renewed the condemnations already pronounced by recent Popes. In fact, the Council explicitly states: "Any act of war aimed indiscriminately at the destruction of entire cities or of extensive areas, along with their populations, is a crime against God and against man himself. It merits unequivocal and unhesitating condemnation" (Constitution: *Gaudium et Spes*, n.80).

(1182) 7. Disarmament is a priority objective for the entire international community. To promote peace, to educate to peace, to safeguard peace in some way - that indeed is a domain in which the *Church can provide its own particular contribution.*

(1183) For the Church never ceases to invite all men, without any distinction whatever, to become engaged in ethical choices that are capable of assuring an enduring peace. The current situation remains distressing. Peace cannot be merely the absence of war. It is more than something technical. It is a spirit. It presupposes the putting into action of spiritual values, such as truth, liberty, justice and solidarity. It is a task for which each one should feel a responsibility.

(1184) Recently the Episcopal Conferences of numerous countries made statements on the problem of armaments. These documents are intended to assist in the formation of Christian consciences, and the titles of several of them are revealing:
"Justice builds peace" (Bishops of Germany).
"The challenge of peace" (Bishops of the United States).
"Earning the peace" (Bishops of France).
"Disarm to build peace" (Bishops of Belgium).
"Peace in justice" (Bishops of Holland).
"The aspiration to peace" (Bishops of Japan).

(1185) All these appeals express the same concern: to awaken spirits and to assist in exercising a "catharsis" of aggressiveness, in order to learn to be more in solidarity and to love more effectively!

(1186) This means that the Catholic Church, spread all over the world, firmly desires peace; for she is convinced, as Pope Paul VI stated at the United Nations in 1965, that "against one another" we proceed to our destruction, while "with one another" we establish peace in the heart of our world.

(1187) During his pilgrimage to Hiroshima, Pope John Paul II expressed the desire that "the international community give itself a system of law that will regulate international relations and maintain peace, just as the rule of law protects national order" (n.4).

(1188) One might think that this is a kind of utopian dream. But one could also consider that it might be a first step towards effective disarmament. In any case, it would be a proof that one can still believe that in man and in his capacities to overcome and conquer his own belligerent instincts in order to place himself at the service of a "civilization of love"!

(1189) 8. In conclusion, I would like to point out that reasons for fighting will be found even in the cause of disarmament! The people of our time, and more particularly the young generations, need to feel that they are mobilized for the sake of great causes. They need to be confirmed in their reasons for living and hoping. Unity, justice, concord; the struggle against hunger, misery and underdevelopment are some of the values which surely do exist, but which risk being obfuscated by ideological confrontation and artificial divisions. For its part, the Church cannot but feel itself responsible to all men of good will - and they are legion, throughout the world - who believe that humanity is not merely a juxtaposition of individuals, and that they aspire with their whole being to form one universal family.

(1190) Disarming to live together! In this arduous task that must be constantly begun anew, the Holy See is conscious of being a voice crying out the message that the victory of disarmament is, in the final analysis, the victory of peace.

X - NUCLEAR WEAPONS

1. The consequences of the use of nuclear weapons

Letter of His Holiness John Paul II to H.E. Ismat T. Kittani, President of the 36th General Assembly of the United Nations Organization. 14 December 1981.

Original: English

(1191) For some months, public opinion throughout the world has been especially preoccupied by the problem of nuclear weapons, particularly in the countries in the possession, or the feared use, of such deadly arms. The reason for this preoccupation is that the men and women of our time are becoming ever more conscious of the terrible and catastrophic consequences connected with the use of such weapons, consequences which would unleash immense death dealing forces which are practically without escape or remedy.

(1192) To this most serious problem of our time, I have already made reference when, on 2 October 1979, it was granted to me to address the Thirty-fourth General Assembly of the United Nations Organization. On that occasion, in speaking of the frightening development of weapons which far exceed the instruments of war and destruction ever before known, I pointed out the risk involved in the possible use of so terrible a means of general destruction.

(1193) Subsequently, on the occasion of the celebration of the Thirteenth Day of Peace, 1 January 1980, I mentioned an overall forecast, given to me some time earlier by a group of scientists, of the immediate and terrible consequences of a nuclear war, with concrete reference to the immediate or delayed deaths caused by such action, the reduction of food resources, dangerous genetic mutations, alterations in the atmosphere and the destruction of all urban services.

(1194) Nor did I consider it possible to remain silent about this distressing possibility when, on 2 June of the same year, I spoke to the United Nations Educational, Scientific and Cultural Organization. On that occasion, knowing of what particular concern the problem is to many scientists, it seemed to me to be appropriate to extend to the scholars and experts in all sectors of modern science gathered there, and through them to their colleagues and friends in all countries and continents, an invitation to commit their moral authority to the saving of humanity from nuclear destruction!

(1195) In recent days, it has seemed useful to me to express my thoughts on this pressing and important question to the Heads of State of the countries which possess nuclear weapons. And given the fact that this is a problem that affects every country of the world, I also wish to express to yourself, and through you to the countries which are members of the United Nations Organization, some specific reflections in this regard. To this end, I have the honour to present to you a Delegation from the Pontifical Academy of Sciences, which will describe the results of a recently completed study on the disastrous immediate and delayed effects which a nuclear war should have on the areas affected. This very accurate study has been made by the same Academy, also assisted by other eminent figures who are not members.

(1196) It is tragically evident that any nuclear war would inevitably inflict humanity with death, disease and suffering in such proportion that there could be no effective recourse therefrom. Medical intervention would be futile. The radiation would provoke irreversible brain damage in huge sectors of the population, and genetics damage would be transmitted to any future generations that would be born after the conflagration. Should a nuclear attack be directed only at military objectives, the entire country would, nevertheless, be devastated: the combined medical facilities could not begin to meet the needs, and the whole population would be immersed in catastrophic social disruption. Food production would subsequently be paralyzed and the water supplies affected; the state of staggering confusion in society would be accompanied by the deleterious biological and geo-physical effects of the nuclear disaster. In view of these and other aspects, the only possible choice is that of total prevention. There is no other recourse conceivable. The last great epidemic of our civilization can be prevented only by putting an end to the arms race.

(1197) A thorough examination of the studies made confirms the conclusion that it is therefore impossible to ward off previously, or to limit afterwards, the disastrous effects that are foreseen as a certain result of the use of such weapons. The destruction caused would be so radical and would so seriously damage the area affected as in fact to leave no alternative to death and no escape therefrom.

(1198) The prospect of such effects reduces to relative insignificance the tragic image of the cities which I visited last February, cities which have the bitter privilege of passing into history as indissolubly liked with the destruction caused by weapons which were in fact less destructive than those available today.

(1199) It is no less worrying to see public opinion seemingly growing accustomed to the idea that the use of such murderous weaponry, previously considered to be quite unthinkable, is now becoming possible, if not probable. I am deeply convinced, and I think that you are too, that our generation has the moral duty to spare no effort to exorcise the spectre of nuclear war and to banish the temptation to yield to the idea that it is something inevitable. This duty falls in a particular way on those whose options and decisions can influence the course of history.

(1200) With deferential regard, and solely by reason of the spiritual and universal mission entrusted to me, I wish, with your help, to address to the Governments of the countries which are members of the United Nations, even if they do not possess nuclear arms, an invitation to do all in their power to smooth the path towards a future in which the probability of such a terrible hypothesis will be definitely removed.

(1201) I am sure that every Government - while having the responsibility of ensuring the defence of its own country - is animated by a sincere desire to avoid for its own people and for the entire world the horrors of nuclear war. The conviction that the same desire animates the leaders of countries in possession of such weapons prompts me to express the hope that a way may be found of encouraging them to promote joint efforts of good will for reaching a notable reduction of such armaments, with a view to their complete elimination.

(1202) This is the hope that I shall continue to express in my prayers, as I invoke the aid of Almighty God in the certainty that the same hope is shared and invoked by millions and millions of human beings throughout the world.

(1203) Trusting that you will favourably accept these reflections, I assure you of my highest consideration.

STATEMENT BY THE PONTIFICAL ACADEMY OF SCIENCES ON THE CONSEQUENCES OF THE USE OF NUCLEAR WEAPONS, attached to the Letter of the Pope to the President of the General Assembly.

Original: English

(1204) On 7-8 October 1981, under the chairmanship of Professor Carlos Chagas, President of the Pontifical Academy of Sciences, at the headquarters of the Academy (Casina Pius IV, Vatican City), a group of fourteen specialized scientists (*) from various parts of the world assembled to

---

(*) Carlos Chagas, Rio de Janeiro; E. Emaldi, Rome; N. Bochkov, Moscow; L. Caldas, Rio de Janeiro; H. Hiatt, Boston; R. Latarjet, Paris; A. Leaf, Boston; J. Lejeune, Paris; L. Leprince-Ringuet, Paris; G.B. Marini-Bettolo, Rome; C. Pavan, Sao Paulo; A. Rich, Cambridge Massachusetts; A. Serra, Rome; V. Weisskopf, Cambridge Massachusetts.

examine the problem of the consequences of the use of nuclear weapons on the survival and health of humanity.

(1205) Although most of these consequences would appear obvious, it seems that they are not adequately appreciated. The conditions of life following a nuclear attack would be so severe that the only hope for humanity is prevention of any form of nuclear war. Universal dissemination and acceptance of this knowledge would make it apparent that nuclear weapons must not be used at all in warfare and that their number should be progressively reduced in a balanced way.

(1206) The above-mentioned group discussed and unanimously approved a number of fundamental points, which have been further developed in the following statement.

(1207) Recent talks about winning or even surviving a nuclear war must reflect a failure to appreciate a medical reality: any nuclear war would inevitably cause death, disease and suffering of pandemic proportions and without the possibility of effective medical intervention. That reality leads to the same conclusion physicians have reached for life-threatening epidemics throughout history: prevention is essential for control.

(1208) In contrast to widespread belief, much is known about the catastrophe that would follow the use of nuclear weapons. Much is known too about the limitations of medical assistance. If this knowledge is presented to people and their leaders everywhere, it might help interrupt the nuclear arms race. This in turn would help prevent what could be the last epidemic our civilization will know.

(1209) The devastation wrought by an atomic weapon on Hiroshima and Nagasaki provides direct evidence of the consequences of nuclear warfare, but there are many theoretical appraisals on which we may also draw. Two years ago, an assessment undertaken by a responsible official agency described the effect of nuclear attacks on cities of about 2 million inhabitants. If a one-million ton nuclear weapon (the Hiroshima bomb approximated 15,000 tons of explosive power) exploded in the central area of such cities, it would result, as calculated, in 180 square Km. of property destruction, 250,000 fatalities and 500,000 severely injured. These would include blast injuries, such as fractures and severe lacerations of soft tissues, thermal injuries, such as surface burns, retinal burns and respiratory tract damage and radiation injuries, both acute radiation syndrome and delayed effects.

(1210) Even under optimal conditions, care of such casualties would present medical task of unimaginable magnitude. The study projected that if 18,000 hospital beds were available in and around one of these cities, no more than 5,000 would remain relatively undamaged. These would accommodate only 1% of the human beings injured, but it must be stressed that in any case no one could deliver the medical service required by even a few of the severely burned, the crushed and the radiated victims.

(1211) The hopelessness of the medical task is readily apparent if we consider what is required for the care of the severely injured patients. We shall cite one case history, that of a severely burned twenty year old man who was taken to the burn unit of a Boston Hospital after an automobile accident in which the gasoline tank exploded. During his hospitalization he received 140 litres of fresh-frozen plasma, 147 litres of fresh-frozen red blood cells, 180 millilitres of platelets and 180 millilitres of albumin. He underwent six operative procedures during which wounds involving 85% of his body surface were closed with various types of grafts, including artificial skin. Throughout his hospitalization, he required mechanical ventilation. Despite these and many other heroic measures, which stretched the resources of one of the world's most comprehensive institutions, he died on his 33rd hospital day. His injuries were likened by the doctor who supervised his care, to those described for many of the victims of Hiroshima. Had twenty score of such patients been presented at the same time to all of Boston hospitals the medical capabilities of the city would have been overwhelmed. Now, consider the situation if, along with injuries to many thousands of people, most of the medical emergency facilities had been destroyed.

(1212) A Japanese physician, Professor M. Ichimaru, published an eyewitness account of the effects of the Nagasaki bomb. He reported: "I tried to go to my medical school in Urakami which was 500 meters from the hypocenter. I met many people coming back from Urakami. Their clothes were in rags and shreds of skin hung from their bodies. They looked like ghosts with vacant stares. The next day I was able to enter Urakami on foot and all that I knew had disappeared. Only the concrete and iron skeletons of the buildings remained. There were dead bodies everywhere. On each street corner, we had tubs of water used for putting out fires after air raids. In one of these small tubs, scarcely large enough for one person, was the body of a desperate man who sought cool water. There was foam coming from his mouth, but he was not alive. I cannot get rid of the sounds of the crying women in the destroyed fields. As I got nearer to the school there were black, charred bodies with the white edges of bones showing in the arms and legs. When I arrived some were still alive. They were unable to move their bodies. The strongest were so weak that they were slumped over on the ground. I talked with them and they thought that they would be O.K. but all of them would eventually die within two weeks. I cannot forget the way their eyes looked at me and their voices spoke to me forever..."

(1213) It should be noted that the bomb dropped on Nagasaki had a power of about 20,000 tons of TNT, not much larger than the so-called "tactical bombs" designed for battlefield use.

(1214) But even these grim pictures are inadequate to describe the human disaster that would result from an attack on a country by today's stockpiles of nuclear weapons, which contain thousands of bombs with the force of one-million tons of TNT or greater.

(1215) The suffering of the surviving population would be without parallel. There would be complete interruption of communications, of food supplies and of water. Help would be given only at the risk of mortal danger from radiation for those venturing outside of buildings in the first days. The social disruption following such an attack would be unimaginable.

(1216) The exposure to large doses of radiation would lower immunity to bacteria and viruses and could, therefore, open the way for widespread infection. Radiation would cause irreversible brain damage and mental deficiency in many of the exposed in utero. It would greatly increase the incidence of many forms of cancer in survivors. Genetic damage would be passed on to future generations, should there be any.

(1217) In addition, large areas of soil and forests as well as livestock, would be contaminated reducing food resources. Many other harmful biological and even geophysical effects would be likely, but we do not have enough knowledge to predict with confidence what they would be.

(1218) Even a nuclear attack directed only at military facilities would be devastating to the country as a whole. This is because military facilities are widespread rather than concentrated at only a few points. Thus, many nuclear weapons would be exploded. Furthermore, the spread of radiation due to the natural winds and atmospheric mixing would kill vast numbers of people and contaminate large areas. The medical facilities of any nation would be inadequate to care for the survivors. An objective examination of the medical situation that would follow nuclear war leads to but one conclusion: prevention is our only recourse.

(1219) The consequences of nuclear war are not, of course, only medical in nature. But those that are compel us to pay heed to the inescapable lesson of contemporary medicine: where treatment of a given disease is ineffective or where costs are insupportable, attention must be turned to prevention. Both conditions apply to the effects of nuclear war. Treatment would be virtually impossible and the costs would be staggering. Can any stronger argument be marshalled for a preventive strategy?

(1220) Prevention of any disease requires an effective prescription. We recognize that such a prescription must both prevent nuclear war and safeguard security. Our knowledge and credentials as scientists and physicians do not, of course, permit us to discuss security issues with expertise. However, if political and military leaders have based their strategic planning on mistaken assumptions concerning medical aspects of a nuclear war, we feel that we do have a responsibility. We must inform them and people everywhere of the full-blown clinical picture that would follow a nuclear attack and of the impotence of the medical community to offer meaningful response. If we remain silent, we risk betraying ourselves and our civilization.

2. Declaration annexed to the instrument of accession to the Treaty on Non-Proliferation of Nuclear Weapons (NPT). The Vatican, 25 February 1971.

Original: French

[On 25 February 1971, the Holy See acceded to the Treaty on the Non-Proliferation of Nuclear Weapons by depositing the official instrument of adherence simultaneously with the Government of Great Britain, the Soviet Union, and the United States, which are the trustees of the Treaty.
At the same time the three representatives of the Holy See read the following additional declaration:]

(1221) 1. This accession by the Holy See to the Treaty on the Non-Proliferation of Nuclear Weapons is inspired by its constant desire, illuminated by the teaching of universal brotherhood and of justice and peace between men and peoples contained in the Gospel message, to make its contribution to undertaking which, through disarmament as well as by other means, promote security, mutual trust and peaceful cooperation in relations between peoples.

(1222) In that perspective, the Holy See judges - as is said in the official document of accession - that the aims of disarmament and detente by which the Treaty is inspired correspond to its own mission of peace, and that the Treaty, although it has its intrinsic limitations, constitutes a noteworthy step forward on the road to disarmament. In fact, in so far as the Treaty proposes to stop the dissemination of nuclear weapons - while awaiting the achievement of the cessation of the nuclear arms race and the undertaking of effective measures in the direction of complete nuclear disarmament - it has the aim of lessening the danger of terrible and total devastation which threatens all mankind, and it wishes to constitute a premise for wider agreements in the future for the promotion of a system of general and complete disarmament under effective international control.

(1223) 2. In the first place, therefore, the Holy See appreciates and shares the following considerations and intentions which the States Party to the Treaty have expressed or declared in the Preamble of the Treaty:

(1224) 1) The awareness of the devastation "that would be visited upon all mankind by a nuclear war and the consequent need to make every effort to avert the danger of such a war and to take measures to safeguard the security of peoples";

(1225) 2) The reaffirmation of the principle that "in accordance with the Charter of the United Nations, States must refrain in their international relations from the threat or use of force against the territorial integrity or political independence of any State, or in any other manner inconsistent with the Purposes of the United Nations, and that the establishment and maintenance of international peace and security are to be promoted";

(1226) 3) The intention "to achieve at the earliest possible date the cessation of the nuclear arms race and to undertake effective measures in the direction of nuclear disarmament";

(1227) 4) The intention "to further the easing of international tension and the strengthening of trust between States in order to facilitate the cessation of the manufacture of nuclear weapons, the liquidation of all their existing stockpiles, and the elimination from national arsenals of nuclear weapons and the means of their delivery pursuant to a Treaty on general and complete disarmament under strict and effective international control."

(1228) 3. The Holy See is furthermore convinced that the Treaty on the Non-Proliferation of Nuclear Weapons will be able to fully attain the noble aims of security and peace which constitute the reasons for contracting it and justify the limitations to which the States Party to the Treaty submit only if it is entirely executed in each of its clauses and with all its implications.

(1229) In the Holy See's view, that actuation concerns not only the obligations to be applied immediately but also those which envisage a process of ulterior commitments. Among the latter, the Holy See considers it suitable to point out the following:

(1230) a) The adoption of appropriate measures to ensure, on a basis of equality, that all non-nuclear-weapons States Party to the Treaty will have available to them the benefits deriving from peaceful applications of nuclear technology, in the spirit of paragraphs 4, 5, 6 and 7 of the Preamble, and in conformity with articles IV and V of the Treaty;

(1231) b) The pursuit of negotiations in good faith "on effective measures relating to cessation of the nuclear arms race at an early date and to nuclear disarmament, and on a treaty on general and complete disarmament under strict and effective international control," in accordance with the commitment foreseen in article VI.

(1232) The Holy See, therefore, expresses the sincere wish that these undertakings will be executed by all the Parties. In particular it declares its special interest and expresses its earnest desire:

(1233) 1) That the current talks between the United States of America and the Union of Soviet Socialist Republics on the limitation of strategic armaments may soon lead to a satisfactory agreement which will make possible the cessation in an effective and lasting manner of the preoccupying arms race in that costly and murderous sector of warlike preparations, both offensive and defensive;

(1234) 2) That the proposals and drafts of agreements which have been put forward for some time past by various sources, especially within the Conference of the United Nations Committee, the prohibition of bacteriological and chemical weapons and the limitation and control of conventional armaments, as well as the draft treaty on general and complete disarmament under strict and effective international control, may attain speedy and concrete results, in conformity with the repeated resolutions of the United Nations Organization and in fulfillment of the justified and anxious expectations of men and peoples of every continent.

(1235) 4. In the spirit of the considerations expressed above, which gave rise to and which accompany this accession to the Treaty, the Holy See is convinced that the attainment of the Treaty's aims of security and peace will be all the more complete and effective according as the extent of its application is the wider and more universal.

3. Statement by Msgr. Achille Silvestrini, Undersecretary of the Council for the Public Affairs of the Church, Head of the Holy See Delegation, at the first Review Conference of the Parties to the Treaty on the Non-Proliferation of Nuclear Weapons. Geneva, 8 May 1975.

Original: French

(1236) When, in February 1971, the Holy See acceded to the Non-Proliferation Treaty, it did so with the purpose of sustaining and encouraging an effort to help humanity to reduce the risks of nuclear destruction. The Treaty represented the first step in the opposite direction to that hitherto pursued towards the multiplication throughout the world of dangers of desolation and death.

(1237) For this purpose, the Holy See, as such, did not have to enter into commitments or give guarantees. It does not have and does not wish to have armies or armaments; its nature and its mission of a religious and spiritual nature place it outside competitions and rivalries between countries. So the State of Vatican City forming its tiny territory is by definition "always and on every occasion neutral and inviolable," and indeed is universally recognized as being, in its entirety a cultural possession of humanity under special protection in the case of armed conflict.

(1238) Nevertheless, the Holy See wished to give its adherence to the Treaty and then, in conformity with article III par. 1, to conclude with the IAEA the agreement extending to the State of Vatican City the controls with regard to the implementation of obligations contracted by the States that were parties to the Treaty.

(1239) Certainly, initiatives such as the NPT, important though they are, do not yet represent the solution of all the problems that endanger international peace. Everyone knows the complex and confused problems that obsess the authorities responsible for the destinies of peoples whenever they discuss control or the reduction of armaments or start projects of general and actual disarmament. Even the dismantling of the military apparatus and the reduction of conventional arms to the minimum could not ensure peace unless it coincided both with determination to suppress the causes of actual or possible conflicts - in particular,inequalities,injustice and oppression - and with the creation of an impartial and effective international authority capable of settling differences in a spirit of superior justice and fairness safeguarding the rights of all.

(1240) All this presupposes a new way of conceiving international safety, nourished by a deep and universal movement of opinion, involving all peoples and all countries. Military disarmament - Pope John XXIII said in the encyclical *Pacem in terris* - is not possible "unless the process is complete and thorough and unless it proceeds from inner conviction: unless, that is, everyone sincerely cooperates to banish the fear and anxious expectation of war with which men are oppressed." The sovereign pontiff Paul VI, addressing the United Nations assembly, during his visit on 4 October 1965, added that the new history of the world, the one that is "truly and fully human," cannot be constructed merely by political means and by the balance of forces and interests, but by a real education of mankind for peace (see above, par. 22 and 23).

(1241) The Roman Catholic Church, a community of millions of believers of all peoples, races and continents, feels her responsibility to contribute to the best of her ability to a convinced service of inspiration, education and stimulation of consciences to spread and develop a real, creative spirit of peace. For this purpose, she takes her place beside all men of goodwill, even though of different faith and convictions, who are endeavouring to obtain for the world a supreme boon that hundreds of millions of human beings of all languages and countries - particularly those who have known the terrible destruction of war - desire and implore.

(1242) Certainly, the universal aspiration of humanity for peace is fully shared by all the delegations of the countries represented here. Nevertheless, I am not presumptuous in considering that it falls precisely to the Holy See, by virtue of its character and its mission, to give particular and emphatic attention to the expectations and wishes that men in general, that all persons eager for peace, address to the representatives of the States with regard to nuclear proliferation. By doing so, the Holy See is aware that it is in harmony with the thought of other Churches and religious communities, even non-Christian ones, and of humanitarian groups and non-governmental organizations - some of which are present here as observers - which have undertaken the difficult and noble work of education to, and promotion of, peace. The expectations, the wishes of public opinion, of the man in the street, concern, of course, the elementary substance of the Treaty, its fundamental political significance, its power of attraction and dynamic action as a possible and desired instrument of safety and peace.

(1243) 1. The man in the street, warned by alarming forecasts of possible atomic destruction, is certainly convinced that it is in the interest of the international community to prevent a wider diffusion of nuclear arms. The fewer the possibilities, the fewer are the dangers. That is the persuasive value of the commitments set in motion by the Treaty which, it must be recognized, represents one of the most important acts recorded in the field of disarmament during these thirty post-war years. The Treaty has obtained ratification by 91 countries and the signature of 17 others. That is an important result. What would be the world situation if the Treaty did not exist? Certainly it would be far more uncertain and dangerous.

(1244) But the object and the purpose of the Treaty require, by their very nature, if not universality - the optimum condition - at least the widest and most complete adherence. Our Conference has, consequently, the duty of increasing the credibility and the persuasive force of the Treaty with regard to the countries that are to ratify it and, with all the more reason, with regard to those whose adherence is desired. That is, above all, the result that everyone claims from our assembly.

(1245) 2. This credibility is strengthened, in the first place, by making the relationship between the Parties to the Treaty easier and more satisfactory. An association is valid and lasting only if it corresponds fairly to the expectations of all those who belong to it. The many considered criticisms expressed in this connection, are shared by wide sectors of public opinion. The Treaty, it is true, came into being by recognizing a situation of disparity that already existed in the world, between countries in possession of atomic weapons and countries not provided with them, and it did not take as its direct and immediate aim to eliminate this disparity. But it is true, nevertheless, that article VI urges nuclear countries "to pursue in good faith negotiations on effective measures regarding the cessation of the nuclear arms race in the near future, and nuclear disarmament, and on a general and complete disarmament treaty, under strict and effective international control."

(1246) No one, of course, cherished the illusion that a programme of this scope could be carried out easily and rapidly. But few people thought that, in spite of the negotiations established and certain results obtained, vertical proliferation would continue to increase, reaching the terrifying levels that we are forced to recognize five years after the Treaty came into force. While not underestimating the partial agreements of the SALT negotiations, it is seen that the initial proportion between horizontal proliferation and vertical proliferation has been changed, in fact, with an imbalance in favour of the latter. That is the most critical point of the reliability of the Treaty, and it disconcerts and disturbs those people who implore from the nuclear powers a gesture of political goodwill capable of stopping the armaments race really and effectively.

(1247) 3. The 1965 resolution of the United Nations recommended that the Treaty should establish "an acceptable balance of mutual responsibilities and obligations" between the nuclear and the non-nuclear powers. This balance concerns, in the first place, the guarantees that can be asked, for their own safety, by non-nuclear States who have accepted the obligations of the Treaty. But it also regards, more generally, all the problems brought into the life of mankind by the possibilities of utilizing atomic energy.

(1248) The ordinary citizen, even when completely devoid of scientific knowledge, is aware of the formidable ambivalence, for good and for evil, that the exploitation of nuclear energy represents. He invokes the ban on nuclear arms, but does not readily agree, particularly at a moment when the search for new sources of energy is becoming a matter of greater concern, to his country being subject to limits and subordinations, in actual fact, as regards the range of possibilities that science and technique are making more and more accessible and feasible for civil life. This is a delicate point that different delegations have stressed with understandable concern and justified remarks, and which will certainly call for a high degree of fair-mindedness and cooperation. But what problem, in international life today, could do without the latter? In spite of disparities and divisions, humanity is one, more and more bound to the same fate. So cooperation is the only way leading to the safeguarding and strengthening of peace.

(1249) A Treaty is always something limited and questionable, for even in the best hypotheses, it represents a compromise between different demands and interests. Now the NPT is a treaty that has been greatly discussed and is subject to different appreciations. The fact remains, however, that a treaty lends itself to being constantly improved and perfected in its application. It is perhaps easier to improve it than to negotiate it.

(1250) To improve the implementation of the Treaty is tantamount to increasing its force of attraction and persuasion and, consequently, its significance as regards detente and peace. When, in 1971, the Holy See gave its adherence to the Treaty, it declared that it was convinced that this pact could "fully attain the noble aims of security and peace" provided it was "entirely executed in each of its clauses and in all its implications". (See above, par. 1228). Four years afterwards, the Holy See is even more convinced that the acceptability of the Treaty as an instrument of safety and peace depends on the political will of all the parties, on their clear-sightedness and wisdom, in order that the Treaty may fully develop the positive potential of all its clauses and of its full significance.

(1251) This is the wish that the Holy See delegation addresses to this Conference. May the hopes and expectations of millions of peace-loving men find in our work confirmation, comfort and encouragement!

4. Statement by Msgr. Audrys J. Backis, Undersecretary of the Council for the Public Affairs of the Church, head of the Delegation of the Holy See, at the Second Review Conference of the Parties to the Treaty on the Non-Proliferation of Nuclear Weapons. Geneva, 13 August 1980.

Original: French

(1252) The presence of the Holy See within these precincts might perhaps astonish the representatives of countries which have only recently given their adherence to the Treaty on the Non-Proliferation of Nuclear Weapons, the examination of which is the object of our Conference. So it is not superfluous to recall that its participation has as its only cause the interest it takes in peace, and therefore in disarmament.

(1253) The Holy See, in fact, is not a "Power" similar to the ones that are gathered here through their representatives: it does not possess technological potential, far less, armaments. But, owing to its conception of man and its spiritual responsibilities with regard to him, it esteems peace, it educates toward peace, it loves peace.

(1254) That is why the Holy See does not try to shirk its responsibilities within the international community, and does not hesitate to commit its moral and spiritual authority to the building of peace, to which the whole of mankind aspires. In this spirit, the Holy See adhered in 1971 to the Treaty on Non-Proliferation; it declared it wished in this way to give its support and bring its moral encouragement to the provisions of the Treaty, "considering that the latter constitutes a considerable step forward towards the desired creation of a system of general and complete disarmament under effective international control," as its instrument of adherence to the Treaty affirmed, for it judged that "the aims of *disarmament* and *international detente* by which the Treaty is inspired, correspond to its own mission of peace" (*ibid.* See above, par. 1222). Today still, disarmament and international detente continue to be at the centre of its concerns.

(1255) If the Holy See was of the opinion that the Treaty on Non-Proliferation represented, on the occasion of its conclusion, a concrete effort of mankind to reduce the risks of nuclear destruction that threaten it, it still reaffirms, ten years after its coming into force, the hope that this Treaty may be consolidated and serve the cause of disarmament more effectively.

(1256) The danger of a nuclear war continues, in fact, to weigh on humanity. While duly appreciating the initiatives taken by the great nuclear powers to limit their quantitative escalation in the area of nuclear armament, it must be recognized that such a high level has been reached in this field that we find ourselves, in fact, up against a "balance of terror," which is an ever present threat.

(1257) For we cannot cherish illusions or accept easily tranquillizing information. The present balance is a frail one, and world peace remains at the mercy of errors of judgement, information, or interpretation, as Pope John Paul II affirmed recently at the tribune of UNESCO. That is why he raised his voice to remind men of culture and of science, and through them also all those who are aware of the situation and of what is at stake, that they have a prime moral responsibility in this field, that they must convince themselves of the priority of ethics over technique, of the primacy of the person over things, of the superiority of spirit over matter (cf. Address to UNESCO, nos. 21 and 22. See above, par. 183-188). It is in such an ethical perspective that it is opportune, in the judgment of the Holy See, not to lose sight of article VI of the Treaty, which makes it binding on the Parties, and in the first place on the powers endowed with nuclear arms, "to pursue in good faith negotiations on effective measures regarding the cessation of the nuclear arms race in the near future, and nuclear disarmament, and on a general and complete disarmament treaty, under strict and effective international control."

(1258) The first step in this process could be the undertaking, on the part of those who possess nuclear arms, to put a definitive end to their *vertical proliferation.* Such an undertaking would constitute a solid foundation for all further progress in disarmament. Would that not be a tangible proof that those who bear the highest responsibilities with regard to peace, have wished to take into account the warnings long launched by eminent persons, and again recently by Pope John Paul II in his Encyclical *Redemptor Hominis* (cf. n. 15) and in his address to the General Assembly of the United Nations (cf. n. 10). Would not a new hope be created in this way for the peoples of this world who rightly perceive the danger that lies in the stocking of nuclear arms, and who are haunted by the spectre of the destruction that such armaments, used even in a limited way, would bring upon humanity, upon so many innocent beings?

(1259) The Holy See is certainly clearly aware of the difficulties to be overcome, and of the fact that negotiations such as the discussions in progress are inseparably linked with negotiations that take place outside these precincts, with the nuclear powers as promoters, and also of the fact that these negotiations progress only very slowly. They must not, however, cause the set goal to be forgotten.

(1260) To the principal peril of a conflict between the great nuclear powers there is added also the danger springing from *horizontal proliferation*, facilitated all the more by scientific and technological progress, and by the fact that it is becoming more and more difficult to establish an adequate distinction between the nuclear experiments carried out for peaceful purposes and others. This problem is taking on new dimensions owing to the more and more extensive use of nuclear energy, with all the risks that this fact entails of the diversion of nuclear material and of specialized knowledge in this field for non-peaceful purposes. So we cannot but encourage all measures of control, already existing or still to be created or perfected, with regard to the transfer of nuclear technology as well as in the field of the processing, sale, or transport of nuclear fuel.

(1261) However, if it is indispensable to find sufficiently reliable solutions, with effective guarantees under international control, to avoid any diversion of nuclear material for military purposes, the thorny problem of *the peaceful use of nuclear energy* cannot be forgotten, however, nor can the means "for giving all peoples access to the immense resources of nuclear energy for peaceful use" be neglected (Paul VI, Message to the extraordinary Session of the U.N. on disarmament. See above, par. 997). The role that IAEA plays in this field cannot be overlooked: its initiatives deserve to be encouraged and supported.

(1262) The clauses contained in the Treaty on Non-Proliferation are very useful at this point. In fact, it clearly calls upon the signatories to share the benefits deriving from the peaceful use of nuclear energy with all peoples and all nations. This sharing is demanded by the sense of fairness understood by the Treaty when it calls upon those who possess nuclear resources and the specialized knowledge connected with them, to share them with all those who can put forward a legitimate right. This must be carried out, therefore, without obliging the beneficiaries to accept conditions that would actually constitute real exploitation, and without forcing them either to pay a cost that they could not afford. The great advantage of this Treaty, furthermore, is that it sets out to make impossible all use of nuclear energy that is not controlled or that is irresponsible. It would be contrary to this purpose, or even to the sense of international justice, if its aim of controlling nuclear energy were diverted in favour of the consolidation of the power of some at the expense of the legitimate needs of the majority.

(1263) The Holy See reaffirms, moreover, that the solution of the serious problems I have just recalled, depends on the climate of international relations, and it also repeats its conviction that the Treaty on non-proliferation can serve the promotion of what is called international detente, it being understood, as Pope Paul VI recalled, that the latter must be understood in its true sense, "that is to say, founded upon a proven willingness to exercise mutual respect" (Message to the extraordinary Session of the United Nations on disarmament. See above, par. 990). Noting, in fact, that "the problem of disarmament is substantially *a problem of mutual trust*," he rightly concluded that "it would therefore be largely useless to seek possible solutions of the technical aspects of disarmament if one were to fail to cure at its source the situation that serves as fertile soil for the proliferation or armaments." (*ibid.* See above, par. 986). That is why, he affirmed, detente "is a condition for setting in motion a true process of disarmament" (*ibid.* See above, par. 990).

(1264) This analysis links up with that of Pope John Paul II before UNESCO, in which he sees the instability of the present international situation connected with not only geo-political reasons and world-wide economic problems, but also with terrible incomprehension and wounded national pride (cf.Address to UNESCO, n. 21. See above, par. 183-184).

(1265) The first step to take certainly consists, therefore, in seeking, with good faith and good will, to improve the atmosphere and the reality of international relations, especially between the great powers and blocs of States.

(1266) Making its own the concerns and the anguish of so many men who aspire to peace, the Holy See, without ever losing sight of the ultimate aim of general and complete disarmament under international control, encourages all efforts undertaken to improve the application of the Treaty, and to help to increase its credibility in the eyes of world public opinion.

(1267) With satisfaction, it sees that the number of the Parties has gone up to 114, and it hopes to see still more States adhere to it, primarily all nuclear powers or those with the capacity of becoming nuclear powers, in order that the Treaty may become a more and more convincing instrument, capable of attaining the noble aims it has set for itself.

(1268) The Holy See therefore renews the hope that the commitments undertaken will be fully respected, and finally it formulates the wish that concrete progress may be realized in the implementation of the Treaty, in an effort of political understanding and will, in order to reconcile the interests that set against each other the States provided with nuclear arms and the countries that lack them or that have renounced them, in such a way as to find, as the final Declaration of the first Conference of the Parties asked in 1975, "an acceptable balance of mutual responsibilities and obligations."

(1269) In spite of the difficulties, this wish is shared by all the Representatives of the different Parties, as the Holy See Delegation is aware: it assures them of all its support in order that the result of their efforts may correspond to the expectation that all men who seek to promote peace place in them.

5. Statement by Msgr. Audrys J. Backis, Undersecretary of the Council for Public Affairs of the Church, Head of the Delegation of the Holy See, at the 3rd Review Conference of the Parties to the Treaty on the Non Proliferation of Nuclear Weapons. Geneva, 30 August 1985.

Original: French

(1270) 1. It is the third time that the States party to the Non-Proliferation Treaty have gathered to review its content and its accomplishments. Certainly positive results which may come from this effort will reflect the commitment of all the participating States, but also will be evidence of the skill and dedication which you and your colleagues bring to this undertaking.

(1271) The participation of the Holy See in this Conference springs from the same desire and convictions which lay at the base of its adherence to the Treaty in 1971. Above all, as a religious and moral authority, the Holy See wishes to bring its own contribution to those initiatives which will promote freedom, security, mutual confidence among nations and that harmonious cooperation which leads to a peaceful world (cf. Additional Note: *L'Osservatore Romano*, 26 February 1971, p.1. See above, par. 1221-1235). Such a commitment takes expression in the activities of the Holy See in various international agencies and meetings. It is exemplified also in the pastoral visits of His Holiness Pope John Paul II to various parts of the world and in his many messages to Heads of State and to special assemblies such as the Second Special Session of the United Nations General Assembly on Disarmament in 1982.

(1272) In all these initiatives, the Holy See is never a party to any particular political bloc. Its voice is a voice devoid of partisan interests. Instead its intention is to use this and every other similar forum to help nations and peoples reflect more deeply on the moral implications of political choices in order to try to place them in the wider context of the wellbeing of individuals and the good of humanity. The observance of the Non-Proliferation Treaty is undoubtedly a moral issue as it is aimed at securing world peace through nuclear disarmament. Therefore, the words which I address to you today are meant to contribute to the cause of peace, which is a supreme good for humanity (cf. John Paul II, Message to the Second Special Session of the United Nations General Assembly on Disarmament: 11 June 1982, n. 13. See above, par. 1067-1076).

(1273) 2. Without deluding ourselves with a false optimism, we can point out certain signs of limited but real progress since the Second Review Conference. The two "superpowers" have reopened their negotiations and have had two sessions in Geneva covering three aspects of nuclear weapons and defence strategies, with a third session already scheduled. More States have accepted and utilized the safeguards that the International Atomic Energy Agency had been developing, and made more precise. It is a fact that, while the capability to produce nuclear weapons is shared by more nations, no new nation, to the best of our knowledge, has actually produced and tested nuclear weapons since the Second Review Conference. Furthermore, the peaceful uses of nuclear energy and nuclear technology have been applied to food production, water resource development, advances in medicine, biology and physics as well as in the promotion of nuclear safety. All these advances are to be praised and, to the extent possible, continued and expanded since they can lead to a more equitable sharing of resources and a greater assurance of the welfare and safety of humanity.

(1274) 3. As we reflect on the experience of the past fifteen years of the Non-Proliferation Treaty, especially within the context of the forty years of research and development of modern arms systems and strategies, all of us can recognize the extent to which our perceptions of each other and attitudes towards each other have affected the decisions which have been made and the programmes which have been carried out. Because the preconceived ideas we have in approaching each other are so decisive for the outcome of any negotiation, it is the earnest wish of this Delegation that all of us might re-examine our own perceptions and attitudes. I say this so that we do not become tied down to biases which may hinder dialogue, or allow ourselves, in the name of "realism", to be satisfied with little or no progress in our efforts. Such a re-examination can create the context for a clear deliberation aimed at furthering the good effects of the Non-Proliferation Treaty and giving new incentive to other elements which need to be reconsidered. If we share the conviction that peace is possible, the first step towards its implementation is to deepen mutual trust.

(1275) 4. We all recognize the importance of treaties as the means for nations to come to terms with their mutual commitments, to strengthen the rule of law and to facilitate peaceful negotiations. Clearly, this Treaty was born in its own time and reflects a number of viewpoints which did not completely coincide during the drafting of the document. Yet what matters is that the good accomplished by the Treaty be confirmed and that its potential be realized in those ways which are diplomatically and politically possible. The world has indeed changed in the past fifteen years, but the same basic components which originally justified this Treaty still exist. The number of countries which possess nuclear arms remains the same, while no new countries in recent times have exploded nuclear devices. The need is still great for the proper development of nuclear resources for peaceful purposes,while the challenge is constant for the realization of ever more effective safeguards. These elements are aided by the fact that this Treaty has addressed the relevant problems and has foreseen that its good results be furthered and its benefits extended. My Delegation would therefore invite the States which have not yet adhered to the Treaty to consider doing so in the future.

(1276) 5. Our meeting here, while a sign of our conviction that this Treaty has contributed to the common good, is likewise a time for honest evaluation of what can be improved and what has not yet been done. Therefore the Delegation of the Holy See would like to call the attention of this Assembly to the three points which deserve a clear statement of purpose and resolve, in order that the potential of this Treaty may be better realized.

(1277) a) The first point refers to Article VI and the question of vertical proliferation. Statistics and facts in their basic configuration are already known. The arguments have been made. Whether it be through negotiations in Geneva or elsewhere, through the development of more effective crisis management, or through other multilateral, bilateral or even unilateral efforts, there must be a reversal to the trend of vertical proliferation. We feel there is a moral link between the limitation of horizontal proliferation and the reversal of vertical proliferation. The nations in possession of nuclear power have the duty to fulfil their responsibilities as enunciated in Article VI of the Treaty. Without presuming to give suggestions of a technical order - which is outside the role of the Holy See - it must be remembered that there are many more weapons and weapons systems than are needed to ensure the security of all nations. Public opinion is aware of this fact and has already made its desire known and its position clear. The people want a reversal of the arms race. In this circumstance, this Delegation reiterates the appeal of His Holiness Pope John Paul II to reverse the current trend in the arms race. This reversal, he said, "involves a parallel struggle on two fronts: on the one hand an immediate and urgent struggle by governments to reduce progressively and equally their armaments; on the other hand, a more patient but nonetheless necessary struggle at the level of the consciences of people to take their responsibility in regard to the ethical cause of the insecurity that breeds violence by coming to grips with the material and spiritual inequalities of our world" (John Paul II, Message to the Second Special Session of the United Nations General Assembly on Disarmament, 11 June 1982, n. 13. See above, par. 1067).

(1278) b) The second point that must be examined at this meeting concerns one of the basic declarations of this Treaty. It is the sharing of the benefits of nuclear technology for peaceful purposes. In this regard, the body of the Treaty, as well as Articles IV and V, provide a clear statement of intent and commitment. It is true that much has already been done. Those nations which have made advances in nuclear technology and in turn have entered into agreements with other nations in the application of these advances deserve our appreciation and esteem. However, is it not possible to admit that more can be done in this area? Nations must be careful in assessing when and where nuclear technology should be applied. It should never be desired only for reasons of prestige. Help in the area of development and transfer of technology could include access to nuclear energy in order to secure legitimate economic interests of non-nuclear countries.

(1279) c) A final point is directed to the non-nuclear nations. Article VII concerns the possibilities of regional treaties to ensure the total absence of nuclear weapons in a region or area. The Tlatelolco Treaty is a significant beginning. Recently some nations in the South Pacific have worked together in this regard. However, simple declarations of intention are not enough. It is incumbent upon all nations to translate their own convictions into specific commitments. Such agreements gave a progressive effect and provide an interlocking set of treaties which can help to guarantee a more peaceful and secure world, taking into account the existing balance of forces and the needs of universal security.

(1280) 6. A few weeks ago, the whole world recalled the Fortieth Anniversary of the atomic explosions on Hiroshima and Nagasaki. In a special radio message to the people of Japan on 6 August, His Holiness Pope John Paul II stated: "Hiroshima is a living witness of what can happen but need not and should never happen ... What is needed is a serious and comprehensive education for peace and a committed response to the inequalities and injustices rampant in our world. If each individual, group and nation is willing, honestly and sincerely, to follow this path, there will never be another Hiroshima" (*L'Osservatore Romano*, 7 August 1985, p. 6). The sentiments expressed by His Holiness are similar to the ones which compelled the nations of the world, in the aftermath of the Second World War, to found the United Nations in June 1945. These two anniversaries can become an incentive for us to renew our efforts and to encourage one another in our attempts to make this Treaty an ever more effective instrument to promote security of nations and peace in the world.

(1281) Those of us who believe with all our hearts that peace is ultimately a gift from God know that here on earth we must strive for that promised goal. With confidence in Almighty God, with firm trust in the capabilities of people of good will to work together, and with a strong desire to see this Treaty promote peace in the next ten years and beyond, this Delegation of the Holy See commends all its distinguished colleagues for the work being accomplished here and encourages all leaders and nations to find the means that will further the good and noble aims of this Treaty "until the hearts of all are won over to those ethical choices which will guarantee a lasting peace" (John Paul II, Message to the Second Special Session of the United Nations General Assembly on Disarmament, 11 June 1982, n. 5. See above, par. 1046).

XI - PEACEFUL USE OF ATOMIC ENERGY

1. Statement by Msgr. Mario Peressin, Head of the Delegation, at 24th Regular Session of the General Conference of the International Atomic Energy Agency (IAEA). Vienna, 24 September 1980.

Original: English

(1282) 1. My Delegation has studied with great care both the materials and publications of the Agency during this past year and the documents which have been prepared for this XXIV General Conference of the International Atomic Energy Agency. Moreover, it has considered seriously the many points made in the report of the able Director, Dr. Sigvard Eklund. It has also taken note of the many interesting statements and propositions made so far in the course of the General Debate. Having reflected on all this material, this Delegation of the Holy See would like to offer some points for consideration to all the distinguished representatives gathered here. These thoughts are based on the work of this Agency, but they stem from the anthropological and social principles which are inspired by our faith, and which have been expressed by His Holiness Pope John Paul II in his addresses to the United Nations Organization on 2 October 1979 and to UNESCO on 2 June of this year.

(1283) 2. In a world increasingly more complex and with exigencies that demand a scientific and technical expertise and that stagger the minds and imaginations of most persons, men and women of science and those who hold political positions of responsibility must be ever more sensitive to the impact which scientific advance and political decisions have on the lives of citizens in this world. There are many forces that can be used, and at times have been used, to reduce the human person, to control whole peoples and to bring about a sense of alienation of man from his true meaning through various manipulations (cf. Address to UNESCO, no.13. See above, par. 169-171). We know that this possibility is not absent from the object of our concern here. It is, therefore, incumbent upon all of us who share this responsibility or who have this expertise to be self-critically conscious of the roles we play and the goals we set for this important element in human life. Pope John Paul addressed this quite succinctly in his Address to UNESCO when he pointed out: "We are well aware, ladies and gentlemen, that the future of man and of the world is threatened - very seriously threatened - despite the unquestionably lofty intentions of scholars and scientists... Whereas science ought to be used for the good of human life, we find only too often that it is subjected to purposes destructive of the true dignity of man and of human life." (Address to UNESCO, no.21. See above, par. 183).

(1284) The spectre of past abuses of science haunts people today. The potential for misuse of scientific advances for purposes of production or greater sophistication of nuclear weapons adds to the apprehension that many people feel. Conscious of this, all of us gathered here have the task first of guaranteeing that the material we deal with is actually employed solely and exclusively for the benefit of mankind. We also have the task of informing people truthfully and honestly of the meaning, purposes, and implications of the choices which come from an Assembly such as this.

(1285) 3. In regard to the first problem, of avoiding misuse and abuse of the power we have, it is incumbent on this Delegation to remind everyone here, as we have done in the past, that the threat of nuclear destruction through the use of nuclear warheads is a grave situation that is contrary to the well-being of humanity. Pope John Paul II, in the above-mentioned address to UNESCO, posed the question whether today we can be sure that the upsetting of the delicate balance upon which international relationships rest "would not lead to war, and to a war in which nuclear weapons would be used without hesitation." And he added: "Nuclear weapons, whatever their scale or type, are becoming more sophisticated year by year, and are being added to the arsenals of an ever-increasing number of countries. How can we be sure that the use of nuclear weapons, even for purposes of national defence or in limited conflicts, will not bring about an unavoidable escalation leading to destruction on a scale which mankind can never either contemplate or accept?" (no.21. See above, par. 184).

(1286) Unfortunately, the current political situation does not give reassurance in the realm of progress towards nuclear disarmament. Unfortunately, the plea for a systematic and mutual reduction in armaments in the name of humanity made by the Pope on 1 January of this year (cf. Homily for World Day of Peace), a plea echoed by religious leaders and religious groups all over the globe, has not alerted those responsible to a degree sufficient to reassure a world that has justified reservations about the current situation.

(1287) 4. In that atmosphere, our responsibility here is a grave one. The peaceful use of nuclear energy, if it is to be rightfully employed, must clearly be separate from, and be seen as separate from, the use of nuclear materials for destruction. The work and the commitment of everyone here must be as scientists and statesmen dedicated to a science "in the service of man's life." To that end, I would like to bring to your attention a twofold consideration, one a vision and the other a means.

(1288) The vision I speak of is in fact a guiding principle for our actions and decisions. It calls, in some cases, for a conversion of outlook and of mentality. It is to find the grounds and develop the attitudes which reflect hope, *hope for mankind, hope for this earth, hope for the future*. Pope John Paul has spoken of hope, saying: "Hope is not a wish. It is not a vague sentiment. It is a category born of our experience of history and nourished by our common desires for the future...It is a future to be built by united efforts to secure the common good through mutual cooperation and collaboration" (Message to the 11th Special Session of the United Nations, no. 6. See below, par. 1405). The kind of hope the Pope speaks of is not naive. It does not ignore the fact that there are tremendous problems and difficulties that must be faced. But it does say that we must share as peoples and nations on this small planet a common outlook and attitude that looks to the defence of humanity, that seeks to build necessary structures,that is willing to work together for the common good of all, while giving up the selfish short-term interest of a few.

(1289) To that positive vision of hope for the common good must be linked the *political will* to bring this about. Political will is the central means to achieve this. In many international forums, and for some years through the work and research of this Agency, we have come to know what are the problems we face and what solutions are available. The key to unlocking the door towards progress is the political will that only those responsible in their respective nations can bring about. If we here seek to provide for a better future for all people on this earth, then we can do it only to the extent that we realistically commit ourselves to setting in motion the structures that respond to the political will of leaders and nations.

(1290) 5. At the recent Conference held in Geneva to review the Non-Proliferation Treaty, the representative of the Holy See called attention to this Agency and the important role it plays. He repeated that the initiatives of this Agency merit encouragement and application (cf. Statement by the Holy See Delegation, in *L'Osservatore Romano*, 20 August 1980. See above, par. 1261). This position is one the Holy See has held for some time and today this Delegation wishes to reassert this. The more this Agency deepens our knowledge of how nuclear materials can be applied for the good of peoples, the more this Agency is a service in making beneficial options available to those who need and want them, the more it will contribute to the strengthening of the forces of life for the well-being of all. The world cannot renounce the atom. But it must ensure that it be used for the good of all. This Delegation wishes to commend those programmes of the Agency that do just that. The possibility of food conservation through radiology as a means to protect the harvest, the various breakthroughs in medicine, genetic research, the programme touching marine biology and marine life today, all these and so many others should be the source of a sense of pride and accomplishment on the part of this Agency.

(1291) All these programmes, however, must always be carried on with a sense of equity and availability to all member States according to their true need, and not merely their power and influence. This Agency and its member States are committed to the principle of equity by the Charter of the IAEA and by the Non-Proliferation Treaty. The well-being of present and future generations in industrialized countries cannot be had at the cost of the well-being of the present and future generations in the developing countries. The Agency can do much in this direction by keeping those responsible informed of what is available and aiding those with fewer resources to use this information for planning their own futures in a reasonable and appropriate way.

(1292) 6. This year the International Nuclear Fuel Cycle Evaluation (INFCE) completed its three years of work. The Agency was an indispensable part of all those studies that culminated in the volumes that have been produced. For experts and for political leaders these reports hopefully will show means of strengthening the "assurance of nuclear supply while minimizing the risk of the proliferation of nuclear weapons" (Bulletin of the IAEA, vol. 22, no. 2, p. 32). Would it be possible for the Agency to simplify some of that and similar material and begin a programme that will make solid and real information more readily available to a public that needs to know? The Agency has prepared a number of fine documents about safety and about preparedness in case of emergencies or accidents. Would these not be helpful as a means of deepening the understanding of a public that wants to know? One of these documents (Document SG-G6 IAEA "Preparedness of Public Authorities for Emergencies at Nuclear Power Plants," p.34) calls for the informing of the public of the arrangements that have been made for their safety... "at public meetings, meetings between the operating organization and representatives of local authorities." It has been a constant position of this Delegation that a well-informed public is a necessity and that together we have an obligation and responsibility to contribute to sound, well-presented, understandable information at the proper levels for people everywhere.

(1293) 7. Two years ago in a message to the Special Session of the United Nations on Disarmament, Pope Paul VI linked together three major problems. He said: "Disarmament, a new world order, and development are three obligations that are inseparably bound together and that by their essence presuppose a renewal of public outlook" (No. 8. See above, par. 1004).

(1294) These words could easily have been addressed to this body today. All three of these concerns touch our work. All three of them demand renewed effort on our part. The Agency must stand for disarmament and it must cooperate in every effort to end the threat of nuclear warfare. The Agency must collaborate with others towards a new world order by ensuring that the advances of this sector of science and technology are made available in appropriate ways, with equity and without consumer self-interest, to all peoples and nations according to rightful need. And in this way, the Agency will find itself committed to development, a development of all peoples, a development of all nations, a development that "will build the common future of the human race and construct the great and lasting edifice of peace." (John Paul II, Message to the 11th Special Session of the United Nations, no. 9. See below, par. 1420).

2. Statement by Msgr. Mario Peressin, Head of the delegation of the Holy See at the 25th Regular Session of the Conference of the International Atomic Energy Agency. Vienna, 5 October 1981.

Original: English

(1295) The Conference is being held at a time when humanity is asking ever more searching questions about the value, significance and use of atomic energy, and its consequences, not only for the present time but also for the generations to come.

(1296) Twentieth-century man has succeeded in producing atomic energy, and in his hands he now has the great but frightening power of either improving the world he lives in or of destroying the whole of humanity. Man has greater power than ever before over the forces of nature; will he be able to control that very power, or will he be dominated by it as by some sort of demonic force? This is the fundamental question that many people are asking today.

(1297) The Annual Report of the IAEA for 1980 indicates that the total installed nuclear capacity in the world increased by about 11 per cent (cf. The Annual Report for 1980. p.17). This development in the exploitation and various applications of nuclear energy has been greeted by some as a great step forward; others however do not agree. The uncertainties and doubts and even the open hostility manifested in certain quarters have forced some governments to cut down, to suspend or at least to slow down the expansion of nuclear power plants.

(1298) The use of nuclear energy, even for beneficial purposes alone, is not immune from certain doubts stemming from the very nature of this energy. In addition, the debate is rendered even more complex by elements of interpretation that not only differ but also diverge. Some people, on the basis especially of ecological considerations, would like to bring nuclear technology into the general process of modern science and technology. Others ask whether it is really a good thing that man should use all the possibilities that science reveals to him; they wonder whether it would not be better, in order to safeguard higher ethical and humanistic values, to renounce the use of these possibilities, either outright or at least until there has been a complete clarification of all their effects and consequences.

(1299) The debate about nuclear energy perhaps shows more acutely than any other areas of debate the uncertainty and in some cases the bewilderment of a society that is scientifically and technologically advanced, but which is not sure what criteria to adopt and what use to make of its knowledge, discoveries and power.

(1300) Since the present questions are so complex, the present debate demands to be tackled on a worldwide scale, on the basis of rigorous scientific research, with alert awareness of the human values involved, and with responsible political orientation.

(1301) The debate likewise calls for an attitude inspired by complete truthfulness. While argumentation has to go beyond mere emotionalism and preconceived ideas, it will also be necessary to avoid one-sided or partial information. It will be especially necessary to make it impossible for the debate to be manipulated for the advantage of particular interests, whether economic or political. It may be thought ingenuous or simplistic to invoke truthfulness in a debate where great vested interests are involved. But one must also realize that, without this objectivity, and without ordinary people really taking part and being accurately informed, one cannot expect people to give their consent, and still less to offer that solidarity needed for the carrying out of options as important and full of consequences as the development of nuclear energy.

(1302) The more one reflects on the information that the Agency has given to us, the more convincing is the argument that the search must continue, the scientific exchange must go on, the advance in our mutual knowledge about the uses, the safety, the capacity of nuclear fuel must be continued. This commitment to continued scientific and technological research obviously is not isolated from the practical realities of political choices and economic considerations. But it is important to stress that one of the great aims of this Agency is to foster that research and to encourage the commitment of talents which will open up not only new capabilities, but which will promote greater safety and sounder understanding of this enormous power that our choices must guarantee will protect and further the good of all.

(1303) Here this Delegation would like to cite and commend the many conferences, scientific and practical, which the IAEA either sponsors or in which it participates to further the advance of this knowledge.

(1304) Of particular interest and importance will be the International Conference of Nuclear Power Experience to be held next year. The Delegation of the Holy See expresses its hope that the Conference will be carefully prepared, with the effective collaboration of scientists, technologists and experts, and also of the leaders of the international community.

(1305) This Agency is called upon to play a part, and an important one, in the present debate on nuclear energy. Through its many programmes, through the activities of its scientific experts, through its setting of standards and enforcement of safeguards, it contributes in so many ways to ensuring that nuclear energy is placed at the service of humanity and of the international community in ways that are peaceful and safe and that promote human well-being.

(1306) This activity will be seen to be of capital and decisive importance for the good of humanity, for the service of the developing countries and for the establishment of an international security system, if the IAEA can convince the international community and public opinion that it has the competence, capacity and means of conducting, developing and controlling the safe, beneficent and peaceful use of nuclear energy.

(1307) Together with other Institutions, the IAEA has drawn up and is carrying forward, in this field, a programme aimed at ensuring that the exploitation and application of nuclear energy does not involve unacceptable risks. In this regard, may I be permitted to state that the notion of risk is to be understood in reference, in the first place and essentially, to man and his environment. This principle, which is self-evident and concerning which there is an ever growing awareness, must constantly be borne in mind in all nuclear choices and activities, and must prevail over all other considerations of the purely economic, industrial and political order.

(1308) The priority given to the human being will, as a logical consequence, ensure the best possible protection, and will likewise favour the constant raising of the standard of professional qualification of those working in this sector. For human life is in itself and per se a good of such value that it cannot be compared or put on the same level with economic interests or advantages, however noteworthy. Human life is of incalculable greatness and cannot be treated in monetary terms.

(1309) The effectiveness of the system of safeguards deserves particular consideration. We have been witnesses, this year, to a singular attack made by one country on the nuclear power installations of another, on the grounds that this other State was developing - in contravention of international obligations undertaken - nuclear facilities for the building of an atomic bomb. Such an event is apt to put in jeopardy the function of the International Atomic Energy Agency as the supervisory institution under the NonProliferation Treaty of 1968. The Agency has the responsibility of clearly establishing that the nuclear power plants constructed in the various countries for the peaceful use of atomic energy are used only, and could be used only, for the said peaceful purposes. The smallest possibility that the safeguard-system administered by the Agency is not foolproof, and the slightest suspicion that a non-nuclear weapon State, could-contrary to the provisions of, and obligations under, the Non-Proliferation Treaty-acquire nuclear weapons to the detriment of its neighbours, would be disastrous for the whole future of the system set up by the said Treaty. On the other hand, if the safeguard-system controlled by the Agency is beyond all reasonable doubt, no State should be permitted, on whatever allegations and invoking whatever national interests, to make a military attack on another State, destroying human lives and industrial installations.

(1310) Under these circumstances, the Delegation of the Holy See can only appeal to all States to remain, by their actions, within the limits dictated by reason and by the need for stable peace in the world, according to the norms established by the Charter of the United Nations and by the other Institutions of the international community.

(1311) The Delegation of the Holy See also wishes to draw the attention of this Conference to the crucial matter of nuclear weapons.

(1312) In the first place it must be noted that today we are living in an international climate different from the cautiously optimistic climate prevailing after the signing of the Tlatelolco Treaty for the proscribing of nuclear arms in Latin America (1967) and the adoption of the Non-Proliferation Treaty (1968).

(1313) A number of observers today are of the opinion that the present international instruments are insufficient or inadequate for stopping the development of nuclear weapons, and no longer represent an effective stimulus for disarmament and peace. Dr. Eklund, the Director General of the IAEA, in his declaration last year at the Twenty-fourth Regular Session of the General Conference, made reference to the crisis of the NPT and expressed the hope that there would be "an early conclusion of a comprehensive Test Ban Treaty", which, on the one hand would be acceptable to those countries that now refuse to join the NPT, and, on the other hand, would put a brake on vertical proliferation. Subsequently, the Secretary General of OPANAL (Organismo para la proscripcion de las armas nucleares en la America Latina), in the statement presented at the meeting of the Organization in Mexico City last April, observed that the failure of the II Conference of revision of the NPT demonstrates the existence of a perhaps insuperable crisis of the system established by this international instrument, and he added that the present situation would encourage a reconsideration of the whole question of nuclear disarmament at the worldwide level.

(1314) The Delegation of the Holy See expresses its own conviction of the need to overcome the present precarious situation of international relations, a situation based upon the balance of terror and the system of dissuasion. The Delegation looks to decisive negotiation for disarmament.

(1315) The hitherto prevailing logic has not only not slowed the nuclear arms race, but has brought about such a development of these weapons that they have become an oppressive burden on the conscience of humanity and an open affront to those suffering from underdevelopment and hunger. In the hands of a small number of leaders there is now the fearsome capability of reducing our planet to a smoking desert, destroying in a flash everything great and sublime that the mind and heart of man has produced in centuries of civilization and progress.

(1316) There is no other rational and profitable path than that of disarmament and the banning of nuclear weapons, by means of worldwide agreements supported by effective guarantees. It could of course be objected that the history both ancient and more recent, of attempts at disarmament has proved to be a series of illusions and delusions. This demonstrates a truth that is fundamental: treaties are not effective unless they arise from and are sustained by a sincere and real desire for peace, because, in the final analysis, the danger and threat come not so much from the weapons as from the one who has them in his hand: man.

(1317) Therefore it is man, and groups and nations, that must abandon ideologies and myths of power and supremacy and be converted to a new order of international relationships based upon mutual respect, trust and collaboration. As John Paul II warned at Hiroshima: "...the future of humanity depends, as never before, on our collective moral choices. ...From now on, it is only through a conscious choice and through a deliberate policy that humanity can survive" (To men and women of science, nn.3-4, 25 February 1981. See above, par. 195 and 196).

(1318) In this spirit, the Delegation of the Holy See asks the IAEA to commit itself resolutely and actively to sustaining and when appropriate, promoting initiatives aimed at overcoming present tensions and at putting an end to the threat of nuclear weapons, from whatever source.

3. Statement by Msgr. Mario Peressin, Head of the Delegation of the Holy See, at the 26th Regular Session of the General Conference of the International Atomic Energy Agency. Vienna, 4 October 1982.

Original: English

(1319) 1. At the beginning of the second quarter of a century of the existence of the International Atomic Energy Agency, it seems proper to reflect upon the Agency's goals and tasks, its past record and the achievements we are all looking forward to in the future. The Director General, Mr. Blix, has indeed done so in his excellent report to this General Conference, and has given us detailed insight into the complexity of the problems with which the Agency has to cope. My Delegation can thus limit itself to some central issues concerning the problem of atomic energy today, the issues of progress, safety and peace.

(1320) 2. The fundamental matrix of reflection on the use or non-use of nuclear energy remains always the diversity of ends to which the atom can be used and its potential for destruction as well as for positive good. The atom, even when harnessed for beneficent and peaceful use, is too easily turned to dangerous purposes, or may become by accident a deadly threat for an unlimited number of people. This is the reason why discussion continues worldwide on the advantages and disadvantages of the peaceful use of atomic energy, even apart from the particular problems relating to its application for military purposes.

(1321) 3. The advantages of the peaceful uses of atomic energy are generally recognized. These peaceful applications represent indeed a wide range of possibilities, be it in the field of food and food conservation, especially through new techniques for plant breeding or through new methods of preservation, be it in the fields of medicine or hydrology. The most important sector is, however, that of providing energy which is so dearly needed and which is becoming more and more expensive in its production and rare in its resources.

(1322) 4. Various specialized agencies of the United Nations which are active in the field of development have stressed over and over again that the economic growth of the Third World countries demands an increasing use of nuclear power. Already today, we are witnessing, for example, a dangerous phenomenon of deforestation in various regions of the world. This brings with it the sad consequence of not renewing the necessary wood supply, and by laying waste the soil contributes, in some regions, to another major problem: that of progressive desertification. Then there are countries where renewable resources of energy are not available. Thus, development - especially industrial development - would seem to be impossible without some application of nuclear energy.

(1323) 5. Therefore, Mr. President, my Delegation believes that all possible efforts should be made to extend to all countries, especially to the developing ones, the benefits contained in the peaceful use of nuclear energy. These countries and their peoples have a just claim to participate in the advantages which human research and ingenuity have brought about in this field. Care should be taken to implement nuclear energy programs always in connection with other complementary energy programs, so that a balance may be maintained and over-dependence on one single energy source can be avoided. Developed and industrialized countries, leading in the field of production and application of nuclear energy for peaceful purposes, should generously share their know-how with the developing countries, without expecting a greater turn than that which may justly be demanded as compensation for the investment in money and human skill previously made by them. Such enlightened policies will do much to foster a progress that all nations can share, a progress that can also further greater understanding among peoples.

(1324) 6. The application of nuclear energy constitutes, however, also a risk for mankind because of the detrimental consequences which accidents in nuclear power plants and nuclear waste storage may entail. This is the reason why so many people today raise the question whether the peaceful use of nuclear energy - viewed over a long range of time - will have a beneficial effect at all for mankind, or whether the already known and yet unknown dangers involved constitute too high a risk for humanity. This view is not only ventured by various groups of naive idealists which would like to proclaim a "return to nature", but is shared also by some scientists, politicians, cultural and religious leaders.

(1325) 7. In this same vein, we are all aware that there has been much discussion recently about the moral and ethical aspects of nuclear energy. While most of these discussions by religious leaders, ethicists and theologians focus on the specific problems that nuclear weapons pose, - a question to which I shall return later - there is no doubt that the ongoing debate affects the evaluation of all forms and uses of nuclear energy.

(1326) Those who hold that nuclear power can be utilized only in a "zero risk" or "no risk" situation, are perhaps applying an unrealistic standard to endeavours which, like all human efforts, necessarily involve some risk. However, the implications of the use of nuclear energy and the necessity for safety in this field are such that no effort should be spared to maximize safety regulations and minimize risk to the utmost. Only a clear and consistent policy that keeps this in mind will permit a nuclear energy program to be responsibly implemented and will offer to the public the assurance, to which they are entitled, that every, possible step has been taken to ensure the safe functioning of a nuclear plant and the secure disposal of nuclear waste.

(1327) 8. My Delegation, therefore, welcomes the fact that the IAEA has expanded its program concerning nuclear safety, something that the Holy See has constantly recommended at General Conferences. We are also happy to note the remarkable fact that scientists and engineers have so far been successful in preventing major nuclear accidents, and that - as a result of all the ingenuity and care which has been put into these efforts - no fatal accident caused by radiation has to our knowledge occurred in nuclear power plants for civilian use. My Delegation feels that these efforts must be continued, in particular with regard to the long-term storage of radioactive waste, which is creating so many serious apprehensions today. Moreover - as the Holy See has stressed again and again - all care should be taken to fully inform the public on the real relation between nuclear plants and the possible dangers, in order not to turn the issues of nuclear policy into an arcane discipline to which only a few scientists and politicians are privy, thereby creating a climate of unnecessary public fear and mistrust.

(1328) 9. Now turning to a third and last issue: namely,the military aspect of the atomic problem, we have to face the fact that human ingenuity has constantly been used to make nuclear weapons still more efficient, and that the nuclear arsenals have constantly been increased. People everywhere feel anguish about a future that might include nuclear war. Demonstrations for nuclear disarmament in many countries testify to this anguish. Not all avenues which nuclear science has opened to mankind lead necessarily to a peaceful progress; some could lead to horror and holocaust.

(1329) 10. In the address delivered on 30, May 1982 during his visit to Great Britain, at the airport of Coventry, John Paul II expressly referred to this dangerous situation. "Our world is disfigured by war and violence", he said. "The ruins of the old Cathedral constantly remind our society of its capacity to destroy. And today that capacity is greater than ever. People are having to live under the shadow of a nuclear nightmare...Today the scale and the horror of modern warfare - whether nuclear or not - makes it totally unacceptable as a means of settling differences between nations. War should belong to the tragic past, to history; it should find no place on humanity's agenda for the future." This applies of course to all wars, but first and foremost to nuclear warfare.

(1330) 11. The IAEA is not only dedicated to the peaceful uses of nuclear energy and nuclear science, but is also committed by its Charter and the decisions of its ruling body to prevent the future spread of nuclear weapons. The Treaty on the Non-Proliferation of Nuclear Weapons, concluded in 1968 and hailed as a milestone in this nuclear century, still constitutes the cornerstone of a system designed to check the nuclear military potential. The future of the Treaty is endangered, however, if the nuclear weapon States do not take serious steps for the implementation of its article VI, where their obligation to a general and complete disarmament is stated. Unfortunately, many people have been disappointed again this very summer, when the United Nations General Assembly's Special Session on Disarmament did not produce the results that had been hoped for. War, and especially nuclear war, continues to hang over this world like a dark cloud.

Among the exigencies to resolve this threat, a comprehensive test ban treaty is a *conditio sine qua non* in a situation where the explosive power of all nuclear weapons in the world has reached insane levels.

(1331) 12. It must be considered a task of utmost importance to prevent any use of nuclear weapons. The Holy See is ready to support any and all efforts aimed at eliminating the risk of nuclear conflict. This commitment was reaffirmed by the Holy Father in his Message to the Second Special Session of the United Nations General Assembly devoted to disarmament.

(1332) I wish to conclude my statement by quoting from that same message:

"To reverse the current trend in the arms race involves therefore, a parallel struggle on two fronts: on the one side, an immediate and urgent struggle by governments to reduce progressively and equally their armaments: on the other hand, a more patient but nonetheless necessary struggle at the level of the consciences of peoples to take their responsibility in regard to the ethical cause of the insecurity that breeds violence by coming to grips with the material and spiritual inequalities of our world" (See above, par. 1067).

(1333) "With no prejudice of any kind, let us unite all our intellectual and spiritual forces those of statesmen, of citizens, of religious leaders, to put an end to violence and hatred and to seek out the paths of peace."

(1334) "... Peace is not a utopia nor an inaccessible ideal nor an unrealizable dream. War is not an inevitable calamity. Peace is possible and because it is possible, peace is our duty: our grave duty, our supreme responsibility" (n. 13. See above, par. 1067-1073).

4. Statement by Msgr. Giovanni Ceirano, Head of the Delegation of the Holy See, at the 27th Regular Session of the General Conference of the International Atomic Energy Agency. Vienna, 12 October 1983.

Original: English

(1335) The Holy See Delegation has studied with great care the various documents which serve as the basis of our general debate. In this connection, we would like to commend the Director-General and his staff for having so well prepared our work, thereby contributing in a decisive manner to the traditional efficiency which distinguishes the activities of the International Atomic Energy Agency and its organs. It has been of particular interest for the Holy See Delegation to listen to the Annual Report which Dr. Blix has given us and which clearly indicates that, even though public debate has somewhat diminished, the utilization of nuclear energy remains a complex question which challenges us all and deserves serious reflection.

(1336) I do not wish to dwell on any of the more technical aspects which are so important for the Agency's everyday activities. Instead, I will address my remarks to some aspects of the Agency's policies and programmes, attempting to draw attention to activities that promote the good of the human person and society in the spirit of the remarks Pope John Paul II made to us here on September 12.

(1337) Originally, our Organization was brought into being for the very purpose of demonstrating that nuclear power need not only be a destructive force but that it could be harnessed for peaceful purposes and for the good of all. The biblical phrase of turning swords into ploughshares has been cited more often in connection with the peaceful use of nuclear energy than in any other context. Today it would seem that nuclear energy is still an ambivalent reality, for it is an instrument that even in peaceful application can be turned for or against its master. In a situation where we have not yet solved the first problem, that of nuclear weapons, we cannot afford to ignore the second problem, the control and the safe use of nuclear energy.

(1338) Unfortunately the first problem, nuclear weapons, has seen no real progress since the last General Conference in 1982. In fact, the present political and military situation in the World, and more particularly in Europe, conveys the impression that the apprehension felt by one side because of the armament efforts by the other side, might lead to a continuing spiral of weapons development and deployment that could exacerbate the world situation unless statesmanlike vision and political will lead to negotiations and agreements that will bring lasting results. The Holy See views with interest and support all the honest attempts at negotiations. This was a major theme of Pope John Paul's message to the Special Session of the U.N. General Assembly on Disarmament in June 1982. It continues to be the foundation of the pressing appeals the Holy See is making to all the interested parties: to negotiate in honesty and integrity; to negotiate with a sense of responsibility to the people; to negotiate in order to reduce tensions and to create freedom, justice and security for every nation, now and in the future.

(1339) For her part, the Church will continue to propose to all interested parties the principles of her tradition. These principles, applied throughout the centuries, can also be applied to the problems of warfare and armaments today as they were in the past, first with the aim of eliminating or at least of minimizing the possibility of war, and secondly to guarantee above all that mass destruction is avoided and innocent people are protected.

(1340) Within the last decade, the possibility and feasibility of the peaceful use of atomic energy has been contested. Those who argue in favour of such a peaceful use assert that this source of energy can be put to use in all countries regardless of the availability of natural or primary resources. Therefore, nuclear energy would seem to be ideally suited especially for the developing countries which have opted for rapid industrialization. For them, to forego nuclear energy, it is said, would mean to forego speedy and certain development. Similarly nuclear energy, it is argued, remains of great value also for the developed countries. High industrialization demands high energy consumption. Countries which today are confronted with great ecological problems, deriving mainly from "unclean" forms of energy used in their industrial processes, would find in nuclear energy a "clean" alternative, which would enable them to keep up their standard of industrial production, and at the same time lessen the negative impact of industrialization on the environment.

(1341) The opponents of nuclear energy state, in contrast, that the risks which the production and the employment of nuclear energy entails are still too great to be undertaken. According to them, these risks are mainly of two kinds: possible malfunctioning of nuclear reactors, which could lead to radio-active contamination of whole regions, and the dangers surrounding the storage of nuclear waste. In this forum I need not develop these basic positions further. Nor do I cite them to resolve a debate which continues to deserve airing. Rather I wish to recognize the legitimacy of the debate as the background and ongoing context that touch and condition the policies and programmes of the Agency itself.

(1342) In 1983, the IAEA provided development aid to more than 70 Member States. This aid took many forms, from research to technical cooperation in fields of agriculture, health care, and geothermal exploration, not to mention the projects that dealt directly with plant maintenance, waste management and all the concerns that touch on nuclear energy development. Two aspects of these activities merit our attention and our encouragement. First is regional cooperation. Given the costs and the available instruments and personnel, regional cooperation in developing countries makes great sense and should, wherever feasible, be encouraged. The Regional Cooperative Agreement (RCA) has already brought benefits to Southeast Asia and the Pacific regions. This type of approach which has for some time borne positive results in research done at CERN in Europe, might well be a model for use in other parts of the world. Devoting personnel, funds and equipment in a greater degree to such initiatives can be one way that the fruits of nuclear energy might be made available for the better good of greater numbers.

(1343) In the past the Delegation of the Holy See has spoken of the need for developing adequate technology and for the improved training of scientists in developing countries. As programmes for regional development and cooperation are being considered, would this not be a crucial element for greater emphasis and commitment? International fellowship programmes, research grants, aid in setting up research facilities, all these could be given greater attention, personnel and funding in regard to the developing nations of the world. It would be a splendid step in the right direction if the cross-fertilization of research and ideas, of scientific skill and knowledge, ever the hallmark of your disciplines,could be strengthened and expanded into an ever greater network of national, regional and international cooperation.

(1344) In May of this year the Pontifical Academy of Sciences organized at the Vatican a symposium on the biological effects of ionizing radiation. While the results of that meeting have not yet been published, I wish to refer to it because it points out in a concrete way what all of us must be committed to. The optimization method was exhaustively examined. One quickly saw, once again,the dedication of the scientific community to protect life and to minimize real or potential threats to life. Here too, the Church plays her role, not by deciding on the merits of a technical process but by aiding all those responsible for such methods to look at the ethical, moral and spiritual implications of whatever method might be under review. Without in any way diminishing the commitment to seek ever greater safety standards, the level of protection against ionizing radiation in current methods demonstrates how scientific expertise, coupled with an ethical reflection on moral responsibility in and to society, can lead to methods and programmes that advance science while protecting the common good and life of everyone.

(1345) The Holy See Delegation is convinced that these are only a few of many difficult questions, questions to which the answers will not be found easily and which therefore will be with us for some time. Our Organization, the International Atomic energy Agency, will have more than ever to concentrate on them. And in so doing, we will have to be ready to respond to the question Pope John Paul II put to us last month: "Does this advance the cause of man as man?" May I close my remarks by directing your thoughts to his words on the meaning of that question: "Such a reflection will not always be easy to make but it is necessary. No one would deny that the complexities of industry, technology, nuclear science and the many organizations of modern society must be approached with full respect for all the components which command our careful attention. In the light of these realities and conscious of the potential they have, I can and must insist that the commitment and effort you rightly give to the intellectual, technical, scientific and educational aspects must always be matched by a sensitivity for and a dedication to the cause of man who we proclaim is formed in the image of God and hence worthy of total dignity and respect" (John Paul II, Address to the International Organizations in Vienna. No. 3. See above, par. 241-242).

5. Statement by Msgr. Giovanni Ceirano, Head of the Delegation of the Holy See to the 28th Regular Session of the General Conference of the International Atomic Energy Agency. Vienna, 26 September 1984.

Original: English

(1346) After having listened attentively to the Report given to us by the Director General, as well as to the statements made so far by various distinguished representatives, we have already had opportunity to view a wide spectrum of problems related to the work of the International Atomic Energy Agency. Given the nature and the role of the Holy See, I will refrain from comment on the more concrete and technical questions and call the attention of this Assembly to some basic and general aspects of the work of IAEA.

(1347) Let me begin, Mr. President, by expressing the satisfaction of my delegation about the fact that our Agency has made, in the course of the last year, an important step towards that universality in membership which is called for by the very matter with which it is concerned. We strongly believe that the various aspects of generating and applying nuclear energy make it imperative that all States, and most particularly those which already possess nuclear power stations, cooperate effectively within the framework set up by the Statute of the Agency.

(1348) This is not to say that it suffices today merely to accept the obligations under a Statute that was drafted almost thirty years ago. Times change, and the safeguards originally contained in a Statute may prove to be inadequate to meet all subsequent challenges arising from the proliferation of the use of the atom for military purposes. Therefore, the Treaty on the Non-Proliferation of Nuclear Weapons signed in 1968, to which the Holy See acceded in 1971, and the safeguard agreements concluded thereafter under different regimes must today be considered as forming an integral part of those regulations which together seek to control the development and use of nuclear energy for the good of all.

(1349) Therefore, Mr. President, my delegation appeals to all members of this Agency to alleviate the fears of humanity by joining together in a common effort to control, restrict and finally to ban nuclear weapons. A universal effort utilizing all the multilateral and bilateral possibilities at the disposal of nations would become a clear sign of a renewed commitment to peace and solidarity in a world too often marred by war.

(1350) Turning now from the military to the peaceful use of nuclear energy, my delegation is concerned about how public opinion reacts to this issue. Only two years ago, the Holy See delegation called attention to the safety and health of those engaged in the entire chain of nuclear power production and the distribution of energy, and to energy development and management with respect to the environment and the protection of the health of humanity. We recognized that the process of developing nuclear energy joins together a high level of knowledge and technical expertise with the economic, social and development priorities of political leaders. Too often, however, the general public is unaware of the safeguards used to monitor the building of nuclear installations and the safety standards that control their operation and the management of nuclear waste. And yet we are faced with the fact that there exists strong opposition to nuclear power in some sectors of public opinion. There are many reasons for this: fear of technological society, fear of reactor accidents, fear of nuclear radiations, fear of nuclear war, fear of genetic damage to future generations, fear of damaging the environment, and also fear for civil liberties, the restriction of which might be called for by safety considerations. Underlying them all is a fear of the unknown. In the face of this, the Holy See would like to reiterate its suggestion that nations make a greater effort to inform public opinion about nuclear power with realism and honesty, and with a sensitivity to the attitudes and mentalities of the people.

(1351) The Church is ready to do its part to give help and moral guidance. Such guidance cannot be given without a careful examination of the matter, as the Pontifical Academy of Sciences has done in Study Weeks in November 1980 on the subject of "Humanity and Energy: Needs - Resources - Hopes", and in May 1983 on the effect of ionizing radiation. Aided by these studies, the Church will offer an ongoing moral reflection on the options available in this field.

(1352) This concern, first to inform public opinion, and then to help people realize the social and ethical options offered through the development of nuclear power, becomes ever more urgent when we recognize that there seems to be a new growth in electrical capacity produced through nuclear power. Recent issues of the "Bulletin" of this Agency speak of 317 units operating in 25 countries, of 209 power reactors being built, and that the 1985 nuclear capacity of 275 gigawatts can develop to between 580 and 850 gigawatts by the turn of the century (cf. Bulletin of IAEA, June 1984, p. 42).

(1353) In order to translate these figures into reality for the majority of people, attention must be drawn beyond the safety measures to the benefits that are being provided to the world, and especially to the developing world, through the proper use of nuclear energy and research. For some time, in international conferences, the Holy See has urged that every country become self-sufficient in foodstuffs and that technology be developed and applied in accordance with the needs and capacities of a people, with due consideration for cultural, social, ethical and spiritual values. In that spirit, it is worthwhile to underline and to publicize the results of the application of nuclear technology in the area of food, in the work that the Agency has been carrying on with FAO, and in the various projects that have brought results in the medical field to alleviate disease and offer a brighter prospect for the health of people especially in tropical climates. Similarly, the commitment of the Agency to supporting institutes in developing countries, so that they can undertake and carry forward research in various scientific fields, merits praise and recognition on a wider scale than at present is the case.

(1354) Finally, in light of the above, I would like to focus on the person of the scientist. In times past the scientist might have evoked mythical images as the solver of all problems. In recent times, certain circles have criticized the scientist and have even castigated him for being unfaithful to the noble aspirations of knowledge and truth. There is no doubt that there are some who use their science for personal gain at the expense of others and of the common good. But science of itself cannot always guard against this misuse. So it is that all of us must be committed to wedding the values of knowledge to the overriding values of the human person in society.

(1355) Under these circumstances, it seems worthwhile to recall the reference made by His Holiness Pope John Paul II in his address to the Members of the Pontifical Academy of Science on 12 November 1983: "There are different ways for men and women of culture to live the precious value of knowledge. Bernard of Clairvaux, one of the strongest personalities in history, who came down from the loftiest peaks of mysticism to share divine and human truth with the ecclesiastical and civil society of his time, as a true master of love and knowledge, described the different types of men and women of culture always found in history. According to Saint Bernard there are five motives that lead human beings to study: "There are people who only wish to know for the sake of knowing: this is base curiosity. Others wish to know in order that they themselves may be known: this is shameful vanity, and such people cannot escape the mockery of the satirical poet who said about their likes: For you, knowing is nothing unless someone else knows that you know. Then there are those who acquire knowledge in order to resell it, and, for example, to make money or gain honours from it: their motive is distasteful. But some wish to know in order to edify: this is charity. Others in order to be edified: this is wisdom. Only those who belong to these last two categories do not misuse knowledge, since they only seek to understand in order to do good".

(1356) In the same address, His Holiness drew the conclusion: "The scientific truth which ennobles your intellect and lifts your research to the level of contemplation of the world and of its Creator, must be transmitted to the whole of humanity for the integral development of each human being and of all nations, for the service of peace which is the object of your reflections and projects".

(1357) These words of His Holiness seem to be particularly apt for the work of scientists in the field of nuclear energy. Fortunately, we already have, in the International Atomic Energy Agency, an organization which is dedicated, on a worldwide scale, to making accessible to all interested states the benefits of nuclear power. It is to be hoped that our Agency will have ever greater success in its efforts to serve humanity in a field where abuse of the matter involved may mean death and destruction to man and culture alike, but where, at the same time, there exists one of the most important sources for the economic and technical progress of future generations.

6. Statement by Msgr. Giovanni Ceirano, Head of the Delegation of the Holy See, at the 29th Regular Session of the General Conference of the International Atomic Energy Agency. Vienna, 25 September 1985.

Original: English

(1358) 1. My Delegation wishes to offer some points of reflection on what we consider to be basic current issues connected with the use of nuclear energy.

(1359) 2. It is the conviction of this Delegation that all members of this Agency must give priority to the whole problem of nuclear weapons and nuclear weapons systems. The constant and abiding presence of the build-up of nuclear power for military uses has made itself felt through and in all the attempts which have been made to secure nuclear energy for peaceful purposes. The work of the Agency and other bodies has been accompanied by the potentially menacing reality that an increasing number of nations have the ability and the expertise to use nuclear energy for harmful rather than peaceful ends. At the recently concluded Third Review Conference on the Non-Proliferation Treaty in Geneva, the Holy See Delegate expressed the position of the Holy See as follows: "...there must be a reversal to the trend of vertical proliferation. We feel there is a moral link between the limitation of horizontal proliferation and the reversal of vertical proliferation. The nations in possession of nuclear power have the duty to fulfil their responsibilities as enunciated in Article VI of the Treaty. Without presuming to give suggestions of a technical order - which is outside the role of the Holy See - it must be remembered that there are many more weapons and weapons systems than are needed to ensure the security of all nations. Public opinion is aware of this fact and has already made its desire known and its position clear. The people want a reversal of the arms race. In this circumstance, this Delegation reiterates the appeal of His Holiness Pope John Paul II to reverse the current trend in the arms race" (*L'Osservatore Romano*, 1, September 1985, p.2. See above, par. 1277).

(1360) 3. In contrast, programmes for the peaceful use of nuclear energy should be enhanced and the Agency should be given the necessary means to play its natural role in the drawing up of the same, in their observation and their co-ordination. As regards these programmes, stress should be laid on the need to ensure that nuclear energy serves man and his spiritual and material development. The extent of this contribution should be the standard by which to judge the quality of any such programme.

(1361) As a general rule, each country should decide for itself whether and to what extent it will have recourse to nuclear energy, always with regard to its own needs and its own resources. However, recourse to nuclear energy must, in any case, safeguard the security of the individual, of society as a whole, and of the ecological needs of the environment. For this reason, programmes for security measures and protection against radiation should be given priority, especially as concerns the need of developing countries to make reasonable and safe choices.

(1362) Apart from producing nuclear energy for peaceful purposes, nuclear technology can and should be utilized for the benefit of all mankind also in other fields, such as agriculture, medicine, geology, scientific research and progress as a whole. In these fields appropriate investments should be encouraged, since it is possible to obtain - with a relatively modest capital input - relatively high returns. Therefore, a special stress should be laid on projects going in this direction.

(1363) 4. In this vain allow me to point out a few of the many programmes and activities of the Agency which illustrate the ideas I have just mentioned.

(1364) The work being done on waste-management is of great importance for the present and future of our planet. The progress being made on low and intermediate level waste-management will serve countries in all parts of the world, while the new concern about high-level waste promises to respond to that real concern for the safety of peoples and nations that must always be at the forefront of our consciences.

(1365) As regards the use of available resources, international justice demands, in general, that they should not be diverted to a few large projects in a small number of countries only, but that a large number of rather small projects should be fostered, projects which are of advantage to the greatest possible number of people and which are adapted to the socio-economic reality and to the actual possibilities of the various countries. It is therefore important to keep in contact with the exigencies and realities at the local level.

(1366) Consistent with the position of stressing the need for intermediate and appropriate technology rather than superfluous high power technologies and installations, the Holy See Delegation is very interested in the results of the research being done on small and medium power reactors (cf. Programme for 1985/86 Gov 2156, p.24). The successful collaboration of buyers, sellers and financing institutions in this type of project will help the integral development of societies that are only beginning to develop their energy capacities and thus beginning to realize the potential that is there.

(1367) Finally, in this same perspective, it is helpful to note the work being done to supply in particular the developing countries "with up-to-date information on the comparative economic performance of nuclear and fossil-fuelled power plants" (*Ibid.*, p.27).

(1368) These and many other efforts which improve performance and which help developing countries to choose and develop the energy systems best suited to their real needs constitute some of the best work which the Agency does.

(1369) 5. At the end of my remarks, permit me, Mr. President, to touch on a current internal question of the Agency. Given its special position as a founding member of the IAEA but one which seeks to play no other part than the moral role consistent with its proper mission, the Holy See would like to say a word about the delicate question of choosing personnel. Two factors must be kept in mind. One is the growing representativity of the membership of the IAEA. This fact naturally leads to the expression by a number of States of a desire that the personnel of the Agency should reflect the geo-political spectrum of the membership. On the other hand, the IAEA, from its inception, has always placed a strong emphasis on the priority of technical expertise. This fact has contributed much to the prestige and effectiveness of the organization and its programme. The Holy See would like to call the attention of all the member States to these two factors. While sympathetic and desirous of having as wide a representation as possible among the personnel, this Delegation is also very much in favour of maintaining the high technical standards that have marked the work of the Agency. Therefore it does not hesitate to commend the example of the past while remaining confident that the good will of all will find the means to respond to current situations without loss of expertise or representativity.

(1370) 6. As this Conference conducts its deliberations and as the Agency seeks to develop even further its programmes and activities for the good of all nations and peoples, I would ask that all of us keep in mind that the real fruit of all this work, apart from the concrete good of this or that project, will be the growth of the spirit of cooperation and harmony among the peoples and nations of this world. Pope John Paul II in his Message to the Special session on Disarmament has enunciated what ought to be our goal: "The building of links among peoples means the rediscovery and reassertion of all the values that reinforce peace and that join people together in harmony. This also means the renewal of what is best in the heart of man, the heart that seeks the good of the other in friendship and love" (John Paul II, Message to the Special Session of the United Nations General Assembly devoted to Disarmament, No. 11. See above, par. 1062).

CHAPTER V

DEVELOPMENT

I - TO MOBILIZE ALL HUMANITY FOR DEVELOPMENT

Address of His Holiness Paul VI to H.E. U Thant, Secretary-General of the United Nations, the Heads of the United Nations Specialized Agencies, the members of the Administrative Committee on Coordination, and to the Diplomatic Corps accredited to the Holy See. The Vatican, 28 April 1969.

Original: French (*)

(1371) It is a joy for us to greet you this morning in our residence. Our welcome goes first of all to U Thant, the indefatigable Secretary-General of the United Nations who received us so graciously in New York on 4 October 1965, and who now presides over your Administrative Committee on Coordination and has just carefully explained to us the precise goals of your meeting in Rome and the purposes of your visit to the Pope. Our greetings also go to the Heads of the specialized agencies of the United Nations and to all the committee members. Gentlemen, you who are in charge of all the international organizations which constitute the family, so to speak, of the United Nations, we know of your competencies and your responsibilities. It is also a great satisfaction at this important meeting this morning to greet among us the distinguished members of the Diplomatic Corps who represent to the Holy See the great family of peoples. To you all, our sentiments of deference and respect.

(1372) This felicitous meeting gives us first of all the opportunity to restate our great esteem for the work of the United Nations and its specialized agencies. It also allows us to affirm our hope for your work whose object is nothing less than the material progress and the social and moral development of peoples which we have so much at heart. We are anxious to thank you, Mr. Secretary-General, for the noble words which you have so kindly expressed to our commitment in this area, particularly for our Encyclical *Populorum Progressio*, and the initiatives which have followed and will follow it.

(1373) If few people speak of your Committee - because few know of its existence - its action however can be decisive in this great work of development. Yours is the coordination of action undertaken and programs executed at different levels and in diverse sectors of international activity. Now, as you know, the gigantic enterprise which is development can only be undertaken with all the strength at the disposal of humanity in service to humanity. We say it again and again without tiring: "The development of which we are speaking does not extend solely to economic growth. To be genuine, growth must be integral, it must clearly provide for the progress of each individual and of the whole man... Consequently not merely this or that person, but all without exception are called to promote the full development of the whole human society" (*Populorum Progressio*, nn.14 and 17).

(1374) Among these forces, it is indispensable to recognize the primary and irreplaceable position held by the mind. You yourself, U Thant, have correctly emphasized that development could not be realized without a radical change in the mentality of many, and in the attitude of peoples and their governments. The issue is awareness and a will to action. The Church, for its part, as you know, commits its energies to help people to better build and manage the earthly city, not from desire for power, nor in search of prestige,but to be "faithful to the teaching and the example of the divine founder" in a desire for disinterested service (cf. *Populorum Progressio*, nn.12 and 13).

(1375) In the words of your noble interpreter, we have noted down the concerns of the Second Decade for Development. To this end, your Committee meeting these days at the headquarters of FAO rightly takes up program planning and the coordination of all of the activities. For ourselves, we would like to say a word, if you allow it, about this Decade. Apparently the success of the first Decade was not very spectacular. Still, at least an awakening took place in the masses themselves that development is an absolute necessity, that it constitutes an irreversible phe-

---

(*) Insegnamenti di Paolo VI, Vol. VII (1969), 285-288.

nomenon, and requires the effort of all, both the developed and under-developed. Because - we reaffirm it - "this is the objective which must be achieved. Since world unity seems daily more operative it must allow all peoples, to use the phrase, to be the architects of their own fortune." (*Populorum Progressio*, n.65). An ever greater awakening is achieved in this way, and it is like a new spirit which must be created in the international community around the concept of integral development in solidarity. We also would want to say that the efficacy of the Second Decade must be directed as much to quantity as to quality. Human resources, human development are the questions-in summary, the human person. When all is said and done, the only true wealth is the human person, and if there is a desire for more, it is to be more (cf. *Populorum Progression,* n.6).

(1376) At the conclusion of this meeting, we are anxious to tell you again, Gentlemen, how much our heart is set on your effort, and how much the Church for its part is devoted to helping human persons to grow in their humanity by appropriate means, enhance their value, and perfect themselves. (*Populorum Progressio*, n. 15).

(1377) In this matter, we want to note the work of our Pontifical Commission "Justice and Peace", a committee fundamentally constituted for human advancement whose members we wanted to be associated with this meeting; the foundation of SODEPAX with the World Council of Churches; and very recently, the organization of the Populorum Progressio Fund which we would like to be a source of new initiatives and generous accomplishments.

(1378) And why not confide in you our joy on the eve of our next visit, in the beginning of June, if God permits, to the International Labor Organization in Geneva on the occasion of its 50th anniversary?

(1379) Gentlemen, from the fullness of our heart, we tell you solemnly today of our great, twofold hope at this moment of human history. First, we hope that the governments of the most developed peoples, or those in conditions of relative well-being, will want to continue or decide generously to contribute always more effectively to the cause of developing countries. For, today, words are tiresome, and more and more, deeds are expected.

(1380) Further, our hope is also in the ardent, generous, enthusiastic and disinterested young people; may they make their own the beautiful ideal of the United Nations, "together with each other, not one over the other, never again some against the others, but always for each other" (Address to the 20th Session of the General Assembly of the United Nations, 4 October 1965. See above, par. 16, 18, 19 and 26). This way, the world will take on a new face; it will be truly human and fraternal in friendship and in peace.

(1381) These are our thoughts this morning which we have had the pleasure of confiding to you at this reception calling the abundance of blessings of the Almighty "Father of all human persons" upon your generous activity in the service of humanity.

II - JUSTICE FOR ALL NATIONS

Message of His Holiness Paul VI to H.E. Mr. Kurt Waldheim, Secretary- General of the United Nations, on the occasion of the Extraordinary Session of the General Assembly on the Problems of Raw Materials and Development. The Vatican, 4 April 1974.

Original: English (*)

(1382) We are happy to take the occasion of this Special Session to send a message of support as the General Assembly embarks on the study of the Problems of Raw Materials and Development. Our deep interest in these important aspects of man's life stems from our spiritual mission at the service of the whole man and of all men.

(1383) We are indeed aware of the importance and urgency of the problems that this General Assembly is trying to solve by reviewing the existing relationships between developed and developing countries, and by endeavouring to create the basis for a new relationship which will eliminate the inequality existing between the rich and powerful nations and those whose true development is hampered by so many obstacles. It is of the utmost necessity for the world community to bridge this ever-growing gap and to alter the situations wherein raw materials do not bring to the people who produce them a just and equitable measure of human well-being.

(1384) It is evident that none of these problems can be solved by policies that serve only national self-interest. Nations are often blinded by egoism and prevented from seeing how their own true interests are compatible with the interests of other States and coincide with the general good of the human family as a whole. It is, therefore, imperative that existing difficulties should be solved through a dialogue undertaken in an international forum in which all work together. We are convinced that only in this way can the interests of the entire human community and of each of its members be promoted; only in this way can the vested interests of nations or groups of nations be overcome for the true benefit of all.

(1385) The Church steadfastly professes the belief that all acceptable solutions must be based on international social justice and human solidarity, and by the practical applications of these principles.

(1386) The developing nations must continue in their efforts to promote the true welfare of their peoples, utilizing all their own energies, working together and sharing among themselves. But international justice demands equally that the wealthy and privileged nations should match that effort by removing any obstacles of economic or political domination, by sharing more equitably economic power with the weaker nations, by allowing developing nations to be the agents of their own development and to exercise their true role in the decision-making that affects the very lives of their peoples. Only when the developing nations will have the means to reach their destiny will they, in turn, be able to discharge the full measure of their responsibility within the brotherhood of nations.

(1387) Convinced as we are that a new order of development will promote peace and serve the genuine advantages of all, we appeal to the developed nations to make greater efforts to forgo their own immediate advantages, and to adopt a new life style that will exclude both excessive consumption and those superfluous needs that are often artificially engendered through the use of the mass media by a limited segment of society in search of riches. Likewise, one should not forget that a life style based on ever greater consumption has deleterious effects on nature and the environment and finally on the moral fibre of man himself, especially the youth.

(1388) Through the good will of all, the riches of this world must serve the true benefit of all - as they were indeed destined by the Creator who, in his bountiful providence, has put them at the disposal of the whole of mankind (cf. John XXIII, *Mater et Magistra*, AAS 53, 1961, p. 430).

(*) AAS 66(1974), 282-285.

(1389) As we call for the application of justice for everyone, we deem it a duty to make a special appeal for the nations most deprived of natural resources or of the fruit of industry. Worthy of particular priority by every honourable standard, these people must be given the means that will enable them to fulfil their human destiny.

(1390) All countries must be aware of their obligation in this field, and of the consequences that their success or failure will produce. Just and equitable relations among all nations can be promoted only if all will agree within an international context to take the necessary measures for revising certain policies heretofore followed. If this is not done, despair will ensue on the part of the poor and powerless, a despair that will spur them to aggressive search of methods - other than international cooperation - to gain what they consider to be their economic rights.

(1391) In this regard we feel constrained to state once again that the giving of aid - however laudable and necessary - is not sufficient to promote the full measure of human dignity required by the solidarity of mankind under the fatherhood of God. The nations must succeed in creating new, more just, and hence more effective international structures in such spheres as economics, trade, industrial development, finance and the transfer of technology. We repeat the challenge that we launched three years ago when we stated that "it is necessary to have the courage to undertake a revision of the relationship between nations ... to question the models of growth of the rich nations and change peoples' outlooks...." (*Octogesima Adveniens*, 43, AAS 63, 1971, p. 432).

(1392) Despite the efforts necessarily involved in such a demanding programme, we are confident in the good will of all. Moreover we are convinced that all those who believe in God will realize more and more that the exigencies of their faith include justice and fraternal love for every man. In the first century of Christianity a great exponent of brotherhood under God expressed the universal challenge of human solidarity, asking: "... how can God's love survive in a man who has enough of this world's goods yet closes his heart to his brother?" (*IJn.* 3:17).

(1393) Because of the profound conviction that we have expressed personally before the United Nations General Assembly "that this Organization represents the obligatory path of modern civilization and world peace" (Address of 4 October 1965, AAS, 57, 1965, p. 878. See above, par. 10), we do not hesitate to repeat the invitation that we subsequently extended in our Encyclical on the Development of Peoples: "Delegates to international organizations, it depends on you to see that the dangerous and futile rivalry of powers should give place to collaboration which is friendly, peaceful and free of vested interests, in order to achieve a responsible development of mankind, in which all men will have an opportunity to find their fulfillment" (*Populorum Progressio*, 84, AAS 59, 1967, p. 298).

(1394) We assure all those pursuing these goals, all those earnestly striving to find just solutions to the pressing problems confronting society today of our prayerful and enduring support.

III - HOPE, THE CONSTRUCTIVE CRITERION IN THE STRATEGY OF DEVELOPMENT

Message of His Holiness John Paul II to H.E. Mr. Salim Ahmed Salim, President of the General Assembly of the United Nations, on the occasion of the 11th Special Session of the General Assembly, dedicated to the New International Development Strategy (*). The Vatican, 22 August 1980.

Original: French (**)

(1395) 1. The importance of this Special Session and of the content of its work prompts me to send to this distinguished Assembly some thoughts and reflections on a subject which has been a constant concern of the Holy See, especially during the past two decades. The Holy See intends, moreover, by this message to pledge its continued interest in this area. The work of preparation for this Session has been long and involved. It has absorbed the energies and the resources of the major organs of the United Nations Organization, and has been the focus of much work and of great expectations on the part of peoples around the world. The Holy See has followed all this work closely and with an earnest desire to be of service.

(1396) Whatever may have been the gains or shortcomings of past efforts, this Special Session should be seen as a new opportunity to set a course which will benefit all peoples and nations. It deserves to be a new opportunity because of the work that has been put into it, but even more because of the needs and just aspirations of so many people who rightfully continue to look for a better and more humane future for themselves and their children.

(1397) 2. To be a new opportunity, this Session of the United Nations Organization must not become submerged in the past. Rather it should be an occasion for everyone to learn from the past and to make new strides forward, being aware of what may have hindered progress in the past, so that sterile checkmates may be avoided in the future. This work cannot afford to be caught by old polarities. It must transcend them. It cannot be the captive of stale ideologies; it must instead bypass them. If the participants in this gathering are of one mind in the desire to look afresh at common problems, then already the atmosphere has been created that will make this one of the most productive Sessions that the United Nations system has seen.

(1398) 3. In these discussions the Catholic Church has her own role to play. She does not seek to speak out on merely economic or technological questions. She does not attempt to give concrete solutions to the complex realities which are not her proper responsibility. This does not mean that the Church is unaware of the complexities of the problems before this Assembly. Nor is she un-knowledgeable about the substance and the content of the issues that must be confronted here by the experts from various parts of the world. But the Church speaks here first of all to give witness to her concerns for everything that touches the human condition. Many of you know already that the Holy See has taken part in various ways in most of the preparatory work for this Special Session, as well as participating in the work of the various organizations whose own concerns figure largely in this Assembly.

(1399) While the Holy See rightly leaves the purely technological and economic matters to those whose proper responsibilities they are, it continues to be present at these meetings in order to add its voice within the discussions themselves. It does so in order to offer a vision of the human person and society. It does so in order to propose some helpful criteria to ensure that human values, values of the spirit, values of peoples and cultures, are not inadvertently made subservient to some lesser goal of merely economic or material gain that ultimately would prove unworthy of the very person and the very society all of us seek to foster.

(*) The Message was delivered to the General Assembly by His Eminence Cardinal Bernardin Gantin, President of the Pontifical Commission "Iustitia et Pax" on 25 August, at the opening of the Special Session.

(**) AAS 72 (1980), 818-824.

(1400) 4. As has been recognized, ever greater importance is now attributed to non-economic considerations in forming new structures of international relations. In this regard, religious and ethnic factors, education and public opinion play a great part. Peace itself becomes a driving force of so many parts of the global community - that peace which is irreconcilable with military or economic wars.

(1401) Such a perspective does indeed lie before us at this Special Session. And if I speak to you out of my Christian inheritance and use a vocabulary that is proper to those of us who follow the one whom we call the Prince of Peace, this is done with the conviction that the words I speak can be readily understood by men and women of good will everywhere and be of benefit to them.

(1402) 5. My first major point is an appeal to all of you here, to all peoples everywhere. It is an appeal to go beyond any static positions that belong to a particular ideology. Let every system and each functioning part of a system look to what in fact it can do, to ask what in fact it can contribute, to see how in fact it can advance the real goals of human living, regardless of whatever positions the stale arguments' ideological bias may wish to impose artificially - positions and biases which may hinder rather than promote real progress and fraternal collaboration.

(1403) There is no question but that this great Assembly has men and women of different, even opposed, systems and ideologies. We cannot, however, afford to let the limitations of ideological biases obstruct our concern for man - man in the concrete, the whole man, every man (cf. *Redemptor Hominis*, 13). Therefore we cannot let these ideological categories imprison us. We cannot let outdated conflicts control us in such a way that we cannot respond to the real needs of peoples everywhere.

(1404) 6. In the place of ideological stalemates that have perhaps prevailed in the past, I would like to suggest a criterion that is an attitude and guiding principle which measures each and every concrete decision that all of you, member States of this Assembly, will make: it is *hope*, a solid, realistic, hope for every man, woman and child, and for society itself.

(1405) This hope is not a wish. It is not a vague sentiment. It is a category born of our experience of history and nourished by our common desires for the future. As such, this hope accepts history as the place of its own operation and declares quite openly and quite realistically that the future is a history to be made, to be made by us with the help of Almighty God. It is a future to be built by united efforts to secure the common good through mutual cooperation and collaboration. This hope is, then, the guiding criterion that tells us that, if there is a history to be made and if we are responsible for the common good, now and in the future, we must together work out and put into practice the modifications that are necessary now so that the future we yearn for will correspond to the hope we share for all individuals, peoples and nations on this earth.

(1406) 7. Viewing this attitude of hope as our common outlook and as a guiding principle in the actions of this Assembly, permit me to point out a few of the items that deserve serious consideration at this Session and beyond. The issues I speak of are not the only ones of great importance. They are, however, some of the more urgent concerns that have already been discussed at various United Nations meetings; and they demand our attention both by reason of the work already devoted to them and by reason of the urgency of the current world condition.

(1407) There is a paramount need for a *greater and more equitable sharing of resources*. This includes the transfer of science and technology, which was the subject of the United Nations meeting in Vienna last year. It means a technology that is appropriate to the needs and best interests of the people and nations involved. But it means much more than just material sharing. There is an urgent need for a sharing of the resources of the mind and the spirit, of scientific knowledge and cultural and artistic expression. Such a sharing is not one-way. It is mutual and multilateral, and it implies that the cultural, ethical and religious values of peoples must always be respected by the parties involved in this sharing. It implies mutual openness to learn from one another and to share with one another.

(1408) In this sharing, there is no question that technological development and economic growth will involve some change in the social and cultural patterns of a people. To a certain extent this is inevitable and must be faced realistically for the sake of the growth of a people. But if we are honest when we say that man is not just *homo economicus*, then all of us must take care to see that any harmful change wherein positive values are sacrificed is minimized and that ethico-moral, cultural and religious values are placed ahead of the merely economic indicators of growth.

(1409) In this sharing, finally, it is good to recognize and to support the many new ways of cooperation among peoples and nations. Not only is there sharing between one group and another; developing nations are also learning to share among themselves, and regional groups are aiding one another to help find the best means to further their mutual interests.

(1410) You Member States of this Assembly cannot rest content with lofty perspectives or ethical ideals alone. You have the responsibility to negotiate together in good faith and mutual respect. The negotiations you carry out should be as all-inclusive as possible, taking into account the advantages to be had from the most complete and far-reaching agreement possible on all the items before you for negotiation. This kind of enlightened realism will do much to construct the necessary modifications for our common future built on our common hope.

(1411) My predecessor Paul VI called on the developed nations to contribute 1% of their Gross National Product (GNP) to the cause of development. The figure that is actually set aside today for this purpose seems very much lower. I recognize that inflation is a worldwide problem affecting the industrialized as well as the developing countries. However, the Holy See wishes to reiterate the appeal of Paul VI that 1% of the GNP is not an unrealistic goal. The contribution of this percentage would greatly aid the Common Fund agreed to through the UNCTAD negotiations as well as a possible World Development Fund.

(1412) For initiatives of this kind to be effective, there must be a renewed effort on the part of all nations, developed and developing, to end all waste, whether material or human.

(1413) On the material level the question of the environment carried on by UNEP and other agencies deserves renewed study and action. The whole problem of energy might well be seen in this context so that the most effective and appropriate energy resources are made available without unnecessary waste and exploitation of materials.

(1414) On the human level, many United Nations conferences have highlighted concern for children, for women, for the handicapped, for so many categories and peoples whose resources are being exploited or not used for their good and the good of society. Once again the commitment to various aspects of human development for the common good can rekindle hope for people, giving them the prospect of a fuller and more fruitful existence.

(1415) Finally I would be untrue to my charge if I did not call attention to the poor and to those on the margin of society throughout the world. There are countries rich in cultural and other spiritual and human resources, but which are among the poorest economically and among those who are suffering most from the current situation. We all know the staggering statistics about the real horror of famine that afflicts so many around the globe. Suffering peoples in various regions cry out to us to give them relief now so that they can survive.

(1416) Can all of us, who have so much, at least commit ourselves to giving new hope to these poor of the world by realizing a pledge- first, to relieve their plight and then to provide for their most basic needs, such as food, water, health and shelter. To relieve the immediate suffering and to provide those elements that will help people become more self-reliant would be a sure indication that we are contributing to the hope that this earth and its peoples need.

(1417) In so many of these matters, what will be needed is the political will that goes beyond immediate self-interest. Such a political will has in the past led to great achievements, such as the Universal Declaration of Human Rights. Such a will must be constantly guided by criteria that exalt the human and social, the ethical and cultural, the moral and spiritual over the solely economic and technological.

(1418) Such a will needs to be developed not only among world leaders but among all peoples at every level of life. Many issues can be solved only on the global level, and you at this Assembly have these tasks before you. But many can and, ought to be brought to fruitful agreement on the continental or regional or other intermediate level. The need for global solutions to many problems should not blind us to the possibilities of resolving problems and building a better future on adequate rather than all-encompassing standards of living. In fact, applying the notion of subsidiarity, we can see that there are many groups and peoples who can solve their own problems better at a local or intermediate level, and that such action moreover gives them a direct sense of participation in their own destinies. This is a positive advance and one to which we all should be sensitive.

(1419) In my pastoral visits in Europe, in North and South America and in Africa, I have spoken often and in varying ways of the need for conversion of hearts. I have stressed the need for each one of us to be converted, to see in the other person a brother or a sister united by the bond of a common humanity under God. My predecessor Paul VI in his Encyclical *Populorum Progressio*, a document which remains one of the enduring and valid contributions to the work of development, said: "There can be no progress towards the complete development of man without the simultaneous development of all humanity in a spirit of solidarity... Man must meet man, nation must meet nation, as brothers and sisters, as children of God. In this mutual understanding and friendship, in this sacred communion, we must also begin to work together to build the common future of the human race." (*Populorum Progressio*, 43)

(1420) May I complete this message to you today by recalling these words and this perspective to your reflection. May I ask that as you seek a change in the structures that will better serve the common good in justice and equity, you will not forget the education and inspiration of your peoples that will help bring about the conversion of hearts. Only through a conversion of hearts can brothers and sisters "build the common future of the human race," and construct the great and lasting edifice of peace. And it is to this peace - the new name of which aptly remains "development" (cf. *Populorum Progressio*, 87) - that all the efforts of this Special Session must be directed. With God's help may it be so!

IV - LOVE, JUSTICE AND POLITICAL DECISIONS

Letter of His Holiness John Paul II to Mr. Alister McIntyre, Deputy Secretary-General of the United Nations Conference for Trade and Development, on the occasion of the 6th Session of the Intergovernmental Group of Experts on the Least Developed Countries. The Vatican, 26 September 1985.

Original: French (*)

(1421) The world economic crisis and various other factors have not permitted the realization of all the objectives defined since the Conference meeting on the Least Developed Countries in Paris, September 1981, and even after the elaboration of the substantial new program of action for the '80s. So, at this half-way point, a general evaluation of the implementation of this programme of action is very appropriate. Further, it is a cause for satisfaction to see the intergovernmental Group of Experts on the Least Developed Countries meeting within the structure of UNCTAD and with its help. I am very happy to express my warm encouragement to all those who

(*) AAS 77 (1985), 1166-1168.

are participating in this session in Geneva. I warmly wish that the political will, based on an objective analysis of the present situation, will be reactivated to adopt more just and effective measures toward the solution of one of the gravest problems of our times.

(1422) During my recent pastoral visit to Africa, I did not fail to emphasize, on several occasions, how I cherish the progress of all peoples; responsibility lies with the governments and the peoples in each country, but also in an interdependent way, with the whole community of nations. Therefore, at Yaounde, for example, I spoke to the President of the Republic, to the constituent bodies and to the diplomatic corps. With the active support of the international community in the areas of food, health and investments, the efforts of African countries, certainly conditioned by limited means, would, however, be capable progressively to meet the economic and social challenge which devastates and humiliates the great majority of their inhabitants. During the work of the session, I do not doubt that the participants, considering attentively the technical reports and the statistics, will have their minds and hearts really captured by the human dramas which millions and millions of our fellow human beings live daily in the poorest countries. All these brothers and sisters are worthy of our solidarity. However, isn't it appropriate to grant a certain priority to those youth without work, without a future and sometimes already suffering in their health and their development?

(1423) Also, I am anxious to touch a delicate, sad question. I am speaking of the torment of the leaders in several countries who do not know how to face the agonizing problem of debt. Without wishing to enter into technical considerations, I would like however to mention this problem which constitutes one of the most complex aspects of the general situation of the international economy. A structural reform of the world financial system is doubtless one of the most urgent and necessary initiatives.

(1424) Nevertheless, allow me to propose two points of reflection for your kind attention. First, it seems to me necessary to search out and to concretize measures capable of helping the indebted and least developed countries to become self-sufficient, or at least largely self-sufficient, in the area of food. Then, I would like to emphasize the specifically Christian value of charity. This value would lead, especially in urgent cases, to political and economic decisions which are not only dictated by considerations of strictly human justice, but inspired by a generosity of a superior order, called love of neighbor by Christians and an expression of the love of God. The Gospel gives us enlightening teaching and striking examples on this subject. In this way, technical adjustments will be at the service of a political decision in the most noble sense of the term. Peace is built or rebuilt among nations thanks to this profound understanding of the common good of humanity and to such courageous decisions. In families, love does not contradict justice but gives it a dimension and a quality which allows trials to be overcome and crises to be surmounted. Thus the great community of peoples can help all the human family to progress in the ways of effective solidarity and to consolidate the deep aspirations for peace.

(1425) Again, I wish that the important and delicate work of this sixth session of the Intergovernmental Group of Experts on the Least Developed Countries will fully meet all expectations.

(1426) The well-being of two-thirds of humanity now confronting insupportable poverty depends on it.

(1427) The honor and the conscience of the peoples who are living in opulence depends on it.

(1428) I invoke abundant light and divine strength on the governments, the experts, the advisers and all the participants in this humanitarian session who can again give hope to our brothers and sisters in the least advanced countries.

May God bless your efforts.

V - SCIENCE AND TECHNOLOGY FOR DEVELOPMENT

Note of the Holy See in preparation to the United Nations Conference on Science and Technology for Development, published by the United Nations on 8 August 1979 (A/CONF.81/6, Vol.I).

Original: English

(1429) 1. The Holy See, consistent with its spiritual mission and its position within the organization of the United Nations, has readily accepted the invitation extended by the Secretary-General of the United Nations to make a contribution for the preparation of the Conference on Science and Technology for Development which is scheduled to be held in Vienna in 1979. The importance of this subject for the development of peoples, a theme which marked the pontificate of Pope Paul VI, cannot escape the concern and interest of the Holy See. Therefore, drawing on its worldwide concern for all peoples and its heritage of ethical and spiritual values as well as its experience of the past in educating peoples, this intervention seeks to make a contribution which will illuminate some of the priorities which, in the Holy See's view, will help advance the well-being of all peoples by providing both material and spiritual benefits for human beings everywhere.

(1430) Science and technology are indispensable elements for any development. While the scope and implications of science and technology cannot be limited just to the economic sphere, *mutatis mutandis*, what the Vatican Council II said of economic life is pertinent here: "The ultimate and basic purpose of economic production does not consist merely in the increase of goods produced, nor in profit nor in prestige; it is directed to the service of man, of man, that is, in his totality, taking into account his material needs and the requirements of his intellectual, moral, spiritual and religious life..." (*Gaudium et Spes*, 64).

(1431) 2. We must face the fact that, when we speak of science and technology, we are dealing with something that is radically ambivalent. Every discovery, every technical innovation has brought negative aspects as well as positive ones. These are so intertwined that it is difficult to determine at what level or at what point the good outweighs the bad or vice versa.

(1432) The fundamental ambivalence in the use of science and technology, the potential it has for good or evil results, lies not in chance or statistical proportions. It rests in the attitudes which we human beings bring to the products of scientific research and technological development. Therefore, before there can be any evaluation of the worth of this or that technique, or the use of this or that scientific achievement, there must be a clarification of the attitudes of ourselves as human beings and as States who carry responsibilities and who have the obligation to ensure that the values which foster the lives of persons and nations actively guide our deliberations and choices in the concerns before us at this conference.

(1433) 3. In union with all people of the world, the Church is ready to support and acclaim the progress that science and technology have already attained, so long as this progress truly serves the good of the inhabitants of this earth and does not deprive anyone of the just fruits of its advances and growth. She does, however, insist that all true progress in science and technology be put at the disposal of people without prejudice or discrimination, and that the value of truth and honesty, equity and fraternity, spirit and religion be advanced by these many forms of progress.

(1434) 4. Real transfer of technology must then meet certain conditions if it is to be effective. Among the conditions that must be met are: (1) the creation of local employment; (2) the improvement of the opportunities for export of goods in equal competition with foreign productions; and (3) that such transfer have a positive effect in inducing development of the local economy. Every realistic plan for development will be successful to the extent that it can be based on a profound understanding of the region involved, its natural resources and its human potential.

(1435) This can come about only through a threefold international action: (a) easier circulation, under equitable modalities, of patent rights and technological application of useful discoveries; (b) freer circulation of technicians and experts at the service of a decentralized regional scientific activity; and (c) effective promotion, with financial assistance, of instruction in those countries which have this need.

(1436) Given these conditions then, there is need to develop *centres for education and research* so that the technological and scientific advances once transferred can be exploited positively by persons in developing countries who will be able in turn to contribute their own expertise to further the advance of science and technology in their own culture. When scientific research is concentrated in a few privileged places, it tends to become separated from the real needs of people and can be turned to useless ends. Scientific research should seek to deepen its links with the economic and social needs of various regions and attempt to harness the resources that are proper to each of these.

1437) 5. Without prejudice to the possibility of highly sophisticated technologies and complex, long flow sheets for productive development where they are legitimately called for, the Holy See would like to see attention drawn to those adapted technologies which combine a certain technological development and advance with the materials and genius proper to a specific culture or society.

(1438) It would be helpful if the Conference could consider the advisability of insisting more directly on "intermediate" or "adapted" technology. Such would be more advanced than the technological skills and installations now in general use by developing counties, but, would avoid the tremendously "capital intensive" and often unadaptable technologies that are highly sophisticated, and which would demand such changes in the ecological and socio-economic environment that they would be counterproductive.

(1439) 6. If intermediate technologies seem at present to offer the best means for ensuring a transfer of science and technology that will guarantee progress and development and also give developing countries the means of assuring a continued role in scientific and technological fields, then the role of food and agricultural development remains the one grand area which needs urgent and serious attention. Self-reliance, the slogan under which many nations are seeking to find their own ability to control their own destinies, comes to the fore when one considers the necessity for every country to be able to produce foodstuff adequate for its needs, and to have an agricultural base that corresponds to the potential that each country has.

(1440) The development of basic water for all peoples in a country or region is a first step of enormous consequence for the movement toward self-reliance. The experiments now going on and the discoveries already developed in water purification, desalination, water drilling techniques, irrigation and the like should be made available at lowest cost as quickly and as widely as possible.

(1441) 7. So, in conclusion, we would repeat that the end of every power and every social action is the human person and the fulfillment of human potential on all levels of family and nation, in such a way that human persons become the free bearer of the values of their culture and their beliefs. Science and technology can be a powerful aid in freeing human beings so that they are ever more the authentic bearers of their culture; it can in unique ways then contribute to the building of a more just and harmonious world, in which peoples can live in peace because the discoveries of the human genius are placed at the service of the development of all peoples everywhere.

VI - INTEGRAL HUMAN DEVELOPMENT

Message of His Eminence Cardinal Maurice Roy, President of the Pontifical Commission "Justice and Peace" to H.E. U Thant, Secretary-General of the United Nations, on the occasion of the launching of the Second Development Decade. The Vatican, 19 November 1970.

Original: English

(1442) 1. The world stands at the threshold of the Second Development Decade. The agonizing question before us is whether it holds more promise than the first for meeting the needs of the poor, the dispossessed, the powerless of our planet. If integral human development must be counted a fundamental right of man, will history record the Seventies as the decade in which, at last, a really serious effort was made to implement this right?

(1443) 2. The Pontifical Commission Justice and Peace, of which I have the honour to be President, was created by Pope Paul VI in the wake of the Second Vatican Council precisely to engage the full energies of the Roman Catholic Church in this project of humanity. Ours is the mission of awakening all within the Church to our common responsibilities for peace, international justice and development.

(1444) 3. As President of the Commission, therefore, I take the occasion of the United Nations' announcement of the Second Development Decade to appeal for world cooperation toward achieving integral human development for all men.

(1445) 4. We begin the new Development Decade with, I believe, deeper insight into the nature of our problems. In the Sixties, both the theory and the practice of development tended to be exclusively economic. Theory drew heavily on the nineteenth century experience of peoples already developed by capital accumulation in the process of modernization. In practice, development was judged to be successful if it achieved rates of growth sufficient to provide both for rising population and rising investment. The essential element in economic assistance was believed to lie in a transfer of capital from rich to poor and, as the Decade advanced, in wider opportunities for the developing nations in international trade. Given these changes, rapid economic growth would prove both possible and largely sufficient.

(1446) 5. These insights of the Sixties - into the need for capital assistance and the necessity of wider opportunities in world trade - are not false. Indeed, the world of the Seventies would be a more stable place if the prime targets of the Sixties had been achieved, in particular the goals of aid equivalent to one per cent of the gross national product of the rich nations, and, for the developing nations, higher export incomes, better access to industrialized markets and more-working capital for trade. We do not dismiss or deny such objectives. They must still be achieved. We simply join in the judgement expressed by an increasing number of development experts and practitioners, and indeed embodied in the international development strategy recently adopted by the General Assembly of the United Nations, that, for truly human societies and a truly peaceful world, these objectives are not enough.

(1447) 6. We would suggest two reasons for this change of view. The first came to the fore during the Annual Meeting of the World Bank and the International Monetary Fund in September 1970; the processes of development of the already industrialized nations, which have been taken as the model for contemporary development, contain too many special circumstances for them to be applicable to the wholly altered conditions of today. Within the early, largely Atlantic, developing societies, epidemics and poor sanitation held back population growth, and greater productivity in agriculture, preceding industrialization, released food and manpower to a growing industrial sector where techniques demanded massive supplies of labour and not too much capital. This capital could in any case be secured by the ability of the entrepreneurs to mobilize for investment the whole productive surplus. In these conditions cities grew as a result of industrial expansion, jobs grew with them and by the time technology demanded more skill and more capital, workers had acquired education, built up mass organizations and stabilized family size. The cities were not utopias. But they were dynamic centres of work and life.

(1448) 7. In any case, external circumstances eased the strain. The European peoples took over all the remaining temperate land of the globe after 1840. Forty million migrants left Europe in the nineteenth century for new land and jobs in the new world. The Europeans could also complete the colonization of virtually the whole of humanity. Their trade and investment in all the continents gave them-although they made up less than 20 per cent of the world's peoples-80 per cent of the world's resources and trade, 90 per cent of the investment, 100 per cent of the services, banking, shipping, research. These proportions have not changed since 1900 and help to explain the vast elbow-room which was available to the already developed nations when they sought to cross the threshold of modernization.

(1449) 8. Today every circumstance in the now developing nations, internal and external, works in the opposite sense. Public health has preceded modernization. Population grows at twice the nineteenth century pace; the work force, if anything, faster. Capital formation, in the farm and factory, is slowed down by rising numbers of consumers, however marginal, and by the new non-saving high consumption habits of the wealthy elite whose standards are now "western" while their societies are not. Under-modernized agriculture cannot feed its own rising millions, so its workers move to the cities ahead of any pull of rising industrial employment. Technology today is based on advanced models. It demands more capital which developing countries lack and fewer workers which they see increase like a flood. Worklessness rises inexorably in the Third World as the poor of the countryside transfer their misery to the fringes of the cities. As Mr. David Morse, former head of the International Labour Organization, recently pointed out, twenty to twenty-five per cent is a standard rate for contemporary unemployment. Among younger workers, it can be higher still. A more detailed and substantial profile of this process as it works in Latin America can be found in the report *Change and Development* recently prepared by Dr. Raul Prebisch, former Secretary General of the United Nations Conference on Trade and Development.

(1450) 9. There are no external safety valves. The world's free land is occupied; the frontier, closed. Political decolonization has not yet altered the overwhelming balance of wealth and power in favour of the already rich. Apart from movements of migrant labour in Europe, the massive migrations today are not across frontiers and oceans to new opportunities. They flow internally, from farm to city, from a rural to an urban misery. And still the numbers rise. Our world will become even more troubled with so great a mass of misery piling up at its base.

(1451) 10. This brings us to the second reason for our belief that economic growth is an indispensable but not sufficient cause of full human development. The reason is quite simply, as Pope Paul underlines in his Encyclical *Populorum Progressio*, that the unfettered working of the market, operating between "partners" of grossly unequal strength, does not secure anything like a proper distribution of the fruits of economic development. In the modern economy, with its premium on skill, drive, capacity and investment, it is the intelligent, the tough, the energetic and the already rich that tend to take all the gains, unless strong political and social policies accompany modernization in order to secure greater justice and greater participation.

(1452) 11. This is the obvious lesson of the nineteenth century. Even with the vast bounties of new continents to develop and a whole planet to colonize, the industrialized nations were racked with crises of social discontent and class war until they introduced the tax systems, the land reforms, the welfare policies and the extension of the vote needed to liberate the mass of people from total dependence upon the dominant classes to give them a sense of participation in society and a share in the wealth they worked every day to produce. Even today, whenever undue reliance on the beneficent workings of an uncorrected market economy persists in developed societies and, as a result, social action is delayed, the weak, the poor, the unskilled, the ethnic minorities tend to fall behind and to relive the squalid miseries of nineteenth century slums and sweatshops.

(1453) 12. These are the facts which underlie the international community's growing disenchantment with purely economic development. At the local level, it can be seen ever more clearly that societies in which little or no political and social action ameliorates the lot of the mass of the people and liberates them sufficiently to take a full part in their own development, no amount of economic growth will lead to satisfactory modernization. On the contrary, it will tend to pile up the riches and consumption of the few and leave a growing mass of "marginal men" at the base of society for whom even the most elementary of human needs and decencies - job, home, school, diet, health, - will be almost completely lacking.

(1454) 13. At the same time, one can see an almost identical process at work at the planetary level. Our technology, our science, our communications all thrust us towards a steadily increasing interdependence. A truly planetary society is, as Pope Paul has never ceased to emphasize, the great imperative of our time. But, as *Populorum Progressio* repeatedly underlines, we have now a world economy in which *all* the positions of strength, all the wealth, all the investment, all the commercial services and above all, the whole crucial apparatus of research are concentrated in the small elite of nations which have already achieved modernization. It is this extraordinary concentration of wealth, of which industrialized nations themselves are all too often largely unaware, that helps to explain the bitterness and resentment which developing nations sometimes display when aid is offered in terms not much removed from patronage and paternalism and recipients are asked to show gratitude for what to them is not generosity but a marginal act of justice.

(1455) 14. To mediate between the wealthy and the developing nations, the international community needs more effective instruments of political responsibility or social good will. The United Nations still lacks the means and support to secure the kind of political participation and commitment required for a truly planetary cooperation. An aid effort which some of the wealthiest nations decreasingly support is not even the beginning, at the world level, of redistributive taxation or a healthy welfare system. In a world of such uneven power, neither justice nor liberation nor cooperation is conceivable so long as the nations are at one only in their cupidities and their fears, spending 200 billion dollars to defend their so-called security and thirty times less to root out the basic causes of insecurity. Unless the Seventies can reverse the widening gap between rich and poor, both within domestic society and in the world at large, it is all but impossible to believe that mankind can reach, in peace, the end of this troubled century.

(1456) 15. The nature of our crisis dictates the policies we must try to formulate and carry out in order to counter it. *all* are not yet accepted. Indeed many still need much more careful research and precise definition. Yet it is possible to see some movement towards a new consensus in which earlier concepts of economic growth are complemented by new ideas of social justice and political participation, and the United Nations international strategy represents the beginning of such a consensus. In short, economic man is beginning to give way a little to the full vision of man as a responsible moral agent, creative in his action, free in his ultimate decisions, united to his fellows in social bonds of respect and friendship and co-partner in the work of building a just and peaceful world.

(1457) 16. At the domestic level there is a growing sense that neither internal modernization nor external economic assistance will be effective:

(1458) a) unless the whole of the people are drawn into active participation in their own improvement and in the liberation of their own energies and skills;

(1459) b) unless the institutions which stultify participation and self-realization are transformed. These include feudal land-holding; non-tax paying, non-saving, wealthy classes; industry without secure wages, opportunity for promotion and wide profit sharing or ownership; education confined to an elite and the acceptance of mass illiteracy; lack of institutions of participation and self-help workers' and peasant organizations, cooperatives; trade unions, saving banks, home loan associations; political systems which allow no play for personal liberty, regionalization and creative experiment.

(1460) c) unless active social policy, within the framework of a large social sector, deals directly with the worst causes of misery among the 25 per cent of "marginal men" whom the processes of modernization tend to leave behind. Direct action is needed for a full employment policy, housing programs, urban renewal and energetic policies to spread rural employment, cooperatives and land ownership as widely as possible in the wake of the Green Revolution;

(1461) d) unless population policies are fully adapted to local needs, traditions and values. Policy will vary according to the actual pressure on family well-being, of rising numbers, or speed of growth. But some principles are universal: that the aim of public policy is to enhance the welfare and quality of families; that life-destroying means or artificial means tending to render procreation impossible be excluded; that full respect is given to parents' God-given right to determine in full responsibility the size of their own family.

(1462) 17. At the international level, in addition to the aims of aid, trade liquidity and debt relief formulated in the Sixties, a number of further policies are gaining wider acceptance:

(1463) a) that all aid should be closely linked to those reforms in domestic structure already outlined above;

(1464) b) that international institutions in which the developing nations are fully represented should coordinate and distribute a larger part of the flow of concessionary finance;

(1465) c) that, as Pope Paul suggests in *Populorum Progressio*, the transfer of a much larger flow of finance to development should be achieved by a phased reduction in the intolerable and inflationary burden of armaments;

(1466) d) that aid flows should be "institutionalized" and accepted as an incipient world tax system in such a way as to underline their essential character not of generosity but of distributive justice. As such, they would be seen as an integrative element in the coming planetary society;

(1467) e) that developing nations, through regional groupings and collective action in the world market, should encourage trade and investment between each other and thus lessen the world economy's imbalance between North and South;

(1468) f) that a fundamental reconsideration of the planet's resource use and management be undertaken so that the increasingly irrational levels of extravagance, waste and pollution of the "high consumption societies" should not jeopardize the poorer nations' hopes of development and humanity's ultimate hopes of survival.

(1469) 18. These are the efforts which we seek, with the deepest urgency and sincerity, to assist and pursue. The Catholic Church hopes to work closely in this field with its Christian brothers in ecumenical programs, and indeed with men of all religions and of none, who are concerned with the future of our troubled humanity. It is our hope that some of our Christian insights may be of use in the great efforts of development. It is an even greater hope that Christian energy and dedication may be mobilized in its service.

(1470) 19. It is, after all, possible to see the planet as an arena in which the fittest survive by virtue of their force or cunning. It is possible to denounce all help to the weak and helpless as a gross interference in the evolutionary process and to proclaim the fitness of conquerors to conquer, simply by the fact that they have done so. It may, therefore, be of assistance to the whole spirit of planetary development in these post-colonial days of vast and deepening inequality if, to the giant disproportions between wealth and poverty, between weak and strong, Christians were to oppose a vision of human responsibility and fraternal love. It is, after all, the fundamental teaching of the Scriptures that we are our brother's keeper and that, if we leave the least of our fellow men to misery, hunger and early death, "the blood of Abel will call from the ground" for judgement and brand us with the mark of Cain. We know, too, how strong are the temptations of wealth and power. We know how much of the world's great surplus of careless and accepted wealth is accumulated among the post-Christian peoples. It is possible that they can still be reminded of God's terrible word to those who selfishly fill their barns with an unshared harvest: "Thou fool, this night thy soul is required of thee."

(1471) 20. Above all, it takes great energy of soul and great fortitude to undo the injustices of centuries and to rise above the ease of comfort and success. Equally, it demands unparalleled generosity to forgive past insults and present oppressions, and join together in the work of building a planet that can be a home to all its children. We do not say that Christians have this energy and generosity. We say only that if they had it, they could add conviction, dedication and staying power to their part in our world-wide task. We will seek by all means to arouse this energy and put it at the service of our human community. For we do not work without hope. We do not believe that "God has despaired of His children." We believe that, on the contrary, we can "work while it is day," and build together a world which is nearer to our Creator's vision and will for all mankind. And we believe that the Almighty Father of our human family will give us all the help we need and seek.

VII - CONCERN OF THE HOLY SEE FOR THE LEAST DEVELOPED COUNTRIES

1. Statement by Msgr. William Murphy, Under Secretary of the Pontifical Commission "Iustitia et Pax", Head of the Delegation of the Holy See, at the United Nations Conference on the Least Developed Countries. Paris, 7 September 1981.

Original: English

(1472) All of us gathered here are aware of the work that has gone into the preparation of this Conference. It is time now to bring the results of that work and study to bear on decisions and programmes that will be fruitful for all. The Church too, while it does not claim special expertise in the technical questions that are at the heart of this Assembly, comes here to work with everyone and to make its proper contribution. That contribution of the Church is founded on its vision of the dignity of every human person and on the fraternity and solidarity of the whole human family.

(1473) Pope John Paul II has demonstrated this in his many discourses and pastoral visits around the world. He expressed it in his first encyclical letter. Continuing in the tradition of Pope Paul VI's letter *Populorum Progressio,* the Pope reflected on the very problems and issues which are the focus of this Conference, when he said: "The principle of solidarity in a wide sense must inspire the effective search for appropriate institutions and mechanisms, whether in the sector of trade, where the laws of healthy competition must be allowed to lead the way, or on the level of a wider and more immediate redistribution of riches and of the control over them, in order that the economically developing peoples may be able not only to satisfy their essential needs but also to advance gradually and effectively" (*Redemptor Hominis* n. 16).

(1474) The basis of my remarks here today is the concern for the whole human person as a member of the human family, united in fraternity and solidarity. It is a concern that is not motivated by any self-interest, but seeks, as the Pope did last year at the Special Session on Development, to offer a solid realistic hope for every person in this world by calling on all of us to grapple with the realities of this world in order to form "a future to be built by united efforts to ensure the common good through mutual cooperation and collaboration" (John Paul II, Message to the 11th Special Session of the General Assembly of the United Nations, dedicated to the New International Development Strategy, No. 6. See above, par. 1405).

(1475) The first step in this process will demand a change or conversion of heart and of mentality. Because the task is not an easy one, and because much has to be done, every person and nation has to look to himself or herself to ensure the attitude of mind and spirit that will lend itself to a real commitment to face these questions together in freedom and solidarity. This change of heart is incumbent on us all, the rich and the poor, the powerful and the weak. Thus, as this Conference tries honestly and realistically to re-think the pressing economic, technical and financial needs present here, it will re-discover and re-assert the values which will advance the fraternity and solidarity of everyone living on this planet earth. In many ways and at diverse levels, the Church has participated and will continue to participate in this process with whatever resources it has to give, consistent with its proper mission.

(1476) The Church has never been satisfied to stop at pronouncements, however valid and important. Its educative task has always been accompanied by concrete programmes and activities. In the Christian commitment to the freedom and dignity of every human person, and in the Christian search for the common good of society, religious groups and religiously inspired agencies, some present at this Conference, have constantly been developing concrete programmes in the areas of health, education, cooperatives, rural development projects and village promotional efforts that sought to improve the lot of people living in some of the poorest and least developed parts of the world wherever they could place themselves in direct contact with those who needed them.

(1477) Because the Christian commitment to the real problems of people everywhere has a long and fruitful tradition, this Delegation would like to share with you, in that same spirit, some of the items which it considers to be of basic importance to the work of this Assembly.

(1478) While the issues being debated here are all interrelated - and thus to look seriously at one will involve the others - it still seems clear that the problem of food remains at the basis of every discussion that has been going on here. The ideal of self-reliance in the area of food and alimentation in the full sense is not an unattainable goal. Self-reliance in providing for the nutritional needs of a people contributes much to the sense of sovereignty and dignity of every country, removing the spectre of famine and allowing greater freedom to confront other questions and build up more diversified economies for the good of people.

(1479) Allied to this is the constant crucial problem of health and the delivery of health care especially to rural areas where, to date, too many suffer needlessly from diseases of many kinds. It is equally important to mention the real needs in the energy field that nations will face as they seek to harness the resources available to them and build up a more healthy, creative and diversified economy. In addition it is wise to give heed to the Least Developed Countries in the area of communications, especially within countries that are geographically spread out or whose topographical situation makes communication difficult. It would be a great step forward if honest, realistic assessments in these areas could be met at this Conference by equally honest, realistic and generous response.

(1480) One final word is in order here about the importance of education. The greatest waste of energy and resources today is the waste of the human intellect and the waste of the creativity of the human person. Malnutrition, lack of resources, lack of infrastructures, especially in the new overcrowded urban centers, all coalesce to hinder the proper and full development of the greatest resource of each and every nation: the human person. The Holy See has already contributed a study on this to the UNCSTD Conference at Vienna in 1979. A commitment at this Conference could bring into action the transfer of learning skills and the building up of the infrastructures that are needed. Ongoing collaboration that would ensure wider and more consistent transfer of learning and its related skills would free millions now locked in illiteracy and give impetus to millions more who want to advance on the road of learning to acquire new skills and expertise that will allow them to fulfill their potential and contribute to the good of humanity itself.

(1481) These are the major points this Delegation would like to put before this Conference today. As the needed judgments and commitments are made about the Substantial New Programme for Action, and as the real needs of the thirty one Least Developed Countries are brought to the fore, it is our hope that as many as possible of the legitimate aspirations and goals of these countries will be realized so that the common good of all humanity will be furthered through the decisions and commitments that are made here by all the participants in accordance with their roles, their capabilities, and their responsibilities.

(1482) May I close with the words of John Paul II who last year told the United Nations Organization: "If there is a history to be made, and if we are responsible for the common good now and in the future, we must together work out and put into practice the modifications that are necessary now so that the future we yearn for will correspond to the hope we share for all individuals, peoples and nations on this earth." (John Paul II, Message to the 11th Special Session of the General Assembly of the United Nations on Development, No. 6. See above, par. 1405).

2. Statement by the Rev. Fr. Roger du Noyer, Secretary of the Pontifical Council "Cor Unum", Head of the Delegation of the Holy See, at the 6th Session of the Intergovernmental Group Charged with the Question of the Least Developed Countries, held in Geneva on 30 September-11 October. Geneva, 2 October 1985.

Original: French

(1483) The least developed countries, we all know, are extremely vulnerable, and in them the least crisis or calamity can have very serious repercussions which are not known in the countries we may call "privileged". Since the meeting which took place in Paris in September 1981, the world crisis has become more intensified, even the Northern countries being deeply affected; natural and man-made disasters have struck Africa, where the majority of less developed countries, are found. I think above all of drought, of famine and of the problem of refugees; but Asia, where Bangladesh was seriously hit by floods, was not spared either. The Holy See wishes that our meeting, by the seriousness of its tasks and the fullness of its undertakings, will return hope to those populations whose distress we can only imagine with great difficulty.

(1484) The agenda we have adopted for today, "the global examination, now half completed, of the progress in the application of a substantial new program of action for the 80's", permits us at this time to consider together the situation in each country that the community of nations has decided to aid with increased means in priority order. We will see then the progress accomplished and also the delays in implementing the program; the objective analysis of the local or external causes, once identified, will be useful in overcoming or at least reducing these obstacles.

(1485) "The examination of measures to be taken in order to assure the application of the program until the end of the Decade" will demand some technical competence and some courageous political decisions at the moment when the world-wide economic crisis strikes everyone. But the poverty of some will not mean the wealth of others; either the future will be constructed together, or injustice and selfishness will only engender violence and war.

(1486) The Catholic Church, in all its international and national components, does not cease lending its support to every initiative tending to ease suffering and famine in the world, and it encourages all the faithful to open themselves to the full advancement and solidarity of humanity. In his Encyclical *Populorum Progressio,* Pope Paul VI declared: "In communion with the greatest aspirations of men, and suffering from seeing them unsatisfied, the Church desires to help them attain their full blossoming, and this is why it proposes to them what is its fundamental possession: a global vision of man and humanity." For we not only speak here of nourishing bodies and protecting health: we have come together in order to permit men and women, and youth of which there are millions, to live in dignity, to develop all their capabilities, to become themselves the free artisans of their future in a solidarity of which they at present feel the need and, in which we hope, they will have decisive fraternal support.

(1487) The Governments represented here recognize, in general, in their respective countries, the social action of Christians, their human and financial participation in development, their commitment; they know the continuing indispensable activity of non-governmental organizations, of which several are under Christian guidance. The financial generosity of Christians from the Northern countries cannot be denied; without racial or religious discrimination for the recipients, they participate in the solidarity among peoples. The words and activities of Pope John Paul II are well-known; the John Paul II Foundation for the Sahel is one example, among others.

(1488) Wishing that our Assembly take concrete decisions, I would like in conclusion, Mr. President, to cite a few of the Pope's recent words which will confirm to you the certitude that he has of the importance of meetings like ours. Last August 15 in Kinshasa, addressing the Members of the Official and Diplomatic Corps, John Paul II said: "...If one must recognize in truth that which heavily weighs on the lives of peoples who aspire to a shared prosperity and to peace, it is also necessary to notice signs of hope. It is not in vain that nations meet to debate the obstacles that they find on their path. It is not in vain that international dialogue continues within the framework of large institutions. It is not in vain that great numbers of men, on all sides, sincerely devote themselves to the great causes of solidarity. The search is possible for a new balance among the peoples of the earth."

VIII - TRADE AND DEVELOPMENT

1. Fraternity to replace paternalism

Statement of the Reverend Louis-Joseph Lebret for the Holy See Delegation at the United Nations Conference for Trade and Development held in Geneva on 23 March-15 June 1964. Geneva, 5 May 1964.

Original: French

(1489) Those who have followed the history of our Conference will not be surprised that the Holy See, responding to the invitation of the United Nations Secretary-General, was anxious to be represented here. Since 14 May 1962, on the occasion of the preliminary consultations of States Members of the United Nations and specialized agencies, the Holy See has spoken out in favor of holding the present Conference as a means of reinforcing international collaboration in development and peace at a moment when it is so necessary. It happens that this response was made between the publications of *Mater and Magistra* and *Pacem in Terris,* the two most important Encyclicals of Pope John XXIII. These documents, as you know, are completely inspired by the profound solicitude of the Holy See for the problems posed by the inauguration of an equitable order intended for the fullest advancement of each member of the human family. Pope Paul VI wanted to dedicate his first Christmas message to this advancement. Among other things, he speaks there about young nations:

(1490) "They do not yet have the possibility of profiting from all the economic and cultural advantages of a fully evolved modern civilization. And so, our love, inspired by the mystery of Christmas, searches for the most serious needs of the world. It shows us, in these young States, the need no longer of self-interested and humiliating charity, but of scientific and technological assistance as well as solidarity based on the friendship of all other nations. May the spirit of fraternity replace paternalism."

(1491) Do not these sentences describe the spirit and the goals of the present Conference? These will inspire the delegation of the Holy See in the part that it takes and will take in the present debates. Its role, no need to mention it, will not be to intervene in the detail of the means proposed to reach these goals, still less to take part in the debates of a purely political nature. Rather, in a spirit of frank and total collaboration we intend to help bring out the ultimate purposes of international exchanges in light of principles of international ethics and of the elementary requirements of equity.

(1492) Several speakers at this podium have already drawn attention to an absolutely fundamental point: development is the ultimate purpose of our Conference. Trade, or more broadly, exchange, is only one way to adapt to this purpose. Further, the full meaning must be given to the concept of development.

(1493) Development, as has been said but perhaps not with enough emphasis, must be distinguished from the simple numerical progress of global quantities, gross national product, or national per capita income. In fact, measured in this way, growth can be only a mask veiling the reality of a population whose privileged classes benefit from a considerable rise in their income, the middle classes of a still important rise, while the great urban or rural majority only benefit a very little without speaking of the cases where income is even decreased. The spread between the standards of living expands considerably, a very small fraction of the population having gone beyond the European or even North American level while a great mass remains behind by several centuries. Growth can also mean the creation of the germ of an economic and social imbalance as, for example, when the attraction of an important industrial or urban pole promotes the exodus from the agricultural areas which become underpopulated in proportion to their normal capacity for production; or again, when an excessive cultivation of the soil from a "get-rich-quick" speculation precipitates erosion of cultivated land; or, another example, when the growth expressed is due in part to construction for the wealthy and privileged classes while housing for the people not only remains poor but becomes increasingly so. Such are the elements demanding, each one, priority in the elaboration of policies for commercial expansion in developing nations!

(1494) In fact, development is indivisible. Progress must take place for each category of the population; in all aspects, the strictly human dimension is primordial. On these requirements for development I had the honor last year on the occasion of UNCSAT to expand at length in the name of the delegation of the Holy See. I will not dwell on them now except to recall that a discipline is defined by its objective; now, the complex discipline of development can only have for primary objective the human uplifting of the people.

(1495) Without having to examine here all the aspects of the methodology of development, it is important only to stress the way in which this conference sees one of the indispensable conditions of development: trade rendered equitable.

(1496) It is a question at one and the same time of trade between countries and between groups of countries, and also of world trade envisaged in its totality. Our battle takes place on this planetary plane, and this obliges us to broaden our goal.

(1497) The term "trade" was chosen because the poorest countries see the present modes of international trade as one of the principle obstacles to their development. Their economy is strangled and their hopes for development vanish if, for example, they receive less currency because of the products they sell, and they must spend more currency to buy either the necessary consumer products or the required means of production; or else, if a considerable contribution of intangible supports and trade accommodations fail to correct the commercial balance and permit stability in the balance of payments.

(1498) So, the problem, in the view of our delegation, is not only trade in the strict sense of the word, but the totality of the relations and exchanges between peoples. We do not underestimate the efforts which have been made here by each more economically developed country or by associations of countries or international organs, and we wish to render homage to them. We must underline, however, that only an evolution in deep-set attitudes will evoke a more intense and more effective altruism and a broadening of perspectives about trade and exchanges until the establishment of a civilization authentically in solidarity is assured.

(1499) This is the great revolution which the present conference must inaugurate, a bloodless, long-term revolution whose first phase will be marked by the resolutions and decisions taken here.

(1500) Mr. President, the delegation of the Holy See knows the difficulties which confront those who wish to change or, at least, profoundly transform an out-dated system of exchange whose harmful effects are not sufficiently compensated by granting gifts and loans.

(1501) Our delegation, as requested by the Secretariat of State of His Holiness communicated to you the text of a letter from the Cardinal Secretary of State expressing the special interest of the Holy Father in our Conference. Allow me to cite now the following passage:

(1502) "The Conference currently opening in Geneva is confronted by problems of a particular gravity. Definitive answers to all the delicate questions asked in Geneva will not perhaps find their answers there. The current problem of international trade could not actually be resolved by solutions as apparently simple as the sole rule of international free market or, at the extreme opposite, of total planning. But, full commitment is necessary through planning appropriate phases and effective institutions in this period of change and transition which will end in full satisfaction of the most legitimate human aspirations within the scope of national independence."

(1503) A perfect regulation of trade could certainly not be obtained overnight. Our knowledge is still fragmentary; we ought not fear the inevitable risks of experimentation.

(1504) In this regard, the delegation of the Holy See would like to pay homage to the modesty and realism of the Secretary-General of our Conference. As he said himself in his speech, he has deliberately contained his personal aspirations and his desires in order to do justice to the search for progressive solutions tried by the test of experience in the good faith of all interested parties.

(1505) We will have to explore new ways. These must fully respect freedom while submitting it to strict disciplines, indispensable at the international plane, so that the disparity disappears between the standards of living of favored peoples and of those scientifically and technologically less advanced. Even more, our delegation esteems that the totality of resources of the world must be exploited so that all humanity is the beneficiary; the exchange of goods produced by all peoples should take place in such a way that all those who do not yet have a decent standard of living or who, because of the impoverishment of their soil, their substratum and their energy resources, cannot hope to escape poverty, nevertheless obtain the satisfaction of their essential needs and achieve a standard of living conforming to human dignity.

(1506) In this context, new rules must be elaborated; on the one hand, equality in exchanges must no longer be considered only in terms of the market, and on the other, financial aid or aid in kind must correspond to the excess available funds varying, of course, according to the degree of development of each more developed country.

(1507) Mr. President, most people recognize today that to modify the methodology for establishing the individual salaries of workers, either by legislation or by collective agreement, is not to grant a privilege to that employee: it is to do justice, recognizing that poverty which affects too many persons. Why not apply the same reasoning to the case of international exchanges? These are a means of basic subsistence for the poor countries and, above all, for those powerless countries at the mercy of ostensibly free sales agreements which are, in reality, imposed.

(1508) Given the degrees in underdevelopment as in development and recognizing also the tasks falling to the poorest countries to direct the revenues of their trade toward an authentic human development of all their populations, the most developed and richest countries must be aware of their special responsibilities here; they must face up to a strict obligation of solidarity and justice in matters of commercial exchange with the third world.

(1509) Moreover, in looking at things close-up, in terms of human values, those who give receive more than those to whom it is given. The civilization of the privileged is menaced by the limitless extension of their desires. They will escape only by committing themselves to a less materialistic and a more humanistic way. According to social justice, all the goods of the rich must contribute to the common good in a community henceforth universal. The poorest, in terms of human values, are those who have a great desire to retain their superfluity for themselves. The greed of nations, denoted by the greed of the greatest number of their members, is a weakness in whatever civilization it is found.

(1510) Finally, Mr. President, the exchange of material goods is only one aspect of the totality of exchanges, and the rules of equitable trade are only a partial expression of a far broader ethic of relationships. These are all the exchanges that must be managed in order that each one gives and each one receives! Everyone agrees now that the least developed countries have extra-economic values to bring to the most developed peoples.

(1511) Gratitude and political friendship, in the sense that Aristotle and Saint Thomas of Aquinas gave to that expression are, in the end, more precious and more efficacious for peace than the material goods which we know how to sacrifice intelligently.

(1512) To use an imperfect image: beyond the strategic combinations and contradictory or inapplicable solutions caused by hidden material or ideological conflicts of interest, beyond even the objectively best solutions for the fleeting period which this meeting inaugurates, the success of this extremely important Conference demands that each one rise up one degree to better understand the problem of "trade and development" in all its dimensions and, even more, to think of "humanity" in its totality.

2. A moral drive to eliminate the inequalities between developing and developed nations

Message of His Holiness Paul VI to Dr. Raul Prebisch, Secretary-General of the United Nations Conference on Trade and Development. The Vatican, 29 January 1968.

Original: French

(1513) We have much pleasure in addressing this message to you and to all present at the second meeting of the United Nations Conference on Trade and Development, in New Delhi. The meeting carries with it the hopes of many peoples in the world. They trust that it will result in some steps towards the improvement of their position in international trade so as to assure them a life more in keeping with their human dignity. We do not hesitate to make this cause our own.

(1514) Although serious economic difficulties exist even in developed countries, the fact that millions of human beings lack the basic necessities of a decent life must not be forgotten. This is fundamentally a moral problem, and it transcends the bare economic aspect of the crisis. The solutions must come from a moral drive to eliminate the inequalities between developing and developed nations. There is no magic formula for solving the extremely technical and complicated problems involved in restructuring world trade on equitable lines, but unwearying good will and determination to succeed should permeate the technical discussions.

(1515) In fact, we are convinced that problems so complex and so important can find proper solutions only if a strong influence of higher thinking and moral energy pervades these discussions and studies and raises them from the merely economic level to one truly human. This implies generous, progressive brotherhood and balanced, inventive wisdom with a view of interests which go beyond the particular difficulties of the moment and look to the future of the peaceful civilization of humanity. This is our thought, as followers of Christ, and we believe that our thinking in these matters coincides both with that of magnanimous men who have the capability to promote justice in the world and with that of the patient and hopeful developing peoples. We feel that this thinking, put into effect, can well result in progress beyond the hopes of all men.

(1516) Our appeal is a reaffirmation of the plea for human solidarity and partnership in economic cooperation in our Encyclical "Populorum Progressio". May it serve as a call to all to labour for the elimination of the dire conditions in which so many of our fellow-men live today.

(1517) Invoking upon the participants of the UNCTAD meeting in New Delhi abundant heavenly blessings, we pray that Almighty God may favour their deliberations with success for the betterment of mankind.

3. Confidence manifest in international economic relations

Statement of His Excellency Msgr. Giuseppe Caprio, Head of the Holy See Delegation at the Second United Nations Conference on Trade and Development, held in New Delhi on 1 February-28 March 1968. New Delhi, 8 February 1968.

Original: French

(1518) Allow me first of all, Mr. President, to congratulate you on your election and to express the high value which the Holy See attaches to the fact that the Government of India was anxious to host this Second United Nations Conference on Trade and Development. Three weeks ago, the Holy Father received the "good-will mission" submitting to him the conclusions of the Algiers Conference. At that time, he recalled the fraternal moments he was given to spend in India thanks to the welcome marked by delicacy and good feelings that the representatives of this great people accorded to him. The Holy Father voiced the wish that "these privileged moments" might be renewed for the participants of the Conference and that our "meeting in New Delhi among representatives of all nationalities, races and religions might become a fruitful dialogue to open the ways to a more fraternal life in a truly universal community." Since then, I have had the honor to read right here the Message addressed by His Holiness: it witnesses to the unceasing interest with which the power that we represent follows the works of UNCTAD since their beginning.

(1519) Four years ago, on the occasion of the first general debate of UNCTAD, the representative of the Holy See spoke of the great revolution which the Conference must inaugurate, a bloodless, long-term revolution whose first phase would be marked by the resolutions and decisions taken in Geneva. The eloquent voice of the great pioneer of development, Father Lebret, is silent now. However, during these years since the Geneva meeting, the doctrine and the thought of the Church of which he wanted only to be the faithful interpreter and authentic commentator, have not ceased to expand and to speak out with vigor and coherence on the majority of the points which constitute the theme of our present meeting. The Second Vatican Council devoted important chapters of its Pastoral Constitution on the Church in the Modern World to them. I do not have to quote them here; our distinguished Secretary-General made adequate application of them to the problems of UNCTAD in his address to the Second Session of the Administrative Council. Adding precision and depth to the teaching of the Church on development, the encyclical *Populorum Progressio,* at the beginning of last year, gave its full weight to the application of principles of charity and justice in international cooperation. Some important paragraphs of this document touch directly "equity in trade relations." The echo that they have met all over the world and, more particularly, in the heart of international meetings proves how opportune were these reminders and this intervention about such a serious question on which - I am quoting the encyclical - "the future of world civilization depends."

(1520) These decisive acts of the Supreme Authority of the Church are not isolated as is seen in the increasingly vivid awareness among Christians of the subject of development and the means to promote it. It is not by chance that the participants of the Third World Congress of the Apostolate of the Laity, held in Rome this fall, devoted so much of their debates to international peace and justice. Furthermore, the Pontifical Commission "Justice and Peace," instituted within the past year to support this awareness, sees itself duty-bound to study immediately the perspectives opened by the preparation of our Conference. UNCTAD helped here, accepting an invitation to be represented by a high-level member of its Secretariat to a session held last December in Brussels. Finally, this ferment which arouses the ranks of Christians leads also to concrete action. On the official level as in private initiatives, actions multiply in the Catholic Church to increase contributions in money, in kind and in human resources for an undertaking which interests all of us because we are in solidarity; charity as well as justice prevent us from working apart from our brothers and sisters of all races and of all religions.

(1521) Supported by this doctrinal effort and this intense activity, our Delegation intends to contribute to this Conference in the form appropriate to the particular function of the Holy See and with the ardent desire to serve which motivates all disciples of Christ; the work of this Conference represents a great hope for the poor and challenges those who think that human will-power, reflecting that of the Almighty, is incapable of correcting the most difficult situations.

(1522) Among the expressions initiated by the documents and discourses just referred to, there is one, pronounced for the first time by His Holiness Paul VI before the Administrative Council of UNCTAD in June 1966, which has had a singular fortune: "Development is the new name of peace." The eminent Secretary-General of the United Nations has taken up that expression several times because it translates so well an essential element of the situation of the contemporary world.

(1523) Is it necessary to clarify that this formula does not signify in any way that peace is uniquely the result of a wise distribution of the economic resources of the universe? Peace does not amount to the stability of trade and commercial balances, no more than to "the absence of war, fruit of an ever precarious equilibrium of forces" (*Gaudium et Spes*). What is understood by this formula is explained clearly when the Encyclical affirms that "the road to peace passes through development." In other words, the contemporary world knows that, in spite of the progress of science and technology, and of the enrichment of the knowledge and capacities of human persons, a drama grips universal attention; the Encyclical describes it in plain language: "The survival of so many innocent children, the access to a human condition for so many unhappy families, the peace of the world, the future of civilization are at stake." What are we talking about here? I refer again to the Encyclical: "The structures" of the developing world "are not entirely suited to cope with the grave economic condition of our time. For unless modern technological civilization is somehow regulated, it necessarily follows that inequalities among peoples in respect to increased production far from being removed will rather grow worse, and that the richer nations will have rapid growth and the more needy peoples will only develop slowly."

(1524) Many examples teach us what the consequences of this situation are. Sporadically but always with increasing frequency, movements of violent unrest appear in the developing world. They translate more than once a true despair in the face of the slowness, not to say the total absence, of a real human advancement for the poor and the little ones. To refuse to confront the underlying causes is to refuse the end of these evils. To pretend to think that it will be possible indefinitely to localize and circumscribe these centers of agitation is to play with fire. The very ones who enjoy the benefits of an economy of abundance would fool themselves by imagining that they are sheltered from such trials: recent upheavals are too powerful witnesses of it.

(1525) Even outside these facts, however incontrovertible, it is true that no national or regional economy will maintain its dynamism and its equilibrium by disregarding the economic difficulties of other nations and of other parts of the world. The dream of a total self-sufficiency in the selfish enjoyment of conquests of intelligence and of science is a dangerous utopia. The political and technological conditioning of the present world make a completely closed-circuit economy unthinkable. Even in the heart of the industrialized zones of the globe, prosperity depends increasingly on the capacities for production, trade and consumption of the immense populations of the poor countries. Let us note it without irony: when preference is given to multilateral over bilateral agreements of international cooperation, there is the risk of arousing sensitivities, and there is the feeling of attacking hard-won positions; is not this reaction the sign of the primordial interest that the developed countries attach to their relations with the developing world?

(1526) The question must be asked with even more insistence since the recent difficulties force the economies of abundance to more than one fundamental revision. These circumstances have been seen as unfavorable for the success of our Conference. We would share this opinion only if the revisions in question would proceed by taking account exclusively of immediate national perspectives and putting off the examination of the effects of world economy on the economies of the most developed countries till later. The latter, they say, are out of breath; could it be, partially at least, because they are involved in a race which is ceaselessly accelerating, where the leader has lost contact with the rest of the mass and, like it or not, remains and will always remain in solidarity?

(1527) The construction of peace through development remains the responsibility of the developing countries, whatever might be the role of the developed countries in it. The international community has perhaps wasted a lot of time and resources for lack of having recognized this fundamental truth; in any event, the evolution of the doctrine of cooperation proves that today it prevails. The Conference of Algiers expressed it in a striking way: "In a world whose elements are always more interdependent, peace, progress and liberty are indivisible and common to all. That is why the development of developing countries will equally profit the developed countries. The developing countries reaffirm that their economic development depends essentially on themselves."

(1528) This truth is confirmed by the programs of assistance and cooperation as they accord an increasingly large place to education in all levels, to professional formation, in a word, to the promotion of human resources. In this way, an original creative imagination is stimulated, permitting the developing world to decide on new ways really adapted to the special requirements of their diverse populations. In effect, we must denounce the menace which weighs on our common undertaking; I mean the pure, simple transposition of procedures and plans which were successful in the old days. It is not only the slogan "Trade, not Aid" which risks being fallacious in this regard. Trade, source of benefits for the developing countries, could not be conceived among the doctrines and mechanisms which assured comfort to the developed world. The misrepresentations and the flaws which accompany this comfort are sufficient to command the caution of those who would like to commit themselves totally to a way which is no longer acceptable. What can we say also about the fascination for certain superficial achievements which neglect the essential for the accessory even when they do not press for operations as harmful as the search for military power or national hegemony. Doubtless, the developing countries are often victims of insinuations and pressures inspired by the least trustworthy foreign interests. Another reason for them to give proof of lucidity, intelligence, balance and maturity!

(1529) There, then, is the price of development, and if it is the condition of peace, development will never be too expensive. The developing world legitimately places its pride in having secured its political autonomy. It fears an economic neo-colonialism. Independence, acquired so dearly, defended so jealously, is given to make a new, more fraternal and more just world. The youth of the world want peace and justice; they reproach their elders for not having known how to assure these for them. By youth we understand first the young nations in search of their own vocation. We must have confidence in them. But, like all youth, they have the duty to make their potential of intelligence and of energy bear fruit; peace is at the cost of their choices. "Artisans of their own development," wrote Paul VI, "the peoples are the first to be responsible for it."

(1530) On the particular agenda points of our Conference, the Delegation of the Holy See has chosen to adopt the same realistic attitude as that of our courageous Secretary-General. What the President of the Fifth Session of the Administrative Council called the "points of crystallization" furnish proof that an effort at conciliation is manifest: it must culminate in immediate resolutions, even if they remain partial. Nevertheless, it is not appropriate to be confined to short term perspectives. These must remain directed toward the long term service of humanity in solidarity. In so doing, we do not lack realism. Insistence on long-term aid helps us to situate the difficulties of the moment in their proper place and to resolve them better.

(1531) For the moment, the major problem is reorganization of trade in primary, particularly agricultural, commodities. The struggle against the risks of famine and of malnutrition which menace entire continents is the responsibility of other organizations. But its success depends in good part on a reform in the trade of agricultural products. Another category of primary commodities, that of petroleum products, has a preponderant place in international commerce. If they receive a separate treatment in the negotiations, consideration of them would not be able to be excluded in the elaboration of a global strategy of gradual reduction of under-development, particularly in the areas of transportation and intangible trade accommodations. For all the other primary commodities, it is indispensable that international accords be concluded and renewed without delay in order to arrive at more stable and more equitable prices. For numbers of developing countries, the revenues coming from the sale of one or two primary commodities are necessary to their subsistence. The word subsistence is to be taken here in the strong sense:

physical survival should almost be used. A requirement of justice is in question here: the prices which are fixed by the raw materials markets must be such that they assure revenues in conformity with human dignity to all producers.

(1532) The general principles and the mechanisms planned for the conclusion of international agreements on primary commodities appear sufficiently elaborated and generally accepted so that at last we might dream of implementing them. Nevertheless, product by product negotiation, however necessary, implies drawbacks and limits. Narrowing the field of negotiation prevents simultaneous planning for compensations for other products, and this does not facilitate impeding selfish interests. Further, this type of negotiations rarely takes into account the global development of the countries in question; they remain purely commercial. Finally, the negotiators still too rarely escape the influence of pressure groups (economic, political, financial, etc.) which with difficulty rise to the vision of general interest. This is why it would be desirable to register the negotiations commodity by commodity in a wider institutional context coming under this global strategy of which our Secretary- General has fixed the principal features.

(1533) For the time being, in regard to the contents of the agreements, the conditions in which their negotiation takes place merit attention. In this matter, *Populorum Progressio* emphasizes that, from now on, "a real equality in discussions and negotiations" must be created. We will not pretend that such a condition has already been realized; often the settlement is practically imposed by the countries or groups enjoying supremacy. A profound reform of commercial customs is thus required. It is essential, among other things, that all the interested parties participate in the negotiations, that these take place publicly, that account be taken of the cost price of the different producers, that recourse be had to independent experts who guarantee the objectivity of the settlements.

(1534) On the question of preferences accorded to manufactured or semi-manufactured products exported by the developing countries to the developed, our Delegation is pleased that the progress since 1964 is such that it is reasonable to expect that this Conference might give the starting signal to conclusive steps. Technical difficulties certainly are not lacking in the implementation of the envisaged systems. They should not serve as a pretext to empty the concessions of their substance or to put them off indefinitely. Furthermore, if the Conference is to arrive at concrete results on this point, it would be illusory to accord it more undue importance given the embryonic status of the process of industrialization in many developing countries.

(1535) Whether the preferences be regional or general, the necessity of a diversification and an intensification of commercial exchanges among developing countries themselves is equally essential. On this point, we salute the willingness affirmed by the countries gathered in Algiers to constitute zones of regional integration suitable to enlarge markets and avoid waste from duplication of work. However, it will be recalled that developing countries do not constitute a homogeneous bloc from the economic point of view. Differences in the level of development exist among the industrialized countries which, in general, it is possible to overcome without too much difficulty as the process of integration of the six countries in the European Community shows. In the less developed countries, the differences are much greater, and the beneficial solutions for some can be harmful for others. It is therefore indispensable to take into consideration the situation of the poorest among the developing countries and find entirely new solutions which cure their difficulties instead of aggravating them. Further, this recommendation concerns also the organization of markets of basic commodities and the institution of a system of preferences as the constitution of zones of regional integration.

(1536) These different measures to be implemented immediately will not have a chance to result in an interdependent development of humanity unless they are joined to a broader, long-term reform of policies and attitudes. Although the Conference has for its specific objective the regulation of commercial problems, the questions posed by the reform of the international monetary system belong to its responsibility. The effectiveness of a simple reorganization of trade would be illusory because the solution to the problems of underdevelopment depend above all on the transformation of structures which will take place only through the invention of new ways for international cooperation.

(1537) In order for this cooperation to become effective, governments and peoples must come to the point of attaching as much importance to the requirements of international development as to national development. This is scarcely the situation now. When the difficulties arising out of economic situations require certain developed countries to reduce their expenditures, foreign development aid is often first to be affected while those developed countries who have been spared such difficulties do not take over to fill the gap. The return to a more flourishing financial situation rarely brings an increase in aid. All this means that international cooperation is out of place in the hierarchy of national priorities. The increasingly urgent aspiration of peoples for a real international disarmament, even if only progressive, will perhaps aid in the re-establishment of a more just hierarchy of government choices. In this context, the appeal in Bombay by His Holiness Paul VI to transform armament expenditures into investments designed to increase cooperation takes on a pressing importance. The common fund constituted in this way "would be at once the symbol and the instrument" of world collaboration; "it would permit sterile rivalries to be overcome and a fruitful, peaceful dialogue among all peoples to be created."

(1538) Long term perspectives are particularly necessary in the reform of the international monetary system. The system in practice during the last century made variations in employment subject to the fluctuation in the balance of payments of the different industrializing countries. This contributed not a little to aggravate the insecurity and the uncertainty of living conditions of the working masses. After the Second World War, thanks to the policies of full employment in all the developed countries, currency was made once again a servant. But, as it is increasingly clear, these policies are always conceived in a strictly national context, and examples abound of monetary and financial measures which consist for one country exporting its own employment problems to its neighbor. Grave conflicts result among industrialized countries, and the system is certainly not a stranger to permanent unemployment and under-employment in developing countries.

(1539) Of course, solutions are not simple, and the acceleration of technical progress can only complicate things. The goal is, nonetheless, clear: beyond trade, beyond aid, it is the full employment of all the resources of the planet, both natural and human, that must be realized. It is appropriate, therefore, to examine carefully the policies which have succeeded in the national context and see why they do not attain the same success at the international level. Following this examination, there is every chance that the necessity of strengthening international cooperation will come to light.

(1540) However carefully this Conference examines certain "points of crystallization", it would not meet the expectations of the world for them if it limits itself to furnish this or that more or less immediate satisfaction. There is more to do, we believe, to avoid or, at least, reduce maximally the frustration which many predict would follow the conclusion of our work. The global enterprise of development in so far as it supposes the reform of international trade relations would not be able to arrive at a good conclusion in seven weeks of the Year of Grace 1968; these seven weeks are at least sufficient, if we wish it, to situate the undertaking in its proper context and improve noticeably the instruments of its construction.

(1541) The appearance of UNCTAD marked the determination of developing countries to obtain consideration of their specific problems by a fundamental revision of the existing, prejudicial system in favor of their short term interests and the long term interests of all. The evolution of UNCTAD during these past four years has proved that, in spite of its imperfections, the formula was good for the establishment of procedures of dialogue among all the partners as much for the evaluation of needs as for the setting of goals and priorities. "The technical problems," said the Holy Father recently in receiving some members of our Assembly, "are complex on all sides. Besides, everyone knows that no magic solution would be able to resolve them without difficulty. Important interests are at stake, and the responsible parties are not always sufficiently aware that finally we are all interdependent."

(1542) We owe it to ourselves to express this spirit of solidarity not by giving a free rein to the experts of the Secretariat of UNCTAD or any other organization but by the clearly expressed will to collaborate, in the context of the Conference, in order to formulate the problems without equivocation, to propose solutions without trickery or dupery and to take decisions that we will be loyally determined to translate into facts. The multiplication of international organisms does not favor their efficiency, and it introduces unnecessary costs. A series of converging steps led to the creation of UNCTAD; it is not appropriate for our Delegation to describe the competencies or identify the technical nature of any organization. But we have the right and the duty to state that, in the heart of UNCTAD, sterile confrontations have a tendency to replace a spirit of dialogue, serene collaboration and harmonious will. Our procedures and methods of work can certainly be perfected. So if we agree to dialogue, will we refuse to conclude in the same forum? And if we conclude, will we escape from the necessary evaluation of the measures adopted?

(1543) The lack of mutual confidence has largely been responsible for the anarchy in the economic relations between developed and developing countries. Without in the least insinuating that confidence is absent elsewhere, it is comforting to see it established in UNCTAD. If this spirit, stripped of all exclusivity regarding other regional or world organizations, takes firm roots on the occasion of the Assembly in New Delhi, the usefulness of UNCTAD will have been demonstrated. The peoples who greeted this meeting with so much hope will not have been disappointed; they will know that our good will is a real determination to work together at the price of sacrifice for the common good of the entire human family created in the image of God.

4. A call for equity in sharing goods of the earth

Letter of His Holiness Paul VI To Mr. Manuel Perez-Guerrero, Secretary-General of the United Nations Conference on Trade and Development. The Vatican, 7 April 1972.

Original: French (*)

(1544) As the Third United Nations Conference on Trade and Development opens in Santiago, Chile, we wish to express to you our profound desire to see the labours of this important Assembly reach a successful outcome in conformity with the hopes that they have rightly inspired.

(1545) We know that this desire, which is shared by the individuals and the peoples of the entire world, is mingled with disquiet in the face of the complexity and vastness of the problems upon your agenda as well as in the face of the differing and, at times, divergent positions represented. For our part, with you we wish to place reliance above all upon the aspiration for justice and the sense of brotherhood which are inscribed in the heart of man; in its own field your Conference would offer an opportunity to these sentiments to find authoritative, mature and effective expression.

(1546) As at New Delhi in 1968, this Conference is being held against the background of an international crisis in currency, exchange rates and even cooperation for development. The resistance inspired by national interests seems to have grown further. Many economic structures that produce domination have not been corrected through the achievement by nations of political independence; inequalities of income and social conditions are tending to increase both between nations and within certain countries.

(1547) Your Conference is aware of the scope and also the limits of the aims to which it so nobly aspires. You are well aware that neither the reform of international trade nor the improvement of aid and cooperation are capable by themselves of ensuring a more united and more human development among peoples. In many cases it is the very structures of power and decision-making that must be altered in order to bring about everywhere, on the political and economic as also on the social and cultural levels, a better sharing of responsibility. Does not justice demand that all peoples, whatever their degree of economic power, should have a real participation in all negotiations of worldwide importance?

(*) AAS 64(1972), 379-381.

(1548) It is natural that the Great Powers and the multinational communities should arouse the special expectations of the countries with the least share in the world's wealth. But it is the particular aim of your Conference to provide a forum in which all voices may make themselves heard in the search for solidarity among nations, realism in solutions and fairness in sharing the goods of the earth. We have not failed to note that your programme accords special attention to the lot of the least favoured among the developing countries. It is indeed desirable that UNCTAD should devote itself to the abolition of systems in which the privileged become steadily more privileged, the rich increasingly engage in trade among themselves and international aid itself often benefits only imperfectly the most poverty-stricken people.

(1549) In this regard we would wish a hearing to be given to the voice of the most deprived, those millions of men, women and children living on the margin of the modern economy, people who are often the victims of sickness, malnutrition, bad housing and working conditions, underemployment, illiteracy and all the other ills that prevent them from sharing fully in one same human condition.

(1550) We send you this message, Mr. Secretary-General, aware of our own responsibilities at the head of a universal Church which desires to march with mankind and to share mankind's lot in the midst of history. The declaration of the latest Synod of Bishops witnesses to this desire and calls for commitment to the service of greater justice both within national communities and on the international level. Be assured that all Catholics and all those who share our common aspiration for an equitable world will follow your deliberations in the conviction that today, to a certain extent, the place of the world is in your hands.

(1551) As we invoke abundant divine blessing upon all those taking part in the Third United Nations Conference on Trade and Development in Santiago, we pray Almighty God to bring to a successful conclusion their work for the benefit of the whole of mankind.

5. World solidarity to allow all peoples to be makers of their own destiny

Statement by H.E. Msgr. Ramon Torrella Cascante, Head of the Delegation of the Holy See, at the 3rd United Nations Conference on Trade end Development, held in Santiago, Chile, on 14 April-20 May 1972. Santiago, 25 April 1972.

Original: Spanish

(1552) The Holy See Delegation has a unique character: we do not represent economic or national interests; we have no privileged position to defend nor claims to present; and, nevertheless, since the establishment of UNCTAD the Holy See has followed with the greatest interest all its endeavours and has actively participated in the first two Conferences held in Geneva and New Delhi because it is convinced that the organic development of peoples is the most important problem of our times; even more, it is a necessity, an opportunity and a challenge.

(1553) Compared to that of nations much richer in population and economic resources, our voice is weak and our power seemingly non-existent; nonetheless we are conscious of expressing here the sentiments of many millions of people who are Christian and who think that their faith compels them to transcend personal and national egotisms in order to build a world of solidarity, of justice and of fraternity.

(1554) We are also aware that we can contribute in giving expression to the profound yearning of individuals and of nations for greater equality, for a more impartial distribution of goods and of power. We would like to make heard the voice of hope, which unceasingly grows in every human heart, for a world in which everyone will be freed from indigence, from want, from ignorance and from all other bondages. In a special way our delegation wants to give voice to the cry of the poorest and the neediest: the voice of the least developed peoples and also the voice of those social classes that live, within each nation, at the margin of the fruits of development. We wish to assure all of these silent victims of injustice whose cry reaches us with difficulty and whose faces tend to disappear behind the complexity of our technical discussions that they can find in our delegation brotherly concern and unselfish support.

(1555) Placing ourselves outside the blocs which can emerge for the defense of particular interests, it becomes easier for us to invite everyone to sincere dialogue and to overcome national particularisms in order that a sentiment of common responsibility may prevail allowing the creation of a true world community, especially by means of fair structures in commercial exchanges, guided by the demands of development and not by the haggling of self-interests.

(1556) For the success of our endeavours, which become more arduous and difficult as we move beyond the initial declarations of intent and tackle specific questions in the pursuit of a common agreement, we believe it necessary to invite all peoples to overcome their national interests and recognize their international responsibilities. Without such attitude it is impossible to build a world community and the chances for international cooperation are drastically reduced while peaceful coexistence itself would rest on a precarious balance under the constant fear of a breach.

(1557) Our delegation offers no technical solutions for the numerous and complex problems faced by our Conference; but we believe that, unless we are all moved by a spirit of effective cooperation, we shall attain no results or poor ones at best. Such a spirit is needed to free the imagination and allow eminent experts to find new and daring solutions avoiding the paralysis created by difficulties and by unnecessary cautions. Such a spirit is needed in order to avoid our Conference resolutions remaining theoretical and ineffective, as all too often happens. Such a spirit is needed if the international organizations are to maintain their original vitality and inspiration without becoming just large fora where words abound while the capacity for action declines. It is time for action; otherwise world public opinion will lose its trust in international conferences and will decide that rights and justice must be obtained through other paths, more direct and perhaps violent.

(1558) The Holy See has always shown great interest in and constant support for the international organizations of the United Nations, particularly for UNCTAD. Evident proof of this is the message of Pope Paul VI to our Third Conference. This Conference must be a forum in which truth will emerge as the conscience of a common responsibility for the future of peoples and for their liberation from the various forms of misery and alienation. For this reason we are of the opinion that UNCTAD should receive more resources and wider powers in order to be more effective.

(1559) Having heard the statements of the delegations which have spoken thus far, we note with satisfaction that many agree, with certain nuances, on the description of the present situation (commercial, economic, financial, etc.), on its seriousness and on the urgent need to find adequate solutions. But we also note that there are differences, at times profound ones, in the study of its causes, i.e. of the mechanisms which engender such situations. Some think that a simple readjustment will suffice. Others, as we ourselves do, believe that it is necessary to change structures since these reflect and maintain inadmissible inequalities. Beyond these structures there is a power system which needs to be clarified and transformed in order to bring about, on all parts, a more equitable sharing of responsibilities.

(1560) Undoubtedly, by bringing forth the question of power we run the risk of going beyond the framework of this Conference, which studies the various forms of commercial exchanges and their impact on development. But we know that the economic, technological and financial exchanges among nations are not the result of automatic mechanisms which must be better tuned for greater justice; they depend, in fact, on the will of groups of people who hold economic and political power and, very often, guide these exchanges according to their own interests. The proof is that these people do not lack imagination in circumventing even the best arrangements whenever these are not of their liking. What is the advantage, for instance, of abolishing custom and tariff barriers if, at the same time, a whole new series of different barriers are covertly introduced?

(1561) We shall not dwell again on the interesting analyses of the outstanding document of the Secretary General, already aptly presented by the majority of the delegations. We want to single out that the structures themselves must be changed; moreover, the relationships and the system of power must be clarified and corrected. In analyzing the present system of power, our delegation, like several other ones, calls attention to a growing phenomenon in regard to which our agenda is so discreet, perhaps even to a fault; it is the invasive power of the large transnational corporations. In a recent document, Pope Paul VI wrote: "Under the impetus of the new systems of production, national boundaries are opening up and new economic forces make their entry, the transnational corporations, which, due to the concentration and flexibility of their resources, are able to carry out autonomous strategies, independently of the national political powers and, consequently, outside of any control from the point of view of the common good" (Letter to Cardinal Roy, 14 May 1971, n.44).

(1562) Nobody ignores the power of these large transnational corporations. They are vast private empires which evade, to a large extent, the national and international political powers. Since their importance is evident to all, would it not be proper to study attentively their conduct and establish a framework to guide and control their activities in view of the common good? Is it not possible to reach at this level an agreement among nations?

(1563) Among the items to which our delegation would like to call attention, we would like to mention the following:

(1564) 1. We single out, in the first place, the disappointment of many, and ours too, who realize that the resolutions adopted in the UNCTAD II and for the Second Development Decade have not been sufficiently implemented. This is serious for two reasons; 1) because many countries have not been able to profit from the measures which were meant to assist in their development, and this represents an objective defect, and 2) because peoples are tempted, with good reason, to lose confidence in the resolutions solemnly adopted by their governments in the assemblies of our international organizations.

(1565) 2. We underscore the necessity on the part of the developed countries to consider effectively the reconversion of their economies with a view to welcoming the products of developing countries into their markets in fair competition. Such reconversion is met by social opposition in the developed countries; industries threatened by this outside competition request protections and assistances of all types. While measures are taken to facilitate this adaptation, it is important that this reconversion be worked out voluntarily and positively in the name of a true solidarity and of a new international distribution of work.

(1566) 3. We are convinced that each developing country must assume its own responsibilities and invest all its natural and human resources to promote development since, as Pope Paul VI affirmed, "world solidarity, each day more efficient, must allow all peoples to be makers of their own destiny" (*Populorum Progressio*, n. 65). However, this economic development aided by more equitable arrangements in international trade must be accompanied by positive policies of distribution in favor of the neediest social classes. This question obviously goes beyond the scope of our Conference. Nevertheless, if we disapprove commercial exchanges where "the rich get richer and the poor always poorer", as it has been clearly shown by the President of the World Bank, shouldn't the same condemnation also be valid within each country where a more equitable distribution of the fruits of development is not sought? This issue is a source of profound preoccupation to us.

(1567) 4. We like to emphasize the present and future importance of technological exchanges among nations. It is not simply a commercial problem: it regards the cost of transmission of technology. Such cost can become exorbitant, too onerous, and must be properly reduced. Moreover one must consider that the different levels of technological development and of the means for innovation give rise to new inequalities and to some subtle and novel power plays among nations. We must be alert on this matter. Scientific discoveries and the resulting technological innovations should be at the service of all mankind and form a common patrimony to which everyone can have access.

(1568) 5. Without overlooking other items on which one can hope that agreement can be reached, like the participation of all countries in the international monetary decisions, on the increase of "assistance", on special measures for least developed countries, etc., we are concerned about the enormous and ever increasing burden upon developing countries of the external debt, whose financing absorbs part of their trade and even of their assistance. It is imperative that measures be taken in this regard, for it would be a scandal to let this situation continue and grow worse. Undoubtedly it is difficult to find the technical solutions, but it is necessary and urgent to make a creative and disinterested effort at a reasonable disposition of the debt.

(1569) The Holy See has always strongly deplored that the majority of developed countries, and also of developing ones, waste huge sums in the acquisition of costly weapon systems which are useless and deadly. We refer here to a problem very deeply felt by our Delegation: that of world peace. We desire that such peace be built by means of harmonious and organic development of peoples; that weapons be silenced and stop being the object of a trade that to some brings wealth and to others struggle and death.

(1570) 7. If we examine realistically the world situation, we are struck by the great diversity in the levels of development. Faced with this, we wish to restate a principle: that of international solidarity. Obviously this generally recognized principle may be applied on a global scale; but it must also be applied, in a proper form, among the various groups according to the different levels of development. International solidarity is everyone's responsibility even though those who possess more have also more obligations. Each people has something to contribute. It is inconceivable that some will only give and others only receive; today such a situation is outdated. It is imperative to foster an international solidarity based upon the mutual and respectful exchange of each one's values and possibilities.

(1571) By expounding some of the items upon which our delegation focuses its particular attention, we wish to express the interest, importance and trust we attach to the work of our Conference. We have all arrived with an open mind and with the expectation of a constructive dialogue. We hope that these attitudes will remain when, going beyond general ideas, we shall discuss the real problems; it is then that national interest can strongly arise in confrontation. It is to be hoped that, at that difficult time, each one will be convinced that progress is possible, even if it may be necessary to give up something which may be perceived as legitimate interest and right. Only then, and at that price, will it be possible to reach solutions.

(1572) Let us not forget the great importance of world public opinion, both at the national and international levels. It expects positive results from this Conference, even if it does not grasp the complexities of the problems we face. Certainly public opinion must receive wider and more objective information and come to know the responsibilities of each nation and of the international organizations.

(1573) We cannot disappoint the tremendous aspiration of all peoples to-day for greater justice. We have the responsibility to give them an effective answer since people will judge us by the hopes that we have given them.

(1574) UNCTAD III must be the forum where truth, dialogue and justice will be the builders of international solidarity.

6. Enlightened self-interest for the common good.

Statement of Lady Jackson (Miss Barbara Ward), a member of the Holy See Delegation at the UNCTAD III Conference. Santiago, Chile, 12 May 1972.

Original: English

(1575) I am most honoured to be permitted as a member of the delegation of the Holy See to address this distinguished body. I only wish that my duties at Columbia University had permitted me to take a fuller part in your deliberations. But even a short exposure is sufficient to show on what critical issues they turn for the future of humanity.

(1576) Perhaps the first and overwhelming impression that I would record is that this assembly brings us together for the first time virtually as the entire human family to discuss the problems of our daily bread. I know that my delegation particularly rejoices in the universality of our encounter. Pope Paul VI has repeatedly underlined his belief that "the social question is now worldwide."

(1577) We are, if you like, the people of earth in search of a community, and I hardly need remind so experienced an assembly that at every level of community - family, institution, State - things do not prosper unless the books are balanced and both ends meet.

(1578) In our world society, today, much of our economic business - our trade, our development - is not doing too well. That two-thirds of humanity command at best a quarter of world investment and income is, of course, the most critical imbalance. But, as we are rather insistently reminded, the rich nations are not doing so well either.

(1579) If anyone thinks that average per capita incomes of 1,500 dollars and more, together with access to the highest science and technology, is the way to human satisfaction and achievement, he has only to look around at the supposedly fortunate lands. And what will he discover? That they are in a really bad way - unemployment, the pressures of inflation, extreme uncertainties about their balance of payments. Clearly they are in deep trouble. Possibly, therefore, this Conference comes at exactly the right moment. It had been chiefly thought of as a means of promoting the fundamental needs and interests of the developing lands. But the happy thought occurs that, in fact, we can do something to help the hard-pressed rich.

(1580) Still, since we are the human family in search of a community, perhaps in helping ourselves rationally, we shall find that we are helping each other, that self-interest, provided it is sufficiently enlightened, can really promote the common good.

(1581) Among the evils of the rich countries which we must seek to alleviate, the worst are clearly inflationary pressures and uncertainties over the balance of payments. Unemployment, fortunately, is on a relatively small scale and tends to be derivative. It is usually caused by the "stop" side of the "stop-go" policies with which governments try to curb domestic demand when rising prices at home put pressure on the balance of payments. So let us concentrate on price inflation and stable currencies.

(1582) I always find it a little strange that those influential and highly qualified financial experts who warn us about the inflationary consequences, of, say, a one per cent transfer of unrequited aid from developed to developing nations or of the issue to developing governments of Special Rights are normally silent on what is surely the most inflationary of all expenditures - the annual bill for armaments. Each year, as we very well know, some two hundred billion dollars are spent on arms. The cost of materials, the wages, the salaries, in some countries the profits, all create streams of purchasing power. But ultimately no useful consumer goods appear to mop it up again. It is the unusual housewife who goes shopping for a sub-machine gun. Even billionaires are doubtful purchasers of supersonic fighters. So the purchasing power storms on to other goods, competing for them, forcing up their price. In order to be able to blow up this small and delicate planet twenty times over - one would have thought once was enough - governments spend each year more than the equivalent of the entire gross national product of the developing world. Yet even a ten per cent reduction in this terrible and inflationary hemorrhage would, if transferred to development assistance, give us close to our immediate goal of 0.7 per cent of gross national product in official aid.

(1583) Controlled progressive disarmament - on this, surely, we can agree. An end to the conflicts that tear us apart and controlled progressive disarmament constitute our first need and chief priority for development and developing peoples alike. But the billions for arms are only a part of the intractable inflationary problems of the rich countries. Every week when the housewife comes back from her marketing her chief annoyance is likely to be that once again this or that item of food has gone up in price, that the familiar bar of chocolate has shrunk once more. She adds up her grocery bill and grimly decides to tell her husband to go on strike for his fifth wage increase in seven years simply to keep pace with the cost of living. And that little domestic argument is what keeps Finance Ministers awake at night. But I wonder how many housewives know that these prices do not reflect the market? They represent the carefully considered policies of reputedly rational governments. Every year, by means of tariffs, to exclude cheaper food or by subsidies to local farmers to make up the difference, the rich market economies pay out between twenty-one and twenty-four billion dollars in order to preserve their people from the terrible risk of lower food prices.

(1584) Nor is this all. According to a survey of the developed world's engineering sector conducted by the Organization for Economic Cooperation and Development (OECD), the annual cost of not using the optimal (or cheapest) resources in the course of production - many of which could be supplied by developing countries - is of the order of fifty billion dollars a year.

(1585) We have to admit that we are beginning to build up a formidable list of wounds suffered by the developed States - even if they are self-inflicted. Put the cost of arms and of food and of manufactures together and the inflationary pressure is not much less than two hundred and fifty billion dollars every year.

(1586) But even this is not the end of the story. The protectionist element in this inflation operates most sharply against the exports of two-thirds of humanity who are still developing. As a result, the combined pressure - of rising prices, of less competitive goods, of strains on the balance of payments - tends to be concentrated within the magic circle of those who already control at least seventy-five per cent of world trade and whose tariff concessions - for instance, the Kennedy Round - are chiefly designed to facilitate the exchanges of high technology. But, as in the rich nations, domestic markets grow more saturated with the second house, third car, fourth TV syndrome, the competitive strains become ever greater. Add a tragic war, and we have the crisis of August 1971.

(1587) Of course I know things are never so simple. Local interests have to be defended and protected. But even here one can point out that with fifty billion dollars annually in saving on engineering costs, local capital and labour can be comfortably redeployed or even pensioned. Recent American computer calculations suggest, I believe, that fewer than one per cent of America's textile workers would have to retrain in the event of lower or no textile quotas. And in agriculture a price policy which subsidizes chiefly the big corporations or private owners is often of dubious social or economic benefit and puts markets under strain. What sense does it make to compel the people to shoulder annually even fifty billion extra dollars in avoidable costs?

(1588) It is at this point, I suggest, that we reach the fundamental convergence of the needs of both developed and developing nations. Three of the basic aims of UNCTAD III show us a clear way forward. The first is a sustained strategy to phase out, over a suitable period of adjustment, the various exaggerated forms of agricultural protectionism into which developed markets have drifted. The second is to extend the system of general specialized preferences to include a wider range of cheaper manufactures of interest to labour-rich developing lands - textiles, clothing, leather goods, electronics - and also processed goods from agriculture.

(1589) The third is the most innovative. It is to take the competitive pressure off the over-strained giants of the developed-market economies, and give the permanent trade surplus they battle for so fiercely and hopelessly (for how can all of them be in surplus?) to the developing lands. In addition to guaranteed aid they should receive new quotas at the IMF and a firm link between Special Drawing Rights and development needs. In all this there is, rightly and inevitably, an element of redistributing world income. But once before, in 1929, the world economy blew itself out by overfierce competition in a restricted market. Let us not repeat the error in 1972. A permanent trade surplus for the developing nations, particularly for the poorest among them, will enlarge their growth and development. As they grow, they will become more effective trade partners in their own right. World markets will widen; the rich nations will breathe again.

(1590) I hope you will forgive my preoccupation with the profound, even heart-rending, difficulties of the rich. I have pursued it because it is their excuse for doing next to nothing about the infinitely more real and heartrending problems of the poor. My basic hope is simply to persuade developed governments and peoples that self-interest rightly conceived will enable them to help both themselves and their neighbour, that enlightened self-interest is not a wholly unworthy object to cherish in our diverse and divided world.

(1591) But community cannot grow from self-interest alone. Interest is primarily rational. For full effect it must be driven forward by drives of emotion and commitment. We can, alas, all too easily begin with fear. If nothing is done to correct the world's imbalance, to eradicate the injustice, to wipe out the deepening misery of half mankind, shall we hope to survive, half slave, half free? You have heard the President of the World Bank eloquently remind you of children without essential protein, families without shelter, men and women without work or hope, and all the time, hour by hour, the extent and depth of degradation increasing. Much of our talk here is, inevitably, technical - quotas, drawing rights, special preferences, multiple exchange rates. But behind the jargon is the fact of deepening misery and static help. This is not, in any culture or tradition, the definition of the good society. And as the towers of technological man grow higher, his dependence on advanced energies systems is greater, his transport and his settlements more vulnerable; rich and poor alike could be heading for the breakdown and anarchy of world-wide civil strife.

(1592) But it is precisely this kind of risk that our assembly has come together to forestall. After all, history does not dictate failure to us. Reforms have been made with imagination and generosity. "The mandate of Heaven" returns; new regimes bring in audacious ideas of renewal. It was not until 1915 that the United States introduced a progressive federal income tax. Is it inconceivable to see in guaranteed international aid the first faint beginning of a tax system on the world scale?

(1593) This generation is, I believe, capable of social inventiveness and generosity of spirit at the planetary level. After hours and days of confusing debates, In a babel of voices, in pressure of time it is perhaps easy to forget that in the broader stream of history of which UNCTAD III is a part, something unprecedented is happening to the human family. A hundred years ago, a few empires would have decided our issues here. Even twenty-five years ago, the relatively small group of the developed States set up the structure of the world economy. Now they are beginning to accept the right of full participation by the developing world - and not one in this hall believes this to be the end of the progress.

(1594) May it not be that we are witnessing - however slow the pace and agonizing the setbacks - the emergence of a world society in which the dignity of men and of nations is becoming part of a wider loyalty to the whole human community of planet earth? Such enlargements of loyalty are not impossible. Men do not cease to love their families when they love their city or their native land. To love this small, beautiful, vulnerable earth as the only home for mankind, does not seem to me an impossible leap of faith. If we can make it, sharing in justice will follow. And after that can come the hope of tranquillity and friendship in a domestic planet.

7. The management of earth's resources

Message of His Holiness Paul VI to H.E. Mr. Gamani Corea, Secretary-General of UNCTAD IV. The Vatican, 28 April 1976.

Original: French (*)

(1595) From the Fourth United Nations Conference on Trade and Development assembled in Nairobi, the peoples - especially the poor - are awaiting decisions which will bring rapid and effective remedies to their most urgent needs and which in attitudes and structures will develop new relationships between nations, thus permitting all of them to contribute to greater solidarity in international life.

(*) AAS 68(1976), 316-318.

(1596) We join our voice to these appeals. We express the deep and confident desire of seeing emerge from your assembly both important activities and new motives of hope for humanity. Since your last Conference in Santiago, the international crisis has amassed sufferings and anxieties. Famine has ravished various regions. Unemployment is sapping energy. Inflation is profoundly disturbing trade relationships. The debts of developing countries are reaching overwhelming and discouraging proportions.

(1597) This situation does not, however, find you unprepared. Thanks to the laborious efforts of the preceding conferences in Geneva, New Delhi and Santiago, which were patiently continued in the intervals between the sessions, a coming to awareness has occurred. The causes of the problems are better known to you in their complexity, which is at one and the same time political, technical, social, cultural and moral. The desire for vast and coordinated action has broken forth beginning with certain convictions that are now widely shared. Courageous decisions based on worldwide solidarity are both necessary and possible, and all are summoned to share in the attainment of this solidarity.

(1598) Is it not a particularly encouraging sign to note that the younger and weaker nations have shown that they are more and more resolved to mobilize their own resources - human as well as material - in order to develop their personality and to engage it responsibly in the creation of closer-knit and more solid networks of solidarity? What we wrote almost ten years ago in our Encyclical on the Development of Peoples we repeat with increased conviction: "Worldwide solidarity, ever more effective, should allow all peoples to become the artisans of their own destiny... The younger or weaker nations ask to assume their active part in the construction of a better world, one which shows deeper respect for the rights and the vocation of the individual. This is a legitimate appeal; everyone should hear it and respond to it." (No. 65)

(1599) Our conviction is nourished on the comforting spectacle of the best experience of individuals and peoples. It is rooted in faith in God "who has willed that all people should make up a single family and that they should deal with one another in a spirit of brotherhood" (*Gaudium et Spes*, 24). The earth has been given to them to share so that they may cultivate it, so that they may manage and multiply material goods in a responsible manner, so that they may impress on them the mark of their own human personality and bring about exchanges of goods between individuals and peoples that should become a constant process of personal advancement in solidarity.

(1600) The management of the earth's resources is thus at the centre of your discussions. You have the legitimate ambition of building trade networks which will ensure more remuneration, more stable and more equitable prices for all, especially for those who are the poorest. To arrive at this point it is necessary that these endeavours, this dialogue between rich countries and less favoured countries, should be inserted within the higher perspective of the individual destination of this world's goods, of the interdependence of peoples, and of co-responsibility in the organization of trade exchanges in the interest of all. This is why it is necessary for you to rekindle incessantly, both personally and through collective effort, the flame of your convictions: material riches exist so that people can have food, clothing, housing, education, and so that assisting one another and developing their solidarity they may build truly fraternal communities which experience true joy in living.

(1601) We address this message to you, Mr. Secretary-General, in the name of the Gospel which, revealing to people the depth of their divine vocation, frees within them irreplaceable forces and an irreplaceable light to orient and sustain their efforts for more humanity in the world - efforts on behalf of that which we have called "the civilization of love". Invoking upon the participants of UNCTAD Conference assembled at Nairobi an abundance of divine blessings, we ask Almighty God that they may find in the wearisome work which will be theirs the joy of opening up together new ways of hope for the peoples of the world.

8. No one can develop in isolation

Statement by H.E. Msgr. Bernardin Gantin, Head of the Delegation of the Holy See, at the IV United Nations Conference on Trade and Development, held in Nairobi on 3-27 May 1976. Nairobi, 14 May 1976.

Original: French

(1601-b) The Holy See Delegation will take an active part in all the debates of this Conference as it has at the previous Conferences of Geneva, New Delhi and Santiago. Although it is conscious of the particular nature - essentially spiritual - of the authority which it represents, the Delegation does not for that reason place itself either on the margin of or above the concrete problems on our agenda. It will examine them in all their aspects and will not dispense itself from following the Assembly's difficult but necessary scientific and technical analyses, which make it possible to study the economic, social and cultural complexity of the questions before us, and to orient action in a realistic and fruitful way. We will be happy to benefit from the presence here of so many experts at the level of theory, experience and action.

(1602) The often strenuous and thankless work we have done together in the past has enabled us to discern more clearly the main questions which now call for new solutions and which our various commissions are examining. But is not the most decisive benefit of our past experience the coming to an awareness that the search for better economic and trade balance between peoples is an undertaking which concerns the whole person and all persons jointly? The *Populorum Progressio* of Pope Paul VI, continuing and implementing the teaching of the Council and the multiple initiatives of the Church in this regard, contributed for its part to this increase of awareness in world opinion.

(1603) Man is not divisible. In their efforts for survival and for a better life peoples are involved with their traditions, their different cultural roots, and their spiritual aspirations. To organize the market for raw materials, to diffuse techniques, to develop industrial products everywhere, to create new financial and monetary structures - all this not only has repercussions on the social and cultural life of peoples but also presupposes that the peoples in question are in a position to engage their full personality therein. In trying to reconcile economic interests - often opposed and sometimes even contradictory - one cannot always hope to obtain a profit on all levels at once. But it is to be hoped that at least certain ones do not register a loss on all levels and that all move forward at the human level. We are sure that we express the preoccupations of this entire assembly in helping, for our part, untiringly to situate economic, trade and financial problems in this perspective of the development of the whole person and of all peoples together.

(1604) From the outset, let us give the word "trade" its full human import and retain it throughout our discussions. All too often this is lost sight of in a purely quantitative perspective or disregarded by practices exploiting the weak. Trade relations between peoples of different customs and cultures, far from being limited to the exchange of material goods, have always conveyed also human values. Generally speaking - at least each time that trade did not deteriorate into a process of domination - the ways boldly opened by merchants permitted the meeting of peoples in their political outlooks, their cultures, their art, their science, and likewise in their religious experiences. Trade has a meaning which is deeply human.

(1605) This Conference, in conformity with its name and its task, intends to give a new impetus to trade relations and specifically to those which exist among countries with different social and economic conditions and systems. No one can develop in isolation. No country can declare itself self-sufficient without considerably limiting its chances of reaching a higher level of well-being. This is said, not to introduce an extraneous and contentious element into our discussions but rather, to situate trade exchange in a wider context - in the field of human experiences and cultures which teach mutual knowledge, mutual respect and which peacefully and reciprocally challenge renewal.

(1606) Moreover, the very logic of trade development demands for its own effectiveness a wider human encounter which alone is capable of thawing out hardened situations, of renewing patterns of thought and of opening up new avenues. Are we not trying to experience this among ourselves when, not betraying our positions and the instructions we have received, we seek in this dialogue, and sometimes in the friendship which springs from it, the help to support the unavoidable tensions and to prepare a favourable climate in which to work out equitable solutions?

(1607) There is another word which needs to find here all its flexibility and its full human forcefulness: "to negotiate". The word denotes a desire for a true encounter and a will to reach an agreement. Some are tempted to conceal themselves remaining entrenched behind inflexible systems by which they impose almost inexorably their conditions in determining prices, in keeping markets open or closed and in the flow of finances. Others are not admitted in any real way to the negotiations where it really counts, or else they are doubtful about taking part, not considering themselves sufficiently powerful. The Holy See Delegation hopes intensely that this Conference will constitute a real forum of negotiation, and that it will create the equitable conditions which will make it possible afterwards to establish networks of exchanges where all peoples may have a voice as free and equal partners.

(1608) The generous solution to the problem of foreign debts is for many developing countries an indispensable prerequisite to granting them access to such networks of exchange. These debts have, in certain cases, reached such crushing and overwhelming dimensions due to a number of causes over which these countries have very little or no control. Neither individuals nor peoples are inclined to make efforts when an excessive debt weighs them down, blocks their horizon and gives them the feeling that new aid has always the bitter taste of a new burden of debts. Such a situation helps no one and undermines world peace. This Conference will do itself honour in reopening to peoples who have debts - and in a way that is generous and without stinginess - a horizon of new hope.

(1609) Another way to create a more equitable balance among the negotiating powers lies in a more active collaboration among the developing countries. The building of the world community, which all of us hope for, comes about little by little, in stages, and by way of regional accords and agreements which unite peoples in a spirit of solidarity and mutual aid. Here too, collaboration among developing countries should not confine itself to material objectives. They themselves desire collaboration to draw up models of development which, while legitimately giving priority to basic needs not yet provided, are in harmony with their cultural and spiritual traditions and do not reproduce the precariousness, contradictions and deadlocks we are witnessing today. The whole world, to build its future, needs to invent new life styles that have greater respect for cultural and spiritual values and that are more careful to eliminate obstacles to their fulfillment. For the greater number the obstacle is poverty; for others it means the sinking into materialism or a pernicious precipitation into unnatural stimulation of artificial needs. The Gospel shows us that man, made in the image of God, does not find his joy in living except when he liberates himself from selfishness and from the domination of money and uses his creativity in the service of others.

(1610) In the message which he addressed to the Secretary-General of UNCTAD, Pope Paul VI stressed that the goods of the earth are destined for all, a truth founded on the unity of the human family. "God ... has willed that all people should make up a single family and that they should deal with one another in a spirit of brotherhood" (Second Vatican Council, Pastoral Constitution *Gaudium et Spes*, 24). What is made clear here in the light of faith is a reality which the best experience of individuals and peoples has rediscovered in our time. Is not the central theme of this Conference a better development and use of the earth's resources with each people actively developing those resources over which it more directly exercises responsibility in a perspective of solidarity at the world level? To enable peoples to provide themselves with food, beginning with a better use of their own riches, to enable them to exchange raw materials and manufactured goods in markets that are more stable, more remunerative, more diversified and more genuinely free, and thus to build more lively and sound economies - this is assuredly a task that deserves all our effort. We shall have all the greater hope of success if we situate the necessary economic growth within a wider context of true progress of individuals and peoples.

(1611) The building of a new international economic order (NIEO) demands from all peoples changes which touch their vital resources far too deeply for it to be possible to impose these changes from outside. Only peoples who have recognition accorded to their full personality and who are assured of becoming "the artisans of their own destiny" (*Populorum Progressio*, 65) will resolutely set out on this path. We can, we must help them. This will be accomplished by the very example of our discussions, where each one ought to be able to give of his best and to enrich his own ideas through invigorating contact with the ideas of others.

9. Solidarity and collaboration among peoples

Message of His Holiness John Paul II to H.E. Mr. Gamani Corea, Secretary-General of the V United Nations Conference on Trade and Development. The Vatican, 26 April 1979.

Original: French (*)

(1612) Human advancement, the upholding of the hope of peoples struggling in precarious and often crushing conditions and helping humanity to regain control of its material and social universe: these are the subjects at the heart of the deliberations of the Fifth Conference of the United Nations on Trade and Development, meeting in Manila.

(1613) These preoccupations are also shared by the Holy See and the whole Church. I am writing to you, Mr. Secretary-General, in order to offer to this common task, together with my fraternal encouragement, a spiritual and ethical contribution drawn from the heritage of the Gospel.

(1614) It is our shared conviction that the courage of the concrete decisions that must be taken and the inspiration of new ideas for directing the future will come from people who have been made more aware of their unsurpassable dignity, more aware of the creative possibilities of their minds, more aware of the potential of their different cultures, more aware of the powerful moral dynamism which impels them to seek justice, peace and fraternal cooperation. These are realities that, in the eyes of a believer, have a depth and a guarantee that come from God. God has made us all in his own image and likeness, and his Son Jesus Christ by becoming man himself has in a certain manner united himself to every human being.

(1615) For development to be both effective and worthy, peoples have to count, first of all, on their work and on exchange. And this poses at the basis of practically all the items on the agenda of the Conference the fundamental questions of the just price and the just contract.

(1616) These are eminently human and moral questions, and they have to be considered in all their constitutive dimensions.

(1617) One of these dimensions is, of course, remuneration for the work actually done by each individual. It is not the only dimension. It is also important to take into account the right of each people to make use of the goods which are more directly entrusted to its management and whose reasonable and farsighted utilization conditions its free development. In addition, since work concerns human beings, their remuneration must enable them to live as befits human beings, to face all the tasks that fall to them, all the needs of human existence, beginning with the need to create, through employment, the very possibility of working. Furthermore, individuals and peoples live in solidarity; their remuneration should manifest this solidarity within each country and between countries, and it must be seen to be a fair sharing in the material and cultural goods which are produced at a given stage of human history and which always have a universal destination.

(1618) It is necessary that all these exigencies, without exception, should be taken into account concretely in the contractual processes which seek to determine the amount of just prices. These

(*) AAS 71(1979), 1018-1021.

processes cannot simply be left to the play of the market forces, which, in fact, are never natural but always constructed by people, nor to the dominant influence of small groups or to that of number. Every contract is a human matter, conducted by people and directed towards serving people. Only then will the market forces, set up and periodically revised and diversified, be able to play their beneficial role: for they will function under the responsibility of individuals and peoples who are free, equal and linked by solidarity, and under the regulation of moral norms that are binding upon everybody.

(1619) Healthy competition of this sort is, in its turn, conditioned by "a wider and more immediate redistribution of riches and of control over them" (*Redemptor Hominis*, 16). It is, thus, in this perspective that one must clarify and resolve the painful problem of the debts that weigh upon the poorer countries, the problem of common funds, the problem of a more adequate and more effective institutional framework of worldwide solidarity.

(1620) While the universal destination of goods is effected in part through the medium of responsible appropriations and of exchanges, it also calls for institutions that more immediately express solidarity and sharing. What still exists, often in such an exemplary way in the practice of hospitality and mutual help by the less advanced peoples, what has been reinstated elsewhere through national budgets and social security systems, namely, the desire to set aside an important part of wealth in order to make it directly available for common use and needs quite apart from any logic of competition and exchange, all this must likewise find its place in the development of the worldwide human community. It is up to the Manilla Conference to explore and stimulate, with realism and generosity, all the opportunities now available for advancing along this path in the order of production as well as in that of distribution.

(1621) Mr. Secretary-General, I express the earnest hope that this Fifth Conference of the United Nations on Trade and Development, which you have prepared with such care and breadth of view, will produce the resolute decisions that the less privileged peoples and, indeed, all humanity await. May this exceptional meeting be, at the same time, the place where new ideas germinate, mature and spread and where these ideas succeed in defining a new long-term strategy, able to halt the gigantic development of the situation referred to in the parable in the Bible concerning the rich banqueter and the poor man, Lazarus (cf. *Redemptor Hominis*, 16). May this exceptional meeting succeed in eliminating a situation which now humiliates mankind and stores up threats for the future, and thus may it infuse new hope into countless human beings.

I pray that God, our common Father, will bless the Manilla Conference.

10. Openness to change, interdependence, development and disarmament, solidarity and self-reliance

Statement by the Reverend Roger Heckel, Head of the Delegation of the Holy See to the Fifth United Nations Conference on Trade and Development, held in Manilla, Philippines, on 7 May-1 June 1979. Manila, 15 May 1979.

Original: French

(1622) Because of the atmosphere of crisis in these recent years, the urgency of economic growth has moved into highest priority among our concerns. Nothing could be more justifiable when we recall the hundreds of millions of men, women, and children whose most elementary needs remain unsatisfied and the hundreds of millions of others who will join them before the end of the century. Let us be wary however of allowing ourselves to be enclosed in a logic that is too excessively economic. If economic growth conditions human and social progress, it does not automatically assure them; even more, it compromises them - and besides, it compromises itself - when, as His Holiness Pope John Paul II said in his recent encyclical *Redemptor Hominis*, "the sole category of economic progress" becomes superior, subordinating all existence to its biased requirements, stifling humanity, dislocating societies, and ending up by sinking into its own contradictions and excesses."

(1623) Because economics is a human and social matter, its growth, however urgent and imperative, can be accomplished only in the context of the development of the entire human person and of society, and this, at every phase. Without prejudice to the specific character of its objects, its appropriate means and the disciplines it demands of all, economic growth must be situated in the vital logic of the integral development of individuals and of interdependent peoples. In its turn, it must agree to accept both the decisive momentum and disciplines from that superior logic. Although the concept of integral and interdependent development emerged during the preceding decades, it has still only insufficiently penetrated and germinated economic thought and practice. It could not justifiably be put aside even temporarily, however urgency presses us on. It is not a luxury for easy times. Its place is in the heart of our debates. I would like to illustrate it by four examples: 1- openness to change; 2- interdependence; 3- link between development and disarmament; 4- vital reconciliation between universal solidarity and self-reliance.

(1624) 1. Under penalty of remaining hesitant and cramped, openness to necessary commercial, financial and monetary adjustments must be fed not only by indications of markets and economic indications in general but also by direct consideration of the essential needs of peoples and their broader aspirations.

(1625) Very authoritative voices right here have made us attentive to the major problem of hunger during the years to come. There are no quick answers to the problem of hunger and the essential needs of humanity. They do not enter spontaneously into economic circulation. The economy must be transformed to make room for them, not only as indirect and derivative objects but as active factors contributing to its orientation and regulation. Thorough studies are necessary to enrich economic thought in this perspective.

(1626) Among the most general aspirations which press the economy to review its performance and structures, I will cite simply the legitimate desire of young nations since their accession to sovereignty and equality in the international society to draw conclusions from it at the world's financial, economic and monetary institutions.

(1627) Yes, the economy - like all the other aspects of existence - must be open to many factors of change, seemingly external, but which, in reality, come from man and, therefore, can contribute precious strength for renewal.

(1628) 2. The second example: interdependence. For the moment, it appears evident from the great majority of the interventions that a new economic growth in developing countries is expected from more ample transfers of financial resources as well as from a larger importation of their products, notably manufactured ones, into the markets of the rich countries. This means that growth takes place by a rapid revival of the rich economies, a boost which it will stimulate and sustain in return. Such a mutually beneficial interdependence is assuredly desirable. To avoid, at the same time, stimulating the world economy with illnesses which undermine it and to prevent excessive dependence by the developing countries on the industrialized economies, two series of questions must be introduced at the start of important qualitative considerations.

(1629) Everyone senses that the models of growth founded on waste and on the motivation to consumption should not become generalized; on the contrary they must be deeply transformed themselves. There, also, authoritative voices have made us attentive to the serious problem of energy, to the excessive part that the rich economies take from the available resources in the world, and to the threats which weigh on the environment. It is thus imperative to orient ourselves toward models of development, and, more profoundly, beginning obviously with the rich countries, toward notions and styles of life which save the limited resources of nations, stimulate, on the contrary, the limitless resources of the human being, and develop in the human persons the taste for creativity more than the instinct for consumption.

(1630) The real and growing interdependence between the rich and poor economies must not conceal from us the excessive dependence of the poor on the rich and also their dramatic vulnerability to the hazards and errors of the privileged. Therefore, the delegation of the Holy See calls for the greatest attention to measures capable of assuring greater independence to the developing economies, especially those which favor their technological advances, their collective self-reliance, and the institution of a common fund as the instrument of an integrated program of basic commodities.

(1631) Briefly, action is appropriate so that the necessary, rapid quantitative growth of the poor economies does not necessarily and always pass through a growth of the same pattern as in the rich countries. This would maintain the present gaps and domination by the rich countries; it would drag the entire world economy toward a deadly waste and would distract the poor countries from the research of new qualitative models.

(1632) 3. Third example: development and disarmament. The arms race directly threatens peace. Indirectly, it endangers peace by the resources that it withholds from development as much in the great powers as in many developing countries.

(1633) Many delegation have suggested instituting a world fund for development with a part of the savings gained from disarmament. Pope Paul VI had already advanced this idea during his trip to Bombay in 1964. UNCTAD cannot remain indifferent to this matter. It would do a very useful work for peace and for the cause for which it has a more direct mission to promote if it obtained a good place for this theme in the development strategy for the '80's. It is a subject which deserves a profound examination and important exploration in two directions: first, the contribution that disarmament can assure to development; and, then, the support to disarmament provided by an international community resolutely determined to promote development and, in this way, to make the absurd arms race more unbearable to world opinion.

(1634) I will be brief on the last example, that of the vital and dynamic reconciliation between universal solidarity and self-reliance, two essential notions which risk discrediting each other for lack of such a concordance.

(1635) For the believer, the universal community of men finds an exceptional strength in the certainty of the common origin, nature and destiny of all persons in God. This community is being built within the frame of nations already assured of their span of responsible liberty and at the same time, within a context yet to be constructed. This is one of the fascinating tasks of our generation - the construction of effective world institutions capable of expressing and promoting the unity of the human family.

(1636) This notion of unity in diversity reflects the ethical concept of the relation between individuals and peoples to material and intellectual goods. These goods are meant for all universally. They must serve all and contribute to unity among peoples. This universal application is actively realized in two complementary ways; on the one hand, responsible management by all of the goods immediately confided to them making them productive and involving them in exchanges useful for all; on the other hand, preservation and cultivation, in appropriate ways, of goods common to all humanity.

(1637) The Message that His Holiness Pope John Paul II addressed to the Secretary-General on these points proposes reflections which can bring new ideas with many ramifications to practically all the points on our agenda.

(1638) The delegation of the Holy See is aware of the complexity of the tasks confronting this Assembly. By helping towards situating them in their full ethical and human perspective, we express the desire to assist in dealing with them without equivocation or delay and finding courageous and realistic solutions.

(1639) Given the particular nature of the participation of the Holy See in this Conference, the delegation abstains from participating in the work of the group to which the Holy See is geographically attached. This decision does not imply any judgment on this group. Its goal is to facilitate a freer dialogue with all groups without exception, in the spirit of disinterested service, with the desire to contribute to the success of this Conference and to the full and solidary development of all peoples.

11. Need to relaunch the North-South dialogue

Letter of His Holiness John Paul II to Mr. Gamani Corea, Secretary-General of the United Nations Conference on Trade and Development. The Vatican, 25 May 1983.

Original: French

(1640) The Sixth Session of the United Nations Conference on Trade and Development is meeting at a time when many questions of grave importance claim the attention of leaders and specialists in the fields of politics, social problems, economics and development. In such an atmosphere in which problems are many and solutions not easy, it is often quite difficult to bring together sufficient resources and energies combined with the necessary political commitment to face up adequately to the many specific challenges in the areas that will be examined by your Conference. Mindful of the very real human factor and informed about the history of previous Conferences, I am writing to you, Mr. Secretary-General, to offer this important meeting some words of support and encouragement which stem from my profound wish that this Conference may contribute to the betterment of the conditions of life and, thus, to the present and future well-being of the developing countries, especially the countries that have the most need for concrete help.

(1641) As you know, the task of the Church is spiritual and religious in nature. Animated by the Gospel message of Jesus Christ, the Church, consistent with that spiritual mission, never hesitates to speak a word and to lend a hand in order to collaborate in the responsibilities we all must face to enhance life and secure a better future for all peoples, especially those who are in the greatest need.

(1642) In my Encyclical *Laborem Exercens*, I spoke of the importance of international organizations in the domain of international collaboration, pointing out that they "must let themselves be guided by an exact diagnosis of the complex situations and of the influence exercised by natural, historical, civil and other such circumstances. They must also be more highly operative with regard to plans for action jointly decided on, that is to say, they must be more effective in carrying them out" (No. 18).

(1643) Many and varied are the studies and analyses that have been carried on by various agencies and governments in the past 20 years concerning development and trade around the word and within individual nations. These have been utilized with varying degrees of success by those responsible. However, what I would want to emphasize today is the need to move from the studies which are already available or which might be readily available when needed, and to arrive at the next point. Aware of their mutual dependence, and in a spirit of solidarity, international organizations and nations should bend their efforts at this UNCTAD VI to plan for action jointly decided upon that might be more effective in furthering the well-being of nations and peoples who come to this forum looking for help.

(1644) To this end, there is a need, I believe, for a relaunching of the North-South dialogue with fresh perspectives and with a renewed political will to carry out programmes that will be mutually helpful. Everyone is aware of the domestic problems that, for some time, have beset all the nations of the world without exception. Great as these are, it would be a pity if the internal difficulties of a developed nation were to be used as an excuse to avoid responsibilities in the international sphere. Thus one can see that, in the area of development, the fundamental step must be the initiation of a dialogue that accepts the other as an equal partner and that seeks to find ways, through sincere and honest negotiations, of resolving real and concrete problems. There can be no substitute for this dialogue. There is no nation which has the right to exempt itself from the demands that such a dialogue presents.

(1645) If the North-South dialogue can be renewed and given new impetus and direction - and this Conference can play an important role in such an endeavour - then a first fruit of that process will be the discovery of a new quality of interdependence. The interdependence of nations is expressed in a number of ways, from the most simple bartering to the most complicated of international economic and trade agreements. These are, however, the plain facts of interdependence which indicate to us that no one nation is able to live solely by itself, looking only to its own interests. Yet, in these facts one can discover a more important reality, namely the quality of interdependence or interchange that must be expressed and developed beyond the mere facts. This must be fostered in the renewal of the North-South dialogue: the quality of the dialogue must be improved. The vision of a world living together in harmony must be emphasized. Esteem for the values of one another's cultures must be deepened. Above all, the full dignity and value of the human person in society must be protected and fostered. The dialogue which you in this Conference must conduct about economics and trade, about development and appropriate technology will be guided by and expressive of the value you place upon the peoples and nations with whom you are dealing. This is, need I add, a mutual discovery and a mutual obligation: to develop a North-South dialogue that embodies and expresses a quality of interdependence that gives to all those involved their true worth and thus opens up the concrete steps to be taken in order to arrive at that sense of the worth of the human person and the common good of all.

(1646) It is my earnest hope that UNCTAD VI will make a real and lasting contribution to this dialogue, a contribution that will find its way in programmes that overcome the current disparities and give new hope to the lives of peoples and nations most in need - a contribution that will press forward to a world in which the worth of every person and nation is fully respected and honoured.

(1647) I pray that God, our Common Father, will bless this Conference, your deliberations and fruit of your work.

12. Interdependence of rich and poor countries

Statement by H.E. Msgr. Edoardo Rovida, Apostolic Nuncio, Head of the Delegation of the Holy See, at the United Nations Sixth Conference on Trade and Development, held in Belgrade, Yugoslavia, on 6 June-3 July 1983. Belgrade, 16 June 1983.

Original: French

(1648) 1. It is strange to find that, for the first time in half a century, the industrially developed countries are facing a severe economic and financial crisis, which has caused mass unemployment and great loss of production not only in these regions but in many countries of the Third World as well. It is also worth noting that the economic crisis does not seem to be just another business cycle which will correct itself within the next few years. It appears to be rather a manifestation of a more fundamental structural maladjustment in the international economy; and, as a consequence, large sectors of the world's population have become "marginalized", with low and inadequate incomes that barely provide them with the necessary purchasing power to buy a sufficiency of the essential commodities for a decent human existence.

(1649) One element that stands out conspicuously in this global picture is the growing realization of the interdependence of rich and poor countries, manifesting itself in the intricate interlocking of their economic systems where, however, the supply of and demand for commodities function haphazardly; where prices of raw materials and manufactured goods are deeply out of balance; where high interest rates immobilize credit; where the transfer of technology from the industrially advanced to the technologically underdeveloped countries is impaired by conflicting interest; and where privileged positions of economic monopoly are strongly defended. Despite all these negative elements, there is no possibility of isolated existence for any country in the world today. The real tragedy is that this interdependence is highly distorted, and the more economically powerful dominate, in a variety of ways, nations that are industrially and technologically less developed. What is required is, therefore, a new type or quality of interdependence. As Pope John Paul II maintained in his message to the Secretary-General of UNCTAD, "If the North-South dialogue can be renewed and given news impetus and direction - and this Conference can play an important role in this endeavour - then a first fruit of that process will be the discovery of a new quality of interdependence" (See above, par. 1645).

(1650) In his Encyclical *Populorum Progressio*, Pope Paul VI drew attention to this type of unbalanced interdependence that manifests itself in the unequal terms of trade in the exchange between manufactured goods and agricultural commodities and raw materials. To quote the Pope's words, "Highly industrialized nations export, for the most part, manufactured goods, while countries with less developed economies have only food, fibres and other raw materials to sell. As a result of technical progress, the value of manufactured goods is rapidly increasing and they can always find an adequate market. On the other hand, raw materials produced by underdeveloped countries are subject to wide and sudden fluctuations in price, a state of affairs far removed from the progressively increasing value of industrial products. As a result, nations whose industrialization is limited are faced with several serious difficulties, when they have to rely on their exports to balance their economy and to carry out their plans for development. The poor nations remain ever poor, while the rich ones become still richer."

(1651) This analysis of the situation between the rich and poor nations is far more true today than when it was first published in 1967. The statistics of the terms of trade available with the United Nations Trade and Development Commission have brought out the continuous deterioration in the exchange value of these two sets of products, especially in the last two years since 1980. To call for free market forces by themselves to improve the international exchange economy appears to be a proposition far too unrealistic in the prevailing circumstances. To quote Pope Paul VI once again, "The role of free trade, taken by itself, is no longer able to govern international relations. Its advantages are certainly evident when the parties involved are not affected by any excessive inequalities of economic power: it is an incentive to progress and a reward for effort. That is why industrially developed countries see in it a law of justice. But the situation is no longer the same when economic conditions differ too widely from country to country" (*ibid.*, 58).

(1652) This structural weakness has been further aggravated by policies adopted by some of the more economically powerful countries to counter rising price trends and increasing costs of living and to safeguard their agricultural sectors through a policy of protectionism. The result has been a calamitous fall in the export earnings of the poor countries, lower production levels, growing unemployment and crippling debt obligations. Besides this, a new and powerful element has entered the international areas in the shape of the transnational corporations that control a substantial proportion of world production and trade for many important primary and processed commodities, particularly in the mining and plantation agriculture sectors. The powerful market position of the transnationals means that they can exercise considerable bargaining power on the market, control and integrate the production process, ensure continuous supplies, transfer their products from one country to another at their own internal price levels and reap the corresponding profits. Thus one may conclude that the burden of global adjustment has fallen disproportionately on the developing countries, which do not possess the strength and the resilience to struggle against these forces.

(1653) 2. When the Holy See Delegation reflects on this situation and offers some observations, it should be realized that these really stem from the basic conception of the absolute and primal importance of man and his dignity as a person, that has been present as part of Church teaching down the centuries ever since the first social grouping of Christians where the unity of all people in and through Christ was demonstrated in a practical way through a common sharing of the goods owned within a harmonious community. This guiding principle has been enshrined in a particular way in the recent social teaching of the Popes in their Encyclicals. In this context one may assert that the guiding principles so clearly spelt out in *Populorum Progressio* provide clear guidelines today as they did some 20 years ago - namely that development cannot be limited to mere economic growth, that it must be integral, that this implies the simultaneous development of all humanity in the spirit of solidarity, that in the area of trade one cannot apply two systems of weights and measures, that development is the new name for peace, that to wage war on misery and to struggle against injustice is to promote the common good. And Pope John Paul II in *Laborem Exercens* goes on to point out: "The fact of the mutual dependence of societies and States and the need to collaborate in various areas mean that, while preserving the sovereign rights of each society and State in the field of planning and organizing labour in its own society, action in this important area must also be taken in the dimension of international collaboration by means of the necessary treaties and agreements" (No. 18).

(1654) 3. In the framework of the United Nations Conference on Trade and Development, laudable efforts have been made to promote just and effective solutions.

(1655) Among the remedies to restore the imbalance in the distribution of the gains from international trade, the Common Fund has been established for providing finance for the buffer stock operations that are required in order to stabilize the prices of the commodities that fall within the international commodity agreements. Such an attempt to prevent, as far as possible, price fluctuations of food commodities are completely in accordance with the concept of solidarity and international cooperation insisted upon by previous representatives of the Holy See at UNCTAD Conferences. It is greatly regretted that the implementation of the Fund's operation has been so long delayed because of the slow process of its ratification and financing by Member Nations. Obviously, it is not a perfect mechanism by itself since the problem of controlling the quantity of the specific commodity to be produced by interested farmers has to be determined at national levels. All the same, it marks the beginning of a series of measures to stabilize supplies and to secure prices that are more equitable to weaker nations.

(1656) One may not trust entirely, however, in the theory of comparative advantage to establish the kind of equilibrium that will benefit all the partner-nations equitably, so as to eliminate the great differences in income that prevail between rich and poor countries. Even if different ways of measuring the well-being of the individuals at the national and international levels are being employed, the gulf that separates the standards of living in the countries at the centre from those at the periphery is still intolerably wide and is an acute cause of the odium and violence that has characterized the last two decades of human existence. Unless such basic injustices are eliminated or, at least, alleviated in the short term world peace becomes an unattainable mirage.

(1657) On the other hand, it is imperative that developing countries should take advantage of their enormous potential for reciprocal trade through preferential treatment among themselves. The internal structures within the peripheral countries, especially for the development and expansion of their agriculture sectors on which the majority of their populations depend, call for urgent transformations. In his address at Cuilapan, in Mexico, Pope John Paul II maintained: "The depressed rural world, the worker who with his sweat waters also his affliction, cannot wait any longer for full and effective recognition of his dignity, which is not inferior to that of any other social being. He has the right to be respected and not deprived, with manoeuvers which are sometimes tantamount to real spoliation of the little that he has. He has the right not to be impeded in his aspirations to share directly in his own advancement. He has the right to be rid of the barriers of exploitation, often made up of intolerable selfishness, against which his efforts of advancement are shattered. He has the right to real help - which is not charity or the crumbs of justice - in order that he may have access to the development that his dignity as a person and as a child of God deserves". These words could well be applied to agricultural workers and cultivators all over the world and much more so in countries where agriculture forms the main source of livelihood for the vast majority of the population.

(1658) 4. Another typical problem for developing countries is created by the fact that their use of the latest technological innovations yields high rewards that are unequally distributed. Because of the weak nature of the labour force, a large amount of the surplus created is absorbed by those who own the land, the natural resources and the means of production. Yet it is out of this surplus that the accumulation of urgently required capital for reinvestment emerges. It is this form of capital that increases employment and productivity. Therefore, it should be used for truly productive purposes, and not on luxury goods or armaments or bureaucratic expenditure or be appropriated by rising global demand.

(1659) Intimately linked with the breakdown of favourable trends in worldwide trade and production levels, and an indirect cause of such a mishap, is the failure of the international community of nations to retain effective control over the creation of liquidity or the requisite financial means. The monetary crisis shows how much more profound has the interdependence between the nations become, and, thus, how much greater is the need for liquidity.

(1660) The international debt problems of the developing countries now loom large on the horizon, and a certain scepticism as to their ability to repay their debts prevails. Though the situation is judged to be serious, it appears to be imperative that a large part of the debt repayment should take the form of increased exports and a fall in the international rates of interest, which are abnormally high. But an increase in export earnings would imply that the industrially developed countries would have to change their "defensive" policies of protectionism.

(1661) Such protectionist policies make it impossible for debtor countries to service their external debts, even when these debts have been rescheduled for countries on the brink of bankruptcy. Those who hold the policies demanding that countries in the Third World should abide by the rules of the open market and allow free entrance to manufactured goods from the developed countries do not seem to take into sufficient account the fact that the weak economies of the poor countries have, perforce, to protect their infant industries against foreign competition in their efforts to produce some of the goods they import, and to diversify their productive capacity precisely in order to service their debts more effectively.

(1662) 5. The Holy See Delegation, therefore, considers that it is of the utmost importance to insist on the need to design a more equitable system of international economic relations that could, at the same time, be combined with the transformation of the international institutional framework so that the system could work much more efficiently. What are the implications of this proposition?

(1663) To make the system more equitable, it is necessary that the fundamental needs of the poor countries be guaranteed.

1. by the speedy preparation and ratification of international commodity agreements to safeguard the "real" value of their exports;

2. by greatly expanding the volume of aid for truly productive purposes. For, despite the many mistaken purposes to which such financial and food assistance has been put by both donor and beneficiary countries, it is an urgent and necessary instrument in the process of development. Rightly used, it could prepare the countries on the periphery to participate gradually on a basis of equality with the countries at the centre in benefiting from the increase in global trade and production;

3. by reducing substantially the existing barriers to the trade of developing countries, barriers which at the same time retard the process of structural change. Obviously, such a policy implies some hardship and sacrifice on the part of developed countries, but it is the best way of manifesting their solidarity with their marginalized neighbours and of safeguarding the long term well-being of all nations;

4. together with these measures, one cannot permit the international monetary system to drift along in the hope of establishing its own equilibrium, or to reverse the world economic recession or stem the tide of rising unemployment. Therefore a positive common agreement on liquidity control or liquidity expansion, as required, should take into account not only national interests but also, and much more, international well-being since the two sets of goals are so intimately linked;

5. finally, there should be flexibility in the application of the prevailing rules regulating economic relations between the developed and developing countries. This would allow for a smoother pro-

cess of adjustment to take place where the existing conflicts between trade policies and monetary policies are reduced or minimized.

(1664) The Holy See Delegation wishes to conclude by insisting that there is a need to establish what might be called a new qualitative interdependence among all nations and among all peoples which, while respecting their identities as sovereign States, would enable them on a basis of equality to share far more equitably in whatever growing prosperity may be brought about by the dynamic advance of technology. To ensure such a favourable outcome, both the system of international economic relations and the international monetary and financial structures need to be remodelled and transformed. At the same time, top priority must be given to immediate action to halt or even, reverse the arms race. World peace thus becomes a necessary ingredient in the entire process of establishing a just society just as much as the establishment of justice in the relations between the nations is necessary to bring about peace. Such justice is only possible if the quality of the interdependence of the nations is radically transformed and inspired by a new sense of mutual solidarity, cooperation and equity, which will ensure the dignity of all human beings and the well-being of all peoples and nations on this planet.

IX - INDUSTRIAL DEVELOPMENT

1. Industrialization: in the service of the human person

Message of His Eminence Card. Maurice Roy, President of the Pontifical Commission "Justice and Peace" for the Extraordinary Conference of the United Nations Industrial Development Organization, held in Vienna on 1-8 June 1971. The Vatican, 1 June 1971.

Original: French

(1665) The United Nations Industrial Development Organization is meeting in an extraordinary Conference. The Pontifical Commission "Justitia et Pax" cannot remain indifferent to this event.

(1666) One overriding concern is manifested both in the preparatory documents and in the agenda of this Conference. You are going to study the means and the measures to take so that your Organization may become a more effective instrument of international cooperation in the area of industrial development. Your debates will bear on precise and technical questions such as: multilateral research, the coordination of all activities of the United Nations in the area of industrial development; the generalized system of preferences; the services of experts, grants for improvements, furnishing of material; cooperation among developing countries at the regional level; the decentralization of the organization's services through creation of regional bureaux.

(1667) In launching the Second Development Decade, the governments of the world have manifested their desire to engage in a more vast, more intense, more coordinated operation. Several international and national organizations, if not all, share this decision and declare themselves ready to commit all their resources to the enterprise of worldwide development.

(1668) The conditions in which our planet finds itself are, to be sure, quite different from the circumstances seen in Western industrialization. On one hand, the industrialized world now dispenses capital, expertise and technical supplies without precedent. On the other hand, the history of industrial growth, the occurrences and experiences of the first Development Decade allow the exercise of a critical judgment on the options taken and a re-evaluation of certain measures adopted to date.

(1669) The increase in economic growth rate no longer suffices either as an objective or as a measure of development. The simple game of economic and commercial techniques is revealed to be insufficient to guarantee the structural elements that would be adequate both for a dialogue between equals and for an equitable redistribution of the fruits of industry. Capital is found concentrated in the hands of industrialized countries who have, by this fact, the power to decide the destiny of others. A growing disparity is being carved out between the rich nations and deprived countries; within the latter, the disparity is manifested between those who, holding the power, are embarked on the path of development, and the great mass that remains a stranger to it.

(1670) For a new undertaking, one needs a new spirit. There will not be true development unless it is focused on man. If the welfare of man is the goal of industry, it is around him alone that industry must orient itself: industry does not attain its ultimate meaning except to the extent that it becomes the work of man's creativity in the service of his evolution and total realization.

(1671) Further, man is a social creature: he blooms in communion with his fellow-man. Every division, whether physical or spiritual, structural or ethical, operates as a countercurrent of fellowship which promotes unification, both in people and in communities that emanate from it. The ambition of UNIDO is to become an effective instrument in the service of these fellowships, and in that regard I express my hearty congratulations. If, in effect, man does not participate fully in the construction of his future; if people do not work out their destiny together; if institutions do not change to function in the service of man; development will not be able to become a reality.

(1672) Your objective, may I say, joins that of the Pontifical Commission which endeavours, for its part, to awaken consciences to their responsibilities in view of a common effort for the full and firm development of man. It is, in effect, with all willing men and women that Christians are called to build a just and fraternal world. The hope they announce is that which comes to them from the Word of Him who renews man, the liberation from fear and egoism so that we may build a better world of which Eternal Love may be the inspiration and the end.

2. Industrialization's problems

Message of His Holiness Paul VI to the President of the Second General Conference of the United Nations Organization for Industrial Development. The Vatican, 12 March 1975.

Original: Spanish (*)

(1673) As the Second General Conference of the United Nations Organization for Industrial Development opens, we wish to express to you our work in the work of this Assembly. This Conference bears witness to the aspirations of people for a more equitable international order, to their impatience at the delays of its realization, but above all to their faith - sustained in the face of all difficulties - in the possibility of a better world being built by the international community.

(1674) It is with all our heart that we express good wishes for the success of these sessions and invoke upon them the blessing of the Almighty. In this year 1975, the Holy Year, we are unceasingly calling Christians to Reconciliation and Renewal. May we exhort the members of this Conference to undertake and continue their dialogue - however difficult it may prove - in a similar spirit, in order that cooperation may overcome confrontation, through the rediscovery of the essential values of human solidarity.

(1675) During the past year, serious circumstances have led the United Nations during its most solemn sessions to study key problems of the international order : the problems of raw materials and development, of food and agriculture, and of economic rights and obligations of States. Your Conference is today considering the subject of industrialization. This is an exciting subject for,

---

(*) Insegnamenti di Paolo VI, Vol. XIII (1975), 224-225.

while "it is a sign of development and contributes to it" (*Populorum Progressio*, 25), it embraces the most specific achievements of modern civilization. It is also a formidable subject, for it is concretely linked with unsatisfactory situations, with benefits which are inequitably shared, with a sometimes inhuman exploitation of the workers - all of which are realities weighing heavily upon international relations.

(1676) Such an examination will call for great clarity of mind, for industrialization runs the risk of promising more than it possesses to those who do not view it as subordinated to the integral aims of an authentic human development. This will also call for each one to consider the more general interests of mankind. A worldwide common good must be developed, to which each nation will be called upon to contribute within the framework of its sovereignty.

(1677) We therefore consider it to be especially indicated, Mr. President, that this present Conference for Industrial Development should give proof of a willingness for renewal in the examination of the very concept of industrialization and its place in the hierarchy of values; it should likewise give proof of a spirit of reconciliation, that is to say, a spirit of listening to one another, of solidarity in seeking the common good, of harmonious attachment to the goal which this present Conference, after so many others, is striving for: the happiness of each individual and the happiness of all.

3. Industrialization and the developing world

Statement by H.E. Msgr. Carlo Furno, Apostolic Nuncio, Head of the Delegation of the Holy See, at the Second General Conference of the United Nations Organization for Industrial Development, held in Lima on 12-26 March 1975.

Original: Spanish

(1678) While our Conference does not claim to deal completely with each of the points raised by the acceleration of the industrialization of the developing countries, it is at least dedicated to encouraging a political impulse and desire in regard to this process. These elements have so far been lacking, and we hope to see them formed in an irreversible manner here in Lima. Resolution 3087 (XXVIII) of the General Assembly has given us two tasks in this respect: an effort at analysis leading to "defining, within a dynamic framework, the contribution of the international community to the process of industrialization of developing countries," and drawing up an *International Declaration* and a *Plan of Action*. The Holy See Delegation intends to make a positive and wholehearted contribution to these vast aims in a way which is consonant with its special character.

(1679) The imbalance which characterizes the distribution of world-production is profoundly unhealthy. In comparison with the world industrial production of countries with a planned economy and of countries with a market economy, the rest of the world, though it forms seventy percent, is responsible for only seven percent of global production.

(1680) No one would deny today that the principal architects of world industrial production are the very countries concerned - and they still need adequate resources for this purpose! Now, without outside aid, one would despair of ever making up for the enormous disparities created between nations by history, geography, climate, culture and so many other factors. Yet however great the volume of this outside aid, it leaves unexploited the most obvious of the potential of the developing countries. To make the fullest use of this potential is not only the most worthy, but also the most profitable solution, in order that these countries may go forward in their development with a chance of success.

(1681) In the world we live in - and even this affirmation calls for explanation - industry appears as a privileged provider of riches. An intelligently conducted industrial production ensures a most substantial contribution to the national revenue, while at the same time ensuring the employment of many citizens. By ensuring all or part of the country's requirements, it allows a reduction in imports, and it is also reasonable to expect that it will increase exports and change their kind. To reserve the advantages which follow from industrial production to a limited category of countries is, therefore, to deprive the other countries forever of a considerable contribution to their wealth, of an important outlet for their human resources, and often too of an equitable utilization of their raw materials.

(1682) But it is not in the profit and loss account that the most serious aspect of the present situation lies. Industrialization represents a conquest by mankind, by all mankind. We will go further: industrialization appears more and more, on the level of society, as a right of man. Pope Paul VI, in his Encyclical *Populorum Progressio* on the development of peoples, devoted a passage to this aspect, a passage which is well known to those familiar with the subject: "By persistent work and use of his intelligence man gradually wrests nature's secrets from her and finds a better application for her riches. As his self-mastery increases, he develops a taste for research and discovery, an ability to take a calculated risk, boldness in enterprises, generosity in what he does and a sense of responsibility" (No. 25).

(1683) Although this does not mean to confer on industry the monopoly of solutions capable of ensuring man's future, no one can fail to see that industry offers contemporary society possibilities of which *a priori* none of its members should be deprived.

(1684) Modern civilization also involves, in a very positive sense, an industrial connotation. Hardly any aspect of progress in methods, work, production, research and science does not call for the intervention of industry, in an elementary or sophisticated form as the case may be, and this too even when one is fearful of its excesses. In the Encyclical already quoted, the Pope opposes the belittling of industry falsely blamed for the "evils which belong to the woeful system which accompanied it. On the contrary one must recognize in all justice the irreplaceable contribution made by the organization of labour and of industry to what development has accomplished" (*ibid.*, no. 26). As is said straightaway in a basic document of the Conference (ID/CONF. 3/5), industrialization has been and remains "the driving force of development" (*ibid.*, 1). The Holy See is profoundly convinced of this, and unstintingly supports the aspirations of the less fortunate peoples to a greater share in industrial production and the exchanges which this makes possible. The preliminary studies which preceded this Conference have demonstrated, if any demonstration were necessary, the complexity of the problems facing us. The industrial process abhors hasty simplifications, and this not only in what concerns its technical aspects. But the human problems also have their own considerations. In the objectives to be chosen and in the strategies to be set in motion, it is therefore necessary to insist on the perspective of a *just social sharing* of the fruits of industrial development. Otherwise one runs the risk of accentuating the inequalities instead of lessening them, and of creating new social categories which will possess industrial goods and power while, at the same time, the exodus from the country and the transfer of activities from one sector to the other will lead to the appearance of masses of unemployed and an acute under-employment, especially among the young. The establishment of new industries is, therefore, a phenomenon that is both socio-cultural and political. The *Declaration* and the *Plan of Action* will have to take these points into account. Otherwise we shall shut ourselves into the closed circle of the economy, and be surprised at not knowing how to get out of it.

(1685) Our Delegation also feels that it will be fulfilling what is expected of it by insisting that all the dimensions of the subject should be taken into consideration. None of the steps taken by the Conference can ignore the exigencies of a higher order and a spirit which, in the terms used by the Pope in his message to this Assembly, we shall describe as a spirit of renewal and of reconciliation.

(1686) When one says reconciliation one is speaking about solidarity. But this solidarity, as we well know, comes up against numerous obstacles; in the first place, the individualism of people and of nations. Solidarity therefore presupposes a change in attitude, a lasting desire for openness and understanding. It is rooted in the affirmation of the unity of the human family, a unity of nature and of destiny. But when one speaks of solidarity one also implies a deliberate intention to remove the obstacles to a possible accord. Among these obstacles to a concerted international effort for development none is worse than injustice, injustice which appropriates to itself what does not belong to it, injustice which holds on to what it knows does not belong to it by right. We all know that industrialization has been, and occasionally continues to be, closely linked with injustice, even if the links are accidental. It is necessary, if there is still time, to urge countries anxious to speed up their industrialization to guard against these evil consequences. But it is also necessary to call on industrialized countries, of all political persuasions, to overcome certain egoisms and to realize that the time has come to make the concessions which equity demands.

(1687) Without any doubt happy developments are, in fact, taking place. In the same way that the world of technology presents a less degrading aspect than that of the early stages of industrialization, the doctrine of production and exchange is tending to abandon the categorical affirmations of the past which authorized the excesses of capitalism, monopolies and technocracy, in favour of a more constructive orientation inspired by solidarity on the national and international levels. There remains the fact that attachment to existing positions, especially to profitable positions, remains tenacious. The cases of reciprocal lack of understanding are not all innocent. But also - why should we not say so - it is the solidarity of all that is in question here. It is not possible to point - in one or other camp - to those especially guilty whose responsibility can serve as an alibi for everyone else's inertia.

(1688) Having said this, let us be fully convinced of the truth that industrialization is neither a magic formula nor an already perfected model for satisfying all needs. Today we are coming round to the idea that we have given it a far too exclusive priority. The world food crisis which has jolted the whole world and which is pressing hard on an ever increasing proportion of mankind is providing us with a salutary, as well as crucial and belated, reawakening in this regard. May we again refer to the affirmation laid down by the Pope when he received on 9 November last the participants in the World Food Conference: "The present crisis appears in fact above all to be a crisis of civilization and of solidarity. A crisis of civilization and of method, which shows itself when the development of life in society is faced from a one-sided point of view, and when only the model of society that leads to an industrialized civilization is considered, that is to say, when too much confidence is placed in the automatic nature of purely technical solutions, while fundamental human values are forgotten. It is a crisis that shows itself when the accent is placed on the quest for mere economic success deriving from the large profits of industry, with a consequential almost total abandonment of the agricultural sector, and the accompanying neglect of its highest and spiritual values" (See below, par. 2105).

(1689) The best way for peoples to protect themselves against these bitter experiences will be to start by adapting their industrial planning to their various possibilities, making it proportionate to a harmonious plan which takes proper account of the men and resources available and does not ignore the rhythm of the adjustments and pace to which they will be subjected; all this in a desire to balance, for all groups and individuals, the satisfaction of their needs, seen according to a truly human scale of values.

(1690) To illustrate our proposal, here are two passages taken from the document ID/CONF. 3/5. The first concerns recourse to techniques, and it observes pertinently: "Advanced techniques are not always adaptable to conditions in developing countries, where unskilled manpower is abundant and capital is scarce" (*ibid.*, 107). With regard to less advanced countries, having enumerated the "many difficult problems of choice and priorities" which must be resolved, the Document shows how progressive and prudent the steps will be: "To eliminate these obstacles, an appropriate strategy is needed, in which the nature and the order of the priority of the measures to be taken to encourage industrialization will be defined. It is necessary, in the first place, to ensure a balanced growth in realizing in each sector appropriate projects which complement one another" (*ibid.*, 114).

(1691) The elements which will determine with priority the choice of methods - or rather policies - are, and must be, the essential terms of what is at stake, that is to say, the human and social factors involved in the undertaking. For industry to be truly human it is not enough for it to be a great success of man. It brings about a real participation for those who are the actual agents of this success only to the extent that their training enables them not only to serve but to act. It was the paradox of a whole century of industrialization that the great victory of mind over matter which industrialization represents was actually such only for a small group of people. The mass of the workers were only associated in it through a physical contribution, most often a very heavy one, and sometimes crushing. This is what education and training are meant to remedy, provided that the task is approached with the utmost seriousness and with no sparing of effort. The Holy See's Delegation has already said this at the Athens meeting, a real beginning of the collective effort of which the Lima Conference forms a decisive step forward:

(1692) "Work is for man a means not only of obtaining the resources for subsistence but also of expressing and developing his personality; he must therefore be able in his work to promote his freedom and exercise responsibilities; and this presupposes structures for participation which, while maintaining the role of authority and the unity of management also calls each one to some initiative. Finally, the problem of professional and human training is essential. Every man must find the means of acquiring, perfecting and renewing the knowledge which he needs for exercising his profession without ever being reduced to the level of a mere robot."

(1693) The progress of industrialization calls then for the creation of civilization in the full meaning of the word. What is today called "industrial civilization" is far from meeting this requirement. There is no doubt that in many advanced societies a positive climate has finally been created: education has been extended to all; professional training multiplies qualifications; remuneration is better spread out among all the strata of the population; recognition is given to the social function and full meaning of leisure; the access of as many people as possible to well-being is far from being alien to a widely held recognition of the fundamental rights of the individual. But what a long time this progress has taken, and at the price of what sufferings have we overcome the consequences of perspectives limited by the fascination of economic profit alone!

(1694) This is why the Holy See Delegation raises its voice here, so that the effort which is awaited from the whole international community in favour of the industrial progress of two-thirds of its members should not remain one-dimensional: limited to an immediate finality and closed to essential values. Let us say frankly that we have been somewhat disconcerted by the fact that the various projects prepared in view of the *Declaration* make only a brief express mention of the human factors as the ultimate goal of development. Nothing, or very little, is said about the social exigencies of industrialization, about the importance of education and training and finally about leisure - the typical product of industrial society, at least in the forms in which it is today accessible to the vast majority. We have it in mind to return to these subjects in more detail in the Commission, but we owe you, Mr. President, at this stage, complete candour regarding the gaps which, were they to be maintained in the conclusions of the Conference, would deprive those conclusions of part of their credibility.

(1695) Before concluding this intervention, we would say a word on the question of the strengthening of the institutions which has been put on the agenda. We share the general conviction that the need for a vast and sustained effort in favour of the industrialization of the developing world should be reflected more effectively in the international institutional system. Let us not forget, however, that structural dispositions carry little weight unless that action is upheld by a firm will to make use of them and to endow them with the necessary resources. As in the past, the Holy See will always follow with sympathy and interest everything which would ameliorate the present arrangement. The Holy See will lend its support, in conformity with its mission, to those bodies which in the future will have to deal with this important sector of the international order. We must however declare at once that, after a mature examination of the subject, the Holy See has become convinced that the international bodies specifically related to industrialization presuppose, on the part of those who intend to take an active part in them, commitments in the economic and commercial order that are foreign to the Holy See's nature and to its possibilities for action. Consequently the Delegation of the Holy See does not intend to enter directly into the debate on the institutions. We are sure that everyone will understand the reasons for this position, and will not see in it a sign of disinterest with regard to the theme of our Conference.

(1696) We are in a difficult period of international economic relations, a period in which there are many uncertainties for the present and for the future, a period in which immediate difficulties risk making us forget more distant objectives. We must overcome this distrust which leads to confrontation. Only a renewed consciousness of human solidarity, applied to the industrial field, will make it possible to enter unhesitatingly into worldwide cooperation.

(1697) And so, once again, we are led to make this Lima Conference a new step on the road to renewal and reconciliation.

4. Industrialization of the Third World

Statement by H.E. Msgr. Luciano Storero, Apostolic Nuncio, Head of the Delegation of the Holy See, at the Third General Conference of UNIDO, held in New Delhi on 21 January-8 February 1980.

Original: English

(1698) This Conference, as the Third General Conference of the United Nations Industrial Development Organization, is devoted to the industrialization of the Third World. Industrialization has for a long time now been regarded as the key to a more prosperous economic future of the developing countries. Far more than a decade ago, the United Nations have realized that a special instrument was needed in order to accelerate industrialization in the Third World. The United Nations then created UNIDO as a sub-organ of the General Assembly, but with much of the structure of a full international organization, and entrusted to it the task of coordinating and supporting all efforts made in the field of industrial development.

(1699) When the international community, at the Second General Conference of UNIDO, held in Lima in 1975, assessed for the first time in the organization's short history the progress made and compared it with the pressing needs existing, it drew up the Lima Plan of Action in order to give a particular impetus to the countries cooperating in UNIDO to make new endeavours in the area of industrialization. Moreover, the Lima Conference called for the transformation of UNIDO into a specialized agency, because it was believed that this would give the organization a freer hand and greater discretion in handling the issues involved, thereby making it a more effective instrument for the purpose it had originally been designed for.

(1700) We all know, Mr. President, how difficult has been the task to work out the Constitution for UNIDO as a specialized agency. While we have luckily finished it last year in Vienna, we are still far from the new organization getting on its way, since very few acceptances of its new Constitution have so far been deposited. At the same time, the progress made in the substance of industrial development lags also behind the previous expectations, and it is certainly not exaggerated when we say that this has given rise to great disappointment throughout the Third World.

(1701) The Holy See has followed all these developments with great attention. While it is not itself an industrialized power, and does not dispose of resources of industrial know-how, it yet believes that it should give the support of solidarity to all efforts in the field of industrialization. Certainly, it would perhaps be improper for the Holy See to serve on the Industrial Development Board, and it intends, in fact, to take up a mere observer position with regard to the new UNIDO, should the latter once come into being. But this is due to the special character of the Holy See in the international community rather than to any disregard of industrialization as an important means to promote human welfare.

(1702) The Holy See therefore deeply deplores the fact that, in the field of industrialization of developing countries, no greater progress has so far been made. One of the reasons for this sad reality must be seen in the continuous arms-race between, not only the superpowers and their various allies but, between the developing countries themselves. This arms-race not only devours more money annually than would be needed to permit the developing countries a great leap forward on their way to economic prosperity, but also diverts the attention of the greater part of mankind from the real needs of the peoples of this world. The late Pope Paul VI,in his famous Encyclical Letter on the Progress of Peoples, *Populorum Progressio*, of 1967, has said that development was only a new name for peace. Now, more than a dozen years later, it seems that the lack of peace, or rather the threat of war, has heavily impeded development. It is the conviction of my delegation, Mr. President, that development cannot be had without peace, and peace not without development.

(1703) This seems to be a vicious circle. If peace cannot come without progress in the field of development, and if such development is dependent upon a status of peace, how will we ever reach both of them, peace and development? The answer is clear enough since peace and development do not lie in the objective connections of the present day situation; this situation cannot be overcome by the force of fact alone. What is therefore needed is a conscious decision of mankind itself in favor of both peace and development. Man is the only being in this world that is able to defeat matter through spirit and to bring about intentionally what would never come by the inherent rationality of things alone. Man, and only man, will be able to arrive at both ends, at peace as well as at development, when he tries to fulfil the command of the gospel: "Thou shallst love thy neighbour as thyself!" If such an attitude could be credibly found among the peoples of this world, modern swords could really be transformed into modern ploughshares; and industrialization could be made to move forward much quicker than it has done so far.

(1704) For such a conversion on a great scale, clear indications on a world-wide basis are needed. How can the developing countries believe in the good-will of the industrialized States if the latter are not prepared to give sufficient signs of that good-will? How can, on the other hand, the industrialized States believe in the good-will of countries of the Third World, if the latter try to bring pressure to bear upon them in an unjustifiable way, as for instance by the constant threat to use the oil-weapon? How can, moreover, the countries of the Western World, which are doubtless still the decisive partners of the developing countries, believe in the good-will of these States if the latter not infrequently show disregard or even contempt for values so dear to the former as personal liberty and the respect for personal property, values for which the peoples of these countries have fought for centuries? How can anybody, finally, believe in a true intention of the developing countries to make all efforts on their way to social and economic progress, if the latter invest so much money in useless things that serve no other purpose than to satisfy national ambition, as for instance prestige projects of doubtful value or even military objects that are out of any proportion?

(1705) The General Assembly of the United Nations, at its Sixth Special Session of 1974, has adopted two resolutions envisaging a New International Economic Order. Some months later, the same General Assembly adopted the Charter of Economic Rights and Duties of States. These three documents, forming together the legal basis for the desired New International Economic Order, have so far remained without great effect. My delegation believes, Mr. President, that there can be found one of the roots of the distrust prevailing as between developed and developing countries.

(1706) The Second Vatican Council, in its Pastoral Constitution on the Church in the Modern World, *Gaudium et Spes*, has clearly and unambiguously proclaimed the duty of the rich countries to give aid to the poorer ones. This cannot just be considered as a matter of charity, but must be seen as a matter of justice. As within the State everybody has a right to just wages in exchange for the work done by him, so in the international area every people has the right to share in the fruits of common efforts and to take a just portion of that wealth which has been, and is constantly, created by the happy combination of natural resources and human work. This does certainly not mean that an immediate transfer of funds has to bring about so rapid a change that by tomorrow all peoples have an even share in the goods of this world. But justice demands that these goods be redistributed in such a way that all peoples are enabled to stand upon their own feet and to run their economy in such a way as to grant them a modest living, as a minimum, together with the chance that, by their own efforts, they might be able to close the gap between themselves and the richer countries. The Holy See, Mr. President, expressly supports all endeavours that are made or are going to be made in the future to bring about such a situation amongst States and peoples as justice demands and the conscience of mankind is pleading for.

(1707) This Third General Conference of UNIDO inaugurates not only a new decade of industrial development, but also the first time in which UNIDO will function as an independent organization dedicated to, and dependent solely on influences directed to, this industrial development. Since we strongly believe that this new decade cannot be under better auspices than those which would be formed by a speedy coming into force of the Constitution of the new UNIDO and its setting up for functioning as soon as possible, my delegation calls upon all States present here in New Delhi to rally to the acceptance of the said Constitution and thereby to demonstrate a common willingness to unite all efforts for the promotion of the common goal of industrial development.

(1708) It is in this sense of solidarity that my delegation wishes this present Third General Conference of UNIDO all possible success!

5. Commitment of the Catholic Church to concrete projects of development

Statement by Msgr. Giovanni Ceirano, Permanent Observer to UNIDO, Head of the Delegation of the Holy See, to the Fourth General Conference of the United Nations Industrial Development Organization, held in Vienna on 2-18 August 1984.

Original: English

(1709) In his address at the thirty-eighth session of the General Assembly last year, the Executive Director, Mr. Khane, called attention to the importance of the Fourth General Conference in which we are participating now. As with the earlier General Conferences, so this one is charged to "assist the accelerated industrialization of the developing countries", a task, Mr. Khane told us, which takes on particular significance "in view of the progress which has been made ... towards the conversion of UNIDO into a Specialized Agency" (Address of Mr. Khane, 25 October 1983, p. 3).

(1710) Here as in other international agencies dedicated to the improvement and development of the living conditions and opportunities of peoples and nations, the Holy See wishes to add its voice to all those who seek to encourage real effort which lead to concrete programmes and actions that are of real benefit to developing nations and their citizens. No opportunity should be lost to make progress for the good of people, even if at times the temptation to discouragement and to loss of commitment can seem to be buttressed by facts and figures that point to lack of progress, even failures.

(1711) Any statement that claims to be a realistic evaluation of the present situation in industrial development, and thus a realistic evaluation of the achievements of the United Nations Industrial Development Organization itself, must start from the fact that industrial development, and therefore the whole process and structure for it, has failed to attain the targets set by the previous General Conferences of UNIDO, especially the Second one in Lima and the Third one in New Delhi. If one compares the annual growth in industrial output of 8% for the period of 1963 to 1973, and, still, of 5% for the period of 1973 to 1980, with only 0.4% for 1981 and only 0.1% for 1982, it is easy to work out how difficult it will be for the developing countries to get from the present little more than 11% of the world's industrial production to the 25% called for by the Lima Declaration of 1975 and repeated by the New Delhi Declaration of 1980. Without any massive changes in the conditions for such industrial development, there is in fact no real chance to come even near, let alone attain, the ambitious targets set by the previous Conferences of UNIDO.

(1712) The reasons for this situation are many and known to all who care to analyze the rising cost of energy in these years, the increased costs for industrial products, tariff problems stagflation, until recently, in the industrialized countries, unemployment problems that differ from country to country but which affect everyone, and the lack of liquidity, especially for countries already carrying sizable debts. Nor can we pass over the enormous consequences of the costs involved in arms development and the vertical proliferation of armaments, both nuclear and conventional, an expenditure of moneys that afflicts developing countries as much as it does the industrialized powers and super powers.

(1713) Without in any way minimizing the effect that these several factors have on development projects and industrial development in particular, it is important that this Fourth General Conference seek to harness the resources available to make progress in the fields of our concern here. This means making the most of the funds and the systems available and to see to it that the various actors, governments, international agencies, non-governmental organizations and institutions be open to mutual help and collaboration so that the goals of industrial development, the realization of the talents and potentials of developing peoples and societies, might be advanced.

(1714) To that end, allow me to point out several elements which must be kept in mind as some of the means and some of the values that will help us travel together on the path that leads to true progress and development.

(1715) To illustrate this concretely, I would begin by reassuring you of the commitment of the Catholic Church and its various aid and development agencies to the problems and the projects under discussion. In every industrialized country, large or small, the Catholic Church has organized agencies whose primary task is to appeal to the generosity of Catholics to lend a helping hand to our brothers and sisters, regardless of race, religion or background, in forging the projects that the local people themselves choose for their own development. This network of "non-governmental organizations" is aided by a coordinating body in the Holy See, the Pontifical Council *Cor Unum.* Let me offer you two examples. In 1983 the Holy See and the various aid and development agencies spent almost 110 million dollars for young Churches and developing societies in every part of the developing world. This past year the Holy Father has established the *John Paul II Foundation* for the Sahel. This foundation will make available to the peoples of that so sorely afflicted region, millions of dollars for programmes of education, agricultural and technological development that ultimately will benefit everyone affected by the scourge of drought there.

(1716) The Holy Father explained the position of the Church in this effort when he addressed the members of that new Foundation on May 26, 1984: "The Church's action, wherever this is possible, is carried out in complementarity with the public Authorities, inter-governmental organisms and non-governmental organizations... For it is men that are at issue, men and women suffering from hunger and thirst, undernourished or badly nourished children; international solidarity can contribute appreciable, even indispensable aid, but in the end, the solution is in the hands of the Africans; to collaborate with them, even on the technical level, does not amount to replacing them" (O.R., Engl. ed., 18 June 1984, p.10).

(1717) This latter aspect holds good as a general approach for development, and especially industrial development, in all parts of the Third World. As Article 2 of the Statute of the *John Paul II Foundation* for the Sahel states: "Foster the formation of competent persons who put themselves at the service of their countries and their brethren, without any discrimination, in a spirit of integral and solidary human promotion for fighting against the desertification and its causes."

(1718) The second element I would submit to you today is at the heart of all the efforts of UNIDO: the centrality of training programmes. The many programmes and courses offered by this Agency and by related groups is one of the best ways to make progress permanent and make the fruits of progress lead to ever greater growth for the good of all. The aims of these programmes include a "multiplier effect", namely they seek to enable those who use these programmes to pass on the fruit of their knowledge and thus multiply the effectiveness of such efforts across the world. Is it too much to ask that this Fourth Conference reaffirm the positive value of such programmes by guaranteeing that they not only be maintained but also expanded in number and in variety? Such emphasis on training and education in the industrial sphere, the ongoing importance of industrial development and the adaptation of technological know how in countries whose people, especially its youth, will make possible those strides forward that will bring to fruition the latent talents that lie untouched. For in the last analysis the most squandered resource in the world today is the intelligence of millions of men and women, old and young, who never have the opportunity of developing their talents, talents that will lead to richer and fuller lives for them, thus enriching the life and the future of us all.

(1719) The Church joins with all of you in recognizing the importance of industrial development as part of the whole interconnecting and mutually supportive development strategy. This positive assessment of the role of industrial development was most forcefully expressed seventeen years ago by Paul VI in his now famous encyclical *Populorum Progressio*: "The introduction of industry", it says, "is a necessity for economic growth and human progress; it is also a sign of development and contributes to it. By persistent work and use of his intelligence man gradually wrests nature's secrets from her and finds a better application for her riches. As his self-mastery increases, he develops a taste for research and discovery, an ability to take a calculated risk, boldness in enterprises, generosity in what he does and a sense of responsibility." (*Populorum Progressio*, n. 25).

(1720) With these few words, this Delegation has sought to reaffirm the commitment of the Catholic Church through its many agencies to concrete projects of development, including industrial development, to stress once again the priority of training and education; a priority we all agree upon and to stress once again that industrial development is one of the indispensable factors in true progress for developing peoples. To that end, all of us have a responsibility to collaborate in fostering true cooperation among industrialized and developing countries in such a way that neither prejudice nor favouritism ever obscure the good that this Agency has been established to pursue, that neither the interests of one group nor the political advantage of another might seem to predominate over the real needs and just claims of those who seek to make their rightful contribution to society and ask that we help them with the means toward that end.

(1721) For in the last analysis, the sole justification for the existence of this Agency and similar bodies is the human person buttressed by our shared conviction that, if we cooperate in helping peoples and nations realize the potential of human beings, then we contribute together to the common good of every person and of society as a whole. Last year, Pope John Paul II spoke in this very centre and said: "It is extremely important that we always maintain the primacy of man as the criteria for our judgments and decisions... Whether the object is industrial projects for developing countries, nuclear reactors, or programmes for the improvement of society, the human person is the guiding criterion. No project, however technically perfect or industrially sound, is justifiable if it endangers the dignity and rights of the person involved". He added further: "Promotion of the common good in your work demands respect for the cultures of nations and peoples coupled to a sense of the solidarity of all peoples and nations..." (Address to International Organizations in Vienna, 12 September 1983. See above, par. 240, 241 and 243).

(1722) If this Conference heeds these words, then we can be confident that the deliberations we carry on and the concrete and realistic projects that are decided on will be marked by the values that will ensure the good and the dignity of persons, realizing their potential in a world that needs the resources of the human mind and the human heart.

X - "DEVELOPMENT IS THE NEW NAME OF PEACE"

1. Letter of His Holiness Paul VI to H.E. U Thant, Secretary-General of the United Nations on the occasion of the meeting in Milan of the Governing Council of the United Nations Development Programme. The Vatican, 26 May 1966.

Original: French (*)

(1723) We have learned that the Governing Council of the United Nations Development Programme is to meet in Milan shortly to hold its second session. On this occasion we are happy to send this message of respectful good wishes and encouragement.

(1724) Pursuing the work previously financed and administered by the enlarged technical assistance programme and the special fund of the United Nations, the United Nations Development

(*) AAS 58(1966), 479-480.

Programme is carrying out its initiatives in order to speed up the economic and social development of least developed countries. How can we fail to rejoice when competent, responsible men meet to pool the resources made available to them by the international community of nations in order to promote the physical, intellectual and spiritual progress of the most needy of its members?

(1725) It is man in his fullest and most harmonious capacity that development seeks to produce, thus a triple longing must be assuaged while ever contending with the growth of daily and most urgent difficulties. The United Nations Development Programme has an increasingly clear view of this physical, intellectual and spiritual need, and the will to remedy it. But for this to be achieved, the whole world must be aware that misery is not only an unbearable evil for its victim but that this must also be so for each and every man worthy of the name. To permit man to survive is not enough, but to give him the means to live fully, as a person capable of establishing a family, and giving a satisfactory education to his children: such are the tasks calling for the disinterested aid of all men of good will, beyond any differences of nationality, race, culture or religion. Thus, man of today must increasingly convince himself that his own existence is involved and that temporary emergency help will not suffice. All human resources must be mobilized, for it is not enough to give of one's means, one must also give of the best of oneself. The peace which the world is aspiring to will not be built on less, for as it has been truly said, "Development is the new name of peace."

(1726) These are the thoughts inspired in us by the coming meeting in Milan and which we have thought worthwhile to communicate, in our ardent desire to spare no effort to ensure, with the collaboration of all men of good will, peace in truth, justice, charity and liberty.

(1727) It is with these sentiments that we invoke for Your Excellency, for Mr. Paul G. Hoffman, Director of the United Nations Development Programme and for all who participate in this session, the abundance of divine blessings.

2. Address of His Holiness Paul VI to Governing Council of the United Nations Development Programme. The Vatican, 25 June 1966.

Original: French (*)

(1728) We would like, Gentlemen, first of all to express our gratitude to your illustrious spokesman for the very kind words that he has just addressed to us. He recalled our interest in the activities of the United Nations: we are happy to have the occasion to prove this, once again, by receiving here, at the conclusion of their deliberations, the members of the Second Session of the Governing Council of the United Nations Development Programme.

(1729) We have followed the development of this work in the press. At the inauguration in the Palais des Nations in Milan, His Excellency Amintore Fanfani, in his capacity as President of the twentieth Session of the United Nations General Assembly, was gracious enough to recall the similarity between your initiatives and our appeal to all nations, made in Bombay in December 1964. At that time we invited all governments to retain a part of the expenditures set aside for armaments and utilize them for development of less favored areas.

(1730) We are thus at liberty to conclude that our humble voice, which seeks to sustain the silent suffering of so many peoples afflicted by famine and the lack of minimal necessities, was not raised in vain. It has found an echo within yourself, an echo rich in promise. As you may well imagine, this is for us a reason for profound satisfaction.

(1731) This satisfaction grows when we find that the "aid" to the developing nations has become a "programme," a "programme of the United Nations." Few facts appear to us more worthy of praise and encouragement than this great gesture of world-wide fraternity. We have here a typical example of overcoming narrow political views. We would like to see in it the sign of a civilization which strives to be truly humane and universal. We applaud this act of intellectual and practical courage,

---

(*) AAS 58 (1966), 587-590.

which fearlessly faces the many evident obstacles in the organization and conduct of the programme and those to be found doubtless even among the future beneficiaries.

(1732) You will without doubt ask us what is our viewpoint on these efforts. Your question is perfectly legitimate. For it is evident to everybody that a religious society such as the Catholic Church is not founded on economic plans alone and does not pursue any aim of self-interest. Thus, its point of view could not be that of a society with temporal objectives. It does, however, observe and favor, with all the means at its disposal, the progress and well-being of humanity. And when we consider, from the point of view of the Church, efforts such as those you are pursuing, we feel led to a double conclusion.

(1733) The first one concerns our duty. What must we do to favour a collective effort like yours, so worthy of support and collaboration? The answer to this first question awakens in us the desire and the taste for generosity. But alas, this only offers us modest means, out of proportion to the depth of the need.

(1734) The second conclusion invites us, on the other hand, to consider the work underway, and to discover the principles which inspire it, and the aims to which it aspires. And when we consider it from this point of view, we see our economic poverty giving way to spiritual riches of which, without any merit on our part, we find ourselves holding and distributing. When, in effect, it is a question of the principles and aims of human activity - even if they are foreign to us by reason of their secular and temporal nature - we always have something important to say.

(1735) Besides, you yourselves, Gentlemen, are you not the first to realize that when you speak of a "programme", you are not merely political and economic men - i.e. men to study and administer but men of thought, of ideology, of philosophy, we are almost tempted to say men of religion? Are you not, in effect, masters ruling on principles and aims which govern practical programme? This view of the principles and aims is the only one that renders justice to the true sense and the full value of your enterprise. It is the only one which answers the question which may legitimately be asked: why these programmes? Why so much trouble? Where to find the drive, the urge, the force for hope which not only justifies and idealizes the arduous and immense task, but renders it morally and practically possible?

(1736) And it is at this point that we feel we are able to insert into your "programme" a contribution which we believe is not useless: the powerful spiritual energy which we derive from the Gospel and which creates in us an immense respect and interest in man, in every man: which makes us recognize him as a brother, and take him to heart with all the great problems he is struggling with and, if he is unhappy and suffering, makes us discover that he has a yet greater right to our love and assistance.

(1737) This is the whole meaning of the great document which emerged from the recent Ecumenical Council on "The Church in the Modern World " which expounds in such great depth the help which the Church wishes to extend to human society today.

(1738) If, as we hope, you have carefully read this text, you will have noted that the questions of development have their place. You will have noticed that the great question of peace among men is discussed also at length. And if we were not afraid of infringing upon your patience, we would wish to confide to you certain thoughts on this gift - supreme in a certain sense - to humanity. For it is Peace, finally, to which your activities witness. They do build peace. They are peace in action. We said this in our recent letter to His Excellency U Thant, Secretary-General of the United Nations; today, "development is the new name of Peace" (See above, par. 1725).

(1739) This beautiful word *peace* has always had more than one meaning, more so today than ever. *Peace* has become, it must be admitted, a propaganda device not always sincere or honest. In certain political and social situations, it is the result of the deprivation of freedom, it has become synonymous with an imposed, oppressive order; peace is also a label for defining balance between opposing forces, contained by fragile agreements or by the accumulation by both parties of ever more dangerous armaments, but *peace,* finally, has become, thanks to God, your association of peoples, resolved to promote among them orderly, profitable relations for all, without recourse to force, without bloodshed. We honour this kind of peace; this is the kind of peace we hope for.

(1740) If we wish this kind of peace to become firm and demonstrate its power of expansion, it is essential that we find a remedy to the great deficiencies still suffered by such a large part of mankind. We must eliminate the all too evident disparities in enjoyment of the benefits of civilization; we must overcome economic systems, perhaps still in force, under which poor people always remain poor and the rich become ever richer.

(1741) Your "programme" is endeavoring to apply this remedy and this is why while we are not competent to judge its practical outcome, we recognize your work as being good, useful to civilization and to peace, and worthy of universal solidarity and applaud and encourage it with all our heart.

(1742) These are the few words we wanted to say to you. We would like to think that you will accept them as the words of a friend, a counsellor, an "expert on Humanity", as we said during our speech to the United Nations. We would, above all, want you to recognize in our voice the echo of Christ's, the great advocate of the poor and the disinherited, Whom we represent in spite of our unworthiness, and Whose message we interpret: this Christ Who will judge us on the ties of love which will have bound us to our brothers; this Christ Who has promised rewards which are neither small nor mean to those who have shown understanding and a heart toward suffering man.

(1743) May these blessings of Christ, of which ours is given as a pledge, descend upon you, Gentlemen, your families and your countries, and enrich your activities so generously devoted to the welfare of mankind.

CHAPTER VI

FOOD AND AGRICULTURE

I - AGRICULTURE

1. Address by His Holiness Paul VI to the World Land Reform Conference. The Vatican, 27 June, 1966.

Original: French (*)

(1744) We extend to you, Gentlemen, the most cordial welcome to the Vatican. Your World Land Reform Conference, with its more than 300 delegates from nearly 80 nations, is an event of far-reaching significance and one that, to be sure, no less authorities than the international organizations of such high competence as the United Nations, the Food and Agriculture Organization and the International Labour Office were instrumental in bringing about. To those Organizations go first of all our salutation and this renewal of our greatest deference and esteem.

(1745) You, gentlemen, are personages of proven competence; you are specialists in the problems of land reform. You are fully cognizant of the need to improve policy and programming in this field which is one of such capital importance for the well-being of countless millions of people of the globe. And you are meeting in order to tell each other of your experiences and to evaluate your action programs. We are greatly honored and deeply touched at your thought in interrupting your labors for a moment to visit us.

(1746) Your deliberations are fraught with consequence. For Land Reform is assigned a vital role in the eradication of hunger and poverty from the countrysides of the world. And the problems to which you are so courageously addressing yourselves are possibly among the most difficult, but also, you may be sure, among the most vital and the most urgent confronting humanity at the present time. Land tenure, redistribution of landed property, changes in the relations between landowner and farmer, the setting of limits to the territorial extension of ownership, consolidation, joint farming and land settlement - there, to mention only a few, are the problems before you.

(1747) Some of you, on this visit to the Vatican, may have wondered what the Pope was going to say on the subject and whether the Catholic Church had an opinion, a solution to offer, in regard to these great problems facing mankind.

(1748) In truth, in all that concerns the purely technical aspects of these problems - administrative aspects, for example, or those of an economic and financial nature - the Church, as such, has no specific competence and, by that token, no solution to propose. But your own efforts reach above and beyond such technical aspects. What you are striving for is to make a worthwhile contribution to the prosperity and welfare of your fellows. And here you join hands with the Church, for She, too, is striving, using methods and means peculiar to Herself, to secure what She considers to be the true good of mankind. She does not promote this, that or the other solution to whatever problem may present itself; rather She professes a doctrine which empowers Her to judge which of the proposed solutions are in keeping with human dignity and of a sort likely to secure true progress for the individual and for society at large.

(1749) This doctrine has been proclaimed afresh by the Ecumenical Council that lately brought together the bishops of the Catholic world. The Council Fathers, numbering over two thousand, adopted the Constitution on the Church in the Modern World. There one may read this solemn affirmation: "God intended the earth and all things in it for the use of all peoples, in such a way that the goods of creation should abound equitably in the hands of all, according to the dictates of justice, which is inseparable from charity. Whatever the forms of ownership, adapted to the lawful institutions of the peoples and in accordance with diverse and changing circumstances, this universal apportionment of goods must be borne in mind at all times."

(*) AAS 58(1966), 591-593.

(1750) It is easy to see, Gentlemen, all the consequences that derive from this basic principle. But the Council, having proclaimed the principle, goes on to consider a number of concrete applications, and there is one of these which we feel is very deserving of your attention:

"In a number of the economically less-developed regions, there are extensive and even vast landed estates which are poorly cultivated or set aside for speculative purposes, while the majority of the population has no land or only a pitiable amount, at a time when agricultural production is patently of the utmost urgency."

(1751) Here, Gentlemen, as you see, we are at the core of the problem. The Council analyses the matter further:

"It often happens that those employed by the owners of these large estates or who cultivate rented plots of land on them receive wages or have an income unworthy of their status as men. They have no decent living quarters and are exploited by the middlemen. Utterly without security, they live in a state of personal dependence such as to deny them practically any possibility of initiative and responsibility, cultural betterment or a share in social and political life. Reform, therefore, is imperative, (the Council concluded) in order, as the case may be, to increase incomes, improve working conditions and security of employment, foster initiative and even to redistribute under-cultivated land among men capable of bringing it into production."

(1752) We ask your indulgence, Gentlemen, for this lengthy quotation. but, as we see it, it is not without interest for you to realize that Land Reform and the efforts of those engaged in that noble undertaking have the care and the solicitude of the Church. Moreover, Her heartfelt support goes out spontaneously to any initiative in this field that is in conformity with the great principles that She herself, but a short time ago, proclaimed afresh through Her bishops in Council.

(1753) It remains for us to thank you once again, Gentlemen, for your kind visit and to say how fervently we wish you a felicitous continuation of your labors. From our heart we invoke upon those labors, as upon you yourselves, your families and your countries, the most abundant blessings of God.

2. Statement by Msgr L.G. Ligutti, Permanent Observer of the Holy See to the FAO, at the World Land Reform Conference held in Rome on 20 June-2 July 1966. Rome, 29 June 1966.

Original: English

(1754) We are about to close a very historic meeting, The World Conference on Land Reform. To all responsible for the planning and conducting of it go our sincerest thanks.

(1755) For ages past and even today, in some localities, this would have meant a study of readjustments to be made because of evidently deteriorated conditions of land tenure and use, with a sequel of social injustices weighing down heavily on a badly patched up economic system. This Conference has come closer to fundamentals. There was some merit in the request that the Conference treat of more than technical questions. To deal with technical questions alone would mean that certain existing present traditions had to be taken for granted as destined to go on to the end of time.

(1756) We must admit that human frailty and weakness do exist but while we can sin we can also make amends for our sins. A dentist will not put filling in a tooth unless the tooth is sound and can support the filling. So there is no sense in promoting a land reform unless the basis is sound, healthy and just.

(1757) Let me give you a very homely illustration. Two little boys were sleeping in the same bed on a cold winter night with no heat in the room and over them a rather skimpy blanket. They were cold and awake most of the night. One pulled and the other pulled, neither enjoying any comfort for any length of time. They could have turned on the light, they could have tucked under the covers and then could have huddled a bit closer, or they could have used some quilts available in the closet. But there was neither peace nor comfort the whole night through because they had not entered into a dialogue and were afraid to get out into the cold for a little while. Let us learn a lesson from the two boys as far as our economic systems are concerned. The bed is any country. The boys: the poor and the rich. The cold is the economic problems. The blankets are the natural resources.

(1758) We must realize that an economic system must exist for man's good, for his welfare, for his advancement and, as Pope Paul said to us the other day, it must respect and develop man's personality and his dignity. It must take into account his right to personal freedom within the limits of his social obligations.

(1759) It is an historical as well as a psychological error to believe that legislative enactments can cure man of his evil tendencies. And it is just as wrong to look upon man as so depraved that he cannot be perfectible hence must be forced into doing good.

(1760) There is a balance in all things, as the Greek philosophers used to say: "neither too much nor too little" or as the Romans put it: "in medio stat virtus". Virtue is the golden mean. Truth is never at the extremes.

(1761) Keeping in mind the nature and extent of the resources available, possessing an understanding of man in his integral and complete makeup, we can come to some conclusions and strike a balance that, while not perfect, will nevertheless be somewhat satisfactory but neither final nor eternal.

(1762) Let me close by quoting an anonymous writer: "New times demand new measures and new men; the world advances and in time outgrows the laws that in our fathers' days were best."

3. Address of His Holiness John Paul II to the World Conference on Agrarian Reform and on Rural Development. The Vatican, 14 July 1979.

Original: English (*)

(1763) Your Conference in Rome is dealing with a subject of extreme importance for the destiny of the human family, and one of lively interest for the Church, which by virtue of her mission feels a commitment to making an impartial contribution, corresponding to her nature, to the human uplifting of those who live and work on the land.

(1764) There can be no doubt that the agrarian reform and rural development that you are dealing with will mark a further step forward along the path that the International Organizations specialized in this matter, among them FAO, have always followed since they were set up.

(1765) I am happy to make use of this special occasion in order to reaffirm, in continuity with my predecessors, the heartfelt appreciation of the Apostolic See for the incisive and efficient action that the Organizations of the family of the United Nations carry out in the sphere of nutrition, agriculture and rural development (cf. John XXIII, *Mater et Magistra*: AAS 53(1961), p.439).

(1766) Your meeting offers you the chance to share with one another information on a great variety of experiences, and it is very probable that from this variety there will emerge orientations that will be an invitation and stimulus to fruitful collaboration in the spheres that you are studying. I express the hope that these orientations will enable you to outline really practical solutions that can be adopted in internal policies, such as to make possible the attainment of a greater harmonization on the international level, taking into consideration the cultural originality, legitimate interests and autonomy of each people, and responding to the right of those living and working on the land to growth in individual and collective life.

(*) AAS 71(1979), 1354-1358.

(1767) The divine command to master nature in the service of life, of course, implies that the reasonable improvement and use of natural resources should be directed towards attaining fundamental human aims (cf. *Redemptor Hominis*, 15). This is also in conformity with the basic principle that all the goods of the earth are meant to benefit all the members of the human family. Undoubtedly, "development demands bold transformations, innovations that go deep" (Paul VI, *Populorum Progressio*, 32).

(1768) With conditions as they are within individual countries, one foresees a land reform involving a reorganization of land holdings and the stable and direct assigning of productive areas to agricultural workers, together with the elimination of forms and structures that are unproductive and damaging to the community.

(1769) The Second Vatican Council's Pastoral Constitution *Gaudium et Spes* has already done justice to these requirements (cf. no.71) by including the legitimate quest for a more effective productive use of the land within the more basic preoccupation that the work of agricultural workers should be carried out in conditions and ways that harmonize with their dignity as persons, and for objectives that are similarly in harmony therewith. The words that I addressed in Mexico to the Indians of Cuilapan hold good here: "The depressed rural world, the worker who with his sweat waters also his affliction, cannot wait any longer for full and effective recognition of his dignity, which is not inferior to that of any other social being. He has the right to be respected and not deprived with manoeuvres which are sometimes tantamount to real spoliation of the little that he has. He has the right not to be impeded in his aspirations, to share directly in his own advancement. He has the right to be rid of the barriers of exploitation, often made up of intolerable selfishness, against which his best efforts of advancement are shattered. He has the right to real help - which is not charity or crumbs of justice - in order that he may have access to the development that his dignity as a person and as a child of God deserves". (AAS 71 (1979), p.209).

(1770) As I said on another occasion, the right to ownership of land always involves a social mortgage (cf. Address to the Third General Conference of the Latin American Bishops, III, 4: Puebla, 28 January 1979). Therefore, in the reform of structures, I permit myself to invite you to take into the deepest consideration all forms of agrarian contracts that make possible efficient use of the land through work, and guarantee the primary rights of workers.

(1771) Reference is made not only to the possibility of working the land efficiently but also to the guarantee of an adequate return from agricultural work.

(1772) It is urgently necessary to attain the objective of the right to work, with all the presuppositions required for widening the possibilities of absorbing the available resources of agricultural manpower and of reducing unemployment. Equally, one must promote among the workers a responsible attitude in the functioning of agricultural enterprises. This will also have the aim of creating, as far as possible, a special relationship between the worker of the land and the land that he works.

(1773) Furthermore, this right to work the land must be guaranteed together with the greatest possible improvement of human and civil life in rural conditions. This is the only way of ensuring the active presence above all of young people in the economy of agricultural development, and of avoiding excessive flight from the land.

(1774) Agrarian reform and rural development also demand that consideration be given to reforms aimed at reducing the gap between the prosperity of the rich and the anxiety and need of the poor.

(1775) However, it has to be borne in mind that to overcome imbalances and the strident inequalities in living conditions between the agricultural sector and the other sectors of the economy, or between the social groups within a given country, the public authorities must have a well-planned policy, one that is committed to the redistribution of income to the advantage of the very poor.

(1776) I think it fitting to repeat what I said on another occasion, namely that a wider reform and a more just and equitable distribution of wealth is foreseen "also in the world in general, ensuring that the stronger countries do not use their power to the detriment of the weaker ones" (Address to the Third General Conference of the Latin American Bishops, III, 4: Puebla, 28 January 1979).

(1777) The reform necessarily extends, therefore, to that of a new regulation of relationships between countries. But for reaching such an objective "it is necessary, in international life, to call upon ethical principles, the demands of justice... Primacy must be given to what is moral... to what springs from the full truth concerning man" (*ibid.*).

(1778) In brief, it is a question of restoring to agriculture its proper place in the sphere of internal and international development, and of modifying the tendency, which, in the process of industrialization, has until recent times tended to give a privileged position to the secondary and tertiary sectors.

(1779) One is pleased to note that it is now clear, on the basis of experience, how necessary it is to correct the one-sided industrialization of a country, and to abandon the utopian expectation that industrialization will certainly and directly lead to economic development and civil progress for everyone.

(1780) The great importance of agriculture and the rural world is obvious from the decisive contributions made by agriculture in providing society with basic foodstuffs.

(1781) But today there is also a growing awareness of the decisive function of agriculture both in preserving the environment and as a valuable source of energy.

(1782) Love for the land and for work on the land is not a nostalgic return to the past, but an affirmation of agriculture as the basis of a healthy economy in the totality of the development and civil progress of each country and of the whole world.

(1783) Active collaboration by the rural population in the whole process of the growth of the community is taking on increasing importance.

(1784) It is obvious that it is always preferable and desirable that collaboration in economic, labour-related and political decisions should take place in a personal and responsible way. This certainty constitutes, in the different economic and political systems, the gradual maturing of an authentic expression of that freedom which is an essential ingredient of true progress.

(1785) One likewise notes the ever clearer importance of various forms of association which can lead to new expressions of solidarity between rural workers, and facilitate the inclusion of all qualified persons,including young people, in agricultural activity and the civic community.

(1786) Naturally, one always has to bear in mind that the suggesting and the carrying out of real and effective reforms presuppose good will and a fundamental change of attitude on the part of everybody, as was recognized by John XXIII in his words to the Directors and Officials of FAO on 4 May 1960: "We are all jointly responsible for the undernourished peoples: people's consciences must be trained to the sense of responsibility that weighs upon the community and upon each individual, especially those who are most favoured" (cf. *Mater et Magistra*: AAS 53(1961), p.440).

(1787) I appeal to all of you who are responsible for the choices and orientations of internal and international policies.

(1788) I appeal to all who are in a position to act as experts, officials and promoters of undertakings that will aid development.

(1789) I appeal especially to all those who are able to work for education and training, particularly of the young.

(1790) Permit me to express my firm confidence that everyone will be moved by this appeal to the generosity of each individual.

(1791) Finally, I ask almighty God to assist all of you, the members of this World Conference assembled in the name of human solidarity and fraternal concern. I pray that the efforts that you are making before the witness of history and in the face of the pressing challenges of this generation will bear abundant fruit for the betterment of humanity - fruit that will last.

4. Statement by H.E. Msgr. Agostino Ferrari Toniolo, Permanent Observer to the FAO, Head of the Delegation of the Holy See, at the World Conference on Agrarian Reform and Rural Development held in Rome on 13-20 July 1979. Rome, 18 July 1979.

Original: English

(1792) The Holy See has carefully followed since its inception the steps leading to the World Conference on Agrarian Reform and Rural Development, in particular the five FAO Regional Conferences, the meetings of experts, and the last Preparatory Meeting with the timely and updated distribution of the introductory documents.

(1793) The Delegation of the Holy See, which I have the honor to represent in its permanent Mission of observation, would like, first of all, to express its satisfaction for the excellent work done by the Secretariat of the Conference under the efficient leadership of Mr. Hernan Santa Cruz.

(1794) The topic of the Conference, which closely links the two issues of agrarian reform and rural development, has guaranteed that the objective of the Conference not be limited to an exclusive reference to land reform changes, but refer more widely to the problems of growth of every aspect of life and activity, non-agricultural as well as of the rural masses.

(1795) This Delegation hopes that the final outcome of the Conference will be fruitful and that it may stay within the scope of its own compelling object without extending over into strictly political issues which are the competence of other qualified assemblies.

(1796) By focussing attention on the human values of the rural world and its truly civil estate, even radical structural changes can be drawn up so that recognition be fully given to the human dignity of rural peoples, which is in no way inferior to that of peoples living and working in other sectors.

(1797) An open and honest debate enables discovery of convergencies among different and even opposing economic, social and political systems which are called upon to co-exist.

(1798) This Delegation trusts that no one intends to impose his own solution or feels that it is valid for all.

(1799) Even less acceptable would be an attempt to overpower the legitimate interests of other countries or to continue forms and methods which, in relations among Nations, contribute to the persistence of a dominant system which has been shown to be incapable of guaranteeing relations that are characterized by principles of justice and international solidarity.

(1800) On the contrary, the convergence in this Conference will be based on a common aspiration: that of satisfying basic human needs and meeting the urgent and basic hope of the poorest peoples.

(1801) To achieve this the Holy See Delegation hopes that the conclusions of the Conference will reflect everyone's commitment and desire evermore to humanize policies, strategies, development models and, particularly, proposals for structural changes. The solutions that will be suggested will have to respect, on the one hand, each country's desire for growth in dignity according to each different cultural context and, on the other hand, the ever-growing interdependence and intensification of relations among peoples.

(1802) After having listened to your statements with great interest, allow me to elaborate on two points made by John Paul II during his recent contacts with farmers in Mexico and Poland.

(1803) Pope John Paul II stated at Novy Targ: "This is the great and fundamental human right: the right to work and the right to the land."

(1804) This statement gives "the right to the land" a broad meaning which is not only that of structural change in previously acquired ownership of the land.

(1805) It implies, above all, the need for the availability of the goods of the earth for productive work. Furthermore, it confirms the priority of forms of access to nature's resources to enable man not only to satisfy his needs, but also to contribute to increased production and improvement of productivity in society for the common good.

(1806) Structural reform, therefore, means making accessible to less endowed and less capable farmers those basic technical services which are indispensable for the transformation of mere ownership or availability of the land into an income producing enterprise.

(1807) The primary designation of the land for everyone's use as a collective good before any particular ownership, has been affirmed since the beginning of creation, according to Biblical texts.

(1808) It is also interesting to note that the culture and life styles inspired by the Koran use water, the irreplaceable source of human, vegetable and animal life as a good of the collectivity, the access to which cannot be denied to those in need of it.

(1809) This same criteria must certainly be applied to all the other resources of nature including everything produced by human inventiveness and initiative.

(1810) Thus the various forms of management of land and water, the availability of all inputs which are premises for a healthy agriculture, all measures which enable working in a rational and efficient way by non-property-owners as well, are of primary importance.

(1811) In this way, the privileged position of those who actually cultivate the land is affirmed, whether they be land-owners or not.

(1812) The various forms of work on the land should be evaluated with the main concern that a personal relation with the land be possible.

(1813) The setting-up of enterprises, even large-scale ones, possibly on a cooperative or associate basis, does not exclude the re-evaluation, as efficient instruments of the economy, of agricultural enterprises which are managed by small-scale or family groups, as long as they enjoy the necessary inputs which assure their functioning for the advantage of the whole society.

(1814) Since in places where the land is the only source of subsistence it often becomes the basis for economic power, a note of preference should be made that the farmer cultivate land which is his own. Preference thus follows for the increase of property-holders as well as for those juridical measures and instruments which facilitate assigning productive land permanently to farmers and the recomposition of the agrarian enterprise according to functional criteria.

(1815) John Paul II further emphasized the urgency of domestic and international reforms adequate for reducing the gap between rich and poor, with the accelerated improvement of the poorest who are, precisely, people in the agricultural and rural sectors.

(1816) He stated that a "more just and equitable distribution of the goods within each Nation" should be foreseen. (Puebla)

(1817) The power connected with property rights needs to be defined, especially the guarantee that its management, whether individual or associative, private or public, be in function of the human needs of all the members of the civil community.

(1818) In this sense, particular interest must be explicitly subordinated to the general interests of a country's economic and social situation.

(1819) Hence, the set of so-called "income policy reforms" take on greater importance since they lead to a real redistribution to the advantage of the poorest and guarantee a social well-being which is harmoniously distributed throughout the various sectors and groups of a society.

(1820) Setting up an efficient and competitive agriculture requires reinforcing and modernizing the productive organization, with the contribution of all suitable inputs for a more dynamic development.

(1821) Reform is, above all, a continuous process which means long-term technical assistance and credit, scientific and applied research, professional training and a welfare and social security system. It also implies the regulation and organization of markets, adequate infrastructures and institutional changes from the villas level to that of greater administrative and political areas.

(1822) During a recent audience Pope John Paul II recalled that a similar distribution should be foreseen "also in the world in general ensuring that the stronger countries do not use their power to the detriment of the weaker ones" (Address to the Third General Conference of the Latin-America Bishops, III, 4: Puebla, 28 January 1979).

(1823) For this purpose, measures appear necessary which will lead to overcoming the international division of labor, thus avoiding the continuation of a situation in which some Countries are destined to remain in a backward economy while others can continue and intensify their industrialization and an ever more rapid increase of their income.

(1824) The tendency toward liberalization without trade regulation, together with recurring forms of protectionism - since these represent further advantages for the more advanced countries - must be avoided when they are in opposition to principles of justice and solidarity.

(1825) The Holy See Delegation favors proposals for measures which correct current tendencies, especially those which have the binding effect of establishing juridical norms.

(1826) Therefore, while this Delegation hopes that the Declaration of Principles and the Plan of Action will be precise and compelling, it reiterates its support for all those conclusions which are limited to specific objectives, with resolutions on individual points or, preferably, with agreements open for signature and ratification. In this sense, it considers as exemplary the agreements on grain trade and the connected food aid convention and awaits their rapid and adequate renewal.

(1827) The Holy See would further like to urge the wider use of multilateral channels to better enable an autonomous development for each country, according to its own desire and in forms which correspond to its particular cultural characteristics and human milieu.

(1828) It also expresses its wish that the process in progress of transferring aid from the more prosperous countries - whether through governmental action or that of the numerous voluntary organizations - be accelerated from occasional and discontinuous aid to an organic security system which is regular and binding.

(1829) This Delegation believes that measures toward limited goals are far more capable of obtaining concrete and wide application. Therefore, it expresses its favor for those proposals which represent steps, even if partial, which are capable of being an effective means of initiating and accelerating the attainment of the required international cooperation. This is necessary for any real reform in the area of overall and continuous economic development and civil progress which is to the particular advantage of the agricultural sector and the rural world.

II - SCIENCE AND TECHNOLOGY FOR IMPROVEMENT OF PRODUCTIVITY

1. Address of His Holiness Paul VI to the United Nations Committee on the Application of Science and Technology to Development. The Vatican, 24 October 1966.

Original: French (*)

(1830) It is a joy and an honor for us to welcome the eminent specialists who compose the Consultative Committee of the United Nations for the Application of Science and Technology to Development. We note the happy coincidence that this meeting is taking place on October 24, the very day of the United Nation's anniversary.

(1831) You are meeting in Rome, gentlemen, chiefly to study two very precise questions: how to increase the production and the use of proteins in food in order to combat malnutrition; and how to obtain, for the same purpose, the maximum use of agricultural and non-agricultural natural resources.

(1832) These are two technological questions about which you do not expect us to offer you advice. As we said on one occasion recently when speaking of Latin America, no claim is made that the Church has expertise in particular disciplines like economics and sociology.

(1833) You have, however, shown a desire to see and hear us because you are aware that beyond the specialized studies in which you are engaged, you, as men of science and technology, and we, as representing moral and religious forces, do meet on common ground - the desire and determination to come to the assistance of our unfortunate brothers and sisters, millions of people, who go hungry for lack of food. This mammoth problem has but recently evoked a cry of alarm from the Director General of the FAO which has caught public attention.

(1834) It is an enormous problem or, rather, an enormous combination of problems of all kinds, which, as any careful observer can see, belong both to the technological and to the moral sphere.

(1835) The unfortunate victims of malnutrition have a right to expect that the resources of human intelligence and human science be put to work to extricate them from their misery. They are just as set upon having their human dignity made the prime consideration of aid; and the aid provided for them cannot consist in just the betterment of their material standard of living, but in their integral development and in the enhancement of their whole human persons with all their faculties.

(1836) The Church is very concerned about this aspect of the problem of development. In the eyes of the Church, human development must progress along both material and spiritual lines; at the same time that the economic order is being improved, the moral order must also be perfected. There are no real prospects for progress, stability, and peace unless moral and spiritual factors are operative.

(1837) We believe that we are not mistaken, gentlemen, in thinking that you, too, are of this opinion. We are equally convinced that the United Nations' generous and far-reaching undertakings have been inspired by the true good of humanity. That is why, following the example of our immediate Predecessors, we have not hesitated to do whatever we can to encourage these enterprises. We feel impelled, too, by the recent decrees of the Second Vatican Council, which once more has affirmed with exceptional solemnity and to the whole world the Church's care for human progress and its readiness to offer its service and support to all who work for human development.

(1838) You, gentlemen, are among those workers and the means at your disposal put you in the happy position of improving the situation of the less fortunate members of our great human family. Science and technology are, as people today readily admit, ambivalent values, capable of effecting great benefits or great evils, depending upon the use to which they are put.

(*) AAS 58(1966), 1153-1155.

(1839) In your capable hands how can they do anything but serve the good, promote progress, and further human development in its most complete sense - economic, social and moral!

(1840) That they will do so is my wish for you as I welcome you today, invoking God's abundant blessings on your countries, yourselves, and the happy continuation of the work in which you are engaged.

2. Address of His Holiness John Paul II to participants in the convention on International Cooperation for Technological Development in Africa, organized by the United Nations Financing System for Science and Technology and the African Regional Centre for Technology. The Vatican, 22 November 1984.

Original: English (*)

(1841) 1. Less than a year ago, members of both State-owned and private organizations in Africa, Asia, Latin America, North America and Europe gathered in Dakar for the first Joint Meeting on International Cooperation for Technological Development in Africa, organized by the United Nations Financing System for Science and Technology and the African Regional Centre for Technology. And now, with the collaboration of ENEA, you have assembled in Rome for a second meeting, sponsored by the Department for Cooperation for Development of the Ministry of Foreign Affairs, by the Ministry of Scientific and Technological Research and by the National Institute for Nutrition, and you have desired on this occasion to meet with the Pope. It is a pleasure for me to welcome you today. And I wish you to know how happy I am to have this opportunity to offer my support and encouragement for the attainment of your important goals. Your collaborative efforts for *the advancement of the peoples of Africa* is a true expression of worldwide fraternal solidarity and concern for justice and peace.

(1842) 2. During the present meeting, you are focusing your attention on ways *to develop and improve food and energy technologies in Africa*, and especially on how to promote effective international cooperation for the achievement of these aims. In these very days when you are engaged in discussion and planning, millions of our brothers and sisters in Africa, and in Ethiopia in particular, are being threatened with death because of drought and famine. Who cannot recognize the immense value, indeed the vital urgency, of joint efforts to assist them? It is for this reason that I have recently launched a pressing appeal on behalf of those suffering from this terrible scourge of catastrophic proportions. In you and the organizations you represent I see a concrete response to deep human needs. For this, I give thanks to Almighty God, and at the same time I pray that your efforts may inspire many others to make a similar response of fraternal solidarity.

(1843) 3. Helping to provide food, health care, shelter and other assistance is a true expression of universal human solidarity and respect for the dignity of every human person. For those of us who are Christians, it is a response to the call of God to imitate the love of our Saviour Jesus Christ. Emergency situations such as those presently affecting numerous countries of Africa call for urgent responses. They require *immediate and sustained international assistance.* But together with these, there is need for more *long-range programmes of international collaboration*, programmes which promote basic scientific research and its technological applications, and which include the economic means to put them into effect. It is in this area most particularly where your meeting can make its greatest contribution.

(1844) Nearly twenty years ago, the bishops of the Catholic Church, gathered at the Second Vatican Council, stated that "advanced nations have a very serious obligation to help developing peoples" (*Gaudium et Spes*, No. 86). In applying this statement more specifically, they went on to speak of how international cooperation is needed in the area of food production: "Some people would greatly better their conditions of life if they could be duly trained to abandon ancient methods of farming in favour of modern techniques. With necessary prudence they should adapt these techniques to their own situations. In addition they need to establish a better social order and reg-

(*) Insegnamenti di Giovanni Paolo II, Vol. VII,2 (1984), 1265-1268.

ulate the distribution of land with fairness" (*ibid.*, No. 87). Cooperation in the fields of science and technology is one of the most effective means not only of contributing to the physical welfare of peoples but also of fostering the dignity and worth of every person.

(1845) 4. As men and women engaged in science and technology, you appreciate the great gift which *human intelligence* is for all peoples. Because of its importance it needs to be cultivated with care, and it is necessary that educational opportunities be made available for gifted persons of every nation, especially for the youth. It is also important that every effort be made to ensure that intelligence and learning not become subject to permanent exportation from poor countries to rich ones because the poor countries lack the adequate cultural, scientific and technical environments and institutions to utilize them. A poor country will always remain in a state of inferiority and subjection as long as it is not in a position to carry out basic scientific research and make technological applications in ways adapted to its own cultural, political and economic system. In view of this, it is necessary that the international scientific community not limit its membership to those coming from countries of high technological development, but that it be comprised of people from all the countries of the world, united in a spirit of mutual collaboration.

(1846) 5. Technological cooperation can pose a serious threat to the culture of developing countries, but it need not be so. And in order to avoid this danger, this cooperation must be carried out in a spirit of fruitful dialogue, one which appreciates the worthy traditions of the peoples concerned and the many different values of each culture. And let us not forget that those nations which are less developed in the scientific field often have much to give from the rich storehouse of their culture to the people of the more advanced nations. Such a *fraternal exchange* enriches all who are engaged in these collaborative efforts.

(1847) 6. In a spirit of admiration and appreciation, then, I address these words to you today. I assure you of the *encouragement and support* of the Catholic Church for such deserving endeavours of international collaboration. From the cooperation and assistance which you are able to promote, I am confident that there will result a growth in knowledge and integral development, a new spirit of fraternity and peace. May God bless you and strengthen you in your work.

III - FISHERIES MANAGEMENT AND DEVELOPMENT

1. Address of His Holiness John Paul II at the World Conference on Fisheries Management and Development. The Vatican, 30 June 1984.

Original: English (*)

(1848) 1. I am very pleased to speak today to those taking part in the World Conference on Fisheries Management and Development, called by the Food and Agriculture Organization of the United Nations.

(1849) As you are aware, our meeting is being held at the time of the religious celebrations marking the origin of the community of Christ's disciples which was founded upon Peter, a simple fisherman who was called to preside over and direct a worldwide spiritual and moral mission. Thus the Catholic Church from the very beginning was in close contact with the world of fishermen. We may think that what particularly attracted Christ to fishermen and caused Him to choose them for a very different kind of work was their courage, their spirit of initiative, and their readiness to face the risks of wind and wave.

(*) Insegnamenti di Giovanni Paolo II, Vol. VII,1 (1984), 1993-1997.

(1850) The Church is well aware of the difficulties and problems of the lives of those connected with the fishing industry, problems that are shared today by those throughout the world who earn their living from the sea.

(1851) 2. It is natural that the main concern of the present Conference is the rapidly increasing need for food resources to satisfy the hunger of millions of people suffering malnutrition in the poorest countries of the world. It is common knowledge that there has been a profound modification of thinking regarding economic and social development in general. Indeed, one notes a comforting return to the primacy of agriculture and the efficient use of agricultural products, following a period of excessive attention to the industrial sector. In this regard it is useful to recall that the Statutes of FAO place under the heading of agriculture the products not only of the earth and the forests but also of the waters.

(1852) It is particularly opportune that emphasis today is being placed on the fisheries sector among the food products demanded by the growing population of the world. This is especially important for responding to the pressing needs of those countries where there is an acute imbalance between demand and actual food resources. In fact, fish resources can still be better and more widely used.

(1853) Fishing thus has enormous importance in the struggle to alleviate malnutrition. Particularly in the smaller centres it is a prime resource for immediate food requirements.

(1854) Your Conference rightly pays particular attention to small-scale fishing, and you insist that the problems connected with it have real priority. Small-scale fishing communities and their needs are to be taken into consideration and integrated into national economies.

(1855) Similarly, the development of the various forms of aquaculture is obviously very opportune. The good results already gained show that this activity not only helps to increase food resources but also creates new employment opportunities, especially in the developing countries. It is also a powerful instrument for protecting and restoring the environment.

(1856) 3. You rightly consider fishing as a whole series of human activities, and you rightly emphasize the social objectives connected with it.

(1857) In order to meet the needs of today's society, it is necessary to apply to the fisheries sector forms required by modern and efficient management.

(1858) Clearly, your Conference has to proceed on the level of the practical solutions made possible by modern technology. Hence the need to take into consideration the actual economic conditions of each individual country, so as to be able to outline realistic targets and specify the financing needed.

(1859) But what you keep constantly in mind and what you use as a constant point of reference are the basic human aspects, especially those experienced by the people whose livelihood is fishing and its connected industry. It is, therefore, the task of your Conference to re-examine the criteria already laid down with regard to agriculture in order to ensure not only technical and economic development but also the human development of individuals and communities.

(1860) Countries are obviously dependent on one another, and it is this fact that makes it necessary to coordinate internal policies with a view to worldwide development. This is why in my Encyclical *Laborem Exercens* I stressed the principle of the priority of human work in the whole economic process (cf. Nos. 4 and 25). Consequently, the public authorities should favour forms of co-responsibility of those working in small-scale and large-scale fisheries, and the different forms of their solidarity in free associations. The active participation of all fishery workers in the decision making that affects their lives and work should be encouraged.

(1861) 4. One of your important tasks is to encourage appropriate use of available resources and to develop new ones. Here too I would like to urge scientists to use all their talents and expertise.

There must also be agreement on the criteria and methods to be applied to fishing in the context of world development.

(1862) A greater availability of financial resources and an improvement in loan and credit facilities are an obvious prerequisite for efficiency of production, and there must also be adequate provision for the replacement of equipment.

(1863) Steps should be taken to facilitate access for fish products to the market, and small-scale communities should be encouraged to improve the treatment and presentation of these products.

(1864) It is, therefore, to be hoped that this Conference will be able to reach an agreement on the major aspects of the management and development of fishing.

(1865) It is also to be hoped that all States and volunteer organizations with all their resources and energies will work effectively together in order to achieve efficient joint action.

(1866) It is to be hoped that your work will confirm the increase in forms of solidarity and mutual aid, not only between the highly industrialized and the developing countries, but also between the countries with limited resources.

(1867) 5. The Church once more repeats that she is ready to assist, in the forms proper to her, all efforts to eliminate hunger and malnutrition in the world, and efforts to raise the living standards of those who are really poor and unable to work for their own economic and social development.

(1868) In particular, it seems opportune to emphasize the Church's readiness to encourage her institutions to collaborate in any appropriate field. The Church is prepared to intensify her own educational work, at both elementary and professional levels, and thus to contribute to the training which is essential for coping with changes in production and selling methods.

(1869) It is with this solicitude for all those working for economic and social development in the fisheries sphere, and likewise for the betterment of those engaged in fishery activities throughout the world, that I express my admiration for your important efforts. Upon all of you I invoke God's blessings in your present and future work for the good of humanity.

2. Statement by H.E.Msgr. Agostino Ferrari-Toniolo, Permanent Observer to the FAO, Head of the Delegation of the Holy See, at the Conference on Fisheries Management and Development, held in Rome on 27 June-6 July 1984. Rome, 4 July 1984.

Original: English

(1870) 1. On behalf of the Delegation of the Holy See I would like, first of all, to extend my compliments to all those who preside over and participate in this World Conference on Fisheries.

(1871) 2. I express my satisfaction at being present at this point which could be decisive in the struggle against hunger.

(1872) I can affirm that I had the privilege during the last 10 years to be present as Head of the Delegation of the Holy See at three significant moments in the sector of food and agriculture.

(1873) Ten years ago the World Food Conference first applied the principles and criteria of the restoration of a New International Economic Order to this domain of agriculture, a forceful movement towards a development inspired by the human value of solidarity. Justice demands a more rational use of resources and a more equitable contractual relationship between States in spite of differences caused by the fact of their power, so as to be free from undue pressure or conditioning from outside.

(1874) 3. Five years later the World Conference on Agrarian Reform and Rural Development had to its credit the making explicit of the inseparable connection between the renewing of structures, techniques, means, methods of work and the basic goal of the human development of all those who work in the rural world.

(1875) 4. In the light of these preceding historic stages, the Delegation of the Holy See considers the World Conference on Fisheries to be opportune and appropriate. This Conference in fact appears to be, above all, an occasion to situate the fisheries sector as an integral part of agriculture.

(1876) This Conference is expected first of all to apply to the fisheries sector the criteria and orientations, both internal and international, adopted by FAO and all the other IGOs with reference to the agricultural sector in general.

(1877) 5. You have certainly followed the recent evolution of facts and trends of the new development strategy based upon auto-development leading to nutritional self-sufficiency.

(1878) In spite of uncertainties and drawbacks, a pattern emerges of international cooperation between States who follow a slow but clear process of more and more precise international rules. Among these the Law of the Sea is a praiseworthy application of the criteria of justice in the relations between peoples whose awareness of their own economic, social and political rights and duties grows ever stronger.

(1879) 6. Moreover this Conference, according to the documentation on the actual situation and the needs of peoples, should recognize both present trends as well as those historically sound and rational criteria for the economic and social development of the fishery sector to contribute to the common welfare of mankind.

(1880) Only thus can one overcome economic tensions that have implicit in them the outbreak of tragic conflicts, causing waste of means and energy.

(1881) In this sense the delegation of the Holy See wishes to point out the absolute priority that each one of us should give to the efforts for world development, a necessary condition for peace and disarmament.

(1882) There must be an organic, continuous and planned development established by a mutual agreement growing out of both internal and international solidarity. Only this can guarantee the concrete application of the fundamental rights and duties of every human being and all peoples.

(1883) 7. This Conference will be a significant step forward if it underlines the importance of the fisheries sector for leaders of Governments, of United Nations Organizations and, above all, public opinion.

(1884) This will become real if the Sovereign States gathered here approve decisions regarding fisheries, based explicitly on the following general criteria: technical solutions cannot be considered separately from the basic goals of humanity; the criteria of solidarity growing out of the interdependence between peoples; harmony within national policies; coordination between common action within the International Organizations and implementation by multilateral means; aims of auto-development according to the models corresponding to the culture and conditions of each Country; the priority given to self-sufficiency in food; the use of up-to-date information supplied by the IGOs, essential for every project established according to the real needs of populations, and requiring precise calculation and strict control; and the coordination between bilateral and multilateral aid from Governments and International Organizations, both official and voluntary.

(1885) 8. Since mine is a multilateral diplomacy in the specific position of "Permanent Mission of Observation", my function is to contribute towards defining common orientations for concrete solutions and real pledges for the welfare of the whole of mankind, in drawing together interests, systems and economic, social and political ideas - even if they are divergent.

(1886) According to its particular nature, the Holy See, being a moral authority, takes part officially in this Conference by indicating and recalling principles. It does not impose its point of view by political vote as the Member-States. Its judgments rise above the level of technical solutions to a basic vision of the criteria of justice and of solidarity aiming at the welfare of peoples.

(1887) 9. In conclusion I might make some basic remarks and orientations. The Delegation of the Holy See hopes that a true "consensus" might be reached constituting a real agreement on the most important aspects of the strategy of management and development of fisheries and on the five concrete programmes of action together with their financing. The least advanced countries should be guaranteed the aid proportioned to their needs, without either domination or pressure by the advanced Countries.

(1888) It is urgent to recognize and apply common rules implying binding commitments and appropriate controls.

(1889) It would be very good if at least an agreement could be reached on the means to achieve an efficient and concurrent common action, followed by everyone: States, Inter-Governmental or Voluntary Organizations.

(1890) From your work is expected, above all, a precise commitment to forms of solidarity between North and South, East and West, especially through technical aid in the widest sense of the term.

(1891) 10. As for conservation of resources, one must recognize that only a small group of Countries, mostly industrialized, benefit from the freedom of fishing conditions. In fact, the absence of rules makes the conservation of biological resources more difficult since uncontrolled use hinders regular reproduction.

(1892) It is all the more evident that the solution of environmental problems in the fisheries sector cannot but be on a universal scale. Both human as well as animal and vegetable growth must be guaranteed a better natural environment.

(1893) 11. The Delegation of the Holy See hopes that the conclusions of this Conference will be inspired by principles flowing from the universal use of fisheries resources so that every human being can satisfy his vital needs. These must be explicitly favouring the poorer countries whether or not they have access to the sea.

(1894) It is the privileged duty of this Conference to affirm a fundamental principle of international justice for the fisheries world: that the distribution of fishery resources, and the result of its consequent economic activity, should be so made as to guarantee the use of all economic and social factors in development of each people, according to their objective needs and taking into consideration their real technical-professional capacity; so too, the contribution of means, expertise and especially investments of every country according to its prosperity.

(1895) A universal use of resources must be understood as a primary right before any particular appropriation. It is a sign of human progress to consider that sea resources are common patrimony for the whole of humanity.

(1896) Any recognition of exclusive zones of management and any particular appropriation is to be subordinated to the common welfare. Property and profits from States or private initiatives must respect the primary right of the universal use of resources in international relations as well as in the programmes of each country.

(1897) 12. Among the measures to sustain countries and groups most in need, credit and loan facilities when granted with conditions appropriate to the various possibilities of those concerned, are the most important.

(1898) As part of aid, the cooperation of scientists and technicians must be underlined: their knowledge must not serve the violence of war but contribute to overcoming the specific violence due to an unbridled use of technological, economic, financial and political power.

(1899) 13. A rational use of fishery resources requires their availability according to the need of each population and above all directed not only to immediate consumption but also to the economic and social development of the country.

(1900) The new rules on the management of the activity for fishing in the open sea and in exclusive zones lead to proposals of new instruments capable of putting the advantages achieved at the disposal of the most needy countries.

(1901) First they must assure the application of the new rules to coastal countries and, in particular, to the small fishermen.

(1902) Aid operations and measures are necessary to make Governments and private firms able to take their own efficient initiatives to contribute directly to the self-development of the country by productive activities including access to market by means suited to conditions of feasibility and self management.

(1903) 14. The Delegation of the Holy See appreciates the new forms of aid, especially monetary, favouring coastal countries which cannot directly take advantage of the new situation. The power they have to grant concessions to other firms and countries make coastal countries able to use these profits as capital for investments for their national development programmes.

(1904) 15. The Delegation of the Holy See expresses special appreciation for the proposals that allow advanced countries or important firms working in ocean resources to grant new forms of aid to other developing countries. In this way, the advantages of the new rules can be applied opportunely, extending the distribution of the profit coming from the use of sea resources, to land locked countries or, more widely, to countries having special difficulties with their balance of payments.

(1905) The Delegation likes to consider these new methods of aid as new forms of modern sufficiency in food, avoiding as they do the control of sea resources by a few and assuring the benefit of food beyond what the economic and social development of each country can support.

(1906) 16. The rational use of available sea resources includes criteria and methods for a rapid increase of production and distribution. The choice of internal and international policies are tied to the possibilities of scientific knowledge and present technology.

(1907) Methods of using resources and models of production, technical solutions beyond the limits of the capacity of the concerned populations, cannot be applied to countries where development is just beginning. This could upset the balance of its total development by destroying particular activities.

(1908) In a situation of total poverty some solution must precede any form of intervention. Development models to be applied in the poorest situation must begin with only limited and partially efficient solutions, and then use more sophisticated forms of productive activities. It must be remembered that an adequate preparation is needed and that this can only be achieved gradually.

(1909) In many interventions we noted that there is an excessive defense of the immediate interests of their own countries in a narrow local and national vision.

(1910) 17. We have to look at trade which is closely connected with production. Specific facilities must be adopted for the marketing of fish products to make possible free access to the market and the treatment of the product by small fishermen before it appears on the domestic market for export.

(1911) The total good of the human person cannot be excluded when choosing models of development designed to increase world production of fish.

(1912) 18. The education of men and women of all ages, who live in fishing communities, is of great importance and must be so done that each one can take part in the process of work and civic and economic progress in liberty and dignity.

(1913) The contribution of women is to be re-evaluated: a contribution made not only to the family and the community, but also to the work of fishing especially in the maintenance of traditional and modern equipment.

(1914) 19. The universal Church adds a new form of contribution to the management of programmes to be formulated: her own numerous and varied personnel whose presence spreads a network in the whole world.

(1915) Her organizations, institutions and associations are available in two ways:

First they participate in the different programmes and projects in the fisheries sector offering their knowledge of the conditions of life and the real needs of local populations according to the different customs and culture.

(1916) Moreover, they provide general instruction and up-to-date professional preparation, as well as fostering development of a civic consciousness.

(1917) They contribute also to specific training indispensable to face the changing models of development and technical and economic methods of fish production and trade; they evaluate external aid so as to assure the effective continuity of economic activities and stable improvement of the conditions of work and life for those who belong to the fisheries sector.

IV - EMERGENCY SITUATION IN AFRICA

Statement by Msgr. Giuseppe Bertello, Delegate of the Holy See, at the United Nations Conference on Emergency Assistance to Africa, held in Geneva on 11-12 March 1985. Geneva, 12 March 1985.

Original: French

(1918) Some days ago, the "Journal de Geneve" headlined one of its articles "Geneva, capital of Africa on 11 March". The presence of so many delegations is the visible proof of the response of the international community to the invitation by the Secretary General.

(1919) Such presence manifests an awareness, at the global level, of the need to guarantee the immediate possibility of survival for millions of people stricken by natural calamities or forced by drought and desertification to abandon their now unproductive lands. Unfortunately these calamities are often worsened by social and economic injustices of various origin, and in particular by ideological or political systems, armed conflicts or guerrilla warfare unleashed by man himself.

(1920) Hunger, destitution and poverty are not only a physical or social problem - no matter what their causes may be. They are also an ethical problem, since a starving man is an individual degraded in all his faculties, whose integral development is in jeopardy: he is marked for the rest of his life at the personal and social level.

(1921) Faced with the gravity of the present situation, as it has been documented during the last few months by the reports of the various organ of the United Nations and illustrated with vivid crudity of televised images by the communication media, the response cannot be dictated by passing emotions, but must take the form of a serious moral responsibility, capable of renewing the political will of mutual aid at the global level, in order to widen and make more effective the thrust of solidarity among peoples.

(1922) On 12 January of this year, in his address to the Diplomatic Corps accredited to the Holy See, in reference to the famine and drought in Africa, Pope John Paul II said: "We know only too well that the countries concerned cannot at the present time - and by themselves - emerge from this tragic situation, prevent millions of people from dying, or stop for tomorrow the expansion of the desert. But the situation can be rectified: not only must we continue to supply the emergency aid, levied, among other things, on surplus crops which some are tempted to destroy for the sake of balancing a too circumscribed economy, but we must place at everyone's disposal the techniques that God has allowed us to discover." (*L'Osservatore Romano*, 13 January 1985).

(1923) The Catholic Church, in all its component parts, has never ceased lending its full support to all initiatives aiming at reducing hunger in the world, and the situation in Africa has been at the very core of its preoccupations during the last few years. The Supreme Pontiff has repeatedly spoken, during the last few weeks, to call attention to this immense tragedy. We could mention his appeal of 9 January and the last message to the Catholics on the occasion of Lent (cf. *L'Osservatore Romano*, 10 January and 21 February 1985). Moreover, he has elected to be present to some of the countries most seriously stricken by sending personal contributions to the local Churches.

(1924) The African delegates to this Conference know what the Catholic organizations of their countries have given in personnel, in financial assistance and food supplies, and in the distribution entrusted to them of the aid which Catholic people from all over the world are sending; and such aid has noticeably increased in 1984.

(1925) Through the initiatives of the Pontifical Council "Cor Unum" and the activities of its voluntary organizations and institutions, the Catholic Church is involved in a direct and practical fashion in this work of solidarity. The Church wishes to continue and develop this humanitarian activity, within its all too limited means, for the good of all peoples, without distinction of religion, race or political ideology, since it regards it as an obligation stemming from the universal paternity of God. (Cf. *L'Osservatore Romano*, January 11, 1985).

(1926) Even though this Conference has as its principal task the definition of the situation by evaluating what has been accomplished and analyzing the current needs, it must also look beyond - as properly emphasized in document SG/CONF. 2/1, in the paragraphs regarding emergency situations and development (p.13) - by seeing that the future activities of the international community are directed to assure not only the survival of the victims of starvation, but also their long-term rehabilitation and advancement through the deployment of all those factors which contribute to the concrete self-development of each nation. In this perspective, the Holy See has created "The John Paul II Foundation for the Sahel". This entity will be managed by its members, the local Churches of the eight countries which the international community recognizes as Sahel. The Foundation proposes to "assist in the preparation of competent people who will place themselves at the service of their country and of their brothers, without any discrimination, in a spirit of integral and cooperative human advancement, for the battle against desertification and its causes" (Art. 2). The Holy Father, in receiving the administrative council of the Foundation, stated: "International solidarity can bring a noticeable, even indispensable aid, but the solution is definitely in the hands of the Africans." (*L'Osservatore Romano*, 26 May 1984). For what pertains to refugees, the Holy See, on the occasion of ICARA II, has elected to give a concrete proof of its solicitude by assuming the financing of a project for the construction and organization of a craftsmen formation center in Rwanda.

(1927) From Ouagadougou, on the occasion of his trip to Africa in May 1980, the Holy Father made an appeal to the world which still maintains all its urgency. My Delegation, not without profound emotion, would like to propose a passage from that appeal, confident that it will be well received by all participants: "let us make sure that the future of these peoples will never again be threatened! Yesterday's solidarity, so extensive and so efficient, has shown that it is possible to listen exclusively to the voice of justice and charity and not to that of individual or collective selfishness".

V - CONCERN OF THE HOLY SEE FOR FOOD PROBLEMS

1. Address of His Holiness Pius XII to a meeting of the Delegates of the European Nations to the FAO. The Vatican, 21 February 1948

Original: French (*)

(1928) We are deeply touched by your presence here, Gentlemen, dedicated as you are to a social task which arises from the conviction and awareness of universal brotherhood. You have also chosen to show Us, in the most delicate way, that you recognize and appreciate in the common Father of all Christians, a heart whose affection and paternal concern extends to all of needy and suffering humanity regardless of nation or background

(1929) We are please to acknowledge and praise the depth of vision which inspired the United Nations to set up an institution especially to deal with food and agriculture problems. We praise also the efficiency which characterizes its management and its methodology, the wisdom and prudence with which it oversees its task. This is done in such a way that each nation, by collaborating with the others, can better attend to the well-being and needs of all through growth, development and the best use of each country's resources.

(1930) By working to increase and balance out the production and distribution of all food and agricultural products, in order to foster general overall economic progress, you are contributing towards freeing nations from the miseries of poverty and from the humiliation of having to beg for alms. You are enabling them all to be, reciprocally and in solidarity, beneficiaries of and benefactors to one another.

(1931) It is only right to concentrate on bettering the living conditions of rural peoples. By their labour these have been the diligent providers to and even the agents of the entire community during years of prosperity. Yet, they are the first victims of penury caused by unpredictable crops and weather, the ravages of war, the uncertainties and complications of the economy which have left the land sterile and impossible to cultivate for long periods in many regions.

(1932) How could we not also rejoice, Gentlemen, in knowing that you wish to take the principles of Catholic social doctrine into consideration. In fact, there is no opposition nor contradiction between Catholic social doctrine and natural social doctrine. Catholic social doctrine only takes into account, in the application of natural social doctrine, the eternal destiny of human beings. In this regard, we can apply to the Church the words of Christ Himself when He affirmed that He had come not to destroy the law, not to change it one iota but to perfect it. If then, the Church, like its Founder and Head, proclaims that man does not live by bread alone, the Church also like Him has the deepest and most loving compassion for the vast multitudes who are hungry.

(1933) We wish to express the interest We have in your work. With all our heart, we entreat God to bless it most abundantly.

(*) Discorsi e Radiomessaggi di Sua Santità Pio XII, Vol. IX (2 Marzo 1947 - 1 Marzo 1948), 461-462.

2. Address of His Holiness Pius XII to the 6th Session of the Conference of the Food and Agriculture Organization. The Vatican, 23 November 1951.

Original: French (*)

(1934) We take with pleasure, gentlemen, the opportunity you offer us today to express to you in heartfelt manner the cordial interest which the Food and Agriculture Organization of the United Nations awakens in Us, and our esteem for those who give themselves to it with ardour. We can not praise too highly your beneficent work and above all the great lesson in courage which you give to the world. For it requires courage to pursue with holy obstinacy a difficult task.

(1935) At the sight of the ruins piled up by wars or revolutions, all over the globe, of cities crushed and of countrysides devastated or deserted; at the sight of the natural scourges which desolated huge regions and of the unheard-of miseries which follow everywhere; at the sight of the populations forced to flee at random, without shelter or resources, before the rising of invading waters often more fearful and more destructive than the volcanic eruptions and the earthquakes of yesterday; the temptation is strong (and many, alas, succumb to it) to give in to discouragement; to waste in lamentations, understandable assuredly, or in unjust recriminations against those who can not help, the strength which would permit one to struggle and to react.

(1936) For you, on the contrary, this general distress is a powerful spur to your initiative; and your Organization sets to work to remedy things with much wisdom, skill and practical methods, and unlimited devotion. Without ever losing sight of the situation in its entirety and in its details, you have given yourselves to analyzing it so as to distribute, among multiple services and various countries, the specialist tasks.

(1937) In truth, this situation is very complex! It is necessary to provide for so many needs, to confront so many difficulties, to triumph over so many obstacles of every sort and in local or regional conditions so widely different!

(1938) In effect your problems concern, all at the same time, the production, conservation,allocation, transport and distribution of the commodities of prime necessity; and the most productive possible exploitation of the immense riches of earth, sea, forests, and watercourses, of agriculture, fisheries and cattle.

(1939) Is it not deplorable to see, since so much time (and in certain cases since the beginning) countries admirably favored by nature but remaining practically unproductive for lack of more advanced methods or tools necessary for the utilization of their natural riches? Or to see other countries completely deprived of these and other indispensable commodities; and burdened with products eagerly wanted elsewhere but for which they have no use and no transport with which to deliver them to markets?

(1940) The list of such anomalies and problems which can only be solved by an active international understanding and by the collaboration of high expertise in every field, is sadly long.

(1941) This, gentlemen, is what your efforts aim toward, with a zeal worthy of every praise, in a spirit of universal brotherhood. You gladly do what is humanly possible; but above human possibility there glides divine power, ready to back up paternally your good will and your effort, awaiting only confident prayers that it be done.

(1942) And so, we urgently raise our petition, calling down upon you, upon your work, upon your co-workers and your families, the benediction of heaven, as a token of which we give you, with all our affection, our Apostolic Blessing.

(*) Discorsi e Radiomessaggi di Sua Santità Pio XII, Vol XIII (2 Marzo 1951 - 1 Marzo 1952), 409-410.

3. Address of His Holiness Pius XII to the 7th Session of the Conference of the Food and Agriculture Organization. The Vatican, 8 December 1953.

Original: French (*)

(1943) It is a fact that, despite the improvements gained in recent times, the problem of food remains crucial for a large part of humanity. As you state in your reports, the current situation of the world from the agricultural viewpoint is characterized by an accentuated imbalance between the developed areas and the insufficiently developed countries. On one hand production is growing rapidly, levels of consumption are rising, exports are increasing; while on the other hand, in the Far East most particularly, production remained weak, food deficient, and imports limited. The possibility of famine and of its terrible consequences does not cease to haunt millions of people and a period of drought suffices to release this fearful scourge. But furthermore, it is necessary also to take account of the steady rise in the population which requires, at the risk of seeing things go from bad to worse, a parallel growth in consumer goods.

(1944) Your organization takes upon itself to face this difficult situation, and to engage in a decisive struggle worldwide to suppress the sufferings and the threats which still today weigh on so many unfortunate people. What courage it requires to dare calmly to envisage an undertaking which without exaggeration can be called gigantic; and to give oneself to it with ardor, when it seems to grow more complex ion direct proportion to one's attachment to it. But you, animated by a zeal which nothing seems to tire, have succeeded in the first place in assuring yourselves an indispensable basis of work, obtaining the necessary information on the agricultural production and exchanges of the various countries. In many cases, in order to procure for yourselves precise indications, it has been necessary to train experts and initiate them in modern statistical methods. You have thus brought together valuable materials which will render great service to the economists.

(1945) The essential part of your work consists of intervening effectively in the domain of agriculture, but also of fisheries and of forest exploitation. Without doubt efforts will be made to direct toward the undernourished peoples, which represent 70% of the world population, the excess production of the more favoured countries, thereby assuring them stable outlets. But it is much more urgent to provide for the increased productivity of those very places where famine is felt. For that, you want first to reduce the sometimes considerable losses due to the inexperience of the growers, and due to epidemics; then to raise yields by improvement of the methods of cultivation, by the use of fertilizers, by the choice of plant species; and finally you are looking toward bringing into use areas still uncultivated, especially by means of irrigation. In all of this, the phases of realization are necessarily preceded by investigations and detailed studies to evaluate the possibilities of success and to avoid the heavy consequences of errors. Let us mention equally, as an example of the cultural impact of your efforts, the task given to you by the United Nations Economic and Social Council, to put into effect an increased production of paper.

(1946) This program, so varied and so broad, certainly raises unusual difficulties. Perhaps the most delicate, you have surely noticed, will consist in creating social conditions which will enable the workers to whom you will be furnishing aid and advice, to acquire a taste for their task, become interested in it, and exploit to the fullest the resources which will be provided to them. It is useless in effect to put in place experts to teach new methods and to perfect the mechanical equipment, if the human conditions in which man moves prevent him from obtaining from his effort the fruit he has a right to expect from it. To arouse interest and personal initiative, to show that the good of the community will not be realized at the expense of the good of individuals but rather to their profit, and to see to it that progress is thereby achieved, this certainly is a capital element of success. Thus, your economic work doubles itself with a social value that is not less decisive and which we love to emphasize. This is why we, desirous of demonstrating to you our support in this enterprise, have wished recently to bring our contribution in favor of the program for extending technical assistance to various countries, especially to the least fortunate regions.

(*) Discorsi e Radiomessaggi di Sua Santita Pio XII, Vol XV (2 Marzo 1953 - 1 Marzo 1954), 495-497.

(1947) In spite of the still limited resources of your organization, you have not hesitated to interest in it all people, who are avid not only to perfect themselves and to obtain economic advantages but also to bring their help to those less fortunate. An action of this sort, as we remarked in an address pronounced on the 21st of February 1948 in circumstances similar to these, obliges nations to feel themselves mutual beneficiaries and benefactors of one another.

(1948) The civilized world looks with a profound sadness at pitiful pictures of victims of famine when the earth is capable of feeding all mankind. To suppress definitively such a wound certainly merits some sacrifice and justifies austere dedication. Was not Christ concerned to satisfy the hunger of the crowds which were following him? Did He not teach to His disciples the prayer which asks of God our daily bread? In pursuing the goal which you have set yourselves, you are realizing without any doubt an intention dear to Him who consecrated Himself to the salvation of humanity. That is why we wish that you may continue your task without weakening. It is no doubt only at its start, but already experience has taught you much; your tools are perfecting themselves, your credit is growing among governments who are appreciating more and more the usefulness and the fruits of your action. If the final term is not yet in view, at least you can hope that a wider comprehension and a more active collaboration will come to re-enforce and multiply the results obtained and to guarantee a more rapid further development.

(1949) We wish this for you with all our heart, at the same time that we call down upon you, your families and upon all who share in your labor the most abundant blessings of Heaven.

4. Address of His Holiness Pius XII to the 8th Session of the Conference of the Food and Agriculture Organization. The Vatican, 10 November 1955.

Original: French (*)

(1950) The Eighth session of the Conference of the FAO in which you, gentlemen, are taking part carries this year a very special meaning, since this organization celebrates at the same time the tenth anniversary of its founding. It was in effect on the 16th of October 1945, that the representatives of twenty States were invited to sign the Constitutive Act of the Food and Agriculture Organization of the United Nations. At the end of the first session of the Conference, forty-two countries had given their official adherence to the new institution. Since then the number has steadily grown and today it stands at seventy-one. In wishing you welcome, we are particularly happy to congratulate you on the progress made during these ten years.

(1951) The objectives which you were proposing for yourselves were and remain primordial: to raise the level of nutrition and the conditions of life of the populations; to increase the yields of production; to facilitate the distribution of food and agricultural products; and to contribute to the expansion of the world economy. The Holy See could not be uninterested in an enterprise so necessary and so beneficial; since 1948 its observer has been at the regional meetings in Rome, and in the following year at a session of the Council; in 1950 the Washington Conference admitted the Holy See as a permanent observer, a status of which, up to now, it is the sole beneficiary.

(1952) You know, gentlemen, with what interest we have followed the various phases of your activity since the day when the FAO was founded. It was, at that time, a case of looking squarely at this terrible fact: more than half of the world's population was undernourished; to satisfy the needs of humanity, it was necessary to double food production. FAO went to work energetically: it set up the International Food Crisis Committee, undertook a world agriculture census, and proposed the creation of a World Food Council; it took charge of the work started in nine war-devastated countries to restore their agriculture. Mentioning only some of the most characteristic results, let us recall that in 1947 the "European Forest Commission" was set up; in 1948 there took place the first regional conference on the problems of nutrition; also starting in 1949 a mixed Committee of experts in these matters has met annually at various points of the globe. Since the increase of productivity and the raising of the standard of living of rural populations are tied to the social conditions

(*) (AAS 48(1956), 53-57.

in which farmers work, the FAO has been working since 1951 on the problems of reforming agrarian structures and on questions related to farm credit; at the same time, numerous meetings on diverse continents are supporting the agricultural co-operative movement.

(1953) Without any doubt boldness was needed to envisage so varied a campaign which extends to such great areas. But these efforts have not been in vain. The report which you published on the situation of agriculture in 1955 notes that world agricultural production reached in 1954 an increase of 25% compared with that of 1946. During this decade the under-developed countries have rapidly improved their land and water resources; thanks to technical assistance they have applied to their animal and plant production new methods tested and developed in more advanced regions. But alongside the positive results it is necessary to note the current shortcomings and the unrests in order to attract the attention of all those responsible and to focus their efforts. You have pointed out among other things the rigidity of productive structures and the difficulty they have in responding adequately to the demand; the stagnation of world commerce in agricultural products, and the inadequate level of farm income compared with other activities. In vast areas of the world we have not succeeded in furnishing to the people the means of acquiring all the nourishment they need. This fact remains, it must be said, the primary motive which stimulates you to pursue your efforts.

(1954) Among the particular studies to which your specialists have given themselves, we should like to point out some particularly indicative ones and first of all, those which concern the very basis of all agriculture, the soil. In the past the utilization, conservation, and improvement of the soil were left to the practical good sense of the farmers; an experience acquired at the price of prolonged labor and not without disappointments showed them how to proceed without ruining the earth from which they drew their living. It is known that if some spared no pains to safeguard this resource, others, pushed by the lure of a quick gain or victims of their own incompetence, caused damage to the soil that quickly became irreparable. In order to understand the consequences of these errors and to prevent their recurrence; and in order also to use to the maximum all the possibilities of these terrains, it was necessary to acquire a rational knowledge of the different soils, of their structure, of their properties, and to set up a map of their geographic distribution. It thus became possible to determine exactly what sorts of planting are best suited for a particular region, what modifications the area should eventually undergo by drainage or by the addition of fertilizers. In particular, it was impossible to neglect the fight against the erosion caused by natural elements but in many cases accelerated by the intervention of persons who, so as to make sloping fields arable, despoiled them of all protective vegetation. It has been found in the United States that the loss of phosphates through erosion was greater than that from harvesting. The publications devoted to this question, such as, for example, that which concerns the map of erosion in Latin America, will contribute much to prevent further damage.

(1955) But soil conservation does not depend solely on erosion control. It is preferable today to see the subject in a larger frame, taking into account modern systems for improving fertility, and economic and social factors capable of raising the well-being of rural populations, of aiding the colonization of waste ground, of slowing the exodus from the countryside and the depopulation of mountain regions in favor of the towns. The impoverishment of the earth can be the result of inadequate land laws, of excessive concentration or subdivision of property, of inadequate value for farm products; hard living conditions discourage the growers and push them to seek to earn their living otherwise. You have not overlooked this aspect, since as we just pointed out you have envisaged a campaign in the field of agrarian reform, as also in the domain of credit and of farm co-operatives.

(1956) Because of the essential part the forests play in the circulation of surface and subterranean water, they merit serious attention; they slow the run-off of water, they assist its penetration in depth and the feeding of springs; they retain the snows, and even if they can not prevent exceptional flooding they regulate river levels. The public authorities, concerned with the development of agriculture, thus have an interest in exercising their vigilance over the manner in which forests are exploited.

(1957) Let us mention again, among many others, the research done on the possibility of using marine algae for human nourishment; until now, however, the exploitation of these resources appears still difficult. These brief reflections make rather clear that the initial program prepared by the Conference at Hot Springs and formulated in the Constitutive Act, is well on its way to execution. Where once the problem of hunger seemed insoluble, it is today possible to confront it squarely, and to count, for its resolution, on the collaboration of governments. The monographs on soil studies have drawn attention to the physical unity of diverse regions, which brings together in solidarity the plains and the mountains. The one who would safeguard the fertility of his fields should carefully note what is going on well beyond their limits. This truth, it seems to Us, has symbolic value; the peoples favored by nature or by the progress of civilization risk hard awakenings if they do not take pains at once to assure to the less fortunate the means of living humanly, with dignity, and the means for them, too, to develop themselves. To arouse further in a large number of individuals and of nations this feeling of collective responsibility, and above all to provoke thereby enlightened and generous intervention, that is a high and noble task; in these times of suspicion, of division, of revolt, the moral force of such a result surpasses by far its material consequences.

(1958) We are pleased above all to recognize, in this worldwide campaign aimed at reaching not a privileged few but the immense mass, often powerless and without defense, an authentic aspect of the charity which Christ illustrated by His life and by His death, and which He wished to make into the distinctive mark of His disciples; this charity - universal, disinterested, demanding to the point of sacrifice - can take root only in the love which God Himself brings to mankind. Such charity makes that love visible and is the most solid proof of it.

(1959) This is why we do not doubt that the Divine Master blesses all that you do for those who belong to Him; it is to Himself that these benefits are addressed; He will know how to recompense them, as He solemnly promised and as we ardently pray Him to do. May the favors of Heaven descend on you and on your work, on your families and on those who are dear to you. We give you, as a token, our Apostolic Blessing.

5. Address of His Holiness Pius XII to the 9th Session of the Conference of the Food and Agriculture Organization. The Vatican, 9 November 1957.

Original: French (*)

(1960) Today we have the pleasure of receiving you, gentlemen, on the occasion of the Ninth Conference of the FAO now being held in Rome. You have under consideration several questions concerning the functioning of this organization, as well as the current difficulties of agriculture and the program of action which you propose in order to bring remedies to it.

(1961) In examining the present situation, you have perceived a disquieting fact and one which requires an urgent solution: the phenomenon of the weakening of agriculture in the world economy. You note that, in internal exchanges as on the international level, the market shows everywhere a tendency unfavorable to the interests of farmers. While the prices of manufactured goods continue to rise, those of agricultural products have been diminishing progressively since 1952. Thus the farmer's purchasing power shrinks little by little, his situation becomes more precarious; and an unfortunate consequence, above all in Europe, the depopulation of the countryside is accentuated, provoking a new series of both social and religious problems. This state of things sharply worries us because it menaces a population which is numerous, brave, and deserving; a population whose qualities of stability and fidelity to the best traditions are more than ever necessary to maintain balance in a society in rapid evolution.

(1962) It is certain that the given elements of the question are very complex and the remedies difficult to apply. But you will render an eminent service to farmers if you succeed in opposing the advance of this phenomenon of deterioration and in starting a movement of rectification. We wish with all our heart that your organization may increasingly unite the participating nations in a gener-

(*) AAS 49(1957), 1023-1024.

ous effort, free of considerations of other sorts that would tend to thwart its action and even at times to render it ineffective. Too many people are still suffering from hunger for us to delay, from motives of special interest, the work which aims at helping them.

(1963) As a token of the support of the Most High, we invoke upon your present Conference and on your activities outside it, for yourselves and all your families and friends, our Apostolic Blessing.

6. Address of His Holiness John XXIII to the 10th Session of the Conference of the Food and Agriculture Organization. The Vatican, 10 November 1959.

Original: French (*)

(1964) You wanted to interrupt briefly the work of your 10th General Conference to come to seek here the encouragement and the blessing of the Pope. We are very happy to receive you because, as you know, the FAO is well-known at the Vatican. The members of your preceding sessions were received in audience more than once by our Predecessor of happy memory, Pope Pius XII, who always offered them the warmest reception. Formerly we used to pass often near the large FAO building, and seeing the many windows lighted at night, we never failed to send a grateful thought to those who were working there for the good of humanity. And now from our own apartment we can see the imposing headquarters of your organization rising on the horizon: so, you see, you are very present to us in mind and in heart.

(1965) We are anxious to tell you that the Church is very interested in the FAO. With maternal concern, the Church looks upon the great and beautiful example you offer with your technicians working all over the world to organize the struggle against hunger, to improve soil, plants, animal species, fishing techniques, dairy organization, forestry development...and all this in order to assist the most unhappy and the most deprived of our brothers and sisters, those who suffer, those who are hungry! This is truly a great and wonderful thing which inspires admiration, edification, confidence in the future.

(1966) You know that, with a full heart, we exhort the pilgrims who come to see us to undertake material as well as spiritual actions motivated by the love of God and neighbor which Church tradition calls the "works of mercy". And, what is the entire activity of the FAO except an immense work of mercy, a work of mercy on a world-wide scale! We scarcely need to exhort you, so eloquent is the very lesson itself which you give to the world. Rather, we want to rejoice with you, to congratulate you warmly, to assure you that we bless your works.

(1967) First, we rejoice sincerely and we thank God that an enterprise like the "Food and Agriculture Organization" could be born, organized and developed following the frightful conflict which bloodied the world. Doubtless, one of the most remarkable and most fortunate facts of the post war years was the recognition by the responsible authorities of the great difference in the standard of living among the nations, of the economic misery of the poorest, - the under-developed, as they were called - in comparison with those who retained the principal sources of wealth. From there, in those noble and dedicated persons concerned with the welfare of humanity, there arose the desire for effective service, a great movement for study, research, exchange of information, placement of technicians was initiated and you have arrived finally at those beneficial achievements which are the result of FAO's activities in recent years and which illustrate so well the booklet which you have offered us: "The FAO at work". How much beautiful and effective energy actually placed intelligently at the service of the good! Allow us to congratulate you most sincerely for it.

(1968) We would like to pick out one characteristic which, in our view, accompanies these fine activities: it is that spirit, wisely realistic and at the same time serenely optimistic, which animates your organization. The FAO does not fear difficulties: it confronts them. It is not discouraged by

---

(*) AAS 51(1959), 865-867.

the number and the size of the obstacles which appear in its way: the ruins and ravages brought about by war, the extent of poverty in certain regions, the epidemics spread by malnutrition and increasing it... without mentioning problems permanently posed by the constant increase of the world population. The FAO wisely saw to the most efficient means to provide, to improve, and to share food through careful distribution, and it put its services at the disposition of interested governments. The Church highly esteems this spirit of positive achievement and of disinterested service; it praises this reasonable boldness,and this confidence in the possibility of solving the great human problems. The Church also is optimistic.

(1969) A precious result of your activities, - and, as we know, also one of the goals of your Organization - is, ultimately, raising the standard of living of those who live in the rural areas. Coming from a rural family, we have seen with our own eyes, during our young years, and we will never forget it, the fatigue and the suffering of those given over to working the land. To contribute to lightening their burden, to giving a bit more material comfort to those who provide the bread for the rest, what a beautiful work of mercy that is also, and how worthy of encouragement and of praise!

(1970) We would also like to add another thought which came to us in reflecting on the broad, strengthening perspectives which the results already achieved by your organization open to the mind. In a world still shaken by war and its consequences, humanity searches for sources of real peace and for those who will be the most effective artisans of peace. The enlightenment from political interaction is still so uncertain, so subject to extinction after having aroused such great hopes! On the other hand, those who promote the practice of good deeds from nation to nation, mutual aid on the economic plane, in a disinterested spirit of friendly benevolence, are not these therefore the ones who set the surest paths to unity and peace among peoples?

(1971) In continuing your beautiful activities, may you also, Gentlemen, work for the peace of the world! In taking our leave from you, we could not give you a greeting which corresponds better, it seems to us, to your wishes as to ours, a wish most surely in conformity, in any event, to that of God the Creator and Savior of humanity. In order to better assure its realization, we grant our paternal apostolic blessing most cordially to all.

7. Address of His Holiness John XXIII to the 10th International Conference of Non-Governmental Organizations, convoked under the auspices of the FAO. The Vatican, 3 May 1960.

Original: French (*)

(1972) You have come to seek the blessing of the Pope on an enormous undertaking which is now the object of your efforts and of your concerns: the organization on a world-wide scale of the "Campaign against Hunger", launched recently through the initiative of the Director General of the United Nations Food and Agriculture Organization. A most cordial welcome to you, because your concerns in this matter coincide with those of the Church, and the tasks with which you concern yourselves seem to us particularly worthy of our approval and our encouragement. In fact, what does the Church do in this world? She continues here the work of Christ, about whom it is written that "he went about doing good and curing" (*Acts* 10:38). Therefore the Church warmly recommends to her children the practice of the spiritual and corporal works of mercy, and among the latter, the one which comes first in the list speaks clearly and precisely: "feed the hungry".

(1973) Of course, the Holy Scriptures teach us that we do not live by bread alone (Deut. 8,3) and experience confirms this for us. However, by the multiplication of this indispensable material food twice during his mortal life, Christ wanted to manifest his power to the crowds who followed him. And if he used a miracle to direct their minds towards spiritual realities, he did not thereby want any less to satisfy their starving bodies. The Gospel which recounts these episodes in detail specifies the profoundly touching sentiments which animated the divine Wonder-worker: "I have compas-

(*) AAS 52(1960), 463-465.

sion on this crowd, because they have been following me for three days, and they don't have anything to eat. If I send them home without food, they are going to faint on the way" (*Mark* 8:2).

(1974) Ladies and Gentlemen, isn't your activity inspired by similar feelings? Certainly, you are animated by the love of justice, by the desire to assure a more equitable distribution of the goods of this world among all peoples; but, also, just like Christ, you feel a profound compassion at the thought of the countless multitude of undernourished people - more than half of the human race - who wait for a gesture of mercy from their more favored brothers and sisters. To draw them from their state of misery and to bring to them an intellectual and moral life more worthy of humanity, more conformed to the will of God, an immense collective effort is indispensable. You have understood this, and you are preparing to collaborate with the United Nations Food and Agriculture Organization to assure the success of this vast Campaign.

(1975) We do not have to say again here all the good that we think of this Organization. Not long ago, we received the delegates to the most recent biennial Conference. We told them "The Church is very interested in the FAO." And we added: "With maternal concern, the Church looks upon the great and beautiful example that you offer with your technicians working all over the world to organize the struggle against hunger, to improve soil, plants, animal species, fishing techniques, dairy organization, forestry development... and all this in order to assist the most unhappy and the most deprived of our brothers and sister, those who suffer, those who are hungry! This is truly a great and wonderful example which inspires admiration, edification, confidence in the future"

(1976) This is what we said to the delegates of the FAO last November.However, it is useless to glory in what has already been accomplished unless we find therein a stimulus for what remains to be done.

(1977) What remains to be done - truly an immense task - is first to draw the attention of the entire world, if that can be done, to the painful problem of hunger and of malnourishment. And here is the first goal of the Campaign to which your organizations will bring their knowledge and active contribution.

(1978) Millions of human beings in the world suffer from hunger; others, without being strictly speaking starved, cannot consume sufficient quantities of the food they need. These are the facts. They must be made known; preach them from the roof-tops, as the Gospel says. (*Matt.* 10:27). Consciences must be awakened to the responsibility which weighs on each and every one, especially on those who enjoy many advantages. Today, in a world where distances no longer exist, no one can offer the excuse that the needs of the distant brother or sister is not known or that bringing help is not everyone's concern. In solidarity with those who are hungry, we are all responsible. There is the firm belief that your organizations will help to spread in a public opinion which, once aware, will demand appropriate measures and will give its support to their implementation.

(1979) The second goal of the Campaign against Hunger is the implementation of those very measures, that is, the direct action to raise levels of production and consumption in zones where the malnourished are. The world today does not produce enough foodstuffs to meet the needs of all the people, especially given the predicted increase in population in the years to come; and, furthermore, the available food is not equally divided. Therefore, new lands must be available for agriculture and the production of food in areas already under cultivation must be increased. Here again, your Organizations - taking into account the goals and the nature of each one - will have to suggest plans of action and of research, cooperate with the implementation, collect among your members the contributions which will permit the attainment of concrete results without too much delay. Such is the extent of the collaboration which is asked of you!

(1980) We feel a great joy in the thought of the immense possibilities of this Campaign, which will have, we are sure of it, the support of all good-hearted people and of all those private and public institutions which are genuinely concerned about the good of humanity. Furthermore, we are confident that by giving our strongest encouragement to you, the echo of our voice will reach beyond those who listen to us now and out to others throughout the world, and to all people of good will; it will be an urgent invitation to take part in this great burst of generosity and in this immense "work of mercy" which the Campaign against Hunger will be. And it is most warmly that we invoke on all who from this very moment participate in it, either individually or collectively, and in a special way on yourselves and your organizations, the choicest blessings of the Almighty and merciful God.

8. Address of His Holiness John XXIII to the 11th Session of the Conference of the Food and Agriculture Organization, during the general audience of 23 November 1961.

Original: French (*)

(1981) We would like to address a few words of welcome to a group of Delegates who have taken part these last days in the Eleventh General Conference of the United Nations Food and Agriculture Organization.

(1982) Last Monday, as a preview of the smoothness of that day's meeting, we already had the pleasure of receiving the President of the General Conference, which includes the representatives of more than one hundred nations, gathered to study the most efficient means of suppressing the rise of famine throughout the world. We receive you here today, dear gentlemen, with particular satisfaction, for the noble goals that the FAO pursues, merit the esteem and the respect of all those who truly have at heart the well-being of their fellow men and women.

(1983) You know all the interest we ourselves have expressed in your work from the beginning. We have even insisted on pointing them out in a solemn papal document, the recent encyclical *Mater et Magistra*, and we have been very sensitive to the sympathetic echo that our remarks have had in your Organization.

(1984) The world of today aspires to two great achievements: peace and bread. Peace finds its source in the faithfulness of human beings to the demands of the Pater Noster; this produces in turn, as its natural fruit, the well-being that we know to be the gift of Providence: *panem nostrum... da nobis hodie*. And it could be said that the one follows upon the other: for those who work to give humanity peace, which is threatened as long as the current serious economic imbalance among nations continues, contribute to peace by the very fact of obtaining bread for hundreds of millions of undernourished men and women.

(1985) Such is the essential condition for your work to be truly effective. Dear gentlemen, may people live in peace on earth and thus find the bread which is necessary for them. This is the wish we express with all our heart and we invoke for you and on your activities choicest divine blessings.

9. Message of His Holiness John XXIII for the Special Meeting of the Food and Agriculture Organization. The Vatican, 14 March 1963.

Original: French (**)

(1986) In our concern with being faithful to the doctrine of Christ and in accordance with the purest tradition of the Church, we have been pleased to promote, since its inauguration in 1960, the "Freedom-from-Hunger Campaign" so laudably launched and pursued by the Food and Agriculture Organization of the United Nations.

(*) AAS 53(1961), 814.

(**) AAS 55(1963), 344-345.

(1987) At a time when, within the framework of this vast Campaign, the "World Freedom-from-Hunger Week" is about to begin, and when the "World Food Congress" is approaching, we want to say how timely are these new initiatives, in our opinion, and how much we wish that they may benefit from universal collaboration.

(1988) The problem is really to put human energies to work on a very large scale . In the minds of its originators, this noble undertaking has only one aim - which would of itself be meritorious and would command respect - to alleviate temporarily what is lacking to peoples who are in the process of development. It aims primarily at encouraging the unanimous effort, of all those in position to do so, to teach human beings how to use fully the superabundant gifts which the Creator has placed at the disposal of humanity.

(1989) How many are the expressions of admiration, in the Holy Scripture, at the marvels of Creation and the bounty of God, who has bestowed upon man "dominion over the works of (His) hands" and "crowned him with glory and honor" (*Ps.* 8:5 and 6).

(1990) This control of man over nature, in the words of the inspired author, is every day revealed to be more widespread. Modern means of investigation provide a glimpse of the still almost undiscovered treasures hidden in the depths of the earth and in the seas. It is man's duty to use the gifts of intelligence and will which he has received in his striving to develop these immense riches.

(1991) But it is also the immediate duty of society, with the resources at its disposal, to bring concrete assistance to those of its members who are deprived of the minimum essential for the normal growth of their personality. St. Paul's warning to the Galatians is still valid, and now more timely than ever: "Bear one another's burdens, and so you will fulfill the law of Christ." (*Gal.* 6:2).

(1992) Considering the prodigious increase in transportation and travel facilities in the modern world, one can no longer say that the hunger and malnutrition prevalent in certain regions of the globe are due solely to the insufficiency of presently available natural resources, since those are superabundant in other regions. What is missing is the coordinated effort of mind and will to organize in such as way as to ensure a fair distribution. Also lacking, among developing peoples, is the adequate development of their own resources.

(1993) May this World Week for the struggle against hunger - and the approaching World Food Congress in Washington - be a call and a stimulant to all men of good will! May they strive hard to speed up projects of agricultural development, to hasten - in line with the conclusions of the recent Geneva Conference - the application of science and technology for the benefit of the less developed regions. In brief, may they strive to promote everywhere a better utilization and a better distribution of human and material resources. In so doing, they will be sure to win the praise and gratitude of all righteous men, and to merit divine blessings in all their fullness. These we personally, wholeheartedly, invoke upon the organizers of these meritorious initiatives, and upon all those - persons and organizations - that will participate in them or benefit from them.

10. Address of His Holiness Paul VI to the 12th Session of the Conference of the Food and Agriculture Organization. The Vatican, 23 November 1963.

Original: English/French (*)

(1994) While we welcome you here today, we cannot begin our discourse without a reference to the tragic death of the President of the United States of America, John Fitzgerald Kennedy. We wish to reiterate here the sentiments to which we have already given public expression: of deploration of the criminal action; of admiration for the man and the statesman; of prayers for his eternal repose, for his country, and for the world, which recognized in him a great leader; and fi-

(*) AAS 56(1964), 40-42.

nally of prayerful wishes that his death may not hinder the cause of peace, but serve as a sacrifice and an example for the good of all mankind.

(1995) We take this occasion to send our greetings to all the nations represented at this audience, especially to those who have recently become members and associates of the Food and Agriculture Organization.

(1996) We pray that God may grant each country prosperity and peace, in international cooperation, and in well-organized modernized work - for work was not cursed by God, when He said: "In the sweat of your brow you shall eat bread" (*Gen.* 3:19); that is, the honest sweat of good labour, according to the example of Christ, Who was Himself a workman.

(1997) To solve the grave problem of the life of human kind, this, then, is the right road: to increase the supply of bread, of food; and not to mortify and destroy the fecundity of life, for the Creator ordered His first creatures to "Be fruitful and multiply, and fill the earth" (*Gen.* 9:1).

(1998) We congratulate you on your notable accomplishments in this regard, we pray that your efforts to help the human race by increasing its food supply may be ever more successful, and to you, your collaborators and your families, we gladly impart a special Apostolic Blessing.

(1999) It is a pleasure for us to receive the President and members of the 12th biennial conference of the FAO. More than one hundred countries are present, together with some forty accompanied by their own Ministers of Agriculture; these figures alone indicate the solid standing of your worthy institution in the cadre of international organizations created after the Second World War.

(2000) We are all the happier to do so as it was our privilege to assist at the birth of FAO and to follow its activity in the modest residence of the Villa Borghese and then to witness the remarkable developments it enjoys today.

(2001) This was a road sown with generous, disinterested initiatives, created for the sole purpose of ensuring human happiness and the means to assure a basic element thereof: to combat the devastating plague of malnutrition, which still, in spite of the tremendous progress of technology, keeps a large part of humanity in a state of painful physical disability and therefore of intellectual and moral weakness.

(2002) It is not surprising that the Church has been the first to applaud activities so directly dedicated to man's well being. It is not surprising that from the very beginning your organization has maintained the most cordial relations with the Holy See which your President has just mentioned.

(2003) You will doubtless recall, as we do, the reception given here by our last two predecessors. Pius XII wanted the Holy See to have a permanent observer accredited to FAO. John XXIII considered your activities as the practice, on an international scale, of the first of the "works of mercy" which he mentioned so often, and, had nothing but goodwill and encouragement towards you. He wished to give the official backing of the Church to your campaigns and to explicitly mention your organization in his memorable encyclical *Mater et Magistra.*

(2004) We were thus not surprised to see in press releases, that at the beginning of your present session your Director-General evoked the memory of this unforgettable pontiff and paid him a public tribute.

(2005) Now it is our turn to bear the heavy yoke of the Supreme Pontificate and we have been mindful not to forget that our solicitude must extend beyond the visible limits of the Catholic Church to everything that concerns true welfare that comes to us from the immense regions of the globe, where developing populations wait for their more fortunate brothers to bring them the help which will indeed deliver them.

(2006) You have heard this appeal and you have undertaken measures to respond. During the current session of your organization, the importance of which your very worthy interpreter has underlined, you will deal mainly with the key problem for any progress in this field, namely agriculture. Our wishes and our prayers, you may be assured accompany your endeavours.

(2007) And if, looking toward the future, we would wish to formulate a desire it would be this: that the efficiency of your Organization be translated increasingly into action: that practical, concrete interventions multiply in all underdeveloped regions and bring to our unhappy brothers, along with the succor they hope for and so ardently desire, the proof that humanity is one large family where the suffering of one is felt by all. That they may thus have the evidence that charity finally triumphs over egoism, that good conquers evil. In this manner, beyond the direct aim of your organization, you will have attained humane and moral objectives to which, you will doubtlessly understand, we are particularly sensitive since they concern not only the material, but also the spiritual progress of mankind.

(2008) We are convinced that God will make your efforts fruitful. We are asking Him to do so with all our heart, while we invoke on the Director-General of FAO, the President of this Conference and on all of you, your families and your countries, the abundance of His divine blessings.

11. Address by His Holiness Paul VI to the Young World Assembly. The Vatican, 15 October 1965.

Original: French (*)

(2009) We are happy to receive you and to extend our welcome to you. As participants in the Young World Assembly, gathered at the invitation of Dr. Sen under the aegis of FAO, your aim is to unite all young people throughout the world in a great campaign against hunger.

(2010) The Food and Agriculture Organization of the United Nations could do no better to celebrate its twentieth anniversary than to turn resolutely towards the young in their millions and ask them to dedicate their energies to the struggle against hunger in the world.

(2011) Today, any man worthy of the name feels personally concerned by the suffering and poverty of others. What greater misery is there than that of the underfed child, too weak to put on the ghost of a smile, or than that of the youth hemmed in by want and doomed never to achieve what others consider a normal existence?

(2012) It is a duty for the whole of mankind to become more keenly aware of the imperative need to secure for all men the first and basic freedom, freedom from hunger, whereby that gift of God, human life, may come to fruition. As the Director-General, Dr. Sen, observed on the eve of the Eucharistic Congress in Bombay on 29 November last, "The half fed are only half alive." And he very rightly added "If the protest of the poor goes unheard for long, the result can only be a large-scale revolt of the dispossessed." May the young who, by God's grace, have enough to eat, hear the cry of distress of all those who are in want; may they place themselves at the service of their less fortunate fellows with generosity and enthusiasm. Let them act boldly to secure for every man the wherewithal of life and a better future. Is there a worthier cause to arouse their zeal and their ingenuity?

(2013) A noble task challenges you in your venture: to move the minds and the hearts of man, to awaken the conscience of nations, to prevail upon public authorities to make the necessary efforts and set apart the necessary resources - in a word, a tide of unanimous opinion and a common will must be aroused so as to put an end to the shocking tragedy of countless mutilated lives. The moral conscience of mankind must be made aware of its duty to worldwide solidarity. For our part, we resolved to address ourselves to this cause by our visit to the United Nations, and we shall do everything in our power to kindle in this field the indispensable "starvingma of Christians and of all

(*) AAS 57(1965), 909-911.

men of good will. We therefore subscribe to the words of encouragement that our predecessor, Pope John XXIII spoke to FAO in similar circumstances: "We want to say how timely are these new initiatives, in our opinion, and how much we wish that they may benefit from universal collaboration." [AAS, 55 (1963), 344. See above par. 1987]

(2014) Yes indeed, it is a dramatic question of life and death for mankind, which must unite to survive and therefore first learn how to share its daily bread. For a Christian, who recognizes the suffering features of his Saviour in any starving man, the well-known text of the Gospel according to St. Matthew remains the fundamental charter for his action: "For I was hungry and you gave Me food ... As you did it to one of the least of these My brethren, you did it to Me" (*Mt.* 25:35, 40 and 45).

(2015) Young people of today, who are fortunate enough to live in a world in which technology is continually placing novel and wonderful instruments in the hands of human beings, it rests with you - for you are the future - to see that these instruments really be used in the service of all mankind, so that the world of tomorrow may be different from that of today, a world where all may be brothers and sisters and at peace with one another.

(2016) Young men, open your eyes on this hungering world and bring your generous contribution to the campaigns of FAO. Give of your money, give of your time and, above all, give of yourselves. Thus you will be truly brethren unto your brethren, and the Lord, the Father of all, shall bless you. This we beg of Him with all our heart, and give you our special Apostolic Blessing.

12. Address of His Holiness Paul VI to the 13th Session of the Conference of the Food and Agriculture Organization. The Vatican, 28 November 1965

Original: French (*)

(2017) You are now meeting in Rome to celebrate the twentieth anniversary of the foundation of your organization. The latter, which the whole world, we may say, has now become accustomed to calling FAO by its initials, appears to us as one of the most benevolent initiatives following the post World War period.

(2018) Without mentioning its other merits, its concern for spiritual and religious values is sufficiently demonstrated by your presence at this Mass, which you elected to attend. And perhaps some of you, as we do, will have evoked on this occasion the memory of another Mass, which at the request of your predecessors, we celebrated in the Vatican grottoes in 1951, shortly after your organization established its headquarters in Rome.

(2019) We were then collaborating with Pope Pius XII, who gave his encouragement to the new born institution as did his successor, John XXIII, at a later date.

(2020) As you see, there is a sort of tradition between the Holy See and FAO of respect and friendship, which has been created over the years and which we are happy today to have another eloquent testimonial.

(2021) If the Church has contributed the weight of its moral authority to an organization such as yours, whose aims appear to be purely temporal and thus seem to be outside of its competence, it is because the Church is fully aware that the fate of all humanity is at stake here. Nothing that affects man's fate is foreign to the Church.

(2022) You have in twenty years done much in a technical and material nature: we congratulate you heartily on these accomplishments, and the people who benefited from your intervention are grateful. Could more and better things have been done? It is possible. Regardless of how noble the aims, no institution in this world is perfect. You have, in any case, achieved a very important

---

(*) AAS 57 (1965), 995-997.

advance on the psychological and moral level: you have contributed towards an awareness in the world of one of the most serious problems of our era which is perhaps the greatest threat to peace in the world: the problem of hunger.

(2023) It has been authoritatively stated in the course of your meetings during these last few days that more than half the population of the world does not eat enough to appease hunger; entire populations are still undernourished; and from the financial mechanisms of the modern world, it would seem that the gap between rich and poor is growing instead of diminishing.

(2024) Your primary mission - to relieve man of hunger - appears now to be conditioned by an even greater problem, of which you are fully aware: that of development. Your task is becoming one of education: you must enable the developing countries to create the economic and technical conditions to assure them of the possibility of feeding their populations. This is the only way in which we can hope to find a final solution to the problem of hunger and misery in the world.

(2025) The immensity of the task, requires from those who work on it, an act of faith. It requires a refusal to admit a fatalistic determinism in the economic evolution of the world and, a belief in the possible success of a strong, coordinated effort to guide and direct this development.

(2026) You have this faith, Gentlemen. You have confidence in man, in society, in the possibilities of production, distribution and the equitable use of the immense resources which the Creator has placed at the disposal of human-kind. Twenty years of intense activity, marked by all sorts of happy initiatives, particularly a resounding world-wide campaign against hunger, prove that you believe in the efficacy of the action undertaken and that you have the will to make it succeed. You also have the means to do so, and you are the only ones to have them on such a vast scale. And this is why, following our predecessors, we encourage you with all our power to pursue and intensify your efforts and we willingly give them the moral backing you are soliciting from the Catholic Church. We also know that the Hierarchy and the faithful consider FAO to be the necessary and effective organization in this field, and that they will continue to cooperate, as they did during the world-wide campaign against hunger, with your activities throughout the world.

(2027) We have confidence that thanks to this support and the support you will receive increasingly from all men of good will, FAO will experience, after the celebration of its twentieth anniversary, a new impulse which will bring it closer to the desirable end we recalled last month at the distinguished United Nations General Assembly: to ensure that "sufficient bread is available for the table of mankind."

(2028) With this wish and this hope in our heart and the pledge of our good will, we invoke upon you, your families, your work and the whole of the United Nations Food and Agriculture Organization the most abundant blessings of Heaven.

13. Address of His Holiness Paul VI to the Intergovernmental Committee of the World Food Programme. The Vatican, 20 April 1967.

Original: French (*)

(2029) Before your departure from Rome, ladies and gentlemen, following the session of your Intergovernmental Committee, you have kindly done us the honor of a visit.

(2030) We are all the more pleased to receive you, because this visit comes for us on the eve of the publication of an important document of our term of Office which very closely concerns the problems and preoccupations that are yours.

(2031) You are the delegates, coming from 24 countries, of the "World Food Program". Your aim is to mobilize the resources of the entire international community in the struggle against hunger,

(*) AAS 59(1967), 423-426.

in such a way that the solution found should be linked to the economic and social development of the under-developed countries.

(2032) What we have proposed to the Church and to the whole human community in the Encyclical *Populorum Progressio* is a vast program of action in favor of the developing countries which takes into account a fact that is major in the view of the Church. That fact is that economic growth alone is not sufficient; that it must be fully human and thus be concerned with the global and balanced development, social, moral and spiritual as well as material, of individuals and peoples.

(2033) You will see, therefore, the profound harmony between your goals and activities and the concerns of the Church for the well-being of her children and of all mankind. And you will understand the pleasure we feel at speaking for some moments with an audience so highly qualified on a subject so near to our heart.

(2034) You will wish no doubt to know what the Church is doing or plans to do in the matter of aid for developing countries.

(2035) Her action is not entirely on the same level as your own, and the convergence of efforts and points of view leaves intact the distinction that exists between a spiritual society like the Church and the temporal society constituted by the countries you represent. (Cf. *Populorum Progressio,* No. 13).

(2036) But you will surely have noticed, particularly in these last years, that the Church more and more exhorts Her children to engage fearlessly in temporal tasks at the service of their brothers and of the common good of the earthly city.

(2037) There is no need to reiterate here the innumerable material and cultural benefits (cf, *ibid,* No. 12) brought by the missionaries, in addition to the spiritual ones, to the countries they have evangelized. The Church has never recognized as hers a conception of religion that is disembodied, purely spiritual, a conception which would keep Christians away from worldly tasks. On the contrary she makes it into a duty for them to accept social and economic responsibilities and to carry them as faithful disciples of Christ - he said it to us Himself - "not in order to be served, but to serve" (*Matt.* 20:28). The conciliar "Constitution on the Church in the Modern World," which is no doubt known to you, is particularly explicit in this regard, and the great movement of renewal, introduced in the Church by the Council, moves in the same direction.

(2038) We ourselves have in our message indicated to the United Nations how concerned we were that our Catholic children should enlarge their hearts and their actions to the immense needs of the world. In several countries, Catholic organizations have been set up, under the direction of the Bishops, for aid to the "Third World." Others, already existing, have enlarged their activities in this direction. We have directed a large international organization to incorporate and co-ordinate this action and to represent it worldwide: *Caritas Internationalis,* which is no doubt not unknown to you.

(2039) Finally, given the importance and the growing seriousness of these problems, we have not hesitated, despite the extra costs to us, to create a new organization within the Roman Curia, a bureau of studies, the Secretariat *Justice and Peace,* the name of which makes clear its program and its goals.

(2040) Here, then, is what the Church is doing in this domain. Its contribution, on the material side, can seem rather modest compared to the contributions of your States. But this is only the least important part of its intervention in the problems which occupy you. The other part is not measured by figures and by balances, and yet it is by far the more notable. It is the part which springs from its spiritual mission.

(2041) In what, it will be asked, can this aspect of the Church's mission influence the problems of under-development? It is in the hearts of people that there exists the deep root of every durable solution in this domain.

(2042) A contemporary thinker has said it in a striking statement, seemingly paradoxical but profoundly exact: "Bread for myself is a material question; bread for my neighbour is a spiritual one" (Nicolas Berdiaeff). Effectively, it is a question first of tearing peoples and nations away from their egoism, their cupidity, their avarice. One can even say that the efforts to resolve the problem of world-wide hunger and poverty are headed for failure if one does not succeed in making a real change in the hearts of the world`s populations and in developing there a deeper and more effective altruism, enlarged to global dimensions.

(2043) It is here, it seems to us, that the Church brings its most effective contribution to your problems. She can act on the hearts of men, for she knows "what there is in man" (cf. *Jo.* 2:25); she has a doctrine on his origin, his nature, his destiny: and it is under this heading that we have taken the liberty of presenting ourself before the United Nations under the title of "expert on humanity".

(2044) If the role of the Church is not to dictate technical solutions for reforming the structures of society, she may, instead, stimulate conscience "which has a new voice for our era" (*Populorum Progressio*, No. 47), awaken conscience to its new duties in today`s world. Thus she can bend the political, social and economic structures of the nations in the direction of real progress. That means the participation of all men in the benefits of development, the elevation of all to living conditions worthy of human beings.

(2045) It suffices to tell you, gentlemen, how much the Church rejoices to see men of warm heart, aware of their responsibilities, devote themselves as you do to increasing the bread on the table of the great human family. We have noted with emotion that the voluntary contributions which come to you from Governments, come not only, as one might believe, from rich countries. No, nations which are themselves on the path of development offer you, they too, their contribution. An admirable example, which would confirm, were it needed, how far your work transcends the simple material level to situate itself at the level of what is greatest, most beautiful, and most elevated in Man: his soul and his heart.

(2046) With our congratulations and warmest wishes for the felicitous continuation of your beautiful task, we assure you, gentlemen, of the deep interest with which we follow its course, and with our whole heart we invoke upon your persons, your families and your activities the most abundant divine blessings.

14. Address of His Holiness Paul VI to the General Committee on Programming between FAO and Industries. The Vatican, 20 March 1969.

Original: French (*)

(2047) We wish, first, to thank your distinguished speaker, Dr. Victor Umbricht, for the words he has just pronounced. They show in a particularly happy fashion the nobility of the sentiments which animate you, and they well define the nature and the breadth of the contribution which your Group of great industrialists can bring, in cooperation with FAO, to the cause of the progress of developing peoples.

(2048) This cause, as you know, holds an important place in the concerns of the Church today. We therefore welcome with lively satisfaction an assembly of personalities so highly qualified, and we thank you for having taken time from your heavy schedule to come to visit us.

(*) AAS 61(1969), 250-252.

(2049) Everything which touches the well-being of humanity and its future finds an immediate and deep echo in the heart of the Church. And it is only right that your representative has evoked the names of our most recent predecessors and recalled their social teachings.

(2050) He also evoked the *specter of hunger*: this terrible word suffices to express the degree of sharpness, of gravity and of urgency which the problem of development today presents, to which our Encyclical *Populorum Progressio* was devoted and to which we have returned very often since. It is, in our eyes, as in those of many, the key problem which governs the temporal future of humanity.

(2051) In effect, according to serious statistics, if things were allowed to go their own way, the gap between the industrialized countries and the developing ones would continue to grow wider. The result would be, by a sort of fate in the current dynamism of production, that the rich nations would get ever richer and the poor, poorer (cf. *Populorum Progressio*, n.8), with the ensuing inescapable aggravation of social tensions.

(2052) It is against this fatality that your action is aimed, and it could show itself to be of capital importance for the poor peoples, and so for the peace of the world and the happiness of mankind.

(2053) You are, in effect, aware that the real problem lies not in assisting the exterior of the poor countries but rather in furnishing to them the instruments necessary to improve by themselves their production, "and to discover, themselves, in faithfulness to their own genius, the means toward their own social and human progress" (*Populorum Progressio*, n. 64).

(2054) You have understood that herein lies a real mission which imposes itself on the industrial nations in the name of human fraternity; and your speaker has pointed out as a positive and encouraging element the fact that the industrial countries are realizing more and more the importance of this mission of theirs.

(2055) Of this task you wish to be the pioneers, in accelerating the rhythm of expansion of the industries related to agriculture in the developing countries. Every person of good will, it seems to us, must applaud this program. "For that is where it must aim. World solidarity, increasingly efficient, must allow all peoples to become themselves the artisans of their destiny" (*Populorum Progressio*, n. 65).

(2056) But a mission presupposes an ideal, and motives that are always elevated and disinterested. Every consideration of personal profit, of competition, of calculated interests must here disappear before the nobility and the urgency of the goal: to enable our less favored brothers and sisters finally to emerge from their humiliating misery and to arrive at conditions of life worthy of Man. It is certainly thus that you will understand it, ladies and gentlemen, and on this path you have gained our most active encouragement.

(2057) No doubt some will be surprised that a society of a supernatural order like the Church attaches such importance to projects of a temporal order. Our predecessor, Pius XII, already many years ago answered this objection, and he did not hesitate to affirm that "a supernaturalism which separates religion from economic and political needs and duties, as if they did not concern the Christian and the Catholic, is a thing unhealthy and foreign to the thought of the Church" (AAS 44(1952), 819). It suffices to say how coherent with faith is an attitude of "engagement" - in the current phrase - in temporal tasks at the service of humanity.

(2058) With all our heart we wish that your efforts, those of FAO and of the Public Powers in favor of the "Third World" may continually grow, and in this sentiment, we bestow on all of you, ladies and gentlemen, as evidence of our goodwill and as a pledge of divine protection our Apostolic Benediction.

15. Address of His Holiness Paul VI to the 15th Session of the Conference of the Food and Agriculture Organization. The Vatican, 16 November 1969.

Original: English (*)

(2059) What can We, the Catholic Church, do with regard to the immense efforts of the Food and Agriculture Organization? Such is the question posed by you and by us today.

(2060) 1. First of all, we have noted with satisfaction how much you are aware of the immense needs of the greater part of mankind, which is underdeveloped. Hunger in the world - this phenomenon is known, is statistically measured, located in its demographic framework, and abundantly provided with estimates for the future. To take an attentive look at this need is in itself a highly valuable humanitarian act, for it follows the example of Christ Who said: "I have compassion on the multitude" (*Mt.* 15:32). Hence our first reaction is one of praise for your admirable efforts.

(2061) 2. We desire, however, to make our appeal to the world also in favour of the hungry, collaborating in your action by our exhortation. To all, then, to all peoples, to the rich, the producers, to politicians and economists, to youth - we address our appeal in favour of the "suffering humanity" (Address to the International Labour Office, June 10, 1969; No. 18. See above, par. 51).

(2062) Woe to those who dissipate their goods and their revenues in scandalous spending, whether for luxuries or for war! Woe to those who selfishly enjoy their wealth without having the slightest care for the poor - for the poor are not only individuals but families, social classes and whole peoples! We must ever repeat, without tiring, the appeal of our Encyclical Letter *Populorum Progressio*: "When so many peoples are hungry... all public or private waste, all ostentatious spending, national or personal, all exhausting armament races become an intolerable scandal. It is our duty to denounce it. May those responsible hearken to our voice before it is too late" (No. 53). This we asked at Bombay, this we requested again in our Encyclical (No. 51), this is the appeal we renew today: That there be set up "a great World Fund derived from a part of the monies used for military expenditures, in order to help the most unfortunate." As for ourself, despite the meagreness of our means, we wished the creation of a "Populorum Progressio" Fund, to show the great importance we attach to this matter, and the urgency attending its realization.

(2063) With all our heart, then, do we greet all those courageous offerings conspiring towards this end, all positive initiatives, all generous undertakings - and we hope that they will become ever more active and attract much imitation.

(2064) 3. So far, then, praise and exhortation. But we can also give you something else, something more specially our own, namely a word of hope. We know that this period immediately following on the first Development Decade is marked by some disillusionment. This shows you how much hope is reposed in you, how heavy a responsibility is yours. But be sure of this: You will succeed if only you persevere. For you are, in fact, promoting a design already prepared in the sector of human destiny - the design of Divine Providence, the beneficent intention of God, Who is always ready to respond to our requests if they are intelligent and courageous. We tell you boldly: Be daring, in wisdom and fearlessness, for thus will you call forth the action of our Father in Heaven. For your action cannot remain a merely profane thing; it is also, in its own way, a prayer: "Give us this day our daily bread" (*Mt.* 6:11).

(2065) 4. Finally, after praise, exhortation and hope, there remains for us to say to you a powerful and mysterious word. All may not, perhaps, be able to understand it in itself, because for this one needs that mysterious knowledge called faith. But all can appreciate it in its consequences; for it is a power-idea, a word which shakes man up, and makes him see and serve Christ in the poor and hungry man: "I was hungry..." (*Mt.* 25:42). This word of love is ours; it is a new and transcendental motive over and above those which civilization proposes to us. This word pushes us to take upon ourselves the burdens of others, and turns our sacrifices into joy. A man works devotedly for an-

(*) AAS 61(1969), 775-777.

other man, because that man is his brother, called like himself "to share, as a son, in the life of the living God, the Father of all men" (*Populorum Progressio*, No. 21).

(2066) 5. This is the message we humbly guard, and which as in duty bound we repeat to you this morning in this Basilica of Saint Peter's. May Christ, Whose first Vicar he was, Whose present representative we are as Peter's Successor, help each and every one of you in your task; may He light in your hearts His own burning love for each of us; may His charity animate your actions. For today charity must be truly international.

(2067) The work you must accomplish, lucidly and generously, is immense. It is up to you to take up the challenge given you, courageously and fearlessly. Such is our wish and hope as we bestow upon you, with all our heart, upon all those who are dear to you, as a pledge of abundant divine graces for the deliberations of FAO General Conference's Fifteenth Session and for the fruitfulness of its results, our paternal Apostolic Blessing.

16. Address of His Holiness Paul VI to the 16th Session of the Conference of the Food and Agriculture Organization. The Vatican, 12 November 1971.

Original: French (*)

(2068) The welcome that FAO gave us on 16 November last on the occasion of its twenty-fifth anniversary, remains as a source of gratitude in our memory, as we are happy to testify to you today on the occasion of the sixteenth session of your general Assembly. This meeting coincides, moreover, with the twentieth anniversary of FAO's establishment in Rome, and in this instance we wish, together with our best wishes for the fruitfulness of your work, to pay a public tribute to those who, these many years were the devoted and efficient Observers of the Holy See to your Organization, our old friend the late Commander Emilio Bonomelli, who often welcomed you at Castel Gandolfo, and dear Msgr. Luigi Ligutti, whose experience and competence you have all long appreciated, in the radiance of his human and priestly virtues, and who has just retired to enjoy a well-deserved rest after so many years of good and loyal service.

(2069) We have studied with great interest some of the preparatory documents for your work: in particular the analysis of the main trends and outstanding facts of the world food and agricultural situation, the prospective study of world agricultural development in the context of the international strategy of the second development decade,the progress of agricultural research, the orientations of the World Food Programme, the balance-sheet and the imperatives of agrarian reform, your relations with the great international organizations on question of common interest; and particularly, your participation in the important U.N. Conference on the Human Environment, which will be held in Stockholm in June 1972, and will deal with very grave questions - some of them really distressing - regarding the future of mankind.

(2070) On reading your work, we were struck by the fundamental concern that inspires your research: an increasingly lively awareness of the solidarity that unites all the members of the great human family and an ever more resolute determination to induce peoples and governments to draw the necessary conclusions to help all men to live a fully human life. How could the Church fail to rejoice in this policy, in such conformity with the demands of her message of universal love, as with the best aspirations of the men of our times? We said so in our encyclical *Populorum Progressio*: "The starving people are becoming aware of their individual hardship" (No. 9).

(2071) The increasing discrepancy of income and the more keenly felt disparity of ways of life, make this realization even more acute today.

(2072) The rising younger generations within the rural world are living this situation with an impatience that is difficult to control, while they claim more and more insistently increased participation,

---

(*) (AAS 63(1971), 875-879.

on the triple plane of property, knowledge and power: "to do more, to know more and have more, in order to be more" (*ibid.* No. 6).

(2073) So it is only right that the problem of "agricultural adaptation", as you define it in point 7 of your provisional agenda (document C 71/41, of 25 August 1971), should claim all your attention. Who does not see that the most remarkable technical progress and the most advanced technological attainments would not be of any use, if rural youth throughout the world did not realize that the progress in question is also within their reach and to their advantage; and that by bringing it about they fulfill themselves. In every village one and all must be interested in his work, given the concrete means of improving it and helped to understand what is at stake. The importation of ready-made techniques would have a short lived effect if this patient and persevering education were not undertaken and carried out by experts deeply concerned about this authentic promotion of man, so true is it that programming and financing are not sufficient: "it is truly the spirit and the heart that first achieve true victories" (Address to the FAO, 16 November 1970, in AAS, 62 (1970), p.835, n.7. See above, par. 65).

(2074) It must be said expressly: economic and social action, however indispensable it may be, is not enough, unless it is sustained and promoted by a plan that is at once psychological, pedagogical and spiritual. We are, in fact, up against radical transformations that are causing upheavals in the life of the world. Rural civilization, which was formerly that of the majority of men and ensured them legitimate development, is now attacked on all sides by the rise of an urban, mechanical civilization, that provides multiple objects intended to make men's lives more comfortable. Frequently isolated in remote country areas, are not the young often losing hope in their future as human beings? Do they not feel that in the last resort, they are working for people in the towns and that there is no real participation for them in what appears to them from far away as a kind of marvellous golden age? The reality, it is true, is quite different from the dream; and disappointment is not long in coming when they are plainly confronted with this reality. But, as everyone knows, the power of myths is such that it shakes mentalities in their most secret depths.

(2075) Young rural people wish to live like other young people today, to exercise a well defined profession, to have a clearly marked social status, a house equipped with a minimum of comfort with surroundings worthy of the name, free time that is a source of legitimate satisfaction, living conditions that they do not blush to share with their mate, schools that educate their children, holidays that make it possible for them to renew their daily horizon.

(2076) In short, it is no longer sufficient to check the growing discrepancy of the situation of the rural populations in the modern world. It is a question of giving them a full place in it, of seeing to it that the rising generations no longer feel the weakening sensation of being left on the shelf, so to speak, living on the fringes of society, deprived of the best elements of modern progress. Who will succeed in convincing them of the value, the interest, the necessity, and at the same time the humanity and the dignity of their toil, in comparison with industrial and bureaucratic work? Who will succeed in giving them the means of living with dignity, and being happy to lead this life, freely taken up? Times have changed, and Georgic and Arcadian poetry is no longer enough - "Beatus ille qui procul negotiis....," Horace, Epodon I, *Vitae rusticae laudes* - to meet the expectation of the rural world. We must help them to construct a whole new society, by giving them the means, economic means, of course, we repeat, but equally cultural, human and spiritual means. On these terms only will it be possible to overcome the present really distressing crisis of the young, only thus will rural families find again their natural balance and will villages become once more animated with cultural and religious life. A noble task, worthy of arousing the enthusiasm of the young and uniting them to carry out a really fascinating project of life!

(2077) It is up to you to meet this legitimate expectation, and in this way to put a stop to the dangerous disenchantment that is spreading all over the countryside as a result of too many frustrated hopes. Men and women, the young especially, need to be helped to obtain means of subsistence with their work and reasons for living through their commitment to the service of a great cause. When it is a question of increasing world food resources, of providing needy populations with the essential foodstuffs, the means strictly indispensable for their subsistence, cannot the same generous impulse be aroused as the one that animates the great achievements of human genius? Is it possible that man is more inclined to direct his inventive skill towards extravagant projects or enterprises of destruction (cf. *ibid.* p. 836, n. 9. See above, par. 67) than to utilize the immense resources of his spirit and his hands to fertilize the earth? May your generous and efficient action bring forth concerned effort among all men of goodwill to exploit so many lands lying fallow and so many productive energies (cf. *ibid*, p. 837, n. 10. See above, par. 68). A fertile land for all men: may this ideal, thanks to your persevering effort, find expression more and more in the reality of the world, on the scale of the dimensions of the international community, the peaceful establishment of which animates the dynamism of all men of feeling.

(2078) This tells you with what esteem we follow your work and what hope it arouses in us, after a Synod that marked the acute concern of the Church to contribute to establishing justice among all peoples. Your mission is a deeply human one, and the ideal that inspires it honours you. Your enterprise is a noble and difficult one; it calls for great courage, and never-failing generosity and perseverance. Far from letting yourselves be discouraged by the vastness of the task to be carried out, may its urgency be for you a stimulus to shoulder your responsibility even more generously and also an appeal to creative imagination, which will inspire liberating solutions. At a time, in fact, when some people feel the insidious temptation to retire within a selfish and absolute nationalism, it is for you to open the ways to increased international cooperation, marking the transition from economies dominated mainly by the pursuit of profit to an economy in the service of the common good. Who does not see that it is on these terms that intelligent mobilization of the innumerable resources of lands and oceans will give all persons what they need to live as human beings?

(2079) This world-wide mission of yours is certainly part of the designs of divine Providence, which invites us to share our daily bread lovingly and see to it that every man can procure it himself by his diligent work. So we warmly call upon your work the abundance of divine graces, in token of which we give you a generous Apostolic Blessing.

17. Address of His Holiness Paul VI to the 17th Session of the Conference of the Food and Agriculture Organization. The Vatican, 16 November 1973.

Original: French (*)

(2080) We are happy to greet first of all the Director General of the U.N. Food and Agriculture Organization, with his collaborators. We thank them for the kind visit they are paying us, in the course of the work of this seventeenth Session of the general Conference. They know how deeply we esteem their tenacious efforts against hunger. Yes, this united work of research, comparison, forecast, organization, mutual help, extended to the whole universe, seeking to cope with the great long-term projects as well as with sudden difficulties, such as the one that Africa has recently met with, deserves our congratulations and encouragement, because it is in the service of the lives of all human beings.

(2081) We are also happy to contact the Delegations of the member States of FAO that are taking part in this Session. This meeting, together with study of their works, enables us, too, to pay new attention to the problems of man-kind, which expects the earth to provide it with enough to eat, and with a harmonious economic development that is a factor of progress. These words just wish to show them how much we take to heart their work, their hopes and the hopes of the peoples they represent. We are all invited to widen our perspectives, to go forward boldly, to meet the increased needs of the world, without falling behind to a dangerous extent.

(2082) At the present Assembly, you are called, Gentlemen to take decisions concerning FAO's internal policies in order to fix, according to the resulting criteria, its ordinary programme for the years 1974-1975; it is a question of implementing concretely in the field the Programmes for the various continents, the campaign against hunger and also the World Food Programme, in agreement with the United Nations. Your decisions must also specify the trends of international policy in the field of agriculture and food, in accordance with the requirements of the present moment.

(*) AAS 65(1973) 656-659.

(2083) In point of fact, the world situation on the agricultural and food planes, such as it appears from the reports recently prepared by FAO, seems to us particularly serious. Anyone who takes to heart the fate of mankind cannot help being concerned by the overall diminution of agricultural and food production on the world scale in the course of the year 1972. World wheat reserves, in particular, seem so much reduced that the minimum level of world food supplies would be dangerously threatened if there were to occur, for different reasons, crises of production in the immediate future.

(2084) Very often, alas, before these worrying facts and forecasts, the international Organizations do not find the real aid or the open support they would be entitled to expect, since it is universal solidarity that constantly prompts their action. There is a contrast here between the growing expectation of the developing countries and the absence of a sufficiently complete and wide commitment on the part of the rich countries.

(2085) We take the opportunity to express this painful impression that we have felt. Recent statistics show that the overall public aid contributed by the rich countries is diminishing. It has not yet been possible to reach the contribution of at least one per cent of the national income that each country should give, according to its degree of development, for effective aid to the countries in the growing stage. Yet the Programme of the United Nations for the first and second development decade referred to this percentage on several occasions. And we ourself, nearly ten years ago, alluded to it during our journey in India.

(2086) The moment has come to strengthen and widen the movement of solidarity between the peoples of the whole world. In view of the acute situation at present, it is necessary to renew the political resolution for world mutual aid. Today, therefore, allow us to launch an urgent appeal for solidarity, an appeal intended for those in charge, but also to the conscience of all men of good will.

(2087) It is not our mission, of course, to suggest the technical solutions or the concrete political choices, in place of the responsible action of the member States of your Organization. But it is up to us to speak in favour of all peoples, for the good of all men, without any discrimination and without any worldly calculation.

(2088) In the name of humanity, we once more ask rulers to show, though their authorized representatives, and even immediately in the course of this FAO conference, that they will not let themselves be confined in the too narrow perspective of the interests of their nations alone nor of the immediate results of particular political enterprises. Rather, let them reach decisions that will oblige them to collaborate more on the international plane to ensure economic development and the progress of society; in this field, they will constantly pay special attention to the developing countries.

(2089) We are aware that the economy and the finances of even highly developed countries are going through a complex and difficult period at present. This does not dispense us, however, from urging them to overcome temptations to isolation, protectionism or direct relations that would make their power weigh on weaker and more exposed countries.

(2090) We appeal to the same effect to world public opinion and to the conscience of the peoples richest in resources, technology and human energies. The latter must take into consideration not only the needs of their own country, but also those of others, and therefore support political choices, demand concrete actions that aim at the good of all men, in the harmony of brotherly understanding.

(2091) We trust that the work of this session of the FAO Conference will open up prospects of real solidarity, which will make it possible to pass from the solution of emergency aid to a more systematic plan to ensure food supplies.

(2092) We very willingly gave our support to the recent "Sahelian zone operation", also receiving several requests, yours, Mr. Director-General, that of the local Churches, that of persons or agencies anxious to respond to both the urgency and extent of this human distress. We then appealed to peoples and governments for rapid and generous collaboration. Furthermore, we saw to it that entities of the Holy See were present actively, particularly our Council *Cor Unum*, the Catholic International Organizations and the institutions of the local Churches.

(2093) But we are deeply convinced that far vaster tasks than mere occasional aid are looming on the horizon for the International Community, and in particular for the Intergovernmental Organizations, in order to draw up long-term plans, in the broader perspectives of multilateral world action.

(2094) We hope that the political will of States will be capable of moving towards an international instrument that will entail a real commitment, inducing them to go beyond the form of generous gifts that are occasional and variable. Thus it would be possible to arrive at forms of permanent commitment in justice, which responding both to the duties of peoples according to their prosperity, and to the needs of the underprivileged countries, would constitute a world food supply system.

(2095) Like all the international Organizations of the family of the United Nations, you are looking, we think to the period of this second decade in which it will be necessary to examine carefully to what extent and how the international Community is attaining the purposes it set itself to satisfy the most imperious needs of the world populations and the most legitimate expectations of a progress guaranteed to everyone, overcoming imbalances and discriminations. Could it not also be desired that greater attention should be given to the possibilities of establishing a situation of justice ensuing from multilateral relations and programmes guaranteed by Intergovernmental Organizations?

(2096) Thus we renew our appeal, with all the hope it permits, in order that, overcoming ever recurring difficulties and false national prestige, decisions may be taken calculated to promote a just world policy for agriculture and food in the service of the urgent needs and real interests of mankind. This is part of that full humanism for which we have so often wished and which entails the complete development of the whole man and every man (*Populorum Progressio*, n. 42).

(2097) On the strength of this hope, we pray to God, the Father of all men, to assist you in your work and inspire those whom you represent, in order that the best possible use will be made of the astonishing possibilities of solidarity that the Lord gives to the men of our time.

18. Address of His Holiness Paul VI to the World Food Conference. The Vatican, 9 November 1974.

Original: French(*)

(2098) It is a pleasure to address this World Food Conference which the United Nations has convened here at Rome. Need we say how fully we share your concerns? Our own mission, after all, is to perpetuate the teaching and activity of the Master from whom the sight of a hungry crowd drew the touching words: "My heart is moved with pity for the crowd... [They] have nothing to eat. I do not wish to send them away hungry, for fear they may collapse on the way" (*Mt.* 15:32).

(2099) 1. In the last few years the situation we sketched in the encyclical *Populorum Progressio* has become even more alarming and the description we gave then is even truer now: "Today no one can be unaware of the fact that on some continents countless men and women are ravished by hunger and countless children are undernourished. Many children die at an early age; many more of them find their physical and mental growth retarded. Thus whole populations are immersed in pitiable circumstances and lose heart" (N. 45: AAS 59(1967), 280).

(2100) The papers prepared for this conference describe the various aspects of hunger and malnutrition, analyze the causes, and attempt, with the help of statistics, market studies and data

(*) AAS 66(1974) 644-652.

on production and consumption, to anticipate consequences. Even the cold figures speak eloquently of tragedy. How much more afflicting it is, then, to be on the scene and experience the reality! Recent catastrophes of every kind - droughts, floods, wars - have led directly to an appalling shortage of food. Less spectacular but equally painful are the difficult situations in which the impoverished classes find themselves because the price of food has risen (a sign that food is less plentiful) and because there has been a steady withdrawal of that international help in the form of food which after the last war contributed so greatly to the recovery and progress of numerous peoples.

(2101) The lack of food has long-range effects that sometimes cannot be foreseen. It has serious consequences for generations still unborn and brings with it dangers of an environmental and hygienic nature which may inflict deeper wounds on whole populations than do the more obvious immediate ills. It is indeed painful to have to face these facts and admit that human society seems incapable as yet of tackling the problem of world hunger, even though it has achieved unprecedented technological progress in all areas of food production - for example, fertilizers, mechanization, distribution and transport.

(2102) Only a few years ago we thought that in one way or another our technological advances, as well as the speed with which we can transmit information and goods, would soon eliminate the danger of that ancient plague, famine, never again to cripple any nation or any large area of the earth for an extended period of time. The expectation has not been fulfilled. Therefore, the atmosphere of this conference is a very sobering one. Therefore, too, the peoples of the earth are filled with anxious hope as they look on. In 1965 we had occasion to address the World Assembly of Youth, which had convened for a world-wide campaign against hunger. What we said then is still relevant: "It is a dramatic question of life and death for mankind, which must unite to survive and therefore first learn how to share its daily bread" which the Lord tells us is meant for us, that is, for each of us. (Address to the Young World Assembly, 15 October 1965: AAS 57 (1965), 910. See above, par. 2014.)

(2103) 2. As you set about your difficult but promising task, we offer two guiding principles. The first is to face the problems squarely without letting panic or discouragement keep you from seeing them as they are. The second is to be sufficiently impressed by the urgency and top priority of the present need that you will not settle for delays and half-measures. The conference will not by itself solve all problems; it is not in the nature of conferences to do that. But either it will reach clear and energetic conclusions that will be the springboard for a series of effective moves, faithfully accepted by all members, or, despite the hopes set on it and the good will of its members, it will have been held in vain. From the rostrum of the United Nations we made the appeal: "Never again a war, never again a war!" (See above, par. 20). We repeat those words now, and we say to you: "*Never again famine, never again famine!*"

(2104) 3. Ladies and gentlemen, the goal can be reached. The threat of famine and the ill effects of malnutrition are not inevitable. At this critical point in our history, nature has not turned into an unfaithful servant. Its potential for production on land and in the seas continues to be vast; indeed, that potential is still largely untapped. According to the generally accepted estimate, 50 percent of the land capable of cultivation has never been exploited. Meanwhile, we have the scandal of some countries periodically destroying a huge excess production of food because we lack a wise economic structure that would have insured the good use of such food.

(2105) These are but illustrations of a fact no one can dispute, even if some doubt that it is possible to exploit the potential of nature quickly enough to allay the hunger of an ever expanding human race. When we speak of "allaying hunger," we all agree that more must be meant than simply prolonging biological existence at a minimal level which is really subhuman. Our real aim is "to provide each individual enough to live, to live a truly human life, to be capable by his own work to guaranteeing the upkeeping of his family and to be able through the exercise of his intelligence to share in the common good of society by a commitment freely agreed to and by an activity voluntarily assumed." (Address to the Food and Agriculture Organization, 16 November 1970: AAS 62(1970), 831. See above, par. 60.)

(2106) 4. The present crisis is really one of civilization and human solidarity. It is a crisis, first, of civilization and method, such as arises when the further development of man's life in society is stymied by a one-sided approach. In the present instance, there is a tendency to focus attention exclusively on the social model that led to our industrialized civilization. This means that we put our whole trust in a purely technological approach to every problem and lose sight of basic human values. The crisis has arisen because exclusive attention has been given to the kind of economic success that depends on huge profits from industry. As a result the agricultural sector has been almost totally neglected and with it the high and human spiritual values which that sector represents.

(2107) The crisis is also one of human solidarity. The imbalances between individuals, groups and people have been maintained and at times even intensified. As is increasingly evident, this state of affairs is due to an unwillingness to contribute to a better distribution of resources at hand, especially to the benefit of less favored countries and of whole areas of the world that are essentially dependent on a still primitive kind of farming.

(2108) It is here that the paradoxical nature of the present situation comes home to us. Mankind is now capable of a hitherto unequaled mastery of the physical universe; it has at its disposal the tools for exploiting the world's resources to the full. Will those, then, who hold these tools in their hands stand paralyzed, as it were, in the face of an irrational situation in which the wealthy, relatively few in number, allow the vast majority to live in wretchedness? In which a few nations enjoying a highly enriched and varied diet are content to see all the others with only a bare minimum to meet vital needs? In which human intelligence is indeed able to change the lot of so many afflicted people, yet refuses to accept the task of guaranteeing the most vulnerable sectors of mankind an adequate nourishment?

(2109) 5. We would not be in this situation if we had not seriously erred in setting our course, even if the mistake was at times one simply of negligence or omission. It is high time to find out what has gone wrong so that we may correct our mistakes or, better, set the whole situation right. The real need, in the last analysis, is to acknowledge, in an effective way, the right of every human being to eat his fill as required by his age and the kind of activities he engages in. This right is based on the fact that all earthly goods are intended, first and foremost, for the use of mankind as a whole and the maintenance of all men, and only secondarily for private appropriation by individuals. Christ bases His judgment of the life of each human being precisely on whether he has respected this right of his fellowmen (See *Mt.* 25:31 ff.).

(2110) If we look at our situation, certain facts are immediately clear. One of the most evident causes of the present disorder is the increased price of foodstuffs and of materials needed for producing them; Think, for example, of fertilizer,the scarcity and high price of which are threatening to reduce the beneficial effects that were rightly expected from the green revolution." But are not scarcity and high prices connected with fluctuations in a production that is regulated with a view to profit rather than to meeting the needs of mankind? The decrease in stocks of food, another cause of our present problem, is at least partially due to commercial decisions that lead to our having no reserves for the victims of sudden and unforeseen shortages.

(2111) We are now confronted with a food crisis which, as far as we can see, will only worsen. Yet in some areas of the world that are especially capable of producing surpluses and reserves for cases of need, an astonishing amount of land has been taken out of cultivation. Here we have the kind of contradiction that shows the deep crisis through which our civilization is passing. Yet, since all these circumstances have resulted from ill-advised action on man's part, it is possible to correct and change them, provided we have the necessary wisdom and courage.

(2112) We mentioned earlier the amount of food each man needs if he is to live a genuinely human life. But the problem of quality of food is no less important and, once again, is caused by economic decisions. The problem is one chiefly for the more industrialized nations. As the atmosphere becomes more polluted and these nations devote themselves ever more eagerly to creating artificial substitutes and increasing production, how will they prudently assure a healthy diet, one that does not seriously endanger the health of those who observe it, especially children and young people? How, moreover, are these nations to break eating habits which are harmful to the eater because the food is so rich and abundant, while also leaving other people with insufficient food? Here again, alertness and courage are needed.

(2113) 6. We would also like to offer some observations about the flow of those resources that could help in the present situation. All are agreed that the multilateral and bilateral help available in the agricultural sector has been inadequate. In preparation for the conference, careful estimates have been made of monetary requirements for stepping up food production in the developing countries and for carrying out measures that would guarantee a world food supply. The monies needed over the next ten years, according to these calculations, are certainly far greater than those committed to the task up to now. At the same time, however, they are small in comparison to the national budgets of the nations that are wealthy or have international assets. A recent crisis has caused a redistribution of these assets but has not reduced their volume.

(2114) As early as 1964, when we visited India, we appealed to the nations of the world to commit themselves generously - chiefly through a reduction of military budgets - to a fund that would decisively help toward the integral development of the least favored sectors of mankind. Now the moment has come for an energetic and unambiguous move in that same direction. The sense of human solidarity, or rather of elementary social justice, which consists not only in not "stealing" but in sharing, has not had the desired effect. Will the dangers of the hour force us at last to move? Or will men stubbornly refuse to see the real situation and look for alibis - such as, for example, an irrational, unilateral campaign against population growth - instead of doing what has to be done?

(2115) We cannot allow those who control the goods and resources of mankind to solve the problem of hunger by forbidding the birth of the poor or letting children die of starvation simply because their parents have not acted in accordance with theoretical plans based on pure hypotheses about the future of mankind. In a past which we had hoped was gone forever, men went to war in order to seize their neighbors' wealth. But is it not simply a new form of war when some nations try to impose restrictive demographic policies on others so that the latter may not claim their just share of the earth's fruits?

(2116) We reaffirm our full moral support of those who have frequently stated at international meetings that they are ready not only to acknowledge every man's right to the goods he needs in order to live but also, through free acceptance of a sacrifice in proportion to their resources and capacities, to put their own goods at the disposal of needy individuals and peoples, without excluding or discriminating against any. Our real need, therefore, is for courageous reforms to eliminate obstacles and imbalances deriving in part from outmoded structures that perpetuate unbearable injustices or hinder production and the effort to assure the adequate flow of vital goods.

(2117) 7. But even the most generous international aid, a more intense research into and application of agrarian technology, and a vary careful planning of food production will be almost useless unless we quickly repair a serious defect in our technological civilization. The worldwide food crisis cannot be overcome without the help of the farmers. That help will not be fully and effectively given unless we radically change the attitude of the contemporary world which attaches little importance to agriculture. Agriculture today is only too readily subordinated to the immediate interests of the other sectors of the economy, even in countries which are now attempting to achieve economic growth and independence.

(2118) Our predecessor John XXIII, in his encyclical *Mater et Magistra*, began a chapter on farming with the words: "Farming has become a depressed occupation. It is inadequate both in productive efficiency and in the standard of living it provides" (N. 124: AAS 53(1961), 432). We need point to only two signs of such depression: the decrease in the number of farmers and, in some cases, in the extent of the land being cultivated in industrialized countries; and the fact that in the developing countries, even though the great majority of people till the soil, agriculture is the most underdeveloped sector of the economy. It follows that, however valuable the technological means available, nothing will be accomplished without the true reform represented by the rehabilitation of agriculture and the reversal of present attitudes towards it.

(2119) We must continually assert and exalt the importance of the farmer and indeed the importance of all who through various kinds of research and its implementation work for the development of agriculture. We ourself made this point in addressing the 1971 Conference of the Food and Agriculture Organization: "It is no longer sufficient to check the growing discrepancy of the situation of the rural populations in the modern world. It is a question of giving them a full place in it, of seeing to it that the rising generations no longer feel the weakening sensation of being left on the shelf, so to speak, living on the fringes of society, deprived of the best elements of modern progress." (Address to the Food and Agriculture Organization, 12 November 1971: AAS 63(1971), 877. See above, par. 2076)

(2120) This goal will be reached only through worldwide, balanced efforts at development, an effort sustained by the political will of governments to give agriculture its rightful place. We must put an end to the pressure exerted by stronger sectors of the economy as they strip the countryside of the human energies that could make farming a highly productive activity. We must inaugurate a policy of guaranteeing the rural young their basic right as persons to choose a worthwhile calling that will provide such advantages as are now to be secured, it seems to them, only by going into the city and industry.

(2121) Here again, there is no doubt that reforms will be effective only if individuals see the point and value of them. That is why education and training are so important if men are to be prepared. "The cooperation of the rural population is essential... Farmers must esteem and be faithful to the way of life they have chosen; they must implement the programs for crop improvement that are indispensable if farming is to escape its age-old sameness and narrowly empirical basis, and to adopt new working methods, new machines and new approaches." (Address to Italian farm workers, 13 November 1966: *L'Osservatore Romano*, 14-15 November 1966.)

(2122) The important thing, from the viewpoint of the world's hungry people, is that governments should make it possible for all farmers to learn how to till and improve the soil, prevent sickness in their animals and produce better crops. Once they are adequately trained, farmers must be able to get the credit they need. In short, the mass of peasants must become artisans responsible for production and progress. This brings us back to the concept of an integral development that embraces the whole man and all men. We Ourself, as far as it has been in our power, have constantly exhorted mankind to work toward that kind of development.

(2123) 9. Such, ladies and gentlemen, are the reflections we offer as our contribution to your work. They proceed from our awareness of our pastoral obligations. They are inspired by trust in the God who neglects none of His children and by trust in man who is created in God's image and capable of magnificent manifestations of intelligence and goodness. When He saw the hungry crowds, the Lord was not content simply to voice His compassion; He also bade His disciples, "You yourselves give them food," (*Mt.* 14:16) and then exercised His power in support of their powerlessness, not their egoism.

(2124) This account of the multiplication of the loaves evidently contains several lessons for us as we face the serious demands of the present hour. But the main lesson we want to insist on today is the call for effective action. There must be a long-range effort to enable each people to secure for itself, in the way best suited for it, all that it needs for a truly human existence. There must also be, however, an immediate sharing that will meet the pressing need of a large part of the human race. Work and charity must go together.

(2125) Such a gradual redirecting of production and distribution implies a further effort that should not be simply a constraint accepted out of fear of scarcity, but a positive determination not to waste resources which ought to promote the good of all. After generously feeding the crowds, the Lord bade His disciples gather up what was left so that nothing might be lost (See *Jn.* 6: 12). What a splendid lesson in thrift, in the noblest and fullest sense of that word, to a wasteful age like our own! It condemns a whole conception of society according to which consumption is an end in itself. Such an attitude is unconcerned with those in need, but it also harms the very people who think they profit by it, for they become incapable of understanding that man is called to a higher destiny.

(2126) Our appeal, therefore, is addressed to both the clear mind and the feeling heart. If nature's potentiality is vast and if the scope of the human spirit's mastery of the universe seems almost limitless , what is it that keeps us from acting in an equitable way for the good of all our human brothers? What is lacking is the noble unrest caused by the sight of the suffering and wretched state of the poor, and the deeply rooted conviction that the whole family suffers when one of its members is in distress. What is lacking is that sense of solidarity which we would like to see prominent in your labors here and especially in the decisions you reach. We earnestly ask the Father of all light to grant you that sense of solidarity as His gift.

19. Address of His Holiness Paul VI to the 18th Session of the Conference of the Food and Agriculture Organization. The Vatican, 14 November 1975.

Original: French (*)

(2127) It is always with special joy that we welcome the members of the United Nations Food and Agriculture Organization. We have a very lively awareness of the importance of the work which brings together political leaders and experts from the whole world, to consider the crucial problems which condition people's lives. This session also coincides with the thirtieth anniversary of FAO; we are happy to renew to this Organization our fervent good wishes and the confident hopes that we went to express in its own headquarters, five years ago.

(2128) The idea of an international agricultural adjustment, which is the central theme of this Eighteenth Session, belongs to the insight which presided over the birth of your Organization. The fact that this idea now influences many with the quiet power of an evident need is surely the best compliment which could be paid to the quality of the work already accomplished. And it is surely the best stimulus for yourselves, at a time when repeated dramatic alarms and the awareness of the precariousness of the world food situation and of general economic balance confer upon you a fresh responsibility.

(2129) In the space of a short period of time, a whole series of international Conferences at the highest level have stressed the need for more equitable international economic relationships. You have contributed to this new awareness. It is now up to you to develop it, and to help it to result in coherent concrete achievements in your particular sphere. Your statutes and the experience which you have gained put you in a leading position to deal with this task.

(2130) In fact, in the course of your present studies you are concerning yourselves directly with the most numerous and too often the most despised and forgotten part of humanity: the rural community, particularly in the Third World. Henceforth, and this may be paradoxical, the elementary economic task that consists in feeding people constitutes a valuable regulator for economic life as a whole. It puts the accent on the scandal of waste - a scandal whose intolerable nature people are becoming more and more aware of at a time when numberless human beings are dying of hunger; it directs efforts towards the real needs, in places where too often the economy is stimulated and diverted by artificial needs; and it invites people to establish new relationships with a view to the true service of man, of every man and of the whole man, in his integral development.

(2131) We rejoice sincerely at these new prospects opening up before you. We congratulate you on the work that has already been accomplished. The history of confident relationships which have not ceased to develop between your Organization and the Holy See illustrates in a significant manner the Church's care to recognize with joy and gratitude all service rendered to people, especially in such a basic matter as that of daily bread.

(*) AAS 67 (1975) 710-713.

(2132) The Church in her turn brings the light and energy of the Gospel to all human activities. Her teaching on the unity of the human family, all the members of which come from God, are created in his image and called to one single end, which is God (cf. *Gaudium et Spes,* 24), enlightens and strengthens what your experience causes you to discover with ever greater clarity: human problems such as international agricultural adjustment, and, more widely, the establishment of more equitable relationships between nations, can only be solved if they are placed within the framework of the effective solidarity of the whole human family.

(2133) This does not mean that a universal framework must be imposed, denying the more individual manifestations of solidarity and seeking to imprison human effort within a single model of development. Universal, living solidarity is built up little by little, starting from the more immediate manifestations of solidarity whereby people and nations develop their personalities in line with their particular creativity, within the environment for which they have more specific responsibility, in the forward movement of a history which enables them to reap the cultural heritage of previous generations and to incorporate it in new constructions. You are in a very special way sensitive to this implantation in a soil and a history: respect for people and the desire for effectiveness come together to demand that peoples should be recognized as having responsibility for their own development, and in the first place an increasing autonomy in food production. But an unflagging effort is needed in order to direct individual groups towards the horizon of wider solidarities, in order to liberate all their energies, or multiply every kind of exchange, to ensure the coherence and effectiveness of everyone's efforts. Agricultural populations will gain by being dynamically inserted into the general movement of economy and civilization.

(2134) The "world conceptual framework" of which your documents speak is therefore, first of all, a question of a mental attitude, an interior dynamism in people and nations which widens their horizons and makes them conceive and achieve their objectives in a setting which provides universal solidarity. This movement from within calls for a true conversion of attitudes, and in this the Church is playing her part. But this movement is endowed with fresh energy for development when universal solidarity succeeds in taking flesh in shared institutions, with shared orientations. You are one of these institutions which already expresses something of the unity of the human family. We trust that the work of your Eighteenth Session will enable you to select orientations capable of bringing about the progress of human solidarity in the common struggle against hunger and for development. This will be your valuable collaboration in the building up of society. Such a building up demands that the quest for more just structures should be rooted in a political desire for peace and brotherhood, both of them being fostered and guided by a firm conviction of the incomparable dignity of the human person; for the human person deserves our tenacious efforts and, when his freedom is respected, reveals a creativity capable of mastering the great problems of our time.

(2135) For our part, we offer you, for this great human work, the inexhaustible resources of the Gospel. These resources have developed, during this Holy Year, new powers of reconciliation, rooting Christians ever more firmly in God and giving them a renewed experience of their brotherhood in God - a spiritual experience which is being lived here and which, throughout the world, is preparing men who are better able to place their efforts in the perspective of the unity of the human family reconciled in our Lord Jesus Christ.

(2136) This is the Church's contribution; this is the meaning of our prayer. We ask the God and Father of all people to assist you in the heavy task which is yours in the service of humanity, in order that the earth may bring forth its fruits in abundance and that these fruits may be available to all.

20. Address of His Holiness Paul VI to the 19th Session of the Conference of the Food and Agriculture Organization. The Vatican, 18 November 1977.

Original: French (*)

(2137) We are particularly happy today to welcome you who are now participating in the Nineteenth Session of the Conference of the United Nations Food and Agriculture Organization. It is truly a joy to see the delegates of so many countries gathered to study the means of responding to the needs of the hungry. We appreciate your efforts and congratulate you for them. However,satisfaction for them cannot prevent consideration being given to what remains to be done. You are all aware of this and, together with our good wishes that your work will be fruitful, we express to you again this morning those hopes which so many who lack the necessities of life would like to place in your Organization.

(2138) Indeed, the food problem is still one of the principal concerns of our time; it is an elementary need of mankind, the satisfaction of which urgently demands large-scale undertakings within the framework of a renewal of the economic and social activities of the international community. The Church has unceasingly shared this pressing anxiety.

(2139) We shall simply recall two particularly tragic and urgent manifestations of this problem. One is the frequent repetition of catastrophes that should be matter for reflection by all mankind: droughts, famines, floods, etc. - catastrophes in which the phrase "died of starvation" is at its most literal. The other is undernourishment and malnutrition, which are major characteristics of underdevelopment and which have so many consequences, such as infant mortality and the lessening or destruction of the ability to work.

(2140) Admittedly there are optimistic reports concerning production. The improved agricultural situation is due not only to climatic reasons but also to the steps taken at various levels, especially since the World Food Conference, and above all to the awareness stirred up by that Conference particularly among policy-makers in the international and national fields. This optimism must however be moderated, for as you yourself remarked, Mr. Director-General, in the field of food and agricultural development, "although spectacular results are obtained, they are often ephemeral: the results do not measure up to what was promised and there has to be a drastic lowering of sights". It is precisely your Organization that has the main task of acting as a catalyst and "moderator" of efforts for international agricultural development, seeing that improvements are consolidated, and that progress rests on a sufficiently sound basis for it to remain constant.

(2141) From this point of view we think it important to recall that FAO has among its primary objectives not only production but also the advancement of rural areas and people, especially in the developing countries. While international production has improved, the same does not seem to hold true for the rural areas of the Third World. This is shown in the clear increase in the proportion of production coming from developed countries in relation to production from the rest of the world. In this can be seen both a structural and institutional problem and at the same time, the need to improve the situation and the training of agricultural workers, especially small farmers and rural youth. We mentioned the need previously, when we addressed the World Food Conference.

(2142) The developing countries also have a choice to make concerning the organization of their economic and social plans. Without any wish to keep perpetually attached to the land the great number of people who now make their scanty living from it, nevertheless it is wise to think of advancing a large proportion of these people in the agricultural sector, rather than to envisage transplanting them into the industrial sector or especially to run the risk of seeing them crowded into suburbs. Furthermore, it is of the highest importance that the developing countries should aspire to the greatest possible self-sufficiency in the field of agricultural consumption by their people. As a result of international trade systems for which they are most often not responsible, too many of

(*) AAS 70(1978) 95-97.

them are living in a dependence that is deeply harmful to their economies, which consequently are heavily in debt.

(2143) Finally, we cannot fail to draw your attention once more to the problem of the distribution of food products and of the balance to be achieved among all the factors governing trade in those products. On the one hand, the cost of importing the agricultural products needed by the developing countries makes a large dent in their meagre resources; on the other hand, receipts from their agricultural exports are not such as to provide them with a fair profit which would constitute a normal contribution necessary for their national budget and an encouragement for the producers. Any speculation exploiting elementary human needs is iniquitous, in a very special way speculation on food and arms. It is to be hoped that in this matter the developed countries, whatever their social and economic system, will finally decide on revisions, however costly, of the practices that they impose on most of the world. Forums for joint efforts, such as FAO, ought to be special centres for success in this regard.

(2144) Nobody can fail to see that the problems with which you are concerned, and of which we have merely mentioned some salient points, are not just technical problems. They are also moral problems. For they imply a concept of the human person that cannot be disregarded in the search for solutions. Therefore, we urge you never to lose sight of the ethical aspect of the problems you are dealing with, and to think of your activities first and foremost as a service - a service to the part of humanity that lacks the most elementary goods, those that ensure subsistence.

(2145) May you have the joy of being counted one day by the Lord himself among those who have truly responded to the needs of their hungry brethren. We ask him now to bless you and your efforts.

21. Message of His Holiness John Paul II to the Director General of FAO, H.E. Mr. Edward Saouma, on the occasion of the first World Food Day. The Vatican, 14 October 1981.

Original: French (*)

(2146) The International Food and Agriculture Organization has decided to promote, on 16 October 1981 - the thirty-sixth anniversary of its institution - the first World Food Day. This initiative should drive home not just to experts but to public opinion, to the whole of mankind, the serious and urgent problems of hunger and malnutrition, and mobilize the energies of everyone to meet them in solidarity.

(2147) I am happy to participate in this event, by becoming the spokesman of all those who are tragically suffering from undernourishment and who appeal to the conscience of their brothers and sisters. I am thinking particularly of the eight hundred million or so men, women and children who are living in a state of absolute poverty, and of all those who subsist under conditions too precarious to ensure bread for the next day. If it is already the duty of every person to be concerned about this, how could those who profess to follow Christ forget that he identified himself with the hungry?

(2148) So I wish to join all those who again proclaim today the necessity of recognizing and guaranteeing every person concretely the exercise of his fundamental right to nourishment. To this right there corresponds the duty of continual, planned action for organic development according to a new international order, capable of ensuring, above all, enough food in the various countries of the world.

(2149) Now a serious imbalance is becoming more and more marked between the needs of populations in vast areas and the food available. How could we fail to be concerned about the acute crises that are foreseen in the near future in several continents? On the basis precisely of the ob-

---

(*) AAS 73(1981) 733-735.

servations of the FAO experts, I had drawn attention to this tragedy at the threshold of this year (cf. Homily on 1 January).

(2150) Certainly, complex factors explain this situation. There are on the one hand natural calamities. But man always has his own share of responsibility. For it is less a question of an overall insufficiency of food products in the world than of a lack of availability and exploitation of the immense riches concealed in nature and intended for common use. Can it not also be said that sometimes the priority character of agriculture has been underestimated in the overall process of development? There is, furthermore, an unfair distribution of the product of work, not to mention excessive expenses to meet superfluous needs or to amass costly armaments in a dangerous way.

(2151) FAO knows better than anyone: the fulfillment of the right to food cannot be limited to aid in the form of immediately indispensable food or to occasional initiatives, although this is of course necessary in emergency cases.

(2152) It is necessary in the first place to secure more widely for the populations that are suffering from malnutrition actual access to the various riches of nature, in the subsoil, in the sea and on the earth. Above all, another agricultural policy and another trade system must be envisaged, because, it is a fact, the efforts of the last two decades of development are far from having solved the problems. New ways unquestionably should be adopted which will permit each country, as far as possible, to provide for its own food needs, without depending too much on foreign exports. As I said in my recent encyclical, "Radical and urgent changes are necessary in order to restore to agriculture - and to rural people - their just value as the basis for a healthy economy, within the social community's development as a whole" (*Laborem Exercens*, n. 21).

(2153) Today a concerted effort must be made by everyone: by governments, whatever their economic and political system may be; by intergovernmental and non-governmental organizations; by various associations of volunteers, and I am thinking in particular of the ones inspired by the Churches and communities of believers. It is in the framework of this indispensable international cooperation that the initiatives of FAO take their place, according to its specific function. The Holy See hopes that this Organization will be able to carry out its mission in a truly ever more efficient manner and in full conformity with the ideals expressed in its statutes. The Holy See also hopes, therefore, that its action will be recognized and supported with increased means by governments and member States.

(2154) On the occasion of this first World Food Day, I express my warm encouragement and my fervent wishes to all those who are working to solve the crucial question of hunger, particularly to all the representatives of these member States and organizations present, especially to the Director-General of FAO, to the officials and the whole staff of FAO. I pray to God - whom we ask every day for the daily bread necessary for everyone - to bless their persons and inspire in them competent and disinterested action in the service of the subsistence of all their brothers and sisters.

22. Address of His Holiness John Paul II to the 21st Session of the Conference of the Food and Agricultural Organization. The Vatican, 13 November 1981.

Original: English (*)

(2155) 1. In keeping with a happy tradition established in previous years, I am pleased today to extend a warm welcome to all of you who make up the Twenty-first Session of the FAO Conference. The importance of your Organization is self-evident, since its objective is to promote agricultural development and the provision of sufficient food for every human being. In this respect, the world situation today is far from satisfactory even though there are hopeful factors. Famine and malnutrition are still all too real for millions of people. The fight against hunger and

(*) AAS 74(1982), 35-39.

malnutrition can and must be continued through the tenacious and harmonious efforts of all: of individuals, groups and volunteer associations, of private and public institutions, of governments and international organizations, especially those that carry out programmes and activities which are multilateral or even totally altruistic, for the sake of those countries which are the weakest and most in need of help.

(2156) As the absolute priority, the strenuous efforts of all should be directed to the elimination of "absolute poverty", that poverty which afflicts the populations of many developing countries. Absolute poverty is a condition in which life is so limited by lack of food, malnutrition, illiteracy, high infant mortality and low life expectancy as to be beneath any rational definition of human decency. The persistence of such degrading poverty, and especially the lack of the absolutely basic minimum of food, is a scandal of the modern world, in which one finds enormous contrasts of income and standards of living between rich countries and countries that are materially poor.

(2157) The conditions of underdevelopment and real dependence which characterize developing countries cannot be attributed solely to a lack of will and commitment on the part of the populations concerned, nor to corruption and undue enrichment on the part of a few people within communities which have recently attained independence. For these conditions are also maintained and fostered by rigid and backward economic and social structures, both national and international, structures which cannot be changed suddenly, but which need to be changed through a long and gradual process, the fruit of a sustained and united effort following the criteria of justice in the relationships between the peoples of the entire world.

(2158) 2. It should never be forgotten that the true purpose of every economic, social and political system and of every model of development is the integral advancement of the human person. Development is clearly something much more fundamental than merely economic progress measured in terms of the gross national product. True development takes as its criterion the human person with all the needs, just expectations and fundamental rights that are his or hers.

(2159) This is the central idea that I presented in my recently published Encyclical *Laborem Exercens*. Its purpose is to highlight "the man who works" and who thus contributes to the economic development and the civil progress of his own country and of the whole world. Human work constitutes in fact the "essential key" of the whole social question. It is a fundamental criterion for a critical evaluation of the choices of internal and international politics which you are called upon to carry out at this General Conference of FAO. It is a criterion for the reform of economic relationships and systems at the worldwide level, always from the point of view of the good of man (cf. *Laborem Exercens*, No. 3).

(2160) 3. The present Twenty-first Session of the Conference of FAO, among other agenda items, is examining and striving to put into effect the concluding resolutions of the World Conference on Land Reform and Rural Development. I have already had the opportunity of expressing my thoughts in this regard during a meeting held on that occasion (Discourse of 14 July 1979. See above, par. 1763-1791).

(2161) At this moment I wish only to confirm, with the words of *Laborem Exercens*, that "In many situations radical and urgent changes are ... needed in order to restore to agriculture - and to rural people - their just value as the basis for a healthy economy, within the social community's development as a whole" (No. 21).

(2162) Therefore I appreciate in a particular way the call which your Assembly intends to make for the recognition of the primacy of agricultural development and food production on a national, regional and worldwide level. This is particularly important at the present time, when we are seeking to devise a strategy for worldwide development in the Eighties.

(2163) Furthermore, great importance must be attached to present political planning for worldwide development, whereby it is desired to encourage developing countries to become self-reliant, and to define and put into effect their own national strategy for development, with a model adapted to actual conditions, capacities and the unique culture of each country. But this should not provide a convenient excuse for more prosperous countries to evade their responsibilities, as though they could leave the burden of development to the needy countries alone; on the contrary, these latter must be guaranteed adequate external support, of a kind which respects their dignity and autonomy of initiative.

(2164) 4. There can be no doubt that the developing countries stand in need of technical and financial assistance in order to become self-sufficient in agricultural production and so be able to feed their own people.

(2165) A few developing countries are beginning to reach a level of self-sufficiency, at least in some basic products, often thanks to their own efforts aided by more prosperous countries. This is an encouraging sign; but there are many other countries with fewer resources and with serious food shortages, which need large-scale and urgent help in order to overcome their poverty.

(2166) The ever more obvious interdependence among the different countries of this world demands that differences of economic and political interests be overcome and that greater expression be given to the solidarity which binds all peoples in the one family.

(2167) But the demands of justice in world solidarity cannot be satisfied merely by the distribution of "surpluses", even if these are adequate and timely. For the demands of solidarity call for an ever greater and more effective willingness to place at the disposal of all people, especially those most in need of help for their development, "the various riches of nature: those beneath the ground, those in the sea, on land or in space" (*Laborem Exercens*, No. 12). The primary destination of the resources of the earth to the common good demands that the necessities of life be provided for all human beings before individuals or groups appropriate for themselves the riches of nature or the products of human skill.

(2168) Hence the need to bring about effective cooperation between highly advanced countries and countries that need their limited capacities and resources to be supplemented from outside. Therefore forms of help must be sought which avoid a continuous recourse to investments obtained through burdensome loans from private sources, or from sources not as sufficiently disinterested as the multilateral methods of the Intergovernmental Organizations.

(2169) 5. I wish above all to make the most earnest appeal possible to people's moral conscience for the concrete affirmation of the objective criteria of justice which must govern relationships among the subjects of the civil community, whether they be individuals, or groups and enterprises, or sovereign countries. In this sense recognition must be given to the obligations which bind, in the first place from the ethical point of view, the more advanced countries such as those of the so-called "North" to the developing countries of the so-called "South." Justice demands that each nation should assume its part of responsibility for the development of the needy nations in true international solidarity, aware that all peoples have equal dignity, and that, together, all the nations constitute a worldwide community. Hard decisions must be taken, with regard to the share that the economically rich nations will have to assume and with regard to the structures that must jointly be set up in order to create new and just relationships in all areas of development. All nations have a claim on the solidarity of all others, but the nations that see the very existence and dignity of their people threatened have a priority claim. Responding to this claim is not a luxury. It is a duty.

(2170) In offering these thoughts to your reflection, I wish to assure you once again of my esteem for your persons and of my total support for your work. As one whose entire ministry is to represent Christ on earth - the historical compassionate Christ who was solicitous for the needy and who fed the hungry - I cannot but testify to my profound admiration for the contribution that you are making, through concerted efforts, to the cause of humanity. May Almighty God sustain you in your mission.

23. Message of His Holiness John Paul II for the Third World Food Day. The Vatican, 12 October 1983.

Original: French (*)

(2171) The Third World Food Day, for which credit belongs to the Food and Agriculture Organization, takes on an importance which should not escape anyone living on this planet. It touches a crucial problem and one which causes divisions among social classes, countries and vast regions of the world. Humanity is becoming more aware of this problem, and it is the Church's constant concern to offer its contribution to its resolution. This is why, in conformity with the specific mission that falls to me on the plane of ethical teaching and of promoting the work of peace-making, I am anxious to launch an appeal to the Governments and to the peoples of all the continents - a new appeal to solidarity, which is especially appropriate within the framework of this Jubilee Year of the Redemption when the Church is extending an invitation to reconciliation with God and among men.

(2172) The Representatives of the Governments and of the various worldwide Organizations which are specialists in this problem are well aware that this sad phenomenon of poverty and hunger of numerous peoples of the globe is not, alas, a thing of the past. To be sure, natural calamities play their part in this tragedy. But we are surely obliged to acknowledge that men themselves contribute to the aggravation of socio-economic injustices which often result from ideological and political systems, or through the outbreak of war or of guerrilla activity.

(2173) The statistics furnished by the Specialized Agencies show that in the course of the last decade, the rate of world food supply has been adequate in a global sense, thanks to the increase of food production which has more than kept pace with that of the population. And discoveries, some of which have occurred recently, allow us to look to the future with confidence, while not losing sight of the foreseen population increases.

(2174) This having been said, it remains a fact that millions of human beings continue to suffer from hunger and even see their situation worsen, notably in Asia, Africa and Latin America. The extremely disturbing question then is that of the imbalances and shortages of food that exist in regions of the world particularly marked by a continuous diminution of available food supplies in the face of rapidly increasing population. Moreover, these truly unfavoured countries seem destined to an ever increasing dependence vis-a-vis the developed nations at the level of imports of farm-food produce. In this I see one of the great scandals of our era. It is indeed a situation of violence inflicted on human populations. And there can be no question of surmounting this situation through other forms of violence against life, but only through the accelerated establishment of an international economic order, truly more just and more fraternal, both on the level of production and on that of the distribution of goods.

(2175) This order requires not only an equitable distribution of the resources necessary to the life, and often to the survival of peoples in misery, thanks, for example, to the gift of surplus foods on the part of wealthy nations, but also a much more effective recourse to all the factors contributing to the concrete self-development of each nation: that is to say, adequate tools and above all investments and loans under conditions suitable for poor countries. To sum up, it is the whole economic system of the entire world that must be remodelled. What is needed is an international economic system that gives moral priority to the development of every country and of every human person.

(2176) Obviously, it is all those countries that are most advanced in their development and their Governments, which are the first called upon by the urgency of such international solidarity, and which have to gear their activity harmoniously with the International Organizations dependent on the United Nations, and also with the Agencies that specialize in the areas of agriculture, food supply, finance and commerce. It is likewise necessary to point out that the non-governmental Organizations that arise from generous and autonomous initiatives have their place as well, often

(*) AAS 76(1984) 136-139.

even an invaluable one. But in order to be fully effective, these organizations need to coordinate their activities with the official agencies.

(2177) The Christian people, for their part, would be unfaithful to the example and teaching of their Founder were they not to bring all their solicitude to their duties of solidarity with those who suffer from undernourishment. Chapter 25 of the Gospel according to Saint Matthew is revolutionary for anyone who reads it with calm objectivity and sincerity. Jesus Christ identifies himself in some way with the least of his brothers who would be able to say: "I was hungry." In every era, Christian communities have endeavoured to live at the service of the poor, of the starving! And often enough in an admirable manner! The honours list of saints and of institutions that came into existence for the relief of human misery would be interminable. I shall take the liberty merely to point out that the Holy See, through its Representative with FAO, was among the first to subscribe to and to launch the "Manifesto" of 14 May 1963 which proclaimed the right of man to eat to satisfy his hunger, and the socio-charitable Organizations of the Church were among the most eager to respond to the appeal of 16 October 1965 for the mobilization of youth in a united front against hunger.

(2178) In this year, dedicated in the whole world to the solemn commemoration of the event of the Redemption, I never cease to exhort the disciples of Christ to become reconciled to God and also to rediscover in a profound way the love of their fellow men, be they near or far away; and especially when they are weighed down by intolerable conditions of life, among which should be numbered undernourishment and hunger. I extend my appeal, beyond the faithful, to all men of good will to work for reconciliation among social classes and among the peoples of the whole world, and to participate very actively in the ever more clearly programmed and more resolute establishment of justice for all, of dignity for all, of happiness for all, thanks to an intense and concerted struggle against misery and hunger on our earth.

(2179) With all my heart, I invoke upon your important Assembly and on its future activity the divine light and power.

24. Address of His Holiness John Paul II to the 22nd Session of the Conference of FAO. The Vatican, 10 November 1983.

Original: English (*)

(2180) I am very happy that so many expert representatives of the States belonging to FAO and to the International Organizations have come from all over the world to take part in this Twenty-second Session of the Conference, and have accepted the invitation to this meeting which has become traditional from the very beginning of the presence of FAO in Rome. It is the second time that I personally have met you, in addition to my visit to the Headquarters of FAO in November 1979, an occasion which remains a happy memory.

(2181) I am glad to have the present opportunity to say once more *how deeply I esteem the work being done by FAO,* and how much I appreciate the recent documentation on the world food situation and on the work programmes and operation aspects of FAO. I am sure that you are more and more aware of the *Holy See's very special interest* in the problem of overcoming hunger and malnutrition, and of the fact of its close study of all undertakings and activities directed towards this humanitarian goal.

(2182) The right to have enough to eat is certainly *an inalienable human right,* and it imposes the obligation to ensure that everyone really does have enough food. It is obvious that the food problem cannot be considered from the point of view of occasional assistance or of the mere increase of production.

(*) L'Osservatore Romano, 11 Novembre 1983, 1.

(2183) I know that *the subject of food security* is at the center of the work programme of FAO, and has been so especially during the last ten years since the World Food Conference of November 1974. But today a more detailed view of food security is rightly being built up. It includes three specific objectives: to guarantee sufficient production; to stabilize as far as possible the flow of resources, especially for meeting emergencies; to make all the resources necessary for continuous and organic development available to all those needing them.

(2184) In order permanently to guarantee adequate supplies for the entire world population, two things must be done: favour the production and availability of food, at accessible prices, for a population that is continually expanding; and, more immediately, face the difficulties and crises in particular countries and regions.

(2185) According to the evaluations provided by your documentation, over the last ten years *food production has increased by a growth index higher than the increase of population.* From the sum of many data on different aspects of production and consumption, there emerges a comforting affirmation of a global sufficiency of food in relation to the present and future demands of the world population, even though this latter is increasing. *But with regard to individual countries* or *certain areas*, one cannot remain silent about the *seriousness of the present situation*, which is also confirmed by the forecasts for the coming decades, of the real problem of the imbalance between population and actual food availability. Particular concern is caused by the ever more obvious divergence, in practically the whole of the developing countries, between the food production growth index and the rate of population growth. This is in particular contrast with the fact that, in the developed countries taken as a whole, food production will continue to increase, resulting in surpluses with respect to the internal demand of these countries with a stable population.

(2186) But it is important to note the statement contained in a study with which you are familiar: "The lands of the Developing World *as a whole* (excluding East Asia) are capable of producing sufficient food to sustain twice their population in the year 1975, and one and a half times their population in the year 2000, even with low level of inputs" (FAO-UNFPA-IIASA Report FPA-INT-513).

(2187) This *contradictory situation* leads one to emphasize the moral duties deriving from the relationships between States and which must be borne in mind as criteria that should also inspire the decisions of your present Session of the Conference of FAO.

(2188) The reaffirmation of the primacy of agriculture and of the whole series of problems concerning the increase of food production certainly continues to be important. But it is clear that, over and above an increase of world production considered on a worldwide scale, *what is urgently needed is to ensure an effective increase in the individual developing countries.* It seems extremely significant, that today emphasis is placed upon the objective of the food self-sufficiency of these countries secured both by their self-development and by external support, but attained according to the now classical definition of self-reliance. Added to this is justified concern to avoid the aggravation of the phenomenon of the new form of dependence upon the developed countries, a phenomenon which has become more marked particularly in recent years, with the developing countries needing to import foodstuffs.

(2189) I therefore repeat a central subject of the Message which I sent for the Third World Food Day: it is a fresh appeal for solidarity addressed to the Governments and peoples of all the continents and involving the "accelerated establishment of an international economic order that is truly more just and fraternal on the level both of production and the distribution of goods" (Message of 16 October 1983. See above, par. 2174).

(2190) There remains the need to restate *the duty of all countries to increase production*: this holds good also for the most advanced. It must also be noted that the concentration of reserve stocks, which also exceed the limit considered by FAO as necessary for minimum security, is found in a restricted geographical area, in which a small number of countries hold almost a half of the world grain reserves. In addition, there are signs of a reduction of the area of cultivated land, not only as a result of erosion and the encroachment of deserts, but also through an artificial reduction of production. An effort must be made to avoid the situation whereby the abandonment of cultivation would lessen the capacity to provide needy countries with basic foodstuffs.

(2191) But it is clear that in this phase *the most obvious objective is certainly that of distribution.* This implies a distribution which is favorable to the developing countries, and an efficient control of commercial exchanges, above all with a reversal of protectionist tendencies.

(2192) Making foodstuffs available on acceptable conditions demands *a reduction of excessive consumption in certain countries.* It also requires an abandonment of the excessive defence of food prices by the high-production countries. Also called for are special measures in favour of countries with a low income and a food deficit, in order to assist ordinary importation of agricultural food products and especially to facilitate imports required by emergency needs.

(2193) It is sad to have to note that in this phase there is a *constant reduction in food aid.* One notes a contraction of the resources made available through the preferable multilateral means, while at the same time one does not see a corresponding increase of bilateral aid. Also with regard to reserves, one notes the praiseworthy favouring of the setting up of national reserves in the developing countries. But this does not mean an abandonment of the willingness to establish effective international reserves placed at the disposal of multilateral Agencies, or at least a system of coordinated national reserves.

(2194) But a fair distribution also calls for a wider access of all countries to all the factors, both proximate and remote, required for concrete development: these especially include *loans on favourable terms* to the poorer countries, thus bringing about an effective redistribution of income between the people. The stabilization of flows of resources and technical assistance programmes have become of primary importance.

(2195) In my Message of 16 October I explicitly stated: "It is clearly all the countries most advanced in their development and their Governments, that are the first to be faced by the urgency of this international solidarity" (See above, par. 2176).

(2196) I would like to add that this also implies *the acceptance of binding commitments.* As in other matters, one cannot fail to call for renewed good will in patiently seeking Agreements and Conventions, if possible also on points that are clearly delineated but concretely fixed and put into practice. In this sense one repeats the invitation to resume the necessary initiatives in the appropriate forums, for renewing the Conventions on grain trade and on the interrelated food assistance programmes; or at least the adoption even in a partial form of the objectives for food security, as in the proposal formulated by FAO.

(2197) The remarks made so far hold good not only *for the produce of the land* but especially at the present moment, they also concern the aspects of *fish production* in connection with the acceptance and putting into practice of the international norms sanctioned in the new Convention on the Law of the Sea.

(2198) A recent proof of *the Holy See's continuing willingness to collaborate* in all suitable initiatives has been given on the occasion of the meeting of scientists of world renown on the relationship between science and the fight against hunger.

(2199) The Pontifical Academy of Sciences has borne and continues to bear witness to the Church's willingness, also on the level of science, to collaborate even in the specific objectives of agricultural and food development (cf. *L'emploi des fertilisants et leur effet sur l'accroisement des récoltes, notamment par rapport à la qualité et à l'économie*, P.A.S. Scripta Varia, 38, 1973; and *Humanité et Energie*, P.A.S. Scripta Varia, 46, 1981).

(2200) Among the points on the agenda of this Session of the Conference of FAO, particular emphasis is given to the *urgent need for more training*: to develop the abilities of people to share in their own development and to prepare competent professionals. In this sphere too, I would like to repeat that the Church's institutions and associations are very willing to make available their various resources for assisting in teaching and training.

(2201) I would also add that the Church is able to collaborate in the proper forming of public opinion, so that not only the developing countries, but especially the advanced ones, will be able *to assume the sacrifices demanded by solidarity* and will work together constructively, using the resources placed at their disposal.

(2202) As I express the hope that the present Session will favour the effective accomplishment of the work programme of FAO for the next two years, I invoke upon your labours the light and the enthusiasm that come from Almighty God, in whom "we live and move and have our being" (*Acts* 17:28).

25. Homily of His Holiness John Paul II during the Mass celebrated in St. Peter's Basilica to commemorate the fortieth anniversary of FAO and the United Nations. The Vatican, 10 November 1985.

Original: French, English, Spanish, Italian (*)

"The Lord keeps faith forever, secures justice for the oppressed, gives food to the hungry" (*Ps*, 145 [146]:6-7).

(2203) These words of the responsorial psalm, which we have listened to in today's liturgy, are more significant than ever in the context of the celebration of the fortieth anniversary of the founding of the Food and Agriculture Organization. I have accepted with great pleasure the invitation extended to me to take part in this celebration.

(2204) I address a cordial and respectful greeting to the experts representing the member States of FAO, and to the senior officials, and I express my appreciation for their work and for the lofty purposes to which they are directing their efforts.

(2205) I greet all the other personalities and the members of the faithful who have wished to join us in this Eucharistic Liturgy of thanksgiving.

(2206) Your presence, distinguished ladies and gentlemen and dear brothers and sisters, reminds us of the efforts made by FAO to eliminate the obstacles and imbalances which impede the dynamism of production, such as is required for a proper distribution of the basic necessities of life. There is no need to say how close the Church is to you in this work of human solidarity. Having as her mission the continuation in time of the teachings and actions of the Divine Master, she does not cease to hear anew that moving exclamation that rose from his heart at the sight of the hungry multitude: "I have compassion on the crowd, because they have...nothing to eat; and I am unwilling to send them away hungry, lest they faint on the way" (*Mt.* 15:32).

(2207) There is no doubt that the present world situation confirms the most important and irreplaceable function of FAO. There is first of all the matter of supporting the continued development of the food self-sufficiency of each people, especially by increasing production and bringing about a fairer distribution of the available resources .

(2208) In addition to this basic action are the exceptional operations for emergency aid. Unfortunately, at present there are ever increasing requests for urgent interventions in particular zones and continents, such as the request of many African countries stricken by drought and famine. Food crises are increasing in number, not only as a result of adverse climatic conditions and natural disasters, but also a result of conflicts caused by economic policies which are not always suitable, and by the forced transfers of populations.

(*) Insegnamenti di Giovanni Paolo II, Vol. VIII,2 (1985), 1233-1240.

(2209) Thus, there are added ever greater commitments in order to meet in an adequate way the obvious needs of the population, including the people yet to be born, to respond to the requests of Governments, and to establish lines of joint and agreed action between member States of the Organization.

(2210) This solemn celebration also reminds me of the fortieth anniversary of the *United Nations Organization*, around which we see the harmonious operating of the whole system of specialized intergovernmental organizations. The Holy See very willingly associated itself with the commemoration of this anniversary, which recalls the coming into force of *the Charter of the United Nations*. Through the Cardinal Secretary of State, I have sent to Mr. Jaime de Piniés, President of the Fortieth General Assembly of the UN, a message reaffirming the moral support that the Holy See has always given to this organization from its very beginning, and I have encouraged specific cooperation aimed at promoting true peace and fruitful understanding between individuals and national communities.

(2211) On various occasions, the Church has expressed her esteem for and affirmation of this supreme forum of the families of peoples, and she constantly supports its functions and initiatives aimed at favouring sincere collaboration among the nations. On this fortieth anniversary, I wish to express once again my gratitude for the invitation extended to me in October 1979 to speak before the representatives to that General Assembly. That invitation was especially significant for me because, as I said at that solemn meeting, it "shows that the United Nations Organization accepts and respects the religious and moral dimension of those human problems that the Church attends to, in view of the message of truth and love that it is her duty to bring to the world" (AAS 71, p. 1146. See above, par. 75). During these forty years the international community has seen the Church and the United Nations Organization in ever increasing cooperation and solidarity, in defence "of man in his wholeness, in all the fullness and manifold riches of his spiritual and material existence" (*ibid.*, p. 1146. See above, par. 75).

(2212) At a moment in history when technology was being directed to the purpose of war, hegemony and conquest, and when man was killing man and nations destroying nations, the birth of this Organization was greeted by those preoccupied about humanity's destiny as a new safeguard of peace and hope; and as the real way destined to lead to the recognition and respect of the inalienable rights of individuals and of the communities of peoples.

(2213) It is my hope that this anniversary will strengthen that conviction and in particular - as I said in the Message of 14 October last - reinforce the moral and juridical authority of this Organization for the safeguarding of peace and for international cooperation in favour of the development and freedom of all peoples.

(2214) The United Nations will fulfil its high mission all the more effectively if in each member State the conviction grows that to govern people means to serve a plan of higher justice. The courageous and hope-filled vision that inspired those who drew up the 1945 Charter must never be disavowed, in spite of the difficulties and obstacles which it has encountered during these forty years. That vision will remain the ideal point of reference until those obstacles have been overcome. This is the fervent desire that I wish to renew at this liturgical celebration, as I pray to the Lord for the success of all efforts in favour of the cause of peace.

(2215) The scene presented by today's Gospel underlines the relationship between rich and poor by illustrating the difference of behaviour between the Scribes and the widow. In the modern world this contrast is being repeated by the disproportionate stages of development in different countries, a contrast which is currently referred to as the North-South relationship.

(2216) The Messiah utters a negative judgment in regard to those who, living in luxury and wealth, despise the poor; in regard to the rich who do not give to the poor as much as they might; or who, even when they do give, do so with an ostentation that betrays the fact that they are seeking their own glory: "Beware of the scribes who like to accept marks of respect in public and have the best seats in the synagogues a.nd the places of honour at banquets" (*Mk.* 12:38-39).

(2217) The words of the responsorial psalm, "The Lord upholds the widow and the orphan" (*Ps.* 145[146]:9), contrast with what the Gospel says about the Scribes, dismissing their external appearance of piety which is contradicted by the arbitrary judgments and injustices which they practise: "They devour the houses of widows and recite long prayers for appearances's sake" (*Mk.* 12:40).

(2218) On the other hand Jesus gives very high praise to the hidden gesture of the poor widow, who generously gives even what she needs for herself, and he contrasts this act with the offerings of so many rich people who give "sizable amounts," but with ostentation.

(2219) Jesus' warning invites us today to examine ourselves: to ask ourselves, that is, if the coming of the Kingdom has really caused the situations of power and extravagance existing in the world to be overturned. This could have happened if each individual had matched his or her faith with logical action, especially with regard to efforts in favour of the very poor, the marginal people and the despised.

(2220) Individuals and whole peoples will be finally judged by history in relation to how they actually fulfil their obligation to contribute to the good of their fellow human beings, in proportion to their own prosperity and in an effective spirit of worldwide shared responsibility according to justice.

(2221) It is to be hoped that everyone - individuals, groups, private undertakings and public bodies - will take proper care of the most needy, beginning with the basic right to satisfy one's own hunger.

(2222) Each individual should prepare, by present actions, so as to be ready to welcome the Messiah when he appears a second time and says: "Come, blessed of my Father, inherit the kingdom prepared for you from the foundation of the world" (*Mt.* 25:34).

(2223) What is being proposed is an examination of conscience that certainly begins with the personal life of each individual, concerning each one's awareness of wealth and poverty.

(2224) Today you are called to acknowledge the privilege of collaborating actively and loyally within the structures of international society. A true sense of responsibility in the proper use of the resources placed at the disposal of FAO demands above all that each person should possess and perfect his or her own professional skill and apply it seriously and accurately to the fulfillment of daily duties.

(2225) But the examination of conscience also extends to the level of the obligation of the member States of FAO to work together in the selection of international policies and concrete proposals that will lead to timely decisions and adequate results.

(2226) It is very important to achieve relationships based on international justice among peoples of the whole world and their States. But it is urgently necessary that solidarity among wealthier countries should also be intensified, with a wider application of multilateral arrangements.

(2227) Reflection on one's obligations as a member of FAO, and more broadly within the United Nations system, should lead to an affirmation of the duty of each people to contribute in proportion both to its own conditions of prosperity and to the needs of others.

(2228) It is desirable that a "World Treaty of Food Security" - such as the one which will be placed before the FAO Conference for its approval - should be considered and recognized as having the value not only of an ethical requirement but also as having juridical force. It is to be hoped that the Act which the Assembly approves will be given such effectiveness, at least vis-a-vis the member States, in the forms considered appropriate according to present-day international law.

(2229) On the other hand, it has to be recognized that there are recurring episodes of distrust and a frequent unwillingness to assume real and definite commitments which would adequately respond to needs and would subsequently be effectively maintained.

(2230) Too often, various forms of nationalism and protectionism hinder both the availability of foodstuffs vital to all without discrimination, and the transfer of the same from high-producing countries to countries less well provided. Such obstacles and modes of conduct openly contradict the principles of real justice in a spirit of solidarity and the putting into practice of the asserted readiness to cooperate with the providential power of God.

(2231) The Eucharistic Liturgy reminds us that Christ, Priest and Victim, offers himself also today without any limits. "But as it is, he has appeared once for all at the end of the age to put away sin by the sacrifice of himself" (*Heb.* 9:26). He immolated himself on the Cross for all humanity, "to bear the sins of many" (*Heb.* 1:28). He gave himself in order to conquer the sin of selfishness that often makes itself felt in the history of human society.

(2232) The Eucharist, which renews the supreme offering of Christ and his immolation for the salvation of his brethren, demands and effects purification of the heart from selfishness, so that the heart opens to others with a spirit of solidarity and of effective fraternal love.

(2233) It is necessary to go beyond the limits of strict justice, in imitation of the exemplary conduct of the widow, who teaches us to give with generosity even that which is meant for our own needs.

(2234) Above all one must remember that God does not measure human actions by a standard which stops at the appearances of "how much" is given. God measures according to the standard of the interior values of "how" one places oneself at the disposal of one's neighbour: he measures according to the degree of love with which one freely dedicates oneself to the service of the brethren.

(2235) The Church, which continues the religious mission of Christ, offers the necessary strength for constantly working according to justice in solidarity. Through Christ, who fully assumes a human nature and links it to the divine richness, living communion with God as Love is possible. This innermost strength of God can sustain human endeavours, in order that the fundamental law of life and of human co-existence according to the twofold principle of love of God and love of neighbor can be realized.

(2236) Just as the Prophet Elijah does not hesitate to ask the widow for her own share of her sustenance, the Pope does not hesitate today to ask the representatives of FAO to continue to support and develop the ordinary activities and the operations to be practically set in motion in favour of the poorest of the world.

(2237) The Church offers the initiatives of her own institutions and associations which operate among the various peoples and on the different continents.

(2238) Above all the Church claims as her obligation and inalienable right the corporal and spiritual works of mercy, especially those charitable works of mutual assistance intended for the alleviation of every human need (cf. *Apostolicam Actuositatem*, n. 8).

(2239) The Church likewise encourages every activity of the non-governmental organizations. In recent times these organizations have been asserting themselves through their growing strength and they are proving to be an efficient element in the concerted action that the whole of humanity must undertake for the benefit of the poorest of the poor. The Church hopes, however, that those voluntary activities will be carried out in a truly disinterested manner and beyond all partisan spirit.

(2240) Finally, the Church wants to share in the updated awareness of the work done by FAO in order to form public opinion in such a way that it will encourage the public authorities and private individuals in each nation to undertake ever broader initiatives in support of food and agricultural development and will secure active and constant sharing by all in worldwide action.

(2241) With this celebration we wish to thank the Lord for the good accomplished and for the generous contributions made hitherto. I hope that this will also be an occasion for a renewed commitment of each individual to ever more efficient and timely action in the future, according to the obligations and degrees of responsibility that each individual has in contemporary society.

26. Statement of the Holy See's Delegation at the World Food Conference. Rome, 11 November 1974.

Original: French

(2242) Last Saturday the Holy Father addressed to those participating in the Conference a Message which the awareness of his deep spiritual responsibility inspired in him at this crucial moment in the life of mankind. In the course of the present intervention, our Delegation will seek to point out certain implications of that Message, and, in its light, to indicate its own position, inspired by the desire to serve, according to the nature of the Holy See, in the face of some of the problems that we are dealing with together.

(2243) We have met here in order to carry out the first stage of the process of liberation from the poverty and famine which afflict an ever growing number of our contemporaries, many of them belonging to the most defenceless classes of society. This first stage can and must be decisive. The future in part depends on the energetic and concrete character that we shall manage to give to our conclusions.

(2244) To undertake, without any turning back, the task of warding off here and now the ravages of hunger and malnutrition in certain parts of the world, and hence to begin a tenacious battle against what causes these scourges and threatens to make them more widespread, is to face without any possibility of avoiding them the demands of international solidarity, above all that of a fair and lasting redistribution of the earth's resources. In a word, this task will meet with no success unless we recognize a possibility for each individual and each people to assume their responsibilities in the community, that is to say, of producing, exchanging and consuming in a measure adequate to their condition - and all this with full respect for the dignity of every person and all peoples. Confidence in the creativity of man and in technological progress must therefore be accompanied by a firm willingness to reform the structures which hold in thrall and render vain every effort towards the authentic construction of a national and international community which will offer to everyone the chance to live a truly human life.

(2245) This implies a resolutely new order of economic and social relationships, a new concept of commerce and its profits, a new civilization marked by frank solidarity in the mutual esteem and total respect of each for the others. Even the urgent measures of ensuring a sufficient supply of food have to be renewed in favor of a more genuine and more unselfish pooling of resources.

(2246) Reserving to itself the right to examine each resolution which will be submitted to us, my Delegation declares itself disposed, from this moment, to support those conclusions which reflect the exigencies that I have just described. We uphold the idea that, to justify such conclusions and to force ourselves to make them become a part of reality, a Declaration should precede the listing of conclusions - a Declaration which would contain principles enunciated in a concise and categorical manner. Starting from the postulate which all political options are proud to adopt - that of the dignity of man - such principles would be expanded by the proclamation, never yet so solemnly made, of the fundamental right of all men to be protected from hunger. It will not be a mere exercise of rhetoric if our conclusions will also mark - and this with a note of urgency - the commitment of all to accept the discipline imposed by the true priorities, those established in accordance with the rules of justice and solidarity and not those of national egoisms and acquired positions. Thus we shall answer the pathetic expectation which this Conference nourishes in so many who are deprived and in so many men of good will who are very ready to act, if they are only told how to do so. Moreover, in this way it will be possible to call the World Food Conference historic.

(2247) Mr. President, however carefully worked out our programmes and projects may prove to be, we will not find a solution if we do not apply themselves to the task of carrying them out: man is the master and artisan of his own advancement. This is applicable also to peoples: everyone knows today that saying this is in no way to undervalue outside assistance. We shall consider those points of our Agenda particularly concerned with the intensification of production. To satisfy a growing need, it is necessary to produce more; in order to respond more effectively to the qualitative demands of our nourishment, it is necessary to produce better. A network of factors and measures will have a part in producing these effects, but it is essential that there be an effort of creative activity from the very start of and throughout the course of all action. It is the mark of and the nobility of man - of every man - to be able thus to contribute to the harmonious development of the various collectivities of which he is part. In the sectors of food development, the artisans of development are above all the agricultural workers to whom the Holy Father devoted a long passage of his address of last Saturday. Without their full participation in the actions advocated by the draft resolution which we have before us, nothing will be done. The Document containing the "Proposals for Action" (E/Conf. 65/4), emphasizes this many times, for example, when it says: "But unless this increase is achieved in a manner that involves the poorest segment of the rural population, that is, the small farmer and the landless worker, in the production and the employment process, they will remain poor and undernourished. Relief assistance of food aid can reach only some of them and for a limited time and is unlikely to provide a permanent solution" (No. 346).

(2248) But when one speaks of associating the rural population in the efforts envisaged, it is in no way merely a matter of thinking of this process from the point of view of the mere perfecting of a work force. It is a matter of supporting and managing well a general action, calling for the collaboration of people who are aware of the meaning and value of their work, even when this work is very hard - people who bring to their work, through a free choice and self-control, judgment and perseverance. Hence the importance of promoting their integral development, in particular through instruction, basic training and preparation for responsibilities that will gradually extend to the different social links that bind each man to his neighbours. One can foresee the importance that women can have in such advancement, once their role and their calling are truly recognized in the rural milieu. It is similarly by thus widening horizons that it will be possible to think of forming, in the rural milieu, a young generation, on the one hand, dedicated to demanding from the land all that it can produce for man; but who, on the other hand, will not tolerate stagnation in the environment into which they find themselves born and in which they have chosen to stay. In this development, the rural family has a special place, for it is from the family above all that there comes concrete application of the principle consecrated by the Universal Declaration of Human Rights: "The family is the natural and fundamental element of society."

(2249) It goes without saying that, if it is to realize these aims, the civil authority must take on indispensable tasks of education and advancement. However, the State, even in its best intentions, would be, left to itself, very lacking in means in the face of this formidable task. The promotion of the well-being of the rural population is equally, if not at the very beginning, the result of community activities, first at the local and then at the regional level, of sharing of responsibility and of actions chosen and undertaken together. Here there fit in groups of a voluntary nature and intermediate bodies, especially if they really have their roots in the rural population itself. In this regard the Document already quoted says in an excellent way, evoking the essential role of agricultural cooperatives: "There really is no effective way to solve the problem of the small farmer until he ceases to be a small farmer by joining a bigger and more viable unity, not as a hired worker but as an active member with a strong stake in its success" (Proposals for Action, No. 353). It is in such units that man is trained to put himself at the service of others, according to the capacities of each one, and that it is possible to establish progressively a civic community marked by the freedom of each individual and the solidarity of all in the tasks undertaken; or, at least accepted no longer in the hope of making a profit, however small, but in the awareness that each individual must make his or her contribution as a person.

(2250) The discussions that have already taken place in our first Committee and the numerous amendments that have been put forward, some by our own Delegation, indicate that each person here is convinced of the need to base all action on a correct estimation of human resources. But if there is any subject that a Resolution text does not exhaust it is this one. After the Conference we shall all have to make an effort to ensure that these intentions do not remain in the state of pious hopes but that they really lead to what the Holy Father called in his address the "rehabilitation of agriculture and the reversal of present attitudes towards it" (See above, par. 2118).

(2251) The demographic problem has been touched upon in this forum, and this is not surprising, since it is the present and future population of the world for whom it is necessary to provide adequate food. It is a question of guaranteeing for this population an increasing availability of foodstuffs, and to do this it is necessary to intensify production within the context of a general development and to avoid wastage. It is here that we must begin. If at Bucharest agreement was reached on any point, it was on this one. It would be a deception to tackle the problem from the other end and to seek to solve the lack of food by reducing the number of those having a right to it. The population problem, which touches the sphere of life and love, finds its solution in the exercise of a responsibility freely assumed. Such a solution is the fruit of an authentic moral development. The Delegation of the Holy See could not therefore, subscribe to proposals of campaigns for birth control; nor to an ambiguous promotion of the limitation of births which would not ensure a just place to full respect of the ethical, cultural and spiritual factors connected with the safeguarding of life and of the laws which regulate its transmission.

(2252) In our opinion, no one will blame this Conference for a lack of clarity on the extent and urgency of this problem; nor will anyone suspect any of its members of lacking in good will or in determination in the search for effective solutions. For it is primarily on the States that lies the responsibility for finding a way out of this distressing crisis. None of us would wish to disappoint the expectations of the victims of hunger, but do we not feel powerless to ensure that our meeting leads to resolutions and actions that will truly respond to everyone's anxious desire not to halt at the very beginning of the road that has to be travelled?

(2253) At the end of this statement we would like to put forward a few modest suggestions to assist towards a successful conclusion. First of all, we venture to think that it is time to remove the mistrust which has been progressively created with regard to international actions organized at the international level; and to unanimously express a strong preference for multilateral actions. If they are well conducted and with sufficient means, such actions have the advantage of being more disinterested and fairer for everyone. It is not up to the Holy See to pronounce itself concretely in favour of one or another international solution in order to ensure the continuation of the effort begun here. However, the crux of the problem surely lies not finally, in the form of institution, but in the degree of confidence that all the States give to the formula of the international community and in the contribution that they make, not as an obligatory concession to the spirit of the times, but as a more substantial sharing in the desire to build a new world. It is rightly said that our problems are dependent in the long run on political will. Is it not on this level that we should begin to exercise it?

(2254) On the other hand, however far-reaching and effective their intention, governmental actions will not succeed in such a situation, if the peoples themselves do not contribute their consent and cooperation. This has just been indicated above in regard to the commitments of the rural population in a complete process of development. It must also be said of the public in general, in both the developed and the developing countries. These are the electorates which accept the decisions of governments: it is the people who must live concretely the actions which are proposed, with all their concomitant difficulties. And often in these great problems of humanity there can also be applied the old adage: *vox populi, vox Dei.* A vigorous impetus from below can inspire those in power with what they sometimes hesitate to conceive of or to carry out. In this regard the responsibility of those who control the media of information and communication is enormous: they owe it to humanity to use them for its greatest good.

(2255) It is also necessary to point out the complementary and indispensable role of private associations - also known as "non-governmental" - which must share in the efforts of the governmental and intergovernmental sector, while at the same time keeping the spontaneity, originality and liberty of action which are proper to them. These are the aid and assistance organizations, the scientific and educational organizations, as well as the consumer groups which play an important role in the improvement of nutrition and in the fight against excessive consumption.

(2256) The Church, for her part, is already engaged in a constant action to stimulate the faithful to realize ever more clearly the problems of the whole human family and to strive to solve them. On the occasion of the recent Synod, the Bishops, united with the Pope, addressed a Message to the world on 23 October, in which we read: "Nations and peoples must undertake a concerted action of solidarity with the coming United Nations World Food Conference. We invite governments to a profound conversion of their attitude towards the victims of hunger, we ask them to accept the imperatives of justice and reconciliation and to find quickly the means of feeding those who are without food."

(2257) I can assure you, Mr. President, that what the Synod asks of governments, the different structures in the Church constantly try to promote among all the faithful. In the entire world there is a network of forces: of the clergy and the laity, of old and young, of citizens of the countries concerned, in union with their brothers and sisters of other nations, all trying to come into direct contact with human poverty and to alert the more affluent Christians to be concerned with this problem with all their heart. These activities will be intensified still more: the Holy Father and the bishops do not cease to urge it; and our young people demand it of us. In union with other Christians and with all men of good will, we are engaged here in a great common task in order that there may be realized the appeal addressed to you by the Holy Father: "*No more hunger, hunger never again!*"

CHAPTER VII

THE DEBT QUESTION

AT THE SERVICE OF THE HUMAN COMMUNITY: AN ETHICAL APPROACH TO THE INTERNATIONAL DEBT QUESTION
Vatican City, 27 December 1986

Document of the Pontifical Commission "Iustitia et Pax", published as an official document of the United Nations General Assembly on 27 February 1987 (Doc.A/42/157).

Original: English

PRESENTATION

(2258) *The phenomenon of international indebtedness has sharply increased in the last few year, presenting new challenges to the international community both because of its size and its implications.*

(2259) T*he remote causes for this phenomenon go back to the time when widely shared opinions about growth possibilities led developing countries to look for capital and commercial banks to offer credits for financial investments, sometimes at high risk. The prices for raw materials were favourable and the majority of debtor nations remained solvent.*

(2260) *The first and second oil crises of 1974 and 1979, the fall in the price of raw materials and the abundance of petrodollars in search of profitable investments, as well as the effects of overly-ambitious development programmes, contributed to the massive indebtedness of many developing countries. At the same time, industrialized countries were taking protectionist measures, while worldwide, interest rates were going up. Debtor countries become increasingly incapable of meeting even the interest on their debt.*

(2261) *In the last three or four years, the accumulation of payments due has reached such a level that many countries are no longer in a position to honour their agreements, and find themselves forced to seek further loans, thus getting caught in a web, escape from which has become very difficult to predict.*

(2262) *Debtor countries, in fact, find themselves caught in a vicious circle. In order to pay back their debts, they are obliged to transfer ever greater amounts of money outside of the country. These are resources which should have been available for internal purpose and investment and therefore for their own development.*

(2263) *The phenomenon of indebtedness brings to the fore the growing interdependence of economies whose mechanisms - capital flows and commercial exchanges - have become subject to new constraints. Thus external factors heavily condition the evolution of the debt of developing countries. In particular, floating and unstable exchange rates, the variations in interest rates and the temptation of industrialized countries to maintain protectionist measures have created an increasingly unfavourable environment for debtor countries that thus become still more vulnerable.*

(2264) *When credit agencies consider the situation solely from the economic and monetary angle, they often impose on the debtor countries terms, in exchange for accrued credit, that can contribute, at least in the short term, to unemployment, recession, and a drastic reduction in the standard of living. This causes suffering, first of all for the poorest as well as for certain sectors of the middle class. In brief, it is a situation that is intolerable and, in the medium term, disastrous for the creditors themselves. Debt servicing cannot be met at the price of the asphyxiation of a country's economy, and no government can morally demand of its people privations incompatible with human dignity.*

(2265) *Faced with demands that are often contradictory, the countries in question have not hesitated to react. Initiatives on both regional and international levels have multiplied. Some have advocated radical unilateral solutions. But the majority have taken into account the globality of the* *problem and its profound implications, not only on the economic and financial level, but also in its social and human dimensions which place before the responsible parties ethical choices.*

(2266) *It is to this ethical aspect of the problem that Pope John Paul II has frequently called the attention of international leaders, particularly on his Message to the 40th General Assembly of the United Nations, October 14, 1985 (n. 5).*

(2267) *Conscious of her mission to shed the light of the Gospel on situation involving the responsibilities of men and women, the Church once again invited all the parties involved to examine the ethical implications of the question of the external debt of developing countries, in order to arrive at just solutions that respect the dignity of those who would be strongly affected by its consequences.*

(2268) *For this reason, the Holy Father asked the Pontifical Commission "Iustitia et Pax" to deepen the reflection on the problem and to propose to the different parties involved - creditor and debtor countries, financial agencies and commercial banks - some criteria for weighing the situation, and method of analysis for "an ethical approach to the international debt question".*

(2269) *The Pontifical Commission "Iustitia et Pax" expresses its fervent hope that this document might contribute to a clarification of the choices to be made by those who exercise responsibility in this area, one which today has become a privileged place for international solidarity.*

(2270) *The Commission also nourishes the hope that these reflections will give renewed confidence to those persons and nations most severely tested, by once again strongly repeating that economic structures and financial mechanisms are at the service of the human person and not vice versa, and that relationships of exchange and the mechanisms of finance which go with them can be reformed before shortsightedness and egoism - be they private or collective - degenerate into irremediable conflicts.*

Roger Card. Etchegaray
President
Pontifical Commission
"Iustitia et Pax"

Bishop Jorge Mejía
Vice President
Pontifical Commission
Iustitia et Pax"

INTRODUCTION

(2271) Political officials and economists, social and religious leaders, as well as public opinion throughout the world, recognize the fact that the debt levels of the developing countries constitute a serious, urgent and complex problem due to their social, economic and political repercussions. The development of the debtor countries and, at times, their very independence are endangered. The living conditions in the poorest countries have become worse, and the international financial system is going through a series of unsettling shocks.

(2272) Creditors and debtors have tried to come up with immediate - and at times even more long term - solutions on a case by case basis. Albeit insufficient and limited, these efforts need to be pursued in a spirit of dialogue and mutual comprehension, in order to see more clearly the rights and responsibilities of each party.

(2273) At the same time that current economic conditions have affected the situation of developing countries to the point that some of them, especially in Latin America and Africa, are on the breaking point because of their inability to meet their debt servicing obligations, the international financial and monetary structures are also being challenged. How did this happen? What changes in behaviour patterns and in institutions will make it possible to establish equitable relations between creditors and debtors and keep the crisis from continuing and becoming even more dangerous?

(2274) The Church shares these concerns, which are international, regional and national in nature, and wishes to reiterate and specify the principles of justice and solidarity which will help in seeking solutions. The Church speaks first and foremost to the principal agents in the financial and monetary worlds. In so doing, she hopes to enlighten the moral conscience of the decision-makers whose choices cannot disregard ethical principles, but she does so without proposing action programmes which would be outside her field of competence.

(2275) The Church speaks to all peoples, especially those most in need, who are the first to suffer the repercussions of these disorders and do so with feelings of fatalism, defeat, latent injustice and sometimes revolt. The Church wishes to rekindle within them hope and confidence in the possibility of resolving the debt crisis with the participation of all parties and in full respect of each party.

(2276) The best way to tackle these serious issues would seem to be in a global perspective which would be at the same time an ethical approach. For this reason, it would seem necessary to highlight the ethical principles applicable to these complex situations before considering the particular choices that those concerned may be led to make, either in emergency situations or in the medium or long term.

(2277) The present text has made use of many studies on the international debt that have already appeared. Ethical in nature, this global perspective allows all the responsible parties, be they persons or institutions, on both a national and international level, to carry out a reflection, adapted to the situations that are within their competence.

(2278) To all those who will heed its words, the Church expresses, from the very outset, its firm conviction that cooperation which goes beyond collective egoism and vested interests can provide for an efficient management of the debt crisis and, more generally, can mark progress along the path of international economic justice.

I - ETHICAL PRINCIPLES

1. Create New Forms of Solidarity

(2279) The debt of the developing countries must be placed in a broader context of economic, political and technological relations which point to the increased interdependence between countries, as well as to the need for international collaboration in pursuing the objectives of the common good. In order to be just, the interdependence should give rise to new and broader expressions of solidarity which respect the equal dignity of all peoples, rather than lead to domination by the strongest, to national egoism, to inequalities and injustices.[1] The monetary and financial issue therefore commands attention today in an urgent and new way.[2]

2. Accept Coresponsibility

(2280) Solidarity implies an awareness and acceptance of coresponsibility for the causes and the solutions relative to international debt. The causes are both internal and external. While they are specific to each country and to each political and economic system, these causes also stem from evolutions in the international environment which depend to a great extent on the actions and decisions of the developed countries. Acknowledgement of the sharing of responsibility for the causes will make possible a dialogue which will seek joint means of solution. Coresponsibility concerns the future of countries and of entire populations, but also the possibilities of international peace based on justice.

3. Establish Relations of Trust

(2281) Coresponsibility will help to create or restore relations based on trust between nations (creditors and debtors) and between the various agents (political authorities, commercial banks, international organizations) for cooperation in the search for solutions. Mutual trust is an indispensable value which must be constantly renewed. It nourishes belief in another person's good faith, even when difficulties prevent that person from respecting his commitments, and makes it possible to continue treating him as a partner. This trust must be based on concrete attitudes which ground it.

4. Know How to Share Efforts and Sacrifices

(2282) In order to emerge from the international debt crisis, the various partners must agree on an equitable sharing of the adjustment efforts and the necessary sacrifices, taking into account the priority to be given to the needs of the most deprived peoples. It is the responsibility of the countries that are better off to assume a larger share.

5. Foster the Participation of All

(2283) Financial and monetary officials have the prime responsibility for finding solutions to the debt crisis, but they share this responsibility with political and economic leaders. All social categories are called to acquire a better grasp of the complexity of the situation and actively to cooperate in the choice and implementation of the necessary policies. In these new ethical domains, the Church is called upon to specify the requirements of social justice and solidarity with respect to the situations of individual countries, seen within an international context.

---

[1] Cf. Paul VI, Encyclical *Populorum Progressio*, March 26, 1967, nn. 64, 65, 80.

[2] Cf. Congregation for the Doctrine of the Faith, *Instruction on Christian Freedom and Liberation*, March 22, 1986, n. 89: "Solidarity is a direct requirement of human and supernatural brotherhood. The serious socio-economic problems which occur today cannot be solved unless new fronts of solidarity are created: solidarity of the poor among themselves, solidarity with the poor to which the rich are called, solidarity among the workers and with the workers. Institutions and social organizations at different levels, as well as the State, must share in a general movement of solidarity. When the Church appeals for such solidarity, she is aware that she herself is concerned in a quite special way."

6. Identify Emergency and Long Term Measures

(2284) The urgent nature of the situation in some countries calls for immediate solutions in the context of an ethics of survival. The main effort will have to be brought to bear on economic and social rehabilitation: recovery of growth rates, productive investments, resource creation, equitable sharing... In order to avoid a return to crisis situations with overly abrupt changes in the international environment, a reform of the financial and monetary institutions also needs to be studied and fostered.[3]

II - ACTION IN EMERGENCY SITUATIONS

(2285) In the case of some developing countries, the total amount of the debts contracted, and especially the interest and principal payments due each year, are so high in relation to available financial resources that meeting these obligations would cause severe damage to their economies and standard of living of their populations, particularly the poorest classes. In addition, this critical situation is worsened by external circumstances which tend to lower their export revenues (drop in the prices of raw materials, difficulties in access to protected foreign markets) or make their debts all the more difficult to service (high and unstable interest rates, excessive and unpredictable fluctuations in exchange rates). Unable to meet their commitments to their various creditors, some of these countries are on the very brink of bankruptcy. International solidarity calls for emergency measures to ensure the survival of these countries.

(2286) The first thing to do is to foster dialogue and cooperation on the part of all for immediate help. It is also necessary to avoid payment defaults which could destabilize the international financial system, with the attendant risks of a generalized crisis. Therefore, an ethics of survival should guide attitudes and decisions: avoid breaches between creditors and debtors as well as any unilateral termination of prior commitments; respect the insolvent debtor and do not burden him with immediate and intolerable demands which he cannot meet. Even if such demands are legal, they can become an abuse. With the Gospel as the source of inspiration, other types of action could also be contemplated such as granting extensions, partial or even total remission of debts, or helping the debtor to regain solvency.

(2287) The immediate needs of countries in such difficulties are a priority, but not to be forgotten are the broader perspectives of the international community and the precedent-setting nature of the solutions adopted.

(2288) The leaders of a given country bear the responsibility for monitoring their foreign debt level in order to avoid having to cope suddenly with such an extreme situation through shortsightedness or careless management.

(2289) One way to contribute to healthier international economic relations and to foster agreement about emergency measures to be adopted would be to foresee, prevent and attenuate such crises which are unfairly advantageous to some, excessively injurious to others, and often lead to unjust speculation. Coordinating structures need to be set up as quickly as possible, and doing so ahead of time would enable them to become operational as soon as needs arise, as is

---

[3] *Ibid.*, n. 91: "International solidarity is a necessity of the moral order. It is essential not only in cases of extreme urgency but also for aiding true development. This is a shared task, which requires a concerted and constant effort to find concrete technical solutions and also to create a new mentality among our contemporaries. World peace depends on this to a great extent."

done in the case of standing security and protection plans in other sectors that deal with possible catastrophes and which have saved many human lives.

(2290) Because of their mandate, certain international organizations bear a special responsibility. For example, the International Monetary Fund (IMF) is responsible for helping member States to redress deficits in their balance of payments and to resolve their monetary difficulties. To this end, the IMF has at its disposal the necessary financial resources. Its role, as well as its methods of intervention, have developed considerably over the last few years. In numerous cases, however, the IMF's decisions have been ill-received by the leaders and the general public of countries in difficulty; the decisions in question may seem to have been imposed in an authoritarian and technocratic way without due consideration for urgent social requirements and the specific features of each situation. It would be advisable to bring out clearly that dialogue and the service of all concerned are values which guide the actions taken by the IMF.

(2291) The various creditors - States and banks - also bear very concrete responsibility in the area of emergency measures. Coordination in necessary if this responsibility is to be carried out justly and efficaciously, with an equitable sharing of immediate duties both in regard to the country in difficulty and to the IMF.

(2292) Coresponsibility comes into play in the search for caused as well as decisions concerning immediate measures to be adopted. In this way, special care needs to be taken to identify, among the various causes of a country's debt situation, those that are attributable to global mechanisms which seem beyond control; for example, the fluctuations of currency used for international contracts, shifts in the prices of raw materials which are often the object of speculation on the major stock markets, or the sharp drop in oil prices.

(2293) Helping whoever is in dire need is indispensable but it is not enough. That type of assistance would even be illusory if at the same time the foundations were not laid for economic and financial recovery in the future. Most often the crisis does not depend on a simple accidental convergence of factors but rather on deeper causes which a crisis brings to the surface. Emergency arrangements must be linked to medium and long term adjustment measures.

III - JOINT ASSUMPTION OF RESPONSIBILITY FOR THE FUTURE

(2294) Financial and monetary relations between countries are complex and in constant evolution. According to the relative value of a country's currency, its trade volume, available natural resources and the technical capacity to exploit them, as well as the degree of confidence it is able to generate abroad, each country occupies a position of weakness or strength, power or dependence which, in turn, is also subject to change.

(2295) An indepth analysis must therefore be made in order to determine the specific responsibilities of each country in terms of both immediate and future action. An initial overview of the situation shows that there is a plurality of agents and organizations, each with specific functions and more or less extensive freedom of action - and therefore of initiative and responsibilities. These agents differ according to their functions and their international positions and can be grouped as follows: the industrialized and developing countries, the creditor and the debtor countries, the national and international commercial banks, the large transnational corporations, and the multilateral financial organizations (e.g. the World Bank, the International Monetary Fund, regional development banks). By reviewing each party's role, resources and margin of freedom of action, it will be possible to bring out more clearly respective responsibilities and propose ethical principles which guide decision-making, alter behaviour patterns, and transform the institutions in view of a better service of humanity. All are called to participate in the building of a more just world, one of whose fruits will be peace. "We see peace", said Pope John Paul II, "as an indivisible fruit of just and honest relations on every level - social, economic, cultural and ethical - of human life on this earth... To you, business men, to you who are responsible for financial and commercial organizations, I appeal: to examine anew your responsibilities towards your brothers and sisters."[4]

This fresh consideration of roles will make it possible to avoid the temptation of fatalism or of powerlessness in face of the complexity of the bonds of interdependence and also to create new spaces of freedom - and therefore responsibility - to be assumed and shared.

III. 1 Responsibilities of the Industrialized Countries

(2296) In a world of increased interdependence among nations, an ethic of expanded solidarity will help to transform economic relations (commercial, financial, and monetary) into relations of justice and mutual service, while, at present, they are often relations based on positions of strength and vested interests.[5]

(2297) Due to their greater economic power, the industrialized countries bear a heavier responsibility which they must acknowledge and accept even if the economic crisis has often challenged them with grave problems of reconversion and employment.[6] The time is over when they can act without regard for the effects of their own policies on other countries. They have to evaluate the positive and negative repercussions of these policies on the other members of the international community and introduce changes if the consequences constitute too much of a burden for other countries and especially the poorest ones. The collective egocentricity of a nation is manifested when it disregards the effects of interdependence or when it does not evaluate such effects and keep them under control. The responsibility for forming public opinion to international openness and to the duties of extended solidarity falls upon social, economic, educational, and religious leaders, and especially upon politicians, who are all too often prone to assign exclusive priority to national interests instead of explaining to their fellow citizens the positive effects of a more equitable international sharing of resources. In his encyclical on "The Development of Peoples" (n. 48) Pope Paul VI had already stated: "Government officials, it is your concern to mobilize your peoples to form a more effective world solidarity, and above all to make them accept the necessary taxes on their luxuries and their wasteful expenditures, in order to bring about development and to save peace." To speak of sharing, even to propose a certain austerity, will be heeded if one appeals to the values of brotherhood and solidarity for peace and development.

(2298) In the face of the challenge of developing countries' increasing debt, the responsibility of the industrialized countries applies in particular to the following areas:

(2299) 1. The debt situation of the developing countries has become even more acute because of the world economic crisis (drop in the standard of living of the poorest classes, increased unemployment...) which weigh heavily on the people in those countries. An enduring and sustained recovery in the industrialized countries will help the world economy to pull out of the crisis and help the debtor countries to honour their debts in the medium and long term without overly jeopardizing their own development. The industrialized countries are trying to develop economic policies which will relaunch economic growth in their own best interests and those of their

---

[4] John Paul II, *Message for the 1986 World Day of Peace*, nn. 4, 7.

[5] Congregation for the Doctrine of the Faith, *Instruction on Christian Freedom and Liberation*, n. 16: "New relationships of inequality and oppression have been established between the nations endowed with power and those without it. The pursuit of one's own interest seems to be the rule for international relations, without the common good of humanity being taken into consideration."

[6] Cf. *ibid.*, n. 90: "The principle that goods are meant for all, together with the principle of human and supernatural brotherhood, express the responsibilities of the richer countries toward the poorer ones. These responsibilities include solidarity in aiding the developing countries, social justice through a revision in correct terms of commercial relationships between North and South, the promotion of a more human world for all".

populations. However, they must measure the effects of those policies on developing countries and, if necessary, modify those current rules of international trade which represent an obstacle to a more just distribution of the fruits of that growth. Otherwise, this very growth will further marginalize the poorest countries and increase the inequalities between nations. The application of economic policies which will lead to growth for all, while keeping a lid on inflation, another source of increased inequality, is a difficult yet challenging task. On the part of political, economic, and social leaders, it demands qualities of expertise and impartiality, an openness to the needs of other countries, and imagination in order to find new courses of action.

(2300) 2. The industrialized countries have to do away with the protectionist measures which hinder exports from the developing countries. This will increase the economic possibilities of those countries, especially if technical know-how is shared as well. The industrialized countries will need to plan a reconversion of their economies with timely buffering of the social effects on their own populations. The current technical and economic competition underway between countries and, above all, between the industrialized ones themselves, is without restraint and is assuming the shape of a ruthless war in no way concerned about the harsh effects on the weaker countries. Ever attentive to their appeals, the Church invites all persons of good will, and especially political and economic leaders, to find the ways and means for improved international sharing of economic activities and labour.[7]

(2301) 3. The interest rates charged by industrialized countries are high and make reimbursement very difficult for the debtor countries. A coordination of the industrialized countries' financial and monetary policies will make it possible to bring these rates down to a more reasonable level and avoid erratic fluctuations in exchange rates. The latter often prompt illicit profits on currency speculation and drains in national capital reserves, a new and additional cause of impoverishment for the developing countries.

(2302) 4. International trade conditions (especially the instability of price of raw material) would need to be carefully reanalyzed in mutual agreement with the countries concerned and with the specialized help of the competent international institutions so that justice and international solidarity would prevail where national interests are overly and exclusively dominant.

Adopting measures to relaunch growth, reducing protectionism, lowering interest rates, ad assigning a just value to raw materials all seem to be the responsibility of industrialized countries in contributing to a "development in solidarity of mankind."[8]

III. 2. Responsibilities of the Developing Countries

(2303) The acceptance of international coresponsibility on the part of the developing countries implies an analysis of the domestic causes behind the increase in their overall indebtedness. It also means planning for the necessary adjustment policies to alleviate the weight of their debt, as much as this depends on them, as well as promoting their own development along the lines of the aforementioned encyclical of Pope Paul VI: "World unity, ever more effective, should allow all peoples to become the artisans of their destiny," with the wish that: "may the day dawn when international relations will be marked with the stamp of mutual respect and friendship, of interdependence in collaboration, the betterment of all seen as the responsibility of each individual."[9]

(2304) A detailed examination of the current debt situation will bring out the specific nature of each developing country, both in terms of internal and external causes, as well as the solutions and the outlook for the future. The evident diversity of these situations is due to numerous factors; e.g. more or less abundant and more or less well managed natural resources (energy re-

---

[7] Cf. John Paul II, Encyclical *Laborem Exercens*, September 14, 1981, n. 18.

[8] Cf. Paul VI, Encyclical *Populorum Progression*, nn. 56-66.

[9] *Ibid.*, n. 65

sources and mines, arable land, climate, ease of communications), the development of human resources, national policy orientations(economy, social affairs, finance, monetary matters). A case by case study would provide for a more equitable evaluation of the coresponsibilities and the solutions adopted, while taking into consideration the bonds of solidarity between all the developing countries, which have every right to consult with one another on a regional and world level.

(2305) It would be highly recommendable for the decision-makers in a given country to take part in an analysis of the situation, especially with respect to the present financial and monetary crisis. In their concern for truth in participation, they will need the civic and moral courage to brief their population on the responsibility which is proper to each individual and each social category in the country. This will serve to build a consensus on the economic adjustment measures to be adopted, on a true distribution of the social efforts to be agreed upon, and on the priorities in the targets to be selected. Especially for the leaders of a country in economic and financial difficulty, it is often tempting to shift full responsibility to other countries, in order to avoid having to explain their own actions, errors, and even abuses, as well as to avoid having to propose any changes which would affect them directly. The denunciation of the injustices of others, be they either committed or tolerated, will fall on deaf ears unless,at the same time, one is willing to explain one's own actions. "It is too easy to throw back on others responsibility for injustices, if at the same time one does not realize how each one shares it personally, and how personal conversion is needed first."[10] This applies to the Church as well.[11]

(2306) The line of demarcation between the rich and the poor does not only cut through nations. It also divides social categories and regions in each country. There are rich people in poor countries and poor people in rich countries. Within the same country , there are poorer regions and more prosperous ones. Pope John XXIII had underlined these new aspects of justice back in 1961. "The evolution of historical situations brings out into ever greater relief how the exigencies of justice and equity not only have a bearing on the relations between dependent workingmen and contractors or employers, but concern also the relations between different economic sectors and between areas economically more developed and those economically less developed within the individual political communities; and on the world plane, the relations between countries with a different degree of economico-social development".[12]

(2307) The various groups in authority in the developing countries must accept having their actions and any responsibilities they may have in their country's indebtedness scrutinized: e.g. negligence in the setting up of suitable structures or abuses in the use of existent ones, tax fraud,corruption, currency speculation, national capital reserve drain,[13] kickbacks in international contracts... This duty of transparency and truthfulness will make it easier to establish individual responsibilities, to avoid unjustified suspicions, and to propose suitable and necessary forms for institutions as well as for personal behaviour. "The structures established for people 's good are of themselves incapable of securing and guaranteeing that good. The corruption which in certain countries affects the leaders and the State bureaucracy, and which destroys all honest social life, is a proof of this. Moral integrity is a necessary condition for the health of society. It is therefore

---

10 Paul VI, Letter *Octogesima Adveniens* to Cardinal Maurice Roy, May 14, 1971, n. 48.

11 Cf. Synod of Bishops, *Justice in the World*, 1971, nn. 42-51.

12 John XXIII, Encyclical *Mater et Magistra*, May 15, 1961, n. 122. Cf. Congregation for the Doctrine of the Faith, *Instruction on Christian Freedom and Liberation*: "New relationships of inequality and oppression have been established between the nations endowed with power and those without it" (n.6). "Whoever possesses technology has power over the earth and men. As a result of this, hitherto unknown forms of inequality have arisen between those who possess technology and those who are simple users of technology" (n. 12).

13 The "drain" of national capital reserves towards other countries does not concern the developing countries alone. However, it does entail more serious consequences for the developing countries in debt, especially when the capital drain involves substantial amounts. A moral judgement in these new areas must begin with an indepth analysis before proposing solutions.

necessary to work simultaneously for the conversion of hearts and for the improvement of structures."[14]

(2308) The improvement of individual and collective behaviour with respect to financial gains and the institutional reforms[15] will strengthen or reestablish national confidence, as well as that of other countries, in accepting the adjustment measures to be adopted and in cooperating in their effective implementation. For political, economic, and social leaders, it is a moral obligation to put themselves concretely at the service of the common good of their respective countries without pursuing personal gain. They must see their function as a service to the community with a direct concern for an equitable sharing of goods, services, and jobs among all, giving priority to the needs of the poor, and carefully monitoring the repercussions on the poor of the economic and financial measures they deem necessary, in all conscience, to adopt. This quest for social justice in political and economic decisions will be all the more credible and effective to the extent leaders themselves adopt a life style in keeping with the one their countrymen are compelled to accept under the difficult conditions of the country. In this sense, Christian leaders will allow themselves to be challenged by the demands of the Gospel.

(2309) In the face of increasing indebtedness and considering the diversity of respective situations, the specific responsibility of the developing countries will apply particularly to the following areas:

(2310) 1. It is advisable to mobilize all the available national resources, material as well as human, to promote sustained economic growth and assure the country's development.

Economic growth is not an end in itself. It is a necessary means of meeting the basic needs of a population, taking into account demographic growth and the legitimate aspirations for an improved standard of living (e.g. public health, education, culture, consumer goods). The creation of wealth is to be encouraged in order to ensure a broader and more just distribution among all.

(2311) The factors inherent in economic growth are numerous, complex, and at time difficult to control and coordinate. The duty of those in positions of responsibility in both the private and the public sectors is to take all this factors into consideration in their decisions. This implies expertise and a concern for the common good. These factors include the choice of priority sectors, strict selection of capital investments, reduction in public spending (especially expenditures for reasons of prestige and armaments), more rigorous management of public enterprises, control over inflation, support of national currency, reform of the tax system, sound agrarian reform, initiatives to private enterprises, and the creation of jobs. All of these are areas in which the Church, by recalling the human and ethical dimension, addresses a particular call to Christians to work on concrete solutions.

(2312) Improved growth rates will make it possible to meet foreign debt commitments (capital and interest) gradually and in a better way, and to reestablish more balanced and confident relations with other countries. The needs of future generations must also be taken into account. This is a duty of solidarity and justice in their regard.

(2313) 2. International solidarity, in the case of developing countries, implies an openness which, if just and balanced, is a good in itself. Pope Paul VI mentioned nationalism among the obstacles to be overcome for the united development of humanity: "Nationalism isolates people from their true good. It would be especially harmful where the weakness of national economies demands rather the pooling of efforts, of knowledge and of funds, in order to implement programmes of development and to increase commercial and cultural exchange."[16]

---

[14] Congregation for the Doctrine of the Faith, *Instruction on Christian Freedom and Liberation*, n. 75

[15] Objective analysis, improved behaviour and institutional reforms relate not only to the authorities in developing countries, but also and in equal degree to those in the industrialized countries in their own domestic activities and in international relations.

[16] Paul VI, Encyclical *Populorum Progressio*, n. 62.

(2314) Rare indeed is it for a country to dispose of all the resources necessary to pursue its development in isolation and satisfy the needs of its people. A country usually receives capital, technology and equipment from other countries. A careful selection of these imports will avoid increasing indebtedness without hampering development.

(2315) Conversely, an immediate and total liberalization of international trade would risk generating competition that would endanger the economies of the developing countries and would oblige them to make overly rapid and destructive adjustments in certain sectors. Equitable rules must be set up in order to eliminate these dangers and to establish better equality of opportunities. "In order that international trade be human and moral, social justice requires that it restore to the participants a certain equality of opportunity. This equality is a long term objective... Who is there who does not see that such a common effort aimed at increased justice in business relations between peoples would bestow on developing nations positive assistance, the effects of which would be not only immediate but lasting?"[17]

(2316) International trade today includes technologies, capital and currency. In each area, the same efforts are required: "Create true equality in discussions and negotiations... establish general norms."[18]

(2317) A particular case in point is evident in modern technologies which promote economic growth if they are adapted to a country's culture and level of development. The nations which invent these technologies have, thanks to these, a capital and power to place at the service of all.[19]

(2318) Regional cooperation, especially among developing countries, is an expression of solidarity which is also to be promoted in financial and monetary matters, in order to find just solutions to the debt problems.

III. 3. Responsibilities of Creditors with Respect to Debtors

(2319) In emergency situations in which debtor countries are unable to service their foreign debts or even meet their annual interest payments, the various creditors need to define their responsibilities within a framework of solidarity for survival. Those provisions, however, do not nullify the respective rights and responsibilities linking creditors and debtors.

(2320) The examination of the internal and external causes behind the debt, its increase, and the amounts to be reimbursed each year by each country will make it possible, in a spirit of dialogue, to determine the responsibilities of the debtor and his respective creditors (States, commercial banks) with a view to finding equitable solutions.

(2321) Except when loans have been granted at usurious rates or used to finance projects overpriced through fraudulent complicity - in which case legal proceedings could be initiated to revise the contracts - creditors have rights, acknowledged by the debtors, relative to interest rates, the conditions and schedule of reimbursement. Respect for the contract by both parties sustains the essential trust factor. However, creditors cannot demand contract fulfillment by any and all means, especially if the debtor is in a situation of extreme need.

---

17 *Ibid*, n. 61.

18 *Ibid.*

19 Cf. John Paul II, Encyclical *Laborem Excercens*, nn. 5, 12; Congregation for the Doctrine of the Faith, *Instruction on Christian Freedom and Liberation*, n. 12.

(2322) 1. The creditor States have to find reimbursement conditions which are compatible with each debtor State's ability to meet its basic needs. Each country has to be left adequate financial leeway for its own growth, which at the same time will help further reimbursement of its debt.

(2323) A decrease in interest rates, the capitalization of payments above a minimum interest rate, a rescheduling of the debt on a longer term basis, national currency payment facilities... these are all concrete measures to be negotiated with the debtor countries in order to lighten the debt service burden and assist in growth recovery. Creditors and debtors need to reach agreement on the new conditions and terms of payment in a spirit of solidarity, sharing the necessary efforts. In the case of disagreements on the precise ways and means, conciliation or arbitration procedures could be requested and acknowledged by both parties. An international code of conduct, with norms of ethical value, would be useful as guideline for negotiations.

(2324) The creditor States will need to pay special attention to the poorest countries. In certain cases, they could convert the loans into grants. This debt remission, however, must not undermine the financial, economic, and political credibility of the "less advanced" countries or put a stop to new flow of capital from banks.

(2325) The amount of public capital transferred from the industrialized countries (public development aid) must return to the level of commitments agreed upon bilaterally or multilaterally. Creditor States should encourage commercial banks to continue lending to developing countries by adopting fiscal and financial provisions and guarantees against possible risks. Coordinated policies in monetary, financial, and commercial affairs on the part of the creditor States will help to keep the developing countries' balances of payments on an even keel and thereby favour debt repayment.

(2326) 2. The commercial banks are direct creditors of developing countries (States and enterprises). Their duties towards their depositors are essential and must be fulfilled if confidence is to be maintained. These duties, however, are not their only ones and must be compatible with respect for their debtors whose needs are often more urgent.

(2327) Commercial banks have an active role to play in the efforts undertaken by creditor States and international organizations in solving the debt problem: rescheduling of debts, revision of interest rates, relaunching investments in developing countries, financing of projects on the basis of their impact on growth in preference to "safer" projects with more immediate investments returns and those of questionable usefulness (e.g. prestige investments, armaments). This approach undoubtedly goes beyond the traditional function of commercial banks insofar as it invites them to undertake a type of discernment which transcends the ordinary criteria of profitability and security for capital invested in the form of loans. Nonetheless, why would they not assume in that way part of the responsibility in the face of this major challenge of our times: promoting the united development of all peoples and thereby contributing to international peace? All persons of good will are called to this task, according to their own expertise, professional commitment, and sense of solidarity.

(2328) 3. Multinational companies are involved in international flows of capital under the form of production-oriented investments and the repatriation of capital (profits and defrayments). Their economic and financial policies therefore have a negative or positive influence on the balance of payments of developing countries (new investments and local reinvestment of profits or repatriation of profits and sale of assets).

(2329) While orienting the activities of these corporations in order to involve them in development plans (national investment code), the public authorities in developing countries could also draw up conventions with them which define mutual obligations, especially in the areas of capital flows and taxation.

(2330) Multinational companies have extensive economic, financial and technological power. Their business plans go beyond and cut across national boundaries. They must be party to the solutions for alleviating the debt of the developing countries. As economic and financial actors on the international stage, they are called to this responsibility and solidarity which is above and beyond their own vested interests.

III.4 Responsibility of Multilateral Financial Organizations

(2331) At the end of the violence and havoc of World War II, the nations of the world joined together to promote peace and international cooperation, to foster the development of peoples, to satisfy mankind's basic requirements (health, food, education, culture) through specialized agencies, and to conduct trade (commerce and industry) on equitable terms. The Church has always encouraged these efforts to construct a more just and more united world.[20]

(2332) Today, international organizations are faced with new and urgent responsibilities: to help solve the debt crisis of the developing countries; to avoid a generalized collapse of the international financial system; to help all peoples, especially those in greatest need, to bring about their own development; to combat the spread of poverty under all its various forms and thereby promote peace by eliminating the threats of conflicts. Among these threats, let us remember, "there is an unpredictable and fluctuating financial situation which has direct impact on the highly indebted countries struggling to achieve effective development."[21]

(2333) The multilateral financial organizations will fulfill their role if their decisions and actions are taken in a spirit of justice and solidarity at the service of all. Certainly, it is not up to the Church to judge the economic and financial theories behind their analyses and the remedies proposed. In these complex domains, certitudes are relative. As her contribution, the Church recalls the need for mutual understanding as a way to shed more light on realities. She also restates the priority to be granted to people and their needs, above and beyond the constraints and financial mechanisms often advanced as the only imperatives.

(2334) Inter-state organizations must take care to respect the dignity and sovereignty of each nation, above all the poorest ones, while remembering that the interdependence of national economies is a fact which can and must become an acknowledged bond of solidarity. Isolation is neither desirable nor possible. "The peoples themselves have the prime responsibility to work for their own development. But they will not bring this about in isolation."[22]

(2335) In order to handle these new tasks, some organization is most assuredly necessary: the adaptation and expansion of their interventions, increased means for action, effective participation of all members in decision-making, contribution to development targets, and priority for the needs of the poorest populations. As early as 1967, Pope Paul VI had expressed hope for this reorganization with a view to "the development of peoples."[23]

(2336) These reorganization endeavours will bolster the confidence to which the inter-state organizations have a right but which they must always justify and, at times, regain. The populations more directly affected by the consequences of the debt crisis need visible signs in order to recognize the equity and effectiveness of the solutions adopted. Confidence, which is a necessary element in generating a national consensus in accepting a fair distribution of sacrifices, and thereby assuring the successful outcome of adjustment measures, is not the result of economic mea-

---

[20] Cf. John Paul II, *Message to the 40th United Nations General Assembly,* October 18, 1985, nn. 2-3 (See above, par, 348-352).

[21] John Paul II, *Message for the 1986 World Day of Peace*, n. 2: Among the suggestions to reduce North-South tensions: "I am thinking of the debt borne by the poor nations and a better and more responsible use of credits in the 'developing countries'".

[22] Paul VI, Encyclical *Populorum Progressio*, n. 77.

[23] *bid*, n. 64: "We hope that multilateral and international bodies, by means of *the reorganization which is required*, will discover the ways that will allow peoples still underdeveloped to break through the barriers which seem to enclose them."

sures alone. It is only granted if impartiality and the service of others emerge as the motives behind decisions, as opposed to the interests of one nation or social category. In this latter case, suspicion creeps in, and, at times without sufficient warning, triggers rejection, denunciation, and even violence.

(2337) It is up to the member States, especially the ones with preponderant influence in the decision-making process because of their economic power and level of contribution, to support these organizations in an active way, to specify their tasks, to expand their endeavours, and to turn these sites of power into centres of dialogue and cooperation for the international common good.

(2338) Each of the multilateral financial organizations - International Monetary Fund (IMF), the World Bank, regional banks - has specific functions, and hence responsibilities in its own right. In order to highlight their inherent character of solidarity and concordance, these bodies will have to acknowledge the need to increase the representation of developing countries and their participation in the major international economic decisions that affect them. It will be the concern of these agencies to coordinate their efforts and policies to respond in a specific and coherent way to the most urgent debt needs with an eye to the future. They will also have to determine, in dialogue with the debtor countries, the measures to be adopted and the distribution of responsibilities, according to each party's functions and possibilities.

(2339) Without going into those details which fall within "the vocation of lay people acting on their own initiative with their fellow countrymen,"[24] the Church draws the attention of multilateral financial organizations and those who work in them to a few points for consideration:

- to examine the loan "conditions" set by the IMF openly in a way which is adapted to each developing country; to integrate the human factor in the "increased surveillance" over the implementation of adjustment measures and the results achieved;

- to encourage new capital, public and private, to finance priority projects for developing countries;

- to foster dialogue between creditors and debtors for a rescheduling of debts and a reduction of the sums due in one or even more years if possible;

- to foresee special provisions to cover financial difficulties due to natural catastrophes, excessive variations in the prices of indispensable raw material (commodities, energy products, mineral resources), and abrupt fluctuations in exchange rates. Because of their unexpectedness, their extent, and financial repercussions, these uncontrolled phenomena disrupt the economic programmes of the developing countries in particular and lead to a state of dangerous and costly international insecurity;

- to prompt a better coordination of the economic and monetary policies of the industrialized countries, encouraging those with the most favourable impact on the developing countries;

- to look into the new problems, current and future, in order to envisage solutions now which can take into account the widely diversified evolution potential of national economies and the future prospects of each country. Such forecasting, difficult and necessary, is a common responsibility in face of future generations and will make it possible to prevent a buildup of serious conflict situations. In a world of rapid and profound changes, "if man lets himself rush ahead without foreseeing in good time the emergence of new social problems, they will become too grave for a peaceful solution to be hoped for;"[25]

---

[24] Cf. Congregation for the Doctrine of the Faith, *Instruction on Christian Freedom and Liberation*, n. 80.

[25] Paul VI, Letter *Octogesima Adveniens* to Cardinal Maurice Roy, May 4, 1971, n. 19.

- to pay close attention to the selection and training of all those who work in multilateral organizations and who take part in situation analysis, and in decisions relative there-to, an their subsequent implementation. Collectively and individually, these people bear a great responsibility. There is always the danger of remaining on the level of theoretical, technical, or bureaucratic solutions, while at stake are human lives, the development of peoples, and solidarity among nations. Economic expertise is indispensable, as is sensitivity to other cultures and direct and concrete experience with people and their needs. To give a firm base to these human qualities, a keen sense of the need to promote solidarity and international justice is also important.

FINAL PROPOSAL

(2340) In order to deal with the serious challenge of the indebtedness of the developing countries, the Church calls upon all people of good will to broaden their conscience to include these new, urgent and complex international responsibilities, and to mobilize the full range of their possibilities for action in order to identify and implement solutions of solidarity.

In particular, has the time not come for the industrialized countries to draw up a broad plan of cooperation and assistance for the good of the developing countries?

Without drawing a parallel with what was done after World War II to accelerate the reconstruction and economic recovery of countries seriously damaged during that conflict, is it not imperative to start working on a new system of aid from the industrialized countries to the less prosperous ones, in the interests of all and especially because it would mean restoring hope to suffering populations? Such a contribution, which would constitute a commitment of several years, would seem indispensable in order to enable the developing countries to launch and conclude successfully, in cooperation with the industrialized countries and the international organizations, the long-term programmes they need to undertake as soon as possible. May our appeal be heeded before it is too late!

CHAPTER VIII

SOCIAL MATTERS

I - CHILDREN

1. COMMON SOLICITUDE FOR ALL CHILDREN

Address of His Holiness Paul VI to Mr. Henry R. Labuisse, Executive Director of the United Nations Children's Fund. The Vatican, 28 June 1978.

Original: English (*)

(2341) With the approach of the International Year of the Child, we are indeed happy to have your visit. We welcome you as the Executive Director of the United Nations Children's Fund, knowing that your organization has been designated by the General Assembly as the lead agency for the International Year.

(2342) We wish to state at once how much we appreciate the great good that UNICEF has done over the years for the children of the world. We have wholeheartedly supported all your worthy activities aimed at providing for the basic needs of children, while at the same time we have repeatedly expressed our dissociation from any involvement in projects that may directly or indirectly favour contraception, abortion, or other practices that do not respect the supreme value of life.

(2343) With regard to the International Year of the Child, it had been the concern of the Holy See that such an event should not be the occasion for multiplying initiatives that would have no direct bearing on the welfare of children. The Holy See is pleased to note that the same concern has been manifested by the General Assembly of the United Nations Organization in determining the general objectives of IYC, which speak of "enhancing the awareness of the special needs of children on the part of decision-makers and the public", and which advocate "sustained activities for the benefit of children" (General Assembly Resolution A-31-169 of 21 December 1976, operative paragraph 2).

(2344) The interest of the Church in this event is in harmony with her constant solicitude throughout the centuries for children's welfare. This solicitude is an expression of her fidelity to the programme enjoined on her by her Founder, Jesus Christ, who stated that "whoever does not receive the kingdom of God like a child shall not enter it" (*Lk.* 18:17). Above all, Christ identifies the child with his own person: "Whoever receives one such child in my name receives me" (*Mk.* 9:37). For the Catholic Church, therefore, service to the child is not a transitory goal, but rather a permanent task invested with dignity and enduring priority.

(2345) A renewed concern for the real needs of children everywhere is furthermore dictated by a realistic awareness of the present situation of the world. Despite technological progress, children still suffer and die from lack of basic nourishment, or as victims of violence and armed conflicts that they do not even understand. Others are victims of emotional neglect. There are people who poison the minds of the young by passing on to them prejudices and empty ideologies. And today, children are exploited even to the point of being used to satisfy the lowest depravities of adults. A despicable aspect of this exploitation is the fact that it is often controlled by powerful forces motivated by financial gain.

(2346) Extending our gaze still further over the world situation, we see that there is another harmful discrimination to which the child is subject and which would worthily engage the full attention of IYC. In our time some people consider the child a burden and restriction of freedom, rather than the living expression of the love of parents. Others deny to the child the fundamental right to have a mother and a father united in marriage. But all society must vigorously reply that the child indeed has the God-given right to be born, the right to a mother and father united in marriage, the right to be born into a normal family. It would be a form of contradiction if, on the occasion of the Interna-

(*) Insegnamenti di Paolo VI, Vol. XVI (1978), 515-518.

tional Year of the Child, activities were to be promoted whose inspiration and purpose were to make children less welcome, or even to prevent them from being born into society.

(2347) In order to fulfil its aim, this Year is called to promote the inestimable value of the child in today's world: the child as a child, as a human person, and not simply as a potential adult. Childhood is an essential phase of human life, and every child has the right to live childhood to the full and to make an original contribution to the humanizing of society and to its development and renewal. All of us personally know this contribution of children to the world. Who has not been struck by children's simple, direct and innocent perception of situations, their open and loving generosity, their lack of prejudice and discrimination, their infectious joy and spontaneous sense of brotherhood, and also by their capacity for remarkable sacrifice and idealism?

(2348) The Church, therefore, stresses that every child is a human person and has the right to the integral development of his or her personality. The role of the family is irreplaceable in attaining this end, since the child cannot be understood and assisted apart from the family, which is the first educator towards physical, psychological, intellectual, moral and religious development. We also wish to encourage endeavours to extend services in favour of children, and to improve the quality of these services, especially on a permanent basis.

(2349) In all these efforts the child remains of central concern: each child and every child throughout the world. We are hopeful that new and revitalized projects will flourish to help needy children everywhere. And we are convinced that in this way the profound exigencies of the young and vulnerable human person will be met: in the first place the right to life, to truth, and to love.

(2350) We are pleased to note that many individual Catholics, Catholic organizations and local Churches are taking part in the preparation of IYC. Their effective contribution will be to rededicate themselves - in the spirit of fidelity to the Gospel message - to the needs of the child, and to develop appropriate programmes that will assist children in various aspects of their lives. We are confident that such programmes will give particular priority to the needs of disadvantaged children, the physically and mentally handicapped, those abandoned and those in special situations of distress and suffering.

(2351) With these sentiments we ask the blessings of God on all who labour to further these high ideals and we pray that the Lord will sustain you and all those who collaborate in this great work of human solidarity.

2. THE CHILD IS A CHALLENGE TO OUR WISDOM

Address of His Holiness John Paul II to Mr. James P. Grant, Executive Director, and to the Executive Council of the United Nations Children's Fund. The Vatican, 26 April, 1984.

Original: English (*)

(2352) I am happy to welcome you this morning to the Vatican and, with you, all those who are associated with the meeting of the Executive Council of UNICEF which is in session in these days in Rome

(2353) Your organization has been entrusted with a very noble and urgent task: that of concern for all the children of the world. The Holy See follows your activities in this field with great attention. Indeed, the Church's mission and duty of service to the human family makes her particularly sensitive to the needs of children, that *precious treasure*, deserving of utmost love and respect, *given*

(*) Insegnamenti di Giovanni Paolo II, Vol. VII,2 (1984), 1120-1126.

to each generation as a challenge to its wisdom and humanity. I am pleased, therefore, to have this opportunity to share with you some reflections related to the task before you.

(2354) 1. Just over four years ago, when I had the honour of addressing the Thirty-fourth General Assembly of the United Nations, I posed the question: "What better wish can I express for every nation and the whole of mankind, and for *all the children of the world* than a *better future* in which respect for human rights will become a complete reality throughout the third millennium which is drawing near." (Address to the General Assembly of the United Nations, 2 October 1979, No. 21. See above, par, 108).

(2355) Concern for the child is concern for that *better future* about which I spoke to the General Assembly. What is at stake in child-hood and in concern for the child is the fate and the destiny of the person, of human life and existence. The child is a sign of mystery of life and a testing-ground of the authenticity of our respect for the mystery of life. Every child is in some way a sign of the hope posited and expressed by the love of parents: a sign of the hopes of a nation and a people.

(2356) The child represents a special sign for the Church. Concern for the child is linked, in fact, with the Church's fundamental mission. As I recalled in my Apostolic Exhortation *Familiaris Consortio* on the role of the Christian family in the modern world, the Church "is called upon to reveal and put forward anew in history the example and the commandment of Christ the Lord, who placed the child at the heart of the Kingdom of God: 'Let the children come to me, and do not hinder them; for to such belongs the kingdom of heaven' (*Lk.* 18:16)" (No. 26). Indeed Christ goes so far as to identify himself with children: "Whoever receives one such child in my name receives me" (*Mt.* 18:5). Every single child in this world is a living sign of that mystery of life and hope that was revealed in Jesus Christ.

(2357) This is why the Church has always considered that every effort invested in the genuine development of the child is an invaluable investment in a *better future* for all of society.

(2358) 2. While one may take comfort in an increasing awareness within public opinion of the need to devote greater resources, and with ever increasing urgency, to the well-being of children, the fact remains that the plight of so many children in today's world is extremely critical. It is certainly one of the great scandals of our society, with the immense progress that it has been able to achieve in technology and science, that so many children are among those who suffer most intensely. And it is even sadder to note that such children, and especially the poorest of them, are often the first to be hit by economic depression and its consequences. The scandalous imbalances which exist within our society are reflected in a particular way amongst our children: while in one sector of our world children are suffering the lack of the most elementary human necessities, in other sectors children from the earliest age are being inserted into a society based on consumerism, possession, and even waste.

(2359) Such a situation is a challenge to the conscience of every man and woman in our world, of every nation and particularly of all those who hold responsibility within the international community. The demands of conscience will not be answered by vague promises, much less by the political exploitation of human suffering. The critical situation of the suffering of the weakest of our brothers and sisters calls for rapid and concerted efforts to assure for all our children the *better future* which is their right.

(2360) 3. The Church's concern for children emerges also from the fact that *the Church is on the side of life.* The Church considers it a priority aspect of her mission in today's world to proclaim the value of each and every human person, especially those who are least able to defend themselves. For this reason the Church will never cease to raise her prophetic voice proclaiming that *human life must be respected and protected* from the moment of conception.

(2361) Is it not possible to notice in the changing demographic trends of many developed countries a changing attitude to the child and to life itself? Is it perhaps possible that some people in their desire that their children should *have* as much as possible, deprive their children of some of the basic, positive elements of what it is to *be* a genuine human person? Can one not detect a certain fear of the child, a fear of the demands of love and human generosity which the procreation and education of children require? Do not love, generosity and self-giving belong to the noblest elements of life itself? The *anti-life mentality* which has emerged in today's society is very often a sign of the fact that people have lost faith in life, have lost sight of the most fundamental elements of human destiny.

(2362) There is a real danger in resorting to solutions which appear to offer short-term results but which, because these solutions are not based on an integral vision of the person, not only will not lead to the desired solution but will lead to an ulterior estrangement of man from himself.

(2363) 4. One example of a false response to the critical plight of children would undoubtedly be to adopt policies that result in a weakening of the *institution of the family*, especially in those developing countries where the traditional family system is truly impregnated with human wisdom and nourished by profound moral values.

(2364) The Church is convinced that one of the most vital answers to the situation of the child in today's world will come through *reinforcing and strengthening* the family as an institution and through policies which will permit families to carry out the irreplaceable role that properly belongs to them.

(2365) Recently the Holy See offered the international community a *Charter of the Rights of the Family*, a document which has been requested by many bishops from all over the world during the 1980 Synod of Bishops held here in the Vatican. This document clearly indicated areas where the rights of families are ignored and undermined. But it is, in the first place, a document which demonstrates the confidence which the Church has in the family, which is *the natural community of life and love* uniquely entrusted with the task of the transmission of life and the loving care and development of the human person, especially in the early years.

(2366) Healthy family life will contribute greatly to the stability of society. It will ensure that children receive a well-rounded personal development in which their needs will be taken into consideration in an integrated manner. You are well aware, I know, of the vital contribution that families can play in health care, in health education and in the developing countries. The love and stability which strong and genuine family life can offer on the physical, cultural and moral levels must also be seen as an important factor in responding to the new forms of malaise which increasingly affect the children of the developed countries.

(2367) In referring to the family, I cannot overlook the important aspect of the *role of motherhood* and the necessity that mothers be afforded all the necessary social protection and assistance during pregnancy and for a reasonable period of time afterwards. An essential element of any policy in favour of the child is that of providing for an effective presence of the mother alongside her young children and of ensuring that mothers are trained to carry out effectively their role in the areas of nutrition and health education. The Holy See has repeatedly advocated appropriate personal and social advancement for women in order to assure the dignity of women and the improvement of the quality of life for the coming generations. Policies aimed at assisting mothers to carry out their task effectively and with satisfaction are based on the principle of giving adequate recognition to the work of mothers in the home because of its value for the family and society.

(2368) 5. Precisely because the Church realizes what a great value the family is, she feels particularly close to all those children who have not had the joy of growing up in a healthy and complete family. As I said in *Familiaris Consortio:* "There exist in the world countless people who unfortunately cannot in any sense claim membership of what can be called in the proper sense a family. Large sections of humanity live in conditions of extreme poverty, in which promiscuity, lack of housing, the irregular nature and instability of relationships and the extreme lack of education make it impossible in practice to speak of a true family. There exist others who, for various reasons, have been left alone in the world." (No. 85)

(2369) Alongside all the efforts which we must make to see that families are helped to carry out their role more effectively, it is important to dedicate urgent and immediate attention to those children who are deprived of family life. In particular I make *an appeal* to other families *to respond to their vocation to hospitality* and to open their doors to children who need temporary or permanent care. At the same time I renew my appeals to authorities to provide legislation which permits suitable families to adopt children or take care of them for a period. Such legislation should at the same time respect the natural rights of parents, also in religious sphere. It is also important to see that all abuses in this field, both on a national and international level, which exploit children and their needs are eliminated.

(2370) Mr. Executive Director, I wish you to know without any doubt that all those who work sincerely for a *better future* for all children of the world will find a staunch ally in the Church and in this Apostolic See. I ask God's blessing on your work and on the work of all those agencies and individuals who, in so many and varied ways, seek to ensure that the gift of God's life in which each child shares is allowed to develop in the fullest manner for the good of all humanity.

3. FOR A BETTER LIFE AND A BETTER FUTURE FOR ALL THE CHILDREN IN THE WORLD

Message of His Holiness John Paul II to the National Committees of UNICEF meeting in Rome. The Vatican, 16 October 1984.

Original: English (*)

(2371) 1. This is the first time in the history of UNICEF that representatives of all the National Committees have met together to reflect on their task and mission. I am particularly happy to greet each of you because, whatever your personal background or country of origin, the principal inspiration which has brought you together in these days is that of a genuine concern and interest in *a better life and a better future for all the children of our world.*

(2372) In that noble task you will always have the support of the Catholic Church in every part of the world. It could not be other-wise with a Church that receives her mission from Jesus Christ, who identified himself with the humblest when he said: "Whoever receives one such child in my name receives me". (*Mt.* 18:5).

(2373) The National Committees which you represent are a sign of the concern and anxieties of many of our fellow men and women - and indeed of many children - for the less fortunate children of the world. One of the original aspects of UNICEF's structure is that it recognizes that the task of successfully working for the good of children all over the world cannot be carried out effectively by a central international agency as it were in isolation, but requires the contribution and the participation of a broad range of the citizens of many countries. Only in this way is it possible to create an awareness of the deeper dimensions of the questions involved and to create the genuine network of human solidarity which is needed to provide integral solutions to those questions.

(2374) 2. UNICEF was set up originally as an "emergency fund", but although the word "emergency" has been removed from the title, the fact remains that the situation of so many children in all parts of the world is more tragic than ever. Indeed, alongside situations in some parts of the world where children lack the most elementary physical necessities even for survival, new forms of suffering are emerging for the children of other parts of the world because of a moral and cultural crisis. As a result of this, children lack that selfless love which is their right to receive from their parents and without which they will never reach happiness and personal development. I am thinking, for example, of the suffering caused by the effects of the breakdown of so many families.

(2375) 3. Our society, in this latter part of the twentieth century, calls a judgment upon itself when, despite all the technological and medical progress and the progress in communications, still every

---

(*) Insegnamenti di Giovanni Paolo II, Vol. VII,2 (1984), 937-940.

day so many of its weakest members suffer and die because they lack simple and basic resources which could, in fact, be made available to them. And notwithstanding this fact which, due to the modern communications media, no one can claim to be unaware of, many men and women still live and transmit a life style based on self-centered consumerism, on exaggerated possession and even on the waste of the earth's potential.

(2376) If we look at the question deeply, we see that the situation in which so many children are deprived of the basic means of survival is linked to a vision of life closed in on itself and which impedes self-giving and solidarity. One of the great crises of conscience of contemporary society is the disregard for the mystery and sacredness of the gift of *life*, which is all too easily manipulated in a manner which does not respect the true nature and destiny of the human person, or which would dare to suppress life itself at the moments in which it is most defenseless.

(2377) Today I appeal to you, who have come to Rome as representatives of the genuine anxieties of many of the people of our world, to see, as a fundamental element of your work for the good of children, the task of the *education of consciences* towards the full appreciation of the value of each and every human life, and especially of the most defenseless.

(2378) 4. You realize well that - without underestimating the urgency of programmes aimed at ensuring the survival of children - your task must lead you further, towards offering all the children of the world the possibility of a genuine physical, moral and spiritual development from the beginning of life onwards.

(2379) In this context, the role of the family, and especially of mothers, is of the greatest importance. You know that the future human development of the child is linked with the health of the mother, right from the moment in which conception takes place, through pregnancy and in the earliest years of the development of the child. You know the value of a strong and loving family environment in which father and mother, brothers and sisters and relatives all contribute to helping the child acquire his or her personal, cultural and religious identity.

(2380) It is not possible to work for the good of the child without, at the same time, being in the front line of those who work for the family, helping all families to realize the potential that is theirs for the formation of mature persons, who will be the strength of the society of tomorrow.

(2381) Just a year ago, the Holy See presented to the international community, and to all those concerned with the mission of the family in today's world, a *Charter of the Rights of the Family* aimed at reinforcing an awareness of the irreplaceable role and position of the family, which "constitutes, much more than a mere juridical, social and economic unit, a community of love and solidarity, which is uniquely suited to teach and transmit cultural, ethical, social, spiritual and religious values, essential for the development and well-being of its own members and of society" (Preamble E). Any violation of the rights of the family, any policy which leads to the weakening of the institution of the family, cannot lead to true human and cultural progress.

(2382) 5. Human problems will be resolved only by solutions that are *integrally human*. To propose anything less would be to treat fellow human beings as possessing a lesser dignity than ourselves. For you, in your work, to overlook *spiritual values*, which are indeed part of the heritage of all the peoples of the world, would be to close the door on the total development of the child and to condemn him or her to a new form of poverty.

(2383) Your task involves bringing much needed material aid, especially to the peoples of the developing nations. One must never overlook, however, that these peoples, despite material poverty, possess a wealth of cultural values affecting human solidarity, love and life, and especially affecting the child. The good of mankind demands that these values not only be respected, but also fostered and recognized as signposts for the many who, by looking upon material progress as an end in itself, lose sight of the deeper values of life itself.

(2384) With these reflections which spring from the Christian understanding of life, which is above all a gift of God who is Life and Love, I wish God's blessing on your work and organizations, and on you and your families.

4. THE FUTURE OF PEOPLES AND NATIONS RESTS WITH THE CHILDREN.

Message of His Holiness John Paul II to Mr James Grant, Executive Director of the United Nations Children's Fund (UNICEF), on the occasion of the Fortieth Anniversary of its establishment. The Vatican, 10 November 1986.

Original: English

(2385) I am very pleased to extend my greetings and best wishes to you and to all those associated with the United Nations Children's Fund on the occasion of the Fortieth Anniversary of its establishment.

(2386) It is particularly appropriate that this Fund, which has done so much for the children of the world over the past four decades, should celebrate its own beginnings at the time of year when much of the world is preparing for Christmas. This season, more than others, focuses on children. It calls to mind the birth of Jesus Christ as a human child; it reminds us too of the children of today, who celebrate this festival with a special sense of wonder and joy.

(2387) All people of good will, whether believers or non-believers, love their children and want what is best for them. We all recognize that children are precious treasures entrusted to the wisdom and humanity of each generation. What is so clearly evident bears repeating: that the future of peoples and nations - and today we must add the very future of our planet - rests with the children. To the extent that they experience love and security in their families and society, they will be disposed to be loving and unafraid as adults. If they grow up without these fundamental human supports, there is always the danger that hostility and insecurity will follow. Humanity must recognize that all have a common interest and a common responsibility to protect and promote the well-being of children everywhere.

(2388) Religious faith confirms the special claim that children have on our love and care. Christians in particular are familiar with their Master's words: "Let the little children come to me, and do not hinder them; for to such belongs the kingdom of God. Truly, I say to you, whoever does not receive the kingdom of God like a child shall not enter it." (*Lk.* 18:16-17). The way that Jesus identified himself with children, exemplified in his statement that "whoever receives one such a child in my name receives me", impels us to a loving concern for children, the living signs of that mystery of life and hope which he revealed.

(2389) Since its inception forty years ago, the United Nations Children's Fund has acted vigorously to promote the life and well-being of the world's children. Originally established as an emergency fund for Europe after the Second World War, UNICEF was later expanded to include the needs of children throughout the world. Today, in addition to war, poverty and famine, children are being subjected to new forms of suffering as a result of moral and cultural crises. These include the plight of refugee and migrant children and those in other high-risk situations; child victims of prostitution and pornography; those dying of preventable diseases; and on the eve of the International Year of Shelter for the Homeless, we must also remember children who, with their families, have no decent and stable place to live.

(2390) The Catholic Church has collaborated with UNICEF throughout the world in Child Programmes for survival and development; in expanded literacy programmes; immunization projects; and in other undertakings which foster both physical health from the moment of conception and likewise the moral ad spiritual development of children. The Church stands ready to continue this promotion of much needed services for all the children of the world. She also remains convinced that one of the most effective responses to the troubled situation of so many children today is the reinforcement of family life through national and international policies enabling families to fulfil the irreplaceable role which properly belongs to them.

(2391) It is my fervent hope and prayer that, in a world in which the survival and growth of millions of children is tragically imperilled by adverse moral, social and economic factors, the United Nations Children's Fund will continue to be an effective instrument for the protection and the development of the unborn, of infants, and of all the children with whom God continues to enrich the human family. On the occasion of this Fortieth Anniversary celebration, I invoke upon you and all those associated with UNICEF abundant divine blessings.

II - YOUTH

1. GIVE YOUNG PEOPLE HIGH IDEALS

Message of His Holiness John Paul II to the Director-General of UNESCO, Mr. Amadou Mahtar M'Bow, on the occasion of World Youth Congress, held in Barcelona on 8-15 July 1985. The Vatican, 1 July 1985.

Original: Spanish (*)

(2392) Because of the cooperation which the Holy See has built up with UNESCO over many years, I received the news of the World Youth Congress to be held in Barcelona from 8 to 15 July 1985 with feelings of joy and hope. As a result, and in response to the wish expressed by your Excellency, I am sending my message to the Congress.

(2393) I have taken up the cause of the young, most emphatically, on many occasions. I have spoken about it, first and foremost, with young people themselves, in the course of the enjoyable meetings I have had with them in various parts of the world. They play the leading parts in their own lives in the fascinating adventure of growing up and becoming men and women. It is only by inspiring them with confidence in themselves and in adults, by instilling in them a capacity for confident expectation, a sense of commitment and of responsibility, that we shall be able to point them towards a future which stimulates their creativity and arouses their enthusiasm. I have talked about this also with parents, educators, men of culture and governments. It is on them that the responsibility falls, for various reasons, for providing the family with cultural and structural conditions needed to produce a future built on justice, respect and the promotion of the rights and lives of all.

(2394) I have spoken of this joyful and sublime duty with particular and understandable insistance, to all those in the Church who are living out their faith in Jesus Christ. I recently proposed to my brothers in the priesthood that, in union with the young people of our own age, they should repeat the gesture so full of implicit humanity and apostolic zeal, made by Jesus to the young man in the Gospel: "He looked at him and loved him" (Mk. 10:21). I have often pointed out the reason for this duty, expressing a widespread and growing concern, touching all men of good will: "youth is a key stage in the life of every individual." It is in the young that the hope of mankind is to be found; and hope, in conjunction with the future, is the expectation of "good things to come". As a Christian virtue it is linked to the active and committed expectation of those eternal good things promised to man through Jesus Christ by God Himself. And at the same time, as a human and Christian virtue, it is the expectation of those good things which man can obtain by making the talents he has received from Providence bear fruit.

(*) Insegnamenti di Giovanni Paolo II, Vol. VIII,2 (1985), 105-109

(2395) But today, young people are under threat, precisely apropos of that destiny of theirs as the hope of mankind and of its future. This happens in different ways but the results are equally sad and worrying. A great many young people find themselves in situations of such despair that they even reach the point of ruling out any reasonable hope of a promising future. Others feel the fears felt by all mankind weighing them down in a tragic way: wars, extermination, famine, manipulation, violence, and aberrant injustices. In Western societies, many young people, disoriented by the unexpected and sometimes uncontrolled wealth of opportunities, of what are often conflicting opinions, are passing through a profound crisis both of identity and about the meaning of life. No reliable and reassuring answers to the fundamental questions about life are put forward. These questions are sometimes evaded by educators, too, giving rise to a depressing basic scepticism or to a restless way of life. An exasperated individualism, existing paradoxically with a high-density society, sometimes ends up by removing all consistency and interiority from the personal life of the individual, even going so far as to ruin his life or reduce it to a mediocre conformism. This dangerous crisis is imprisoning a great many young people in a present without prospects, or is forcing them to look for outlets which are nothing but retreats from life, prejudicial to mankind and frequently ending tragically in death.

(2396) Happily, however, there are also a great many positive reactions and hopeful signs. The many young people I have met during my apostolic journeys and the many also who came to Rome to celebrate the Holy Year of Reconciliation with me and also this present International Youth Year, sustain my hopes. They are many, and they are of fine quality, these young people who are involved at the present time in the reform of society, in building the "civilization of love", devoted to Jesus Christ to whom they have joyfully opened the already approaching. But I cannot contemplate these young people without thinking at the same time about all the others.

(2397) It is with these feelings in mind that I join UNESCO in expressing my satisfaction at the timely idea of organizing this World Congress, with the collaboration of devoted educators and distinguished experts. A further subject for satisfaction on my part concerns the themes included in the agenda. Education, work, cultural development, and international development are, undoubtedly, matters of fundamental concern in the lives of the young, and sensitive points in the process of social change. Many of the existing problems preoccupying those who value the young have their roots here. For example, how can these young people look to the future with hope when they see the possibility of earning their daily bread and building up a decent life by means of steady and satisfying work growing gradually fainter and fainter? Differences do not put obstacles in the way of collaboration, in which the barriers erected between different social groups or between nations, because of hatred, deep-seated discrimination, nationalistic distrust or hegemonic pretensions, give way to a serene and constructive conviviality oriented towards the good and the integral human development of all. But alas, every day they come up against news and events of war, of absurd disputes, against power tactics which increase the distances between the rich countries and poor countries. Despair arises from deeper and more long-term causes which must be identified clearly and courageously. The study of these problems in all their essential dimensions could give everyone a more critical awareness, a well-founded realism, and at the same time open up new and enterprising prospects. It may happen that you reach the conclusion that difficulties exist which are beyond your strength and that we shall have to wait a long time before we see our hopes realized. The analysis of such important themes, solutions for which often lie outside the range of action available to the young, because they are the concern of higher authorities, could also provide a further reason for disillusion, for scepticism and even for a split between the generations. The Congress, showing great wisdom, has given special attention to education.

(2398) I should like here to point out that education is far more than just mere practical preparation; it cannot be reduced to the acquisition of a science or a technical training. True education certainly embraces science, culture and technology, but it is oriented towards the very noble objective of training the individual, in his integral human dimensions and from the point of view of his highest purposes. Consequently, education consists of both the propounding and the assimilation of "values" which are the basis of the identity, the dignity, the vocation and the responsibilities of man as an individual and as a member of society. Young people have every right to expect their educators to be genuine teachers able to orient them towards high ideals and to give them an example of these in their own lives. An attitude and climate of relativism and permissiveness, which have frequently grown into a loss or erosion of spiritual and ethical values, have certainly not produced good fruit and are of no help in the development of the true personality of the young.

(2399) I should like to say this to you: have the courage to propose high goals to the young people of today and also to ask them - while providing them with the motivations for so doing - to make the sacrifices needed to achieve those goals. In this way you will stimulate the forces often latent within young people, forces which are awaiting for convinced and expert educators to bring them to the surface and guide them in a creative manner. By this means, it will also be possible to regenerate ossified structures and ways of life and to develop the meaning - and the joy - of life and of work.

(2400) Your Excellency, in sending my heartfelt and most sincere good wishes to you and to all those attending this important Congress, I ask Almighty God to bless the efforts of all those who are working for the good of the young, whom we value so highly.

2. RESPONSIBILITIES AND CONTRIBUTIONS OF THE YOUNG FOR A MORE HUMAN WORLD

Address of His Holiness John Paul II to young Muslims. Casablanca, 19 August 1985.(*)

Original: French (**)

My dear young people, I greet you most warmly and, through you, the entire population of this noble country.

(2401) 1. I give thanks to God and glorify Him who has enabled me to be with you today. His Majesty the King honoured me with a visit to Rome a few years ago, and he was kind enough to invite me to visit your country and to meet with you.

(2402) I gladly accepted his invitation to come to speak to you in this Youth Year.

(2403) I often meet with young people, usually young Catholics. This is the first time that I am meeting with young Muslims. We Christians and Muslims have many things in common, both as believers and as human beings. We live in the same world, a world that is marked by numerous signs of hope, but also by many signs of anguish. For us, Abraham is the same model of faith in God, of submission to His will and of confidence in His goodness. We believe in the same God, the one God, the living God.

(2404) It is therefore towards God that my thoughts turn and to whom I lift up my heart. It is of God Himself that I wish above all to speak to you, since it is in Him that we believe, you Muslims and we Catholics, and I wish to speak to you also of the human values which have their foundation in God, the values which concern our development as persons, but also the development of our families and our societies, and the development of the international community.

(2405) Is not the mystery of God the highest reality on which the very meaning which man gives to his life depends? And is this not the first problem which a young person faces when he reflects on the mystery of his own existence and on the values which he intends to choose to build his developing personality?

(*) At the request of the Permanent Mission of the Kingdom of Morocco, the Address has been published as a document of the General Assembly of the United Nations (A/40/570, 22 August 1985).

(**) AAS 78(1986), 95-104.

(2406) In the Catholic Church, my office is that of successor of Peter, the apostle whom Jesus chose to confirm his brothers in the faith. Following in the unbroken line of popes down the ages, today I am Bishop of Rome, called to serve among his brothers in the world as a witness to the Christian faith, responsible for the unity of all the Church's members.

(2407) It is thus as a believer that I have come to be among you today. My purpose is simply to testify here to what I believe in, to my hopes for the happiness of my fellow man, to what, based on my experience, I consider useful for everyone.

(2408) 2. First of all I invoke the Most High, God the Almighty, who is our Creator. He is the origin of all life, as He is the source of all that is good, all that is beautiful, all that is holy.

(2409) He brought light out of darkness. He has made the entire universe unfold according to a marvellous plan.

(2410) He made us, us human beings, and we are His. His holy law guides our lives. It is God's light that serves as the beacon of our destiny and enlightens our conscience. He makes us capable of loving and of transmitting life. He asks all men to respect every human creature and to love every man as a friend, as a companion, as a brother. He invites us to come to the aid of our fellow man when he is injured, when he is abandoned, when he is hungry and thirsty, in short, whenever he no longer knows how to find his way on the path of life.

(2411) Yes, God asks us to listen to His voice. What He expects of us is obedience to His holy will in the free acceptance of the intelligence and the heart.

(2412) That is why we are answerable to Him. It is He, God, who is our judge, He alone who is truly just. But we know that His mercy is inseparable from His justice. When man returns to Him repentant and contrite after having fallen into sin and the works of death, it is then that God reveals Himself as one who pardons and grants mercy.

(2413) To Him, therefore, go our love and our adoration. For His blessings and for His mercy, we give Him thanks at all times and everywhere.

(2414) 3. In a world which yearns for unity and peace and yet is racked by a thousand tensions and conflicts, must not believers foster friendship and unity among the men and peoples who form a single community on earth? We know that they have one and the same origin and one and the same final end: the God who made them and who waits for them, because He will gather them together.

(2415) The Catholic Church for its part undertook, 20 years ago at the Second Vatican Council, through its bishops, that is, its religious leaders, to strive for co-operation among believers. It issued a *document on dialogue between religions* (*Nostra Aetate*). It affirms that all people, especially active believers, must respect one another, be above discrimination of any kind; live together and promote universal brotherhood (cf. document cited above, n. 5). The Church gives special attention to Muslim believers, in view of their belief in one God, their feeling for prayer and their regard for life. It hopes "to promote together, for all people, social justice, moral values, peace and freedom" (*ibid.*).

(2416) 4. The dialogue between Christians and Muslims is more necessary now than ever before. It is necessitated by our faithfulness to God and presupposes that we acknowledge God by our faith and bear witness to Him by word and deed in a world that is becoming increasingly secularized and sometimes even atheistic.

(2417) The young can build a better future if they put their faith in God first and commit themselves to building this new world according to God's plan, with wisdom and trust.

(2418) Today we must bear *witness* to the spiritual values which the world needs. First of all to *our faith in God.*

(2419) God is the source of all joy. We must therefore bear witness to our *worship of God*, our adoration, by our prayers, our praise and our supplications. Man cannot live without prayer any more than he can live without breathing. We must bear witness to *our humble efforts to ascertain His will.* It is He who must inspire a more just and more united commitment on our part. The ways of God are not always our ways. Considering that our actions are always incomplete, and the innermost intentions of our hearts imperfect, God can never be used for our own ends because He is above everything.

(2420) This demonstration of faith, which is vital to us and which cannot tolerate disloyalty to God or indifference to the truth, is made with respect for other religious traditions, because all people expect to be respected for what they really are, and for what they believe in their hearts. We wish that all may arrive at the plenitude of divine truth, but can achieve that only by the free exercise of one's beliefs, free from external constraints which are unworthy of the free tribute of reason and of the heart which characterizes the dignity of man. That is the true meaning of religious freedom, which respects both God and man. It is from such worshippers that God expects sincere worship, worshippers in spirit and in truth.

(2421) 5. It is our conviction that we cannot invoke God, the father of all men, if we refuse to behave fraternally towards some of these men created in God's image. (Declaration *Nostra Aetate*, n. 5)

(2422) We must therefore *respect, love and help every human being* because he or she is a creature of God and, in a certain sense, His image and His representative, because that is the way that leads to God and because one cannot develop fully without knowing God, accepting Him with all one's heart and obeying Him even as we follow the path to perfection.

(2423) This obedience to God and this love for mankind must therefore lead us *to respect human rights*, those rights which are the expression of God's will and the requirement of human nature, as created by God.

(2424) Respect and dialogue therefore require reciprocity in all fields, particularly as regards fundamental freedoms, and particularly religious freedom. They promote peace and understanding among peoples. They help to solve all the problems of men and women today, and especially those of youth.

(2425) 6. Normally, the young look towards the future, they aspire to a more just and more human world. God has made them so, precisely in order that they may help to transform the world according to His plan of life. But to them, too, the situations often seems dark.

(2426) In this world, there are boundaries, there are divisions between peoples and misunderstandings between generations; there is also racism, there are wars and injustices, just as there is hunger, waste and unemployment. These are the tragic evils which affect all of us, and particularly young people the world over. Some might be discouraged, others might be resigned, others might wish to bring about change by violence or by extreme solutions. Wisdom teaches us that self-discipline and love are the only instruments for achieving the desired renewal.

(2427) *God does not want people to remain passive.* He has given them the earth so that they, together, may master it, cultivate it and make it bear fruit .

(2428) You are responsible for the world of tomorrow. It is *by assuming your responsibilities fully and courageously* that you will be able to overcome existing difficulties. It is therefore incumbent upon you to take initiatives and not to expect everything from your elders and your authorities. It is for you to build the world, and not merely dream about it.

(2429) It is *by working together* that one can be effective. Work, of course, means service to others. It creates bonds of solidarity. The experience of working together helps one to purify oneself and to discover the merits of others. This will give rise, gradually to a climate of trust that will enable each one to grow, to develop and to "be something more". Do not fail, dear young people, to cooperate *with the adults*, and especially with your parents and your teachers, and with the "leaders" of society and the State. Young people must not be isolated from others. Young people need adults, just as adults need the young.

(2430) In this joint work, human beings, whether men or women, must never be sacrificed. *Each person is unique* in the eyes of God, and irreplaceable in this work of development. Every one must be recognized for what he is and, consequently, respected as such. No one must use his fellow man; no one must exploit his equal; no one must despise his brother.

(2431) Only thus can we have a more human world, more just and more brotherly, in which each person can find his place in dignity and freedom. This twentieth century world is in your hands. It is you who will shape the centuries to come.

(2432) 7. This future world will depend on the *youth of all countries of the world.* Our world is divided, and even torn asunder; it is experiencing many conflicts and grave injustices. There is no true North-South solidarity; there is not enough mutual aid among the nations of the South. There are cultures and races in the world that are not respected.

(2433) Why is all of this so? *It is because human beings do not accept their differences*: they do not know enough about each other. They reject those who are not of the same civilization. They refuse to help one another. They are unable to rid themselves of selfishness and complacency.

(2434) Yet God created all men equal in dignity, but different in gifts and talents. Mankind is a whole in which each group has its own role to play. The values of different peoples and different cultures must be recognized. The world is like a living organism; each one has something to receive from others and something to give to others.

(2435) I am happy to be meeting you here, in Morocco. Morocco has a *tradition of openness*; your scholars have travelled and you have welcomed scholars from other countries. Morocco has been a meeting-place of civilizations: it has permitted exchanges with the East, Spain and Africa. Morocco has a tradition of tolerance: in this Muslim country there have always been Jews and almost always Christians; they have lived in respect, in a positive manner. You have been and will remain a hospitable country. You, young Moroccans, are therefore ready to become citizens of tomorrow's world, of this *brotherly world* to which you aspire together with the young people of the whole world.

(2436) All of you young people, I am sure, are capable of this dialogue. You do not wish to be conditioned by prejudices. You are prepared to build a civilization based on love. You can work to break down the barriers resulting partly from pride and, more often, from weakness and from fear of men. You wish to love others regardless of national frontiers, race or religion.

(2437) To achieve this end, *you want justice and peace.* "Peace and youth go together," as I stated in my message for World Peace Day this year. You want neither war nor violence. You know the price they exact from innocent people. Nor do you want an escalation of armaments. That does not mean that you want peace at any price. Peace goes hand in hand with justice. You do not want anyone to be oppressed. You want peace with justice.

(2438) 8. First of all, you wish that people should have enough on which to live. Young people who have the good fortune to pursue their studies, have the right to be solicitous about the profession that they will be able to exercise on their own behalf. But they also must concern themselves with the living conditions, often more difficult, of their brothers and sisters who live in the same country, and indeed in the whole world. How can one remain indifferent, in fact, when other human beings, in great numbers, die of hunger, of malnutrition or lack of health care, when they suffer cruelly from drought, when they are reduced to unemployment or to emigration through economic laws that are beyond their control, when they endure the precarious situation of refugees, packed into camps, as a consequence of human conflicts? God gave the earth to the entire human race so that peoples could derive their livelihood from it in solidarity, and so that each people might have the means of feeding itself, caring for itself and living in peace.

(2439) 9. However, important as economic problems may be, man does not live by bread alone; he needs an intellectual and spiritual life, and it is there that you will find the soul of this new world to which you aspire. Man needs to develop his mind and his conscience. This is often lacking to the man today. Forgetfulness of values and the crisis of identity which frustrate our world oblige us to outdo ourselves in a renewed effort of research and investigation. The interior light which will thus be born in our conscience will enable us to give meaning to development, to orientate it towards the good of man, of every man and of all men, in accordance with God's plan.

(2440) The Arabs of the Mashreq and the Maghreb, and the Muslims in general, have a long tradition of study and scholarship, in literature, science and philosophy. You are heirs to that tradition, you must study in order to come to know this world that God has given you, to understand it, to discover its meaning, with love and *respect for the truth*, and to come to know the peoples and human beings created and loved by God, in order to prepare yourselves to serve them better.

(2441) And what is far more important, the search for truth will lead you, beyond intellectual values, to the spiritual dimension of the inner life.

(2442) 10. Man is *a spiritual being*. We believers know that we do not live in a closed world. We believe in God. We are worshippers of God. We are seekers after God.

(2443) The Catholic Church views with respect and *recognizes the quality of your religious progress* and the richness of your spiritual tradition.

(2444) We Christians, too, are proud of our religious tradition.

(2445) I believe that we, Christians and Muslims, must joyfully acknowledge the religious values that we have in common and give thanks for them to God. We both believe in one God, the only God, who is ever just and all-merciful. We believe in the importance of prayer, of fasting, of almsgiving, of repentance and of pardon. We believe that God will be a merciful judge to us at the end of time, and we hope that after the resurrection He will be satisfied with us, and we will be satisfied with Him.

(2446) Loyalty also requires that we recognize and respect our differences. The most fundamental is obviously the regard which we have for the person and works of Jesus of Nazareth. You know that for us Christians, this Jesus led us to require an intimate knowledge of the mystery of God and to share His gifts in a filial communion, so that we recognize Him and proclaim Him Lord and Saviour.

(2447) Those are the important differences, which we can accept with humility and respect, in mutual tolerance. That is a mystery on which God will one day enlighten us, I am sure.

(2448) We Christians and Muslims have generally misunderstood each other, and sometimes, in the past, we have opposed each other and even exhausted each other in polemics and wars.

(2449) I believe that God invites us, today, *to change our old practices*. We must respect each other and stimulate each other in good works, following God's ways.

(2450) With me, you know what is the reward of spiritual values. Ideologies and slogans cannot satisfy you nor can they solve the problems of your life.
Only the spiritual and moral values can do it, and they have God as their foundation.

(2451) I hope, dear young people, that you will be able to help to build a world in which God has first place in order to aid and save mankind. In pursuing that goal, you may be sure of the esteem and cooperation of your Catholic brothers and sisters, whom I represent here this evening.

(2452) 11. I should now like to thank His Majesty the King for inviting me, and also to thank you, dear young people of Morocco, for coming here and listening trustingly to my message.

(2453) But even more, I wish to thank God who has made this meeting possible. We are all watched over by Him. He is the first witness of our meeting today. It is He who places in our hearts the feelings of mercy and understanding, of forgiveness and reconciliation, of service and cooperation. Should we not, as believers, reproduce in our lives and in our communities the qualities reflected in the good names which our religious traditions have granted to Him? May we, therefore, be available to Him and submit to His will and to the appeals which He addresses to us! Thus will our lives acquire a new dynamism.

(2454) Then, I am convinced, a world can be born where men and women of living and effective faith will sing to the glory of God, and will seek to build a human society in accordance with God's will.

(2455) I should like to conclude by invoking Him personally in your presence:

O God, you are our Creator.
You are limitlessly good and merciful.
For you is the praise of every creature.
O God, you have given to us men an interior law
by which we should live.
To do your will, is to perform our task.
To follow your ways, is to know peace of soul.
To you, we offer our obedience.
Guide us in all the steps that we undertake on earth.
Free us from evil inclinations which turn our
heart from your will.
Do not permit that in invoking your Name
we should come to justify the human disorders.
O God, you are the One Alone.
To you goes our adoration.
Do not let us stray from you
O God, judge of all mankind,
help us to belong to your elect on the last day.
O God, author of justice and peace,
grant us the true joy and the authentic love, as
also a lasting fraternity between the peoples.
Fill us with your gifts for ever. Amen!

3. THE CHARACTERISTICS AND CONCERNS OF YOUTH TODAY

Statement of the Holy See Delegation by Ms. Mary Reiner to the United Nations World Conference for the International Youth Year. New York, 12 November 1985.

Original: English

(2456) It is with special satisfaction that the Holy See intervenes at this Conference on Youth as the International Youth Year moves to its climax in this 40th Session of the United Nations General Assembly.

(2457) The preparations everywhere have been extensive and the collaboration of the Catholic Church has been marked by the vitality and joy that characterize many young people in the Church today. Youth activities of the Church have included the International Meeting of Youth in Rome with the participation of about 250,000 young people who demonstrated the great openness and interest of Catholic young people in the task of building a society of justice and peace inclusive of the spiritual dimension of human persons. Further, an annual World Day of Youth has been designated by the Catholic Church to direct attention to the contributions and the potential of youth in creating a better future. Finally, I would like to recall the numerous programs, seminars and meetings initiated by the many international Catholic non-governmental organizations with the participation of young people.

(2458) The Holy See would, therefore, express appreciation to all the delegates of the Third Committee who for many years have guided the planning for this momentous occasion and also to the Secretariat for their work culminating in this important event.

(2459) As the member of this delegation appointed for this agenda item, I would like to contribute from my research and my experience with my peers on three continents to the international dialogue here in three areas: the importance of International Youth Year, the situation of youth today, and some major concerns of contemporary youth for consideration by the United Nations in the future.

(2460) The significance of International Youth Year needs to be exposed fully in order to enrich and to guide the actions of the international community in behalf of youth. Careful reflection on the truth about International Youth Year is a means of renewal and rededication.

(2461) Although the attractions and the stresses of this moment in history command intense attention, the future of youth imposes an overriding importance because the future of youth signifies the future of all humanity. There is no tomorrow without the youth of today. The tomorrow of the world lies in the minds and hearts and hands of today's young people. Youth is the state of the future, and they are the society of tomorrow. The destiny of all humanity is the destiny of this present generation of youth. When we ask ourselves, what do we want for our future, the accuracy of our answer hinges on what we are doing with and for our youth today. For these reasons, International Youth Year appears before us as a time of action to prepare the adulthood of the millions of youth of the world. My delegation insists most emphatically that the world of tomorrow and its society are created out of the actions for and with the youth of today.

(2462) Therefore, we say that the youth of today hold the key to the transformation of society. The hopes and plans made during this International Youth Year pass into the hands of my generation for implementation. The improvements envisioned and sought by adults will be realized as they are molded by today's young people. And, in turn, my generation needs to learn this same lesson immediately, for the rapidity of social change is a reality we must cope with. We will have to be ready to prepare for our tomorrow which is in the hands of my generation for implementation. The improvements envisioned and sought by adults will be realized as they are molded by today's young people. And in turn, my generation needs to learn this same lesson immediately, for the rapidity of social change is a reality we must cope with. We will have to be ready to prepare for our tomorrow which is in the hands of the children of today. Therefore, communication among generations assumes increasing importance, and the openness of heart and mind, and that willingness to learn from others characteristic of little children, as proclaimed by Jesus in Christian Scripture, becomes essential for the happiness of all.

(2463) Most importantly, International Youth Year moves all of humanity closer to what we want to be. This year must be the beginning of the coordination of long-term programs to confront the grave problems which menace the very existence of humanity by threats to environment, and which attack human creativity by unemployment, and which diminish the fullness of humanity by erosion of the spiritual dimension of life.

(2464) The initiatives in behalf of youth must help us to deepen and broaden the concept of the free person, called to realize the project of growth and self-realization which God has written in the human heart without withdrawing from personal aspirations that are honest and beautiful, but always remaining open within the community and society to whose progress we young people are committed.

(2465) International Youth Year is an opportunity for youth and for adults together to renew themselves. It provides an impetus for all generations to overcome marginalization and divisions of all kinds in order to unite to make a new world where participation, development and peace flourish. It is a challenge to address jointly the uncertainties of the new century and to construct together the new civilization of truth and love.

(2466) Certainly one of the achievements of the International Youth Year for which the world community can already be pleased is the amount of research undertaken through the United Nations Secretariat on the situation of youth. For the first time,as the documentation shows, we know more about the conditions of youth of the world than before. The results of the research are alarming: the health, the education, the unemployment, the situation of young women, of young refugees, migrants and prisoners, so-called street and abandoned youth, young prostitutes, both male and female, homeless young people and those victims of violence are often in perilous situations and, we might say, unjust situations when compared with the attention, talent and finances devoted to armaments and to destruction. The Holy See has called attention to this injustice on many occasions, and at this time, we bring the attention of this International Youth Year Conference to such a scandal in the hopes of action in behalf of these particular youth groups.

(2467) Furthermore, Mr. President, this delegation would supplement the research on youth today with some characteristics based on the Church's service to and contact with youth all over the world.

(2468) In the matter of peace, a theme and priority of International Youth Year, young people today are in the front row. More acutely than others, for whom they are often the privileged expression, youth longs to live. And yet, they are the first to be forced to take up arms, the first to be indoctrinated and manipulated in favor of violence and war. Many young people are convinced that war is not preparation for peace, and it is not a road to peace. Yet, often in the quest for peace,our ready good will is rebutted and looked upon with condescension. Young people must often overcome the snubs of cynics and the indifference of those unwilling to listen to them and to encourage their participation in matters concerning themselves and their future, for example, peace. The willingness to participate must be given encouragement in each young person, for otherwise we will not develop our abilities to help attain universal peace. Moreover we will not achieve fulfillment as persons, for peace means the fullness of being. The words of the Holy Father give us confidence and strength here: "I believe in youth wit hall my heart and the strength of my conviction," he said.

(2469) The youth of today are very demanding, sometimes falling into exaggeration and succumbing to personal selfishness. In us, there is a desire for honesty, truthfulness, justice and consistency. There is widespread dissatisfaction among us evoked by the widely evident lack of justice and generosity. Very sensitive to the tension between good and evil in the world and in ourselves, many of my peers suffer intensely at the victory of falsehood and injustice and at our powerlessness to make truth and justice triumph. Like youth of every age, we are searching for truth, for ideals to live by, for responsible participation, moral beauty and innocent joy.

(2470) The suffering of young people results also from the contradictory nature of the ideologies that impinge upon us and from the continuing emptying of ideals which we witness. Professional integration in societies where pleasure is the purpose of life demands compromises which, for many of us, sometimes inspire revolt, escape or resignation. But employment is not even available to so many, even though they have the necessary skills and are animated by good will to contribute to society. Young persons without work are exposed to every type of temptation: violence, drugs, even despair and suicide.

(2471) Also we are a questioning youth, wanting to account for what is happening, looking for the meaning of our own lives and the significance of humanity and of the whole universe. We are a youth which invoke certainty and clarity on our own destiny and with regard to our own conduct. Ours is a period of transition when uncertainties abound. Questions arise among us: what meaning does the life we are living have? is it possible to hope? Certainly clear ideas, well-defined goals and concrete proposals respond best to our needs. We sense the necessity of finding a reality that may give a decisive and ultimate meaning to our fragmented reality.

(2472) Finally we are a youth filled with fear: fears about the threat to survival of our human species, anxiety about the threat to peace in our world because of atomic armament, worry about the destruction of our ecological balance and our beautiful planet earth, and concern for the problems of our nations which remain unresolved for so long.

(2473) These then, are some characteristics of youth today: critical, demanding, suffering, questioning, and fearful.

(2474) An initial concern of my generation can be phrased this way: What will be the meaning of existence in the future? In the third millennium, the time of maturity for the youth of today, many of us believe that we will find our meaning in truth,the possession of truth and the possibility to live in truth. This is truth in thought and truth in action. To experiential and scientific truth must be added a profound moral and religious formation that will be deeply lived and will bring about an increasingly harmonious synthesis between faith and other human dimensions: reason, culture, life. In his Apostolic Letter to the Youth of the World on the occasion of International Youth Year, Pope John Paul II explains: "Truth is the light of the human intellect. If the intellect seeks, from youth onwards, to know reality in its different dimensions, it does so in order to possess the truth, in order to live the truth." Youth seeks the meaning of human life in truth, the Truth that, as the Church teaches, will make us free.

(2475) A second concern of my generation is: how to arrive at goodness? how to pass through sacrifice, effort and struggle to a final triumph? The importance of the family cannot fail to be recognized as teacher of good and mentor of the good life. The stable family can provide for the young members loving patience, understanding and support so that they can discover their own infinite capacity for love, trust and sharing. This aspect of the family's educative role is particularly relevant to young people as they approach the age of marriage. The responsibilities of raising a family are enormous and in order to establish a solid and loving family relationship, the necessary qualities must already have been cultivated. Thus the importance of the family as educator in morality, conscience, and the discovery of love is easily recognized. As the young person grows and develops, so too does the family. However, "growing up" can be difficult for the family as well as for the young person. Both will face obstacles and will need support to overcome them. The family that encourages its younger members to persevere in the face of difficulty must itself be encouraged by society.

(2476) However, in many instances today we find that the ideal of mutual support and development between society and the family is non-existent, and the two are often in opposition to each other. If the family must fight for its own survival it cannot also give the necessary guidance to the young persons within it. Consequently, society suffers the double loss of breakdown in the family and the young person's frequent engagement in anti-social behavior. Moreover, because their sense of self-esteem has not developed within the family, or because they did not have the benefit of family protection, young people are exploited in degrading occupations such as prostitution. The Holy See strongly defends the rights of the family against undue interference in its structure and functioning and condemns those situations that debase the fundamental integrity of the person.

(2477) Finally, a concern of ours is how to explain to the world why we young people are filled with hope. How do we explain to the world the hope that lies at the very root of youth? Pope John Paul II and many others refer to us as "the hope of society" and "the hope of peace". In fact, youth is a sign which tells people of all ages something about themselves and about what it is to be a creation of God. The images of youth, such as beauty, strength and enthusiasm, symbolize qualities potential within every human person. Youth then is a precious possession, available to each one, not merely to those in the 15 to 24 age bracket. It is a timeless state defying death, and it is a reminder that death is not the end and that death has been conquered. If the folly of youth is to cling to materialism,the wisdom of youth delves into a deeper vision of life where love,beauty, strength, enthusiasm, courage and resilience flourish. These youthful qualities and spiritual powers live within persons of all ages, and International Youth Year is, above all, a call to honor such youthful qualities of human nature.

(2478) In conclusion I return to an appreciation of International Youth Year as an impetus for the years ahead. This moment marks a determination not to leave the future to chance. It signals a time of commitment: the adults of today commit themselves to youth for a transformation of society into a better world tomorrow. Today's youth, my generation, commit ourselves to children, the youth of tomorrow and to the society we begin in collaboration with the adults of today. Basic to our future together is the assumption that work for youth must be done with youth. We urge a greater investment of human resources to prepare youth for the tomorrows and the optimism, dedication, and good will of the adult generation to prepare with us for a future beyond this great International Youth Year.

III - THE VALUE OF OLD AGE

Message of His Holiness John Paul II to the World Assembly on the problems of the aging population. The Vatican, 22 July 1982.

Original: English (*)

(2479) Already on a number of occasions the Holy See has greeted with considerable interest and hope the initiative of the United Nations to promote a World Assembly on the problems of the aging population and of its consequences for each person and for society. Once that decision was confirmed, one witnessed a development and a deepening of the awareness of this demographic phenomenon of our times which obliges the nations and international society to question themselves concerning the destiny,the needs, the rights, the specific capacity of the aging generations whose number is increasing. Even beyond persons, this reflection must extend to the very organization of society with regard to this group of the population.

(2480) The attentive study of the preparatory work of this World Assembly and of the Plan of Action, at present submitted to the examination of all the member Nations of the United Nations, allows one to see a number of points which encounter a particular support on the part of the Holy See. I will quote some: the attention brought to elderly people as such and to the quality of their lives today; respect for their right to live as active members of a society which they have helped to build; the will to foster a social organization in which each generation can bring its contribution in line with the others; finally an appeal to the creativity of each socio-cultural milieu, so that they can find satisfying responses which enable the elderly to carry out activities which correspond to their great diversity of origin and education, of capacities and of experience, of cultures and of belief. The themes already mentioned are sufficient to indicate that we are not dealing here simply with abstract or technical problems, but much more with the destiny of human persons, with their particular personal history characterized by family roots, social links, professional successes or failures which have marked, or which still mark, their existence.

(2481) To your important Assembly, oriented as it is towards these realities in order to deepen them and to find concrete and balanced solutions, the Church wishes to offer the contribution of its reflection, of its experience and of its faith in man. Practically speaking, it wishes to propose its human and Christian vision of aging, its conviction concerning the family and of institutions of family type as the most favourable place for the development of the elderly and to sustain, through its interest, contemporary society in the service of the aging generations.

(2482) I recall with great emotion my meeting with the elderly in November 1980 in Munich Cathedral. I underlined on that occasion that human aging is a natural stage of existence, which generally must be considered its crowning. This vision presupposes obviously that old age - when one arrives at it - is considered as an element having a particular value within human life considered as a whole. It also requires an exact concept of the person who is, at the same time, body and

(*) AAS 74(1982), 1172-1179.

soul. It is in this perspective that the Bible speaks of old age and of the elderly with respect and admiration. The book of Ecclesiasticus, for example, after praising "judgment in grey-haired men" (25:4-6) begins a long panegyric of the ancestors whose "bodies were buried in peace, and whose name lives to all generations" (cf. chap. 44 to 51). And the New Testament is full of veneration for the elderly. Saint Luke, with great emotion, presents the image of the elderly Simeon and the prophetess Anna who receive Christ in the temple. And, in the era of the early Christian communities, we find the Apostles designating Elders to watch over their young foundations. The Church earnestly hopes that the Plan of Action will be open to this conception of old age considered not only as an inexorable process of biological degradation or as a period detached from the other seasons of existence, but rather as a phase which is capable of natural development of the life of the entire human being, for whom it represents fulfillment.

(2483) It is indeed true that life is a gift of God to men, created through love in His image and likeness. This understanding of the sacred dignity of the human person leads one to attribute a value to all the stages of life. It is a question of coherence and justice. It is, in effect, impossible to appreciate in truth the life of an old person without appreciating in truth the life of an infant at the beginning of its conception. It is impossible to know at what point one will arrive if life is not any more respected as an inalienable and sacred good. One must firmly affirm with the Congregation for the Doctrine of the Faith in its Declaration on Euthanasia of 5 May 1980 that "no person may authorize the suppression of the life of an innocent human being, fetus or embryo, child or adult, old person, incurably sick or dying... It is a violation of the Divine Law, an offence against the dignity of the human person, a crime against life, an attempt against humanity". It is very opportune to add further what the same Declaration says of the use of therapeutic means: "It is today very important, at the moment of death, to protect the dignity of the human person and the Christian conception of life against the application of technical advances which risk becoming abusive". Death is a part of our human horizon and gives it its true and mysterious dimension. The contemporary world, especially in the West, needs to learn to reintegrate death into human life. Who could not augur for others and desire for himself to accept and assume the final act of his earthly existence in the dignity and serenity that is certainly possible for believers?

(2484) I wish now to look once again with you at the characteristics of old age. On the one hand, they are sad and difficult to accept,especially for the person who is alone. On the other hand, there are characteristics which are a source of wealth for oneself and for others. Taken together, they form part of the human experience of those who are old today and of those who will be old tomorrow.

(2485) The fundamental aspects of the third and of the fourth age are linked naturally with a certain frailty of the physical forces, with a reduced vivacity of the spiritual faculties, with a progressive separation from the activities to which one was attached, with sickness and with an incapacity which overcomes one, with the perspective of affective separations linked with death. These saddening characteristics can be transformed through philosophical convictions and, above all, for those who have the good fortune to believe, through the certitude of faith. For believers, in fact, the final stage of earthly life can be seen as a mysterious accompaniment of Christ the Redeemer, along the dolorous path of the Cross, leading to the radiant dawn of Easter. But in a more general sense one can affirm that the manner in which a civilization copes with old age and with death as a constitutive element of life, and the manner in which it helps its elderly members to live their death,are decisive criteria of the respect it bears for man.

(2486) There are also positive aspects of old age. It is the time in which men and women can gather the harvest of the experience of their entire lives, making the choice between what is accidental and essential, and achieving a level of great witness and of profound serenity. It is the period of life in which they dispose of a great deal of time, even of all their time, to love their habitual or occasional companions with a disinterest, a patience and a discreet joy of which the elderly act as admirable examples. For believers, further, it offers the happy possibility to meditate on the splendours of the faith and to pray in a deeper manner.

(2487) The fecundity of these values and their survival are linked with two conditions which cannot be dissociated. The first requires that the elderly themselves deeply accept their age and appreciate its possible resources. The second condition refers to today's society. It must become capable of recognizing the moral, affective and religious values which exist in the spirit and in the heart of the elderly and it must be open to the integration into our society which suffers through a disturbing gap between its technical and ethical levels. The elderly, in fact, can live only with difficulty in a world which has become unaware of its spiritual dimension. They arrive at a point in which they disregard themselves, in that they see that it is the productivity of citizens which seems to count most, while the other resources of the human person are ignored or undervalued. Such a climate goes against the fulfillment and the fecundity of old age and necessarily engenders a turning in on self, the sad feeling of being useless and finally despair. But one must underline once again that it is society as a whole which deprives itself of enriching and guiding elements when it begins to consider as valid for its development only its young or adult members in full possession of their strength and when it considers the others as unproductive, even though numerous experiences, judiciously carried out, prove the contrary.

(2488) In my Apostolic Exhortation *Familiaris Consortio* I recalled, in the light of the divine origins of the human family, that its essence and its tasks are defined by love: "Established as 'an intimate community of life and love' the family ...has the mission to guard, reveal and communicate love.... All the members of the family, each according to his or her own gift, have the grace and responsibility of building, day by day, the communion of persons, making the family 'a school of deeper humanity'" (nn. 17 and 21).

(2489) Allow me to look at the possibilities that are offered through the family to old people, both with regard to the faithful support which they have the right to expect from the family and with regard to the possible contribution which they can make to its life and mission. It is quite true that the conditions necessary for the integration of the elderly into the home of their children or other relatives do not always exist and that such integration occasionally reveals itself as impossible. On such occasions, then, one must envisage another solution, with the responsibility for the children and the other members of the family to maintain warm and regular bonds with the one who has had to go to a home for the elderly.

(2490) Having said this, it is also certain that, living with their own flesh and blood, the elderly can, with the appropriateness and the discretion that this will always require, bring to their relatives the benefit of that affection and wisdom,that understanding and indulgence, of advice and comfort, of faith and of prayer which are, for the most part, the charisma of the twilight of life. Living in this manner they will equally contribute to giving their due place, especially by example,to attitudes which are often undervalued today, like listening,self-effacement, serenity, self-giving, interiority, discreet and radiant joy ... it is worth noting also that the habitual or occasional presence of the elderly among their own relatives is often a precious factor in the linking and mutual understanding between the generations, which are necessarily diverse and complementary. Indeed this strengthening of the family, along the lines that I have just recalled, and according to its possible manner, can be a source of balance and of vitality, of humanity and of spirituality for that fundamental cell of all society which bears the most expressive name which exists in all the languages of the world: "the family".

(2491) With the current demographic evolution, society sees opening before itself a new field of action in the service of the human person in order to guarantee for the elderly the place that belongs to them in the civil community and to foster their specific contribution to its development.

(2492) The aging generations who, in certain legislative and social systems, see themselves retiring earlier and earlier from the area of economic production, ask themselves - often with anguish - about the place and function that is reserved for them in this new type of society. How does this early retirement which is imposed on them help them themselves? Does current society in its evolution and orientations still expect something from aged and retired members?

(2493) It appears that, faced with this new and vast problem, society as a whole, and particularly those who bear responsibility, must envisage solutions capable of responding to the aspirations of aged persons. These solutions cannot be of one single type. If it is normal that society should foster the maintenance of the elderly with their family and their own environment, as long as this solution is possible and can be supported, other means must also be offered to the third and fourth age. In this domain a society which is truly aware of its duties towards those generations who have contributed to making the history of nations must set up appropriate institutions. To maintain continuity with that which the elderly have known and experienced, it is most desirable that these institutions have a family character; that is to say, that they try to provide the elderly with human warmth, so necessary at any stage of life but particularly for the stage of advanced age. These institutions must equally provide for a certain autonomy, compatible with necessities of community life, as well as possible activities which correspond to their physical and professional capacities.

(2494) Finally these institutions must care for all the needs of an age which advances. Certainly, there already exist institutions of this kind. But they must be developed. You will permit me, on this subject, to call to mind the charitable action of the Church through so many institutions dedicated to the care of the elderly, for such a long time. May they be congratulated and encouraged! A society brings to itself singular honour when it makes these paths of service for man converge in what is best in respect for the elderly and for the varying institutions which receive them. It seems useful to me to draw attention briefly, once again, to some of the new services which society could render to retired persons and to the elderly to assure them a place and a role in the human community. I think, for example, of the permanent practical formation in many countries which generates, for those who benefit from it, not only personal enrichment, but also capacities of adaptation and of participation in the daily life of society. Truly, the elderly possess reserves of wisdom and experience which, maintained and at the same time completed by a well-adapted process of permanent formation,could be inserted into those lively sectors of education to humble socio-charitable services. On this level new initiatives could be sought with the interest of the elderly themselves or with the associations which represent them. I equally think that society should seek, in taking careful account of the individual capacities of the elderly and of the strongly varying situations in the different continents, to establish a possibility of a certain diversification of activities. Between boring uniformity and continuous fantasy, it is possible to find a judicious balance between professional and other work, between reading and study, leisure, organized or individual encounters with other persons and other milieux, a time for serene and prayerful meditation.

(2495) There is another service which society can render to the aging generations. It is that of encouraging the creation, when this is called for, of associations for the elderly and of supporting those which already exist. They already are bearing fruit, especially combating isolation and the painful impression of being rendered useless which often pervade the stage of retirement and old age. Such associations need to be recognized by those with responsibility in society as a legitimate expression of the desires of the elderly and, among them, the desires of the most marginated.

(2496) Finally, I think of the role which the means of social communication and particularly of television and radio can and should play in order to create a more just and renewed image of aging, and its possible contribution to the vitality and balance of society.

(2497) This requires that those responsible for audio-visual means and for the press must be convinced, or at least respectful, of a conception of human life founded no longer only on economic or purely material utility but on its fuller sense which can admit of development and an admirable expansion until the end of the earthly course, especially when the environment favours such a possibility.

(2498) At the conclusion of these reflections and suggestions, it remains for me to express the hope that the Vienna World Assembly on the problems of aging will progressively bring about abundant and enduring fruit. In this domain, as in many others already studied and fostered by the United Nations, e.g.childhood, the world of the handicapped, etc., we are dealing with questions which touch the ultimate realities of the present and future of human civilization. All culture, in whatever continent or country and for the entire era of history, cannot find its value and its radiance except in always assigning primacy to the integral development of the human person, of the first and final stage of his earthly course, and this encounters the temptation of a society taken up with the dizziness of the production of things and of their consumption. May those who are responsible for the world today open themselves unitedly for the true advancement and maintenance of their people in this manner! This is not only the object of my ardent wishes but also of my constant prayer to God, the Author of all good things.

IV - WOMEN

1. INTERNATIONAL WOMEN'S YEAR: A CALL OF THE SPIRIT

Address of His Holiness Paul VI to Mrs H. Sipila, Secretary-General of the International Women's Year. The Vatican, 6 November 1974.

Original: English (*)

(2499) We very willingly greet in you, this morning, the representative of the commitment assumed by the United Nations for the "International Women's Year", proclaimed for 1975; this meeting offers us the opportunity to express the goodwill and attention with which we wish to follow this initiative.

(2500) In fact, the initiative does not find the Church inattentive to the problem or lacking in a clear desire to solve it. On the contrary: in the contemporary effort to promote the advancement of woman in society, the Church has already recognized "a sign of the times", and has seen in it a call of the Spirit. The Study Commission which we set up, accepting a wish expressed by the 1971 Synod, has precisely received the mandate to study, in a comparison with the aspirations of today's world and the enlightening doctrine of the Church, the full participation of woman in the community life of the Church and of society.

(2501) The programme of International Women's Year, well summed up in the theme "equality, development and peace", is thus not extraneous to the most lively interest of the Church herself.

(2502) Equality can be found only in its essential foundation, which is the dignity of the human person, man and woman, in their filial relationship with God, of whom they are the visible image.

(2503) But this does not exclude the distinction, in unity, and the specific contribution of woman to the full development of society, according to her proper and personal vocation.

(2504) In this way the woman of today will be able to become more conscious of her rights and duties, and will be able to contribute not only to the her self-improvement but also to a qualitative progress of human social life, "in development and peace".

(2505) And since the fundamental and life-giving cell of human society remains the family, according to the very plan of God, woman will preserve and develop, principally in the family community, in full co-responsibility with man, her task of welcoming, giving and raising life, in a growing development of its potential powers.

(2506) To all those collaborating in the preparation of International Women's Year in the most worthy purpose of strengthening ever more the dignity and mission of woman, we indicate as a solid point of reference the figure of the Blessed Virgin. As we stated in our recent Exhortation *Marialis Cultus*, our age is called upon to verify and to "compare its anthropological ideas and the problems springing therefrom with the figure of the Virgin Mary as presented by the Gospel. The reading of the divine Scriptures, carried out under the guidance of the Holy Spirit, and with the discoveries of the human sciences and the different situations in the world today being taken into account, will

(*) Insegnamenti di Paolo VI, Vol. XII (1974), 1054-1055.

help us to see how Mary can be considered a mirror of the expectations of the men and women of our time ... [she] offers them the perfect model of the disciple of the Lord: the disciple who builds up the earthly and temporal city while being a diligent pilgrim towards the heavenly and eternal city, the disciple who works for that justice which sets free the oppressed and for that charity which assists the needy; but above all, the disciple who is the active witness of that love which builds up Christ in people's hearts" (37).

(2507) And with this bright vision before our eyes, we wish the undertaking harmonious and profitable work, upon which we invoke the intercession of the Mother of God and the fullness of divine blessings.

2. CHURCH ACTIVITIES FOR WOMEN

Message of His Holiness Paul Vi to Mrs. H. Sipila, Secretary-General of the World Conference of the International Women's Year. The Vatican, 16 June 1975.

Original: Spanish (*)

(2508) It is a pleasure for us to greet the World Conference of International Women's Year which is opening in Mexico City and to express our best wishes for its work, which can happily contribute to the future of humanity.

(2509) We have already had the opportunity - on the occasion of your visit - to emphasize the goodwill and attention with which we intended to follow the International Women's Year proclaimed by the United Nations. We recognized, in fact, in the threefold theme of the Year - equality, development and peace - the synthesis of a vast network of problems that the world community must face today and which expresses aspirations with which the Church herself manifests her solidarity. The present Conference, however, marks a genuinely new stage in progress of nations in their constant search for more just and more human conditions of life.

(2510) On the one hand, it is a question of doing justice to women, who too often in the course of history and still today have found or find themselves relegated to a position of inferiority with regard to men, and the victims, to a greater degree than men, of the scourges of underdevelopment and war. But on the other hand, as we have been happy to note in the goals assigned to the International Women's Year, it is also a question of ensuring concretely the full integration of women in the global effort for development and of recognizing and encouraging their contribution to the strengthening of peace. What a great hope for humanity it would be, if, by the concerted effort of all people of goodwill, the hundreds of millions of women in all parts of the world could finally place at the service of these great causes and of the "reconciliation in families and in society" not only the strength of their numbers but also the irreplaceable contribution of their gifts of mind and heart! This hope we evoked still more recently, on the occasion of the World Day of Peace.

(2511) It is not only in recent times that the Catholic Church has called for the accomplishment of these goals assigned to International Women's Year. Already nearly twenty years ago (not to mention still earlier periods), our predecessor Pius XII said to the women of the whole world: "You can and must make your own, without restriction, the programme of the advancement of women - a programme which upholds with an immense hope the unnumbered throng of your sisters who are still subjected to degrading customs or who are the victims of poverty, of the ignorance of their milieux and of the total lack of means of culture and formation" [Address to the World Union of Catholic Women's Organizations, 29 September 1957: AAS 49(1957), p. 907). This advancement was to be conceived "in Christian terms, in the light of faith"; but this was certainly not in order to diminish its scope. On the contrary, for it is in this light that there emerges most clearly the true

(*) AAS 67 (1975), 437-439

equality between man and woman, each in his or her proper way endowed with the dignity of the human person and created in the image of God.

(2512) Thus it is that, in his Encyclical *Pacem in Terris*, Pope John XXIII hailed as a "sign of the times" the fact that "women are gaining an increasing awareness of their natural dignity ... they are demanding both in domestic and public life the rights and duties which belong to them as human persons" [AAS 55(1963), pp. 267-268). At the same time, the Second Vatican Council, recognizing the solidarity of the whole Church with "the joys and hopes, the sadnesses and anxieties" of the modern world, hastened to condemn the injustices of a discrimination based on sex and to vindicate for women, with reverence for their rights and duties in accordance with their own specific aptitudes, a responsible and fuller share in the whole of the life of society (cf. Pastoral Constitution *Gaudium et Spes*, 29 and 60).

(2513) It is not possible to recall here all the efforts whereby the Catholic Church seeks to contribute effectively to the integration of women into the works of development and peace. It will suffice for us to mention just one sphere which we have particularly at heart: the campaign against illiteracy, the illiteracy which plays an evil role, especially among women in rural areas, constituting an obstacle to development and offending essential rights, for, as we recalled in our Encyclical *Populorum Progressio*, "hunger for education is no less debasing than hunger for food: an illiterate is a person with an undernourished mind" [35; AAS 59(1967), p. 274].

(2514) Emphasizing the disinherited masses' elementary need for teaching does not imply forgetting the importance for the goals of International Women's Year of education in all its forms - the education of men as well as of women - and of the action to be undertaken at the level of public opinion. It is, moreover, by a healthy effort of education that it will be possible to bring into operation the necessary discernments in order that "liberation" may not lead to new and worse forms of servitude, and in order that the struggle against discrimination may not base itself upon a "false equality which would deny the distinctions laid down by the Creator himself" [*Octogesima Adveniens*, 13; AAS 63(1971), p. 411], or which would risk attenuating the exact idea of the privileged mission of women.

(2515) In order to promote and orientate this action for a salutary change of attitudes, we have made it our task to set up a Committee of the Holy See for International Women's Year. We have also suggested to the local Churches throughout the world that they should make use of this occasion in order to examine themselves regarding the effective participation of women in the Church's life and regarding the Catholics' contribution to every effort aimed at the harmonious collaboration between men and women in the great tasks facing society.

(2516) We wish in this way to make our contribution towards ensuring that International Women's Year may truly be, in accordance with the happy idea of its promoters, the point of departure for long-term action.

(2517) We finally turn to Almighty God. It is He who created woman, no less than man, in His own image (cf. *Gen.* 1:27); it is also He who wished to call a woman, the Virgin Mary, in order that she might give "her active and responsible consent" [*Marialis Cultus*, 37; AAS 66(1974), p. 148] to the decisive event of the coming of Christ into the world, the good news of the fullness of life and of true liberation for all mankind. May Almighty God bless the work of this Conference, may He grant strength and enlightenment to all those responsible for it, in the service of the human family.

3. INTERNATIONAL WOMEN'S YEAR: A STEP FORWARD

Statement made by H.E. Msgr. Ramon Torrella Cascante, Vice President of the Pontifical Commission "Justice and Peace", Head of the Holy See Delegation to the World Conference of the International Women's Year, held in Mexico City on 19 June - 2 July 1975.

Original: Spanish

(2518) The Delegation of the Holy See has pleasure in reiterating the deep interest of the Catholic Church in International Women's Year, an interest that was clearly evident in the Message of His Holiness Pope Paul VI to this Conference.

(2519) We are also pleased to express our deep appreciation of the positive action for the effective promotion of women undertaken over nearly thirty years - in fidelity to the principles laid down in the Charter of the United Nations and the Universal Declaration of Human Rights - by the United Nations Organization and its specialized Agencies. This intergovernmental action has been well supported and completed by many forms of private initiative, among which are those of Catholic international organizations and of the Catholic Church itself.

(2520) It is therefore gratifying, today, to observe, not only concrete results, but also an ever more widespread awareness of the rights, as well as the duties and responsibilities of women in every walk of life. International Women's Year, on the one hand, crowns and reveals the extent of these efforts; on the other hand, and especially, it gives them fresh impetus, inserting them in the wider context of the threefold theme of the Year: equality, development and peace. In this way it marks indeed - we sincerely hope - an entirely new stage in the progress of the nations towards a more just and more human society.

(2521) This global character of International Women's Year - affecting men as well as women, the individual as well as the whole of society, and its dynamic thrust towards the future of a world in the throes of radical transformation - is the first point we would like to emphasize. We have, therefore, concentrated particular attention on the aims and objectives of IWY and on the draft World Plan of Action (E/CONF/66/5), which seems to summarize and link the various aspects of the theme, while at the same time providing a basis for long term action. We shall have to express some reserves, some concern that we feel as a result of our study of this draft, but our primary intention is to give the measures proposed their full human scope and value.

(2522) If we are entitled to speak here, it is in the name of the Church's mission to humanity, a mission that seeks to be universal, that must be so. Our first appeal to this Conference is, then, to ask it to be fully itself: to be truly the voice of the persons, cultures and situations present or represented here, in all their rich diversity. So that it may speak as it should, we ask it to listen to the authentic voices of all peoples, seeking to integrate their spiritual and moral riches; to listen - with the heart, when voices are too weak and far away to reach the ear - to the cries of the women, the men and women, who are most deprived: voices stifled by want, ignorance, loneliness, fear, degradation and oppression of every sort; and finally to lend an attentive ear to the voices of the younger generation. At this turning point in history, their freshness of outlook and vital dynamism can give us precious assistance in overcoming, on the one hand, unconscious prejudices, and, on the other, any temptation to discouragement, any attitude too conditioned by what may have been bitter experience; in regaining interest, if need be, in the true values of life.

(2523) To seek for woman equality with man can, in fact, have meaning only in the context of a plan for society that will offer both women and men the necessary conditions for truly human fulfillment. As a preliminary step, we must therefore ask ourselves what sort of society we want to establish by this new cooperation, in equality, between men and women, that is the aim of International Women's Year.

(2524) For us, only one reply holds good: a society focused on the human person, who, created in the image of God, "is and must be the beginning, subject and goal of all social institutions"

(*Gaudium et Spes*, 25); and which is not, therefore, merely a means of collective promotion or economic production; a society which gives its rightful place to the family, "the natural and basic element of society" according to the Declaration of Human Rights (Art. 16).

(2525) A society of this kind that would recognize in woman, as in man, the dignity and value of the human person, proclaimed by the Charter of the peoples of the United Nations, would be open to a process of genuine development, a development that would be "integral, that is, promoting the good of every man and of the whole man" (*Populorum Progressio*, 14).

(2526) But, and we regret having to say so, it seems to us that the development advocated in the draft Plan, is not always genuine in this sense. Too often it would seem to be based on quantitative criteria, with excessive concern for what might be called the "profit-motive" of the promotion of woman. This concern may lead to forgetfulness of "genuine progress" which is "to be found in the development of moral consciousness, which will lead man to exercise a wider solidarity and to open himself freely to others and to God" (*Octogesima Adveniens*, 41). Promotion of this kind can only be achieved progressively, leaving all the time necessary for human maturation. Legislative measures, however indispensable, will not suffice. And where woman is oppressed, marginalized, or merely deprived of the means necessary for her personal fulfillment, man will suffer too, and his diminished humanity will reflect on woman. It is a circle from which we must find a way out, a hill to be climbed, together, if mankind is to reach a fully human "quality of life".

(2527) To insist in this way on the development to be achieved by men and women, together, does not mean ignoring unjust discrimination against woman because of her sex. On the contrary, the whole of society must be given the means of eliminating this injustice, and encouraged to do so.

(2528) Vatican Council II, in its Pastoral Constitution on the Church in the Modern World, after asserting the "essential equality" of all human beings, however diverse their individual capacities, asks that "every type of discrimination, whether social or cultural, whether based on sex, race, colour, social condition, language, or religion, be overcome and eradicated as contrary to God's intent"; and, adding "it must still be regretted that fundamental personal rights are not yet being universally honoured", the Council quotes "the case of a woman who is denied the right and freedom to choose a husband, to embrace a state of life, or to acquire an education or cultural benefits equal to those recognized for men" (*Gaudium et Spes*, 29).

(2529) The affirmation of the fundamental equality of persons must, however, respect their diversity. We have to build "a world that will not be levelled down to uniformity, but harmoniously unified according to the plan of the Creator" (Paul VI, Address to the Committee for the International Year of Women, 18-IV-1975). Man and woman were created with equal dignity, but also with "effective complementarity", by divine act and intention ("and God saw that it was good", says Genesis). To ignore this diversity in favour of new "unisex" stereotypes would be a tragic impoverishment for mankind, just at the moment when it is becoming possible to enjoy fully the riches of woman's, as well as man's, original contribution in all social relationships (family, work, culture, politics...); when "God's image" may emerge more completely, no longer obscured by a too partial, too exclusively masculine view.

(2530) The "complementarity" willed by God will doubtless be expressed differently in different cultures, but that is in itself a richness. Today we are accustomed to studying on a world or "planetary" scale the problems of physical and material life: food, environment, habitat, health... We must equally seek out and develop for the benefit of all humanity the riches of moral dignity, of wisdom and culture peculiar to each people. In all cultures, we see an effort to renew the concept of man-woman relationships to meet the rapid and deep changes affecting the various societies. This presents a challenge to contemporary mankind, and we shall need all the wisdom of all the peoples to answer it. The Catholic Church wishes to contribute to this effort from its age-old and universal experience; and also on the basis of the evangelical principles, which - like beacons - can light the path of the human family.

(2531) For two thousand years the Catholic Church has shared the ups and downs of the successive generations. Throughout the course of its history, it has indeed shared the conditioning related to factors of discrimination against women. But it stands in solidarity with the present-day hopes for effective equality according to God's plan. As "expert on humanity" (Paul VI, Address to the United Nations, 4 October 1965. See above, par. 10) it seeks to place at the disposal of all humanity the resources of its wisdom and experience.

(2532) It is not a question - as we have already said - of an equality of persons considered in isolation within the context of a global society. Between the person and society there is, first of all, the family, the basic unit, the place where personal growth begins from real interpersonal relationships. In every society that is in any way dynamic, there are also many other intermediary groups in which women should participate for their own fulfillment and in the service of the common good. But we must, first of all, insist on the primary importance of the family: for woman herself, as also for man, in her personal vocation, and for the contribution of women and men to society. It seems to us that the Plan of action should state more clearly, at the outset, and not only in a special chapter, the need to bear in mind, this importance of the family in all the measures to be envisaged.

(2533) In spite of the attention given to responsibilities within the home, the Delegation is concerned to see how, more than once, woman's maternal role is felt as being rather an obstacle to her fulfillment (cf. 76, 123). We are anxious when we see maternity presented in a chiefly negative aspect, of risk (125), and in a way that does not respect moral principles that govern human life and that the Catholic Church has the duty to reassert. "This Plan - it is said in n. 127 - "endorses the recommendations of the World Population Plan of Action." As at the Conference of Bucharest, the Delegation of the Holy See must then express its anxiety at the fact that the plan proposed for our study provides no distinction of a moral order between the "means of contraception and birth control" which are advocated and which have only to be "efficient and compatible with cultural values prevailing in different societies" (130). The Plan also seems to accept implicitly (125) the legalization of abortion; and it is well known that the Catholic Church categorically condemns abortion in the name of the respect due to all human life from its very conception.

(2534) In this context we should like to insist on the need for a formation for responsible fatherhood and motherhood, which are also to be rightly understood, with respect for moral law; and therefore, the need for an education that is first and foremost a moral education, for the responsibilities of married life and parenthood.

(2535) We were pleased to note that the draft Plan recalls the principles laid down by ILO with regard to maternity protection, specifying that: "Provisions relating to maternity protection should not be regarded as unequal treatment of the sexes" (87). It is also requested that "special attention be given to the need for multilateral approaches to facilitate the combination of family and work responsibilities" (88). We should like to see this respect for family tasks, and the recognition of their irreplaceable value to society (113), given greater emphasis in the whole of the Plan.

(2536) Arrangements made to facilitate family tasks, must have particular features for women in rural districts of developing countries. How many women who are also engaged in work that is recognized as "productive" have to bear heavy burdens - both literally and figuratively - in their household tasks, or are deprived of elementary needs (drinking water, for instance) when many problems might be solved by a minimum of technical assistance, setting the women free also for access to values, not only of economic efficiency, but of responsible participation in the life of society.

(2537) Again with regard to the needs of the most deprived, the Delegation noted with satisfaction the stress in the draft Plan (132) on the need, in order "to improve the status of women" and "enable them to contribute fully to social and economic development," to take into account "migration and the ways it affects the family and working lives of women."

(2538) We should like to see a deeper study of the problem raised here, in its various aspects: the wives of migrant workers, and migrant women who work themselves, whether married or not.

(2539) The migrant woman does, in fact, often find herself in an extremely unfavourable situation of discrimination, marginalization and isolation. Often she has only a minimum of culture, and no professional training: her family responsibilities may be doubly heavy when she has to face up to them in an entirely new context and in the insecurity that is usually inherent in the situation of migrants.

(2540) In view of the gravity of the situation for a growing number of women, it seems to us that measures to be taken in this respect should be included among the priorities listed (35), both for home countries and host countries.

(2541) We should also like to mention what is certainly a primary aspect of the concerns of the International Women's Year: the access of women to an education adequate for their human fulfillment, at all levels, and in basic equality with men.

(2542) Only one aspect can be touched on here, and that very rapidly: women's illiteracy which is still such a plague, particularly in rural districts.

(2543) Pope Paul VI, in his Encyclical *Populorum Progressio*, already in 1967, insisted that literacy was "a fundamental factor of social integration, as well as of personal enrichment," while "for society it is a privileged instrument of economic progress and of development" (35). He saw here, too, a field of action of particular importance for the Church: "True to the teaching and example of her divine Founder, who cited the preaching of the Gospel to the poor as a sign of His mission, the Church has never failed to foster the human progress of the nations. However, local and individual undertakings are no longer enough. The present situation of the world demands concerted action based on a clear vision of all economic, social, cultural and spiritual aspects...." The Holy See has, therefore, never spared its expressions of esteem for the initiatives undertaken in this field, especially by UNESCO; and, with the means at its disposal, it has sought to multiply within the Church activities for the education of adults, and lifelong education corresponding to the real needs of the most underprivileged populations.

(2544) In this context, women have benefited to a great extent, and there has been real progress towards general - personal, family and community - education. We should, however, like to point out also the active, responsible, creative role played by Religious Sisters in this field, either through their collaboration with the Governments of developing countries, or through their own activities for the education and promotion of woman. Sometimes they are working in a cultural milieu where they are the only ones who can exercise any such action among the women.

(2545) If we have stressed illiteracy, it is also because this field seems to illustrate the close link between equality of opportunities for men and women and that development which is "the new name of peace". Once they have had new horizons opened up to them through instruction and a first initiation into a new quality of life, women will be able to make a real contribution towards peace in the world; not only in posts of public responsibility to which a certain number of women already, exceptionally, have access, but in the family, through education to respect and mutual understanding, at grass-roots level and in the intermediary structures of society.

(2546) What a source of hope, indeed, for mankind would be even the quantitative contribution to peace of hundreds of millions of women keenly sensitive to injustice and integrated into public and community life at all levels. But we should think, above all, of what could be the contribution in quality of this half of mankind, altering not only the balance of power but the very fabric of relations between peoples.

(2547) It is difficult to foresee and impossible to define this "irreplaceable contribution" of women "to the peace of the world and the building of a more just and fraternal society" (Paul VI, Address to the Committee for the International Year of Women, 18-IV-1975). Woman is not automatically a peace-maker, all sweetness, devotedness, patience and love. She, too, must learn to dominate her egoism, maybe her aggressiveness, her ambition for power, even her hatred. She, too, must develop in the service of peace, the so-called "virile" qualities of strength, creativity and breadth of vision.... It is, therefore, not a question of "sharing " peace between men and women - of discrimination within peace itself - but rather of seeking an indivisible peace in "effective complementarity" (ibid) of the two branches, male and female, of mankind. It is the whole peace for which the whole woman and the whole man, all women and all men must strive.

(2548) What will this total participation mean for woman herself? There again, it is impossible to forecast; no doubt, it will mean a new way of life, new openings and responsibilities: for herself, for the couple, for the family and for the various communities. Is this merely a dream, a Utopia? We think not, if women want it sincerely: if, at all levels, men and women organize themselves for these new roles of peace, if educators, both men and women, prepare for them, and public authorities provide for the necessary adjustments.

(2549) Before concluding, we should like to express our satisfaction with the importance given in the Plan (161ff) to mass communications media, their influence in forming public opinion and the image of men and women they portray. We hope that there will be extensive collaboration with the enquiries proposed in this field (163) and an assessment of their findings in serious interdisciplinary studies.

(2550) May we insist, once more, on the primary role for International Women's Year and its continuation in the years to come of the non-governmental organizations and of bodies working at the grass roots, especially of those which are motivated by an integral view of human reality and the moral and spiritual values without which woman - and man - can find no true fulfillment.

(2551) May this Conference, at the half-way point of International Women's Year, be a decisive moment, so that the Year, with all the efforts it comprises, may mark an irreversible step forward in the march of humanity towards the full development of persons, and of a world of justice, peace and love. And may young people look with hope to our assembly and regard it as an invitation to accept generously, in mutual respect and common commitment, the gift of human life they have received - whether masculine or feminine - from the hands of the Creator.

4. THE DECISIVE MISSION OF WOMEN

Statement made by H.E.Msgr. Paul J. Cordes, Head of the Delegation of the Holy See to the World Conference of the United Nations Decade for Women. Copenhagen, 22 July 1980.

Original: English

(2552) The Holy See delegation thanks you for the opportunity offered to it to transmit to you and to your Assembly the feelings of esteem of Pope John Paul II for the activity of the United Nations in general, and for that of their specialized agencies in particular, feelings which he himself has had the opportunity to express personally to you several times, particularly on the occasion of his visit to the headquarters of the U.N., on 2 October 1979, and of UNESCO, on 2 June last.

(2553) Right from her origin and throughout the course of her history, the Church has often manifested her concern for the good of humanity; let it suffice to mention the work of persons such as St. Elizabeth of Hungary, St. Louise de Marillac, and the presence, so active, of Mother Teresa of Calcutta in our time. By her very nature the Church is in the service of "man in all his truth, in his full magnitude ... 'concrete,' 'historical' man" (*Redemptor Hominis*, 13). She cannot be indifferent to anything that concerns the human person and its full development.

(2554) Well today, numerous rights recognized as inalienable by the Universal Declaration on Human Rights, are ignored, despised, and even mocked. The profound changes through which humanity has lived are modifying the human person's ways of thinking and acting, bringing about a real social and cultural metamorphosis, a psychological, moral and religious evolution. This leads to considerable imbalances at the level of the individual, the family, social environments and nations.

(2555) Yet, in the midst of such upheavals, there can be noted a growing awareness of the dignity of the human person - man and woman - whose fundamental aspirations are expressed with ever greater forcefulness: "Man as an individual and as a member of society craves a life that is full, autonomous, and worthy of his nature as a human being; he longs to harness for his own welfare the immense resources of the modern world" (*Gaudium et Spes*, 9).

(2556) This longing for a fully human and free life is at the root of the great women's liberation movement. And it is certainly not by chance that this movement is set in a context of civilization's crisis. Have not women often carried out a decisive mission at the great turning-points of history? And today, as yesterday, it is precisely they who can grasp with deepest insight the possibilities and risk of a world capable of acting for the better or for the worse, while there opens up before it the way to freedom or to slavery, to progress or to regression, to brotherhood or to hatred (cf. *Gaudium et Spes*, 9).

(2557) If the Catholic Church and her members emphasize the value and the dignity of woman, it is not only because we have become aware of the importance of her social role, but above all out of faithfulness to Revelation itself, to the foundation of our Christian faith. The narrative of the Creation stresses, in fact, that man and woman are absolutely equal on the level of dignity. The Holy Bible teaches us that woman, like man, is created in the image of God; and it tells us clearly that the two sexes were created together and that neither can claim for itself any superiority over the other.

(2558) The conviction of the equality of man and woman has always been present in the teaching of the Church, and is sometimes expressed forcefully: "In their personal dignity as children of God, man and woman are absolutely equal, as also with regard to the ultimate purpose of human life, which is eternal union with God" (Pius XII, quoted by John Paul II at the Audience granted to the Italian Professional Association of Family Collaborators on 29 April 1979. See *L'Osservatore Romano* of 30 April - 1 May 1979).

(2559) It is quite clear, therefore, that woman as such is the image of God and reflects His divine perfection. To fulfil her personality completely, she must grow and progress as a woman. Her model cannot be man but only God because she was created in His image. Man and woman were created together and between them there exists a relationship of reciprocity without any discrimination. They complete each other. Each finds fulfillment in exchange and in giving.

(2560) Beyond the narration of the creation of man, Jesus Christ himself makes us appreciate better the dignity and the value that Christian faith confers on woman. Baptism, which is the rite of initiation into the Christian community, is administered both to men and to women, thus creating a new basis which transcends the specific sex of every human being, whether it is a question of a man or of a woman.

(2561) For this reason, in the New Testament, man and woman belong to the same people of God. At Pentecost, which marks the birth of the Church, women are part of the group of those who receive the gifts of the Holy Spirit.

(2562) Jesus himself has not left any particular doctrine with regard to woman. But with his novel esteem for woman and his attitude towards her, he scandalized his contemporaries and also his disciples (cf. *Jo.* 4:27). It is they who tell us so in the Gospel: they inform us of his surprising conversations with women, of his miracles in favour of women, of his readiness to accept their hospitality and their demonstrations of veneration. He specifically addresses women, who at that time were not always recognized by society as having the rights that were due to them.

(2563) One woman deserves quite special mention: Mary, the mother of Jesus. She embodies, from before the birth of Jesus, the ideal image of the woman believer: she accepts the word that God addresses to her through his messenger. Mary accompanies the Lord during his life, not remaining silent and taking no initiative, but rather asking questions, seeking, being active. She is his best witness.

(2564) Can we say today that woman is accepted as the Creator wished and as Christ accepted her, that is, for her own sake, as a fully responsible human person? Can it be said that she carries out her decisive role, in particular in the sphere of work, health, and education? It is precisely these questions that the Conference is trying to answer, drawing up a balance sheet of the progress made and the obstacles encountered after the Mexico City Assembly.

(2565) Some reports written in preparation for this Conference have been negative. They show, among other things, that the measures for the advancement of woman, taken in a perspective of mere assistance and considering woman only as a "passive user of progress", are ineffective. But a certain number of initiatives are more positive. Therefore the Holy See expresses its satisfaction with the founding of an international Institute of research and training for the advancement of woman.

(2566) There can be noted some progress in going beyond claims of a purely equalizing character (women must do everything that men do) or even "anti-male" ones, in favour of the aspiration towards a society in which every person, woman or man, respecting real differences, can contribute freely to improving the quality of human life. At the same time the fact is discovered or rediscovered that some values considered as "feminine", and some activities traditionally assumed by women, can be given new value and lived by both women and men in the service of the whole community. Finally, there can be noted an awareness of the importance, even economic, of women in the home and of all the human riches that a healthy and well-balanced family life can and must bring to society. These renewed ideas should encourage the complete education of persons, collaboration between men and women, the organization of work and the socio-cultural planning of the community, efforts for a well-balanced development of the populations, the increase and progress of the spiritual values of individuals and of collectivities.

(2567) The Church, for her part, particularly through her specialized organizations, has set up various programmes which contribute to the advancement of the human person and which, in many cases, mark out new ways and can give rise to other initiatives. Among these programmes continually being implemented and developed, we can recall, for example, the literacy plans, assistance for refugees, the promotion of peace, especially with the institution of Peace Days, and also some specific programmes concerning work, health, and education.

1) Men and women with respect to work.

(2568) To look for a job, to keep one's job, not to lose it ... this is the distressing concern of a large number of men and women. The evolution of conditions in the world of production is such that even rural people in developing countries have to enter new economic circles and cannot live on their harvest. One or more members of the family - very often the father - have to look for work far from home.

(2569) In this context women encounter particular problems: their wages, frequently considered as supplementary earnings, are still often less than those of men doing the same work.

(2570) Many of them have no vocational training and are, therefore, deprived of any hope of improvement. At a very young age, they are sometimes obliged to accept tasks that take up all their time (just think, for example, of domestic help, completely in the service of the families that have engaged them, and where they do not receive any training). Women who are not so young, and who have to or wish to seek employment after having brought up their children, encounter great difficulties both in retraining themselves and in finding a position.

(2571) In spite of the tension caused by unemployment, which does not always facilitate reflection, it is necessary to consider a certain number of fundamental questions, beyond mere economic criteria of advancement and success.

(2572) Today, when we ask ourselves questions about a new distribution of wealth, we must ask how to distribute work among everyone: according to what criteria at the level of individuals and at the level of States? What will be the place of women in this distribution? Is it possible to hope for real freedom of choice for everyone?

(2573) To study these complex questions, it is necessary to take into account the place that work itself has in the lives of men and women. Work must be considered not only as a means of earning a living, but also as a possibility for the person to develop his own creative capacities; a participation in the process of the construction of a more just society; a place where solidarity with others can live and develop; an opportunity for mutual research and progress; an environment which serves as a link between the "private" and the "social".

(2574) The entry of women into the world of work can be a possibility of renewal and can permit greater enrichment and greater opening of their personality and of that of men. But it is also necessary that the activities of women who stay at home be considered "noble work", in particular the upbringing of children, which is a task of prime importance. In this sense it is necessary not only to give new value to this type of work and ensure housewives an adequate training, but also to enable them to have the free time they need to dedicate themselves to their spheres of interest and to increase them. The result will be real human growth, from which the family itself, among others, will benefit.

2) Health for everyone

(2575) In the field of health and food, the Commission on the Status of Women points out a concrete improvement in the space of the last five years, in particular a reduction of mortality among mothers and infants, which varies, however, according to social groups and countries. But a great deal still remains to be done to improve health structures: to struggle against hunger, malnutrition, under-nourishment, and paradoxically, also against overfeeding in industrialized countries.

(2576) Health is not something that concerns only doctors; as a matter of fact each one is responsible, in his own sphere, for his own health and for that of others. To defend health and improve it signifies the deep meaning of human life in all its dimensions, including the spiritual one.

(2577) This human life is too often threatened by the lack of hygiene, by inhuman living conditions, and also by practices that offend the dignity of the person and especially of women: systematic sterilization, sexual mutilations which lead to serious psychological and pathological consequences. It is important that the Conference, examining the subject of health, should give its support to programmes that protect and help both mother and child, before and after birth. It should denounce practices such as abortion, which are opposed to physical, moral and social health. Abortion, in fact, kills the embryo which is, right from the moment of conception, a human being; it also diminishes the esteem the mother has of herself and often constitutes a danger for the woman's health and for the possibility of future conception.

(2578) It is important, moreover, that the Conference should promote women's education in the health field. Women's role is, in fact, of particular importance to improve the first elements of health care, for education in prevention, for food hygiene, and for the psycho-physiological knowledge of the person.

(2579) We would also like to stress the activity of women in health services. It is necessary to pay tribute to their dedication, to encourage them, and offer them means of training and improvement on the professional and ethical levels. Their possibilities of involvement in health services must be expanded so that they can have access to managerial posts, not only in order to operate at the executive level, but also to contribute to drawing up health policies. We regret that the Convention concerning the hiring and the work conditions and life of nursing personnel, adopted by the International Labour Organization on 21 June 1977, has found hardly any place in national legislations.

(2580) Health improvement consists also in helping the sick to take an active part in their cure. No real progress can be made in this field unless society first recognizes de jure and de facto the inestimable value, as well as the rights and the duties, of the sick, old, or handicapped person.

3) For an ongoing education for everyone

(2581) If we must rejoice because the proportion of children of both sexes in school is increasing on the world plane, we must also note that of 700 million illiterates, two thirds are women, and that women represent only 39 percent of university students.

(2582) It is necessary to combat the prejudices, habits, and economic conditions which today still exclude or limit the possibilities of schooling for women. Scholastic programmes, and other instruments which permit overall education, must be urgently set up. Scholastic programmes, in fact, are geared only to economic life and to obtaining jobs (at a time when work itself is in crisis). School gives little or poor preparation for life. School texts still present the various social roles in a traditional and stereotyped way. It is necessary, therefore, to multiply the few studies in progress in order to give men and women real preparation for their responsibilities in society.

(2583) Let all education, which must necessarily be ongoing, therefore, have as its purpose the human and spiritual growth of persons set in their context and in their relationships. It is to be an education which must take into account their lives and their complete development.

(2584) Of all these problems, it seems to us that some should particularly hold our attention:

(2585) - The search for criteria to harmonize professional and family obligations. This agreement calls for the full acceptance of, and deep respect for, the fundamental values of life: recognition of the family as the basic cell of society; economic life and real service of the human person; the participation of all: young people, adults, old persons, men and women, in the implementation of this harmony which calls for imagination and creativity to construct new social models.

(2586) In this way the regulation of daily working hours and the possibility of interrupting work in the course of a professional life, must certainly take into account the demands of a profession, but also those of family life. It is important, for both man and woman, that there be safeguarded "a time for work, a time for the family".

(2587) - The pursuit of a simple life corresponding to the real needs of each one. It has already become the object of study by groups in various countries, which are aware that such a choice conditions all deep changes in society in view of the real progress of the whole human person. Women, especially, are sensitive to this problem and can become fervent promoters of its solution. To struggle against any form of super-consumerism in order to enable the majority of mankind, who are living in poverty, to arrive at a decent existence, is a possible and fundamental endeavour. It consists in giving "priority to the poorest", that is, in revising all the values of life in accordance with the complete fulfillment of humanity.

(2588) - Education for peace. Everyone: women, men, parents, children, are called to believe in peace, to establish it and preserve it and live in it. Women must be convinced that it is up to them, also to them, to think of how to prevent war and establish peace; to have an active role in the building of peace, which consists not only in the absence of armed conflicts, but is, above all, a fair distribution of economic goods, respect for minorities, the recognition and protection of the rights of the human person, the determination to solve peacefully the inevitable conflicts that spring from the limitations of human nature. Instead it can be noted that today women in many countries are participating, more and more, in situations and acts of terrorism and violence. Why? This question cannot be left unanswered, and yet it cannot conceal the positive contribution of hundreds of millions of women who, with their husbands, educate their children to nonaggressiveness, dialogue, and respect for others. They take part in political and international life, trying to promote respect for the rights of the human person and to eliminate injustices of which racial discrimination is a particularly odious manifestation. Examples of this participation are the birth of the peace movement in Ireland, and the Nobel peace prize conferred on Mother Teresa of Calcutta.

(2589) In conclusion, we would like to stress that the fundamental question is a problem of humanity to be set in the wider context of the construction of a "civilization of love", which will expose and overcome the idolatrous images of power, riches, and sex that are widespread in our modern societies nowadays, and which will permit the liberation of all human energies.

(2590) Technical progress alone, in fact, is very far from wiping out all disparities. As John Paul II says: "This difficult road of the indispensable transformation of the structures of economic life is one on which it will not be easy to advance without the intervention of a true conversion of mind, will, and heart. The task requires resolute commitment by individuals and peoples that are free and linked in solidarity" (*Redemptor Hominis*, 16).

(2591) May this Conference be, in this sense, an important stage of the United Nations Decade for Women, in order that the recognition and advancement of woman's status may enrich the whole of humanity, and so that together, "men and women may make the contribution of their peculiar riches and dynamism for the construction of the world, not levelled and uniform, but harmonious and unified according to the Creator's plan" [Paul VI, Address to the Committee for the International Year of Women, AAS, 67(1975), p. 264].

[The World Conference of the United Nations Decade for Women on 30 July 1980, adopted a Programme of Action for the second half of this decade. In abstaining from the vote on the Programme of Action, the Delegation of the Holy See expressed some specific reservations which were explained in the following statement]

(2592) The Holy See is pleased to be associated in the deliberations on the Programme of Action for the second half of the United Nations Decade for Women. This is because the Holy See attaches great importance to the main objectives of the Decade - Equality, Development, and Peace - by promoting a fuller participation of women in the total contribution of people, male and female, towards the realization of the above-mentioned objectives.

(2593) The Delegation of the Holy See has also appreciated the effort of the Conference to concretize these objectives in the practical domain of Health, Employment, and Education.

(2594) Arising from the primary and compelling mission of the Catholic Church, the Holy See, by its emphasis on the ethical, spiritual, and religious perspectives, strives to foster every initiative which contributes to a fuller realization by all women and by each woman in the social-economic, political, cultural, and religious dimension of human life, and to the attainment of a greater solidarity between all human persons and all nations in peace, justice, truth, and love.

(2595) Recognizing the many differences of opinion on political and economic structures that were the topics of intense debate during this Conference, the Delegation of the Holy See notes that it is primarily interested in human values, in ethical and moral principles, and in a recognition of the spiritual dimension of the human person, female and male, which are important for Equality, Development, and the attainment of a lasting Peace. In abstaining from the vote, the Delegation of the Holy See does not wish to be seen as accepting or endorsing one or the other viewpoints on those disputed questions that remain unresolved.

(2596) The Delegation of the Holy See is especially interested in giving its moral support to those proposals concerning women in particularly difficult situations: in conditions of poverty and underdevelopment, migrant and refugee women, women in rural areas, women who suffer racist discrimination, handicapped or disabled women, the aged or isolated, those who are victims of forced prostitution or other forms of violence. Having participated in the deliberations of this Conference, the Delegation of the Holy See desires to make three critical observations:

(2597) 1) It would have been desirable for the objectives of the second half of the Decade, which bring out very clearly and richly the "total development" and "integral perfection" (Art. no 4) in the personal and collective life of the human person, to be translated more effectively in the Programme of Action;

(2598) 2) The general propositions, more often than not, have tended to reduce the participation of women to the sole domain - even if very important - of an economic development that does not sufficiently take into consideration the potential of women or their contributions in other areas of human and social development;

(2599) 3) The Programme of Action could have had a more global and deeper perspective on the family. Even with a minimum degree of realism, one cannot ignore the family milieu as a fundamental dimension of human experience. If it is important to stimulate a greater participation of women in public life as well as to promote a greater participation of men in family life, it is also important to remember that the family is the source of the real growth of human persons, a growth which has ramifications and repercussions in every domain of social life. To reduce in any way the position of the family is to ignore the very basic foundation for the realization of the major objectives envisaged in the United Nations Decade for Women. It is primarily in the family that men and women learn to recognize each other's dignity as equals, enriched by their differences. It is in the family that they find the opportunity to develop the quality of their personality in interpersonal communion; it is in the family that they are gradually educated to live in peace, based on freedom, mutual understanding, and love.

(2600) It is in this perspective that the Delegation of the Holy See has been obliged to reserve its position with respect to some references concerning family planning (par. 88 [i], 120, 186 [d]). The interpretation and utilization of these recommendations could lead to indiscriminate use of methods which violate human dignity and responsible parenthood.

2601) It is important to appreciate the essential and unique role of woman which can best be exercised in partnership with man, whether in the intimacy of a family or in a wider social or political domain. Hers it is to shape and nurture, to animate and inspire the new generations to build a world according to the objectives of the U.N. Decade for Women.

5. THE CHURCH CALLS FORTH WOMEN

Statement made by H.E.Msgr Paul J. Cordes, Vice President of the Pontifical Council for the Laity, Head of the Delegation of the Holy See to the World Conference to Review and Appraise the Achievements of the United Nations Decade for Women: Equality, Development and Peace, held in Nairobi (Kenya) on 15-26 July 1985. Nairobi, 19 July 1985.

Original: French

(2602) The participation of a Delegation of the Holy See in this Conference is - as was its participation in the United Nations Conferences in Mexico City and in Copenhagen - the expression of the strong interest and commitment in solidarity which it brings to the Decade for Women, as it has been promoted by the United Nations.

(2603) The achievements which have been realized during the Decade have been enormous, and they will doubtless bring forth much fruit. For example, the new formulation of civil law in many countries has meant equality between men and women.

(2604) More and more competent and professionally trained women have taken their places and assumed their responsibilities in all aspects of the life of society, at the same time filling their familial mission. Important juridical improvements have been made to the socio-economic status of women. Education at all levels, considered a necessity in our times, is more and more accessible to women. Finally, through appropriate culture and policy, conditions are being created which allow women to leave contemporary limiting structures and to decide responsibly for their own lives.

(2605) On the other hand, all that remains to be done must be accounted for. It is true that the activities of the United Nations furnished valuable means of elaborating laws in different countries in the areas of women's concerns. But, in many cases, the way to use them is not yet known. What has been written in the documents has not yet produced any results at the level of real life. This is due to the fact that the problem, in many circumstances, cannot be resolved by law because it has its roots in a mistaken mentality regarding women. Society cannot recognize more deeply the value and dignity of women if it does not take into account the relationship between men and women. It is in this relationship that the heart of the women's question lies.

(2606) It is unfortunately true that women are still among the principal victims of the dramatic situations or events such as: the scourge of war, economic crisis, hunger, forced immigration, the tragic fate of the refugees, the misery of organized prostitution, and so on.

(2607) We cannot consider the closing of the women's Decade as ending the presentation of the drama of women on which a curtain will fall, and afterwards we have only to applaud the actors.

(2608) The drama continues if only because the directions given up to this point, seem to have accounted for only a part of the problem concerning women.

(2609) The primary criterion for the work of the Decade and its permanent reference point has been the socio-economic progress of women. Unquestionably, this is a problem which, in the totality of the drama, confronts us, and no one can set it aside. Who would dare deny the importance of the economic resources to assure an existence which respects the dignity of the human person! Therefore, throughout its history, Christianity has never ceased to combat poverty and misery. The Gospel commits every Christian to adopt such an attitude.

(2610) The Gospel announces that, at the end of time, all our actions will be judged. The judge will be the very Christ who in proclaiming the Kingdom of God during His earthly life left no doubt about the decisive criterion of His judgement: everything will be measured by the good deeds that we have done to men and women, our brothers and sisters (*Mt.* 25:31 ff.). Thus, the history of Christianity is filled with men and women who tried to confront the socio-economic situations of their contemporaries in order to improve them. Allow me to cite some examples in the recent past:

(2611) Jacques Desiré Laval (†1864); Francesca Saveria Cabrini (†1917); Madeleine Debrel (†1964); Dorothy Day (†1980); Barbara Ward (†1981); Mother Theresa of Calcutta.

(2612) It would be impossible to cite here the names of all those who, in our times in the countries of the so-called Third World, commit themselves to serve the human dignity of every person. Their service involves also a concern for the improvement of the material conditions of life. But I want at least to cite their number: statistics speak to us of 212,584 women religious in the service of humanity in the Third World without counting the men religious and the lay volunteers. All of them are aware of being sent and supported by the Church in their work.

(2613) I think we also must mention the financial help given by the Church to the service of humanity: collections for material assistance; initiatives aiming at development; collections for all sorts of programmes of training and education.

(2614) Because I am of German origin, I can give you some figures from my country which are better known to me and therefore, better verified. In 1984, the different organizations of the Catholic Church (Misereor, Adveniat, Missio and Caritas) made a contribution of about 250 million dollars for work in the Third World. Compared to a population of 27 million Catholics, this means that, on the average, the contribution represents almost $10 per person.

(2615) Even if aid to development is contested because it does not definitely change the situation of persons; even if the material contributions to some countries are sometimes categorically refused because they would support a corrupt system, the facts just given confirm, at least, that the Catholic Church takes the material needs of humanity seriously, that is, the economic dimension of the existence of men and women.

(2616) Still, the question must be asked: can there be any real progress, in the full sense of the word, without reference to a total vision of the human person in being and in becoming? Is there real progress if the infinite value of each human person in all its consequences is not considered: respect for human dignity, the fundamental equality of all, freedom of conscience, and sacredness of life?

(2617) This is why the Holy See would like to bring a few reflections concerning the dignity of women into the framework of this Decade:

(2618) a) - Without doubt, the human person is, from a certain viewpoint, a material being, one of the animals of the earth, subject like them to an infinite variety of instincts and conditionings which are inherent to its diverse individual factors, both natural and social: race, language, sex, position in the social hierarchy, etc. But at the same time, the human person is capable, by reason of intelligence and freedom, of transcending these conditions to affirm and to realize what is objectively just, true, and good in conformity with the specific human destiny.

(2619) It is exactly in this capacity for transcendence of these conditions to which the human person is subject that the dignity of that human person resides.

(2620) Like others among the greatest religious traditions of humanity, the Catholic Church sees, in this permanent process of the transcendence of all the conditions which limit human freedom, a dialogue established between the human person and a divine presence guiding towards truth. Out of this capacity for the transcendence, which is characteristic of the human person, is born a duty: that of combatting and abolishing all the situations where the human person is humiliated and offended, violated in its sacredness, reduced to one dimension of being, in sum, all those situations where the human person is not treated as a person and is denied the recognition of full human dignity because of race, sex or other natural or social factors. Is it not gravely oppressive to consider a woman only as a means of production or as an indispensable element of a consumer economy?

(2621) The struggle to guarantee a minimum of material support must, therefore, be animated by a conviction of the irreplaceable value of the human person and it must be built on that foundation. Otherwise, we will see the reappearance of those old enemies of the dignity of women: sexual discrimination, women reduced to objects or to instruments deprived of a transcendent good and accorded importance by conditions determined by sex.

(2622) b) - In limiting the advancement of women to the socio-economic perspective, there is also the risk of destroying some great human values which are specific to women's contribution to society.

(2623) In many situations, women have been able to conserve some essentially human values, transmitting them to the next generations and preserving them for universal human culture. Frequently rejected in a relative way by a competitive society, where human relationships are determined almost exclusively by the exchange of goods or by war, women have conserved, much more deeply than men, an ethic of giving, of free offering, in a disinterested spirit, simply motivated by an admiring astonishment before the miracle of the person that is 'the other' or by a pure desire of goodness toward the others. Therein lie the fundamental attitudes characteristic of the mother to the child.

(2624) These attitudes, of course, are not exclusively feminine. But, women have conserved fundamental human values which little by little have been erased in the masculine world, so the advancement of women must not be promoted by means of the "masculinization" of women into self-centered bourgeois who forget the reality of humanity.

(2625) If this were so, not only that essential and mysterious dimension of femininity would disappear, but men also, that is, every human being would be deprived of a certain vitality. It is very necessary that, thanks to a correct evaluation of the specifically feminine, these values become common to all humanity, that they should not be depreciated and considered at a lower level, nor serve as an alibi for the perpetuation of the subjection of women. However, it is true that the mother has a special and privileged access to these non-competitive values of communion where sharing appears most clearly as an essential law of being. This is, of course, the experience of childbirth, of bringing a child into the world, and of maternity. Here, to welcome another person into one's self becomes a personal experience of particular significance involving completely the body and the spirit of the woman.

(2626) The oldest culture and religious tradition as well as modern human sciences confirm for us that here is a definitive experience constituting the identity of the woman as well as of the child.

(2627) However, during this experience, the woman needs the help and support of her culture and society. Each woman has the right to a stable family during pregnancy, to a loving relationship with her husband, the father of her child, which is defended and guaranteed by law. Each woman has the right to be protected against the attacks of a society or a State that wishes to deprive maternity of its fundamentally sacred character, reviling feminine sexuality, or destroying the fruit of conception by abortion. Each woman also has the right both to a complete knowledge of her own body and of its biological functions so that she has a better understanding of her vital experience of the conception and birth of her child and also to a rational control of her own fertility so that the dignity given by God to human sexuality as a material expression of the mutual gift of persons not be diminished but rather magnified.

(2628) c) - The work of women as well as men must be considered as built on human dignity. Certainly, work is a means of earning one's living, but it is equally true that it cannot be separated from nor opposed to family life. Necessarily, aspects of work must be studied so that, neither by their hours, their schedules nor their organizations, would they be obstacles to parenting in such a way that maternity might imply an automatic or unjust exclusion from work.

(2629) It is necessary to ensure forms of protection for family income which, recognizing the service rendered by parents to all of society, allow the mother to devote herself completely to family life when the demands of the family so require.

(2630) In order to attain a genuine human emancipation, a woman should not have to give up her own femininity and the experience of maternity in marriage where she finds fulfillment and her greatest significance. Instead, our societies must be opened to those non-competitive values of peace, sharing in suffering, spontaneous and free self-giving which are preserved and transmitted among women through a woman's culture which, although never officially recognized, has nevertheless profoundly marked our culture.

(2631) For Christians, and also for Moslems, the highest expression of this feminine principle in culture is found in the person of Mary, mother of Jesus. In confiding to her the destiny of the world, we affirm our conviction that only a cultural change aiming at restoring this feminine dimension to the roots of our culture can save humanity from the threats and dangers which today darken the horizon.

(2632) Many times the philosopher Karol Woytyla has spoken on human growth and the full development of the human person. He shows how the human person realizes the potential in and through action. On one hand, evidently, it is through action that the person enters into relationship with the outside world.

(2633) It is by means of action that each person exercises an influence on the surrounding people and world. On the other hand, by means of action human persons transform themselves and grow. Isn't it true that each one of us is the image of what we have lived and done?

(2634) It is in this perspective that we must understand the following passage of the Encyclical of Pope John Paul II on human labour (Section 9):

(2635) "Work is a good thing for man - a good thing for his humanity - because through work man not only transforms nature, adapting it to his own needs, but he also achieves fulfillment as a human being and indeed, in a sense, becomes 'more a human being.'"

(2636) The study of the theme which concerns us here cannot bring forth worthy fruit unless women commit themselves, more and more, to action. No one - neither at the level of Governments nor at the level of social structures - can either think or decide for them. Forms for their development cannot be imposed from outside. Women must, on the contrary, be allowed the freedom in which they themselves can search out their own way.

(2637) The demand contained in paragraph 10 of the Conference document concerning the forward - looking strategies of implementation for the advancement of women (A/CONF. 1/16/12) cannot be considered as a feministic battle-cry.

(2638) It is rather the fruit of an anthropological analysis that we can only underline: "The Copenhagen World Conference interpreted equality as meaning not only legal equality, the elimination of *de jure* discrimination, but also equality of rights, responsibilities and opportunities for the participation of women in development, both as beneficiaries and as active agents."

V - THE VALUE AND DIGNITY OF DISABLED PERSONS

Document of the Holy See for the International Year of Disabled Persons. The Vatican, 4 March 1981

Original: French

(2639) From the very beginning the Holy See received favourably the United Nations' *initiative* of proclaiming 1981 the "International Year of Disabled Persons". These persons deserve the practical concern of the world community, both by reason of their numbers (it is calculated that they exceed four hundred million) and especially for their particular human and social condition. Therefore, in this noble enterprise, the Church could not fail to show her caring and watchful solicitude, for by her very nature, vocation and mission she has particularly at heart the lives of the weakest and most sorely tried brothers and sisters.

(2640) For this reason, the Church has followed with close attention everything that has been done up to the present time on behalf of the disabled on the legislative level, both national and international. Worthy of note in this regard are the United Nations Declaration of the rights of the disabled, and the Declaration concerning the rights of the mentally retarded, as also the progress and future prospects of scientific and social research, plus the various new proposals and initiatives now being developed in this area. These initiatives show a renewed awareness of the duty of solidarity in this specific field of human suffering; also to be borne in mind is the fact that in the Third World countries the lot of the disabled is even graver, and calls for closer attention and more careful consideration.

(2641) The Church fully associates herself with the initiatives and praiseworthy efforts being made in order to improve the situation of the disabled, and she intends to make her own specific contribution. She does so, in the first place, through fidelity to the example and teaching of her Founder. For Jesus Christ showed special concern for the suffering, in all the wide spectrum of human pain. During His ministry He embraced them with His merciful love, and He showed forth in them the saving power of the Redemption that embraces man in his individuality and totality. The neglected, the disadvantaged, the poor, the suffering and sick, were the ones to whom He specially brought, in words and actions, the proclamation of the Good News of God's Kingdom coming into human history.

(2642) Through the centuries, the community of Christ's disciples, following His example, has caused to flourish works of extraordinary generosity, works that witness not only to faith and hope in God but also to an unshakable love and faith in the dignity of man, in the unrepeatable value of each individual human life, and in the transcendent dignity of those who are called into existence.

(2643) In their view of faith and in their concept of man, Christians know that in the disabled person there is reflected, in a mysterious way, the image and likeness which God Himself impressed upon the lives of His sons and daughters. And as they remember that Christ mystically identified Himself with the suffering neighbour and took as done to Himself everything done for the least of His brethren (cf. *Mt.* 25:31-46), Christians feel a call to serve, in Him, those whom physical accidents have affected and disabled. They are resolved not to omit any of the things that must be done, even at the cost of personal sacrifice, in order to alleviate their disadvantaged condition.

(2644) At this moment, one cannot fail to think, with lively gratitude, of all the communities and associations, all the men and women religious and all the lay volunteers who spend themselves in work for the disabled, thus manifesting the perennial vitality of that love that knows no barriers.

(2645) It is in this spirit that the Holy See, while expressing its gratitude and encouragement for what has been done by those responsible for the common good, by the international organizations and by all those who work for the handicapped, considers it useful to recall briefly a few principles that may be useful guides in dealing with the disabled, and also to suggest some practical points.

I BASIC PRINCIPLES

(2646) 1. The first principle, which is one that must be stated clearly and firmly, is that the disabled person (whether the disability be the result of a congenital handicap, chronic illness or accident, or from mental or physical deficiency, and whatever the severity of the disability) is *a fully human subject, with the corresponding innate, sacred and inviolable rights.* This statement is based upon the firm recognition of the fact that a human being possesses a unique dignity and an independent value, from the moment of conception and in every stage of development, whatever his or her physical condition. This principle, which stems from the *upright conscience* of humanity, must be made the inviolable basis of legislation and society.

(2647) Indeed, on reflection one may say that a disabled person, with the limitations and sufferings that he or she suffers in body and faculties, emphasizes the mystery of the human being, with all its dignity and nobility. When we are faced with a disabled person, we are shown the hidden frontiers of human existence, and we are impelled to approach this mystery with respect and love.

(2648) 2. Since the person suffering from handicaps is a subject with full rights, he or she must be *helped to take his or her place in society in all aspects and at all levels, as far as is compatible with his or her capabilities.* The recognition of these rights and the duty of human solidarity are a commitment and task to be carried out, and they will create psychological, social, family, educational and legislative conditions and structures that will favour the proper acceptance and complete development of the disabled individual.

(2649) The Declaration of the Rights of the Disabled states, in Section 3, that "disabled persons have the right to respect for their human dignity. Disabled persons, whatever the origin, nature and seriousness of their handicaps and disabilities, have the same fundamental rights as their fellow-citizens of the same age, which implies first and foremost the right to enjoy a decent life, as normal and full as possible."

(2650) 3. *The quality of a society and a civilization are measured by the respect shown to the weakest of its members.* A perfect technological society which only allowed fully functional members and which neglected, institutionalized or, what is worse, eliminated those who did not measure up to this standard or who were unable to carry out a useful role, would have to be considered as radically unworthy of man, however economically successful it might be. Such a society would, in fact, be tainted by a sort of discrimination no less worthy of condemnation than racial discrimination; it would be discrimination by the strong and "healthy" against the weak and the sick. It must be clearly affirmed that a disabled person is one of us, a sharer in the same humanity. By recognizing and promoting that person's dignity and rights, we are recognizing and promoting our own dignity and our own rights.

(2651) 4. The fundamental approach to the problems connected with the sharing by the disabled in the life of society must be inspired by the *principles of integration, normalization and personalization.* The principle of *integration* opposes the tendency to isolate, segregate and neglect the disabled, but it also goes further than an attitude of mere tolerance. It includes a commitment to make the disabled person a subject in the fullest sense, in accordance with his or her capacities, in the spheres of family life, the school, employment, and, more generally, in the social, political and religious communities.

(2652) As a natural consequence there derives from this principle that of *normalization,* which signifies and involves an effort to ensure the complete rehabilitation of the disabled person, using all means and techniques now available, and, in cases where this proves impossible, the achievement of a living and working environment that resembles the normal one, as much as possible.

(2653) Thirdly, the principle of *personalization* emphasizes the fact that in the various forms of treatment, as also in the various educational and social means employed to eliminate handicaps, it is always the dignity, welfare and total development of the handicapped person, in all his or her dimensions and physical, moral and spiritual faculties, that must be primarily considered, protected and promoted. This principle also signifies and involves the elimination of collectivized and anonymous institutions to which the disabled are sometimes relegated.

II OPERATIVE LINES

(2654) 1. One cannot but hope that such statements as those of the Declaration cited will be given full recognition in the international and national communities, avoiding limiting interpretations and arbitrary exceptions and perhaps even unethical applications which end by emptying the statements of meaning and import.

(2655) Developments in science and medicine have enabled us today to discover in the foetus some defect which can give rise to future malformations and deficiencies. The impossibility, at present, of providing a remedy for them by medical means has led some to propose and even to practice the suppression of the foetus. This conduct springs from an attitude of pseudo-humanism, which compromises the ethical order of objective values and must be rejected by upright consciences. It is a form of behaviour which, if it were applied at a different age, would be considered gravely anti-human. Furthermore, the deliberate failure to provide assistance, or any act which leads to the suppression of the new-born disabled person, represents a breach not only of medical ethics but also of the fundamental and inalienable right to life. One cannot, at whim, dispose of human life, by claiming an arbitrary power over it. Medicine loses its title of nobility when, instead of attacking disease, it attacks life; in fact, prevention should be against the illness, not against life. One can never claim that one wishes to bring comfort to a family, by suppressing one of its members. The respect, the dedication, the time and means required for the care of handicapped persons, even of those whose mental faculties are gravely affected, is the price that a society should generously pay in order to remain truly human.

(2656) 2. A consequence of clear affirmation of this point is the duty to undertake more extensive and thorough research in order to overcome the causes of disabilities. Certainly much has been done in recent years in this field, but much more remains to be done. Scientists have the noble task of placing their skill and their studies at the service of bettering the quality and defence of human life. Present developments in the fields of genetics, foetology, perinatology, biochemistry and neurology, to mention only some disciplines, permit us to foster the hope of noticeable progress. A unified effort of research will not fail, it is hoped, to achieve encouraging results in the not too distant future.

(2657) These initiatives of fundamental research and of application of acquired knowledge deserve, therefore, more decisive encouragement and more concrete support. It is the hope of the Holy See that international institutions, the public powers in individual nations, research agencies, non-governmental organizations and private foundations will, more and more, foster research and allot the necessary funds for it.

(2658) 3. The priority to be given to the prevention of disabilities should also make us reflect on the distressing phenomenon of the many persons who undergo stress and shock that disturb their psychic and interior life. Preventing these disabilities and fostering the health of the spirit signifies and implies unified and creative effort in favour of integral education, and an environment, human relations and means of communication in which the person is not damaged in his more profound needs and aspirations - in the first place moral and spiritual ones - and in which the person is not submitted to violence which can end by compromising his interior balance and dynamism. Spiritual ecology is needed as much as natural ecology.

(2659) 4. When, notwithstanding the responsible and rigorous application of all the techniques and cures possible today, the disability cannot be remedied or reversed, it is necessary to seek and bring about all the remaining possibilities of human growth and of social integration which remain open for the person affected. Apart from the right to appropriate medical treatment, the United Nations Declaration enumerates other rights which have as their objective the most complete possible integration or reintegration into society. Such rights have very wide repercussions on the whole of the services which exist at present or which must be developed, among which might be mentioned the organization of an adequate educational system, responsible professional training, counselling services and appropriate work.

(2660) 5. One point seems to merit particular attention. The United Nations Declaration on the Rights of Disabled Persons affirms: "Disabled persons have the right to live with their families or with foster parents" (no. 9). It is extremely important that this right be put into effect. It is in the home, surrounded by loved ones, that a handicapped person finds the surroundings which are most natural and conducive to his development. Taking account of this primordial importance of the family for the development of the handicapped person and his integration into society, those responsible for socio-medical and orthopedagogical structures should make the family the starting point in planning their programmes and make it the principal dynamic force in the process of social care and integration.

(2661) 6. From this viewpoint, it is necessary to take into account the decisive importance of offering help at the moment when parents make the painful discovery that one of their children is handicapped. The trauma which derives from this can be so profound and can cause such a strong crisis that it shakes their whole system of values. The lack of early assistance or adequate support at this phase can have very unfortunate consequences for both the parents and the disabled person. For this reason, one should not rest content with only making the diagnosis and then leaving the parents abandoned. Isolation and rejection by society could lead them to refuse to accept or, God forbid, to reject their disabled child. It is necessary, therefore, for families to be given great understanding and sympathy by the community and to receive from associations and public powers adequate assistance from the first discovery of the disability of one of their members.

(2662) The Holy See, conscious of the heroic strength of mind required of those families that have generously and courageously agreed to take care of, and even adopt, disabled children, wants to assure them of its appreciation and gratitude. The witness which these families render to the dignity, value and sacredness of the human person deserves to be openly recognized and supported by the whole community.

(2663) 7. When particular circumstances and special requirements for the rehabilitation of the disabled person necessitate a temporary stay or even a permanent one away from the family, the homes and institutions which take the family's place should be planned and should function in a way as near to the family model as is possible and should avoid segregation and anonymity. It must be arranged that, during their stay in these centres, the bonds linking the disabled persons with their families and friends should be cultivated with frequency and spontaneity.

(2664) Apart from professional competence, the loving care and dedication of parents, relatives and educators have obtained, as many have testified, results of unexpected effectiveness for the human and professional development of disabled persons. Experience has demonstrated - and this is an important point for reflection - that in a favourable and human family setting, full of deep respect and sincere affection, disabled persons can develop in surprising ways their human, moral and spiritual qualities and even, in their turn, bring peace and joy to others .

(2665) 8. The affective life of the disabled will have to receive particular attention. Above all when their handicap prevents them from contracting marriage, it is important, not only that they be adequately protected from promiscuity and exploitation, but that they also be able to find a community full of human warmth in which their need for friendship and love may be respected and satisfied in conformity with their inalienable moral dignity.

(2666) 9. Handicapped children and young people obviously have the right to instruction. This will be assured them, to the extent possible, either through an ordinary school or a specialized school for people with their handicap. Where home schooling is required, it is hoped that the competent authorities will supply the family with the necessary means. Access to higher learning and opportune post-school assistance ought to be made possible and aid should be given for this purpose.

(2667) 10. A particularly delicate moment in the life of the disabled person is the passage from school to placement in society or professional life. In this phase the person needs particular understanding and encouragement from various sectors of the community. Public authorities should guarantee and foster with effective measures the right of disabled persons to professional training and work, so that they can be inserted into a professional activity for which they are qualified. Much attention should be focused on working conditions, such as the assignment of jobs in accordance with the handicaps, just wages, and the possibility of promotion. It is highly recommended that advance information be given to employers regarding the employment, the situation and the psychology of the disabled, who often encounter various hindrances in the professional sector: for example, a sense of inferiority about their appearance or possible productiveness, worry about having accidents at work, etc.

(2668) 11. Obviously, the disabled person posses all the civil and political rights that other citizens have, and it should, as a general rule, b e made possible for him or her to exercise them. However, certain forms of disability - for instance, the numerically important category of those who have mental handicaps - constitute an obstacle to the responsible exercise of these rights. Even in these cases action should be taken, not in an arbitrary manner or by applying repressive measures, but on the basis of rigorous and objective ethical and juridical criteria.

(2669) 12. On the other hand, the disabled person must be urged not to be content with being only the subject of rights, accustomed to receiving care and solidarity from others, with a merely passive attitude. He is not only a receiver; he must be helped to be a giver to the full extent of his capabilities. An important and decisive moment in his training will be reached when he becomes aware of his dignity and worth and recognizes that something is expected from him and that he, too, can and should contribute to the progress and well-being of his family and community. The idea that he has of himself should, of course, be realistic, but also positive, allowing him to see himself as a person capable of responsibility, able to exercise his own will and to collaborate with others.

(2670) 13. Many individuals, associations and institutions are today dedicated by profession, and often by a genuine humanitarian and religious calling, to helping the disabled. In many cases they have demonstrated a preference for "voluntary" personnel and educators, because they see in them a particular sense of unselfishness and solidarity. This observation makes clear that, although technical and professional competence is certainly necessary and ought indeed to be cultivated and improved, it is not sufficient by itself. A rich human sensitivity must be added to competence. Those who commendably dedicate themselves to the service of the disabled should have scientific knowledge of their disabilities, but they should also comprehend with their hearts the person who bears the handicap. They should learn to become sensitive to the special signs with which the disabled express themselves and communicate. They should acquire the art of making the proper gesture and saying the right word. They should know how to accept with calmness possible reactions or forms of emotion and learn to dialogue with the parents and families of the disabled. This competence will not be fully human unless it is sustained by inner suitable moral and spiritual dispositions: attentiveness, sensitivity and particular respect for everything in the human person that is a source of weakness and dependence. Care and help for disabled persons then becomes a school of genuine humanity, a demanding school, a noble school, an uplifting school.

(2671) 14. It is very important and even necessary that professional services receive material and moral support from the public authorities, with a view to being organized in the most adequate way possible and to having the specialized interventions function effectively. Many countries have already provided, or are in the process of providing, exemplary legislation that defines and protects the legal status of the disabled person. Where such legislation does not yet exist, it is the duty of the government to provide an effective guarantee and to promote the rights of the disabled. To this end, it would be advantageous for families and voluntary organizations to be associated in drawing up juridical and social norms in this matter.

(2672) 15. Even the best legislation, however, risks having no effect on the social context and not producing full results if it is not accepted into the personal conscience of the citizens and the collective consciousness of the community.

(2673) Handicapped persons, their families and relatives are part of the whole human family. However large their number may unfortunately be, they form a minority group within the whole community. This is enough to entail the danger that they may not be given sufficient public attention. Add to that the often spontaneous reaction of a community that rejects and psychologically represses that which does not fit into its habits. People do not want to be faced with forms of existence which visibly reflect the negative aspects of life. This gives rise to the phenomenon of exclusion and discrimination as a kind of mechanism of defence and rejection. Since, however, man and society are truly human when they enter into a conscious and willing process of accepting even weakness, of solidarity and of sharing in others' sufferings, the tendency referred to must be countered by education.

(2674) The celebration of the International Year of Disabled Persons, therefore, offers a favourable opportunity for a more precise overall reconsideration of the situation, of the problems and of the requirements of millions of those who make up the human family, particularly in the Third World. It is important that this occasion not be allowed to pass in vain. With the contribution of science and of all levels of society, it should lead to a better understanding of the disabled person and of his dignity and rights; and above all it should foster sincere and active love for every human being in his or her unique and concrete situation.

(2675) 16. Christians have an irreplaceable mission to carry out in this regard.

(2676) Recalling their responsibility as witnesses to Christ, they must adopt as their own the Saviour's sentiments towards the suffering and stimulate an attitude of charity and examples of it in the world, so that there is never any lack of interest in our brothers and sisters who are less endowed. The Second Vatican Council identified in that charitable presence the essential core of the apostolate of lay people. It recalled that Christ made love of one's neighbour His personal commandment "and enriched it with a new meaning when He identified Himself with His brothers as the object of charity.... For, in assuming human nature, He united all of humanity to Himself as His family, and He made charity the distinguishing mark of His disciples in the words: 'By this all men will know that you are my disciples, if you have love for one another' (*Jn.* 13:35). In the early days the Church linked the agape to the Eucharistic supper and by so doing showed herself entirely united around Christ. So too, at all times, she is recognized by the distinguishing sign of love and, while rejoicing at initiatives taken elsewhere, she claims charitable works as her own inalienable duty and right. That is why mercy to the poor and the sick, and works of charity and mutual aid for the alleviation of all kinds of human needs, are held in special honour by the Church" (*Apostolicam Actuositatem,* 8).

(2677) In this International Year of Disabled Persons Christians will, therefore, stand side by side with their brothers and sisters of all organizations in order to foster, support and increase initiatives suitable for alleviating the situation of the suffering and for inserting them harmoniously into the context of normal civil life, to the extent that this is possible. Christians will make their contribution in personnel and resources, especially through the deserving institutions that - in the name of Christ and of his love and with the marvellous example of people wholely consecrated to the Lord - devote themselves especially to giving education, professional training and post-school assistance to young disabled persons and to caring generously for the worst cases. Parishes and youth groups of various kinds will give special care to families in which one of these children marked by sorrow is born and grows to maturity; they will also study, continually apply and, if necessary, revise suitable methods of catechesis to the disabled, and they will pay attention to their insertion into cultural and religious activities, so as to ensure that they will be full members of their Christian community, in accordance with their clear right to appropriate spiritual and moral education.

(2678) 17. Celebrating the Day of Peace at the beginning of this year, the Holy Father mentioned publicly in the Vatican Basilica the initiatives of the International Year of Disabled Persons and called for special attention to solving their serious problems. He now renews his call to show concern for the lot of these brothers and sisters of ours. He repeats what he said then: "If only a minimum part of the budget for the arms race were assigned for this purpose, important successes could be achieved and the fate of many suffering persons alleviated" (Homily on 1 January 1981). His Holiness applauds the various initiatives that will be undertaken on the international level and also those that will be attempted in other fields, and he urges especially the sons and daughters of the Catholic Church to give an example of total generosity. Entrusting the dear disabled persons throughout the world to the motherly protection of the Holy Virgin, as he did on that occasion, he repeats his hopeful trust that, "under Mary's maternal gaze, experiences of human and Christian solidarity will be multiplied, in a renewed brotherhood that will unite the weak and the strong in the common path of the divine vocation of the human person" (*ibid.*).

VI - POPULATION

1. POPULATION PROBLEMS AND HUMAN DEVELOPMENT

Address of His Holiness Paul VI to Mr. Antonio Carillo-Flores, Secretary-General of the World Conference on Population, and Mr. Rafael Salas, Executive Director of the UN Fund for Population Activities (UNFPA). The Vatican, 28 March 1974.

Original: Italian (*)

(2679) We would like, first of all, to thank you for coming to see us. You wished to have this meeting in order to speak to us about the high responsibilities that the United Nations Organization has given you in connection with the World Population Year and the World Population Conference. We avail ourself of the occasion to assure you of the interest with which the Holy See follows the international community's efforts in favour of justice and peace.

(*) AAS 66(1974), 253-256.

(2680) The numerous activities being organized within the framework of the World Population Year and in connection with the World Population Conference, to be held in Bucharest next August, cannot leave the Holy See indifferent. Although the quest for solutions to the problems posed by population growth will, for many years ahead, call for the generous commitment of all men of good will, the World Population Year and Conference present particularly important occasions for alerting world opinion to the needs of individuals and peoples.

(2681) When the Church concerns herself with population problems, she does so by reason of fidelity to her mission. This concern stems from her commitment to work for the promotion of the integral good, both material and spiritual, of the whole man and of all men. The Church knows that population means people, human beings. Since she is the depositary of a revelation in which the Author of life speaks to us about man, his needs, his dignity and his human and spiritual destiny, the Church takes a profound interest in everything that can serve man. But at the same time, she concerns herself with everything that might compromise the innate dignity and freedom of the human person.

(2682) We are aware that the growing number of people, in the world taken as a whole and in certain countries in particular, presents a challenge to the human community and governments. The problems of hunger, health, education, housing and employment become more difficult to solve when the population increases more rapidly than the available resources.

(2683) For some people, there is a great temptation to believe that there is no solution and to wish to put a brake on population growth by the use of radical measures, measures which are not seldom in contrast with the laws implanted by God in man's nature, and which fall short of due respect for the dignity of human life and man's just liberty. Such measures are, in some cases, based upon a materialistic view of man's destiny.

(2684) The true solutions to these problems - we would say the only solutions - will be those that take due account of all concrete factors taken together: the demands of social justice as well as respect for the divine laws governing life, the dignity of the human person as well as the freedom of peoples, the primary role of the family as well as the responsibility proper to married couples (cf. *Populorum Progressio*, 37; *Humanae Vitae*, 23, 31).

(2685) We do not wish to repeat here in detail the principles that are at the basis of the Church's position in the matter of population. These principles have been clearly set forth in the Constitution *Gaudium et Spes* of the Second Vatican Council and in our encyclical letters *Populorum Progressio* and *Humanae Vitae*. These documents, the contents of which are well known to you, demonstrate that the Church's teaching on population matters is both firm and carefully enunciated, respectful of principles and, at the same time, deeply human in its pastoral approach.

(2686) No pressure must cause the Church to deviate towards doctrinal compromises or short-term solutions. It is not, of course, for the Church to propose solutions of the purely technical order. Her role is to bear witness to the dignity and destiny of man, and to enable man to rise to greater moral and spiritual heights. The Church's teaching, which we do not cease to reaffirm, assists the faithful to understand better their individual responsibility and the contribution that they are called upon to make to the solution of these problems. In this search they must not allow themselves to be influenced by the affirmation of individuals or groups who claim to present the Church's position while omitting certain essential aspects of the teaching of the genuine 'Magisterium'.

(2687) The Church has always emphasized, and she still does so today, the need to deal with the problems of population in the objective reality of their various aspects. These problems have of course economic and social aspects, but they are above all human problems.

(2688) In fact, discussion of the population problems involves the very finality of the human person. God's creative and redemptive will with regard to man can be recognized, confirmed or rejected in a debate that touches upon man's very existence. And this existence of man is only fully human to the extent that, "master of his own acts and judge of their worth, he is the author of his own advancement, in keeping with the nature which was given to him by this Creator and whose possibilities and exigencies he himself freely assumes" (*Populorum Progressio*, 34).

(2689) Any population programme must, therefore, be at the service of the human person. It must "reduce inequalities, fight discrimination, free man from various types of servitude and enable him to be the instrument of his own material betterment, of his moral progress and of his spiritual growth" (*Populorum Progressio*, 34). Hence it must remove everything that is opposed to life itself or which harms man's free and responsible personality.

(2690) Any population policy must, likewise, guarantee the dignity and stability of the institution of the family by ensuring that the family is provided with the means enabling it to play its true role. The family unit is at the service of a life that is fully human; it is the starting-point for a balanced social life, in which self-respect is inseparable from respect for others. Married couples must therefore exercise their responsibilities with a full awareness of their own duties towards God, themselves, the family and society, in a correct hierarchy of values. The decision regarding the number of children they will have depends upon their right judgment, and cannot be left to the discretion of the public authorities. But because this judgment presupposes a rightly-formed conscience, it is important that there should be realized all the conditions which will allow parents to attain a level of responsibility in conformity with morality - a responsibility which is really human and which, without neglecting the sum total of the circumstances, takes account of the law of God (cf. *Humanae Vitae*, 10; *Gaudium et Spes*, 50, 87).

(2691) One of the great themes that must be examined is, therefore, the theme of social justice. A fully human life, one endowed with freedom and dignity, will be assured to all men and all peoples when the earth's resources have been shared more equitably, when the needs of the less privileged have been given effective priority in the distribution of the riches of our planet, when the rich (individuals as well as groups) seriously undertake a fresh effort of aid and investment in favour of the most deprived.

(2692) The Population Year should proclaim a renewal of the commitment of all in favour of full justice in the world, in order to work together to build the common future of the human race (cf. *Populorum Progressio*, 43).

(2693) One often hears it said that, in order to make possible the development of the less privileged countries and to guarantee to future generations a healthy environment and a life worthy of man, population growth must be radically slowed down, and that the public authorities must concern themselves with this matter.

(2694) The public authorities, within the limits of their competence, can certainly intervene by favouring the availability of appropriate information, and especially by adopting suitable measures for economic development and social progress, provided that these measures respect and promote true human values, both individual and social, and provided that due respect is paid to the moral laws (cf. *Mater et Magistra* in AAS, 53 (1961) p. 447; *Populorum Progressio*, 37; *Humanae Vitae*, 23).

(2695) Dear friends: the fundamental attitude of the Church in this Population Year is one of hope. The history of the world proves that man can succeed in finding correct answers to the questions which face him, when he applies to this task all his creativity and all his gifts of heart and mind in a sincere collaboration in favour of his brothers and sisters, in order to assure for all a truly human life in freedom and responsibility. The Church has been the witness to this truth down the centuries.

(2696) The Church's hope is, of course, based on realism, but also upon the certitude that the sphere of what is possible can always increase when one goes forward with God.

2. A GENUINE POPULATION POLICY

Statement of H.E.Msgr. Eduard Gagnon, President of the Pontifical Committee for the Family, head of the Delegation of the Holy See at the World Conference on Population. Bucharest, 23 August 1974.

Original: French

(2697) The responsibilities of the present Conference are heavy, but we are sure that all of us here have decided to share them. We shall do so with more assurance if we let ourselves be illumined by a hope which is grounded both in a realistic knowledge of the difficulties and in the belief that it is possible to overcome them. It is in a spirit of service that the Holy See takes part in this Conference, wishing faithfully to offer that contribution which corresponds to its own mission and nature.

(2698) Rarely have international gatherings concentrated on a subject graver than that of population, such as is posed today. The problem of population touches the primary and fundamental relationship between man and woman and their fellowmen, a relationship of vital importance, for it is from a man and a woman that a person receives his existence and his insertion into the human community. The recommendations which this Conference will make will be capable of affecting man in his most intimate being and in the exercise of his most sacred rights. Their impact will affect the future of generations and of societies, in their life, their culture, their structure, and their equilibrium.

(2699) A great unrest is at the root of this Conference and the World Year of Population. Undoubtedly this unrest is nourished by artificial elements, but, primarily, it is based on the reality of two great human problems: underdevelopment which is so difficult to eliminate, and growth which is difficult to control.

(2700) To this first unrest is added another: fear, always a bad counsellor, fixes our attention on apparent information rather than on deeper causes, tends to give superficial solutions rather than well proven and fully human ones. "And man is only truly man in as far as, master of his own acts and judge of their worth, he is author of his own advancement, in keeping with the nature which was given to him by his Creator and whose possibilities and exigencies he himself freely assumes" (*Populorum Progressio*, 34).

(2701) This Conference has been preceded by an immense effort in research and exchange of ideas, to which the vast amount of documentation put at our disposal bears witness. The four symposia in particular have been a new way of getting to know the difference of positions on such a delicate and highly controversial subject.

(2702) The Secretary-General of the Conference has completed the enquiries with a symposium on Human Rights, and the report of that Symposium must be the inspiration for all our debates. The tone and the whole outlook of the documents serve to show that, without it, the Conference would run the risk of limiting itself to socio-economic considerations, without confronting the much more basic problems of *values* and *motivations*. These realities of the intellectual, moral and spiritual order, which it is the practice of the United Nations summarily to denote as "cultural factors", contain elements of fundamental importance for our subject, such as the desire for happiness, love and the value of life.

(2703) Allow me to pause for a moment at this latter notion. Our documents highlight it from two points of view: the struggle against illness and mortality - the intangible ideal of every society - and the preservation of the *quality of life*, that is to say, to use a phrase from one of the Symposia, the seeking for "a life more full of meaning", protected against "the exclusive anxiety for economic development" (E/CONF/60/ CBP/4/134). However, on the whole, even when there is reference to the motivations behind procreation, there is scarcely any mention of the role and of the respect for life or the laws which govern the unfolding of procreation itself.

(2704) The documentation displays a certain reluctance to speak of children, who, according to the First World Health Assembly, "represent all the hope of future humanity" (WHA, 1, 43). If our reading has been correct in the basic reports there is only one mention of the satisfaction to be found in the children's call to life (E/CONF/60/4/85).

(2705) Certain affirmations about the relationship between the prolongation of life and the birth-rate give the impression that interest for fecundity is to be measured by concern over the rate of replacement (the equilibrium which must be struck between the birth-rate and death-rate: cf. E/CONF/60/7/17). Is it not true that, at the bottom of things, one has opted for a certain type of well-being which does not comprise the whole of happiness, for a world where the children will find themselves overwhelmed by adults, always more grown up, always more serious and calculating!

(2706) Let us be attentive to what our Conference will bring to the young who are weary of a certain ideal of security, of spiritless modernization and with confidence wish for things which may be better, but will certainly be different. They are prepared to assert their control of the universe by making it human and joyful.

(2707) One will understand the satisfaction with which the Holy See's Delegation observed the special attention given to the family in the preparation for this Conference and in the arrangement of its work, but careful study of the documents leaves us somewhat perplexed. It is often difficult to know whether the family is being considered for its own intrinsic values or simply as an ally in pursuing certain policies. The family would appear to have been considered almost exclusively in its socio-economic aspects; few references are made to the profound realities which give it birth, which give reason to its proper function and permit its development.

(2708) The affirmation of the family's place in society and of its rights would appear to be a step backwards if one compares it to the clear pronouncements of the *Universal Declaration of Human Rights* and the much more recent Declaration on Social Progress and Development (United Nations, 11 December 1969, Art. 4). The projected World Plan of Action, instead of referring in a simple and straight-forward manner to these principles, turns them into nothing more than recommendations. This can be seen in No. 37, a, with reference to article 16, 3 of the Universal Declaration: "The family is the natural and fundamental group unit of society." And again in No. 37, c, with reference to article 16, 2 relative to the freedom of matrimonial consent.

(2709) It would not have been out of order, on the other hand, to analyse the bonds which knit the family together in its intimate life, the total complex of the realities which the family naturally assumes and because of which it has a right "to the protection of society and of the State" (cf. *Universal Declaration*, art. 16, 3).

(2710) It is in the family that many of the problems of population are experienced, that there is decided the fate of childhood, of youth, and to some extent of old age. Lest it should become impossible for the family to carry out its task, it should be assured of all the material, intellectual and spiritual resources which it needs to fulfil its vocation with generosity.

(2711) Over the last twenty-five years or so the situation of that two-thirds of the world's population which is less favoured than the rest has become the major problem which faces the human family at every level. At first, without fanfare and only in certain countries, then in an ever more incisive and general way, the question was asked whether the growth of the world's population, particularly that of the developing world, did not constitute a serious problem for development policies. The very fact that we are taking part in this Conference obliges each one of us to take a stance in this regard.

(2712) The two basic documents which we have on the subject, E/CONF/ 60/4 and 5, try to clarify the relationship between demographic growth, development, resources and environment. In general, the findings, the fruits of careful analysis, are characterized by a moderation and a desire for objectivity which we are happy to recognize. We ourselves subscribe to this conclusion of the Report on Development"As long as one poses the problem of population and of development, it is essential to realize that one is not dealing with unrelated elements. Demographic growth is not the principal cause of the problems of development. Demographic policies can contribute in a very important way to a more rational development; they are not sufficient to solve these problems" (E/CONF/60/4, n. 118).

(2713) We are well aware of the negative effects which are most probably connected with demographic growth: the constant increase in the gap which separates the 'per capita' income of those living in the developed countries and that of countries still in the course of development; the slow progress of productivity in relation to demand, above all in agriculture; the increased cost in certain sectors, notably that of education.

(2714) On the other hand, we must make known our disappointment at the perspectives put forth in the same report (E/CONF/60/4). The imbalance which affects or threatens developing countries seems to be defined as being dependent solely on national potential, as though one were not considering international social justice and solidarity between peoples. We would be the last to deny that often things happen as though these were utopian ideas. However, international cooperation and technical assistance are no longer mere hypotheses, nor have they been so for many years. If, to refer to the terms of the Project of a World Plan of Action, we are not to be afraid of envisaging "vast social, institutional and structural reforms, which can have repercussions on the whole of society" (E/CONF/60/7, n. 29), then should we not include in our balance sheet the whole of the international potential, faced as we are with this "challenge" posed by "the increasing number of men ... for the community of peoples and for their governments"? - these are the words which Pope Paul VI addressed to the Secretary-General of our Conference. To proceed in such a way is to respect the chronological and ethical priority of our solutions.

(2715) Bearing in mind the "demographic inertia," often spoken of by experts, and of the reduced efficiency which they attribute to the systematic campaigns for planning the birth rate which have been carried out so far, we must, at the same time, give full consideration to the other term of the equation. If development is primarily of importance to the interested parties and if, in a sense which must be closely defined, each country has a responsibility in determining policies regarding population, then nothing will be achieved by countries left to themselves. In such a case, one can ask if such countries would manage any better with less inhabitants. We agree that, broadly speaking, the means of progress already existing for some must be made available to all. The first thing which the peoples have a right to expect from our Conference is, therefore, an energetic appeal, backed up by suitable recommendations, for the inauguration of a new development order, called for by Paul VI in his letter to the Secretary General of the United Nations on the occasion of the Special Session of the General Assembly last April (see above, par. 1382-1394). The repercussions of the present economic crisis have led States to undertake, yet again, a drastic revision of international economic and commercial policies. It would be lamentable if the "crisis of existence", the true population problem, did not have the same stimulating and, we would readily say, compelling effect. The confusion which is at present affecting the developed world reminds it that it is on a wrong path. Will it accept the invitation to bring a remedy to the formidable "social inequality" of today - that of individuals, called to mind by the Report on Development (ibid. nn. 110-115), and that of entire nations which is still more striking? The egoism of the rich plays a larger part in this than the fertility of the poor.

(2716) All this takes on an increased importance because of the place we should give in our calculations to the availability of resources in the face of consumption demands. The Report on Resources and the Environment, E/CONF/60/5, is neither too utopian nor overpessimistic in this regard: there are the possibilities of creating both food and energy resources for a population much greater than that which the most reliable calculations lead us to predict. Instead of insisting solely on an abundant exchange of the technology and capital required for the utilization of these resources, should we not, first of all, denounce the inequality in consumption which has quite a different effect on the figures our predictions are based on? I will quote just one statement from the Document E/CONF/60/5: "Eighty-seven percent of the energy used in the world today is consumed by the rich countries and only thirteen percent by the rest of the world." The report puts some pertinent questions: "Is it possible, or indeed opportune, to leave the utilization of energy to follow its present rhythm in the developed countries? ... Can the poor countries attain a sufficient level of energy consumption to escape from poverty and misery?" This is the sense in which Pope Paul made his appeal to Mr. Waldheim in the letter already mentioned"... we appeal to the developed nations to make greater efforts to forego their own immediate advantages, and to adopt a new life style that will exclude both all excessive consumption and those superfluous needs that are often artificially engendered ... by a limited segment of society in search of riches. Likewise, one should not forget that a life-style based on ever greater consumption has deleterious effects on nature and the environment and finally on the moral fibre of man himself, especially the youth." (See above, par. 1387).

(2717) It will soon be thirty years since, with an unprecedented wave of "displaced persons" scattered over Europe, a special class of people was formed to whom any future seemed closed, even their acceptance into a new national community. This was the hard core, the residue of this mass of people, with reference to which the author of a vigorous plea launched the formula: "the unwanted men". This is certainly not the whole of the contemporary demographic problem, but do we not give the impression that there are "unwanted men" in relation to the monopolization of resources and their consumption by a small number?

(2718) In a desire to concentrate our thoughts with the aid of a precise text, and to avoid the danger that fifteen days of work should render no concrete results, the Secretary General of the Conference has submitted a "Project for a World Plan of Action" (E/CONF/60/7). The introduction to the document shows what the Plan hopes to be"a parallel in the field of population to the plans established in other sectors by different international agencies within the framework of the Second Development Decade." To this end, it seeks "expressly to modify the demographic variables" (*ibid.* 1). Is this the whole of a population policy or rather is it only a part? As we understand it, a genuine population policy will seek to establish the equitable sharing of resources and dwelling spaces; the contribution of different age groups and classes to the national and international life of today and of tomorrow; the responsibilities and tasks of States and of the world community with regard to populations already in existence and those yet to come. It is within this framework that there is integrated the consideration of the demographic variables, of their influence and of the eventual measures to be taken.

(2719) The perspectives of the "Project for a World Plan of Action" are so wide; could it not be that this is the origin of its short-comings? True, one finds here excellent comments on the struggle against illness and mortality, on study and research, and especially on migration. These are topics where a gradual consensus is seen to be emerging. Our Delegation wishes that the question of migration should receive all the attention that is its due. The sections of the Plan which refer to this are largely inspired by the "Symposium on Human Rights", itself well informed and to the point in its suggestions.

(2720) The main concern of the Project is in relation to the reduction, as rapidly as possible, of the birth rate, while repeatedly affirming the many limitations which are imposed by the sovereignty of States. On many occasions, most recently in the address of the Holy Father to Mr. Carrillo Flores and Mr. Salas and the intervention of our Delegation at the Geneva consultation, the Holy See has declared that it shares in the preoccupations which arise from the actual problems of population. But it does not think, for all this, that the actions to be taken should be guided by a too exclusive attention to the whole problem of demographic variables. The draft of the plan seems to us, in this respect, to be one-sided. We will explain this in more detail in the relevant working group. But we must mention here and now the considerable reservations which would be called forth on our part by the establishment of direct and indirect measures to obtain an urgent decrease in the birth rate. The Delegation of the Holy See has already said at Geneva: "We fear that to concentrate exclusively on demographic growth, to make it a privileged subject in campaigns on development, to channel huge resources into the solution of this one problem, is to upset the perspectives and only to prepare for mankind new frustrations." The Plan should have given an example of accuracy in determining the competence of the State regarding the first principle of the freedom of choice of married couples (cf. E/CONF/ 60/CPB 10, n. 52). This principle is repeated all through the Plan but is only interpreted as a right to "the limitation of birth". The intention of those who were the first to insert this in international texts was, above all else, to protest the freedom of the married couples against the intrusion of an indiscreet policy for the reduction of fertility (WHA 18, 49 and General Assembly 2211, XXI).

(2721) Many seem to believe that "modernization" assures a perfectly sound, and therefore in this matter they would say, restrictive judgment. But it is to self-control and to the perfect exercise of responsibility that we should aim. We are convinced that a healthy development contributes to this, especially since experience shows that the less well-to-do and even the poor, are often superior to the rich in this. This much at least is certain, that the education and the formation which develop such attitudes go well beyond the socio-economic perspectives and the competence of the State itself.

(2722) Finally, we will not pass over the fact that the passages of the Plan relative to contraception and the methods of preventing birth are not acceptable to us. They are not acceptable in what concerns contraceptives, in regard to which the Catholic Church has already made her position clear, and is aware of the need to reaffirm and maintain her teaching without ambiguity. Nor are these passages acceptable because we have no guarantee that those who have recourse to abortion and to its legalization will not appeal to them. The uncertainties expressed during the "Symposium on Human Rights" (E/ CONF/60/CPB/4, n. 24, nn. 76-82), do nothing to still our apprehensions.

(2723) Such are the principal positions which the Holy See's Delegation has the task of presenting to this Conference. We shall make an effort in the Commissions to make certain points more explicit and more precise; we shall, above all, apply ourselves to bringing our spirit of complete cooperation to our colleagues in the Conference. We remain convinced that a largely constructive work can be accomplished here, and that it will be that much better if we do not compromise on the firmness of our principles and do not stint ourselves in the generosity of our commitments. May the Lord, from whom all fatherhood takes its name, help us in this.

N.B. The World Conference on Population concluded its work on 30 August 1974. A majority of 138 Delegates agreed to the amended text of the "World Plan of Action on population". After the adoption of the Plan, the Head of the Holy See Delegation, Archbishop Eduard Gagnon, made the following statement:

(2724) The text of the World Plan of Action, which has been submitted for the approval of the Conference, represents a substantial improvement on the draft presented to the delegates at the beginning of our work. This is the result of some hard work, the quality of which has, in part, made up for the procedural difficulties and for the shortness of time available for drawing up a text charged with political and ethical implications for the public life of nations and for the private life of families and of every individual. Some of the changes which have been made constitute a notable correction of the previous situation. Thus, above all else, there is the affirmation that the problem of population can only be confronted within the more general perspective and overall priority of a global policy of integral human development. To this there must be added insistence on the fact that development policies require the setting up of a new socio-economic order in a spirit of international justice and of a new balance in world consumption.

(2725) The Holy See's Delegation has not ceased during the course of this Conference to defend these same theses, and congratulates those whose initiative has made it possible for them to be stated so expressly in the Plan. May all who make use of the Plan find inspiration in these points.

(2726) We regret, however, that even in this new perspective the Plan, rather than embracing the breadth of a true population policy, remains essentially on the level of a demographic policy. We explained this during our intervention in the general debate. Such a wider approach would have avoided the disproportionate emphasis given to a single one of the demographic variables. It would have allowed some qualification to be given to references made in some passages to facts and hypotheses which, in our view, are presented in a manner which is too absolute for a document of this kind.

(2727) If the Holy See Delegation does express its satisfaction with this re-orientation of the World Plan of Action, it nevertheless is gravely concerned about other points which are at stake in the Plan as a whole. The Delegation has never hidden its feelings about them: the family, respect for life, and indiscriminate recourse to means of birth prevention. We gladly recall here that a notable effort to meet our wishes regarding the above-mentioned points was made in the course of the negotiations, which were themselves conducted in an excellent spirit. It was because of a desire to work with our colleagues in a spirit of loyalty that we tabled precise amendments formulating our positions. Thus, we were able to find out just how far agreement was possible. We also recognized the point at which our propositions did not meet with the assent of the majority. Furthermore, some proposals or expressions retained from the original text, some changes introduced during the session, and the result of some of the voting create, in regard to these sectors of capital importance, ambiguities to which our Delegation is not able to give its assent. Everyone will understand that we are here dealing with principles concerning which the very nature of the Holy See prohibits any compromise. The Holy See owes this fidelity to Him from whom it receives its mission; equally it owes it to the whole community of man, to which, in a spirit of fraternal service, it offers its teaching.

(2728) In these circumstances, our Delegation considers itself obliged not to associate itself with the consensus regarding the adoption of the Conference's World Plan of Action. Another formula of agreement, that of approval with reservations, would undoubtedly seem more appropriate to many people, especially after two weeks of stimulating collaboration. It is not, however, possible for us to use this formula. States will defend themselves against what seems to them unacceptable in the Plan, thanks to their recognized right to exercise full sovereignty in defining their national population policy. People expect a basic stand from the Holy See . It is known that recourse to distinctions about what in the Plan has been accepted and what has not been accepted scarcely retains any meaning for those who accept a doctrine or ask for advice. We recognize that the persistence of ambiguities, the introduction of unfortunate expressions, the omission also of certain essential elements, are subject to too many interpretations and harmful consequences to allow us to approve, as a whole, the Plan which embodies them and which logically could inspire them.

(2729) It is in these circumstances, while not failing to recognize the value of some of the changes incorporated into the Plan, that the Holy See's Delegation declares once more that it does not participate in the consensus and requests that the text of the present statement be included in the Conference Report.

3. EVERY DEMOGRAPHIC POLICY MUST RESPECT MAN.

Address of His Holiness John Paul II to Mr. Rafael M. Salas, Secretary-General of the 1984 International Conference on Population, and Executive Director of the United Nations Fund for Population Activities (UNFPA). The Vatican, 7 June 1984.

Original: English (*)

(2730) 1. I am pleased to welcome you here today and to share with you some reflections on the coming 1984 International Conference on Population, for which you have been designated Secretary General. This Conference, to be held in Mexico City in August 1984, provides an opportunity for a re-examination of many important issues related to population growth or decline some ten years after the World Population Conference in 1974. The Holy See has followed the

---

(*) Insegnamenti di Giovanni Paolo II, Vol. VII,1 (1984), 1625-1631.

discussions of population during these years, and has studied *the implications of the demographic factor for the entire human family*. It is readily apparent that the worldwide population situation is very complex and varies from region to region. Behind the demographic facts there are many interrelated issues that have to do with improving the circumstances of living so that people can live in dignity, justice and peace, so that they can exercise the God-given right to form families, to bear and bring up children, and so that they can pursue their eternal destiny, which is union with the loving God who has created them. Thus, the Catholic Church takes positive note of the concern for improving systems of education and health care, recognizing the roles of aging persons, obtaining greater opportunities for people to be active participants in the development process and in constructing a new global economic system based on justice and equity.

(2731) 2. The Church recognizes the role of governments and of the international community to study and to face with responsibility the population problem in the context of and with a view to the common good of individual nations and of all humanity (*Populorum Progressio*, 37). But demographic policies must not consider people as mere numbers, or only in economic terms, or with any kind of prejudice. They must respect and promote the dignity and the fundamental rights of the human person and of the family.

(2732) The dignity of the human person - of each and every person - and his or her uniqueness and capacity to contribute to the well-being of society are of primary importance to the Church when entering into discussions about population. For the Church believes that human dignity is based on the fact that God has created each person, that we have been redeemed by Christ, and that, according to the Divine Plan, we shall rejoice with God forever. The Church must always stand as a sign and safeguard of the transcendent character of the human person (cf. *Gaudium et Spes*, 76), restoring hope to those who might otherwise despair of anything better than their present lot. This conviction of the Church is shared by others and is in harmony with the most secret desires of the human heart and responds to the deepest longings of the human person. The dignity of the person, then, is a value of universal importance, one that is upheld by people of differing religious, cultural and national backgrounds. This emphasis on the value of the person demands respect for human life, which is always a splendid gift of God's goodness. Against the pessimism and selfishness which cast a shadow over the world, the Church stands for life and calls for ever greater efforts to correct those situations that endanger or diminish the value and appropriate enjoyment of human life. Thus, I recall the words of my Apostolic Exhortation *Familiaris Consortio*, which reflect the consensus of the 1980 World Synod of Bishops on the family in the modern world:

(2733) "The Church is called upon to manifest anew to everyone, with clear and stronger conviction, her will to promote human life by every means and to defend it against all attacks, in whatever condition or state of development it is found.

(2734) "Thus, the Church condemns as a grave offence against human dignity and justice all those activities of governments or other public authorities which attempt to limit, in any way, the freedom of couples in deciding about children. Consequently any violence applied by such authorities in favour of contraception or, still worse, of sterilization and procured abortion, must be altogether condemned and forcefully rejected. Likewise to be denounced as gravely unjust are cases where, in international relations, economic help given for the advancement of peoples is made conditional on programmes of contraception, sterilization and procured abortion" (no. 30).

(2735) The experiences and trends of recent years clearly emphasize the profoundly negative effects of contraceptive programmes. These programmes have increased sexual permissiveness and promoted irresponsible conduct, with grave consequences especially for the education of youth and the dignity of women. The very notion of "*responsible* parenthood" and "*family* planning" has been violated by the distribution of contraceptives to adolescents. Moreover, from contraceptive programmes a transition has in fact often been made to the practice of sterilization and abortion, financed by governments and international organizations.

(2736) 3. The Church stresses *the importance of the family*, which is "the natural and fundamental group unit of society, and is entitled to protection by society and the State" (cf. Universal

Declaration of Human Rights, 16,3). At the request of the international Synod of Bishops, the Holy See itself has issued a Charter on the Rights of the Family in which it "urges all States, International Organizations, and all interested Institutions and persons to promote respect for these rights and to secure their effective recognition and observance" (Preamble). In this document, the family is recognized as "a community of love and solidarity which is uniquely suited to teach and transmit cultural, ethical, social, spiritual and religious values, essential to the well-being of its own members and of society" (Preamble, E). The family is truly a community of persons bound together by love, by mutual concern, by commitments to the past and to the future. While the primary members of the family are the spouses and their children, it is important to maintain an awareness of the family as a community where the different generations come together, and whose strength it is to provide a place of identity and security for relatives and for those who are assimilated into it.

(2737) The family has a unique and irreplaceable role in handing on the gift of life and in providing the best environment for the education of children and their introduction into society. It is primarily in the family that the child finds love and acceptance from the moment of conception and throughout the process of growth and development. Insecurity about the future should not diminish our hope and joy in children. Now, more than ever before, we must reaffirm our belief in the value of the child, and in the contributions that today's children can make to the entire human family.

(2738) As I said before the United Nations General Assembly: " In the presence of the representatives of so many nations of the world gathered here, I wish to express the joy that we all find in children, the springtime of life, the anticipation of the future history of each of our present earthly homelands. No country on earth, no political system can think of its own future otherwise than through the image of these new generations that will receive from their parents the manifold heritage of values, duties and aspirations of the nation to which they belong and of the whole human family. Concern for the child, even before birth, from the first moment of conception and, then, throughout the years of infancy and youth, is the primary and fundamental test of the relationship of one human being to another." (See above, par. 107)

(2739) 4. Yet, we all know that the spouses' decision in favour of childbearing and childrearing is not always easy and often occasions sacrifice. The Church is realistically aware of this, and her teaching on responsible parenthood concerns married couples - who alone have the right to procreation - to assist them in making what must be a free, informed and mutual decision regarding the spacing of births and the size of the family. This decision should be based on their prayerful and generous appreciation of their association with God in the work of creation, and their responsibilities to themselves, to their children, to their family and to society. It should be a decision that is based on morally acceptable methods of spacing or limiting births, about which it is the right and duty of the Church to speak. On the other hand, it is the role of governments and of international organizations to assist married couples by creating a socio-economic order conducive to family life, childbearing and childrearing, and by providing accurate information on the demographic situation so that couples may properly assess their duties and their capabilities.

(2740) 5. Special attention should be given to the role of women in modern society. Improving the status of women is important. In this regard we should not overlook the contributions that women make in the home and in their unique capacity to nurture the infant and guide the child in the earliest phase of education. This particular contribution of women is often ignored or diminished in favour of economic considerations or employment opportunities, and sometimes even in order to decrease the number of children. Continued efforts should be made to ensure the full integration of women in society, while giving due recognition to their important social role as mothers. This should include maternal and child health care, proper maternal leave, and family income supplements.

(2741) The Church is also aware of the initiatives in favour of the aging sponsored by the UNFPA. The number of aging persons is increasing in most countries. Their needs are often overlooked, and also the contribution they make to society. They bring experience, wisdom and a special patience to the solution of human problems, and they can and should be active members of contemporary society.

(2742) 6. Much attention is given to the relationship of population to development. It is widely recognized that a population policy is only one part of an overall development strategy. Once again, the Church emphasizes that the needs of families should be a primary consideration in development strategies, that families should be encouraged to assume responsibility for transforming society and be active participants in the development process. Yet, development itself should be more than a pursuit of material benefits; it should involve a more comprehensive approach that respects and satisfies the spiritual as well as the material needs of each person and of the whole of society. In a word, development strategies should be based on a just worldwide socio-economic order directed towards an equitable sharing of created goods, respectful stewardship of the environment and natural resources, and a sense of moral responsibility and cooperation among nations in order to achieve peace, security and economic stability for all. Above all, development should not be interpreted simply in terms of population control, nor should governments or international agencies make development assistance dependent on the achievement of family planning goals.

(2743) At this time, Mr. Secretary General, I would appeal to you and through you to all those participating in the 1984 International Conference on Population, to face the issues of population with renewed confidence in the human person, and in the power that moral and spiritual values have to contribute to the true solution of human problems in our day. May God Himself assist you to fulfil this important task.

4. PROGRESS MUST FIND NEW WAYS TO SERVE MAN IN DIGNITY, IN SOCIAL COHESION AND IN PEACE

Statement by H.E. Bishop Jan Schotte, Vice-President of the Pontifical Commission "Justice and Peace", Head of the Delegation of the Holy See, at the International Conference on Population, held in Mexico City from 6 to 13 August 1984.

Original: English

(2744) The Holy See is pleased to participate in the 1984 United Nations International Conference on Population and to consider, along with the Member States, observers and international organizations and agencies, the implications of population trends and policies for the future of the entire human family. The Holy See wishes to bring to such meetings and discussions an ethical or moral perspective on the human problems which are under consideration. The viewpoint of the Holy See is obviously shaped by its faith conviction - notably that the universe and each human being is created by God, that each person has been redeemed by Jesus Christ, and through God's providence enjoys a temporal existence and an eternal destiny. But, flowing from this conviction, the Holy See is also inspired by an understanding of the human person and his or her involvement in society that is profoundly humanistic, that is, that focuses on the person in his or her wholeness, respecting all human capacities and potentialities and respecting the need to create a global community where all may live in truth, justice and peace. It is, in a word, a commitment to "making life more human" for all. In this perspective, the Catholic Church, entirely free from every form of political, economic and ideological conditioning, wishes to render a service to man and to the international community, carrying out its prophetic mission for the good of the person and of humanity.

(2745) The Holy See recognizes the complexities of the questions involved in population issues, as well as their seriousness for the present moment and for the future. Realizing that these issues, if they are to be satisfactorily resolved for the good of mankind, must be looked at from an ethical perspective, it wishes to draw attention, in the first place, to some of the basic values involved in our discussion: the sacredness of human life and its transmission, the dignity and importance of each person, the inviolability of all human rights, the value of marriage as the natural institution to which the transmission of life is exclusively entrusted, and the need for a global commitment to social justice and socio-economic development. It is in the light of these values -

universally recognized by people of various cultures, religions and national backgrounds - that all policies and strategies must be evaluated.

(2746) At the 1974 World Conference on Population, the Holy See did not associate itself with the consensus regarding the adoption of the World Population Plan of Action. While it took an active part in the Bucharest Conference and appreciated much of the content of the Plan of Action, it was seriously concerned by some of the currents of reflection which underlay the document, especially those in regard to the family, respect for life and an indiscriminate recourse to means of birth regulation. The questions involved were - and still are - questions concerning fundamental aspects of a basic understanding of the person.

(2747) It is in the light of this position that the Holy See has studied the *Recommendations for the Further Implementation of the World Population Plan of Action* and offers the following comments.

(2748) The Holy See has carefully studied the demographic events and projections since the World Population Conference in 1974 in Bucharest, and has taken part in the preparatory meetings for this Conference throughout the past year. Many of the more pessimistic projections of the past have not materialized, and some trends have developed that were not forecast. Indeed, the world still faces a variety of population problems particular to various regions and nations, and often, very much related to the overall process of development. We know that, in general, the rate of world population growth has declined, as have fertility and mortality rates. In some developed nations the rates of population growth and fertility have fallen to alarmingly low levels with a corresponding increase in the proportion of elderly persons while, in some developing nations, rates of growth remain quite high. We have seen improvements in data gathering and analysis, and an extension of census-taking to an increasing number of countries, but, at the same time, experience reminds us of the complexity and uncertainties of long-range projection.

(2749) *The Recommendations for the Further Implementation of the World Population Plan of Action* tell us that the basis for solving population problems is socio-economic transformation, and that population policies should be part of overall policies of socio-economic development, and not a substitute for them.

(2750) The *Holy See wishes to stress* that in all areas of development, and particularly in population policy which touches on aspects of human behaviour which are profoundly linked with the nature and happiness of the person, it is necessary to undertake a critical analysis of the various theories of development, and to challenge them at their very basis. Population policies, and the development policies of which they are a part, have to do with the well-being of individual persons and the common good. The dignity and welfare of the person constitute a central part of the foundation on which population policies are built. Accordingly, the Holy See notes that the spiritual as well as the material well-being of the person must be taken into account in the development process, because spiritual values give meaning to material progress, to technical advances and to the creation of political and social structures that serve the community of persons we call society. Spiritual values enable people to see the real worth of material goods, to work for their attainment without sacrificing other values, and to enjoy life even when some material advantages are absent. Socio-economic development, then, is not simply a matter of economic philosophy or strategies, but it must be an ongoing process that respects the value and individuality of every person and in which each person is free to take responsibility for his or her own destiny and growth.

(2751) The person is, however, not absolutely autonomous, isolated from all others. Every person is a member of some, often many, communities - the family, the tribal community, the neighbourhood, the social and religious communities, the national and global communities. At the same time, each person has responsibilities towards the community. Socio-economic development is intended to broaden the basis for an equitable sharing and appropriate enjoyment of material goods. Scientific and technological progress should find new ways to make it possible for increasing numbers of people not simply to survive, but to live together in dignity, in social unity, harmony and in peace. This requires international cooperation, particularly in economic affairs, in technology, in dialogue among nations, in constantly searching for and discovering new ways to ensure development and progress for all. To see all progress as dependent on a decline in population growth betokens a shortness of vision and a failure of nerve, and it often results in policies or initiatives that violate human dignity and threaten the common good. On the contrary, in the light of the great disparities between rich and poor, it is a challenge to the global community to pursue social justice and to find new ways to accelerate the process of development, to assist all nations in developing their resources - human and material - and to develop an appropriate international economic system that is open to all nations and enables all to participate freely and equitably, with due regard for cultural traditions and differences.

(2752) The Holy See expresses its concern about the setting of quantitative population growth targets. There is always the danger that the achievement of such targets, especially in terms of declines in population growth and/or fertility rates, will be used as a condition for economic assistance. Bilateral or multilateral economic aid for the advancement of peoples should never be conditioned on a demonstrated decline in birth rates, nor depend on participation in family planning programmes.

(2753) The *Recommendations* recognize the worldwide decline in mortality and propose a number of specific measures to further reduce morbidity and mortality. The dignity of the person and the value of human life call for strategies to improve health and to ensure a longer life span. The Holy See agrees that continued efforts should be made to control infectious and contagious diseases and to improve nutrition and health care systems and ensure greater access to health maintenance and primary health care for both adults and children. Particularly important are programmes to reduce maternal and infant mortality and to assist in the physical and psycho-social development of children in their early years.

(2754) The family, based on marriage, is the basic unit of society which the State must juridically protect, support and foster. At the same time, the family is a community of love and solidarity, which is uniquely suited to teach and transmit cultural, ethical, social, spiritual and religious values, essential for the development and well-being of its own members and society. The status and roles of the family unit should be given highest recognition, and governments should establish appropriate social policies emphasizing the benefits that accrue to the individual couple and to society from stability in marriage.

(2755) In fact, it is not possible to treat the question of population seriously, or to indicate valid proposals for a solution to the problems involved, while prescinding from the *institution of the family*. The *Recommendations* mention the irreplaceable role of the family which the *World Population Plan of Action* recognizes as the "basic unit of society", and they refer to other important functions of the family. Unfortunately, this affirmation of principle is not taken up consistently and in detail by the *Recommendations*. Indeed, in some points the affirmation in principle is later denied or contradicted. The fundamental concept which underlies the text is, in reality, marked by a noticeable individualism. The very notion of *family* planning is falsified when it is used and applied not just to married couples but also to individuals and even to unmarried adolescents.

(2756) In this context the Holy See calls attention to the wording of the *Recommendations* with regard to responsible decisions on the spacing and limiting of births. Prior to the Bucharest Conference, the decision was recognized as a prerogative of married couples in their exercise of responsible parenthood. The *World Population Plan of Action* speaks of "individuals and couples," thereby endorsing a viewpoint which accepts sexual intimacy and parenthood as appropriate for unmarried individuals. In doing so, it diminishes the special and exclusive position which belongs to marriage and the family. Moreover, to some degree, the increased incidence of extramarital sexual activity and out of wedlock pregnancy during the last decade, especially in developed countries, can be attributed to the absence of an internationally accepted ethical principle that gives unique status to marriage as the only place in which both sexual intimacy and parenthood are appropriately and responsibly pursued.

(2757) The Delegation of the Holy See invites the Conference to reflect on the consequences of this undermining of the family institution. Development programmes which would contribute in any way to the weakening of the family institution or which would infringe on the inalienable rights of families do not lead to genuine human development, but rather to a weakening of the social and cultural fabric and to an alienation of the person from one of the principal dimensions of his or her humanity. Some societies are already having to face the harmful effects of this weakening of the family, with the serious consequences it brings for married couples and, especially for women and children.

(2758) It is in the light of this situation that the Holy See recently published and distributed a *Charter of the Rights of the Family* with the aim of reaffirming the essential rights of the institution of the family.

(2759) In particular, it is the positive duty of governments to create conditions that enable couples to exercise responsibly their fundamental right to form families, to bear and rear their children, without coercion or pressure to conform to the small family model or limit childbearing to one or two children per family. It is the right of the married couple to make a free, informed and mutual decision, in accordance with objective moral principles, regarding the spacing of births and the size of the family. This decision should be based on their recognition of their responsibilities to God, to themselves, to their children, to their family and to society. In pursuing these decisions, couples should be able to rely on those morally licit methods of family planning that are in accordance with the dignity of the person and with the authentic expression of conjugal love. It is the role of governments and international organizations to assist married couples by creating a socio-economic order conducive to family life, childbearing and childrearing, and by providing accurate information on the demographic situation so that couples may properly assess their duties and responsibilities. Couples should be protected from all forms of coercion such as loss of maternal and child health benefits, educational assistance and tax benefits or the imposition of penalties for going beyond a given number of children. They should also be protected from the sometimes subtle pressure that results from antinatalist propaganda campaigns or from quotas assigned to family planning workers for new acceptors. The freedom of poorer couples is often weakened by the offering of incentives which are, in the short term, attractive, but, in the long term, are dangerous to conjugal unity and family stability.

(2760) The Holy See must also express its opposition, on moral grounds, to abortion, sterilization and contraception. Among all human rights, the most fundamental is that of the right to life itself: human life must be respected and protected from the moment of conception, and abortion, which is the destruction of a human life during its earliest stages of development, should not be permitted either as a demographic strategy or as a way of dealing with problems related to pregnancy. The practice of abortion has not, in fact, been arrested by the massive introduction and distribution of contraceptive means. Indeed, abortion constitutes today a problem of such gravity for the human conscience that society cannot ignore it or cover it up. The question cannot leave this Conference indifferent. Despite affirmations to the contrary, and often contrary to the explicit formulations of national legislation, abortion is more and more used as an integral part of family planning programmes, financed even by governments and international organizations. The Holy See makes an appeal to all governments and international organizations to affirm clearly and explicitly the value, the inviolability and the dignity of human life from the moment of conception and, therefore, to prohibit and exclude abortion - not just in theory but in fact - as an element of family planning.

(2761) Sterilization and contraception must also be considered as morally illicit because, through their use, the inherent connection between intimacy and procreation is violated, and it is this inherent connection that gives meaning to human sexuality as a unique and exclusive expression of conjugal love. The *Plan of Action* and the *Recommendations* presented to this Conference make no explicit reference to sterilization, which, in the ten years since Bucharest, has become more and more widely used in family planning programmes in many nations. The Holy See has constantly opposed the practice of sterilization because of the finality with which it destroys one of the person's greatest prerogatives, the ability to procreate, and because as a demographic measure it can be too easily used in violation of human rights, especially among the poor and uninformed. The Holy See urges this Conference to find safeguards that protect all, and especially women - who are most vulnerable - from any coercion or pressure to undergo sterilization. It is well known that the Catholic Church has always rejected contraception as being morally illicit. That position has not changed but has been reaffirmed with new vigour.

(2762) The Holy See supports the proposal in the *Recommendations* which proposes access to natural family planning and which suggests that governments should in this manner provide concrete assistance for couples, which respects their religious values, in making responsible decisions regarding the spacing of births. Recent scientific studies underscore the validity and reliability of the newer natural methods, and pedagogical techniques have been developed that can be properly implemented and evaluated in various cultures. Women achieve a better understanding and appreciation of their sexuality from instruction in the natural methods, and couples who commit themselves to natural family planning strengthen their communication, mutual respect and shared responsibility in regard to parenthood. Respect for conscience, as well as the value of these natural methods in fostering stable marriage, require access to instruction in the proper use of these methods. Continued research is helpful to understand better the female fertility cycle.

(2763) In matters pertaining to family life and sex education, the Holy See calls attention to the rights of parents to impart values and to establish standards of conduct for their children in the context of ethical principles and a commitment to family life. Educational programmes, either in schools or under the auspices of voluntary agencies, must respect parental rights, and should be carried out only under the supervision and with the participation of parents. Education in responsible parenthood and the imparting of information regarding family planning to their children is also primarily a parental right and responsibility. The provision of such information and services in schools and other agencies generally fails to impart ethical standards and values, and at times can encourage sexual behaviour that is in conflict with the values and principles set down by parents. Such programmes should not be established or encouraged by governments or public authorities.

(2764) The Holy See has repeatedly advocated appropriate social and personal advancement for women in order to assure the dignity of woman and to provide for genuine human development for future generations. While supporting programmes which aim at the advancement of women in all areas of their life, it is important to remember that the advancement of women is not to be identified exclusively with work outside the home. Adequate recognition must be given to motherhood and the work of mothers in the home because of their value for the woman herself, for the family and society, not only on the material level but also in other aspects, particularly in the field of education.

(2765) Mothers must be afforded all the necessary social protection and assistance during pregnancy and for a reasonable time afterwards so that they can be with their children during this vital period of their development. Education of women, and particularly of mothers, is one of the critical determinants of the health, welfare and development of children. Mothers should receive the necessary training so that they can carry out their roles in the areas of education, nutrition and primary health care with both competence and satisfaction. Policies should aim at reducing the heavy work load which many women have to bear in various societies, both developed and developing, and programmes of education for fathers should lead them to assume fully their role of effective collaboration in family and parental duties and responsibilities.

(2766) The Holy See recognizes the difficulties involved in internal and international migration patterns, and urges that the human rights of migrants and refugees, as well as their families, be recognized and adequately protected. Migrants and their families have the right to respect for their own culture and to receive support and assistance towards their free integration into the community to which they contribute. In particular, migrant workers have the right to see their family united as soon as possible.

(2767) In the area of internal migration, special problems are caused by the flight from rural areas and from agricultural activities towards the large cities, thus increasing the social problems associated with rapid urbanization and often leading to a decrease in agriculture, with negative effects on food supply and economic growth. The Holy See supports suggestions which, while respecting the rights of freedom of movement, promote regional and rural development and provide adequate incentives for those involved in agriculture.

(2768) The Holy See supports the *Recommendations* in regard to respect and recognition of the place and proper role of aging persons in the development of society. It stresses that policies oriented towards ensuring the health, well-being and security of the aging should not limit themselves solely to technical and economic assistance. They should stimulate all to discover and appreciate the role of the aging as protagonists in the social community in which they should be considered as an integral part of society and as agents in its development. Their contributions to younger families and to other members of the extended family and their voluntary contribution of time, special competence and personal energy to many community interests and efforts, are of special value to the overall society.

(2769) These references to the problems of specific sectors of the population draw our attention once again to the fact that when we are dealing with population estimates and trends we are dealing in the first place with people. Demographic information is valuable because it informs us of events and trends which touch the lives and future security of living people and of the coming generations, and because it highlights the significance of population factors in the search for a better future in freedom and dignity for all persons. It is simplistic and unreal to identify population policy with population control: at the heart of population policies is the good, the health and the well-being of the human person, who must always be looked upon as an active participant in the life of society, as a precious good to be cherished, and not as a mere object of government policies.

VII - HUMAN SETTLEMENTS

1. Address of His Holiness Paul VI to Dr. Enrique Peñalosa, Secretary-General of the United Nations Conference on Human Settlements. The Vatican, 24 September 1975.

Original: Spanish (*)

(2770) We are very happy to take advantage of the opportunity offered us to indicate the importance we attribute to the United Nations Conference on Human Settlements, which is to take place in Vancouver next year, and to express to you our deep satisfaction with the ardour and competence with which you are assuming responsibility for its preparation.

(2771) The problem of the human environment is one of the most urgent and serious ones that face humanity today. In the course of the next few years, the general conditions of the human environment will change in many countries, not just in the town areas, but also in the country and in the different forms of rural life. The rapid growth of the population, its concentration, the accelerated exodus of rural populations towards the towns, the changes in economic life, the new mobility of men, the extension of a basic education and greater cultural possibilities for the whole population are, in our opinion, the main factors of this change. Man's aspiration, such a legitimate one, to a better quality of life calls for a dwelling that is not just a shelter against bad weather, but also favours man's own fulfillment in his material, cultural and spiritual needs, and contributes in this way to the growth of the most human side of man.

(2772) However different the forms may be, the dwelling, to be really human, must satisfy fundamental needs, which have not been sufficiently recognized hitherto. These needs belong to two categories: one concerns private, personal and family life; the other, social life. In the first place, it is necessary to ensure the possibility of privacy, calm and intimacy indispensable both for personal and for family life. Families must be given houses proportionate to the number of their children, which will permit a normal life and the cultural and spiritual development of all, without causing a limitation of births. Other needs are connected with the necessity of being open to others, meetings, interchange and mutual enrichment. All this implies a suitable conception of cities, towns, villages and their layout.

(2773) It is true that the environment is not sufficient to satisfy these needs. Facilities providing collective services are also necessary, some for material needs and others that meet cultural and spiritual requirements. These collective facilities must pro-vide the individual and the family with the services that are lacking in their homes; at the same time, they must offer the opportunity for meetings and contacts that meet the needs of private life on the plane of openness towards others and permit more personalized forms of social life. Some of these facilities deserve special mention, owing to their human and social importance, and because they are often forgotten: nurseries where working women's children are looked after during the day; sports grounds and facilities, cultural centres, centres for old people, meeting places of different kinds, especially for the young. In this context, provision should also be made for places of worship, since man has spiritual and religious needs that are not fully satisfied except in concrete community expressions.

(2774) However desirable it may be to offer man a dwelling that meets his legitimate aspirations as far as possible, it is clear, however, that, as regards the human environment, absolute priority must be given to ensuring everyone the minimum conditions for a decent life. We are aware that, at present, this need is not satisfied in most cases and that the realization of adequate living conditions continues to be one of the most serious social problems. We are thinking of the large number of human beings who still have no homes, or who have only wretched hovels, lacking the most elementary comforts, such as we see springing up in the outskirts of the large cities. We are thinking especially of the large number of families, young people, old people, migrant workers liv-

(*) Insegnamenti di Paolo VI, Vol. XIII (1975), 980-982.

ing in conditions unworthy of man. These situations are all the more deplorable when, as often happens, luxurious residential areas are found not far from these wretched shanty-towns. Nor should it be overlooked that these deplorable situations are made worse by those who speculate in the field of real estate in order to make excessive profits.

(2775) To put an end to this state of affairs is one of the most imperious and urgent demands of justice, since the right to a dwelling is one of man's fundamental rights.

(2776) We are happy, Mr. Secretary, to note on the agenda of the Conference concern for an environment that will fully meet all man's needs. Count on our full support in order that this United Nations Conference on Human Settlements may contribute to prepare all the inhabitants of the earth a suitable and really human habitat.

2. Message of His Holiness Paul VI to the President of the United Nations Conference on Human Settlements. The Vatican, 24 May 1976.

Original: French (*)

(2777) We are happy to address our greeting to you today and to express to the United Nations Conference on Human Settlements our profound satisfaction at seeing - as the preparation and organization of your labours prove - that the international community is acquiring an ever greater consciousness of the importance of the questions submitted for your study.

(2778) Periodically, the drama of earthquakes recalls to public opinion the place which a dwelling occupies in the life and in the hearts of people. You know that individuals, groups, entire sectors of people live permanently - either always, or under the pressures of social changes - in the situation of those whom nature suddenly deprives of their home and their living environment. The preparatory works of this Conference tell us that it is no longer possible to ignore such a situation or to grow accustomed to it or to tolerate it. Nor has your Conference assembled in order to deplore with resignation the enormous and growing deficiencies in the matter of the habitat, but to reanimate and sustain the courage of builders, and to seek original and magnanimous solutions to the most urgent problems, so that each person can have - together with a worthy and attractive dwelling - the normal services of health, hygiene and communication, within a framework of life that permits his or her full physical and spiritual progress.

(2779) In this message, it is not for us to suggest technical solutions, but we wish before all else to reiterate to you our confidence in the person and in his capacity to enlarge ceaselessly the area of what is possible, if his intelligence and heart are committed to a truly human existence for all his brothers and sisters. And we would also like to recall certain essential principles which can inspire and stimulate the reflection of this Conference and the competent work of those who will subsequently be called upon to put these programmes into practice.

(2780) "Human beings constitute the most important element in the universe." We rejoice to see this affirmation heading the General Principles which guide your labours. In effect the centre and fundamental priority of all programmes must be the person: the person in all his dimensions and all his dignity, the individual and social being, natural and historical, corporal and spiritual.

(2781) But all persons share in the same dignity. All life bears in itself an intrinsic quality. And this demands that conditions for fully human progress should be ensured for all people in their habitat.

(2782) The home, that is to say, the centre of warmth in which the family is united and the children grow in love, must remain the first concern of every programme relative to the human environment.

(*) AAS 68(1976), 503-406.

(2783) But this presupposes that the family and all its members are helped to be educated about the meaning and value of life, about the means of reaching true happiness. How many parents shower their children with secondary and passing things, but take little interest in giving them, in the home, a little space and peace for their balanced development? How many parents do not know how to arouse in their children an interest in the running and embellishment of their home, and do not prepare them to collaborate tomorrow in the perfecting of the human environment?

(2784) It also seems to us important that the Conference, while noting the primary role of technicians and creative geniuses with an enlightened social sense, should show a great confidence in the active and constructive participation of people; that it should mobilize the material and moral energies of all, even the apparently most humble, in the framework of programmes proportioned to their real possibilities, their legitimate aspirations and their particular cultural conditions.

(2785) We have already on several occasions manifested our conviction that international Organizations are necessary in order to specify the exigencies of justice between peoples and to render effective the good resolutions of solidarity among individuals. The present Conference fulfills this role by making once more possible the affirmation by all the nations of a clear political will and a serious spirit of collaboration; by enabling international cooperation to be expressed in bold, realistic and precise programmes; by ensuring that these programmes will be taken up and sustained by the decisions of the United Nations and that they will be integrated, as an essential element, into this new international economic order that has to be ceaselessly built up.

(2786) Finally, it seems to us important for a Conference like yours to form for itself a complete vision of reality by looking at the past, the present and the future.

(2787) The past, in order to take note of the valid and diverse experiences left to us by the tradition of peoples, for, even in accepting lights coming from outside, each people has always had a special insight in order to solve the problems proper to it.

(2788) The present, in order to appreciate the gravity of the present phenomena regarding the habitat, but by going beyond immediate appearances and seeking the real causes, moral or physical, of the present ills: it is at this price that fresh errors of orientation will be avoided.

(2789) The future, in order to challenge people's imaginations and to call forth great and original projects that will measure up to the future: for there is a new civilization, very close, in which we shall face the alternative either of the accumulation of calamities that destroy the human environment or of the courageous establishment of a habitat, worthy and honourable, for all.

(2790) Mr. President, we express our warm good wishes that this Conference will respond to the hopes placed in it. We know that the efforts of all its members will be directed towards giving to each individual the chance of finding a dwelling in a fully human setting. In anticipation, we thank you and invoke the blessings of heaven upon your work.

3. Note by the Holy See in preparation for the Conference on "Habitat" in Vancouver, Canada. The Vatican, 25 March 1976.

Original: English

(2791) In the course of the coming 50 years the general conditions of the human habitat will change in many countries, no doubt more than they have changed during the past millennium. The change will affect not only areas of urban settlement but also the countryside and the lifestyles of the rural habitat. Its principal factors are the rapid growth and the concentration of population, the transformations of economic life, a new type of human mobility, due in particular to migration, to the automobile and to employment instability, mass dissemination of information and the extension to the entire population of basic education and greater cultural opportunities. The result will necessarily be a profound modification of social life, which will inevitably have psychological and spiritual repercussions on both individuals and communities.

(2792) While it appears that the change in material, external conditions will be swift and compelling, it should nevertheless be recalled that it will affect human beings who carry within themselves a collection of permanent needs and a natural potential for self-fulfillment which will, to a large extent, continue to be what they were in the past, as much at the psychological and spiritual level as the biological level. No doubt, man knows better than any other living creature how to adapt to extremely varied conditions of life, and that will certainly continue to be true at a time when the growth of human population on the surface of the earth brings about a profound change in the human and social conditions of every individual's existence. However, just as the past has taught human beings to adapt to the earth's various climates and resources by finding the means to become increasingly human, so must the present allow adaptation to the new forms of social environment of favouring, rather than restricting or hindering, the growth of the most human qualities in man.

(2793) Thoughtfulness and firmness are, therefore, required of those entrusted with shaping the necessary transformation of the human habitat; and the Vancouver Conference becomes particularly valuable. The Holy See notes with satisfaction that the specifically human questions have been included explicitly among the many habitat problems on the Conference agenda. The Conference is to define a habitat which can meet the spiritual needs of man, offer adequate space for private life and social life and allow family and children's activities in satisfactory conditions.

(2794) It is the specifically human aspects of the habitat problem which will be stressed here. The Church has always been anxious to see full recognition and respect given to man's true nature, his roots in the universe and in history, his dignity and his spiritual calling; and in its recent teaching, for example in the Constitution *Gaudium et Spes* of Vatican Council II, the Encyclical *Pacem in Terris* of Pope John XXIII and the Encyclical *Populorum Progressio* and the Letter *Octogesima Adveniens* of Pope Paul VI, it formulated fundamental principles for the healthy development of man, society and social justice in which the basis of a sound doctrine of the habitat must be sought. On several occasions and especially at the time of the housing crisis which was particularly acute following the Second World War, the Popes have been moved to stress a number of major requirements which human habitat design must satisfy. [*]

(2795) In view of the seriousness of the housing problem today, and also of heightened aspirations for a better quality of life, the Holy See will set out here a series of principles and specific requirements for a habitat truly worthy of man. It appears all the more necessary to recall such requirements since often a narrow and even materialistic view of the human habitat continues to prevail. It would seem from many programmes and finished works that man's habitat needs are thought to have been met once he has merely been offered shelter against the elements and a minimum of conveniences (water, electricity); and even that minimum is not always provided. Such a view fails to recognize psychological, aesthetic and spiritual needs which are by no means a luxury but represent vital human requirements essential to health and physical and psychological stability.

(2796) Naturally, there cannot be a uniform proper habitat design to meet all man's needs in life. It cannot claim to be valid for all time and everywhere. As in the past, it may today have a number of variants according to the climate, the type of settlement (rural or urban), the culture and the style of life which is currently undergoing such significant changes. No country and no social class can claim that what suits it must be adopted by others.

(2797) Furthermore, in a number of poorer countries, or in large areas of those countries, communities are so lacking in the essentials of life or survival that it may seem inappropriate to enumerate all the requirements of an ideal habitat without first meeting other physical needs, such as food or basic health, and a minimum level of cultural and spiritual needs (see below). The Holy See, therefore, wishes to draw the attention of the Vancouver Conference to these situations of

(*) See for ex.: Speech of Pius XII on 15 November 1939; Message of Pius XII to the International Labour Organization, 25 April 1949; Message of Pius XII to the Institut pour les habitations populaires, 21 November 1953; Letter by H.E.Msgr. G.B. Montini, Acting Secretary of State to the Spanish Social Week, 25 June 1954.

poverty throughout the world, which urgently call for wide-spread cooperation, and in which the question of habitat is raised in quite different terms than in countries which have reached a certain level of economic development.

(2798) Nevertheless, the phenomenon of urban concentration - and hence of the proliferation of new housing to shelter thousands of migrants and persons who have been uprooted or have left the countryside - appears to be spreading to all continents. Housing is part of the essential minimum in life, corresponding to a biological need, together with food and health, not to mention the major psychological effects indicated above. It is therefore right to be concerned about the quality of life for all, enhanced or diminished by housing. It therefore seems indispensable, despite the diversity of customs and the disparity of means, to define a series of basic requirements to satisfy truly and fully the desire for comprehensive and interdependent development. It is timely, in any event, to consider a habitat policy geared to man which is free of superfluities, by specifying a number of appropriate measures, even if it is not yet possible to implement them all. That is the purpose of this preliminary document.

(2799) These requirements are of two kinds. Some concern individual and family private life, others concern social life. These two categories of needs are closely related. The individual and the family must find in their habitat and in its complements and environment both the opportunity to be isolated and the opportunity to be open and have contact with others. Individual housing must be such, both in its design and in its situation with regard to other housing and human settlements, that it allows both private life and collective life in suitable conditions. A habitat which is not sufficiently isolated to guarantee privacy and one which is so isolated that it does not allow easy participation in social life are thus both excluded.

(2800) An essential function of the habitat is to provide human beings, both those who live alone and childless couples or families, with sufficient isolation. Isolation from the outside physical environment rain, wind, cold or heat. But that is not sufficient. For private life to be really possible, the habitat must first be designed in such a way that the neighbors cannot hear what is said or done in it. Housing must also provide peace and quiet, which implies suitable isolation both from the noise of neighbours and from outside noise. These two requirements raise problems of sound-proofing which are still very often settled in a most unsatisfactory way, either because of builders' negligence and lack of concern or through lack of funds.

(2801) Space is a second fundamental requirement of a really human habitat. Cramped housing is a major obstacle to individual and still more to family life. The quality of life of the couple and of the family unit grouped around it, is such an essential value, rooted in the nature of the human race, that it cannot be sacrificed under the pretext of technological and social necessity. Housing units must, therefore, contain enough rooms to allow family members, parents and children, both the opportunity to communicate and temporary isolation which seems vital for psychological stability and for the various activities of private life. It should be stressed that children in particular need to be able to be by themselves, either to relax or to work and, more deeply, to assert and develop their personalities. With regard to children's work at home, attention should be given to the fact that many young people, unable to find at home the necessary and other requirements for individual work, have not been able to reach the educational level to which they aspired and for which they none the less had the necessary ability.

(2802) Attention should be given here to a point to which the builders of cheap mass housing do not appear to give sufficient thought: the minimum number of bedrooms required by a family with children or expecting to have children, as is usually the case. All family housing should have at least three bedrooms: One for the parents, one for the boys, one for the girls. To ignore this elementary need for a number of bedrooms allocated according to sex is to prevent proper and peaceful family life and encourage the older and younger children, brothers and sisters, in a promiscuity which is intolerable for their character and which even endangers the rectitude of their feelings and of their morals. It often causes them to leave home prematurely. Is it not, unwittingly, to set them on the path of juvenile delinquency and even of prostitution? Sufficient space is truly a major requirement in a home.

(2803) It is desirable that a private or public open-air space should adjoin the housing space proper. Of course, in urban areas, the addition of a garden to the habitat cannot easily be reconciled with aesthetic architectural requirements, at least in town centres. Greater emphasis should, therefore, be placed both on the need to design the habitat in such a way that wide, pleasant views may be obtained and on the creation of public areas near the housing which contain not only greenery but also playgrounds, since children, far more than adults, need a great amount of space for their stability and physical and psychological development.

(2804) The habitat, however, even extended by such private or public areas, cannot alone guarantee individual and family fulfillment. Community services, those indispensable complements to housing, are also needed. They have two purposes: they provide the individual and the family with services which cannot be supplied in the home and which, for various reasons, must be collective; and they provide opportunities for meetings and contacts which satisfy the need for openness of private life, complementary to the need for isolation. It is not merely a question of helping the family cell - which is not an end in itself - to find what it lacks, but also of fostering coexistence and interchange in wider circles which are still on a human scale, limited to the reasonably close neighbourhood of each person. Modern forms of urbanization tend not to give due attention to this intermediate level of existence, and modern planning now tends to take into account only the isolated human individual or the very general abstract whole. An effort should be made to provide people with opportunities for intermediate levels of social life which are more personalized, with all the necessary facilities for such neighbourhood life.

(2805) Particular attention should be given to certain of these facilities because of their human and social importance and also because they are often the most overlooked: day-care centres for the children of working women, sports grounds and establishments, cultural centres, old people's centres and various kinds of meeting places, particularly for the young.

(2806) People do not seek to satisfy only their material needs through or around such community facilities: they also seek, more or less consciously, to find opportunities for putting down roots, which enhance the identity and stability of individual and family life, and also landmarks which help to give their neighbourhood a familiar, intimate and original quality and link it to traditions which are an integral part of its history. Naturally, the opportunities which a predominantly rural habitat provided in the past, with its small shops and craftsmen, its art and its traces of the past, are less and less conceivable today in an increasingly urban life, with high mobility and widespread replacement of householders by tenants. No solution has been found to the problem of how to humanize the large new complexes, which are too often uniform and unsettled, and thus satisfy man's need for stability, failing which the ceaseless uprooting and the anonymity imposed on him will take its toll in instability or despair.

(2807) In a similar realm of ideas, particular importance should be given to the planning of places of worship. The Holy See cannot fail to stress their importance. It is true that in many regions history has bequeathed to the Catholic Church religious buildings which, by their size and beauty, are privileged places for self-recollection and prayer, where even those who do not share the Christian faith often come to meditate and seek peace. Urban development has resulted in the creation of districts and even of new towns where the problem of building places of worship is acute. Sometimes the need for such buildings is questioned, either on the ground that priority should be given to housing construction, or because it is considered that the practice of religion and the expression of faith do not signify that closed spaces should be exclusively given over to religious services. The Holy See wishes to speak out against such arguments. Neither personal nor social life can find fulfillment in purely earthly activities. Man does not live by the bread of his own civilization alone: he has spiritual needs. Moreover, we are made of flesh and blood, we are not pure spirit; our lives and desires can be completely fulfilled only in tangible forms, of which architecture is one of the most fundamental and indispensable.

(2808) Thus the Church asserts that the town should reserve a place beside the houses of men for the house of God; and, according to custom, mere "premises" will not suffice. To a reasonable degree, consonant with financial possibilities and taking into account the fulfillment of other needs, it must be, by its interior and exterior beauty, a symbol of man's faith and hope in his supernatural destiny, and it must blend harmoniously with the city's other monuments. Cooperation between the Church and the town planning authorities is both possible and desirable (cf. the symposium held in 1965 at UNESCO on the inclusion of places of worship in physical planning).

(2809) Man, as an organism, is inseparable from sub-human nature as a whole - animals, vegetation, countryside - and it is undesirable for him to become over-civilized to the extent that a barrier is created, psychologically and culturally as much as biologically, between him and the natural universe from which he originates and which is his first environment. Urbanization began spontaneously, implying a sort of rejection of the natural world in favour of the world of human creations: houses, streets, workshops and factories, public buildings... The natural universe was relegated to the "countryside", outside the "towns". We are reaching the point, however, where the systematic pursuit of that spontaneous process would lead to a form of urban development which would be psychologically, sociologically and culturally most harmful. Future physical planning and habitat development will have to find new relationships between all the necessary technological aspects of the habitat and the "natural" segment of the universe and of the earth's environment which must be permanently accessible. The solution does not reside merely in a few of the open spaces mentioned above. It means that the countryside must be nearby, and perhaps that habitats should be further apart, and there should be nature reserves.

(2810) Thus whether it is a question of isolation, space, community services, humanization of neighbourhoods or man's relationship with God and with nature, all these requirements are fundamental for a human habitat.

(2811) The great majority of people, however, do not yet have a habitat which meets the requirements listed above. The creation of such a habitat, not only for the privileged but for all, even the poorest, is currently one of the most serious social problems. A great many persons are still homeless, or have for a home only wretched shanties lacking even the most elementary conveniences, which proliferate on the outskirts of cities. The situation is all the more shocking since often, at no great distance from those sordid shanty towns, is found the ostentatious luxury of magnificent homes.

(2812) In this unacceptable situation, contrary to the dignity and common destiny of all men, the Holy See reaffirms that the habitat is also a fundamental human right.

(2813) Some inequality of resources, and thus of habitat "status", is in itself certainly not to be condemned. However, in view of the vital nature of the need to be satisfied, far less inequality is acceptable in respect of the habitat than for less essential needs. To be precise, the inequality which is wholly intolerable is that which creates the situation in which the privileged take possession of the best sites (the best parts of towns and of the coastline) and secure large areas for their own residence with its private environment. As a result, those with few means are relegated to the outskirts of towns or far from the coast, since the land and the best buildings in such areas are not accessible to them because of their very high price. There is, therefore, a segregation which runs absolutely counter to a healthy attitude towards human communities, in which social classes must be mixed. In regions which are very densely populated, this inequality may be heightened by the fact that land on which good-quality housing may be built is increasingly scarce. Furthermore, this state of affairs leads to construction programmes of excessive density which do not meet the requirements described above, particularly as concerns isolation and the provision of sufficient space for private life, and of surrounding public areas, chiefly open spaces.

(2814) To what may so unjust and deplorable a situation be attributed? This is a complex problem with many causes, and one which is certainly hard to solve, since it is found in almost every country. One can certainly blame the selfishness of those who take over the best areas for themselves; and still more those who speculate in housing to obtain outrageous profits. It is also certainly true that the various social categories have not been sufficiently aware of the value of a more human habitat, compared with other necessities of life.

(2815) Beyond such ethical causes, which should be remedied by education, blame also attaches to an economic system which has not thought to temper the legitimate right to private property by placing reasonable limits on the exercise of that right with regard to the acquisition of building-land. Attention should also be given to the short-comings both of buildings and of their environment, resulting from anarchial urbanization due to neglect on the part of the authorities, which for a long time did not perceive that it was dangerous to leave the construction of large housing complexes to individual initiative alone. Today there are many sociological jurists who rightly admit that this matter is also the concern of the authorities inasmuch as there are common interests at stake. It would be desirable, for example, to avoid building neighbourhoods for the rich and others for the poor, which is so much against the tradition of the city in European civilization. In addition, the authorities should not allow the areas needed by all citizens, whatever their social class, for their rest and enjoyment, to be taken over for private use, such as the seacoast, lakeshores, woods, forests... They should also intervene to prevent the construction of the countless housing estates of a drab uniformity or a variety quite lacking in stylistic unity, and of agglomerations with very few community services or facilities, which are often nothing but dormitory towns, towns which are half dead.

(2816) Having enumerated these causes of hardship, the Holy See wishes, without going into any detail, to mention the basic requirement s to be taken into account in policies to remedy this deplorable situation.

(2817) While the authorities have a major role to play, as described below, in the formulation and implementation of better guidelines for housing construction, individual citizens also have responsibilities. The creation of an acceptable habitat for all depends largely on their behaviour and on their aspirations. It is true that, often, they cannot by themselves attain that result, or even contemplate doing so, because of a lack of resources. Often, however, it is clear that if they do not have the habitat which their personal and family life demand, it is because they are injudicious in establishing priorities among their needs and do not hesitate to sacrifice their habitat to an inordinate need to travel, for example by auto-mobile, or to types of consumption which are far less necessary to their real well-being. They must therefore be educated, but such education is still very often wanting.

(2818) Use can also be made of many kinds of local initiative before the authorities become involved. Through the many kinds of associations which they can form, the persons concerned in a neighbourhood, an area or a town have their say in the construction, improvement and management of their habitat. They cannot be bypassed without serious harm: neither the State nor any other social class should do violence to their human potential and disposition, by requiring that they should accept living conditions which were prepared for them but without them. It is for them to become aware of their needs, to organize, to initiate a dialogue with the local authorities and to cooperate among themselves in patience and solidarity to improve the collective services and general conditions of their habitat. Many tenant associations, for example, have already undertaken encouraging work.

(2819) As for the authorities, chief among their occupations should be the definition of a land use policy, reserving sufficiently large areas for the social habitat by means of judicious purchases. Clearly that presupposes sufficient funds, which in turn implies that the authorities must establish a sounder hierarchy of needs, and a policy of redistribution of wealth which, while avoiding the excesses of total, paralysing and inhuman socialization, should have the effect of reducing by suitable means exaggerated inequality of income and wealth. The formulation of a sound housing policy is admittedly no easy task. It is often necessary to choose between conflicting requirements. Thus the attempt to give an aesthetic quality to housing, housing complexes and the towns containing them results in higher construction costs, which may lead to a smaller number or smaller size of housing units. Certain necessities which may on no account be sacrificed could also be noted.

(2820) First among these necessities is the obligation to provide families with housing which is sufficiently large for the number of their children. The tendency in certain housing policies to sacrifice the family, without hesitation, on the ground that the need for sufficiently large housing is incompatible with the need to build in great quantity, should be emphatically condemned. The consequences of such policies are that families live in conditions which do not allow a normal life and still less the cultural and spiritual development of their members, with the serious psychological disturbances which ensue (see above); or else families are obliged to reduce the number of children they had intended to bear.

(2821) Another concern of a sound housing policy should be to remedy the great difficulties encountered by disadvantaged categories, such as young married couples, old people and migrant workers, in their search for housing.

(2822) Whether for these categories or for the families, it is unacceptable to settle for easy solutions which consist of building housing in areas at a great distance from places of work, recreation or administration of towns, and whose community services are wanting in number and quantity. Here again the requirements may appear to be contradictory. Dormitory towns do not seem to be a good solution, and they do not solve the problem of long and tiresome commuting which is a cause of nervous stress and of dispersal. On the other hand, it is no more human to continue to create dense tentacles of population around industrial centres which are themselves enormous and close together. Would the solution not be to encourage the decentralization of enterprises and towns, which has been attempted in places? There must be a search for bold policies calling for enthusiasm, competence and persistence in the regions where the creation of new towns has caused a sharp rise in population. If such policies encounter many obstacles, it is because they require prior in-depth studies which are often still lacking. Nevertheless, outstanding successes have been achieved in many countries, demonstrating that improvement is possible when there is a sincere desire for a more human apportionment of the habitat.

(2823) All that has been said here about the policy which a given country should follow to develop its human settlements presupposes that the entire population of the country must have the same access to the essential goods which support material and cultural life. The Vancouver Conference should not merely consider the problem of an ideal habitat, when there are whole regions in which the people do not even have the proper shelter and cannot satisfy other fundamental needs: food, health, sanitation, employment, family stability, literacy, social justice, peace, opportunities for a spiritual life (cf. *Populorum Progressio*, 21, 35-38, 45 etc.).

(2824) It is the honour and the duty of an international organization such as the United Nations to consider the situation throughout the world and give priority to the poorest communities in defining the most urgent and essential needs as well as the strategies and resources needed to meet them. Its role is to replace the question of human settlements in the framework of all other human needs and, within the sphere of the habitat itself, to define the fundamental and universally valid rights which guarantee the biological, psycho-logical, social, cultural and spiritual stability of human beings. In any event, it is important to ensure, at least, that family life may develop in dignity, since the home is the basic cell, the centre and, as it were, the heart not only of the first years of a life but of every truly human life. All peoples, whoever they may be, must be helped to adopt a policy geared to man. The harmony and success of human settlements will depend on such a policy, which cannot be the marginal corollary of decisions inspired primarily by economic considerations. In the face of the shocking disparities in populated areas and resources, the Vancouver Conference-Exposition should foster realistic and effective international cooperation, as other institutions have done for hunger, literacy and health.

(2825) The Church needs to take part in this effort to provide people, particularly the neediest, with a habitat which meets their material and spiritual needs. It first wishes to make its children aware of the urgent need for them to commit themselves alongside their brothers to the improvement of the habitat. Furthermore, through its institutions the Church itself willingly collaborates, to the best of its ability, in this essentially humanitarian under-taking. History shows that the Church has been pressured by Christ's charity to heed the call of the great number of homeless or badly-housed persons. It knows that Christ identifies with them at the Last Judgement: "I was a stranger, and you took me in" (*Mt.* 25:35). Its action throughout the world has very often taken the form of initiatives for housing. In recent times, for example, improvement of the habitat occupied an important position in the great social movement created among Catholics by the encyclical *Rerum Novarum* of Leo XIII (1891) and the great social encyclicals of his successors, chiefly those of John XXIII and Paul VI: action in favour of the habitat of the people, workers' gardens, and young and old people's homes. The personal contribution Pope Paul VI made to solving the housing crisis in 1973 in Acilia, in the suburbs of Rome, is well known. There are many examples of priests and laymen whose activity helped to orient housing construction towards serving the greatest number, with the participation of the persons concerned, and to foster a habitat particularly designed to meet the needs of large families. Two typical cases, among many others, will serve as examples. A priest in Brescia (Fr. Ottorino Marcolino, a Doctor in Mathematics and engineering) has built, in the course of the last 20 years, and without State aid, some 15,000 housing units in the north of Italy for badly-housed persons, organizing them in co-operatives with quick access to ownership, thanks to the work of the tenants. In Chile, in the suburbs of Santiago, for over 15 years a priest has provided a humble but adequate and well-designed habitat for families who were living in the most abject conditions.

(2826) The Church, for which the Holy See is speaking here, thus gives its full attention to action in favour of human settlements, as an undertaking which answers one of the most pressing demands of justice and charity. It wishes to attempt to foster a habitat which fully meets human requirements and material and spiritual needs, while at the same time supporting many undertakings with the generosity which it derives from the message of the Gospel. It is in this spirit that the Holy See has ventured to contribute, in conformity with its moral and spiritual position, to the work of the Vancouver Conference-Exposition by preparing this preliminary document. It sincerely hopes that a broad consensus will be forth-coming on the subject of the fundamental requirements which must be satisfied, and that effective measures will be adopted and recommended to the participants, so as to prepare a more human habitat for all the earth's inhabitants.

4. Statement of H.E. Msgr. Eduard Gagnon, President of the Committee for the Family, Head of the Delegation of the Holy See at the United Nations Conference on Human Settlements, held in Vancouver (Canada) on 31 May-11 June 1976. Vancouver, 2 June 1976.

Original: French

(2827) The Holy See Delegation confirms once again the importance which the Catholic Church attributes to this Conference of the United Nations on Human Settlements, and her lively interest in it, as was clearly expressed in the words which His Holiness Pope Paul VI addressed to the Secretary General, Dr. Enrique Peñaloza, on the occasion of the audience granted to him on 24 September last year.

(2828) Sharing "the joys and hopes, the grief and anxieties of the people of our time" (Second Vatican Council, *Gaudium et Spes*, I) the Church proclaims the Gospel and offers her contribution in the midst of the problems affecting the existence and destiny of individuals and peoples. And when all the problems and challenges implied in the human "habitat" - the theme of the International Conference that unites us - are considered, who can doubt that the existence and destiny of humanity is faced with a singularly serious and complex perspective of vast magnitude?

(2829) It is evident today that the general conditions of the human habitat will, in the next decades, undergo profound changes which will affect civilization itself. Under multiple influences combined with the accelerated growth of the world's population, with the vertiginous and concentrated rhythm of urbanization, with the change from agrarian societies to various forms of industrialization, with the complex process of migration in new contexts of human mobility, with the diffusion on all levels of scientific, technological and educational developments, with the creation of new political and economic conditions and situations, etc., new and qualitatively different horizons open up in regard to the "habitat" of individuals and peoples. The immensity of the challenges which this perspective reveals, as well as of the tasks and resources which it requires "to prepare for all the inhabitants of the earth a suitable and truly human habitat" (Paul VI, Address to Dr. Enrique Peñaloza, 24 September 1975. See above, par. 2776), is such as to appear, at first sight, disconcerting. Is technical, political and spiritual preparation being made to face serenely such urgent problems of the human habitat, in order to overcome the oppressive avalanche of spontaneous events which ceaselessly feed these problems, and in order to be raised above habits and vested interests and thus to dominate evolutionary tendencies by controlling them and orienting them towards fully human solutions?

(2830) Given the magnitude and velocity of such processes of change in the human habitat, the complexity of the implantation and adaptation of the human communities in this context, the unconcern for, ignorance of or resistance to this challenge, there is needed a deliberate strategy, at a national and international level, clearly programmed to create the conditions for substantially improving the dwelling of people in their historical existence.

(2831) In the face of the problems of the human settlement which are glimpsed in the previsions and predictions for the year 2000, who today can trust the regulating and "salvific" effects of material progress left to change? The opposite of an irresponsible liberal optimism is a despairing pessimism manifested in catastrophic and apocalyptic predictions. Moreover, on all sides there are the noticeable effects of an uncontrolled, unbalanced and unequal growth following its manifest course through the evident injustices that call for the establishing of a "New International Economic Order", through the chaotic and anarchical development of urbanization on the ecological border of vast settlements of people (barrios, rural areas and towns) who are kept at the margin of the profits of civilization, where life is contaminated.

(2832) Likewise evident are those evils affecting the human habitat that spring from the massive and depersonalized buildings that are expressions of a collectivism which, in theory or practice, denies sufficient dignity to the person or to the human structure of the family.

(2833) Essentially there results a dilemma. Either the capacity will be acquired and the real will affirmed, according to a deliberate plan - by which the growth of construction will be controlled and its organization and proper use regulated - to build a habitat substantially different from that which the present conditions produce; or the new generations will receive the sad inheritance of a human habitat incapable of satisfying the aspirations for a life that is worthy and happy for everyone.

(2834) For this reason the problem of the habitat necessarily looks to the inspiration and effective actualization of models of integral development, if which policy with respect to human settlements is a strategic priority and is not relegated as a simple marginal corollary of economic decisions.

(2835) In regard to this particular point, it is not up to the Holy See to enter into technical considerations or turn to political solutions, even though it is not unaware of the difficulties, problems and real possibilities at such levels. But the Holy See wishes to sensitize public opinion, to manifest appreciation and support for and to stimulate a just "habitat policy geared to man" (Document A/CONF. 70/RPC/BP/15, "Contribution of the Holy See", 6) and which tends to be "integral, that is, it has to promote the good of every man and of the whole man" (Encyclical, *Populorum Progressio*, 14).

(2836) "To promote the good of every individual and of the whole individual": in this twofold direction and perspective it becomes possible to develop and deepen the basic requirements and priorities for a policy of housing - an essential condition in the human habitat.

(2837) "Every individual!" In the first place the Holy See reaffirms its conviction - in the words of Pope Paul VI to Dr. Peñaloza - that "absolute priority must be given to ensure to everyone the minimum conditions for a decent life" (See above, par. 2774). And for everyone this minimum of life requires housing that takes into account the essential biological requirements (in nutrition, hygiene, health, etc.) and the basic social needs for a life worthy of individuals and peoples (employment, family stability, literacy, justice in structures and in social relations, peace and respect for human rights in coexistence, the possibility for spiritual life, etc.).

(2838) It is not acceptable to suggest that the legitimate aspiration for a better "quality of life" in the matter of the habitat should be filled according to the false standards of consumerism, hedonistic refinements and aesthetical and sumptuous luxuries when, for vast sections of humanity, life itself is at stake being menaced as it is by miserable living conditions. In this sense, it is necessary to attend particularly to the poor, this "large number of human beings who still have no homes, or who have only wretched hovels, lacking the most elementary comforts, ..." (Address to Dr. Peñaloza. See above, par. 2774). Permit us in this regard to recall all the most underprivileged human categories: the multitudes cramped on the outskirts of the great cities, condemned to live in abject crowding; the vast sectors of rural dwellers whose habitat is a clear sign of that technical, social and socio-economic delay in which extensive rural areas are maintained; the young people held in the demoralizing state of having continually to wait before establishing a family, being subjected to the scarcity and instability of employment and the penury of housing for this purpose; the old people alone and passed over - and some times relegated together and unattended -according to rapacious criteria of what they can yield; the workers who have emigrated in search of a better and stable home; the sick who are suffering from the lack of sanatoria and of medical and hygienic infrastructures; the victims of natural calamities who must remake their habitat from its foundations.

(2839) As happened in Bethlehem, which "had no place in the inn" (*Lk.* 2:7) for the poor one who was the Son of God, on a planetary level we are seeing such situations which are all the more regrettable in so far as they frequently coexist at a short distance from the luxury and waste of sumptuous residences established in the districts of privileged minorities. In the words of Pope Paul VI to the Secretary-General of this Conference: "To put an end to this state of affairs is one of the most imperious and urgent demands of justice, since the right to a dwelling is one of man's fundamental rights" (See above, par. 2775).

(2840) Attention, therefore, must be directed to "every individual", but also to "the whole individual". Better quality of life demands a housing that is not only a shelter against inclemency but also fosters the very realization of people in their material, cultural and spiritual needs. Beyond the distinct forms which can be adapted to physical, climatic, socioeconomic and diverse cultural situations, all housing - to be truly human - must satisfy certain fundamental requirements: some that concern private, personal and family life; and others that concern life in society.

(2841) In the whirlwind of the agglomeration, congestion, contamination and noise of the cities, it is necessary to ensure, today more than ever before, the possibilities for privacy, tranquillity and intimacy indispensable both for personal as well as for family life. Sight cannot be lost of the essential importance that the home presupposes for the harmonious realization of conjugal life, the wholesome and integral education of children, the affirmation of a serene and receptive family climate. Families have the right to count on a dwelling that is appropriate to the number of children. It must not remain in the domain of a utopia that the children should be the most privileged in the construction of the human habitat. Would that they were taken into account!

(2842) The exigencies of private life - personal and family - require that housing should also be the basis for personal exchanges and mutual enrichment in the order of life in society. And all of this implies a distribution and appropriate conception of cities with human dimensions, a development of neighbourhood units and new community forms of relation and cooperation, an adequate system of transport and communications, the reduction of oppressive distances between homes and places of work, an aesthetic concern for the beauty of housing and its surroundings, a new synthesis between technical creations of the human habitat and a natural environment which ensures open spaces and those for recreation, as well as ecological and psychological balance; finally a new plan is required for physical, social, economic and cultural space for the life of the human communities.

(2843) A special mention should be made of the necessary settlements dedicated to community services of the material, cultural and spiritual order, which may cooperate in the social assistance of problems that individuals and their families cannot solve by them-selves in their own dwellings, and which may be the occasion of an encounter, contact and popular cooperation and may permit forms of more personalized social life to help moderate the tendencies towards the massiveness and anonymity of the great modern human conglomerations. It is necessary to pay special attention to some of these groups "owing to their human and social importance, an because they are often forgotten: nurseries where working women's children are looked after during the day; sports grounds and facilities, cultural centres, centres for old people, meeting places of different kinds, especially for the young".

(2844) "In this context provision should also be made for places of worship, since man has spiritual and religious needs that are not fully satisfied except in concrete community expressions" (Address to Dr. Peñaloza. See above, par. 2773).

(2845) The Holy See hopes that this conference will be the place and occasion for the launching of collective mobilization of the cooperation of international institutions, of the renewed programming of the public powers of the various States and of the creative participation of peoples in order to create conditions for a human habitat that fosters the development of the material cultural and spiritual potentialities of all people. Is this not a veritable challenge to the wisdom of people, to their capacity for organization and to their imagination? (cf. Apostolic Letter of Pope Paul VI, *Octogesima Adveniens*).

(2846) The Catholic Church is disposed to participate actively in such an endeavour - as she has been doing throughout all her history - animating and stimulating all Christians to contribute their efforts at remaking a world that is more human, just and fraternal, promoting all those of her programmes and institutions that present a vast and immense contribution in the construction of housing and in the management of community services necessary in the life of the most diverse human communities and, in particular, for the multitude of the most needy and helpless - those with whom Christ will identify Himself in the final judgment: "I was a stranger and you made me welcome" (*Mt.* 25:35).

(2847) Let us do what is possible to construct a habitat worthy of the individual and of all people in our temporary dwelling on this earth - a habitat which may become the sign, in obscure anticipation, in the greatness and fragility of the human realizations and limitations - of the definitive "habitat" of heaven, which, already in this world, we must proclaim, prepare for, and confidently await.

VIII - REFUGEES

1. Radio Message of His Holiness John XXIII for the opening of the "World Refugee Year". The Vatican, 28 June 1959.

Original: French (*)

(2848) We learn with great satisfaction of the designation, through the efforts of the United Nations, of the World Refugee Year: June 1959 - June 1960, and most willingly we bring the moral support of our encouragement to this noble initiative.

(2849) The fate of those who live exiled far from their homeland has always attracted the maternal solicitude of the Catholic Church in a special way because the Church could not forget the words of Christ, her divine Founder: "I was a stranger and you welcomed me, naked and you clothed me, a prisoner and you came to see me" (*Mt.* 25:35).

(2850) Now, today, hundreds of thousands of refugees - no one can be unaware of it - victims in diverse ways of the upheavals of these recent years, are still kept in camps and lodged in barracks, humiliated in their dignity as human persons, exposed sometimes to the worse temptations of discouragement and of despair.

(2851) What good-hearted person could remain indifferent to this sight: so many men, women, even children, deprived, not because of their fault, of certain of the most fundamental human rights, families separated against their will, husbands separated from their wives, children kept far from their parents. In modern society, so proud of its technological and social progress, what a sad

(*) AAS 51(1959), 481-483.

anomaly! Each person has the duty to awaken to this and do what he or she can to make it disappear.

(2852) Earlier, what was not done in favor of the refugees of the first world war by Pope Benedict XV, whose generous heart was so open to all distress? And in his turn, at the time of the last conflict, what did our immediate predecessor Pius XII not do, he who was so compassionate to human suffering, so sensitive to any attack on natural law? How many interventions on the international level, how many initiatives of the Holy See, how much aid of all kinds sprang from Vatican City during these tragic years: beneficial activity in many respects of which we ourselves were, to some extent, the witness filled with emotion and also the instrument.

(2853) Called to take note of this precious heritage of charity and of defense of the poor, which is one of the most beautiful jewels of the Catholic Church, we too raise our voice in behalf of refugees, and we paternally exhort our children of all parts of the world to bring their generous and effective collaboration to the success of this "World Refugee Year", which is of such noble and disinterested inspiration that we would like to render homage to it. Let everyone then, according to their means, devote themselves to assuring a better fate for their unfortunate brothers and sisters, recalling that their present trials, in many cases, are not unknown to the Church and to Christ to whom they remain attached. And if any one - God forbid - was tempted to close their heart to this appeal, let that person recall the serious warning of our predecessor: "And you who remain insensitive to the anguish of the homeless refugee, should you not feel in solidarity with those whose pitiable fate today could be yours tomorrow?" [Pius XII: Christmas Radio Message 1950, AAS 43 (1951), p. 56].

(2854) Above all, we exhort the Pastors of souls to call to the attention of their faithful this invitation of Providence to manifest their feelings of Christian charity.

(2855) Since, on the other hand, private initiative is powerless by itself, alone, to resolve problems of such size, we are confident that public authorities will make a point, during this year, of continuing and intensifying, still more, such praiseworthy efforts undertaken in this matter. Important results, as we know, have already been obtained on the international level, notably the elaboration and adoption by a rather large number of States of the Convention of 1951 on the Status of Refugees. May these States, and others following them, always open ever more generously their frontiers and assure promptly the humane relocation of so many unfortunate people in a way that they are integrated into their new society! May these persons find without delay what they long for so ardently: a worthy life in the heart of a hospitable adopting country, in the peaceful enjoyment of their personal and family rights.

(2856) On all those individuals and groups who will hasten the realization of this greatly desired goal by participating in some way - as we will do so ourselves, according to our means - to the success of the World Refugee Year, we invoke most warmly the protection and the special favors of the Almighty and merciful God.

2. Address of His Holiness Paul VI to participants in the XII Session of the Executive Committee of the Programme of the United Nations High Commissioner for Refugees. The Vatican, 30 October 1964.

Original: French (*)

(2857) We are happy to receive you in Our residence, and we thank you with all Our heart for this visit which honors Us and permits Us to participate, in some measure, in the 12th session of the Executive Committee of the Programme of the United Nations High Commissioner for Refugees.

(2858) We truly feel associated with your meeting, not only because this time you elected, exceptionally, to meet in Rome, but because We are so deeply touched by the painful human prob-

(*) AAS 56(1964), 996-997.

lem of refugees. We experienced this same anguish of so many people torn from their first home and roots when We were working in the State Secretariat and following the beginning of the International Office for Refugees, and later the founding of your High Commission. In this, We were merely executing the wise instructions of our unforgettable predecessor Pius XII to serve suffering humanity.

(2859) It is a comfort for Us to know that your organization - under the auspices of the United Nations and with the effective aid of many deserving benevolent associations - has been able to provide, during more than ten years of your activity, the conditions needed to permit hundreds of thousands of unfortunates to survive. This humanitarian work continues, and your faith in the justice of this cause permits you to triumph happily over the inevitable difficulties you encounter.

(2860) In fact, we should all recognize that aid to refugees is an extremely complex undertaking, for not only must it afford legal protection, but likewise financial and social support, coupled at times with medical and psychological treatment to the oppressed; to which we should add the necessary training of youth and the adaptation to new professions for older members of the human community.

(2861) Your Executive Committee, gentlemen, in its firm wish to help all the various categories of refugees has been able to obtain the confidence and approval of the United Nations General Assembly for programmes allowing you to meet ever-growing needs. Thus, the Office of the High Commissioner has been able to convene highly useful conferences. And it is about to conclude success–fully a series of steps which have enabled it to intervene almost anywhere when a difficult situation has been created by the appearance of refugees. The fact that these new groups of refugees have instinctively appealed to you for help is, in itself, a clear recognition of the effectiveness of your moral and humanitarian aid.

(2862) As your twelfth session draws to a close and another important stage in assistance to refugees has been reached, We are pleased to tell you how agreeable to Our ears are the noble words of your President and of the High Commissioner, interpreters of your sentiments. You have clearly confirmed your willingness to continue, as intensively as in the past, the efforts needed to provide the asylum of a safe haven to refugees and the warmth of a hearth, which so many unfortunates still lack.

(2863) Yours is an act of love toward your neighbors, and your efforts will call forth a world more caring, in which each and all may live in peace, in a safe and well oriented community, imbued with the spirit of reciprocal respect and friendship.

(2864) It is from the depth of Our heart that We congratulate you on your devotion to the cause of refugees and formulate the most cordial wishes for the happy conclusion of your task and that We invoke for you, your families and all refugees - unfortunately still so numerous - the abundant grace of Almighty God.

3. Address of His Holiness John Paul II to Mr. Poul Hartling, United Nations High Commissioner for Refugees. The Vatican, 25 June 1982.

Original: French (*)

(2865) 1. I was very pleased to have had today's meeting with you. Last year, and again this year, you had expressed the desire that I should pay a visit to the Headquarters of the High Commission in Geneva. Unfortunately, other engagements did not permit this, but I myself heartily regretted it and hastened to express the appreciation and encouragement of the Catholic Church for the efforts which your institution makes on behalf of refugees.

(*) Insegnamenti di Giovanni Paolo II, Vol. V, 2 (2982), 2398-2401.

(2866) 2. Your competence extends to all refugees - in the strict sense of the United Nations Convention of 1951, the Protocol of 1967 and numerous other Conventions and texts - that is to say, to people who have had to leave their own country because of a well-founded fear of persecution for reasons of race, religion, nationality or political conviction, or to escape violence and war. They are legion, more than ten million of them, perhaps fifteen, and whole new waves of populations are ceaselessly uprooted from their environment for various reasons. Lebanon is once more in the limelight, in a sudden and dramatic fashion, but one cannot allow the other Middle Eastern refugees to be forgotten, the very numerous Palestinian refugees, particularly the Cambodians and the "boat people", who continue to flee under very risky conditions, or are waiting in camps in Thailand, Malaysia, Indonesia and Singapore; nor the Somali refugees, and all those on the African continent; nor those of Central America, etc. It is really a disgraceful scourge of our times the way so many countries and governments are no longer capable of granting a just freedom and a decent living to all their citizens. The international community is genuinely concerned about this tragedy, and especially the United Nations High Commission for Refugees.

(2867) 3. There is of course no question, when seeking a solution for these refugees, of dispensing their countries of origin from doing their duty, nor of encouraging their negligence or ill-will, still less of taking sides in matters which have men at their origin. But you, rightly, look at the facts; you observe that these populations are, *hic et nunc*, threatened or stateless, often deprived of everything which might help them to live, their whole patrimony. And this extreme physical, psychological and moral misery simply will not wait. Thanks be to God, public opinion still understands this quite well, and lets itself be moved whenever the mass media describe the tragedy, but interest quickly wanes and generosity dries up, or does not reach the point of getting to grips with it in a steady fashion, with long-term solutions. It is there that your organization makes its irreplaceable contribution.

(2868) 4. You do, in fact, seek to give back to these refugees the conditions of their human dignity: you help them to become self-sufficient. In the short-term, they need protection, security, basic assistance, food, somewhere to stay, at least under a tent, medical assistance and educational opportunities. In this area, you contribute the necessary aid. But at the same time, and above all else, you seek a permanent long-term solution, the best possible, either by helping the refugees to return to their country by free and personal decision, which is much to be desired if a viable living can be made possible there for them , or at least to become genuinely integrated, with conditions more secure than simply precarious and temporary asylum, in the country that first received them, or, finally, by enabling them to emigrate and integrate themselves in a third country. As you know better than anyone, certain countries make efforts in this direction which would merit being quoted as examples.

(2869) 5. You have, then, a key role to play in the country of origin and in the country of acceptance, assisting those who are in transit, departing or settling in. In this task of assistance, other agencies may work alongside you, starting with those within the United Nations Organization, as we have just seen in Lebanon, or Governments and governmental organizations, or the International Red Cross Committee and the League of Red Cross Societies, or any of many other aid organizations. I know that the High Commission looks for such cooperation, rejoices in it and encourages it, for the task of humanitarianism requires manifold and concerted effort.

(2870) 6. The Catholic Church, for her part - and this above all is the scope of my remarks - considers aid to refugees an essential labour, and she extends a pressing invitation to all her Christian children to collaborate in it, for the Bible in general and the Gospel in particular, do not allow us to let go unaided those displaced persons who seek asylum.

(2871) Moreover, a goodly number of Catholic organizations are trying, according to their abilities and opportunities, to alleviate the suffering of refugees, as you yourself have had the kindness to testify. I can assure you that the Pontifical Council "Cor Unum" takes an active interest in this, since it is designed to attract the attention, and in certain circumstances to stimulate and coordinate the initiatives , of other Catholic organizations, and thus give expression to the charity of the Pope.

(2872) 7. Over and above this concrete assistance, the Church also deems it her duty to exhort those in charge to change this situation, as I did for example when I visited the Bataan Refugee Processing Centre near Morong in the Philippines on 21 February 1981, or when I received the Diplomatic Corps in Nairobi in 1981, or quite recently in Lisbon. It must be said again that here we are dealing with abnormal situations which must be cured at their source by seeking to convince nations that refugees have a right to freedom and to a dignified human life in their own country. It is also necessary to make an ever wider appeal for hospitality and welcome on the part of those countries which can take in refugees. Lastly, it is necessary to organize international mutual assistance, an assistance which does not dispense the refugees from looking after themselves little by little, for that too is a pathway to human dignity.

(2873) In short, Mr. High Commissioner, I am happy to tell you that the Holy See warmly appreciates the work which has been entrusted to you, and to assure you that the members of the Church, and especially the Catholic charitable organizations, will continue their commitments in this field with eagerness and generosity, and will make their contribution to alleviating suffering and forming consciences in a disinterested, by which I mean impartial, fashion, guided only by the viewpoint of the good of those people, whoever they may be, who know the distress of life as a refugee, for whatever reason.

(2874) And we always join to our concrete actions that of prayer, imploring the Holy Spirit to enlighten men's spirits and open their hearts, so that this world might be more human and more true to the plan of brotherhood which God has assigned to humanity.

4. Message of His Holiness John Paul II to the Second International Conference on Assistance to Refugees in Africa (ICARA). The Vatican, 5 July 1984.

Original: French (*)

(2875) I address you a respectful and trusting greeting. It is to your credit as men, as government leaders and as senior officials of organizations, that you began preparations long ago for this important meeting and that you have come to it with the firm purpose of improving still further standards of reception and living conditions and, thus, to reaffirm the hope of a more human future for the millions of our brothers and sisters who are refugees or have been displaced in the African continent.

(2876) As I said recently in Thailand when I addressed the refugees in the Phanat Nikhom camp and in my statement to the members of the Government and the diplomatic corps, it is the human person's dignity - a gift of God - which is at stake. May this thought preside over your work and inspire your decisions!

(2877) The very large number of refugees should not mean that their problems can be regarded as those of masses of humanity who must merely be sheltered, fed and protected against epidemics, pending their departure for other places. These are our brothers and sisters whom countries have decided to take in, desiring to alleviate their suffering and give them hope. But the heavy financial burden that this involves cannot be borne by the host countries alone; this is why the international community is called upon to give its generous aid.

(2878) When you will study the projects submitted, may you look beyond the refugee problem as a whole and think of the individual tragedy of each refugee, of the distress of each family; the causes of these situations will, of course, have to be studied objectively, for they must be eliminated as quickly as possible: they wound adults and young people seriously and sometimes fatally in their human dignity by uprooting them from their cultures and families, by imposing on them physical hardship and idleness, and by denying them the exercise of their social rights. Our own human dignity, as beings whom God has created brothers, would be seriously impugned if we were to ignore these sufferings.

(*) Insegnamenti di Giovanni Paolo II, Vol. VII,2 (1984), 26-28.

(2879) Your participation in this meeting, the purpose of which is to consider projects which are not aimed at mere survival but rather at human promotion and social integration, is already a first response offering hope to the millions of refugees who have turned to you: you will thus show them that they are welcome, respected and loved, and that with your help they themselves will prepare their own future, so that one day they will be able to resume their places in their own countries - an imprescriptible right - with the increased skills acquired during the time of their exile.

(2880) When men of good will wish to work together for the benefit of those who suffer, when they are in agreement and combine their efforts for greater effectiveness, our humanity is rendered more fraternal; when we listen to words such as those of the Sermon on the Mount and the Beatitudes, we all of us, men and women of every religion, are preparing a world in which life will be better.

(2881) The Secretary-General of the United Nations, the Office of the United Nations High Commissioner for Refugees, the Organization of African Unity, all participating Governments and all non-governmental organizations represented here are to be congratulated on their initiative and praised for the generosity of their commitments.

5. Letter of H.E. Cardinal Agostino Casaroli, Secretary of State, to Mr. Poul Hartling,UN High Commissioner for Refugees on the occasion of the round table on the subject: "The Refugee Child", held in Geneva from 21 to 23 October 1980.

Original: French (*)

(2882) The United Nations High Commissioner's Office for Refugees, which you direct, is organizing in Geneva, from 21 to 23 October l980, a round table on the subject: "The Refugee Child". Sharing your concern to drive home to international public opinion this serious problem which has long held the attention of the Holy See, Pope John Paul 11 has entrusted to me the task of expressing to you the deep interest of the Church in anything that may improve the fate of these children, too often abandoned, as well as his approval of this initiative of the High Commissioner's Office and his best wishes for its success.

(2883) How could one fail to express, in the first place, great concern at the growing numbers of refugees? Already a considerable number in the past, it has reached enormous proportions in the last few years, both because of natural catastrophes such as drought and floods or, more often than not, for political reasons, internal conflicts, or invasions.

(2884) Now it is certain that the child is a victim of these situations in a quite particular way. Certainly, he feels less directly and less violently than the adult the sufferings of uprooting and the difficulties of becoming integrated into a new society, but the depth of their repercussions on his physical and psychic development cannot be doubted.

(2885) Children are deprived of security and stability, traumatized by being torn from their usual environment and from everything that was dear to them, at the very moment when they most need calm and serenity. This situation is made even more difficult when the children are, furthermore, torn away from their families and in particular from their parents.

(2886) Finally, children are too often deprived of adequate religious, moral, and intellectual formation during the period which is precisely the most favourable one to receive it. To this moral handicap, physical deficiencies are nearly always added: lack of food and care, which cause disorders in children that accompany them all their life.

(2887) That is why, if it is not always possible to remedy completely the sufferings of refugee children, especially from the psychological and moral point of view, the duty of society is to alleviate at least the main difficulties of their situation. Every effort must be made to help them to form

(*) Insegnamenti di Giovanni Paolo II, Vol. III,2 (1980), 1020-1022.

their personality and to find a place in society, preventing them from sinking, for lack of interest, into a life on the fringes of society, deprived of culture and almost asocial.

(2888) The first effort in this direction concerns children separated from their parents. As far as possible, the attempt must be made to replace the parents, endeavoring, however, not to uproot the child from his family environment, and while waiting to be able, as soon as circumstances permit, to find his family again for him or, if this is impossible, an adopted family, for the greatest thing that can be done for an abandoned child is to give him the possibility of uttering again the name of "mamma".

(2889) The school, for its part, is of major importance to direct the child's energies and prevent him from withdrawing into himself in uncertainty and anxiety. A suitable scholastic activity, with the social relations that spring from it, will greatly help the child to become integrated into society, to the point of becoming capable even of helping his parents to adapt themselves better to the new realities.

(2890) In all these fields, the problems that arise with regard to the refugee child, are not simple or easy to solve, due to their many social, moral, and economic implications. It is impossible, however, to ignore them or to remain impassive before the tragedy that strikes so many little ones, the victims of misfortune.

(2891) In faithfulness to the teaching of her Divine Founder, the Church, for her part, has always believed that the education and training of children were one of her main duties. With all the more reason she considers that she has duties towards refugee children, who deserve even more attention due to their situation.

(2892) However, the duties of society towards them concern the whole of mankind. That is why the Holy See considers with sympathy and gratitude all public and private organizations which endeavor, with the resources at their disposal, to assist them. Among these organizations, the United Nations High Commissioner's Office for Refugees puts at their service not only important means, but also its competence and dedication. The refugee child, the subject of your forthcoming round table, will, however, be physically absent, His voice will not be able to make itself heard except through the voices, the hearts and the deep sense of responsibility of the participants. Assured of their complete commitment to the service of so many innocent victims, the Holy Father expresses his best wishes for the course of the work of this round table and asks the Lord that it may achieve results that are useful for the future of "the refugee child".

(2893) Happy to transmit this message to you, I beg you to accept, Mr. High Commissioner, with my personal regards, the assurance of my very high consideration.

6. Statement by Msgr. Silvio Luoni, Head of the Delegation of the Holy See, at the United Nations Conference on Territorial Asylum, held in Geneva on 10 January - 4 February 1977.

Original: French

(2894) First of all, the Delegation of the Holy See wishes to congratulate most sincerely the Group of Experts who prepared the draft of the Convention on Territorial Asylum. The result of its work is a good overall instrument whose positive points are evident. If this convention were adopted, the humanitarian law relating to refugees would have come a long way.

(2895) With the Convention relating to the status of refugees in 1951, the refugee succeeded in rounding a real "Cape of Good Hope" so to speak. If the new Convention is adopted, the refugee will be very close to having a sure place of asylum and, whenever possible, the one of his choice.

(2896) It is not our intent at the moment to demonstrate the interest of the Holy See in the many aspects of the refugee problem. The concern of the Church has always been manifest in the past, but it is all the more so today when the refugee problem is of such magnitude that it often goes beyond the capabilities of the States concerned.

(2897) The 1963 Encyclical *Pacem in Terris* dealt, among other matters, with the rights of refugees: "At this point it will not be superfluous to recall that such exiles are persons, and that all their rights as persons must be recognized, since they do not lose those rights on losing the citizenship of the States of which they are former members."

(2898) "Now among the rights of a human person there must be included the one by which a man may enter a political community where he hopes he can more fittingly provide a future for himself and his dependents" (John XXIII, *Pacem in Terris*, Nos. 105-106).

(2899) This is why the same Pope John XXIII proposed: "...for the attention and gratitude of all right-minded persons the manifold work which specialized international agencies are carrying out in this very delicate field" (*ibid.*, No. 108).

(2900) It should come as a surprise to no one that the Holy See is present at this diplomatic Conference on Territorial Asylum and that it is ready to make a contribution emanating from its experience in the humanitarian sphere, with the intent of putting an instrument at the disposition of the High Commissioner, which is both simple and efficacious, for accomplishing the very noble task of relieving human suffering.

(2901) While the moral support of the Holy See is total, it is evident that practicalities must be taken into consideration. The City State of the Vatican, which the Holy See represents, occupies a very particular geographical location: it is a very small territory with very limited means.

(2902) As regards the articles in the draft of the Convention, the Delegation of the Holy See reserves the right to intervene as the need arises. For the moment, the Delegation will confine itself to one general comment which, in its opinion, must be expressed without delay; that is, the particular way in which the refugee is viewed in the draft of the Convention. The reality is frequently more complicated.

(2903) For this reason after having expressed well-deserved congratulations to the Group of Experts, the Delegation of the Holy See wishes, at the very outset, to voice a concern: at the 1951 Conference of Plenipotentiaries of the United Nations which related to the status of refugees, the resolution on "the reunification of the family, this natural and basic element of society... a reunification constantly threatened" was termed "an essential right of the refugee" (Convention Relating to the Status of Refugees HCR/INF/ 29, p.12). This resolution was unanimously adopted.

(2904) It is perhaps good to recall the text of this Convention concerning this right:

"This Conference...

"declares with satisfaction that, from the official commentary of the special Committee on Statelessness and connected problems (E/1618, p.38) the rights of refugees are extended to members of their family...

"recommends that Governments take the necessary measures to protect the family of the refugee and in particular to:

"1) ensure the reunification of the family of the refugee especially in the case where the head of the family has fulfilled the conditions necessary for his admission in a country;

"2) assure the protection of refugees who are minors, especially of separated children and young girls, specifically in what concerns guardianship and adoption".

(2905) We feel obliged to mention that nothing further has been added to this recommendation in the new draft of the Convention. This is all the more surprising when we consider that other recommendations of the 1951 Conference have been given a juridical formulation in the draft. I refer, for example, to the recommendation concerning the spirit of international solidarity which, very fortunately, can be found in Article 5 of the new draft.

(2906) Of course, we are all aware that asylum seekers often arrive with their family at the frontier of a country where they hope to find refuge. What will happen in such a case? Will the authorities at the frontier apply the principle of "non-refoulement" in a selective way by granting asylum to the head of the family and by rejecting the other members? What will happen to the reunification of the family, so formally affirmed at the 1951 Conference?

(2907) The possibility of facilitating family reunification must also be foreseen in the case where the members of the family have remained in the country of origin and desire to join the head of the family.

(2908) All of us are also familiar with cases where the family of the refugee is detained as a kind of hostage, "manipulated" and pressured in an effort to change the refugee's mind. How can the omission of a subject of such vital importance in the new draft be explained? Will there be a turning back, a shift with regard to the 1951 Convention? Did the Group of Experts forget to deal with the principle of family reunification or did it simply take it for granted?

(2909) In any case, it is better for this Conference to deal with it. For highly humanitarian reasons, as well as by virtue of being a Member of the Executive Committee of the Programme of the United Nations High Commissioner for Refugees, the Holy See hopes that this omission will be rectified. We must also remember that the Holy See was party to the 1951 Convention and adhered to the 1967 Protocol. Its basic concern is none other than to put an efficacious juridical instrument at the disposition of the High Commissioner for Refugees.

(2910) On this matter, the rights of the refugee, including the one on family reunification, defined as essential, must be recognized without any ambiguity whatsoever, through norms of humanitarian law, norms that do not provide an easy means of escape to those who do not wish to apply them.

(2911) Unfortunately, experience teaches us that, very often, the recommendations of international conferences remain nothing but declarations of good intentions if they are not followed up with juridical formulations.

(2912) Moreover, twenty-six years after the 1951 Conference's unanimous approbation of the right of the refugee to family reunification, we can ask what practical steps have been taken to effect the recommendation? How many countries would willingly question themselves on this point? It seems wise to remove the recommendation from the simple domain of an appeal to the good will of the States. Such is the advice, such is the wish of the Delegation of the Holy See.

(2913) To conclude, the Delegation of the Holy See would like to see a new article added to the draft of the Convention, an article concerned with the reunification of the family of the refugee. Uprooted from his country, the refugee would at least have the consolation of not being uprooted from his most natural milieu, his own family.

7. Statement by Msgr. Audrys Backis, Undersecretary of the Council for the Public Affairs of the Church, Head of the Delegation of the Holy See, at the "Meeting on refugees and emigrants of South East Asia. Geneva, 21 July 1979.

Original: French

(2914) In the evening of 20 June last, Pope John Paul II addressed a crowd of visitors in St. Peter's Square in Rome in the following terms: "Urged on by the love of Christ - 'Caritas Christi urget nos' - this evening I wish to raise my voice to invite you to turn your minds and hearts to the drama that is taking place in the countries and on the distant seas of South-East Asia, a drama that is involving hundreds of thousands of our brothers and sisters. These people are looking for a homeland, because the countries that at first received them have reached the limits of their capacities, while at the same time the offers to accept them permanently in other countries are, so far, proving insufficient."

(2915) Besides those who were present, the Pope was really addressing all men and women, when he added: "I appeal to the conscience of humanity, that all should take their share of responsibility, both the peoples and those who govern them, in the name of a solidarity that goes beyond frontiers, races and ideologies."

(2916) I recall these words of the Pope because they indicate the profound reason why the Holy See is concerned with the problem that is the subject of this International Conference. The Catholic Church knows that, at every moment of history and in an ever new way, she is being challenged by the message of love that the Founder left her. It is a love that must be able to bring help, whatever the causes, immediate or remote, of the distress. It is a love that sees only the man, woman or child in need, and that does not allow itself to be disturbed by other considerations. Such was the attitude of the Good Samaritan in the Gospel: he brought help to the wounded stranger, abandoned at the side of the road and ignored by the passers-by. Such is meant to be the reason for the Holy See's presence here.

(2917) The Holy See is well aware that this attitude is also shared by all people of good will, including those who do not count themselves among those who believe in God. The International community itself is not insensible to this ethic: does one not find an expression of its convictions in the principles enunciated in the Universal Declaration of Human Rights and sanctioned by the States that have adhered to the Covenant on Civil and Political Rights, a Covenant that has already come into force? The reason why we are all meeting here is that each of us firmly believes in the principle of the first Article of the Universal Declaration, which states that "All human beings are born free and equal in dignity and rights", which implies that every person has the right to live in freedom, in his own country. It is because each of us recognizes, as is also stated by Article 13 of the same Declaration, that "everyone has the right to leave any country, including his own, and to return to his country". And again it is because each of us admits, in accordance with Article 14 of the Declaration, that everyone has the right to seek and to enjoy asylum in other countries.

(2918) Such are the reasons that led Pope John Paul II to encourage the convening of this Conference. Over and above the concrete results which should flow from it, and which we profoundly desire, the Conference, even before its opening, has already caused a veritable avalanche of generosity. This has manifested itself, both within the official bodies and in society as a whole, by a new readiness to undertake the humanitarian obligations imposed by this problem, which is one of such dimensions "that the weight of it cannot be left for long upon the shoulders of only a few" (John Paul II, *ibid.*).

(2919) The Holy See shares the view of the High Commissioner for Refugees, according to which, for resolving the problems in the region, it would be essential to take into consideration the situation in its totality, and to seek comprehensive solutions at all levels. We shall limit our intervention to the humanitarian aspects, as was decided upon by the Secretary-General of the United Nations Organization in convening the present meeting.

(2920) For one cannot ignore any longer the fact that the tragic lot of the refugees in Indo-China poses a humanitarian problem whose nature is without precedent. A considerable number of men and women have already met death in various ways. Some hundreds of thousands of people, especially those who have been led to take the sea route, are facing dangers and taking enormous risks to save their own lives, even before they reach a friendly country that is ready to accept them.

(2921) The reason why the Holy See, and the Catholic Church all over the world, feel involved in this problem and for some years have already been devoting special attention and efforts to it, is that they are challenged by man.

(2922) In the countries which have provided first asylum, the Christians have taken practical measures, with the help of their brothers and sisters in every country, and with full respect for the competence of the Governments and for the role of the intergovernmental institutions. Over the course of the years, one sees that this contribution manifests a considerable financial generosity. The Catholic bishops in the countries providing first asylum have, themselves, launched appeals to all the bishops of the world, to bring to their attention the burden borne by their countries. Recently too, there has been held in Bangkok a meeting of the bishops and all the Catholic charitable organizations in Asia to reflect on the measures to be taken, in the hope that our present meeting will lead to concrete pledges, within which these organizations will be better able to situate their own actions.

(2923) In the countries offering permanent settlement, as the government authorities will be able to testify, considerable efforts in manpower and financial means have also been made by numerous Catholic organizations, to participate along with the Governments in receiving the refugees and inserting them into the community. In response to the Pope's appeal, Catholics are examining the reception possibilities of families, parishes and religious communities, to enable the States to open their frontiers still wider.

(2924) For the Holy See it is clear that any solution, to be effective and lasting, must start with man and his dignity. It is desirable that the formulas adopted for coping with the present crisis should not deal merely with considerations of economic, ethnic or political order, for such formulas would run a great risk of not leading to a real solution and would only prolong, indeed perpetuate, this inhuman situation.

(2925) Every refugee has the right to live and, therefore, in the first place, the right to survive. The Holy See appeals to all the nations not to let any more of the refugees die by shipwreck, and to find the means to rescue them on the high seas. When people are in danger of death, it is not the moment to dwell on distinctions between "refugees" and "migrants". The loss of a single child, a single human life, weighs on our consciences as human beings.

(2926) The efforts of the international community should secure a permanent settlement for all of them, without discriminating against the aged, the handicapped, or others that some people would consider unproductive. With good will and with an increased respect for human dignity, means ought to be found to put a stop to the exodus taking place in the midst of confusion and extreme danger, while safeguarding the principles of free migration and reunification of families, without physical or moral constraint.

(2927) If our meeting must decide, in order to meet the immediate urgent need, to arrange for special centres recognized and respected by the international community and where the refugees will be assured of being received, it will have to be clearly understood that these centres will not become places of permanent asylum, for such a situation would not make possible social integration for individuals and families who have the right to find work and earn their living in normal human conditions.

(2928) For its own part, the Holy See is resolved to pursue all efforts that are within its possibilities. The Catholic Church throughout the world wishes to be ever more present and available. Her organizations will continue to work in liaison with the Governments, if so desired, complementing the actions of the Governments and of the international institutions.

(2929) May I be permitted here to pay homage to the remarkable results already achieved, thanks to the collaboration of so many nations, the action of the United Nations, and especially that of the Office of the High Commissioner for Refugees.

(2930) The task is immense, and time is pressing. A problem with such tragic dimensions demands worldwide and immediate solutions. Men, women and children in distress are turning their anguished arms towards this Conference. We cannot disappoint them.

8. Statement by the Rev. Fr. Roger du Noyer, Secretary of the Pontifical Council "Cor Unum", Head of the Delegation of the Holy See, at the Second International Conference on Assistance to Refugees in Africa (ICARA II), held in Geneva on 9-11 July 1984. Geneva, 10 July 1984.

Original: French

(2931) The Holy See is delighted to note that the preparation and the aim of this Conference mark a truly new approach to the problem of refugees and of returnees. This step should also be valid for continents other than Africa. The Holy See would like to point out two things regarding this new vision: the first is the mutual accord among the principal intervening parties, not neglecting also to dialogue with non-governmental organizations. The second is the involvement of the refugees themselves in their own situation. This means a better recognition of their dignity; it means making them partners in projects which concern their own human promotion and in the preparation of a better future for themselves and their families.

(2932) This Conference, Mr. President, must concentrate its work on the evaluation of "Programmes for Relief, Rehabilitation and Resettlement" for refugees and returnees in Africa; but the participants should also take note of other proposals intended to identify the causes which have led to such a situation. Africa, a land so rich in its youthfulness, is already grappling with critical economic difficulties which are aggravated by an all-pervasive drought, striking unceasingly at an ever more significant population, where the victims of famine are all too numerous, forcing thousands of persons to leave their unproductive lands in the hope of finding a little water and food elsewhere. To these natural catastrophes, human beings add other calamities which force their compatriots to go into exile in order to save their lives or to maintain some modicum of freedom and dignity. When will African fraternity be stronger than hatred, than political divisions or ideological options? All this exacts a high toll on Africa and retards its development. This is an assault on all of humanity; these situations must be denounced.

(2933) The Holy See Delegation is very grateful to the Office of the High Commissioner for Refugees for its untiring activities devoted as much towards the protection of the rights of persons as towards setting up programmes and coordinating activities. In a particular way, Africa, these days, attracts the attention of the international community which, for many years, has displayed a deep solidarity towards refugees of all continents. In general African nations do not refuse asylum, but they beg us help them cope with the burden they carry.

(2934) Strengthening the infrastructures and providing for lasting solutions does not mean, Mr. President, that the refugees give up the right of voluntary return to the country of their origin. This is "an inalienable right" as the Pope said in his Message. This means, however, that the host countries must facilitate their reception better so that the refugee will feel himself accepted as a brother, integrated into the economic and social life and able to contribute to the development of the country granting asylum.

(2935) Moreover, idleness is demoralizing and devaluates human persons in their own eyes; labour is necessary for human promotion and for a person's fulfillment. To know that one is useful to society is a source of comfort. For the refugee, training means acquiring additional competences and being prepared, when he returns to his country of origin, to participate more efficaciously in its economy and social life.

(2936) All the participants at this meeting, Mr. President, have already collaborated towards alleviating certain conditions of refugee life. The African States present here know the commitment, in terms of personnel and finances, of their Catholic compatriots. This effort will continue; we are sure of it. The National Caritas offices, the International Commission for Migration and other organizations can offer some rather impressive figures when we recall that all they do is voluntary.

(2937) For its part, the Holy See, which does not have a government budget augmented by taxes, continues and will continue to manifest its concern for refugees in a concrete way. Within the limits of its possibilities, and without ceasing to give assistance to activities that service refugees in most countries of Africa, and in other places around the world, the Holy See chooses, on the occasion of this Conference, to participate in a special way towards the financing of Project No.4, presented by Rwanda: "The Construction and Installation of Craft Training Centres". In the next few days, Caritas Rwanda will receive the sum of $50,000 to strengthen the action it had already undertaken in this sector, in full and trusting collaboration with the responsible authorities. Some Catholic organizations, which are an expression of the generosity of Catholics of other nations, have also agreed to contribute to the financing of this project, whose total cost is approximately $300,000.

(2938) The Holy See is confident of the kindly interest nations are bringing to this Conference and of the commitments they will make to realize its objectives.

IX - MIGRANTS

Proposals by the Holy See concerning the drafting of the "International Convention on the Protection of the Rights of All Migrant Workers and Their Families", submitted on 6 February 1984 to the United Nations Working Group charged with the elaboration of the above mentioned Convention. The Vatican, 17 December 1983.

Original: English

(2939) In times like ours, marked by persistent economic recession and by a crisis of values, the temptation emerges occasionally among nations and their leaders to center on the search for their own welfare and national security, ignoring the duties of international solidarity in pursuing the well-being of all the peoples of the earth.

(2940) Governing implies meeting the needs of the common good. This principle was expressed thus by Pope John XXIII when he stated that "the attainment of the common good is the very reason for being of public authorities" (cf. John XXIII, Encyclical *Pacem in Terris*, 11 April 1963, nn. 44-78). And the common good requires the creation of an environment centered upon respect for humanity and embodying the rights of each person, group or associative entity.

(2941) In this context the Holy See cannot fail to praise the international community for its efforts to elaborate, in clear and precise form, an "International Convention on the Protection of the Rights of All Migrant Workers and Their Families", since these persons are, more than others, exposed to conditions detrimental and harmful to their personal dignity.

(2942) The Convention must aim not only at preventing the forced exoduses and the clandestine recruitment of foreign workers - a phenomenon which seems to assume structural characteristics on the international labour market - but also at protecting the fundamental rights of the migrants and of their families: these are inalienable and inviolable rights rooted in the dignity of the human person and not simply on the working ability of each individual.

(2943) Nations and governments must support the formulation of a personal freedom expressed by responsible participation in the service and growth of the human community.

(2944) This presupposes the existence of material and spiritual conditions favorable to "the becoming conscious of one's own dignity and the fulfilling of one's vocation" (II Vatican Council, Pastoral Constitution *Gaudium et Spes*, 7 December 1965, n. 31). The migrant person, on the contrary, is often forced, by complex structural and superstructural reasons, to move away from his place of origin for the sake of survival, and in the new environment often remains socially, politically and culturally isolated.

(2945) "Where there is not respect, defense and protection of the rights of man, his inalienable freedom becomes subject to violence and fraud; there cannot be true peace where man's personality is ignored or degraded, where there is discrimination, slavery and intolerance" (Paul VI, Message for the Day of Peace, 8 December 1968).

(2946) It becomes evident, even in the international documents and in the Declaration of the Universal Human Rights, that there is no agreement between the acknowledged right to migrate and the lack of a precise statement of the corresponding duty of the wealthy nations to receive the foreign workers whose manpower they employ. Every person has the right to work, which is the ordinary means of subsistence and of cooperation in God's creation (cf. *Gaudium et Spes*, n. 72), and this right demands working conditions and remuneration consistent with the dignity of the person (cf. *Gaudium et Spes*, nn. 66-67). From this fundamental principle, sanctioned by the Declaration and universally recognized, derives the right to seek work in those places where true working possibilities exist or can be made to exist. Migration constitutes a fundamental test stand for the application of the Declaration of the fundamental human rights, to such an extent as to require the restructuring of inter-national relations and "profoundly innovating and bold changes" (Paul VI, Encyclical Letter *Populorum Progressio*, 26 March 1967, n. 45).

(2947) The phenomenon of migration, as it is now taking place, shows that a satisfactory international economic and political order has not yet been achieved. One continues to encounter "migrant people ... still waiting for recognition of the fullness of their rights" (John Paul II Homily for the Mass at Curitiba, Brazil, L'Osservatore Romano, suppl. n. 151, 1982).

(2948) The new international order must face up to three obligations: "the duty of solidarity, i.e. the assistance which wealthy nations must lend to the developing countries; the duty of social justice, i.e. the restructuring in fairer terms of the faulty relations between powerful and powerless peoples; and the duty of universal charity, i.e. the promoting of a more human world for everyone" (Paul VI, *Populorum Progressio*, n. 44).

(2949) The establishing of a "civilization rooted in love", the overcoming of extreme rigidities and nationalisms, the achieving of conditions of parity among the citizens of the world must lead also to a courageous convention in favor of all migrants, who form the clearest indicator of the weaknesses of our society.

(2950) In justice, many appeals are heard for a deeper knowledge of the labour market and for the dissemination of more detailed information on available employment. Many calls are rightly made for the punishment of traders in clandestine labour as warning example to others. Frequently heard also is the just plea for a market economy which rejects illegal labour practices and bestows equal dignity on every type of work.

(2951) The drafters of the Convention cannot underestimate the new phenomenon of clandestine migration, which seems to mark the eighties. The importation of foreign manpower, provided with regular contracts, is being blocked in many countries and ways are established to favor forced repatriations, while at the same time the importation of a new working force without legally recognized contracts is on the rise. The economic, political and cultural conditions of some countries are serious factors in causing these ever more clandestine exoduses.

(2952) These workers, truly "economic refugees", cannot enjoy the recognition accorded by the international community to political refugees; they, therefore, become a community of persons deprived of juridical protection. Their number is on the rise in spite of repressive measures which seem to have augmented rather than decreased the phenomenon of clandestine work.

(2953) The pretended safeguarding of migrants' rights simply on the base of legal working contracts turns out to be restrictive and discriminatory for a large segment of workers deceitfully enticed and ignorant of the labour market legislations of the receiving countries.

(2954) It is, therefore, necessary that the Convention take into account the economic refugees for the respect of their dignity as human persons and of their rights as contemplated in the Universal Declaration on Human Rights. The points of Parts I and II of the proposed Convention must, therefore, be applied to all the migrants. The Church supports the efforts aimed at widening the definition of migrant so as to include the various categories and to insure that the labour legally recognized by the laws of a country will not be the sole motivation for the protection of migrants' rights and duties.

(2955) Humanity has a spiritual dimension which transcends material aspects and economic and political structures; the migrant, as well, has a right to the spiritual goods. This right not only demands the absence of coercion in the religious field, but also the real possibility of worship and of religious practice.

(2956) In its Declaration on Religious Liberty the II Vatican Council stated that "the human person has a right to religious freedom. Freedom of this kind means that all men should be immune from coercion on the part of individuals, social groups and every human power so that, within due limits, nobody is forced to act against his convictions in religious matters in private or in public, alone or in association with others. The Council further declares that the right to religious freedom is based on the very dignity of the human person as known through the revealed word of God and by reason itself. This right of the human person to religious freedom must be given such recognition in the constitutional order of society as will make it a civil right" (II Vatican Council, Declaration on Religious Liberty *Dignitatis Humanae*, 7 December 1975, n. 2).

(2957) For this reason "the Church strictly forbids that anyone should be forced to accept the faith, or be induced or enticed by unworthy devices; as it likewise strongly defends the right that no one should be frightened away from the faith by unjust persecutions" (II Vatican Council, Decree on the Church's Missionary Activity *Ad Gentes Divinitus*, 7 December 1965, n. 13).

(2958) The proposed Convention explicitly mentions the right to religious liberty. Particularly in times past, migrants have been discriminated against and prevented from professing their religious faith when it differed from the official religion. In numerous cases they were forced to practice their religion in secrecy. It is, there-fore, opportune that the Convention restate expressly and for today's society the freedom to worship and the right to association for religious purposes.

(2959) The Convention should, moreover, explicitly mention the freedom of movement to be accorded to the clergy who intend to minister and to assist the migrant workers and their families. Their presence has historically proven to be a constant catalytic agent in promoting a positive insertion of the migrants in the new country.

(2960) The proposed Convention corroborates one of the fundamental tenets of the migrant worker's rights: the respect for the culture of ethnic and linguistic minorities (cf. *Gaudium et Spes*, n. 86). Such respect must find expression in positive steps by the receiving country in the cultural and educational fields. The State must provide to the migrant all the means usually supplied for the safeguarding of cultures so as to avoid the harmful effects of an assimilative policy aiming at the elimination of minority cultures.

(2961) "It is through culture that man lives a truly human life" (John Paul II, Address to UNESCO, Paris, 2 June 1980. See above, par. 154). The right of every one and every people to culture translates itself also in the teaching of the language and culture of origin, integrated in the normal schooling programmes. The Convention should, indeed, encourage the participation in such courses also by the indigenous student population so that future generations will acquire greater knowledge, and consequently greater respect, for the values and riches of every culture, and thus the human family may draw closer even within the diversity and richness of all cultures.

(2962) The migrant workers not only contribute with their labour to the wealth of the receiving country, but also by bringing their own cultural heritage. In conjunction with the respect for the migrant's culture, there must also be a guaranty for continuing education.

(2963) Likewise, the Convention should promote the offering of language and cultural programmes of study especially for the migrant women, frequently excluded - particularly if employed in domestic work - from contacts with the local society, thus running the risk of acute isolation for themselves and their families. Civilized nations must regard, as a priority goal, the protection of the migrant women against all conditions of exploitation and marginalization.

(2964) The receiving countries should not regard cultural problems as an economic liability, but rather as a long-term investment which will bring a cultural enrichment and guaranties of peace and harmony among various ethnic groups.

(2965) The right of the migrant worker to rejoin the family, already underlined in the Convention's draft, must be accompanied by practical indications and measures (e.g. providing adequate housing) which will allow the union of the family and its educational tasks in today's society. Discrimination between local and migrant families must be avoided, as well as circumstances leading to possible breakings of family ties. The Convention should condemn some common policies which sanction extended seasonal work without the presence of one's family, and thus by law do not allow, and in fact prevent, a rejoining of the family.

(2966) Participation in the social, cultural and political life is one of the conquests of modern democracies, but it is, in fact, almost always denied to the migrants. It will be opportune for the Convention to restate, both for the countries of departure and those of arrival, the obligation to foster involvement in political life, through local and administrative elections and, at least in the country of origin, through participation in general political elections, with provisions for a truly free and secret ballot. The receiving countries should feel bound to promote the free flow of information and political opinions in order to cultivate an ever more authentic self-determination.

(2967) The drafting of the Convention stands as an occasion of hope for the migrant workers and their families, for the full recognition of their fundamental rights. The Convention must formulate new directions for a better future in the world of migration, offering advanced proposals as an answer to the changed conditions and the new aspects which migration, especially when it is forced, is assuming nowadays.

(2968) We hope that the work of the preparatory Commission may expeditiously reach its conclusions and that, in a short time, a Convention on the rights of all the migrants may be supported by all the countries which make up the United Nations and become a decisive impulse for programmes in favour of migrant workers and their families.

X - VICTIMS OF WAR

Addresses of His Holiness Pius XII to the United Nations Relief and Rehabilitation Administration (UNRRA).

Original: English

1. The Vatican, 8 July 1945[1]

(2969) You will understand, gentlemen, what a great pleasure it is for us to receive such a distinguished representation of UNRRA led by its esteemed and worthy Director General.

(2970) During the past year tens of thousands of people have visited the halls of the Vatican. Every day, with very few exceptions, we have met them, we have talked with so many of them, of all ages, of all classes, of many nationalities. Behind and beyond them we could see with the mind's eye millions of others throughout the world, who like them are looking to the future with eager

[1] Discorsi e Radiomessaggi di Sua Santità Pio XII, Vol VIII (2 Marzo 1945 - 1 Marzo 1946), 117-118.

hope, yet not without misgiving, even fear; some perhaps with little, too little, hope. And they are asking themselves the question: has man certain God-given rights which the State is obliged to protect, may not infringe upon? Or is the notion to prevail, which assigns unlimited power to the State, leaving to the individual only what rights and prerogatives the State may find it useful to confer? Who does not see the fatal consequences of such an error? It leads inevitably to the despotic rule of one or of few who, without pity or conscience, have been able to seize the ascendancy and block or poison the natural channels of a people's national life. True freedom stagnates there, and dies. Moreover, such a claim of absolute, irresponsible power for the State leaves the stability of international relations at the mercy of the same capricious despotism; and the foundations of any lasting peace are shattered.

(2971) No wonder, then, that many right-minded men are anxious about the future, and the high hopes of many peoples of the world begin to droop. It is for the responsible leaders of political thought and government in all nations today to sustain these peoples; to encourage them in their efforts to rise from the ruins of an unhappy past to a new, a better, a more stable national life; above all to make it abundantly clear to them, even to national minorities, that they will enjoy complete and genuine liberty in what is dearest to them - their cultural and religious life.

(2972) Your splendid Organization, gentlemen, is making a powerful and necessary contribution towards just this end; and Europe will never cease to bless you for it. May God strengthen your hand, give light and courage to the promptings of your heart, and grant you the precious consolation of doing untold good to your fellow-men in their piteous need and sufferings: a truly Christ-like work.

(2973) For you, the Director General of UNRRA, and all your collaborators, we invoke God's choicest blessings; and may He bless all here present and those who are near and dear to you.

2. The Vatican, 22 October 1945[2]

(2974) We recall with pleasure the visit which your Director General, Mr. Lehman, paid us several months ago; and it is no less a joy for us now to say a word of welcome to his able and devoted colleagues. We have followed the activities of your admirable association with very great interest and high hopes. It is a beautiful thing, is it not, to contemplate nations, which differ from each other in many respects, united in a work of brotherly love, pooling resources so as to bring relief and succour to the victims of heartless war. Your enterprise is the more admirable for its vastness and all-embracing charity. Difference of race or colour or political belief do not obscure the guiding truth that shows up all as members of one grand family under God.

(2975) But for all the noble beauty of your undertaking, it has its prosaic side, too, with many annoying problems. The best of human endeavours will meet with obstacles and in more ways than one will fall short of the ideal proposed, of the hopes conceived. We know it well. At all times, but especially when the desolation consequent on war or natural catastrophes overwhelms peoples, we ourselves are literally assailed, as we are today, by thousands of piteous pleas for help; and few suspect how deeply our paternal heart suffers for our inability to alleviate all the sufferings and sorrows of men as we would wish. It is only right that they should expect assistance from the common Father of all. But our resources are so limited; with all our efforts we feel how little is accomplished in comparison with the enormous needs. You may draw on an immensely larger and deeper source; yet even that source is limited, and at times perhaps leaves you empty-handed in the presence of hungry children. This is an added stimulus for all to re-dedicate themselves to a task that is deserving of all that is best in human nature; and the Lord of heaven and earth will bless them for what they have done to the least of His brethren, whom He loves with an eternal love. May His choicest favours descend upon all the nations whose generosity has made your association possible. For yourselves in particular, and for all your dear ones at home, we pray God's abiding blessing.

---

[2] Discorsi e Radiomessaggi di Sua Santità Pio XII, Vol. VII (2 Marzo 1945 - 1 Marzo 1946), 243-244.

3. The Vatican, 6 April 1947[3]

(2976) In receiving such a distinguished gathering of high-ranking officials of UNRRA, one might easily yield to the temptation to descant rather at length on the words that make up the title of your organization. "United Nations": nations of the world united; surely the fond and holy hope of mothers and wives and sisters, and of all men of good will; united, moreover, for the purpose of bringing relief to their less fortunate neighbours; and, what is more, united to inflame in them anew a flickering courage or a smothered sense of personal respect and responsibility to arise and take their place with dignity among their peers: what a worthy and ennobling aim! But time will not permit us to delay on these thoughts and we must content ourselves with the sincere expression of our welcome to you all.

(2977) You have gathered in Rome to prepare the passing of your Organization into the history of these eventful days. Its book of life is to be closed. But the spirit that wrote its best pages must not pass. There are nations still crippled; they cannot stand unaided. There are peoples still struggling in the battle for existence; they must succumb to the agony they have been enduring in body and soul these long, endless postwar years, unless the granaries of their more prosperous fellow-men continue, for yet a while and increasingly, to supply life's sustenance. We speak to those whose experience has taught them how tragically true are these conditions. We feel certain that they will not be abandoned.

(2978) This is Easter day. There is no quarter of the world but where men are commemorating today the Resurrection of the Saviour of mankind. His was an all-embracing love, as is that of the Church He founded. For His followers there were to be no strangers; but all men were to be made brothers through Him. The spirit of brotherly love still thrives in the heart of the common man. Its generous manifestations have been the one bright and cheering colour in a very dismal picture. Men do not want to be pitted ruthlessly against each other; they want to love one another, and they know that there lies the road to peace. It is in this universal brother-love we place our confidence that help will continue to come to those in need. In its ability to triumph over self-seeking sowers of hate or disunion we see the sole hope of a just and enduring peace. Let no one cease to work and pray that peace may come and come soon; the peace of Christ in the hearts of men and concord among nations.

(2979) May God bless you abundantly for the good that you have been able to accomplish through your organization. As a token of heavenly reward, we are happy to impart our Benediction to you and your dear ones at home.

XI - DRUGS

Statement by Msgr. Giovanni Ceirano, Observer of the Holy See, at the 31st Session of the United Nations Commission on Narcotic Drugs, held in Vienna on 11-20 February 1985. Vienna, 13 February 1985.

Original: English

(2980) I wish to take the floor in order to express the thoughts and concerns of the Holy See with regard to the very grave problem which is being examined by this the Thirty-first Session of the Commission on Narcotic Drugs.

(2981) The phenomenon of the growing use and abuse of narcotic and psychotropic substances has assumed dimensions that no responsible people can fail to describe as tragic. Especially serious is the fact that the problem particularly involves thousands of young people, and therefore has

[3] Discorsi e Radiomessaggi di Sua Santità Pio XII, Vol. IX (2 Marzo 1947 - 1 Marzo 1948), 11-12.

enormous implications and consequences for the future of society. It is not my intention to deal with the numerous and complementary aspects of the matter, which is clearly vast and complex. May I just be permitted to recall the fact that Pope John Paul II, as also various Bishops' Conferences of the Catholic world, have repeatedly spoken on the subject. My purpose is simply to offer some points for reflection, together with some practical suggestions.

(2982) In the view of many experts, there is no doubt that the narcotic drugs phenomenon is linked to a crisis of civilization and to a great malaise. Why do so many young people take drugs? One of the principal answers - and one which concerns the duties of educators and those responsible for society - is that the decision to do so reflects a rejection of a model of society incapable of offering valid reasons for living or strong motives for undertaking commitments. The taking of drugs challenges a human and cultural outlook that lacks sufficient ideals; it challenges paradoxically the permissive way of life, the materialistic mentality and the consumer society - all of which are unaware of, or ignore, essential elements and genuine aspirations of the human person. Therefore, to speak of a moral and spiritual crisis when we speak of the narcotic drug phenomenon is in no way to evade the problem. It is putting one's finger on a wound that calls for the attention of us all. Drug taking is really an alarm bell for our entire society and for human civilization. And into this crisis - this vacuum, this state of unpreparedness on the part of society to face it properly - there has crept, for its own ignoble ends, "a gigantic international plot of high finance, pitiless and cruel" (cf. Statement of Father Pedro Arrupe, S.J. at the 1980 Synod of Bishops).

(2983) Everyone knows that the drug traffic is one of the biggest illegal and criminal businesses in the world today. But it continues to prosper. There is yet another question that has been raised and that weighs upon the tragic phenomenon of drug abuse. In an international society, marked by political and military tensions, is it possible that certain people might be tempted to use the weapon of drugs as a means for causing instability and the destruction of society? Public opinion would like to be reassured on this point.

(2984) A first priority is to discover and analyze realistically the reasons -and if possible all the reasons - for the phenomenon of drug abuse. Then it will be necessary to adopt resolutely the necessary remedies. Pope John Paul II has summed up in the following terms the programme to be undertaken: prevention, suppression, rehabilitation (cf. Address to the Eighth World Assembly of Therapeutic Communities, 7 September 1984).

(2985) All political and social leaders, all those concerned with the world of education, on the national and international levels, are called upon to act with promptness, clarity and courage. In the speech I have just mentioned the Pope stated: "In the sphere of mutual efforts between nations and supranational organisms, as in legislation and laws on a national level, severe regulations are needed which discourage the vile traffic from the start and, at the same time, other regulations are needed concerning the recovery of those who have become entangled in the distressing slavery".

(2986) We note with gratitude that some governments and institutions have adopted exemplary measures. We recognize and express our admiration for the competent work and self-sacrifice of those who devote themselves to the rehabilitation of drug addicts, and especially for what is being done by the healing communities and various voluntary bodies. But we also have to listen to the voices of those who still complain that, in this field of prevention, suppression and rehabilitation there is still too much complacency, superficiality and fear of facing the problem at its roots and providing answers matching the gravity of the situation.

(2987) As Pope John Paul II has said: "Drug abuse is an evil and there can be no yielding to evil. Even partial legalizations, in addition to being at least questionable in relation to the character of the law, have not achieved the results which were desired". (*ibid.*)

(2988) There still remains much to be done. The Holy See wishes to seek and to stimulate the competent and effective commitment of all governments and international bodies working in a delicate sector that involves the defence and promotion of man, especially the young, and the building of a genuinely human civilization. If what so many young people are trying to say through their tragedies and anguished appeals is listened to, then this deadly phenomenon of narcotics abuse may prove to have had a positive significance for our time: paradoxically, it will become a sign of hope, a life-giving stimulus for bringing about a change that must involve all men and women of good will.

XII - HEALTH

1. Address of His Holiness Pius XII to the World Health Assembly. The Vatican 27 June 1949.

Original: French (*)

(2989) It is distressing to continue seeing, long after the cessation of hostilities, misunderstandings, prejudices, conflicting interests and ideologies still preventing the resolution of grave problems, the settlement of troubling consequences of the war. Yet a basis for confidence and joy is to be found in a matter of major importance: the great number of nations which, in spite of the tensions that endure among them on economic, social, political and moral grounds, are nonetheless united in working together for the general health. They are prompted not only by a quite justified preoccupation with reciprocal defense but also by a praiseworthy spirit of mutual help and solidarity. With deep satisfaction we welcome you on this occasion when you are engaged in your common task and we thank you for giving us the opportunity to do so.

(2990) Often, sad to say, all too often, fear is the origin of many wise measures which because of their origin go beyond the limits set by wisdom. In the present context, what is in it self legitimate defense against the imminent danger of infection, has led, during the course of history, to the adoption of harsh laws and an even harsher application of them. Carried to the point of cruelty, this can only be explained by panic among a whole populace. We do not need to go back as far as the Milan plague of 1630. Among many more recent memories is the deplorable odyssey that occurred in the fall of 1884 when the ship Matteo Bruzzo and its passengers roamed the sea, driven from ports everywhere, even by cannon fire, because cases of cholera on board created panic along the whole Atlantic coast.

(2991) Without going to that extreme, at one time did not quarantine measures, terrible because of their length and severity, subject poor passengers to a deplorable situation, from both a physical and moral standpoint, not to mention the damage done to the public economy? Thanks be to God, in creating human beings to His image, He has placed in their hearts natural instincts of benevolence, of goodness. Once past the first movement of irrational terror and again self-possessed, people do try to reconcile, as well as they can, their duties toward humanity with their duties for public security. Little by little, progress in science, hygiene, prophylaxis and therapy, have made it possible, without prejudice to security, to mitigate the treatment inflicted upon travellers suspected of the least possibility of carrying contagion. Moreover, reason argues that it is not enough to spare innocent people, our brothers and sisters, who have already been subjected to unhealthy conditions or some temporary health crisis in their country, punishment only appropriate for criminals. It is our duty to do more, to give them, and them first of all, the help which will protect them from harm and at the same time prevent them from harming the rest of the world.

(2992) A just human sentiment of this kind has dictated an initiative which has gradually taken on such vast proportions, that today delegates or observers from almost all nations as well as representatives of intergovernmental organizations connected with the World Health Organization attend its meetings.

(2993) Among many peoples, either because of poverty and powerlessness or because their civilization or their science and technology are not yet highly developed, the level of health and

(*) Discorsi e Radiomessaggi di Sua Santità Pio XII, Vol. XI (2 Marzo 1949 - 1 Marzo 1950), 131-136.

sanitation in their countries are far below those of other countries. Periodically recurring epidemics and lasting endemic diseases are destroying them by degrees. Statistics, however recent and imperfect they may still be, attest to the ravages threatening to wipe out tribes, whole peoples. Could we find it tolerable to see our brothers and sisters suffering from diseases and physical defects, sometimes serious enough to bring them to extinction, while many other societies in the world have reached such a degree of good health that early deaths have progressively diminished and one-time unyielding plagues are now gradually giving way?

(2994) Private and particular initiatives cannot be too highly praised. By dispensing financial resources and giving inexhaustible devotion, they have improved health in less favored countries, thanks especially to the work of missionaries; yet by themselves they fall short of what is needed, and the World Health Organization brings to this eminently human and social undertaking a more universal, more concerted and, consequently, a more effective collaboration with quicker and surer outcomes.

(2995) In responding to the noble impulse of benevolence and human solidarity, you serve as well the interests of each of your own countries, even those with the finest equipment and best trained personnel, where the people's health and physical fitness are most diligently promoted, where legislation makes provisions for safeguarding, maintaining and improving public health.

(2996) Vigilance, care, institutions, however perfect they may be presumed to be in any one country, cannot suffice to put an end to the ever increasing risks occasioned by the frequency of international relations, the movement of populations, and the voluntary or forced displacement and migration of peoples. To accomplish that, general and concerted action is needed.

(2997) Is there a better way of reducing these risks than by working ceaselessly and simultaneously for the improvement of health in all regions and in all classes of humanity? That is what you are doing, gentlemen, and that is what you are devoting yourselves to, particularly during the days of the congress that has just brought you together.

(2998) On reading over your program and proceedings one point particularly caught our attention: the broad and deep meaning that you give to the expression "health". In your eyes it is not simply negative, as if health, in general, consisted in the simple exclusion of bodily sickness and physical impairment, as if mental health, in particular, meant no more than the absence of alienation or abnormality. Health encompasses the positive spiritual and social well-being of humanity and, on this ground, is one of the conditions required for universal peace and common security.

(2999) It follows that the question of health goes beyond the bounds of biology and medicine; of necessity it has its own place in the moral and religious sphere.

(3000) The Church, far from considering health as a subject of the exclusively biological order, has always emphasized the importance of religious and moral forces in order to maintain health and has always numbered among the conditions requisite for the dignity and the complete well-being of human beings, their corporal and spiritual, temporal and eternal good.

(3001) The social doctrine of the Catholic Church lets no doubt remain that health of body and mind, in the case when healthy social relations also exist, can contribute effectively to establishing a most favorable atmosphere for people's inner and mutual peace. Everything that can effectively serve the cause of true peace is assured of receiving the Church's encouragement and support.

(3002) As an expression of that encouragement and support, we offer you our felicitations and good wishes on the increasingly gratifying results of your work, and we ask for God's best blessings on your charge.

2. Message of His Holiness Paul VI to Dr. Marcolino Candau, Director-General of the World Health Organization, on its 20th anniversary. The Vatican, 28 April 1968.

Original: French (*)

(3003) At this time when the World Health Organization is preparing solemnly to commemorate the twentieth anniversary of its founding, it is a special pleasure for us to express the respect we feel for this international organization and all those who so generously unite their research and efforts to help in this difficult task.

(3004) Within the family of the United Nations the World Health Organization has a fundamental place, even if its action is not as fully known as it deserves to be. What would be the task of "the integral development of man and the united development of mankind" (*Populorum Progressio*, no. 5), if it did not imply that every human being enjoy good health, this "state of complete physical, mental and social well-being", as defined so well by the WHO Constitution? Pope Pius XII when on June 27, 1949 he received the participants in the second World Health Assembly, forcefully affirmed this concept: "The Church, far from considering health as a subject of the exclusively biological order, has always emphasized the importance of religious and moral forces in order to maintain health and has always numbered among the conditions requisite for the dignity and the complete well-being of human beings, their corporal and spiritual, temporal and eternal good". (*L'Osservatore Romano*, June 29, 1949). And our venerable predecessor, John XXIII, in his encyclical *Pacem in Terris* cited among the universal, inviolable and inalienable rights of human beings the right to life and physical integrity, while we ourselves, in our encyclical *Populorum Progressio* emphasized how much the battle against endemic diseases and access for all to health is one of the aspirations of present-day man (nn. 1 and 6). We can only rejoice that this anniversary of the founding of WHO is celebrated this year, when the whole world is invited to honour human rights more authentically. The profoundly charitable mission of your Organization will thus, no doubt, be emphasized and its action approved even more wholeheartedly.

(3005) The fight against disease, in all its forms, throughout the world, entails difficult, costly operations which are demanding of men and resources both for laboratory research and all the health campaigns launched in the furthest corners of the globe. This activity can bear fruit only if we all unanimously cooperate and if there is a fertile dialogue between experts and those they come to relieve. For the Christian, it means following Christ Who, during His life-time, never ceased to deplore human misery and sought to alleviate and heal it. And every man of good will who ponders the moving parable of the good Samaritan, will surely also be induced to "love and help each and everyone as his neighbour, his brother" (*ibid.*, n. 82), bringing him help without sparing efforts. We also wish to honor the work of mercy done by WHO, and all those who support its activity, and thus facilitate its effectiveness.

(3006) Let it also be understood by all responsible parties that any reduction in governmental budgets for public health will unfailingly affect the most needy and the most disinherited. Finally, it is certainly obvious that for the young nations, where health problems are often serious and perplexing, one of the most necessary tasks - among other urgent ones - is the training of a sufficient number of competent persons, from among their citizens, to meet their health needs. This task cannot be improvised; it requires courageous choices and demands disinterested support from the more favoured countries. It demands also an awakening of the consciences of individuals who will not hesitate to sacrifice legitimate aspirations of their own prosperity, in order to dedicate themselves to restore health to people condemned to premature death, if no one comes to their aid. Is not this the best proof of the moral development of mankind, that the more fortunate members of the human family lend themselves to the service of their brothers in pain and need?

(3007) The impetus given to WHO during these last two decades by its directors, members and experts, and the extent and quality of the work done, are pledges that this great international Organization will continue to pursue this activity in favour of mankind in full respect of the laws of its

(*) AAS, 60(1968), 349-351.

nature, as established by its Creator. In forming this wish, we call down the fullness of divine blessings on all those who, under the auspices of WHO, work in the service of health for all mankind.

3. Message of His Holiness Paul VI to Dr. Marcolino G. Candau, Director-General of the World Health Organization, on its 25th anniversary. The Vatican 30 April 1973.

Original: French (*)

(3008) On several occasions, particularly in February 1966 on the occasion of your visit to us in the Vatican, and in 1978 on the twentieth Anniversary of the World Health Organization, we have expressed to you the esteem and interest with which we follow the activities of that body. On this twenty-fifth anniversary of the coming into effect of its Constitution, we are anxious to join in the tribute and good wishes which are reaching it from all sectors of the International Community.

(3009) An essential function devolves upon the World Health Organization in the concerted effort of the family of the United Nations and Specialized Agencies with a view to the complete development of mankind - "of the whole man and of all men" - to repeat the formula that ran through our Encyclical Populorum Progressio on the development of peoples. The first article of your Constitution assigns you the purpose "of bringing all peoples to the highest level of health possible"; and assuring for every human being the exercise of this fundamental right, "the possession of the best state of health he is capable of reaching", as the preamble of this same Constitution says.

(3010) To watch over man's health, improve it, prevent disorders, cure them, should they arise, is that not dedication to the service of the Creator's first gift to man: life? This life, the source of joy when it gushes forth, the beginning of a destiny that is unique each time and, in spite of appearances, always admirable, since it is called to bloom in endless happiness! That is why the professions which dedicate themselves to the health of men carry out a lofty and redoubtable task and are among the noblest vocations in the service of man.

(3011) It is true that the specific work of the World Health Organization concerns public health: you tackle the problems of human life, its promotion and protection, in the fields of health administration, training and research, epidemiology and improvement in sanitation, large-scale prophylactic measures. But you are well aware that you are always in the service of individuals whose lives, or in any case the "quality" of their lives, as is said today, often depends on your steps, your activities and your decisions. The value and the respect for individual life in the eyes of the World Health Organization can rightly be illustrated by the place it gives in its programmes to the outcasts of society such as the mentally impaired, the handicapped, the victims of drug addiction, and so many others.

(3012) In the preface of the book published by the Organization at the end of its second decade of existence, you spoke, Mr. Director-General, of the "sense of the irreplaceable value of every human life". It is this sense which, after twenty-five years of life, must win for an Organization such as the one you direct, the gratitude of many, the esteem of all. At a moment when the outbreak of violence on so many points of the globe, on the one hand, and on the other hand the giddy whirl in which modern society is so often caught up and which dims true values, seem to undervalue life, all life, from its origin on to its decline, it is our most fervent wish on this twenty-fifth Anniversary, that the World Health Organization to which the International Community has entrusted the preservation and promotion of men's health, should maintain on all occasions the primacy of life and keep for mankind the complete contribution of an authentic deontology in regard to it.

(3013) We are aware, Mr. Director-General, that in the course of this Assembly, you are preparing to hand over to some one else a general management which has identified you with the Organization for twenty years. So we would like, in conclusion, to express to you and to the one who will be called upon to succeed you our most fervent wishes, accompanied by our prayer to the Lord, on

(*) Insegnamenti di Paolo VI, Vol XI (1973), 383-385.

behalf of the entire Organization and yourselves, that He may bless the work begun twenty-five years ago.

4. Statement by Msgr. Silvio Luoni, Permanent Observer of the Holy See to the Office of the United Nations and specialized Agencies in Geneva, at the 27th Assembly of the World Health Organization. Geneva, 15 May 1974.

Original: French

(3014) The short time at my disposal does not allow me, unfortunately, to make an in-depth analysis of Dr. Mahler's report, a document that is both rich and stimulating. It shows, if that were still necessary, the happy choice made by the World Assembly in the election of its Director-General.

(3015) So I will make a few reflections:
- first, on basic health problems:
- second, on protection of human life;
- third, on WHO's "research programme on human reproduction".

(3016) 1. The Holy See Delegation shares first of all with WHO the idea that health is a fundamental right of all men. This means that basic health protection must be ensured at all levels, so as to guarantee all essential services. It does not mean, however, that there is one single model valid for all situations.

(3017) Just as there is not one model of development applicable in all economic situations - as experience shows, more and more clearly - in the same way there is not one model of health service valid for all countries.

(3018) This was realized by renowned physicians, such as the late Dr. Schweitzer, who endeavored to adapt his methods to the local conditions. It was also the ideal that inspired the action in favour of African populations carried out by Dr. Aujoulat, a familiar figure to this Assembly, whose premature death everyone regrets.

(3019) Among the initiatives of the developing countries that are worthy of mention, the Director-General cites in particular those of certain countries, which "have aroused great interest in Asia, Latin America and Africa" (Director-General's Report, page X).

(3020) At first sight, the Holy See Delegation considers WHO's new policy a very positive one. This policy aims at stimulating and supporting the initiatives of the countries themselves to set up health systems in conformity with the basic needs of their populations, their economic possibilities and their socio-cultural nature.

(3021) This is what could be called the replacement of imported health methods by indigenous methods and formulas in accordance with the genius of the population.

(3022) 2. The second reflection concerns the protection of human life. What would seem self-evident - speaking of the defence of human life before the greatest world conclave on health - actually becomes necessary, since measures have been adopted in certain countries to liberalize abortion. These provisions, whatever be the reasons adduced and the often dramatic situations to which they refer, are always tantamount to authorizing the physician to cause the death of a living being.

(3023) What a tragic contradiction, to wish to protect the mother's health by doing away with clandestine abortions, while refusing the child in her womb the same right to life!

(3024) The clandestine nature of the act of killing is attacked, but not the act of killing in itself, as if it were the fact of being clandestine that made it a crime.

(3025) But is a crime no longer a crime when it is no longer committed clandestinely but openly?

(3026) Is a crime no longer a crime just because the law does not punish it and even grants its protection?

(3027) Does error become truth because of a sanction authorizing its free circulation?

(3028) There exists a law of nature that precedes positive laws and the latter would be neither just nor binding if they were in contradiction with natural law.

(3029) It is necessary to deplore strongly the discrimination and other form of moral pressure exerted in some countries against physicians, health personnel and clinics that refuse to cooperate directly or indirectly in the suppression of life. Thus we arrive at the absurdity that faithfulness to the Hippocratic oath, which should be the fundamental rule of medical ethics, is considered blameworthy.

(3030) Are there, by chance, forms of life to be given preference as regards protection while others may be destroyed?

(3031) Where would the principle of discrimination between different forms of human life lead us? Have we measured the consequences that could be derived from such a principle?

(3032) But why have we reached this point? This is the problem that must be raised because it is necessary to seek the underlying causes of social pathological phenomena by tracing the evil back to its source.

(3033) The leaders of society should make it their business to find remedies for these causes instead of permitting the legal elimination of innocent victims.

(3034) As for the Church, she will never cease proclaiming her convictions. Her choice has already been made. She has always been and will always be on the side of life.

(3035) 3. The third reflection concerns a subject that is extremely relevant in this Population year, namely WHO's programme "of research, development and experimentation on human reproduction" for the purpose of setting up "safe, effective and acceptable methods for the regulation of human fertility".

(3036) We cannot but rejoice that an Organization with the prestige of WHO, and with such a noble and elevated humanitarian ideal, has undertaken such an important and necessary task. That should guarantee the thoroughness and objectivity of the research.

(3037) Even if "family planning is only one of the numerous aspects of human reproduction which the research Programme will study" (Report, page 117), this does not prevent it from being considered one of the most important aspects.

(3038) As Pope Paul VI said to the Director-General of the World Conference on Population and to the Executive Director of the United Nations Fund for Population Activities (28 March 1974): "When the Church concerns herself with population problems, she does so by reason of fidelity to her mission. This concern stems from her commitment to work for the promotion of the integral good, both material and spiritual, of the whole man and for all men. The Church knows that population means people, human beings" (see above, par. 2681).

(3039) The attitude of the Church to the population problem consists in avoiding all unjustified optimism and all excessive pessimism; it is based on healthy realism. She is not insensitive to the consequences of an indefinite and uncontrolled increase of the world population, but neither does she share the artificial and selfish alarmism of some sectors.

(3040) The Church asks, first and foremost, that family planning should respect the dignity of the human person.

(3041) Planning will not be really human unless it respects the dignity of the human person, and the freedom and responsibility of the couple.

(3042) Nevertheless, "it is important that there should be realized all the conditions which will allow parents to attain a level of responsibility in conformity with morality - a responsibility which is really human... That is why "the Church has always emphasized, and she still does so today, the need to deal with the problems of population in the objective reality of their various aspects" (Paul VI, *ibid.* See above, par. 2690 and 2687).

(3043) It is necessary to avoid any incomplete or biased view or stand; it is clear that the solution to the population problem must be found in an overall framework, in the context of social justice, development, environment and human rights (cf. *Encyclical Humanae Vitae*, n. 23). In this sense, the efforts of researchers to study and make possible the use of natural methods for the regulation of births are to be warmly encouraged (cf. *ibid.* n. 24).

(3044) Such are the few reflections suggested by a reading of the Director-General's report.

(3045) My Delegation is happy to assure WHO of the support and cooperation of the Holy See in order that it may attain the humanitarian purposes for which it was set up, in respect of the laws of life and of moral values.

5. Statement by Mons. Silvio Luoni, Permanent Observer of the Holy See to the Office of the United Nations and Specialized Agencies in Geneva, at the 28th Assembly of the World Health Organization. Geneva, 22 May 1975.

Original: French

(3046) It is hardly necessary to repeat from this rostrum the interest that the Holy See takes in the activities of the World Health Organization, which is in charge of one of the most fundamental services rendered to mankind in its struggle against disease, ignorance and want.

(3047) So the reports of the Organization and the documents of its various sessions are the object of careful study on our part, in a spirit that is *a priori* sympathetic. An examination in depth of the Director-General's very valuable report would certainly be more complete, but speaking in the framework of the general discussion, the Holy See Observer will limit himself, for lack of time, with the deference but also the frankness due to you, to reflections on the chapter dealing the family. A subject in which our interest is constant, but which seems to us to take on a particular significance in this Women's International Year and immediately after the World Population Conference in Bucharest where it was at the centre of the work of a special Commission and of discussions within the Working Group charged with drawing up the World Plan of Action. It is with pleasure, therefore, that the Holy See Delegation congratulates the Director-General on the importance given to the subject of Health and the Family, an importance emphasized by the place given to it in the annual Report.

(3048) Although it is contested in some quarters today, the family certainly remains, according to the excellent definition of the Universal Declaration on Human Rights, art. 16, par. 3: "the natural and fundamental element of society" which "is entitled to the protection of society and the State". It is hardly necessary to stress the importance of health in the family; the health of each member is the business of them all; and among the essential needs is that of competent and proven resources to meet the problems raised by the physical evolution of the members of the family, the accidents that may occur, the more or less serious illnesses to which they are exposed.

(3049) Referring to WHO's conception of its role at present, the Director-General writes in his introduction: "Today it endeavours to express this principle defining health in its Constitution, in actual facts seeking the means of ensuring a lasting balance between man and his environment, which would certainly make him less vulnerable to disease and would enable him to lead a more productive and attractive existence" (p. X). Although - let it be said with all respect - the terms "productive" and "attractive" seem to us to fall far short of the definition of an authentic "quality of life", we agree without question to the idea of ensuring a lasting balance between man and his environment.

(3050) We are happy t o read in this regard in the chapter on the "Health of the Family", in the Director-General's Report that "the Organization is doing everything in its power to seek and promote new ways for the health education of mothers, children and youth in particular for the purposes of their protection against the harmful factors of modern life" (2. 63). The context from which this sentence is taken shows that, very rightly, the factors envisaged here are not merely physical or biological ones.

(3051) It also seems to us that, in this perspective, concern for the health of the family, one of the main victims of the aggressions of the contemporary environment, would have a place of prime importance. The approach of the Conference on Habitat, to which WHO expects to make the contribution that its functions call for, draws our attention to one of the essential problems of environment for the family, a problem in which health aspects are fundamental. Is not the family's exercise of its basic rights often hindered by the fact of the conditions of habitat imposed on it by the prevailing culture, contemporary economic systems or sometimes even by the political authority itself?

(3052) To come to the sectors specifically touched upon by the chapter of the Report on the health of the family, it is certainly the interdisciplinary approach advocated that is the most promising one: to give the family the guarantees it is entitled to expect from medicine and auxiliary sciences. In the light of the work of the recent World Food Conference in Rome, the vital role of food and nutrition problems, and consequently of the education of married couples, and particularly of wives and mothers, should be stressed. We recall here that many voices were raised in Rome to indicate that an improvement and drastic revision of practices in this matter concerned not only the developing countries, but were to be urgently envisaged in countries in which abundance and consumer societies prevail. In this field WHO owes it to itself to work out and promote clear and convincing indications; for habits contracted and strengthened by a whole complex of economic and social factors, will not be easy to transform.

(3053) In connection with mother and child care services, the Introduction to the Report admirably states that "their mission consists above all in caring for the health of the pregnant woman, satisfactory confinement and health protection of the infant and young child" (p. XIII). But, according to the Introduction, the services aimed at "helping parents to space out births and the size of the family" (*ibid.*) are at a far less important level.

(3054) Hence, is there not a certain imbalance in the chapter on "Family Health" where preponderance is clearly given to family planning problems? Without questioning the importance of the health aspects of the regulation of births, a world medical organization cannot assign such preeminence to it in its programme for family health as to give it precedence over other subjects; we do not think we are misinterpreting this chapter when we speak in this way. A reading of the entire text shows how frequently family planning is mentioned, in different connections, in addition to the numerous paragraphs expressly dedicated to it.

(3055) The subject thus takes on an importance and special position that do not agree with one of the points that won unquestionable acceptance at Bucharest, namely, that the regulation of births, rather than being considered an end in itself, should be carried out in respect of the rights of the individual and the family, as the fruit of an overall pursuit of complete development and fully human balance.

(3056) In this connection, we deeply regret that the research of WHO in the field of human reproduction seems to be directed almost exclusively to medical technology and not sufficiently by the sense of human dignity and responsibility, in respect of principles and moral values.

(3057) Since, in developing countries particularly, the programmes are often carried out in communities that have not yet won their struggle against illiteracy, research should take this into consideration and pay more attention to health education and the psychological aspects of the regulation of births. It is necessary, in fact, to make sure that couples clearly understand the repercussions and impact of the interventions they are induced to accept.

(3058) Above all, it is with the greatest concern that we note the increasing radicalization in the recourse to birth control methods whose moral value is more and more questionable. Formerly, at least a certain gradation was established among contraceptives, sterilization and abortion; today, as is seen in par. 2,013 and 2,104 of the Report, sterilization is classified directly among contraceptive methods and in par. 2,113 a process which is an abortion is recorded in the midst of a series of methods for regulating fertility. This is all the more worrying when it is known that large sums are allocated to research on abortion processes. Our Delegation has already pointed out from this rostrum on several occasions that abortion constitutes a most serious violation of human and medical ethics. It also rejects, as is known, sterilization and all non-natural methods of regulating births.

(3059) In this connection, the Delegation of the Holy See cannot conceal a certain surprise at the hasty way in which paragraph 2,117 states that "little progress has been made and few practical ideas have been put forward" in the field of natural regulation. According to our information and the opinions of our experts, such a negative view is far from being justified by the facts.

(3060) But the astonishment of the Holy See Delegation is even greater at the complete indifference that the activities described in the Report show with regard to the ethical factors concerned.

(3061) It would be normal, however, that the World Health Organization should promote observance of medical ethics, which guarantees all health activity and constitutes its honour.

(3062) We have reached a moment in history when many people like to question the doctrine accepted by the finest minds of mankind and of the medical profession on respect of life and its laws. The Holy See, owing to the esteem it has for WHO, presses its concern to see it in this field in the vanguard of the defence of fundamental values, which a certain purely technological research often does not take into sufficient consideration.

6. Statement by Msgr. Joseph Geraud on behalf of the Delegation of the Holy See, at the 29th Assembly of the World Health Organization. Geneva, May 1976

Original: French

(3063) It is fortunate that we are given the possibility, at regular intervals, of becoming acquainted in detail with the activities of the World Health Organization, and of thus gauging, through a thorough study of the report of the Organization and of the documents emanating from its commissions, the quality as well as the importance of the work accomplished.

(3064) The Holy See Observer, a witness among you to the spiritual and human significance of the Church at the heart of the daily activities of men and women and of society, expresses satisfaction with the positive elements contained in the Director-General's report. It is also up to the Observer, you will easily understand, to communicate to you the reflections he draws from it and to stress the critical observations that certain passages suggest to him.

(3065) How could one fail to be sensitive to the first words of the Introduction to the Director-General's report? Referring to the resolution unanimously adopted by the United Nations General Assembly, which advocates "a new economic order", he points out, in fact, that it "is a concrete expression of the deep change of atmosphere which at last puts an end to the opposition between rich countries and poor countries".

(3066) As it is a question of problems in which the health of the family and, more exactly, the family itself, is involved, the Church knows what is the vigorous contribution of the poor countries in the real life of nations, and she perceives in it an application of the Beatitudes taught by Christ. Indeed, in this field as in many others, are not the poor very often our teachers and those who awaken our conscience?

(3067) In the chapter entitled "Health of the family", a first aspect holds our attention: in its presentation, unidisciplinary and specialized projects are replaced by wider multidisciplinary and multisectoral programmes. Moreover, together with this concern there is that of the respective dimension to be observed between the services destined for the individual and the ones geared to the community.

(3068) It seems to us increasingly necessary to consider the approach to problems in the widest possible or global aspect. The family is a case in point: it is directly involved in a whole set of situations, and numerous points raised in various parts of the report concern it essentially (for example in the prophylaxis of diseases or with regard to the environment...). But it is also, in itself, a privileged source of dialogue and a factor in the reciprocal education of its members. This is also important in the field that interests us here, for, to the extent to which it comes into play, it is an element of the "health of the family."

(3069) Likewise, when talking about the question of the relationship between the individual and the community, this chapter coincides with a constant concern of the Holy See. Already the Pastoral Constitution *Gaudium et Spes* on the Church in the Modern World, had dealt with this situation in the chapter dedicated to the human community (nn. 24, 25). More recently, the Declaration of the Congregation for the Doctrine of the Faith on Procured Abortion said: "In regard to the mutual rights and duties of the person and of society, it belongs to moral teaching to enlighten consciences, it belongs to the law to specify and organize external behaviour. There is precisely a certain number of rights which society is not in a position to grant since these rights precede society; but society has the function to preserve and enforce them. These are the greater part of those which are today called 'human rights' and which our age boasts of having formulated. The first right of the human person is his life. He has other goods and some are more precious, but this one is fundamental - the condition of all the others. Hence, it must be protected above all the others. It does not belong to society, nor does it belong to public authority in any form to recognize this right for some and not for others: all discrimination is evil, whether it be founded on race, sex, colour or religion. It is not recognition by another that constitutes this right. This right is antecedent to its recognition; it demands recognition and it is strictly unjust to refuse it."

(3070) The bearing in mind of these convictions will enable you to understand better the agreement of our views on a good number of steps proposed in this chapter of the report; it will also guide us, at the appropriate moment, to express our reservations and fears.

(3071) We are in agreement on the four priority sectors proposed and you will allow me, in concord with the feeling of the Organization, to underline the effort carried out by certain governments and teaching establishments to "stress the family considered as a basic social unit". It is by endeavouring to draw out the consequences of this proposition that one can make a great step forward because the fundamental problem is viewed in a positive perspective: the family is dealt with in itself, in its human and social function and no longer as an object of sterile controversies or struggles.

(3072) Another series of positive aspects lies in the importance attributed to the development and growth of the foetus and the exigencies that are involved on the nutritional and psycho-social plane (cf. 2.7-2.15). In this way, the value of this period of life is affirmed and the respect and concern with human life in its prenatal period is stressed. This part of the report cannot, therefore, but meet with our approval.

(3073) The Observer also notices the place granted in this report to the five paragraphs (2.95 to 2.99) which deal with natural methods of regulation and fertility. International information is more enlightened on this subject today and the positive presentation of the question is noted with interest. The support of the World Health Organization in research and concrete applications of these methods receives our full encouragement.

(3074) The positive elements contained in the report cannot conceal from us, however, some serious preoccupations which we felt on reading it. The Holy See Observer owes it to himself, therefore, to express his fears frankly, hoping in this way that the parties concerned will feel supported in their positive action. He is aware of the difficulties that any educative step presents. He knows what it costs. And it is for this reason that he attaches such importance to demonstrating it benefits.

(3075) It is not without anxiety that he sees appearing under the title "Health of the family", alongside positive steps in favour of life, its growth and its development, what is called "the struggle against uncontrolled fertility," considered as a defective health state and a "human waste". In this perspective, therefore, all methods of family planning are introduced and, it seems, on an equal footing. How can we fail to recall, then, before going further in our critical observation, the position expressed by Pope Paul VI in his Encyclical *Humanae Vitae* (n. 16): "The Church is the first to praise and recommend the intervention of intelligence in a work that associates the rational creature so closely with his Creator, but she affirms that this must be done in respect of the order established by God. If there are serious motives to space out births, which derive from the physical or psychological conditions of husband and wife, or from external conditions, the Church teaches that it is then licit to take into account the natural rhythms in the generative functions, for the use of marriage in the infecund periods only, and in this way to regulate birth without offending moral principles."

(3076) The fears we have are confirmed by a careful reading of the paragraphs dedicated to human reproduction in this same chapter of the report (2.79 to 2.139). They reveal, in fact, the anxieties and even more the numerous uncertainties that exist in the whole of this field and regarding the different methods of regulation.

(3077) Is it certain that the persons in charge of action will be attentive to the serious facts noted throughout the report? We can quote, for example, what is said regarding "the distant effects of the use of oral contraceptives for girls, especially as regards their future reproductive capacity", or regarding "the psychosocial aspects of abortion and the health implications of the fall of the birth rate and the dwindling of families in certain industrialized countries" (2.7), regarding sterilization (2.100) or again regarding abortion practised more and more often as a method of regulating fertility (2.102). Will they not be tempted, on the contrary, to see only the immediate technical facilities?

(3078) The situation is serious enough to arouse our concern, which we know, moreover, is shared by many.

(3079) How can one fail to be concerned, in fact, on seeing the World Health Organization carry out family planning programmes everywhere? The Organization has prepared two series of directives for the use of administrations and organizers of family planning programmes so that they may be able to choose priorities, the cost of implementation and the workload for supporting services. Now no mention is made, in the choice of these priorities, of the health problems of the mothers to whom these programmes will be applied, and one of these series is dedicated to the different techniques of sterilizing women (2.18)!

(3080) A glance at the balance-sheet of the activities of the health services in countries and regions shows stress laid, above all, on the importance attached to the development of family planning programmes. The question is raised how to induce the young to take part in these programmes (2.24). The progression of programmes for the interruption of pregnancy is emphasized.

(3081) This orientation of the Organization towards the promotion of family planning that does not take into account human principles as a whole, and moral exigencies in particular, is, therefore, a source of serious concern for us: the human person is not envisaged in all his components, in all his rights and all his values.

(3082) It is the technological aspect which prevails over the educative aspect.

(3083) Now, in this field of procreation, it is impossible to ignore systematically the dignity, the destiny, the freedom of the human person. Likewise, can it be considered acceptable when a balance sheet of activity in the service of the health of the family fails to mention: respect for life, respect for man and woman as persons and as a couple, the responsibility of man and woman in the gift of life, the role of society as protector of these values?

(3084) The future of an agency such as the World Health Organization rests on the generosity of men, on their sense of responsibility, and even on acceptance of self-denial in the service of others. These attitudes are based on a scrupulous respect for reality, for the essential values of human nature, such as conscience has transmitted to us and defended against the ever repeated attacks of selfishness, opportunism, and even violence in all its disguises.

(3085) We wonder if it is not contributing to the deterioration of consciences and even gradually of the creative ideal to change the meaning of essential words, such as life, health and well-being; to mask abortion under the name of interruption of pregnancy; sterilization, which destroys vital faculties, under the name of health care; punitive measures against large families under that of social progress? To ignore or conceal the dangers of certain forms of medicine diffused without discernment, is that not to be responsible for new forms of tyranny?

(3086) Youth is thirsty for justice and peace. It calls for authenticity. Can we say that we are serving our young people, that we are meeting their expectations, when we facilitate their pursuit of selfish pleasure, dispensing them from reflecting on the consequences of their acts? Even if today's youth lets itself be swept along into the temptations that some people propose, there is no doubt that we will witness painful and explosive awakenings. For the force of life will always prevail!

(3087) The Church has confidence in man, in his capacity for love. That is why she defends and proclaims the holiness of marriage and procreation. She recognizes and supports the search for quality of life as an expression of her holiness, as a sign of true love.

XIII - CRIME

Document of the Holy See concerning arbitrary and summary executions, submitted to the United Nations Committee on Crime Prevention and Control, published in the Report of the Secretary-General of the United Nations E/AC.57/1982/4/Add.1, 11 March 1982.

Original: French

(3088) The problem of arbitrary and summary executions needs to be considered in the broader framework of relations between a human being and those institutions of the State whose task it is to guarantee his protection. In the last resort, the reason for any authority and any political activity, both national and international, is service to man, the protection of his dignity and the effective promotion and safeguarding of his rights. Conversely, any human being, along with his inalienable and indefeasible rights, has corresponding duties towards other human beings and society.

(3089) Arbitrary and summary executions are a tragic and typical example of the aberrations which exist within some political regimes; they reflect the loss of the values which should be the foundation of any social organization, and they involve the destruction of human life, which is sacred in its origin and destiny. The Catholic Church has repeatedly made its voice heard on this serious problem.

(3090) The position of the Catholic Church was stated most clearly and fully in the famous address of Pope Pius XII to the Sixth International Congress on Criminal Law (1953). He explained the State's right to punish, and then placed this right in the context of present-day national and international requirements. He spoke of the State's right to demand punishment commensurate with the crime committed and he explained the significance of legal safeguards as an intrinsic and necessary part of the whole legal process: "Even arrest, which is the first step in punitive action, must not be arbitrary but must be in accord with legal norms. It is unacceptable that even the most blameless person can be arrested arbitrarily and simply disappear in a prison. To send someone to a concentration camp and keep him there without proper trial is to make a mockery of the law... The safeguarding of proper legal procedure requires that the actions of Governments and courts should not be arbitrary nor depend on purely personal judgement, and should receive a firm basis of clear legal rules, a basis which is in conformity with sound reason and the universal sentiment of justice, at the disposal of which contracting Governments can place their authority and coercive power... ."

(3091) Pope John Paul II gave first place to "the right to life, freedom and personal security" among the rights he mentioned in his address to the thirty-fourth session of the United Nations General Assembly (1979; see above, par. 89); also, referring to the tragedy of people who had been lost or had disappeared, in his address before the "Angelus" (1979), he urged that "information on the situation of prisoners should be given speedily and that, in all circumstances in which one is seeking to ensure that the law is respected, there should be a strict commitment to respect the physical and moral integrity of the person, even in the case of those guilty or accused of having broken the law".

(3092) The Holy See's position is clear and consistent. It recognizes the State's right and need to punish the guilty in order to safeguard security and order in society. It insists that the punishment should be proportionate to the crime. It explains very clearly the safeguards which the penal code should contain to ensure respect for the rights and dignity of accused persons. It thus offers the basic doctrine which can help in the formulation of a penal code providing real safeguards against arbitrary and summary executions, contrary to human dignity and the dignity of the State, whose function is to serve the common good of all citizens in a world where harmony reigns between peoples.

XIV - UNIVERSAL PERPOSE OF CREATED THINGS

A - ENVIRONMENT

1. ENVIRONMENT, COMMON PATRIMONY OF MANKIND

Message of His Holiness Paul VI to Mr. Maurice F. Strong, Secretary-General of the Conference on the Environment. 1 June 1972.

Original: French (*)

(3093) On the occasion of the opening of the United Nations Conference on the Environment, which you have prepared zealously and competently, we would like to tell you and all participants of the interest with which we follow this great enterprise. The care of preserving and improving the natural environment, like the noble ambition of stimulating a first gesture of world cooperation in this field, so precious for everyone, meets needs that are deeply felt among the men of our times.

(3094) Today, indeed, there is a growing awareness that man and his environment are more inseparable than ever. The environment essentially conditions man's life and development, while

(*) AAS 64(1972), 443-446.

man, in his turn, perfects and ennobles his environment through his presence, work and contemplation. But human creativeness will yield true and lasting benefits only to the extent to which man respects the laws that govern the vital impulse and nature's capacity for regeneration. Both are united, therefore, and share a common temporal future. So man is warned of the necessity of replacing the unchecked advance of material progress, often blind and turbulent, with new-found respect for the biosphere of his global domain, which, to quote the fine motto of the Conference, has become "one Earth", to quote the fine motto of the Conference.

(3095) The shortening of distance by the advances in communications; the establishment of ever closer bonds among peoples through economic development; the growing subservience of the forces of nature to science and technology; the multiplication of human relations beyond the barriers of nationalities and races are so many factors of interdependence - for better or for worse - for the hope of safety, or the risk of disaster. An abuse, a deterioration in one part of the world has repercussions in other places and can spoil the quality of other people's lives, often unbeknownst to them and through no fault of their own. Man now knows with absolute certainty that scientific and technical progress, despite its promising aspects for the advancement of all peoples, bears within it, like every human work, a heavy measure of ambivalence, for good and for evil.

(3096) In the first place intelligence can apply its discoveries as means of destruction, as in the case of atomic, chemical and bacteriological arms and so many other instruments of war, large and small, for which moral conscience can feel only horror. But how can we ignore the imbalances caused in the biosphere by the disorderly exploitation of the physical reserves of the planet, even for the purpose of producing something useful, such as the wasting of natural resources that cannot be renewed; pollution of the earth, water, air and space, with the resulting assaults on vegetable and animal life? All that contributes to the impoverishment and deterioration of man's environment to the extent, it is said, of threatening his own survival. Finally, our generation must energetically accept the challenge of going beyond partial and immediate goals in order to prepare a hospitable earth for future generations.

(3097) Interdependence must now be met by joint responsibility; common destiny by solidarity. This will not be done by resorting to facile solutions. Just as the demographic problem is not solved by unduly limiting access to life, so the problem of the environment cannot be tackled with technical measures alone. The latter are indispensable, it is true, and your Conference will have to study them and propose means to rectify the situation. It is only too clear, for example, that industry being one of the main causes of pollution, it is absolutely necessary for the industrial operators to perfect their methods and find the means, as far as possible without harming production, to reduce, if not eliminate completely, the causes of pollution. In this task of purification it is clear, too, that chemical research workers will play an important role, and that great hope is placed in their professional capacities.

(3098) But all technical measures would remain ineffectual if they were not accompanied by an awareness of the necessity for a radical change in mentality. All are called to clear-sightedness and courage. Will our civilization, tempted to increase its marvellous achievements by despotic domination of the human environment, discover in time the way to control its material growth, to use the earth's food with wise moderation, and to cultivate real poverty of spirit in order to carry out urgent and indispensable reconversions? We would like to think so, for the very excesses of progress lead men, and significantly the young, to recognize that their power over nature must be exercised in accordance with ethical demands. The saturation caused in some people by a life that is too easy and the growing awareness in a large number of the solidarity that links mankind, thus contribute to restoring the respectful attitude on which man's relationship with his environment is essentially based. How can we fail to recall here the imperishable example of St. Francis of Assisi and to mention the great Christian contemplative Orders, which offer the testimony of an inner harmony achieved in the framework of trusting communion with the rhythms and laws of nature?

(3099) "Everything created by God is good," the Apostle St. Paul writes (*ITim.* 4:4), echoing the text of Genesis that relates God's satisfaction with each of His works. To rule creation means for the human race not to destroy it but to perfect it; to transform the world not into a chaos no longer fit for habitation, but into a beautiful abode where everything is respected. No one can take possession in an absolute and selfish way of the environment, which is not a "res nullius" - something not belonging to anyone - but the "res omnium" - the patrimony of mankind. Those in possession of it - men in private or public life - must use it in a way that redounds to the real advantage of everyone. Man is certainly the first and truest treasure of the earth.

(3100) For this reason the responsibility of offering everyone the possibility of access to a fair share in the resources, both existing and potential, of our planet must weigh particularly on the conscience of men of goodwill. Development, that is, the complete growth of man, presents itself as *the* subject, the keystone of your deliberations, in which you will pursue not only ecological equilibrium but also a just balance of prosperity between the centres of the industrialized world and their immense periphery. Want, it has rightly been said, is the worst of pollutions. Is it utopian to hope that the young nations, who at the cost and efforts are constructing a better future for their peoples, seeking to assimilate the positive acquisitions of technical civilization, but rejecting its excesses and deviations, should become the pioneers in the building of a new world, for which the Stockholm Conference is called to give the starting signal? It would be all the more unfair to refuse the young nations the means to do so, in that they have often had to pay a heavy, unjustified price for the degradation and impoverishment of their common biological patrimony. Thus, instead of seeing in the struggle for a better environment the reaction of fear of the rich, they would see in it, to the benefit of everyone, an affirmation of faith and hope in the destiny of the human family gathered round a common project.

(3101) It is with these sentiments that we pray to the Almighty to grant to all the participants, together with the abundance of his Blessings, the light of Wisdom and the spirit of brotherly Love for the complete success of their work.

2. ENVIRONMENT AND DEVELOPMENT

Statement by Rev. Fr. Henri de Riedmatten, O.P., Head of the Delegation of the Holy See, to the United Nations Conference on the Environment, held in Stockholm on June 1972.

Original: French

(3102) The Message from His Holiness Paul VI, which I had the honour to read here the day before yesterday, expresses the fundamental positions of the Holy See on the important problems we are gathered here to study. It is in the light of these principles that I will now set forth the precise points on which the Delegation of the Holy See regards itself capable of making a contribution to the work of the Conference. Strong in the hope which, in our opinion, animates every really human project, we cannot reduce our common effort merely to establishing salvage and recovery measures; we firmly intend to make it a positive stage in the pursuit of the complete development of man, a pursuit which, as far as we are concerned, our faithfulness to Christ's message obliges us to undertake.

(3103) Fascinated by the exclusive concern *to have more*, technological civilization has compromised the fundamental symbiosis between man and his environment; it is only by the determination *to be more* that the harmony between man and nature, his first matrix, will be restored. It is nonsense, in fact, to oppose or unite environment and development, as if they were two independent values. Every inroad on the environment reveals a mutilated perception of development. The very confusion into which the environment crisis throws the industrialized world shows that there are no developed countries; there are only developing countries and, as regards the environment, the ones that top the list according to some indices of progress, appear much further down here. The environment and its good use are, in fact, part of development, with a decisive influence on the satisfaction of man's fundamental needs: the subsistence, health and education of the individual - the cultural and social equilibrium of nations.

(3104) It remains to be determined more precisely what degree of priority the problems of the environment have in the projects of human advancement. Our Delegation considers that this is the point at which we will be able to reconcile our views on the relationship between development and environment. Some people are frightened by the fact that the environment has, apparently and suddenly, acquired absolute priority. If it is set in its proper place in real development, it will be possible to define more accurately national and international policies with regard to it, and to draw more than one practical conclusion for the purpose of our Conference. For example, the nature of the institutional entity to be set up to coordinate and stimulate the environmental activities of the international Community will vary greatly according to whether other sectors of development are considered to fall under them or whether, on the contrary, these activities are regarded as elements within these sectors, which are already covered by the different agencies of the United Nations family.

(3105) Likewise, the so-called developing countries will cooperate to a better discovery of the dimensions of the environment if they include it in the model of civilization that they set for themselves. Uniting fully with the whole international Community to cope with the problem of the environment, they will control, through the very needs of the developed countries, the quality of the merchandise offered to them. Finding themselves in this way in solidarity with the developed countries, they will prevent the latter from withdrawing into contemplation of their affliction and using it as a pretext to restrict their contribution to the overall enterprise of development.

(3106) Certainly, as has already been pointed out several times from this platform, to decide correctly about ecological problems and their relative importance, it is necessary to acquire an ever more extensive and well-ordered knowledge of them. Many things, it is true, have been or are about to be undertaken; the scope of the perspectives that have been opened up in the course of the preparation of the Conference, cannot be ignored. But, how long the road ahead still is! However exhaustive our documentation on other chapters, it remains scanty indeed on subjects such as the biological impact of the elementary factors (light, noise, infrasound and ultrasound, living space); the breaking of rhythms acquired in the course of generations; the weakening of certain reconstitution, recuperation and adaptation forces of the organism; and, even more, the exact description of what is meant by "quality of life". It would also be necessary to study to what extent industrial and technological civilization is responsible for the undeniable crises through which - for good or for evil, we are not called upon to decide - young people are passing, not satisfied with a happiness that we fondly imagined ensured for them.

(3107) I have spoken of the young and this is an opportunity for me to express what I think is a disappointment for many of us. In spite of the efforts made to get the young to take part in the preparation of our Conference; in spite, in particular, of the enthusiasm with which Mr. Maurice Strong, a great motivator, set about it, we are compelled to recognize that the young are keeping us at a distance. We are dealing with a new subject where constructive elaboration depends far more on the younger generation than on ourselves, and it has not been possible to bring about the needed full cooperation of the generations. It is not a matter here of blaming anyone, but of becoming aware of a very regrettable gap at the present stage of our enterprise. The disagreement to which it is due has its origins partly in conditions of the social, cultural and economic background; but it is also connected, it seems, with the very conception of life, of man and therefore of the environment.

(3108) We would like to conclude by saying that our approach to the draft Declaration of Principles prepared for the Conference, must go to the root of the problems. It is possible and probably desirable to accept the text as it stands, in order to provide a platform for immediate work in Stockholm,. This text, the fruit of long labour, reflects not only divergences skillfully reduced to ingenious compromises, but also the tenacious effort of governments and men of goodwill to agree on at least a first outline of the ideals envisioned, an instrument that can be used to implement them.

(3109) We hope that the imperfections, even incoherences, of the proposed text will not make us lose sight of this generous intention and will not prevent legislators on the environment from drawing widely on all the substantial elements it contains. Its key point is the solemn affirmation of the responsibilities of States and individuals as regards the environment. We would have liked an even clearer formulation of this principle and we would have liked the underlying principle, recalled in Pope Paul VI's message, to be mentioned. The environment and resources are for everyone; they are the inalienable property of everyone, and there does not exist, over this universal property, any discretionary sovereignty exempting anyone from responsibility towards the humanity of today and tomorrow.

(3110) We also regret a certain ambiguity in the text as regards the notion of development. We said above how we conceived the relationship between development and environment, but such a conception holds good only if development means the complete promotion of man, comprising his highest aspirations. By saying this, we do not mean to suggest that the Declaration should have introduced, unduly, some contested philosophical or religious thesis, but that it should set the problems both of the environment and of development in their true dimensions. Those who prepared the Conference became increasingly aware of these dimensions. Rarely do international documents appeal so much to ethics, will-power, courage and clearsightedness. We would have liked to find a more explicit echo of this precious realization in the affirmations of the Declaration, rather than the mention contained in the draft of the Preamble.

(3111) Without expatiating further, we will recall in connection with principle 21 the strong statements in the Pope's Message about armaments and war: the text proposed is in full agreement with the spirit that dictated them. Finally, after it has been repeated so often that the worst of pollutions is want and that those in greatest need suffer most from deteriorations in the environment, one would have expected to see them mentioned - these underprivileged people - with greater emphasis in what is presented to us, at least for now, as the Charter of the environment. If this text comes to the knowledge of the inhabitants of shanty towns, workers in exhausting and degrading conditions, innocent victims of wars and conflicts, will they be satisfied with an affirmation as general as the one in Principle 6 on the relationship between development and the environment? You will understand that our Delegation, however much it wishes to respect compromises reached with great difficulty, hopes that this silence will be corrected one day.

(3112) The speakers who preceded me have described in varying degrees of detail the activities and plans of their Governments as regards the environment. The Holy See, in view of its particular nature and the tiny territory of the State of Vatican City, cannot draw up any environmental programme properly speaking. Nevertheless, it takes an active interest in one sector. This interest is expressed in concrete achievements to which you will allow me to refer briefly, in conclusion. The different territories that make up the State of Vatican City or come under its jurisdiction for different reasons, possess, in proportion to their extent, a unique cultural and artistic patrimony. Aware of its mission of administering this patrimony for the benefit of the whole of mankind, the Holy See feels responsible for the delicate problems which the increasing deterioration of the environment creates for monuments and works of art. The Department of the Vatican Museums has entrusted its own scientific research laboratories with the task of studying this damage and these threats. These laboratories are constantly carrying out treatments to reconstitute and protect the items affected. To quote only one example, the Vatican Laboratories have developed an electrochemical treatment for bronzes which reduces the effects of corrosion and restores its original grain to the metal. The success of these methods can be seen in their application to Donatello's bronzes, in Padua; to Philaret's door at St. Peter's Basilica; to the Byzantine door of St. Paul's Basilica. On 23 May last, you will remember, there occurred in St. Peter's Basilica an attack on one of the most famous pieces of the artistic heritage common to mankind, Michelangelo's "Pietà". Our competent services set to work at once and those in charge of them were able to announce, on the basis of delicate analyses and a study of the fragments collected, that it would be possible to repair the statue almost completely. This restoration will be due to modern techniques and to the degree of efficiency and precision that can be attained today. Allow me to see in this a symbol of what mankind can expect from wise policies for the environment. For if the facts established in this connection impose heavy responsibility on our civilization, its scientific resources, together with nature's power of regeneration, give us the right to advance with optimism, now that we recognize the harm that has been done, and we are boldly preparing to redress it.

(3113) If the International Community takes this path at Stockholm, the work of the Secretary-General and his collaborators, to whom I am happy to express once more the deep esteem of the Holy See, will find its best justification and highest reward. The Swedish Government will have the honour of having initiated the enterprise by suggesting it in the first place, and then by contributing with generous hospitality to ensuring its first implementation. Personally, we are happy to have the privilege of taking part in it under your enlightened chairmanship.

3. GIVE FUTURE GENERATION A HEALTHY ENVIRONMENT

Message of His Holiness Paul VI on the occasion of the Fifth World Day of the Environment. The Vatican, 5 June 1977.

Original: English (*)

"And God saw everything he had made and behold it was very good" (*Gen.* 1:31).

(3114) This ancient text, so simple and yet so profound, is a reminder to all of us today that the world we live in, this creation, is to be seen and embraced by all people in its totality as good: good because it is a gift from God: good because it is the environment in which all of us have been placed and in which we are called to live out our vocations in solidarity with one another.

(3115) In recent years there has arisen around the world an increasing awareness that "the environment essentially conditions man's life and development, while man, in his turn, perfects and ennobles his environment through his presence, work and contemplation" (Message to the Conference on the Environment, Stockholm, 1972. See above, par. 3094).

(3116) Because of this, it is very heartening to see the members of the United Nations setting aside a world-wide Environment Day so that people everywhere can take this opportunity to celebrate the good things of this earth and to share them more consciously and more equitably with all their brothers and sisters.

(3117) This consciousness of the environment around us is more pressing today than ever. For men who have the means and the ability to construct and ennoble the world about them can also destroy it and squander its goods. Human science and technology have made marvelous gains. But care must be taken that they are used to enhance human life and not to diminish it. Human effort has brought forth much wealth from the earth. But this wealth should not be squandered superfluously by a small minority nor selfishly hoarded for a few at the expense of the rest of mankind in need.

(3118) For these reasons, this day of celebration of the environment we live in should also be a day of appeal to all of us to be united as stewards of God's creation. It should be a day of rededication to the enterprise of preserving, improving and handing over to future generations a healthy environment in which every person is truly at home. (Cf. Message to the Conference on the Environment, Stockholm, 1972; above, par. 3094-3097).

(3119) The intent of such an appeal demands more than just a renewal of effort. It calls for a change of mentality, for a conversion of attitude and of practice so that the rich willingly use less and share the earth's goods more widely and more wisely. It calls for a simplicity of life style and a society that intelligently conserves rather than needlessly consumes. It calls finally for a universal sense of solidarity in which each person and every nation plays its proper and interdependent role to ensure an ecologically sound environment for people today, as well as for future generations.

(*) Insegnamenti di Paolo VI, Vol. XV (1977), 561-562.

(3120) "Everything created by God is good" wrote the apostle Paul. It is our earnest prayer that this Environment Day may be a time in which all people everywhere rejoice in the wisdom of that cry and commit themselves to a fraternal sharing and protection of good environment, the common patrimony of mankind.

B - DESERTIFICATION

Statement by H.E.Msgr. Agostino Cacciavillan, Apostolic Nuncio, Head of the Delegation of the Holy See, to the United Nations Conference on Desertification, held in Nairobi (Kenya) on 29 August-8 September 1977. Nairobi, 31 August 1977.

Original: English

(3121) From the very beginning, when the first announcement was made about this United Nations undertaking, the Holy See showed its special interest by submitting a preparatory statement. Its lively concern was reiterated by His Holiness Pope Paul VI during the audience he granted to Dr. Mostafa K. Tolba, Secretary-General of this conference, on 13 July last.

(3122) The problems of lands plagued by drought are not new to the Church. Within the framework of her missionary activity, the Church has often carried out, and continues to carry out, pioneering works in desert regions. His Excellency Mzee Jomo Kenyatta, President of the Republic of Kenya, in a Message of 14 July 1976, to the Association of Member Episcopal Conferences in Eastern Africa (AMECEA), said: "...in the dry and sometimes very remote areas of our country we find personnel of your Church teaching in humble schools, devotedly working in small dispensaries and maternity clinics, and even making the desert bloom with crops that never grew there before."

(3123) 1. At the time of the tragic drought which ravaged the Sahel and its neighbouring zones five years ago, the Church and her institutions were often among the first to sound the alarm and to start relief efforts. The initiatives taken on that occasion are now being submitted to critical evaluation by a Working Group in the Pontifical Council *Cor Unum* in order better to assess the perspective of development in emergency actions. It is, then, with great satisfaction that the Holy See - after the admirable effort of international solidarity to give immediate help to the victims of the catastrophe - views the holding of this Conference, which intends to examine the deep causes of such disasters and to prepare a broad strategy of action to combat the growing phenomenon of desertification. And so, the Holy See has charged me to convey its warmest encouragement and the assurance of its total support. It hopes that, in the light of the conclusions of this Conference, the Catholic relief agencies will be spurred on and better guided in the part - be it ever so modest - that they are resolved to play in such a necessary undertaking.

(3124) 2. Turning to the "Draft Plan of Action to Combat Desertification", permit me to express the Holy See profound appreciation of the impressive work which the preparation and subsequent elaboration of this document required. Various bodies of the Holy See have studied with care the different working papers; they note with satisfaction the high quality of the text which is now before us. The richness of the document is contained not only in its recommendations but also, and even more, in its detailed commentaries, which describe the measures to implement these recommendations and which form a compendium of actions to be launched for a decisive battle against desertification, its progression and its consequences for the peoples affected. The countries concerned will have to determine their priorities according to their most pressing needs and the available, though often limited, resources of personnel and material. I am happy to point out that the present text of the Draft Plan contains in Chapter III a set of recommendations and a description of the stages that are obligatory in any undertaking of this nature. These will be of great help in establishing options, which by their nature are extremely complex.

(3125) The project brings us face to face with a desolate, hostile and indeed vitiated environment that calls man to a struggle for domination according to the commandment of Genesis (*Gen.* 1:26-27, cf. *Gaudium et Spes*, 34). Man is the sole agent capable both of halting the advance of the desert, and of making things worse by unwise interventions. But in success or in failure, it is in the final analysis always man who benefits or suffers.

(3126) Looking at land affected by this process, the Church sees in the foreground man, who is sometimes a contributing cause to the process of desertification, and always a victim affected by it, and who, above all, is called to become the protagonist in the struggle against the desert.

(3127) Public attention has recently been directed in an unprecedented manner to the serious droughts that have taken the lives of numerous human beings. But one should not forget that even apart from tragic events, the man of the desert is always living in extreme hardship. His existence is precarious. The prevailing conditions of underdevelopment prevent him from effectively combating not only the advance of the desert, but also disease, hunger, poverty and ignorance, thus imprisoning him in a dramatic vicious circle.

(3128) In the spirit and with the concern of the Encyclical of Paul VI *Populorum Progressio*, whose tenth anniversary was recently celebrated, the Holy See and the entire Church cannot but feel highly pleased to see that priority is given in the Draft Plan of Action to the human dimension of the phenomenon of desertification: "All measures are to be primarily directed toward the well-being and development of the peoples affected by, or vulnerable to, desertification" (p.7,f); the struggle against desertification is considered part of a broad programme for promoting social and economic development; numerous detailed proposals are made for a great common effort to assist the man in the desert through material help and education.

(3129) Thus the Draft Plan considers financial and technical means, as well as education, counsel and training, in the fields of health, nutrition, livestock, vegetation, irrigation, the use of land and resources in general, settlements and resettlements, migration, drought, etc.

(3130) 3. Population problems deserve special attention, and have to be treated in the objective reality of their various aspects. They should be seen in the context of social justice which demands a more equal sharing of the resources of the earth and new efforts to provide aid and investments in favour of the less well-off. (cf. Address of Paul VI to the Secretary-General of the World Conference on Population, 28 March 1974. See above, par. 2684-2685). One entire section of the plan (Chapter II, C, nos. 39-52) is devoted to these questions under the title of "Population and the Human Condition". The text of Recommendation 8, gives the broad outlines of a population policy in the desert zones, including the maintenance of an adequate rural labour force, permanent settlement of the nomads, and provisions called for by the migratory movements. The text of the Recommendation itself is much more satisfactory and far more balanced than the paragraph which introduces it (no.39) and which seems to reduce the problem to a question of excessive demographic growth in the desert and subdesert zones. A generalization, such as this one, would require much more exhaustive analysis than the rather hasty affirmations in the following paragraph (no. 40) regarding the birth and death rates among nomads. On the other hand, one must concur with what Recommendation 10 states, that health care for these peoples ought to be intensified, better suited to their conditions, and made the object of sustained attention. With regard to measures taken at the time of, or in anticipation of, crises - touched upon in Recommendation 11 - care should be taken that the remedies chosen do not, in the long run, cause new difficulties. This is true not only in the case of the hasty transfer of peoples, but also when poorly planned and insufficiently spread out distribution points create the risk of unhealthy and irreversible concentrations of population.

(3131) Where the Draft fore sees the introduction of family planning among its health care proposals, the Delegation of the Holy See wishes to stress what is rightly recalled in no 44: the "parental right to decide on the number and spacing of their children". "The right to marriage and procreation" - as stated in the Encyclical *Populorum Progressio*, 37 - "is an inalienable right, without which there would be no human dignity. In the final instance, it is for the parents to decide on the number of children they wish to have, with full knowledge of all the circumstances, and having regard for their responsibility to God, to themselves, to the children they have already brought into the world and to the community to which they belong, following the dictates of their conscience enlightened by the law of God authentically interpreted, and supported by their confidence in Him" (cf. also *Gaudium et Spes*, 87).

(3132) 4. In line with ethical standards, respect is always due to the peoples involved, with regard to their social and behavioural patterns, their social and economic institutions, their traditional systems, and their indigenous science and technology. Such respect - based on adequate knowledge, which is the fruit of opportune studies and research - does not at all exclude advancement towards better forms of existence, or the promotion of a sound evolution of institutions and traditional systems. On the contrary, respect for man in his unique personality and his social milieu demands that efforts be made towards his steady advancement, but the changes that are necessary should be effected with his cooperation. This can only be achieved through education - an education adapted to existing conditions, and aimed at promoting the initiatives of peoples towards their own self-development.

(3133) Care must, therefore, be taken to exclude an abrupt change-over or a forceful intervention. Besides being a violation of the dignity of man in the desert, it would also be counterproductive of the true, gradual and lasting success of the great task which the United Nations is praiseworthily setting out to accomplish. Hence, a wise and definite national policy is necessary in the context of "community development", and of course it is primarily at this level that account must be taken of the requirements already mentioned. The Draft Plan devotes several particularly pertinent lines in regard to this subject in no. 22(b). Permit me, nevertheless, to insist on the following: the measures provided for or suggested by the Draft Plan - cattle raising, water management, respect for vegetation, the selection of crops - will never be realized in an enduring fashion if the smallest communities and their members do not assume responsibility for them with full awareness of their own true interests. This is in no way to minimize the role of the public powers, but indeed to guarantee their complete success through the acceptance by and the collaboration of the peoples concerned. The importance of a national commitment to the struggle against desertification is brought out well in the Draft Plan, and emphasis is rightly placed, among other things, on formal and informal education, on information and the formation of public opinion. The Holy See, in its preoccupation with the "ecology of the spirit", i.e. the spiritual and moral environment, expresses the hope that the content of this education and information process will always be compatible with ethical principles.

(3134) It is also necessary to emphasize the fact that there remains a great need for assistance, on both the national and local level, since we are often dealing with countries which, as the Draft Plan points out, do not have sufficient resources (p. 9), and which lack sufficient scientific and technological capabilities (p. 47).

(3135) Attention is also rightly directed by the Draft Plan to the regional dimension of the problem, proposing a whole series of measures eventually to be applied at that level, in the spirit of a much wider collaboration.

(3136) 5. Desertification, however, not only affects human life in the area where it occurs, but has consequences for the whole interlocking global ecosystem, creating dangers that threaten humanity in the short and long term. This gives another reason - apart from urgent assistance to the most needy - for international collaboration at the level of research and action between individual governments, various units of United Nations agencies, and governmental and non-governmental organizations. It is well known to what extent the Holy See encourages collaboration among peoples, because it firmly believes that all men and women are children of God and that they are all brothers and sisters.

(3137) May these reflections show the interest and support which the Holy See gives this Conference, for whose full success I express its best wishes. The Holy See hope that excellent results will derive from this Conference to the advantage of the peoples and nations most directly concerned, and for the material and spiritual progress of the whole human race.

C - WATER

Statement by H.E. Msgr. Pio Laghi, Apostolic Nuncio, Head of the Delegation of the Holy See, to the International Water Conference, held in Mar del Plata (Argentina) on 14-25 March 1977. Mar del Plata, 22 March 1977.

Original: Spanish

(3138) The Holy See has accepted the invitation to participate in the United Nations Conference on Water in the conviction that the Conference represents - in the words of its Secretary-General - "an indispensable stepping-stone to a better life".

(3139) In recent years increasing attention has been paid to water, which is the quintessential ingredient of life and such a fundamental part to our environment. Much is now being done to curb former large-scale misuse of this vital element, but there remains a great need for harmonizing human activities with the preservation of our natural heritage for posterity.

(3140) We are convinced, also, that a study of water on the scale contemplated by the Conference must inevitably include the total environmental context and the dynamic ecological interrelationship between water and man. Questions of water are inseparable from those of development and we are all aware that the true significance of development lies in the contribution it makes to man and to the alleviation of the daily difficulties of the most needy.

(3141) Since water has a considerable impact upon the life and well-being of man and on his livelihood - in the Middle East water is called "sister of the soul" - human considerations must consequently outweigh all others in the efforts to provide community water supplies, especially to the rural world where hundreds of millions still live mostly without it.

(3142) The Holy See Delegation wishes to emphasize also that access to a sufficient supply of water for all individuals, families and communities is a matter of justice. Very few of those who have only to run the tap to get as much safe water as they want realize that - according to statistics - more than 80% of the world population does not as yet have access to a public water supply. Only 20% enjoy this privilege. Even then such supply is often defective, either in quantity or in quality or in both. A little less than half the urban dwellers of the world have their house connected to a communal piped system, while others are served by reasonably close public water stand-pipes.

(3143) In a new world based on distributive justice, development objectives must be man-centered and intended primarily to give him dignity and a better way of life through access, as a minimum, to those natural resources which it is his human right to have.

(3144) Church related programs of assistance have always given a paramount importance to water. They have been motivated not so much by the fact that since time immemorial water has played a most fundamental function in all symbolic and religious rites, but above all by the promise of Christ, that not even a glass of fresh water given in His name will remain without recompense. At the end we shall be judged for having shared, or refused to share, our bread with the hungry, our water with the thirsty, our dwelling with the homeless brother.

(3145) It is in the light of these centuries-old convictions that one should evaluate the contributions made by Church-related organizations in promoting and financing programs of assistance in this sector in various parts of the world, as it is documented in the paper presented by the Holy See to this Conference (Doc. E/CONF.70/TP61 and Add. 1). The document is a synopsis containing a concise description of the policies and programmes of several organizations in their large and small projects.

(3146) The help of experts - often so precious - can at times be less useful than one would wish, when superspecialists recommend extremely costly and complicated projects, without considering, for instance, that sometimes a first modest step represents an enormous progress in certain areas. We find enlightening, for the problem of water which we are considering, a statement by Pope Paul VI in his Encyclical *Populorum Progressio*, where it is said that for an authentic progress are not only necessary technicians in ever greater number, but also deep thinkers, seeking after a new humanism where man will be allowed to discover himself by assuming the superior values of love, friendship, prayer and contemplation.

(3147) Nor it is possible for a super-bureaucrat to define at his desk immediate solutions to the problems of all rural areas and urban slums of the world. We like to state, that in our view, the solutions must be sought on a smaller scale, beginning with an adequate education, without, however, loosing sight of the need to program comprehensive solutions to the water problems of a country or a region.

(3148) And we think it is important to restate what is already obvious to all the Delegates, that man is the fundamental subject of all the concerns and cares of the community in its assistance projects. Water is only the object of our interest: a "means", an element, indeed indispensible, to assist man in reaching for his integral development.

(3149) Nor should development be just alms, or a gift, offered to a brother less well provided; to the contrary, with great sensitivity, every man must be brought to participate with his own work, within all reasonable limits, in his own advancement, and thus to fulfill the ancient saying that "Each one must by his efforts be the author of his own redemption". In this way, and only in this way, the programmes which are planned will reach the proposed goal.

(3150) Among the grave problems which require immediate attention by the international community, we must mention the until now unresolved difficulties posed by the transporting, storing and disposing of radioactive waste. According to a recent publication, it will take 25 thousand years for these materials to lose half of their radioactivity. It is imperative to face this tremendous problem and assure ways of adopting adequate safeguards in protecting water sources from such contamination.

(3151) It will also be necessary to furnish a response to the proposal stated by the United Nations Conference on Human Settlements, to provide "pure water to the whole world by 1990". Mindful of the saying "When you drink water, think of its springs", we shall certainly not alleviate the sufferings of the thirsty simply by thinking and reflecting on the sources of this precious element, but we shall perhaps increase our sensitivity to their needs, awaken to the human dimension of the problems and enhance our capacity to solve them.

(3152) With the decision makers of the world's nations, we are aware of our collective responsibility for finding effective solutions to the problems of the world's poor. The Conference's true significance lies in the contribution it can and must make towards raising the living standards of the masses, especially of developing countries, through improvement in their water resources and supply.

(3153) In connection with the suggestion for the promotion of educational programmes that will provide for active public participation and emphasize the value and the scarcity of water in the urban, rural and industrial areas - as it has been recommended in the documents and resolutions of the Vancouver Conference on the Human Habitat - the Holy See wishes to reaffirm her readiness to cooperate in promoting all initiatives aimed at publicizing the objective of the Conference, calling at the same time for the cooperation of the non-governmental relief and assistance organizations at all levels.

(3154) We assure you of the willingness of the Church's organizations - whose purpose include human development - to cooperate fully in the various sectors pertaining to water. These organizations will be delighted to seize the opportunity to continue to serve the International Community, within the sphere of their competences, "with disinterestedness, humility and love" (Paul VI, Address to the United Nations General Assembly, 4 October 1965. See above, par. 5).

(3155) In conclusion, our Delegation is convinced that by keeping the human dimension as the ethical mainspring of its deliberations, in addition to its scientific and technological considerations, the Conference will direct its efforts to the heart of the problem, and the world will be much richer for its findings.

D - ENERGY

Address of His Holiness John XXIII to the United Nations Conference on New Sources of Energy. The Vatican, 28 August 1961.

Original: French (*)

(3156) We are very grateful for the kind visit which you have paid to us during the United Nations Conference on New Sources of Energy which has brought you together in Rome from so many different countries and at which you have been working all these days.

(3157) Your visit demonstrates to us that, apart from the scientific and technical aspect of your learned research, you are also aware of the human, moral and spiritual aspect which it assumes by the very fact of being focussed on man and his genuine well-being.

(3158) The Creator has bestowed abundant energy on the world, and over the ages man has applied his genius to harnessing and using it for his needs. But in our times, in what may be called the technical age of man, the possible uses of energy are increasing enormously: not only energy of the "traditional" kind but also energy which comes from sources which have so far been used little or not at all, such as the sun or the wind or even the waters and vapours hidden in the bowels of the earth: solar energy, wind energy, geothermal energy.

(3159) Your discussions will focus on these new possibilities, not so much in order to consider the abstract principles as to draw up an inventory of existing concrete achievements in various regions of the universe which may be applied with success elsewhere.

(3160) And you are concerned above all, we know, with the well-being of mankind and you wish in particular to help the peoples of the underdeveloped countries, whose enormous needs constitute today a ceaseless appeal to all men of feeling.

(3161) On many occasions, and most recently at considerable length in the Encyclical *Mater et Magistra* on the social question, we exhorted our sons of the Catholic Church, and with them all men of good will, to show a greater awareness of their duties towards these less favoured brothers.

(3162) We feel, in fact, an intimate and profound satisfaction at the thought that your work, generously focussed on serving the poorest, will also contribute to this "great work of mercy". People will rightly praise you for it and - what is even more important - God will reward you: for whoever works for the good of his brothers in a nobly selfless spirit gives glory to God and gains His grace.

(3163) Indeed, does not your work keep you in constant contact with His almightiness? Are not the still deeply mysterious forces which you are investigating His work? True men of science - as experience teaches - easily recognize the immensity of the Creator and are quite ready to practice Christian humility. They practice with simplicity and uprightness this "fear of the Lord" - *timor Domini* - which the Holy Scriptures never cease to praise and which they teach everyone is the alpha and omega of true wisdom. This very morning, during the reading of the Breviary and while Our spirit was already moving among you, We came on these words so full of meaning and en-

---

(*) Discorsi Messaggi e Colloqui del Santo Padre Giovanni XXIII, Vol. III (28 Ottobre 1960 - 28 Ottobre 1961), 390-392.

couragement from the book of Ecclesiasticus, which We would like to leave with you in conclusion: "*Corona sapientiae timor Domini*: Wisdom's garland is fear of the Lord, with blossoms of peace and perfect health. Knowledge and full understanding she showers down; she heightens the glory of those who possess her. (...) If you desire wisdom, keep the commandments and the Lord will bestow her upon you" (*Sirach*, 1:16-17 and 23).

(3164) We could not formulate a better wish for you at the end of your kind visit. And it is with all Our heart that, as We assure you again of the pleasure that it has given Us, We call down God's best blessings on you, on your work, on your families and on the countries which you represent.

E - SEA

1. Statement of H.E. Msgr. Antonio Del Giudice, Apostolic Nuncio in Venezuela, Head of the Delegation of the Holy See, to the First Session of the Third Conference of the United Nation on the Law of the Sea, held in Caracas (Venezuela) on 12 June-29 August 1974. Caracas. 12 July 1974.

Original: English

(3165) The Holy See is deeply aware of the importance of the subject under consideration, and in particular of the complex problems inseparably connected with it. A rapid survey of some of these matters may not be out of place.

(3166) Of special concern is the rapidity with which technology is making possible the utilization of ocean spaces, at ever increasing depths, for military purposes. Even the ocean floor can be measured in this way. Experimental nuclear explosions, for instance, always carry with them the frightening possibility of widespread destruction of the marine ecosystem, Equally frightening and unthinkable is the prospect that the ocean floor be turned into a launching pad for missiles with atomic warheads and that the sea become the hunting-ground of increasing numbers of submarines bearing nuclear weapons. We are aware that there exists a Treaty prohibiting the emplacement of nuclear weapons on the sea bed and the ocean floor, but this Treaty does not prohibit their use for a variety of other military purposes, such as bases for nuclear submersibles. The stark terror that this prospect holds must catalyze the nations into inscribing, into whatever treaty or agreement results from this conference, exclusion of the sea to all but peaceful uses.

(3167) The sea is the last considerable patrimony belonging to mankind, with a potential of resources that may well be decisive for mankind's very future. There arises, inevitably, the crucial question: are the enormous benefits to be drawn from the sea at the disposal of all nations without discrimination, or are they the exclusive claim of the rich nations which have the means of actually winning those benefits? The problem is an urgent one, for the swift pace of technology has suddenly confronted the world with new questions regarding the sea, its bed and subsoil, questions that require a thorough airing in the interest of the economic, political and environmental concerns of individual States and of the common-wealth of nations as a whole.

(3168) The urgency of these problems, and their impact on the present and future well-being of all the peoples, impels the Holy See to take a profound interest in this Conference, as an expression of its dedication to the service of all mankind.

(3169) The United Nations has already, in its twenty-fifth General Assembly, moved a considerable way towards establishing the principles that ought to guide this Conference: "The sea bed and subsoil, together with their resources, form part of the "common heritage of mankind" to be explored and exploited for the benefit of mankind as a whole, irrespective of geographical location of States, whether landlocked or coastal, and taking into particular consideration the interests and needs of the developing countries".

(3170) This concept has the strong support of the Catholic Church, as may be seen from her social teaching. Pope John XXIII in his Encyclical *Mater et Magistra* stated: "According to the plan of creation, the goods of the earth are above all destined for the worthy support of all human beings" [AAS 53(1961), p.430].

(3171) To the Secretary-General of the United Nations International Conference on the Environment Pope Paul wrote: "No one can take possession in an absolute and selfish way of the environment, which is not a "res nullius" - something not belonging to anyone - but the "res omnium" - the patrimony of mankind, so that those in possession of it - men in private or public life - must use it in a way that redounds to the real advantage of everyone... For this reason the care of offering everyone the possibility of access to a fair share in the resources, both existing or potential, of our planet must weigh particularly on the conscience of men of good will" [AAS 64(1972), p.445. See above, par. 3099-3100].

(3172) Recently Pope Paul VI in his message to the Secretary-General of the United Nations on the occasion of the Special Session of the General Assembly in April of this year said: "Through the good will of all, the riches of this world must serve the true benefit of all - as they were indeed destined by the Creator who, in His bountiful providence, has put them at the disposal of the whole of mankind" [Message to Dr. Kurt Waldheim, 4 April 1974, AAS 66(1974), p.283. See above, par. 1388].

(3173) One of the major tasks entrusted to the common effort of the Nations to come to a concrete under-standing of what constitutes this common patrimony with regard to the sea, the sea bed and its subsoil It also seems that the world community will have to agree that, just as absolutely open seas without control can lead only to ultimate disaster for all, so also an absolute control of wide waters by coastal States is an inadequate solution to humanity's common claims to their use, to protection from pollution and to safeguarding marine ecology. The Conference will have to weigh the interest of the whole of mankind, giving just consideration to the rights and needs of the landlocked States, coastal States poor in offshore resources, the developing nations as a whole, all other States and generations to come.

(3174) It will be for the world community to work out, indeed to create, a new jurisprudence that will give proper weight to the claims of individual States and to those of the world community itself, taking into account the universal destination of the riches of this earth as intended by its Creator.

(3175) The fitting pursuit and effective realization of the universal common good require of the community of nations that it organize itself in a manner suited to these present responsibilities. This goal undoubtedly requires the progressive establishment of some form of universal public authority, acknowledged as such by all and endowed with the power necessary to safeguard, on behalf of all, security, regard for justice and respect for rights (cf. Second Vatican Council, *Gaudium et Spes*, nn. 82-84).

(3176) Some might consider this ideal as a utopian vision. Indeed, the establishing of a world authority is no easy process and the full achievement of this goal might still be far off. And yet, is it not also true that nothing great has ever been achieved except by the persevering and inspired action of men and peoples with vision who dare to take a few small steps at a time? This Conference, we believe, can take such a step.

(3177) As we review the issues at stake, it is clear that the heads of States who have agreed to the present Conference, and the govern-mental and international experts who must seek solutions, have assumed great responsibilities before men. To all of them we would recall the words which Pope Paul VI addressed to them once before at the conclusion of his Encyclical *Populorum Progressio*: "Delegates to international organizations, it depends on you to see that the dangerous and futile rivalry of powers should give place to collaboration which is friendly, peaceful and free of vested interests, in order to achieve a responsible development of mankind, in which all men will have an opportunity to find their fulfillment" [No. 84, AAS 59(1967), p. 298).

(3178) Specifically, as they address themselves to these new problems, with new conflicts of rights and a new need for world authority, their efforts must be imbued with a sense of the urgent need to seek "a justice that is less and less imperfect" (*Octogesima Adveniens*, no. 22). Likewise, all narrow national egoism should be put aside, as Pope Paul VI said to the Special Session of the United Nations on Natural Resources and Development held in April of this year: "Nations are often blinded by egoism and prevented from seeing how their own true interests are compatible with the interests of other States and coincide with the general good of the human family as a whole" (cf. also *Octogesima Adveniens*, no. 46).

(3179) We are confident that the "forward-looking imagination" of this Conference and its "courage to revise existing systems and institutions" (*Octogesima Adveniens*, nos 42 and 52) will bring forth a new Law of the Sea, offering to all of mankind greater justice and a more stable peace.

2. Statement by Msgr. Silvio Luoni, Head of the Delegation of the Holy See, to the Seventh Session of the Third United Nations Conference on the Law of the Sea, held in Geneva (Switzerland) on 28 March-19 May 1978. Geneva, 5 May 1978.

Original: French

(3180) The attendance of the Holy See at the Conference on the Law of the Sea, convened for the purpose of establishing legal norms for the use of the sea, which cover four-fifths of our planet, is a confirmation of the international character of the Holy See itself. Exactly on account of this characteristic, the Holy See anxiously looks toward the adoption of measures capable of guaranteeing the common good as such, that is the peace of the international community.

(3181) The problem is that of abolishing existing injustices and of removing possible causes of future injustices. The contribution which the Holy See can make to the Conference does not contain proposals of a technical nature, but rather the enunciation of principles which can guarantee just and balanced solutions for the whole international community, and first of all, the statement of that tenet universally accepted, at least in theory, that the sea is "a common heritage of all mankind".

(3182) Moreover, this principle is part of the wider concept of the "universal purpose of creation". It has already been applied to the States in regard to their own national territory, not as a restriction to their sovereignty, but for the exploitation and use of their natural resources in such a fashion as to take into account the needs of all mankind and, especially, of that part of mankind belonging to States with limited resources. It is the principle of justice among nations, which is universally accepted like the one of justice among individuals.

(3183) For these reasons, the Holy See delegation cannot hide its uneasiness when faced with the tendency, emerging more and more at each session of the Conference, whereby the delegates press charges on the use of the sea, which are in open contradiction with the above-mentioned principles, and even try to justify them with an inadmissible legal concept, particularly when they invoke the "consuetudinary" quality of certain practices. In fact consuetudinary law does not establish a legal foundation, especially when it is recognized by only one segment of the international community. It could certainly guide toward the formulation of rules of law, but only on condition that it be critically examined in the light of ethical and legal principles.

(3184) Under certain circumstances, the rejection of existing norms is all the more necessary inasmuch as a notable evolution of the world economic situation has taken place and more refined analyses have clearly shown the injustices of the present system: hence the need to define the "New Economic Order".

(3185) Why would this Conference miss the unique opportunity of providing with the Law of the Sea the foundation to the New Economic Order?

(3186) This is at the same time a requirement and an appeal. Will this Conference have sufficient imagination, understanding and courage to lay the foundation for a legislation on the sea that will be based upon the same principles upon which the assembled States are building their concept of a New Economic Order, namely, above all, the abolition of the claim to ownership of natural resources by those countries privileged by their geographical location, and the equitable distribution of resources among peoples, in accordance with their need?

(3187) In the light of the above observations, the Holy See has formulated the following considerations.

(3188) The fact that the sea is "a common heritage of all mankind" does not imply at all that the sea must be administered on a joint basis, but only that its exploitation must be conducted in accordance with the interests of all the States which make up the international community. In this regard, the principle of the delimitation of sea areas adjacent to the shores of countries as economic zones entrusted to them, would seem acceptable, since a collective sovereignty is not applicable. On the other hand, however, a strictly interpreted claim to the resources living in those zones contiguous to the coastal countries is inadmissable, because such resources are not *"res nullius"* (nobody's property), but belong to the inter-national community and, moreover, the principle of "being contiguous" on which that claim is founded does not offer a sufficient basis for acceptance.

(3189) This idea of delimitation of sea areas adjacent to the coast-lines was born of a legitimate desire to satisfy the needs of some coastal States and to put an end to unlawful exploitation of the sea. However, such concept, even with its justification, cannot be interpreted simply in a geometric and uniform fashion, but rather by taking into account the geographical, physical and biological differences of such areas, as well as the various degrees of social and economic development of the coastal States, while not overlooking the needs of those countries which are not adjacent to the sea.

(3190) Consequently, the jurisdiction of the coastal States on the economic zones must be subjected to notable restrictions, such as are already - in what pertains to the migration of fish - generally accepted for the sea areas adjacent to the coast and even more for the economic zones.

(3191) It would seem logical to affirm that such restrictions on sovereignty apply also to the resources living in an economic area. That means that the coastal States with an abundance of living resources have the duty to share them with other States, particularly the less fortunate, and therefore that the latter acquire some rights on these resources.

(3192) According to all the above, the criterion of distribution and its actual realization must not depend upon the discretionary powers or the good will of coastal States, but be ensured by detailed provisions of law which can withstand the controversies that could ensue.

(3193) These are some of the considerations which the Holy See delegation submits to the members of this Conference, with the wish that the Conference may reach those goals of equity and universality which are at the basis of an eventual International Convention on the Law of the Sea.

3. Statement of H.E. Archbishop Giovanni Cheli, Apostolic Nuncio, Head of the Delegation of the Holy See, to the Eleventh Session of the Third United Nations Conference on the Law of the Sea, held in New York on 8 March-30 April 1982. New York, 31 March 1982.

Original: English

(3194) In his Message to the 34th session of the General Assembly of the United Nations, Pope John Paul II said: "Since...material goods by their very nature provoke conditionings and divisions, the struggle to obtain these goods becomes inevitable in the history of humanity." And he added: "If we cultivate this one-sided subordination of man to material goods alone, we shall be incapable of overcoming this state of need." But he did not stop on this material aspect which is divisive, and he brought out the spiritual dimension of human existence and of goods which "does not divide people but puts them into communication with each other, associates them and unites them." (2 October 1979, no. 16. See above, par. 92)

(3195) Based on this vision of humanity and of the world, the Delegation of the Holy See wishes to contribute to the advancement of this communication, of this concrete association, and of this union of efforts for the good of all: herein lies the irreplaceable condition for the establishment of a Convention on the important question that unites us, and such a Convention, in return, will serve the wider cause of peace, will strengthen the common will to answer the challenges which war, poverty, and ignorance thrust before all nations. At this moment when we have come to the end of a long journey and we have only to surmount the last obstacles, it is useful to situate our particular task in a renewed awareness of the overall mission of the United Nations, which is to bring about the union of efforts for the service of greater international justice.

(3196) With other delegations, we have followed with interest all the sessions and their laborious negotiations, and we made our own appropriate contribution. It is not our responsibility to propose technical and financial solutions. However, the Holy See wishes to draw the attention of this Assembly to the hope which the Conference on the Law of the Sea represents as an example of peaceful labor and as an original, innovative institutional structure capable of contributing effectively to the birth of a more generous and more just international community.

(3197) The third Conference on the Law of the Sea, after ten years of work, is a powerful symbol of an international society in the process of organization. The draft of this great international Convention is ambitious because it proposes to make all that is related to maritime zones, and everything linked to them the object of a large consensus. The creation of the Seabed Authority is a vast innovation among existing juridical structures. Six years ago, the Holy See welcomed this proposal with interest and gave it support as an instrument enabling unity among all Nations in a common effort to manage all resources destined for all of humanity, especially for the poorest.

(3198) In its own way, the Conference on the Law of the Sea contributes to the birth of a legal system adapted to the problems of our times. In this light, our first concern must be to act so that the institution to be born favors a convergence of interests. The viability of the Authority will result from its internal coherence and its ability to resolve problems arising from the necessity of achieving the convergence of the interests of all parties. The search for such a convergence should be concerned with the future and with the future of the projected institution. This latter is called to be the expression of the highest principles of organization of the international community for the purpose of the solution of an important concrete problem. Its success will reinforce these principles and its future decisions will reveal their richness. The authority can and should be a precious instrument to manifest clearly the universal purpose of the goods of the earth and to serve that same goal. The new institution, like others, will allow, with the participation of all, the management of important resources with a view to contributing to the survival and the development of a great number of men, women and children. The anxiety for their fate must stimulate our efforts to arrive at a necessary compromise. It is true that the newness of this institution, its unique character in history, means that it will find its stability only in the exercise of its mission. That is why the establishment of this ambitious project requires a profound examination, and its implementation an exceptional sense of responsibility. By means of and beyond the immediate goal of the Law of the Sea, there is here an exceptional opportunity to assure for the United Nations that revival of favor in the world public opinion which the organization needs to fill its mission, now more indispensable than ever.

(3199) Let us, then, keep present to our minds: the occasion which is offered to us to do something new; the goal of the projected institution in the frame of the development of humanity; the way to follow which is that of convergence. At this grave moment in international life, we do not have the right to fail. The final realization of the objectives clearly fixed for the future at this Conference require of all those responsible parties, along with a legitimate preoccupation for respective national interest, a clear and generous awareness of the interest of the entire humanity. Men and women expect from the third Law of the Sea Conference those deeds which awaken hope because they constitute progress along the paths of wisdom and of peace.

F - OUTER SPACE

1. Message of His Holiness Paul VI to the Conference on the Peaceful Use of Outer Space. The Vatican, 6 August 1968.

Original: French (*)

(3200) At a time when, for the first time in the history of the world, an International Conference is meeting on the exploration and peaceful use of outer space, we greet with feeling the highly qualified delegates from all the participating nations. We desire to offer them our best wishes as they begin their work and assure them of the profound interest with which the Catholic Church will follow its course.

(3201) With the exploration and utilization of outer space it can be said that human life is acquiring a kind of new dimension. Thanks to artificial satellites, which will probably continue to multiply and improve even further, hitherto unsuspected possibilities are now opening up before men and peoples for the transmission of knowledge and information in all fields; this is a new road which is opening up and it may prove to be enormously speedy and effective as a means of progress in education, cultural exchanges and inter-national assistance; it is perhaps - God wishes it! - a herald of the imminent collapse of the barriers which still impede peaceful relations among certain social and national groups, a sign of a forthcoming era of sincere cooperation among all the nations of the globe, a turning-point - and perhaps a decisive one - in mankind's anguished march towards peace.

(3202) Although the Church is not competent to give an opinion on the technical and scientific aspects of the exploration of space, it is nevertheless directly interested in the educational, cultural, moral and social consequences which will flow from this sudden expansion of the scope of human activity. It is concerned that the enormous progress in space technology, which the world has witnessed with admiration for some years now, should be put to the service of peace and the common welfare of mankind. And it believes that, by giving a timely reminder of the principles of moral and spiritual order so often proclaimed by Sovereign Pontiffs in recent years, it can make also in this field a useful contribution to the true good of society.

(3203) For it is clear to any impartial observer that forgetfulness or transgression of moral rules would have particularly serious consequences in this area. If, for example, the benefits of the use of outer space should be put, in disregard of justice, to the profit of only one group of nations to the exclusion of the others; if the free circulation of information should produce the uncontrolled propagation of false news; if the increased transmission facilities became an instrument for ideological propaganda tending to spread subversion, stir up hatred, perpetuate racial discrimination and set peoples or social classes against each other instead of uniting them: who can fail to see that the recent and marvellous discoveries of science would then turn against man and work for his unhappiness rather than his happiness?

(3204) It has often been noted that scientific and technical progress is not always followed by comparable progress in morality, law and international cooperation. Yet, remarkable efforts have already been made and we sincerely wish to pay a tribute to them. A Treaty was concluded last year which defines the principles governing the activities of States in the exploration and use of space. This is a first step, to which the Holy See has given its support and which the Church wel-

(*) AAS 60(1968), 570-572.

comes. But the Church, without exceeding the limits of its mission, thinks that it can draw the attention of persons in authority to the urgent need for progress along this road. There must be no delay in drafting a whole body of "space law" to coordinate and discipline initiatives in these matters; any forthcoming conquests of science - and science is advancing swiftly - must already find in place the legal framework and the institutional arrangements to ensure that these conquests will be used for the common good and protected against abuse.

(3205) If this done the space age will advance in order and not in confusion and rivalry. If this is done it will benefit all peoples and not just the privileged few. We are thinking, in particular, of those whose low level of cultural and economic development has kept them, up till now, in an invidious and unjust state of inferiority and who now see opening up before them opportunities for rapid progress along the roads of educational and cultural development. Using for their benefit the resources offered by the exploration of outer space means working simultaneously for the advancement of mankind, for justice and for peace.

(3206) These are the wishes and recommendations which we make bold to put forward at the opening of the first United Nations Conference on the Exploration and Use of Outer Space. With all our heart we call down on its organizers and on all those who will take part in its work God's most abundant blessings.

2. Statement by Msgr. Mario Peressin, Head of the Delegation of the Holy See, to the 2nd United Nations Conference on the Exploration and Peaceful use of Outer Space, held in Vienna on 9-21 August 1982. Vienna, 10 August 1982.

Original: French

(3207) The Holy See is fully aware of the importance and the complexity of the questions studied by this Conference. On the one hand, the progress of humanity, of science and of technology in the conquest of outer space can be brought to light, and, on the other, many questions are addressed to the ethical, juridical human conscience.

(3208) 1. Today the conquest of space fascinates public opinion less than at its beginnings. And yet, when we think about it, what a fantastic scientific and technological adventure has gone on for the entire duration of the last decade!

(3209) The arrival of satellites is going to shape the future of our societies. In the domain of intercontinental telecommunications, the Intelsat system has continued its expansion at two levels, one, of ground stations and the other, of spatial segment, allowing the development of television circuits and thousands of telephone circuits. The arrival of geostationary satellites has been instrumental in meteorology. The use of satellites for navigation is making remarkable progress. Satellites for remote sensing have provided valuable information in agriculture (notably harvest forecasting), cartography, hydro-geology, forestry development and marine resources etc. What does the decade which has just begun hold for us?

(3210) On February 7, 1971, before the *Angelus*, Paul VI did not hesitate to express in a lyrical meditation his enthusiasm for the success of the Apollo 14 mission with the landing of its extraordinary lunar vehicle; he cried out: "What is man, this atom of the universe, not capable of! Honors to man, to thought, to science, to technology, to work, to human boldness. Honors to the synthesis that man knows how to make between science and its implementation, and, different from all the other animals, knows how to give instruments of conquest to human intelligence and hands. Honors to man, ruler of the earth and of the skies."

(3211) In his eyes, even a fundamental anthropological requirement characterized this remarkable scientific and technological accomplishment; more precisely: "Man sees reflected in himself its invisible mystery, the immortal spirit, and obeys the natural destiny pushing it to progress. No vain ambition, but the response to the vocation of being."

(3212) Could this not be, however, an excessive enthusiasm? Wouldn't the conquest of space bring the most powerful States and the scientific community to forget our fundamental human problems (the tragedy of poverty and of hunger for the hundreds of millions of human beings, the scourge of unemployment which spreads more and more in industrial society without forgetting the chronic under-employment in the poor countries, etc)? Wouldn't it be necessary first to make a great effort to resolve these tragic problems? Isn't the conquest of space perhaps a costly, useless luxury as well as a dangerous diversion?

(3213) The objection is pertinent if we turn it around. Examination of the facts in no way allows consideration of outer space conquest as a costly, useless luxury. Quite on the contrary, the very interest of humanity makes it essential to continue. And it is precisely humanity which asks the decisive question in a new light: capable of such scientific and technological feats, why would not contemporary humanity be capable, if it so desired, of solving the great problems of employment and of sharing of resources? What would be necessary is only a very strong sense of solidarity and a strong desire to implement it at the national and international levels.

(3214) 2. Alas, these magnificent perspectives are darkened by the transfer of our military confrontations into space. At the time when there were still only two thousand satellites, more than half were estimated to be for military purposes. The fraction grows larger each year. It is true that the greatest part of their missions is not directly for "destruction" but for "detection" (telecommunications, electronic eavesdropping, reconnaissance, remote sensing, and alert). Unfortunately, during these recent years, missions to intercept satellites have appeared. And it is not without reason that satellites loaded with nuclear devices are being discussed. From a technological point of view, the range of "killer" satellites could be enlarged. Sensational newspapers are not the only ones to describe space as the "battlefield of the future". The possibility is even more serious since military preoccupations have, until now, played an essential role in the considerable effort which has been spent for space conquest. Isn't it evident that it is vital to avoid this for the peace of the world and in the very interest of the great powers?

(3215) Reaction in this direction is essential, especially since the use of space for military purposes is absolutely contrary to the stipulations of the Treaty (1967) on Principles Governing the Activities of States in the Exploration and Use of Outer Space, including the Moon and Other Celestial Bodies. Not only does its preamble affirm "the common interest of all mankind in the progress of the exploration and use of outer space for peaceful purposes", but further, its article 4 prescribes that "the Moon and the other celestial bodies shall be used by all States Parties exclusively for peaceful purposes." It even specifies that "States Parties to the Treaty commit themselves not to place in orbit around the Earth any objects carrying nuclear weapons or any other kinds of weapons of mass destruction, install such weapons on celestial bodies, or station weapons in outer space in any other manner." Article 3 specifies the extension of international law, including the Charter of the United Nations, into space: in particular, this means forbidding "the threat or use of force" (art.2, par.4 of the Charter).

(3216) The prescriptions of international law are clear. Naturally, it is important to settle the details and adapt a system of guaranties and of verification. Already, article 12 of the Treaty on Outer Space takes a step in that direction when it specifies that "all the stations, installations, equipment and space vehicles on the Moon or other celestial bodies shall be open to representatives of other States parties to the Treaty..." However, since this accessibility is not expected for stations and vehicles outside of the celestial bodies, and since every treaty must be interpreted in a restrictive way, the existence of spy satellites is not surprising.

(3217) Certainly, it can be objected that article 11 of the said Treaty imposes a general obligation to inform about the "activities in outer space". But, it is expected that this is only "to the greatest extent feasible and practicable..." Practically, such a reserve leaves the field open to the concerned States. A much more efficient international verification would have to be anticipated, for example, with a system of observers like that organized by the Treaty on the Antarctic.

(3218) Hypothetically, as a young American asked, "there ought not to be any reason why the nations of the world would not use space peacefully." Everyone must understand that its military use can lead to the worst catastrophes and that the terrible dangers which already threaten humanity would only be reinforced as the weapons would be placed there. Only in peace and mutual cooperation can the conquest of space definitively be beneficial for humanity. It will remain a fantastic adventure only if it is peacefully shared, potentially by all the peoples of the world.

(3219) 3. Thus we are coming to a decisive stage in our reflection, one which emphasizes forcefully a cardinal point of the new international law now developing under the auspices of the United Nations, and which manifests, at least theoretically, a watershed: the introduction of the concept of "humanity" not only as the horizon of international activity but even as "subject", properly speaking, of international law, as the inclusive and decisive "actor" in international life.

(3220) Already, the Treaty on Antarctica (December 1, 1959) recognized, in the preamble, "that it is in the interest of all mankind that Antarctica shall continue forever to be used exclusively for peaceful purposes and shall not become the scene or object of international discord...." The Treaty on Outer Space uses the same expression in the preamble: "...the common interest of mankind". Its first Article states that "the exploration and use of outer space shall be carried out for the benefit and in the interests of all countries... and shall be the province of all mankind". This last expression, whose theoretical impact is startling, is found in article 11 of the Treaty on the Moon of 1979. It is also found in the draft convention on the Law of the Sea which the United Nations just adopted, last April 30.

(3221) Let's say it plainly: if we are willing to acknowledge the real meaning of the words, we are witnessing in certain domains a real change in international law: it is becoming a Law of Humanity (Jus humanitatis), or Planetary Law. At least theoretically, the problem is profoundly new: no longer is the "State" from now on the decisive actor looking primarily for its own interests and binding itself juridically only insofar as is advisable; now, for example "humanity" is considered as the one to whom sea or outer space belong. All the other actors (notably the States) are juridically obliged to respect these fundamental rights and interests. The change is genuinely revolutionary. Did the signatories to the texts where it is registered sign sincerely or half-heartedly? Are they really committed to honor it? The common ideal of humanity requires this and demands that national egoisms recede before this primary requirement.

(3222) All the stipulations of the Treaty of 1967 (as well as those of 1979 for the Moon) are conditioned by the law of outer space whether it might be a matter of equality among all States, of their freedom of peaceful exploration and use, the requirement of non-appropriation imposed on them, as well as their responsibility and duties of assistance and restitution. These are all, finally, the concrete implementation of the same fundamental law: belonging to all humanity (*res communis humanitatis*). Such an evolution corresponds perfectly to the deepest conviction of the Christian faith concerning the unity of origin, of nature and of vocation of the human family which embraces, in solidarity, all human beings in time and in space; and, particularly, to the essential principle to be inferred concerning the original universal destination of the Earth's goods and thus of their availability for all peoples and for every person based on their legitimacy.

(3223) Strongly affirmed in the patristic period, this principle was taken up later by Saint Thomas Aquinas, then by Francisco de Vitoria, and strongly emphasized by Pius XII in his message of June 1, 1941; he declared then: "Every human person, as a human being endowed with reason, holds by nature the fundamental right to use the material goods of the Earth, although it is left to human will and the juridical forms of peoples to regulate in greater detail the practical implementation of this right." The Second Vatican Council spoke in the same way: "God has destined the Earth and all it contains to the use of all humanity and of all peoples so that the goods of creation should equitably flow into the hands of all, according to the rule of justice which is inseparable from charity." (Constitution *Gaudium et Spes*, n. 69) In his encyclical *Laborem Exercens*, John Paul II recalled that "the right to private property is subordinate to that of common use, to the universal destination of goods" (n.14).

(3224) The above are only a few particularly meaningful quotations. This ethical principle has general consequences for the social doctrine of the Catholic Church, as much in regard to international life as to the internal affairs of States. In the eyes of the Church, the resources of the

Earth and those which can be put to work in cosmic space belong, first, to all of humanity and must therefore be used in the common interest. It is readily recognized that there may result some immediate sacrifices for certain groups (for example, the great powers) and for all of industrial society. But isn't it to their advantage in the long run? In other respects, shouldn't one be guided by the fundamental ethical requirements of justice and solidarity?

(3225) Let us add that, in this use, in solidarity, of the resources of land and of outer space, it is crucial to think of future generations, to take into account their interests as much as ours. If each generation thinks only of its greatest wellbeing and comfort, it is witness to irresponsibility and egoism, and it risks becoming guilty of injustices to tomorrow's humanity.

(3226) Although implementation of this central principle of sharing common resources to the benefit of all of humanity is delicate, and although it poses a quantity of practical problems and can move forward only by trial and error, how can it not be recognized? With good will,the difficulties are not insurmountable. What is fundamental is the awakening of a world conscience.

(3227) 4. In practice, if the orientation is not in the direction just specified, that is, from the central concept of "humanity", the victims of the conquest of space - as of the totality of scientific and technological development - will be the poor countries, made unable, by their very poverty, to participate in it. In this way, the unfavorable gap which separates them from the rich countries will not cease to grow. In the name of solidarity and justice, the international community must, therefore, be ready to take into account their legitimate interests.

(3228) This precise requirement is imposed by the international law of outer space, since the Treaty of 1967 stipulates that "the exploration and use of outer space... shall be carried out for the benefit and in the interests of all countries, irrespective of their degree of economic or scientific development..." (Article 1). It is a question there of a preferential option in favor of the developing countries: at least, in the sense that recognition of their legitimate interest must be deliberately sought and constantly examined. Better yet, concern must be given so that they, like others, draw a real benefit from the conquest of outer space. Without that, they will be once more the victims of industrial society's forward thrust.

(3229) As has been very well said, "to the sharing of the world we must substitute, gradually but surely, the world of sharing". Such a perspective radically challenges the fantastic expenses for armaments in the contemporary world. Development in the sense given in the encyclical Populorum Progressio is clearly the new name of peace. For the rich countries not to enter into these perspectives would be as much blindness as egoism.

(3230) 5. As we have noted, space technology has already provided remarkable results, in themselves eminently positive, regarding remote sensing and data messages.

(3231) Remote sensing has already provided valuable service for general cartography, notably for areas of difficult access, geological cartography, the inventory of hydrographic resources, harvest forecasting, etc.

(3232) As for data broadcasting, (telephone, television...) doesn't it considerably facilitate communication among human beings and their mutual human enrichment?

(3233) It is true that real problems arise in these two areas. Different States have complained that remote sensing allows an unchecked examination of their activities. Further, foreign broad-casting can result in a serious cultural imposition on a given population. In both cases, it would be a violation of sovereignty. What solutions can be envisaged? Two principles must be taken into consideration at the same time: first, each State enjoys a legitimate independence and has the right to act freely, although respecting the rights of others and on the basis of universal human solidarity; and then, sovereignty - which might, among other things, impede free cultural exchanges - is not an absolute right because it also must be based on the same foundation of universal human solidarity.

(3234) Advances in present technology easily convince us that remote sensing and data transmission will only progress. How can we regret the positive results here? Given the negative results, what matters is, in concrete terms, respect for a code of good conduct and, at the same time, the organization of international regulations.

(3235) From many ways, we arrive at the same conclusion: the necessity of organizing institutions indispensable to international regulation of the peaceful uses of space.

(3236) Certainly, some institutions already exist: in particular the United Nations Committee on the Peaceful Uses of Outer Space, the World Meteorological Organization, and the International Telecommunications Union. They have great juridical or technical relevance. But their authority is not sufficient to assure the harmonization of programs and still less the supranationality for which the international law of outer space logically calls.

(3237) The contemporary papacy has insisted for a long time on the necessity of providing the international community with institutions to facilitate cooperation among countries and the solution of the great social problems, which are, from now on, world problems. As the Second Vatican Council has said, "an adequate pursuit and a more efficient realization of the universal common good require, from now on, that the community of nations organize according to an order which fits contemporary tasks" (Constitution *Gaudium et Spes*, n. 84,). Every effort to organize international cooperation for the peaceful use of outer space will thus receive the warm support of the Holy See which, because of its mission of disinterested service to humanity, wishes that the needs of the developing countries, and especially of the poorest among them, also be generously recognized.

3. THE IMPACT OF SPACE EXPLORATION ON MANKIND

Conclusions of the Study Week held by the Pontifical Academy of Sciences (1-5 October 1984, Vatican City) on "The Impact of Space Exploration on Mankind", published also as United Nations Doc. A/40/272, 30 April 1985.

Original: English

Introduction

(3238) The second half of the twentieth century has witnessed the beginning of space exploration by man.

(3239) Human understanding of the universe has been much advanced by close observation of other planets - Venus, Mars, Jupiter, Saturn - of the moons of these planets and our own as well, and by space observation of the cosmos unavailable from the earth. Orbiting telescopes and detectors operating in the ultraviolet, infrared, visible, x-ray and gamma-ray spectral ranges are offering a new, more complete view of the universe.

(3240) From the technological viewpoint, one of the most important achievements concerns the use of artificial satellites. After 27 years of experience with artificial earth satellites, we have however only a taste of the benefits humanity will receive from the exploration and utilization of space. Satellites have contributed to national and international security by providing assurance of no undetected launch of intercontinental-range ballistic missiles, as well as by helping to ensure that nations comply with their commitments under international or multinational agreements which limit the nature or number of tests of nuclear weapons or their delivery systems.

(3241) *Space communications* have included international telephone and point-to-point data communication, dissemination of television and radio signals for retransmission by terrestrial transmitters, and direct reception of such space broadcasts by the end user. Reliable communications to mobile users have been provided from space for civil and military users.

(3242) *Satellite remote sensing* provides continuous near-global environmental data as well as frequent information on local conditions and crops, available to any user. The global observation of the earth's gravity fields, of the ocean surface, and the details of the atmosphere, provides information on the structure and functioning of the earth's system.

(3243) For mobile users, not only communication but also accurate, flexible navigation capabilities are available from space, and enhanced safety is provided by the first-generation, satellite-aided search-and-rescue system, KOSPAS-SARSAT.

(3244) In summary, it may be said that satellites in their variety of uses, have provided mankind with new, powerful means of transporting information of all kinds on large and small scale from one part of the earth to another without the major constraints that often affect the terrestrial telecommunication network. In fact, the distance on earth between two ends of a satellite telecommunication link has no effect on the cost of providing the service. Moreover, satellites offer simultaneous access to a large number of stations, thus realizing a full communication network, in contrast with the terrestrial media, which are essentially able to link two single points and can form a network only through complex communications and switching nodes.

(3245) Following are the conclusions and recommendations that the participants of the Study Week have arrived at the end of their discussions. They have been divided into three groups:

(1) Telecommunication Satellites.
(2) Space Technology.
(3) Future Uses of Space.

Telecommunication Satellites

(3246) The participants of the Study Week noted that the future evolution and development of satellite telecommunication systems were bound to be increasingly affected in the future by non-technical issues.

(3247) Although technology will continue to evolve, the choice of systems, the extent of their coverage and the types of service they will provide are likely to be more a function of the context in which the sponsors of the systems want to use these, rather than what is technically achievable.

(3248) This evolution has given rise to new concerns which will need to be addressed in a systematic way if the interaction between the political, economic, technical, cultural, and last, ethical factors involved are to be adequately understood and discussed.

(3249) 1) The present array of civil satellite communication systems for international, inter-regional and national use operates as a result of intergovernmental negotiations which, even if these were carried out separately, are to a greater or lesser extent interrelated but certainly fully coordinated from the technical and economic point of view.

This fact should be given its full importance and more attention should be paid to the possible consequences of actions not coordinated on an international basis which are likely to affect the use and operation of satellite communication systems, the operation of which is the result of international agreement, which reflects the broadest form of policy and interest.

(3250) 2) Satellite telecommunication systems are capable of having considerable economic, social or cultural impact. They are, further-more, likely to be conceived to have a life span of many years.

The effects of such systems will in most cases be felt over large areas and for long periods of time so that millions of people can be affected, possibly to the extent of becoming dependent on such services.

Those responsible for establishing such satellite communication systems, especially when they provide services not available to the public by other means, should be aware of the political and social responsibility they incur.

(3251) 3) The present evolution of satellite communication could place increased importance on the economic and social issues involved, especially as one cannot overlook the "public utility" aspect of some of the telecommunication services offered.

A better understanding of the economic and social dependence, both existing and potential, of mankind on telecommunications, including satellite telecommunication systems needs further study.

Space Technology

(3252) The participants of the Study Week noted that, while using space technology for various applications, there is a need to develop new *configurations* and *new ways* of integrating the *new technology* with the existing economic and cultural variables of society in different parts of the world. The problems of hunger, lack of facilities for basic education and health care, unequal opportunities for continuous learning and access to resources, *cannot* be solved through space technology alone, and certainly not through the use of a uniform version of the technological configurations evolved to meet the needs of affluent developed societies. One has to respect and build on the local talent and existing institutional infra-structure. Wisdom of the poor and the deprived is not inferior for the fact of being powerless; it should be integrated with the new knowledge and information and not drowned in a flood of standardized prescriptions from far away. The long reach of space communication should not lead to homogenization and indoctrination; rather, it should open windows to the big wide world and enrich the living and action within the community, with the respect for political, economic, cultural and moral identities of all nations and people.

(3253) Fortunately, space technology is now extremely versatile and flexible. While using it under different conditions obtaining on the earth, we need to, and can, use it in different ways. In some parts of the world, community receiving facilities may be used for information dissemination and education. Microprocessor-based modern techniques, and small ground stations may provide two-way communication between communities and between people and sources of vital information. Some of the new possibilities in this regard may not have been possible even five years ago.

(3254) Even while terrestrial services are being improved, some of the vital needs of modern industry, banking, transport, education, etc., could be quickly met through digital satellite systems, using customer-based ground stations if good end links are not available. Many developing countries can overcome their "last mile problem", namely the need for good terrestrial links and efficient switching systems, through some version of packet switching networks. In some circumstances, low rate data services could be established even before the telephone service, due to lower cost. Nevertheless, a cheap, efficient telephone system does remain a very desirable intermediate objective, as we move towards integrated services networks.

(3255) Some countries may decide to acquire their own satellite systems, while others might employ satellite capacity from an international common carrier or a neighboring State. The increasing success of international cooperatives in space systems is a positive factor in this regard.

(3256) Satellite remote sensing is proving to be an almost essential technology for locating, managing and caring for our renewable and non-renewable resources, particularly mineral exploration, agriculture, forestry and land use, even though the ultimate objectives are realized only after a great deal of additional work on the ground. The large view from above illuminates the relational aspects, so essential for environmental management, and understanding of the weather.

(3257) Even while the use of remote sensing expands, there is in-creasing concern among many countries whether the required data would be continuously available on an affordable and equitable basis and whether some vital information about their resources, derived by a few entities, may not be equally accessible to the countries concerned. In any case, the countries' central concern is related to having preferential rights to the strategic information of their respective territories and to making certain that the natural resources of space are exploited for the benefit of mankind. It is also necessary in this and other applications of space technology to be consistent with the concept of common heritage of mankind of Outer Space.

(3258) We urgently need to work towards a direction where the basic needs of the whole world in respect to weather and remote sensing services are assured through an appropriate mechanism. (Some of the existing mechanisms of international telecommunication systems may provide suitable examples in this regard.)

(3259) For all uses of space, in communication, broadcasting, education, resources management, etc., it is essential to keep the focus on the ultimate objective, namely the well-being of all people, especially the poor, the isolated and the underprivileged.

(3260) The Pontifical Academy of Sciences might consider organizing a study group to explore how remote sensing and information systems could be best developed and used to assure food security, including aspects of production, distribution and protection of the poor from exploitation. The stratification of various land uses over large areas can best be done by satellite images. From these various land strata, crop fields can be efficiently sampled on the ground to provide precise estimates of total crop production. This information is essential for the poorer countries to understand their food needs.

The Future Uses of Space

(3261) Progress in the exploitation of space for the benefit of humanity will depend upon the effective use of technology, organization, and management tools. One should consider the following observations:

Space Sciences

(3262) Space science has provided marvelous and inspiring insights and surprises. The braided rings of Saturn, the vulcanism of Io, and (it seems so long ago) the nature of the surface of the moon, of Mars and of Venus have provided a point to fix the imagination and a base for further conjecture. The space probe observation of Martian dust storms has contributed to the recognition that fires set by nuclear war on earth could lead to winter temperatures and perhaps consequences even more catastrophic than the direct effects of nuclear war.

(3263) Some fundamental experiments of physics and observations of cosmological relevance can be done only in space, and a truly scientific study of the effects of the zero-g environment on human health and performance is long overdue. Some science and perhaps some technology can be done more cheaply in space: the fabrication and operation of precision radio antennas of kilometer or multi-kilometer size, the construction and use of very large composite optical mirror systems and very-long-baseline interferometry. In addition, advanced technology for space services (communication, navigation, remote sensing) may have to be demonstrated or verified in space experiments before it can confidently be included in a worldwide system.

(3264) Without recommending specific missions or even fields, we express our admiration for the results of planetary and space science thus far, and the feeling that a substantially larger component of research on space science and technology is warranted to speed the availability of new space services.

Benefits from Space Explorations

(3265) A) The spectacular achievements of space exploration have not as yet fully contributed their potential to the reduction of poverty, of illiteracy, or to the improvement of public health among the poorer nations of the world, or to improving food production and food security. Not only must developing countries participate in the acquisition of information and technology for weather forecasting, detection of new mineral resources, water management, and improved communication, but major efforts must be made in providing means to ensure that the benefits of economic and human development are actually available to the vast numbers of people in need.

To this end, regional mechanisms of cooperation could aid the realization of these benefits, and nations and international and multinational organizations should encourage the establishment of such mechanisms as appropriate.

(3266) B) To ensure the continual availability to all nations of the benefits of space exploration and exploitation, and to preserve the contribution to international security and national security made by existing satellite systems and those which might augment them, it is essential to prevent a spiral of competitive deployment of weapons in space.

To this end, an international treaty is required, with the purpose of banning the placement and testing of *all* weapons in outer space, on the moon, and all other celestial bodies, and in banning tests of anti-satellite weapons, wherever located. The necessity for an eventual international multilateral agreement should not delay an urgently needed bilateral agreement to this end between the two leading space powers.

Decision Procedures

(3267) In order to provide benefits of human and economic development to people throughout the world, one must select missions, to be fulfilled by technological approaches, with appropriate choice of reliability and response time. The choice of mission, approach, and performance must be guided by efficiency - both near-term and long-term. It is important to do the research, development, and analysis required to make these judgments, including generic work not associated with a commitment to a particular mission.

(3268) Tradition provides a candidate (traditional) approach, but it must not be allowed to define or limit the technological candidates for accomplishing a particular mission or to define the missions themselves.

(3269) Development has provided and experience has demonstrated the utility of manned reusable spacecraft for satellite launch and in-orbit repair; it has also provided a basis for unmanned launch, rendezvous, resupply in various orbits and for large and small payloads.

(3270) Key Directions for Better Performance

a) Burgeoning capability for computation and signal processing based on the last decade's progress in microprocessors to give ten-million to 1,000-million operations per second in a few micro-chips;

b) the application of microprocessors and microwave integrated technology to flexible communication systems such as phased-array antennas which can make possible efficient satellite communication systems and appropriate space information relay (and especially satellite-to-satellite relay) by radio or laser link. Just as the Tracking and Data Relay Satellite (TDRS) is replacing many ground stations, so can the output of low-earth-orbiting satellites be made available more economically by radio relay via geostationary satellite. INTELSAT space cross-links would be valuable and, for instance, search-and-rescue satellite signals can be acquired by low-earth-orbit satellites and relayed by a geosynchronous-orbit satellite whose phased-array antenna occasionally looks at the SARSATs and requests the transmission of any stored signals;

c) the use of telecommunication to provide more effective linkage of scientists in their laboratories with experiments or observing facilities in orbit;

d) the increasingly powerful augmentation of human ability by local computing power and instruments;

e) the perfection of reliable reusable transportation of people and things to and from orbit, and, complementarily, the availability of automated or remote-managed orbital resupply, repair, or adjustment;

f) the evolution of a capability for cost-benefit analysis, project management, system engineering and design choice which can provide a more solid groundwork than intuitive choice - among potential applications as different as remote data communications and vehicle monitoring - while retaining the possibility of accepting and evaluating proposals of intuition and genius;

g) the experience of productive collaboration in which real decisions are made and real hardware and capabilities created - such as the INTELSAT cooperative and the Canadian provision of the remote-manipulation arm for the U.S. space shuttle.

(3271) Recommendations

a) For a given mission, an informed choice should be made as to the proper mix of human intelligence and machines, and the optimum location of the human furnishing the intelligence.

b) Society must choose among a homogeneous system in which all obtain the same communications service at the same price; a heterogeneous system in which concentrated users obtain a better service or lower cost; and a heterogeneous system in which there is internal or external subsidy.

c) Planning for an evaluation of accomplishing a SET of missions must consider t he options of a large space station on the one hand, in comparison with a set of smaller satellites on the other. Such analyses must include the unconstrained application of feasible technologies such as satellite-to-satellite communications, reusable or expendable launchers and re-entry vehicles, manned or automated docking and resupply, and the like. The benefits and costs of international collaboration must also be considered, with likely net benefit for collaboration in the planning and technology phase, as well as in operation.

d) Much research and development would be justified and should be performed to provide additional options for reduction of cost in performing space tasks now feasible and in providing new and competitive technological options (e.g., robotics, expert systems, and artificial intelligence) for accomplishing new tasks.

e) As for manned space flight, each person traveling to space and returning safely is testament to the magnificent achievement of the men and women who have created the technology, the organizations, and the operational systems which make space flight possible. Nations providing the capabilities for manned space flight or participating in manned space flight should take into account the essentially human and spiritual response to the human adventure in space. Flight opportunities should be provided to people, such as writers and artists, who can better transmit those adventures to the multitudes who cannot personally participate.

f) Efforts should be undertaken to maximize the economic and social benefits available from the exploitation of space by the use of manned missions or unmanned missions as are best suited to the specific tasks to be accomplished.

g) Analysis of space missions should be extended beyond the planned end of useful life of the satellite, to include the ultimate fate of the space debris. Ideally, no debris should be left in near-earth space, but in any case the amount of debris should be minimized in order not to prejudice the future use of space by others. A possible criterion might be to ensure that the debris from a century of anticipated space operations should not shorten the expected operational life of additional satellites by 0.1%. One must balance the costs of controlling debris against the cost of damage if debris is not controlled.

h) In cases in which centralized organizations are used to increase efficiency of *building* and *operating* systems of satellites, special means and care are needed to ensure that new technology is introduced whenever it can reduce the overall cost of providing a given level of service. Alternatively, care must be taken to avoid introduction of technology which can unwarrantedly increase costs to consumers who cannot control the total system.

i) The availability of global communications should be accompanied by means for improvement of local communications, with a view to allowing individuals and groups to maintain cultural diversity and to retain and enhance a sense of community.

Conclusions

(3272) Increasing human capabilities in space could bring forth an era where distance stands abolished and all humans on the planet truly begin to feel and function like members of one global family. The very same space awareness could make us live hereafter in greater harmony with our beautiful and fragile home in the solar system and to monitor, use and care for its resources for the common good of us all.

(3273) We could share the richness of our cultures, the increasing fund of our knowledge and understanding, the new techniques of bettering the conditions of life, and the delights of our intellectual and spiritual adventures - all this again because we could all have a voice a nd might be able to talk to whomsoever we want.

(3274) Such a world has now become possible. How much more desirable it would be to use our magnificent tools of space technology and operation to work toward this goal rather than to slide toward the unthinkable possibility that much, if not the whole, of the human race may be wiped out from the surface of this planet, perhaps within the lifetime of our children.

Address of His Holiness John Paul II to the participants to the above mentioned Study Week. The Vatican 2 October 1984

Original: English (*)

(3275) 1. I am very grateful to the Pontifical Academy of Sciences and to its President, Professor Carlos Chagas, for having arranged this interesting Study Week on the subject of "The Impact of Space Exploration" being held in the Casina of Pius IV.

(3276) For me it is a source of great satisfaction to meet you, the members of the Pontifical Academy and scientists from all over the world. The present assembly gives me an opportunity to express my admiration at the exceptional developments which have taken place in space technology. At the same time, it enables me to expound the guidelines of a moral, social and spiritual order which belong to the mission entrusted to the Successor of Peter by Christ.

(3277) 2. Centuries have passed since Galileo's telescope penetrated the heavens and gave mankind a new vision of the universe. In his brief but fundamental work entitled Sidereus Nuncius, published in Venice in 1610, he spoke of the discoveries made by means of his telescope, but he added, being both a scientist and a believer, that he had made them "divina prius illuminante gratia", preceded by the enlightenment of divine grace.

(*) Insegnamenti di Giovanni Paolo II, Vol. VII,2 (1984), 721-726.

(3278) Other great scientists such as Kepler and Newton likewise searched the heavens with the spirit of believers. Poets and philosophers such as Pascal contemplated with awe the mysterious silence of outer space.

(3279) 3. Today, your gaze is directed at the heavens not only in order to study and contemplate the stars created by God, as was done by the great figures I have just mentioned, but in order to speak of the space probes, space stations and satellites made by man. I am with you in your work, for I regard the presence in space of man and of his machines with the same admiration as that of Paul VI at the time of the Apollo 13 undertaking, when he invited those taking part in the Study Week on "The Nuclei of the Galaxies" to "pay homage to those who, by their study, action and authority have once more shown the world the unlimited powers of the sciences and of modern technology. With us also you will raise an ardent hymn of gratitude to God, the Creator of the universe and Father of humanity, who in these ways also wishes to be sought and found by man, adored and loved by him".

(3280) 4. Today, years after those first events, we can see the immense path covered by man's intelligence in knowing the universe, and we rejoice in this by reason of our very faith, for the perfection of man is the glory of God. Scientific research on the nature of our universe has progressed and will progress still more, with the use of highly sophisticated systems, such as those perfected by the late member of the Pontifical Academy, Professor Giuseppe Colombo. Instruments are capable of going into space and avoiding the disturbances connected with the earth's surface and the lower layers of the atmosphere. Space probes, a new challenge by man to the distances of space and a symbol of his ever restless desire for knowledge, are coming ever closer to the heavenly bodies, in order to reveal their inmost secrets. Permanent space stations will in their turn be centres of observation making possible experiments never before attempted and the study of new techniques. All these new space instruments have been achieved thanks to the great progress of fundamental scientific research in mathematics, physics and chemistry, and through the development of the telecommunications techniques discovered by a great member of the Academy, Guglielmo Marconi.

(3281) 5. These various modes of man's presence in space lead us to ask a question: to whom does space belong? While space was something merely observed and studied by the human eye, though with the aid of powerful astronomical instruments, this question was not yet asked. But now that space is visited by man and his machines, the question is unavoidable: to whom does space belong? I do not hesitate to answer that space belongs to the whole of humanity, that it is something for the benefit of all. Just as earth is for the benefit of all, and private property must be distributed in such a way that every human being is given a proper share in the goods of the earth, in the same way the occupation of space by satellites and other instruments must be regulated by just agreements and international pacts that will enable the whole human family to enjoy and use it. Just as earthly goods are not merely for private use but must also be employed for the neighbour's good, so space must never be for the exclusive benefit of one nation or social group. The questions of the proper use of space must be studied by jurists and given a correct solution by governments.

(3282) The presence of man in space with his satellites and other instruments also involves other matters of a cultural, moral and political nature which I would bring to your attention.

(3283) 6. One of the biggest tasks that can be carried out by the use of satellites is the elimination of illiteracy. About one billion people are still illiterate. Again, satellites can be used for a wider spreading of culture in all the countries of the world, not only in those where illiteracy has already been eliminated, but also in those where many can still not yet read or write, for culture can be spread with the use of pictures alone. I hope that the scientific and technological progress which you are now discussing will contribute to the spreading of a culture that will truly promote the integral development of man.

(3284) But the transmission of culture must not be identified with the imposition of the cultures of the technologically advanced countries on those still developing. Peoples with ancient cultures, though sometimes still partly illiterate but endowed with an oral and symbolic tradition capable of passing on and preserving their own cultures, must not fall victim to a cultural or ideological colonialism that will destroy those traditions. The rich countries must not attempt, through the use of the instruments at their disposal, and in particular modern space technology, to impose their own culture on poorer nations.

(3285) 7. Satellites will carry out a beneficial task when, instead of imposing the culture of the rich countries, they favour a dialogue between cultures which means a dialogue among the nations, essential for the peace of the world. Nations have cultural frontiers that are more deeply rooted than geographical and political ones: it must be possible to cross them, for every human being is a citizen of the world, a member of the human family. These barriers must not, however, be altered in a violent way. Similarly, cultural frontiers must not impede a fruitful dialogue between cultures, nor must they be violated by forms of cultural or ideological dictatorship. Modern space technology must not be used by any form of cultural imperialism, to the detriment of the authentic culture of human beings with the legitimate differences that have developed in the history of individual peoples.

(3286) 8. Modern space technology, properly understood, also provides observations useful for the cultivation of the earth, far beyond what can be accomplished by any system working on the earth`s surface. Through the use of satellites it is possible to obtain exact data regarding the condition of tracts of land, the flow of water and weather conditions. These data can be used for the purpose of improving agriculture, checking the state of the woodlands and forests, evaluating the condition of individual zones or of the whole earth, thus making it possible to draw up particular or global programmes in order to meet concrete situations.

(3287) This so-called "remote sensing" is of fundamental importance in the fight against hunger, provided that the economic and political powers that possess special means of observing the world situation help the poorer countries to draw up programmes of economic development and help them in a practical way to carry out these programmes.

(3288) 9. With your knowledge and practice of modern space technology, you are well aware of how it would be possible to work out adequate programmes for helping the world to overcome the imbalance of agricultural practices, the advance of deserts, ecological disasters caused by human rapacity against the earth, in the waters and in the atmosphere, with the ever more alarming destruction of animal and plant life, and with grave and mortal illnesses affecting human life itself.

(3289) Order and justice must be re-established; harmony between man and nature must be restored. We must strive for a technology that will free the poor peoples and relieve oppressed nature, that will promote projects and agreements. Space technology can make a highly effective contribution to this cause.

(3290) 10. Ladies and Gentlemen, true peace is born from the heart of those who are open to the gift of God, that God who, at the coming of Christ, promised peace to people of good will. In your scientific researches and technological inventions I invite you to seek the God of peace, the Invisible One who is the source of everything that is visible. I exhort you to seek Him by listening to the silence of space. Heaven and earth proclaim that they are only creatures, and they urge you to rise into the supreme heaven of transcendence, in order to open your minds and hearts to the love that moves the sun and the other stars. Thus, you will be the creators not only of ever more perfect instruments but also of that civilization which is the only one desired by God and by men and women of good will: the civilization of truth and love, so necessary to guarantee peace among the nations of the world.

4. MPACT OF REMOTE SENSING ON DEVELOPING COUNTRIES

Conclusions and recommendations of the Study Week held by the Pontifical Academy of Sciences (19-21 June 1986, Vatican City) on the "Impact of Remote Sensing on Developing Countries", published as United Nations Doc. A/42/62, on 22 December 1986.

Original: English

Introduction

(3291) The face of the earth looks to the sky. It follows that the sky is the most favorable vantage point from which to look at the face of the earth. Remote sensing with aerial photographs and space imagery at many different wavelengths from the visible to the infrared and microwave regions, exploits this principle. Perhaps the most important applications of remote sensing for the benefit of all mankind are through the use of it in monitoring the earth's natural resources and environments - important steps leading to the intelligent management of such resources.

(3292) By the end of the 1920's, there was clear evidence that aerial photographs of the earth's surface often could be used effectively by those at regional and national levels who wished to monitor key environmental variables, and to inventory, monitor, and manage natural resources. More than two decades passed, however, before there was a general acceptance and use of this capability at regional and national levels.

(3293) Similarly, by the end of the 1960's, there was clear evidence that space photographs of the earth's surface and its atmosphere (when augmented by other forms of remote sensing data acquired from aircraft and spacecraft) often could be used even more effectively than aerial photos alone at the national, regional and global levels, for environmental monitoring and resource inventory purposes. Nearly two decades have passed since the start of investigating and using remote sensing techniques. Many programs and countries have effectively used the technology. However, additional programs could benefit by using the technology, especially if decision makers were better informed on the potentials of techniques and if they accepted the use of remote sensing.

(3294) This Study Week on the Impact of Remote Sensing on Developing Nations was a direct outcome of the Study Week held on the Impact of Space Exploration on Mankind, October I - 5, 1984.

(3295) Through our economic and technological activity, humanity is now contributing to significant global changes on the Earth within the span of a few human generations. We have become part of the Earth System and of one of the forces for Earth changes.

(3296) The use of available information holds the key for the effective use of renewable and nonrenewable resources, and for protection of, and from, the environment. Research holds the key to our global future. Recent studies of the earth's components have revealed a complex and dynamic world. Analyses have also delineated, with increasing clarity, the fundamental interactions among these components and their profound effect upon Earth's history and evolution. With new insight and technology, humanity can gain a deeper understanding of the Earth and of the consequences of global changes.

(3297) The following were the primary reasons for convening this Study Week and bringing to it remote sensing experts from many of the world's developed and developing countries:

(1) to consider the impact, both present and potential, of modern remote sending technology on developing countries, particularly with respect to the effective monitoring of the environment, and the inventory, and management of their natural resources, and

(2) to determine, for certain instances in which such effective use obviously could be made, various means by which the rate of acceptance and adoption of this remote-sending-based technology might be accelerated.

(3298) The subject matter for this Study Week was organized under the following four headings:

(1) The present status of remote sensing technology;

(2) Its potential usefulness in developing countries with respect to the environment and *renewable* natural resources such as marine, timber, forage, water, minerals, soils, and agricultural crops;

(3) Its potential usefulness in developing countries with respect to such *non-renewable* natural resources as minerals and fossil fuels; and

(4) Related economic, social, and legal considerations.

It seemed apparent that, once our Study Week participants had systematically considered these four aspects, we would be in a favourable position to draw conclusions with respect to the theme of this Study Week: Remote Sensing and its Impact on Developing Countries.

(3299) Summary of Findings

1. Satellite remote sensing is becoming more and more useful in the monitoring of the environment and the inventory and monitoring of natural resources to facilitate their management. The synoptic global view with frequent coverage provides compliment to airborne remote sensing and surface-based measurements.

2. The case examples presented by participants in this Study Week show that various satellite and airborne remote systems, including environmental/meteorological satellites, have been successfully applied in providing management solutions to a variety of environmental and natural resource problems at the local, national, and global levels.

3. Global efforts are being actively pursued to apply this technology in searching for answers to the world's major problems of environmental hazards, food production, desertification, deforestation, soil degradation, and the destruction or improper use of coastal and marine resources.

4. Full utilization of remotely sensed data in the developing countries has been and is constrained by:

   a) the limited access to, and availability of, remotely sensed data, especially from satellites,
   b) the increase in costs of satellite data to the user for products and in certain elements of the infrastructure, such as ground receiving operations,
   c) the inappropriate and incomplete transfer of the technology including inappropriate equipment for understanding and using remote sensing,
   d) the ineffective efforts by scientists to communicate to decision makers the demonstrated advantages of remote sensing,
   e) in many cases, the inadequate appreciation by decision makers of what remote sensing can do has resulted in a consequent lack of its acceptance,
   f) the continuing lack of adequate training,
   g) the slow diffusion of the technology between users and user agencies, and,
   h) the inability of remote sensing techniques to provide all types and levels of information required for complex resource and environmental problems.

5. Users should derive greater benefits from the application of this technology through:

   a) use of optimal combinations of remote sensing methods,
   b) the formation of national, regional, and international data/information management facilities and training programs,
   c) the development of indigenous and self-sufficient remote sensing programs, and
   d) ncreased use of remotely sensed data from new generations of earth observing satellites and airborne instruments.

6. Countries which have developed the remote sensing technology should pro- vide the proper environment in which developing countries can fully utilize the technology for the management of their natural resources. Continuity and stability of data should be encouraged while costs associated with applications should be held to a minimum.

7. Overall there continues to be only a moderate rate of acceptance for using modern remote sensing technology among the world's developing countries. Remedies to this difficulty should begin with a better understanding of the factors involved in gaining acceptance and use of a new, rapidly growing technology such as remote sensing.

8. The Committee on the Peaceful Uses of Outer Space of the United Nations General Assembly (COPUOS) adopted a draft of "Principles Relating to Remote Sensing of the Earth from Space" at its twenty-ninth session in June 1986. The participants support these principles and consider them of primordial importance.

9. To protect the legitimate rights and interests of sensed countries, legal regulation of dissemination of the data and information of remote sensing is essential. Dissemination of remote sensing information should be regarded as constituting wrongful acts when such activities violate the Declaration of Principles of International Law concerning Friendly Relations and Cooperations among States in accordance with the Charter of the United Nations adopted by the United Nation General Assembly in 1970.

10. The peaceful uses of outer space and international cooperation in economic and humanitarian spheres are indispensable to provide for wider participation of developing countries in remote sensing activities.

11. Remote sensing may affect economic, social and strategic interest of sensed countries and the international community as a whole. Together with positive effects, it may cause negative effects on developing countries. To eliminate possible negative effects further, development of international cooperation in this field is required at all levels - bilateral, regional, and multilateral.

(3300) Recommendations

1. Remote sensing, by providing information, can make a unique contribution to global food security by monitoring conditions during the growing season, and monitoring the occurrence and intensity of natural disasters such as drought, floods, and plagues of locusts. In this respect, the holding of an international meeting on remote sensing for food security in the next decade is timely and is recommended. Particular attention should be paid to such staple crops, e.g., rice in the developing countries of Asia, the home of majority of the world's population.
2. Measures must be taken to ensure long-term continuity and availability of remotely sensed data.

3. There should be a continued effort to formulate and/or strengthen international cooperation, coordination, and programs which study earth processes, productivity, and resources on a global basis.

4. Developed countries should assist developing countries in using information and data analysis systems to assure that all information is available for their decision makers and for their future resource mapping and monitoring programs. An advanced information and data analysis system should be established for use on an international basis. This will permit the use of new and existing remotely sensed data for critical national resource mapping and monitoring programs. It will also facilitate the transfer and cooperative use of data and information to evaluate earth resources and processes on a regional and global basis.

5. There should be a vigorous effort made to promote a clear understanding of the factors that govern the acceptance and use of a new, sophisticated, and potentially very consequential technology, such as remote sensing.

6. Policy makers must be convinced of the need to action through remote sensing with respect to development and management of national resources and protection of the environment. Policy makers should be briefed at a special meeting organized by the Pontifical Academy of Sciences or the Third World Academy of Sciences. Brief but effective training programs and seminars could be offered to high level decision makers and planners of developing countries to ensure their support of remote sensing pro- grams.

7. Greatly increased efforts must be made to educate potential and existing users. Workshops and training programs should be held for agriculturist, environmentalists, foresters, hydrologists, climatologists, geologists, data collectors, data reducers, data analysts, and other users.

8. Development goals and resource management priorities should be clearly stated so that proper remote sensing techniques can be defined and used.

9. Developing countries should be encouraged to develop self sufficient and indigenous national remote sensing programs based on their financial and scientific capabilities addressed to their national development needs. National remote sensing programs should be developed to the extent necessary to meet national planning and development needs and, in the case of developing countries, international agencies and donor countries, should be urged to support those programs.

10. Remote sensing efforts, as applied to the developing countries, should be regionally coordinated as appropriate.

11. Developing countries often share the same situations and problems in resource management. Transfer of technology between these countries should be encouraged (in terms of pilot projects, exchange of specialists, technology assessment, software/hardware, training, seminars, etc.).

12. Efforts should be continued to develop all-weather operational capabilities (e.g. utilization of both active and passive microwave techniques).

13. There should be a program to measure costal zone and ocean productivity, an area in which remote sensing capabilities are now deficient.

14. Standards should be defined for remote sensing related hardware and software to insure maximum capability between satellites and user systems.

15. Attention should be directed to the use of data from environmental monitoring satellites. Regional and international efforts in this program should be encouraged.

16. Countries possessing remote sensing technology should facilitate the following:

    Techchnology transfer in Remote Sensing.
    - through training,
    - through the distribution of applicable equipment and software,
    - through assistance to national/regional mappings and exploration, thereby helping t\e programs of developing countries which use remote sensing.

17. Developed countries should assist developing countries to locate, archive, and make available existing resources information in order to improve the quality of resource survey and management programs.

18. More funds should be directed to the production of high quality, affordable products for use in resource development and environmental monitoring.

19. Commercialization of satellite remote sensing systems could compromise the national development of national resources in developing countries and thus it is of a grave concern. It is recommended that the impact of commercialization, especially with regard to copyright and cost of these data, should be carefully evaluated in the near future.

20. We recommend that all States support principles relating to remote sensing of the earth from space, adopted by the Committee on Peaceful Uses of Outer Space (COPUS) on June 13, 1986. In particular, we recommend that States should bear international responsibility for damage caused by the dissemination of remote sensing information about other countries.

21. Further action by States should be taken to maintain outer space for peaceful purposes and thus to promote international cooperation on a non- discriminatory basis in the field of remote sensing.

22. The study team, in their role as scientists, recognizes that continued applications of remote sensing for development require an ongoing program of research and training. This group strongly recommends that the international university community be encouraged and supported to provide remote sensing training and research.

23. The institutional and organizational frameworks of international cooperation in the fields of remote sensing and information systems should be further studied.

CONCLUSION

(3301) The benefits to mankind of remote sensing have been demonstrated over the past twenty five years. Through international cooperation these benefits will continue to be available in the interest of peace and for welfare of all men and nations but particularly for those who suffer from hunger and disease.

Address of His Holiness John Paul II to the participants to the above mentioned Study Week. The Vatican, 20 June, 1986.

Original: English (*)

Mr. President, Ladies and Gentlemen, It is a pleasure to receive today those taking part in the *Study Week organized by the Pontifical Academy of Sciences, on the subject of "Remote Sensing and Its Impact on Developing Countries"*.

(3302) An ever deeper knowledge of the earth, and in particular of its poorest zones, is the purpose for which the Pontifical Academy and its distinguished President have brought you together in order to study this theme.

(3303) 1. The new technique of remote sensing makes it possible to survey anything from a few square metres to huge expanses of the earth's surface. Certain areas, the home of hundreds of thousands of people, are being affected by the *terrible phenomenon of desertification*, with consequent famine and disease. The causes of this phenomenon vary from unsuitable methods of farming to climatic factors such as cyclones and other atmospheric disturbances.

(3304) Survey carried out *with the aid of satellites* linked with a network of ground tracking stations can provide a detailed and exact picture of crops, including their increase or deterioration, and can offer the chance of using *technical means of combatting the encroaching desert*, which imperils the livelihood of a high percentage of the world's population.

(3305) With the help of remote sensing, it is possible to give useful advice for many schemes. These latter include the improvement of soil condition, forecasting and increasing the development of crop harvesting both in quantity and quality, the introduction of new crops, the prevention of the destruction of forested areas needed for ecological balance and the taking of measures to meet possible atmospheric conditions, both harmful and beneficial.

(3306) By means of remote sensing it is likewise possible to detect the presence of concealed sources of energy, both renewable and non-renewable, as also the presence of food resources on the seabed and in rivers and lakes, together with the mineral wealth lying in the subsoil.

(3307) 2. Your meeting has highlighted the possibility of aiding all peoples, with the help of advanced technological methods, to attain a *more just form of worldwide coexistence, so that the earth's resources,which are the patrimony of all, may be fairly distributed and shared.* This is in accordance with the will of the Creator who made man and woman in his own likeness and said to them, "...have dominion over the fish of the sea and over the birds of the air and over every living thing that moves upon the earth... I have given you every plant yielding seed which is upon the face of all the earth, and every tree with seed in its fruit; you shall have them for food" (*Gen.* I:28-29).

(3308) The resources of science make it possible to feed the whole human family, with the remedying of past and present mistakes and short-comings. Nevertheless, one cannot help noting that there is still a lack of firm determination in political circles to make proper use of the technological means which you have been examining during these days of study and of service to human welfare. We know that *progress must not be the exclusive privilege of the favoured few.* We should not forget the words of Pope Paul VI who said that development is the new name of peace.

(3309) 3. It is a source of satisfaction that the conclusions of your previous Study Week, held in October of the year before last, on the subject of "The Impact of Space Exploration on Mankind," have been published by the United Nations and sent to all Member States. This is indeed a sign of

(*) L'Osservatore Romano, 21 Giugno 1986.

profound respect for the relevance and importance of the work being done by the Pontifical Academy.

(3310) It is my hope that by means of joint agreement and commitments all Governments will promote the *peaceful uses of space resources, for the sake of the unification of the human family in justice and peace*. I take this occasion to express once more my conviction that national and international economic powers should serve all peoples and every individual, but with special preference for those whose lives are particularly threatened and who need assistance for securing their very survival and the means of living in a manner consonant with human dignity.

May the Lord of heaven and earth look kindly upon you and grant to you and your families the abundance of his blessings.

APPENDIX

I - THE HOLY SEE AND PEACE

Lecture by His Eminence Cardinal Agostino Casaroli, Secretary of State, at the University of San Francisco, San Francisco, CA (USA). 18 November 1983.

Original: English

I have been asked to speak on this occasion about the Holy See and peace.

(3311) 1. I am pleased to accept this task, although - I must confess -with some misgivings.

(3312) So much has been said about peace, everywhere, and for so long, in so many situations, in so many different ways and in so many tones, that one can reasonably fear sounding, to say the least, not very original in approaching a theme that has been so widely explored and about which it seems difficult to say something that has not already been said again and again.

(3313) Much is also said about the declarations and actions of the Holy See with regard to peace, in favour of peace, particularly because of the powerful consensus evoked by the words and actions of the person who has occupied the See of Peter for the past five years, Pope John Paul II.

(3314) But the question of peace and war is so important and is so relevant - today especially - with its pressing weight of fear, and involving such hopes and anxieties for millions and millions of men and women everywhere, that it can never appear trivial when it is approached with the seriousness that it deserves. I mean when it is not treated in a rhetorical or one-sided way, but objectively and with an effort to be concrete, as befits a subject that is of vital importance for people everywhere and for the whole of humanity. Fine words and lofty sentiments are not enough. What is required is clarity of mind and firmness of will (even though it must be recognized that not even these are always sufficient to put an end to war and to ensure peace: not always sufficient, it is true, but always indispensable).

(3315) I wish, therefore, to avail myself of the opportunity which this pleasant and significant encounter offers me in order to explain, in some way, the present position of the Holy See with regard to the question of peace and war as it presents itself today, with an immediacy and dramatic urgency that no epoch of the ancient or more recent history of the human race has ever known, or perhaps even approached.

(3316) There is no need for me to emphasize that what I have to say is not an official statement of the Holy See's position but strictly elements already publicly known.

(3317) 2. The work of the Holy See in the area of peace and war follows essentially three lines of development:

(3318) 1) a doctrinal approach, on the level of the moral teaching which the Catholic Church - as, indeed, other Christian Churches and communities - considers to be among her specific and most fundamental tasks and duties;

(3319) 2) the influencing and orientation of public opinion, particularly among Catholics, by means of a constant call to reflection, prayer, and the proper use of the rights and opportunities of citizens to act, individually or collectively, in favour of peace (as in other fields in which politics, in the widest sense of the word, are linked to morality);

(3320) 3) by direct action addressed to the decision-making centres of Governments and International Organizations, both as a recognized moral force of worldwide extension, and as occupying a legitimate place in the international Community. This latter element makes it possible for the Holy See, in direct contact with the parties involved and always from the moral point of view in which it is competent, to enter into concrete questions regarding peace and war. These questions are always difficult and complex, even when it might appear that they affect only "minor" problems, as it were.

(3321) 3. The documents in which the Holy See and, more directly, the Popes, have expressed their thoughts regarding peace are quite numerous. Not all of them are of the same level or importance from the point of view of what I have called the doctrinal approach.

(3322) To limit ourselves to our own times, beginning, that is, from the pontificate of Pius XII, one may recall his Christmas Radio Messages in which he sought to outline, somewhat systematically and in spite of the lapses of time between them, a consistent "doctrine of peace", in response to the new situation brought about by the Second World War and the post-war period, with its corresponding developments in terms of political tensions and new weapons.

(3323) One might say that the clear analyses of Pius XII and his repeated appeals, which were certainly not without profound emotion, were somewhat overshadowed, at least in the mind of the man in the street, and also in worldwide public opinion, by the luminous, warm, and at the same time serene clarity of the words of Pope John XXIII, especially in the Encyclical Pacem in Terris, the twentieth anniversary of which occurred this year.

(3324) The pontificate of Paul VI is particularly rich in doctrinal insights and developments, with numerous public and diplomatic interventions in favour of peace in a world increasingly exposed to the danger of forgetting the horrors of the last war and of being carried away by the logic which, in spite of the declared willingness to disarm, has led progressively to an increase of opposing stockpiles of weapons, extravagant both in quantity and quality.

(3325) As well as remembering that the signature of Paul VI is the first to appear at the foot of the great Pastoral Constitution Gaudium et Spes of the Second Vatican Council, one recalls his speech to the General Assembly of the United Nations on 4 October 1965; the Encyclical Populorum Progressio, with its well-known affirmation that "development is the new name for peace"; the various messages and homilies for the annual World Day of Peace, which he instituted to awaken consciences and to encourage people to want to serve peace. These have followed each other at the dawn of each new year since 1 January 1968. The annual meetings with the Diplomatic Corps accredited to the Holy See often gave him the opportunity to return to this theme, which is so closely linked to the very nature of diplomatic activity. His last great intervention against the spectre of war was the solemn Message which he sent to the General Assembly of the United Nations convened in Special Session on Disarmament, on 27 May 1978. Little more than two months later, Paul VI reached the end of his hardworking earthly existence.

(3326) His successor - Pope John Paul II - after the short interval of the pontificate John Paul I - has taken up and carried forward Pope Paul's intense doctrinal activity and concern for the cause of peace.

(3327) As Paul VI did, the present Pontiff too has addressed the General Assembly of the United Nations, in October 1979. On the occasion of the Second Special Session on Disarmament, in June 1982, he sent a long Message which he had carefully reflected upon. Just like Paul VI, he too speaks to the entire human family on the occasion of the annual World Day of Peace.

(3328) His visit to Hiroshima and Nagasaki, in February 1981, presented him with a singular opportunity to admonish the whole world solemnly against the danger of a nuclear holocaust. John Paul II has also endeavoured to stimulate the consciences of the men and women of science regarding their responsibility in this field, and he has made use of, and continues to make use of, the valuable contribution of their experiences and ideas. It is sufficient to recall here the very recent discourse on 12 November to the Pontifical Academy of Sciences, in which the Pope requested "in this so very grave moment of history ... the charity of wisdom which builds peace".

(3329) 4. If we now try to extract from this vast "literature" the essential and basic lines of the position of the Holy See in the matter in question, we can, in my opinion, summarize them in a number of fundamental points which, in turn, would then, naturally, need to be accurately defined and developed:

1) Peace is a supreme good for humanity;
2) Peace is necessary;
3) Peace is possible;
4) Peace is a duty.

(3330) 5) Peace has various indispensable premises or conditions. In particular, true peace cannot even be built without true justice, in which the immense resources of the world are utilized for all peoples and for the good of humanity, instead of being diverted for constructing weapons.

(3331) 6) Closely connected to the problem of peace, there is the question of the build-up of weapons. The arms race and the level that weapons have reached in various parts of the world, with particular reference to the major Powers with their respective alliances, represent:
a) an evil (especially with regard to the use of human potential and material resources), and
b) a grave danger to peace.

(3332) 7) The problems raised by nuclear weapons require a separate and absolutely urgent consideration. They call for a particularly exhaustive and serious examination of a whole range of general and specific moral questions which these weapons pose for the human and Christian conscience. In effect, the concern of the Popes during the past decades - and they are not alone in this - has been deeply marked by the emergence of this new situation which raises questions about the traditional doctrine concerning war. This has not made them forget the problems arising out of the existence of other particularly cruel and harmful weapons, such as chemical, bacteriological and biological armaments.

(3333) 8) There is, therefore, a clear moral obligation incumbent on everyone, to the extent of each one's respective responsibilities, to make every effort to achieve real disarmament, progressively but without delay, especially in the area of nuclear weapons. The Popes hope that this disarmament will be complete, on the part of all nations, in a way, obviously, that is balanced and mutually guaranteed through the necessary systems of control.

(3334) 9) The problem of nuclear and non-nuclear disarmament, while it is of primary importance and urgency, cannot - in fact - and should not - in principle - be considered as a question unto itself. By itself it does not offer a complete answer to the problem of peace, which has much wider implications and requirements. Nor does it have any real possibility of success if, in the first place, other means than those of conflict cannot be found to resolve the questions that divide or will divide peoples and nations. Speaking more generally, disarmament cannot be achieved if international relations are not based on mutual trust and cooperation leading to the elimination, or at least the gradual lessening, of the gap between the rich and poor countries, favouring the development of all peoples, members of the great human family, inseparably bound to each other and interdependent in good as in bad.

(3335) 5. Without claiming to cover every point, I believe that this brief outline describes, fairly adequately, the essential line of thought that is to be found in the teachings and declarations of the Popes closest to us in time.

(3336) The doctrinal and practical approaches of John XXIII, Paul VI and John Paul II in the area of peace, disarmament and international cooperation have been, and are still, the object of many positive judgments coming from various quarters, sometimes even from quarters opposed to each other.

(3337) The teaching of these Popes, which has been respectfully received by millions and millions of persons including non-Catholics, has been repeatedly acknowledged and praised by statesmen and politicians as a great "inspiration".

(3338) We may ask ourselves whether they also find it sufficiently "realistic".

(3339) "Realism" is a word that can have different meanings and interpretations. Those who are concerned primarily with the moral aspect of the problem and who rightly consider that this aspect prevails over all others, have an almost instinctive fear of this word: as if "realistic" tended to be in contrast not only with a sentimental and ethereal idealism but also with a just recognition of the supremacy of moral values in judgment and in consequent actions.

(3340) It would be wrong to assert, in an a priori and indiscriminate way, that politicians, statesmen and others responsible for public life, who are confronted daily by the reality of difficult and complex problems, including those that refer to the security of their respective countries, and who in this sense are almost "condemned" to a strict and watchful realism, are less sensitive to moral exigencies and accept the idea, which was in vogue at one time but which today no one would explicitly support, that moral norms apply to the individual while States are governed exclusively by the rule of self-defence and victory in the "struggle for existence".

(3341) It is understandable, at any rate, that they should experience a certain, sometimes unspoken, perplexity, with respect to the affirmation that in spite of whatever difficulties, it is always possible to maintain peace and avoid war. Or, what is the same thing, that the necessary conditions for reaching peace are capable of being achieved.

(3342) In a well-known passage of the Encyclical Pacem in Terris, four values arising out of the requirements of the moral law in relations between peoples and States are enunciated and developed: truth, justice, effective solidarity, and freedom. These values have been reiterated and further developed by the successors of John XXIII. It is certainly true that, were these conditions to be realized, a peaceful and harmonious coexistence would be ensured on the international plane. But how can it be achieved that peoples and States which are different from each other in race, history, power and interests, will always and everywhere observe these moral norms, in such a way as not to destroy the tranquillitas ordinis, according to Saint Augustine's well-known definition of peace. Justice, the first condition for peace among nations - Opus justitiae pax! - itself becomes a source of conflict when the arrogance of one State towards another elicits a justified reaction on the part of the offended party.

(3343) 6. John XXIII was well aware of the difficulty. And he indicated a solution in the establishment of "universal public authorities in a position to take efficient action" (no. 137), "with sincere and effective impartiality" (no. 138).

(3344) The establishment of "some universal public authority acknowledged as such by all, and endowed with effective power to safeguard, on behalf of all, security, regard for justice, and respect for rights" was recommended by the Second Vatican Council (Gaudium et Spes, 82) and by Paul VI in his Address to the United Nations (no. 3. See above, par. 16). This idea represents, as it were, a permanent aspect of the views of the Holy See and of the Catholic Church -and not only of them - on the question of peace.

(3345) But such a solution seems, for the moment, to be far away and difficult to achieve. Nor should it be forgotten that even when a higher authority is established, such as the power of the State in a country, this higher authority of itself is not always capable of preventing disputes among citizens and social groups, or even sometimes of preventing a revolt against the authority of the State itself. Nor does the activity of the various International Organizations, including the United Nations, which nevertheless enjoy the confidence and support of the Holy See, seem sufficiently effective. Consequently the problem of what can be done in a situation in which the fulfillment of the conditions that can ensure peace among the different States or blocs of States is left to the good will of the parties involved and to their capacity or incapacity to resolve their differences peacefully, still remains in all its acuteness.

(3346) Precisely because of these difficulties, which too often seem insurmountable, the persuasion that military action is lawful when necessary for the "defence of the just rights of peoples," as Gaudium et Spes phrases it (no. 79), has not yet been abandoned. This is the classical "just war" theory, the principles of which are often useful for discerning various aspects of the problem, and which the Holy See considers it cannot, in principle, condemn absolutely and unconditionally, until such time as mankind develops some other effective means of safeguarding justice in relationships between peoples.

(3347) In principle, I have said, and under strict conditions, to which the Popes, since the beginning of the First World War, have not ceased to draw attention with increasing insistence. In particular, it is necessary in every case to try all possible, sincere, tenacious and generous efforts to arrive at a peaceful solution, also with the help of allies and existing international mechanisms. It is required, too, that there be a proportion between the good to be defended and the evils of war in the concrete circumstances of each individual case.

(3348) 7. This latter condition has become more relevant in relation to the constant progress made in the development of new systems of weapons. This is especially so in the case of nuclear weapons, with their tremendous capability of inflicting destruction and suffering lasting long after the actual moment of armed conflict. This fact, confirmed by the tragic experience of Hiroshima and Nagasaki and the statements which science itself has made with a forcefulness that impresses even more than the legitimate emotional response of millions of people around the world, arouses fear and appeals to our sense of responsibility. All of which, as I have already indicated, obliges us to make a profound revision of traditional principles of evaluation, a revision which takes into account the difficulty - many would say, the practical impossibility - of controlling those immense forces which man succeeds in releasing, but which he seems incapable of containing and regulating according to his wishes and according to the dictates of his conscience.

(3349) 8. The specific problems raised by nuclear weapons and the terror caused by their rapid and progressively more menacing development, in a race that appears to have no foreseeable end, have almost made us forget the horror of other weapons and other wars. Such wars have followed one another in many parts of the world since the end of World War II, causing increasing slaughter and destruction.

(3350) Not only are these situations totally unjust towards the people caught up in them; they are also extremely dangerous. A limited war, in fact, especially in certain strategic points around the globe, could give rise to a widening series of involvements leading eventually to a regional or even worldwide conflict.

(3351) In any case, it is understandable that the fear produced by the ever more menacing line-up of nuclear armaments capable of destroying so much life on the face of the earth, or at least in vast regions of the earth - as at present, for example, in Europe - is much greater than the fear produced by other means of destruction and death which, by comparison, appear less terrifying in extension and consequences.

(3352) Scientists warn about the consequences of a nuclear conflict. Churchmen anxiously examine the many moral questions that the possible use of these weapons poses for man's conscience, from the merely human as well as the religious and Christian points of view. Mass movements are organized against the nuclear threat. Politicians and people in government ask what can be done.

(3353) The Holy See, for its part, has not ceased to give attention to these complex questions (without overlooking at the same time the questions posed by other kinds of weapons, such as the bacteriological and biological weapons already mentioned).

(3354) 9. The positions of Pius XII, John XXIII, of Paul VI and John Paul II re-propose, one could say, on a higher level both quantitatively and qualitatively, the principles that apply to all weapons, especially the most dangerous among them.

(3355) While maintaining as an essential point of reference what the Second Vatican Council solemnly declared, that "any act of war aimed indiscriminately at the destruction of entire cities or of extensive areas along with their population is a crime against God and man himself" (Gaudium et Spes, 80), the effects and consequences of a nuclear war are always such as to exclude even the hypothesis of recourse to them. It would really be a type of collective murder-suicide, notwithstanding the efforts made to limit the harm and consequences, by making the nuclear arms more precise and more limited in their effects.

(3356) On this point there seems to exist a general consensus. There also seems to be a general agreement that nuclear weapons, used once for the first time to win a prolonged war, given that science and technology have put them in the hand of nations or alliances opposed to each other, may now be produced and stockpiled, not in order to be used, but to prevent or forestall their use by the other side. There are those who think that nuclear weapons have marked the end of the epoch of war: War with a capital "W" at least, if not of "limited" wars. Not wanting to face collective suicide, mankind will be forced to seek the path of co-existence, perhaps of peace.

(3357) Notwithstanding this thesis, or these hopes, there remains the grave human and moral problem of the danger that these weapons, because they exist, will at some point be used.

(3358) And there remains the problem, no less serious from the moral point of view, of how to react when one side becomes the object of a nuclear attack: does one respond and "defend oneself" with the same "suicidal" arms?

(3359) And how does one behave in the case of an attack with overwhelming conventional weapons, or even with genocidal biochemical or bacteriological weapons?

(3360) 10. The spectre of a possible transition from "deterrence" to actual use includes other hypotheses as well.

(3361) These seem to appear less and less improbable as tension grows in international relations and as more countries and opposing blocs feel that their security or the values that they consider vital are jeopardized.

(3362) The ensemble of these questions is the object of serious and concerned examination and discussion, not only on the part of men and women in politics, of experts, and of public opinion, but in particular of moralists and of entire Bishops' Conferences in different parts of the world.

(3363) Humanity hopes and dreams of being free from the nightmare of a nuclear holocaust that threatens, as if in revenge, those who have violated the mysterious secrets of matter's innermost composition, releasing its unimagined forces.

(3364) The mass demonstrations continually taking place in so many parts of the world, even if they are sometimes affected by unilateralism and unjustified oversimplification, correspond nevertheless to people's deepest feelings.

(3365) We all know that science is not to blame for the present situation. Science is to be admired and encouraged in its conquests. It is man's abuse of these conquests that is at fault.

(3366) More than a question of physical forces, no matter how terrible their unleashing, it is a moral question: a question of wisdom and of will.

(3367) 11. That is to say, man, who is free and who is the master of his own decisions, in spite of the conditioning that he receives from the forces or the resistances of the physical world that he finds himself living in, is the one who can and who must decide his own future and the future of the earth that has been given to him as his home.

(3368) Man: a being who is small and yet immense, weak and yet capable of dominating forces immeasurably greater than himself! Man: the king of the universe!

(3369) The Popes tirelessly recall and emphasize this sovereignty, against the recurring temptations to a more or less explicit abdication from a dignity which is, at the same time, an almost frightening responsibility.

(3370) But when one says "man" one is really saying "men": millions, tens of millions of men and women, organized in ethnic and political groupings differing from one another and too often at odds.

(3371) A common responsibility is divided among them. There thus returns the problem of how one can ensure a common harmony of wills, in order to avoid a common destruction.

(3372) Bearing in mind the real possibilities available, mankind does not seem to have, for the moment, any other choice than between the path of agreement and the path of fear, or of "deterrence".

(3373) The atomic weapon is precisely considered the typical and most effective weapon of "deterrence" existing today.

(3374) There are many who do not hesitate to attribute to it the "merit" of having prevented, for almost four decades, the outbreak of a new world conflict.

(3375) In reality, the nuclear weapon, had it remained the monopoly of a single Power, would have enabled this Power to exercise uncontested dominion over the world. Having come into the possession of others as well, it destroys any dream of absolute predominance, except perhaps over an earth reduced to a desert, and it may be an encouragement to seek some reasonable agreement.

(3376) Naturally, the nuclear threat is not the only means of deterrence: but it does seem to sum up, and raise to a sort of symbol, the other means which, from the earliest days of man's turbulent living in society, have in their various forms been a part of our history. In its radical nature, this threat emphasizes the essential irrationality of a relationship between individuals and peoples based not on the dominance of law and justice - which are often on the side of the weakest - but on the dominance of force, which, no less often, assists those who are in the wrong, or who wish to oppress others, as in the saying recorded in the Book of Wisdom (2:11): "But let our might be our law of right, for what is weak proves itself to be useless."

(3377) The Popes and the Church are of course in favour of a mode of life based upon a mutual commitment to sincere respect for law and justice. But, in view of a reality that unfortunately seems a long way from being capable of change, they recognize that one cannot condemn recourse to a not indiscriminate deterrence, as a means for trying to defend one's own security and to resist unjust aggression, and in the meantime to prepare to change the situation which for the moment justifies the use of deterrence.

(3378) Everybody knows the statement of Pope John Paul II in his Message to the Second Special Session of the General Assembly of the United Nations on Disarmament:

"In current conditions 'deterrence' based on balance, certainly not as an end in itself but as a step on the way toward a progressive disarmament, may still be judged morally acceptable" (See above, par. 1053).

(3379) 12. This statement is of a general nature, and, with regard to the actual ways of exercising this deterrence, one has to have recourse to the familiar principles of moral teaching: taking into due consideration what is at stake, that is to say the values that may be endangered and which have to be protected.

(3380) In itself, deterrence does not require a mathematical "balance" of forces of terror, because deterrence can prove to be effective also in some other way. But, in practice, balance is being sought today, by both the blocs that divide humanity, as an element considered necessary. On the other hand, the principle of balance, political or military, is a classical one in the relationships between States and alliances; and any attempt to destroy the balance to one's own advantage is interpreted as a sure sign of a desire to oppress.

(3381) But, as Pope Paul warned in his Message to the First Special Session of the General Assembly of the United Nations on Disarmament: "The logic underlying the search for the balances of forces impels each of the adversaries to ensure a certain margin of superiority, for fear of being left at a disadvantage" (See above, par. 977).

(3382) This logic leads not to real balance but to a successive imbalance -or at least to a fear of imbalance - which, in the quest for a restoration of balance, fosters an ascending spiral which creates growing costs and growing dangers.

(3383) At any rate, in the papal teaching, deterrence cannot be considered "an end in itself". It has an essentially provisional nature, and, so to speak, an instrumental one. As well as serving in the meantime to avoid the worst, it also has to serve to give time for seeking agreement and understanding, which represent, not only on the moral level but also on the level of the true interests of peoples and of humanity, what I would call the "realistically ideal" condition for human existence in society. It is an ideal that one must make every effort to get ever closer to.

(3384) 13. In the eyes of the Popes, agreement has two purposes. The first, which one could call a negative one, without this definition in any way detracting from its vital importance, is the elimination or at least the limitation of the means which enable men to wage war and which, in some way, can be an encouragement to war; in other words, disarmament.

(3385) The declarations and exhortations of the recent Popes on this subject are, in number and warmth, one of the most eloquent proofs of their concern for the prevention of bloody conflicts between peoples.

(3386) The insistent invitation and exhortation to sincere dialogue, without surrendering to exhaustion or discouragement, mainly concern this first condition for forestalling dangers to peace. The most recent example is the Letter of 26 October last which Pope John Paul II addressed to the President of the United States of America and to the Chairman of the Presidium of the Supreme Soviet of the Soviet Union, in order to urge them not to desist, in spite of the grave difficulties, from the Geneva talks on the reduction of strategic weapons (START) and on intermediate nuclear forces (INF). The Holy See, while remaining on the strictly religious and moral level proper to it, just as it had supported the Treaty for Nuclear Non-Proliferation and had acceded to the same, is now taking part in the preparatory meetings for the Conference on Confidence and Security Building Measures and Disarmament in Europe, which is to be held in Stockholm in January 1984.

(3387) But as well as this "negative" purpose, indeed - in a wider historical view - above and much more than this, the Holy See looks to the positive aspects of peace, which, in the words of the Second Vatican Council, "is not the mere absence of war" (Gaudium et Spes, 78).

(3388) The space created by the hoped-for absence of war must be filled by cooperation for human well-being and progress, backed by the energies and resources thus saved, but backed especially by the generosity and spirit of self-sacrifice of which mankind has so often given such splendid examples on the field of battle.

(3389) Winning true peace demands no less valour and commitment than winning a war.

(3390) The progress of all peoples, a more just and constructive relationship between the developed and the developing nations, between North and South, between States with different political and social regimes - these are the objects of attention and action on the part of the Holy See. In this spirit, the Holy See wished to be a party with full rights and responsibility of the Helsinki Conference on European Security Cooperation.

(3391) 14. We all know the difficulties of dialogue, whether for disarmament, for seeking political solutions for the problems dividing the peoples, or for ensuring harmonious international cooperation. The complexity and difficulty of the problems which are almost inextricably interwoven and which touch upon vital rights and interests, deep feelings and strongly rooted convictions, constitute an obstacle that, too often, can appear in practice unsurmountable.

(3392) On the other hand, dialogue requires sincerity, frankness, a spirit of understanding, firm and patient openness, and generosity, as Pope John Paul II recalled in the Message for the 1983 World Day of Peace. Above all it requires each side to succeed in having confidence in the other side's frankness and good will: something, at least today, which seems almost unattainable, also by reason of invincible ideological differences.

(3393) In order to facilitate dialogue between Governments, much can certainly be done by the support, or pressure, of public opinion, itself trained to understand and be generous to others, sensitive to the needs of those with least resources, and not closed up within nationalistic egoism or racial and cultural prejudices.

(3394) Hence the importance of education for peace: a task of primary importance, both individual and social. The Popes have always made this one of the main concerns of their Magisterium - which is directed beyond ecclesiastical frontiers to all those capable of listening to the voice of conscience that this Magisterium wishes to interpret. It has, likewise, always been part of their ministry to the sons and daughters of the Church. Since, in the last analysis, what will matter is that people are educated to become peacemakers, it is imperative that peace studies be even more developed in all centres of higher learning, in particular in Catholic colleges and universities, and that peace research become, more and more, an integral part of the commitment and contribution that Catholics make in the academic community.

(3395) Dialogue often needs mediators: not always, of course, in the technical sense that this word has in international law.

(3396) The Holy See, for its part, does not shrink from the duty of offering its help, in accordance with its specific nature and possibilities.

(3397) Interest in the cause of peace is so vital that neither difficulties nor disappointments can stop the Holy See in its desire to serve humanity or individual countries.

(3398) 15. What I have tried to say fails to convey the profoundly religious and almost "prophetic" tone that distinguishes the interventions of the Popes in the field of the problems of peace. Nor does it render the profound emotion that accompanies their efforts to set forth, with the rigour of truth and the warmth of their pastoral charity, the demands of the moral conscience and the divine law, the principles that must rule the relationships between individuals, between social classes, peoples and States. It likewise fails to convey the almost painful tension of having to reconcile justice, fundamental human and national rights, freedom and dignity, with the need to safeguard peace, especially in the state the world finds itself living in, in the nuclear age. There is, in fact, a real change of direction in the age-old history of humanity, faced today with the danger of its own self-destruction.

(3399) From the anguished warning of Pope Pius XII at the beginning of World War II: "Nothing is lost with peace, everything can be lost with war", to the cry of Pope Paul VI before the General Assembly of the United Nations: "No more war, war never again!", from John XXIII's impassioned defence of peace to the insistent appeals of Pope John Paul II against the nuclear peril and on the need for constructive dialogue between peoples and the leaders of the nations - all of this tells us how the universal desire for peace finds an echo and a voice in the hearts of the Popes. Peace: "most ardently in every age all people have longed for" - these are the first words of the Encyclical Pacem in Terris.

(3400) This desire finds particular expression in their insistent invitation to prayer: peace is, in fact, a "gift of God".

(3401) But since this gift is "entrusted to us" (Message for the World Day of Peace 1982), the Holy See is equally insistent in appealing to the concrete responsibilities of all.

(3402) The Holy See reminds everyone that it is not enough to proclaim loudly the general desire for peace; it is also necessary to cooperate in creating the conditions that make peace possible.

(3403) To everyone, particularly to believers, the Popes and the Church do not cease to address the pressing appeal to "conversion". They warn that hatred, injustice, conflicts and wars are the "social" fruit of man's departure from the moral order willed by God or, in other words, they are the fruit of what in Christian language is called sin.

(3404) Over sin there is victory: the Redemption. There is a victor: Christ the Redeemer.

(3405) It is Christ whom the Popes, and the Church of which they are the first servants, wish everyone to know, in every clime, in every continent. It is Christ whom they wish everyone to listen to and to follow.

(3406) For they know that, as He is the life of the world, He is also "the Prince of Peace" (*Is.* 9:5); indeed, He is "our peace" (*Eph.* 2:14): "the one desired by all the nations" (*Haggai* 2:8).

II - Address of His Holiness John Paul II to the United Nations Economic Commission for Latin America and the Caribbean (ECLA/CEPAL). Santiago, Chile, 3 April 1987.

Original: Spanish

(3407) 1. It is a great pleasure for me to meet with you here in the Chilean headquarters of the Economic Commission for Latin America and the Caribbean. I would like to begin by expressing my most cordial greeting and gratitude to all those present, particularly to the Executive Secretary of CEPAL for his kindness in inviting me here and for his friendly words of welcome.

(3408) My greeting goes as well to the staff of this center, which is the main office of the United Nations in this region, to the representatives of the organizations, agencies and entities here represented, and to the distinguished guests here present.

(3409) My presence here today continues and reaffirms the support and collaboration which my predecessors, whom we fondly remember, have already offered to the United Nations, a support which I too have made a point of firmly establishing from the very beginning of my papacy.

(3410) 2. Your primary purpose is to study the socioeconomic situation of the region, to formulate and suggest economic policies, and to carry out projects of international cooperation for the good of this vast area of the globe, whose fifth centenary of evangelization we are about to celebrate.

(3411) Simply my standing here and describing the scope of your task is an indication of the great interest the Church has in your work. We share the same problem from different but complementary perspectives. In fact, what constitutes a concern for you is also a motive for continued efforts by the Church, whose mission consists of service to man in all his many dimensions as a creature of God to whom will come Christ's salvation. It is in light of natural and divine law and of the social doctrine of the Church that I wish to contemplate with you this afternoon a few of the more urgent issues that affect all of us.

(3412) 3. Your studies have shown that, despite diverse national economic situations, the crisis that the region as a whole experienced between the years l981 and l985 was the worst, most serious of the last half century and that, despite some signs of recovery in recent times, it is still a dramatic situation. During this period, the gross national product for each country in the region dropped greatly in real terms, while the population increased considerably and obligations on the foreign debt became more critical. You indicate also that, as was foreseeable, the sector most cruelly affected was the mass of people living in conditions of poverty, and that the phenomenon of critical poverty tends to repeat itself, as you put it, in a disheartening vicious circle. Naturally you have not limited yourselves to making a purely negative diagnosis of the problem. I am happy to see that you see possibilities for readjustment and progress. Progress which, with heartening courage,you have expressed in the formula of the opposite "virtuous circle" of production, employment, growth and equality.

(3413) 4. However, the general picture is still dark. I am sure you have discerned as I have the living, pain-filled faces behind the concise language of numbers and statistics. The face of each unemployed and underprivileged human being, with his grief and joy, his frustrations, his anguish and his hope for a better future, stares out from the sheets of statistics.

(3414) It is man, the whole man, each man in his unique being created and redeemed by God, who looks at you with his individual face, with his indescribable poverty and exclusion stamped clearly on his features. Behind all the statistics, *Ecce homo*!

(3415) 5. Faced with this perspective of pain, I can do no less than make an appeal to the public authorities, to private enterprise, to whatever persons or institutions in the entire region within range of my voice, and naturally, to the developed nations, summoning them to meet this formidable moral challenge which was described a year ago in the Instruction on Christian Freedom and Liberation in the following terms: "The aim of this in-depth reflection is to work out and set in motion ambitious programs aimed at the socioeconomic liberation of millions of men and women caught in an intolerable situation of economic, social and political oppression" (No. 8l).

(3416) In this respect and in basic principle, the first problem presents itself regarding the role of the State and that of private enterprise. As a doctrinal matter I shall limit myself to citing a well-known postulate in the teachings of the Church regarding social matters: the principle of subsidiarity. That is, the State must not supplant the initiatives and the responsibilities that individuals and smaller social groups can assume in their respective fields. On the contrary, the State should actively support those areas of liberty, and at the same time it should take care of its own commitments and watch over its own contribution to the common good.

(3417) Within this framework many positions can be taken in the relationship between public authority and private initiative. Faced with the drama of intense poverty, there must exist between the two a mentality of decisive cooperation. Work together, integrate your efforts, do not let a question of ideology or the interest of a given group take precedence over the needs of the poor.

(3418) 6. The challenge of poverty is so vast that in order to overcome it one must have recourse to all the dynamism and creativity of private enterprise, to all of its potential, to its capacity to use resources efficiently and to the fulfillment of renovative energies. Public authority, for its part, cannot abdicate its administrative responsibilities in the economic process nor its power to mobilize the forces of the nation, to cure certain deficiencies characteristic of developing economies and, in short, its ultimate responsibility for the common good of all society.

(3419) However, the State and private enterprise are constituted ultimately by people. I want to underline this ethical and personal dimension of these two economic forces. My call to you, then take on a moral imperative: Be united, above all! Whatever your role is in your social and economic life, construct in your region and economy of solidarity! With these words I propose for your consideration what I called in my message for the most recent World Day of Peace, "a new relationship, the social solidarity of all" (No. 2) In this regard I would like to repeat today the conviction expressed in the recent message of the Pontifical Justice and Peace Commission concerning the handling of the foreign debt: "Cooperation which goes beyond collective egoism and vested interests can provide for an efficient management of the debt crisis and, more generally, can mark progress along the path of international economic justice" (Introduction. See above, par. 2278).

(3420) 7. Solidarity as a basic attitude implies a feeling of empathy with the poor. Feel the misery of the underprivileged as your own and thereby you will act with rigorous consistency. This is not just a question of professing good intentions, but the decisive will to find effective solutions in economic technology with the clarity of vision of that love and creativity that spring from solidarity. I believe that in this economic solidarity we put our greatest hope for the region. The most appropriate economic mechanisms are those that lie at the heart of the economy: The dynamism that gives them life and makes them effective (their "internal mystique") is this sense of solidarity. This, in substance, is the meaning of the repeated teachings of the Church on the predominance of the person over things and of moral conscience over social institutions.

(3421) Your technical reports deserve dual consideration on my part. On the one hand, the fact that fundamental solutions to poverty are not in sight unless there is a substantial increase in production, and hence, a sustained drive in economic development for the entire region. On the other hand, this solution, because of its duration in time and its internal dynamics, may be totally insufficient in the face of immediate urgent needs of the dispossessed. Their condition cries for extraordinary measures, urgent help, imperative monetary aid. The poor cannot wait! He who has nothing cannot wait for relief to arrive as a kind of rebound from the general prosperity of society.

(3422) I know that in complex economic structures it is difficult to combine both of these imperatives without one nullifying the other. The pastor who speaks to you cannot offer technical solutions to this matter: They lie totally in your competence as experts. The common father of all the dispossessed is convinced that the appropriate application of a consistent economic policy is possible - must be possible - through so much will power that is morally united and therefore technically creative.

(3423) 8. It consoles me to know that your latest studies contemplate a strategy for the combination of these two economic imperatives, the long-range and the immediate. It also pleases me to know that your strategy has, as its high-priority goal, the reduction of the high unemployment index in so many countries in this region.

(3424) An unquestionable priority must be given to the policy of reducing unemployment and to the creation of new sources of employment. This priority, as your reports indicate, has purely technical reasons in its favor. There is a reciprocal relation, a mutual causality, a fundamental dynamic of the previously mentioned "virtuous circle", between the creation of jobs and economic development.

(3425) Permit me, nevertheless, to insist on the profoundly moral reason for this priority of maximum employment. The health, nutrition and food subsidies granted to the most indigent person are indispensable, but the person receiving aid is not the propagator in this laudable act of welfare. To offer him work is to activate the essential mechanism of his human activity, by virtue of which the worker takes possession of his own destiny, integrates with all of society and even receives other aid, not as alms, but in a way as the living and personal fruit of his own labor.

(3426) The studies made on the "psychology of the unemployed" confirm this priority. A man without work is wounded in his human dignity. When he is made into an active worker he not only receives a salary, but he recovers that essential condition of human nature that is work, and this, for a Christian, is his everyday road to grace and perfection. Your recent graphs on unemployment in the region are frightening. Do not rest until everything has been done so that each inhabitant of the region has access to that authentic, fundamental right which is, for human beings, the right and correlative responsibility to work.

(3427) 9. A job, justly compensated, offers the intrinsic possibility of reversing that circular process you have called the "repetition of poverty and marginalization." This possibility can be realized only if the worker reaches a certain level of education, culture and work capacity and has the opportunity to pass it on to his children. And it is here, as you well know, that we are touching the nerve of the whole problem. Education, the master key to the future, the read to the social integration of the underprivileged, the soul of social dynamism, is the essential duty and right of every human being. Let the State, the intermediary groups, individuals, institutions, the varied forces of private enterprise, concentrate their best efforts on the promotion of education in the entire region.

(3428) The moral causes of prosperity have been well known throughout history. They reside in a constellation of virtues: industriousness, competence, order, honesty, initiative, frugality, thrift, spirit of service, keeping one's word, daring - in short, love for work well done. No system or social structure can resolve, as if by magic, the problem of poverty outside of these virtues. In the long run, both the projects of institutions and their functioning reflect the habits of human beings - habits that are acquired during the education process and that form an authentic work ethic.

(3429) 10. Finally, a word concerning the important work developed by the Latin American Demographic Center, an organ of CEPAL. I know that the increase in population seems to augment the regional problems we have already spoken of and is felt as a heavy burden. In this regard I shall repeat the words that Pope Paul VI pronounced at the Food and Agriculture Organization in l970: "Surely, faced with the difficulties to be overcome, there is a great temptation to use the power of the State to diminish the number of guests at the table rather than multiply the bread to be shared." (See above, par. 64). Even within the problematic context of the economy, human life conserves, with its most intimate and sacred nucleus, that intangible character that no one has the right to manipulate without giving offense to God and injury to all society. Let us defend it in the face of easy solutions based on destruction. No to the artificial prevention of fecundity! No to abortion! Yes to life! Yes to responsible parenthood!

(3430) The demographic challenge, like all human challenges, is ambivalent, and we have to redouble our concentration on the best efforts of human solidarity and collective creativity so as to convert population growth into a formidable potential for economic, social, cultural and spiritual development.

(3431) 11. I would have liked speaking to you at this meeting of other themes shared by CEPAL and the Holy See, but I wanted to concentrate on the question of extreme poverty, which is at the center of your concern and which is a painful thorn in my heart as father and pastor of so many faithful in the beloved nations of this vast region of the world.

(3432) I reiterate my thankfulness for your kind invitation, which I accepted with great pleasure. And I raise my prayer to the almighty Father, to Jesus Christ, Lord of history, and to the Holy Living Spirit, through the intercession of Our Lady of Guadalupe, patron of Latin America, than an abundance of holy light and energy may fall upon those concerned with the social and economic progress of the developing nations, so that the greatest concentration of intelligence, good will and creative labor may be possible - a concentration demanded imperatively by the present interaction among the countries of Latin America and the Caribbean.

III - Address of His Holiness John Paul II to the United Nations Committee on Coordination. The Vatican, 24 April 1987.

Original: English

(3433) I wish to thank you for the kind sentiments which the Secretary-General, Mr. Pérez de Cuéllar, has expressed on your behalf. I am pleased that this meeting in Rome of the *United Nations Administrative Committee on Coordination* has made possible your presence here today, and I extend to each of you my welcome and cordial greeting.

(3434) 1. The United Nations Organization, which you serve, has a vital role in today's world. We are all aware that *increasing global interdependence and intercommunication* create an ever greater potential for peace and understanding, but also multiply the risks of wider conflict. Your Organization is uniquely suited to fostering the possibilities for peace and to reducing the dangers created by injustice and aggression. It serves as a *useful forum for discussion and an effective instrument for action,* in promoting the common good of the human family. It owes its very existence to the desire of people of good will for peace, security and the freedom to seek legitimate human development for themselves, their families, and their communities. Each of the agencies and activities you represent was initiated in order to ensure true human progress, that is, progress based on respect for fundamental God-given rights, on mutual cooperation, and on the promotion of justice and peace.

(3435) The United Nations Organization deserves praise for its *service to humanity on many levels.* As part of its regular activities, it has drawn international attention in recent years to such issues as poverty, homelessness, human rights, the plight of the refugees, the needs of children and of the handicapped, and the contribution of women to society. It has likewise drawn attention to issues related to the spheres of culture, economics, science and public health. Among its many positive achievements I would also mention the Conventions signed last year in Vienna on collaboration in the event of nuclear accidents. Each of the problems just mentioned and many others as well, can only be remedied by *cooperation that transcends national and regional boundaries and interests.* The initiatives of the United Nations are a sign of hope that such cooperation is indeed possible.

(3436) As we know so well, the *search for worldwide consensus and cooperation in establishing peace and solving problems is not always an easy one,* given the many social, political and economic differences that mark the human family, and given the constant temptation for individual nations to pursue excessive self-interest at the expense of the greater good of all. For this reason, the work of the United Nations requires patience and perseverance in continuing along the path of cooperation.

(3437) 2. But there is an even deeper challenge to be faced from within. All those who administer and carry out the programmes of the United Nations must continue to find their *inspirations in the ideals and moral values* upon which it was founded. Only in this way will the Organization *project a sense of purpose* which is a genuine service to the world community. Only in this way can it maintain a *vision which inspires international trust and cooperation.* The highest standards of personal integrity are required on the part of all. Any falling short would mean sacrificing credibility in the urgent task of promoting ethical solutions to the world's problems.

(3438) *The ethical approach is crucial,* for without it one can lose sight of the dignity and rights that belong to every human being. If that dignity is not recognized, and if those rights are not respected, there can be no genuine progress nor any lasting solution to the problems that beset us. For too long in this century *humanity has been conditioned by the clash of competing ideologies and economic interests,* a conflict in which the individual is disregarded or subordinated to profit-making or to ideological concerns. This has been the cause of much division and hatred, of much violence and warfare, and it continues to hamper efforts for justice and peace. The human family has also been profoundly affected by scientific and technological developments, and these also raise ethical questions about the nature of progress as it relates to the human person.

(3439) 3. It is my conviction that at this moment in its history the United Nations Organization faces a twofold challenge: *to overcome ideological competition* and *to foster an ethical approach* to human development and the resolution of social problems. When I speak of the ethical approach, I mean to say that man, and the truly human quality of life which one wishes him to have, should be at the center of thought and action. Man and his rights; the right to life, the right to a dignified existence, the right to profess his religious beliefs freely, the right to work, and so forth. It is not only a matter of observing certain moral standards in the carrying out of United Nations business and activities, but also of consciously adopting an approach which is recognized as ethical because it is *truly at the service of the individual and respects human dignity and human rights.* The recent publication by the Pontifical Commission for Justice and Peace of reflections on the international debt question is an attempt to articulate such an approach with regard to a particular problem of pressing concern to all nations.

(3440) 4. The Catholic Church, whose members come from many different lands and nations, appreciates the worldwide efforts of the United Nations as well as the magnitude of the problems that call for ethical solutions. For the Church has a *message that transcends human divisions and national boundaries.* She deeply believes in peace. She works for development and progress, while insisting that they are truly human only when they are rooted in the truth of the divine creation and redemption of the world. For these reasons, *the Church is always ready to cooperate* with the United Nations in any worthy initiative which promotes and protects the dignity of the human person and the peace, justice and well-being of all.

(3441) I pray that God will bless you and your collaborators in your service to humanity through your work in the United Nations Organization. May he also bless your families and all your loved ones with his grace and peace.

IV - Message of His Holiness John Paul II to Dr. Arcot Ramachandran, Executive Director of Habitat, for the International Year of Shelter for the Homeless, The Vatican, 20 March 1987.

Original: English

(3442) In this International Year of Shelter for the Homeless, I extend my cordial greetings to you and to all those taking part in the Tenth Commemorative Session of Habitat, the United Nations Centre for Human Settlements.

(3443) From the beginning, the Church has taken an active interest in the goals and activities of the Centre. On this Tenth Anniversary of its founding, I assure you that this interest has increased with the passing of the years, as has the conviction of the vital urgency of co-ordinated efforts to assist in an effective way those who are homeless or whose housing is inadequate.

(3444) It has become increasingly apparent that the housing problem, like so many other human problems in our world today, can be solved only through cooperation on the part of the whole international community. Thus I stated in my 1987 World Day of Peace Message: "The underlying challenge for all of us is to adopt *an attitude of social solidarity with the whole human family* and to face all social and political situations with this attitude" (No. 3).

(3445) Habitat is in a position to encourage and foster precisely such an attitude and to assist in efforts to put it into practice, particularly for the well-being of those suffering from inadequate housing. Even though the number of the homeless and those lacking proper shelter continues to grow, may we not hope that the desire to help them will grow even more? It is my prayer that we shall see many sectors of the world community engaged in planning and implementing effective housing strategies, efforts which will manifest a practical attitude of social solidarity with all those in need.

Upon yourself and upon all attending the Session in Nairobi I invoke God's gifts of wisdom and peace.

V - Message of His Holiness John Paul II on the occasion of the International Conference on Drug Abuse and Illicit Trafficking. The Vatican, 4 June 1987.

Original: English

(3446) The phenomenon of drug abuse is one of the greatest tragedies plaguing society today, a tragedy of ever-widening proportions that strikes both industrialized and developing countries with devastating effects on individuals, families and the whole social fabric. The fact that the abusers are predominantly young people poses a particular threat to the future stability of society as we advance towards the end of the Second Millennium.

(3447) Unfortunately there are indications that this human tragedy is steadily worsening: a) illegal drugs are being produced in ever-increasing quantities; b) illicit drug trafficking which produces immense profits continues unchecked; c) the vastly widespread character of drug abuse which, although concentrated mostly among young people, is also found at every level of modern society, in rural as well as urban areas, among both men and women, among all races and cultures.

There is no country which is now immune from this modern scourge, either in the East or the West, in the northern or southern hemispheres, in the poorer or the richer countries.

(3448) Many factors contribute to the dramatic increase in drug abuse. Surely a primary one is the breakdown of the family. In addition, there is a steady weakening of traditional ways of life which for generations have passed on cultural values and given meaning to daily existence; there are increasing tensions in human relationships, rising unemployment, sub-human standards of living, fears engendered by the threat of nuclear war and numerous other social factors, not the least of which is a psychological need to escape from the hardships and painful responsibilities of life. But at the root of this evil is the loss of ethical and spiritual values. If it is true that the youth of today are the greatest consumers of hard drugs, then it is legitimate to ask if this is due to the kind of society in which our young people are being reared.

(3449) Drug abuse impoverishes every community where it exists. It diminishes human strength and moral fibre. It undermines esteemed values. It destroys the will to live and to contribute to a better society. Drug abuse is indeed a scourge, just as much as a famine, a drought or an epidemic. Every year it reaps an increasing harvest of human lives.

(3450) But the modern plague of drug addiction has not gone entirely unchecked or unopposed. We cannot close our eyes to the immensity of the evil inflicted on humanity by this tragic problem; but neither should we fail to see the many efforts, even heroic ones, which are being made to counter it.

(3451) The United Nations Organization, as well as other institutions both governmental and non-governmental, have called attention internationally and regionally to the consequences of drug abuse. Conventions have been held, studies have been undertaken and other means have been employed, and the Holy See has been pleased to take an active part in these initiatives.

(3452) The continuing growth of illegal production and sale of drugs makes even more urgent the duty to expand those initiatives which seem now to be achieving concrete and positive results. It is imperative that the criminal activity of drug production and trafficking should be directly opposed and ultimately stopped. In this regard, my encouragement and admiration go to all those countries in which government leaders and citizens are truly committed to combatting the production, sale and misuse of drugs, sometimes paying a very high price, even sacrificing their own physical integrity. And I applaud all those who are working with equal determination to impart preventive education in the home, at school and in places of work. This requires some form of collaboration with agencies at the national and international level.

(3453) But all of this would still not be sufficient if such political, legal and educational efforts were not accompanied by other initiatives, such as making crop substitution a feasible alternative in areas where illicit plant cultivation seems to be the only profitable or viable option available to the farmer. To provide such an alternative requires comprehensive rural development programmes, with stable infra-structures, appropriate technology and the fundamental community facilities of health care, education and so forth. Clearly, the problem of drug addiction and illicit trafficking is not unrelated to the question of human development.

(3454) Special consideration must also be given to the treatment and rehabilitation of those who have become addicted to drugs or dependent on them in an unhealthy way. This requires the establishment and maintenance of institutions which can meet the specific needs of each individual victim of drug abuse. The great variety of needs represented requires the possibility of a threefold treatment: medical, social and legal. In this, the Church is ready to be of assistance, especially through the centres which she has herself established and by her cooperation with centres which are provided by other agencies.

(3455) A key factor in successful rehabilitation, particularly in the case of young people, is the restoration of self-confidence and a healthy self-esteem, which provide fresh motivation based on solid moral and spiritual values. Drug abusers must be helped to re-establish trusting relationships with their families and friends. They must also be helped to resume their work, education or job-training. Families play a vital role in this process, as do educational, social and cultural institutions. Rehabilitation requires team work, and thus each of these should collaborate willingly with families and all concerned.

(3456) I assure you that the Church wishes to offer every possible support to the many and varied efforts being made. And I wish to add a word of personal encouragement to you and the Governments and organizations that you represent. The common struggle against the plague of drug abuse and illicit trafficking is motivated by a serious spirit of mission, on behalf of humanity and for the very future of society, a mission whose success demands a mutual commitment and generous response on the part of all.

May God bless your efforts and may this Conference be for the rest of the world a beacon of encouragement and hope.

INDEX OF THE DOCUMENTS

INDEX OF THE DOCUMENTS

Pius XII:

JOHN XXIII

PAUL VI

JOHN PAUL II

H.E.MSGR. GIOVANNI BENELLI
SUBSTITUTE OF THE SECRETARIAT
OF STATE, SPECIAL ENVOY.

HOLY SEE

PONTIFICAL COMMISSION
"IUSTITIA ET PAX"

PONTIFICAL ACADEMY OF SCIENCES

HOLY SEE DELEGATION

TOPICAL INDEX

TOPICAL INDEX

Abandonment

systematic a. of the **ambition of being a human person**: 171; judicious a. of **arms**: 916; of the mentality of **relations based upon fear** of mutual destruction: 1105; of **ideologies and myths of power and supremacy**: 1317; of the categorical affirmations of the past which authorized the excesses of **capitalism, monopolies and technocracy**: 1687; of the **agricultural sector**: 1688; of the **utopian expectation** that industrialization will certainly and directly lead to economic development and civil progress for everyone: 1779; of the **excessive defence of food prices** by the high-production countries: 2192. See also: 191; 417; 611; 1085; 1844; 1919; 2190; 2193; 2350; 2410; 2466; 2661; 2882; 2888; 2916; 2977; 3346.

Aberration

exaggerated **nationalism**, **racism** engendering hate, **lust for unlimited power**, unbridled **thirst for domination**: 67; **destruction of innocent human life**, at whatever stage it may be, through the heinous crimes of abortion or euthanasia: 647; **arbitrary and summary executions**, example of the a. which exist within some political regimes: 3089.

Ability

human person's a. to triumph over self-seeking sowers of hate or disunion: 2978; **to adapt**, particular characteristic of true culture: 697; of **judgement**: 770; **nations' a. to control their own destinies**: 1439; to **work**: 2139; 2942; of the **entrepreneurs** to mobilize for investment the whole productive surplus: 1447; of **each debtor State** to meet its basic needs: 2322. See also: 053; 65; 275; 1241; 1359; 1660; 1682; 1719; 2761; 2801; 2824; 3117; 3198; 3270/d.

Abolition

of **classes** and discrimination: 630; of **systems** in which the privileged become steadily more privileged: 1548; of the **claim to ownership** of natural resources by those countries privileged by their geographical location: 3186;

Abortion

1. constitutes today **a problem of such gravity for the human conscience** that society cannot ignore it or cover it up: 2760;
is opposed to physical, moral and social health; in fact it kills the embryo which is, right from the moment of conception, a human being: 2577;
diminishes the esteem the mother has of herself: 2577; often constitutes **a danger** for the woman's health and for the possibility of future conception: 2577;
has **not been arrested** by the massive introduction and distribution of contraceptive means: 2760;
it is **more and more used** as an integral part of family planning programmes, financed even by governments and international organizations: 2760; 3058; 3077;

2. the **Catholic Church**: **states** that no person may authorize the suppression of the life of an innocent human being, foetus or embryo,...: 2483; will **never cease** to raise her prophetic voice proclaiming that **human life must be respected nd protected from the moment of conception**: 2360; 2483; 2533; 2760; 3023; 3072; see also *Life/11;*

categorically condemns *abortion in the name of the respect due to all human life from its very conception: 2533; 3429; and suppression of the foetus in the presence of some defect which can give rise to future malformations and deficiencies: 2655;*

considers *it a massive aberration, an heinous crime 647; 2483; 3024-3026; a most serious violation of human and medical ethics: 3058;*

opposes *its legalization: 2533; 2722; 3022-3034;* ***condemns and*** *forcefully rejects any violence applied by governments or other public authorities in favour of contraception or, still worse, of sterilization and procured a.: 2734;*

denounces *as gravely unjust cases where, in international relations, economic help given for the advancement of peoples is made conditional on programmes of contraception, sterilization and procured abortion: 2734-2735; see also Family/6;*

makes an **appeal** to all governments and international organizations to affirm clearly and explicitly the value, the inviolability and the dignity of human life from the moment of conception and, therefore, to prohibit and exclude abortion - not just in theory but in fact - as an element of family planning: 2760; 2360; see also *Life/1-5*;

strongly **deplores the discrimination and other forms of moral pressure** exerted in some countries against physicians, health personnel and clinics that refuse to cooperate directly or indirectly in the suppression of life: 3029;

3. see also: 432; 2342; 2627; 2759; 3080; 3085; *Population/5; Suppression.*

Accord

common a. in building up social justice: 47; **international a.** to arrive at more stable and more equitable prices: 1531; the building of the world community comes about little by little through **regional a.**: 1609; needed **among member States of the United Nations** to seek appropriate means of dissuasion and intervention, to avoid recourse to the force of arms: 354; in renouncing the weapons that threaten to kill peace while claiming to serve it: 1010; **close a.**: between the Holy See and the United Nations to protect the freedom and dignity of every person, without discrimination: 434; 605. See also: 119; 324; 478; 1121; 1686; 2931; 3090; *Agreement.*

Action

1. of **God in history**: 398; of the **Church/Holy See**: for the cultural promotion of peoples: 774; educational a.: 781; 2543; against racial discrimination: 612; 616; 619; 627; for the elderly: 2494; for the disabled: 2641; for the improvement of the habitat: 2825-2826; for refugees: 2848; 2922-2923; 2928; 2937; for peace: 3313; 3316-3320; see also: 043; 073; 088; 64; 177; 709; 733; 771; 1520; 1695; 1716; 2014; 2032; 2035; 2038; 2153; 2206; 2274; 3390;

2. of the **United Nations**: 310; 2929; priority objectives of international common action: 359; of **ILO**: 47; of **FAO**: 58; 60; 69; 114-115; 118; 130; 132; 143; 1960; 1962; 2007; 2026; 2052; 2061; 2066; 2087; of **UNESCO**: 594; 705-706; 723; 733; 776; 887; 890; 894; 895; 910; 923-924; 928; 933; to eliminate illiteracy: 780; 784; 789; 790; 795; 1480; 2543; of the **WHO**: 3004;

3. of **States**: 349; of a **world authority**: 16; 68; 3343; for the **realization of the legitimate aspirations** of the people of our day: 411; 413;

4. of the **human being**: 159; 165; 728; 1456; the human person realizes its potential in and through action: 2632-2636; **contrary to one's conscience**: 522;

5. **repressive and discriminatory**, against vast numbers of citizens: 456; against **apartheid**: 606; 611-612;

6. concerted, common a. of the **workers**: 225; collective a. **to win the cause of peace**: 717; immediate a. **to halt arms race**: 1664; **military**: 3346; **social**: 1441; 1452-1453; 1460; 1487; 2074;

7. for **development**: 1374; 1406; 1413; 1418; 1435; 1467; 1481; 1484; 1557; 1597; 1601/b; 1631; 1642-1643; 1653; 1664; 1678; 1684; 1695; 1699; 1710;

8. in the sphere of **nutrition**, **agriculture** and **rural development**: 60; 1765; 1826; 1828; 1865; 1884; 1887; 1889; 1947; 1948; 1966; 1979; 2007; 2032; 2035; 2038; 2052; 2061; 2064; 2074; 2077; 2084; 2090; 2093; 2111; 2124; 2148; 2153-2154; 2208-2209; 2219; 2222; 2234; 2239-2241; 2247-2250; 2252-2256;

9. for the solution of the **debt question**: 2274; 2280; 2286; 2290; 2295; 2299; 2305; 2307; 2333; 2335; 2340;

10. in behalf of **youth**: 2460-2461; 2466; educative a. of **women**: 790; 2544; for the **promotion of women**: 2514-2516; 2519; 2521; 2532-2533; 2537; 2549; 2592; 2597; 2599; for **aging population**: 2480; 2482; 2491; 2494; to improve the situation of the **disabled persons**: 2641; 2668; for **refugees**: 2929;

11. in the field of **population**: 2708; 2714; 2718-2720; 2724; 2727-2728; 2746-2747; 2749; 2755-2756; 2761; 3047; in the field of **health**: 2996; 3004; 3018; 3074; 3077; to combat **desertification**: 3123-3124; 3128; 3136;

12. see also: 05; 026; 028; 123; 159; 691; 699; 709; 863; 875; 1036; 1061; 1183; 1193; 1242; 1288; 1310; 1373; 1406; 1413; 1738; 1994; 2397; 2474; 2610; 3090; 3176; 3249; 3252; 3279; 3300/6; 3300/21; 3313; 3339, and *Activity*.

Activity

1. **of the Church**, in education: 687; temporal aspect of its a.: 947; humanitarian: 1925; missionary: 3122; of the Christians: 688; of the **Holy See**: in the service of peace and of a more just and brotherly social order, in and among all nations: 074-082; 086; for refugees during the First and the Second World Wars: 2852; doctrinal: 3326;

2. **human** a.: 37; 53; 219; 221; 265; 692; 1734; 3202; 3425; of the **spirit**: 916; **social**: 667; **economic**: 667; 3295; **political**: 76; 667; its reason is service to the human person, the protection of its dignity and the effective promotion and safeguarding of its rights: 3088; **professional**: 680; **technological**: 3295; **aimed at discovering the very roots of hatred**, destructiveness and contempt: 86; **extra-conjugal sexual activity**: 2756; **guerrilla** a.: 2172;

3. **of parents** in the education of their children: 840; of **women** in health services: 2579; professional activity of **disabled persons**: 2667; scholastic a. of **children**: 2889; in the service of the **health** of family: 3083;

4. **international**: 3219; of **International Organizations**: 3345; of **governments**: 2176; **diplomatic**: 3325; of **non-governmental organizations**: 1487; 2239; **of the UN**: 74; 939; 2552; 3345; for peace: 1069; disarmament: 1076; of **FAO**: 60; 63; 123; 125; 1952; 1966; 1974; 2000; 2026; 2105; of **ILO**: 212; 214; of **UNESCO**: 747; 749; 894; 939; against illiteracy: 787; 800; of **IAEA**: 1306; of **WHO**: 3005; 3007; 3061;

5. see also: 40; 42; 46; 253; 480; 620; 698; 741; 1094; 1132/4; 1167; 1373; 1381; 1521; 1794; 1855; 1894; 1900; 2098; 2120; 2179; 2247; 2824; 2859; 3005, and Action;

Admiration

respect and a. for the **elderly**, in the Bible: 2482; admiring astonishment before the miracle of the **person that is "the other"**: 2623; for the rich **creativity of the human mind**: 161; a. and gratitude for **savants, research workers** and **technicians**: 870; for the **cultures** of the new societies: 173; for

science: 3365; for the results of planetary and space science: 3202; 3264; 3276; 3279. See also: 40; 59; 245; 456; 689; 741; 747; 1847; 1869; 1965; 1975; 1989; 1994; 2170; 2986.

Advancement

human a.: 1377; 1612; 1626; 3104; concern of the Holy See: 1156; 2567; **of the human person**: 209; 798; 927; 930; 1489; 1599; 1758; 2158; 2247; 2467; 2688; 2700; 3132; 3149; **of humanity**: 202; 1486; 3205; **of women**: 883; 2248; 2367; 2500; 2511; 2565; 2591; 2622; 2624; 2637; 2764; **of a nation**: can never be realized at the expense of another: 243; **of peoples**: 930; 2498; 2734; 2752; 3095; **peoples of Africa**: 1841; **least favoured**: 685; **poor**: 1524; **rural workers/areas**: 1657; 1769; 2141; **starving people**: 1926; **peace a.**: 193; **social**: 102; 781; 2367; 2764; **professional**: 815. See also: 278; 582; 617; 694; 749; 927; 2249; 2571; 3195; *Development; Progress.*

Affirmation

of the **primacy of the human factor** over the product of work: 45; **sense of a.**: 170; 205; progressive a. of **human rights**: 425; of **duties**, correlated with the **a. of rights**: 863; of the **being** of each person and people: 930; **concrete a.** of the objective criteria of justice: 2169; of the **family's place in society** and of its rights: 2708; of the **unity of the human family**: 1686; of the **fundamental equality of persons**: 2529; of **agriculture** as the basis of a healthy economy: 2169; 2188; of **technology** as a basic coefficient of economic progress: 238; of the **juridical equality of all the member States** of the United Nations: 382; **and appeals** for justice and peace: 861; reaffirmation of the plea for human solidarity: 1516; of **faith and hope in the destiny of the human family**: 3100; **that it is always possible to maintain peace and avoid war**: 3341; of the **responsibilities of States and individuals** as regards environment: 3109. See also: 013; 162; 207; 809; 1225; 1681; 1687; 1688; 1749; 2185; 2211; 2227; 2656; 2686; 2705; 2724; 2755; 2760; 2780; 2785; 2841; 3110; 3111; 3130; 3325.

Africa

particularly affected by the ecological problems: 277; **John Paul II appeal from Ouagadougou** on behalf of all those suffering from drought: see *Ougadougou*; **its peace depends also on** the reconciliation of people in each country: 289; it **requires the solidarity of all Africans** at the service of the whole African family: 289; **its future** depends on the African peoples themselves: 284; **cultural maturity**: 741; **African countries** will be capable progressively to meet the economic and social challenge which devastates and humiliates the great majority of their inhabitants: 1422; the **solution** of its nutritional problems is in the hands of Africans: 1715-1716; **emergency situation**: 1842-1843; 1918-1927; 2080; 2208; **international cooperation for its technological development**: 1841-1847; **refugees**: 2866; 2875-2881; 2931-2938; **situation in Southern Africa**: see *Apartheid.* See also: 044; 884; 1419; 1483; 2174; 2273; 2435; 3018-3019; 3122.

Aggression

we are still living too often with **reflexes of suspicion and a. which are detrimental to relations between nations**: 251; one cannot condemn **recourse to a not indiscriminate deterrence**, as a **means** for trying to defend one's own security and **to resist unjust a.**: 3377, see also *Deterrence.* See also: 580; 975; 3051; 3434; *Attack/3; Deterrence; War.*

Aging

right to live as active members of society: 2480; **old age in the Bible**: 2482; **characteristics**: 2485; **values**: 2486; **society must be able to recognize the moral, affective and religious values of the el-**

derly: 2487; must be **integrated** in family and society life: 2489-2493; **care of the Church** for the elderly: 2494; associations of elderly: 2495. See: **2479-2498**; 2596; 2730; 2741; 2748; 2768; 2926; Life/9; *Euthanasia.*

Agreement

1. **between States**: 68; regional: 1609; between different countries in Southern Africa: 658; **international** a. to ensure indispensable reserves of cereals: 137; **commodity** a.: 1532; 1655; 1663/1; **sales** a.: 1507; **preference given to multilateral over bilateral** a. of international cooperation: 1525; **trade** a.: 1645; 2302; on **grain** trade: 1826; on **liquidity control**: 1663/4; on the **management and development of fishing**: 1861; 1864; 1887; 1889; for **development:** 1882; **among creditors and debtors**: 2323;

2. **aimed at reducing the arms race**: 85; 1233; on the complete and effective banning of the preparation, manufacture and stockpiling of **all chemical weapons**: 1160; for **effective control of the reduction and spread of conventional weapons**: 1176; 1234; wider a. for the **promotion of a system of general and complete disarmament** under effective international control: 1222; partial a. of the **SALT negotiations**: 1246; **worldwide a. for disarmament and the banning of nuclear weapons**: 1316; see also: 3356; 3372; 3375; 3383-3384;

3. for the **use and operation of satellite communication systems**: 3249; **banning the placement and testing of all weapons in outer space**: 3266; for the **regulation of the occupation of space by satellites**: 3281; 3289; for **peaceful uses of space resources**: 3310;

4. see also: 20; 50; 73; 149; 231; 328; 359; 432; 439; 470; 513; 594; 611; 701; 792; 836; 877; 953; 996; 1133; 1178; 1181; 1238; 1278; 1279; 1338; 1342; 1348; 1410; 1418; 1533; 1556; 1562; 1568; 1607; 1739; 2082; 2196; 2251; 2261; 2289; 2727-2728; 2880; 2946; 3070-3071; 3107; 3111; 3166; 3240; *Accord; Law.*

Agriculture

1. may be considered the **most important sector in the world economy**: 116; 1780; **basis of a healthy economy**: 1782; 2152; 2161; **primacy**: 1851; 2150; 2188; **progress made**: 201; 1953; **development**: 2119-2120; 2767; **under-modernized** a.: 1449; **difficulties**: 1960; **weakening**: 1961; **in developing countries** calls for urgent transformations: 1657; 2055; **need to promote a just world policy for a.**: 2096; **subordinated** to the immediate interests of the other sectors of economy: 2117; **the most underdeveloped sector of the economy**: 2118; 2250;

2. **accelerated increase of production**: 131; 1820; **slow progress of productivity in relation to demand**: 2713; need to regulate **trade and external assistance** to countries which need it to ensure their economic trade-off: 131;

3. **place in** the sphere of **internal and international development**: 1778; **function in preserving the environment** and as a valuable source of energy: 1781; utilization, conservation, improvement of the **soil**: 1954; exploitation of **forests**: 1956, and: 61; 277; 1322; 1938; 1945; 1965; 1975; 2815; 3209; 3256; 3286; 3299/3; 3305;

4. **benefit from remote sensing**: 3209; 3256; 3286 and 3291-3310;

5. see also: 1342; 1362; 1447; 1587; 1588; 1652; 1675; 1744-1829; 1859; 1873; 1875; 1929; 1938; 1945; 1979; 2006; 2082; *Developing Countries/3; Development/5; FAO; Food.*

Aid

1. to **underprivileged peoples**: 777; 1548; 1887; 2340; 3130; the **least favoured**: 784; the **developing countries**: 836; 1389-1391; should be **imbued with respect** for indigenous cultures:

836; to **development**: a condition for peace: 1101; must not take on the forms of neo-colonialism: 1101; should be closely linked to reforms in domestic structure: 1463; the **least advanced countries** should be guaranteed the a. proportioned to their needs, without either domination or pressure by the advanced countries: 1887; a. for the advancement of peoples **should never be conditioned** on a demonstrated decline in birth rates, nor depend on participation in family planning programmes: 2752; 2115; 2734; *Family/6;*

2. however laudable and necessary, is **not sufficient** to promote the full measure of human dignity required by solidarity of mankind: 1391;

3. is **not even the beginning**, at the world level, **of redistributive taxation** or a healthy welfare system: 1455; a. flows **should be "institutionalized"** and accepted as an incipient world tax system, to underline their essential character not of generosity but of distributive justice: 1466; 1592; from occasional and discontinuous **should be transformed into an organic security system**, regular and binding: 1828; 2091; international a. **often benefits only imperfectly the most poverty-stricken people**: 1548; new a. has always the bitter taste of a **new burden of debts**: 1608;

4. a. programmes **to guarantee food**: 134; see also: 1826; 2093; 2151; 2193; 2208; 2247; in **emergency situations**: 134; **launched by FAO**: 137; **given by the IAEA**: 1291; 1342-1343;

5. to **refugees**: 2852; 2859-2861; 2868-2870; 2877; see also Refugees;

6. the Second Vatican Council has clearly and unambiguously proclaimed the **duty of the rich countries to give aid to the poorer ones**: 1706; **action of the Church**: 1715-1716; 2034; 2038; 2852; 2870-2872;

7. see also: 46; 63; 256; 398; 590/a; 770; 1202; 1275; 1345; 1351; 1409; 1411; 1441; 1446; 1462; 1484; 1506; 1528; 1530; 1537; 1539; 1547; 1566; 1582; 1589; 1609; 1663/2; 1680; 1725; 1835; 1866; 1884; 1890; 1898; 1902-1905; 1917; 1921-1922; 1924; 1926; 1946; 1955; 1970; 2084-2086; 2117; 2165; 2255; 2284/3; 2297/6; 2325; 2383; 2410; 2432; 2451; 2615; 2666; 2676; 2691; 2824; 3006; 3265; 3307; 3421; 3425; *Assistance; Developing Countries/9-11; Development/3;*

Alienation

and fragmentation, **characteristic of modern societies**: 266; **caused by** a political activity cut off from its fundamental relation to the human person: 76; of **education**, which accustoms the human being to becoming the object of a host of manipulations: 169; 1283; **liberation of peoples** from various forms of misery and a.: 1558. See also: 152; 224; 2757; 2998.

Ambition

for **power**: 897; 2547; **national**: 1704; see also: 5; 171; 272; 696; 699; 1600; 1671; 3093; 3211; *Power/2; Selfishness;*

Anxiety

1. of **youth** at the invasion of technocracy: 56; 681; of the **human beings** to solve to dominant problem of their living together: 744; a. and need of **the poor**: 1774; pressing a. **for the food problem**: 2138; exclusive a. for **economic development**: 2703;

2. **about the threat to peace** in our world: 2472; **of the scientific world** in the face of an irresponsible use of science: 195; serious a. **at the persistence and aggravation of situations of racial and ethnic discrimination**: 432;

3. see also: 2533; 2889; 3075; 3198; Fear.

Apartheid

1. the **Catholic Church/Holy See proclaims**:
the dignity of the human person and the brotherhood of all human beings: 637; see *Person, Brotherhood;*
that whatever impedes human freedom or dishonours it, such as the evil of *apartheid* and all forms of prejudice and discrimination, is an affront to the human being's vocation to shape its own destiny: 276;
that its opposition to *apartheid* derives from the incompatibility existing between systematic racial discrimination and basic tenets of Christianity, according to which all men and women are equal by reason of their common origin, nature and destiny: 655;
that for Christians no system of *apartheid* or separate development will ever be acceptable as a model for the relations between peoples or races: 260;
that it is inconceivable for anyone who receives the Gospel message to deny fundamental human equality in the name of a pretended superiority of one race or one ethnic group: 614; 626;
that within a country which belongs to each one, all should be equal before the law, find equal admittance to economic, cultural, civic and social life and benefit from a fair sharing of the nation's riches: 643;
that power, responsibility and decision-making cannot be the monopoly of one group or race or segment of the people: 643; that humanity rightly considers unjustifiable and rejects as inadmissible the tendency to maintain or introduce legislation or behaviour systematically inspired by racist prejudice: 642;
considers *apartheid* an unjust system: 664; which must be eliminated: 665;
deplores existing social situations based on racial discrimination, which constitute **a manifest and inadmissible affront to the fundamental rights of the human person**: 642; 664;
condemns the attempt to create juridical and political structures in violation of the principles of universal suffrage and the self-determination of peoples: 653; 653;
is following with close attention the development of the situation in Southern Africa and has repeatedly shown its concern that the rights of the individuals and peoples living there be respected: 654;
expresses its concern and hopes that a different policy will be established: 660; is at the side of the United Nations Special Committee against *Apartheid* and is ready to support every effort aimed at removing the temptation to violence and at helping to solve the problem of *apartheid* in a spirit of dialogue and fraternal love that respects the rights of the parties involved: 661.

2. **protest of the local Catholic Church** against the displacement of vast numbers of South African citizens: 659; **joint ecumenical initiative** of the Southern Africa Catholic Bishops Conference and the South African Council of Churches: 660; **condemnation by the Southern African Catholic Bishops' Conference**: 670;

3. **United Nations Committee against *Apartheid***: its work demands firmness in the defence of principles and prudence in the choice of the means suitable for attaining its purpose: 661; see also: 635; 649-651.

4. see: 605-606; 634; 635-674; 757; and *Discrimination/2; Equality/1-2; Segregation; Struggle/2.*

Arbitration

the Church has consistently supported the **development of an international administration of justice and a. as a way of peacefully resolving conflicts** and as part of the evolution of a world legal system: 248; the **Holy See** sometimes has been asked to arbitrate: 053; **Permanent Court of Arbitration**: has contributed to settling a number of conflicts and to averting the use of armed force: 252; see: 246; 247; 248; 253; 267; 268; see also: 255; 258; 268; 2323.

Armaments/Weapons

1. their **production and possession** are a consequence of an ethical crisis that is disrupting society: 1063; they engender bad dreams, feed evil sentiments, create nightmares, hostilities, and dark resolutions even before they cause any victims and ruins: 24;

so long as man remains the weak, changeable, and even wicked being that he so often shows himself to be, **defensive arms will, alas, be necessary**: 24;

2. deep **feeling of distress** in face of tragic absurdity of devoting enormous sums to a. which would have been enough to rescue numbers of countries from poverty: 67; see also: 1175; 1569; 1582; 1585; 3229; 3330; **contrast** between the enormous sums invested in the production of a. and the increasing material distress of more than half of mankind: 955; 1017; **humanity spends immensely more money on arms than on development**: 203;

3. the **recourse to a.** and to violence of all kinds, to terrorism and reprisals, degrades the human being and is unworthy of its rational nature and of its calling to a destiny beyond itself: 1151;

4. **production and exportation to developing countries**: permanent incitement to have recourse to violence: 385; 1102; new rise in the sale: 1016; see also: 1056; 1176;

5. of **mass destruction**: 514; 978; 1171; **conventional**: 1176; 3359; 80 percent of the expenditure for weapons are devoted to conventional arms; its traffic directed most of all toward developing countries: 1056-1057; **chemical**: 183; 1016; 1160; 1181; 1234; 3096; 3332; 3359; **bacteriological**: 183; 1234; 3096; 3332; 3353; 3359; **biological**: 3332; 3353; 3359;

6. **nuclear**: developments in quality and quantity: 184; 194; 978; 1058; 1284-1285; 1292; 1315; 1328; 3348-3349;

unacceptability of the actual use and also of the threat of their use: 1105; 3355; their use for purpose of national defence or in limited conflicts: 184; 1285;

the fear of nuclear weapons acts as an impulse to the arms-race: 385;

are considered the typical and most effective weapon of "deterrence" existing today: 184; 3373, see *Deterrence*;

call for a particularly exhaustive and serious examination of a whole range of general and specific moral questions which the pose for the human and Christian conscience: 3332; 3352;

consequences of their use: 1180; **1191-1220**;

see also: 183; 264; 290; 1160; 1311-1313; 1318; 1325; 1328; 1331; 1338; 3166; 2472; 3096; 3240; 3332; 3351-3352; 3356-3357; 3375; *Science/2,11; Scientist/3*

7. **Treaty on Non-Proliferation of Nuclear Weapons**: reasons of the accession of the Holy See: 1221-1235; 1236; 1254-1255; 1271-1272; 3386; acceptability: 1250; power of attraction: 1242; 1250; see: 1170-1171; 1221-1281; 1290-1291; 1309; 1312; 1330; 1348; 1359; 3386; **Tlatelolco Treaty** for the proscribing of nuclear arms in Latin America: 1279; 1312;

8. weapons **in outer space**: 1181; 3215; 3218; 3266;

9. **balance of a.**, seen almost as the sole guarantee of mutual security: 378; the danger is always present to see the search for balance turned into a search for superiority of a type that sets off the arms-race: 1031;

10. **even the terror of new weapons runs the risk of being ineffective**, to the extent that other guarantees are not found for the security of States: 987;

11. see also: 012; 077; 318; 544; 645; 671; 752; 916; 933; 991; 994; 1036; 1040-1041; 1059; 1237; 1274; 1339; 1359; 1658; 2143; 2150; 2311; 2327; 2466; 2468; 3322; *Force/3; Peace/10; Security/2; Violence/1-4; War.*

Arms race

1. an **intolerable scandal**: 67; 1001; 2062; an **evil**: 3331; an **absurdity**: 1633; a **grave danger to peace**: 3331; an **oppressive servitude**: 953;

2. in a **continual escalation**, in quantity and in quality: 977; 3324; **vertical and horizontal**: 1246; **between not only the superpowers** and their various allies but **between the developing countries** themselves: 1702; 1712; with an **immense expenditure** of men and means: 977; to think that it can go on indefinitely, without causing a catastrophe, would be a **tragic illusion**: 979;

3. the increase in arms budgets **can stifle the economy of countries that are often still at the developing stage**: 1000;

4. to **reverse the current trend** involves a parallel struggle on two fronts: On the one side, an immediate and urgent struggle by governments to reduce progressively and equally their armaments; on the other hand, a more patient but nonetheless necessary struggle at the level of the conscience of peoples to take their responsibility in regard to the ethical cause of the insecurity that breeds violence by coming to grips with the material and spiritual inequalities of our world: 1067; 1277; 1332

5. **nuclear arms race**: the hitherto prevailing logic has not only not slowed the nuclear a.r., but has brought about such a development of these weapons that they have become an oppressive burden on the conscience of humanity and an open affront to those suffering from underdevelopment and hunger: 1315; see also: 1208; 1226; 1231; 1245; 1256-1257; 1285; 1348; **vertical** (1258; 1277; 1313; 1359), **horizontal** (1260; 1277; 1359) **proliferation**;

6. see also: 85; 109-110; 183; 318; 378; 986; 996; 1031; 1045; 1058; 1066; 1106; 1170-1171; 1196; 1233; 1246; 1338; 1359; 1664; 2437; 2678; *Developing Countries/6; Development/11; Food; Hunger/8; Peace/11.*

Asia

religious traditions: 209; **refugees of South-East Asia**: 2914-2930. See also: 044; 1342; 1483; 1841; 2174; 3019; 3300/1.

Aspiration

1. deep a. **of mankind to peace** established and strengthened in justice: 0108; see also: 94; 300; 835; 967; 1095; 1184; 1242; 1424; increasingly urgent a. **of peoples for a real international disarmament**: 1537; unanimous a.: **to be able to enjoy human dignity**: 335;

2. for **liberty**: 322; for **justice**: 1545; 1573; of all persons **to enjoy human rights**: 637; to **build a fraternal world**: 686; legitimate a. of **oppressed peoples**: 631-632; for a **better and more just** (329), **equitable** (1550) **world**, where force no longer dominates with its blind and selfish weight: 341; for a **better an more humane future**: 1396; a **more equitable international order**: 1673; an **improved standard of living**: 2310; 2771; 2774; better quality of life: 2795; 2838; for a **life that is worthy and happy** for everyone: 2833;

3. of **youth** to take their place as men and women in society: 56; see also: 834; widespread a. that **all men and women be guaranteed equal dignity**: 477; of **women**: 2500; 2509; 2566; of **aged persons**: 2493; of the **rural worker** to share directly in its own advancement: 1657; 1769; **scientist's** noble aspirations to knowledge and truth: 1354;

4. of **governments**: 86; of **peoples**: 86; of **young nations**: 1626; of **the least developed countries**: 1481; of the **less fortunate peoples** to a greater share in industrial production: 1684;

5. see also: 76; 107; 411; 419; 435; 614; 619; 705; 722; 729; 771; 926; 963; 1022; 1087; 1123; 1124; 1133; 1164; 1486; 1502; 1504; 1603; 1624; 1800; 2070; 2464; 2500; 2555; 2658; 2738; 2784; 2817; 2982; 3004; 3006; 3110.

Assimilation

of ever increasing **treasures of science and technology**: 695; of **values**: 2398; of the **positive acquisitions** of technical civilization: 3100; **assimilative policy** aiming at the elimination of minority cultures: 2960; see also: *Culture/5,6; Migrants/1; Minorities/2.*

Assistance

1. the **fundamental subject** of all the concerns in assistance projects is **the human being**: 3148; is **indispensable but not enough**; it would even be illusory if at the same time the foundations were not laid for economic and financial recovery in the future: 2293;

2. **external**, to countries which need it to ensure their economic take-off: 131; conditions for its effectiveness: 1459-1461; **international**: for development: 135; 140; 1445-1446; 1582; **should not be made dependent on the achievements of family planning goals**: 2742; 2759, and *Family/6*; to face **ecological problems**: 280-281; to **regions stricken by drought**, in order to provide food: 285-286; **food a.**: 1663/2; 1833; 1843; 2196; 2247; **to developing peoples** and those in need of defence and promotion: 296; **to less favoured peoples**: 1175; **to least developed countries**: 1568;

3. **religious**: 492; 529; **cultural** assistance: 787; to **eradicate illiteracy**: 789; 818, and *Literacy;* **mutual** a. among peoples: 940; **financial**, for effective promotion of instruction in countries which have this need: 1435; in order to become self-sufficient in agricultural production: 2164; **technical**: 1490; 1724; 1821; 1946; 1953; 2194; 2536; 2714; **to combat desertification**: 3134; 3136, and Desertification;

4. **to parents**, in order to perform their educational role properly: 590/a; **for access to natural family planning**: 2762; **to mothers during pregnancy**: 2367; 2765; **to migrants and their families**, for integration into the community to which they contribute: 2766; **to disabled persons**: 2655; 2661; **post-school a.**: 2666; 2667; **to the aging**: should not be only technical or economic: 2768; to **refugees**: 2862; 2868;

5. **a. programmes of the Church**: 2567; for the refugees: 2872; 2937; to solve water problems: 3144-3145; 3153;

6. see also: 047; 229; 1208; 1470; 1565; 1736; 1843; 1847; 1924; 1991; 2182; 2238; 2255; 2315; 2340; 2522; 2565; 2843; 2948; 2975; 3148; 3201; 3222; 3300/4,16,17; 3310; *Aid; Collaboration; Solidarity.*

Association/Assembly

1. **right to** freedom of a.: 89; one of the basic rights: 232; right to association **for religious purposes**: 2958;

2. the right to associate freely is a fundamental one **for all those who are connected with the world of work** and who constitute the work community; it expresses the **solidarity** of all workers in the defense of their rights; it affords **a normal channel for participating actively** in the performance of work and everything related to it, while being guided at the same time by a concern for the common good: 226; 232; 1860; International Association for the Legal Protection of Workers: 327; **for the elderly**: 2494-2495; **for helping the disabled persons**: 2670; **professional**: 323; 694;

3. **Church's** associations: 1915; 2200; 2237;

4. International Social Association: 217; International Association for the Defense of Religious Liberty: 516; Association of the Member Episcopal Conferences in Eastern Africa (AMECEA): 3122;

5. **non-governmental**: 2255; **voluntary** a., **of volunteers**: 2153; 2155; 2670; **of individuals in society** demands the acceptance of one fundamental principle: that each individual is truly a person, with inalienable rights and duties: 447;

5. an a. is **valid and lasting** only if it corresponds fairly to the expectations of all who belong to it: 1245;

6. see also: 011; 16; 74; 92; 195; 237; 244; 354; 492; 753; 755; 1459; 1498; 1739; 1785; 1813; 1817; 2153; 2558; 2644; 2661; 2818; 2859; 2940; 2974-2975; 3195; and *Trade/11.*

Asylum

1. **nations who provide a.** are often no longer in a position to provide refugees with adequate shelter and help them to fit into society: 386; **temporary** a.: 2868; **first** a.: 2922; **permanent** a.: 2927;

2. **right to seek and to enjoy a. in other countries**: 2917; Convention on Territorial Asylum: 2894-2913.

3. see also: 2933-2934, and *Refugees.*

Attack

1. no one can dare to a. **human life**: 27; **attacks of human life**: 432; 2655; 2733; **dignity**: 656; **rights**: 413; 622; **of the inviolability of conscience**: 534; against the **causes of racial discrimination**: 609; of the material and human **environment**: 832; **of rural civilization**: 2074;

2. **military**: 970; 1027; 1309; 3359; **nuclear**: 1196; 1205; 1209; 1214-1215; 1218; 1220; 3358; on **nuclear installations**: 1309;

3. **protection against the a. of a society or a State** that wishes to deprive maternity of its fundamental sacred character: 2627;

4. see also: 0104; 79; 446; 1525; 2463; 2852; 3084; 3112; *Abortion; Aggression; Euthanasia; War.*

Attempt

1. **against humanity**: 2483; **to impose on the human being** a set of apparent imperatives: 170; of **one people or race to dominate another**: 259; to **impose beliefs and convictions** by force: 534; to **introduce or maintain legislation or behaviour based on racial discrimination**: 653; to **limit the freedom of couples** in deciding about children: 2734;

2. to settle the conflict in the Middle East: 84; at disarmament: 1316; at negotiations: 1338; to secure nuclear energy for peaceful purposes: 1359;

3. to put our world aright, to **eliminate spiritual confusion**: 1064; **to guarantee food for all**: 134; to **prevent price fluctuations of food commodities**: 1655; to **overpower the legitimate interests of other countries**: 1799;

4. see also: 138; 241; 248; 778; 1280; 1336; 1398; 1436; 2100; 2117; 2678; 2819; 2822; 2826; 2888; 3280; 3284; 3380.

Attention

1. to the **spiritual realities**: 94; 100; 141; human values of the **rural world**: 1796; to religious freedom: 452; 474; **human rights**: 459; 893; 903; **discriminations**: 609; religious and moral **meaning of the equality** of all human beings: 625; to the **inequalities within each nation**: 891; activities that **promote the good of the human person and society**: 1336; to **Muslim** believers: 2415;

2. to the development of the **situation in Southern Africa**: 654; 660; the **Middle East**: 1146; 1149; to the **nuclear threat**: 183; 1311; disastrous **effects of war**: 1042;

3. to the problem of **hunger**: 138; 1923; 1977; 2081; **food and agricultural development**: 1439; **food distribution**: 2143; 2149; **development**: 1523; 1630; 1640; 2073; 2095; 2106; **unbalanced interdependence**: 1650; the invasive **power of transnational corporations**: 1561; situations of **poverty**: 2797;

4. to **work/workers**: 218; 230; 328-329; particular a. to the **poor/poorest countries**: 614; 619; 1415; 2324; **migrants and minorities**: 616; 2719; immediate attention **to children deprived of family life**: 2369; to the **contributions and potential of youth** in creating a better future: 2457; 2461; to the **elderly**: 2480; 2494; to issues related to: the **situation and role of women**: 2499; 2509; 2521; 2533; 2535; 2584; 2740; **disabled persons**: 2640; 2660; 2665; 2667; 2673; 2678; **family**: 2707; 3051; 3057; 3067; **demographic variables**: 2720; **relation between population and development**: 2742; **basic values in population issues**: 2745; 3130; **rights of parents**: 2763; **refugees**: 2854; 2871; 2882; 2891; 2899; 2921-2922; 2933;

5. to issues related to **habitat**: 2801; 2802; 2804; 2805; 2815; 2826; 2840; 2843; **drugs**: 2982; **drought**: 3127; 3135; **water**; 3139;

6. to the **ethical problems** of the technological society: 206; **ethical principles** 1023; **ethical aspects of the debt problem**: 2266;

7. see also: 033; 45; 73; 75; 76; 218; 239; 242; 291; 294; 526; 761; 803; 836; 855; 887; 888; 927; 933; 949; 960; 1016; 1035; 1058; 1123; 1138; 1141; 1157; 1219; 1242; 1276; 1287; 1290; 1342; 1343; 1345-1346; 1350; 1353; 1369; 1409; 1424; 1437; 1429; 1533; 1548; 1563; 1571; 1701-1702; 1709; 1750; 1833; 1842; 1851; 1854; 1953; 1956; 1957; 2088; 2279; 2339; 2346; 2353; 2397; 2466; 2499; 2509; 2521; 2756; 2769; 3150; 3196; 3204; 3249; 3282; 3300/1,15; 3347; 3353; 3390, and Care.

Auschwitz

one of the places that are most distressing and **overflowing with contempt for the human being** and its fundamental rights; should be a **warning sign** on the path of humanity, against any kind of concentration camp: 80; see also *Concentration/1.*

Authenticity

minds' movements toward human fulfillment and a.: 615; **youth**, athirst for a.: 690; 709; **call for a.**: 3086; **the child is a testing-ground of the a.** of our respect for the mystery of life: 2355;

Authority

1. the fitting pursuit and effective realization of the **universal common good require of the community of nations that it organize itself in a manner suited to these present responsibilities**. This goal undoubtedly requires the progressive establishment of some form of **universal public a.**, acknowledged as such by all and endowed with the power necessary to safeguard, on behalf of all, security, regard for justice and respect for rights: 3175-3176;

impartial and effective **universal public/world a.**: 090; 16; 68; 317; 349; 3178; **absence**: 1054; 1178; **necessity**: to ensure peace: 1239; 3343; security: 3344; disarmament: 1239; respect for justice: 3344; rights: 3344; and law: 1103; represents a **permanent aspect of the views of the Holy See on the question of peace**: 3344; for the moment **far away** and **difficult to achieve**: 3345;

2. the **reason for any a.** and any political activity, both national and international, is service to the human being, the protection of its dignity and the effective promotion and safeguarding of its rights: 3088; **democracy** in its exercise: 622; its **temptation** to favour birth control: 64; 3429;

3. **moral**: of the human being: 165; of parents: 167; of scientists: 188; 1194; **civil**: 2249; bound to respect religious freedom: 455; **public authorities**: primary guarantors of the inviolable rights of the human person: 64; 3069; relation between **public a. and private initiative**: 3417-3418; **political**: 3051;

4. see also: 67; 101; 464; 498; 632; 690; 757; 864; 996; 1239; 1692; 2307; 3090; 3204; 3236; 3279;

Autonomy

1. distinctive and **autonomous value of the human being**: 162; **its craving** for a life that is full, autonomous: 2555; its **not absolute a.**: 2751;

2. **right of peoples to aspire to their own a.**: 644; **political** a. of developing countries: 1529; **a. of each people**: 1766; **autonomous development** for each country: 1827; a. **in food production**: 2133; external support must respect the dignity and **a. of initiative of the needy countries**: 2163; **autonomous strategies** of transnational corporations: 1561;

3. of **culture**: 710; of **learning**: 871; of **intergovernmental organizations**: 114;

4. see also: 836; 875; 977; 2176; 2493; *Independence/1,6;Person/6; Self-Determination; Society/1,2.*

Availability

1. restricted a. of **material goods**: 850; of the **goods of the earth** for productive work (1805), for all peoples and for every person (3222); of **natural** or primary **resources**: 1340; **lack of a.** and exploitation of the immense riches concealed in nature: 2150; of financial resources: 1862;

2. of **food**: 2184-2185; 2230; 2251; of **resources** in the face of consumption demands: 2716;

3. of **new space services**: 3264; continual **a. to all nations of the benefits of space exploration and exploitation**: 3266;

4. see also: 1291; 1806; 1810; 1899; 2694; 3270/e; 3271/i; 3299/4/a; 3300/2.

Awakening

of **conscience**: 3006; see also: 319; 699; 709; 1672; 1978; 2013; 2044; 3226; 3325; **peoples favoured** by nature or by progress of civilization **risk hard awakenings** if they do not take pains at once to assure to the less fortunate the means of living humanly,...: 1957. See also: 793; 928; 1375; 1443; 3086.

Awareness

1. general a. **of the dignity of the human being**: 89; 2555; growing a. **of the duty to respect human rights**: 258; see also: 334; 413; 429; 431; 450; 583; 609; 612; 624; 638; 656; 671; **human beings' a.** of their liberty: 726; mission in society: 781; of what they are living and of what they are: 794; that society exists for the human being: 266; **development of the human being a.**: 224; need for a **higher religious a.**: 992;

2. **of the urgency of uniting the efforts of everyone** for the cause of peace: 077; see also: 717; **Church's a. of her native vocation** to be the teacher of universal peace: 744; of service to the whole humanity: 793;

3. **of the grave problem of illiteracy**: 772; 780; 789; 820; 828;

4. **of uniting for a more just and brotherly social order**, in and among nations: 077; that the social question has become world-wide: 39; enhanced a. **of social justice**: 225; of the **universal common good**: 56;

5. of the subject of **development and the means to promote it**: 1520; of the **duty of solidarity with the underprivileged peoples**: 777; 1390; 1520; 3161; of **world-wide solidarity**: 2013; 2070; 2169; 2249; 2279/2; 2280; 3152; of **those who are hungry**: 1978; of the imperative **need to secure for all people freedom from hunger**: 2012; see also: 2022; 2024; 2045; 2053; 2060; 2089; 2099; 2128-2130; 2137; 2140; 2171-2172; 2181; 2223; **of universal brotherhood**: 1928;

6. of the **common responsibility** vis-a-vis the challenges of the future: 878; world's increasing a. of the **mutual dependence of all peoples**: 1143; 1541; 1643; of the **decisive function of agriculture**: 1781;

7. **that the future of the human being and of the world is threatened**: 183; 1283; of the **devastation of a nuclear war**: 185; 1224; 1257; of the **formidable ambivalence**, for good and for evil, **of nuclear energy**: 1248;

8. growing a. **of the need to protect and conserve certain non-renewable natural resources**: 274; growing awareness **that the human being and his environment are inseparable**: 3094; 3098; 3110; 3115;

9. of the **special needs of children**: 2343; 2345; 2358; 2373; of the **irreplaceable role and position of the family**: 2381; see also: 2690; 2736; 2739; 2741; **women's a. of their natural dignity**: 2512; widespread a. **of the rights, duties and responsibilities of women**: 2520; see also: 2557; 2566; 2587; 2612; renewed a. of the **duty of solidarity with the disabled persons**: 2640; 2669; of the **refugees' problem**: 2850; 2906;

10. see also: 030; 064; 072; 095; 8; 11-12; 19; 47; 64; 97; 210; 212; 307; 346; 394; 398; 695; 697; 737-738; 830; 841; 852; 873; 886; 938; 941; 952; 993; 994; 1131; 1144; 1242;

1259; 1269; 1277; 1300; 1307; 1359; 1374; 1383; 1397; 1454; 1550; 1554; 1597; 1602; 1614; 1644; 1833; 1850; 1878; 1919; 2021; 2123; 2127; 2240; 2242; 2248; 2397; 2479; 2713; 2722; 2774; 2814; 2818; 2835; 2982; 3107; 3112; 3140; 3166; 3195; 3199; 3250; 3272; 3288; 3343.

Balance

1. peace is not built merely by means of politics and a b. **of power** and interest: 23; 977-978; 1060; 1240; it is built upon a new b. **of cooperation and trust**: 1108; peace is a dynamic b. **between diverging interests**: 1096;

2. the quest for the b. **of power** impels adversaries to seek to ensure a certain margin of superiority, 977; 1030-1031; 3381-3382; **of forces** between the different States or group of States: 970; 1029; 1279; 1285; b. **of armaments** now seen almost as the sole guarantee of mutual security: 378; 971; 1171; security through b. **of fear**: 978; **of terror**: 098; 979; 1029; 1256-1257; 1171; 1256; 1314; 3380; "deterrence" based on b. 1053; 3378: see Deterrence; it is essential to find **means of replacing the b. of terror by the b. of trust**: 988; **balanced and controlled disarmament** assist detente to progress and grow stronger: 359; 990; 1054-1055; 1205; 3333; it is indispensable to plan and **promote a b. yet courageous strategy of peace and disarmament**: 995; acceptable b. **of mutual responsibilities and obligations** between the nuclear and the non nuclear powers: 1247; 1268;

3. b. **in justice** on the social level; **conditions**: 1097; awareness that the search for better **economic and trade b.** between peoples is an undertaking which concerns the whole person and all persons: 1602; **general economic b.**: 2128; **commercial b.**: 1497; 1523; more **equitable b. among the negotiating powers**: 1609; b. to be achieved **among all factors governing trade in food products**: 214; balanced **development**: 2032; world-wide balanced effort at development: 2120; need to ensure a balanced **growth**: 1690; b. **of payments**: 1538; 1581; 1586; 1904; 2290; 2328;

4. violence which can end by compromising the **interior b.** and dynamism of the person: 2658; **psychological** b.: 2842; family is the starting-point for a **balanced social life**: 2690; **human being finds its own b. in culture**: 156; consequences of human intervention (61), of the irresponsible use of science (195) in the b. **of nature**; worry about the destruction of our **ecological** b.: 2472; 2842; 3305;

5. see also: 38; 61; 281; 293; 687; 751; 842; 1257; 1323; 1488; 1515; 1529; 1556; 1689; 1739; 1760; 1761; 1907; 1930; 1961; 2040; 2076; 2312-2313; 2325; 2358; 2481; 2490; 2494; 2496; 2546; 2566; 2783; 3049; 3055; 3049; 3100; 3181;

Bank

commercial banks: active role for the solution of the debt problem: 2327; see also: 2268; 2281; 2295; 2320; 2325-2326; **regional**: 2338; **development** banks: 2295; **International Monetary Fund**: 2338; the **World Bank**: 2338; see also: 1448; 1459; 2291; 2324; 3254; and *Debt*.

Behaviour

1. of **human beings**: 170; 265; 550; 830; 2307; 2750; of **society**: 170; 550; of **States**: inspired more by the "reason of State" than ethical norms: 027; **oppressing** human persons and groups: 615; **anti-social** b.: 2476; **anti-human**: 2655; **sexual** b. in conflict with the values and principles set down by parents: 2817; education assures the **transmission** of knowledge and behaviour: 679; ethical principles which alter **b. patterns**: 2295; need for a world-wide **programme to educate** conscience and b.: 552-553; latest fashion in b.: 170;

2. sent by Jesus Christ, **the Church wants to help form the conscience and the b.** of human beings: 265; radically **renounces any b.** that could be resented outside the Church as manifesting hegemony: 509; **urges to refrain from all forms of b.** that may suggest coercion, dishonesty or insincere persuasion: 561;

3. **violence and criminal b.** in nations and culture encourages violence and criminal b. in international relations: 266; multi-faced **causes producing and supporting behaviours of racial discrimination**: 609-610; **justification** for racist b.: 613; see also: 623; 642;

4. see also: 195; 556; 573; 580; 616; 879; 2215; 2273; 2308; 3069; 3132; and *Permissiveness.*

Belief

1. the **human being can be wounded in its most personal b.**: 101; **respect** for individual beliefs: 457; **diversity** of b.: 927; 2480; **religious** b.: 141; **liberty to profess personal b.** alone or with others, in private and in public: 458; 516; 519; 2420; see also: *Freedom/2;*

2. **Christian** b.: 557; 561; **that all human beings are brothers and sisters**: 514; see *Brotherhood*; **incompatibility between racial discrimination and basic b. of Christianity**: 665; **fundamental equality** of the human beings, whatever their belief: 724;

3. **in the human being's future**: 207; **in the value of the child**: 2737;

4. see also: 369; 524; 536; 541; 564; 577; 1208; 1385; 1441; 1451; 1576; 1978; 2025; 2281; 2697; 2674; and Faith;

Believers

1. **sustained by** the awareness of the presence of God in history: 398; **right to religious freedom**: 072; see *Freedom/2*; **non-believers**: 082; 522; 563; 566; 963; 2387;

2. **for the b.** the universal community of people finds an exceptional strength in the certainty of the common origin, nature and destiny of all persons in God: 1635;

3. **Christians and Muslims** have many things in common, as believers: 2403; 2414; 2415; 2453; cooperation among b.: 2415; **Mary**, the mother of Jesus, embodies the ideal **image of the woman believer**: 2563;

4. see also: 177; 450; 735; 892; 1111; 1133; 1139; 1147; 1148; 1154; 1241; 1614; 2153; 2407; 2483; 2486; 3277; 3403; and Faith.

Belligerent

Benedict XV appeal to the belligerents: 349; human being's capacities to overcome and conquer its own **b. instincts**: 1188; see also: 385; 1102.

Benefit

1. call to dominate the earth **for the b.** of all: 226; the riches of this world (1388; 3172), the goods of the earth (1767) must **serve the true benefit of** all; **b. from peaceful use of nuclear technology** for all the countries: 1230; 1262; 1275; 1278; 1284; 1323-1324; 1342; 1353; 1357; 1362; 1384; enormous **b. from the sea**, at the disposal of all nations: 3167; 3169; the **b. of the**

use of outer space for the profit of all nations: 3203; 3205; 3218; 3220; 3226; 3228; 3240; 3257; 3261; 3266; 3281; 3291; 3301; international b. of the solution of ecological problems: 280;

2. **peace and rights are two b. directly related** to each other as cause and effect: 422; the **free exercise of religious benefits both individual and governments**: 455; b. **proper to a civilization of well-being**: 875; **b. of civilization**: 1740;

3. **mission of the Church for the b. of** the human being and peoples: 886, and *Church/4*; **material, spiritual and cultural b. brought by the missionaries** to the countries they have evangelized: 684; 2037; 3122;

4. within a country which belongs to each one, **all should benefit from** a fair sharing of the nations's riches: 643; better distribution of resources at hand, especially **to the b. of less favoured countries**: 2107; rural populations still remain those who derive **the least b. from progress**: 891; science and technology **for the b. of the less developed regions**: 1993; **privileged classes b. from** a considerable rise in their income: 1493; **rural majority b. very little**: 1493; **trade, source of b.** for developing countries: 1528; see also *Aid/3;*

5. **participation** of all persons in the b. of development: 2044; **b. available** to the vast number of people in need: 3265; 3267; development should be **more than material b.**: 2742;

6. see also: 07; 052; 25; 42; 195; 468; 471; 529; 581; 643; 691; 707; 717; 722; 790; 801; 864; 869; 910; 914; 973; 1002; 1101; 1172; 1290; 1298; 1306; 1320; 1401; 1429; 1452; 1535; 1551; 1587; 1602; 1618; 1628; 1656; 1663/2; 1675; 1710; 1715; 1731; 1838; 1891; 1905; 1930; 1934; 1947; 1951; 1959; 1967; 1987; 2031; 2022; 2064; 2110; 2239; 2343; 2476; 2490; 2494; 2528; 2530; 2544; 2574; 2638; 2754; 2759; 2852; 2880; 3074; 3094; 3100; 3112; 3125; 3270/f; 3271/c,f; 3285; 3293; 3299/5.

Birth control

1. **United Nations task** is so to act that there will be enough bread at the table of mankind and not to support an artificial, irrational, birth control, aimed at reducing the number of those sharing in the banquet of life: 27; see also *United Nations/6;*

2. the Church is firmly opposed to a birth control which would be **accomplished with methods and means unworthy of human beings**: 64; **proclaims the right of the couple to make a free decision** regarding the spacing of births and the size of the family, see *Family/8*; **urges** not to allow those who control the goods and resources of mankind to solve the problem of hunger by forbidding the birth of the poor: 2115; **states that the right road** to solve the problem of the life of human kind is to increase the supply of food and not to mortify and destroy the fecundity of life: 1997;

3. see also: 852; 1461; 2251; 2533; 2720; 2727; 2756; 2759; 2772; 3058; 3097; 3429; *Aid/1; Assistance/2; Contraception; Development/12; Family/6-8; Life/3; Population/5-7; Sterilization.*

Bombay

Appeal made by Pope Paul VI in B. on December 4, 1964, to devote to the benefit of developing countries at least a part of the money that could be saved through a reduction of armaments: 25; 951; 1002-1003; 1537; 1633; 1729; 2114.

Broadcasting

favorable effects of **b. by satellite**: 847; 3232; 3241; see also *Education/12*, and *Space.*

Brotherhood/Fraternity

1. **Jesus' message of b.**: 331; 866; 926; **the Catholic Church** unhesitatingly proclaims the dignity of the human person and the brotherhood of all human beings: 637; efforts in educating to b.: 630; see also: 426; 637;

2. **spiritual**: 866; **human and supernatural**: 2279/2; effective: 892; **progressive**: 1515; **among human beings**: 46; 400; 614; 626; 798; 1475; **peoples**: 400; 751; 1139; 2455; among **nations**: 293; 1386; **universal**: 518; 669; 743; 926; 1145; 1221; 1928; 1941; world-wide: 1731; **building a world of b.**: 56; **a world of f.**: 341; **promotion of**: 2415;

3. **sense of**: 58; 1545; 2347; **spirit of**: 1599; 1610; 1847; economy of **service and b.**: 67; **search for** f.: 209; **aspiration for** f. 834;

4. see also: 17-18; 533; 574; 584; 597; 604; 646; 651; 673; 710; 757; 779; 804; 819; 1042; 1392; 1433; 1472; 1474; 1490; 1553; 2054; 2134; 2135; 2297; 2556; 2678; 2874; 2932; Creation/2; Humanity/1-2; Solidarity/3.

Budget

peace is built up when **national budgets** are finally **diverted from** the creation of more powerful and deadlier weapons to provide food and raw materials to meet basic human needs: 290; the most astonishing opportunities for progress thrown away on **war b.**: 337; enormous **military b.**: 971; 1176; 2114; **arms b.**: 1000; **for the arms race**: 2678; **national** b.: 1620; 2113; 2143; governmental **b. for public health**: 3006.

Buildings

places of worship: 528-529; 2807; see: 2778; 2800; 2802; 2809; 2813; 2815; 2820; 2822; 2832; 2833; and *Habitat*.

Building up

peace: 22; 31; 94; 188; 196; 287; 396; 1042; 1151; 1162; 1184; 1254; 2588; **world**: 55; 563; 695; 1471; 2529; 2601; the **world community**: 1556; 1609; **a world** of dignity and justice: 200; of justice and peace: 226; 1456; more just and harmonious: 1441; 2295; of solidarity: 1553; fraternal: 56; 686; 709; better: 1672; new: 2253; 2417; 2428; 3100; in which God has the first place: 2451; **society**: 57; 329; 1374; 2506; new society: 196; 459; 590/f; 701; 2134; 2454; 2480; of justice and peace: 2457; more just and fraternal: 2547; community of life: 628; fraternal community: 414; 1600; **common future**: 63; 1294; 1419; 1420; 2692; better future: 1418; peaceful: 86; f. of justice: 565; **well-being**: 63; **more human existence**: 175; **a genuinely human civilization**: 2988; a civilization based on love: 2436; **communion of persons**: 2488; **links** that unite people together: 1060; 1062; 1370; **international cooperation**: 352; more **just world** order: 353; diversified **economies**: 1478-1479; sound economy: 1610; **trade networks** which will ensure more remuneration, more stable and more equitable prices for all, especially for the poorest; conditions: 1600; new international **economic order**: 1611; 3186. See also: 32; 51; 148; 233; 237; 832; 1039; 1085; 1167; 1288; 1480; 1574; 1585; 2405; 3386.

Campaign

against **hunger**: 59; 1972; 1974; 1977; 1979-1980; 1986; 2003; 2026; 2082; against **illiteracy**: 723; 749; 782; 783; 788; 789; 791; 799; 802; 2513; in the field of **agriculture**: 1953; 1955; 1958; unilateral (2251), systematic (2715) c. **for birth control**; anti-natalist propaganda c.: 2759; see also 2720; **health** c.: 3005; see also: 706; 2016.

Capability/Capacity

1. of the **human being**, to understand the demands of reality: 0101; **inventive**: 646; 673; **to promote justice**: 1515; **harmonious**: 1725; **for transcendence**: 2619; 2620; **to contribute to the well-being of society**: 2732; **to enlarge the area of what is possible**: 2779; **for love**: 3087; of **humanity**: 396;

2. of **children**, for remarkable sacrifice and idealism: 2347; for confident expectation, to be instilled in **young people**: 2393; their infinite c. for love: 2475; specific, of the **aging**: 2479; **technical-professional**, of each people: 1907; of a country: 2294; to **promote justice** in the world: 1515;

3. limited c. of **material goods**, for satisfying the needs of the human being: 90; of **communication media** to penetrate minds and distance: 844; for **improving** and for **destroying** the environment: 275; **nature's** c. for regeneration: 3094; of **agricultural areas**, for production: 1493; 1661; to **provide needy countries** with basic foodstuffs: 2190;

4. to produce **nuclear weapons**: 1273; installed nuclear c.: 1297; tremendous destructive c.: 1315; 1329; 3348;

5. see also: 029; 046; 051; 090; 365; 956; 978; 1048; 1302; 1267; 1306; 1352; 1451; 2740; 2833; 2845; 3077; 3151; 3255; 3270/a,f; 3292; 3300/14; 3345; 3348; 3418; 3427.

Capital

antinomy which may set human labour against c.: 230; "**capital intensive**" technologies: 1438; **transfer** of c. from rich to poor countries: 1445; c. **assistance**; 1446-1447; c. **concentrated** in the hands of industrialized countries: 1669; **drains** in national c. reserves, caused by fluctuations in exchange rates: 2301; 2307; see also: 1449; 1587; 1658; 1668; 1687; 1690; 1903; 2259; 2263; 2311; 2314; 2316-2317; 2323; 2324; 2325; 2327-2328; 2329; 2339; 2716.

Care

for the **common good** of humanity: 205; of preserving and improving the **natural environment**: 272; 279; 3093; 3117; that ethico-moral, cultural and religious **values** are placed ahead of the merely economic indicators of growth: 1408; of the **Church** for human progress: 1837; **social** care: 2660; for the **poor**: 2062; most **needy**: 2221; the **elderly**: 2494; for the **disabled** persons: 2655; 2664; 2669; 2670; 2677; to identify the causes of a country's **debt situation**: 2292; see also: 273; 336; 887; 1176; 1210-1211; 1218; 1323; 1327; 1752; 2365; 2369; 3133; 3171; 3271/h; 3272; 3416 and *Attention*.

Changes

1. in the c. taking place at the present time, so **far-reaching and so rapid**, the human being discovers itself anew each day, and it queries the meaning of its own being and of its collective survival: 830; the **profound** c. which humanity has lived are modifying the human person's ways of thinking and acting: 2554;

2. **international situation** is too exposed to the ever possible c., and caprices of tragically free wills: 991; **social and cultural** c., affect in a particularly painful way agriculture: 116; c. **needed** in the socio-economic domain: 176; social system, living conditions: 229; people cannot be liberated merely by c. **in their external conditions of life**: 391; of the general conditions of the **human environment**: 2771; 2829; profound **c. that disturb our times** render communication between generations more difficult: 680;

3. **urgent** c., needed in order to restore to agriculture and to the rural people their just value: 2161; the building of a **new international economic order** demands from all peoples c. which touch their vital resources: 1611;

4. **structural**, demand clarity and courage in planning in order to promote justice and solidarity: 583; 1796; 1801; **scientific and technical**, call for the constant study of methods of education: 683;

5. see also: 275; 597; 759; 794; 809; 829; 844; 860; 1096; 1438; 1445; 1171; 1746; 1794; 1796; 1821; 1868; 2273; 2284; 2297; 2305; 2587; 2778; 2796; 2946; 3132; 3295.

Character

of the **Catholic Church/Holy See**: 019; 1242; religious, moral, 74; supranational, 918; non-temporal, 1009; of **Jerusalem**: particular, 1117; sacred, 1129, 1131; as a sacred heritage shared by all three monotheistic religions, 1132; universal, special, 1137; of the **human person**: transcendent, 2732, social, 155; see also: 27; 46; 78; 215; 228; 280; 315; 463; 613; 927; 942; 1466; 1552; 2150; 2338.

Characteristic

particular characteristics and aims of the **Holy See**: 043; 046; **cultural** c. of each nation: 836; 1827; of **modern societies**: increasing fragmentation and alienation: 266; salient c. of **humanity**: freedom: 453; 484; **special c. of each nation**: not ignored in the work of education of the Church: 633; the problems of **work** share one c., solidarity: 220-221; major c. of **underdevelopment**: undernourishment and malnutrition: 2139; c. of **youth**: 2467-2472; of **old age**: 2484-2485; of the **mother**: 2627; see also: 013; 054; 060; 0101; 16; 59; 154; 158; 197; 237; 689; 926; 1968; 2157; 2620; 3418.

Child

1. has the God-given **right** to be born, to a mother and father united in marriage, to be born into a normal family: 2346; 2367-2369; to integral development of his or her personality: 2348; 2378; a **precious treasure**, deserving of utmost love and respect, given to each generation as a challenge to its wisdom and humanity: 2353; 2387; **considered** by some people **a burden** and restriction of freedom: 2346; **fear** of the c.: 2361;

2. the **future of peoples and nations** rests with children: 2387; 2462; 2704; **its future**: 1167; **survival:** 1523; 2378; **right to a better future**: 2359; see also: 1396; 2355; 2371; now, more than ever before, **we must reaffirm our belief in the value of the c.** and the contributions that today's children can make to the entire human family: 2737;

concern for the c., even before birth, from the first moment of conception and then throughout the years of infancy and youth, is the primary fundamental test of the relationship of one human being to another: 107;

one of the **most vital answers to the situation of the c. in today's world** will come through reinforcing and strengthening the family: 2364-2367; 2379-2380; 2737;

an essential element of **any policy in favour of the c.** is that of providing for an effective presence of the mother alongside her young children and of ensuring that mothers are trained to carry out effectively their role in the areas of nutrition and health education: 2367;

3. the c. and the adolescent **ask** for nothing more than **to live in mutual relationship with their equals**, whatever be their race and social origin, beyond the differences arising from wealth and power: 696;

4. **education: parents are the first and foremost educators** of their children: 590,a,e; they must assure the harmonious development of the affective faculties of the c.: 695; 2740; obstacles to **religious instruction** of children: 528; **moral** education, based on the spiritual dimension of the human being, should characterize the whole process: 843; 2382; **to non-aggressiveness**: 2588; see also: 790; 801-803; 828; 840; 1725; 2075; 2588; 2763; 2841; 3427;

5. decision about the **number of children**: 2690; 2734; 2739; 2759; 3131; see *Family/8*;

6. many children in today's world are **among those who suffer most intensely**: 2358; see also: 1549; 1591; 1622; 1716; 2011; 2099; 2115; 2147; 2345; 2358; 2373-2376; 2389; 2975;

7. **disabled** c.: 2661; 2662; 2666; 2677; **migrant** c.: 2389; 2925; **refugee** c.: 2389; 2851; 2853; 2870; 2882-2893, 2904; 2925; children and **habitat questions**: 2772; 2773; 2782-2783; 2793; 2800-2803; 2805; 2820; 2824; 2841; 2843;

8. International Year of the Child: 107; 801; 2341-2351, passim;

9. for the **Catholic Church** service to the c. is not a transitory goal, but rather a permanent task invested with dignity and enduring priority: 2343-2344; 2353; 2356-2357; 2360; 2372; 2388;

10. see also: 54; 81; 102; 108-109; 111; 177; 203; 282; 284-285; 492; 590; 695; 790; 828; 1549; 2038; 2112; 2462; 2483; 2753; 3435; *Family/3*.

Christianity

in a multiplicity of ways, all Europe - from the Atlantic to the Urals - **testifies to the links between culture and Christianity** in the history of each nation as well as in that of the community as a whole: 47-48; 160-164; see also: 062; 44; 84; 94; 154; 160; 162; 540; 588; 666; 917; 1112; 1128; 1392; 2609; 2610.

Christians

take part with all their heart in the combat for the promotion of the human being: 57; **face the challenges of the present life**: 399-405. See also: 57; 208; 260; 311; 343; 399-400; 403-404; 505; 508-509; 512; 522; 526; 529; 532; 540; 558; 559; 561; 566; 579; 616; 626; 688; 764; 926; 963; 1082; 1125; 1128-1129; 1131; 1424; 1470-1471; 1487; 1520; 1553; 1653; 1672; 1674; 1843; 1928; 2013-2014; 2037; 2057; 2135; 2177; 2257; 2311; 2388; 2403; 2416; 2435; 2444-2446; 2448; 2631; 2643; 2675; 2677; 2846; 2922; 3005; 3426.

Church/Holy See

1. **sent by Jesus Christ**, wants to help form the conscience and behaviour of human beings: 265; see also 75; is anxious to help human beings recognize that they are brothers and sisters in a humanity advancing towards its full development: 687; has a doctrine on the human being's origin, nature, destiny: 2043;

its kingdom is the kingdom of conscience: 014; **its words** meant to be the echo of the moral conscience of humanity: 1020-1021;

wishes to exert itself unceasingly to improve consciences and open hearts: 311; to form consciences: 2873; to interpret to voice of conscience: 3394; to set forth the demands of moral conscience and the divine law, the principles that must rule the relationships between individuals, between social classes, peoples and States: 3398. See *Teaching*;

is well aware of the specific nature of its possible contribution to the international community, which is essentially that of appealing to the conscience of humanity in the face of the forces which divide individuals and nations, in order tirelessly to seek new paths to peace, understanding and cooperation between peoples and communities: 346; see also 543; 1070; 1083; 2915;

sides with what is essential and inviolable in the human person: conscience, and relationship to God: 533;

unarmed, its strength is that of truth, of solidarity with all victims of intolerance, of protection of conscience and even of those who practice intolerance, so that they may renounce it: 544;

feels its responsibility to contribute to a convinced service of inspiration, education and stimulation of consciences to spread and develop a real, creative spirit of peace: 1241; see *Responsibility/12;*

endeavours to awaken consciences to their responsibilities in view of a common effort for the full and firm development of the human being: 1672; to stimulate, to awaken conscience to its new duties in today's world: 2044; 3006;

speaks for of all those who are tragically suffering from undernourishment and who appeal to the conscience of their brothers and sisters: 2147; see also 11; 1554;

appeals to people's moral conscience for the concrete affirmation of the objective criteria of justice which must govern relationships among subjects of the civil community, whether they be individuals, groups, enterprises, or sovereign countries; 2169; to people of good will: 2340; (in the debt problem);

expert on humanity: 10; 603; 740; 1742; 2531; see also *Humanity/6*; **shares** the hope, the grief and the anguish of people of our time: 410; see also *Solidarity/13*;

2. **proclaims** the message of salvation: 656; 684; the human dignity: 656; the value of each and every human person: 2360; 656; always **claims respect** for the inviolable rights of the human person: 64; **condemns injustices and attacks** on human dignity: 656; see also *Dignity/1; Person/1,19; Rights/2,3; Teaching/1-8;*

3. ***committed*** *to the promotion of human dignity: 651; 864; to assisting today's men and women in advancing the cause of justice and peace so as to make our world ever more hospitable and human: 476; 1254; see also Commitment/1*; **solicitous** for the true good of the human being: 60; **not involved in** the inevitable conflicts of interests between peoples and States: 059; 088; 746; **not pursuing temporal interests** of its own, but concerned about those legitimate ones that are common to all: 059; 746; see also *Interest/9;* **at one with the entire family of nations** in the fundamental purpose of promoting the progress of mankind: 213; **radically renounces any behaviour** that could be resented as manifesting **hegemony**, and **profoundly respects**, in theory and in practice, each person's religious and philosophical convictions and also the freedom of personal conduct of each individual: 509; 534;

4. **authority**: moral: 603; 1254; 1271; 1886; spiritual: 1254; 1520; religious: 1271; see also: 016; 017; 085; 090; 464; 495; **power**: spiritual: 07; 1008; moral: 023; **mission**: universal: 213; 2522; religious: 74; 123; 213; 476; 769; 1237; moral: 74; 123; 213; 1849; spiritual: 294; 947; 1237; 1429; 1641; 1849; 2040; of peace: 1008; 1222; 1254; of ethical teaching: 046; 2171; 2594; prophetic, for the good of the person and of humanity: 2744; of continuing in time the teaching and actions of the Jesus Christ: 2206; see also: 064; 494; 684; 2235; 2372; 2543; 2727; **mission and duty of service** to the human family: 2353; to the human being in all its dimensions: 3411; see also: 219. See also: 020; 075; 72; 94; 160; 162; 177; 207; 218; 223; 322; 346; 570; 612; 656; 762; 886; 1242; 1369; 1475; 1695; 1763; 2041; 2267; 2356; 2639; 2697; 3038; 3204;

5. **attitude/spirit**: of **respect and dialogue**: 505; 540; 554; 568; with the international community: 050-051; 060-082; 313; with other Christian Churches: 505; 555; 064; other religions: 556-557, in particular Judaism 558-559 and Islam: 559-560, unbelievers and atheists: 563; firmly rejects all proselytizing activity: 561; 2957; of engagement in temporal tasks: 2057; at the **service** of humanity: 593; 2057; 2353; 2612-2613; 3168; 3237; of the human being: 656; 2553; 2744; 3411; of peace: 075; 1241; 1374; 3202; of a more just and brotherly social order, in and among all nations: 075; 1374; 1550; 2036; of development: 1469; 1837; of the underprivileged: 776; 2177; 2390;

6. and the **United Nations**: the universality of the Catholic Church seems in a way to be reflected from the spiritual sphere into the temporal sphere of the UN: 294;

esteem: 73; 345; **very high conception**: 293; **support**: 10; 73; 295; 349; 603; 3409; **approval**: 10; **agreement**: 73; **faith**: 305; **confidence**: 091; 74; 305; **trust**: 317, see *trust/3*; **appreciation**: 1019; 3440;

convinced: that the United Nations **represents the obligatory path** of modern civilization and world peace: 10; 316; 332; 348; the **last hope** for peace and harmony: 10; 348; that it is **uniquely suited** to fostering the possibilities for peace and to reducing the dangers created by injustice and aggression: 3434; and of the need to **organize international society globally** in order to achieve a common international good and to realize the need for a world authority: 317; 257; 349;

considers it: an **irreplaceable institution** in the present phase of the history of humanity: 348; to be the **fruit of a civilization** to which the Catholic religion gave the vital principles: 293; an **instrument of brotherhood between nations**, intended to favour progress and peace among men: 293; **a steadily developing and improving form of the balanced and unified life of all humanity** in its historical and earthly order: 293;

efforts to support the human work of **justice**, **peace** and **development** which remains the **ideal** of the UN: 307; see also 3437; homage and encouragement to its effort for **disarmament**: 954; 964-966; 1018; moral support for its **institutional principles and basic goals**: 316; 420; esteem and hopes for its **fundamental programmes**: 296; support, encouragement, **collaboration**, above all in whatever serves the cause of peace, the defence of human rights, international justice and the development of peoples: 321-322; 354; 421; 3440; **support**, **encouragement**, and **even exhortation**, if such is the case, **to do more and better**: 372 (cf. 370-372);

is conscious of the **limits which reduce its possibilities of effective intervention** in difficult situations: 308; 350; 3436; of the **challenge** that has to be faced from within the Organization: 3437; has seen its **shortcomings and suffered the disappointments** which have marked its development: 350; 372; would like its **resolutions** to be determined always by the objective good of all, above all of the populations most affected by want, hunger, injustice or ill-usage, and not by selfish or nationalistic perspectives or by purely economic interests: 308;

expresses the conviction that at this moment in its history it faces a **twofold challenge**: to overcome ideological competition and to foster an ethical approach to human development and the resolution of social problems: 3439;

wishes that the UN **possibilities of action** may be further improved: 310; that it be "par excellence" the **expression and the rampart** of the **human rights** it has so solemnly proclaimed: 310; confidence that it will be able to meet the **immense hope of a world fraternal community** in which each one can live a really human life: 343;

although at a different planes and with different means, both **converge** towards the same aim: **peace**: 300; 346; in **defending the freedom and dignity** of every human person and every group, without discrimination: 434; 605; 634; meet in the defence of **human rights**: 302; 416; 421; 439; 443;

follows with great interest and profound understanding its activities: 960; **is associated** in its work and the objectives which it pursues, to the extent that these are in accordance with the demands of its mission in the world: 346; its **participation** in the activities of the Organization is different from that of the States: 72;

its possible **contribution to the work of the UN** is essentially that of **appealing to the conscience of humanity** in the face of the forces which divide individuals and nations, in order tirelessly to seek new paths of peace, understanding and cooperation between peoples and communities: 346; **special bonds** of cooperation: 72; 274; ever increasing **cooperation and solidarity**, in defence of the human being in its wholeness, in all the fullness and manifold riches of its spiritual and material existence: 2211; **objectives of common action**: 359; considers extremely important the **dialogue** with the UN: 313; the Holy See **presence**, through the intermediary of a **Permanent Observer** at the headquarters in New York as also in Geneva and at the specialized organisms in Rome, Paris and Vienna, attests to its interest in the work of the United Nations and emphasizes the convergence of the aims pursued, each in the sphere proper to it: 346; 72; 123; 160; 218. See also: 344-362; 1019; 1558; 2211.

7. and the **FAO**: **praise, interest**, disinterested **support**: 58-60; **special relationship**: 123-124; **respect and friendship**: 2020; **profound harmony** between FAO's goals and activities and the concerns of Church: 2033; at the fourth session of FAO, on 23 November 1948, granted the unique status of Permanent Observer: 126. See also: 1928-2257, *passim*; in particular: 1929; 1934; 1965; 1968; 1975; 2003; 2026; 2128; 2181; 2206; 2211.

8. and the **IAEA**: stresses the importance, **commends and encourages the initiatives of the Agency**: 1261; 1290 and 1282-1370, *passim*;

9. and the **ILO**: **sympathy**: 39; **encouragement and agreement**: 50; 216-218; **concern** for its basic objectives: 213; 329; see also: 51; 57; 233; 331; **HABITAT**, see *Habitat/5;* **UNDP**, see *UNDP*; **UNIDO**, see *UNIDO*;

10. and the **UNESCO**: **esteem**: 901; 936; **support**: 901; **close ties**: 760; **close and trusting relations**: 703; 712; **collaboration** in the fields of education: 682; 761; 2392; **sincere interest** for its ideals and activities: 761; 885-887; the **presence of a Permanent Observer** to the UNESCO is entirely in keeping with the very nature of the Apostolic See: 160-164; between the two institutions there is a **community of intentions** in their concern over the destiny of mankind on earth: 732; **both converge** in giving priority to the development of the spiritual dimension of the human being: 734-735; **come together** in the effort of recombining the unity of the human family: 737; desires to see UNESCO extend its **peaceful activities for human development**: 678; both **meet** along the road to peace; 742. See in particular: 713-755;

11. and the **UNICEF**: **appreciates** the great good it has done over the years for the children of the world; **has wholeheartedly supported all its worthy activities** aimed at providing for the basic needs of children, while at the same time has repeatedly expressed dissociation from any involvement in projects that may directly or indirectly favour contraception, abortion, or other practices that do not respect the supreme value of life: 3242; has **collaborated with UNICEF throughout the world** in Child Programmes for survival and development; in expanded literacy programmes; immunization projects; and in other undertakings which foster both physical health from the moment of conception and likewise the moral and spiritual development of children, and is stands ready to continue this promotion of much needed services for all children of the world: 2390;

12. and the **International Court of Justice/of Arbitration**: interest and support: 247-248;

13. see also: *Abortion/2; Action/1; Activity/1; Advancement; Aging; Aid/6; Apartheid/1,2; Armaments/7; Assistance/5; Association/3; Authority/1; Awareness/2; Behaviour/2; Belligerent; Benefit/3; Birth Control/2; Bombay; Brotherhood/1; Care; Child/9; Collaboration/6; Communication/5; Community/E; Complementarity; Conversion; Creation; Culture/3; Deterrence; Developing Countries/6; Detente; Development/15; Disabled Persons/4; Disarmament/8; Discrimination/1,2; Drugs/3; Duties/4; Education/6,7,9,10,11; Educator/2; Energy/3; Environment/3; Euthanasia; Faith/2; Family/B,4,5; C,3,6-9; FAO/2; Freedom/1,2; Habitat/5; Health/1; Heritage/2; Holy See; Hunger/9; Industrialization/5; Instruction; Law/3,6; Life/11; Literacy/4; Love/2; Marriage/1,3; Mass Media/4; Migrants/5; Minorities/3; Nation/2; Nature/4; Ougadougou; Peace/13,15; Peoples/7; Poor/3; Population/1; Progress/11; Redemption; Relation/2; Refugees/5; Rights/2,3; Sahel; Science/15; Solidarity/13; Space/1,3; Sterilization; Subsidiarity; Teaching/1-8; Trade/10; Traditions; Training/1; War/4,5; Women/4,5,10; Work/1; Youth/10.*

Civilization

1. has **to be built on spiritual principles**: 34; the development of c. must be **at the service of the human being**: 90; attempts to impose on human being a set of **apparent imperatives** which its spokesmen justify by appealing to the principle of development and progress: 170-171; marches towards the **recognition** of the equality and the freedoms demanded by reason of the human dignity and equality proper to the human person: 638; the most advanced civilizations **collapse** when they no longer either respect or protect the human person: 724; **criterion** of really true c.: respect for rights: 311; for the weakest of its members: 2650;

2. in the last hundred years **has contributed** as never before to the development of material goods, but has also given rise to attitudes in which sensitivity to the spiritual dimension of human existence is diminished: 91; partly **based** on the assumption that scientific and technical progress would automatically bring moral and human progress: 391;

3. **crisis**: 56; 1688; 2106; 2556; 2982; **threats** to, failure, annihilation of modern c.: (armaments, war): 068; 099; 0104; 183-184; 194; 352; 396; 1028; 1315; **future:** 1515; 1519; 1523; 2789; **dialogue** between civilizations: 710;

4. of **well being**: 875; c. of **human labour**: 233; 329; of **solidarity**: 233; 1498; of **peace**: 350; of **love**: 233; 1188; 1601; 2396; 2436; 2949; **new** c.: marked by frank solidarity in the mutual esteem and total respect for each other: 2245; of truth and love: 2465; 3290; **rural** c.: 2074; **technological**: 1523; 2117; 3100; 3103; **industrial**: 1693; 3106;

5. see also: 10; 41; 44; 101; 173; 197-198; 293; 316; 332; 348; 376; 581; 628; 630; 686; 688; 701; 709; 725; 741-742; 751-752; 927; 1050; 1509; 1675; 1684; 1731; 1740; 2433; 2485; 2498; 2807; 2829; 2988; 2993; 3098; 3105.

Collaboration/Cooperation

1. at no time in history has there been greater **need** for dialogue and collaboration at the international level and for joint efforts by nations to promote integral human development and to further justice and peace: 270; 3435; is still cruelly **contradicted**, in many parts of the world, by racial, ideological and religious discrimination, by forceful subjection of weaker nations, by political regimes which deprive citizens of just freedom, by recourse to threats and violence to resolve conflicts of self-interest: 417; **cannot exist without freedom** of each nation, at the international level, or of each person, at national level: 893; is **inconceivable so long as the nations are at one only in their cupidities and their fears**, spending 200 billion dollars to defend their so-called security and thirty times less to root out the basic causes of insecurity: 1455;

2. among all **human groups**: 341; **peoples**; 352; 1221; 1271; 1370; **men and women**, in tasks facing society: 2515; 2523; 2566; with **those who follow other religions**: 557; 782; to **promote human rights**: 428; 431;

3. **cultural**: 759; must be carried out in a spirit of sincerity and disinterested service, with respect for the cultural differences of every people, with the determination to avoid everything that would be undue attempt at influencing or a subtle form of domination: 778; **for education**: between parents, teacher and school authority: 590/e; of diverse human communities: 699; of Religious Sisters in developing countries: 2544; **to combat illiteracy**: 776-778; 782; 784; 788-789; 791; 809; 1480;

4. **technical**, in the field of agriculture: 1342; 1343; **economic**: 1516; see also *Aid, Assistance*; **among developing countries**: 1527; 1609; **among developed and developing countries**: 2168; 2340; **leading to** the gradual lessening of the gap between rich and poor countries: 3334;

5. for **peace**: 149; 416; 1042; 1069; 1098; 1103-1104; 1108; 1158; 1171; 1248; 1317; 1726; 2210; 3201; 3436;

for **development**: must be friendly, peaceful and free of vested interests: 1393; 3177; see: 86; 142; 201; 359; 873; 1444; 1489; 1519; 1536-1537; 1539; 1542; 1546-1547; 1556-1557; 1614; 1642; 1653; 1655; 2047; 2213; for industrial development: 1666; 1696; 1713; 1720; for the advancement of peoples of Africa: 1841-1846; for the good of Latin America and the Caribbean countries: 3410; 3417;

for the **common good**: 320; 330; 1288; 1405; 1474; 2337; **common progress**: 382; to solve the **environment**: 272; 281; and **food** problems: 99; 1948; 1957; 1979; 2013; 2092; 2121; to face the **debt** question: c. which goes beyond collective egoism and vested interests can provide for an efficient management of the debt crisis and can mark progress along the path of international economic justice: 2278; 3419; see: 356; 2279; 2281; 2286; 2303; 2318; to create conditions of **habitat** that foster development: 2845; in favor of **refugees**: 2853; 2869; 2929; for the exploration and peaceful uses of outer space: 3237; 3265; 3270/g; 3271/c; 3299/9.10; 3300/3.4.21; 3301;

6. **of the Catholic Church/Holy See**: with the international community: 020; 025; 070; 071; 091; with the United Nations and related Organizations: 72-73; 124; 218; 247; 322; 343-344; 346-347; 715; 900; 2211; 2392; 3045; 3409; 3440;

7. **promoted by the United Nations and related Organizations**: 1; 26; 48; 74; 137; 193; 220; 308; 315; 702; 709; 756; 878; 914; 948; 1402; 1455; 2078; 3435-3437;

8. see also: 47; 119; 149; 326; 328; 334; 632; 916; 942; 1147; 1525; 1829; 1848; 1878; 1898; 1940; 2134; 2248; 2254; 3231; 2397; 2478; 2695; 2714; 2751; 2765; 2785; 2797; 3218; 3237; 3336; 3388; 3391.

Commitment

1. **of the Church/Holy See**: for the conservation and improvement of our environment: 273; in support of the United Nations: 603; to the victims of racial discrimination: 617; to the cause of promoting human dignity: 651; 1476; to work for the promotion of the integral good, both material and spiritual, of the whole human being and of all human beings: 2681; 2744; 3038; to peace: 3394; to the material progress and the social and moral development of peoples: 1372; 1487; 1715; 1720; 1763; to the real problem of people: 1477; to the assistance of refugees: 2873; 2936; personal c. of the believers: 398-399; 405; see also: 057; 398; 478; 1083; 1237; 1271; 1372; 1695, *and related voices;*

2. to the **cause of the human being**: 1345; to **serve others**: 882; **in favour of human rights**: 421; 439; 494; 861; **to peace**: 067; 216; 368; 1349; 3389; **to justice**: 632; 1550; 2692; 2745; **to solidarity**: 1349; to forms of solidarity between North and South, East and West: 1890; to the struggle **against illiteracy**: 176; 788; 809; 820; for the solution of the **problem of work**: 220; **to development**: 65; 1414; 1801; 2745; **to solve the food problem**: 60; 117; 2049; 2105; 2196; 2209; 2241; 2246; 2254; **in favour of the developing countries**: 1353; 1481; 2157; **to creditors**: 2286; 2312; 2325; 2340; to the struggle **against desertification**: 3133; **political** c.: 1455; 1640; 1710;

3. made **by nuclear powers** in promoting the NPT: 1170; according to the NPT: 1229; 1231; 1243; 1268; 1270; 1275; 1278-1279; for the **peaceful use of nuclear energy**: 1287; 1302; 1331; 1343; 1344; 1345;

4. **to youth**: 2478; **of youth**: 2551; **to disabled persons**: 2648; 2651; to **refugees**: 2881; 2892; to the problems posed by **population growth**: 2680; to **family life**: 2763; to respect for the **physical and moral integrity of the person**, even in the case of those guilty or accused of having broken the law: 3091;

5. see also: 057; 130; 237; 240; 261; 352; 369; 901; 1121; 1475; 1480; 1502; 1591; 2077; 2084; 2281; 2499; 2590; 2602; 2723; 2736; 2982; 2988; 3240; 3267; 3310; 3377; 3416; 3456.

Commodities

international agreements on **primary c.**: 1532; 1655; 1663/1; trade in primary c.: 1531; unequal terms of trade in the exchange between manufactured goods and **agricultural c.** and raw materials: 1650; see also: 61; 1535; 1630; 1648-1649; 1652; 1938-1939.

Communication

1. **right to freedom of c.**, today so threatened; **concern for authentic c.** as a source of communion among all and implying honesty founded on truth: 931; **dangers**: lack of quality, moral degradation, excess of messages: 932;

2. **between generations**: rendered more difficult by the profound changes that disturb our times: 680; its importance: 2462;

3. difficulty of c. **in least developed countries**: 1479; **through satellites**: 3209; 3214; 3232; 3236; 3241; 3243-3245; 3249-3253; 3258-3259; 3263; 3265; 3270/b,c,f; 3271/b,c,i;

4. **media of social c.**: see *Mass Media;*

5. the **Catholic Church**: **claims** freedom for religious authorities to communicate with those belonging to their religious denomination and to use media of social c.: 494-495; 528; **proclaims** the right of the family to expect that the means of social c. will be positive instruments for the building up of society and will reinforce the fundamental values of the family; and the right to be protected, especially with regard to its youngest members, from the negative effects and misuse of the mass media: 590/f.

Community

A. civil

the **human being is the fundamental subject** of all the concerns and cares of the c. in its assistance projects: 3148; **forms its members** as citizens: 112; **cannot grow from self-interest** alone: 1591; **marked by the freedom** of each individual and the solidarity of all in the tasks undertaken; or, at least accepted no longer in the hope of making a profit, however small, but in the awareness that each individual must make his or her contribution as a person: 2449; see also: 1577; 1580; 1783; 1817; 2249 and *Society;*

B. scientific

its task can be decisive for the future of humanity: 197; dedication to protect life: 1344; see also *Scientists;*

C. universal/world

need to build a **fraternal world c.**: 343; 414; 437; 630; 1518; 1594; **comes about little by little**, in stages, and by way of regional accords and agreements which unite peoples in a spirit of solidarity and mutual aid: 1609; 1620; **finds an exceptional strength in** the certainty of the common origin, nature and destiny of all persons in God: 1635;

D. international

1. **lacks a system of moral and legal means to establish and maintain the rights of everyone**: 247; cannot tolerate that States members of the United Nations should systematically and openly violate fundamental human rights: 360; 543; during the last decades has shown interest in the safeguarding of human rights and fundamental liberties and has carefully concerned itself with respect for freedom of conscience and religion in well-known documents: 479; legitimately seeks effective ways within the framework of laws and binding conventions to eliminate injustices and uphold efforts that the oppressed themselves undertake to have their rights recognized: 615;

2. a sense of i.c. **calls for the provision of useful aid** of all kinds, particularly to the least favoured countries: 784; needs more effective instruments of political responsibility or social order, to mediate between the wealthy and the developing nations: 1455; it must be ready to take into account the legitimate interests of the developing countries to share in the benefits of the conquest of space: 3227; its **contribution** to the economic and social development of the developing countries: 1724; and to the process of their industrialization: 1678; 1698; 1701; its **future activities** are directed to assure not only the survival of the victims of starvation, but also their long term rehabilitation and advancement through the deployment of all those factors which contribute to the concrete self-development of each nation: 1926;

3. **its role** to study and face with responsibility the population problem in the context and with the view to the common good of individual nations and of all humanity: 2731; its **genuine concern** about the tragedy of the refugees: 2866; 2917; 2926-2927; and for the protection of the migrants: 2941; its **interest** about issues related to health: 3012; environment; 3104;

4. see also: 0103; 13; 129; 200; 893; 969; 1116; 1134; 1148; 1182; 1243; 1254; 1305; 1424; 1527; 1556; 1633; 1659; 1673; 2031; 2077; 2095;

E.organization

Pius XII already in 1939 was calling for the creation of a new world organization, on the basis of international law: 349; see *United Nations*

F. The Holy See and the I.C.

1. **right to belong to it**: is centuries old: 03-04; **unique situation**: 012-016; in relation to other forces operating in the sphere of the spirit and conscience: 015-016; in relation to the States: 026-027; in relation to other non-national or non-governmental organizations: 028-029; as representative of moral values: 031; recognized by the international community: 032-044; placed in and accepted by the i.c. almost as the "conscience of humanity": 045;

2. committed to full **collaboration** with the i.c., in order to carry out the latter's aims: 020; 045-049; 0108; in certain cases playing the role of intermediary and, if requested, of "**mediation**" and "**arbitration**": 050-053; 248;

3. **relationship** of cordiality: 054-059; and trust: 056-059; 077; **attitude**: of respect, understanding, interest and sympathy, readiness to cooperate: 060; of **dialogue**: 060-082; with: no limits except the ones imposed by a persistent refusal on the part of the others: 066; no illusions about the real possibility of making determinant contributions: 077; **deliberate position of neutrality**, of equidistance between the opposed parties or blocs: 079-082; 1237; gives **due respect** to the sovereign prerogatives of any State: 502;

4. **aware that its first and fundamental duty** is to protect and vigorously promote the cause of the Church, the rights of all believers to religious freedom, and respect for the fundamental rights of the human person and individual conscience (072), but **considering also no less fundamental part of its mission** to operate in the service of peace and of a more just and brotherly social order, in and among all nations: 075; 0108;

5. not full **fledged Member** but Observer of the International Organizations: 087-089; active **participation** in international organizations: 257; **continues to proclaim** the necessity of: a world organization of peoples: 090; 3237; a world legal system: 256; a world authority, accepted by everyone and respected by everyone, and endowed with the power necessary to safeguard, on behalf of all, security, regard for justice and respect for rights: 090; 098-0105; 349; 3175; see also *Authority/1;*

6. **participation in the international conference**: demonstrates the concrete interest with which the Holy See follows the problems of the international c.: 01; see also *Holy See/6.*

Complementarity

distinction and c. ***among nations****: 228; among individual and community, private and public aspects* ***in the expression and practice of religious freedom****: 491;* ***of schooling*** *in relation to the primary educative task of parents: 695;* ***of cultures****: 697; 878;* ***among the rights of the individual and the rights of peoples****, with due consideration of the primacy of the human being: 925; complementary and indispensable role* ***of private associations****: 2255;* ***of the generations****: 2490; equal dignity and effective c.* ***between men and women****: 2529-2530; 2547; of the* ***action of the Church***

in relation to that of the public authorities and the private associations: 1716; 2928; 3411;
10. see also: 1636; 2799; 2804; 2981 and Relation.

Concentration

1. c. **camps**: to send someone to a c. camp and keep him or her there without proper trial is to make a mockery of the law: 3090; see also: 80; 526(*); 592, and *Auschwitz*;

2. **c. of research apparatus** in small elite of nations which have already achieved modernization: helps to explain the bitterness and resentment which developing nations sometimes display when aid is offered in terms not much removed from patronage and paternalism...: 1454;

3. excessive c. or subdivision of **property**: 1955; **urban population** c.: 2771; 2798; 3130; a greatest c. of **intelligence, good will and creative labour** required for the social and economic progress of the developing nations: 3432.

Conflicts/Confrontation

c. which **rend our era**: 54; **labour** c.: 46; 49; **between those who possess and those who are without material goods**: 90; **structures which cause** injustice and c.: 196; between **social groups**: 196; 583; 632; **racial**, in South Africa: 653; in certain countries, **between various cultural groups**: 909; possible c. **of rights**: 903; 3178; conflicting **situations**: 615; **opinions**: 2395; **requirements**: 2819; of **interests**: 334; 385; 632; 725; 1512; 1649; 2989; **between trade and monetary policies**: 1663/5; **caused by economic policies**: 2208; 2270; **prevention**: 21; 26; 973; 1178; 1239; 2332; 2339; **armed** conflicts: 83; 184; 334; 973; 1000; 1026; 1028; 1097; 1102; 1103; 1141; 1161; 1176; 1919; 2345; 3342; 3348; 3350; 3374; **peaceful solution**: 21; 248; 249; 252; 262; 971; 1171. See also: 580; 1403; 1583; 1880; 2414; 2432; 2438; 2588; 2763; 3403;
confrontation: between the **religious view of the world and the agnostic** or even atheistic view: 105; 489; **in the midst of the worst confrontations** there appears ever more strongly the **aspiration towards a world where force no longer dominates**...: 341; values obfuscated by **ideological** c. and artificial divisions: 1189. See also: 580; 614; 619; 658; 971; 987; 1026; 1139; 1542; 1571; 1674; 1696; 3214; *Contrast; War; Work; Workers.*

Conscience

1. the appeal to the **moral** c. of the human being has never before been as necessary as it is today, for the danger comes neither from progress nor from science but from the human being: 33; the efforts of **people's** c, must be increased to match the rising tensions between good and evil to which humans are being subjected at the close of the twentieth century: 185; our generation is faced by a great moral challenge, one which consists in **harmonizing the values of science with values of c.**: 210; when science advances from success to success, its use places ever greater demands upon the c. of the human being: 338; 3328; **by c. the human being marshals its conquests** for the service of the human family: 701;

2. new ethical choices are necessary; a **new world c.** must be created; each of us must regard him or herself as a member of the world community: 227; an **extra effort of c.** would be necessary to make human rights the criterion of human civilization, and to really bring about, not excluding any race or any people, the solidarity that is necessary among brothers and sisters, all created in God's image: 311; 879; 1142; the **spirit of brotherhood appeals to c.**: 631; 643;

3. c. **of a common responsibility for the future of peoples** and for the liberation from various forms of misery and alienation: 1558; peoples c. **must be trained** to the sense of responsibility that weighs upon the community and upon each individual, especially those who are most favoured: 1786; 1978; 2013;

4. in relation to the **problems of distribution of goods, hunger, development, sharing of natural resources**: 53; 1672; 1706; 2044; 2086; 2090; 2147; 2169; 2223; 2225; 2274; 2308; 2340; 3100; 3171; 3226; 3325; in relation to **armaments/peace/war**: 069; 397; 1065; 1067; 1070; 1083; 1241; 1277; 1315; 1332; 1364; 3096; 3225; 3332; 3348; 3352; 3420;

5. Christ (1165), God (2410; 3131), moral teaching (3069) **enlighten the c.**; the human being **needs to develop its mind and its c.**: 2439; **education of c.**: 552-553; 578; 602; merit of non-Catholic organizations and religions in proclaiming principles and **forming and guiding c.**: 028; **has a new voice for our era**: 2044; the c. of humanity **makes its heard** clearly in the United Nations: 333;

6. **one of the great crises of c. of contemporary society** is the disregard for the mystery and sacredness of the gift of life: 2376-2377; **professional c.**, in matter of information: 473; **convictions firmly rooted in c.**: 1011; **deterioration**: 3085;

7. **rights**: 072; 105; 360; 500; **right to freedom of c.**: 101-102; 454; 478-479; 481; 489; 496; 516-517; 522; 526(*); 534; 551; 589; 593; 2616; to **worship according to one's c.**: 339; 483; 487; see *Freedom/2;*

8. see also: 32; 78; 153; 188; 194; 261; 813; 849; 2475; 2646; 2655; 2672; 2690; 2762; 2925; 2970; 3084; 3207; *Church/1 and Science.*

Consumerism/Consumption

society based on c.: 834; 1468; 2358; struggle against any **form of super-c.**: 2587; **self-centered c.**: 2375; **unrestrained** c.: 889; 1387; **false standards of** c.: 2838; **high c. habits**: 1449. See also: 91; 1453; 1629; 1899; 1943; 2125; 2192; 2255; 2498; 2716-2717; 2724; 2817; 2982.

Contraception

the experience and trends of recent years clearly emphasize the **profoundly negative effects** of contraceptive programmes: 2735; effects of the **use of contraceptives**: 3077. See also: 2342; 2533; 2722; 2734; 2760; 2761; 3058; *Abortion; Birth Control; Family/6-8; Population/5-7; Sterilization.*

Contrast

1. **growing** c. between the prodigious **increase of the goods** at the disposal of the human being and **their distribution**, so easily made unjustly: 53; **in the sphere of the "possession"**: 99;

2. between the **enormous sums invested in the production of ammunitions** and the immense, **ever increasing material distress** of more than half of mankind: 955;

3. **today's world is ever more marked by c.**: 1173; c. **in peoples' conditions**: 1174; between the **growing expectation of the developing countries and the absence of** sufficiently complete and wide **commitment** on the part of the rich countries: 2084; enormous c. of income and standards of living **between rich and materially poor countries**: 2156; 2185; 2215. See also *Conflicts; Disparities; Gap.*

Control

1. of **reason over nature**: 78; **self-c.**: 2248; 2721; human being's c. **of its life**: 726; 932; **of the forces of nature**: 686; 709; 1296; 1990; **of the forces it has succeeded in releasing**: 094; 3348;

2. **over riches**: 1473; 1619; **of the creation of liquidity**: 1659; 1663/4; **of commercial exchanges**: 2191; **inflation**: 2311;

3. developing countries' **ability to c. their own destiny**: 1493; **of the activities of trans-national corporations**, see *Corporations*;

4. strategies of peace which only **verify c.**: 1060; **c. of nuclear energy**: 094; 1262; 1337; 1350; of its safe use: 1306; in its transfer: 1260-1261; of armaments: 1044; 1234; 1239; 1349; **of production and traffic of nuclear weapons**: 1056; **of disarmament**: see *Disarmament*;

5. of **human fertility**: 2627; 3075; of the **population growth**: 2699; 2742; 2769; 2829; 3039; see also *Birth control*

6. see also: 135; 235; 1283; 1403; 1586; 1608; 1612; 1652; 1655; 1659; 1884; 1888; 1955; 2072; 2292; 2297; 2345; 2395; 2438; 2753; 2833; 3098; 3105; 3173; 3203.

Conversion

Paul VI appeal to c., personal transformation, interior renewal: 32; **need for personal c.**: 2305; 3403; c. of **outlook and mentality**: 1288; of **hearths**: 1419-1420; 1475; 2307; true c. of **mind, will,** and **heart**: 2590; of **attitude and practice**: 3119; human being's c. **of attitudes in favor of peace and development**: 1703-1704; **towards the victims of hunger**: 2256; see also: 2134;

Corporations

trans-national/multinational: due to the concentration and flexibility of their resources, are **able to carry out autonomous strategies**, independently of the national political powers and, consequently, outside of any control from the point of view of the common good: 1561; **would be proper to study attentively their conduct and establish a framework to guide and control their activities in view of the common good**: 1562; control a substantial proportion of world production and trade for many important primary and processed commodities: 1652; see also: 2295; 2328-2330.

Creation

1. **teaching of the Bible**: 37; **God created all things** and intrusted them to the care of human beings: 273; everything created by God is good: 3099; 3114; 3120;

2. **human beings c. by God**, in His image: 144; 263; 273; 302; 311; 424; 511; 601; 651; 666; 701; 911; 1543; 2123; 2132; 2421; 2423; 2524; 2557; equal: 416; 2557; 2511; 2557; 2559; children of the same Father: 57; 614; 626; children of God: 343; 419; 1419; 1471; 1657; 1769; 2123; 2558; 3136; creature of God: 688; 1997; 2410; 3411; established lord of the c. 701; to rule c. 3099; steward of c. 3118;

3. **universal purpose of c.**: 3170; 3182; 3223; created goods, directed to the good of all humanity: 274; 279: 1749; 1807.

Crime

State's right to demand **punishment commensurate with the c.** committed: 3090; 3092; abortion, euthanasia, war, **are c.**: see: *related voices*.

Crisis

which **shakes modern civilization**: 56; of civilization: 2556; 2982; above all one of civilization and human solidarity: 2106-2107; 1688; **specific c. of the human being**, in which it has less confidence in its own humanity in the meaningfulness of being a person and in the sense of affirmation and the joy that stem therefrom and are a source of creativity: 170; distressing c. **of the young**: 2076; both of identity and about the meaning of life: 2395; see also: 1167; 2439; **of humanity**: 1065; **world** c.: 1483; crises **of the more affluent milieux and societies**: 165; **moral**: 194; **cultural**: 857; moral and cultural: 2374; 2389; c. **of existence**: 2715; **ethical** crisis: 1063-1064; **of values**: 2939; **spiritual**: 2982; c. **of conscience**: 2376; **economic**: 136; 227; 319; 1485; 1514; 1596; 1622; 1648; 2297; 2299; 2606; 2715; 3412; **financial**: 1648; 1659; 2305; **debt c.** 2273; 2275; 2278; 2282-2284; 2286; 2293; 2299; 2332; 2336; 3419; **world food** c.: 1688; 1952; 2111; 2113; 2117; 2208; 2252; **housing** c. 2794; 2824. See also: 84; 321; 829; 857; 930; 1277; 1313; 1424; 1452; 2083; 2149; 2184; 2260; 2289; 2661; 2924; 3103; 3106;

Culture

1. is **a characteristic of human life as such**; it is through c. that human being lives a truly human life: 154; 2961; can come to an authentic and full humanity: 704; is **an essential part of the being of each person and people**, a major factor of their affirmation, advancement, development and spiritual growth: 930; 2498; is **a specific mode of the human being's "existing" and "being"**: 155; 197; it is **therein** that **is grounded the fundamental distinction between what the human being is and what it has**: 197;

2. **the human being**, in the entirety of its spiritual and material subjectivity, **is c.'s only subject, only object and end**: through it the human being becomes more humane: 156; 157-159; 161; 765-766;

3. **relation between** c. and the world of human production: 156-157; between spiritual and material c.: 158; organic and essential bond between religion and c.: 160; fundamental link creative of c. between the Gospel and human being: 162; between Christianity and c. in Europe: 160-164; uniqueness and value of the heritage of other continents, deriving from other sources of religious, humanistic and ethical inspiration: 161; **Catholic Church/Holy See and c.**: 160-163;

4. **right**: 894; 904; **to freedom**: 89 its primary and indispensable duty is education: 165; see *Education*; its prime and fundamental dimension is sound morality: 168; one of its **loftiest achievements** is peace: 196; the right of the nation must be situated at the root of c. and education: 172-173; see *Nation*;

5. **value** of, **respect** for different cultures: 243; 630; 697; 710; 762; 1614; 1645; 1721; for **minority cultures**: 2960; **migrant's** c.: 2962; **cultural pluralism**: 878-880; 909; 2434; 2530;

6. technological cooperation can pose a serious **threat to the c. of developing countries**: 1846; development according to the models corresponding to the c. and conditions of each country: 1884; 1915; 2163; 2317;

7. **dialogue among cultures**: 581; 3285; **convergence** of c.: 881-882; cultural **discrimination**: 260; 640; 2432; cultural **cooperation, progress**: 759; 878-880; cultural progress is closely connected with the construction of a more just and more fraternal world: 759;

8. **cultural policies**: must be concerned with human being in its integrity, that is to say, in all its personal dimensions, not forgetting the ethical and religious aspects, and its social dimensions: 766; see: 765-766;

9. **spreading of c. through satellites**: 3283; **must not be identified with the imposition of the c.** of the technologically advanced countries on those still developing: 3284-3285;

10. **basic c.**: see *Literacy*; **ethical c.**: 168; **c. of peace**: 376; **on it depends the future of mankind**: 189; 376;

11. see also: 30; **146-191**; 196; 204; 204-205; 259; 260; 266; 281; 330; 693; 702; **704-704-706**; 709; 751-752; 781; 783; 797; 822; 829; 1060; 1257; 1357; 1399; 1436-1437; 1441; 1614; 2498; 3051; 3435; *Assimilation; Education; Heritage; Riches; Traditions* and *UNESCO.*

Debt

1. the **problem of the Third World global indebtedness** and of new relationships of dependence which it creates, cannot be posed solely in economic and monetary terms; it has become more widely a problem of political cooperation and economic ethics: 356; **neither the creditor countries nor the debtor countries have anything to gain from the development of situation of despair that would be uncontrollable**: 357; **cooperation** which goes beyond collective egoism and vested interests can provide for an efficient management of the d. crisis: 2278; 3419;

2. **ethical approach** to the question: principles: 2279-2284; action in emergency situation: 2285-2293; **joint assumption of responsibility** for the future: 2294-2295; **responsibilities** of the industrialized countries: 2296-2302; of the developing countries: 2303-2318; of creditors with respect to debtors: 2319-2330; of multilateral financial organizations: 2332-2339;

3. see 355-358; 1101; 1423-1424; 1462-1468; 1568; 1608; 1652; 1660-1661; 1712; 2142; **2258-2340**; 3412; 3439 and *Bank.*

Defence

1. all those who desire the **d. and the progress of the human being** must love it for its own sake: 208; of the human being: 460; 636; 725; 737; 2211; 2988; of its dignity: 322; 460; and its rights: 302; 322; 359; 422; **of workers**: 232; 325; of **humanity**: 1288; of the **right to education**: 894; of **human life**: 2656; 3022; of **principles**: 661; of **fundamental values**: 3062; of **peace**: 935; 3399;

2. **legitimate d.**: 969: 975; 983; 1027; 1176; 1201; 1285; 3340; of the just **rights of the peoples**: 3346; legitimate defence **against the imminent danger of infection**: 2990; use of nuclear weapons for purpose of **national d.** in limited conflicts: 185; 1285; *Armament/1;*

3. of particular, immediate **interests**: 1555; 1909; excessive d. of **food prices** by the high-production countries: 2192; d. of **ideological claims**: 1064; **defenceless people**: 1958; 2243; 2376-2377;

4. see also *Interest; Rights; War.*

Degradation

of **nature**: 889; of the **biological patrimony**: 3100; **biological d.**: 2482; **social**: 46; **moral**: 845; 908; 932; **of the human being**: 195; 1591; 2522; **of the human being as the subject of work**: 225.

Dependence

human being although dependent on the resources of the material world for life, cannot be their slave, but must be their master: 97; **relationships of d.** and exploitations foster frustrations and reaction which are at the root of many wars of liberation or of internal revolts: 1100; **need and means to avoid excessive d. by developing countries** on industrialized economies: 1628-1631; d. **resulting from the international trade system**: 2142; increasing d. **at the level of imports** of farm-food produce: 2174; 2188; **personal**: 1751; **economic or political**: a form of neocolonialism: 99; **on ad-**

vanced energies systems: 1591; **economic and social d. of mankind on telecommunications**: 3251. See also: 72; 156; 356; 726; 1323; 1452; *Developing Countries.*

Desertification

see: 277; 382; 1322; 1717; 1919; 1922; 1926; 1935; 2190; **3121-3137**; 3288; 3299/3; 3303-3304; *Ougadougou; Sahel.*

Detente

in the real sense, that is to say, **founded upon a proven willingness to exercise mutual respect**, is a condition for setting in motion a true process of disarmament: 990; 1263-1265; **its aims correspond to the Holy See mission of peace**: 1222; 1254. See also *Trust.*

Deterrence/Dissuasion

1. justice and the interest of peace demand a **rapid abandonment of the mentality of relations based upon the fear of mutual destruction**: 1105; **strategy for a precarious and uncertain peace**: 1104; 1314;

2. "in current conditions **deterrence based on balance**, certainly not as an end in itself but as a step on the way toward a progressive disarmament, **may still be judged morally acceptable**": 1053; see: 1053-1055; 1106; 3378; **as an end in itself encourages the arms race**: 1106;

3. **nuclear deterrence**: hitherto it has been said that nuclear weapons represented a deterrent which has prevented the outbreak of a major war; and this is very probably true. But at the same time we may wonder if it will always be so: 184; "The Popes and the Church are of course in favour of a mode of life based upon a mutual commitment to sincere respect for law and justice. But, in view of a reality that unfortunately seems a long way from being capable of change, they recognize that one cannot condemn recourse to a non indiscriminate deterrence, as a means for trying to defend one's own security and to resist unjust aggression, and in the meantime to prepare to change the situation which for the moment justifies the use of deterrence": 3377; see **3356-3383**; see also: 354; 978; 1029 and *Fear.*

Developing Countries

1. **justice demands** that each nation should assume its part of responsibility for the development of the needy nations in true solidarity, aware that all peoples have equal dignity, and that, together, all the nations constitute a worldwide community: 2169; the construction of **peace through development** remains the responsibility of the d.c., whatever might be the role of the developed countries in it: 1527;

2. the **structures** of the d. c. are not entirely suited to cope with the grave economic condition of our times: 1523; **structural weakness**: 1650-1652; rigid and backward economic and social structures: 2157;

3. **under-modernized agriculture**: 1449; 1844; 2118; 2142-2143; lack of adequate development of their own resources: 1992; should aspire to the greatest possible self-sufficiency in the field of agricultural consumption by their people: 2141; need technical and financial assistance in order to become self-sufficient in agricultural production: 2164-2165; need to ensure an effective increase of food production in the individual d. c.: 2188; a distribution favorable to d. c.: 2191; see also 2113; FAO must enable the d.c. to create the economic and technical conditions to assure them of the possibility of feeding their populations: 2024; 2141; see *FAO, Food, Hunger;*

4. increasing burden of the **external debt** whose financing absorbs part of their trade and even of their assistance: 1568; see also: 355-358; 1608; 1660; 2258-2340; **dependence** of the poor economies on the rich; their dramatic vulnerability to the hazards and errors of the privileged: 1630; 2142; 2157; 2188; fear of an **economic neo-colonialism**: 1529;

5. their **intention to make all efforts** on their way to social and economic progress cannot be believed if they invest so much money in useless things to satisfy national ambition, like military equipments: 1704; 1712;

6. **Catholic Church/Holy See**: because of its mission of disinterested service to humanity, the Holy See wishes that the need of developing countries, and especially of the poorest among them, be generously recognized: 3237; has always strongly deplored that the majority of developed countries and even of developing ones, waste huge sums in the acquisition of costly weapon systems: 1569; see also: 1582; deeply deplores the fact that, in the field of industrialization of developing countries, no greater progress has so far been made, due also to the continuous **arms race** between not only the superpowers and their allies but between the d. c. themselves: 1702; see also 1720; states that advanced nations have a very serious obligation to help developing peoples: 1844; awakes conscience to its new duties in today's world: 2041-2044; see: 1715; 2032-2040; 3390;

7. **relationship between developed and developing c.**: the d. nations must continue in their effort to promote the true welfare of the their peoples, utilizing all their own energies, working together and sharing among themselves; 1386; international justice demands that the wealthy and privileged nations should match that effort by: removing any obstacles of economic or political domination, 1386; sharing more equitably economic power with the weaker nations, 1386; 1409; allowing d. nations to be the agents of their own development and to exercise their true role in the decision-making that affects the very lives of their peoples, 1386; to mediate between the wealthy and the d. nations, the international community needs **more effective instruments of political responsibility or social good will**: 1455; lack of mutual confidence largely responsible for the anarchy in the economic relations: 1543; distrust prevailing between developed and developing c.: 1705; see also: 1525; 1588; 1663/5; 2169;

8. moral drive to eliminate the **inequalities** between d. and developed countries: 1514; **consequence** of the present situation: movements of violent unrest: 1524; controlled progressive **disarmament** constitute chief priority for developed and developing peoples alike: 1583;

9. **transfer of technology to d.c.**: cannot be expected to have lasting results if training is not provided for technicians and scientists from these countries themselves: 281; need of centres for education and research in d.c.: 1436; "adapted" technology: 1438-1439; 1449; technological cooperation can pose a serious threat to the culture of d. c.; to avoid this danger it must be carried out in spirit of a dialogue which appreciates the worthy traditions of the peoples concerned and the many different values of each culture: 1846; the fact that the whole apparatus of research is concentrated in the small elite of nations which have already achieved modernization helps to explain the **bitterness and resentment** displayed sometimes by d.c. when aid is offered in terms of **patronage** and **paternalism**: 1454;

10. **industrialization** is one of the indispensable factors in true progress for d. c.: 1720; if things were allowed to go their way, the gap between the industrialized countries and the developing ones would continue to grow wider: 2051; see also: 1665-1722, *passim*; **training and education**: 1718

11. **capital assistance**: aid equivalent to one percent of the gross national product of the rich nations: 1446; see also: 1582; aid effort supported by some of the wealthiest c. is not even the beginning, at the world level, of redistributive taxation or a healthy welfare system: 1455; should be "institutionalized" and accepted as an incipient world tax system, to underline their essential character of distributive justice: 1466; 1589; should lead to self-reliance: 1101;

12. **wider opportunities in world trade**: 1446; **higher export incomes**: 1446; **better access to industrialized markets**: 1446; **trade and investment between each other**, through regional grouping and collective action in the world market: 1467; **good will and determination** in trying to restructure world trade on equitable bases: 1514; **commercial exchanges** among d.c.: 1535; **reciprocal trade** through preferential treatment: 1675; **protectionism**: 1652; 1586; 1663/3; see also: 1535; 1565; **reforms** needed at the national level: 1458-1461; **policies** needed at the international level: 1462-1468;

13. **collaboration** among d.c.: 1609; **solidarity** with and among d. c.: 1866; 2948; **interdependence**: 1454; 1525-1527; 1628-1629; 1653; **self-reliance**: 1439; 1527; 1630; 2163; **self-development**: 1529; 1566;

14. concern must be given so that d. c., like others, draw a real benefit from the conquest of **outer space**: 3228; see also: 3237; 3254; 3265; 3284; 3291-3310;

15, **family**: 2363; 2366; **children**: 2363; 2383; **women**: 2536; 2544; 2568; 2765; **population growth**: 54; 2711; 2714; 2748;

16. see also: 25; 64; 229; 235; 241; 277-278; 281; 296; 385; 546; 777; 813; 836; 897; 928; 1002; 1056; 1101; 1291; 1306; 1323; 1340; 1342-1343; 1353; 1361; 1367-1368; 1379; 1383; 1386; 1411-1412; 1445; 1449; 1464; 1473; 1493; 1515; 1528; 1531; 1534; 1538; 1541; 1579; 1584; 1588-1589; 1593; 1628; 1638; 1640; 1652; 1658; 1731; 1855; 1904; 2005; 2032; 2047; 2055; 2084; 2088; 2193; 2156; 2254; 2948; 3019; 3052; 3057; 3103; 3105; 3152; 3169; 3173, and *Solidarity*.

Development

1. is for each and all the transition from less human conditions to those which are more human: 685; **focused on, at the service of the human person**: 90; 1670; 2158-2159; 2430; 3143; 2750; see 1653;

2. **right**: of all human beings to pursue their material well being and their spiritual d. in conditions of freedom and dignity, of economic security and equal opportunities: 41; of all peoples to their integral d.; to become artisans of their destiny: 55; see also: 423; 628; 1442; 1445; 1682;

3. **needs** wise human beings, new humanism: 198; a radical change of mentality of many and in the attitude of peoples and their governments; 1374; conversion of hearts: 1419; a new spirit, 1670; see also: 129; 762; 1408; 1644-1645; **solidarity**, international **cooperation/collaboration**: 86; 119; 142; 228; 940; 1474; 1486; 1537; 1546; 1570; 1598; 1609; 1620; 1642; 1666; 1677; 1873; 1882; 1929; 1940; 1948; 2120; 2133; 2134; 2167; 2176; 2195; 2213; 2751; 2284; 2297; 2302; 3177; 3178; 3299/11; **aid**: an exigency of justice: 1101; must not take the form of neo-colonialism; should lead to self-reliance: 1101; see: 1342-1343; 1537; 1663/2; 1680; 1788; 1903; 2085; 2325; 2615; at domestic (1458-1462) and international (1462-1468) level;

4. **of the individual**: entails social progress/d.: 60; 129; simultaneous d. of all humanity in a spirit of solidarity; 1419; 1653; see also: 64; 140; 142; 208; 224; **of society**: all human beings are called to promote the full d. of the whole human society: 1374; **of peoples**: integral and united: 39: taking into account spiritual values: 140-141; involves equality of races and the right to aspire to their own legitimate autonomy: 644; interdependent: 067; 336; 1536; 1540; 1623; 1650; 1653; 1860; and *Interdependence*; see also: 201; 319; 322; 359; 644; 1372; 1547; 1552; 2133; 2327; 2331; **of each country**: global: 1532; necessitates organic and worldwide overall d.: 137; **self/auto-d.**: 1884; 1902; 1926; 2175; 2188; 2200; 2207; 2334; 3132; 3149; see also: 140-141; **of needy peoples/countries**: criteria: bilateral relations must be increasingly replaced by a multilateral system: 135: its aim must be the satisfaction of real human needs, those which are really basic: 136; see: 55; 136; 1468; 1472-1488, passim; 1724; 1907-1908; 1988; 1992; 2114; 2163; 2167; 2194; 2332; 2693; 2713; 3205; 3227-3228; 3265; 3287; 3299; **worldwide**: 139; 1470; 1667; 1860-1861; 1881; 2163; of the **civilization**: 90; of **humanity**: 687;

5. **integral**: d. does not extend solely to economic growth; to be genuine, growth must be integral, it must clearly provide for the progress of each individual and of the whole human being: 1373; see: 39; 55; 90; 270; 274; 287; 289; 336; 478; 568; 644; 687; 771; 799; 807-808; 1356; 1366; 1373; 1375; 1414; 1442; 1444; 1494; 1623; 1653; 1717; 1835; 1847; 1920; 1926; 2096; 2122; 2130; 2158-2159; 2248; 2348; 2397; 2398; 2498; 2525-2526; 2551; 2553; 2597; 2632; 2724; 2834; 3004; 3009; 3055; 3100; 3110; 3148; 3283; **spiritual**: 41; 483; 707; 723; 734; 930; 2742; **moral**: 90; 2251; 3006; **cultural**: is closely connected with the construction of a more just and more fraternal world: 759; see also: 705; 708; **social**: must be obtained by calling on the free participation and the sense of responsibility of all, in the public and in the private sphere, both nationally and internationally: 129-130; 1374; see also: *Progress, Collaboration,* Participation, *Solidarity*; **material/economic**: can be accomplished only in the context of the d. of the entire human person and society: 1623; see: 65; 90; 91; 278; 1445-1453; 1653; 1669; 1851; 2025; 2081; 2088; 2742; **scientific and technical**: technical d. however necessary it may be, is not everything; it has to find its place in a wider, fully human plan: 141; if it was bent on dispensing with ethical values would gradually turn against the destiny of human being itself: 766; see: 65; 90; 141; 766; 1567; **industrial**: utopian expectation that industrialization will certainly and directly lead to economic d. and civil progress: 1779; would seem impossible without some application of nuclear energy: 1322; 1340; 1719; see: 238; 1391; 1665-1722; *Industrialization*; **food and agricultural**: 68; 1439; 1675; 1773-1774; 1956; 1993; 2069; 2119; 2140; 2150; 2162; 2199; 2240; 2247; **food and energy technologies in Africa**: 1841-1847; basic **water** for every people: 1440; **urban**: 2807-2809; **rural**: 1476; 1774; 1746; 1794; 1874; 2074; 2160; 2215; 2248; 2767; 3453;

6. of the **international law**: 246-269, *passim*;

7. of **armaments:** 978; 1055; 1061; 1192; 1274; 1313; 1315; 1338; 1712; 3348-3349; of **nuclear resources for peaceful use**: 1275; 1297; 1301; 1350; 1352;

8. **First D. Decade**: marked by a certain disenchantment of public opinion in the face of frustrated hopes: 58; 2064; see also: 1668; 2085; 2152; **Second D. Decade**: 55; 337; 698; 778; 1375; 1442; 1564; 1667; 2069; 2085; 2152; 2718; **Third D. Decade**: 131;

9. **human rights and d.**: their concrete enjoyment necessitates organic and worldwide overall d.: 129; essential for the free and integral d. of the human person: 478; human dignity and rights constitute the active criterion inspiring and guiding all efforts for d.: 143; see also: 90; 137; **justice**: d. is the indisputable exigency of justice: 644;

culture: brings human being full d. by making it familiar with the past, rooting it in the present and opening it to the future: 705; major factor of the affirmation, advancement, d., and spiritual growth of each person and each people: 930; see: 705; 759; 930; 945-946; 2283, and *Culture*;

education: has as its object the full d. of the individual: 882; there is no education without the harmonious d. of the mind and body: 691; must contribute to the d. of the best potentials of each person: 696; see also: 691; 695-696; 698-699; 882; 927; 1480; 2024; 2583;

literacy: is a privileged instrument of economic progress and d. for society: 770; only this basic education makes it possible to ensure d.; hunger for education is no less debasing than hunger for food: an illiterate is a person with an undernourished mind: 707; see: 771; 780; 788; 793; 797; 799; 803; 807; 808; 813; 817; 820; 2513; 2543; 2545, and *Literacy*;

10. **peace and d.**: world peace and d. depend on a common effort of understanding, a convergence of will, and a worldwide commitment: 067; the initiatives aimed at international cooperation for the fostering of d. serve the cause of peace: 86; by helping to remove tensions: 127; integral d. is a condition for peace: 278; see also: 098; 39; 206; 259; 287; 289; 291; 722; 835; 942; 1091; 1101; 1294; 1387; 1420; 1489; 1522-1529; 1569; 1664; 1702-1704; 2327; **d. is the new name of peace**: 067; 39; 86; 287; 644; 722; 1091; 1522; 1653; 1702; 1725; 1738; 2545; 3308; 3325; **d. and "a new heart"** are new names for peace: 291;

11. **arms race and d.**: humanity spends immensely more money on arms than on d.: 203; see also: 337; 1315; **economic growth**: is an indispensable but not sufficient cause of full human d.: 1451-1453; 1623; 1669; **environment**: essentially conditions the human being's life and d.:

3094; 3115; **industrialization**: it is a sign of d. and contributes to it: 1675; 1694; (see also above **industrial d.**) **natural resources**: their use must aim at serving integral d. of present and future generations: 274; see: 274; 1629; **nuclear energy**: need to ensure that it serves man and his spiritual and material d.: 1360; see also: 1340; 1342-1343; 1348; 1356-1357; **progress**: 60; 65; 142; 205; 228; 231; 235; 278; 782; 1851; **row material**: 1382-1394; 1650; 1675; **science and technology**: the most dynamic factor of the d. of society today, provided that are avoided three temptations: to pursue technological d. for its own sake; of subjecting it to economic usefulness in accordance with the logic of profit; to subject it to pursuit or maintenance of power: 204-205; basic coefficient of economic progress: 238; the scientific truth must be transmitted to the whole of humanity for the integral d. of each human being and all nations: 1356; their tremendous resources could be more effectively used for the d. and growth of peoples: 201; see also: 275-276; 278; 351; 1429-1441; 1830-1839; **trade**: equity in trade relations: indispensable condition of d.: 1495; 1497; 1519; 1653; 1655; see also: 1512-1513; 1555; 1560; 1589; 1603; 1606; 1615; 1650; 1663; **desertification**: 3127; 3128; 3133; **disarmament**: world d., a necessary condition for peace and disarmament: 1881; see also *Disarmament/7*; **environment**: steps must be taken to ensure that economic, material and social d. include proper consideration of the impact on the environment, both immediate and in the future: 278; see also: 3094; 3100; 3102-3113;

12. **family and d.**: 2707; 2742; 2754; 2757; 2772; 2820; **family planning**: opinion held in international organizations which extol planned birth control as a radical solution to the problems of developing countries: 64; the work for the integral human d. will favour a rational control of birth by couples who are capable of freely assuming their destiny: 64; see also: 2734; 3035; 3055; 3075; **population**: 2693-2694; 2699; 2703; 2711-2712; 2715; 2718; 2720-2721; 2724; 2733; 2742; 2745; 2748; 2749-2751; 2760; 3035; 3043;

13. the exploration of **outer space and d.**: 3205; 3209; 3227; 3228; 3246; 3265; 3267; 3269; 3271/d; 3276; 3280; 3287; 3299/11; 3300/6,8,9,18,19,22; 3305;

14. d. of the **unborn**: 2391; 3072; the **children**: 2347-2348; 2357; 2365-2366; 2374; 2378-2379; 2382; 2390-2391; 2737; 2753; 2765; 2783; 2883; the **disabled persons**: 2648; 2653; 2660; 2664; **youth**: 2397-2398; the **aged**: 2481-2482; 2487; 2491; 2768; **women**: 2501; 2503-2505; 2510; 2513; 2520; 2527; 2537; 2566; 2595; 2598; 2636-2638; **refugees**: 2883; 2932; 2934;

15. **Catholic Church/Holy See** and d.: **calls all those responsible** to work for integral d., the d. of the whole human being and every human being: 64; 568; 687; 1373; 1382; 2096; 2122; 2130; 2525; 3009; plays an effective part in human being's harmonious d.: 141; **intends to help mankind** to attain its full d.: 854; urges the integral united d. of all peoples: 39; **wants to contribute** to the d. of each nation in cultural, social and political expressions which are always truly human: 633; all over the world **contributes to authentic d.**: 685; **is convinced** that the organic d. of peoples is the most important problem of our times; even more, it is a necessity, an opportunity and a challenge: 1552; gives priority to the d. of human being's spirit: 734; proclaims d. "the new name of peace": 067; 39; 86; 287; 644; 722; 1091; 1522; 1653; 1702; 1725; 1738; 2545; 3308; 3325; see also: 067; 307; 322; 359; 568; 628; 676; 685; 771; 1061; 1374; 1411; 1429; 1443; 1469; 1476; 1519-1520; 1552-1454; 1569; 1653; 1702; 1715; 1717; 1719-1720; 1836-1837; 1867; 1881; 1926; 1965; 1975; 2032; 2044-2045; 2050; 2053; 2331; 2513; 2553; 2613; 2730; 2742; 2794; 3102; 3123; 3255.

16. see also: 12; 39; 65; 173; 142; 170-171; 198; 208; 227; 235; 248; 259; 260; 270; 341; 372; 676; 782; 790; 801; 830; 834-835; 841; 847; 873; 883; 1041; 1103; 1104; 1107; 1132; 1153; 1273; 1277; 1278; 1322; 1366; 1386; 1411; 1474; 1480; 1487; 1494; 1495; 1508; 1535; 1566; 1570; 1582; 1589; 1591; 1598; 1657; 1676; 1694; 1715-1719; 1778; 1782; 1788; 1839; 1851; 1859; 1877; 1916; 2050; 2106; 2134; 2148; 2161-2162; 2183; 2194; 2215; 2247; 2254; 2260; 2262; 2271; 2297; 2299; 2303; 2304; 2306; 2310; 2313-2314; 2317; 2329; 2381; 2404; 2430; 2439; 2465; 2476; 2655-2656; 2708; 2750-2751; 2794; 2798; 2803; 2831; 2842; 2845; 2932; 3017; 3095; 3102; 3140; 3143; 3189; 3198; *Participation; Responsibility/9;*

Dialogue

need: 270; **creates brotherhood**: 710; represents a **condition for peace**: 1142; 3386; d. for **disarmament**: see *Negotiation*; in **economic** and development issues: 1488; 1518; 1537; 1541; 1555; 1574; 1600; 1606; 1639; 1641; 1669; 1674; 1757; 1846; 2751; 2818; in the quest for the solution of **the debt** question: 2272; 2280; 2286; 2290; 2320; 2337; 2338-2339; **North-South** d.: 1644-1645; 1649; of the **Holy See** with the international community: see *Community/E*; **requires** sincerity, frankness, a spirit of understanding, firm and patient openness, generosity: 3392; **difficulties**: 3391; **biases** which may hinder it: 1274; among all those who believe in human being's spiritual calling: 209; see also *Church/5;* See: 220; 226; 476; 579; 661; 730; 775; 948; 1085; 1106; 1115; 1142; 1274; 1384; 2588; 2620; 2670; 2751; 3005; 3068; 3285; 3391-3397.

Dignity

1. of the **human person**: the dignity and value of the human person is clearly one of the root convictions of the Christian f. at the basis of every educational effort by the contemporary Catholic Church: 571; see also *Person/1;*

is based on the fact that the human being: has been **created by God in His own image and likeness**: 2732; see also: 242; 453; 510; 525; 614; 626; 651; 666; 1345; 1657; 1769; 2511; 2529, and *Creation*; has been **redeemed by Christ**: 2732; see also: 614; 626; 651; **is called**, according to the Divine Plan, to rejoice with God forever: 2732; see also: 614; 626; 651;

is equal for all human beings: 46; 477; 603; 605; 614; 640; 651; 666; 667; 2434; 2502; 2781; for men and women: 477; 641; 2502; 2558; 2599; and for all peoples: 614; 2169; 2279; 2434;

is the base of **solidarity**: 188; 582; **human rights**: 408; 426; 447; 449-450; 478; 515; 637; **religious freedom**: 452; 483; 510; 2956;

is invoked in dealing with issues related to: **primacy of the spiritual** in the human being: 152; its worth: 162; **religious freedom**: 103; 106; 488; 490; 525; 2420; **racial discrimination**: 412; 434; 605; 631; 634; ***apartheid***: 635-637; 640; 641; 644-645; 648; 651; 656; 660; 662; 665-667; 669; 672-673; 674; **education**: 701; 761; 927; 2398; **illiteracy**: 799; 802; 808; 820; 821; 826; **peace**: 477; 835; 3398; **justice**: 477; the **need to assure to each person the indispensable material good**, especially food: 28; 283; 407; 1835; 1843; 1844; 2178; 2244; 2246; 2264; **development**, personal and social progress, the progress of humanity, of peoples: 135; 143; 200; 206; 241; 286; 296; 644; 1391; 1472; 1486; 1513; 1531; 1594; 1614; 1645; 1653; 1657; 1664; 1721; 1722; 1748; 1758; 1769; 1912; 1957; 2076; 2134; 2163; 2751; 2764; 2769; 3143; 3310; **external debt**: 2267; 2279; 2334; **human labour**: 45; 97; 214; 215; 223; 225; 231; 233; 2628; 2946; 3426; the **mass media**: 175; **information**: 471; the **responsibility of science**: 183; 195; 1283; the **construction of a new social order**: 207; **environment**: 274; 279; **youth**: 2431; **aging**: 2483; 2619;-2620; **disabled persons**: 2642; 2646; 2647; 2662; **family planning**: 2600; 3040-3041; 3083; 3131; population: 2600; 2681; 2684; 2686; 2690; 2691; 2730; 2731; 2732; 2734; 2735; 2745; 2750; 2751; 2753; 2759; 2760; 2764; 2769; **habitat**: 2812; 2824; 2832; health: 3000; 3004; **refugees**: 1154; 1156; 2872; 2876; 2924; 2926; 2931; 2932; migrants: 2941; 2954; **summary executions**: 3088; 3092;

awareness: 89; 638; 2555; **respect**: 88; 2616; gives birth to effective protection of human rights: 449; **protection**: unthinkable without good will: 27;

is still an **aspiration** for many people: 58; is **violated**: by exploitation of labour and many other abuses: 97; when human rights are flouted: 826; 893-894; 2620;

is **proclaimed** and defended by: the **Church/Holy See**: 219; 347; 423; 455; 502; 510; 605; 620; 635-636; 637; 644; 651; 656; 864; 1476; 1486; 1653; 2794; 3369; the **United Nations** and its related Organizations: 021; 27; 41; 93; 296; 322; 334; 335; 339; 347; 364; 407; 409; 416; 448; 460; 571; 574; 718; 724; 2525; 2917;

see also: 76; 88; 384; 2612; 2642; 2790; 2976;

2. of **every country**: 502; 1478; 1801; 2334; of **each people**: 2530; of **rural peoples**: 1769; 1796; of **child**: 590/a; 1657; of the service to the child: 2344; of **women**: 2367; 2382; 2506; 2512; 2557; 2560; 2577; 2605; 2609; 2617; 2621; 2735; 2764; **disabled persons**: 2649; 2650; 2653; 2665; 2669; 2674; of **refugees**: 2850; 2868; 2887; **migrants**: 2942; 2944; 2946; **accused**

persons: 3092; **people in the desert**: 3133; of **work**: 37; 232; 233; of **human sexuality**: 2627; **human life**: 2683; from the moment of conception: 2760; of the **family**: 2690; 2832;

Dimension

1. **the person is the fundamental d. of human existence**, the human person in its entirety, living simultaneously in the sphere of material values and in that of spiritual values: 150-152; **the human being is threatened** with becoming a part of itself, with being reduced to one d. only: 53; 89; 1694; 2620; **full human**: 89; 489; 2398, **spiritual**: 103; 188; 765; 843; 2457; 2595, **social**: 766, **economic d.**: 2615, **of the human being**;

2. **spiritual**: 91-94; 2463; 3194, **religious**: 2594, **social d. of the human existence**: 76; **of life**: 454; 2441; 2576; spiritual d. of **humanity**: 2955; **human d. of the phenomenon of desertification**: 2128; **of the problem of water**: 3151; 3155; mysterious d. **of femininity**: 2625; **feminine d. in culture**: 2631; **human d. of peace**: 110; **full positive d.** of peace: 1141; **of justice**: 1424; connected and complementary d. **of religious freedom**: 491-495; d. **of contemporary manifestations of religious intolerance**: 521;

3. see also: 75; 155; 168; 204; 219; 229; 283; 257; 482; 489; 651; 759; 927; 1063; 1494; 1653; 2042; 2211; 2311; 2373; 2397; 2474; 2483; 2487; 2599; 2653; 2757; 2780; 2842; 3201; 3411; 3419 and *Dignity*.

Disabled Persons

1. the d. person **is a fully human subject**, with the corresponding innate, sacred and inviolable rights: 2646; **must be helped** to take his or her place in society in all aspects and at all levels, as far as it is compatible with his or her capabilities: 2648; **its sharing in the life of society** must be inspired by the principles of integration: 2651; normalization: 2652; personalization: 2653;

2. **inadmissibility of the suppression of the un-born or new-born d. person**; furthermore, the deliberate failure to provide assistance, or any act shich leads to suppression of the new-born disabled person, represents a breach not only of medical ethics but also of the fundamental and inalienable right to life: 2655; see also *Euthanasia*;

3. **duty to undertake research in order to overcome the causes of disabilities**: 2656; **the quality of a society and a civilization are measured by the respect shown to the weakest of its members**: 2650;

4. United Nations Declaration of the Rights of the Disabled: 2649; 2660; concern of the Church: 2639-2645; 2678;

5. see also: 647; 685; 2350; 2580; 2596; **2639-2678**; 2926; 3011.

Disarmament

1. first **pathway to peace**: 23-25; is **a priority objective** for the entire international community: 1182; clear **moral obligation**: 3333; **responds to the needs and the expectations of peoples**: 984; the world wants d.; the world needs d.: 1034-1038; justice requires d.: 1003; **even small steps can have a value**: 1048; see also: 995;

2. **armaments, nuclear weapons and d. are too important** in themselves and for the world ever to be made part of a strategy which would exploit their intrinsic importance in favour of politics or other interests: 1047;

3. **there will be no d. of weapons if there is no d. of hearts**: 1011; true d., that which will actually guarantee peace among peoples, **will come about only with the resolution of the ethical crisis that is disrupting society** in all its political, social and economic dimensions; to the extent that the efforts at arms reduction and then of total d. are not matched by parallel ethical renewal, they are doomed in advance to failure: 1063; see also: 1062-1064; 1370;

4. is essentially a problem of **mutual trust**: 986-993; 1179; 1263; 3334; **calls for** an extraordinary effort of intelligence and good will: 985; **requires** the remotion of the situation which serves as fertile soil for the proliferation of armaments: 986; 1263; **dialogue**: 3386; **would require a system of law** that will regulate international relations and maintain peace: 1187; **a world authority**: see *Authority/1;*

5. its prospect is a **great hope**: 1001; **would create a climate of confidence**: 1172; **by itself does not offer a complete answer to the problem of peace**: 3334; must be: **mutual, simultaneous, organic, progressive**: 359; 953; 995-996; 1033; 1054; 1107; 1160; 1172; controlled: 337; 359; 688; 953; 955; 996; 1033; 1054; 1107; 1176; 1178; 1222; 1227; 1231; 1245; 1254; 1257; 1266; 1583; 3333; **reduction of armaments**: effective, general, controlled: 955; 971; 973; qualitative and quantitative: 1058; final goal: **general and complete d.**: 995; 1033; 1055-1056; 1160; 1170; 1234; 1245; 1254; 1257; 1266; 1330; 3333;

6. **nuclear**: has the first place: 997; 1166; 1170-1171; 1222; 1226-1227; 1231; 1245; 1257; 1272; 1286; 1313; 1315-1316; 1328; first step: to put an end to the vertical (1258-1259) and horizontal (1260) proliferation; **weapons of mass destruction** (chemical, bacteriological, etc...): 998; 1181; **conventional weapons**: 999-1000; 1176;

7. **relation between d. and development**: 337; 1061; Paul VI appeal from Bombay: to devote to the benefit of developing nations at least a part of the many saved through a reduction of armaments: 25; 951; 1002-1003; 1537; 1633; 1729; 2114; **d., a new world order, and development are three obligations that are bound together** and that by their essence presuppose a renewal of public outlook: 1004; 1293; by cutting down on military expenditure, **a substantial part of the immense resources that it now absorbs can be employed in a vast world development project**: 1001; see also: 098; 1001; 1014; 1061; 1175; 1465; 1582-1583; 1623; 1632-1633; 1712; 1729; 3229; 3334;

8. **contribution of the Church/Holy See**: does not enter in the technical and political aspects of d.: 1023; **the teaching of the Catholic Church in this area has been clear and consistent**; it has deplored the arms race, called nonetheless for mutual, progressive and verifiable reduction of armaments as well as greater safeguards against possible misuse of these weapons; it has done so while urging that the independence, freedom and legitimate security of each and every nation be respected: 1045; see also: 349; 952-953; 955; 1006-1012; 1042; 1182-1183; 1189; 1254; 1271; 1286; 3336; 3386;

9. see also: **959-1076**; **1158-1189**; 1239; 1240; 1243; 1258; 1314; *Negotiations; Obligation/3; Responsibility/7; Trust.*

Discrimination

1. **the Catholic Church insists that all forms of social or cultural discrimination in basic personal rights on the ground of sex, race, color, social conditions, language or religion must be curbed and eradicated as incompatible with God's design**: 410; it can **never** be acceptable: 260; see: 101; 260; 276; 335; 339; 417; 442; 525-526; 601; 609; 622; 639; 640; 641; 719; 894; 1156; 1487; 1715; 1725; 1925; 2436; 2528; 3069; all discrimination **is evil**, whether it be founded on race, sex, colour or religion: 3069; it is **bitterly deplored**: 432; Christian universality requires the abolition of classes and discrimination: 630-630; it is of capital importance that it be **banished from education environment**: 696; 775-776; *Segregation.* See also: 102; 289; 360; 500; 592; 597; 634; 647; 724; 894; 916; 1433; 1717; 1926; 2087; 2095; 2116; 2230; 2397; 2415; 2689; 3029;

2. **racial discrimination/racism**: is **absolutely unacceptable**: 651; the **scourge of r.d., in all its many forms, still disfigures our age**; it denies the fundamental equality of all men and women, proclaimed by the different Declarations of the United Nations, but above all rooted in God: 652; **multi-faced causes**: 609-610; **evil consequences**: social injustice, economic misery, ideological oppression, revolutions: 412; is a threat to peace: 671; has at the moment great relevance because of the **tension it stirs up** both within certain countries and on the international level: 642;

effective pressure made by individuals and governments is more constructive than violence: 634; the temptation is great to respond with violence to such wrongs to human dignity; **but real evil should not be fought against at the cost of greater misery**: 412; **violence as a solution is illusory**; is not an acceptable solution, it must give way to reason, mutual trust, sincere negotiations and fraternal love: 646.

concern of the Catholic Church/the Holy See: the Church cannot be silent concerning its teaching that all racist theories are contrary to the faith and Christian love: 626; it is resolutely committed in the common effort to combat them: 605; 607; its specific contribution: 611-617; 619-622; effort in educating to brotherhood, justice and peace while respecting different cultures and civilizations: 630; 637; see: 412; 432; 434; 442; **594-674**; 2588; 2596; 3203; *Apartheid*;

3. **ethnic**: 432; **social**: 775; **ideological**: 417; **religious d.**: 339; 417; 456; 492; 525; 526(*); 528; 537; 894; 1487; 2958; **based on sex**: 2512; 2514; 2527; 2528; 2531; 2547; 2559; 2638; against **migrants**: 2593; 2953; 2958; 2965; against **unproductive members of society**: 2650; **handicapped**: 2673; 2926; **aged**: 2926.

Disparities

between **excessive rich individuals and groups and the majority** made up of the poor and the destitute: 98; 1066; between **areas of satiety and areas of hunger and depression**: 99; see also: 176; 1066; 1669; 2751; **in socio-economic progress**: 176; in the **standards of living**: 1505; 2071; in **enjoyment of the benefits of civilization**: 1740; in **basic culture**: 176; between **countries in possession and not of atomic weapons**: 1245-1246. See also: 1248; 1646; 1680; 2590; 2798; 2824; *Dependence; Imbalance; Inequalities.*

Distrust

great d., **based on the fear of the wish to exercise power**, or of a "crusading" spirit, on the part of one or other of the blocs: 380; mutual d. **causes arms-race**: 1027; **leads to confrontation** in international economic relations: 1698; prevailing **between developed and developing countries**: 1705; **nationalistic distrust**: 2397; recurring **episodes of d.** and frequent unwillingness to assume real and definitive commitments: 2229.

Drugs

1. the phenomenon of d. abuse is **one of the greatest tragedies plaguing society** today: 3446; unfortunately it is steadily worsening; no country is now immune from this modern scourge: 3447; it **challenges** a human and cultural outlook that lacks sufficient ideals; it challenges paradoxically the permissive way of life, the materialistic mentality and the consumer society: 2982;

2. among the factors that contribute to the dramatic increase in **d. abuse**, a primary one is the **breakdown of the family**; in addition a steady weakening of traditional ways of life; tensions in human relationships; rising unemployment; sub-human standards of living; fear; psychological need to escape from the hardships and painful responsibilities of life; but at the root of this evil is the **loss of ethical and spiritual values**: 3448;

3. **effects**: 3449; **efforts** to counter the plague of d. addiction: 3450-3451; 2984; preventive education at home, at school and in places of work: 3452; **treatment of the addicted**: medical, social and legal: 3454; a key factor in successful rehabilitation, particularly in the case of young peo-

ple, is the **restoration of self-confidence and a healthy self-esteem**; role of the family in this process: 3455; the **Church** wishes to offer every possible support to the many and varied efforts being made: 3456;

4. duty to expand initiatives aimed at stopping the continuing growth of the **illegal production and sale**: 3452; need to make crop substitution a feasible alternative: 3453; 2983;

5. the common **struggle against the plague** of d. abuse and illicit trafficking is motivated by a serious spirit of mission, on behalf of humanity and for the very future of society, a mission whose success demands a mutual commitment and generous response on the part of all: 3456;

6. See: 387; 1176; 2470; **2980-2988**; 3011; **3446-3456**.

Duties

1. **rights and d.** of the person: 090; 27; 39; 409; 416; 436; 447; 459; 651; 802; 824; 827; 842; 1097; 1878; 1882; 3069; of each individual to seek the truth, and corresponding d. of other persons and civil authority to respect the free spiritual development of each person: 483; to consider the human being not according to whether or not it is useful in its work, but to consider work in its relation to the human being: 224;

2. **to respect human rights**: 52; 258; 431; 426; 431; 708; to respect **the dignity of each person**: 863; of respect, love, for every member of the human family: 400; of improving one's self: 841; of combatting and abolishing all the situations where the human person is humiliated and offended: 2620; **imperative, sacred d. of the building of a more just humanity**, a more united international community: 200; **of the nations** to discover and bring to ever greater perfection the institutional mechanisms, which ensure their peaceful relationships: 348; **deriving from the relationships between States**: 2187; **to promote peace**: 754; 1010; 1073; 1084; 1162; 1334; 3329; **to do away with war**: 76; 1199; **d. of justice**: 407; 2312; 2948; **of love**; 866; **of charity**: 2948; **of solidarity**: 319; 777; 791; 1143; 2013; 2169; 2177; 2297; 2312; 2640; 2648; 2939; 2948; **of co-operation**: 791; **of rich countries** to give aid to the poorer ones: 1706; see also: 2012; 2147; 3161; **of society** to bring concrete assistance to those of its members who are deprived of the minimum essential for the normal growth of their personality: 1991;

3. **of Christians** to accept social and economic responsibilities: 2037; **of youth** to make their choice: 1529; **towards youth**: 2394; **the aging**: 2493; **disabled**: 2671; **rights and d. of women**: 2504; 2512; **d. and responsibilities**: 2520; **of married couples**: 2690; 2759; positive d. **of governments** to create conditions that enable couples to exercise responsibly their fundamental right to form families, to bear and rear their children,...: 2759; **towards refugees**: 2851; 2867; 2872; 2887; 2891; 2892; **migrants**: 2946; 2951;

4. the **Catholic Church/Holy See considers its d.**: to bring to the world the message of truth and love: 75; 2211; to denounce arms race: 67; 2062; to reveal more fully the range of the goods that are linked with the spiritual dimension of human existence: 94; to proclaim the moral teaching concerning peace: 3318; to echo the legitimate aspirations of the people of our day: 411; to make a special appeal for the nations most deprived of natural resources or of the fruit of industry: 1389; to reassert the moral principles that govern human life: 2533. See also: 491; 593; 947; 1005; 2066; 2872; 2739;

5. see also: 046; 063; 073; 76; 86; 107; 165; 221; 304; 313; 315; 467; 473; 592; 789; 808; 821; 822; 823; 841; 862; 897; 913; 927; 1244; 1277; 1359; 1520; 1542; 1733; 1894; 1990; 2044; 2057; 2094; 2190; 2224; 2227; 2307; 2311; 2353; 2676; 2738; 2765; 2824; 2851; 2867; 2982; 2991; 3191; 3161; 3191; 3222; 3396; 3427.

Ecology

the vastness and complexity of many ecological problems **demand** not only a combined response at local and national levels but also **substantial assistance and coordination from the international community**: 280; **e. disasters caused by human rapacity** against the earth, in the waters and in the atmosphere: 3288; worry about the **destruction of e. balance**: 3472; **forest areas needed for e. balance**: 3305; **spiritual e. is needed as much as natural e.**: 2658; e. of the spirit: 3133. See also: 61; 274; 275; 277; 279; 282; 427; 1298; 1340; 1438; 2472; 2831; 2842; 3100; 3106; 3140; *Environment, Nature/3.*

Economy

1. **need for transformation** of an e., too often tainted by power, waste and fear, into an e. of service and brotherhood: 67; the **transition from selfish and exclusive profit-based e.** to an e. which will voluntarily undertake the satisfaction of mutual needs calls for the adoption of an international law based on justice and equity, at the service of a truly human universal order: 68; 2078;

2. **should aim at and be guided by the satisfaction of real human needs**, not the artificial needs, partly created and always increased by publicity, by the play of market forces and by the position of power acquired in the economic, financial and political fields: 136; 1625; 2130;

3. world e. in which all the **positions of strength**, all the **wealth**, all the **investment**, all the **commercial services** and above all, the whole crucial **apparatus of research** are **concentrated in the small elite of nations** which have already achieved modernization: 1454; **world e.'s imbalance between North and South**: 1467;

4. of the **poorest**, the **developing countries**: 1497; 1630; 1631; 1648; 1650; 1661; 3418; necessity on the part of the developed countries to consider effectively the **reconversion** of their economies with a view to welcoming the products of developing countries into their markets in fair condition: 1565; 2300; **interdependence** between the poor and rich economies: 1628; 1630-1631; 2263; 2334; **crisis**: 136; 227; 319; 1485; 1514; 1596; 1622; 1648; 2297; 2299; 2606; 2715; 3412; **structural maladjustment** in the international e.: 1648;

5. see also: 97; 116; 137; 688; 1000; 1423; 1451; 1452; 1478; 1479; 1524; 1525; 1526; 1549; 1583; 1589; 1593; 1610; 1625-1631; 1651; 1679; 1773; 1782; 1813; 1823; 1854; 1922; 1931; 1961; 2089; 2117; 2118; 2120; 2152; 2264; 2285; 2299; 2313; 2315; 2950; 3419; 3420; 3429; *Market; Order/4; Power/10; Relation/8.*

Education

1. **to educate is to help the human being become more fully a human being, to enable it to "be" more, not only to "have" more**: 165; 679; 691; its **aim** is to form human beings, teach them to live, bring the young a wisdom that is a project of life rooted in a specific civilization: 709; to help them to take their proper place in the community where they live, and in this community exercise in their turn their free and responsible activity: 692; 882; 2398; towards the **conquest of truth**: 688-689; its ultimate goal is **wisdom**: 701;

2. is a **community task**: 694; 839; primacy of the **family**: see *Family/4;* educational environment: all **segregation** must be banished from it: 696;

3. need: **hunger for education** is no less depressing than hunger for food: 682; 707; 2513; see also: 58; **lifelong** e.: 839; 841; 883; 927; 2494; 2543; **parallel** e.: 839; **integral** e.: 842; 2658; 2841; **moral** e.: 843; 879; 2534;

4 its unilateral movement towards **instruction** in the narrow sense of the term, exclusively geared to possession leads to its **alienation** and accustoms the human being to become an object of a host of manipulations: 169-170; e. **must not be just transmission of knowledge** but must in-

volve a formation which proposes, makes understood and esteems the values of life, the true values and their hierarchy: 602; 692; 697; 700; 896;

5. **must promote** a **civilization of the universal** as well as a **dialogue of the cultures**, for each one has its own wealth: 581; must promote the **advancement of interpersonal solidarity** beside that of the dignity of the human being: 582-584;

6. contribution of the **Catholic Church**: 684-687; 699-700; 1476; 1868; 2567; 2613;

7. e., the **master key to the future**, the read to the social integration of the underprivileged, the soul of social dynamism, is the **essential duty and right** of every human being: 3427; **right**: 89; 790; 894; 904; **freedom**: 492; 494; to promote **human rights**: 896; **religious** e., see *Freedom/2*; **to promote religious tolerance**: 538-581; educational contribution of the Catholic Church to the promotion of tolerance and respect, esteem and friendship in pluralistic societies: 567-571; see also: 554-563; e. of **conscience**: 553; 573; 578; 2377; and **behaviour**: 553; 573; for **peace**: 22; 83; 1011; 1140; 1182; 1240; 1241; 1242; 1253; 1280; 2588; 2599; 3394; for **development**: 698-700; 1429; 1436; 1480; 1528; 1691; 1693; 1694; 1715; 1718; 1720; 1725; 1845; 1868; 2024; 2073; 2075; 2121; 2249; 2368; 3132; 3147; 3153; for the **elimination of racism**: 602; e. of mentalities and conscience: 612; 613; educational effort of the Catholic Church: 616-617; 630; 633; **equality in educational opportunities**: 622; 2528;

8. **children**: 2361; 2368; 2377; **youth**: 2397-2398; 2399; 2466; 2475; **aging**: 2494; **women**: 2514; 2528; 2541; 2544; 2564; 2566; 2578; 2581-2588; 2604; 2740; 2764; 2765; **disabled**: 685; 2648; 2653; 2658; 2659; 2664; 2670; 2673; 2677; **refugees**: 2841; 2868; 2891; **migrants**: 2960; 2962; 2965;

9. **health e.**: 2366; 2367; 3050; 3052; 3057; 3068;

10. **sex e.**: is a basic right of the parents and must always be carried out under their close supervision: 590/c; in matters pertaining to family life and sex e., the Holy See calls attention to the **right of parents to impart values and to establish standards of conduct for their children** in the context of ethical principles and a commitment to family life: 2763;

11. e. in **responsible parenthood** and the imparting of information regarding family planning to their children is also primarily a parental right and responsibility; **the provision of such information and services in schools and other agencies** generally fails to impart standards and values, and at times can encourage sexual behaviour that is in conflict with the values and principles set down by parents: 2763; see also: 2735; 2756; 3053; 3131; 3429.

12. **relation with the other problems of human existence**: 150; **mass media** and e.: 201; **space technology** and e.: 682; 847; 3201; 3202; 3205; 3252; 3253; 3254; 3259;

13. **formation** cannot be limited to preparation for a job: 907-908; professional f.: 1528; 1717; moral and religious f. of youth: 2474. See also 139; 590/d; 615; 680; 803; 905-906; 1184; 2380; 2494; 2511; 2534; 2721; 2886.

14. see also: 047; 102; 150; 162; 168; 177-178; 203; 240; 552; 567-568; 579; 683; 703-704; 705; 928; 1120; 1129; 1132; 1156; 1420; 1459; 1912; 2514; 2541; 2544; 2545; 2682; 2713; 2730; 2735; 2771; 2783; 2801; 2815; 2817; 2829; 2985; 3074; 3103; 3129; 3252; 3428.

Educator/Teacher

1. e. **must use all possible means to develop the faculties of judgment and discernment**, and give to those concerned the desire and the means to pursue their own education by themselves later on: 683; **the personality of the e. is irreplaceable**, for **its task** is not only that of transmitting knowledge, but also of communicating values and discovering truth: 689; **training of teachers**:

927; **true e.** are those who are stimulated by constant concern for study, research and adaptation, who are preoccupied in preparing a future, and who are always alert to the demands of the times and events: 692;

2. the **Church "mother and teacher"**: 046: 684; **of truth**: 046; of truths transcending the horizon of time and history: 0107; **of universal peace**: 744; **her numerous e.** have largely contributed in many countries to the advancement of the least favoured, and notably women: 685; **catholic e.** wish to work in close relationship with all e., in loyal collaboration with those who are responsible for the common good of the community: 699;

3. **the family**: 173; 927; **first e.** towards physical, psychological, intellectual, moral and religious development: 2348; **its importance** as e. in morality, conscience, and the discovery of love: 2475; as first e. of their children, **parents should be aware of the leading trends in the field of teaching**: 695; see also: 590; 801;

4. **e. sometimes evade the fundamental questions about life** put forward by young people, giving rise to a depressing basic skepticism or to a restless way of life: 2395; **young people** have every rights to expect their e. to be genuine teachers able to orient them towards high ideals and to give them an example of these in their own lives: 2398; 2399;

5. **the poor are our teachers** and those who awaken our conscience: 3066;

6. see also: 22; 613; 690; 693; 694; 700; 701; 2393; 2548; 2664; 2982.

Employment

1. **the human person is the first and ultimate criterion in the planning of e.**: 230; e. has become **one of the major problems of our present society** and one with harsh consequences for the workers which are too often overlooked: 229; a **positive solution** to the problem of e., and more particularly of e. for young people, presupposes **solidarity** of the highest degree within and among all peoples: 231; see 229-231;

2. **discrimination in e. on religious ground**: 492; **youth e.**: 56; 2470; 2838; **women** who are not so young, and who have to or wish to seek e. after having brought up their children encounter great difficulties both in retraining themselves and in finding a position: 2570; 2740;

3. unquestionable **priority** must be given to the policy of reducing unemployment and to the **creation of new sources of e.**: 3425; **moral reason for this priority of maximum e.**: to offer a person work is to activate the essential mechanism of its human activity, by virtue of which the worker takes possession of his or her destiny, integrates with all of society and eve receives other aid, not as alms, but in a way as the living and personal fruit of his or her own labor: 3425, see 3423-3426;

4. see also: 60; 227; 328; 813; 1449; 1460; 1538; 1617; 1658; 1681; 1751; 1855; 2247; 2297; 2651; 2667; 2682; 2823; 2837; 2950; 3213; 3412.

Energy

1. a **severe shortage** of e. and natural resources impedes the progress of developing nations and results in harsh living conditions: 277; **real needs** in the e. field that nations will face as they seek to harness the resources available to them and build up a more healthy, creative and diversified economy: 1479; there are the **possibilities of creating both food and e. resources for a population much greater than that which the most reliable calculations lead us to predict**; 2716; see also 3158; the problem is the **inequality in its consumption**: eighty-seven percent of the e. used in the world today is consumed by the rich countries and only thirteen percent by the rest of the world: 2716; **new sources of energy**: 3156-3164; by **remote sensing** it is possible to detect the pres-

ence of concealed sources of energy, both renewable and non-renewable: 3306; **e. technologies in Africa**: 1842; **crisis**: 857; **problem**: 1629; rising **cost**: 1712;

2. **nuclear** e.: **ambivalence**, for good and for evil: 1248; 1337; **peaceful use**: 997; 1248; 1261-1262; 1273; 1275; 1282-1370; **need to ensure that it serves the human being and his spiritual and material development**: 1360; **applied to** food production, water resource development, advances in medicine, biology and physics: 1273; **access to** nuclear e.: 1278; **necessity of sharing its benefits**: 1262; 1278; 1323; 1365; calls for a **conversion of outlook and mentality** (1288); **political will** (1289); **contested**: 1297-1298; 1340; **strongly opposed**: 1350; **safety**: 1292; 1302; 1319; 1326; 1327; 1344; 1350; 1353; 1364; **protection against radiation**: 1308; 1344; 1361; **safeguard**: 1275; 1305; 1309; 1348; 1350; 1361; **benefits**: 1284; 1290; 1320-1321; 1353; 1362; **risks**: of nuclear proliferation: 1292; for persons and environment: 1307; 1324-1326; 1341. See also: 094; 194; 235; 1247-1248; 1260-1262; 1282-1370: *passim*;

3. **moral, spiritual**: it takes great e. of soul and great fortitude to undo the injustices of centuries and to rise above the ease of comfort and success: 1471; the Church brings the light and e. of the Gospel to all human activities: 2132; **the greater waste of e. and resources today** is the waste of the human intellect and the waste of creativity of the human person: 1480; see also: 1469; 1515; 1529; 1736; 1967; 2134; 3432;

4. see also: 337; 1505; 1596; 1781; 2304.

Environment

1. growing awareness that the **human being and its e. are more inseparable than ever**: 3094; **is not "res nullius"**, something not belonging to anyone, **but "res omnium"**, the patrimony of mankind: 3099; 3171; **care of preserving and improving natural e.**: 272; progressive **deterioration** of the e.: 61; **threats to** e.: 277; 2463; deleterious **effects** caused by a life style based on ever greater consumption: 1387; 2716; with the rapid acceleration of science and technology in recent decades, e. has been **subjected to far greater changes than ever**: 275; the **capacity for improving the e.** and the capacity **for destroying it** increase enormously each year: 275; **the ultimate determining factor is the human person**: 276; 832; steps must be taken to ensure that the economic, material and social development include **proper consideration of the impact of modern industry and technology on the e.**, both immediate and in the future: 278; human e.: 2771; 2773-2774; 2776; 2789; **consequences on the e.** of the use of nuclear weapons: 290; 1180; 1191-1220, *passim*; of nuclear energy: 1307; 1340; 1350; 1361; e. **data provided by space technology**: 3242; 3263; 3291-3293; 3296; 3297/1; 3298/2; 3299/1,2,3,4/h; 3300/6,7,15,18;

2. **the home must remain the first concern of every programme relative to human e.**: 282-283; 2782; 2783; living e.: 2778; 2799; private: 2813; e. **programmes for food and housing** are concrete ways of promoting peace: 287-288; **culture-creating** e.: 167; 176; educative e.: 696; **social environments**: 813; 2554; 2792; **socio-economic**: 1438; **international**: 2280; 2284; **family**: 2379; 2888; **working**: 2652; **spiritual and moral**: 3133;

2. **Catholic Church/Holy See**: for many years now has taken **active interest** in question concerning e.: 272-273; **its commitment to the conservation and improvement of e.** is linked to a command of God: 273; **it approaches this problem from the point of view of the human person**, for the ultimate purpose of e. programmes is to enhance the quality of human life, to place creation in the fullest way possible at the service of the human family: 279; for that reason they must include also the **problems of housing and shelter**: 282;

3. see: **279-291**; 290; 423; 1413; 1629; 1781; 1845; 1855; 1892; 2069; 2101; 2133; 2248; 2263; 2493; 2497; 2573; 2658; 2693; 2712; 2737; 2742; 2800; 2809; 2815; 2842; 2866; 2885; 2944; 3043; 3049; 3051; 3068; **3093-3120**; 3139-3140; 3167; *Ecology; Nature/3.*

Equality

Equity

Ethics

Euthanasia

is a **heinous crime**: 647; it is today very important, at the moment of death, to **protect the dignity of the human person and the Christian conception of life against the application of technical advances** which risk becoming abusive: 2483; See also *Life/1-2,3-4.*

Exexutions (Arbitrary and summary executions)

are a tragic and typical example of the **aberrations** which exist within some political regimes: 3089; **even arrest must not be arbitrary** but in accord with legal norms: 3090; in all circumstances there should be a strict commitment to respect the physical and moral integrity of the person: 3091. See: 3088-3092, *Oppression, Violence.*

Exploitation

1. **the God of Christians** is a liberating God and **calls on all believers to struggle against all e.**, all oppression of any person by another: 532; any **speculation exploiting elementary human needs** is iniquitous, in a very special way speculation of food and arms: 2143; **of the human being**: 97; 363; 622; no one must exploit its equal: 2430; of **labour**: 97; rural workers: 1657; 1751; 1769; of **migrant workers**: 783; migrant **women**: 2963; of the **weak**: 1604; of **children**: 2345; 2369; **young people**: 2476; of **disabled persons**: 2665; political e. of **human suffering**: 2359; **relationships of dependence and e.** foster frustrations and reactions which are at the root of many wars of liberation or of internal revolts: 1100;

2. **e. of the results of scientific discoveries**, particularly in the natural sciences, for purposes which have nothing to do with the requirements of science, and indeed for purposes of destroying and killing: 183; **of the riches of nature**, must take place according to criteria that take into account not only the immediate needs of people but also the needs of future generations: 274; by its **thoughtless e. of nature**, the human being is in danger of destroying it and of being, in its turn, the victim of this destruction: 832; disorderly e. **of the physical reserves of the earth**: 3096;

3. **of the resources of nature, for the benefit of the whole humanity**: 1505; 2150; 3182; see also: *Creation; Goods,* of **nuclear energy**: 1248; 1297; 1307; of the immense **riches of earth**, 1838; **sea**, 1838; 1957; 3189; to be exploited for the benefit of mankind as a whole: 3182; 3188; 3257; **forests**, 1938; 1945; 1956; **watercourses, agriculture**, 2077; 2104; **fisheries**, 1938; 1945; **cattle**: 1938; **space**: 3271/f; for the benefit of humanity: 3261; 3266;

4. see also: 51; 99; 538; 615; 1047; 1262; 1414; 1436; 1675; 1680; 1938; 1645; 1946; 1956; 1957; 2105; 2108; 2294, and *Speculation.*

Faith

1. f. **supports hope** and, at the same time, sharpens in the heart the sense of one's own responsibilities and the consequent personal commitment: 398;

2. the Church strictly **forbids that anyone should be forced to accept the faith**; likewise it strongly defends the **right that no one should be frightened away from the f.** by unjust persecution: 2957;

3. every person must be given: the **opportunity to profess** his or her f. and belief, alone or with others, in private and in public: 458, 485; **freedom to hold or not to hold a particular f.**; freedom **from any form of coercion** to perform acts contrary to one's f.: 492; freedom **to receive and publish religious books** related to f. and worship, and to have free use of them; **to proclaim and communicate the teaching of the f.** by the spoken or written word, inside as well as outside places of worship: 494;

4. there are today hundreds upon hundreds of thousands of **witnesses to the f.**; they include parents who are refused the right to have their children educated according to their f.; men and women, manual workers, intellectuals, or those carrying out other occupations, who, simply be-

cause they profess their f., run the risk of being deprived of interesting opportunities for their careers or their studies: 526(*); **a regime which tries to extirpate f. in God cannot safeguard respect for the human person and the human fraternity**: 533; see also 493; 495; 560; *Freedom/2;*

5. **according to Christian f.**: all human beings are brothers and sisters: 532; **Christian f. calls for the deepest respect of other faith**: 560; 2420; far from leading Christians astray, **f. stimulates their search** in every field: 688;

6. **spiritual principles**, on which has to be built modern civilization, **cannot rest on anything but f. in God**: 34; **unity, brotherhood**,... these **are realities** which are the common patrimony of all humanity, **whose foundation is seen by believers to be God**, and **which Christians see in their f. in Christ**, the saviour of all human beings: 892; **Christian f. concerning the unity of origin, of nature and of vocation of the human family** which embraces, in solidarity, all human beings in time and space: 3222; for "**f. in God**", see also: 34; 350; 369; 483; 511-512; 892; 1123; 1392; 1599; 2403; 2417; 2418; 2642; 2917; see also: *Brotherhood, Dignity, Creation, Family/B, Humanity; Solidarity*; the **exigencies of f. in God** include justice and fraternal love for every human being: 1329; their **f. compels Christians** to transcend personal and national egoisms in order to build a world of solidarity, of justice and of fraternity: 1553; see also: 1599; 1610; 1673; **Christian engagement in temporal tasks** at the service of humanity is coherent with their f.: 2057;

7. "**common monotheistic tradition of f.**", base of the hope for a solution of the question of Jerusalem and the Middle East: 1123-1124; 1133; 1139;

8. **those who have f.** in a higher Providence **cannot forget that peace is a gift of God** intrusted to everyone: 369; all who carry in their hearts the treasure of a religious f. **must share in a common work for human being's development**: 208; all those who have f. in the human being's spiritual calling **are invited to a common task**: to constitute a real science for the total advancement of the human being: 209; 568;

9. religious **f. confirms the special claim that children** have on our love and care: 2388; **dignity and value that Christian f. confers on woman**: 2560; **youth** and f.: see *Youth/1;*

10. harmonious **synthesis between f. and other human dimensions**: reason, culture, life: 2474;

11. **f. in the human being**: 2481; in the destiny of the human family: 3100; unshakable Christian love and f. in the dignity of the human being, in the unrepeatable value of each individual human life, and in the transcendent dignity of those who are called into existence: 2642; in their view of f. and in their concept of the human being, Christians know that in the disabled person there is reflected, in a mysterious way, the image and likeness which God Himself impressed upon the lives of His sons and daughters: 2643; **f. in life**: see *Life/3;*

12. **in the fundamental human rights**: 021; 93; 364; in the United Nations: 305;

13.
good f.: 462; 989; 1231; 1245; 1257; 1265; 1410; 1504; 2281;

14. see also: 016; 94; 101; 233; 311; 400; 403; 457; 561; 684; 1021; 1282; 2025-2026; 2065; 2178; 2219; 2316; 2394; 2406; 2416; 2454; 2485; 2486; 2490; 2744; 2807; 2808.

Family

A. f. of **peoples**: 011: 1371: of the **United Nations**: 116; 1371; 1765; 2095; 3004; 3009; 3104; of **nations**: purpose: of promoting the progress of mankind: 213;

B. great, whole, **human f.**

1. need to strive to preserve it from the terrible prospect of nuclear war: 186; 194; 195; morally cannot go on much longer employing about half of the world's research-workers for military purposes: 201;

2. each one, without renouncing its origins and its membership of its f., its people and its nation, or the obligations arising therefrom, must regard itself as a member of this great f., the world community: 227; 3285;

3. it is a requirement of our human dignity, and therefore a serious responsibility, to exercise dominion over creation in such a way that it truly serves the h.f.: 274; 279;

4. God has willed that all people should make up a **single f.** and that they should deal with one another in a spirit of brotherhood: 1599; the Catholic Church will not remain indifferent to responsibility towards the **unity of the h.f.**: 418; her teaching on the unity of the h.f.: 2132; unity of origin, of nature and of vocation: 3222; humanity is one large f. where the suffering of one is felt by all: 2007; 2126; see also: 639; 737; 744; 1610; 1635; 1686; 2134; 2135; 2166; common destiny: 1142; fraternity and solidarity: 1472; 2070; see *Brotherhood, Solidarity;* **unification** of the human f.: 3310;

5. there is an immense task incumbent on all people of good will: of restoring the relations of the h.f. in truth, in justice, in love and in freedom: 755; **progress** by each member of the great h.f. will be to the advantage of progress by all and will serve to give more solid foundation to **peace**: 1003: the situation of that two-thirds of the world's population which is less favours than the rest has become the major problem which faces the human f.: 2711; 2730; all the **goods of the earth** are meant **to benefit all the members of the h.f.**: 1767; see: *Goods; Heritage/5; Humanity/10; Resources/1; Riches/2; Sea/2; Space/1*; **Church's mission and duty** of service to the human f.: 2353;

6. see also: 400; 419; 437; 617; 637; 659; 686; 701; 705; 709; 793; 794; 882; 1384; 1471; 1489; 1543; 1576; 1580; 1593; 1763; 1838; 2045; 2256; 2417; 2530; 2673; 2674; 2738; 2744; 2961; 2974; 3006; 3104; 3178; 3272; 3281; 3388; 3334;

C. **Family as an institution**

1. is the **natural community of life and love** uniquely entrusted with the task of transmission of life and the loving care and development of the human person, especially in the early years: 2365; see also *Love/5;* a community of love and solidarity which is uniquely suited to teach and transmit cultural, ethical, social, spiritual and religious values, essential to the well-being of its own members and of society: 2381; 2488; 2736; a fundamental dimension of human experience: 2599; the f., based on marriage, is the **basic unit of society** which the State must juridically protect, support and foster: 2754; see also: 2524; 2532; 3048; 3071; the importance of f. as teacher of good and mentor of the good life cannot fail to be recognized: 2475;

2. **right to found a f.** and to enjoy all conditions necessary for f. life: 89; it is a positive **duty** of governments to create conditions that enable couples to exercise responsibly this right, to bear and rear their children, without coercion or pressure to conform to the small family model: 2759; no system can be justified that violates the universal brotherhood by **impeding the exercise of the natural rights of marriage or by prohibiting normal f. life** on grounds of colour or race: 669;

3. **right of all f./of the parents**: to have their children educated in schools reflecting their own view of the world, **absolute right** of believers not to have their children subjected to atheist-inspired curricula in their schools: 177; since they have conferred life on their children, parents have the original, primary and inalienable **right** to educate them; hence they must be acknowledged as the first and foremost educators of their children: 590: to educate their children in conformity with their moral and religious convictions: 590/a; to choose freely schools or other means necessary to

educate their children in keeping with their conviction, without incurring unjust burdens: 590/b; to ensure that their children are not compelled to attend classes which are not in agreement with their own moral and religious convictions: 590/c; their **rights are violated** when a compulsory system of education is imposed by the State from which all religious formation is excluded: 590/d; the **Holy See** urges all States, International Organizations, and all interested Institutions and persons to promote respect for these rights and to secure their effective recognition and observance: 2736; **Charter of the Rights of the Family**: 590; 2365; 2736; 2758; see also *Education/10,11;*

4. **primacy** of f. in the process of **education**: 166-167; 172-173; 175; 590; 694-695; 839-840; 927; 2348; 2366-2367; 2475; 2737; see also *Educator/3*; **in population policies**: 2684; 2690; 2710; 2731; **role of the f.**: irreplaceable in attaining the integral development of children: 2363; 2366; 2348; 2368; 2369; 2379; 2380; 2390; 2391; 2737; importance of the f. educational role for youth: 2393; 2475-2476; women: 2505; 2532; 2539; women's f. tasks: see *Women/3; possibilities offered to old people: 2481; 2489; 2490; 2493; to disabled persons: 2648; 2651; 2660; 2663; 2664; 2669;* ***weakening*** *of the institution of the f.: 2363; any policy which leads to the weakening of the institution of the f. cannot lead to true human and cultural progress: 2381; 2757; the* ***breakdown of the f.*** *is primary factor contributing to the increase in drug abuse: 3448; need to* ***reinforce the f. as an institution****: 2364; 2390;* ***healthy f. life*** *will contribute greatly to the stability of society: 2366; 2380;* ***aim of public policy*** *is to enhance the welfare and quality of f.: 1461; see also 1725; duties of the media of social communication towards f.: 175; 590/f; see Mass Media;*

5. importance of the **role of motherhood**; necessity that mothers be afforded all the necessary social protection and assistance during pregnancy and for a reasonable period of time afterwards; principle of giving adequate recognition to the work of mothers in the home because of its value for the f. and society: 2367; 2740; see also: 2379; 2533; 2535; 2577; 2625; 2627; 2628; 2629; 2630; 2740; 2753; 2759; 2764; 2765; 3053;

6. **f. planning**: its very notion is falsified when it is used and applied not just to married couples but also to individuals and even to unmarried adolescents: 2755; small family model: 2759; in pursuing their decision regarding the spacing of births and the size of the family, couples should be able to rely on those morally licit methods of f. planning that are in accordance with the dignity of the person and with the authentic expression of conjugal love: 2759; **indiscriminate use of methods which violate human dignity and responsible parenthood**: 2600; 2727; 2735; 2742; 2746; 2752 2760; 2761; 3054; 3075-3087; 3429; and *Contraception*; the Church asks, first and foremost, that f. planning should respect the dignity of the human person: 3040; see 3037-3043; 3081; 3083; 3131; and should not be made a condition for granting economic assistance to developing countries: see *Aid/1, Assistance/2, Development/12;*

7. **natural f. planning**: recent scientific studies underscore the validity and reliability of the newer natural methods, and pedagogical techniques have been developed that can be properly implemented and evaluated in various cultures; women achieve a better understanding and appreciation of their sexuality from instruction in the natural methods, and couples who commit themselves to natural family planning strengthen their communication, mutual respect and shared responsibility in regard to parenthood: 2762; 2763; 3073-3075;

8. **responsible parenthood**: the Church **proclaims the right of the couple to make a free, informed and mutual decision**, in accordance with objective moral principles, regarding the spacing of births and the size of the family and relying on morally licit methods of family planning that are in accordance with the dignity of the person and with the authentic expression of conjugal love: 2739; see also: 1461; 2759; 2762;

this decision cannot be left to the discretion of the public authorities: 2690; it should be based on their prayerful and generous appreciation of their association with God in the work of creation, and their responsibilities to themselves, to their children, to their family and to society; it should be a decision that is based on morally acceptable methods of spacing or limiting births, about which it is the right and duty of the Church to speak: 2739;

the Church **condemns as a grave offence against human dignity and justice** all those activities of governments or other public authorities which attempt to limit, in any way, the freedom of couples in deciding about children: 2734;

couples should be protected from all forms of coercion such as loss of maternal and child health benefits, educational assistance and tax benefits or the imposition of penalties for going beyond a given number of children; they should also be protected from the sometimes subtle pressure that results from antinatalist propaganda campaigns: 2759;

need for a **formation for responsible fatherhood and motherhood**, which are to be rightly understood, with respect for moral law; and therefore, the need for an education that is first and foremost a moral education, for the responsibilities of married life and parenthood: 2534; see *Education/11;*

9. **habitat**: 2772-2773; 2782-2783; 2793; 2799; 2801-2802; 2804; 2806; 2817; 2820; 2823; 2824; 2832; 2837; 2838; 2840; 2841-2842; **refugees**: 2855; 2878; 2888; 2903; 2904; 2906-2908; 2910; 2912-2913; **migrants**: 2766; 2965; **health**: 3048; 3050-3055; 3066-3068; 3075; 3083;

10. see also: 46; 60; 220; 221; 224; 227; 282; 446; 849; 908; 1441; 1447; 1577; 1813; 1913; 1969; 2105; 2365; 2529; 2544; 2548; 2554; 2568; 2574; 2627; 2628; 2648; 2655; 2684; 2707; 2708; 2736; 2739; 2768; 2751; 2756.

FAO

1. its **purpose** is to free human family from hunger: 117; it **aims at "furthering separate and collective action... and thus at contributing towards an expanding world economy" and the promotion of the common welfare**: 118;

2. it is the first intergovernmental organization with which the Holy See established regular diplomatic relations; in fact, by unanimous vote on 23 November 1948, at the fourth session of its Conference, it accorded the Holy See the unique status of permanent observer: 123; support of the Catholic Church/Holy See: see *Church/7*;

3. see: **58-70; 113-145**; 1353; 1744; 1764; 1786; 1833; 1848; 1851; **1928-2257**, *passim*; 3429.

Fear

of a true "biological death" in the near future, because of the progressive deterioration of the environment: 61; in this decisive moment of its history, **humanity**, faced with the question of its survival, **hesitates between f. and hope**: 62; 338; 681; **peace is not born from f. of the bomb**: 264; is above all **absence of the f. of war**: 942; **the threat of nuclear weapons is the great f.** which hangs over humanity and essentially conditions its mode of conduct; it acts as an impulse to the arms race: 378-381; 977; 989; 1027; 1030; 3381; 3382; see also: 319; 933; 997; 1044; 1050; 1191; 1315; 3348; 3351; 3448; **f. of the use of nuclear energy**: 1346; 1350; quest for **security through the balance of power and f.**: 978; 1104; 1105; 1108; 1455; 1556; 3372, and Deterrence; **f. of differences**, cause of intolerance: 535; 537; 580; **developing countries' f.** of an economic neo-colonialism: 1529; **of youth**: 2395; 2436; 2472-2473; **"f. of the Lord"**: 3163. See also: 047; 0104; 67; 365; 375; 790; 875; 1022; 1078; 1082; 1161; 1327; 1503; 1591; 1672; 1684; 1935; 1943; 1968; 2036; 2125; 2361; 2522; 2700; 2866; 2970; 2986; 2990; 3070; 3100; 3314; 3339; *Balance/2; Peace/5.*

Fisheries Management

see: 1848-1917.

Food

right to f.: 89; it impose the obligation to ensure that everyone really does have enough f.:2182; despite the improvements gained in recent times **the problem of f. remains crucial for a large part of humanity**: 1943; **f. crisis are increasing in number**, not only as a result of adverse climatic conditions and natural disasters, but also as a result of conflicts caused by economic policies which are not always suitable, and by the forced transfer of populations: 2208; **effects of a nuclear war on f. resources and production**: 1193; 1196; 1215; 1217; **nuclear technology applied to f.** production and conservation: 1273; 1290; 1321; 1353; benefit from remote sensing: 3260; 3265; 3300/1; 3306; 3307; it is necessary to search out and to concretize measures capable of helping the indebted and least developed countries to **become self-sufficient**, or at least largely self-sufficient, in the area of food: 1424; 1439; 1478; 1610; 1884; 2133; 2165; 2207; **international cooperation needed** to transform ancient methods of farming in favour of modern techniques: 1844; 2117; justice demands a **more rational use of resources and a more equitable contractual relationship between States** so as to be free from undue pressure or conditioning from outside: 1873; hope that the political will of States will be capable of moving towards an international instrument that will entail a **real commitment, inducing them to go beyond the form of generous gifts, and would constitute a world f. supply system**: 2094; 2113; **scandal of some countries periodically destroying a huge excess production of f.** because we lack a wise economic structure that would have insured the good use of such f.: 2104; 2111-2112; **f. security** includes three specific objectives: to guarantee sufficient production; to stabilize as far as possible the flow or resources; to make all the resources necessary for continuous and organic development available to all those needing them: 2183; 2184-2201; 2228; too often, various **forms of nationalism and protectionism hinder both the availability of foodstuffs vital, and the transfer of the same** from high-producing countries to countries less well provided: 2230. See also: 48; 60; 98; 116; 127; 134; 138; 193; 285-288; 290; 1416; 1422; 1583; 1585; 1600; 1655; 1663/2; 1688; 1780; 1826; 1831; 1833; 1842-1843; 1851-1853; 1855; 1872; 1905; 1924; 1930; 1951; 1952; 1967-1968; 1972-1974; 1978-1979; 1986-1988; 1993; 1997; 2014; 2069; 2077; 2083; 2091; 2096; 2098; 2100-2102; 2105; 2110; 2123; 2128; 2138; 2140-2141; 2143; 2148-2156; 2171-2177; 2237-2240; 2244-2245; 2247; 2251; 2256; 2767; 2797; 3052; 3098; 3425; 3429; *Abandonment; Aid/4; Anxiety/1; Assistance/2; Attempt/3; Attention/3; Autonomy; Availability; Balance/3; Birth Control/2; Budget; Capability/3; Collaboration/3; Commitment/2; Crisis; Defence/3; Dependence; Developing Countries/3; Development/5; Dignity/1; Energy/1,2; Environment/2; Imbalance/1; Obligation/4; Order/4; Peace/10; Reduction/3; Resources/4,8; Responsibility/9; Riches/2; Rights/6; Security/1; Self-Reliance; Society/11; Solidarity/9; United Nations/9.*

Force

1. **forces** operating in the sphere of the **spirit and conscience**: 015; of **nature**: 093; 28; 45; 686; 688; 709; 1296; 3095; **natural** f.: 884; of the **physical world**: 679; 3367; 3368; that aim at emphasizing **moral values** in conduct of international affairs and in relations between States: 031; **unleashed by the human being**: 095; 53; 3348; 3363; at work in the human dynamics of **modern labour**: 48; 220; making for **division and opposition**: 226; destructive, of **contestation and "babelization"**: 54; **human**: 57; 306; of **society**: 232; of the **community**: 694; **greater**: 698; **new**: 796; **market**: 136; 1618; 1651; **against which developing countries are unable to struggle**: 1652; that **serve to orient the spiritual dimension of human existence**: 152; **economic**: 169; 1561; 3419; of the **private enterprise**: 3427; of **dissolution and discord**: 329; **hostile**: 334; of **division**: 342; 346; of **selfishness**, of **hatred** and of **war**: 403; working for **peace**: 750; **creative**: 1060; **spiritual**: 1068; 1333; **UN f. in Lebanon**: 1086; **devastating**: 1166; **death dealing**: 1191; 1214; which can be used **to reduce the human person, to control whole peoples** an to bring about a sense of **alienation of the human being**: 1283; of **life**: 1290; **moral**: 3000; 3004; **irreplaceable** to orient people and sustain their efforts: 1601; a **network of f.** trying to come into direct contact with human poverty and to alert the more affluent Christians: 2257; **powerful f.** motivated by financial gain: 2345; often **latent within young people**: 2399; frailty of the **physical f.**: 2485; **recuperation and adaptation f.** of the organism: 3106; **mysterious**: 3163; for **earth changes**: 3295; of the **nation**: 3418;

2. **work force**: 1449; 2248; **labour f.**: 1658; 3130; **working**: 2951; **physical**: 173; of **culture**, more powerful than all other f. combined: 173; **moral**: 112; 1957; 3320; **moral and religious**: 1833; of **law**: 324; **juridical**: 2228; of the **Spirit**: 57; 210; of the **mind**: 1374; of **life**: 3086; **driving f.** 58; 1400; 1684; **dynamic f.**: 2660; for **hope**: 1735; economic systems, perhaps still **in force**, under which poor people always remain poor and the rich become ever richer: 1740; of **conviction**: 051; of **attraction and persuasion**: 1250; of **right and reason**: 068; of **fact**: 1703; **by virtue of f.**: 1470; **imposed by f.**:349; 534; 645; 671;

3. **threat of use of f.**: 3215; **use of f.**: 247; **against the territorial integrity or political independence** of any State: 1225; **recourse to f.** 352; to **f. of arms**: 354; **armed f.**: 252; **brute**: 632; **destructive**: 1337; **military**: 1020; **without recourse to f.**: 1739; **forceful subjection** of weaker nations: 417; must not be a means of regulating relationships between nations: 13; 3376; conflicting interests: 0102; 350; instead of serving as a guarantee of justice may become a tyrannic instrument for violation of justice: 953; **balance of forces between the different States of group of States**, as protection for peace: 970; 1029-1030; 1279; 3380; 3381; b. of forces and interests: 1240; precarious equilibrium of f.: 1523; between opposing f.: 1739; the search for balance turns into a search for superiority: 1031; see also Deterrence; we must strive untiringly to substitute relationships based on f. with relationships of deep understanding, mutual respect and creative collaboration: 334; 341;

4. **forced labour camps**: 526(*); **emigrations**: 543; **transfers of populations**: 2208; 2996; **exoduses**: 2942; **migrant**: 2944; 2967; **repatriations**: 2951; **immigration**: 2606; **prostitution**: 2596; **to act against its convictions**: 2956; **to accept the faith**: 2957; **to practice religion in secret**: 2958.

Freedom

1. **right to f.**: 89; 445; if there is a right to f., there is a duty to make human beings free: 827; the human being has need of l.; there is no respect for its dignity, for its vocation as a person, artisan and master of its destiny, if the rights which guarantee its liberty are not acknowledged: 893; right to **f. of association**: 232; of **expression**: 98; 102; **education and culture**: 89; **movement**: 89; 2959; of **thought, conscience** and **religion**: 89; 102; 451; 454; 478; 479; 481; ... and **belief**: 516; 517; 551; f. of **opinion and conscience**: 360; of **information**: 464; 472; of **communication**: 931; of **choice**: 882; 2572; 2720; of **action**: 2255; 2295; **freedoms** of the human being: 89; 90; 645; spiritual, personal: 259; of workers: 46; 49; is the first and inalienable human prerogative: 49; true f. is the **salient characteristic** of humanity: it is the fount from which human dignity flows; it is the exceptional sign of the divine image within the human being; it is offered to us and conferred on us as our own mission: 453; 484; **is the first requirement for peace**: 723; 925; **essential ingredient of true progress**: 1784; 1527; **whatever impedes human f. or dishounours it is an affront to the human being's vocation to shape its destiny**: 276; one of great paradoxes of our time is that in fact the **freedoms demanded by reason of the human dignity and equality are all too frequently restricted, violated and denied**: 638; 1739; nations and governments must support the formulation of a personal freedom expressed by responsible participation in the service and growth of the human community: 3943; 3945; **the Church desires to cooperate with all people of good will to build a world where every person no matter of what race, religion or nationality can live a fully human life, where f. is not an empty word**: 414; see also: 434; 593; 607; 634; 1271; 1476; 1726; 2415; **freedom of peoples means civil independence, political self-determination, emancipation from the domination of other powers**: 644; see also: 1045; 2213; 2684. See also: 021; 090; 11; 14; 27; 41; 45; 55; 72; 79; 139; 195; 224; 257; 279; 322; 342; 347; 364; 409; 516; 417; 443; 636; 665; 679; 689; 726; 755; 808; 875; 894; 1141; 1143; 1183; 1338; 1475; 1478; 1505; 1635; 1692; 1704; 1758; 1891; 1912; 2012; 2134; 2249; 2346; 2424; 2431; 2528; 2556; 2599; 2616; 2618; 2620; 2636; 2681; 2683; 2691; 2695; 2708; 2734; 2769; 2866; 2872; 2917; 2932; 2970; 2971; 3041; 3083; 3091; 3222; 3342; 3398; 3416.

2. **Religious freedom**: springs from the dignity of the human person, who experiences the inner and indestructible exigency of acting freely according to the imperatives of his own conscience, 483; see also: 103; 510-514 and *Human Rights*; is at the basis of all other freedoms and inseparably tied to them all, 452;

Catholic Church/Holy See: is aware that its first and fundamental duty is to protect and vigorously promote the right of believers to religious freedom, 072; does not cease to appeal for religious freedom as a basic right, 533, and to denounce its violations and the consequent discrimination: 46; 101; 260; 335; 410; 417; 442; 525-526; 601; 609; 622; 640; 641; 719; 894; 1156; 1487; 1715; 1725; 1925; 2436; 2528; 3069; regrets the absence of international agreement supporting this right and specifying its consequences, 432 and 101; 339; appeals for dialogue and the participation of religious authorities when the exact tenor of the exercise or the right to r.f. is being discussed or determined: 106; 490; 496; see also *Church/5*; is contrary to any form of "proselytizing" as understood in the current negative sense of the word, 561; 2420; 2957. See in particular: 27; 101-107; 339; 432-433; 452-457; 476-503.

right to r.f.: is a primary and inalienable (496), the most sacred (339; 432) right of the human person; touches the very essence of the human person and expresses fully its dignity, 339; recognized by the United Nations among the fundamental rights of the human person (339) and by most State Constitutions (481); its exercise cannot be reduced to the purely private sphere (104; 458; 485); is not to be impeded, provided that just requirements of public order are observed, 484; see also: 89; 103; 106; 454; 483-484; 641; **implications of its exercise**: at the personal level, 492; at the community level, 493-495; 3439;

respect: an obligation which falls on everyone, both private citizens and legitimate civil authority, 455; see also: 561; 2420; 2975; should be effectively guaranteed by any political regime or system, 102; 454; 457; 478; 533; **beneficial effects**: favours the common good of society; benefits both individual and governments, 455; brings serenity to individuals and peace to social community; strengthens a nation's moral cohesion; improves people's common welfare; enriches the cooperation among the nations, 497; will contribute to the formation of citizens who will be obedient to lawful authority and lovers of true freedom: 498; helps to ensure the order and common welfare of each nations, of each society, 499; contributes to strengthening international peace, 500;

violations: with no possibility of appealing to a higher authority or of obtaining an effective remedy, 101; with impunity, 339; even if freedom of religious worship receives constitutional recognition, 454; see in particular: 102; 339; 432; 454-458; **522-531**; **consequences**: suffering and bitterness, moral and material hardship (497; 531), persecution, discrimination (526(*); **intolerance**: 543; 548-551; causes: 535-540;

right of the parents, 177; 590; 839-840; see also: *Family/3*;

principles contained in international documents: 451; 478-481; **Declaration of the Elimination of all Forms of Intolerance and Discrimination based on Religion or Belief**: has marked a big step forward, 519; might become an International Convention: 520; 586; see also: 586-589;

references to and quotations from the II Vatican Council: 103-104; 339; 410; 454-455; 484; 486; 488-489; 507; 557-558; 561; 2956-2957;

see also: 072; **101-106**; 409; 416; **451-458**; 474; **476-593**; 1115; 1119-1120; 1132; 2424; 2616; 2866; 2955-2958; *Association/1; Attention/1; Authority/3; Belief/1; Benefit/2; Church/3; Child/4; Collaboration/1; Communication/5; Complementarity; Community/D,1; E/3; Dignity/1; Dimension/2; Discrimination/1,3; Education/7; Employment/2; Faith/3-4; Family/3; Force/4; Information/1; Instruction; Liberation/1; Love/5; Migrants/1; Obligation/2; Opinion/2; Oppression/1; Participation/1; Peace/7; Peoples/1; Power/3; Reaction; Reduction/1; Responsibility/6; Segregation; Society/2; Solidarity/6; State/3; Structure/2; Suppression; Training/1; Truth/2.*

Gap

which separates the juridical norms set up to assure respect for human rights **from their effective implementation**: 334; 893; **between law and reality** (in order to neutralize threats to peace): 1104; widening g. **between rich and poor countries/persons**: 1174-1175; 1455; 1631; 1706; 1774; 1815; 2023; 3227; 3334; **developed-developing countries**: 1383; 2051; **between the "per**

to make use of the g. which are more directly entrusted to its management: 1617; **according to social justice, all the g. of the rich must contribute to the common good in a community henceforth universal**: 1509; **exchange** of material g.: 1505; 1510; 1604; 2623; of manufactured g.: 1610; 1649; 1661; 1961; **natural g.**: 704;

4. **we cannot allow those who control the g. and resources of mankind solve the problem of hunger by forbidding the birth of the poor**: 2115.

5. See also: 94; 134; 704; 802; 906; 1392; 1430; 1434; 1511; 1582; 1586; 1588; 1600; 1653; 1658; 1648; 1805; 1943; 2062; 2102; 2116; 2144; 2310; 2823; 3069; 3117; *Resources; Riches.*

Growth

to be genuine, g. **must be integral**, it must clearly provide for the progress of each individual and the whole human being: 1373; 3100; **of the human person**: 208; 811; 841; 890; 1991; 2574; 2583; 2632; 2659; 2750; begins in the family: 2532; has ramifications and repercussions in every domain of social life: 2599; **spiritual**: 342; 930; 2583; 2689; **of ideas**: 728; **economic**: should be accompanied by social: 60; 1610; ethical and moral progress: 62; must be situated in the logic of the entire human person and of society: 1623; 1653; **economic g. alone is not sufficient**: 2032; importance that so many countries attach one-sidedly to the pursuit of purely material economic g.: 777; is an indispensable but not sufficient cause of full human development: 1451; is not an end in itself: 2310; no amount of economic g. will lead to satisfactory modernization: 1456; factors inherent in economic g.: 2311; **g. can also mean the creation of the germ of an economic and social imbalance**: 1493; **appeal for a world freed from the obsession with quantitative g.**: 834; 1408; **g. in consumer goods**: 1943; **food production g.**: 2185; see also: 1322; 1373; 1445; 1456; 1523; 1622; 1629; 1631; 1669; 2117; 2299; 2317; 2767; 2831; 3098; the **orderly and sustain g. of each country necessitates organic and worldwide overall development**: 137; 2299; 2302; developing countries g.: 1589; 1628; see also: 928; 940; 1391; 1690; 1929; 2259; 2284; 2322; 2323; 2327; **right of those living and working on the land, to g. in individual and collective life**: 1766; see also: 1783; 1794; 1801; **of science and technology**: 204; 1433; **industrial g.**: 1668; 1711; 1718; 1719; **population g.**: see *Population.* See also: 064; 38; 126; 197; 201; 205; 722; 867; 883; 946; 1042; 1370; 1725; 1847; 1892; 2099; 2312; 2391; 2833; 2943; 3072; 3075; 3412, and *Advancement; Development; Progress.*

Habitat/Human Settlements

1. is **one of the fundamental human rights**: 89; 2775; 2812; **the home must remain the first concern of every programme relative to the human environment**: 282; 2782; 2824; 2841; should be not just a shelter against bad weather; it should favour the fulfillment of the human being in its material, cultural and spiritual needs: 2771; **problems created by the rapid increase of urbanization and industrialization**: 283; 2792; 2798; 2809; 2829; the housing problem, like so many other human problems in our world, **can be solved only through cooperation on the part of the whole international community**: 3444;

2. **absolute priority must be given to ensuring everyone the minimum conditions for a decent life**: 2774; 2837; situation of people living in absolute destitution: 283; 1416; 1453; 2368; 2774; 2797; 2811; 2838; 2813; 2838; 2839; difficulties encountered by disadvantaged categories: 2821-2822;

3. to be really human, **must satisfy fundamental needs**: 2772; 2795; 2824; 2840; 2835-2838; **needs which concerns private**, personal and family life; 2772; 2798; necessity to ensure the possibility of privacy, calm and intimacy: 2772; 2783; 2800; houses proportionate for the number of children: 2772; 2801-2802; 2820; **needs which concern social life**: 2772; 2799; 2842;

4. facilities providing **collective services**: 2773; 2804; 2843; **places of worship**: 2773; 2807-1808; 2844;

5. **United Nations Center for Human Settlements**: is in a position to encourage and foster international cooperation for the solution of the housing problem, and to assist in efforts to put it into practice: 3445; see also 271; 282; 3442-3444; **Church/Holy See** concern for the problem of housing: 282; 2794; 2825-2826; 2846;

6. see: 67; 282-283; 288; 1460; 1493; 1549; 2682; 2718; **2770-2847**; 2965; 3051; 3130; *Homeless.*

Handicapped see *Disabled Persons*

Health

1. sufficient h. care, **among the fundamental human rights**: 89; 904; 3016; this means that **basic h. protection must be ensured at all levels**, so as to guarantee all essential services: 3016; **one of the fundamental needs of the person**: 2798; 2823; 2837; 3103; to defend h. and improve it signifies the deep meaning of human life in all its dimensions, including the spiritual ones: 2576; **lack of h. care**: 382; 2438; 2797; 2993-2994; 3252; **teaching of the Church**: 3000-3001; 3004;

2. **contradiction between "protection of human life" and abortion**: 3022-3034; h. of the mother and of the child: 2367; 2379; 2390; 2577; 2740; 2765; see also Abortion;

3. **World Health Organization**: should maintain on all occasions the primacy of life and keep for mankind the complete contribution of an authentic deontology in regard to it: 3012; should promote observance of medical ethics, which guarantees all health activity and constitutes its honour: 3061; see also: 2992; 2994; 3003-3004; 3007; 3008-3013; 3046; its programmes: of research, development and experimentation on human reproduction: 3035-3043; on health and the family: 3050-3060; 3067-3086;

4. see also: 047; 30; 75; 1174; 1342; 1416; 1453; 1479; 1843; 2310; 2366; 2367; 2379; 2390; 2466; 2564; 2575-2580; 2682; 2753; 3129; 3130; 3265; 3425.

Hegemony

h. and imperialism cannot be the fundamental criterion for comparing social, economic and political systems: 97; the **Nation** must not become victim of totalitarianism, imperialism or h.: 174; **harmful search for national h.**: 1528; technology directed to the purpose of war, h. and conquest: 2212; the **Catholic Church** renounces any behaviour which could be resented as manifesting h.: 509.

Heritage

1. **Jerusalem**, a h. sacred to the veneration of millions of believers of the three great monotheistic religions, Judaism, Christianity and Islam: 84; 1111; 1132; common h. of humanity: 1134;

2. **of values, duties and aspiration of the nation, transmitted by parents** to their children: 107; 2738; the Catholic Church respects, protects and honours the h. of values of each nation: 633; 1429;

3. **spiritual** h. of humanity: 154; **Christian h. of Europe**: 160; **h. of other continents**: 161; **cultural**: 279; 695; 2133; 2962; **scientific and cultural** h., at the service of the true progress of

humanity: 200; **world-wide h. of the human being,** enriched by religious traditions of Asia: 209; **h. of the Gospel**: 636; 1613;

4. **common h. of humanity**: 565; 797; 912-913; 927; 3282; 3112; sea bed and subsoil: 3169; 3188; outer space: 3257;

5. see also: 635; 636; 710; 866; 2853; 3139.

Hiroshima/Nagasaki

a living witness of what can happen but need not and should never happen: 1280; see also: 194; 195; 290; 1164; 1187; 1209; 1211; 1317; 3328; 3348.

Holy See

1. **supreme organ of government of the Catholic Church**: 08; **the perpetual and visible principle and foundation of the unity of the Catholic Church**; dedicated in an original, fitting and constitutional way to the promotion of peace: 743;

2. **nature**: see *Church/1-5;* **authority/power**: spiritual, religious, moral: 012; 052; not involved in the inevitable conflicts of interests between peoples and States: 059; 746; not committed to supporting or opposing the conflicting parties: 088; see also *Power/16*;

3. **sovereignty**: **territorial**: limited to the small State of Vatican City: 72; the minimum needed in order to be able to exercise its spiritual mission in full freedom, without dependence on other sovereignties: 07 (see 05-07); 5; 72; **spiritual**: recognized to the H.S. as the supreme organ of government of the Catholic Church; was accepted in the period 1870-1929 when the Holy See was deprived of territorial sovereignty: see: 08-019; 8; 11; 160;

4. **Holy See-Vatican City**: not to be confused: 05-011;

5. presence in the **international community**: see *Community/E;*

6. participation in the **international conferences**: the Holy See always regards the ethical and juridical aspects of the question under discussion: 02; 083-084; its frankly moral approach may sometimes seem disturbing, but the spiritual inspiration that it can bring to the work of the great international conferences is received respectfully and positively appreciated: 085; see also Community/E;

7. see also: *Accord; Arbitration; Church; Dialogue; Equality/3; Independence/4; Mediation/2; Namibia;*

Homeless

a great many persons are still h., or have for a home only wretched shanties lacking even the most elementary conveniences, which proliferate on the outskirts of cities; the situation is all the more shocking since often, at no great distance from those shanty towns, is found the ostentatious luxury of magnificent homes: 2811; the number of h. and those lacking proper shelter continues to grow: 3445. See: 282; 283; 2389; 2466; 2825; 2853; 3144, and *Habitat; Refugees.*

Humanism

need for a new h. which would enable modern human being to find itself anew by embracing the higher values of love and friendship, of prayer and contemplation: 198; **seeks to develop all of the**

human being's potentialities, both material and spiritual: 220; **complete h. is the integral development** of the whole human being and of all human beings: 687; see *Development/4,5; Person: 1-11;* attitude of **pseudo-humanism** which compromises the ethical order of objective values and must be rejected by upright consciences: 2655. See also: 709; 876; 880; 2096; 3146.

Humanity/Mankind

1. **God creator** of the universe and **Father of h.**: 3279; **Jesus Christ**, in assuming human nature, **united all of h. to Himself as His family**: 2676;

2. the **fundamental reality today** is m. as a whole: 227; in spite of disparities and divisions, **h. is one**, more and more bound to the same fate: 1248; this unity shows itself more and more in the very rejection of injustice and war in the very hope of a world of fraternity: 341; see also: 791; 911; 912; 926; 939; 1419; 1635; is not merely a juxtaposition of individuals: 1189; **must unite to survive** and therefore first learn how to share its daily bread: 2014; is **interdependent**: 572; 584; for long time has been **conditioned by the clash of competing ideologies and economic interests**: 3438;

3. an ever **greater part continues to hunger** for bread and education: 58; 1943; 2171; most humiliated section of m.: 336; most vulnerable sectors of m.: 2108; 2114; most forgotten part: 2130; majority of m. living in poverty; 2587; 2838; extremely poor: 2368; that lack most elementary goods: 2144;

4. it is **surrendering m. to an uncertain and perhaps catastrophic future** to continue to throw away on war budgets the most astonishing opportunities for progress that it has ever known: 337; 1176; its **future**: depends on our collective moral choices: 195-198; see also: 63; 186; 684; 751; 1026; 1069; 1167; 1317; 1329; 1469; 1515; 2069; 1575; 2461; 2508; 2704; 3225; better future for m.: 49;

5. the **progress** of h. must be measured not only by the progress of science and technology, but also and chiefly by the primacy given to spiritual values and by the progress of moral life: 78; see also: 98; 196; 200; 213; 884; 977; 1732; 3207; cultural progress: 731; moral progress: 79; 283;

6. the **Catholic Church, expert on h.**: 10; 603; 740; 1742; 2531; puts no limits to its dialogue with the international community when it is a question of problems that concern h.: 066; appeals to the conscience of h.: 346; desires to march with m. and to share m.'s lot in the midst of history: 1550;

7. need of a **conscious decision** of m. itself in favour of both peace and development: 1703; deep aspiration of m.: a peace established and strengthened in justice: 0108; universal aspiration of f. for peace: 1242; see also: 300; 1254; march towards peace: 3201;

8. what **nuclear war could mean for the whole of m.**: 184; nuclear holocaust: 1028; see 1166; 1194-1196; 1205; 1236; 1258; 3363; h. must make a moral reversal; take a major step forwards, in civilization and wisdom, to avoid the risk of being destroyed: 198; 981;

9. not wanting to face **collective suicide**, m. will be forced to seek the path of co-existence, perhaps of peace: 3356; for the moment does not seem to have any other choice between the path of agreement and the path of fear, or of "deterrence": 3372;

10. concerted **action**: 2239; **advancement**: 3205; **assault** on all h.: 2932; **anguish**: 994; **appeals in the name of h.**: 1070; 1286; 2088; **attempt against**: 2487; **beneficial** for: 3218;
benefit of/to: 1284; 1362; 1551; 2530; 2591; 3112; 3261; 3301; benefits h. will receive from the exploration and utilization of space: 3240; **better** m.: 921; right to expect a better m.: 11; **betterment** of: 1517; 1791; **brotherhood** which should unite all m.: 892;

capacity: 396; **cause of** m.: 13; 2170; **causes** of m. 057; **challenge to** contemporary m.: 2530; profound **changes**: 2554; **civilized** h.: 698; **claims** of h.: 3173; **commitment**: 1033; **concept**: 294; 624; 3227; **concept** of h. **as subject of international law**: 3219; **concern**: 2892; need for a radical change in the **conduct** of h.: 62; **conquest by** m.: 1682; **conscience**/moral conscience: 47; 290; 333; 346; 674; 1020; 1315; 1706; 2013; 2646; 2915; **crime against h.**: 975; **crisis**: 1065; **crucial** to m. today: 175;

danger: 1256; 2631; **defence**: 1288; **dependence**: 3251; **desire**: 785; **destiny**: 322; 469; 732; 1005; 2212; 2461; 2828; **destiny and happiness**: 883; **detrimental** to: 195; **devastation**: 1224; **development**: 12; 771; 286; 336; 834; 854; 1339; 1356; 1419; 1443; 1468; 1536; 1586; 1653; 2302; 2313; 3004; 3006; 3177; 3199; **advancing towards its full development**: 687; **dignity**: 339; **dignity and grandeur**: 927; at the **disposal** of h.: 1388; 2531; 3172; increasing **material distress** of more than half of m.: 957; 1591; 1688; 1740; **duties** toward h.: 2991; **duty**: 2012;

education for peace: 1240; **efforts**: 1255; **end to h.**: 366; new **era**: 28; **experiences**: 706;

fate: 2083; in **favor** of: 245; **fear**: 378; 681; 1349; **fears**: 2395; **freedom**: 875; **frustrations** for m.: 2720; **fulfillment**: 2587; **for** all h.: 2231;

goals: 1884; **good**, common/great/true good of: 81; 141; 183; 205; 274; 1272; 1306; 1424; 1480; 1481; 1505; 1748; 1837; 1869; 1994; 2254; 2296(5); 2370; 2383; 2553; 2731; 2744; 3230; **goods and resources**: 2115; **goods** common to: 1636;

health: 1350; to **help** h.: 185; 210; 569; 1612; **heritage**/common heritage: 565; 805; 892; 912; 927; 930; 1134; 1895; 2625; 3112; 3169; 3182; 3188; 3257; **history**: 44; 51; 62; 76; 90; 92; 94; 348; 580; 3194; 3398; **hope** of/for: 681; 994; 957; 1069; 1167; 1596; 2394; 2510; 2546; **hope and desire**: 949; **horizons**: 993;

ideal: 26; 340; 409; **idealism**: 365; **impoverishment** for m.: 2529; **interest**/common interest of: 1676; 2096; 2173; 3213; 3215; 3220; 3383; **awareness of the interest** of the entire h.: 3199; great **interests and great causes** of m.: 077;

more **just** h.: 200;

liberation for all m.: 2417; **love** for: 2423;

masses of h.: 2877; **march** of: 2551; **message for all m.**: 8; **mission** to h.: 2522;

needs: 727; 738; 749; 764; 780; 1625; 1952; 2138; 2331; 2615; **needy and suffering h.**: 1928; **new h.** : 1011;

path of h. today: 80; **patrimony**: 413; 3099; 3120; 3167; 3171; **possession**: 1237; **prejudicial to**: 2395; **present** and future of m.: 0105; **problems**: 066; 067; 33; 1746; 1747; 2254; 2589; 2771;

quality of: 2387;

reality of: 2624; **respect for**: 2940; **resources** destined to all h.: 3197; **responsibility** toward/before h.: 200; 992; towards the h. of today and tomorrow: 3109;

risk: 198; 1324; **ruin**: 890;

safety: 1273; **salvation** of: 1948; **service** of/to: 021; 59; 119; 144; 206; 245; 593; 1305; 1357; 1373; 1381; 1530; 1567; 2015; 2136; 2295; 2612; 2613; 3167; 3237; 3397; **service of health** for all m.: 3046; 3046; **significance**: 2471; present **situation**: 092; 0106; 62; 85; 1104; **solidarity with**: 188; **solidarity of**: 745; 878; 1391; 1486; 1530; 3098; **stifling**: 1622; **suffering h.**: 51; 63; 2858; **sufferings**: 1155; **support from**: 633; **survival**: 376; 1204; 1468;

task: 262; **threat to**: 186; 378; 514; 2463; 2631; 3136; 3218; **threats**: 997; 1222; **traditions**: 2620;

unworthy of: 698; for the **use** of m. as a whole: 2109;

values common to the whole of m. 031; **vision** of: 1486; 3195; **vocation**: 599;

warfare against h.: 94; **welfare**/common welfare: 186; 1273; 1743; 1879; 1885; 3202; well-being: 662; 1285; 1426; 1732; 2998;

11. with the meaning of "**human nature**", "**quality of being humane**": 10; 39; 55; 76; 156; 162; 163; 165; 170; 172; 173; 178; 179; 197; 207; 221; 224; 354; 394; 453; 466; 613; 666; 670; 704; 927; 953; 1166; 1376; 1419; 1601; 2353; 2378; 2394; 2463; 2488; 2490; 2526; 2635; 2650; 2670; 2757; 2880; 2955.

Hunger/Starvation/Famine

1. **fundamental right of all human beings to be protected from h.**: 2246; **freedom from h. is the first and basic freedom**: 2012; see also *Food/1; Nourishment/1;*

2. is the **most serious and most urgent problem**: 132; perhaps the greatest threat to peace in the world: 2022; more than half the population of the world does not eat enough to appease h.; entire populations are still undernourished: 2023; see also: 1415; 1978; 2060; 2099; 2146; 2172; 2174; 2208; 2243; 2438; 2932; 3303; no country and no system in the world can remain indifferent when confronted with the "geography of h.": 152;

3. **it is an ethical problem**, since a **starving person is an individual degraded in all its faculties,** whose integral development is in jeopardy: 1920; **the half fed are only half alive**: 2012; "bread for myself is a material question; bread for my neighbour is a spiritual one": 2042;

4. **consciences must be awakened** to the responsibility which weighs on each and every one, especially on those who enjoy many advantages; in solidarity with those who are hungry, we are all responsible: 1978; 2155; 2221; in response to the demands of international solidarity, above all that of a fair and lasting redistribution of the earth's resources: 2244;

5. **the fight against h. can no longer be conducted by appeals to sentiment**, by sporadic and ineffective outburst of indignation: 132; **the only way to find a final solution** to the problem of h. in the world: **development leading to self-reliance**: 1478; 2024;

6. we cannot allow those who control the goods and resources of mankind **to solve the problem of h. by forbidding the birth of the poor** or letting children die of starvation simply because their parents have not acted in accordance with theoretical plans based on pure hypotheses about the future of mankind: 2115; see also: *Birth control*;

7. **struggle against h.**: 31; 1189; 1531; 1871; 1965; 1975; 2010; 2031; 2134; 2155; **Freedom-from-Hunger Campaign**: 59; **1972-1980**; **1986-1993**; 2026; 2082;

8. **scandal of arms race**: 1175; 1315; see *Arms race*; and **waste**: 2130; **frightful disparities between excessively rich individuals and groups and the majority** made up of the poor and the destitute, condemned to h. and disease: 98; 99; 176; 382; see *Disparities; Gap;*

9. **appeal to the youth**: 2009-2016; appeal made by John Paul II from Ougadougou: see *Ougadougou*; **references to the action of the Church**: 1486; 1923; 2177; 2181; 2198; 2256; 2257;

10. see also: 46; 58; 60; 117; 227; 285; 1003; 1470; 1625; 1716; 1746; 1842; 1867; 1922-1923; 1945; 1948; 1957; 1962; 1982; 2014; 2016; 2050; 2070; 2080; **2098-2126**; 2139; 2154; 2252; 2575; 2606; 3287; 2389; 3301; *Food; Nourishment.*

IAEA:

dedicated to the peaceful use of nuclear energy: 1360; **committed to development** of all peoples, of all nations: 1294; committed **to prevent the future spread of nuclear weapons**: see: 1261; 1282-1370, *passim; Church/8.*

Illiteracy

the **elimination** of i. is essential for the promotion of human dignity: 820; 2513; the **struggle against i. should be intensified** in a renewed spirit of cooperation, even, in a certain sense, a new one, which will unite the individual, the family and local community, public and private infrastructures, governments, and, beyond them, the whole international community: 788. See also: 30;

99; 176; 769; 773-774; 780; 788-789; 790-792; 795; 800; 816; 818; 821; 827-828; 1003; 1459; 1480; 1549; 2156; 2542; 2544; 3057; 3265; 3283.

ILO

1. **origin**: 38; 216; 326-327; **structure**: 328; its **activities** aim at making work more human: 218; can contribute to the creation of a better future for mankind by being actively and inventively true to its **ideal**: universal and lasting peace, based on social justice: 41; 47; 49; 216;

2. **vocation**: 46; **action**: 47; **spirit** in which it has carried out its mission since its foundation: universalism, humanism, community spirit: 220; **contribution** to the building up of a civilization of human labour, of solidarity and of love: 233; **achievements**: has woven an ever closer fabric of juridical rules which protect the labour of men, women and youth, ensuring its proper remuneration: 54; see also: 43-46; 233; 324; 328; **authority**: 329; **difficulties**: 48; **encouragement** of the Holy See: 50-51; 57; 233; 331;

3. **method** of work: harmonization of the three forces at work in the human dynamics of modern labour: men of government, employers, workers, so that they do not oppose each other, but combine in a courageous and productive collaboration: 48; 220; 324;

4. **tasks**: must **defend the human being against itself**, because it is threatened with being reduced to one dimension only: 53; must **struggle against the abuses and the injustices**: 52; must **ensure the participation of all workers in the economic and social responsibilities** upon which their future and the future of their children depend: 54-55; must **express in rules of law that solidarity** which is becoming ever more definite in the conscience of human beings: 55; 220; see also: 228-232; must **master the rights of strong peoples and favour the development of weak** peoples: 55; **training programmes for youth**: 56;

5. see: 35-57; 212-233; 323-331; 2535; 2579; *Church/9; Work.*

Imbalance

1. **world's** i.: 1591; economic, between **North and South**: 1467; **developed and developing countries**: 1943; which affects or threatens **developing countries**: 2714; imbalances **between individual, groups and people, nations**: 2107; 2554; scandalous imbalances **within our society**: 2358; **in living conditions** between the agricultural sector and the other sector of the economy, or between the social groups within a given country: 1775; between **demand and actual food resources**: 1852; between rapidly increasing **population and food** availability: 2149; 2174; 2185; imbalances which **impede the dynamism of production**: 2206;

2. **economic i.** among nations, threaten peace: 1984; growth can also mean the creation of the germ of an **economic and social i.**: 1493; uncontrolled, unbalanced and unequal growth: 2831; that two thirds of humanity command at best a quarter of world investment and income is the **most critical i.**: 1578;

3. **prices of raw materials and manufactures goods** are deeply out of b.: 1649-1650; in the **distribution of the gains** from international trade; remedies to restore it: 1655; which characterizes the **distribution of world-production**: is profoundly unhealthy: 1679;

4. imbalances caused **in the biosphere** by the disorderly exploitation of the physical reserves of the planet: 3096;

5. in the **proliferation of armaments**: 1246; **successive i.** caused by the logic underlying the search for the balances of forces: 3382;

6. see also: 681; 2095; 2116; 2724; 2831; 3288; *Inequalities; Injustice.*

Imperialism see *Hegemony*

Inability

to **communicate** with others: 722; **of developing countries to meet their debt servicing obligations**: 2273. See also: 212; 382; 2675; 3299/4/h.

Independence

1. of the **Pope with regard to any State**: 07; 5; 72; of the **Church**: 753; of the **International Court of Justice**: 261; cohesion among the forces of society must be the outcome of free decisions by those concerned, taken **in full i. from the political authorities**: 232;

2. peoples which have recently acceded to **national i.**: 14; 351: 879; 940; 1529; 1546; i., acquired so dearly, defended so jealously, is given to make a new, more fraternal and more just world: 1529;

3. many economic structures that produce domination have not been corrected trough the achievement by nations of **political i.**: 1546; 1529; **economic i.**: 2157; 2271; **national i.**: 1502; **threat or use of force against** territorial integrity or political i. of any State: 1225; legitimate i. of each State: 3233;

4. the **Holy See stresses the right of peoples to** self-determination and i.: 257; 644; 645; **calls for the respect of the i.** freedom and legitimate security of each nation (1045), of the i. and territorial integrity of Lebanon: 84; **for the speedy i. of Namibia**: 655; 657; **for measures capable of assuring greater i. to developing economies**: 1630;

5. see also *Autonomy; Freedom; Self-determination.*

Industrialization

1. appears more and more, **on the level of society**, as **a human right**: 1682; **is a sign of development and contributes to it**: 1675; the driving force of development: 1684; **modern civilization involves**, in a very positive sense, **an industrial connotation**: 1684; 1688; the **progress of i.** calls for the creation of civilization in the full meaning of the word: 1693; see *Civilization*;

2. **runs the risk of promising more than it possesses** to those who do not view it as subordinated to the integral aims of an authentic human development: 1676; is **neither a magic formula nor an already perfected model** for satisfying all needs: 1688; social exigencies of i.: 1694; **one-sided i.**: 1778; **has been**, and occasionally continues to be, **closely linked with injustice**: 1686-1687; 1691;

3. the **rapid increase of urbanization and i.** creates complex problems of housing and environment: 283; **high i.** demands high energy consumption: 1340;

4. **of the developing countries**: see in particular: 277; 1340; 1694-1695; 1698-1708;

5. **concern of the Catholic Church/Holy See**: 1695; 1701-1702; 1715; give priority to training and education: 1720;

6. see: 201; 1447; 1534; **1678-1722**.

Inequalities

1. **in the possession and enjoyment of material goods**: various of its forms can often be explained by different historical and cultural causes and circumstances, but are all the same marked by injustice and social injury: 96;

2. i. of **income and social conditions**: tend to increase both between nations and within certain countries: 1546; of **economic power**: 1651; **economic**, **social** and **cultural**, within each country and **between the privileged and the less privileged countries**: 891; see also 726; 1383; between **the rich and the poor**, increasing: 681; **developing and developed nations**: 1514; **among peoples**, in respect to increased production, growing worse: 1523;

3. **harmful i.** an flagrant injustice, which stimulate the temptation to revolt against the inefficiency of institutions: 697; **new relationships of i.** and oppression between the nations endowed with power and those without it: 2306(12); **hitherto unknown forms of i.** between those who possess technology and those who are simple user of it: 2306(12);

4. in the **distribution of wealth**: 176; in the distribution **of the benefits of technological innovations**: 1658; **of terms of trade** in the exchange between manufactured goods and agricultural commodities and raw materials: 1650;

5. **material and spiritual**: 1067; 1277; 1332; **social**: 2715; **in consumption**: 2716; **of resources** and thus of habitat "status": 2813; **exaggerated i. of income and wealth**: 2819;

6. see also: 224; 775; 1003; 1065; 1239; 1280; 1470; 1559; 1567; 1648; 2279; 2296(5); 3252; *Disparities; Gap; Imbalance; Injustice.*

Information

1. **right to objective information**: 465-466; 904; 931; it is a fundamental right which proceeds directly from the vocation of man in his capacity as a spirit thirsting after truth and knowledge: 846; **entails the free flow of i.**: 846-847; 2966; **freedom of exchange of religious i.**: 480; 494; 495; 524;

2. **role**: to assist the human being to better undertake its own destiny and that of the human community: 469; 468;

3. to supply **exact i.** about international affairs demands intellectual and moral qualities of high order: 462; **duties, professional conscience**, of the informant: 467; 473; **mediocrity and excess of the "messages"**: 932;

4. an i. worthy of the name **should not ruin anyone**: 462; **must be true and honest** in fidelity to the event in order to fill its social role: 470; 846; **should shape things rather than misshape them**: 845; **must impose upon itself limits demanded by a higher good**; **must be respectful of others** and of their personal well-being, and of the common good: 471;

5. **the content of i.** is still too much a means of dominating, an instrument for instigating violence, war, social hatred, moral degradation; it can be an efficient means of widening everybody's horizons, it can weave solidarity, develop a peaceful spirit among the nations, contribute to the spiritual and material progress of all: 845; **should always be compatible with ethical principles**: 3133; **demographic i.**, must be accurate: 2700; 2759; 2769;

6. **benefits from and responsibility of the use of artificial satellites**: 3201; 3203; 3253; 3260; 3265; 3270/b; 3296; 3299/4.h,5.b,9; 3300/1,4,17,20;

7. **i. media**: see *Mass Media;*

8. see also: 747; 790; 791; 829; 836; 1179; 1275; 1291; 1292; 1301-1302; 1367; 1572; 1884; 1944; 2102; 2667; 2694; 2739; 2763; 2950; 3091; 3257; *Communication; Opinion.*

Injustice

1. in all its various aspects, **as cause of war**; this i. **first attacks human rights**, destroying the organic unity of the social order, **then affects the whole system of international relations**: 87; great i., the violation of human rights: 383; 432; 444; 615;

2. in the **possession and enjoyment of material goods**: 96; **in the field of the spirit**: 100; both are a threat to peace: 95;

3. **in the world of labour**: 51, 52; **social, economic i.**: is the worse obstacle to a concerted international effort for development: 1686; see also: 412; 1471; 1485; 1554; 1591; 1653; 1755; 1919; 2116; 2172; 2217; 2275; 2279; 2305; evident **injustices** that call for the establishing of a "New International Economic Order": 2831; 3184; injustices **are the "social" fruit of the human being's departure from the moral order** willed by God: 3409; **towards youth**: 2466; **women**: 1512; 2527;

4. see also: 028; 080; 45; 96; 116; 196; 308; 341; 604; 631; 656; 697; 1239; 1280; 2395; 2426; 2546; 2588; 3181; 3434.

Insecurity

its **root cause can be found in the ethical crisis of humanity**: 1065-1067; **generate arms race**: 1066; **breeds violence** by coming to grips with the material and spiritual inequalities or our world: 1067; 1277; 1332; usually **inherent in the situation of migrants**: 2539. See also: 46; 1538; 2339; 2387; 2737.

Instability

of our **world**: 183; of the **present international situation**: 1264; of **price of raw material**: 2302; of **relationships**: 2368; of **employment**: 2838. See also: 2806; 2983.

Instruction

has always been **closely bound up with the Church's mission**: 177; 1915-1916; **systematic growth of i. exclusively geared to possession**: 169; **right of the parents** to have their children attend catechetical and religious i. as provided by their faith community: 492; **hindrances to religious i. of children**: 528; **effective promotion**, with financial assistance, of i. in those countries which have this need: 1435. See also: 162; 176; 790; 2248; 2545; 2762; *Education; Literacy.*

Integration

1. **scholars in search for an i.** between their science and their desire to serve the whole human being: 209;

2. **of educators within the community**: 693; **in a distinct culture**: 697; of **literacy** in the overall movement for the development of the individual: 771; **social i.** through literacy: 707; 770; 781; 2543; **education**, the **read to the social i.** of the underprivileged: 3427; **employment**, **means of i.** of the indigent person with society: 3425;

3. **of youth in society**: 56; 681; 684; 2470; **of migrant workers** in the social and professional activities of the host country: 783; 2766; of **refugees** into their new society: 2855; 2868; 2879; 2884; 2927; 2934; of **elderly people** into our society: 2487; their i. into the home of their children or other relatives: 2489; full i. of **women** in the global effort for development: 2510; 1513; and for peace: 2513; women integrated into public and community life at all levels: 2546; 2740; of the **disabled persons** in the life of society: 2651; 2659; 2660; **reintegration of death into human life**: 2483;

4. of small-scale **fishing communities** and their needs **into national economies**: 1854; **zones of regional i.**: 1535.

Interaction

between the human person and technology: 239; among the countries of **Latin America and the Caribbean**: 3432. See also: 1970; 3248; 3296; *Relation.*

Interdependence

1. more than ever before, **the fate of individual nations are bound up with one another**: 250, **and interdependent in good as in bad**: 3334; it is **keenly felt** when it is a question of facing natural disasters: 280;

2. **given the present degree of interdependence among peoples, it is needed**: to organize international society globally, in order to achieve a common international good and realize the need for a world authority: 317; the contribution of all to solve the great problems of mankind: 067. See also: 1454; 1527; 1536; 1600; 1645; 1659; 2166; 3095; **increasing global i.** and intercommunication create and ever greater potential for peace and understanding, but also multiply the risks of wider conflict: 3434;

3. **i. of humanity**: 584; its interdependent **development**: 336; 1422; 1536; 1623; 1628; 2798; growing i. of **economies**, brought to the fore by the debt crisis: 2263; 2295; 2296; 2297; 2303; 2334; **between the rich and poor** economies, countries: 1630; **cultural identity of each country and ever-growing i.**: 1801;

4. the real tragedy is that **i. is highly distorted**, and the more economically powerful dominate nations that are industrially and technologically less developed: 1649; unbalanced i.: 1650; justice in the relations among nations is possible if **the quality of the i. of the nations is radically transformed** and inspired by a new sense of mutual solidarity, cooperation and equity: 1664; 1884; in order to be **just**, the i. should give rise to new and broader expressions of solidarity: 2279;

5. **must now be met by joint responsibility**: 3097; every nation plays its proper and interdependent role **to ensure an ecologically sound environment** for people today, as well as for future generations: 3119;

6. the **i. of all forms of aggressiveness and of discrimination** does not thereby signify confusion: 610; **i. of questions**: 1047; **mutual dependence of all people**: 1143; **of international organizations and nations**: 1643; **of societies and States**; its meaning for the planning and organizing of labour: 1653;

7. see also *Solidarity.*

Interest

1. **of the nations and disarmament/peace problems**: 1047; 1060; 1064; 1096; 1097; 1099; 1101; 1105; 1116; 1121; 1240; 1243; 1249; 1268; 1309; 3214;

2. **political**: 027; **81**; **88**; 1047; 2166; **nationalistic** 130; 337; **clash** of national i.: 259; of **different i.**: 1000; **national self-i.**: 350; 1384; 3436; **consumer self-i.**: 1294; **many-faceted i.** of nations: 1047; **criteria of self-i.**: 175; 320; **narrow self-i.**: 699; **politics of self-i.**: 261; **individual i.** 207; **diplomacy determined more by self-i.** than by the requirements of the common good: 352; **immediate i.**: 756; immediate self-i.: 1417; to seek **self-i. even against justice**: 393; **enlightened self-i.**: 1590; **the community cannot grow from self-i. alone**: 1591;

3. **vested i.**: 1301; 1393; 2278; 2296; 2330; 2829; 3177; **partiality of those who defend particular i.**: 47; it is by sacrificing these i. for the sake of peace that we serve them best: 88. See also: 1546; 1556; 1579; 1580; 1645; 1663/4.; 2296(5); 2297; 2336; 3199;

4. **defence of legitimate i.**: 090; defence of i. by violence: 350; legitimate i. of workers: 226; awareness of one's own i.: 394; each individual is tempted to retire within itself, defending its own i., asserting its rights rather than its duties: 842; **collective i.** should not harm in any way the uniqueness of the human being: 925; **spiritual i.** of the human being: 946; **legitimate i. and autonomy of each people**: 1766;

5. **organizations intended to** foster peaceful coexistence and **reconcile conflicting i.** under the aegis of law: 0102; the **United Nations was set up to serve the highest i. of nations and peoples**: 321; 947; **supreme i.** of the world community: 349; **real i.**: of mankind: 2096; **best i.** of the people: 1407;

6. **conflicting i.**: 334; 632; 1649; 2989; conflict of i.: 385; of self-i.: 417; self-interested exploitation of conflictive situations: 615; **joint i.**: 697; **mutual i.** of developing nations: 1409; developing countries, victims of **foreign i.**: 1528; **particular i.**, to be submitted to the wider vision of the common good: 46; 217; 1288; 1818; national **true i.**: are compatible with the i. of other States: 1384; 3178; **local i.**: 1587; **general i.**: 1003; 1532; 1532; 1541; 1676; 3188; **economic i.**: 308; 1278; 1308; 1603; **human i.**: 746;

7. **common i.** of mankind in the exploration and use of outer space for peaceful purposes: 3215; 3220; 3221; 3224; 3225; 3228; 3249; 3301; 3383; i. of the sensed countries: 3299/9,11;

8. **Interest rates**: 2260; 2263; 2285; 2301; 2302; 2312; 2319; 2321; 2323; 2327;

9. the **Church/Holy See**: above opposed interests: 049; not bound to party i.: 050; does not represent economic or national i.: 1552; 1555; does not pursue any aim of self-interest: 1732; free of selfish aims or concerns other than those prompted by healthy common i.: 052; not involved in the conflicts of i. between peoples and States: 059; an ally of all those with responsibilities regarding great i. of mankind: 077; offers discreet, reserved and disinterested intermediary: 050; disinterested service to humanity: 5; 593; 603; 733; 776; 1020; 1272; 1374; 3154; 3237;

10. **Jerusalem embodies i. and aspirations shared by different peoples** in different way: 1123; 1124; 1131; 1133;

11. see also: 23; 174; 250; 357; 360; 777; 778; 982; 1490; 1555; 1560; 1720; 1885; 2117; 2299; 2387; 2815; 2995; 3133; 3213; 3214; 3417; 3435-3436; *Nationalism; Peace/4; Selfishness.*

Inviolability

of **conscience**: 534; of **human rights**: 64; 329; 408; 431; 447; 465; 533; 592; 1237; 2646; **2745**; 3004; and **the dignity of human life**, from the moment of conception: 2646; 2760. See *related voices.*

Jerusalem

1. **the Holy See advocates a special statute** that, under international guarantees, would respect the particular nature of J., a heritage sacred to the veneration of millions of believers of the

three great monotheistic religions, Judaism, Christianity and Islam: 84; 1111; 1116-1118; 1133; 1137; **sovereignty over** J.: 1117; 1137; 1139;

2. J. has been and continues to be **the most important centre of all three monotheistic religions**, the site of shrines and memorials venerated by their followers, who regard J. as a common sacred patrimony: 1114; 1122; 1123-1129;

3. **requirements for an equitable, stable and peaceful solution** of the problem: 1115; 1119-1121; 1130; 1132; 1133; 1137; **failure to find a solution** to the it, or an adequate solution, could bring into question the settlement of the whole Middle East crisis: 1109. See: 1109-1139.

Jesus Christ

1. **revelation** made by J. concerning God: 34; fundamental **link between the message of Christ and of the Church and the human being** in its essential humanity: 162; love for the human being as such is at the centre of the message of J.C.: 207;

2. **Son of God**, by becoming man Himself has in a certain manner united Himself to every human being: 1614; was **known as "the son of the carpenter"**: 37;

3. **preached a Kingdom of truth, love and peace**: 264; proclaimed **a message of salvation**: 420; no person is excluded from the possibility of being saved by C.: 614; 626; 2744; in the **Redemption effected by J.C. the Church sees a further basis of the rights and duties of the human person**: 651; 684;

4. **will judge** us on the ties of love which will have bound us to our brothers and sisters: 1742; 2610; **made love of one's neighbour His personal commandment**: 2676;

5. **was concerned to satisfy the hunger of the crowds** which were following Him: 1948; 1973; 2060; 2170; identified Himself with the hungry: 2065; 2147; 2177; with the humblest: 2372; with the multitude of the most needy and helpless: 283; 2824; 2846; showed special concern for the suffering, in all the wide spectrum of human pain: 2641; 2643; 2676; **placed the child in the heart of the Kingdom of God**: 2344; 2356; 2388;

6. **chose the apostle Peter** to confirm His brothers in the faith: 2406;

7. see also: 57; 75; 207; 219; 283; 401; 402; 512; 532; 544; 636; 670; 690; 743; 793; 911; 1128; 1641; 1653; 1843; 1849; 1932; 1958; 2037; 2109; 2125; 2135; 2178; 2218; 2219; 2232; 2344; 2386; 2394; 2396; 2446; 2462; 2482; 2485; 2506; 2517; 2560; 2563; 2564; 2677; 2853; 2914; 2978; 3005; 3405; 3432.

Justice

1. **supreme norm of all human and international coexistence**: 1108; j. is always the **higher norm** which the law is entrusted with interpreting and sanctioning: 1097; **aspiration of youth**: 56; 1529; 2437; 2457; 2469; 3086; **of all peoples**: 698; 748; 1573; 1614; **demands the halt of the arms race and disarmament** duly obtained by joint agreement and effective controls: 953; see also: 1105; 1107;

2. **social**: 38; 39; 41; 47; 49; 216; 225-226; 445; 1385; 1456; 1509; 2114; 2308; 2315; 2684; 2691; 2714; 2745; 2751; 2794; 2823; 2948; 3043; 3130; balance of j. in the social level: 1097; at national and international level: 1097-1098; **distributive**: 1466; 3143;

3. **international**: 315; 322; 353; 1262; 1386; 1894; 2226; 2278; 2339; 2724; 3195; the principles of justice establish juridical equality of all States and also the rights of peoples: 1099; in the economic relations: 1100;

4. **criteria of j.** in the relationships among the subjects of the civil community: 2157; 2169; 2315; **exigencies of j.** and equity: 2306; duty of solidarity and j.: 2312; 2785;

5. **and peace**: j. in the relations between nations is necessary to bring about peace: 1664; see also:091; 51; 87; 216; 716; 724; 835; 884; 1066; 1095; 1099; 1100; 1101; 1102; 1104; 1108; 1141; 1152; 1183; 1184; 1189; 1726; 2280; 2437; 3330; 3342: see Peace; and **the question of Jerusalem**: 1117; **Middle East**: 1152; 1156; 1157;

6. in matters related to **development**, 1385; 1386; 1389; 1392; 1420; 1424; 1443; 1451; 1454; 1455; 1485; 1769; 1777; 1799; 1841; trade, 1507; 1508; 1515; 1519; 1531; 1545; 1547; 1560; 1657; 1824; 2297(6); 2302; **in the redistribution of the goods of this world**: 1706; 1749; 1927; 1974; **in the use of the resources**: 1873; 1878; 2167; 3223; 3224; and the **food situation**, 2094; 2095; 2230; 2233; 2256; **water**: 3142; debt, 357; 2274; 2283; 2296; 2312; 2333; 3419; **use of outer space**: 3203; 3205; 3227; 3289; 3310; **pursuit of the common good on the basis of j.**, according to the norms of a true world legal system: 262;

7. **International Court of Justice**: 247-248; 252-255; 261-262; 267-269;

8. **commitment of the Catholic Church/Holy See to the promotion of justice**: 476; 630; 646; 864; 1520; 1550; 1553; 1886; 2078; 2235; 2283; 2415; the Holy See **speaks for those who long for j.**: 11; **the cult of j.**, which is part of the Christian heritage, is implanted within the adhesion to a higher moral and spiritual realities: Love, Charity, Fraternity: 866;

9. see also: 021; 025; 079; 080; 13; 49; 57; 68; 78; 112; 125; 209; 249; 257; 270; 307; 308; 327; 333; 345; 347; 350; 354; 364; 365; 381; 385; 391; 402; 407; 448; 455; 458; 477; 478; 496; 565; 583; 615; 632; 644; 662; 673; 719; 726; 755; 818; 842; 861; 872; 884; 904; 925; 952-953; 992; 1003; 1152; 1156; 1221; 1239; 1338; 2178; 2214; 2220; 2246; 2393; 2412; 2483; 2506; 2510; 2512; 2551; 2594; 2679; 2692; 2730; 2734; 2744; 2775; 2826; 2837; 2839; 2859; 2950; 3090; 3175; 3178; 3179; 3203; 3344; 3346; 3376; 3398; *Accord; Affirmation; Aid/3; Arbitration; Aspiration/1,2; Authority/1; Awareness/4; Balance/3; Building up; Capability/1,2; Changes/3; Church/1,2,3,6; Collaboration/1,5; Commitment/2; Community/E,5; Deterrence/1,3; Developing Countries/1,7,11; Development/3,9; Dignity/1; Dimension/2; Disarmament/1; Discrimination/2; Duties/2; Economy/1; Equality/4; Faith/6; Family/B,2; Food; Force/3; Goods/2,3; Humanity/7; ILO/1; Interest/2; Law/3,6,11; Love/4,6; Obligation/4; Order/1,3; Peace/3,8; Peoples/4; Power/13; Progress/10; Relations/4,5,7,8; Rights/7; Scientists/3; Sea/4; Selfishness; Society/3; Solidarity/8,9; State/5; Structures/5; Struggle/1; Teaching/7; Trade/7; Truth/4,8; Underprivileged; United Nations/2,4,7; Worker/2; Youth, 2.*

Knowledge

1. **human being's restless curiosity for k.**: 093; the human being naturally desires to know: 775; it is a spirit thirsting for truth and k.: 846; **misuse of k.**: 1355; is **no longer something acquired once and for all**: 683;

2. **spheres of k. open to spiritual values**: 206; **rational science** and the human beings **religious k.** need to be linked together: 209; **link between technological k. and moral k.**: 209; **development** of the human being's k. and awareness: 224; commitment to facilitate the **spreading of exchange of k.** and experience in the field of education, included in the Helsinki Final Act: 494; education assures the **transmission of k.** and behaviour: 679; **it is not enough to give a taste for k.** and the means for power, it is also necessary to add reasons for living: 709; **k. of truth**: 176; 178; 181;

3. **youth seek k.** that taches how to live rather than k. which is continually undergoing evolution: 690; 709; the **acquisition of k.** and the training of the will are directly focused on persona and social action: 691;

4. **scientific k.** is one of the foundations of the evolution of society, but is not the only one: 876; **scientists' and technicians' k. must not serve the violence of war**: 1898; 1908; 2670; 2697; **k. of the consequences of a nuclear war**: 1205; 1208;

5. see also: 680; 689; 692; 700; 701; 710; 795; 830; 836; 840; 842; 844; 867-869; 874; 1407; 1692; 1718; 1915; 1954; 2065; 2446; 2578; 2627; 2657; 2950; 2961; 3131; 3132; 3163; 3252; 3273; 3280; 3288; 3302.

Labour see Work

Law

1. **equality** before the l.: 640; 643; **gap** between law and reality: 1104;

2. **peace, through the application of l.**: 091; 0102-0103; **the cause of peace and l. is sacred**: 305; 352; 354; **the international community should give itself a system of l. that should regulate international relations and maintain peace**, just as the rule of l. protects national order: 1187; 1275; 3376; 3377; **l. of humanitarian and criminal responsibility** towards the international community: 257;

3. **international**, based on justice and equity: 68; is becoming the Law of Humanity: 3221; the **development** of new norms of i.l. will be impeded as long as the States do not agree on its fundamental principles and general rules: 254; it is of vital importance today: 262; **the Church points out the criteria which the development of an international system of l. must satisfy**; in legal terms, these can be expressed as the recognition of human rights; in moral terms: truth, love, freedom, justice and solidarity: 257; 258; 262; 329; 611; 615; **international l. of labour**: 55; 329; diplomatic l. 039. See also: 021; 252; 349; 364; 598; 657; 2228;

4. without an understanding of the **source** of l., the **reason** for l. and the **object** of l., a proper legal system cannot exist: 262;

5. the **l. of God** written in peoples' hearts and proclaimed by the Church provides the norms and impulses for the improvement of human l., for God's l **transcends** time: 263;

6. **universal moral** laws of unconditionally binding moral character: 613; **moral** l. that **God has written in the depths of human hearts** and that **must govern peoples' mutual relationships** on the basis of truth, justice and love: 992; His holy l. guides our lives: 2410; interior l.: 2455; violation of divine l.: 2483; 2683; **natural l.**: 2852; 3007; precedes positive laws: 3028;

7. **Jesus came not to destroy the l.**, not to change it but to perfect it: 1932;

8. absolute **respect for the innermost l. of life**: 764; 3045; **safeguard of life and of the l. which regulate its transmission**: 2251; **respect for moral l.**: 2534; respect **for the divine laws governing life**: 2684; 2690; 2694; 2703; respect **for the laws that govern the vital impulse and nature's capacity for regeneration**: 3094; 3098;

9. **it belongs** to moral teaching to enlighten conscience, **to the l. to specify and organize external behaviour**: 3069; conscience enlightened by the l. of God: 3131;

10. requirements of **moral l.** in relations between peoples and States: 3342; 3398; 3411;

11. **scientific** laws: 874; purely **economic**: 230; 2438; **trade l.**: 235; l. of healthy competition: 1473; l. of the **market**: 1176; l. of **justice**: 1651; Law of the Sea: see Sea; of the space: see Space; **humanitarian**, relating to refugees: 2894; 2910;

12. **International Law Commission**: 041; **International Law Academy**: 253;

13. see also: 013; 021; 090; 13; 47; 55; 106; 163; 226; 267; 305; 324; 326; 490; 526(*); 1097; 1098; 1103-1104; 1932; 1955; 1991; 2235; 2603; 2605; 2625; 2627; 2954; 2965; 2985; 2987; 2990; 3026; 3090; 3091; 3183; 3204; *Norms; Obligations.*

Lebanon

see: 84; 1077-1088; 2866; 2869.

Liberation

1. **from present oppression in the domain of freedom of thought, conscience, religion and belief**: 551;

2. **spiritual l. of people shut up inside the walls of under-development**: 723; conscience of a common responsibility for the l. of peoples **from various forms of misery and alienation**: 1558; **from poverty and famine**: 2243;

3. need for programs aimed at the **socio-economic l. of millions of men and women** caught in an intolerable situation of economic, social and political oppression: 3415;

4. see also: 617; 793; 1100; 1458; 1672; 2514; 2517; 2556; 2589; *Freedom.*

Liberty see *Freedom*

Life

1. **human l. is sacred**; no one can dare to attack it: 27; sacred in its origin and destiny: 3089; is **a gift of God**: 2012; 2483; 2551; 2732; 3010; sacredness of l. 2745; mystery and sacredness of the gift of l. which is **so easily manipulated** in a manner which does not respect the true nature and destiny of the human person, or which dare to suppress life itself at the moment in which it is most defenseless: 2376; 3029; even within the problematic context of the economy, **human l. conserves that intangible character that no one has the right to manipulate without giving offense to God and injury to all society**: 2439; it is impossible to know at what point one will arrive if life is not any more respected as an inalienable and sacred good: 2483; 3031; one cannot, at whim, dispose od human l., by claiming an arbitrary power over it: 2655;

2. **right to life**, the first right of the human person: 3069; the most fundamental of all human rights must be affirmed anew, together with the condemnation of that massive aberration which is the destruction of innocent human l., at whatever stage it may be, through the heinous crimes of abortion or euthanasia: 647; see also: 89; 257; 416; 423; 445; 628; 647; 849; 2349; 2655; 2760; 3004; 3439; right refused to the child in its mother's womb: 3023; if there is a right to life there is a **duty** to favour and protect l.: 827; 3022;

3. **transmission** of l.: 679; 2365; 2410; 2703; 2745; right to responsible procreation: 445; 1461; see also *Birth Control*; *Family/8*; the **anti-life mentality** which has emerged in today's society is very often a sign of the fact that people have lost faith in l., have lost sight of the most fundamental elements of human destiny: 2361

4. **value of human l.**: 927; 2702; 2732; 2753; 2783; unrepeatable value of each individual human l.; transcendent dignity of those who are called into existence: 2642; practices that do not respect the supreme value of l.: 2342; forms of violence against l.: 2174; **dignity**: 183; 1308; **primacy**: 3012;

5. **respect for the sacredness of life**: 2616; respect for the mystery of l.: 2355; absolute respect for the innermost law of life: 764; 2251; 3045; 3062; respect for the divine laws governing

l.: 2684; respect for l., replaced by the "imperative" to snuff out and destroy l.: 170; attacks on human l., especially on l. in the womb: 432; threats to human l.: 2577; respect of a conception of human l. founded no longer only on economic or purely material utility: 2497; wish that the work of the living never be used against l., but to feed that l.: 337; see also: 766; 2703; 2727; 2732; 2746; 3011;

6. **right to enjoy a decent l.**: 2649; minimum conditions for a decent life: 2774; 2837; people who long for dignified l.: 11; those subjected to humiliating l. conditions: 894; a life more in keeping with human dignity: 1513; means of living with dignity: 2076; intolerable conditions of l.: 2178; see also: 60; 275; 286; 392; 765; 776; 808; 882; 1205; 1514; 1603; 1641; 1688; 1718; 1844; 1951; 1974; 2014; 2056; 2070; 2106; 2112; 2130; 2137; 2150; 2156; 2167; 2174; 2175; 2206; 2244; 2371; 2386; 2397; 2504; 2509; 2526; 2556; 2590; 2612; 2691; 2695; 2744; 2764; 2771; 2774; 2781; 2792; 2795; 2797; 2824; 2833; 2838; 2840; 2843; 2846; 2873; 2880; 2977; 3115; 3117; 3273; **effort to improve the quality of human l.**: 279; 789; 881; 1640; 2367; 2545; 2566; 3049; 3087; 3106; 3439; psychological need to escape from the **hardships and painful responsibilities of l.**, a factor which contributes to the increase in drug abuse: 3448;

7. **intellectual/moral/spiritual/religious**: 78; 106; 418; 458; 483; 490; 492; 684; 726; 817; 927; 932; 1430; 2076; 2349; 2439; 2441; 2463; 2804; 2823; 2837; 2971;

8. **life styles**: 1387; 1609; 1629; 1808; 2308; 2375; 2716; 2796; 3119; ways of l.: 2071; 2121; 2399; permissive way of l.: 2982; deeper/fundamental/true/ **values** of l.: 017; 896; 2383; 2522; 2585; 2587; highest and spiritual values of l.: 1688; deeper vision of l.: 2477; spiritual dimension of the inner l.: 2441; its erosion: 2463; religious dimension of l.: 2594; conception of l.: 3107; **meaning of human l.**: 91; 223; 224; 263; 687; 802; 817; 993; 2395; 2405; 2471; 2474; 2576; 2783; a life more full of meaning: 2703; purpose of l.: 2470; 2558;

9. **final stage** of human life: 2485; the contemporary world, especially in the West, needs to learn to reintegrate death into human l.: 2483; one can affirm that the **manner in which a civilization copes with old age and with death** as a constitutive element of life, and the manner in which it helps elderly members to live their death, are decisive criteria of the respect it bears for the human being: 2485; Christ' **judgement** of the l. of each human being: 2109;

10. respect for the laws that govern the **vital impulse and nature' capacity for regeneration**: 3094; mastery of l.: 62; of nature in the service of l.: 1767; assaults on vegetable and animal l.: 3096;

11. the **Catholic Church** is on the site of l.; she will never cease to raise her prophetic voice proclaiming that human l. must be respected and protected from the moment of conception: 2360; 2483; 2533; 2760; 3023; 3072; stands for life and calls for ever greater efforts to correct those situations that endanger or diminish the value and appropriate enjoyment of human l.: 2732-2733; 3034;

12. see also: 021; 28; 107; 144; 154; 188; 219; 235; 245; 364; 403; 412; 414; 437; 494; 501; 622; 641; 643; 689; 709; 841; 862; 1180; 1283; 1344; 1773; 2109; 2355; 2356; 2378; 2450; 2482; 2485; 2488; 2490; 2505; 2517; 2533; 2548; 2555; 2566; 2658; 2673; 2689; 2738; 2763; 2772; 2773; 2778; 2793; 2799; 2807; 2820; 3139; 3141; 3201; 3420; *Abortion; Birth Control; Euthanasia; Family/6-8; Law/8.*

Literacy

1. **must not be an isolated process**, a purely technical objective, but ought to be integrated within an overall movement for the development of the individual: 771;

2. **it is a fundamental factor of social integration**, as well as of personal enrichment; for society it is a privileged instrument of economic progress and development: 2543;

3. it is for nations themselves to define and promote l. through appropriate policies; **the problem is, however, a vast one and necessitate the collaboration of all, going beyond cultural and territorial boundaries**: 784; see also: 776-778; 788-789; 791; 809; 1480;

4. **action of the Church**: is intended at the moulding of the individual as a whole and at its human and social advancement: 781; see also: 769; 771; 774; 776; 778; 782; 797; 2543-2544; 2567;

5. see also: 176; 415; 723; **769-829**; 883; 2390; 2542-2545; 2823; 2837; *Migrant/3; Women/8.*

Love

1. **God is l.**: 2384; God of l.: 686; loving God: 2730; **asks all human beings to l. every person as a friend**: 2410; **l. of God**: 603; 614; 626; 911; 1424; 1958; 1966; 2440; 2975; **l. for God**: 263; 1966; 2413; 3279; **design of God's love for the world**: 53; 26;

2. **l. of the human being**: 58; if unhappy and suffering, he has yet greater right to our l.: 1736; **l. is due to the human being by virtue of its special dignity**: 162; 207; see also: 2178; 2422; 2423; **duty of l.** for every member of the human family: 400; **l. for the human being as such** is at the centre of the message of Jesus Christ and His Church: 207; 208; 418; 2916; **message of truth and l.**, that is Church's duty to bring to the world: 75; 607; 656; 2070; 2211;

3. **twofold principle of l. of God and l. of neighbour**: 2234; Jesus' commandment: 866; 1703; 2676; l. of one's neighbour: 263; 494, particularly for those most in need: 496, expression of the l. of God: 1424; see also: 2863; 3005; **fraternal/brotherly l.**: 646; 661; 673; 1392; 1470; 2232; 2978; 3101; **mutual**: 911; **fraternal l. among races and peoples** as well as between classes and generations: 54; **God measures human actions according to the degree of love with which one freely dedicates oneself to the service of brethren**: 2234;

4. **civilization of l.**/rooted in l.: 233; 1188; 1601; 2396; 2436; 2465; 2589; 2949; 3290; **l. will overcome the growing menace of hatred and destruction**: 188; **peace in mankind's future depends on l.**: 189; 197; 245; truth, l. and peace: three indivisible elements: 264; peace among the nations based on liberty, justice, truth and l.: 716; 729; 755; 992; 1141; **a person cannot l. with offensive weapons in his hands**: 24;

5. **young people wish to l. others regardless of national frontiers, race or religion**: 2436; their infinite capacity for love, trust and sharing: 2475; 2477; **l. of parents for their children**: 2346; 2355; **children's right to love**: 2349; 2374: see also: 2353; 2361; 2387; 2388; 2737; **children's growth in l.**: 2782; **family, community of l.**: 2365; 2366; 2381; 2488; 2736; 2754; **conjugal l.** 2759; 2761; **for disabled persons**: 2644; 2647; 2660; 2665; 2674; 2676; 2677; for **refugees**: 2879; 2916;

6. **l. as the responsible communion of persons, replaced by the "imperative" of maximum sexual enjoyment** devoid of all sense of responsibility: 170; **for justice**: 268; 327; **first duty of l.: to see that justice is done**: 866; **l. for the land**: 1782;

7. see also: 57; 112; 198; 257; 282; 283; 284; 311; 402; 498; 557; 684; 700; 866; 874; 918; 1062; 1126; 1167; 1185; 1370; 1490; 1594; 1672; 1742; 1843; 2065; 2066; 2251; 2383; 2394; 2426; 2455; 2483; 2486; 2506; 2547; 2551; 2594; 2599; 2641; 2642; 2914; 2974; 3087; 3146; 3154; 3420; 3428.

Market

demands: 91; **play**: 136; **laws**: 1176; **access to industrialized m.**: 1446; **unfettered working of the m.**: 1451; **m. economy**: 1679; **uncorrected m. economy**: 1452; **world m.**: 1467; 1589; **international free m.**: 1502; **raw materials m.**: 1531; 1603; **developed markets**: 1588; **developed-m.**

economies: 1589; **more stable m.**: 1610; **forces**: 1618; **free m.** forces: 1651; **powerful m. position of the trans-nationals**: 1652; **rules of the open m.**: 1661; **unfavorable to the interests of farmers**: 1961; **protected foreign markets**: 2285; **stock m.**: 2292; **labour m.**: 2942; 2950; 2953. See also: 67; 1506; 1535; 1565; 1583; 1586; 1587; 1607; 1624; 1650; 1821; 1863; 1902; 1910; 2100; *Economy/4; Trade.*

Marriage

1. **natural right to m.**: 669; 3131; **the Church defends and proclaims the holiness of m. and procreation**: 3087; **value of the m. as the natural institution** to which the transmission of life is exclusively entrusted: 2745; **benefits from the stability of m.**: 2754;

2. **absence of an internationally accepted ethical principle** that gives unique status to m. as the only place in which both sexual intimacy and parenthood are appropriately and responsibly pursued: 2756;

3. if these are serious motives to space births, which derive from the physical or psychological conditions of husband and wife, or from external conditions, the Church teaches that it is then licit to take into account the natural rhythms in the generative functions, for the **use of m. in the infecund periods only**, and in this way to regulate birth without offending moral principles: 3075;

4. see also: 2346; 2475; 2630; 2762; *Family.*

Manipulations/Experimentations

1. **in the field of genetic m. and biological e.** there is evidence of a scientific research directed to purposes contrary to the good of humanity: 183; 195; **social and behavioural sciences utilized to m. people**: 195;

2. **manipulations of which the human being is both the object and the outcome**: ideological and political, through public opinion; m. operating through the monopoly or control of the media by economic forces or political powers; m. whereby people are taught that life is the specific manipulation of the self: 169; 622; see: 169-171; 776; 830; 1283; 2395; 3035; *Life/1.*

Mass Media

1. since these media are the "social" means of communication, **they cannot be the means of domination over other** wielded by the agents of political or financial power who set out to dictate their own programmes and their own models: 175; see also 169;

2. progress made in the **social communication m. applied to education**: 201; their educational purpose: 682; 770; 815; 917; m. and peace: 291;

3. **influence**, **power**, **responsibility** of those who possess this power: 844; 2254; 2658; **superfluous needs often artificially engendered through the m.**: 1387;

4. see also: 250; 681; 2375; 2496-2497; 2549; 2867; *Communication/5;Information; Opinion; Peace/10; Riches/3.*

Mediation

1. m. and arbitration, **most appropriate way to avoid recourse to the use of force**: 247; see *Arbitration;*

2. the **Holy See does not claim to play a role of "mediation"** in the technical sense of the word on the international plane, **unless it receives proposals to do so**, but it **does not refuse to accept requests, and does not itself hesitate to take initiatives of rapprochement and conciliation**: 053; traditionally has played the role of mediator: 248; m. of the Popes: 620; intervention in the case of the tension between Argentina and Chile: 83;

3. **effort of m. of the Secretary General of the United Nations**: 310; **mediators**: 385; 3395;

4. to mediate **between the wealthy and the developing nations**, the international community needs more effective instruments of political responsibility or social good will: 1455.

Middle East

question of Palestine: respect for the rights of all peoples concerned: 84; 1152; Palestinian refugees: 1154; 1156; Pontifical Mission for Palestine: 1156; see: 1146-1157; **question of Jerusalem**: see *Jerusalem*; **Lebanon**: see *Lebanon*.

Migrants/Migrations

1. the **phenomenon of m.**, as it is now taking place, shows that a satisfactory international economic and political order has not yet been achieved: 2947;

2. **right to internal and external m.**: 89; 2926; 2946; lack of a precise statement of the corresponding duty of the wealthy nations to receive the foreign workers whose manpower they employ: 2946; **rights of the m.**: 2942; 2947; 2953; 2954; right to **respect for their own culture**: 2767; 2960-2962; **to receive support and assistance** towards their free integration into the community to which they contribute: 2767; 2966; **to see their family united as soon as possible**: 2766; 2926; 2965; **to spiritual goods**: 2955; **to a real possibility of practice of their religious faith**: 2955-2958; **to freedom of movement**: 2959; there is **discrimination** when the m. worker is treated as second-class citizen: 622; looked down upon: 641;

3. **causes**: 116; 2438; **uncontrolled immigration**: 386; 2951; **forced emigration**: 543; 2606; 2944; 2996; problems caused by the **flight from rural areas** towards the large cities: 2767;

4. **literacy programmes for m. workers**: 782; 783; 787; **advancement** of m. workers: 883; **m. children**: 2389; **young**: 2466; **women**: 2537-2539; 2596; 2606; 2963;

5. International Convention on the Protection of the Rights of All Migrant Workers and Their Families: 2939-2968;

6. **constant attention of the Church/Holy See to the situation of the migrants**: 616; 2936; urges that human rights of m. and their families be recognized and adequately protected: 2766; 2954;

7. see also: 1450; 2774; 2798; 2821; 2829; 2838; 2925; 3129; 3130; Refugees.

Minorities

1. **rights of ethnical m.**: 302, **minority groups**: 423, **ethnic or religious m.**: 546; they call for protection: 647; **discrimination**: 622; **intolerance** towards m. of belief or conviction: 541; **persecution of m.**, among the causes of the increasing flow of refugees: 386;

2. **respect for the culture of ethnic and linguistic m.**; **assimilative policy** aiming at the elimination of minority cultures: 2960; **national m.**: 2971; **privileged m.**: 99; 2839; 3117; **handicapped persons form a minority group** within the whole community: 2673;

3. concern of the **Holy See and of Christian communities** for the situation of minorities: 616.

4. see also: 629; 1452; 2588; *Refugees.*

Motherhood see *Family/5.*

Namibia

independence: 656; **the Holy See** does not put forward proposals of political nature (656); it expresses the hope that the negotiations which have been going on for a long time may be translated, without too much delay, into clear decisions which will recognize without ambiguity **the right of this nation to be sovereign and independent**: 657; in the meantime, it is of capital importance that the conduct of **the civil and military authorities in Namibian territory should be inspire by respect for the rights of the inhabitants**, even in the situations of confrontation that may exist: 658. See also: *Negotiations/1; Independence/4.*

Nation

the **right of the nation must be situated at the root of culture and education**: 172-173; the n. is indeed the broad community of men and women who are united by a variety of ties but are above all joined, in fact, by culture: 173; nation's sovereignty: see *Sovereignty/1;* **rights of the n.**: 102; 224; **equal rights**: 364; 417; 445; 497; 878; **equality of all n.**: 624; 643; **respect for the culture of nations**: 243; see *Culture/5;* sacred **egoism of the n.**: 027; **temptation** for individual n. to pursue excessive self-interest at the expense of the greater good of all: 3436; see also *Interest/2;*

2. the **Catholic Church has a deep concern for the dignity and rights of every nation**; she has the desire to contribute to the welfare of each one and she commits herself to do so: 502; see also: 619; 620; 633; 1045;

3. see also: 097; 74; 80; 98; 160; 227; 228; 234; 361; 577; 836; 842; 882; 891; 893; 913; 953; 1529; 1598; 1626; 2943; 3285; *Developing Countries; Peoples; State*

Nationalism

among the obstacles to be overcome for the united development of mankind: 2313; hinder both the availability of foodstuffs and the transfer of the same from high-producing countries to countries less well provided: 2230;

exaggerated n., an aberration: 67; temptation to retire within a selfish and absolute n.: 2078; see also: 173; 2949. See also *Interest/2; Selfishness.*

Nature

1. **human**: 156; 2423; 2470; 2588; 2676; 2801; 2975; 3007; 3084; 3426; common n. of human beings: 601; 637; 665; 1635; unity of n. of the human family: 1686; 3222; human being's n.: 0101; 103; 447; 466; 484; 488; 599; 601; 1151; 2376; 2555; 2683; 2688; 2700; 2750; 2794; 3223; social n.: 104; 465; 488; spiritual n.:223; sacred n.: 894; uniqueness with regard to n.: 78;

2. **sub-human**: 2809; forces of n.: 097; 45; 679; 686; 688; 709; 1296; 3095; secrets: 701; 1682; 1719; resources: 098; 423; 1805; 1809; riches: 274; 2167; access to the riches of n. 2152; countries/peoples favoured by n.: 1939; 1957; n.'s capacity/power for regeneration: 3094;

3112; 195; nature reserves: 2809; oppressed n.: 3289; degradation: 889; effects on n.: 1387; 2716;

3. **relationship** with n.: 775; 2810; harmony between the human being and nature: 3103; stewardship over n. 274; 701; control over n.: 78; 1990; power over n.: 3098; conquest of n.: 53; 62; balance of n.: 61; 144; mastery of n. in the service of life: 1767; transformation: 2635; exploitation of n.: 832; of the potentiality of n. 2105; 2126; of the riches of n.: 2150; n. has not turned into an unfaithful servant; its potential for production on land and in the seas continues to be vast; indeed, that potential is still largely untapped: 2104; return to n.: 1324;

4. specific/special n.; n. of the **Church/Holy See**: 020; 022; 043; 046; 088; 160; 346; 611; 628; 1346; 1601/b; 1695; 1886; 2242; 2553; 2639; 2697; 2727; 3112; 3396; n. of its mission: 72; 123; 476;

5. see also *Creation; Ecology; Environment; Goods; Resources; Riches; Sea.*

Negotiation

1. **to resolve tensions**, neutralize threats to peace: 13; 308; 417; 632; 646; 673; peace negotiations for the Middle East: 1110; on the question of Namibia: 657;

2. **for disarmament**, the only realistic response to the threat of war: 1054; see: 318; 1055; 1056; 1103; 1107; 1158; 1163; 1178; 1231; 1245; 1246; 1249; 1257; 1259; 1273-1275; 1277; 1314; 1338;

3. **economic/trade n.**: 1410; 1411; 1531; 1532; 1533; 1547; 1607; 1609; 1644; 2316. See also *Dialogue.*

Neocolonialism

economic: 99; 1101; 1529; **cultural or ideological** colonialism: 3284.

Norms

ethical: 027; 2323; **moral**: 1618; 3340; 3342; **of morality**: 407; **of moral life**: 418; of **the natural law**: 236; **higher/supreme norm**: see *Justice*; **model norm**: 695; **of international law**: 254; 598-599; **international**: 2197; **general**: 2316; **legal**: 3090; 3180; **juridical**: 418; 1825; **social**: 599; 2671; **constitutional**: 494; **of humanitarian law**: 2910; **of precedence in the Diplomatic Corps**: 033; 042; 044; **fundamental**: 1098; **of a true world legal system**: 262; **arbitrary**: 490. See also: 084; 47; 205; 329; 1310; 3184. See also *Ethics; Law; Obligations.*

North-South

relationship: 382; 2215; 2297/6; 3390; **dialogue**: 1644-1645; 1649; **contrast**: 1173-1174; 2332(21); **economic imbalance**: 1467; **solidarity**: 1890; 2432; **moral obligation** which bind the countries of the "North" to those of the "South": 2169.

Nourishment/Malnutrition

1. necessity of recognizing and guaranteeing every person concretely the **exercise of its fundamental right to n.**: 2148; **right to eat**: 2109; 2177; 2182; 2221;

2. the **unfortunate victims of malnutrition have a right to expect** that the resources of human intelligence and human science be put to work to extricate them from their misery: 1835; **they appeal to the conscience** of their brothers and sisters: 2147;

3. **the threat of famine and the ill effect of malnutrition are not inevitable**; at this critical point in our history, nature has not turned into an unfaithful servant: 2104; it is necessary in the first place to secure more widely for the populations that are suffering from malnutrition actual access to the various riches of nature, in the subsoil, in the sea and on the earth: 2152;

4. n./nutrition/nutritional needs/malnutrition/under-nourishment, see: 60-61; 99; 117; 756; 828; 1174; 1478; 1480; 1531; 1549; 1765; 1831; 1835; 1851; 1853; 1867; 1877; 1951; 1952; 1953; 1957; 1968; 1977; 2001; 2100; 2108; 2139; 2140; 2155; 2156; 2177; 2178; 2181; 2244; 2247; 2255; 2345; 2367; 2438; 2575; 2753; 2765; 2837; 3052; 3072; 3129; 3425. See also *Food; Hunger.*

Nuclear Energy see *Energy/2*; **N. Weapons** see *Armaments/6,7; Arms race/5; Deterrence/3.*

Obligation

1. obligations **arising from treaties and other sources of international law**: 021; 364; deriving to States from the signature of the NPT: 1229; 1238; 1247; 1268; 1330; 1348; arising **from one's membership of its family, its people, its nation**: 227;

2. **work o.**: 98; human work is a right and an o.: 831; moral o. **to seek truth**: 103; 484; 488; **to respect human right**: 459; 861-862; 893; **religious freedom**: 455; **to building peace**: 396-397;

3. **disarmament, a new world order and development are three obligations bound together**, 1004-1005; 1293; moral o. incumbent on everyone, to the extent of each one's respective responsibilities, to make every effort to achieve real disarmament: 3333;

4. moral o., **for the rulers of rich nations**, to make their fellow countrymen become aware of their important duty of solidarity with the underprivileged peoples: 777; **o. of solidarity** and justice in matters of commercial exchange with the third world: 1508; **to help developing countries**: 1844; **connected with the mutual dependence of all people**: 1143; **which bind the more advanced to the developing countries**: 2169; to ensure that everyone really does have enough food: 2182; **economic rights and o. of States**: 1675; **debt o.**: 1652; 2273; 2285; 3412; **social o.**: 1758; **humanitarian o.**: 2918; o. which the **new international economic order** must face: 2948;

5. for **political, economic, and social leaders**, it is a **moral o.** to put themselves concretely at the service of the common good of their respective countries without pursuing personal gain: 2308;

6. criteria to harmonize **professional and family o.**: 2585; **o. to provide families with housing** sufficiently large for the number of their children: 2820;

7. see also: 237; 486; 1292; 1309; 1390; 1432; 1570; 1645; 1925; 2123; 2220; 2225; 2227; 2238; 2241; 2329; 2585; 2966; 3217; Duty; Law; Norms

Opinion (Public Opinion)

1. evolution of the **question of human rights in the p.o.**: 481; **its strength**, when upheld by solid ideals: 1011; **appeal to the p.o.** for the birth of a truly universal consciousness of the terrible risks of war: 1052; is **growing accustomed** to the idea that the use of nuclear weapons is now becoming possible, if not probable: 1199; **responsibility of forming p.o.** to international openness and to the duties of extended solidarity: 2297;

2. in questions related to: **religious freedom**: 524; 526(*); **literacy**: 789; 791; 828; **armaments/peace/nuclear energy**: 1168; 1242; 1266; 1350; 1359; 3319; 3323; 3362; 3393; **social/economic/financial questions**: 58; 1400; 1572; 1883; 1978; 2090; 2146; 2201; 2240; 2271; **children**: 2358; **women**: 2514; 2549; **habitat**: 2635; **refugees**: 2867; 2882; **drugs**: 2983; **desertification**: 3133.

3. see also: 169; 944; 3208; *Communication; Information; Mass Media.*

Oppression

1. **various kinds of torture and o.**, either physical or moral, carried out under any system, in any land, should disappear forever from the lives of nations and States: 80; **terror and o. of inhuman ideological and practical systems**: 138; o. **of a person by another**: 195; 532; the world today offers too many examples of **situations of injustice and o.**: 444; vast number of citizens who have had to suffer all sorts of o., even death, **in order to preserve their spiritual values**: 456; present o. **in the domain of freedom of thought, conscience, religion, and belief**: 551; recourse to **violence as a result of a prolonged o.**: 335; **ideological o.**: 412;

2. new **relationships of inequality and o.** have been established between the nations endowed with power and those without it: 2296(5); 2306(12); intolerable **situation of economic, social and political o.**: 3415;

3. see also: 336; 456; 622; 672; 724; 1239; 1471; 2522; *Power; Security.*

Order

1. o. **in conformity with justice**: 952-953; o. **of justice** universally recognized: 248; o. **and justice** must be re-established: 3289; **equitable** o.: 1489;

2. **public**: 484; **constitutional** o. of society: 2956; **national** o.: 1187;

3. **social**: 017; 232; 330; **better** social o.: 1844; **new** social o.: 207; 231; **socio-economic** o. marked by justice and humanity: 39; **new** socio-economic o.: 2724; socio-economic o. **conducive to** family life, childbearing and childrearing: 2739; 2759; **new o. of economic and social relationships**: 2245;

4. **economic**: 1836; **new** economic o.: 914; 3065; 3184-3186; **New International Economic O.**: 1611; 1705; 1873; 2831; **international** economic o. truly more just and more fraternal: 2174; **new international** economic and social o.: 885; new international o., **capable of ensuring**, above all, **enough food** in the various countries of the world: 2148; establishment of an **international economic order more just and more fraternal**, on the level of production and on that of the distribution of goods: 2174-2175; 2189;

5. **international** o.: 991; 1675; 1695; **true** international o.: 896; **new** international o.: 809; 812; 994; 1293; 1294; 2148; 2948; new o. **of international relationships** based upon mutual respect: 1317;

6. **truly human universal o.**: 68; **more just world o.**: 353; **new world o.**: 794; 1004;

7. o. **established by God**: 755; 1145; 3075; **moral o. willed by God**: 3403; **moral**: 0100; 498; 1836; 2533;

8. see also: 47; 499; 645; 671; 744; 1037; 1424; 1685; 2057; 2702; 2843; 2924; 3202; 3276; 3428; *Economy; Justice.*

Disorder: 537; 2110; 2275; 2455; 2886; 3010.

Ougadougou

***appeal to international solidarity**, launched by Pope John Paul II from Ougadougou on 10 May 1980, on behalf of the victims of drought and desertification: 284-285; 1927; see also: Desertification; Sahel.*

Parenthood (**Responsible P.**) see *Family/C,8.*

Participation

1. **right to political p.**; right **to participate in the free choice** of the political system of the people to which one belongs: 89; **in decisions** that affect people and nations: 445; everybody must participate **in the life of the nation**: 643; 668; right to participate **in the culture of one's people**: 781; see also: 783; 828; **political p.**: 1455; 1456; p. of those most concerned, **when the exact tenor of the exercise of religious freedom is being discussed or determined**: 490; see also 106;

2. of all peoples **in the building of the world**: 55; responsible participation of all in the building of **a new world order**: 794; **of a more just world**: 2295; a new world where p., development and peace flourish: 2465; in **civic** and **social responsibilities**: 492; **in the life of society**; 828; in social life: 2799; **social and political** life: 928; in **social political and cultural** life: 2966;

3. freely organized and socially disciplined and organic p. **in the responsibilities and in the profits of work**: 47; 54; p. **in the whole process of production** and in the social life that grows up around that process: 97; 232;

4. in **development/growth/advancement**: 136; 232; 1451; 1458-1459; 1487; 2247; 2335; 2751; 2784; 2943; calling on the free p. and the sense of responsibility of all, in the public and in the private sphere, both nationally and internationally: 129; full p. of the developing countries in the making up of the world economy: 1593; 2338; in remote sensing activities: 3299/10; p. in the process of industrialization: 1691; 1692; of all concerned, for the solution of the debt crisis: 2275; 2305; 2335; in commercia negotiations: 1533; 1547; in the benefits of development: 2044; of all countries in the international monetary decisions: 1568;

5. **youth**, see *Youth/2*; **women**, see *Women/4*;

6. of the **Holy See** in the international organizations and conferences: see Holy See/6; very different of that of the States: 72; 257; 616;

7. see also: 590/e; 1086; 1323; 1418; 1452; 1663/2; 1671; 1860; 1915; 2373; 2585; 2752; 2763; 2845; 2846; 2935; 3153; 3198.

Peace

1. **is a gift of God**: 1281; 3400; **intrusted to us**: 3401; intrusted to everyone: 369; **a supreme good for humanity**: 3329; **a light-house guiding civilization**: 742; **our duty**; our **common responsibility**: 1073-1075; 1334; 1441; **a right**: 445; 827; **an urgent and universal duty**: 754; 827; **a positive and inexpressible hope**: 754; **a necessity**: 1024-1027; 3329;

2. **has more than one meaning**; it has become **synonymous with an imposed, oppressive order**; it is also **a label for defining balance between opposing forces**, contained by fragile agreements or by the accumulation by both parties of ever more dangerous armaments: 1739; p. **based upon the balance of nuclear terror**; its dangers: 1104;

3. there is an **immense aspiration for peace** in everyone's heart, for social peace as well as for international peace, for p. based on justice and on the recognition, in all its rights and in its development, of the dignity of the human being; dream, the **deepest aspiration of the peoples**: 300; 967; 1069; 1242; 1488; 2414; 3399; **not a utopia**, an inaccessible ideal, an unrealizable dream: 1071; 1334; p. **is possible**, because it is inscribed in the human being's hearts: 835; possible: difficult, indeed very difficult, but possible; **it requires** a higher wisdom, a sense of humanity, perseverance which does not flag or become discouraged; awareness of one's own interests: 394; 3329; 3341;

p. movements: have been developing everywhere; their ideological basis are multiple; their projects, proposals and policies vary greatly and can often lend themselves to political exploitation; however, all those differences of form and shape manifest a profound and sincere desire for p.: 1051;

4. is something **greater and more important of any particular interest**, including political; it is by sacrificing these interest for the sake of p. that we serve them best: 88; **fruit of universal reconciliation**, more specifically, of universal brotherhood, a brotherhood called for by a condition shared by all humanity and by its close solidarity: 926; solidarity may be regarded as a step along the path of peace: 1143; p. **must be built on the foundation of the intellectual and moral solidarity of mankind**: 747; 226; see also: 1380; 2284(3);

5. is **not born from fear of the bomb** or the power of one over another: 264; is not only absence of war 942; 3387; it **is above all absence of the fear of war**; it has also other synonyms such as: reconciliation, international cooperation, development and integral progress of mankind: 942; **the road to peace passes through development**: 1523; see *Development/10,15;*

6. is the **result of respect for ethical principles**: 1063; **depends on the primacy of the spirit**; on love: 189; 197; **on moral an political choice**, that of putting all the resources of mind, science and culture at the service of p.; **we shall build p. by building a more humane world**; p. is **one of the loftiest achievements of culture**: 196; **comes only when human beings strive for truth and love** in their dealing with one another, when they discover who they really are and recognize one another purpose: 264; truth is an essential ingredient of peace: 727; see also: 463; we are far from that **"culture of peace" which alone can guarantee the survival of humanity and its civilization**: 376;

7. there is a **direct relation between human rights and p.**; it is impossible to have true and lasting p. where human rights are unrecognized, violated and trampled upon: 417; p. and rights are two benefits directly related to each other as cause and effect: there can be no peace where there is no respect for, defence and promotion of human rights; while promotion of the rights of the human person leads to peace, at the same time peace contributes towards the realization of this aim: 422; **promotion of human rights is the path towards peace**: 418; see also: 86-88; 94; 101-103; 188; 302; 347; 360; 416; 419; 426; 436; 448; 477; 478; 645; 657; 660; 662; 671; 674; 861; 925; 1066; 1096; 2945; 2970; 3398; **the recognition, guarantee and respect of religious freedom bring serenity to individuals and p. to social community**: 497; will contribute to strengthening international p., which, on the contrary, **is threatened by any violation of human rights**: 500;

8. **there can be no p. without justice**, without acknowledgment and respect for fundamental equality between human beings, whatever their race, beliefs, cultural level or social position: 724; 726; **p. as an indivisible fruit of just and honest relations on every level** - social, economic, cultural, and ethical - **of human life** on earth: 2295; see also: 50; 90; 92; 724; 1089-1108; 1664; 2280; 3330; 3342; universal lasting p. based on social justice, the ideal of ILO: 41; 49; 216;

9. **to guarantee p. among the nations of the world is necessary a civilization of truth and love**: 3290; **clarity of mind and firmness of will**: 3314; **education** for p.: 1141; 1240-1241; 1280; 3394; **dialogue**: 1142; 3386; 3391-3397; **conversion**: 3403; **the establishment of an impartial and effective international authority**: see Authority/; **struggle against hunger** and towards the main needs of the world: 31; 1984; 2022; **elimination of**: inequalities and injustices: 95; 1089-1108; 1239; 1280; 1656; 1740; 1984; discrimination: 622; 639; oppression: 1239; tensions/conflicts: 1239; distrust: 380-381;

10. p. **is built slowly trough good will, trust and persevering effort**: 288; p. is built by Heads of States and politicians when they rise above divisive ideologies and cooperate in joint efforts free of prejudice, discrimination, hatred and revenge; is fruit of reconciliation: 289; **when national budgets are finally diverted from the creation of more powerful and deadlier weapons to provide food and raw materials to meet basic human needs**: 290; 1585; **by men and women of the mass media** when they bring to the attention of the public the facts about those who suffer, about refugees and the dispossessed, when they stir up in others a determination and generosity to respond to all those in need: 291; **is to be found at the end of an indispensable process of rapprochement by the parties involved**, desirous as they are of basing their relations upon a new balance of cooperation and trust: 1108; **"winning true peace demands no less valour and commitment than winning a war"**: 3389.

11. **to live in real peace, nations must be liberate from the oppressive servitude of the arms race**: 953; 3331; the arbitrary sale of arms, especially to poor countries, remains one of the gravest threats to p. at the present time: 1102; see also: 777; 953; 1632; 3331; **no stable peace can be established among human beings until there is effective, general, controlled armament reduction**: 955; 1182-1186;

12. the **great enterprises designed to promote peace** and the progress of mankind throughout the earth **must necessarily be founded on the Union of Nations**, on mutual respect and on international cooperation: 149;

13.**International Year of Peace**: suggestions by and hopes of the Holy See: 1140-1145.

14. **United Nations**: see *United Nations/1-4,9;* **UNESCO**: see *UNESCO/1,2,4*; **Youth**, see *Youth/2,4,7*; **Women**, see *Women/4,8*;

15. **Catholic Church/Holy See**: the Catholic Church **sees in this domain its own particular task**: 94; **her native vocation to be the teacher of universal p.**: 744;

that the Holy See should be in an original, fitting and constitutional way dedicated to the promotion of p. in the world will surprise no one: 743; p. **is the programme of its apostolic presence in the world**: 746; **its contribution is essentially that of appealing to the conscience of humanity in the face of the forces which divide individuals and nations**, in order tirelessly to seek new paths to p., understanding and cooperation between peoples and communities: 346; **never a party to any particular political bloc**: 1272; **intends to help nations and peoples reflect** more deeply on the moral implications of political choices: 1272; 3397; is **keenly aware of** the fact that the violation of basic rights and freedoms constitutes a threat to true p.: 671; does not enter into the technical and political aspect of the problem, **calls the attention to ethical principles**: 996; 1023; 1165; **loves p.**: 1253; **in every place on earth proclaims a message of peace, prays for peace, educates for peace**: 83; will continue to educate for peace: 1011; 1241; 1253; 3394; does not shrink from the duty of offering help (mediation): 3396; will continue to pray for peace: 1012; see also: 404; 405;

doctrinal approach: 3318; 3321-3328; influencing and orientation of public opinion: 3319; direct action addressed to the decision-making centres of Governments and International Organizations: 3320; **basic lines of its position**: 3329-3334; **encouragements and hopes**: 1039; 1042; 1266-1269; **appeals**: 1070-1076; 3399;

see also: 047; 053; 067; 070; 075; 080; 11; 25; 265; 293; 346; 455; 476; 501; 630; 671; 713; 717; 744; 918; 1008-1012; 1042-1046; 1253-1254; 1222; 1254; 1272-1273; 1936; 2567; 2592; 2594; 2595; 2679; 2744; 3180; 3311-3406;

16. see also: 025; 025; 80; 85; 193; 244; 245; 250; 251; 270; 349; 352; 365; 376; 391; 396; 402; 546; 565; 597; 755; 819; 864; 884; 916; 1400; 1511; 1520; 1608; 1841; 1970-1971; 2415; 2455; 2664; 2730; 2751; 2800; 2823; 2837; 2863; 2964; 2978; 2998; 3001; 3195; 3199; 3290; 3356; 3436; *Accord; Action/1,6; Activity/1,4; Advancement; Affirmation; Africa; Aid/1; Anxiety/2; Arbitration; Arms race/1; Aspiration/1; Authority/1; Awareness/2; Balance/1,2; Benefit/1,2; Building up; Church/1,3,4,5,6,8; Civilization/4; Collaboration/1,5; Commitment/1,2; Community/E,4; Conflicts; Conscience/4; Control/4; Conversion; Culture/4,10; Defence/1; Detente; Deterrence/1; Developing Countries/1; Dialogue; Dignity/1; Dimension/2; Disarma-*

ment/1,3-5; Discrimination/2; Duties/2,4; Education/7; Educator/2; Energy/2; Environment/2; Faith/8; Family/B,5; Fear; Force/1,3; Freedom/1,2; Humanity/7; Hunger/2; ILO/1; Imbalance/2; Injustice/2; Interest/1,3,5,7; Law/1,2; Love/4; Mass Media/2; Negotiation/1; Obligation/2; Opinion/2; Participation/2; People/4,7; Person/1,7,11; Power/5; Progress/1,4,5,10; Relation/1,5,7,8; Responsibility/7; Rights/6,7,10,11,13; Science/4; Security/2; Society/3; Solidarity/5,9; Space/1,3; Structure/2,3,7; Teaching/6,7; Tensions/1; Trust/1,3; Truth/4; UNDP; Values/7,10; War/2.

Peoples

1. **rights**: 79; 137; 259; 383; 431; 645; 654; 925; 1099; 1152; 1154; 1704; 1706; 2212; 2715; 3346; **rights and duties**: 1882; **duties**: 2094; **common right of p. to their integral development**: 55; right **to self-determination and independence**: 257; 432; 645; 653; **freedom**: 2684; 2691; **religious freedom**: 455;

2. **equality**: 597; **equal dignity**: 614; 636; 2279; **values**: 140; 1399; 1407; 2434; **culture**(s): 173; 174; 243; 770; 2434; **sovereignty**: 310; 1487; 2714; **conscience**: 1067; 1332; 1427; 2169; **aspirations**: 86; 1537; 1573; 1684; **interests**: 360; 3383; **needs**: 127; 984; 1403; 1416; 1624; 1702; and **expectations**: 984; 1234; 1395;

3. **underprivileged**: 777; 1621; 1684; 2052; 2282; 1800; **less favoured**: 1175; 1684; 2282; **least advanced/developed**: 806; 1554; 1620; 1786; **oppressed**: 631; 3289; **more needy**: 1523; 1595; 1621; 1646; 1800; 2332; **undernourished**: 1786; 1945; 1974; **suffering**: 1415; 1730;

4. **community of**: 0108; 79; 753; 1424; **family**: 011; 1371; 1599; 1610; **assembly** of: 13; **relations**: 260; 1145; 1636; 1801; 1878; 2246; 3342; 3376; 3398; **interdependence**: 067; 097; 317; 1600; 1623; 1664; 1801; 1884; **justice among p.**: 024; 2078; 2157; 2226; 2279; 2315; 2785; **love/fraternity**: 53; 64; 400; 751; 926; 2455; **conflicts of interests**: 059; 1174; **inequalities**: 1523; **reconciliation**: 189; 2178; **solidarity**: 63; 231; 243; 777; 910; 1487; 1609; 1886; 1921; 2086; 2714; **collaboration/cooperation**: 346; 756; 1158; 1221; 1370; 1409; 1069; 2254; 3133; 3136; **spiritual fusion**: 751; **balance**: 1488; **trade balance**: 1602; trade **relations**: 1604; **peace**: 50; 300; 1063; 1537; 1970; **understanding**: 1323; 2424; **security**: 365; 1224; 1364;

5. **development of/among**: 098; 39; 198; 201; 322; 359; 793; 854; 890; 1061; 1101; 1294; 1372; 1379; 1429; 1441; 1547; 1569; 1598; 1639; 1682; 1841; 2327; 2331; 2335; 2339; 2734; 2752; 3009; 3334; development of p. **involves**, beside the equality of races, **the right to aspire to their own legitimate autonomy**: 644; **participation of all p. in the building of the world**: 55; all p. **must become the artisans of their destiny**: 55; 1375; 1566; 1598; 1611; 2055; 2303; **developing**: 296; 1482; 1515; 1583; 1713; 1720; 1844; 2047;

6. United Nations vocation: **to bring p. together**: 16; **seat of freedom of p.**: 127;

7. Holy See, **eager to contribute**, to the best of its ability, **to the welfare and peace of peoples**, especially the weakest and most vulnerable: 053; see also: 047; 048; 0107; 346; 614; 1422; 2275; 2828;

8. see also: 043; 070; 13; 24; 53; 67; 76; 93; 112; 149; 244; 263; 284; 294; 307; 308; 334; 350; 639; 657; 680; 772; 776; 795; 886; 918; 993; 997; 1000; 1012; 1026; 1040; 1050; 1060; 1062; 1075; 1096; 1116; 1123; 1125; 1133; 1139; 1239; 1240; 1241; 1258; 1261; 1262; 1272; 1283; 1288; 1290; 1294; 1374; 1402; 1405; 1418; 1488; 1505; 1556; 1564; 1590; 1599; 1601; 1607; 1608; 1611; 1615; 1618; 1689; 1703; 1706; 1710; 1721; 1749; 1845; 1846; 1886; 1925; 2062; 2070; 2092; 2116; 2133; 2172; 2175; 2220; 2297; 2339; 2383; 2387; 2414; 2426; 2530; 2546; 2590; 2734; 2752; 2787; 2824; 2845; 2939; 2948; 2971; 2975; 2993; 2996; 3009; 3095; 3100; 3124; 3128; 3130; 3132; 3186; 3201; 3203; 3205; 3222; 3223; 3284; 3289; 3307; 3310; 3330; 3385; 3390; 3391; 3399; *Advancement; Collaboration/2; Development/4; Progress/10; Solidarity/8.*

Permissiveness

1. an **attitude and climate of relativism and p.**, frequently grown into a loss or erosion of spiritual and ethical values, have not produced good fruit and are of no help in the development of the true personality of young people: 2398;

2. contraceptive programmes have increased **sexual p.** and promoted irresponsible conduct, with grave consequences: 2735;

3. **drugs addiction challenges paradoxically the permissive way of life**: 2982.

Person (Human Person/H. Being/Man)

1. **dignity***: every h. b. is endowed with a dignity that must never be lessened, impaired or destroyed but must instead be respected and safeguarded, if peace is really to be built up: 88; 89; see also: 021; 024; 76; 93; 97; 106; 143; 225; 231; 233; 296; 322; 364; 407; 418; 426; 447; 449; 452; 455; 478; 483; 490; 510-511; 515; 533; 571; 574; 582; 604; 614; 635; 637-638; 644; 651; 662; 701; 821; 849; 863; 927; 1472; 1645; 1843; 2134; 2502; 2525; 2554; 2555; 2560; 2609; 2616; 2619; 2621; 2646; 2647; 2662; 2681; 2684, and Dignity/1*; **primacy over things**: 185; 1257;

2. is **unique, complete** and **indivisible**; it cannot be considered solely as the result of all the concrete conditions of his existence, as the result - to give one example - of the production relationships prevailing at any given time: 157; 1603; constitute the most important element in the universe: 2780; the first and truest treasure of the earth: 3099;

3. **spiritual dimension intrinsic in the human individual**: 765; it is impossible to have the concept of the human individual without coming back to the spiritual and moral dimension of the human person itself: 765; is a spiritual being: 2442; needs intellectual and spiritual life: 2439; has spiritual and religious needs: 2773; cannot live without prayer any more than he can live without breathing: 2419; has need to **shed light on its future** by means of **permanent, eternal verities**, which are beyond its grasp, certainly, but traces of which it can discover for itself, if it really wants to: 831;

4. is not an individual shut away within his own destiny; it is an **essentially social person, member of a universal community** within which it has the right to be recognised, listened to and respected, because it is an irreplaceable, active element of that community: 737; 227; 1474;

5. it is essential for human being to realize that they have been **created in God's image** and that therefore they must respect one another instead of exploiting, torturing and killing one another: 263; 2123; 2410; 2422; 2483; 2524; 2559, and *Creation/2*;

6. must be **affirmed for its own sake**, and not for any other motive or reason: 162; 207; must be **loved because it is a human being**; love **is due** to the human person because of its special dignity: 162; 207-208;

7. must conquer his **selfishness**: 68; 2433; it is an historical as well as a psychological error to believe that legislative enactments can cure the human being of his evil tendencies; and **it is just as wrong to look upon the human being as so depraved that he cannot be perfectible** hence must be forced into doing good: 1759; **should transcend itself by its own effort** so as to dominate its aggressive and possessive instinct and to give the necessary breath and priority to the life of its spirit: 726; **the more advances into the realms of "being more"**, the more it becomes an agent and factor for peace: 726; must **love** other persons because recognizes in them its brother or sister: 70;

8. must be considered in its **wholeness**, in all the **fullness and manifold riches of its spiritual and material existence**: 75; 158; in its **entirety**, that is to say, in all its personal dimensions - not forgetting the ethical and religious aspects -and in its social dimensions: 766;

9. the h. b. in its entirety, living at the same time both in the **world of material values** and in that of **spiritual values**, is the fundamental dimension of human existence: 90; 151; 158; in this relationship **spiritual values are pre-eminent**: 90;

10. it must be **defended** against itself, because it is threatened with becoming only part of itself, **with being reduced to one dimension only**: 53; against the one sided **subordination** to material good alone: 91-92; can be accustomed, by an alienating education, to becoming the **object of a host of manipulations**: 169-171; 830; 1283; and *Manipulation*;

11. the "economic" human being is beginning to give way a little to the **full vision of the human person** as a responsible moral agent, creative in its action, free in its ultimate decisions, united to his fellows in social bonds of respect and friendship, and co-partner in the work of building a just and peaceful world: 1456; see also 1408;

12. although dependent on the resources of the material world for life, it cannot be their **slave**, but it must be their **master**: 97; has succeeded in subduing the earth, now must dominate his domination: 62;

13. is the end of every power and every social action: 1441; the fundamental subject of all the concerns and cares of the community in its assistance projects: 3148;

14. **rights**: there is no respect for the dignity of the human being, for its vocation as a person, artisan and master of its destiny, if the rights which guarantee its liberty are not acknowledged: 893; all h. b. in every nation and country should be able to enjoy effectively their full rights under any political regime or system: 102, the most advanced civilizations collapse when they no longer either respect or protect the individual: 724; and *Rights*

the **priority of the human person over every political or ideological system** the equality of every human being must be accepted and respected by all and everywhere: 384; political activity, whether national or international, comes from the h.b., is exercised by it and for it: 76;

15. **aspirations**: to build a fraternal world: 686; to enjoy the rights which flow from its dignity as human person: 637; to a life that is full, autonomous, and worthy of its nature as a human being; to harness for his own welfare the immense resources of the modern world: 2555;

16. is the **only subject of culture**, its **only object** and its **end**: 156; see: 154-159; is always present in any form of culture: 161; it can come to an authentic and full humanity only through culture: 154; 156; 704; 765; see also Culture; is a human being through **truth**, and becomes increasingly a human being through an ever more perfect knowledge of truth: 176;

17. is the **subject of all work** and **all our intellectual and scientific disciplines**: 241; see *Work*; is the **criterion** of all our judgments and decisions: 240; under God, it is the **measure and end** of all the projects that we attempt in this world: 241-242; must be the **active criterion inspiring and guiding all efforts for development**: 143; 241; 1721; is the **master and artisan of its own advancement**: 2247; 2688; 2700;

18. its **future is threatened,** because the results of scientific research and discoveries have been and are still being exploited for the purposes of destroying and killing: 183; 185; 1283; 1315; see also 093-097;

the appeal to its **moral conscience** has never before been as necessary as it is today, in an age marked by such great human progress; for the real danger comes from the human being, which has at its disposal ever more powerful instruments, fitted to bring about ruin or to achieve lofty conquests: 33; 1296;

it is the human person, and especially groups of persons, communities and nations, freely choosing to face the problems together, **who will, under God, determine the future**: 276; its **trust**

must be sustained against all the temptations to fatalism, to paralysing passivity and to moral dejection: 200;

19. **Catholic Church/Holy See**: by her very nature the Church is at the service of the human being in all its truth, in its full magnitude, of the concrete, historical human being: 2553; sent by Jesus Christ, she wants to help form the conscience and behaviour of human beings: 265; 2044; considers the human being the **first road which she must travel in fulfilling its mission**: 219; 570;

cannot afford to let the limitations of ideological biases obstruct its **concern for the individual human being, for the whole human being and every human being**: 1403; 1486; profoundly attached to the promotion of human dignity on a world-wide scale: 605; 637; 864; 1376; 1653; 2360; 2686; calls all those responsible to work for the development of the whole human being and of every human being: 64; 2096; 2122; 2130; 2365; 2525; 2587; 2594-2595, and *Church*;

Pope John Paul II addresses to the International Organizations reflect, in a coherent way, one fundamental idea and one basic preoccupation: the **cause of the human being**, its **dignity and the inalienable rights flowing therefrom**: 219;

20. see also: 093-097; 28; 44; 45; 64; 80; 90; 92; 103; 153; 155; 165; 173-174; 186; 198; 206; 221-242; 336; 279; 459; 649; 665; 668; 687; 699; 723; 725; 771; 798-799; 808; 819; 852; 872; 890; 1015; 1028; 1066; 1074; 1096; 1151; 1161; 1181; 1188; 1253; 1307; 1336; 1345; 1354; 1356; 1360; 1375; 1382; 1387; 1399; 1419; 1429; 1441; 1480; 1514; 1591; 1617; 1623; 1629; 1664; 1670; 1682; 1692; 1703; 1719; 1721; 1761; 1805; 1835; 1882; 1911; 1920; 1989; 1990; 2011; 2065; 2074; 2077; 2096; 2150; 2159; 2144; 2158; 2109; 2220; 2175; 2178; 2244; 2246-2248; 2362; 2376; 2382; 2398; 2405; 2430; 2420; 2457; 2482-2483; 2498; 2550; 2555; 2616; 2618; 2620; 2632; 2635; 2673; 2681; 2689; 2695; 2898; 2917; 2924; 2935; 2961; 3000; 3049; 3094-3095; 3115; 3146; 3148-3149; 3289; 3439.

Poor

1. **countries/peoples**: 56; 66; 136; 681; 1102; 1174; 1390; 1415; 1507; 1525; 1631; 1652; 1661; 1663; 1757; 2052; 2053; 2175; 2306; 2716; 3066; 3212; 3227; 3334; **poor/rich**: 67; 1445; 1475; 1566; 1649; 1845; 2279; **differences/gap**: 1175; 1455; 1650-1651; 1656; 2156; 2397; **the poorer/poorest**: 1422; 1468; 1476; 1497; 1508; 1535; 1589; 1600; 1619; 1706; 1750; 1851; 1893; 2194; 2271; 2297; 2299; 2324; 2332(21); 2334; 2797; 3237; 3260; 3265; 3284; 3287; 3302; Rich;

2. **individual/groups**: 282; 287; 622; 641; 1415; 1416; 1442; 1449; 1452; 1493; 1521; 1524; 1590; 1595; 1621; 1742; 1757; 2012; 2065; 2115; 2216; 2219; 2236; 2306; 2308; 2676; 2721; 2761; 2838; 2839; 2991; 3152; 3252; 3259; 3260; 3417; 3420; 3421; **rich/poor**: 67; 1475; 1566; 1591; 2215; 2279; 2715; 2815; **disparities/inequalities**: 98; 681; 1066; 1455; 1740; 1774; 1815; 2023; 2051; 2751; **poorest**: 1509; 1800; 1815; 1819; 1967; 2239; 2247; 2264; 2285; 2299; 2335; 2358; 2587; 2811; 2824; 3162; 3197;

3. **Catholic Church/Holy See**: speaks for the poor: 11; 1554; gives privileged attention to the poor/poorest: 614; 619; 685; 1867; 2062; 2126; 2177; 2543; 2641; 2853.

Population

1. **the dignity of human person**, of each and every person, and his or her uniqueness and capacity to contribute to the well-being of society are **of primary importance to the Church when entering into discussions about p.**: 2732; see also: 2681; 2685; 2732; 2744-2746; 3038-3039;

2. **need to take into account the totality of data in a scientific study on p.**, without excluding moral principles, and **not only the quantitative aspect**: 848-852; 2687-2988; 2702; 2752; 3042;

3. **population policies** should be adapted to local needs, traditions and values, always respecting universal principles: that life-destroying means or artificial means tending to render pro-

creation impossible be excluded: 1461; see *Birth Control*; that full respect is given to parents' God-given right to determine in full responsibility the size of their own family: 1461; 2690; 2759; see *Family/;* **must not consider people as mere numbers**, or only in economic terms: 2731; they **must respect and promote the dignity** and the fundamental rights of the human person and of the family: 2731; see also: 849; 2689; **must guarantee the right to life**: see *Life/*; **the dignity and stability of the institution of the family**: 2690; and **enhance the welfare and quality of the families**: 1461; 2095; 2750; 2755; at the heart of population policies is the good, the health and well-being of the human person: 2769;

4. **growth**, more rapid than the available resources: 2682; demographic growth and development: 2712-2714; demographic growth **is not the principal cause of the problems of development**: 1712; to concentrate exclusively on demographic growth, to make it a privileged subject in campaigns on development, to channel huge resources into the solution of this one problem is to upset the perspectives and only to prepare for mankind new frustrations: 2720; 2742; 2751; **demographic variables**: 2718; 2720; 2726; **the "crisis of existence" is the true p. problem**: 2715; **it is simplistic and unreal to identify p. policy with population control**: 2769; see also: 776; 1445; 1447; 1449; 1968; 1979; 2173; 2174; 2184-2185; 2310; 2699; 2748; 2771; 2792; 2829; **irrational, unilateral campaign against population growth**: 2114; 2115; **"demographic inertia"**: 2715;

5. **temptation to put a brake on p. growth by the use of radical measures**, which are not seldom in contrast with the laws implanted by God in the human being's nature, and which fall short of due respect for the dignity of human life and the human being's liberty, based, in some cases, upon a materialistic view of the destiny of the person: 2683; 2693; see also *Birth Control;*

6. the **population problem**, which touches the sphere of life and love, **finds its solution in the exercise of a responsibility freely assumed**: 2251; 2684-2690; see also it can only be confronted within the more general perspective and overall priority of a global policy of integral human development: 2724; see also 64; 2749-2751, and *Family/, Development/;*

7. the **demographic challenge is ambivalent**, and we have to redouble our concentration on the best efforts of human solidarity and collective creativity so as to convert population growth into a formidable potential for economic, social, cultural and spiritual development: 3430;

8. see: 2679-2769; *Abortion; Birth Control; Contraception; Family/C; Sterilization.*

Power

1. **the end of every p. and every social action is the human person** and the fulfillment of human potential on all levels of family and nation: 1441;

2. **human being's thirst for p.**: 097; human being's growth in its being and not just in its possessions or its knowledge of its p.: 197; **lust for unlimited p.** 67; idolatrous images of p., riches, and sex widespread in our societies nowadays: 2589; **saving p. of the Redemption**: 2641; **arbitrary p. over life**: 2655; **p. contributed by moral and spiritual values**: 2743;

3. **no merely human p. can either command or prohibit internal acts of religion**: 104; 488;

4. p. responsibility and decision-making **cannot be the monopoly of one group or race or segment of the people**: 643; 668;

5. peace is not born from fear of the bomb or the **power of one over another**: 264; **p. of expansion of peace**: 1740;

6. science and technology are not capable of providing the **p. that would bind culture together**: 204; unlimited **powers of the sciences and of modern technology**: 3279;

7. various **systems based on ideology and on p.** have allowed flagrant injustices to persist or have created new ones: 225;

8. **temptation of resorting to violence to impose aims of p. and supremacy**: 090; thirst for p. regardless of needs of others: 81; collective evil always ready to employ material p. in the lethal conflict of man against man and nations against nation: 152; bloody struggles for p.: 176; politics of p. struggles: 261; p. of constraint: 354; ambition for p.: 897; 2547; p. of communications media: 844; 847;

9. **fearsome p. of armaments**: 933; great but frightening p. of twentieth-century human being, of either improving the world it lives in or of destroying the whole humanity: 1296; peoples fearful of their own p. to destroy themselves: 365; great distrust based on the fear of the wish to exercise p.: 380; abusive p. of arms: 645; 671; balance of p.: 977; p. of dissuasion: 978; 1105; p. of true negotiation: 1054; p. of decision: 1084; misuse or abuse of the p.: 1285; search for military p.: 1528; consolidation of the p. of some at the expenses of the legitimate needs of the majority: 1262; it is the human being, and groups and nations, that must abandon ideologies and myths of p. and supremacy: 1317;

10. **economic p.**: 1386; 2297; 2317; 2330; 2337; p. of the strong: 55; differences arising from wealth and p.: 696; inequalities of economic p.: 1651; rivalry of powers should give place to collaboration: 1393; balance of wealth and p. in favour of the already rich: 1450; uneven p.: 1455; temptations of wealth and p.: 1470; structure of p. and decision-making that must be altered: 1547; 1559; 1561; profound yearning of individuals and of nations for greater equality, for a more impartial distribution of goods and of p.: 1554; invasive p. of the large transnational corporations: 1561-1562; industrialized countries who have the p. to decide the destiny of others: 1669; 1684; need to ensure that the stronger countries do not use their p. to the detriment of the weaker ones: 1776; 1822; 2089; differences between States caused by the fact of their p.: 1873; p. connected with property rights: 1814; 1817; new relationships of inequality and oppression have been established between the nations endowed with power and those without it: 2296(5); 2306(12); p. tactics which increase the distances between the rich and the poor countries: 2397;

11. notion which assign **unlimited p. to the State**: 2970; coercive p. of governments: 3090; most powerful States: 3212; the p. of the State in a country: 3345; p. to mobilize the forces of the nation: 3418;

12. p. over nature: 3090; nature's p. of regeneration: 3112;

13. **the powerful**: 1475; the more economically powerful dominate: 1649; the powerless: 1442; 1507; 1958; 2123; 3252; faulty relations between powerful and powerless peoples: 2948; powerlessness to make truth and justice triumph: 2469;

14. **will-power**: 1521; 3110; **power-idea**: 2065; **p. of myths**: 2074; **quiet p. of an evident need**: 2128;

15. **superpowers**: 010; 1273; 1702; 1712; space powers: 3266; great powers: 361; 378; 980; 989; 1027; 1102; 1265; 1548; 1632;

16. the international community as a whole sees in the **Holy See** today a p. on whose resolute desire for good and on whose commitment all nations can rely absolutely when it is a question of defending and promoting the great causes of mankind: 057; characteristic of the p. of the Holy See: 011; 017; spiritual: 07; moral: 023; moral and spiritual: 108; has no military or economic p.: 052; no temporal p.: 5; lacking political p., but rich in a spiritual and moral influence: 059; is not a world p. nor has political p.: 1008; 1020; 1253; 1553; commits its energies to help people, not from desire for p.: 1374;

17. see also: 051; 052; 47; 67; 175; 187; 188; 200; 331; 431; 575; 620; 709; 832; 1027; 1200; 1291; 1299; 1471; 1560; 1567; 1652; 1776; 1898; 1973; 2072; 2219; 2230; 2254; 2294; 2546; 2956; 3175; 3342; 3344; 3429; *Oppression*.

Primacy

1. **of the labour of the human being** over the other elements of economic life: 39; **of the human factor over the product of work**: 45; of human work over the means of production, of the individual at work over production requirements of purely economic laws: 230;

2. **of the spirit**: 183; 189; 197; **given to spiritual values**: 78; **to the latest fashion in behaviour** instead of the truth: 170; **of the cultural realities of** the human being, communities, peoples and nations: 174; **of the person over things** and superiority of the spirit over matter: 185; 210; 226; 1257; **of the human being** as the criterion for our judgments and decisions: 240; 1721; p., uniqueness of the human being, which collective interest should not harm in any way: 925; in the international life, **p. must be given to what is moral**, to what springs from the full truth concerning the human being: 1777; culture cannot find its value and its radiance except in always assigning **p. to the integral development of the human person**: 2498; **of human life**: 3012;

3. p. **of the family** in the whole process of educating a person: 172; in the task of education: 175; **of ethics** in all the spheres of science: 186;

4. see also: 860; 1851; 2162; 2188; *Ethics/1; Person/1.*

Progress

1. **always requires an assessment and a value judgement**: one must ask whether a given p. is sufficiently "human" and at the same time sufficiently "universal"; whether it helps to level out unjust inequalities and to promote peaceful future for the world;...: 224;

2. **the p. of humanity must be measured** not only by the p. of science and technology, which shows the uniqueness of the human being with regard to nature, but also and **chiefly by the primacy given to spiritual values and by the p. of moral life**: 78; **genuine p. is to be found in the development of moral consciousness**, which will lead the human being to exercise a wider solidarity and to open itself freely to others and to God: 2526; concerted p. **towards more truth and brotherhood**: 757; **of human solidarity** in the common struggle against hunger and for development: 2134;

3. **for an authentic p. not only technicians are necessary** in ever greater number, **but also deep thinkers**, seeking after a new humanism where the human being will be allowed to discover itself by assuming the superior values of love, friendship, prayer and contemplation: 3146;

4. **p. by each of the members of the great human family will be to the advantage of p. by all** and will serve to give a more solid foundation to peace: 1003; peace, p. and liberty are indivisible and common to all: 1527;

5. **scientific and technological** p. should find new ways to make it possible for increasing numbers of people not simply to survive, but to live together in dignity, in social unity, harmony and in peace: 2751;

6. the key to unlocking the door towards progress is the **political will** that only those responsible in their respective nations can bring about: 1289;

7. the very **excesses of p.** lead human beings, and significantly the young, to recognize that their power over nature must be exercised in accordance with ethical demands: 3098;

8. there can be **no p. towards the complete development of the human being** without the simultaneous development of all humanity in a spirit of solidarity: 1419;

9. which is **measured and recognized** first and foremost on a quantitative basis: 850;

10. **agriculture**: 201; 2006; 2069; constant p. made in the development of **new systems of weapons**: 3348; **in broadcasting by satellite**: 847; **civil and social**: 456; **civilization**: 1957; poor countries, **social and human** p.: 2053; **cultural**, closely connected with the construction of a more just and more fraternal world: 759; 731; **disarmament/peace**: 973; 990; 1064; 1160; 1258; 1259; 1268; 1273; 1274; 1286; 1338; in the field of **ecology**: 274; the finest technical achievements and **the greatest economic p.** cannot effect by themselves the development of a people: 65; **economic p. does not automatically assure human and social p.**: 1622; see also: 238; 1120; 1704; economic, **of the developing nations**: 3432; **economic and social**: 29; 1912; 1930; p. **in education, cultural exchange and international assistance**, thanks to artificial satellites: 3201; 3205; educational planning: 927; **harmonious** p.: 025; **human and cultural**: 2381; **total p. of each individual**: 196; real p. **of the whole human person**: 2587; see also 195; 208; 1373; 2616; **human being's moral p.**: 723; **genuine human p.**: 233; see also: 275; 973; 1719; 1895; 2781; important p. **in the domain of the protection of human rights**: 353; 894; of the **human society**: 26; **industrial**: 45; 1693; 1694; 1700; 1702; along the path of **international economic justice**: 2278; 3419; p. in disinterested **knowledge**: 181; of knowledge: 868; **moral p. of humanity**: 79; **true p. of humanity**: 200; **material and spiritual**, 2007, **complete**, 884, **integral**, 942, p. **of mankind**: 213; of the entire human family: 882; aimed at the integral betterment of mankind: 762; **spiritual p. of the whole human race**: 3137; **material**: 1372; 2393; 2750; 2831; 3094; the most extraordinary scientific p., the most astounding technical feats and the most amazing economic growth, **unless accompanied by authentic moral and social progress, will in the long run go against the human being**: 62; see also: 383; 2689; **autonomous p. of each nation**: 836; nations, in their constant search for more just and more humane conditions of life: 2509; **towards a more just and more humane society**: 2520; **civilization**: 752; **international community**: 0103; **peace or the survival of the human race is henceforth linked indissolubly with p.**, development and dignity for all people: 206; 209; **religious**: 2443; **rural population**: 2119; 2073; 2122; assumption that scientific and technical p. would automatically bring moral and human p.: 391; at **the service of arms race**: 977; see also: 068; 64; 337; 351; 910; 1260; 1523; 3095; social, of men and women: 142; **social**, without which there is no true development: 60; social: 021; 024; 364; 1101; 2694; society: 41; 2088; 2464; **literacy source of p.** for the individual and for society; privileged instrument of economic p. for society: 770; see also: 771; 782; 789; 793; 805; 813; 819; 828; p. made in the action against illiteracy: 795; 798; **socio-economic**: 176; **space technology**: 3205; 3207; 3209; 3215; 3234; 3261; 3280; 3283; 3308; **spiritual and material p. of all**: 845; **spiritual p. does not stem for material p.** as the effect from its cause: 338; see also 2778; technical p. alone is very far from wiping out all disparities: 2590; **technical** p. in the field of nuclear energy: 094; **technical, one-sided p. towards goals of war**: 79; technical: 682; 689; 832; 1539; 1650; 2001; 2101; 2244; 2345; 2358; technological and social: 2851; **women p. in general education**: 2544; see also: 2564; 2566; 2573; 2609;

11. **the Church is ready to acclaim the p.** that science and technology have already attained, **so long as this p. truly serves the good of the inhabitants of the earth** and does not deprive anyone of the just fruits of its advances and growth; She does, however, **insist that all true p. in science and technology be put at the disposal of people without prejudice or discrimination**, and that the value of truth and honesty, equity and fraternity, spirit and religion be advanced by these many forms of p.: 1433; care for human p.: 1837; see also: 2543; 3390;

12. see also: 11; 33; 53; 98; 149; 170; 223; 254; 277; 293; 382; 547; 549; 555; 680; 706; 744; 885; 891; 930; 1315; 1319; 1323; 1328; 1357; 1362; 1364; 1397; 1402; 1422; 1439; 1484; 1493; 1494; 1515; 1593; 1610; 1651; 1684; 1703; 1710; 1714; 1718; 1720; 1724; 1732; 1748; 1779; 1782; 1784; 1828; 1829; 1836; 1839; 1946; 2044; 2047; 2073; 2076; 2081; 2095; 2100; 2140; 2158; 2159; 2375; 2504; 2556; 2580; 2640; 2656; 2669; 2713; 2715; 2991; 3059; 3199; 3211; 3412; 3438; *Advancement; Development; Growth; Science; Scientist; Technology.*

Propriety/Ownership

right: 89; 636; 1119; **respect** for personal p.: 1704; **the right to ownership of land always involves a social mortgage**: 1770; the right to private p. is **subordinated to that of common use, to the universal destination of goods**: 3223; 1749; 1803-1811; 1814; 1817-1819; 1896. See also: 1459; 1460; 1746; 1955; 2072; 2109; 2815; 3109; 3281.

Racism see *Apartheid, Brotherhood; Discrimination/2; Equality; Person; Rights.*

Reaction

of the **workers** to injustices: 225; passionate reactions **against religious intolerance**: 538; **of those who claim the right to self-determination and independence**: 645; **fostered by** relationships of dependence and exploitation: 1100; **against the use of space for military purposes**: 3215. See also: 844; 1525; 2060; 2396; 2670; 2673; 3100; 3342.

Redemption

in the Redemption effected by Jesus Christ the Church sees **a further basis of the rights and duties of the human person**: 651; Jesus' saving power of r. **embraces the human person** in its individuality and totality: 2641; **human being's thirst for r.** and immortality: 209; **over sin** there is victory: the r.; there is a victor: Christ the Redeemer: 3149.

Reduction

1. erroneous r. **of religion to the purely private sphere**: 458;

2. **r. of armaments**: 25; 955; 1002; 1045; 1054-1055; 1063; 1163; 1170; 1176; 1178; 1201; 1239; 1286; 1465; 3386; of the **expenses for armaments**: 1582; of military budgets: 2114;

3. **of food resources**, as a consequence of a nuclear war: 1193; gradual r. **of under-development**: 1531; **in imports**: 1681; of the area **of cultivated land**: 2190; **of excessive consumption** in certain countries: 2192; constant r. **in food aid**: 2193; drastic reduction **in the standard of living**: 2264; **in public spending**: 2311; rescheduling of debts and a r. **of the sums due** in one or even more years: 2339; **of poverty**: 3265; **of the high unemployment** index: 3423;

4. **of mortality among mothers and infants**: 2575; r. **of the birth rate**, of fertility: 2720; **in governmental budgets for public health**: 3006.

Reform

1. effective reforms **presuppose good will** and a fundamental change of attitude on the part of everybody: 1786;

2. structural r. of the world **financial system**, one of the most urgent and necessary initiatives: 1423; of the international monetary system: 1536; 1538; of relationships of exchange and mechanisms of finance: 2270; financial and monetary institutions: 2284; of the tax system: 2311;

3. **land r.**: 1452; 1744-1762; agrarian r. and rural development: 1763-1829; 2118; 2311; vital role in the eradication of hunger and poverty: 1746; imperative: 1751; demand that consideration be given to reforms **aimed at reducing the gap** between the prosperity of the rich and the anxiety and need of the poor: 1774; 1776; 1815; **income policy** r.: 1819;

4. **in the trade** of agricultural products: 1531; of commercial customs: 1533; of international trade relations: 1540; long-term r. of policies and attitudes: 1536;

5. r. in **domestic structures**: 1463; of **economic relationships** and systems at the worldwide level: 2159; **structural**: 1806; 2244; **institutional** r.: 2308; institutional and structural: 2714; **of the society**: 2396.

Refugees

1. **flow** of r.: is daily increasing in most parts of the world, as a consequence of wars, revolutions, the denial of human rights, the persecution of minorities, the uncertainty about the future: 386;

2. it is really **a disgraceful scourge of our times** the way so many countries and governments are no longer capable of granting a just freedom and a decent living to all their citizens: 2866;

3. it must be said that we are dealing with abnormal situations which must be cured at their source by seeking to convince nations that **r. have a right to freedom and to a dignified human life in their own country**; it is also necessary to make an ever wider appeal for hospitality and welcome on the part of those countries which can take in r.; it is necessary to organize international mutual assistance: 2872;

4. r. **child**: 2389; 2882-2893; **Palestinian** r.: 1154; assistance to the **r. in Africa**: 2875-2881; 2931-2938; r. **of South East Asia**: 2914- 2930;

5. the **Holy See urges** that the human rights of r., as well as their families, be recognized and adequately protected: 2766; 2897; 2925; 2934; **concern for and activity in favor of** r.: 2852-2854; 2870-2871; 2873; 2891; 2896; 2923; 2936-2937;

6. see also: 291; 1483; 1926; 2438; 2566; 2567; 2596; 2606; 2848-2874; 2894-2913; 3435; *Minorities/1; Migrants; Society/6; Solidarity/12; Training/2.*

Relation/Relationship

1. **human being's r. with God**: 101; 221; 500; 512; 515; 525; 533; 2502; 2526; 2810; **inner r. with truth**: 101; with culture; with its possessions:156; with technology: 239; with nature: 775; **human rights** concern human being's r. with others: 89; direct r. between human rights and peace: 417; see also 478;

2. **production r.** is not the basic, decisive key to the understanding of the historic quality of the human being and its culture: 157; **r. between culture and Christianity**: 160; between the Church and culture: 762; fundamental importance of education in developing **human and social interrelationships**: 165;

3. **human r.**: 2623; 2658; 3095; interpersonal: 2532; 2583; 2623; family: 2475; 2627; between men and women: 849; 2530; 2559; 2605; 2698; the child, test of the r. of one human being to another: 107; 2738; between the individual and the community: 3069; social: 2529; 2837; 2889; 3001; r. of political activity with the human being: 76; **social r.**, conceived not in terms of uncompromising opposition between classes, but in terms of solidarity: 226-233;

4. **r. between nations** must be regulated by reason, justice, law and negotiation, and not by force, violence, war, nor indeed by fear and deceit: 13; reflexes of suspicion and aggression, detrimental to r. between nations: 251; courage to undertake a revision of the r. between nations: 1391; **need to substitute r. based on force with r. of deep understanding**, mutual respect and creative collaboration: 334; r. motivated by reciprocal collaboration and by constructive sincerity: 632; r. **based upon the fear of mutual distraction**: 1105; **upon a new balance of cooperation and trust**: 1108; the principle of balance, political or military, in the r. between States: 3380; moral duties deriving from the r. between States: 2187; r. **between disarmament and development**: 1061; see *Disarmament/7*;

5. **r. between peoples or race**, inacceptability of the system of apartheid: 260; people's mutual r., on the basis of truth, justice and love: 992; 2157; 2169; 2226; mutual trust and peaceful cooperation: 1221; requirements of moral law in r. between peoples and States: 3342;

6. r. between the **Great Powers**: 378; 989; **East and West**: 1095; 1173; 2809; **North and South**: 1173; 2215; 2297(6); between different countries in Southern Africa: 658;

7. **international r.**: affected by injustice: 87; international r. and human rights: 95; 97; exigencies of justice, peace and promotion of common good in the international r.: 248; ways in which the judicial element can play a wider role in international r.: 255; see also: 258; violence and criminal behaviour: 266; efforts to improve its atmosphere: 989; 1265; regulated by a system of law: 1187; based upon mutual respect, trust and collaboration: 1317; 2303; 3334; restructuring of international r.: 2946; international r. at the mercy of capricious despotism: 2970; tension grow in international r.: 3361; threat or use of force in the international r. among States: 1225

8. **bilateral r.** must be increasingly replaced by a multilateral system, in the fields of international assistance and investments: 135; **direct r.**, that would make highly developed countries weigh on weaker and more exposed countries: 2089; **multilateral r.** guaranteed by Intergovernmental Organizations: 2095; **between developing and developed countries**: 1383; 1525; 1543; 1663/5; 3390; equity in trade r.: 1519; see also: 1540; 1596; 1604; 1605; 1651; need for a more equitable system of **international economic r.**: 1662; 1664; 1675; 1696; 1799; 1878; 1896; an ethic of expanded solidarity will help to transform economic r. (commercial, financial and monetary) into r. of justice: 2296; **justice in r. between peoples**: 3346; 3376; new r. on inequality and oppression have been established between nations endowed with power and those without it: 2296(5); 2306(12); a new r., the social solidarity of all: 3419; in order to have peace among nations justice must preside over their economic r.: 1100; 2295;

9. **r. of dependence and exploitation** foster frustrations and reactions which are at the root of many wars of liberation or of internal revolts: 110; new r. of dependence created by indebtedness: 356;

10. r. between individuals and peoples **to material and intellectual goods**: 1636; faulty r. **between powerful and powerless peoples**: 2948; r. between **workers and employers**: 328; reciprocal r. between the creation of jobs and economic development: 3424; r. between landowner and farmer: 1746; the worker of the land and the land that he works: 1772; 1812;

11. between **science and armaments**: 1181; **science and the fight against hunger**: 2198; between **demographic growth, development, resources and environment**: 2712; 2713; 2717; 2720; 2734; 2742; between **prolongation of life and birth-rate**: 2705;

12. **of the human being with its environment**: 3098; between development and environment: 3104; 3110; see also 279; ecologic inter-r. between water and the human being: 3140;

13. between the human being and those institutions of the State whose task it is to guarantee its protection: 3088;

14. United Nations: **a network of r. between States**: 16;

RELIGIOUS FREEDOM see *Freedom/2.*

Resources

1. **universal destination of r.**: 913; 1767; 1805; 1895; 3197; 3226; 3307; the totality of r. of the world must be exploited so that all humanity is the beneficiary: 1505; a universal use of r. must be understood as a primary right before any particular appropriation: 1895; 1896; **primary destination of the resources of the earth to the common good** demands that the necessities of life be provided for all human beings before individuals or groups appropriate for themselves the riches of nature or the products of human skill: 2167; sea r. common patrimony for the whole humanity: 1895; 3167; 3188; sea and subsoil: 3169; environment r. are for everyone; they are the inalienable property of everyone: 3109; of earth and outer space: 3224; of space for the benefit of mankind: 3257; 3272; 3310;

2. **use and management**: 193; 1468; 1480; 1610; 1946; 1957; 2026; 2107; 2201; 2224; 2304; 3129; 3418; use for the development/advancement of peoples: 098; 201; 202; 274; 1001; 1061; 1175; 1566; 1598; 1667; 3205; for the personal welfare: 30; 176; 1692; 2555; 3143; for the common good: 176; 2125; 3182; 3272;

3. **equitable/fair sharing/distribution**: 206; 423; 1097; 1407; 2026; 2107; 2175; 2244; 2284; 2297; 2691; 3129; 3171; 3186; 3307; 3313;

4. there are the possibilities of creating both **food and energy r. for a population much greater** than that which the most reliable calculations lead us to predict: 2716;

5. **human r.**: 66; 69; 1375; 1415; 1480; 1520; 1528; 1566; 1681; 1722; 1725; 1835; 2077; 2250; 2304; 2478; 2531;

6. **natural r.**: 193; 227; 230; 274; 277; 278; 423; 889; 913; 1340; 1389; 1434; 1658; 1706; 1757; 1767; 1805; 1831; 1992; 2294; 2304; 2742; 3096; 3143; 3178; 3182; 3186; 3257; 3291; 3292; 3297; 3298/2,3,; 3299,2,3,6; **fishery**/marine/sea: 1895; 1896; 1899; 1904; 1906; 1907; 1957; 3209; 3231; 3299/3; water: 1953; 3134; 3152; 3231; **land**/sea: 337; 1954; 2078; earth: 1600; 1610; 2167; 2244; 2691; 3224; 3300/4; 3307; **earth**/space: 3224; 3225; **space**: 3205; energy: 1413; 1480; 1505; 2304; 2716; **of nuclear energy**: 997; 1061; 1175; 1261; 1262; 1275; 1351;

7. **hidden r. of the universe**: 832; of the planet/world: 1468; 1539; 1505; 2108; 2555; 3330; **available r.**: 1689; 1713; 1724; 1761; 1772; 1861; 2207; 2682; 2716; limited r.: 1629; 1866; 2975; 3124; 3182; 3393;

8. **economic**: 202; 1175; 1523; 1553; 2609; **food** r.: 193; 1193; 1217; 1851; 1852; 1855; 3306; **financial**: 1628; 1861; 2285; 2290; 2994;

9. see: Goods; *Nature; Riches; Sea; Space.*

Responsibility

1. **of the family in education**: 175; 840; of **science and technology**: 194; 195; **of scientist towards society and humanity**: 200; 3328;

2. in regard to the many problems inherent in the reality of **human work**: 212; of the worker for defending the truth, the true dignity of its work: 232;

3. serious r. **to exercise dominion over creation** in such a way that it truly serves the human family: 274;

4. of those materially favoured **towards the more needy**: 319; moral r. of people today **concerning the situations of inequality**: 96;

5. of the **great powers**: 361; moral r. **of those who control the media of information** and communication: 844; 2254; common r. **vis-a-vis the challenges of the future**: 878;

6. for the **respect of human rights**: 304; **for religious freedom**: 490; **for action against illiteracy**: 776; 789; for **the destiny of the nations**: 963; **of mankind**: 1005;

7. **for nuclear disarmament**: 997; for the non proliferation of nuclear weapons: 1247; 1257; 1258; 1268; 1277; for the **peaceful use of nuclear energy**: 1283; 1287; 1292; 1309; 1326; 1344; 1359; **in regard to the ethical causes of the insecurity**: 1067; 1277; 1332; **for peace**: 1073; 1075; 1144; 1183; 1239; 1334; 3401; every government's r. **of ensuring the defence of its country**: 1201;

8. of the international community **in the question of Palestine**: 1150;

9. in matters related to **development**: 1386; 1405; 1410; 1422; 1432; 1455; 1470; 1481; 1482; 1508; 1527; 1529; 1547; 1555; 1558; 1559; 1566; 1570; 1572; 1573; 1600; 1610; 1618; 1620; 1635; 1636; 1644; 1682; 1687; 1692; 1719; 1720; 1751; 1784; 2133; 2142; 2169; 2251; 2742; 2750; 3152; 3175; 3418; 3426; in facing the **food problem**: 1786; 1921; 1953; 1957; 1978; 2045; 2062; 2064; 2078; 2122; 2128; 2150; 2163; 2244; 2252; in relation with the **debt question**: 2272; 2280; 2281-2283; 2288; 2290-2292; 2295; 2297-2298; 2303-2305; 2307; 2309; 2311; 2319-2320; 2327; 2330; 2332; 2334; 2338; 2339-2340;

10. common r. **towards children**: 2387; towards **young people**: 2393; **of young people**: 2428; 2475; of the members of the **family**: 2488; for the members of the family: 2489; of women: 2505; 2520; 2533; 2534; 2539; 2545; 2548; 2582; 2600; 2604; 2638; of **married couples/parents**: 1461; 2251; 2684; 2686; 2690; 2739; 2759; 2762; 2763; 2765; 3041; 3042; 3083; 3131; of **States** and of the world community with regard to population question: 2715; 2718; 2731; **towards refugees**: 2915;

11. of States and individuals as regards **environment**: 3109; in the **exploration and use of space**: 3222; 3250; 3300/20;

12. the **Catholic Church** will not remain indifferent to r. towards the unity of the human family: 418; it appeals to the r. of the international community when acts of religious intolerance are due to governments: 543; r. vis-a-vis the human beings: 764; see also: 01; 030; 411; 1241; 1253-1254; 1398; 1399; 1550; 1641; 1679; 2037; 2087; 2267; 2269; 3196; 3390; of Christians in whatever sectors they work: 764;

13. see also: 027; 030; 0107; 69; 182; 185; 231; 255; 280; 286; 330; 341; 352; 411; 476; 488; 643; 661; 668; 757; 947; 992; 1133; 1144; 1860; 2669; 2676; 2976; 3097; 3100; 3133; 3369; *Obligation*.

Rich

1. r. **countries** buying at the lowest possible prices the produce of poor countries, and selling their own produce to these poor countries at a very high price: 67; it is necessary to question the models of growth of the r. **nations**: 1391; duty of the r. countries to give aid to the poorer ones: 1706; there are countries r. in cultural and other spiritual and human resources, which are among the poorest economically: 1415; political decolonization has not yet altered the overwhelming **balance of wealth and power in favour of the already r.**: 1450;

2. according to social justice, all the **goods of the rich** must contribute to the common good in a community henceforth universal: 1509; commercial exchange, economic systems where the rich get richer and the poor always poorer: 1566; 1740; 2051; 2397; among the evils of the r. countries the worst are clearly inflationary pressures and uncertainties over the balance of payments: 1581; 1583;

3. the **people richest in resources**, technology and human energies must take into consideration not only the needs of their own country, but also those of others: 2090; eighty-seven percent of the energy used in the world today is consumed by the rich countries and only thirteen percent by the rest of the world: 2716;

4. see also: 56; 681; 777; 778; 1445; 1446; 1451; 1453; 1508; 1548; 1583; 1590; 1628; 1629; 1631; 1845; 2084; 2085; 2112; 2169; 2218; 3167; 3229; 3284; 3285; Poor.

Riches

1. there are no true r. but the **r. of human being**: 45; see also: 75; 120; 161; 764; 795; 869; 2211;

2. the **exploitation of the r. of nature** must take place according to criteria that take into account not only the immediate needs of the people but also the needs of future generations: 274; the r. **of earth**: 144; through the good will of all, the r. of this world **must serve the true benefit of all**, as they have been put by the Creator at the disposal of the whole of mankind: 1388; 3172; 3174; of nature: 1719; lack of availability and exploitation of the immense r. concealed in nature and intended for common use: 2150; 2167; wider and more immediate redistribution of r. and of control over them: 1619; 2691; 3119; it is necessary to secure for the populations that are suffering from malnutrition actual access to the various riches of nature, in the subsoil, in the sea and on the earth: 2152; 2167; within a country all should benefit from a fair sharing of the nation's r.: 643; material r. exist so that people can have food, clothing, housing, education, and so that assisting one another and developing their solidarity they may build truly fraternal communities which experience true joy in living: 1600; **material riches exist so that people can have food**, clothing, housing, education, and so that by assisting one another and developing their solidarity they may build truly fraternal communities which experience true joy in living: 1600; 1843; 2785; 2845;

3. control of the mass media by a limited segment of society in search of r.: 1387;

4. **cultural** r.: 707; value and r. of every culture: 2961; 3273; **spiritual** r.: 1734; spiritual and moral: 2522; r. **of moral dignity**, of wisdom and culture peculiar to each people: 2530; human r. **of a healthy and well-balanced family**: 2566; peculiar r. and dynamism of men and women: 2591;

5. see also: 1473; 1610; 1682; 1938; 1939; 1990; 2589; Resources.

Rights (Human Rights)

1. flow directly from and are inherent to the human being's dignity and therefore **universal, inviolable and inalienable**, 39; 64; 71; 79; 86; 88-89; 127; 219; 329; 335; 347; 349; 408; 411; 426; 431; 449 (see 447-450); 465-466; 477-478; 484; 510-513; 515; 525; 571; 592; 637; 1066; 1096; 2212; 2512; 2745; 2757; 2942; 3004; see also: *Dignity/1; Person/1*; **antecedent to their recognition**, 3069; entitled to obligatory protection by the State, 2970; a **common good for all human beings**, 414; 436; see also: Good; not to be subjugated to political interest, 81; see also: *Interest/2*; **indissolubly linked together**, 608; 825; **linked to duties**, 090; 27; 39; 224; 231; 426; 708; 802; 821; 824; 827; 841-842 1097; 1882; 2148; 2504; 2512; 2520; 2580; 2676; 3069. See also: *Duties/1*; **would require the establishment of a world authority**, endowed with effective power, 090; 16; 101; 349; 3175; 3344; see also: *Authority/1*;

2. **Catholic Church**: in every domain of human action **always claims respect for the inviolable rights of the human person**, 64; 546; **can never dissociate herself from the rights of man**, created in the image and likeness of his Creator, 302; 424; **feels injured** when the rights of a person, whoever it may be, and wherever it may be, are ignored and violated, 302; 424; **desires to cooperate** with all people of good will to build a world where every person no matter of what race, religion, or nationality, can live a fully human life where freedom is not an empty word, 414; **insists that** juridical norms be inspired by the principle of respect for human rights and by promotion and preservation of these same rights, 418; **has a deep concern for** the dignity and rights of every nation, 502;

3. **Holy See**: **is aware that its first and fundamental duty is to protect and vigorously promote the rights of believers to religious freedom**, and the respect for fundamental rights of the human person and individual conscience, 072; **has a constant interest and solicitude** for fundamental h.r., 438; 507-510; 520; 533; **wants to make an honest contribution** to building a community of life which guarantees to individuals and to groups everywhere the right to life, to personal and social dignity, do development, to a just sharing of natural wealth an the advantages of civilization, 628; **cannot**, without grave danger to society, **resign itself** to the infliction of so many wounds upon

these rights today, in several countries, despite so many eloquent proclamations, 302; 423; 432; **meets** with the United Nations in the field of the defence of h.r., the rights of human groups, and particularly of ethnical minorities, 302; **gives full moral support** to the common ideal contained in the Universal Declaration of Human Rights, 425; **wishes** that the UN may be "par excellence" the expression and the rampart of the h.r. it has so solemnly proclaimed, 310; **ready to continue to offer the UN its loyal collaboration in whatever serves the defence of h.r.**, 322; 347; 416; 443; **expresses great confidence and firm approval** of the continuing commitment of the UN to promote, in an ever clearer, more effective manner, respect for the fundamental h.r., 421; 439, and 296.

4. **United Nations: proclaims the basic rights and duties** of the human person, 27; 93; 416; the **Secretary General** is the guarantor in a way, before the whole of mankind, of the respect for h.r., 303;

5. **r. of the peoples**: to **self-determination** and **independence**, 257; 432; 1099. See *Autonomy/2;* Self-determination/1, *Independence/4; see also: 137; 256; 423; 622; 644; 645; 925; 1617; 1766; 3346; and Development/2;* ***of the nation****, see Nation/1,2;* **of minority groups**, 302; 423; 546; 622; 647; and *Minorities/1*; **of the child**: see *Child/1,2*; **of the women**: see *Women/1*; **of the family**: see *Education/10,11*; Family/C,2,3,8; **of the aging**: see *Aging*; ***of the Disabled Persons****: see Disabled Persons/1,2;* **of the migrant**: see *Migrants/1,5*; **of the refugees**: see *Refugees/1,3,5;*

6. **fundamental H.R.**: **spiritual**: 101; 188; 641; 1066; **economic, social, cultural**: 128; 188; 925; 1390; 1887; **political**: 89; 445; 925; 1099; 1887; **r. to be born**, **r. to responsible procreation**, 445; **r. to life, liberty, and security of person**, 79;89; 257; 423; 445; 628; 647; 849; 1758; 2655; 2760; 2925; 3004; 3023; **r. to personal and social dignity**, 423; 628; **r. to food, clothing, housing, sufficient health care, rest and leisure**, 89; 257; see also *Food, Hunger/1, Nourishment/1,2; Habitat/1; Health/1*; **r. to education and culture**, 89; 708; 781; 790; 822; 893. See also *Culture/4, Education/7,* ***r. to choose a state of life, to found a family*** *and to enjoy all conditions necessary for family life, 89; 669; 2730; 2759; see also Marriage/1*; **r. to property and work, to adequate working conditions and a just wage**, 89; 445; 1706; see also *Property, Work/2*; **r. to freedom**, see *Freedom/1*; of **thought, conscience and religion**: see *Freedom/2*; of **expression**, 89; of **information**: see *Communication/1,5; Information/1*; of **assembly and association**: see *Association/1,5*; of **movement**, to internal and external **migration**, 89; 622; 2767; **r. to nationality and residence**, 89; **r. to political participation and to participate in the free choice of the national political system**, 89; 445; **r. to protection by the law**, 257; **r. to material well-being**, 41; 1693; **r. to peace**, 445; 827; **r. to development**: see *Development/2*; **r. to an equitable division of nature's resources and the fruits of civilization**, 423; 628 and 257; 1706.

7. **recognition**: constitute the criteria which the development of an international system of law must satisfy, 257 and 311; is the foundation of freedom, justice and peace in the world, 347; see also: 79; 335; 349; 415; 615; 644; 991; 2588.

8. **respect**: underlies everything, 151; universal duty, 426 and 52; 258; 413; 426; 431; 436; 459; 708; 827; is more than esteem and mutual tolerance; it implies a positive affirmation that these rights exist, a total commitment not to infringe them, every effort to promote and extend them, 861; see 860-867; requires a political will of the States, 308; the cooperation of everyone, 431; 518; see also, 072; 79; 102; 108; 112; 131; 137; 188; 224; 241-242; 329; 349; 546; 719; 816; 863; 872; 894; 991; 1598; 1721; 2110; 2354; 2423; 2588; 2945; 3009;

9. **defence, protection**: 024; 302; 322; 329; 349; 353; 359; 647; 2588.

10. **promotion**: is the path towards peace, 418 and 426; does not constitute interference in the internal affairs of States, 428; 518; see also: 427; 508; 611; 752; 2393; 2588; 2945.

11 **threats**: do violence to the human person, 152; endanger peace, 90; 500; are linked in an overall sense with the unjust distribution of material goods, 96; see 94-99); and with various forms of injustice in the field of the spirit, 100-106;

12. **violation**: due to the fact that in our world today there is no programme that puts human being first, 592; constitute a great injustice, 383; are a form of warfare against humanity, 94; cause of tensions and disturbances even in the international sphere, 86-88; 426; see also: 80; 101; 360; 384; 386; 393; 410; 411; 413; 417; 431-433; 444-446; 518; 592; 601; 622; 826; 893-894; 1066; 2528; 2554; 2761.

13. **International juridical instruments of protection of h.r.**: are endeavouring to create general awareness of the dignity of the human being, and to define at least some of its inalienable rights, 89; see: 81; 256; 263; 334-335; 359; 435; 551; 571; 575; 591; 2640;

Universal Declaration of: indicates a course that cannot be abandoned if mankind sincerely wishes to achieve peace, 417; 422; was paid for by millions of people at the cost of their suffering and sacrifice, 81; is a milestone on the long ad difficult path of the moral progress of humanity, 78-79; 383; the basic inspiration and the cornerstone of the UN, 81; remains one of the UN greatest claims to fame, 335; 422; must remain the basic value in the UN with which the consciences of its members must be confronted and from which they must draw continual inspiration, 81; must not be subjugated to political interest, 81; has struck a real blow against the many deep roots of war, 86; marked an important step towards the establishment of a juridico-political organization of the world community, 407; remains the expression of a more mature and more definite awareness of the question of the rights of the human person, 429; not to be reduced to an empty recognition of values or to an abstract doctrinal principle without a concrete and increasingly coherent application in the contemporary world, 430; is an ideal for the human community, 416; see also: 114; 128; 151; 153; 347; 359; 386; 406; 408; 417; 419; 421; 435; 438; 479; 507; 584; 589; 598; 608; 708; 925; 1098; 1417; 2248; 2519; 2524; 2554; 2708; 2709; 2736; 2917; 2946; 2954; 3048.

International Covenant on Economic, Social and Cultural Rights: mark a significant step forward in making effective one of the basic principles which it has adopted as its own from the very foundation of the organization: namely, to establish juridically binding means for promoting the h.r. of individuals and for protecting their fundamental liberties, 441; see also: 18; 128; 479; 925; 2917;

14. **h.r. and peace**: see *Peace/1,3,7,15*; **h.r. and development**: see *Development/4,9*; **equality of r.**: see *Equality/2*;

15. see 021; 068; 097; 11; 55; 84; **86-106**; 123; 127-129; 143; 172; 174; 177; 223; 225; 227; 232; 241; 247; 252; 259; 267; 296; 315; 352; 364; **406-674**; 698; 709; 724; 737; 757; 763; 788; 801; 805; 818; 835; 839; 846-847; 878; 903-905; 911; 931; 969; 975; 1008; 1115; 1119-1120; 1132; 1137; 1152; 1154; 1239; 1262; 1435; 1442; 1461; 1557; 1582; 1589; 1591; 1593; 1644; 1653; 1657; 1675; 1682; 1686; 1705; 1736; 1769; 1770; 1772-1773; 1803-1804; 1817; 1835; 1878; 1895-1896; 1946; 2109; 2116; 2120; 2158; 2177; 2221; 2230; 2246; 2251; 2272; 2319; 2321; 2336; 2346; 2347-2349; 2359; 2398; 2365; 2369; 2374; 2379; 2381; 2393; 2476; 2479; 2480; 2489; 2513; 2528; 2565; 2627; 2638; 2646; 2648; 2649; 2650; 2659-2660; 2666-2669; 2671; 2674; 2677; 2698; 2720; 2731; 2739; 2761; 2763; 2766; 2775; 2812; 2815; 2824; 2837; 2839; 2841; 2851; 2855; 2872; 2878-2879; 2897-2898; 2903-2904; 2910; 2912; 2927; 2933-2934; 2940; 2947; 2953-2958; 2960-2961; 2965; 2967; 2970; 3016; 3043; 3051; 3055; 3081; 3088; 3090-3092; 3131; 3143; 3173; 3178; 3191; 3121; 3223; 3233; 3257; 3299/9; 3391; 3398; 3435; 3439; *Affirmation; Apartheid/1; Aspiration/2; Asylum/2; Attack/1; Attention/1,4; Auschwitz; Authority; Awareness/1,9; Believers/1; Benefit/2; Civilization/1; Collaboration/2; Complementarity; Commitment/2; Community/D,1; E/1,4,5; Conflicts; Conscience/2,7; Crime; Defence/1,2; Discrimination/1; Educators/4; Faith/2,4,12; Force/2; Gap; Goods; Growth; Humanity/10; ILO/4; Industrialization/1; Justice/1; Instruction; Interest/4; Inviolability; Law/4; Life/1,2,3,6; Love/2,5; Middle East; Namibia; Obligation/2,4; Opinion/1; Participation/3; Peoples/1,5; Person/4,14,15,19; Population/3; Power/10; Progress; Reaction; Redemption; Relation/1,7; Resources/1; Responsibility/6; Sea/4; Security/1; Selfishness; Sensing; Society/2; Solidarity/6; Sovereignty/2; State/3,5,6; Sterilization; Structures/2; Struggle/2; Tension/1,2; Trade/4; Truth/6; UNESCO/3; United Nations/5; Wealth/2; Worker/2; Youth/1.*

Sahel

1. **appeals of Pope John Paul II on behalf of all those suffering from the devastating drought**: 284-285; see also *Ouagadougou*; **relief efforts** of the Catholic Church: 2092; 3132;

2. **John Paul II Foundation for Sahel**: is a sign of the Church's love for the men, women and children who have been stricken by the continuing tragedy of drought: 284; its aim is to assist in the preparation of competent people who will place themselves at the service of their country and of their brothers, without any discrimination, in a spirit of integral and cooperative human advancement, for the battle against desertification and its causes: 1926; see also: 1487; 1715-1717.

Satisfaction

of mutual (68), essential (89; 1505), fundamental (3103), real human, basic (136), most elementary (955; 2138) **needs** (1689); of the needs **in the field of education**: 777; of the most legitimate **human aspirations**: 1502; **material** s.: 889. See also: 728; 1520; 1579; 2367; 2704; 2765;

Science

1. s. **is to be admired and encouraged in its conquests**; it is man's abuse of these conquest that is at fault: 3365; concern at everything which would turn s. into an instrument to attain goals alien to it: 181-182;

2. the **future** of the human being and of the world is **threaten because the results of the research and discoveries, particularly in the natural s.**, have been and are still being **exploited for purposes which have nothing to do with the requirements of s.**, and indeed for the purposes of destroying and killing, purposes destructive of the true dignity of the human being and of human life: 183; 1283; **for production of armaments**: 24; 184; 1059; 1180-1181; 1257; 1283-1284; **for personal gain at the expense of others and of the common good**: 1354; **nuclear s.**: 242; 1330; 1345; **space s.** 3262;

3. the **cause of mankind will be served if s. and conscience are allied**: 185; 210; when s. advances from success to success, its use places ever greater demands upon the conscience of the human being which sets it to work: 338; **appeal to respect the primacy of ethics in all the sphere of science**: 186; 1257; 3203;

4. as **instrument of life**: 28; its use for **development**: 098; at the **service of peace** and of the building of a new society: 196; for the **common good**: 3204; relationship between **s. and the fight against hunger**: 1835; 2198; 2199; 2358; the resources of s. make it possible to feed the whole human family: 3308;

5. the social and economic s. and the s. of planning could combine **to direct in a more humane and effective way the process of industrialization and urbanization**, and to promote the new models of international cooperation: 201;

6. **rational s. and the human being's religious knowledge need to be linked together**: 209; the reasons for the **condemnation of racism cannot be sought in s. alone**: 597; 613; **each s. should learn to recognize its limits**, in its own field; it cannot claim a monopoly so far as the meaning of the human being is concerned; it must respect other approaches and remain open to the possibility of a transcendent factor: 833;

7. education forms the human being, **s. provides it with means to act**, culture brings it full development: 705;

8. see also: 178; 193; 342; 830; 832; 1344; 1454; 1525; 1604; 1684; 2626; 2674; 3052; and *Scientists.*

and technology:

9. show the human being's uniqueness with regard to nature, but **cannot be the only criterion to measure the progress of humanity**: 78; are a **wonderful product of God-given creativity**, since they have provided us with wonderful possibilities, and we all gratefully benefit from them: 195; **have always formed part of the human being's culture**, but today we are witnessing the speedily increasing growth of a technology which seems to have destroyed its equilibrium with the dimensions of culture by acting as an element of division: 204;

10. are **the most dynamic factors of the development of society today**: 204; are indispensable elements for any development: 1430; 1429-1441; 1830-1840; find their justification in the **service that they render** to the human being and to humanity: 206; 885; their resources **could be more effectively used** for the development and growth of peoples: 201;

11. research and t. must always be at the service of the human being; in our days, the **use and misuse of s. and t.** for other purposes is a too well known fact; a significant percentage of the research currently expended in the field of arms t. and s. should be directed towards life and the welfare of the human being: 1059; **ambivalence**, potential for good or for evil results (1432; 1838), **depending upon the use to which they are put**: 1838; care must be taken that they are used to enhance human life and not do diminish it: 3171; see also: 30; 977; 1058-1060; 1180; 3356; responsibility: 194; 195;

12. **powerful aid in freeing human beings** so that they are ever more authentic bearers of their culture: 1441; our t., our s., our communications all **thrust us towards a steadily increasing interdependence**: 1454;

13. sharing, **transfer of**: 1407; 1436; 1439; **cooperation** in the fields of s. and t. is one of the most effective means not only of contributing to the physical welfare of peoples but also of fostering the dignity and worth of every person: 1844; **for the benefit of the less developed regions**: 1993; 2090;

14. **progress of**: 275; 351; 910; amazing progress of humanity in the spheres of s. and t., at the service of the discovery of ever more sophisticated and powerful instruments of destruction: 977; immense progress, and the scandal of the critical situation of so many children in the world today: 2398; scientific and technological progress should find new ways to make it possible for increasing numbers of people not simply to survive, but to live together in dignity, in social unity, harmony and peace: 2751;

15. **the Church is ready to support and acclaim the progress that s. and t. have already attained**, so long as this progress truly serves the good of the inhabitants of this earth and does not deprive anyone of the just fruits of this advance and growth; she does, however, insist that all true progress in s. and t. be put at the disposal of people without prejudice or discrimination, and that the value of truth and honesty, equity and fraternity, spirit and religion be advanced by these many forms of progress: 1433;

16. see also: 276; 342; 706; 1294; 1298; 1345; 1523; 1579; 1845; 1993; 2398; 2993; 3095; 3210; 3211; 3213; 3227; 3263; 3264; 3279; 3283; 3420; *Progress; Ethics; Primacy.*

ß

Scientists

1. **serve the truth with utmost dedication**; concern when they are required to serve their purposes without having the opportunity of judging and deciding, quite freely, whether such aims are honest in human and ethical terms, or when they are threatened with the consequences if they refuse to have any part in them: 181-182;

2. **will truly help mankind if they preserve a sense of transcendence of the human being over the world and of God over the human being**: 185; 210; 242; all who generously dedicate their knowledge to the progress of the people and all those who have faith in the human being's spiritual calling are **invited to a common task**: to constitute a real science for the total advancement of the human being: 209;

3. **John Paul II appeal to s. to institute an respect the primacy of ethics in all the sphere of science**, and to preserve the human family from the terrible prospect of nuclear war: 186-188; see also 183-185; 1194; 1204; 1257; 1283; **to study more deeply the ethical problems of the technological society**: 206; to join in placing the scientific and cultural heritage **at the service of the true progress of humanity for the building of a world of dignity and justice for all**: 200; to study the link which must be established between **scientific and technological knowledge and the human being's moral knowledge**: 209;

4. **assistance and cooperation of s.** in the transfer of technology to developing countries: 281; 1898; need for **improved training of s. in developing countries**: 1343;

5. see also: 1204; 1287; 1304; 1324; 1327; 1354; 1357; 1861; 2656; 3277; 3278; 3352; *Ethics.*

Sea

1. **riches**: 144; 1938; **resources**: 337; 1904; 1906; modern means of investigation provide a glimpse of the still almost undiscovered **treasures hidden in the depths of the earth and in the seas**: 1990; nature's potential for production on land and in the seas continues to be vast: 2104; riches of nature in the s.: 2152;

2. the sea bed and subsoil, together with their resources, **form part of the common heritage of mankind to be explored and exploited for the benefit of mankind** as a whole: 3169; see also: 1895; 2167; 3173; 3178; 3188;

3. frightening prospect that the **ocean floor be turned into a launching pad for missiles with atomic warheads** and that the sea become the hunting-ground of increasing numbers of submarines bearing nuclear weapons: 3166;

4. **Law of the Sea**: is a praiseworthy application of the criteria of justice in the relations between peoples whose awareness of their own economic, social and political rights and duties grows ever stronger: 1978; **Seabed Authority**: 3197-3198. See also: 3165-3199; *Resources; Riches.*

Security

1. **right to s. of person**: 89; 334; 1152; 3091; **economic s.**: 41; **social s.**: 328; 1620; 1821; s. **of employment**: 1751; **organic s. system**: 1828; **food** s.: 2183; 2190; 2196; 2228; 3260; 3265; 3300/1; **criteria of profitability and s.** for capital invested in form of loans: 2327;

2. **s. of international community, without any recourse to arms**: 24; 991; 1044; 1045; see also: 365; 375; 381; 702; 982; 1220; 1225; 1228; 1235; 1250; 1271; 1279; 1280; 1306; 1338; 2742; 3175; 3240; 3266; 3340; 3344; 3386; 3390; **hatred still imperils the s.** peace and prosperity of peoples: 639; **based on armaments**: 378; 777; 978; 983; 987; 1277; 1359; 1455; 3361; 3377; **disarmament and s.**: 1107; 1221; **in the use of nuclear energy**: 1361;

3. internal s., **as a pretext for torture and oppression**: 80; **national** s.: 2939; **in society**: 3092; experience of s. **in the family**: 2387; 2736; **young people** weary of a certain ideal of s.: 2706; of the **aging**: 2768; of **refugees**: 2868; 2885; **common** s.: 2998. See also: 2769; 2991.

Segregation

struggle against any form of s. which generates inferiority on any ground, slavery, caste, race, religion or class: 46; **to be banished form educational environment**: 696; of the **disabled persons**: 2663; **social s. in the cities**: 2813; see also: *Apartheid; Discrimination.*

Self-Determination

right of peoples to: 257; 645; 1099; freedom means... **political s.**: 644; attempt to create juridical and political structures in **violation of the principles of universal suffrage and the s. of peoples**: 778; **obstacles** to s.: 432; see also *Autonomy.*

Self-Reliance

the goal of international aid should be progressively to **lead developing countries to a position of s.**: 1101; in the area of **food and alimentation** is not an unattainable goal; it contributes much to the sense of sovereignty and dignity of every country: 1478; 1439; 2188; **the development of basic water** for all peoples in a country or region is a first step of enormous consequence for the movement toward s.: 1440; **reconciliation between universal solidarity and s.**: 1634-1636.

Self-Sufficiency

s. **in agricultural production; nutritional s.**: 1353; 1424; 1877; 1884; 2142; 2164; 2165; 2188; 2207; **the dream of a total s.** in the selfish enjoyment of conquests of intelligence and of science is a dangerous utopia: 1525; **no country can declare itself self-sufficient** without considerably limiting its chances of reaching a higher level of well-being: 1605; s. **of the refugees**: 2868; see also *Autonomy.*

Selfishness

reason and a will enable us to overcome the **instincts of s.** which cause us to seek our own interest even against justice and the rights of others; **s. which is the root of divisions and wars**: 393; **forces of s.**: 403; **selfish appetites**, generators of conflicts of interests and ever-deepening rifts: 725; **selfish short-term interest** of a few: 1288; 1532; **the human being does not find its joy in living except when it liberate itself from s.** and from domination of money and uses its creativeness in the service of others: 1609; **intolerable**: 1657; 1769; woe to **those who selfishly enjoy their wealth** without having the slightest care for the poor: 2062; temptation to retire within **a selfish and absolute nationalism**: 2078; against the **pessimism and s.** which cast a shadow over the world, the Church stands for life...: 2732. See also: 052; 097; 18; 23; 67; 68; 207; 226; 274; 308; 333; 341; 382; 697; 1470; 1525; 1657; 1927; 2231; 2433; 2469; 2814; 3039; 3084; 3086; 3099; 3117; 3171; *Interest; Nationalism.*

Sensing (Remote Sensing)

benefits from: 3209; 3230; 3231; 3233; 3234; 3242; 3256; 3258; 3260; 3287; 3297; 3298; 3300/1; 3303-3307; **impact on developing countries**: 3291-3301; **for the benefit of all mankind**: 3291; to protect the **legitimate rights and interests of sensed countries,** legal regulation of dissemination of the data and information of r. s. is essential: 3299/9; 3300/20; 3257; *Space.*

Society

1. fundamental **sovereignty** of s. which is manifested in the culture of the nation: 173; 175;

2. **exists for the human being**: 266; any well-regulated and profitable **association of human beings in s. demands the acceptance of one fundamental principle**: that each individual is truly a person, and as such endowed with rights and duties which together flow as a direct consequence from its nature: 447; there is a certain number or **rights which s. is not in a position to grant since they precede s.**; but **s. has the function to preserve and enforce them**: 3069; **civil s.** has the duty to respect the free spiritual development of each person: 483; 637; religious freedom will help ensure the **common welfare of each s.**: 499; we must all contribute our share to the **building up of a s. that makes possible and feasible the enjoyment of rights** and the discharge of the duties inherent in those rights: 459; 701; 712; promote a **"moral" s.**: 551; **international s.** is directly concerned by the violation of human rights and in promoting them: 518; **discrimination affects the harmony of s.**: 639; 645; 671;

3. a **new s.**, which will succeed in eliminating the causes of wars by generously pursuing the total progress of each individual and of humanity: 196; 198; **a s. where each one may be recognized**, respected, and supported in its efforts to achieve spiritual growth towards a greater mastery of self in genuine freedom: 342; emergence of a **world s. in which the dignity of human beings and nations** is becoming part of a wider loyalty to the whole human community of planet earth: 1594; 1645; a **s. lives in peace** when it has reached a consensus on the transcendent and unassailable character of justice: 1097; 1664; 2134;

4. a **s. of solidarity** is built up day by day, first by creating and then preserving the conditions on which the free participation of all in common effort effectively depend: 232: **solidarity refuses to conceive of s. in terms of struggle "against"** and of social relationships in terms of uncompromising opposition between classes: 226;

5. **need to organize international s. globally**, given its present degree of interdependence, in order to achieve a common international good and to realize the need for a world authority: 317; a truly **planetary s.** is the great imperative of our time: 1454; 1466;

6. modern societies are characterized by **increasing fragmentation and alienation**: a s. seen as a mere system cannot provide people with a decent human existence: 266; **disintegration** of human s.: 53; 204; one of the great **crises of conscience of contemporary s.** is the disregard for the mystery and sacredness of the gift of life: 2376; 3083; 3429; **bewilderment of a s. that is scientifically and technologically advanced**, but which is not sure what criteria to adopt and what use to make of its knowledge, discoveries and power: 1299; **rejection of a model of society incapable of offering valid reasons for living** or strong motives for undertaking commitments: 2982;

7. plan of God for the **progress** of human s. on earth: 26; see also: 41; **good** of s.: 42; human being's share in the **common good** of s.: 60; 226; 232; 243; 455; 765; 1336; 1344; 1414; 1476; 1721; 2105; 2742; 3202; 3418;

8. **industrial** s.: 45; 3212; 3224; 3228; when only the model of s. that leads to an industrialized civilization is considered, we experience a crisis of civilization: 1688; 1694; ethical problems of the **technological** s.: 206; fear of technological s.: 1350;

9. **s. and aging**: s. as a whole deprives itself of enriching and guiding elements when it begins to consider as valid for its development only its young or adult members in full possession of their strength and the others as unproductive: 2487; see also: 2479; 2480; 2481; 2491; 2492; 2493; 2494; 2495; 2498; 2499; 2768; **disabled persons**: the quality of a s. and a civilization are measured by the respect shown to the weakest of its members: 2650; see also: 2646; 2648; 2651; 2655; 2659; 2660; 2661; 2667; 2673; 2674; **refugees**: duty of s. is to alleviate at least the main difficulties of their situation: 2887; see also: 2884; 2889; 2892; 2903; 2918; 2935;

10. **families** should be encouraged to assume responsibility for transforming s. and be active participants in the development process: 2741; family entitled to the protection of s.: 2709; 2736; 2754; 3048; see also *Family*; **women**: see *Women*; a s. which has not succeeded in integrating **youth** into itself: 56; 681; 834; 2396; which does not offer enough space and hope to the **weak and poor**: 387;

11. **duty** of society to avoid the possibility of provoking a war: 86; our s. must realize that the future of humanity depends as never before on our collective choices: 195; it is the **immediate duty of s. to bring concrete assistance to those of its members who are deprived of the minimum essential** for the normal growth of their personality: 1991; it is painful to have to admit that **human s. seems incapable as yet of tackling the problem of world hunger**, even though it has achieved unprecedented technological progress in all areas of food production: 2101; 2358; 2375;

12. deficiencies in the **organization** of s., which prevent personal initiative, even by terror and the oppression of inhuman ideological and practical systems: 138;

13. **mass media** and s.: 175; 465; 468; 844;

14. see also: 78; 229; 241; 276; 302; 330; 391; 468; 621; 647; 770; 781; 830; 1143; 1721; 2035; 2057; 2076; 2346; 2347; 2744; 2949; 2956; 2958; 2963; 2965; 2981; 2983.

Solidarity

1. is becoming **ever more definite in the conscience of human beings**: 55; 3098; duty of s.: 319; 1143; the serious socio-economic problems which occur today cannot be solved unless **new front of s.** are created: s. of the poor among themselves, s. with the poor to which the rich are called, s. among the workers and with the workers...: 2279(2); international s. **is a necessity of the moral order**: 2284(3);

2. s. **broadens horizons** to include not only the interests of individuals and particular groups but the common good of society as a whole, whether nationally, internationally or worldwide; seeks to struggle for a just social order in which all tensions can be absorbed and in which conflicts can be settled more easily; for that, it must remove the foundations of hatred, selfishness, and injustice: 226;

3. the need for interpersonal s. **derives, as an essential requirement, from the Christian belief that all human beings are brothers and sisters** because they have a single Creator and Father: 510; 514; 518; 911; 912; 926; the Christian name for s. is fraternity: 584; s. is a direct requirement of human and supernatural brotherhood: 2279(2); it is essential to raise consciousness of the unity of mankind in order to perceive clearly the precise duties imposed by s., not only within the local or national community, but also on the universal plane: 791; fraternity and s. of the whole human family: 1472; 1474; is rooted in the affirmation of the unity of the human family, a unity of nature and of destiny: 1686;

4. promotion of the advancement of **interpersonal** s.: 582; 583; all of humanity has become interdependent, and, if we do not deliberately promote s., we shall be incapable of resolving the great problems we must face: 584;

5. **international**: 63; 227; without frontiers: 228; universal: 228; 1143; of all peoples and nations under the guidance of a common Father: 243; is progressing too slowly as far as actual behaviour and decision-making is concerned; it should result, in part, from the education of the moral conscience...: 879; 1185; **may be regarded as a step along the path of peace**: 1143; the **absence of s. within a country** encourages a lack of s. in the world: 266;

6. **religious** s.: 495; **with the victims of religious intolerance**: 530; 532; 544; the need for interpersonal s. derived from our universal fraternity clearly leads to the conclusion that all of interna-

tional society is directly concerned by the violation of human rights, particularly religious liberty, regardless of where it occurs, and in promoting these rights: 518;

7. **of the world of labour**: 220-233; is inherent in one way or another in the very nature of human work: 220; 221; 223; between workers: 225; 229; need to forge a new s. based on the true significance of human work: 225; it derives its strength from the nature of human work: 226; s. for work: 226; with work; in this sense, it casts a special light on the problem of **employment**: 229-230; is the key to the employment problem: 231; as **an imperative of social order**: 232; work creates bonds of s.: 2429;

8. a new spirit must be created in the international community **around the concept of integral development in s.**: 1375; see also: 1391; 1392; 1419; **economy of s.**; a new relationship, the social s. of all: 3419; 3420; the principle of s. in a wide sense **must inspire the effective search for appropriate institutions and mechanisms**, whether in the sector of trade, or on the level of a wider and more immediate redistribution of riches and of the control over them, in order that the economically developing peoples may be able not only to satisfy their essential needs but also to advance gradually and effectively: 1473; 1475; 1486; 1487; 1488; 1599; international s. is everyone's responsibility even though those who possess more have also more obligations; it is imperative to foster international s. based upon the mutual and respectful exchange of each one's values and possibilities: 1570; 1574; 1595; 1597; 1600; 1609; 1610; 1617; 1618; 1619; 1620;

with developing countries: 546; 1490; 1498; 1516; 1565; should not lead to the domination of certain countries by other countries: 836; 1799; 2279; in a world of increased interdependence among nations, an ethic of expanded s. will help to transform economic relations (commercial, financial, and monetary) into relations of justice and mutual service, while at present, they are often relations based on positions of strength and vested interests: 2296; justice among nations is only possible if the quality of interdependence of the nations is radically transformed and inspired by a new sense of mutual s., cooperation and equity: 1664; **with the underprivileged countries/peoples**: 777; 1422; 1663/3; all nations have a claim on the solidarity of all others, but the nations that see the very existence and dignity of their people threatened have a priority claim: 2169; strict obligation of s. and justice in matters of commercial exchange with the third world: 1508; 1655; 1824; these peoples possess a wealth of cultural values affecting s.: 2383; world s., each day more efficient, must allow all peoples to be artisans of their own destiny: 1566; 1598; 2055; vital reconciliation between universal s. and self-reliance: 1634-1636;

comes up against numerous obstacles, in the first place the individualism of peoples and nations; therefore it presupposes a change in attitude, a lasting desire for openness and understanding: 1686;

other references in connection with problems of development: 1520; 1526; 1530; 1542; 1548; 1553; 1643; 1674; 1677; 1687; 1688; 1696; 1701; 1708; 1721; 1741; 1841; 1866; 1873; 1882; 1884; 1886; 1890;

9. **s. between rural workers**: 1785; s. in free associations of **fishery workers**: 1860; in the **emergency situation in Africa**: 1716; 1842; 1843; 1921; 1925; 1926; 1927; in relation to **agriculture and food problems**: 1930; 1957; 1978; 2013; 2070; 2084; 2086; 2091; 2097; 2106; 2107; 2114; 2126; 2132; 2133; 2134; 2146; 2166; 2171; 2176; 2177; 2189; 2195; 2201; 2206; 2211; 2226; 2230; 2232; 2235; 2244; 2245; 2246; 2249; 2256; God gave the earth to the entire human race so that peoples could derive their livelihood from it in s., and so that each people might have the means of feeding itself, caring for itself and living in peace: 2438; the demands of justice in world s. cannot be satisfied merely by the distribution of "surpluses", even if these are adequate and timely; for the demands of s. call for an ever greater and more effective willingness to place at the disposal of all people, especially those most in need of help for their development, the various riches of nature: those beneath the ground, those in the sea, on land or in space: 2167;

10. s. implies an awareness and acceptance of co-responsibility for the causes and the solutions relative to **international debt**: 2280; see also: 2269; 2274; 2279; 2283; 2285; 2297; 2302; 2304; 2312; 2313; 2318; 2319; 2323; 2327; 2330; 2333; 2334; 2338; 2339; 2340;

11. in the struggle against **illiteracy**: 777; 791; 818; in the realm of **education**: 836; 842; **information**: 845; **culture**: 878-880;

12. genuine network of human s. for the good of **children** all over the world: 2373; 2376; towards **disabled persons**: 2640; 2648; 2669; 2670; 2673; 2678; the **refugees**: 2853; 2905; 2915; 2933; **migrants**: 2939; 2948; the family, a community of love and s.: 2381; 2736; 2754;

13. s. **of the Church** with the joys and hopes, the sadnesses and anxieties of the modern world: 410; 2512; 2531;

14. see also: 24; 26; 63; 66; 129; 188; 257; 280; 285; 289; 308; 345; 467; 565; 593; 597; 617; 630; 706; 717; 747; 910; 940; 941; 1083; 1165; 1183; 1301; 1349; 2432; 2438; 2509; 2529; 2531; 2573; 2590; 2594; 2602; 2714; 2785; 2818; 2989; 2995; 3097; 3105; 3119; 3123; 3213; 3222; 3224; 3225; 3227; 3233; 3342; 3430; *Brotherhood; Collaboration; Developing Countries/13; Development/3.*

Sovereignty

1. **of peoples**: 310; **national community**: 13; fundamental s. possessed by **every nation** by virtue of its culture: 174-175; of nations over their natural resources: 913; **nations** that do not yet enjoy full s.; those that have been forcibly robbed of it: 112; fundamental s. **of society** which is manifested in the culture of the nation, through which, at the same time the human being is supremely sovereign: 173; the Popes tirelessly recall and emphasize the s. **of the human being**: 3369, see 3367-3370;

2. the development of laws and mentalities in a **community based on the principle of the absolute s. of individual States** has lagged behind other developments in an era in which destructive violence and all-embracing communication determine the picture of the world: 251; governments do not have the right to invoke their s. in order to evade practising the basic requirements of the United Nations Charter and the great documents on human rights connected with it: 518;

3. principle of the "universal purpose of creation" and the s. **of the States**: 3109; 3182; 3188; s. of the States, direct broadcasting and remote sensing: 3233;

- of the Holy See, see *Holy See*; s. over Jerusalem, see *Jerusalem*;

- see also: 5; 228; 354; 543; 1478; 1626; 1653; 1664; 1676; 2720; 2728; State.

Space (Space Exploration/Outer Space)

1. **the Church is concerned that the enormous progress in s. technology should be put to the service of peace and the common welfare of mankind**: 3202-3204; space belongs to the whole humanity, is something for the benefit of all: 3281; see also: 2167; 3219-3228; 3257-3261; 3239-3290, *passim*;

2. **benefits** from the exploration of outer s.: 847; 3201-3202; 3205; 3239-3290; see also *Sensing*;

3. every effort to organize international cooperation for **its peaceful use** will receive the warm support of the Holy See: 3237; **need to develop a world legal system to coordinate and discipline initiatives** in these matters: 3204-3205; 3237; for **military purposes**: 3214-3218;

Speculation

any s. **exploiting elementary human needs** is iniquitous, in a very special way s. on food and arms: 2143; **currency s.**: 2301; 2307; on the **stock markets**: 2292. See also: 132; 1493; 2289; *Exploitation.*

Stability

psychological: 2795; 2801; **spiritual**: 2824; **of individuals, families** and **societies**: 116; of society: 2366; of individual (2806) and of family life (2366; 2806); of the institution of the family: 2690; 2759; 2823; 2837; in marriage: 2754; in the **balance of payments**: 1497; **of trade** and commercial balances: 1523; **of rural population**: 1961; **economic**: 2742; of **international relations**: 2970. See also: 1836; 2803; 2885; 3198; 3299/6.

State

1. **undue ascendancy of the S. over the individual**: 330; the human being must be prevented from becoming only the mechanized servant of a S. tempted to subject all energies to its service alone: 53; governments and their leaders cannot carry on the affairs of S. independent of the wishes of their peoples: 1050; arbitrary actions of S.: 349; **the S. must not supplant the initiatives and responsibilities that individuals and smaller social groups can assume** in their respective fields: 3416;

2. States **can no longer ignore each other**: 13; the United Nations works not just to eliminate conflicts between States, but to make it possible for States to work for each other: 26; wish that S. not only promulgate the principles of the United Nations in their constitutions but have public authorities put them into operation so that every person may live a life worthy of the same: 412; S., as units in which people live together, must respect and support one another: 263; juridical equality of all S.: 382; 1099;

3. if it is in the interest of S. to cooperate in scientific, economic, technological and ecological matters, it is even more **in their interest to collaborate in the safeguarding and promotion of human rights**: 427-428; 478; people must become aware that economic tensions within a country and in the **relationship between States** and even between entire continents contain within themselves substantial elements that restrict or violate human rights: 97; today **most S. constitutions recognize the principle of respect for freedom of conscience and religion** in its fundamental formulation as well as the principle of equality among citizens: 481; **violation of religious freedom by States**: 457; 590/d; 591; see also *Freedom/*; arbitrary procedures, torture, disappearances, banishments, forced emigrations of families, executions after hasty trials, are not worthy of **self-respecting sovereign S.**: 543; God-given rights which the S. is obliged to protect: 2970; right of the S. to demand punishment commensurate with the crime committed: 3090; 3088-3092;

4. **means of common extermination in the hands of the modern States**: 109; **rivalry between S.** to develop military strength: 247; **balance of force** between different S. or groups of S.: 970; 3380; **relationships between S.**: 975; 1040; 3390; **confrontation** between S.: 987; **blocs** of S.: 989; S. must refrain in their international relations from the threat or **use of force**: 1225; **trust** between S.: 1227; today no one would support the idea that moral norms apply to the individuals while S. are **governed exclusively by the rule of self-defence** and victory in the struggle for existence: 3340; **requirements of moral law in relations between peoples and S.**: 3342; 3398; **the power of the S.** in a country is not always capable of preventing disputes among citizens and social groups: 3345;

5. **responsible for common good**: 909; the objective good of all supposes a political will of States, impartial and clear sighted, firmly resolved to prevent conflicts or find reasonable solutions for them, and to put into practice, effectively, what is demanded by human rights and solidarity: 308; the common good of nations demands that S. should rise above their merely nationalistic in-

terests: 337; 1384; 1410; 1432; 3178; **young S. need no longer self-interested and humiliating charity**, but scientific and technological assistance as well as solidarity based of friendship of all other nations: 1490; 2279; **mutual dependence of S.**: 1653; **industrialized S.**: 1704; **within the S. everybody has a right to just wages** in exchange for the work done: 1706; **international cooperation between S.**: 1878; **property and profits from S.** or private initiatives must respect the primary right of the universal use of resources in international relations as well as in the programmes of each country: 1896; 3182; 3188; **moral duties deriving from the relationships between S.**: 2187; relationships based on international justice among peoples of the whole world and their S.: 2226; corruption which in certain countries affects the leaders and the S. bureaucracy: 2307; **creditor S.**: 2322; 2324; 2325; 2327;

6. the family has the right to the protection of the S.: 2709; 2736; 2754; 3048; responsibilities and tasks of States and of the world community with regard to population already in existence and those yet to come: 2718; responsibilities of S. and individuals regarding the environment: 3109; coastal, 3173; 3189; 3190; 3191; 3192; landlocked S.: 3173; activities of S. in the exploration and use of outer space: 3204; 3212; 3215; 3216; 3217; 3221; 3222; 3224; 3233; 3255; 3299/9; 3300/20,21;

7. of **Vatican City**: always and in every occasion neutral and inviolable: 1237; cultural possession of humanity: 1237;

8. see also: 79; 80; 2249; 2252; 2253; 2290; 2291; 2337; 2429; 2572; 2721; 2818; 2845; 2855; 2896; 2917; 2923; 3419; 3427; 3429; *Authority; Equality; Sovereignty.*

Sterilization

s. and contraception must be considered as **morally illicit because**, through their use, the inherent connection between intimacy and procreation is violated; the Holy See has constantly opposed the practice of s. because of the finality with which destroys one of the person's greatest prerogatives, the ability to procreate, and because as a demographic measure it can be too easily used in violation of human rights, especially among the poor and uninformed: 2761. See also: 2577; 2734; 2735; 2760; 3058; 3077; 3085; *Birth Control; Contraception.*

Structure

1. ideological s. **of mankind**: 16; neither the absolutization of matter in the **s. of the human subject**, nor, conversely, the absolutization of the spirit in that s., expresses the human being's truth or serves its culture: 159;

2. structures **of social life** in which the practical exercise of the freedom of the spirit, such as freedom of thought and expression, religious freedom. and freedom of conscience, condemns the human being, in fact if not formally, to become a second-class or third-class citizen: 102; s. which cause injustice and conflict: 196; social s. oppressing human persons and groups: 615; 631; 634; international trust presupposes s. that are objectively suitable for guaranteeing, by peaceful means, security and respect for or recognition of everyone's rights: 991;

3. confidence in the creativity of the human being and in technological progress must be accompanied by a firm **willingness to reform the s.** which hold in thrall and render vain every effort towards the authentic construction of a national and international community which will offer to everyone the chance to live a truly human life: 2224; **economic s.** and financial mechanisms are at the service of the human person and not vice versa: 2270; the **s. established for people's good** are of themselves incapable of securing and guaranteeing that good: 2307; the difficult road of the indispensable transformation of the **s. of economic life** is one on which it will not be easy to advance without the intervention of a true conversion of mind, will, and heart: 2590; the **quest for more just s.** should be rooted in a political desire for peace and brotherhood, both of them being fostered and guided by a firm conviction of the incomparable dignity of the human person: 2134;

4. **the nations must succeed in creating new, more just, and hence more effective international s.** in such spheres as economics, trade, industrial development, finance and transfer of technology: 1391; 1514; 1555; 1652; 1663/3; **backward** economic and social s.: 2157; s. **of the developing countries**: 1523; 1536; 1657; **economic s.**: 217; 1626; 3104; 3422; of the world economy: 1593; economic s. that produce domination: 1546; which reflect and maintain inequalities: 1559; fundamental **structural maladjustment in the international economy**: 1648; **structural reform of the world financial system**: 1423; 1603; 1664; 2273;

5. reform of the **s. of society**: 2044; 2714; reforms **in domestic s.**: 1463; **intermediary** s. of society: 2515; **social** s.: 3428; s. **of participation**: 1692; s. **of power and decision-making** that must be altered: 1547; 1561; s. **that will better serve the common good** in justice and equity: 1420; **new s. of international relations**: 1400; 1595; 2946; **restructuring in fairer terms** of the faulty relations between powerful and powerless peoples: 2948; **structural consequences of universal solidarity**: 228; 231; 583;

6. elimination of **agrarian s. that are unproductive** and damaging to the community: 1768; see also: 1770; 1801; 1804; 1806; 1874; 1952; 1953; 1954; outmoded s. that perpetuate unbearable injustices or hinder production: 2116;

7. **dialogue s.**: 337; **political** s.: 115; s. **which would help ensure peace**: 1042; 1044; **economic and political** s.: 2955; **institutional** s. : 3196; **juridical** s.: 3197; **health** s.: 2575;

8. **infrastructures**: 788; 1480; 1821; 2838; 2934; 3252;

9. see also: 214; 418; 611; 616; 653; 1288; 1289; 1669; 1671; 2141; 2169; 2224; 2289; 2393; 2399; 2476; 2595; 2604; 2648; 2660; 2698; 2750; 2837.

Struggle

1. **between those who supply work and those who execute it**: 47; 49; **for justice and for the truth** of social life: 226; **workers' s.**: 325; **class** s.: 647; see also *Solidarity/4*; **to obtain material goods**: 92; 3194; **for power**: 176; 261;

2. for the **promotion of human rights**: 510; **against** any form of **segregation**: 46; against **racism and racial discrimination**: 434; 603; 605; 608; 609; 611; 612; 616; to banish ***apartheid:*** 673; against all **exploitation or oppression** of any person by another: 532; against **discrimination towards women**: 2514; against **illiteracy**: 774; 787; 788; 809; 825; 3057; against **drug**: 3456;

3. **for disarmament**: 1064; 1067; 1277; 1332; **at the level of the conscience of people** to take their responsibility in regard to the ethical cause of the insecurity that breeds violence: 1067; 1277; 1332; see also 3340; **armed s.**: 632;

4. **against hunger**: 31; 1189; 1871; 1965; 1993; 2010; 2134; 2178; 2575; the risk of famine and of malnutrition: 1513; to alleviate malnutrition: 1871; **injustice**: 1653; see also: 1944; 2621; against **overfeeding** in industrialized countries: 2575; **any form of super-consumerism**: 2587; against **illness and mortality**: 2703; 2719; 3046; "against uncontrolled fertility": 3075;

5. for a better **environment**: 3100; 3125; against **desertification**: 3126; 3128; 3133;

Subordination

one sided s. **of the human being** to material goods alone: 91-92; 3194; of **all existence to** the biased requirements of economic progress: 1622; of **industrialization** to the integral aims of an authentic human development: 1676; of **particular interest** to the general interests of a country's economic and social situation: 1818. See also: 024; 1130; 1248; 1896; 2117; 3223.

Subsidiarity

well-known **postulate in the social teaching of the Church** regarding social matters, according to which the State must not supplant the initiatives and the responsibilities that individuals and smaller social groups can assume in their respective fields: 3416; see also 1418.

Suppression

of **religious freedom**: 497; 531; no person may authorize the s. **of the life of an innocent human being**: 2483; 3029; s. of the **new-born disabled person**: 2655; **drug abuse** s.: 2984; 2986; *Freedom; Life.*

Survival

of the weak: 55; **of humanity**: 62; 197; 206; 397; 1204; 1468; 2472; **collective** s.: 830; of **the modern world**: 338; of **certain nations**: 337; 2285; of **Lebanon**: 1081; means of **nourishment for s.**: 1081; of **so many innocent children**: 1523; **physical** s.: 1531; **effort for** s.: 1603; of million **of people stricken by natural calamities**: 1919; of **peoples in misery**: 2175; 2797; 3310; **ethics of s.**: 2284; 2286; **solidarity for s.**: 2319; children deprived of the **basic means of s.**: 2374; 2376; see also: 2378; 2390; 2391. See also: 2476; 2487; 2879; 2944; 3096; 3198.

Syndicates see *Association, Trade/11.*

Teaching/Doctrine

1. the Church's mission is the **continuation in time of the t. and actions of the Divine Master**: 414; 2206; 2543; 2686;

2. **Catholic d.** has always been engaged in looking for ethical criteria that could be recognized by all: 575; puts forth the religious and moral meaning of the equal dignity of all human person: 614;

3. the Church **cannot be silent concerning her t. that all racist theories** are contrary to the faith an Christian love: 626; her t. **on the human dignity** and the fundamental equality of all human beings, and, in particular, on the issue of discrimination, reflects a whole Christian concept of the human being itself, created in God's likeness and redeemed by Christ: 635; t. **on development**: 1519; **concerning contraceptive**: 2722; **responsible parenthood**: 2739;

4. the Church **has a d. on the human being's** origin, its nature, its destiny: 2043; her t. **on the unity** of the human family: 2132; 2794; repeated t. **on the predominance of the person** over things and of moral conscience over social institutions: 3420;

5. **social d. of the Catholic Church**: 212; 328; 3001; 3170; 3224; 3411; 3416; of the Popes: 1653; there is no opposition nor contradiction between Catholic social d. and natural social d.; Catholic social d. only takes into account, in the application of natural social d.. the eternal destiny of human beings: 1932;

6. Christian **d. of work**: 223; the Church and confessional communities in general need to enjoy freedom to proclaim and communicate the **t. of faith**; to make known their moral **t. on human activities** and **on the organization of society**: 494; **moral t.** which the Catholic Church considers to

be among her specific and most fundamental tasks and duties: 3318; **constant d. of peace**: 3322; **t. on disarmament**: 1045; **concerning war**: 3332; **deterrence**: 3383; see also: 3335; 3337;

7. **fraternity is the great t. which Christians received from Christ**: 926; t. of universal brotherhood and of justice and peace among human beings and peoples contained in the Gospel message: 1221; **enlightening t. of the Gospel**: 1424; **fundamental t. of the Scripture**: 1470;

8. **Holy See**: proposes **points of moral d.**; its discretion, when it acts as a member of the international community, in carrying out the functions of ethical teaching: 046; its **t. in defence of the human being**: 636; t. of the Church and the Holy See **on racial discrimination and *apartheid***: 650; 670; its mission is to perpetuate the t. and activity of Jesus Christ: 2098; its specific mission on the plane of **ethical t.**: 2171;

9. evolution of the **d. of cooperation**: 1527; d. **of production and exchange**: 1687; **legal d.**: 481; **moral d.**: 3062;

10. see also: 08; 012; 87; 192; 464; 517; 556; 626; 682; 695; 814; 896; 1374; 1602; 1748-1749; 1986; 2177; 2200; 2961; 3062; 3092.

Technology

1. is the **fruit of science**: 195; directed in its **one-sided progress** towards goals of war, hegemony, and conquest: 79; 2212; concern for the fact that t. **is making possible** the utilization of ocean spaces, at ever increasing depths, for military purposes: 3166; that the enormous **progress in space t.** should be put to the service of peace and common welfare of mankind: 3202; 3214;

2. temptation to pursue **technological development for its own sake**, imposing on the human being the inevitable realization of its ever new possibilities, as if one should always do what is technically possible; temptation of **subjecting technological development to economic usefulness**, in accordance with the logic of profit or nonstop economic expansion, with no care for the true common good of humanity; temptation **to subject technological development to the pursuit or maintenance of power**, as happens when it is used for military purposes, and whenever people are being manipulated in order that they may be dominated: 205; **t. exists to serve mankind**: 766; must be used in the service of all mankind: 2015;

3. the achievements of t., like those of science, enjoy a **legitimate autonomy** so long as they do no harm: 875; **priority of ethics over technology**: 210; 1417;

4. correct affirmation of **t. as a basic coefficient of economic progress**: 238; points of **interaction between the human person and t.**: 239; the human being is the subject of all work and of all our intellectual and scientific disciplines: 241; see: 238-243;

5. **transfer of t.**: 1391; 1407; 1649; **conditions** to be met in order for it to be effective: 1434-1435; **intermediate technologies**: 1439; t. **based on advanced models**: 1449; **technological exchanges**: 1560; 1567; 1586; 2716; the **transfer of technological skills to developing countries** cannot be expected to have lasting results if training is not provided for technicians and scientists from these countries themselves: 281;

6. **need to adapt technology** in a way that fully respects the cultural and social fabric of the local community: 281; danger of the transference of poorly-adapted technologies, imposed to the detriment of the nation's original culture, and used with the aim of dominating that country: 877; 1437; 1438; 1845; **technological cooperation** can pose a serious threat to the culture of developing countries, but it need not be so: 1846; **cooperation for technological development in Africa**: 1841-1847;

7. **in spite of the tremendous progress of t.**, the devastating plague of malnutrition still keeps a large part of humanity in a state of painful physical disability: 2001; 2101; 2102; 2375; 2751; de-

spite technological progress, children still suffer and die from lack of basic nourishment: 2345; **involvement of rural youth in the use of t.**: 2073; help of the farmer: 2117; technological progress must be accompanied by reform of structures: 2118; 2244;

8. **whoever possesses t. has power over the earth an the human being**; as a result of this, hitherto unknown forms of inequalities have arisen between those who possess t. and those who are simple users of t.: 2306(12); 2316; technological power: 2317; 2330; scientific and **technological assistance**: 1490;

9. peaceful applications of **nuclear t.**: 1230; 1273; 1278; 1299; 1302; 1343; 1345; 1353; 1362; 1366;

10. **space t.**; its benefits: 3230; 3240; 3252; 3253; 3256; 3263; 3265; 3270/b; 3271/c,d,e,h; 3274; 3276; 3279; 3286; 3288; 3289; 3290; 3293; 3296; 3297; 3298; 3299/3,4,5,6,7; 3300,5,11,16; 3307; 3308; the rich countries must not attempt, through the use of modern space t., to impose their own culture on poorer nations: 3284; space technology for the benefit of mankind: 3257; 3261; 3267;

11. fascinated by the exclusive concern to have more, **technological civilization** has compromised the fundamental symbiosis between the human being and its environment: 3103;

12. see also: 45; 65; 207; 275; 278; 427; 836; 1447; 1560; 1591; 1645; 1658; 1664; 1687; 1718; 1858; 1898; 1906; 2090; 2106; 2279; 2650; 2801; 2829; 2851; 3056; 3062; 3132; 3134; 3167; 3202; 3420; *Science*.

Tensions

1. principal t. which, **in connection with the human rights**, can weaken the construction of peace: 88; t. **caused by material goods**: 90; t. and disturbances, caused by the violation of human rights: 426; **racist** t.: 610; 623; 632; 642; 670; t. **between groups** which are often liable to break into open conflict: 226; in **human relationships**, and drug abuse: 3448.

2. **economic t.** within countries and in the relationship between States and even between entire continents contain within themselves substantial elements that restrict or violate human rights: 97; have implicit in them the outbreak of tragic conflicts: 1880; **social**: 2051; **caused by unemployment**: 2571; rising t. **between good and evil**: 185; 210; 2469; **ideological**: 705; **political and military**: 2983; 3322; **international** t.: 319; 1227; **East-West**: 1104; 1173; **North-South**: 1173-1174; 2332(21);

3. **creative t.** between nations' effort to develop their own spiritual and material resources and universal solidarity: 228; **negotiation to reduce t.**: 1338;

4. see also: 18; 76; 88; 127; 341; 351; 1141; 1163; 1318; 1606; 2414; 3398.

Terrorism see *Violence.*

Torture see *Violence.*

Trade

1. **wider opportunities for the developing countries** in international t.: 1445; 1446; 1513; the developing countries should take advantage of their enormous potential for reciprocal t. through preferential treatment among themselves: 1657;

2. **fair terms** of t.: 914; t. rendered **equitable**, one of the indispensable condition of development: 1495; 1497-1498; beyond t., beyond aid, it is the full employment of all the resources of the planet, both natural and human, that must be realized: 1539; see in particular the section *Trade and Development,* 1489-1664;

3. **t. problems** in the perspective of the development of the whole person and of all peoples together: 1603; **t. relations** between peoples of different customs and culture, far from being limited to the exchange of material goods, have always conveyed also human values: 1604-1606;

4. a permanent **t. surplus** for the developing nations, particularly for the poorest among them, will enlarge their growth and development; as they grow, they will become more effective t. partners in their own right: 1589;

5. even in the heart of the industrialized zones of the globe, prosperity depends increasingly on the **capacity for production, t. and consumption** of the immense population of the poor countries: 1525;

6. **rules of equitable t.** are only a partial expression of a far broader ethic of relationships; these are all the exchanges that must be managed in order that each one gives and each one receives: 1510; **co-responsibility in the organization of t. exchanges** in the interest of all: 1600;

7. the problem of **international t.** could not be solved through the sole rule of international free marked nor, at the extreme opposite, through total planning: 1502; 1651; new ways must be explored: 1505-1506; 1514; 1528; problems so complex and so important can find proper solutions only if a strong influence of higher thinking and moral energy pervades discussions and studies and raises them from the merely economic level to one truly human: 1515; the tendency towards **iiberalization** without t. regulation, together with recurring forms of **protectionism**, must be avoided when they are in opposition to principles of justice and solidarity: 1824; an immediate and total liberalization of international t. would risk generating competition that would endanger the economies of the developing countries; in order that international t. be human and moral, social justice requires that it restore the participants a certain equality of opportunity: 2315;

8. **protectionist element** operates most sharply against the exports of two thirds of humanity who are still developing: 1586; need to reduce the **existing barriers** to the trade of developing countries: 1663/3;

9. reorganization of t. **in primary**, particularly agricultural, **commodities**: 1531-1536; **unequal terms of t.** in the exchange between manufactured goods and agricultural commodities and raw materials: 1650; in the area of t. one cannot apply two systems of weights and measures: 1653; remedies to restore the imbalance in the distribution of the gains from international t.: 1655-1656; **powerful market position of the transnational corporations**: 1652; **weapons t.** 999; 1176; 1569;

10. **Church's appeals** for human solidarity and partnership in economic cooperation: 1516; equity in trade relations: 1519; better sharing of responsibilities: 1547; world-wide solidarity: 1598; 1617-1620; relaunching of the North-South dialogue: 1644-1645; more equitable system of international economic relations: 1662-1663:

11. **T. Unions**: cohesion among the forces of society **must be the outcome of free decisions by those concerned**, taken in full independence from the political authorities and arrived at in full freedom as regards the determination of the internal organization of t. u., their operating methods and their activities: 232. See also: 238; 1459, and *Association; Worker.*

12. see also: 131; 1391; 1448; 1462; 1467; 1473; 1826; 1917; 2142; 2143; 2152; 2196; 2294; 2299; 2302; 2316; 2331.

Traditions

legitimate **pluralism of t.**: 016; various traditions that make up the spiritual heritage of humanity: 154; **Christian t.**: 165; 267; **religious t. of Asia**: 209; **cultural** t. of each nation: 228; 2751; 3284; **of the family**: 590/a; **t. penetrated by racism**: 616; t. **of the community**: 693; expansion of a new culture and **living faithfulness to the heritage of t.**: 710; cultural and spiritual t. **of the developing countries**: 1609; dialogue which appreciate the **worthy t. of the peoples** concerned: 1846; **rural populations' fidelity to the best t.**: 1961; **respect for other religious t.**: 2420; religious t.: of the Catholic Church: 2620. See also: 816; 909; 1461; 1603; 2453; 2806.

Training

1. freedom for the Church and for confessional communities in general to have their own **institution for religious t.** and theological studies: 494;

2. **of teachers**: 927; **of technicians and scientist** of developing countries: 281; 1343; **professional**, without which a country cannot control its own destiny: 928; **professional and human**: 1692; see also: 1693; 1821; t. and education **in the industrial sphere**: 1718; 1720; 1789; **essential** for coping with changes in production and selling methods: 1868; 1917; t. **of agricultural workers**: 2121; 2141; 2200; 2248; of those who work in multilateral organizations: 2339; **of women**: 2539; 2570; 2574; 2579; 2613; 2765; **of the disabled persons**: 2659; 2667; 2669; 2677; **professional t. of youth**: 56; 66; 681; 2860; education and t. of **children**: 2891; **of adults** for professional advancement: 815; **of refugees**: 2935; **for space technology**: 3299/3.f,5.a; 33/6,7,11,16,22; **advanced t.**: 193; **of the will**: 691; **vocational**: 2570. See also: 240; 1691; 1694; 1718; 2398; 3006; 3011; 3129.

Transnational Corporations see *Corporations*

Trust

*1. **between States**: condition for peace: 288; 1108; 1163; 1221; and for effective disarmament: 986; in order to make substantial progress along the road to **disarmament** it is essential to find means of replacing the "balance of terror" by the "balance of t.": 988, see 986-993; 1179; 1227; 1263; 3334; **presupposes a new international order**: 991; 994; 1317;*

*2. relations based on t. between nations and between the various agents, **for cooperation in the search for solutions of the debt question**: 2281; 2321*

*3. **of the Holy See in the United Nations**: 308; the **reason for such t.** are not accidental, they are intentional; they are based on deep convictions: the need to organize international society globally, given its present degree of interdependence among peoples, in order to achieve a common international good and to realize the need for a world authority; and thus the conviction of the intimate, essential link between the world organization and the safeguard of peace and concord among all peoples of the earth: 317; relations of t. **with FAO**: 126; close and trusting relations **with UNESCO**: 703; 712;*

*4. **mistrust**: 310; 984; 1327; 2253; see also Distrust;*

5. see also: 052; 058; 077; 17; 126; 200; 317; 321; 457; 646; 673; 1042; 2123; 2429; 2475; 3437.

Truth

1. full dominion of reason, through t., in the behaviour of the individual and of society: 78;

2. **all human being are impelled by their nature and bound by a moral obligation to seek the t.**, especially religious t.; they are also bound to **adhere to the t.** once they come to know it: 103; 483; 484; 488; **concern for t.**: 728;

3. the human being, in its entirety, **in all the t. of its spiritual and bodily subjectivity**: 159; in the innermost **t. of its humanity**: 173; **as a spirit thirsting after t.**: 846; see also 176; 178; 244; 1777; 2553;

4. **peace comes only when human beings strive for t.** and love in their dealing with one another: 264; 463; based on liberty, justice, t. and love: 716; 1141; 1183; 1726; 3342; t. essential ingredient of peace: 727;

5. **work helps the human being to live in t.** and freedom, in a freedom built on t.: 224;

6. **t. of social life**: 226; **t. and information**: 462-463; 470; 844; t. and **education**: 689; t. and **learning**: 869; 871; **ultimate aim of knowledge**: 178; knowledge of t.: 181; orientation of culture towards a **disinterested search for t.**: 766;

7. **children's right to t.**: 2349; **youth, in search for t.**: 690; 709; 2469; 2474;

8. **honesty founded on t.**: 931; **people's mutual relationships on the basis of t.**, justice and love: 992; solidarity, in t.: 2594; need to create a global community where all may **live in t.**: 2744; **civilization of t. and love**: 3290; **rigour of t.**: 3398;

9. the full development of the human being and of humanity opens to all the **way to t.**; **t. of science** as well as moral and **spiritual t.**, which alone is capable of fulfilling the human being's aspirations: 771; **scientific t.**: 1356;

10. see also: 101; 112; 163; 164; 170; 257; 265; 354; 402; 505; 509; 530; 536; 544; 556; 593; 688; 755; 766; 1433; 1760; 2211; 2305; 2420; 2440; 2465; 2483; 2620; 3027.

Underdevelopment:

1. **cannot be automatically resolved** by exporting the industrial models and the ideologies of the developed countries: 133;

2. **nuclear weapons** have become an oppressive burden on the conscience of humanity and **an open affront to those suffering from u. and hunger**: 1315;

3. the problems of u. **depends above all on the transformation of structures** which will take place only through the invention of new ways for international cooperation: 1536;

4. **transfer of technology** from the industrially advanced **to the technologically underdeveloped countries** is impaired by conflicting interests: 1649; **raw materials produced by underdeveloped countries** are subject to wide and sudden fluctuations in price, a state of affairs far removed from the progressively increasing value of industrial products: 1650;

5. see also: 99; 723; 1003; 1189; 1508; 1531; 1953; 1967; 2007; 2031; 2041; 2060; 2118; 2139; 2157; 2335(23); 2510; 2596; 2699; 3127; 3160; *Development; Technology.*

Underprivileged

the imperative requirements of justice call for **special solicitude for the u.**: 904; **duty of solidarity with the u.** peoples: 777; 3420. See also: 776; 778; 794; 797; 904; 2094; 2543; 2838; 3111; 3259; 3413; 3427; *Justice; Solidarity; Subordination.*

UNDP

is carrying out its **initiatives in order to speed up the economic and social development of least developed countries**: 1724; **satisfaction of the Holy See** for the fact that "aid" to developing nations has become a "programme of the United Nations": 1731; **encouragement** for the work of the UNDP, useful to civilization and to peace, worthy of universal solidarity: 1741. See 1723-1743.

Unemployment

is **in all cases an evil** and when it reaches a certain level, **can become a real social disaster**; it is **particularly painful when it affects young people**: 231; **a man without work is wounded in his dignity**: 3426; **one of its causes** may lie in the improvement in the instruments of production which progressively curtails the direct share of people in the production: 230; u. and **drug abuse**: 3448. See also: 933; 1449; 1538; 1549; 1581; 1596; 1648; 1652; 1663/4; 1684; 1772; 2264; 2299; 2426; 2438; 2463; 2466; 2470; 2571; 3212; 3423; 3424.

UNESCO

1. is **the creation of nations impelled by a desire for peace, union and reconciliation**: 149; established by the Organization of the United Nations as an agency for specialization in education, science and culture: 682;

2. has principally the **vocation** of contributing to peace and security by promoting collaboration among nations through education, science and culture: 702; 719; of working for the complete development of the human being: 710; has the **mission** of encouraging the growth of ideas capable of enlightening mankind: 728;

3. its **activities** are orientated towards the primarily cultural and spiritual liberation of those people who are shut up inside the walls of underdevelopment: 723; its activities **on behalf of human rights**, its unceasing fight against all forms of racial discrimination, oppression and nationalistic domination, and against everything which undermines the dignity and integrity of the human individual: 724; **concerned not only with the defence of the human being but also with its promotion**: 725; 734-735; 737; involved in reducing the scandalous inequalities between the rich and the impoverished countries: 726;

4. its **contribution to the cause of peace**: 713-755, *passim*; on 30 November 1974, it was **awarded by Pope Paul VI the John XXIII International Peace Prize.**

5. **action in favour of literacy**: 769-828, *passim*; difficult **problems confronting the Organization today**: 936-948; **intervention with the aim of safeguarding the artistic and religious riches represented by Jerusalem** as a whole, as the "common heritage of humanity": 1134; **support of the Catholic Church/Holy See**, see *Church*;

6. see: 146-191; 675-948; 2392-2400.

UNICEF

since the beginning it **has acted vigorously to promote the life and well-being of the world's children**; originally established as an emergency fund for Europe, after the Second World War, has later expanded to include the needs of children throughout the world: 2389; 2375; **one of the original aspects of its structure** is that it recognizes that the task of successfully working for the good of children all over the world requires the contribution and the participation of a broad range of citizens of many countries (National Committees of UNICEF): 2373; **collaboration of the Catholic Church**: see *Church*. See: 2352-2391, *passim*.

UNIDO

created by the United Nations (on 1965) as a sub-organ of the General Assembly, but with much of a structure of a full international organization, with the **task of coordinating and supporting efforts made in the field of industrial development**: 1698; its conversion into a Specialized Agency: 1699-1700; 1707; 1709; **the Holy See has taken an observer position with regard to the new UNIDO**, but this is due to its special character in the international community rather than to any disregard of industrialization as an important means to promote human welfare: 1701. See: 1665-1722, *passim*.

Unions see *Trade Unions in Trade/11.*

UNITED NATIONS

1. came into existence to be **against war and for peace**: 20; it aims at the study of means that can guarantee the security of international life without any recourse to arms: 24; its functions and initiatives are aimed at peaceful coexistence and collaboration between nations: 73; it endeavours with the means at its disposal and the methods in its power to exclude war, division and mutual destruction within the great family of humanity today: 74; people turn to the UN as if it were their last hope for peace and harmony: 11

2. its **increasing importance** becomes more evident every year; at no time in history has there been a greater need for dialogue and collaboration at the international level, and for joint efforts by nations to promote integral human development and to further justice and peace, precisely the goals to which the UN is dedicated: 270; 315;

3. educates them for **peace**: 22; has a key function and a guiding role in the titanic labour of building up the peaceful future of our planet: 86; peace is the essential goal of its efforts: 88; its first aim: 300; its **raison d'être**; 354; the supreme goal of its activity: 1069; it is a special place for the effort of building peace: 397;

4. offers the many States which can no longer ignore each other a form of coexistence that is extremely simple and fruitful; it recognizes the and distinguishes them **from each other**: 13; brings them together **with each other**: 16; it is the **supreme forum** for the international life of humanity today: 73; 78; 112; it unites and associates nations and States; it seeks the ways for understanding and peaceful collaboration: 74; 149; 237; works to make it possible for them to work **for each other**: 26; within it the desire of governments and peoples to work together efficaciously for the establishment of brotherly unity is most surely followed up; in it governments and peoples find a bridge to link them, a table around which they can gather, and a tribunal where they may plead the cause of justice and peace: 333;

5. proclaims the basic **rights and duties** of the human being, its dignity, its liberty and above all its religious liberty: 27; vast amount of work done devising juridical instruments of protection: 353; see *Rights/*; strives to assure each human being **a life in keeping with its dignity**: 28; 338; 341-343; 1414; works with ardor to conquer **illiteracy**, to spread **culture**: 30, see UNESCO; must be **preserved**, **improved upon** and **adapted** to the demands which the history of the world will make upon it: 12;

6. in its **Assembly respect for life** ought to find its loftiest profession and its most reasonable defense, even where the matter of the great problem of birth rates is concerned: 27; the task of its **General Assembly** must be to lend the voice to those who are not able to make themselves heard, to denounce, without care for ideologies, all oppression, whatever its source, and to ensure that cries of distress receive a hearing, just requests be taken into consideration, the weak be protect-

ed against the violence of the strong and the flame of hope thus be kept burning in the breast of the most humiliated section of mankind: 336;

7. **authority**: 354; 956; 2213; should be endowed with juridical and political means: 354; 359; must increase: 24; moral authority of the Secretary-General: 1088; still **lacks the means and support** to secure the kind of political participation and commitment requires for a truly planetary cooperation: 1455; will **fulfil its high mission** all the more effectively if in each member State the conviction grows that to govern people means to serve a plan of higher justice: 2215;

8. **Administrative Committee on Coordination**: can be decisive in the great work of development: 1371; 1373;

9. **University of the United Nations**: seeks to place science and research at the service of the great humanitarian ideals of peace advancement, development, the improvement of food resources, the proper use of natural resources and cooperation between nations: 193;

10. **activity**: the **question of Jerusalem** and the **Middle East**: 1135-1136; 1144; 1153; **disarmament**: 337; 949; 954; 956; 959; 961; 1013; 1018; 1200; 1234; 1221-1281; **use of force** in the settlement of conflicts: 354; in the international relations between States: 1225; **development**: 1372-1374; 1376; 1380; 1382-1383; 1393; 1395-1398; 1418; 1421; 1444; 1446; 1456; 1472; 1481; 1483-1485; 1488; 1848; 1870; 1918-1919; 2085; 2098; 3407; 3410-3412; 3421; see also: *FAO, ILO; UNCTAD, UNDP, UNIDO*; **science and technology** for development: 1407; 1410; 1429; 1830-1831; 1837; 1839; 1841-1842; 1847; **children**: see *UNICEF*; **youth**: 2392; 2397; 2456; 2466; **aging**: 2479; 2480; 2498; **women**: 2499; 2508-2509; 2518-2519; 2552; 2591; 2592; 2599; 2602; 2605; **disabled persons**: 2639; 2640; 2659-2660; **population:** 2679; 2697-2729; 2730; 2744-2769; 3429; **habitat**: 2770; 2777; 2785; 2824; 2827; **refugees**: 2848; 2857-2864; 2865-2869; 2873; 2875; 2881; 2882; 2892; 2894-2895; 2903; 2917-2919; 2929; 2931-2933; **migrants**: 2941-2942; 2951; 2954; 2958-2960; 2965-2968; **victims of war**: 2969-2979; **drugs**: 2980; **health**, see *Health*; **environment**: 1413; 3093; 3102; 3116; **desertification**: 3121; 3133; 3136; **water**: 3138; **energy**: 3156; **sea**: 3165; 3169; 3180; 3195; 3196-3199; **outer space**: 3200; 3207; 3216-3217; 3219-3220; 3222; 3236; 3299/8;

11. see in particular: 1-34; 71-112; 232-343; 344-362; 1185-1186; 2210-2214; 3433-3441; 3434; 3435.

Urbanization

began spontaneously, implying a sort of rejection of the natural world in favour of the world of human creations: 2809; **rapid increase** of: 283; 2767; 2829; anarchical development of: 2815; 2831; **modern forms** of u. tend not to give due attention to the community level of existence; modern planning tends to take into account only the isolated human individual or the very general abstract whole: 2804, see also 201; *Habitat*.

Values

1. **human being's** true v.: 198; individual's higher v.: 725; 802; system of v.: 830; of the human person: 3081; 3083; human nature: 3084; v. of **life**: 896; 2587; fundamental v, of life: 2585; true v. of life: 2522; **temporal and eternal** v. of the soul: 882; v. which proceed fundamentally from the recognition of the **dignity** and the **grandeur** of humanity and of the relations between human persons: 927;

2. **human**: 243; 577; 621; 766; 1300; 1399; 1509; 1604; 1688; 2106; 2404; 2595; 2622; 2633; 2624; 2694; the pre-eminence of the **spiritual** v. defines the proper sense of earthly material good and the way to use them: 90; see also 78; 129; 140-141; 151; 206; 329; 456; 1183; 1353; 1429; 1688; 2018; 2382; 2450; 2566; 2750; v. of **the spirit**: 208; 836; 1399; **spiritual and moral**: 043; 0107; 557; 2450; 2550; 2743; **religious**: 017; 710; 1407; 2018; 2445; 2762;

supremacy of **moral** v. in judgment and in consequent action: 3339; see also: 031; 183; 354; 2363; 2415; 3045; 3056; **ethical**: 572; 574; 576; 578; 793; 1353; 1407; 1429; **spiritual and cultural**: 1609; **cultural**: 243; 557; 1407; 2533; of **culture**: 330; 1143; 1353; **ethical and humanistic**: 1298; **intellectual**: 2441; higher v. of **love** and **friendship**, **prayer** and **contemplation**: 198; 3146; essential v. of a modern form of **humanism**: 876; attitude of pseudo-humanism, which compromises the ethical order of objective v.: 2655;

3. human v. of the **rural world**: 1796; see also: 2106; authentic v. of the different **religions and beliefs**: 565; v. and riches of **every culture**: 2961; 1846; v. of **peoples and cultures**: 1399; 1645; the v. that are the honour of the cultures brought forth by mankind: 710; **peoples of developing nations** posses a wealth of cultural v. affecting human solidarity, love and live, and especially the child: 2383; see also: 1704; v. of **each nation**: 633; v. represented by **Lebanon**: 1087;

4. **fundamental**: 221; 3062; **essential**: 1694; **true**: 700; 3012; true v. and their proper **hierarchy**: 896; 904; 1677; 1689; 2690; **material**: 90; 151; **material and economic**: 90; **natural**: 704; **social**: 793; 1353; of **work**: 233; **common** v. necessary to the progress of the entire human family: 882;

5. spiritual v. which the **world needs**: 2418; **erosion** of spiritual and ethical v.: 2398; **forgetfulness** of v. and the crisis of identity which frustrate our world oblige us to outdo ourselves in a renewed effort of research and investigation: 2439; **loss** of the v. which should be the foundation of any social organization: 3089;

6. great moral challenge of harmonizing the v. of **science** with the v. of **conscience**: 210; science and technology, **ambivalent** v.: 1838;

7. v. **on which peace rests**: 261; 1062; 1141; 1370; 3342; v. to develop in order to foster cooperation, mutual trust, fraternity and peace: 1042; v. that will help travel together on path that leads to true progress and development: 1714; v. that ensure the good and dignity of persons: 1722; v. of brotherhood and solidarity for peace and development: 2297; essential v. of human solidarity: 1674;

8. God measures according to the **standard of the interior** v. of "how" one places oneself at the disposal of one's neighbour: 2234;

9. affective and religious v. which exist in the spirit and in the hearth of the **elderly**: 2487;

10. values considered as "**feminine**": 2566; see also: 2595; 2622-2625; our societies must be opened to those non-competitive v. of peace, sharing in suffering, spontaneous and free self-giving, which are preserved among **women** through a woman's culture: 2630;

11. the **family**, constitutes a community of love and solidarity, uniquely suited to teach and transmit cultural, ethical, social, spiritual and religious v.: 2381; 2736; 2754;

12. education consists of both the **propounding** and the **assimilation** of v. which are at the basis of the identity, the dignity, the vocation and responsibilities of the human being as an individual and as a member of society: 2398;

13. see also: 91; 107; 173; 240; 279; 281; 330; 430; 433; 550; 689; 748; 844; 850; 905; 1037; 1060; 1096; 1189; 1354; 1408; 1432; 1441; 1461; 1475; 1510; 1570; 2290; 2536; 2661; 2702; 2707; 2738; 2745; 2763; 2939; 3103; 3361; 3379; *Culture; Heritage; Tradition.*

Violence/Terrorism/Torture

1. temptation of resorting to **violence** to impose aims of power and supremacy: 090; of destructive v.: 55; see also 69; 412; recourse to v. to resolve conflicts of self-interest: 417; tendency of individuals and peoples to settle their conflicts by force and to defend their interests by v.: 350;

2. **forms of collective v.** ; use of physical and psychological **torture** perpretated against prisoners or political dissenters: 446; see also 592; **egotistical** v.: 834; resentment that can turn to v.: 1066; **insecurity that breeds v.**: 1067; 1277; 1332; injustice and selfishness will only **engender** v. and war: 1485; see also: 1656; specific v. **due to an unbridled use of technological, economic, financial and political power**: 1898; situation of v., which must not be surmounted with other forms of v. **against life**: 2174; **suspicion** which triggers rejection, denunciation, and even v.: 2336; v. **applied by authorities in favour of contraception**: 2734;

3. **not a means to regulate relations between nations**: 45; to settle clashes of ideologies, aspirations and needs: 1164; not an acceptable solution of racial discrimination: 412; 646; 661; 673; wish to bring about change by v.: 2426;

4. the **recourse to arms and to v. of all kinds**, to **terrorism** and to reprisals, degrades the human being and is unworthy of its rational nature and of its calling to a destiny beyond himself: 1151;

5. the **content of information**, still too much an instrument for instigating v.: 845; elimination of all propaganda in favour of war, violence, racism and apartheid: 757;

6. **v. and criminal behaviour in nations and cultures** encourages v. and criminal behaviour in international relations: 266;

7. we are witnessing a **worldwide spread of v.** among individuals and groups for political or other motives: 387; our world is disfigured by war and v.: 1329;

8. **terrorism**, sometimes with the backing of public powers, has become one of the plagues of our society; it is often linked with the commerce of drugs and the **explosion of sordid v.** of all kinds, before which political communities often stand helpless: 387;

9. everything that is a continuation of the experiences of the extermination camps like the one of Auschwitz, under different forms, namely, the various kinds of **torture** and oppression, either physical or moral, carried out under any system, in any land, should disappear forever: 80; arbitrary procedures, **torture**, disappearances, banishments, forced emigration of families, executions after hasty trials, all this is not worthy of self-respecting sovereign States: 543;

10. see also: 45; 152; 251; 310; 333; 336; 360; 432; 1068; 1084; 1141; 1147; 1148; 1176; 1333; 2331; 2345; 2395; 2437; 2466; 2468; 2470; 2588; 2596; 2658; 2818; 2866; 2945; 3012; 3084; *Attack; Oppression; Power;*

Vulnerability

countries whose poverty renders them dependent and vulnerable: 471; 1483; debtor countries which become still more vulnerable: 2263; of the poor **economies** to the hazards and errors of the privileged: 1630. task of guaranteeing the most vulnerable **sectors of mankind** and adequate nourishment: 2108; **youth**: 471; **children**: 2349; **women**: 2761; see also: 053; 1591; 1594; 2761; 3049.

War

1. **a supremely unacceptable means** of regulating the relationships between States, 975; totally unacceptable as a means of settling differences between nations, 1329; mankind must put an end to war, or war will put an end to mankind: 20; 366;

2. **absurd**: 1065; **irrational**: 1171; act of war direct to the indiscriminate destruction of whole cities or vast regions with their inhabitants: **a crime against God and humanity**: 975; 3355; **preparation to**: 1026-1028; **"just war" theory**: 3346-3348; **local war**: constitute a threat to general peace: 385; 999-1000; 1025; 1102; 3350;

3. **appeals to the General Assembly of the United Nation**: of Paul VI: 19-20; 24; John Paul II: 82; 85-88; 92-94;

4. **nuclear war**: a **collective suicide**: 1104; **threat**: 1256; 1330; **prevention**: 1164; 1166; **consequences**: 1180; **1191-1220**; 3352; **concern of the Holy See**: 1331; 3332; 3353-3355;

5. **John Paul II appeal to the scientists** to preserve the human family from the terrible prospect of nuclear war: 182-186; 195-196 (**check with scientist)**

6. see also: 061; 062; 068; 091; 74; 78; 149; 245; 248; 249; 294; 318; 325; 327; 328; 337; 341; 344; 349; 351; 352; 364; 365; 366; 386; 393; 396; 403; 416; 752; 757; 835; 845; 942; 967; 971; 974-976; 1042; 1050; 1054; 1056; 1072; 1080; 1100; 1162; 1167; 1176; 1181; 1183; 1233; 1240; 1241; 1256; 1280; 1285; 1294; 1328; 1330; 1334; 1339; 1349; 1400; 1452; 1485; 1523; 1538; 1702; 1898; 1931; 1935; 1970; 2062; 2100; 2103; 2115; 2212; 2389; 2395; 2426; 2437; 2468; 2510; 2588; 2606; 2623; 2852; 2866; 2974; 2989; 3096; 3111; 3262; 3314-3315; 3317; 3320; 3322; 3324-3325; 3341; 3349; 3356; 3384; 3387; 3388-3389, and *Armaments; Arms Race; Contrasts; Defence; Disarmament; Rights; Science; Scientists.*

Waste

1. the greater w. of energy and resources today is the w. of the human **intellect** and the w. of the **creativity** of the human person: 1468;

2. there is a whole **economy**, too often **tainted by** power, w. and fear, which must be transformed into an economy of service and brotherhood: 67; the increasing irrational levels of extravagance, w. and pollution of the **high consumption societies** should not jeopardize the poorer nations' hopes of development and humanity's ultimate hopes of survival: 1468; models for **growth** founded on w.: 1629; 1631; of **resources** which ought to promote the good of all: 2125; **scandal** of w.: 2130; 2358;

3. of huge sums in acquisition of **costly weapons**: 67; 1569; 1880; **radioactive** w.: 1324; 1326; 1327; 1341; 1342; 1350; 1364; 3150;

4. see also: 1322; 1412; 1413; 1535; 1955; 2062; 2297; 2375; 2839; 3075;

Water

the **development** of basic w. for all peoples in a country or region is a first step of enormous consequence for the movement toward self-reliance: 1440; 1273; 1953; questions of w. are inseparable from those of development: 3140. See also: 61; 277; 285; 1196; 1215; 1416; 1808; 1851; 1935; 1938; 1956; 2536; 2795; 2932; 3096; 3133; **3138-3155**; 3265; 3286; 3288; 3298/2.

Wealth

1. when all is said and done, the only true w. is the **human person** and if there is a desire for more, it is to be more: 1375; **human** w.: 551; of each **culture**: 581; 696; of cultural values: 2383;

2. every people has the **right to take a just portion** of that w. which has been, and is constantly created by the happy combination of natural resources and human work: 1706; human effort has brought forth much w. from the earth, but it **should not be squandered** superfluously by a small minority nor **selfishly hoarded** for a few at the expense of the rest of mankind in need: 3117; **distribution**: 176; 1776; 2310; 2572; redistribution: 2819; fair **share** in world's economic w.: 257; 622; 628; 1452; 1548; **balance**, in favour of the already rich: 1450; **concentration**: 1454; **dispro-**

portion between w. and poverty: 1470; desire to set aside an important part of w. in order to make it directly available for **common use and needs** apart from any logic of competition and exchange: 1620; Jesus Christ utters a **negative judgment** in regard to those who, living in luxury and w., despise the poor: 2216;

3. **the wealthy**: nations/countries: 1386; 1455; 2113; 2175; 2226; 2946; 2948; elite: 1449; classes: 1459; 1493;

4. see also: 230; 1485; 1569; 1681; 1967; 1967; 2062; 2108; 2223; 2395; 2484; 2962; 3167; 3306; *Balance; Poor; Rich; Riches.*

Welfare

of **peoples** 053; 1886; **nations/countries**: 502; their communities: 058; their peoples: 1386; 1748; search for their own w.: 2939; of **humanity**: 186; 1273; 1743; 1885; 1967; **common**: 118; 497; 499; 1879; 1896; 3202; 3301; **human**: 1701; 3308; of the **human being**: 223; 1059; 1180; 1670; 1758; 2555; 2750; 3425; of **families**: 1461; **children**: 2343; 2344; 2765; **handicapped**: 2653; **physical**: 1844; **centres** for w. 1132; **policies**: 1452; **system**: 1455; 1821.

Well-being

1. is **within our grasp**, but we must want to build it together: individuals for others, individuals with others and, never again, individuals against others: 63;

2. the w. of present and future generations in **industrialized countries** cannot be obtained at the cost of the w. of present and future generations in the developing countries: 1291;

3. the **media** of communication/**information** must have regard for the human being's w. and its dignity: 175; 471; w. in which material factors are predominant: 850;

4. youth's desire to go beyond a **society** of simple w. where the essential task would consist of producing and consuming: 834;

5. the road which leads **from w. to happiness** is difficult to define because of the diverse types of mentality, of their freedom of choice and of their personal destinies: 882;

6. see also: 41; 152; 220; 224; 655; 662; 723; 729; 868; 869; 875; 1272; 1285; 1290; 1305; 1379; 1383; 1426; 1429; 1461; 1605; 1640; 1643; 1656; 1663/3,4; 1664; 1693; 1732; 1745; 1819; 1819; 1955; 1982; 1984; 2033; 2049; 2249; 2358; 2381; 2387; 2389; 2669; 2705; 2732; 2736; 2750; 2754; 2768; 2769; 2817; 2939; 2998; 3000; 3004; 3085; 3128; 3141; 3157; 3168; 3225; 3259; 3388.

Women

1. **equality** can be found only in its essential foundation, which is the **dignity** of the human person, man and w., in their filial relationship with God, of whom they are the visible image: 2502; 2555-2563; 2618-2621; see *Creation/1; Dignity/1, Equality/1-3*, practices that offend the dignity of women; 2577; **equal rights** of men and w.: 021; 93; 364; without discrimination: 442; there is discrimination when the equal dignity of w. is not respected: 641; see *Discrimination*; widespread aspiration that all men and w. be guaranteed equal dignity in sharing material goods, in effectively enjoying spiritual goods, and consequently in enjoying the corresponding inalienable rights: 477;

2. equality does not exclude the **distinction, in unity**, and the **specific contribution** of w. to the full development of society, according to her proper and personal vocation: 2503; 2504; human values which are specific to women's contribution to society: 2622-2625; claims of a purely

equalizing character: 2566; **cooperation** in equality between men and w.: 2523; fundamental equality of persons must respect their **diversity**: 2528-2529; true meaning of the **complementarity**: 2529-2530;

3. since the fundamental and life-giving cell of human society remains the family, w. will preserve and develop, principally **in the family community**, in full co-responsibility with man, her task of welcoming, giving and raising life, in a growing development of its potential powers: 2505; 2532; **w.'s family tasks**: 2535-2537; 2545; 2566; 2586; 2628; 2629; **w.'s maternal role**: 2533; see 2367; 2533-2536; 2599; 2625-2627; 2630; 2765; the **particular contribution of women at home** and in their unique capacity to nurture the infant and guide the child in the earliest phase of education, is often ignored or diminished in favour of economic considerations or employment opportunities: 2740;

4. full **participation** of w. in the community life of the Church and of society: 2500; 2515; 2532; 2536; 2548; 2573; 2588; 2592; 2598; 2599; 2638; 2740; full **integration** of w. in the global effort for development: 2510; 2513; into public and community life at all levels: 2546; 2740; contribution to the strengthening of **peace**: 2510; 2547-2548;

5. **promotion**: 2519; profit-motive of the promotion of w., genuine progress: 2526; 2566; 2589-2591; 2597-2598; 2609; 2616; **elevation** of women to their rightful place in society: 415; **advancement** of v. 883; 2622-2627;
- the Holy See has repeatedly advocated appropriate personal and social advancement for w. in order to assure the dignity of w. and the improvement of the quality of life for the coming generations: 2367; in the contemporary effort to promote the advancement of w. in society, the Church has already recognized a "sign of the times", and has seen in it a call of the Spirit: 2500; see also: 2511-2513; 2515; 2518; 2531; 2553; 2764;

6. necessary **discernments** in order that **liberation** may not lead to new and worse forms of servitude, and in order that the struggle against **discrimination** may not base itself upon a false equality which would deny the distinctions laid down by the Creator himself, or which would risk attenuating the exact idea of the **privileged mission** of w.: 1514;

7. young w. who are **denied the possibility of consecrating themselves** to a common life dedicated to prayer or to works of charity: 526(*);

8. w. and **literacy**: 787; 790; 2513; and access of w. to an **education** adequate for their fulfillment: 2541-2545; 2581-2583; contribution in **health** services: 2564; 2575-2580; 3053; education for **peace**: 2588; w. and **culture**: 2630-2631;

9. regulation of the **work** of w.: 328; w. in relation with work: 2568-2574; 2628-2635; 2773; 2805; 2843; harmonization of **professional and family obligations**: 2585-2586; pursuit of a life-style corresponding to the real needs of each one: 2587; **migrant** w.: 2537-2540; 2963;

10. **International Women's Year**: see 2499-2551, passim; programme: equality, development and peace: 2501; synthesis of a vast network of problems that the world community must face today, which expresses aspirations with which the Church herself manifests her solidarity: 2509-2510; see also: 2520; **World Plan of Action**: 2521; 2526; 2532; achievements of the **United Nations Decade for Women**: 2602-2638, passim.

11. see also: 1913; 2248; 2466; 2735; 2757; 2761; 2762; *Abortion, Contraceptives, Sterilization.*

Work

1. the reality of w. in the **Bible**; 37; teaching of the **Church**: 39; 218-219;

2. the modern concept of w. is based on a fundamental principle which has been brought out conspicuously by Christianity: in labour is **the human being** which **comes first**: 44-45; 219; 226; **primacy** of the **labour** of the human beings over the other elements of economic life: 39; 1860; at all costs the human being must be prevented from becoming the mechanized servant of a blind machine which devours the best of itself: 53; w. in any of its forms deserves particular **respect** because it represents the output of a human being and because behind it there is always a live subject: the human person; that is the source of its value and its dignity: 214-215; the **w. of agricultural workers** should be carried out in conditions and ways that harmonize with their dignity as persons, and for objectives that are similarly in harmony therewith: 1769; labour is necessary for human promotion and for a person's fulfillment: 2935; a person without w. is wounded in its human dignity; **right** and correlative **responsibility** to w.: 3426; 3439;

3. the problems of w. share one characteristic, which is at one and the same time a condition and a programme: **solidarity**, inherent in one way or another in the very nature of human w.: 220-232, see *Solidarity*;

4. the problem of w. has a very **profound link with that of the meaning of human life**; this conviction is the whole foundation of the Christian doctrine of w.: 223;

5. like each human being, **each people must be able by its w. to develop itself**, to grow in humanity, to pass from less humane conditions to more humane ones: 55;

6. w. is still **ambivalent**, and its organization may easily depersonalize the one who performs it, if he becomes its slave, abdicates intelligence and freedom, and even loses his dignity through it: 45; **labour camps** organized as institutions, which have been the shame of the civilized world: 45; 526(*); miserable **proletarian condition**, in which hunger is joined to social degradation to create a state of real insecurity: 46; **fragmentation** of labour in contemporary society: 45;

7. the **labour movement** cannot content itself with material successes, with achieving a perfect system of guarantees and insurances, with acquiring a greater share of influence in the economic sphere; it must seek an end on the universal level, in a social order where material prosperity is engendered by the collaboration by all for the general good and support is given to the highest values of culture and, above all, to a consummate union of minds and hearts: 330; **Labour associations**: see *Association, Unions;*

8. labour **conflicts** cannot be remedied by artificially imposed conditions which fraudulently deprive the worker and whole social community of their first and inalienable human prerogative, which is freedom; nor can they be remedied by solutions which result solely from the free play of the determinism of economic factors; it is only when the deepest reasons of these conflicts are understood, and the just claims they express are satisfied, that it is possible to avert their dramatic explosion and avoid its ruinous consequences: 49; 46; the solution of the problems of w. has been seen to lie in a commitment by all the parties involved, and in peaceful bargaining aimed at the well-being of the human being at its work, and peace between societies: 220; **exploitation** of labour: 97; labour **market**: 2942; 2950; 2953; **clandestine, illegal** labour practices: 2950; rural labour **force**: 3130;

9. contemporary **labour legislation**: 325-327; International Labour Convention: 232; International Labour Code: 328-329;

10. see also *ILO, Worker.*

Worker

1. an end has been put to the priority of labour over the labourer, to the supremacy of technical and economical necessities over human needs; never again will work be superior to the w., **never again will work be against the worker**; but always work will be for the w., work will be in the service of human being: 44; 223;

2. despite the greater and more **effective respect** for worker's fundamental rights in many countries, various systems based on ideology and on power have allowed **flagrant injustices** to persist or have created new ones: 225; the struggle for justice must not ignore the **legitimate interests** of w. associated in the same occupation: 226; w. which are too often **overlooked**, especially when they receive no assistance from society: 229; no system can be vindicated that deprives the w. of their just rights and of their personal and corporate dignity by reason of their **colour or race**: 669; **exploitation** of the w.: 1675;

3. drama of the modern w.: 46; organic **participation** of all w. not only in the fruits of their labour, but also **in the economic and social responsibilities** upon which their future and the future of their children depend: 54; 330; solidarity among w.: 225; of w.: 229; with w.: 2279, see *Solidarity*; unions: 328;

4. **research w.**: 178; 195; 201; 870; 3097; **professional**: 229; **migrant w**. 622; 641; 782; 783; 883; 2766; 2774; 2821; 2941; 2959; 2960; 2962; 2965; 2967; 2968; see *Migrants*; **rural w.**: 229; 1657; 1768; 1769; 1770; 1772; 1785; 1838; 2121; 2141; 2247;

5. Pope Leo XIII had an acute perception of the great importance of w. engaging in international collaboration: 326;

6. see also: 37; 38; 39; 329; 1447; 1449; 1459; 1587; 1691; 1860; 1942; 1946; 2249; 3311; 3426; 3427; *Associations; ILO; Solidarity; Struggle; Trade/11;Work.*

Youth

1. ardent, generous, enthusiastic, disinterested: 1380; have the right to expect a better mankind: 11; they will build the world of tomorrow: 56; 2461-2462; feel more than others the contradictions evident in society, since they are **particularly concerned about the future**: 834; it is only by inspiring them with confidence in themselves and in adults, by instilling in them a capacity for confident expectation, a sense of commitment and of responsibility, that we shall be able to point them towards a future which stimulates their creativity and arouses their enthusiasm: 2393-2394; today, they are **under threat**, precisely apropos of their destiny as the hope of mankind and of its future: 2395; see **2395-2399**; the young can build a better future if they put their faith in God first and commit themselves to building this new world according to God's plan, with wisdom and trust: 2417; 2464;

2. **willingness** to participate: 2468; 2469; 2494; **aspiration** to take their place in society: 56; their aspirations, utopian though they sometimes are, betray the desire to go beyond a society of simple well-being where the essential task would consist of producing ad consuming: 834; the y. of the world want **peace** and **justice**; they reproach their elders for not having known how to assure these for them: 1529; they aspire to a more just and more human world: 2425; to justice and peace; **peace and youth go together**: 2437; see also: 2468; 3086; youth's support for peace movements: 1051; their concern for **disarmament:** 1162; 1167; 1189;

3. **expectation**: anxious and impatient: 56; 681; **refusal** to become part of a world of dominant interests and egotistical violence: 834; **appeal** for a world freed from the obsession with quantitative growth, aspiring to fraternity and sharing, looking for ways leading to the solidary development of mankind: 834;

4. **agony** in the face of unemployment, before the madness of armaments and their increasingly fearsome power; more fundamentally, agony in facing a life to which so many young people are unable to give meaning: 933; the **suffering** of young people results also from the contradictory nature of the ideologies that infringe upon them and from the continuing emptying of ideals which they witness: 2470; **fears**, about the threat to survival of the human species; anxiety about the threat to peace in the world because of atomic armament; worry about the destruction of the ecological balance of the earth; concern for the problems of the nations which remain unresolved for so long: 2472;

5. **in rich countries**, their anxiety at the invasion of technocracy, their rejection of a society which has not succeeded in integrating the into itself; 56; 681; bored because they lack an ideal worth of claiming their support and galvanizing their energies: 66; **in poor countries**, their lament that, for lack of sufficient training and fitting means, they cannot make their generous contribution to the tasks which call for it: 56; 66; 681; the **combination** of these young resources can change the future of the world if the adult can prepare them for this great task: 66;

6. **crises** which affect, above all, the younger generations: 165; 338; 3106; youth's **minds poisoned** by people passing on to the prejudices and empty ideologies: 2345; **drug abuse**: 3446; 3447;

7. y. **in quest of truth**, athirst for **authenticity** and **distrustful** of all authority, **often rebellious** to lessons of the past, seek **knowledge** that teaches how to live: 690; 709; difficult task of **educating** y. and preparing them to face their future tasks: 695; education for peace: 1141; **literacy** programmes for y: 774; 787; 788; 790; 795; 815;

8. **unemployment**, particularly painful when it affects young people: 231; 1422; 1449; 1684; **misery** of the y. hemmed in by want and doomed never to achieve what others consider a normal existence: 2011; the y. who have enough to eat should hear the cry of distress of all those who are in want and place themselves at the service of their less fortunate fellows with generosity and enthusiasm: 2012; see also 2009-2010; 2015-2016; 2061; 2177; 2257;

9. the rising younger generations within the **rural world** claim more and more insistently increased participation, on the triple plane of property, knowledge and power: to do more, to know more and have more, in order to be more: 2072; the most remarkable technical progress and the most advanced technological attainments would not be of any use, if the rural youth throughout the world did not realize that **the progress in question is also within their reach and to their advantage**, and that bringing it about they fulfill themselves: 2073; frequently isolated in remote country areas, the y **are often losing hope in their future** as human beings: 2074; young rural people **wish to live like other y.** today, to exercise a well defined profession, to have a clearly marked social status,...: 2075-2077; 2120; 2248; need to improve the **training** of rural y.: 2141;

10. **Catholic Church**: eager to help young people and adults, not only for the needs of their physical and intellectual life, but also for those of their moral and spiritual life: 684; religious institutes, whose specific goal is to prepare y. for their future task: 693;

11. see also: 54; 69; 338; 471; 528; 590/f; 1486; 1718; 1773; 1785; 1789; 1845; 2112; 2424; **2426-2432**; **2436-2438**; 2451; **2456-2478**; 2522; 2551; 2570; 2585; 2666; 2677; 2706; 2710; 2716; 2735; 2738; 2773; 2774; 2801; 2805; 2838; 2843; 2860; 2878; 2981; 2982; 2983; 3050; 3080; 3098; 3107.